Philadelphia Remembers World War II

This book has been produced from archival material. HBI has made every effort to reproduce this book using state-of-the-art equipment. However, due to the condition and/or quality of the original material available to us, some pages have not reproduced as well as others. Since HBI did not want to omit the historical material, we included the pages in spite of their condition.

Credits:
We gratefully appreciate the contribution of ***The Philadelphia Inquirer*** for its assistance in putting this book together as well as the tireless efforts of the **Historical Briefs** staff for bringing it to life.

Developed under agreement with
Historical Briefs, Inc., Box 629,
Sixth St. & Madalyn Ave., Verplanck N.Y. 10596

Printed by
Monument Printers & Lithographer, Inc.
Sixth St. & Madalyn Ave., Verplanck, N. Y. 10596

Foreword

It has been said that nothing is staler than yesterday's newspaper. Well, yesterday's newspaper may be pretty stale today, but just wait 50 years. It will dazzle you.

There's a reason that time capsules always contain a newspaper or two. For an instant slice-of-life glance at what the world – and your little corner of it – was like decades ago, no other medium even comes close.

You're holding a time capsule. The time that it capsulizes is, beyond argument, the most fascinating and earth-shaking that the 20th century has to offer: the World War II years. That holds true whether you lived through it or know it only from someone else's war stories.

The American people have always been taken with round-number anniversaries. Since 1989, Anniversary No. 50 has brought World War II back into the national consciousness in a major way. For many of the participating survivors, those years never left the mind. As you leaf through these pages, you'll see why. From the days leading up to Pearl Harbor through the aftermath of Hiroshima, the searing power of these events is apparent.

Quite intentionally, this collection of pages from The Philadelphia Inquirer is not just a sequence of front-page banner headlines. Although Philadelphia and the rest of the United States paid an extraordinary price during the war, this country was spared the physical devastation that many of its allies and enemies suffered. That's why we've gone deeper into The Inquirer than just Page 1.

Newspapers were very different 50 years ago, and some of the differences are ugly. The blatantly racist "Japs" references and the stereotypes of American blacks found in every day's paper; the press' failure to aggressively ferret out vague reports of the Nazis' annihilation of the European Jews and to quickly and fully tell the story once the facts were known; the inaccurate hyping of the victories and downplaying of the defeats of the war – these are hardly high points in the history of the American press or of The Inquirer.

Nonetheless, the story told in these pages is gripping. The horrors are all here, with all their death, destruction and heroism. And so are the more mundane things. Strawbridge & Clothier had its Clover Day ads, just as today, but the merchandise was quite different. Spacious suburban houses were selling for $6,500 and could be yours for $650 cash - about the price of a new car. Savor the movie ads (there were dozens of theaters in Philadelphia), the photo spreads (The Inquirer ran them frequently), the fashions of the day, the exploits of the pathetic Phillies and Athletics, the food-page recipes, the comic strips and the dozens of other snippets of life during a time when very few comforts or possessions were taken for granted.

The Editors of The Inquirer

U.S.

The Philadelphia Inquirer

PUBLIC LEDGER

6 A. M. EDITION

CIRCULATION: December Average Daily 341,994, Sunday 1,036,393 — PHILADELPHIA, THURSDAY MORNING, JANUARY 5, 1939 — abdefgh — VOL. 220, No. 5 — THREE CENTS

ROOSEVELT WARNS DICTATORS

Today

Symbolic Parleys
Cautious Democrats
Hopkins an Issue
Senatorial Dignity
Mending a Breach

By Mark Sullivan

WASHINGTON, Jan. 4.

THESE conferrings and maneuverings between President Roosevelt and Vice President Garner are like the recent conference at Munich. And they have the same kind of outcome.

At Munich, Hitler didn't care very much whether there would be war or not. Mr. Chamberlain, on the other hand, desperately wished to avoid war. So Hitler won. In that kind of conference, the man who wishes desperately to avoid war will make great concessions. The man who doesn't much care will make few concessions.

So it is with this series of conferences and maneuvers between Mr. Roosevelt and Mr. Garner about the course of the Democratic Party in Congress.

Mr. Garner wishes desperately to avoid a split in the party. Mr. Roosevelt does not care much whether there is a split or not—certainly he does not care as much as Mr. Garner does. Consequently, Mr. Roosevelt wins the conferences.

Mr. Roosevelt wanted to make Mr. Harry Hopkins of WPA a Cabinet member. Ordinarily that would meet resistance from the conservative Democrats in the Senate, symbolized by Mr. Garner. They had abundant grievances against Mr. Hopkins. Next to Mr. Roosevelt himself, Mr. Hopkins was the official leader of the purge.

Long before the President personally took a hand, Mr. Hopkins made a direct, public effort to prevent renomination of Senator Gillette of Iowa, who had opposed President Roosevelt's Court measure. That was the beginning of the attempted purge.

For that, most of the Democrats in the Senate ordinarily would have been disposed to resist Mr. Hopkins' appointment. Even some of the so-called liberal Democrats would have joined in the resistance, for what Mr. Hopkins did was a threat to all Senators at all times, an offense to the Senate's dignity and to its spirit of fraternity.

And if the Senate Democrats did not wish to put opposition to Mr. Hopkins on the ground of his political hostility, they could put it on the ground that Mr. Hopkins is quite without experience to equip him to be Secretary of Commerce—no one pretends he is chosen for fitness.

But apparently the Senate Democrats are not going to oppose Mr. Hopkins. From persons who share Mr. Garner's point of view, come expressions which say in effect, "Oh, well, maybe he'll work out all right."

The Senate Democrats, those of the Garner type, don't like the Hopkins appointment. But they aren't willing to split with Mr. Roosevelt. They want to hold the party together, or at least create the illusion of solidarity until the 1940 Presidential election. They don't want to give offense to Mr. Roosevelt. They want him to support the ticket in 1940.

The concession of the conservative Senate Democrats on the Hopkins appointment is, as party strategy, useful all round. It not only avoids a row with the President. It saves the party from some unpleasant experiences that otherwise might have happened.

By getting Mr. Hopkins out of WPA the threat of an unpleasant agitation, possibly of a Congressional investigation, is partly averted. There is not much point in investigating Mr. Hopkins' administration of WPA—after Mr. Hopkins is in a different office. And there is less point in investigating WPA after Mr. Hopkins is out of it.

WPA, it can now be said, is in different hands, the hands of an Army officer. Further, in the shifts of posts attending Mr. Hopkins' departure from WPA, two minor officials of WPA who might have been subjects of critical agitation are removed to other departments.

By this series of maneuvers,

Continued on Page 6, Column 3

ROPER 'PARTY' SHIP'S CAPTAIN OUSTED HERE

U. S. Commissioner Suspended; Merely Obeyed Superiors' Orders, He Asserts

Suspension of Captain William T. Coad, local United States Shipping Commissioner, in connection with charges that former Secretary of Commerce Daniel C. Roper staged private parties at Government expense aboard the ship Eala, was revealed here yesterday.

Captain Coad, who by his own admission "knows more about what happened on the Eala than anyone else," commanded the Bureau of Marine Inspection and Navigation vessel at the time Roper and other officials assertedly used it for private celebrations.

FOLLOWED ORDERS

At these parties, according to a report by Acting Comptroller General Richard N. Elliott, mineral water, flowers, cigars and cigarettes were furnished by the Government through the expedient of vouchering them as "paint, provisions and supplies."

"I've done nothing I'm ashamed of," Captain Coad said yesterday.

Continued on Page 6, Column 1

Dr. Dafoe Hits Omission Of Quints on King's Trip

CALLANDER, Ont., Jan. 4 (U. P.).—Dr. Allan Roy Dafoe criticized today as showing a lack of "courtesy" to French Canadians the failure of the program for the visit of King George and Queen Elizabeth to include a stop at the home of the Dionne quintuplets.

Commenting on the Dominion government's scheduled itinerary for the British monarchs' Canadian visit next spring, Dafoe said:

"The Government is not showing much courtesy to the French in Canada. The quins are the pride of the French-Canadian race."

He said he "did not believe for one minute" that Their Majesties were responsible for Callander being left out of the program. He suggested that as the girls are wards of the King a "private visit" might be arranged.

Ickes Cancels Attack on Rep. Dies

By GEORGE E. REEDY

Inquirer Washington Bureau

WASHINGTON, Jan. 4.—A radio address entitled "Playing With Loaded Dies," which was to have been made here Friday night at a dinner for the American League for Peace and Democracy by Secretary of the Interior Harold L. Ickes, was canceled today.

Apparently the speech was to have been an attack on Rep. Martin Dies (D., Tex.), chairman of the House Committee Investigating un-American activities.

Ickes, approached for an explanation as he left a Cabinet meeting today, refused to amplify his announcement of the cancelation.

"The speech has been canceled," Ickes said, "and that is all there is to say."

Asked by reporters if the Nazis had scared him out of it, the generally voluble and explosive Interior Secretary looked toward the skies and said, "It isn't raining, is it?" and refused further comment.

Later, neither Ickes nor his asso-

Continued on Page 7, Column 1

REPUBLICANS SEEN SURE OF REGAINING 3 SEATS IN SENATE

By JOSEPH H. MILLER

Inquirer Harrisburg Bureau

HARRISBURG, Jan. 4.—Seating of the three Republican Senators-elect who were denied the right to take their oaths of office by a Democratic minority at yesterday's organization meeting of the State Senate, appeared assured today.

IN COMMITTEE'S HANDS

Senator William J. Eroe, Jr., Lawrence county Democrat who helped the Republicans capture the prized president pro tempore post, which controls committee assignments, said he would vote to seat the three Senators who were compelled to step aside under a ruling of retiring Lieutenant Governor Thomas Kennedy.

The fate of the three Republican members-elect will be placed in the hands of a Republican-controlled elections committee, which will rec-

Continued on Page 27, Column 4

'BIAS' CHARGES SNARL BALDWIN NLRB HEARING

Attorney for Works Assails Examiner On Record Order in Turbulent Session

Robert Denham, examiner for the National Labor Relations Board, who is hearing charges of unfair labor practices against the Baldwin Locomotive Works, was openly charged yesterday with being "biased and prejudiced" in favor of the NLRB.

The accusation, made by Gilbert H. Montague, attorney for the Baldwin concern, came in the midst of the second day of the hearing—a day almost entirely devoted to bickering, objections, threats of citation for contempt, and attacks of one side upon the other. Virtually no evidence was taken during the hearing, which was held at the Board of Education Building, 21st st. and the Parkway.

RULES ON RECORDS

Montague's attack upon the examiner came after Denham had ruled that original copies of the company's records, rather than photostatic reproductions, must be left in the hands of NLRB attorneys after they were introduced as evidence.

The Baldwin attorney announced that he would seek a ruling from the U. S. Circuit Court of Appeals, which has right of review over NLRB cases. Then he faced Denham and said:

"You are so obviously acting as counsel for the board, fortifying the board's testimony, that I must object that you are denying due process of law."

WARNS OF 'CONTEMPT'

In reply, Denham warned the attorney that he was "verging very close upon the area of contempt," and added:

"This hearing has been marked by more unnecessary interruptions than by facts, in the few short hours we have been sitting. There have been more interruptions than I could possibly have conceived of until now. These hearings are not conducted captiously or with any desire to infringe upon the rights of anyone."

AGREES TO OBEY RULING

At this juncture, Jack Davis, one of the NLRB attorneys, rose and declared that the Baldwin firm was trying to "impede and delay" the hearing as long as possible, "in the hope that the new Congress will in some way amend the National Labor Relations Act."

Denham clarified matters by declaring he would abide by a Circuit

Continued on Page 6, Column 6

'True Love Flight' Melts Kremlin; Couple Reunited

MOSCOW, Jan. 4 (A. P.).—Bryan Grover, whose flight for love landed him in a Soviet jail, got his wife back today, proving again that faint heart never won fair lady.

What diplomatic experts had failed to achieve in four years of effort, the square-jawed Englishman accomplished in a few weeks by making a "one-man invasion" of Soviet Russia from Stockholm last November in a second-hand plane with only three weeks' flying instruction.

OFFERED TO BECOME CITIZEN

On top of that, he carried his case to the doorstep of Josef Stalin and offered to become a Soviet citizen if necessary to regain his wife.

Whether the 37-year-old engineer would be allowed to take his wife out of Russia still was not certain, but he was with her tonight "somewhere in Moscow" after having been released by Soviet authorities.

She, too, had definitely been released from jail, and all optimists who knew anything about the case declared the Soviet Government surely would not spoil everything now by separating them again.

The impression gained in official circles was that henceforth she could do as she pleased. Apparently Grover's willingness to dare anything for the sake of a Russian girl rather pleased the Kremlin.

Grover worked in Russia as an oil specialist, fell in love with Eleana Petrovna Golius and married her in 1933. After he went to Iran to work in 1934 he was not permitted to enter the country to rejoin her or bring her out of the country.

Opposes Slash in Spending, Favors Defense Expansion

Urges Italy And Reich To Aid Jews

ROME, Jan. 4 (U. P.).—President Roosevelt has appealed to both Premier Benito Mussolini and Reichsfuehrer Adolf Hitler to aid in a general settlement of the Jewish problem, it was reported in an authoritative source tonight.

The same source said Mr. Roosevelt expressed belief that, with good will on all sides, the problem could be solved with a minimum of bitterness.

PROBLEM DISCUSSED

The appeal was made through American Ambassador William Phillips in a long conversation with Premier Mussolini, who was understood to have been asked particularly to use his influence with Hitler to facilitate efforts to reach a settlement.

An official communique confirmed that the Jewish problem had been discussed, but did not mention reports, from unimpeachable diplomatic circles, that the President had also expressed the hope that there would be no new developments which would jeopardize European or world peace.

PROPERTY RIGHT BACKED

Diplomatic sources emphasized that the general situation as well as the Jewish problem was discussed.

"Il Duce received at Venice Palace in the presence of Foreign Minister Count Galeazzo Ciano the United States Ambassador, Mr. Phillips, who conveyed a message from President Roosevelt concerning the European Jewish problem and its possible solution of a general character," the official announcement said.

The President was reported to have suggested through Phillips that Italy and Germany could facilitate the emigration of their unwanted Jews by granting them permission to take at least a portion of their worldly goods with them.

REMEDY URGED

There were certain territories in which Jewish refugees might be allowed to settle if they had funds, it was suggested.

Attention was also called to the promise made by the Fascist Grand Council in September that subject to certain conditions Jews might settle in Ethiopia. The President was said to have inquired if these conditions could be made as lenient as possible.

It was understood that Phillips described the Jewish problem as a "canker" irritating international relations and suggested that it was advisable to remove it as soon as possible.

It was understood Mussolini received the suggestions "sympathetically" and promised careful consideration.

Chamberlain, Halifax To Visit Pope Jan. 13

VATICAN CITY, Jan. 4 (U. P.).—Pope Pius will receive Prime Minister Neville Chamberlain and Foreign Minister Lord Halifax Jan. 13 at noon in his private library.

(A. P. Wirephoto)

President Roosevelt as he addressed Congress yesterday and warned the Nation that arms must be expanded to prepare for any possibility of attack.

Makes Plea For Harmony Within U. S.

Text of the President's message is on Page 4.

By WILLIAM C. MURPHY, JR.

Inquirer Washington Bureau

WASHINGTON, Jan. 4.—President Roosevelt today coupled a ringing denunciation of the dictator nations with a plea for harmony within the United States—a domestic peace which he asserted would insure ultimate victory in the event of attack by "another form of government."

The President's declaration, made in his annual message, which he delivered in person before a joint session of Congress, was generally considered to be the most forthright statement of policy in the international field made thus far during his occupancy of the White House.

Mr. Roosevelt told the legislators that world conditions made an expanded national defense program imperative.

HINTS JOINT ACTION

In one portion of his speech he hinted that the United States might be willing to co-operate in economic sanctions directed against the dictator States—a hint construed in some quarters as an amplification of his famous "quarantine" suggestion made at Chicago in October, 1937.

"We have learned that God-fearing democracies of the world which observe the sanctity of treaties and good faith in their dealings with other nations cannot safely be indifferent to international lawlessness anywhere," the President said. "They cannot forever let pass, without effective protest, acts of aggression against sister nations—acts which automatically undermine all of us.

'WAR NOT ONLY MEANS'

"Obviously they must proceed along practical, peaceful lines. But the mere fact that we rightly decline to intervene with arms to prevent acts of aggression does not mean that we must act as if there were no aggression at all.

"Words may be futile, but war is not the only means of commanding

Continued on Page 4, Column 6

DEFICIT OF 3 BILLION DUE IN NEW BUDGET

Inquirer Washington Bureau

WASHINGTON, Jan. 4.—President Roosevelt's defense of New Deal spending in his annual address to Congress today made it certain that his budget message, scheduled to go to Capitol Hill tomorrow, would presage a Federal deficit of around $3,000,000,000 in the 1939-1940 fiscal year starting next July 1.

Although details of Mr. Roosevelt's financial estimates were kept a closely guarded secret, indications were that his expenditures would total around $8,500,000,000 to $9,000,000,000, against anticipated revenue of from $5,750,000,000 to $6,250,000,000 for the period.

MAKES STAND PLAIN

The pre-judgment of the budget figures was based on United States Treasury statistics issued today to show that the Administration filed up a gross deficit of $1,601,920,303 during the first six months of the present fiscal year ending Dec. 31.

In the period from last July 1 the Government spent $4,529,205,700. In-

Continued on Page 5, Column 3

CONGRESS UNITED BEHIND ARMS PLAN

By RICHARD L. HARKNESS

Inquirer Washington Bureau

WASHINGTON, Jan. 4.—President Roosevelt's message to Congress today produced the practical effect of uniting the Senate and House behind the Administration's new foreign affairs policy of rearmament, with reservations, while driving a new political wedge between New Dealers and orthodox Democrats and Republicans over his plan to continue spending.

Comment from Senators and Representatives revealed a general stand behind the President's recommendation for a national defense program against dictatorships, but plainly showed that a stubborn bloc of anti-New Dealers would fight his determination to seek prosperity through continued expenditures from the United States Treasury.

MILD RECEPTION

Even the support pledged to rearmament was tempered by demands that Mr. Roosevelt's plans be kept within bounds, a feeling emphasized by the generally mild reception Mr. Roosevelt's words received as he spoke them into a battery of radio microphones before the ceremony and pomp of the joint session of the Senate and the House.

The historic House chamber was jammed to its very eaves for the President's message, a speech considered so important throughout the world that it was translated into German, Italian, Spanish and three other languages tonight and rebroadcast by short wave to all of Europe and South America.

The President spoke from a small platform directly in front of the Speaker's rostrum, from which Vice

Continued on Page 5, Column 1

Chair for 'Oven' Deaths Barred as Trial Opens

The Commonwealth will not press for conviction in the first degree of any of the five officials of Holmesburg County Prison who were indicted for murder in connection with the four isolation block "heat deaths" of last August.

Judge Robert E. Lamberton so instructed the jury in Room 653, City Hall, where Frank A. Craven, 39-year-old deputy warden of the prison at the time of the deaths, went on trial.

He will be tried on two bills of indictments, one charging murder and the other manslaughter, in the death of Frank Comodeca, 46-year-old prison inmate. Craven entered a plea of not guilty.

An entire day and one full panel of 47 veniremen was spent yesterday in selecting the first 10 jurors, including six men and four women. Four of the jurors are Negroes—two men and two women.

The Court's direction that no element of first degree murder was contained in the case came during the afternoon, when Assistant District Attorney John A. Boyle was questioning a prospective juror, Mrs. Kathryn Minnick, of 1150 Woodlawn ave.

Mrs. Minnick disclosed that her husband was a first cousin of Thomas J. Minnick, an attorney representing one of the other defendants in the "heat death" case—Prison Guard Francis J. Smith.

However, Boyle asked her whether she knew of any reason, including that relationship, which would pre-

Continued on Page 7, Column 2

Mrs. Roosevelt Attends Jo Davidson Showing

WASHINGTON, Jan. 4 (A. P.).—Mrs. Franklin D. Roosevelt tonight attended a benefit exhibition of busts of Spanish Loyalist Government leaders sculptured by Jo Davidson. The showing was sponsored by the Washington Sons of Spanish Democracy to aid the Spanish Children's Milk Fund.

IN TODAY'S INQUIRER

THE WEATHER

Official forecast: Eastern Pennsylvania—Rain, with slowly rising temperature today; warmer tonight; rain tomorrow, warmer in east portion.

New Jersey and Delaware—Rain, with slowly rising temperature today; warmer tonight; rain and warmer tomorrow.

Sun rises	7.22 A.M.	Sets 4.48 P.M.
Moon rises	5.01 P.M.	Sets 6.45 A.M.

Other Weather Reports on Page 2

Mark Sullivan

Democrats in Congress Worried Over What Roosevelt Will Do

WASHINGTON, Jan. 21.

The attitude of the Democratic leaders in Congress toward President Roosevelt is like the attitude of the elders of a family toward a high-spirited and somewhat wilful young child. They treat Mr. Roosevelt with a mixture of fondness and gingerliness. They aren't going to let him have his way—but they worry about what he may do.

The wish of the leaders, first and all the time, is to avoid a row, to hold the party together for the Presidential election of 1940; and that wish on their part is constantly threatened by anxiety about Mr. Roosevelt.

Mr. Roosevelt's notion about holding the party together is that the party should go his way— that was the spirit of his Jackson Day dinner address.

Mr. Roosevelt told the diners that the only path for the Democratic Party is to be wholly New Deal and always more and more New Deal. "Do this," he seemed to say, "or else"—

BACKING AWAY CERTAIN

This the party leaders will not do. They will make many concessions for the sake of unity. They will be careful to avoid repudiating the New Deal—but their idea about this session of Congress is a program which shall back a little away from the New Deal rather than go farther with it. The backing away will be cautious, with care not to hurt Mr. Roosevelt's pride—but it will be a backing away.

The attitude of the Democrats in Congress toward Mr. Roosevelt and the New Deal is accurately measured by what the House did about the first measure that came up.

Mr. Roosevelt asked for $875,000,000 for WPA. The House voted him $725,000,000—about 17 per cent. less than he asked. And just about that, to reduce the New Deal as a whole by 17 per cent., is a roughly mathematical measure of what the Democratic leaders in Congress want to do.

WHAT WILL HE DO?

But as they do it they are eternally anxious, jittery. Every time they lop a little off the New Deal they look anxiously toward the White House to see if fireworks emerge.

Mr. Roosevelt did not like the House's 17 per cent. reduction of his request for WPA money. To a press conference he spoke with resentment, and rather incited the newspaper men to take a line that would stir up resentment in the public.

Always, to the Democratic leaders in Congress, the question is, what will the President do?

What are Mr. Roosevelt's possible courses? What are the "or else's" which Mr. Roosevelt can threaten? Let us list them.

WOULD FACE BATTLE

1. He could take a determined stand that the Democratic Party in Congress must go his way. Then, to make good his stand, he could determine to run for a third nomination in 1940. Could he get the nomination? Probably he could. Certainly he could if James Farley united with him.

And if Mr. Roosevelt asked Mr. Farley to help, the request would be a strong pull on the quality of loyalty that Farley prizes greatly and has always practiced.

But, while Mr. Roosevelt could probably get the Presidential nomination from his party, winning the election would be a different matter. He would encounter the country's traditional reluctance to give a third term to any President. And he would encounter something more concrete than that. Demand for a third nomination, or seizure of third nomination, is the point at which many of the Democratic leaders would turn.

MIGHT BACK HOPKINS

That "walk" that "Al" Smith once talked about would surely take place. A considerable group of the Democratic leaders would form some kind of rump party. As a party it would not amount to much; it might not get more than a few hundred thousand votes. But the effectiveness of this gesture would lie in the very large number of Democratic voters who would be led to support the Republican ticket.

2. Mr. Roosevelt could make war on the Democratic leaders, in the form not of going after the Presidential nomination himself, but of getting it for some one whom he favors, such as Harry Hopkins, who is frequently mentioned in this connection.

This program by Mr. Roosevelt would hardly succeed. It is so unlikely to succeed that he is unlikely to attempt it. That is the point at which Farley's loyalty would feel entitled to a release.

Besides, a large majority of the regular Democratic leaders would unite in opposition to giving the nomination to any such Presidential favorite as Hopkins.

DEFEAT INEVITABLE

The Democratic leaders wish strongly to get along with Mr. Roosevelt in peace. To that end they will be willing to treat with Mr. Roosevelt about choice of the next Presidential candidate.

It is part of their program to nominate some one not repugnant to him, some one whom he will support. But if Mr. Roosevelt should, during the session of Congress, make war on the Democratic leaders and, as an incident to that war, try to nominate some outright favorite of his own he would not succeed.

3. Mr. Roosevelt can form a third party. Or can he? Starting a third party is a formidable business. The nearest example was the attempt Theodore Roosevelt made in 1912. The outcome of that was merely that Theodore Roosevelt split his own party, the Republican, and presented the Presidency to the Democrats.

In that 1912 election Theodore Roosevelt's third party carried six States, the Republicans carried two States, the Democrats carried 40 States. Something like that, with the Republican Party as the beneficiary, would happen next year if Mr. Roosevelt should undertake to start a third party.

CHANCES STRENGTHENED

All these possible courses of resentful action by Mr. Roosevelt, it will be observed, lead to the same result—a strengthening of the chances of Republican victory in 1940.

That is why none of them is likely to be attempted. The Democratic leaders do not need to fear Mr. Roosevelt as much as they do. Mr. Roosevelt, like it or not, is in the same boat with the Democratic leaders.

With this exception: Quite likely Mr. Roosevelt does not fear a party split as much as the Democratic leaders do. Mr. Roosevelt has had his two terms, as much as any President ever had. In the normal course he is at the end of his political career. Whether the Democrats win or lose in 1940 Mr. Roosevelt has his career rounded out, "in the bag," as Mr. Farley would say.

MATTER OF LIFE OR DEATH

On the other hand, to the Democratic leaders winning the 1940 election is a matter of political life and death, to each of them individually.

In any given controversy over a specific measure Mr. Roosevelt psychologically is able to make a stronger bluff than the Democratic leaders. He has comparatively little to lose. They have everything to lose.

Yet in actuality the Democratic leaders have not much to fear from Mr. Roosevelt. Nor do they have much to fear from the men around Mr. Roosevelt, the radicals.

These minor New Dealers may not like what the Democratic leaders in Congress do. They may not like the Presidential candidate the Democrats nominate in 1940. But what can the minor New Dealers do? Have a tantrum and vote the Republican ticket? Hardly that. They can join one of the existing third parties—Farmer-Labor, the La Follettes' Progressive Party, the American Labor Party.

But that, again, would be to help the Republicans.

(Copyright 1939)

Business Is Invaded By Microphotography

A year's file of a standard-size newspaper preserved for eternity in a cigar box—compression of 7000 square feet filing space into 50 achieved by microphotography, is considered by many one of the most important contributions to business research in the last decade.

Discussion of this new business method is the feature of the open forum at Gibson Institute, 12 S. 12th st., Wednesday evening, James C. Torrey, auditor, The Philadelphia National Bank, and R. A. Fliske, Controller, Gimbel Bros., will talk on the subject.

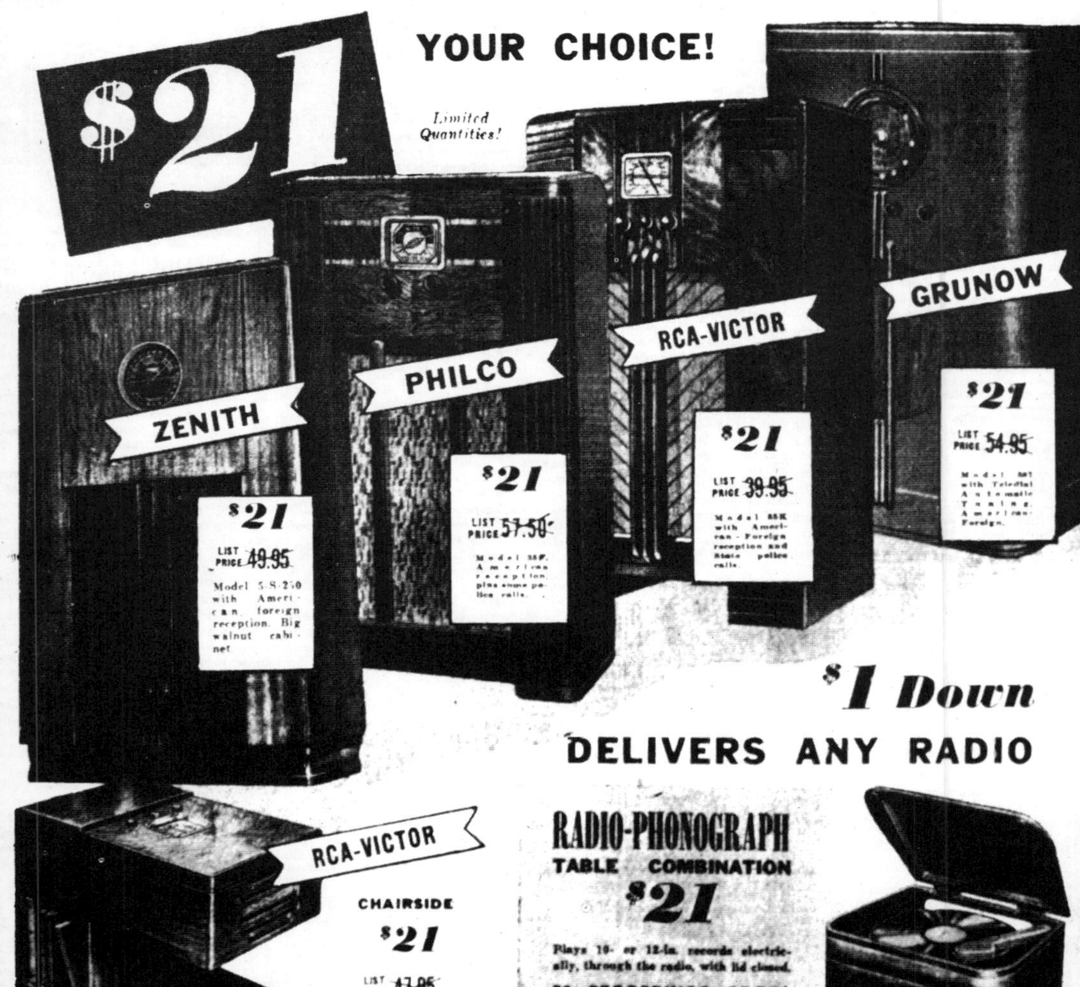

AMERICAN STORES CO.

48th Anniversary Sale!

BIG MONEY SAVING EVENT

Sensational Values!

We are gratified to see the throngs of our old friends and many new ones visiting our stores this week. Our Big Birthday Celebration is the talk of the town—value high-spot of the hour in food buying. Don't miss this big money-saving event. We mention below a few of the many big values available in our stores. Our Producer to Consumer Plan of Merchandising offers lower price levels on quality foods and you profit not only in bigger values but also in greater variety. Visit your convenient American Store today and help us celebrate; it will pay you well in real savings.

Stock Up and Save!

Your Opportunity to Save Money on Your Food Bills!

ASCO Fancy CORN 3 No. 2 cans 25c

Specially priced. Your choice of Golden Bantam or Shoe Peg.

ASCO Apricots	California Peeled	3 tall cans	25c
Calif. Apricots	Choice Whole Unpeeled	2 largest No. 2½ cans	21c
ASCO Tomatoes	Selected Hand Packed	2 No. 2 cans	19c
SPRY Shortening	pound can 18c	3 lb can	49c

Louella Sweet Cream Butter Pound Carton **32c**

America's Great Prize Winning Butter

Richland Butter pound **30c**

Creamery Prints of Quality

Gold Seal Quality Family Flour 12-lb bag **31c**

5-lb bag 15c

The ideal all-purpose family flour. Its uniformity makes your baking results dependable.

ASCO Baking Powder lb can 15c

Hi-Test Pure Phosphate Powder

Eat More Eggs for Health and Economy

EGGS Carefully GRADED doz **23c** | Gold Seal "DATED" Carton of 12 **28c**

Gold Seal Cartons are Dated for Your Protection—Assuring Eggs of Fine Quality.

Bacon ASCO Sliced No-Waste 2 ½ lb pkgs **25c**

ASCO California Golden Peaches 2 largest No. 2½ cans **25c**

Calif. Cling Peaches 2 largest No. 2½ cans 21c

Beardsley's Shredded Codfish Pkg **11c**

ASCO Cut Red BEETS 3 large No. 2½ cans **25c**

Delicious Wholesome Energy Food for Children and Grown-ups

Victor Sliced BREAD Formerly 7c NOW **5c**

Golden Valentine Layer Cake each **29c**

Wilbur's Breakfast COCOA 2 one pound cans **21c**

Wilbur's Baking Chocolate ½-lb bar **10c**

FANCY BLUE ROSE RICE	2 lbs		9c
EXTRA FANCY RICE ASCO Whole Long Grain	pound carton		9c
TOMATO JUICE COCKTAIL ASCO	2	20-oz. Jars	29c
ASCO TOMATO CATSUP Hot or Regular	10-oz bot		10c
DRIED LIMA BEANS Calif. Large	2 lbs		15c
Glenwood Fancy Grapefruit	2	No. 2 cans	19c
ASCO Pancake Flour	pkg		5c
MOTHER'S JOY SYRUP	pint bot		15c

A Blend of Pure Cane and Maple

FARMDALE TOMATOES Extra Standard	2	No. 2 cans	15c
Tender Lima Beans	3	No. 2 cans	25c
APPLE BUTTER Glenwood	2	28-oz jars	25c
APPLE SAUCE Glenwood	2	No. 2 cans	15c
BREAD CRUMBS ASCO	12-oz pkg		5c
GELATINE DESSERTS ASCO	3 pkgs		10c
FLORIDA ORANGE JUICE	2	No. 2 cans	15c
N. B. C. CAKES & CRACKERS	pkg		9c

Premium Crackers, Oreo, Social Teas, Butter Cookies, Fig Newtons

Repp-U-Tation Sweet Mixed Pickles 24-oz Jar **15c**

Re-Umberto Pure Olive Oil 3-oz bot **12c**

Picknick Sour or Dill Pickles 2 quart jars **25c**

R&R Boned Chicken 6-oz can **41c**

H-O Rolled OATS 20-oz pkg **12c**

PRINCESS Candies Chocolate Straws or Walnut Chips 6-oz pkg **10c**

King Midas Golden-Egg Noodles pound pkg **10c**

King Midas Spaghetti Dinner pkg **22c**

Hormel's SPAM 12 oz Can **29c**

Serve as is or fried with Gold Seal Eggs.

PHILLIPS Delicious BEANS 6 1-lb cans **25c**

With Pork and Tomato Sauce

Tomato or Vegetable Soup	4 10½-oz cans	19c
Vegetable Soup	large No. 2½ can	10c
SPAGHETTI	15½-oz can	5c

ELASTIC STARCH The Complete Powdered Mixture for INSTANT HOT STARCH

Special OFFER Get a New Stretch-on Ironing Board COVER

Keeps smooth ironing surface by tension of elastic cord on under side. Washable muslin. Reversible—does double duty. Mail this ad with your name and address and one Elastic box top, enclosing 10c for mailing costs to: The Hubinger Co., Keokuk, Iowa

12-oz pkg **8c**

SHEFFORD Cheese Chevelle, American or Pimiento 8-oz pkg **15c**

Heat-flo Roasted COFFEES

Heat-flo roasting ensures better, fuller flavor. With the very first cup you'll taste the difference!

Win-Crest	Mild and Satisfying	lb 15c
ASCO	Blend of the World's Finest Coffees	lb 18c
Mother's Joy	Winey and Different	pound can 20c

ASCO Orange Pekoe TEA BALLS 2 pkgs of 15 **25c**

Tea Peps You Up!

CRAX Educator Crackers **2** 1-lb pkgs **25c**

Special for Friday and Saturday Only!

PRINCESS Assorted Chocolates pound box **25c**

PRINCESS Peppermint Patties Chocolate Covered lb box 19c

OAKITE 2 10½-oz pkgs **19c**

ASCO Stuffed Large Queen Olives 7½ oz. bot **29c**

FANCY Rich, Full Cream Cheese lb **25c**

Princess Margarine 2 1 lb Prints **21c**

2 Cakes Octagon Toilet Soap for 1c

With purchase of large pkg. Soap Chips at reg. price.

Octagon Laundry Soap 5 Giant Bars 19c

Octagon Soap Powder 2 14-oz. pkgs. 9c

Herb-Ox Bouillon CUBES Beef and Chicken **2** tins of 5 cubes **15c**

Very Handy and Economical. For Soups and Sauces.

Lykit Dog Food 6 1-lb cans **25c**

Give Your Pet a Treat.

Blue Ribbon Hop Flavor—Light or Dark Malt Extract 3 lb can **55c**

Quality MEATS—New Regular LOW PRICES!

MORRELL'S PRIDE

Smoked Picnics lb **15c**

Pork Shoulders Lean Fresh Country Style lb **14c**

Long Cut Sauer Kraut	3 lbs 10c
Sliced Cooked Ham or Dried Beef	¼ lb 13c
Armour's Assorted Meat Loaves	½ lb 10c
Codfish Batter Ready to Fry	lb 12c
Sliced Lebanon Bologna	½ lb 13c
Shoulders of Lamb	lb 17c
Neck of Lamb	lb 17c

Shank End Smoked **Large Hams** (up to 8 lbs) lb **15c**

Slices of These Hams lb 32c

Canadian Style Back Bacon	¼ lb 12c
Spiced Luncheon Meat	½ lb 13c
Rich, Creamy Rice Pudding	1¼ lb pan 15c
Fish Cakes Ready to Eat	4 for 10c
Fresh Country Sausage Chester County	lb 16c
Meaty Scrapple Chester County	2 lbs 15c
Boneless Bacon Dry Cured—Hickory Smoked	lb 25c

Whole Cuts Chuck **Pot Roast** lb **17c**

Cross Cut or Boler Roast lb 29c

No. 1 Canadian Large Smelts lb 12c | Fancy Sea Trout lb 10c | Fresh Fillets Haddock lb 17c | Fresh Opened Select Oysters doz 15c

Fresh Fruits and Vegetables

Sweet Juicy Florida ORANGES	doz 15c
Large Juicy Florida GRAPEFRUIT	4 for 15c
Tasty Juicy TANGERINES	doz 12c
Stayman Winesap and Greening APPLES	4 lbs 19c
Tender, Crisp CELERY	2 big stalks 15c
Ripe Slicing TOMATOES	2 lbs 25c
Red Bliss Variety NEW POTATOES	3 lbs 14c
California BROCCOLI	2 bunches 25c

SHOP IN YOUR NEIGHBORHOOD ASCO STORE WHERE QUALITY COUNTS AND YOUR MONEY GOES FURTHEST

Prices Effective in Our Stores in Philadelphia and Vicinity

Picture Record of 'Columbia Lou' Gehrig as Fans Saw Him During His Career

Lou Gehrig, the "Iron Horse" of baseball, who set the practically unassailable record of playing in 2130 consecutive games before benching himself this spring in what was a prelude to probable permanent retirement, is shown going through the motions that made him one of the outstanding stars of all time. Left, the Yankee first baseman is seen in his most famous role—smashing out a prodigious home run. Centre, he is displaying a bit of fielding artistry around the initial sack. Right is depicted the payiff of that sock on the left, with Lou crossing the plate. An ailment diagnosed as "chronic infantile paralysis" apparently has terminated the career of the New York star.

Sportlight

Gehrig Courageous
Golf 'Hall of Fame'
Great Names of Links
First Selections Hard
Room for Women, Too

By Grantland Rice

NEW YORK, June 21.

ONLY an amazing amount of courage could have carried Lou Gehrig as far as he went in the last 18 months. This was especially true of his spring campaign, where he was trying desperately to beat down some unknown and invisible foe. He knew something had to be wrong, but he knew there was no answer.

I asked him one night in Florida if he was out of gear physically in any way.

"Not that I know about," Lou said. "I just can't seem to handle myself on the field. I just can't seem to swing a bat the way I once did. There's no reason, at least, why one can't swing a bat."

Only a slight touch of infantile paralysis, affecting the spine, is needed to break up all co-ordination, to wreck both timing and balance. Yet, week after week, Lou fought back with everything he had, trying out every scheme, hoping against fading hope that he would finally break through the bonds that kept him tightly bound. It is easy enough to see now why no one, not even Manager Joe McCarthy, could guess the answer, to what at one time looked to be one of the greatest mysteries of sport.

Golf's Hall of Fame for the United States is now getting under way. The Professional Golf Association has agreed to sponsor and support the idea we advanced some time ago and within a short while will announce the names of a nominating committee of golf writers and golf officials who will cast the opening and the annual votes.

The main scramble will come in connection with the first list selected.

You can see the possibilities ahead from such names as these—Bobby Jones, a 12-time National champion—Walter Hagen, a 12-time National or major champion—Francis Ouimet, who rode over the bodies of Vardon and Ray to bring golf back to the kids—John J. McDermott, the first of the home-borns to break up the foreign domination of English and Scotch—Gene Sarazen, winner of the U. S. and British Opens and the P. G. A.—Jerry Travers, four-time winner of the U. S. Amateur and also first in the U. S. Open.

And Chick Evans, winner of the U. S. Amateur and Open—Ralph Guldahl, consecutive National Open winner and triple Western champion—Walter J. Travis, who started golf at 36 to prove older men could win beyond 40, first to surround the British Lion at Sandwich.

With so many highlights of golf from which to pick, the hardest selections will undoubtedly be the opening group—to choose from Jones, Hagen, Sarazen, Ouimet, McDermott, Armour, Barnes, Travers, Evans and many others.

There is no reason why the women golfers should not carry out the same idea. This is a matter that should be handled and will be handled by the Women's Golf Association, which has a parade of stars to work with.

They have such champions as Glenna Collett Vare, Alexa Stirling, Marion Hollins, Mrs. Ogden Hill, the Curtis sisters, Patty Berg, Marion Miley, Katherine Hemphill, Helen Hicks, Virginia Van Wie—and on and on.

St. Louis Rallies To Defeat Phils

Continued From First Sports Page

the left field bleachers for a home run, scoring behind Slaughter and Crespi. Brown doubled to left and scored on Moore's two-bagger to the same spot. Pearson replaced Mulcahy and Mize scored Moore with a double to right-centre. Medwick flied to Marty to end the inning.

Moore, who was safe on Brown's second error of the game, was the only Phillie runner in the sixth, while Brown's single, walks to Mize and Medwick, and Owen's single was good for another pair of Red Bird runs in the sixth.

After the Phils were out in order in the seventh, C. Davis greeted Kerksieck's second pitch squarely on the nose and it landed in the bleachers.

Arnovich's double was wasted in the eighth, while a walk to Owen and Crespi's double was good for the final Cardinal tally in the eighth.

Phils Battered

PHILLIES

Bolling, 3b; Mueller, 2b; Scott, rf; Arnovich, lf; Marty, cf; May, 3b; [illegible], ss; Millies, c; Mulcahy, p; Cohle, c; Pearson, p; Kerksieck, p; aMartin; b-Young [illegible]

Totals [illegible]

ST. LOUIS

Gutteridge, 3b; Brown, ss; Moore, cf; Mize, 1b; Medwick, lf; Slaughter, rf; Owen, c; Crespi, 2b; C. Davis, p; Lang? [illegible]; King, cf [illegible]

Totals [illegible]

a-Batted for Pearson in 5th.
b-Batted for Kerksieck in 9th.

Phillies [illegible]
St. Louis [illegible]

[illegible] Runs batted in—Medwick, Mueller, Brown, Moore, Mize, Arnovich, Crespi. Home runs—[illegible] C. Davis. Sacrifices—[illegible] Double plays—[illegible] Left on bases—Phillies [illegible] St. Louis [illegible]. Base on balls—Off Mulcahy 1, Pearson 2, Kerksieck 1, Davis 2. Struck out—By Mulcahy 1, Pearson 1, Davis 1. Hits—Off Mulcahy 10 in 3 2-3 innings; off Pearson 5 in 2 1-3 innings; off Kerksieck 1 in 2 innings. Losing pitcher—Mulcahy. Umpires—Goetz, Reardon and Pinelli. Time of game—1.51.

Cleveland Beats Washington Again

WASHINGTON, June 21 (A. P.)—In a game which featured most everything except baseball, the Cleveland Indians today nosed out the Washington Senators, 9 to 8.

Enjoying a one-run lead in the 9th, Joe Krakauskas gave up a triple to Cleveland's Ken Keltner, a double to Bruce Campbell, a single to Julius Solters, threw to the wrong base and balked in a run.

In Washington's half of the 7th Cleveland's pitchers looked almost as bad. Four of them saw duty—including Bob Feller—before they stopped the Senators with three [illegible]

[illegible box score]

Totals 42 [illegible]

a Batted for [illegible]
b Batted for Appleton in 9th.
c Ran for [illegible]

Cleveland [illegible]
Washington [illegible]

Errors—[illegible] Lewis, Earl, 2, Webb, Keltner 2, Harder 2, Chapman, West, Trosky, West 2, Lewis, Campbell, Prichard. Three base hits—Keltner 2, Harder, Stolen bases—Heath, Weial, Chapman. Sacrifices—Bloodworth, Estalella, Myer. Left on bases—Cleveland 12, Washington 14. Bases on balls—Off Haynes [illegible] off Zuber [illegible] Struck out—By Harder [illegible] By Haynes 2; by Harder 1; by Krakauskas 4; by Zuber 1. Hits—off [illegible] innings; off Harder 11 in 8 innings; off Haynes [illegible]; off Hudlin 1 in [illegible]; off Zuber 0 in 1 2-3; off Krakauskas 1 in 1-3. Balk—Krakauskas. Winning pitcher—Zuber. Losing pitcher—Krakauskas. Umpires—Quinn, McGowan and Pipgras. Time—2.34. Attendance 3000.

Team's Interests Always First With Gehrig; Benched Self Because He Wasn't Helping

By PERRY LEWIS

Continued From First Sports Page

able will that marked Gehrig's entire athletic career.

REPLACED PIPP IN 1925

It was on June 1, 1925, that Gehrig, who had been seasoned with the Hartford club of the Eastern Association, replaced Walter Pipp at first base for the Yankees. From that day until May 2 of this year he was never out of the New York line-up.

During the training period this spring, Columbia Lou played far below form. He had trouble bending over for the low ones, and at the plate he was awkward as well as ineffective. With the opening of the regular season the big first baseman showed no improvement, but he played out his string until he came to its end on Sunday, April 30.

On that day Gehrig played his 2130th, and last, consecutive game. He went to bat four times against Washington, and on each occasion left men on base. That settled an issue long debated in Gehrig's own mind, and that night, in his hotel room, made up his mind to voluntarily withdraw from the line-up.

ANSWER 'OBVIOUS'

Discussing his decision two days later, Gehrig remarked:

"After blowing those four chances to do something for the team last Sunday, I went to the hotel and added things up in my own mind. The answer was obvious. It wasn't fair to the boys, to Joe, to the baseball public or to myself to stay in there any longer.

"It got to be plenty tough walking up to the plate with winning runs on the bases and leaving them there. Joe would have left me in there until the cows come home, I guess, but it wasn't doing any good."

Gehrig's final smack at the ball on April 30 in Washington was a long fly that, had it gone to right, might have nestled into the grandstand seats for a homer. But Fate ruled otherwise, and one of baseball's greatest hitters threw down his bat, probably for the last time.

UNUSUALLY STRONG

Gehrig was born of sturdy German stock in congested Upper Manhattan, and was one of a sickly family of four children. Three failed to make the grade in a struggle of the parents to rear a family in their constricted home, but Henry Louis grew from a sickly tot to a robust youngster.

As the years passed, he developed unusual strength and stamina, and early in his boyhood went in for all branches of sport, baseball, football, basketball, skating and swimming.

In 1920 he was graduated from the High School of Commerce, New York, where he was a leader in sports activities. In an inter-city championship baseball game between his school and Lane Tech, of Chicago, young Gehrig amazed baseball men by hammering a home run over the right field fence of Wrigley Field. Some years later, in 1932, he duplicated this feat twice in a game between the White Sox and the Yankees.

Aided by the privations and sacrifices of his parents, Lou was able to enter Columbia University in 1921, remaining until his junior year. He was scholastically ineligible for freshman sports, but in 1922 was a member of the Columbia grid squad and the following year alternated as pitcher and first baseman on the Lions' diamond.

At the conclusion of the college season he signed with the Yankees, playing in 13 games that year after being with Hartford most of the season. He was recalled by the Yankees late in 1924, and the following year started a consecutive game streak which will probably never be equalled.

SET MANY RECORDS

Gehrig compiled an amazing record in his 16 full years in the majors. He led the American League batsmen in 1934 with an average of .363, he scored 100 runs or more for 13 years, and shares with Babe Ruth the record for driving in more than 100 runs a year for a 13 year span leading the American League in that department five times.

At the end of the 1938 season Gehrig was second to Ruth in the greatest number of long hits—with 1190. He hammered out 535 two-base hits, 161 three basers and 494 home-runs over the 16 year span.

In 1922 he homered in six consecutive games, twice with the bases full. He was second only to Ruth in the most bases on ball in his lifetime, getting 1505 passes to Ruth's 2056.

The records credit Gehrig with a lifetime batting average of .341 for 2717 hits in 7973 times at bat. He drove in a total of 1990 runs, and struck out 787 times.

IRON IN HIS MAKE-UP

ROCHESTER, Minn., June 21 (A. P.)—Lou Gehrig, baseball's "Iron Man" showed he had iron in his makeup when Mayo Clinic physicians told him he had chronic poliomyelitis and could never again play baseball, it was disclosed today.

Discovery that he could not return to the Yankee lineup was made several days ago. Neither physicians nor Gehrig would announce the findings here, the Yankee slugger preferring to tell club officials first.

Announcement of the findings were not made to Gehrig abruptly. His knowledge of his complaint came about gradually.

Gehrig bravely received the news, merely saying:

"I suspected something was wrong." He realized, he said, that he was slowing up and seemed not greatly shocked.

The former Yankee slugger was cheerful throughout further examinations.

On Tuesday he was a guest at an informal birthday party and at no time did he show any evidence that he had heard the verdict that probably would permanently retire him from active baseball.

One of his last acts at the airport yesterday before leaving was to autograph a 10 cent baseball for a small boy.

Gehrig told clinic representatives he is prepared to adjust himself to his new condition in life.

Diagnosis

CHICAGO, June 21 (A. P.).—Dr. Morris Fishbein, editor of the Journal of the American Medical Association, made the following comment today on the diagnosis of the illness which has possibly ended Lou Gehrig's career as a baseball player.

"The diagnosis of chronic infantile paralysis used to describe a wasting of the muscles of the neck and upper parts of the body.

"It passed from general use when infantile paralysis was better known and segregated as a separate disease.

"The diagnosis of amyotrophic lateral sclerosis is a well established scientific diagnosis of a condition in which there is a hardening of the tissues in the spinal column and a wasting of the muscles dependent upon it.

Big League Baseball Facts

Continued From First Sports Page

WHAT MAY HAPPEN TODAY

AMERICAN LEAGUE

	Win	Lose
New York	.800	.782
Boston	.585	.565
Cleveland	.554	.536
Detroit	.534	.517
Chicago	.518	.500
Athletics	.400	.382
Washington	.390	.373
St. Louis	.304	.286

NATIONAL LEAGUE

	Win	Lose
Cincinnati	.661x	
St. Louis	.574	.556
New York	.544	.526
Chicago	.517	.500
Brooklyn		.500x
Pittsburgh	.463	.444
Boston	.418	.400
Phillies	.365	.346

x—not scheduled.

RUNS FOR THE WEEK

AMERICAN LEAGUE

	S.	M.	T.	W.	T.	F.	S.	Tl's
Athletics	[illegible]							11
Boston	[illegible]							18
Chicago	[illegible]							21
Cleveland	[illegible]							20
Detroit	[illegible]							18
New York	[illegible]							35
St. Louis	[illegible]							10
Washington	[illegible]							18
Totals	[illegible]							154

NATIONAL LEAGUE

	S.	M.	T.	W.	T.	F.	S.	Tls
Boston	[illegible]							12
Brooklyn	[illegible]							12
Chicago	[illegible]							19
Cincinnati	[illegible]							17
New York	[illegible]							10
Phillies	[illegible]							2
Pittsburgh	[illegible]							4
St. Louis	[illegible]							22
Totals	[illegible]							94

INTERNATIONAL LEAGUE

	S.	M.	T.	W.	T.	F.	S.	Tls.
Baltimore	[illegible]							17
Buffalo	[illegible]							24
Jersey City	[illegible]							15
Montreal	[illegible]							18
Newark	[illegible]							26
Rochester	[illegible]							16
Syracuse	[illegible]							37
Toronto	[illegible]							22
Totals	[illegible]							185

A's Option Wagner

Hal Wagner, A's third-string catcher, has been sent to Newark, of the International League, on option, it was announced yesterday. His departure made room for Harry O'Neill, young backstop recently graduated from Gettysburg College. O'Neill was coached at Gettysburg by Ira Plank, brother of the late Eddie Plank, onetime A's southpaw ace.

TEN LEADING HITTERS

NATIONAL LEAGUE

PLAYER-CLUB	G	Ab.	R	H	P.C.
ARNOVICH, PHILS	52	201	36	80	.398
BONURA, N. Y.	54	199	41	69	.347
McCORMICK, CIN.	55	219	41	75	.342
J. MARTIN, ST. L.	30	100	22	33	.330
HASSETT, BOSTON	50	183	20	60	.328

AMERICAN LEAGUE

PLAYER-CLUB	G	Ab.	R	H	P.C.
McQUINN, ST. L.	55	224	41	80	.357
FOXX, BOSTON	47	174	44	59	.339
HOAG, ST. L.	51	214	39	72	.336
HIGGINS, DETROIT	37	134	15	45	.336
SULLIVAN, ST. L.	41	131	20	44	.335

By Associated Press

HOME RUNS

AMERICAN LEAGUE

GREENBERG, TIGERS	16
FOXX, RED SOX	11
SELKIRK, YANKEES	10

NATIONAL LEAGUE

CAMILLI, DODGERS	12
LOMBARDI, REDS	11
McCORMICK, REDS	11

RUNS BATTED IN

AMERICAN LEAGUE

GREENBERG, TIGERS	55
WILLIAMS, RED SOX	54
WALKER, WHITE SOX	47

NATIONAL LEAGUE

McCORMICK, REDS	47
GOODMAN, REDS	45
CAMILLI, DODGERS	43
MEDWICK, CARDINALS	43

STOLEN BASES

AMERICAN LEAGUE

CASE, WASHINGTON	26
CHAPMAN, CLEVELAND	9

NATIONAL LEAGUE

HANDLEY, PITTSBURGH	11
HACK, CHICAGO	7

HOW THEY STAND

INTERNATIONAL LEAGUE

YESTERDAY'S RESULTS

Baltimore, 2; Jersey City, 0.
Syracuse, 4; Newark, 2 (first).
Syracuse, 11; Newark, 3 (second).
Rochester, 4; Toronto, 3.
Montreal, 8; Buffalo, 7.

HOW THEY STAND

	W.	L.	Pc.
Rochester	37	23	.617
Jersey City	36	26	.581
Syracuse	36	28	.563
Newark	33	30	.524
Baltimore	27	32	.458
Montreal	27	32	.458
Buffalo	26	33	.441
Toronto	21	39	.350

TODAY'S SCHEDULE

Montreal at Toronto.
Rochester at Buffalo.
Jersey City at Newark.
Baltimore at Syracuse.

EASTERN LEAGUE

YESTERDAY'S RESULTS

Hartford, 6; Wilkes-Barre, 5 (first).
Wilkes-Barre, 2; Hartford, 0 (second).
Williamsport, 3; Albany, 0.
Scranton, 5; Springfield, 4 (first).
Springfield, 1[illegible]; Scranton, [illegible] (second).
Binghamton, 7; Elmira, 6 (11 innings).

HOW THEY STAND

	W.	L.	P.C.
[illegible]	[illegible]	[illegible]	.608
[illegible]	[illegible]	[illegible]	.574
[illegible]	[illegible]	[illegible]	[illegible]
[illegible]	28	[illegible]	[illegible]
Albany	[illegible]	[illegible]	.482
Scranton	26	28	.481
Wilkes-Barre	25	34	.424
Hartford	19	35	.352

TODAY'S SCHEDULE

Elmira at Binghamton.
Williamsport at Albany.
Scranton at Springfield.
Wilkes-Barre at Hartford.

Dickey's Homer Wins for Yanks

NEW YORK, June 21 (A. P.)—Solving Southpaw Thornton Lee's slants for five runs in the fifth, the New York Yankees bunched all their runs into three consecutive innings today to come from behind and nose out the Chicago White Sox 9 to 8.

The clincher was Bill Dickey's seventh homer of the season with Joe DiMaggio on base in the seventh. DiMag had singled to score Tom Henrich, who had doubled.

NEW YORK	ab.	r.	h.	o.	a.	CHICAGO	ab.	r.	h.	o.	a.
Crosetti, ss	4	0	0	2	3	Hayes, 2b	5	0	2	3	4
Rolfe, 3b	5	1	2	2	3	Kuhel, 1b	4	2	0	11	1
Henrich, rf	4	2	3	3	0	K'vich, cf	4	2	2	1	0
DiMaggio, cf	4	2	2	1	1	Rad'ff, rf	5	1	2	3	0
Dickey, c	4	1	2	3	2	Walker, lf	2	3	2	3	0
Gordon, 2b	4	0	1	2	4	Appling, ss	2	0	1	1	3
Selkirk, lf	2	2	0	2	0	M'N'r, 3b	5	0	2	0	4
Dahlgren, 1b	2	1	1	12	1	Tresh, c	4	0	1	1	1
Gomez, p	1	0	0	0	2	Lee, p	2	0	0	1	0
aPowell	1	0	1	0	0	Brown, p	1	0	0	0	0
Sundra, p	2	0	1	0	1	xM'cum	1	0	0	0	0
Murphy, p	0	0	0	0	1	Rigney, p	0	0	0	0	0
Totals	33	9	13	27	18	Totals	35	8	12	24	13

a—Batted for Gomez in 5th.
x—Batted for Brown in 8th.

Chicago	0	2	2	0	2	0	2	0	0	—8
New York	0	0	0	0	5	1	3	0	x	—9

Errors—Kreevich, Gordon. Runs batted in: McNair 4, Walker 2, Appling 2, Rolfe, DiMaggio 2, Dickey 4, Sundra. Two-base hits: Kreevich, Appling, Sundra, McNair, Henrich. Three-base hit: Gordon. Home run: Dickey. Sacrifices: Dahlgren, Walker. double-plays: Appling, Hayes and Kuhel; McNair, Hayes and Kuhel; Crosetti, Gordon and Dahlgren. Left on bases: New York 5, Chicago 8. Bases on balls: Off Gomez 2; off Lee [illegible] off Brown 1, off Sundra 4, off Rigney 1, off Murphy 1. Struck out: By Rigney 1. Hits: Off Gomez 10 in 5 innings; off Sundra 2 in 3 innings (none out in 9th); off Murphy 0 in 1 inning; off Lee 9 in 4 2-3 innings; off Brown 4 in 2 1-3 innings; off Rigney 0 in 1 inning. Wild pitch: Brown. Balk: Lee. Passed ball: Dickey. Winning pitcher: Sundra. Losing pitcher: Brown. Umpires: Hubbard, Rommel and Kolls. Time: 2.20.

St. Louis Rookie Blanks Red Sox

BOSTON, June 21 (A. P.).—Rookie Jack Kramer kept 10 hits and four bases on balls well scattered today while pitching the St. Louis Browns to a 6-0 shutout over the Red Sox.

BOSTON	r.	h.	o.	a.	e.	ST. LOUIS	r.	h.	o.	a.	e.
Carey, 2b	4	0	2	3	1	Hoag, cf-rf	4	1	1	3	0
Finney, zz	1	0	1	0	0	Sullivan, rf	4	2	2	1	0
Cramer, cf	5	0	2	5	0	Laabs, cf	0	0	0	0	0
Vosmik, lf	4	0	1	2	0	McQ'nn, 1b	4	1	2	13	0
Foxx, 1b	4	0	0	10	0	Gal'her, lf	4	1	2	2	0
W'l'ms, rf	4	0	0	3	0	Clift, 3b	4	0	1	0	3
Cronin, ss	3	0	2	1	5	Glenn, c	4	1	1	2	0
Tabor, 3b	4	0	2	1	1	Ber'no, 2b	4	0	1	4	5
Peacock, c	2	0	0	2	1	Chr'an, ss	4	0	2	2	5
Heving, p	0	0	0	0	1	Kramer, p	4	0	0	0	1
Dickman, p	3	0	0	0	4						
Non'amp, z	1	0	0	0	0						
Totals	35	0	10	27	13	Totals	36	6	12	27	11

z—Batted for Dickman in 9th.
zz—Batted for Carey in 9th.

St. Louis	0	2	2	0	0	0	0	2	0	—6
Boston	0	0	0	0	0	0	0	0	0	—0

Errors—Hoag, Heving. Runs batted in—Gallagher 2, Sullivan, Clift, Glenn, Christman. Two base hits—McQuinn, Gallagher, Clift, Finney. Stolen base—Tabor. Double plays—Berardino, Christman and McQuinn; Christman, Berardino and McQuinn. Left on bases—St. Louis 3, Boston 12. Bases on balls—off Kramer 4. Struck out—by Kramer 2, by Heving 1, by Dickman 1. Hits—off Heving 8 in 2 innings; off Dickman, 4 in 7. Losing pitcher—Heving. Umpires—Summers, Grieve and Ormsby. Time—1.51.

ChicagoCubs Blank Bees, 3-0 In Tilt Halted by Rain in 8th

CHICAGO, June 21 (A. P.).—Chicago's Cubs and the Boston Bees had to suspend play at the end of eight and one-third innings on account of rain today, but not before Chicago had scored a 3-to-0 victory for its fourth straight triumph.

Bill Posedel was the losing pitcher, although he gave up only five hits, while the Bees made seven off Earl Whitehill. The Cubs, however, bunched three of their blows in the first inning, scoring two runs on singles by Stanley Hack and Billy Herman, Galan's sacrifice fly and a triple by Carl Reynolds.

The Cubs counted their third run in the fourth when Reynolds walked and Hartnett doubled. The game was called in a downpour in the ninth after Max West had doubled and Simmons had fouled out to Hartnett.

The Box Score

CHICAGO	ab.	r.	h.	o.	a.	BOSTON	ab.	r.	h.	o.	a.
Hack, 3b	4	1	1	1	2	W'ler, 2b	4	0	0	0	3
Herman, 2b	4	1	2	3	4	C'ney, cf	4	0	1	1	0
Galan, lf	3	0	0	5	0	H'sett, 1b	4	0	1	10	0
Reynolds, cf	3	1	1	2	0	West, rf	3	0	1	3	0
Hartnett, c	3	0	1	3	0	S'mons, lf	4	0	0	3	0
G. Russell, 1b	3	0	0	7	0	Ma'ski, 3b	3	0	2	0	1
Gleeson, rf	2	0	0	3	0	Miller, ss	3	0	0	3	7
Bartell, ss	2	0	0	1	2	Lopez, c	2	0	1	4	0
Whitehill, p	2	0	0	0	0	Posedel, p	3	0	1	0	1
Totals	26	3	5x25	8		Totals	31	0	7	24	12

x Game called account rain after 8 1-3 innings.

Boston	0	0	0	0	0	0	0	0	0	—0
Chicago	2	0	0	1	0	0	0	0	0	—3

Error—Herman. Runs batted in—Galan, Reynolds, Hartnett. Two-base hits—Hartnett, West. Sacrifice—Galan. Double plays—Bartell, Herman and G. Russell 2; Warstler, Miller and Hassett 2. Left on bases—Boston 7, Chicago 4. Bases on balls—Off Posedel 4, off Whitehill 1. Struck out—By Posedel 4, by Whitehill 1. Passed ball—Hartnett. Umpires—Magerkurth, Stewart and Stark.

THE TOPS IN BASEBALL

Factual biographies of the lives and accomplishments in the national pastime of baseball's selected heroes for permanent memorialization in the Baseball Hall of Fame at Cooperstown, N. Y., are contained in the new booklet "Baseball's Immortals," now ready at The Inquirer Service Bureau in Washington.

To get your copy, fill out the coupon below, enclose a dime (carefully wrapped), to cover return postage and other handling costs:

CLIP COUPON HERE

F. M. Kerby, Director,
The Philadelphia Inquirer Service Bureau,
1013 Thirteenth Street, Washington, D. C.

Here's my dime, send my copy of the booklet "Baseball's Immortals" to

Name ____
St. & No. ____
City ____ State ____

I am a reader of The Inquirer.

P1

WAR EXTRA

The Philadelphia Inquirer

PUBLIC LEDGER

An Independent Newspaper for All the People

9 A. M. EDITION

CIRCULATION: July Average Daily 381,815, Sunday 1,004,236 — PHILADELPHIA, SATURDAY MORNING, SEPTEMBER 2, 1939 — a b d e f g h i j — VOL. 221, No. 64 — THREE CENTS

LONDON, PARIS VOTE ON WAR

Nazis Batter Poland With Army, Navy, Planes; Bombed Cities Report Heavy Casualty Lists

Today

Subtle Propaganda
Britain Big Spender
Stand on War Bills
Political Fences
Treasury Inquiry

By Paul Mallon

WASHINGTON, Sept. 1.

A REALISTIC exposure of subtle propaganda methods in this country—British as well as Nazi, Japanese as well as Communist—will be tossed right into the middle of this crisis of power politics in Europe shortly.

It will indicate the British spend more money to influence our public opinion than any other nation, but all are amazingly alert in developing shrewd methods of steering American thoughts their way.

Dies Committee investigators have just finished a draft of this evidence which they have accumulated privately during the past two years and have planned to make it public at once.

Propaganda is effective only when people are unaware that it is propaganda. Acting on this theory, the investigators concentrated on producing the inside background on the distribution of foreign movie films in this country and the short-wave broadcasting from abroad. They claim to have the goods on one British film now being released.

But on the other side of the world political fence in the camp of the Communists, popular front, fellow travelers or just-strolling-along-behinds, they found a more amusing, if equally amazing, situation.

Organizations have been set up whose distribute information to the variety of strollers as to just what pictures they should see and whoop up in their neighborhoods to create a good box office—and what pictures should be boycotted.

All Bundiers, Commies and others under subpena to the Dies Committee were still in this country when the latest check was made. Committeemen rechecked when they heard about the mysterious couple boarding the German freighter Wiegand in the Delaware River, but found none of their troublesome boys and girls missing.

A canvass of the scattered Congress has been started privately by business representatives here to ascertain how far the legislators might go with Mr. Roosevelt in event of war. Results can only be superficial because a majority is out of reach, but returns so far indicate an unusual situation might arise.

The legislators polled suggest they would consider it their patriotic duty to stand by the President, but they would take extreme steps to see that the arbitrary powers granted him would last only for the duration of the war.

Each bill passed would carry a proviso requiring automatic repeal when peace arrives. Also some suggest a joint Congressional committee be appointed to work with the executive branch.

No one can tell what will happen, however, when the bands start to play.

That all-important inquiry into the Treasury's fiscal policies by the Wagner Committee seems to be developing ennui before it starts. Creditable inside reports indicate the fatigue will continue indefinitely, so no decision will be reached before the Presidential elections.

Committee authorities say the membership is strung out around the world, cannot be reassembled before Oct. 1, but the common authoritative guess is the inquiry may not start until Congress does, Jan. 1.

This means the Eccles plan of absorbing Treasury credit influences in his own Federal Reserve Board is blocked.

Presidential Secretary "Pa"

Continued on Page 6, Column 2

Two Parliaments Meet for Fateful Decision Today

LONDON, Sept. 2 (Saturday) (A. P.)—Passed through British censorship—Great Britain and France have given Germany her final warning and the British press today, virtually with one voice, accepted war as inevitable.

The press charged the responsibility to the ambitions of Fuehrer Adolf Hitler.

Both Britain and France were in full readiness to go to war in defense of Poland.

'WAR THERE MUST BE'

Typical of the British press comment was this today in the Times of London:

"Since Herr Hitler has chosen war, in spite of the many chances given to him up to the last hour to avoid it, war there must be.

"There was abundant evidence yesterday that, in Mr. Chamberlain's words, we are ready."

The newspapers proudly pointed out the smoothness with which the removal of children, women, invalids and the aged was carried out in London and other metropolitan centres.

SPIRIT IS PRAISED

It said British efficiency and spirit were better than in 1914 or 1938.

The only hope of escape was for Germany to cease her aggression and

Continued on Page 2, Column 1

PARIS, Sept. 2 (Saturday) (A. P.)—Authoritative French sources said today that Parliament would decide unanimously to support Poland by making war on Germany.

Typical comments of French leaders as Parliament assembled for the historic session:

Leon Blum, former Premier—"All is irrevocably lost. One man wished war; one man unchained it."

Henri de Kerillis, Rightist deputy—"Cannon are going to speak. Long live eternal France!"

A French-British ultimatum delivered in Germany and demanding the immediate withdrawal of German troops now invading Poland went unanswered.

France's powerful fighting forces, strengthened by general mobilization, were prepared to go to the aid of her Polish ally in war against Germany. They awaited only the word to move.

France, like Great Britain, yesterday sent Germany an ultimatum demanding an immediate halt of aggressive action and the withdrawal of German troops from Poland.

But the Nazi answer, even before the message was delivered to German diplomats preparing to leave Paris, was practically certain to be a flat "no."

SIEGE PROCLAIMED

A state of seige was proclaimed yesterday throughout France. But the fact is that the Army, Navy and Air Force have been in control of everything necessary for days in a smooth, orderly change-over from normal control by civil authorities.

In official Paris interest waned in diplomatic efforts to keep peace or find a settlement in view of the German invasion of Poland.

In spite of the situation on the German-Polish border, however, the Daladier Government found the time

Continued on Page 3, Column 4

British Anthem on Air Marks 'Crisis' Growth

LONDON, Sept. 2 (Saturday) (U. P.)—Indicative of the imminence of war the British Broadcasting Co closed its program at midnight with the National Anthem. The anthem is put on the air by B B C only on the most solemn occasions.

Bulletins

Poland Counts 130 Air Raid Dead

LONDON, Sept. 2 (Saturday) (A. P.).-(By Radio)—The British Broadcasting Company, in a news summary today, said that a Polish telegraph agency report declared 130 persons had been killed, 12 of them soldiers, in 94 German air raids on Polish territory. The number of seriously wounded, the report added, "is large."

Soviet Relieves Envoy to Reich

MOSCOW, Sept. 2 (Saturday) (A. P.).—Soviet Russia has "relieved" her Ambassador to Germany, A. S. Merkaloff, of his duties, it was disclosed today. A. A. Shkvartzeff was appointed to succeed him.

Merkaloff, who handled much of the important negotiations for the recently-signed non-aggression pact between Russia and Germany, was relieved "in connection with his appointment to other work."

Oslo Group to Stay Neutral

OSLO, Sept. 2 (Saturday) (U. P.).—The Government today announced that Norway, Denmark, Finland, Sweden and Iceland would remain neutral.

Hint Churchill Call to Duty

LONDON, Sept. 2 (Saturday) (A. P.).—(Passed Through British Censorship).—The British Press Association said today "there is a strong impression in political circles that Mr. Winston Churchill will join the Government shortly."

It added: "Mr. (Anthony) Eden's return is not regarded as so probable and it is at present too early to say what is likely to be the position of opposition leaders such as Mr. (Arthur) Greenwood (Labor), and Sir Archibald Sinclair (Opposition Liberal)."

Britain Limits Food Exports

LONDON, Sept. 2 (Saturday) (U. P.).—The Government today prohibited the export, except under license, of ground wheat and flour, tinned meats, poultry, game, condensed and dried milk, fruits and conserves, fish, sugar, exposed films and sound tracks, phonograph records, raw silk and silk yarns.

WARSAW GIRDS FOR BIG PUSH BY HITLER TROOPS

Reich Army Hurled Back on Border, Poles Assert; Gdynia Reported Shelled

WARSAW, Sept. 2 (Saturday)—(U. P.)—Poland steeled herself today in anticipation of a mighty blow from Fuehrer Adolf Hitler's war machine if Great Britain and France make their expected declarations of war against Germany.

Outwardly the Poles were jubilant at their success in repelling the first day's German attacks yesterday, but heads of the armed forces and the Government secretly were preparing for the worst.

It was believed that Hitler would strike immediately with all his power if Britain and France came in—as Poland contended they were bound to do under terms of their pledges to this country.

NATION SERENE

The Nation continued to face the situation serenely, however, and there was complete confidence that Polish defenses could take the beating sure to come.

The Government last night proclaimed a state of war and invoked the aid of Great Britain and France against German armies smashing across the frontiers and Nazi bombing planes alleged to be killing women and children mercilessly.

'FORMALLY AT WAR'

A Government spokesman said that Poland considers that she now is formally at war with Germany, but added that fighting up to midnight largely was confined to the border, with both sides making some small gains.

He said the Germans so far have lost 16 planes, an armored train and several tanks, and that Poland has lost two planes and possibly some tanks.

The spokesman said that towns bombed yesterday by German planes include Warsaw, Raomosko, Torun, Kutno, Tunel, Krakow, Krosno, Gdynia, Jaslo, Katowice, Tomasow, Puck, Tczew, Broadnica, Orotrow, Nowydwor, Augustow and others.

CHURCHES STRUCK

Catholic churches were hit at Grodno and Bidla Polaska.

The spokesman had no figures as to dead and wounded throughout the Nation but said: "They are numerous."

United Press border correspondents confirmed the statement that the fighting up to midnight was confined to border points.

No large Polish units had been engaged.

WEAKEST IN CORRIDOR

The German p sh was the heaviest in Silesia and comparatively strong in the southeast corner of East Prussia.

It was weakest in the Polish Corridor—which Adolf Hitler is determined to regain.

A spokesman said that Gdynia—modern Polish port near Danzig—was bombed continuously all day yesterday. Casualties there were "heavy."

(An Associated Press dispatch said

Continued on Page 2, Column 3

Warning

Censorship has been established over the news dispatches now being received from the major European capitals, and in the countries involved in the present crisis propaganda departments often control the news.

Although reliance may be placed in the integrity of American correspondents in their efforts to perform first class factual reporting, propaganda departments may often exert efforts to color the news.

Of these conditions The Inquirer wishes to remind its readers.

Hitler Rejects Allies' Ultimatum; Duce Decrees Italian Neutrality

LONDON, Sept. 2 (Saturday) (A. P.)—(Passed through British censorship)—The belief was general in diplomatic circles today that a British declaration of war was imminent and for the second time in 25 years, Britain looked to war to halt the march of Germany.

The parliaments of Great Britain and France were gathering this morning in the most solemn sessions they have held since 1914, as both nations awaited the official declarations of war against Germany which virtually all sources agreed were inevitable.

The entire armed forces of both allies were completely mobilized, ready to strike in behalf of invaded Poland.

These grave moves followed Fuehrer Adolf Hitler's flat Defiance of a joint ultimatum sent by Paris and London, giving him last warning that unless he immediately withdrew his troops from Poland, Britain and France would fight.

GERMANY PRESSES 'LIGHTNING WAR'

Meanwhile, Germany pressed her 'lightning war" against Poland from land, sea and air. Wave after wave of airplanes rained bombs on Warsaw and scores of other Polish cities, leaving the streets littered with non-combatant dead. There were six air raids on Warsaw alone.

Nazi troops swarmed against the Poles from three frontiers simultaneously, and ambulances began their fateful shuttling to and from the battle fronts.

REICH FLEET BOMBARDS GDYNIA

The German fleet in the Baltic Sea, blockading Poland's key port, Gdynia, was reported already bombarding the city.

To all intents and purposes the second World War was on. London newspapers were virtually unanimous in their acceptance of war as now unavoidable. High French sources stated unequivocally that the French Parliament would vote unanimously for war against Germany.

Although the actual conflict was still limited to Germany's attack upon Poland, every country in Europe, even those traditionally neutral, was mobilized down to its last man.

ITALY RULES OUT INITIATIVE

Italy declared, however, she would refrain from taking any initiative in military operations growing out of the German-Polish hostilities. Rome's declaration, although coming after Hitler's message to Premier Benito Mussolini that he did not need his help at this time, was interpreted in many foreign circles as meaning Italy would remain inactive unless her own territory was attacked.

Rumors spread of British "appeasement" on the Duce's claims in Djibouti or the Suez Canal to keep Italy neutral.

Even Bulgaria, Germany's World

Continued on Page 2, Column 1

War Summary

A full page of radioed pictures on Page 14. Additional radioed pictures on Pages 3, 4 and 9.

LONDON—The British Parliament was gathering this morning, simultaneously with the Parliament of France, for a session from which virtually every newspaper in England agreed must come a declaration of war against Germany.

PARIS—High French officials declared this morning that the French Parliament would vote unanimously for war against Germany.

WARSAW—Poland awaited a big push today after the Polish capital and scores of other cities were bombed from the air by German planes, with hundreds of civilians killed. Gdynia, key port on the Baltic, was reported bombarded and blockaded by the German fleet. Nazi troops pressed their attack on three frontiers.

BERLIN.—Declaring Germany was prepared for a 10-year war, an official spokesman voiced defiance of the ultimatum from France and England. He charged Britain was an aggressor. German officials claimed their armies were "deep in Polish territory" and that their warplanes "controlled Polish air."

ROME.—The Italian Government declared it would refrain from taking any initiative in military operations growing out of the German-Polish hostilities. The statement was interpreted in foreign circles as meaning Italy would remain inactive until her own territory is attacked.

WASHINGTON — President Roosevelt said he was confident America could keep out of the war and promised every effort in his power to do so. His appeal that warring nations refrain from bombing civilian areas brought quick agreement from Britain, Poland and France. Italy pointed out she planned no armed action. Germany did not answer.

ITALIAN NEUTRALITY DECREED BY DUCE

ROME, Sept. 1 (A. P.).—The Italian Government declared today it would refrain from taking "any initiative" in military operations growing out of the German-Polish hostilities.

The announcement, issued after a brief Cabinet meeting was called by Premier Benito Mussolini, was interpreted in foreign circles as meaning that Italy intended to stay out of war until her own territory was attacked.

The Government announced it considered that the precautionary measures of a military nature already taken were adequate.

ITALIANS RELIEVED

Announcement of the Cabinet's decision relieved Italians, whose hope of avoiding conflict had dwindled with the outbreak of fighting between Germany and Poland. They had taken some comfort earlier from Fuehrer Adolf Hitler's declaration that he did not intend calling on Italy for aid.

The official communique said the Cabinet had examined the Polish situation, "the origin of which goes back to the Versailles Treaty."

PEOPLE PRAISED

The Cabinet, said the statement, took cognizance of all documents presented by Foreign Minister Count Galeazzo Ciano which showed "the work carried out by Il Duce to assure Europe of a peace based on justice."

The communique addressed "high praise to the Italian people for the example of discipline and calm of which it has given—as always—proof."

Reflecting the general Italian hope that Great Britain and France would let Germany and Poland

Continued on Page 3, Column 1

ALLIES' ULTIMATUM DEFIED BY GERMANY

BERLIN, Sept. 1 (U. P.).—An official German spokesman tonight defied a virtual ultimatum from Great Britain and France to call off the invasion of Poland and warned that Germany is "ready to wage a 10 years' war" against what was described as British aggression.

The defiant answer to London and Paris was made by D. N. B., official German news agency, while the Reich's high command announced that three armies were smashing deep into Poland "with complete supremacy."

'PUNITIVE MEASURE'

The invasion, marked by shattering aerial bombardments of Polish

Continued on Page 3, Column 7

Roosevelt Vows Every Effort To Keep U. S. Out of War

By WILLIAM C. MURPHY, JR.
Inquirer Washington Bureau

WASHINGTON, Sept. 1.—President Roosevelt today called upon the Nation to remain calm in the face of the outbreak of European war and pledged his Administration to do everything possible to prevent American involvement in the catastrophe touched off by Nazi Germany's attack on Poland.

The White House announced tonight that the President would deliver a radio message to the Nation at 10 P. M. Sunday (E. D. T.) which would be designed to relieve so far as possible the suspense and anxiety growing out of the European crisis. The President's address will be carried on the Nation-wide chains of the three broadcasting systems.

MAY REVEAL PLANS

It was considered possible—but by no means definite—that Mr. Roosevelt might announce in his address his plans for proclaiming United States neutrality and for convening Congress in a special session to revise neutrality laws.

At his press conference, following a sleepless night during which he set in motion some of the machinery designed to protect American interests and avoid entanglement in the war,

Continued on Page 6, Column 7

THE WEATHER

Official forecast: Eastern Pennsylvania, New Jersey and Delaware—Generally fair today and tomorrow; little change in temperature.

(Daylight-saving Time)

Sun rises	6.27 A.M.	Sets 7.32 P.M.
Moon rises	9.13 P.M.	Sets 9.56 A.M.

Other Weather Reports on Page 3

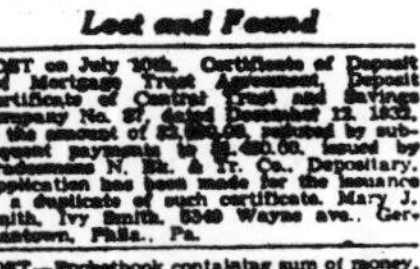

Westgate Hills

A Residential Community of Character

$4990

$490 CASH

$35.26 Total Cost Per Month

4½% F. H. A. Mortgage

Single Colonial Homes
Only 5 Minutes From 69th St. Terminal

With Twenty Outstanding Features

* Living Room 11.6x19 Feet * Spacious Colonial Dining Room * Large Kitchen with Plenty of Built-in Cabinets * Three Generously Proportioned Bedrooms * Colorful Tile Bath with Shower * Full Basement—All Stone Foundations * Large Garage—Over 20 Feet Deep * Quality Automatic Console Gas Range * Armstrong's Lifetime Inlaid Linoleum * Built-in Venetian Crystal Mirror Medicine Cabinet * Plenty of Hot Water for Domestic Use * Hardwood Floors Throughout * Finest Interlocking Zinc Weatherstripping Throughout * Built-in Recessed Sun-Ray Radiation with Hot-Water Heat * Rockwool Insulation * Copper Tubing Throughout * Abundant Closet Space with Large Guest Closet and Linen Closet * Finest Colonial Lighting Fixtures * Large-Sized Lots * Choice of 16 Distinctive Architectural Types

16 Exquisite Sample Homes Open Daily & Sunday, 10 A. M. to 9 P. M.

Furnishings in Authentic Colonial by Geo. B. Davis & Co.

DIRECTIONS: From Sixty-ninth and Market Streets drive or trolley out West Chester Pike (just three and one-half miles) to Westgate Hills, only two squares past Eagle Rd. on West Chester Pike. Follow signs to operation. 5 minutes from 69th St. Terminal.

WARNER-WEST Corporation Builders of Master-Kraft Homes — Delaware County's Foremost Home Builders — **W. S. PEACE, Inc.** Sales Agent

BUY NOW—FOR THE FUTURE AT TODAY'S LOW COST!

AMERICAN HOMES

in the 69th St. Section

SECURITY! That's a mighty important word these days. Protect your family against what the future may hold by buying an "American Home" on the new 4½% F. H. A. mortgage basis. You'll love the 3 spacious bedrooms, the breakfast nook, tile bath with shower, recreation space and garage. And you'll agree that nowhere is there a better buy in a beautiful new home.

No greater saving... **ANYWHERE**

DOWN PAYMENT—Lower than any of the five major competing homes in this price class.

MONTHLY CHARGES—Probably less than your present rent. Everything included—no extras!

UPKEEP—Solid masonry construction, copper piping, gutters, flashing, downspouting. Ten-year guarantee roof. Nothing to wear or deteriorate with age.

TAXES—Low taxes for economy. No high city taxes to burden your budget.

TRANSPORTATION—Just a step to the 69th St. Terminal served by trolleys, busses, and the subway-elevated system. One fare—only 7½c—to the center of the city.

HEATING—Quiet May oil burner included in the price. Insulated second floor makes for savings.

Only **$33.50 Monthly**

Total price $4750

Furnished Exhibit Home, 208 Wingate Road

Other "AMERICAN HOMES":

Only $35.00 Monthly

Total price $4990

Exhibit Home, furnished by Lit Brothers, at 208 Hampden Road

JOHN H. McCLATCHY, Builder

WEST PHILADELPHIA
Continued From Page 5

BUY NOW BEFORE PRICES RISE

[illegible]

"AS YE SOW— So Shall Ye Reap"

[illegible]

THE CLARKE WAY AND SAVE ON OUTLAY

W. A. CLARKE CO. SHE. 4000

OVERBROOK SECTION

THE CLARKE WAY AND SAVE ON OUTLAY

[illegible]

W. A. CLARKE CO. SHE. 4000

$3500—1741 N. 61ST ST.

[illegible]

ADOLPH B. CASPAR

[illegible]

REAL BUYS

[illegible]

Brookline Park

Overlooking the Grounds of the Haverford Township High Schools

TREMENDOUS VALUE

Brings Fine Living Within Your Reach

* A charming, restricted home community.
* Landscaped garden lots 142' deep.
* 3 bedrooms PLUS a study or nursery.
* Kitchen to delight the lady of the family.
* Large living room for beauty and comfort.
* Total monthly on 25-yr. FHA plan $41.65.

SIX DIFFERENT TYPES OF COLONIAL AND ENGLISH ARCHITECTURE

$6490

$690 DOWN 4½% FHA Mortgages

TYSON CONSTR. CO., Bldrs. — THOMAS & GRISHON, Sales Agts.

Single Homes in Sweetgum Forest Secane, Delaware County

Your Inspection Invited Open Until 10 P. M. Daily

Spring Hill

$5245 $35.15 Per Month Moderate Down Payment

Lots 56x125

Only 19 Minutes on P. R. R. to Central Phila.

Nearby Golf Courses, Tennis Courts, Etc.

Three comfortable bedrooms, tile bath, shower; living room with real log-burning fireplace, convertible into game room; big closets. Oak hardwood floors throughout.

DIRECTIONS: Baltimore Pike through Clifton Heights, turn left on Bishop Ave. Follow signs to sample furnished house.

SPRING HILL CORPORATION

Secane, Ridley Twp., Pa., Swarth. 560. — 1530 Chestnut St., Spr. 5272

Announcing...

SUCH AMAZING VALUES

IT'S HARD TO BELIEVE POSSIBLE!

LOTS 250' DEEP

Plenty of room for a tennis court, flower and vegetable gardens and a playground. The most sensational value ever heard of in Delaware County. Such features as log burning fireplaces, overhead garage doors and complete insulation are included. An extra bath or a charming sun deck can easily be added. 4-bedroom homes with 2-car garage, $500 additional.

Phone: Hilltop 737

$6490

Including OIL BURNER **$690 CASH**

Sample House Open Until 9 P. M.

HARVARD & MANOR RDS.

BROOKLINE GARDENS

STEPHAN SCHIFTER—Builder

DELAWARE COUNTY'S LANSDOWNE GARDENS — **2** — OUTSTANDING VALUES RIDLEY FARMS

LANSDOWNE GARDENS $5990

590.00 CASH, 43.65 MONTHLY

New homes in established residential community, exceptionally well constructed, with Warner waterproof concrete foundations, slate roofs, tile baths and oil burner. No extras needed.

Directions—From Baltimore Ave. turn south on Lansdowne ave. ½ mile to development. Turn left on Providence rd. to sample house.

RIDLEY FARMS $3990

390.00 CASH, 27.17 MONTHLY

Only Eight left at original Low Price. Conditions abroad are forcing material costs higher and our price must follow.

The Biggest Dollar Value in Delaware County

Westinghouse Electric Kitchen
Full Cellar — 55'x150' Lot
Paved Streets — Sewers

2 rooms from Phila.—Out Baltimore Pike to Springfield Swimming Pool. Turn left on Woodland Ave. and follow signs. About one mile to development, or out McDade Blvd. from Darby to Amosland Road, turn right 1½ blocks. Bus and Penna. R. R. transportation.

ARLEN CORPORATION

1604 WALNUT STREET — KIN. 3000

OPENING Today!

SINGLE ALL BRICK HOMES

ON EXCEPTIONALLY LARGE LOTS

In Yeadon

ONE FARE FROM CITY HALL

$300 G. E. OIL BURNER Included

$5990

$590 Cash — CARRYING CHARGES LESS THAN RENT

The most sensational home value ever offered in Delaware County. Act quickly, only 3 at this price. Large living room with 3 exposures slate roof, large unfinished third floor 3 fine bedrooms, colored tile bath with stall shower, spacious garage. In a community of new single homes.

RUNDALE AVE. at MacDADE BLVD.

Drive out Baltimore Ave. or Whitby Ave. to Church Lane, turn left to MacDade Blvd. (1000), turn right to Rundale Ave.

AGENT ON PREMISES UNTIL 9 P. M.

EVERDUR HOMES, INC. BUILDER

a HOME to Suit Every Family

242 FAMILIES HAVE BOUGHT EASIER-TO-OWN HOMES THIS YEAR

They have found Easier-to-Own homes exceptional in value—attractive, well built, located in established neighborhoods. They have found the Easier-to-Own plan suited to their budget—and giving greatest economy and protection. Investigate Easier-to-Own homes!

SEE THESE EXHIBIT HOMES • OPEN TODAY

7505 Germantown Ave. Six rooms, tile bath with stall shower, large kitchen, basement garage. Only $525 down. Total monthly carrying costs less than rent. Open Sunday 3-6 P. M.
Priestman-Helmetag Co. 18 W. Chelten Ave. Vic. 8000

4741 WHITAKER AVE. Attractive, modern home on wide street, 6 rooms, tile bath, garage. Only $450 cash. Open Sunday 2-4 P. M.
Associate Brokers Co. 3708 N. Broad St. Rad. 2050

HIGHLAND PARK Half stone single home on corner lot. Well-planted lawn. First-class condition. Only $595 cash. Can be seen by calling
KERSHAW & RANEY 51 Long Lane, Upper Darby, Pa. Gra. 1700 Blvd. 1700 Open Sun. 1-6 P. M. and Evgs.

156 MIDWAY AVE. (Lansdowne) Quiet section. 6 rooms, tile bath, garage. Out Marshall Road to Wycombe, left 2 blocks to Midway. Open Sunday 2-6 P. M.
Walnut Management Co. 1528 Walnut St. Pen. 0000

5700 BLOCK HADDINGTON ST. West Phila. Only 3 left. Modern 6 rooms, tile bath, enclosed porch. Near Overbrook High School. $500 cash.
Wm. H. W. Quick & Bro. 8 S. 40th St. Eve. 2330

7523 TABOR RD. (Burholme) Beautifully reconditioned, attractive red brick twin home. Only $510 down. Open Sunday 2-6 P. M.
HEYER-KEMNER CO. 7319 Rising Sun Ave. Pil. 7300

a PLAN to Suit Every Budget

Up to 200 Months to Pay
• Small Down Payment
• Real Savings
• No Financing Charges
• Minimum Settlement Charges
•
Sponsored by One of America's Great Financial Institutions

EASIER to OWN HOMES

SEE CLASSIFIED COLUMNS FOR OTHER EASIER-TO-OWN HOMES

WEST PHILADELPHIA

BUY THE CLARKE WAY AND SAVE ON OUTLAY
ONLY $250 DOWN
5521 Larchwood Ave.

EIGHT ROOMS. A reconditioned home with hot water heat, sun porch & breakfast room. FINANCED FREE. See it today.
W. A. CLARKE CO. SHE. 4000
111 S. 52nd St.

6824 HAZEL AVE.—3-sty., twin, h. w. ht., hdwd. flrs. $500 below assessment. Joe. Allen Potts, 4905 Baltimore Ave.

SPRUCE ST. 5844, 8 rms. & b., hot air ht. Bargain at $2500. Wm. Mack, 5238 Spruce st. Sh. 1622.

WEST PHILADELPHIA

BUY THE CLARKE WAY AND SAVE ON OUTLAY
6580 BEAUMONT AVE.

Overlooking Cobbs Creek & the Parkway. A splendid, modern home with sun porch, tiled bath & garage. $500 DOWN, financing FREE. See this "stand out" buy TODAY.
W. A. CLARKE CO. SHE. 4000
111 S. 52nd St.

GARAGE & dwelling, 12,000 sq. feet, main highway West Phila., to settle estate. K-226 Inquirer.

SACRIFICE, 48th & Greenway ave., cor., 7 rms. & bath, suitable for apts. $2500. TRIESTER, 6622 WOODLAND. SAR. 3200.

WEST PHILADELPHIA

5223 LITCHFIELD ST.

VIC. 52D ST. BELOW BALTIMORE AVE. Mod. 2-sty. home, encl. pch., 6 rms. & bth., h. w. ht., hdwd. flrs., newly papered & painted, new elec. fixtures, gas range, etc. $2350, 20% cash. Open Sun. 1 to 4. M. L. LIFSHETZ, 1318 LOCUST. PEN. 3698

LOW COST—NICE HOME

5519 Saybrook at 55th & Woodland. 6 large rms., bath, porch front, end home, excellent condition. Price only $2250. Occupant will permit inspection.
LEVITT, 1500 CHESTNUT ST. LOC. 2105

4539 SANSOM ST. Only $300 cash, balance like rent, buys this fine 6-bedroom house with 2 tile baths, porch, h. w. heat. In perfect condition. Close to transportation and schools. FULL PRICE, $4500. Immed. possession. Open for inspection.
LEVITT, 1500 CHESTNUT ST. LOC. 2105

$200 CASH buys this modern pch. home on nice wide st. Bal. amort. mtg. All chgs. paid monthly. Pen. 2488.

SACRIFICE, N. E. cor. 78th & Chelwynde ave. 2-sty. brick dwlg., lot 50x100, $1700. TRIESTER, 6622 WOODLAND. SAR. 3200.

WEST PHILADELPHIA

WYNNEFIELD AVENUE, 5411—Modern, 5 bedrooms, 3 baths, 2-car garage, oil heat, perfect condition. Owner moving out of town, must sell. Inspection and price upon request.
CABALLERO, Cyn. 1804, Gre. 1804.

OVERBROOK section, will sacrifice beaut. stone & brick home, 6 large rooms & sun parlor, real log burning f'place, tile b., stall shower, garage. Only $600 cash, monthly charges less than rent. J. W. RYAN, 23 S. 52D ST. ALL. 1411.

NOT A MISTAKE. Our price of $6500 for property in 6100 block Oxford st. is correct and we will take offer. Large lot. Stone, semi-det. 8 rooms, 2 baths, 2-car gar. LEROY A. WORRELL, Realtor-Appraiser, GRE. 4000.

$400 DOWN buys 1811 S. Cecil st. 6 r. & b., mod., vacant, move right in. Newly renovated. Key 5609 Chester ave.

7400 BLK. Elmwood ave. Mod. brick dwlg., basement gar., good cond. Bargain, $3100. TRIESTER, 6622 WOODLAND. SAR. 3200.

HAZEL AVE., 5108, 3-sty. twin, 9 r., 2 b., oil ht., comp. renov. Open Sun., 2 to 5. Small dn. payment, bal. like rent. Bar. 2217

WEST PHILADELPHIA

SALE

1455 N. Robinson st. 5 rms. Bath	$2100
1542 N. Robinson St. 6 rms. Bath	$3000
5238 Walnut st. Bargain	$3600
6022 Lansdowne av. Store & dwell.	$7000

Quinn, 6218 Lansdowne ave. Tri. 2333.

5624 WESTMINSTER AVE. Cor. of FRAZIER. Modern, enclosed porch, h. w. ht., with 2-car detached garage, with apt. above. Total monthly rent $54. Price $3000. Ebbert, Land Title Bldg. Rit. 4273

OPEN TO-DAY, 2 TO 6

Great sacrifice in price. 5237 Upland (nr. 53d Chester), 7 large rms. & bth., newly renovated basement to roof, parquetry flrs., small amount of cash. Rit. 1179.

SEE these newly decorated HOLC homes, only 10% down, 15 yr. mtg. 5948 Chester Ave. 6 rms. & bth. 5908 Oxford St., 6 rms., bath, gar. 1838 S. 68th St., 6 rms. & bath. JOSEPH H. KASS CO. RIT. 1179.

433 N. 32D ST. 3-story, 2 bath rooms; 11 rms.; lot runs to rear street. Ripe for apts. for quick sale, $1000. SLOANE, 502 Land Title Bldg. Rit. 4273.

5943 NASSAU RD.—Mod. sun parlor home, h.w. ht., gar. On one of the nicest sts. in Overbrook, $4500. May consider offer. Harry J. Perry, Land Title Bldg. Spr. 7980.

MORTGAGEES Sale. Only $300 cash required, balance same as rent. 6018 Greenway ave., desirable 2-sty., side yard, modern porch dwelling. Cresse, 1328 Chestnut.

WEST PHILADELPHIA

117 N. Edgewood, vacant, renov.	$350 cash
5838 Carpenter st., vacant	$600 cash
5213 Lebanon ave., gar., mod.	$500 cash
5617 Litchfield st., modern	$500 cash

J. Lipschutz, 521 S. 60th st. Gra. 5803.

42 N. HIRST, A-1 condition	$2300
727 N. 67th, 6 rms., tile bath, gar.	Offer
824 Marlyn rd., C. P. heat, beaut.	Offer
5125 Master, 6 r., det., gar., oil burner	$4200

CELLA MANAGEMENT, ALL. 7611

SACRIFICE

To settle estate. Corner store & 14 garages, 2 apts. Make offer. 432-34-36 N. 61st st. Call Wav. 3832.

CONESTOGA, S., 531, near 54th & Cedar ave.—Modern 2-sty. porch-front dwelling. 6 rms. & b., hot water heat, newly renovated, $2950. Financing arranged. Samuel Stern, N. E. cor. 15th & Locust sts. Pen. 8247

6101 ELLSWORTH STREET, 4 bedrooms, tile bath with shower, enclosed porch. Attractive modern decorations. Thoroughly reconditioned. William Pugh, 5713 Market St. Gra. 3300.

5450 MEDIA Street, 4 bedrooms, 1st floor lavatory, h. w. heat, tile bath, model kitchen. An unusual bargain, $2750. Raymond S. Erb, 1474 N. 52d st. Tri. 3560.

5844 DELANCEY ST. 6 rms. & bath. Porch. Hwd. flrs., h. w. heat, convenient to transportation & shopping. $2600. Will finance. LEVITT, 1500 CHESTNUT ST. LOC. 2105

Continued on Page 10

GERMANTOWN

7505 GERMANTOWN AVE.

Facing acres of beautiful lawns this modern home is convenient to schools, stores, churches, trains, trolleys, and buses. It contains 6 good size rooms, tile bath with stall shower, an exceptionally large kitchen and basement garage. It has been thoroughly reconditioned and re-decorated, and can be bought for only $525 down and total monthly carrying charges less than rent. No finance or conveyancing chgs. Open for inspection 3 to 6 today. Many others in Gtn. and West Oak Lane on equally easy terms. This is the time to buy. Priestman-Helmetag, Vic. 8000.

405 W. MT. AIRY AVENUE

will be open for inspection today from 3 to 6—and it's well worth seeing. There's a centre hall, large living room with enclosed sun porch, well proportioned dining room, full size breakfast room, 4 bedrooms, tile bath with stall shower, garage. Entire house reconditioned like new and decorated in quiet taste. At $5950 it's the best buy on the west-side. Many others in Gtn. and West Oak Lane at today's prices. Priestman-Helmetag, Vic. 8000.

BARGAINS!

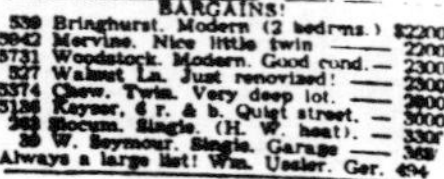

539 Bringhurst. Modern (2 bedrms.)	$2200
5942 Mervine. Nice little twin	2200
5731 Woodstock. Modern. Good cond.	2300
527 Walnut La. Just renovized!	2300
5374 Chew. Twin. Very deep lot.	2800
5126 Kayser. 6 r. & b. Quiet street.	3000
283 Slocum. Single. (H. W. heat).	3300
39 W. Seymour. Single. Garage	[illegible]

Always a large list! Wm. Ussler. Ger. 494

YANKS BEAT REDS, 7-4, TO SWEEP SERIES

The Philadelphia Inquirer
PHILADELPHIA, MONDAY MORNING, OCTOBER 9, 1939

DiMaggio
Sullivan
Werber
Pinelli
Dickey
Lombardi
Crosetti

(A. P. Wirephoto)

Here's the daffy finale of the Series at home plate in the 10th inning yesterday. Lombardi, Cincinnati catcher, is still sprawled on the ground after doing a flip-flop in trying to tag Keller (not shown). Crosetti had scored in front of Keller. Di Maggio, whose single on which Goodman erred, had sent in the two runners, sensing Lombardi's predicament, also has raced across the plate. Werber has rushed in to aid the catcher, but it's too late. Sullivan is the batboy.

La Salle College Gridders Beaten by Scranton, 12-7

Invaders Triumph by Scoring Two Touchdowns in First Half; 68-Yard Drive Features Explorers' Attack

By EDWARD J. KLEIN

Scranton University's football forces came down from the coal region yesterday and exploded La Salle College's hopes of enjoying its first unbeaten season since 1934 by whipping the Explorers, 12 to 7, before 7500 spectators at McCarthy Stadium, 20th st. and Olney ave.

Led by the punting and passing of Joe Flaherty and Lester Dickman, two brilliant backs who played together at Scranton Central High before entering college, the Tommies whirled over two touchdowns in the opening half to record their sixth victory in the eight-year-old rivalry.

Halted on Scranton's one-yard line late in the first period and stopped at the Tommies' 30 in the second session, LaSalle's gallant gladiators marched 68 yards on just three plays in the third quarter to score their only touchdown.

BYNON LEADS ATTACK

Fleet-footed Bill Bynon, sophomore halfback from Kingston, Pa., was the spearhead of the Explorers' scoring surge. Bill flung a perfect pass to John Pilconis, junior left end, for a first down on the Tommies' 34, then sliced 33 yards through centre to the one. Then, Steve Brody, senior quarterback, crashed into the end zone. With Brody holding, Bynon converted the extra point with a placement that split the uprights. Since Scranton has missed the con-

Continued on Page 21, Column 3

The Lineup

La Salle.	Positions.	Scranton
Pilconis	Left end	Tomasello
Meno	Left tackle	Bove
Loughney	Left guard	Cerra
Baddick	Centre	Solfanelli
Mandarino	Right guard	Patrick
Pisanic	Right tackle	Yantorn
Biezup	Right end	Turley
Deschak	Quarterback	Dickman
Prettyman	Left halfback	Stascavage
Kosteva	Right halfback	Flaherty
Lochetto	Fullback	Rogalla

La Salle	0	0	7	0 - 7
Scranton	6	6	0	0—12

Touchdowns—Turley, Shonesky, Brody. Point after touchdown—Byon. Substitutions—La Salle, ends, Hunt, Zatoris; centre, Lacek; backs, Sullivan, Cairns, Brody, Bonder, Gidjunas, Williams; tackles, Petro, Pakenas; guards, Filipone. Scranton tackles, Martinelli, Cippicani, Andrejack; backs, Barnscheuer, Shonesky; ends, Falkie, Wasnetsky; guards, Kenosky, Moran.

Officials Referee, J. A. Glascott, Catholic U.; umpire, H. S. Herzog, Temple U.; head linesman, C. S. Rogers, U. of Penna.; field judge, John H. Brinton, U. of Penna.

STATISTICS

	Scranton	La Salle
First downs	12	8
First downs (rushing)	7	4
First downs (passing)	5	4
Yards gained (rushing)	152	83
Penalties, against,	4 for 50 yards	2 for 10 yards
Total yards gained	335	170
Total yards lost	32	7
Forwards attempted	17	11
Yards gained forwards	182	83
Passes intercepted by	1	3
Number of punts	9	10
Average distance (from line of scrimmage)	34.3	42.7
Kicks returned	86	52
Fumbles	1	3
Own fumbles recovered	0	2

Pro Redskins Hand Dodgers 41-13 Defeat

WASHINGTON, Oct. 8 (A. P.).—The Washington Redskins piled up their biggest score in three years today in a 41-13 victory over the Brooklyn Dodgers, before 27,092 and stayed in a first place tie with the New York Giants in the National Football League.

Sammy Baugh, the Redskins' passing star, was out because of injuries, but Frank Filchock ably filled his place. Andy Farkas and Dick Todd, a freshman on the squad, carried the brunt of the running attack. Another freshman, Bob Russell, a big tackle from Auburn was a standout in the Washington line.

The game was close for three periods, but the Redskins ran wild for 20 markers in the final quarter.

REDSKINS TAKE LEAD

Washington took a 7 to 0 lead when Filchock collected a touchdown with a short plunge on the end of a 42-yard advance. Bob Masterson added the extra point. In the second period, the Reds made it 14 to 0 when Jimmy German, rookie from

Continued on Page 21, Column 5

Canisius Defeats Niagara Eleven

BUFFALO, N. Y., Oct. 8 (A. P.).—A fast, scrappy and outweighed Canisius College football team snapped at every opportunity and upset Niagara University, 19 to 0, on a rain-soaked field here today.

Niagara (0)	Pos.	Canisius (19)
	Left end	Haber
	Left tackle	Zaso
	Left guard	Frank
	Centre	Toth
	Right guard	Mazuca
	Right tackle	Centofanti
	Right end	Propis
	Quarterback	Quarantillo
	Left halfback	Marinaccio
	Right halfback	Coniglio
	Fullback	Colella

Score by periods:

Niagara	0	0	0	0— 0
Canisius	0	13	0	6—19

Canisius scoring—touchdowns, Colella, Frank, Haber. Point after touchdown, Coniglio (place kick).

Referee, W. H. Friesell, Princeton; umpire, ... Goodwin, Washington and Jefferson; head linesman, H. J. Benzoni, Colgate, field judge, Dr. W. E. Bachman, Buffalo.

Sigel-Dudley Win Lady-Pro Golf Crown

By FRED BYROD

Helen Sigel and Ed Dudley, Philadelphia Country Club's long-hitting team had to play nine holes before they could gain an advantage yesterday at Old York Road in the final of the Philadelphia Lady-Pro golf championship, but then they finished out the match with customary celerity, winning by 3 and 2 from Mrs. Frank O'Neill, Jr., and Joe Kirkwood, Huntingdon Valley.

While Mrs. O'Neill and Kirkwood, the medalists, twice had been carried extra holes, the Country Club team never had to play past the 16th and finished the selective drive-alternate stroke tournament's four 18-hole match play rounds 13 up and 12 to play.

On the front nine, the Country Club cannoneers matched men's par. But even so, they were never up until Mrs. O'Neill, who had been doing some remarkable "pressure" putting, finally missed a two-footer for a par and a half at the 9th.

WINS FOUR IN ROW

Miss Sigel and Dudley carried their winning streak to four consecutive holes by taking the 10th with a par four and the 11th with a one-over-par five. This put them three up and they coasted home. With a

Continued on Page 22, Column 3

On Series Firing Line

By JAMES C. ISAMINGER
Inquirer Sports Reporter

CINCINNATI, Ohio, Oct. 8.—Cincinnati was banished from the World's Series tournament by the butter-fingers route today. The Yankees tabbed three soiled runs in the 10th to win their fourth straight classic in straight sets.

Both teams were malefactors on the defense and Red Rolfe was a sinful Yankee, for his fumble on a hard chance in the 7th gave the Reds three unearned runs that kept New York from winning in regulation innings.

Only one hit was concocted by the Yankees in the winning 10th and it scored three runs, because a brace of boots was attached.

Cincinnati is baseball mad tonight. Mad at the Reds, especially Shortstop Bill Myers, who betrayed Bucky Walters with two hideous errors that meant runs to the Yankees.

Looked as if the Reds were going to win as they came from behind to get a two-run lead at the end of the eighth.

Johnny Murphy, who followed Hildebrand and Sundra on the peak, was the winner, and Bucky Walters, Philadelphia boy, the loser. Of the five runs scored off Bucky, three were unearned.

The Series ended in solemn silence.

Continued on Page 20, Column 2

4th Game Box Score

NEW YORK YANKEES

	Ab.	R.	H.	2b	3b	HR.	TB.	Rbi.	SB.	SH.	O.	A.	E.
Crosetti, ss	4	1	0	0	0	0	0	0	0	0	2	3	0
Rolfe, 3b	4	0	0	0	0	0	0	0	0	1	1	3	1
Keller, rf	5	3	2	0	0	1	5	3	0	0	2	0	0
Di Maggio, cf	5	2	2	0	0	0	2	1	0	0	3	0	0
Dickey, c	5	1	1	0	0	1	4	2	0	0	10	0	0
Selkirk, lf	4	0	1	1	0	0	2	0	0	0	1	0	0
Gordon, 2b	4	0	1	0	0	0	1	0	0	0	0	3	0
Dahlgren, 1b	4	0	0	0	0	0	0	0	0	0	11	0	0
Hildebrand, p	1	0	0	0	0	0	0	0	0	0	0	0	0
Sundra, p	1	0	0	0	0	0	0	0	0	0	0	0	0
Murphy, p	2	0	0	0	0	0	0	0	0	0	0	3	0
Totals	38	7	7	1	0	2	14	5	0	1	30	12	1

CINCINNATI REDS

	Ab.	R.	H.	2b	3b	HR.	TB.	Rbi.	SB.	SH.	O.	A.	E.
Werber, 3b	5	0	2	0	0	0	2	1	0	0	0	1	0
Frey, 2b	5	0	0	0	0	0	0	0	0	0	3	4	0
Goodman, rf	5	1	2	1	0	0	3	0	0	0	4	0	1
McCormick, 1b	4	1	2	1	0	0	3	0	0	1	7	1	0
Lombardi, c	5	0	1	0	0	0	1	0	0	0	5	0	1
Craft, cf	1	0	0	0	0	0	0	0	0	0	1	0	0
Berger, lf-cf	5	0	0	0	0	0	0	0	0	0	4	0	0
Myers, ss	3	1	1	0	1	0	3	0	0	0	2	1	2
Derringer, p	2	0	1	0	0	0	1	0	0	0	1	0	0
Simmons, lf	4	1	1	1	0	0	2	0	0	0	3	0	0
a-Hershberger	1	0	1	0	0	0	1	1	0	0	0	0	0
Walters, p	1	0	0	0	0	0	0	0	0	0	0	0	0
Totals	41	4	11	3	1	0	16	3	0	1	30	8	4

a-Batted for Derringer in 7th inning.

NEW YORK YANKEES	0	0	0	0	0	0	2	0	2	3—7
CINCINNATI REDS	0	0	0	0	0	0	3	1	0	0—4

Left on bases: New York Yankees 5, Cincinnati Reds 9. Base on balls: Off Derringer 2, Sundra 1, Walters 1. Struck out: By Hildebrand 3, Derringer 2, Sundra 2, Murphy 2, Walters 1. Hits: Off Hildebrand, 2 in 4 innings; off Sundra, 4 in 2 2-3 innings; off Murphy, 5 in 3 1-3 innings; off Derringer, 3 in 7 innings; off Walters, 4 in 3 innings. Winning pitcher: Murphy. Losing pitcher: Walters. Umpires: Pinelli, plate; McGowan, first; Reardon, second; Summers, third. Time of game: 2.04.

Champions Jubilant, Reds Quiet, Wait for Next Year

By CHARLES DUNKLEY

CINCINNATI, Oct. 8 (A. P.).—Joseph Vincent McCarthy, kindly 51-year-old leader of the New York Yankees, was the happiest man in the baseball world tonight.

Deacon Bill McKechnie, boss of his vanquished Royal Reds, was the saddest.

McCarthy, with just a trace of a tear in his eye, joined with the Yankees in the noisiest clubhouse victory celebration they have ever staged. He was supremely happy because his players had just presented him with a fourth world's championship and their ninth consecutive World's Series victory.

First of the Yankee players to storm into the dressing room were Shortstop Frank Crosetti, Left Fielder George Selkirk, and Second Baseman Joe Gordon. After yelling out a few piercing "yippees" and "hurrahs," the real celebration started.

Graying Art Fletcher, one of the coaches and McCarthy's first lieutenant, jumped on a trunk and broke out into the familiar song "The Sidewalks of New York."

Al the players joined in, with McCarthy standing beside Fletcher. After the last words of the song bounded into the rafters Fletcher jumped from the trunk to McCarthy's back.

In walked William Harridge, president of the American League, extending his hand in congratulation.

Continued on Page 20, Column 2

New York Takes 4th Game in 10th Inning As Three Cincinnati Errors Ruin Walters

National Leaguers Lead in Eighth, But Defense Collapses in Last Two Sessions as Champions Tie and Capture Contest; Murphy Winning Hurler; Keller and Dickey Crash Home Runs

By CY PETERMAN
Inquirer Sports Reporter

CINCINNATI, O., Oct. 8.—The bloom is off the rose, the class has left "October's Classic" and the New York Yankees have stalked to their fourth straight world's championship at baseball.

While history repeated itself like a busted phonograph record,. the Cincinnati Reds, maladroit stooges to the greatest band ever assembled on the diamond, today thrust a fourth victory in a row upon the men of McCarthy, and, 20 years after, repaid in clumsy fashion that gift of 1919.

The score of the final game was 7-4 in 10 innings, with the Reds descending to low comedy and bush tactics to insure their loss.

FAIL HURLING MATES

Those Reds threw down, before the grief-stricken gaze of 32,794 loyal Cincinnati burghers, their pitching ace, Paul Derringer, and his partner in pennant triumph, Bucky Walters, and that after three American League castoffs had arisen from the slough of despond to snatch apparent victory from the Yankees.

It was the poorest exhibition of sandlot jitters since the 1938 Cubs went rubber-kneed in this same finale, and when the patrons walked in profound silence from Crosley Field they had indeed been the victims of a gigantic fraud. For they had paid as high as $100 for admission to what is billed as the "cream of baseball," and they were treated to anything else but.

In the seventh inning, thanks to the resurrected Al Simmons, Bill Werber and the rookie obtained from New York's A-A farm in Newark, Will Herschberger, the Reds had overcome a 2-0 Yankee lead compiled on homers by "King Kong" Keller and Bill Dickey, and added in the eighth one more marker to make it 4-2.

DEFENSE MELTS

But in the ninth, with Walters relieving the arm-weary Derringer, heroic figure amid a bunch of stumblebums, the Reds' captain, Billy Myers, blew a double play throw and in the 10th the whole Red defense went to jelly.

In that critical session, which will live long and somberly in the memories of all Redland, the huge and stolid catcher, home-run hitter and civic hero of Cincinnati, Ernesto Schnozzola) Lombardi, a pathetic figure throughout the four games, reached a crossroads in his relations with our national pastime.

A tired and distraught man, his spirits ebbing like the wind from a punctured tire and with the abandon of a man diving off a cliff, he sat down on home plate while the runs poured in.

BLUSH FOR FANS

The incident deserves more than passing mention, for it forms, possibly, the nadir in another National League performance, over which every right-thinking fan must hide a blush.

Here's what happened:

Walters, the score tied 4 to 4 as a result of Myers' dropping Lonnie Frey's throw in the ninth for a dou-

Continued on Page 20, Column 3

Yankees Get $5,614.26 Each

CINCINNATI, Oct. 8 (A. P.).—The $5,614.26 each of the New York Yankees won today as the winner's individual share of the World Series playing pool fell only $168.50 short of equaling the all-time high for players shares in a four-game series.

The record of $5,782.76 was set last year as the Yankees took four straight from the Chicago Cubs. Players share only in receipts of the first four games.

Each of the losing Cincinnati Reds received $4,282.58 compared to the four-game series record of $4,674.87 which each Cub received last year as "consolation" for the same kind of four straight drubbings the Reds took.

In 1938 there was no sale of radio rights such as that which added $60,000 to the players pool this series.

The all-time record winning players' share was $6,544.76, by the Detroit American League club in 1935 when the series went six games.

The players pool this series was $380,117.84, the third highest in history. The largest pool was $460,-002.66, in 1936, when the Yankees played the New York Giants six games.

Reading Germans Beat Upper Darby Booters

READING, Oct. 8.—With Francis Nelis, former Philadelphia Phoenix forward, pacing the National Soccer League champions, the Reading German Americans defeated the Upper Darby booters, of Philadelphia, 7-1, here in today's exhibition match on the Germania Stadium pitch.

Series Facts

YESTERDAY'S RESULT

New York, 7; Cincinnati, 4 (10 innings).

HOW THEY FINISHED

	W.	L.	P.C.
New York	4	0	1.000
Cincinnati	0	4	.000

SERIES AT A GLANCE

FIRST GAME

		R.	H.	E.
Cincinnati	000 100 000	1	4	0
New York	000 010 001	2	6	0

Batteries: Derringer and Lombardi, Cincinnati; Ruffing and Dickey, New York.

SECOND GAME

		R.	H.	E.
Cincinnati	000 000 000	0	2	0
New York	003 100 00x	4	9	0

Batteries: Walters and Lombardi, Hershberger, Cincinnati; Pearson and Dickey, New York.

THIRD GAME

		R.	H.	E.
New York	202 030 000	7	5	1
Cincinnati	120 000 000	3	10	0

Batteries: Gomes, Hadley and Dickey, New York; Thompson, Grissom, L. Moore and Lombardi, Hershberger, Cincinnati.

FOURTH GAME

		R.	H.	E.
New York	000 000 202 3	7	7	1
Cincinnati	000 000 310 0	4	11	4

Batteries: Hildebrand, Sundra, Murphy and Dickey, New York; Derringer, Walters and Lombardi, Cincinnati.

ATTENDANCE AND RECEIPTS

FOURTH GAME

Attendance	32,794
Receipts	$150,243.82
Players' Pool	$ 76,624.35
Commissioner's Share	$ 22,536.57
Clubs' and Leagues' Share	$ 51,082.90

FOUR GAME TOTALS

Attendance	183,849
Receipts	$745,329.09
Players' Pool	$380,117.84
Commissioner's Share	$111,799.36
Clubs' and Leagues' Share	$253,411.89

abdef

CLOUDY

The Philadelphia Inquirer

PUBLIC LEDGER

An Independent Newspaper for All the People

6 A. M. EDITION

CIRCULATION: November Average Daily 397,095, Sunday 1,073,541 a b d e f g h MONDAY MORNING, DECEMBER 18, 1939 Second Largest 3c Morning Circulation in America THREE CENTS

NAZIS SCUTTLE GRAF SPEE

Today

Draft-Pepper Move

Heartening Thought

Duty to Respond

Close-Up of Dewey

James as Compromise

By John M. Cummings

NEW YORK, Dec. 17.

IN the last sentence of his speech at the dinner of the Pennsylvania Society of New York last night, George Wharton Pepper gave expression to a thought encouraging to Republicans who have launched a drive to draft him as their candidate for United States Senator.

Recipient of the Society's gold medal for distinguished public service, the former Senator said: "I am going to hang it (the medal) up where every morning it will radiate inspiration for the day's work. And the lesson which I shall learn from it is this—Pennsylvania expects every man to do his duty."

It is quite well known, of course, that Mr. Pepper does not relish the prospect of again running for public office.

It is equally well known that several other Republicans of renown are quietly nursing an ambition to sit in the Senate, and because of this situation there is a growing fear the party is driving into a cat and dog fight.

Since Pennsylvania, as Mr. Pepper has so well said, expects every man to do his duty, the implication is plain insofar as he is concerned. A considerable number of his fellow citizens believe it is his duty to respond to the call.

As these Republicans scan the political landscape they see in the Philadelphia lawyer the one hope of avoiding a primary contest which unquestionably would impair party prospects in the State in the election next November.

It so happened that the gold medal was presented to Mr. Pepper in the name of the Society by former Senator David A. Reed. He and Pepper served together in the Senate. Mr. Reed is one of several outstanding Republicans with an eye on the Senate nomination.

Chief Justice Kephart, who has been taking soundings in the State, was among the several hundred Pennsylvanians here for the dinner. Another prospective candidate, State Senator G. Mason Owlett, a member of the Republican National Committee, was not on deck.

It is no reflection on the fitness or the capability of the more or less active candidates to suggest that as of this day and date Mr. Pepper looks like the one man most likely to harmonize the party for the primaries.

If Mr. Pepper should respond to the draft, Mr. Reed would drop out of the picture. It can be put down as a certainty they would not enter a contest. It is felt, too, that neither Justice Kephart nor Senator Owlett would care to challenge Mr. Pepper.

Should Pepper refuse to run, however, it would take a lot of maneuvering to clear the field in favor of any one of the candidates now marshaling their forces.

The draft-Pepper movement, therefore, results from the widely held conviction that as a compromise candidate he would not invite opposition of a serious nature and the party would be spared a lot of unnecessary blood-letting in the spring campaign.

It is not expected Senator

Continued on Page 36 Column 2

6 Shopping Days Until Christmas

NEEDY MOTHER ADMITS TORSO KILLING OF SON

Smothered Him, Cut Up Body, She Says; Inquirer Puzzle Leads to Capture

A picture story of the torso murder appears on Page 16 and the mother's own story of how and why she killed her son is on Page 9.

By GEORGE M. MAWHINNEY

Just 24 hours after the headless, legless torso of a little boy was found in Berks st. west of 45th, a phlegmatic sergeant in the 19th and Oxford sts. police station last night dipped his pen in the ink and inscribed the following line:

"Tillie Irelan, 35, 15th st. near Montgomery ave.—charge, murder."

Tillie Irelan is the baby's mother.

PICTURE PUZZLE IS CLUE

She was "booked" last night on a charge of suffocating the child and dismembering its body after she had been tracked down through a single clue provided by a picture puzzle in The Inquirer—one of the newspapers in which the body was wrapped.

At the same time police arrested as a material witness Theodore Thompson, 43, of Park ave. above Oxford st., a gas station employee who they said had been a close friend of the woman. Detectives emphasized belief that he knew nothing of the killing.

Police said it appeared likely the woman killed her child because she wanted more time to devote to her friendship with Thompson. Weeping at the police station after her arrest, Thompson himself declared: "I didn't even know she had a kid. I just asked her to come live with me and she said she would."

HOMICIDE CHARGED

A charge of homicide was lodged against Mrs. Irelan after she had confessed killing the baby "because I couldn't support him" and after police had found in her room a suitcase containing the child's head and limbs.

Last night she was taken to City Hall, fingerprinted and photo-

Continued on Page 9, Column 1

'Mysterious Mrs. Peck,' Adviser of Wilson, Dies

NORWALK, Conn., Dec 17 (A. P.).—Mrs. Mary Allan Hurlbert Peck, known to the world as "the mysterious Mrs. Peck" when she was mentor and adviser of the late President Woodrow Wilson, died today in a hospital here after a five-week illness.

Few, if any, knew the true identity of the 75-year-old woman who lived in virtual obscurity during the last five years in Westport although at least two biographers of Mr. Wilson credited her with moulding the life and political career of the World War President.

(A. P. Wirephoto)

CROWDS WATCH GRAF SPEE'S LAST MOMENTS AFLOAT

This picture, radioed from South America and received here at 2 A. M. today, shows the battle-scarred Admiral Graf Spee steaming out past the Montevideo breakwater toward her watery grave. Crowds on shore, visible in the foreground, had no way of knowing what the outcome of the tense drama would be. A few minutes after the photograph was taken the pocket battleship was scuttled, on orders from Fuehrer Adolf Hitler.

Hitler's Orders Send Battleship to Bottom; Crew Safe

Thousands in Montevideo Watch As Explosions Wreck Craft; Germany Protests Uruguay's Ban

A full page of pictures on the Graf Spee on Page 18

By HAROLD K. MILKS

MONTEVIDEO, Dec. 17 (A. P.).—Proud and powerful marauder of the high seas, the Nazi pocket battleship Admiral Graf Spee was blown up and sunk tonight to save her from defeat and destruction at the point of British naval guns. Official Berlin sources declared the scuttling was done at the personal order of Fuehrer Adolf Hitler.

Captain Hans Langsdorff and "every member of the crew" which went out to scuttle the Graf Spee were reported by officials to have reached safety aboard other boats before the 10,000-ton war monster, her hull shattered and her wreckage aflame from the explosions of internal mines, sank in 25 feet of water three miles from shore within sight of the city.

FREIGHTER CAPTAIN ARRESTED

The German freighter Tacoma, still carrying two or three hundred members of the crew, anchored in Montevideo harbor late tonight. The captain immediately was arrested for violating a port-closing order earlier in the day, and Uruguayan authorities said they would intern all Graf Spee crewmen who remained in Uruguayan waters. The remainder of the crew—about 700 men—were reported en route to Buenos Aires aboard tugs and launches and will surrender to the Argentine Government.

Capt. Langsdorff and other ship's officers also were reported headed for Buenos Aires aboard a Graf Spee launch.

CAPTAIN LAST TO LEAVE SHIP

Langsdorff, last to leave his ship, sent a bitter wireless ashore from the bridge before he gave the order to abandon ship, protesting that Uruguay's refusal to let the Graf Spee remain in the harbor later than this evening "leaves me no alternative than to sink my ship near the coast and save my crew."

The alternatives he refused were to resume the battle with British warships outside the harbor from which he fled last Wednesday night, his ship split by British shells, or to let his ship be interned for the rest of the war.

The pocket battleship, which had sunk at least nine British freighters in far-ranging raids, was blown up less than two hours after she had steamed slowly away from her anchorage and headed south out of Montevideo harbor.

CREW TAKEN ABOARD FREIGHTER

Capt. Langsdorff and the other ship's officers were reported to have escaped by ship's launch. Other members of the crew tumbled over the side into a small fleet of rescue tugs and

Continued on Page 2, Column 1

72 BRITISH KILLED IN FIGHT WITH SPEE

Illustrated on Page 6

LONDON, Dec. 17 (A. P.).—The three British cruisers which engaged the German pocket battleship Admiral Graf Spee suffered 72 killed and 31 wounded in the battle, the Admiralty disclosed today.

"In the severe and well-fought action of the 13th (Wednesday)," the Admiralty said, 61 men were killed and 23 wounded on board the cruiser Exeter.

Five officers were killed and three

Continued on Page 6, Column 3

IN TODAY'S INQUIRER

Eye-Witness Stories

Vivid Descriptions Of Graf Spee Scuttling Given by Observers

Editor's note: The following eye-witness description of the sinking of the Admiral Graf Spee is by a United Press staff correspondent who circled over the German pocket battleship in an airplane as she was blown up.

By ROSCOE SNIPES

MONTEVIDEO, Dec. 17 (U. P.).—I watched from the vantage point of an airplane while explosions wrecked the doomed German pocket battleship Admiral Graf Spee and she sank in the estuary of the River Plata.

The pilot with whom I flew risked his life and mine to get as near the Nazi sea raider as possible. We were about 2000 feet high and less than half a mile from the Graf Spee when the first explosions came—apparently from time bombs placed in the ammunition magazines.

GREAT FLASH OF FLAME

We were drawing nearer the Graf Spee, after a dash out over the sea to re-check the location of waiting British warships, when the battleship exploded.

I was looking directly at the ship which floated, to all appearances peacefully, on the water.

Suddenly a great flash of flame leaped high in the air from her single funnel amidships.

THICK, BLACK SMOKE

A column of thick black smoke belched up after the flame.

I had just looked at my watch, which read 7.52 P. M. (5.52 E. S. T.).

Because of the roar of the plane's motors, we could not hear the explosions which we knew were taking place.

We had followed the Graf Spee's every move from the moment she pulled her anchors and put out towards the sea.

I was at the Montevideo Airport when word was telephoned the pocket battleship would leave the harbor as

Continued on Page 3, Column 4

By FRED G. HYDE

By overseas telephone an eye-witness in Montevideo gave The Inquirer last night a vivid first-hand account of the sinking of the crippled German pocket battleship, Admiral Graf Spee, three miles outside Montevideo harbor.

The eye-witness, Harry Stanley Smith, former Boston business man, watched the ship's destruction with binoculars from the ninth floor of the Hotel Nogaro, in Montevideo's central square.

SAILED AT TWILIGHT

"It was twilight and we were having tea in the hotel," he said, "when word came that the Graf Spee had lifted her anchor and was about to make her dash outside.

"I scrambled to the ninth floor with eight British sea-captains, former prisoners of the Spee, who had been

Continued on Page 3, Column 6

ORDER TO SINK SPEE CAME FROM HITLER

BERLIN, Dec. 18, Monday (U. P.).—Fuehrer Adolf Hitler personally ordered that the pocket battleship Graf Spee be blown up and sunk at Montevideo because the Uruguayan Government "declined to grant the time necessary to make the ship seaworthy," it was announced early today.

Although the news of the scuttling of the 10,000-ton pride of the German navy took the German people by surprise there had been a hint of such action last night when an official statement asserted that the pocket battleship had "fulfilled her task."

NAVY HEAD CONSULTED

Hitler took the decision after conferring lengthily with Admiral Erich Raeder, commander-in-chief of the navy, and other high advisers at the Chancellory.

"Regarding the sinking of the armored cruiser Admiral Graf Spee it is made known that the Fuehrer and the highest commander gave the order to Capt. (Hans) Langsdorff to destroy the ship through its own explosion inasmuch as the Uruguayan Government declined to

Continued on Page 3, Column 5

The War on Pneumonia

Greatest of Mass Killers Target of Penna. Offensive

First of a Series

By JOHN M. McCULLOUGH

Pennsylvania has declared war on one of the greatest mass-murderers in the history of mankind!

Survey the campaigns of history's great captains — Genghis Khan, Tamerlane, Philip of Macedon, Alexander, Caesar, down to the modern era—and there is one captain before whom all must bow in respect to his untiring superiority in the art of murder—

Pneumonia!

He strikes with deadly savagery at the two extremes of the human scale—infancy and old age—but his worst devastation is the most productive period—the middle years.

For centuries beyond number pneumonia regularly has killed from 25 to 40 out of every 100 persons who fall its victims.

POWERFUL WEAPONS

By the middle of next year the State Department of Health, through the co-operation of private physicians and their organized medical groups, hope to have effectively treated a minimum of 12,000 cases of the disease in Pennsylvania with either or both of the two most power-

Continued on Page 36 Column 1

Spee's Captain Safe on Launch

MONTEVIDEO, Dec. 17 (A. P.).—Three hours after the German raider Admiral Graf Spee had been scuttled by her crew outside Montevideo harbor, the port inspector tonight wirelessed the Uruguayan cutter Huracan these instructions:

"The German launch may proceed wherever the German commander desires."

This apparently placed Capt. Hans Langsdorff, the Spee's commander, aboard one of the scuttled vessel's launches, somewhere in the mouth of the River Plata. Other reports had hinted he had blown himself up with his ship.

Report Hitler Offered Reward to Save Spee

LONDON, Dec. 18 (Monday) (U. P.)—The Daily Sketch in its "Inside Information" column asserted today that Fuehrer Adolf Hitler offered Capt. Hans Langsdorff a reward of 1,000,000 marks if the Graf Spee reached home safely.

The Fuehrer said, however, according to the column, that he preferred the warship be scuttled rather than fall into British hands or that anything happen which would permit the British to claim "a great naval victory."

THE WEATHER

Official forecast—Eastern Pennsylvania: Partly cloudy today; cloudy followed by rain tomorrow; not much change in temperature.

New Jersey and Delaware: Fair today; increasing cloudiness tomorrow, followed by rain in afternoon or night; not much change in temperature.

Sun rises—7.16 A. M. Sets—4.36

Moonrises—11.48 A. M. Sets——

Other Weather Reports on Page 3

Trotzky Analyzes World Chaos From Mexican Haven

Interview Bares Stalin's Motives

Nazi Pact Unpopular, Finland Invaded to Save Face

Continued From First Page

days over them, then wrote the answers in Russian. Next they were translated by an aide into English, after which Trotzky edited them. One of his American secretaries, James O'Rourke, a New Yorker and university graduate, next went over them for clarity—and Trotzky edited them again.

The questions and his roundly developed answers of the causes behind the present world conflicts and of what may be learned from these conflicts to date follow:

In discussing the present conditions in the Soviet Republic, Leon Trotzky 12 years after he was forced by Stalin into exile has this to say: "It would be childish to think that the collaboration of Stalin and Hitler is founded on mutual confidence. These gentlemen understand each other too well."

Did Stalin Have to Make Alliance With Hitler?

WHAT is your opinion of the German-Russian alliance? Did Stalin have to make it? If so, what could he earlier have done to avoid it? Russia, in going into the Baltic States and Finland, contended it was compelled to do so to properly defend itself against aggression. Do you believe there was any likelihood of Nazi aggression? Do you believe there was any likelihood of an attack by the capitalist democracies?

TROTZKY:

FOREIGN policy is an extension and development of domestic policy. In order to understand correctly the Kremlin's foreign policy, it is always necessary to take into account two factors: on the one hand, the position of the U. S. S. R. in capitalist encirclement and, on the other, the position of the ruling bureaucracy within the Soviet society.

The bureaucracy defends the U. S. S. R. But above all it defends itself inside the U. S. S. R. The internal position of the bureaucracy is incomparably more vulnerable than the international position of the U. S. S. R. The bureaucracy is merciless against its disarmed adversaries inside the country.

But it is extremely cautious and sometimes even cowardly before its well-armed external enemies. If the Kremlin enjoyed the support of the popular masses and had confidence in the solidity of the Red Army, it could assume a more independent position in relation to both imperialist camps. However, reality is different. The isolation of the totalitarian bureaucracy in its own country threw it into the arms of the nearest, the most aggressive and therefore the most dangerous imperialism.

Already in 1934 Hitler said to Rauschning: "I can conclude an agreement with Soviet Russia whenever I wish." He had categorical assurances on this account from the Kremlin itself. The former chief of the foreign G. P. U. agency, General Krivitsky, revealed extremely interesting details of the relations between Moscow and Berlin. But, for the sensitive reader of the Soviet press, the Kremlin's real plans have been no secret since 1933. Above all Stalin was afraid of a great war. In order to escape it he became an irreplaceable aid to Hitler.

'United Front' Drive Not a Sheer Swindle

However, it would be incorrect to conclude that the five-year campaign of Moscow in favor of a "united front of the democracies" and "collective security" (1935-1939) was a pure swindle as is represented now by the same Krivitsky who saw from the quarters of the G. P. U. only one side of the Moscow policy, not perceiving it in its entirety. While Hitler spurned the extended hand, Stalin was compelled to prepare seriously the other alternative, that is, an alliance with the imperialist democracies.

The Comintern naturally did not understand what was involved; it simply made "democratic" noises, carrying out the instructions.

On the other hand, Hitler could not turn his face toward Moscow while he needed the friendly neutrality of England. The spector of Bolshevism was necessary above all in order to prevent the British Conservatives from eyeing with suspicion the rearmament of Germany. Baldwin and Chamberlain went even further; they directly aided Hitler in forming Greater Germany as a powerful base in Central Europe for world-wide aggression.

Hitler Had No Choice But Pact With Moscow

Hitler's turn toward Moscow in the middle of the past year had a substantial basis. From Great Britain Hitler had received all that was possible. One could not expect Chamberlain to grant Hitler Egypt and India in addition to Czecho-Slovakia. Further expansion of German imperialism could be directed only against Great Britain itself.

The Polish question became a turning point. Italy stepped cautiously aside. Count Ciano explained in December, 1939, that the Italo-German military alliance, signed 10 months before, excluded the entrance of the totalitarian Allies into a war within the next three years.

However, Germany, under the pressure of its own armaments, could not wait. Hitler assured his Anglo-Saxon cousin that the annexation of Poland was on the road to the east and only to the east. But his conservative adversaries grew tired of being duped. War became inevitable. Under these conditions, Hitler had no choice; he played his last trump, an alliance with Moscow. Stalin finally attained the handshake of which he had dreamt unceasingly for six years.

Frequent assurances in the democratic press that Stalin deliberately sought to provoke a world war by his alliance with Hitler are to be considered absurd. The Soviet bureaucracy fears a great war more than any ruling class in the world; it has little to win, but everything to lose.

Counting on the world revolution? But even if the thoroughly conservative obligarchy of the Kremlin were striving for the revolution, it knows very well that war does not begin with revolution, but ends with it, and that the Moscow bureaucracy itself will be thrown into an abyss before the revolution comes in the capitalist countries.

During the Moscow negotiations of the past year, the delegates of Great Britain and France played a rather pitiful role. "Do you see these gentlemen?" the German agents asked the rulers of the Kremlin.

"If we divide Poland together, they will not so much as move their little finger." While signing the agreement, Stalin, with his political limitations, could expect that there would not be any great war. In any case, he bought himself the possibility of escaping for the next period the necessity of involvement in a war. And nobody knows what is beyond "the next period."

Invasions Inevitable Results of Alliance

The invasions of Poland and of the Baltic countries were the inevitable result of the alliance with Germany. It would be rather childish to think that the collaboration of Stalin and Hitler is founded on mutual confidence; these gentlemen understand each other too well.

During the Moscow negotiations last summer, the German danger could and had to appear not only very real but also quite immediate. Not without Ribbentrop's influence, as was said, the Kremlin supposed that England and France would not make a move against the accomplished fact of the subjugation of Poland and that consequently Hitler might gain a free hand for further expansion toward the east. Under these conditions the alliance with Germany was completed by material guarantees taken by Russia against its ally.

Quite probably the initiative, even in this sphere, belonged to the dynamic partner, that is Hitler, who proposed to the cautious and temporizing Stalin that he take guarantees by force of arms.

Naturally the occupation of Eastern Poland and the formation of military bases in the Baltic did not create absolute obstacles for the German offensive: the experience of the last war (1914-18) testifies sufficiently to this.

Alliance With Nazis Unpopular in Russia

However, the moving of the border to the west and the control over the eastern Baltic coast represents indubitable strategic advantages. Thus in his alliance with Hitler and on Hitler's initiative, Stalin decided to take "guarantees" against Hitler.

Not less important were the considerations of internal policy. After five years of uninterrupted agitation against Fascism, after the eliminations of the old guard Bolsheviks and of the general staff for their alleged alliance with the Nazis, the unexpected alliance with Hitler was extremely unpopular in the country.

It was necessary to justify it with immediate and brilliant successes. The annexation of Western Ukraine and White Russia and the peaceful conquest of strategic positions in the Baltic States were designed to prove to the population the wiseness of the foreign policy of "the father of nations." Finland upset these plans a bit.

determine the question of invasion of neighboring States.

The defense of an isolated workers' State depends much more on the support of the laboring masses all over the world than on two or three supplementary strategical points. This is proven incontrovertibly by the history of foreign intervention in our civil war of 1918-20.

Robespierre said that peoples do not like missionaries with bayonets. Naturally that does not exclude the right and duty to give military aid from without to peoples rebelling against oppression.

Police Methods Repel Masses of World

For example, in 1919 when the Entente strangled the Hungarian Revolution, we naturally had the right to help Hungary by military measures. This aid would have been understood and justified by the laboring masses of the world.

Unfortunately we were too weak . . . at present the Kremlin is much stronger from the military point of view. However, it has lost the confidence of the masses both inside the country and abroad.

If there were Soviet democracy in the U. S. S. R.; if the technological progress were accompanied by the increase of Socialist equality; if the bureaucracy were withering away, giving place to the self-government of the masses, Moscow would represent such a tremendous power of attraction, particularly for its nearest neighbors, that the present world catastrophe would inevitably throw the masses of Poland (not only Ukrainians and White Russians but also Poles and Jews) as the masses of the Baltic border States on to the road of union with the U. S. S. R.

At present this important precondition for revolutionary intervention exists, if at all, in a very small degree. The strangling of the peoples of the U. S. S. R., particularly of the national minorities, by police methods, repelled the majority of the toiling masses of the neighboring countries from Moscow.

The invasion of the Red Army is seen by the populations not as an act of liberation, but as an act of violence, and thereby facilitates the mobilization of world public opinion against the U. S. S. R. by the imperialist Powers. That is why it will bring in the last instance more harm than advantage to the U. S. S. R.

Strategy Was Right But Weather Wrong

WHAT is your opinion of the Finnish campaign from the military standpoint: as to strategy, equipment, leadership both military and political, the matter of keeping up communications and the general training of the Red troops? What is likely to be the result of the Finnish campaign?

TROTZKY:

AS FAR as I can judge, the strategical plan, abstractly considered, was sufficiently correct; but it underestimated Finland's power to resist and ignored such details as the Finnish winter, conditions of transportation, supplies and sanitation. In his satirical verse on the Crimean campaign of 1855, the young officer, Leo Tolstoy, wrote:

"Easily written on paper,
But the gullies forgotten.
And we had to march in them."

Stalin's decapitated and demoralized General Staff repeats textually the strategists of Nicholas I.

On the 15th of November last I wrote to the editor of one of the most widely read American weeklies: "During the next period Stalin will remain Hitler's satellite. During the coming winter he will in all probability make no moves. With Finland he will conclude a compromise."

Shameful Defeats Compromise Kremlin

Facts showed that my prognosis was incorrect on this final point. The error was provoked by the fact that I ascribed to the Kremlin more political and military sense than it demonstrated in reality. Finnish resistance, it is true, placed the prestige of the Kremlin at stake, not only in Estonia, Latvia and Lithuania, but also in the Balkans and Japan. Having told A, Stalin was compelled to tell B.

But even from the point of view of his own ends and methods, he didn't have to attack Finland immediately. A more patient policy could never have compromised the Kremlin as much as have its shameful defeats in the course of 11 weeks.

Moscow discovers now that no one expected a rapid victory and makes references to the frost and blizzards.

Astonishing argument! If Stalin and Voroshiloff can not read military maps, they can, one should expect, read the calendar; the Finnish climate could not have been a secret to them.

Stalin is capable of utilizing energetically a situation that has ripened without his active participation, when the advantages are without question and the risk at a minimum. He is a man of the apparatus. War and revolution are not his element.

When foresight and initiative are necessary, Stalin knows only defeat. Such was the case in China, Germany and Spain. Such is the case of Finland.

Not the physical climate of Finland is decisive, but the political climate of the U. S. S. R. In the Russian Bulletin edited by me, I published in September, 1938, an article in which I subjected to an analysis the causes for the weakening and direct decomposition of the Red Army.

It clarifies sufficiently, according to my opinion, both the present failures of the Red Army and the growing difficulties in industry. All the contradictions and defects of the regime always find a concentrated expression in the army. The enmity between the laboring masses and the bureaucracy corrodes the army from within.

Personal independence, free investigation and free criticism are no less necessary for the army than for the economy. Meanwhile the Red Army officers are put under the control of political police in the form of careerist commissars.

Independent and talented commanders are being exterminated; the others are destined to constant fear. In such an artificial organism as the army where preciseness of rights and duties is inevitable, nobody in reality knows what is permissible and what is tabu.

The thieves and chiselers operate behind a patriotic front of denunciations. Honest people become disheartened. Alcoholism spreads and more vividly. Chaos reigns in the military supplies.

Parades celebrated on Red Square are one thing, the war is quite another. The planned "military stroll" into Finland converted itself into a merciless accounting of all aspects of the totalitarian regime. It uncovered the bankruptcy of the leadership and the inadequacy of the high commanding staff appointed because of its servility rather than for its talent and knowledge.

Besides, the war uncovered an extreme lack of proportion in the different branches of Soviet economy, in particular the poor state of transportation and various kinds of military supplies, especially of provisions and clothing.

The Kremlin constructed, not without success, tanks and planes, but neglected sanitations, gloves and boots. The living man who stands behind all machines was completely forgotten by the bureaucracy.

The question of whether the defense of "one's own" from foreign invasion or an offensive against another country is involved, has an immense and in some cases decisive importance for the mood of the army and the nation.

Genuine Zeal Needed For Offensive War

For an offensive revolutionary war are necessary a genuine enthusiasm, extremely high confidence in the leadership and great skill in the soldier. Nothing of this was shown in the war Stalin undertook without technical and moral preparation.

The final result of the struggle is predetermined by the relation of forces. The half million of the Red army will strangle the Finnish army in the end if the Soviet-Finnish war does not resolve itself in the next few weeks into a general European war. Possibly the shift in the military situation will come about even before these lines appear in the press.

In this case the Kremlin, as has occurred already during the ephemeral successes in the beginning of December, will try to supplement the military aggression by a civil war inside Finland. In order to include Finland in the framework of the U. S. S. R.—and such is now the obvious aim of the Kremlin—it is necessary to Sovietize her, i. e., carry through an expropriation of the higher layer of landowners and capitalists. To accomplish such a revolution in the relations of property is impossible without a civil war.

The Kremlin will do everything in order to attract to its side the Finnish industrial workers and the lower stratum of the farmers. Once the Moscow oligarchy finds itself compelled to play with the fire of war and revolution, it will try at least to warm its hands. It will undoubtedly achieve certain successes in this way.

But one thing can be said now with assurance: No subsequent successes can blot out from world consciousness what has happened so far. The Finnish adventure already has provoked a radical re-evaluation of the specific weight of the Red army which had been extraordinarily idealized by some foreign journalists devoted—we suppose disinterestedly—to the Kremlin.

All partisans of a crusade against the Soviets will find in the military failures of the Kremlin a serious argument. Doubtless the impertinence of Japan will increase and that may create difficulties along the road toward a Soviet-Japanese agreement which actually constitutes the main task of the Kremlin.

Already one can assert that if exaggeration of the offensive capacities of the Red army characterized the former period, now begins a period of underestimation of its defensive strength.

It is possible to foresee also other consequences of the Soviet-Finnish war.

Army Failure May Force Retreat of Bureaucracy

The monstrous centralization of the entire industry and commerce from top to bottom such as the compulsory collectivization of agriculture, were determined, not by the needs of Socialism, but by the greed of the bureaucracy to have everything without exception in its hands. This repugnant and by no means necessary violence against the economy and the man that disclosed itself clearly enough in the Moscow "sabotage" trials, found its cruel punishment in the Finnish snow drifts.

It is quite possible, consequently, that under the influence of military failures the bureaucracy will be compelled to make an economic retreat. It is possible to expect the re-establishment of a kind of NEP, that is, of the controlled market economy on the new, higher economic level. Whether the bureaucracy will succeed in saving itself by these measures is another matter.

Invasion of Balkans Awaits Hitler Word

WHAT would be the wisest action for Stalin to take today in Rumania, considering the possible political, social and military implications?

TROTZKY:

I THINK that the Kremlin itself, particularly after the Finnish experience, will consider in the next period as "wisest" not to touch Rumania. Stalin can move against the Balkans only in agreement with Hitler, only in order to aid Hitler—at least until Hitler's strength is not undermined, and this is not at all near. At present Hitler needs peace in the Balkans in order to obtain raw materials and to maintain his ambiguous friendship with Italy.

From both a military and political point of view, Rumania is another edition of Poland, if not worse. The same semi-feudal oppression of peasants, the same cynical persecution of national minorities, the same mixture of lightmindedness, impertinence and cowardliness inside the ruling stratum personified by the King himself.

However, if the initiative of the hostile camp compels Hitler and Stalin to upset the unstable peace of the Balkans, the Red Army will enter Rumania with slogans of agrarian revolution and probably with greater success than in Finland.

Red Invasion of India Not Impossible Feat

WHAT can or must Stalin do in the Balkans generally, in the light of present events? In Persia? In Afghanistan?

TROTZKY:

THE Soviet armed forces have to be ready to defend a vast area with insufficient means of communication. The world situation dictates the necessity, not of dispersing the army in separate adventures, but of maintaining it in powerful concentrations.

If, however, Great Britain and France — with some co-operation from Germany—consider it necessary to undertake a war against the Soviet Union, the situation will be radically changed. In this case it is not excluded that the Soviet cavalry may try to invade India through Afghanistan; technically the task is not unrealizable.

The former Sergeant-Major of the Czarist Army, Budenny, may be destined by history to ride a white horse in the role of a "liberator" of India. But this is in any case a rather distant perspective.

Bolshevism's Napoleon: Ex-New York Tailor

If Lenin was the father of the Russian Revolution, then Leon Trotzky was its uncle. But the uncle was exiled when Stalin came to power, and Trotzky for the past 13 years has charged that his and Lenin's revolution was betrayed by Stalin.

The fiery orator and military tactician who organized Russia's Red Army and became known as "the Napoleon of Bolshevism" has found a haven in Mexico, and there he dwells in a suburban villa, writing all day long at his monumental "life of Lenin" and innumerable other books and articles.

The police guard his home, which is the headquarters of his Fourth Internationale, set up in opposition to Stalin's Third Internationale. He lives a scholar's life, but all his hopes and ambitions are bound up in the desire to oust the Stalin regime. He has followers all over the world, and they have reportedly increased recently, because of the turn of events in Russia.

Like those of other Bolshevik leaders, Trotzky's name is an assumed one. He was born Lev Davidovitch Bronstein and as a youth was an active revolutionary in Russia, and served several terms in prison. He escaped from Siberian exile in 1902, obtained a false passport, sardonically assumed the surname of his most recent jailer, and fled to London.

He was a New York tailor when the Russian Revolution broke out, and he returned to his native land. He attained high place among the Soviets, was the first Commissar of Foreign Affairs, became War Minister, and directed the Red Army through the civil war of 1919-20. But he made many enemies, and when Lenin died in 1924, Stalin came to power, and Trotzky was stripped of his offices, expelled from the party, and sent into exile in 1927.

His exile carried him through Turkestan, Turkey, France, Sweden and Norway to Mexico. Now 60, he lives peacefully with his wife, Natalia, and an entourage of secretaries, writing and hoping for "the day."

Invasion Hurt Soviet In Opinion of World

DO YOU, as the former head of the Red Armies, feel it was necessary for the Soviets to move into the Baltic States, Finland and Poland, to better defend themselves against aggression? Do you believe that a Socialist State is justified in extending Socialism to a neighbor State by force of arms?

TROTZKY:

IT cannot be doubted that control over the military bases on the Baltic coast represents strategical advantages, but this alone cannot

Little Hope Held For Quick Peace

Contradictions Between Rivals 'Too Irreconcilable'

CONSIDERING Russia's vastness and its numerous borders and actual and potential enemies, what is its immediate future?

TROTZKY:

THE invasion of Finland indubitably provokes a silent condemnation by the majority of the population in the U. S. S. R. However, at the same time, the minority understands and the majority feels, that behind the Finnish question, as behind the question of the errors and crimes of the Kremlin, stands the problem of the existence of the U. S. S. R.

Its defeat in the world war would signify the crushing not only of the totalitarian bureaucracy but also of the planned State economy; it would convert the country into a colonial booty for the imperialist States.

The peoples of the U. S. S. R. themselves have to crush the hated bureaucracy. They cannot bestow this task on either Hitler or Chamberlain.

The question is whether as a result of the present war, the entire world economy will be reconstructed on a planned scale, or whether the first attempt of this reconstruction will be crushed in a sanguinary convulsion, and imperialism will receive a new lease on life until the third World War which can become the tomb of civilization.

THE Soviets are generally credited with having made a strong defense and having, in effect, defeated the Japanese at Changkufeng in the summer of 1938. Do you believe this was a test case of Soviet arms and, if so, do you believe it caused Hitler to look in other directions than the Ukraine?

TROTZKY:

THE Red Army, as was said above, is incomparably more powerful on the defensive than on the offensive. Besides, the popular masses, particularly in the Far East, understand well what Japanese domination would mean for them. However, it would be incorrect, following the Kremlin and the foreign correspondents attached to it, to over-estimate the importance of the fighting at Changkufeng.

In the past years I have referred several times to the fact that the Japanese army is the army of a decomposing regime and has many traits resembling the Czarist army on the eve of the revolution.

Conservative governments and general staffs overrate the army and navy of the Mikado in the same way that they overrated the army and navy of the Czar. The Japanese can be successful only against backward and half-disarmed China.

They will not endure a long war against a serious adversary. The success of the Red army near Changfukeng thus has a limited significance for its evaluation. I don't think that this episode had any influence on Hitler's strategical plans. His turn to Moscow was determined by much nearer and more powerful factors.

Red Rulers Called New Aristocracy

CONCERNING the Communist Party of the Soviet Union—what do you think of the rank and file of the Party? You have said that the leadership of the party does not follow Marxist-Leninist lines. Do you believe, if that leadership were removed, that the Party would proceed in the Socialization of Russia, and to what extent do you believe Russia already has been Socialized? Is it possible for the Russian people to change leadership now without violence? If a change in the leadership were made, would it lay Russia open to attack from other Powers? Would it risk the loss of what the people have gained?

TROTZKY:

OUR differences with the leadership of the so-called Communist party of the U. S. S. R. ceased a long time ago to carry a theoretical character. The "Marxist-Leninist" line is not at all the issue now.

We accuse the ruling clique of having transformed itself into a new aristocracy, oppressing and robbing the masses. The bureaucracy answers with accusations that we are agents of Hitler (as it was yesterday) or agents of Chamberlain and Wall Street (as of today). All this bears very little resemblance to theoretical differences between Marxists.

It is about time that serious people cast aside the spectacles which the professional "friends of the U. S. S. R" put on the nose of radical public opinion. It is about time to understand that the present Soviet oligarchy has nothing in common with the old Bolshevik party, which was a part of the oppressed. Degeneration of the ruling party, supplemented by bloody purges, was the result of the backwardness of the country and the isolation of the revolution. It is true that the social upheaval brought important economic successes.

Nevertheless, the productivity of labor in the U. S. S. R. is five, eight or 10 times lower than in the United States. The immense bureaucracy devours a lion's share of the modest national income. The second part is consumed by the armed forces. As before, the people are compelled to fight for a piece of bread. The bureaucracy plays the role of distributor of goods and retains the choicest morsels for itself. The higher layer of the bureaucracy lives approximately the same kind of life as the well-to-do bourgeois of the United States and other capitalist countries.

Twelve to 15 millions are privileged—these are the "people" who organize the parades, manifestations and ovations which create such an enormous impression on liberal and radical tourists. But apart from this "pays legal" as was once said in France, there exist 160,000,000 who are profoundly discontented.

What is the evidence? If the bureaucracy had the confidence of the people, it would strive to maintain at least its own Constitution; in reality it tramples it underfoot. Antagonism between the bureaucracy and the people is measured by the increasing severity of the totalitarian rule.

Nobody can say with certainty—not even themselves—what is wanted by the Communists who are doomed to silence by the Kremlin with even greater brutality than the rest of the population.

However, there can be no basis for doubting that the overwhelming majority of the Communists and the population do not wish the return of capitalism, particularly now when capitalism has thrown humanity into a new war.

The bureaucracy can be crushed only by a new political revolution that will preserve the nationalized means of production and the planned economy and will establish on this basis a Soviet democracy of a much higher type.

This profound transformation would increase immensely the authority of the Soviet Union among the laboring masses all over the world and would make practically impossible a war of the imperialist countries against it.

Russian Reaction Part of World Trend

IF YOU had been the leader of the Soviet State, what would have been your international policy from the time Hitler came into power in Germany, thereby adding German Fascism to Italian Fascism to form a Fascist bloc in Europe?

TROTZKY:

I CONSIDER this question internally contradictory. I could not have been the "leader" of the present Soviet State: only Stalin is fit for this role. I did not lose power personally and accidentally, but due to the fact that the revolutionary epoch was superseded by a reactionary one.

After prolonged efforts and innumerable victims, the masses, tired and disillusioned, retreated. The vanguard become isolated. A new privileged caste concentrated the power in its hands and Stalin, who played before a secondary role, became its leader.

The reaction inside the U. S. S. R. proceeded parallel to the reaction over the entire world. In 1923 the German bourgeoisie strangled the unfolding proletarian revolution. In the same year the campaign against the so-called "Trotzkyists" began in the Soviet Union. In 1928 the Chinese Revolution was strangled.

At the end of 1928 the "Trotzkyist Opposition" was excluded from the party. In 1933 Hitler takes power and in 1934 he carries through his purge. In 1935 begin the tremendous purges in the U. S. S. R., trials against the Opposition, liquidation of the old guard Bolsheviks and of the revolutionary staff of officers.

Such are the main milestones which show the indissoluble connection between the strengthening of the bureaucracy in the U. S. S. R. and the growth of world reaction.

The pressure of world imperialism upon the Soviet bureaucracy, the pressure of the bureaucracy upon the people, the pressure of the backward masses upon the vanguard, such are the causes of the defeat of the revolutionary faction which I represented.

That is why I cannot answer the question what I would have done if I had been in Stalin's place. I cannot be in his place. I can be only in my place.

My program is the program of the Fourth International which can come to power only under the conditions of a new revolutionary epoch. I recall, by the way, that at the beginning of the last war, the Third International was incomparably weaker than the Fourth is now.

Another Interview with LEON TROTZKY Will Appear Next Sunday

N. Y. Yankees Put on Block for $7,000,000

Strictly Sports

Jockey's Dream of Derby Is Jack Flinchum's, Too

Craves a Mount at Churchill While Quietly Disclaiming Present Honors

By CY PETERMAN

MIAMI BEACH, Fla., March 14.

IT was cool and breezy up there above the offices of the Coral Gables Racing Association, and the bare-waisted little men swarmed amid a welter of silk tunics, open trunks, cluttered lockers and Pinkerton agents as we invaded the jockeys' room to view a prodigy.

"Flinchum, hey Flinchum," bawled the doorman, the last of a half dozen tough officials one must penetrate to reach this sanctum.

There was a moment's quiet as the kids all turned toward the door, but then a vest-pocket youngster stepped from behind a post and Roy Jack Flinchum, Jr., leading rider of Florida tracks and tomorrow full-fledged jockey without apprentice allowance, was giving the answers. We drew him aside lest he blow away in the draft from an open window.

* * *

HE'S only 17 years old, weighs just 90 pounds, and today was celebrating the first anniversary of breaking his maiden.

"That was at Oaklawn, near Hot Springs," he said. "I remember it well cause all jocks got a thrill with that first winner."

Roy Jack, as he prefers to be known, is the only son of a hoss-training father who breeds and races a couple head from the family farm near Miamisburg, O. It is a riding family, moreover, with two older sisters taking it cross-pasture on the steeds with no more trepidation than their illustrious kid brother. Pop himself could make the weight until a few years ago, for he beams only 150 pounds today.

Father and son work together at the tracks, however, for the jockey's engagements are handled by the elder Flinchum, and to him go currently those who seek to sign Roy Jack to a regular contract. The rush began during the Hialeah meeting in which Flinchum won 49 races in 46 days, took the gold watch and a big lead for the year's riding honors.

* * *

ACCORDING to horsemen here, Jackie is considered one of the smartest prospects to come along in years. Weighing so little, he can still make any of the required scale.

Right now, however, Flinchum Jr. is eager to see America's leading race tracks, having confined his activities to those around Chicago and the Miami sector the first year.

"I'd like to see some of Maryland, of New York, and Kentucky," he confessed, adding that Churchill Downs in May must be pretty fine. "You mean on Derby Day especially, don't you, Jack?"

"Gee, yes. I wonder if I'll ever have a mount in that race?"

It is this naivete that captivates those who know the boy, and which earned him more publicity than anyone since Sonny Workman and Willie Munden rode helter-skelter across the running horse horizon. "Clinch em with Flinchum" will be remembered as the motto of many in Miami this season of 1940.

Having never seen the famous "Run for the Roses" at Col. Winn's capital of the Mint Julep, Flinchum, like every rider in the country, is burning up with desire to get to the Derby. And while a $75,000 pot of gold and the prestige that goes with it may put experience ahead of him for a year or so, there is little doubt that Jack some day will be tossed up on a blue grass hopeful.

* * *

FOR the present, however, he's eager to see how he does without that "five pounds apprentice allowance."

The one-year career has not been all winners and applause for Flinchum. Already he has taken six trips to the dust with flying hooves thundering by, and last spring, at Buelah Park, while booting Sheriff Eugene, he came near completing a promising young life.

"One of the horses hit me with a shoe and it took 40 stitches to close up my leg," he told us, adding that was the only serious fall. Here another rider made bold to differ, however.

"How about that one at Dade Park?" said A. Loturco, a half-mile pilot of long experience. "If I don't snatch up that time, you're maybe not sitting there laughing off those tumbles."

To this, Jackie solemnly agreed, explaining he only counted as real dangerous those falls in which he came out scarred as well as scared.

Standing in his linen breeches, size 4½ boots and fluttering silks, he looks exactly like what he probably is—a truant from grade school. For it is well known the average jockey cares little for books and erudition once the smell of the barn is in his nostrils, once the feel of straining withers courses up through his knees.

* * *

FLINCHUM Jr., like all riders of note, goes in for other games, including pool.

"He's pretty hot with that cue," Loturco told, "so don't let him kid about bowling or fishing. He don't need an apprentice allowance at rotation or billiards, either."

Jackie's nearest approach to a calamity this winter came not on the race tracks, he said. He was deep sea fishing one Sunday and enjoying it as much as a 20-to-1 winner, when suddenly, whappo. He was almost over the side.

"I'd hooked a 25-pound barracuda, and it was too much for me," he confessed. "I hung on long enough to save the tackle, and with some help we got him in. That was the biggest fish I ever saw and I don't want to handle another like it."

Getting back to horses, the riding star disclaimed any personal charm with them, denying the praise on his form and courage. He brought in Mucho Gusto, for instance, in a race where Merrill Packer on Piccolo seemed to have all the best of the stretch duel. But at the finish, there was Flinchum and his mount, a nose in front and the boy not yet gone to the whip.

"I'm not much for whipping horses," he said simply; "mostly it does as much good just shaking the stick at 'em."

* * *

AND like most good riders, he doesn't urge you to back his mounts, gives no tips.

"It isn't us that does the running," he explained patiently, "it's always the horse. If he's got enough speed, I'll try to do my part. That's all any rider can do."

Which isn't bad information, if you're inclined to follow the bangtails.

BEULAH BUEK SWIMS TO VICTORY FOR TEMPLE IN RECORD TIME FOR 50-YARD BREASTSTROKE (Story on Page 34)

The Philadelphia Inquirer

PHILADELPHIA, FRIDAY MORNING, MARCH 15, 1940 abdefg 31

Eight World Records Set In Dartmouth Track Meet

John Woodruff Runs 1.47.7 Half-Mile; Herbert, Borican, N. Y. U. Four in Stride

HANOVER, N. H., March 14 (U. P.).—In the greatest record-breaking carnival in indoor track and field history, eight new indoor world marks were established tonight during the third annual invitation Dartmouth games.

One of the new figures, long John Woodruff's 1:47.7 for the half-mile, proved the fastest time ever registered indoors or outdoors for that distance.

New York University's one-mile relay team concluded a night of record-making over Dartmouth's over-sized board track by covering the distance in three minutes 15 seconds flat. This established two new board marks, bettering Fordham's 3:15.2 for the mile and also for the 1600 meters established last year.

In addition to the New York U. mile relay and 1600-meter records, and the new half-mile mark established by Woodruff, former Pittsburgh U. Negro runner, these five records also were hung up:

In running the half-mile, Woodruff's time for the 800 meters was 1:47, a new indoor mark.

Jim Herbert, New York U. Negro, opened the competition with new figures of 0:48.4 for the quarter-mile and 0:47.9 for 400 meters. This was the first time a runner had been timed for the 400 meters indoors.

MILE RELAY CLOSE

New York University's half-mile relay team registered a new figure of 1:27.7 for that event.

John Borican, New York Negro, set a new mark of 3:01.2 for the three-quarter miles.

Although Herbert's quarter-mile figure broke the recognized record, it was not as fast as the 0:48.2 or 0:48.3 set last week by Roy Cochran, of Indiana U., at the Big Ten meet in Chicago. Should either of Cochran's marks be recognized later, Herbert's claims to a new record naturally will be tossed out.

A capacity crowd of 1500 fans witnessed tonight's historic competition. In all the events except the mile relay the runners were paced by Dartmouth handicap men. In the mile relay New York U.'s quartet of speedsters were pushed throughout b ya veteran four from the Boston Athletic Association. At the third exchange of batons in this relay Douglas Raymond, of Boston, was actually ahead of Harold Bogrow, of N. Y. U.

HERBERT IN STRIDE

Herbert, speedy New York University Negro, established new records for the 400 metres and quarter-mile in winning the first event.

Herbert strode around Dartmouth's huge indoor saucer in 47.9 seconds for the 400 meters as he stepped off the full 440 yards in 48.4. His quarter-mile figure or 0.48.4 bettered the 27-year-old mark of

Continued on Page 33, Column 3

Finns Undecided

HELSINGFORS, March 14 (A. P.).—Vice Mayor Erik von Frenckell, chairman of the Helsingfors Olympic Committee, said today, "It is too early to give out a final decision whether we intend to hold the Olympic Games this summer."

"In a house of sorrow there is no time to think of future celebrations," said the vice mayor. "After we have recovered from the first shock of present events, perhaps we can say something more definite."

The various Olympic sites, including the main stadium and Olympic village, all escaped damage from bombs. They were nearing completion when the war with Russia started last fall. Finland has until April 1 to announce its intentions regarding the games.

Tilden Defeats Richards In Swarthmore Net Match

By DORA LURIE

Big Bill Tilden, disdaining his 47 years, spanked his former protege, Vinnie Richards, last night before an overflowing crowd of 3000 in the Swarthmore College Field House.

While the heavy rain beat down on the roof, Tilden stroked his way to victory by scores of 7-5, 8-6.

The crowd included 800 college boys and girls, who added a real rah-rah touch to the evening.

Against Richards, the volleying New Yorker, 10 years his junior, whom he discovered at the age of 15, Tilden continued to display his unquenchable desire for triumph.

MANY SERVICE BREAKS

The first set found Tilden racing off to a 3-0 lead before Richards caught up with him at 3-3; from here it was a matter of service breaks with Richards failing to sustain his 5-4 advantage in games. Tilden broke Richards four times and lost three of his own services.

The second set was a decided contrast. Richards opening up service to take the first game. The pair traded delivery for 14 games before Tilden broke through in the 15th and pocketed the 16th after the game had been deuced four times.

After the matches, Tilden left for California by automobile to open a tennis school where he will be in charge of eight new courts. The lanky Philadelphian expects to re-

Continued on Page 33, Column 7

Lewis Kayoes Collins in 4th

Fight fans at the Olympia were early to bed last night, since every bout ended in a knockout. Tiger Red Lewis mowed down Billy Collins in the fourth round of the featured bout, scheduled for eight periods.

Lewis, 169, a clownish slugger from Richmond, Va., was the winner at 1.42 of the session when Collins, 163, Chester youngster, sank floorward for the second time in the round. Referee Matt Adgie, who had just finished tolling nine over Collins on the first knockdown, dispensed with the formality of a count on the second flooring.

COLLINS TWICE FLOORED

Collins, outpunched, took a sound beating for three rounds, while Lewis, a wild hooker-swinger, hit him at will. Rights that boomed into the body accomplished the first knockdown in the fifth; a right swing to the jaw was the finishing punch.

Lewis, substitute for Roxie Forgione, had been knocked out by Jersey Joe Walcott, to whom he conceded much weight in a previous appearance here.

Hard-hitting Joe Brickle, burly Negro product of C. C. C. battles, knocked out George Estock, giant Camden novice, in the fourth round

Continued on Page 33, Column 5

Mrs. Vare Loses

BELLEAIR, Fla., March 4 (U. P.).—Dorothy Kirby, Atlanta, upset Mrs. Glenna Collett Vare, Philadelphia, 5 and 3, today in the semi-finals of the Belleair women's golf tournament.

In the other match, Jane Cothran, Columbia, S. C., won from National Champion Betty Jameson, San Antonio, 4 and 2.

The championship match will be played tomorrow.

No Bar to U. S. Participation If Finland Holds Olympics

By BILL BONI

NEW YORK, March 14 (A. P.).—If Finland should decide to go through with the 1940 Olympic Games, as originally scheduled for July 20 to Aug. 4, there would be nothing to bar United States participation, Dan Ferris believes.

The secretary-treasurer of the A. A. U., also active in Olympic circles, said today he thought both the games and U. S. representation in them might be on a smaller scale than was planned before the outbreak of the Finnish-Russian war.

Finnish officials announced not long ago they would go through with the games, on a curtailed basis if necessary, if their country was not actually at war on April 1. Cutting the size of the American team, Ferris said, might be necessitated by lack of time in which to raise sufficient funds.

"But even that latter point would not necessarily be true," he added. "There might be so much enthusiasm among American sports lovers to pay Finland tribute by sending a truly representative team that there'd be no financing difficulty."

The simplest way for an American team to go to Finland probably would be by steamer to a Norwegian port, possibly Bergen, and then overland through Sweden. Direct travel by ship to Helsingfors would be impossible, since the entrance to the Baltic Sea lies in belligerent waters barred to American-flag ships.

JOHN WOODRUFF
Who ran to new indoor 800-metre and half-mile records in a sensational performance at Dartmouth College last night.

Phillies' Rally Beats Rochester

By STAN BAUMGARTNER
Inquirer Sports Reporter

WEST PALM BEACH, Fla., March 14.—Power—the long-distance hitting that Doc Prothro says he needs to win ball games — coupled with some gilt-edged hurling by Recruits Dale Jones and Clyde Smoll, gave the Phils a 7-4 conquest over Rochester of the International League here today before 1500 fans.

It was a victory gained in an uphill battle against odds after Hugh Mulcahy gave the Red Wings a 4-0 lead in the first three innings.

Apparently angered by this humiliation, the Phillies tore into three Rochester hurlers. They did not make many hits—only seven in all—but four of these were for extra bases. One was a home run by Letchas, one a triple by Bragan and Levy and Arnovich both contributed doubles.

This display of power, however, would have been useless if Dale Jones and Clyde Smoll had not turned on shut-out pitching for the final six innings.

Jones was a bit wild. He hit one and walked five, but he did not allow a hit and got into most of his trouble after two were out. Smoll, on the other hand, allowed three singles, but did not walk a man.

Such twirling as this, coupled with some old-fashioned Phil slugging of

Continued on Page 34, Column 3

Ruppert Heirs Seek Cash to Pay Taxes

Syndicate Headed by Murphy Said To Be Ready to Close Deal for Club; 'Nothing Even Semi-Definite'—Barrow

By LESLIE AVERY

NEW YORK, March 14 (U. P.).—The New York Yankees are for sale, the United Press learned today.

The greatest team in organized baseball will be sold in order to raise cash to meet inheritance taxes on the $50,000,000 estate of the late Col. Jacob Ruppert, who loved the Yankees so much he spent a fortune building them to their present peak.

It was reported in New York today that a syndicate headed by Gov. Francis P. Murphy, of New Hampshire, already had closed a deal to purchase the club.

But Ed Barrow, president of the Yankees, said in Sebring, Fla., that "no deal has been completed."

"As president of the club, I would be in a position to know if the Yankees were to be sold," he said. "The club certainly is for sale, but at the present time there is nothing definite, or semi-definite."

Barrow said that three or four tentative bids had been received in the last six months.

In Boston, Gov. Murphy said that discussions for the purchase of the club "are still in the preliminary stage."

"It is correct to say that the deal is brewing," he said. "It is absolutely wrong to say that purchase had been made."

ASKING $7,000,000

Barrow said, however, that Gov. Murphy was not among those who had made bids for the club. Barrow pointed out that Gov. Murphy had been reported as trying to buy a major league club for 10 years.

The Ruppert estate is reported asking $7,000,000 for the Yankee team, the Yankee Stadium and the far-flung Yankee farm system that includes the Newark Bears in the International League and the Kansas City Blues of the American Association.

The Yankee Stadium and the land upon which it is located in the Bronx is assessed at $2,550,000, while the present Yankee squad of players is worth at least $1,500,000.

COL. RUPPERT'S DESIRE

In his will Col. Ruppert, who died on Jan. 13, 1939, said that it was his desire that the Yankees be "perpetuated." Ruppert and Col. Tillinghast Huston purchased the Yankees in 1915 for $450,000; Ruppert later became sole owner.

When he died Ruppert owned 2990 of the 3000 shares in the capital stock of the club and he left it to be divided equally among his two

Continued on Page 34, Column 6

Athletics Beat Pirates in 14th

By JAMES C. ISAMINGER
Inquirer Sports Reporter

SAN BERNARDINO, Calif., March 14.—Two Pennsylvania teams training in California met under snow-topped mountains here this afternoon and the Athletics collected three runs in the 14th inning to overcome Pittsburgh, 10 to 7.

Connie Mack's first game this year with a major league opponent was a spectacular success after three hours and thirty-five minutes of tense battling.

With the game deadlocked, Sam Chapman, the hero of the long fight, opened the 14th with a pass and quickly stole second. Miles fanned and Gantenbein walked. So did Brancato, filling the bases.

Fred Chapman forced Brancato, Garms to Gustine, Sam Chapman scoring, and when Gustine threw wild to first trying for a double play, Gantenbein raced home. Fred took second on the error.

UNNECESSARY RUN

Earle Brucker then slapped a solid two-bagger to left to admit F. Chapman and clinch the victory.

Sam Chapman's bat figured in the scoring earlier. The strong boy of California blasted a single, triple and home run to be responsible for the first six runs tabbed by the Macks.

In the sixth he put the Athletics in the game by lashing a 360-foot

Continued on Page 34, Column 5

Medalists Serafin, Allan Beaten in St. Augustine Golf

ST. AUGUSTINE, Fla., March 14 (U. P.).—Upsets marked first round play today in the national amateur-professional match play championship.

The tournament medalists, Felix Serafin and Frank Allan, were defeated 1 up by Paul Bell, Torrington, Conn., and Peter Gruntal, Scarsdale, N. Y., while another team of favorites, Paul Runyan, White Plains, N. Y., and Charles Whitehead, Plainfield, N. J., lost to Herman Keiser, Springfield, Mo., and Dick Doeschler, Jacksonville, Fla., 1 up in 21 holes.

Other results:

Dutch Harrison, Little Rock, and Bill Stark, Jacksonville, defeated Byng Good and Charles Bennett, St. Augustine, 6 and 5.

Johnny Revolta, Evanston, Ill., and Billy Coffey, Fort Worth, Tex., defeated Willie Goggin, San Francisco, and Ray O'Brien, Larchmont, N. Y., 1 up.

Henry Poe, Reading, Pa., and Harold Mandly, Weatherfield, Conn., defeated Frank Moore, Reading, Pa., and Oscar Evers, Jacksonville, 1 up.

Rod Munday, White Plains, N. Y., and Bobby Walker, Jacksonville, defeated Vic Ghezzi, Deal, N. J., and Roy Salmen, New Orleans, 4 and 3.

Sam Snead, Shawnee-on-Delaware, Pa., and Wilford Wehrle, Racine, Wis., defeated Ben Loving, Springfield, Mass., and Jack Mitchell, Hartford, Conn., 3 and 1.

Clyde Usina, Jr., West Palm Beach, and Walter Burkemo, Evanston, Ill., defeated Henry Picard, Hershey, Pa., and Frank Ford, Charleston, 1 up.

Harold McSpaden, Winchester, Mass., and Tommy Aycock, Jacksonville, defeated Ted Luther, Wilkinsburg, Pa., and Don Allan, West Pittston, Pa., 5 and 4.

Craig Wood, Winged Foot Club, N. Y., and Dave Mitchell, Augusta, Ga., defeated Lloyd Mangrum, Oak Park, Ill., and Morton Bright, Daytona Beach, Fla., 1 up, 20 holes.

Chandler Harper, Portsmouth, Va., and Al Dollins, Roanoke, Va., defeated Harry Cooper, Chicago, Ill., and Fred Haas, New Orleans, La., 1 up.

Gene Sarazen, Brookfield Center, Conn., and Ellsworth Vines, Pasadena, Calif., defeated Milton Trish, East Aurora, N. Y., and Bob Montague, Jr., Saginaw, Mich., 1 up.

Jimmy McHale, Saranac Inn, N. Y., and Powell Crichton, Jr., Winged Foot Club, N. Y., defeated Lee Kosten, Eustis, Fla., and Warren Dawson, Chicago, Ill., 3 and 2.

Horton Smith, Oak Park, Ill., and Martin Ward, Spokane, Wash., defeated A. B. Thorne, Lancaster, Pa., and Ben Stegal, Daytona Beach, Fla., 5 and 4.

Military Expert's Views

Nazis Should Sit Tight, But Does Hitler Think So?

Chafing at Inaction, He Knows Reich Must Have 'Miracle' Tonic Even Though Main Object Is Won

By MAJ. GEO. FIELDING ELIOT

Formerly a reserve officer in the U. S. Army's Intelligence, author of the non-fiction best seller, "The Ramparts We Watch," and one of America's most lucid interpreters of military tactics.

OF recent days, there has been increasing evidence available that the Allied blockade of Germany is not especially efficient; probably, all things considered, not efficient enough to set a time limit within which Germany must attain victory on the battlefield or abandon hope of it.

This being so, the tendency of a writer with military training is to try to put himself in the place of a high German staff officer making an estimate of this situation, and to determine what the decision of his superior, based on this estimate, would be.

PRIME OBJECT WON

From that point of view the answer is plain: sit tight, take no risks, let the Allies have the ball.

Germany has gained her immediate object, the elimination of Poland; she has closed the threatening breach in the Northern Front; she is completely surrounded by neutral States save the short stretch of the heavily fortified Western Frontier; given time, she can possibly make available Russian supplies in decisive quantities; meanwhile she must avoid exhaustion of her reserve supplies.

NO REASON FOR RISKS

There is no conceivable military reason (unless the blockade is in fact more effective than appears) why she should take the terrific risks (without any assurance of victory) of an attack by land in the West, or an attack by air against the British Isles (which, being a bid for a decision, would necessarily involve risking her whole air force).

There is every reason to believe that the above represents the considered opinion of most of the higher officers of the Army General Staff and of the Navy.

HITLER WILL DECIDE

And yet the final decision is not in the hands of these. It is rather in the hands of a man whose decisions and reactions have never been predictable with any degree of accuracy: Adolf Hitler.

So far as any opinion may be formed from available evidence, Hitler tends to chafe under inaction.

Moreover, he has to take into account factors other than military; factors having to do with the internal state of the German nation. It is quite possible that he may have reason to believe the German people are not likely to endure the stresses of a long war without periodic "miracles."

There is certainly advice being given to him that the time to strike is now; this advice comes less from military than from party sources, and may well have its origin not only in military ignorance and overconfidence, but also in a growing fear on the part of politicians of the expanding power of the military leaders necessarily arising from the fact that the flower of German manhood is under military command.

ADVANTAGES WILL SHRINK

There are certain present points of German superiority which will dwindle with time—that is, proportionately. One is their enormous reserve of ammunition, in which they are far ahead of the Allies.

Another is their present numerical superiority in airplanes, which will probably be reduced to equality in 1941.

A third is their numerical superiority in available divisions on the Western Front, which will diminish as British divisions are trained, equipped and take the field, and may be still further diminished if inaction permits the Allies time to organize diversions in the Near East or the Balkans.

Thus a case can be built up for action now, but it is not a sound case, for it seems probable that inaction will have even worse effects on the Allies, affecting neutrals adversely to their cause.

RISKS ALREADY TAKEN

While it is perfectly true that one cannot, as Napoleon remarked, make war without the taking of risks, it is also fair to observe that the Germans have taken their risks, won their victory, and are now concerned not with destroying the Allies, but with resisting the attempts of the Allies to deprive them of their spoils.

But it is not the estimate of the situation prepared by the great General Staff which will determine the fate of the Third Reich; it is rather the decision of Hitler, who, in every crisis, has formed his own estimate of the situation and action on it—thus far with complete success, but, being human, with also the possibility of fatal error.

Pope Expected to Ask Funds for Finland

VATICAN CITY, April 6 (U. P.).—Authoritative Vatican quarters said today that Pope Pius II soon would instruct all bishops in all non-belligerent countries to collect funds for aiding in the reconstruction of Finland.

It was said that the Pontiff would confer regarding the fund with Myron C. Taylor, President Roosevelt's personal representative to the Vatican.

WORLD BLOCKADE WIDENED BY ALLIES

Pacific Included As Trade War On Reich Is Tightened

BY FREDERICK KUH

Continued From First Page

night and again today. They worked out details for sealing leaks and loopholes in the blockade.

It was understood that Britain had taken the stand, first, that any attempt by Norway and Sweden to reach an understanding with Germany against future Russian aggression would be viewed as an unfriendly act toward Britain; secondly, that any Russian move to extort or conquer new Atlantic ports from Scandinavia would be considered a threat to Britain.

From outside of this country, there were reports today that a 2819-ton Jugoslav freighter, the Dubac, bound for Italy, had been seized by British warships off the coast of Greece and taken to the blockade station at Malta, and that a British cruiser and three destroyers were in the Adriatic to head off any attempts by Germany to use neutral waters there for a sea route for Balkan products which could be trans-shipped by rail from Italy to the Reich.

Moreover, persons who profess to be in the know in London contended that Britain's use of money in the Balkans to stop German supplies is proceeding favorably.

Planes Machine-Gun 3 Belgian Fishing Boats

BRUSSELS, April 6. (U. P.).—Three Belgian fishing boats were machine-gunned by airplanes while fishing 30 miles north of Zeebrugge Wednesday, it was reported today from Ostend. None of the vessels was hit. The nationality of the planes was not known.

Berlin Calls on Scandinavia To Pick Sides in Blockade

By LOUIS P. LOCHNER

Continued From First Page

tions and declarations by the British and French blockade ministers in London and on the new Allied notes to Norway and Sweden.

Germany stands by as a decidedly interested observer of all this—and it is taken for granted here that the Reich is not standing by idly.

Again and again, especially in the last few days, the statement has been heard that "Our Fuehrer isn't sleeping."

EXPECT COUNTER-MOVE

It may be taken as certain that Germany will make some counter-move should Britain attempt forcibly to prevent Swedish ores from reaching her by way of neutral waters or neutral railways.

Germans claim also that it shows "Our enemies have a senile conception of war. To them the intensity of war is merely proportionate to the amount of blood shed. That women and children starve is not war to them."

REICH PRESS IRATE

The Saturday evening press gave these bannerlines to French Blockade Minister Monnet's declarations that the Allies would choke German economy "more and more:"

Nachtausgabe: "Brutal declaration by French Blockade Minister: Germany's women and children are to be struck! War preparations against neutrals completed."

Der Angriff: "Week-end Plot by Enemy Blockade Ministers."

Lokalanzeiger: "Starving Out Women and Children. Announcement by French Blockade Minister. He received command by Churchill."

WAR FILM PRAISED

These headlines, together with glowing praise of the film, "Baptism of Fire," first shown last night, in which the German Air Force on the basis of the Polish campaign was depicted as invincible, seemed to neutral observers to be calculated to prepare the German people for coming events of the first magnitude.

At the same time it was said that no matter which side decided "to take over" Norway and Sweden for the duration of the war, if such a course should become inevitable, neither country was regarded as a military factor so far as resistance is concerned.

STRENGTH MINIMIZED

Military experts held that Sweden could not possibly mobilize more than six divisions (approximately 75,000 men). Three of these were reported taken to the extreme north to guard the frontier against any possible Soviet Russian move, and it was believed here that, with limited rail facilities, it would take considerable time to bring them south should that area become a theatre of war.

Norwegian strength also was minimized. (Norway has an army of six combat divisions.)

Graf Spee Sailors Ordered Interned

BUENOS AIRES, April 6 (A. P.).—Following the flight of three interned officers of the scuttled German pocket battleship Admiral Graf Spee, police announced today their comrades in Buenos Aires would be interned Monday at the naval base on Martin Garcia Island, 80 miles off Buenos Aires in the River Plata.

Miguel Viancarlos, chief police investigator, made the announcement. More than 500 members of the crew already have been sent to the interior.

The German Ambassador was reported advised of this and other steps to prevent further escapes.

BLOCKADE OF NAZIS PUSHED BY FRANCE

Economic, Military Plans Discussed by Reynaud and Aides

PARIS, April 6 (A. P.).—The Allied program for tightening the economic and military blockade of Germany was reflected today in a full program of conferences at Premier Paul Reynaud's office.

Among those who conferred with the Premier, who also holds the Foreign Ministry portfolio, were General Maxime Weygand, commander of Allied forces in the Near East; General Auguste Nogues, supreme commander of French defense forces in North Africa; Andre Francois-Poncet, Ambassador to Rome; Raymond Brugere, Minister to Jugoslavia; Louis Oscar Frossard, Minister of Information; Jean Mistler, President of the Chamber of Deputies, and August Zaleski, Polish emigre Minister of Foreign Affairs.

Reynaud, acting in concert with Great Britain, earlier handed a note to the Swedish and Norwegian Ministers bearing on relations between the two Scandinavian countries and the Allies.

Pope Is Host for First Time At Brilliant Musicale

By JAMES M. MINIFIE

Special Cable to The Inquirer and New York Herald Tribune

ROME, April 6.—The Papal Court held its first social occasion under the present Pontificate this afternoon, when the finest orchestra in Rome gave a musicale at the Vatican in the presence of Pope Pius XII.

The Pope received a tremendous ovation. It was a unique occasion. To find a comparison one must go back prior to the "Vatican Captivity" to the days when the Popes were not only spiritual heads of the Catholic Church, but also temporal rulers of Rome and the surrounding territories.

After the concert the Pope took occasion to refer to the spiritual harmony which unites men of creative genius the world over, and expressed the wish that this could be extended.

Besides the Pope there were present members of his family, 15 Cardinals, the former Queen of Spain, the Infante Christine, the Prince of the Asturias and his wife, the grand master of the Sovereign Order of the Knights of Malta, members of the Italian royal family and court, the diplomatic corps accredited to the Holy See, and some 1200 Roman patricians and prominent personalities of the Church and State.

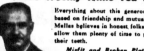

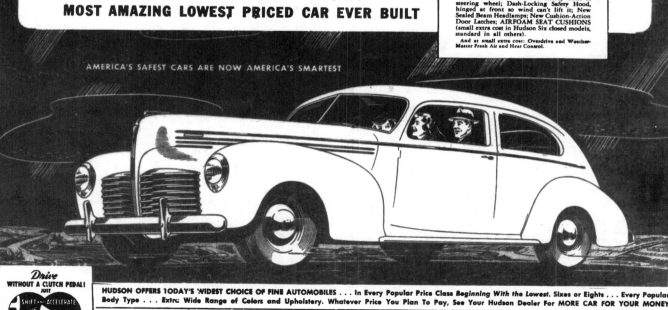

The Philadelphia Inquirer

PUBLIC LEDGER

An Independent Newspaper for All the People

6 A. M. EDITION

CIRCULATION: March Average Daily 403,590, Sunday 1,140,332 abdefgh TUESDAY MORNING, APRIL 9, 1940 Second Largest 3c Morning Circulation in America THREE CENTS

 VOL. 222, NO. 100

DENMARK, NORWAY INVADED BY NAZIS; COPENHAGEN TAKEN

Today

Problem Is Brewing
U. S. Demands Dollars
British Supply Limited
What When It's Gone?
Will We Ban Credit?

—By Mark Sullivan—

WASHINGTON, April 8.

THERE is a condition which the United States will be obliged to meet if the war in Europe continues a year or more. This condition is just dawning upon Government officials and thoughtful persons. It may become tangible and need to be met in a shorter time than a year.

Britain and France are buying supplies in the United States. For these supplies they are paying cash, because our neutrality law forbids American citizens to sell goods to a nation at war on any basis except cash.

The cash which Britain and France pay for supplies from America is in a sense a special kind of money. (I put it thus to avoid the mysteries of international exchange.) It is the kind of money that one country can send to another country. In the present case, it must be dollars—Britain cannot pay an American manufacturer with pounds.

Internally—within Britain—the Government can buy from its own citizens with pounds. For her internal purchases the Government can, in one way or another, produce as many pounds as it needs.

If the war lasts long enough, the British Government (and also the French) may be obliged to organize its currency and economy much as Germany has, on a semi-Communist basis. By these methods there is practically no limit to what a country can buy within its own borders.

But buying from America is a different matter. For purchases made in America Britain must produce dollars. How to get these dollars will in time become a problem to Britain. After that, it will give rise to a problem for the United States to decide for itself.

For procuring dollars, Britain has three main methods. One is to send gold to America and turn it into dollars.

By a second method, the British Government requires its citizens to turn over to the Government such stocks and bonds of American corporations as they possess. The British Government takes these stocks and bonds and sells them in America. Thus it acquires dollars.

A third method of acquiring dollars is by sending goods here, just as in the ordinary course of peace time trade—such goods as textiles, hardware and the like.

Now all these methods of getting dollars are limited and will in time peter out to almost nothing.

The amount of gold Britain has is limited. The amount of American stocks and bonds it has taken over from its citizens is a fixed quantity. The amount of goods it can send to America is limited, because its labor and factories are absorbed in making war supplies.

When and if Britain comes to the end of its capacity for getting dollars, how can it buy anything in America? As things stand, it can buy nothing here. The only other way would be to buy on credit. And it cannot buy on credit.

Two of our American statutes stand in the way. Under our Neutrality Act, no American can sell goods to Britain except for cash. Under a second law, the so-called Johnson Act, no American can lend money to Britain, which would be the same as selling to it on credit.

The Johnson Act forbids any American citizen to lend money to any nation which in the past has been indebted to the Government of the United States and has defaulted in payment. This

Continued on Page 2, Column 2

Oslo Goes to War After Beating Off Attack From Sea

STOCKHOLM, April 9 (Tuesday) (U. P.).—The Norwegian radio said today that German troops had landed on the southern coast of Norway.

WASHINGTON, April 8 (A. P.).—Mrs. J. Borden Harriman, American Minister to Norway, notified the State Department tonight that the Norwegian Foreign Minister had informed her that Norway is at war with Germany.

The State Department issued the following statement:

The American Minister to Oslo, Mrs. J. Borden Harriman, telegraphed to the Department of State tonight that the Foreign Minister had informed her that the Norwegians fired on four German warships coming up the Oslo fjord and that Norway is at war with Germany.

"In response to a request by the British Minister to Norway, the American Legation at Oslo has been authorized to take over British interest in Norway in case he is obliged to evacuate."

The Norwegian Minister to the United States, Wilhelm de Morgenstierne, was in conversation with the State Department shortly before midnight.

NORSE ENVOY ACTIVE

The department, where a night watch has been maintained constantly since the outbreak of the European war, stirred quickly to activity.

Across the street, lights burned in the White House executive offices although President Roosevelt was at his Hyde Park home.

There was no comment from officials here as to whether the President would take immediate steps to issue a proclamation under the Neutrality Act adding Norway to the list of belligerents.

When the State Department issued its dispatch from Mrs. Harriman, the Norwegian Minister said he had received no direct word yet from the Government at Oslo.

BATTLE AT OSLO FJORD

STOCKHOLM, April 9 (Tuesday) (A. P.).—Oslo, the capital of neutral

Continued on Page 2, Column 1

LATE FLASHES

LONDON, April 9 (Tuesday) (U. P.).—Reports reaching here from Oldenzaal, Holland, said travelers from Germany reported heavy concentrations of German troops near the Dutch frontier.

PARIS, April 9 (Tuesday) (A. P.).—The Oslo radio announced early today that the Norwegian Government had ordered general mobilization after an all-night meeting of the Cabinet.

STOCKHOLM, April 9 (Tuesday) (U. P.).—It was announced here that German transports were unloading troops in Jutland, Denmark.

WASHINGTON, April 9 (Tuesday) (U. P.).—Secretary of State Cordell Hull notified his office early today that he was cancelling his vacation at Atlantic City and would return to the Capital as soon as possible.

Cardinal Verdier Dies

PARIS, April 9 (A. P.).—Jean Cardinal Verdier, Archbishop of Paris, died today.

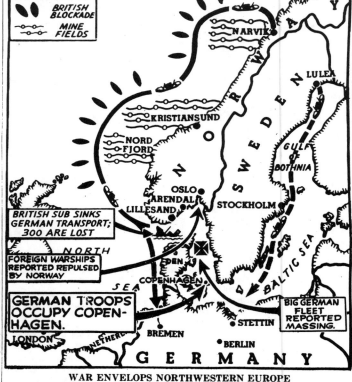

0 100 200 Miles
BRITISH BLOCKADE
MINE FIELDS
NARVIK
LULEA
KRISTIANSUND
NORD FJORD
NORWAY
SWEDEN
GULF OF BOTHNIA
OSLO
ARENDAL
LILLESAND
STOCKHOLM
BRITISH SUB SINKS GERMAN TRANSPORT; 300 ARE LOST
NORTH SEA
FOREIGN WARSHIPS REPORTED REPULSED BY NORWAY
COPENHAGEN
BALTIC SEA
GERMAN TROOPS OCCUPY COPENHAGEN.
BIG GERMAN FLEET REPORTED MASSING.
LONDON
STETTIN
BREMEN
BERLIN
GERMANY

WAR ENVELOPS NORTHWESTERN EUROPE

Almost simultaneously with the German invasion of Denmark and occupation of Copenhagen, Norway notified the United States Minister that it was at war with the Reich. The action of Oslo followed an attempt by warships to penetrate Oslo fjord, water gateway to Oslo, which was repelled by shore batteries. Other events which formed a prelude to these developments are indicated on this map.

Germans Swarm Over Little Nation By Land, Air, Sea

LONDON, April 9 (Tuesday) (A. P.).—A special announcement of the German radio intercepted today by Reuters, British news agency, said German troops had invaded Denmark and Norway.

Reuters said that the following announcement was made by the German radio:

"The High Command of the German Army announces that in order to counteract the actions against Denmark and Norway (apparently the Allied minelaying along the Norwegian coast) and to prevent a possible hostile attack against these countries, the German Army has taken these two countries under its protection.

"The strong forces of the German Army have therefore invaded these countries this morning."

The intercepted Oslo radio report said that the Norwegian Government had abandoned its capital and was moving to Hamar.

German forces were said to have occupied Bergen and Trondheim.

LONDON, April 9 (Tuesday) (U. P.).—British sources reported today that German forces had invaded Denmark and that troops landed from three German warships had occupied parts of the Danish capital, Copenhagen.

The Danes apparently made no resistance.

The German invasion, the British Exchange Telegraph Co. reported, was carried out by land and sea.

Airplanes earlier had scouted over all Denmark.

Three large German ships, reportedly transports, were in the Copenhagen Harbor.

TROOPS LANDED FROM BARGES

The troop transports anchored in the Little Belt and men started coming ashore in barges.

Ordinary communications between London and Copenhagen were interrupted.

Fragmentary messages, however, indicated that the Germans were swarming in with such speed that the occupation of key centres in the little Danish State might be completed within 24 hours.

A Danish garrison at Sonderborg was reported retreating to avoid contact with the Germans.

GERMAN DOUBLE STROKE INDICATED

The German moves followed earlier reports that unknown warships, believed to be German, had attempted to force an entrance into the Oslo fjord, water entrance to the capital of Norway.

A fleet of 100 or more German ships, including heavy cruisers, was reported making its way slowly through Kattegat.

It was not clear, however, whether these operations were connected with the Danish invasion.

The possibility was suggested here that the Germans were planning a double stroke—against both Denmark and Norway in retaliation for Great Brit-

Continued on Page 3, Column 1

IN TODAY'S INQUIRER

Illinois Governor Defies Aide's Seizure of Rule

Illness Given As Reason for Ouster Effort

Illustrated on Page 5

SPRINGFIELD, Ill., April 8 (A. P.).—Lieut. Gov. John Stelle proclaimed himself "Acting Governor" in a melodramatic move today but ailing Gov. Henry Horner refused to relinquish the reins of the State Government.

Steele, insurgent candidate for the Democratic nomination for Governor, strode into the Governor's State House office, seated himself at a secretary's desk and issued the proclamation.

CALLS LEGISLATURE

He signed himself "Acting Governor" and called the Legislature into special session April 30—the same date listed in a similar call by Gov. Horner filed less than an hour earlier.

Stelle told reporters he was as-

Continued on Page 5, Column 4

F.D.R. and Dewey Face Test Today In Two States

By WILLIAM C. MURPHY, JR.
Inquirer Staff Reporter

CHICAGO, April 8.—Illinois and Nebraska tomorrow will serve as political speedometers to measure the approach of President Roosevelt and Thomas E. Dewey toward the 1940 Democratic and Republican Presidential nominations.

The President is certain to win an overwhelming victory in the Nebraska preferential primary where he is unopposed and equally sure to win by a substantial majority in the Illinois, "advisory" primary where he is opposed by Vice President John N. Garner.

HEAVY VOTE SOUGHT

But the question in the minds of politicians here is the size of the vote which can be piled up in this State for a third term. The efficient Cook county (Chicago) political machine headed by Mayor Edward J. Kelly and Pat Nash, national committeeman, is straining all of its many and varied resources to pile up such an overwhelming majority for the President that the result will look

Continued on Page 5, Column 6

DAVIS RETIREMENT SLATED BY COUNCIL

By CHARLES H. ELLIS, JR.

Ross B. Davis, veteran chief engineer of the Fire Bureau, is slated for retirement, it was reported yesterday.

Under terms of an ordinance which has the approval of City Council leaders, Davis and other officers of the police and fire bureaus who heva reached the age of 65 will be forced to quit. Davis was 65 last year.

While he did not say there is any plan to push through the ordinance, Mayor Lamberton lent strength to the reports yesterday by declaring he approved the principle.

Several members of Council, the Mayor said, have discussed the matter with him since the first of the year, and all have indicated they favor the move.

Last Saturday, at the Army Day parade, the possibility of introducing the ordinance was brought up by several Councilmen, Lamberton said.

Rank and file police and firemen

Continued on Page 8, Column 4

Bridegroom-to-Be Makes Nervous Bandit

The bandit's hand trembled last night as he pressed a revolver against Mrs. Edith Graff, wife of the proprietor of a drug store at 20th st. and Medary ave.

"I wish you wouldn't be so nervous," Mrs. Graff remarked.

"He's got a right to be, lady," said the bandit's confederate, helping himself to $30 at the till. "He's getting married next week."

Airliner Fights Fog 5 Hours To Land Its 14 Passengers

A TWA airliner with a Hollywood star and a three-month-old baby among its 14 passengers made a safe landing last night on an emergency field near Altoona after a dramatic trip which kept it aloft for more than seven hours.

The tale of that perilous journey will be found on the log-book of Flight 10, which tells of five thrill-packed hours in the air above fog-bound airports of three States on a trip which should have taken less than two hours.

The log would tell how the plane circled LaGuardia Airport, at North Beach, Long Island, for more than three hours—"stacked up" with other planes ploughing through cloud banks at different altitudes waiting for a "break" in the weather.

It would record orders to return to Pittsburgh, if necessary, and attempts to land at Newark, Camden and Harrisburg—but it wouldn't record the nervous tension in the cabin as the minutes slipped into hours, nor the feeble crying of an infant.

HENRY FONDA ABOUND

The plane took off from Pittsburgh Airport at 2.37 P. M. with Pilot Eugene Klose, of Kansas City, at the controls, bound for New York City. Among the passengers was Henry Fonda, movie star, and three-months-old Barbara Jane Williamson, with her mother, Mrs. J. Wood Williamson, of Waynesburg, Pa.

Flight 10 was due at LaGuardia

Continued on Page 8, Column 3

THE WEATHER

Official forecasts: Eastern Pennsylvania—Rain in north and cloudy preceded by rain in south portion today, slightly cooler tonight, tomorrow generally fair.

New Jersey—Cloudy preceded by occasional light rain in north portion, slightly cooler in south portion today; tomorrow fair.

Sun rises 5.32 A. M. Sets 6.32 P. M.
Moon rises 6.30 A. M. Sets 8.26 P. M.

Other Weather Reports on Page 2

WORRY HERE WANES FOR WAR ZONE KIN

Officials Believe All U. S. Citizens In Norway Safe

Tension among Philadelphians who have friends and relatives trapped in the Norwegian war-zone eased somewhat yesterday with official State Department assurances that all U. S. citizens are believed safe. Some worry persisted, however, when efforts at direct communication failed.

Among those who did receive first-hand news was the family of Mrs. Raymond E. Cox, wife of the First Secretary of the U. S. Legation to Norway, who cabled she had left Oslo for the interior of the country.

MRS. COX FROM RADNOR

Mrs. Cox is the former Margaret Berwind, daughter of Mrs. Henry A. Berwind, of Radnor, and sister of Henry Berwind, of Chestnut Hill. She has a son, Allan, 10.

"We got a cable from Mr. Cox the first day there was trouble, saying that my daughter had been sent with other women and children from the danger zone into the interior," Mrs. Berwind said. "While we feel she is probably safe, naturally we are deeply concerned over all of them."

NO WORD OF MORAN

No word, however, has yet been received from John T. Moran, of Malvern, since he arrived in Norway three months ago, his sister, Mrs. Elizabeth Miller, also of Malvern, informed Matthias J. Moe, Norwegian Consul, yesterday.

Meanwhile, the number of seamen from the Philadelphia area aboard three U. S. ships in the danger zone was raised to seven with the listing of Joseph Dean, of Atlantic City, as a seaman on the Mormacsea, last reported at Trondheim.

OUT OF BERGEN

The other ships are the Flying Fish and the Charles R. McCormick, both last reported at Bergen. Moore-McCormack line officials said yesterday they understood their three freighters had been ordered out of the harbor before British planes bombed German land forces.

Worry also was expressed at the home of Charles Martin, foreman at the Philadelphia Electric Co. plant in West Conshohocken. His wife, Bergliot, said she had a brother and three sisters in Norway in towns in the fighting zone.

"There are six sons in their families, all eligible for war calls," Mrs. Martin said.

Quebec Speeds Women's Vote

QUEBEC, April 11—(A P)—By a vote of 67 to 9 Premier Adelard Godbout's measure to grant women the right to vote in provincial elections and to sit in the Legislature passed second reading in the Legislative Assembly today.

LOGICAL EVACUATION ROUTES

This map shows the most logical routes Americans can follow in the evacuation of U. S. citizens from Norway. From the ports of Trondheim or Bergen they could be transported by freighter to Britain. Another plan under consideration is for the refugees to go south to Germany and then on down to Italy, where the United States Lines touches.

U. S. Arranges to Evacuate 3000 Citizens in Scandinavia

By JOHN C. O'BRIEN

Continued From First Page

known to be residing in the Scandinavian countries—1067 in Norway, 552 in Denmark and 1752 in Sweden. Of those living in Norway, 777 were listed in the Oslo consular district and the others in the Bergen district. More than half of those living in Sweden—987—were listed in the Goteborg district and the others in the Stockholm district.

VIA REICH TO GENOA

The State Department instructed its representatives in the three countries to arrange for the transportation of Americans by rail through Germany to Genoa, where American ships would be waiting to transport them to the United States.

Although the German Government has not been asked to grant safe conduct for the refugees, State Department officials said they anticipated no difficulty on that head.

Americans wishing to leave Norway would cross into Sweden and proceed by rail to ferry connections with Germany. State Department officials said refugees unable to pay their passage could borrow from the contingency funds of the American Legations and Consular offices.

NOT ORDERED TO LEAVE

The State Department made it clear it was not ordering Americans out of the Scandinavian countries. How many would desire to leave was not known, but it was thought few in Denmark or Sweden would feel any anxiety for theri safety under present conditions.

At his press conference this morning Secretary of State Cordell Hull said this Government was still hampered by lack of official information necessary for determining whether a state of war existed in Norway and Denmark.

Until the inquiry is completed, he indicated, there would be no decision as to whether the Neutrality Act should be invoked.

ICELAND-GREENLAND ISSUE

Hull added that no inquiries had been addressed to either Germany or Denmark with respect to the status of Iceland or Greenland. He refused to discuss the bearing of the Monroe Doctrine in the event the Allies or Germany attempted occupation of either of the Danish possessions lying within the Western Hemisphere, asserting that no diplomatic issue had yet arisen.

It was assumed in State Department quarters, however, that if either Iceland or Greenland were occupied, this Government would serve notice that any permanent extension of new sovereignty in those countries would not be tolerated.

DIFFICULTIES DISCLOSED

The difficulties experienced by the department in communicating with its representatives on the zone of hostilities was disclosed in an announcement that none of a dozen telegrams filed by Raymond E. Cox, first secretary of the American Legation at Oslo, in an 18-hour period between Tuesday and Wednesday had been received.

From Frederick A. Sterling, American Minister to Sweden, the department learned that Mrs. J. Bordon Harriman had deported by telephone to Stockholm that she was with the Norwegian Government at an undisclosed interior point in Norway. This was the first message she had been able to get through in more than 24 hours.

ASSIST BRITISH STAFF

The legation at Oslo informed the department the staff had assisted the members of the British Legation and Consular staff in departing last night by rail for Stockholm.

The interests of the French and British Government have been taken over by the American Minister, both at Oslo and at Copenhagen.

Meanwhile, Treasury officials completed plans for carrying out President Roosevelt's executive order freezing Danish and Norwegian funds and credits in this country so that Germany could assert no claim to them.

Orders were issued to all holders of Danish or Norwegian wealth in this country to list their holdings with the Treasury under penalty of a heavy fine. The Treasury estimated the holdings would run into several hundred million dollars, mostly in short-term bank balances and "ear-marked gold."

Secretary of the Treasury Henry Morgenthau said that he would be guided by the "rule of reason" in issuing licenses for withdrawal of the funds by their rightful owners. He added that he would do all in his power to expedite such transactions.

ALL SWEDISH SHIPS ORDERED OFF SEAS

Special to The Inquirer

NEW YORK, April 11.—Sweden's merchant fleet of more than 1200 vessels, aggregating approximately 1,500,000 gross tons, was ordered off the high seas tonight.

This extraordinary precautionary measure, paralyzing the shipping of a neutral nation, was taken by the Swedish Government because of the uncertainty of Germany's aims in Scandinavia, it was learned officially.

Sweden followed the lead of the Danish Government representatives, who on Tuesday cancelled all sailings, directing Danish ships in neutral havens to remain there, and ordering all of their ships at sea to rush to neutral ports.

Some Norwegian ships began reloading today, although the decision as to whether they will remain in service rested on the Norwegian shipmasters, in lieu of no communications with the owners.

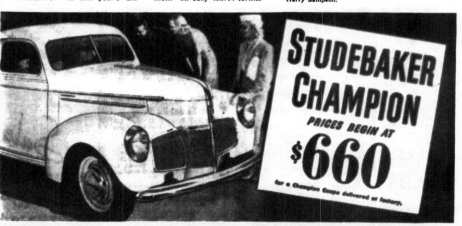

Danes May Seek to Transfer Registry of Ships to U. S.

WASHINGTON, April 11 (U. P.). —Discussions were in progress here late today regarding the possibility of transferring to American registry numerous Danish merchant vessels now in America or other neutral waters.

Danish Minister Henrik de Kauffmann was in conference on the subject, reportedly with representatives of Danish shipping lines.

It was reported in one quarter that there was a proposal for the transfer of at least 60 vessels to American registry. Such a move would be designed to permit Danish vessels to operate as neutrals, whereas if they remained under Danish registry they might be subject to German orders and considered by British and French authorities as "enemy" property.

SEEK U. S. ADVICE

A number of Norwegian ships in American waters have sought advice from the Norwegian Legation regarding what to do in view of the German invasion of their country, but the Norwegian Legation said it could not instruct ship operators until it received information from the Norwegian Government.

Private Norwegian ship owners could enter into arrangements with American shippers or the American Government without official permission of Norway, however, they said.

WOULD HURT ALLIES

Norway and Denmark are among the largest shipping nations in the world, with merchant fleets vastly greater in proportion to their size than most other countries.

They operate vessels in many parts of the world on regular lines and have many "tramp" vessels which take cargoes wherever there is business. Their ships have transported great amounts of supplies to Great Britain and France, and would be of much use to Germany if that country could obtain control of them.

Archbishop Coins Term For Unwed War Mothers

Special Cable to The Inquirer and New York Herald Tribune

LONDON, April 11.—The Archbishop of Canterbury, Dr. Cosmo Gordon Lang, coined a new phrase today to describe the unmarried mothers of children whose fathers are men in the service. Under new war regulations these mothers can draw pensions from the Government in the same manner as legally married mothers.

"The women irregularly allied to men in the forces" was the description voiced in the House of Lords by the Archbishop in the course of a debate.

"Nothing is more distasteful to me," he remarked on the subject.

(Copyright, 1940)

BOB FELLER PITCHES NO-HIT, NO-RUN GAME

The Philadelphia Inquirer

PHILADELPHIA, WEDNESDAY MORNING, APRIL 17, 1940 abdefgh★ 27

Strictly Sports

This Handy Horsey Guide Will Tell How and Why

Easy Definitions on Track Expressions May Dispel Your Daze

By CY PETERMAN

NOW that the income tax is out of the way and the gallopers back in Maryland, it is appropriate that we introduce our 1940 edition of McGoofey's First Reader, that indispensable handbook for race track chumps.

It is true, of course, some few may stumble through the spring meetings without need of this valuable volume, but as the Derby and Preakness, not to mention the Belmont and summer stakes approach, you will find it increasingly helpful in explaining how, where and why your good money was burned.

We have encountered in the course of our race track explorations no less than a dozen poor oafs who went flat broke without knowing a "goodie" from a "stiff," for instance. This seems downright uncharitable; not so much the fact they went broke but because they didnt realize how it happened.

• • •

THEREFORE let us to the meaning of certain expressions, terms and, insofar as printable, the language of all and sundry at the hoss parks:

"Coming out cold"—No Aunt Aggie, this has nothing to do with the weather or Cynthia Lou's debut. It means the nag you backed went into the race like Norway, unprepared. We hope Norway does better at the finish.

"Riding acey deucey"—Highly technical term having nothing to do with bridge or poker, used to identify short and long stirrup for the jockey. Supposed to provide an advantage on sharp turns, preventing Andy K's from running over the hills and far away as the rider leans in toward the rail.

"Playing the chalk"—Favorite pastime for favorite players, very discouraging at Hialeah the past winter. When long-shots cavort chalk players play the breadlines after hours.

• • •

"UNDER wraps"—Track equivalent for under restraint, indicating jockey has looped half-hitches around wrists to keep horse from loping into adjoining county. Considered most unethical when horse is trying to catch up with pace and is then referred to as . .

"Pulling"—The fine art of keeping a likely chance from getting up there, so some other gee can win. Also called . .

"Quitting With Mouth Open"—A phenomenon viewed with disfavor by most stewards as horse fights against bit and quite often leading to . .

"Summoning the Trainer"—American version of the Gestapo, a star chamber quiz to find out "what goes on here."

"Coming in on the Bill Daly"—Archaic expression denoting a long lead and easy victory without need of photo finish. Obsolete.

• • •

"CLIMBING aboard a stiff"—Most painful exercise at a race track. Involves deep study of form, esoteric connections, considerable discussion beforehand, careful scrutiny of odds board and lasting chagrin as the animal jogs home last.

"Pressing your luck"—Once-in-a-lifetime opportunity (usually unrecognized at the time) wherein horse player gets hot with streak of winners. If he wakes up in time to press his luck, can make it unpleasant for bookie or even knock down the odds at mutual track.

"Looked him in the eye"—Being challenged by another steed which draws even. Steeds rarely look each other in the eye during a race, however, and those with blinker equipment never. Just another silly colloquialism.

"He'll run off and hide"—One of many glib phrases used by touts when building up a prospect. Refers to excessive speed of their selection, indicating race will be run in two sections, tout's selection and rest of field. Smart prospects will "run off and hide" when approached by such salesmen.

"Coming down like trained pigs"—Fatuous reference to parade of favorites. Mostly used by civic-minded boosters of the track.

• • •

"GOING for Sweeney"—Very bad way of going, too. Sort of race suggesting Sweeney doesn't care.

"Throw out last"—Handicapper's casual method of dismissing a bum guess.

"Going sore"—Always refers to the horse, not the player, and we've always wondered why.

"Like money from home"—World's grossest exaggeration.

"Clockers special"—Caveat emptor. Take this in small doses.

"What do you hear?"—Salutation from a guy not doing so well.

"Straight from the stable"—And into the barnyard.

"Out of the clouds"—Where long shots come from.

"Round robin reverse"—Like the three-horse parlay, proof that hope springs eternal.

"A trifle short"—Which your horse was out of breath and you now are of cash.

"Blowout"—Trial ventilation of colt's lungs. Serious rent in bankroll if you bet him.

"Sleeps with the jockey"—The Charlie McCarthy posture, sometimes paying dividends.

"Took a bath"—Honest confession of a gent fresh out of funds. One who sent in the roll on a loser.

"Showed startling improvement"—Thinly veiled hint that owner or trainer had change of heart.

"Form flop"—Defter treatment of above.

"Paying the feed bill"—Snatching a part of the purse.

183,957 See Openers

NEW YORK, April 16 (A. P).

UNCERTAIN weather held down attendance at some games, but the total turnout of 183,957 fans in eight cities sounded a cheerful signal for baseball's 1940 major league season today.

The campaign was five days old last year before conditions permitted eight games on a single day and it was July before any one-day count equalled today's. The opening day attendance record was set in 1931 by 249,010 fans.

Led by Detroit with 49,417, the American League had all the best of the patronage today with a total gate of 114,604. This included the Nation's No. 1 fan, President Roosevelt, at Washington.

The figures:

AMERICAN LEAGUE	
At Detroit	49,417
At Washington	31,000
At Philadelphia	20,187
At Chicago	14,000
Total	114,604

NATIONAL LEAGUE	
At Cincinnati	34,342 (Capacity)
At St. Louis	16,600
At New York	14,840
At Boston	3,571
Total	69,353

Phils and A's Win Openers

MOSES STARTS TOWARD FIRST AS SELKIRK SPEARS HIS SMASH TO RIGHT (Another picture on Page 29)

Suhr's Homer Beats Giants

14,840 Watch Higbe Outpitch Hubbell for 3-1 Victory in N. Y.

By STAN BAUMGARTNER

Inquirer Sports Reporter

NEW YORK, April 16. A mighty home run by Gus Suhr, coupled with three-hit pitching by Kirby Higbe, gave the Phillies a surprise 3-1 triumph over Carl Hubbell and the New York Giants before 14,840 opening day fans at the Polo Grounds here today.

Suhr's glamorous circuit clout came in the eighth inning with the Phils trailing, 1-0, and two of his mates on base and one out.

HIT FIRST PITCH

The first baseman hit the first ball hurled by Hubbell, a high fast one, and it sailed against the upper wall of the rightfield stand as the entire Phillies bench danced with glee.

Joe Marty started off the inning with his third hit off Hubbell, a sizzler to left. Klein fanned and the jig looked up when Arnovich bounced what should have been a putout to Witek. The expensive sacker from Jersey City, made a $40,000 boot and tossed the ball over Jurges' head, all hands being safe. Suhr then leveled his bat at Hubbell's first pitch, and away it went.

FIRST SINCE 1930

It was the Phillies first opening triumph at the Polo Grounds and the initial kick-off victory on New York loam, which includes Brooklyn,

Continued on Page 29, Column 5

Suhr's Big Day

PHILLIES

	*B.Avg.	Ab.	r.	h.	rbi.	o.	a.	e.
Schulte, 2b	.200	5	0	1	0	3	3	0
Marty, cf	.750	4	0	3	0	2	0	0
b Benjamin	.000	0	1	0	0	0	0	0
Martin, cf.	.000	1	0	0	0	1	0	0
Klein, rf.	.000	4	0	0	0	1	0	0
Arnovich, lf.	.250	4	1	1	0	5	0	0
Suhr, 1b.	.500	2	1	1	3	9	0	1
Warren, c.	.000	4	0	0	0	4	1	0
May, 3b.	.000	4	0	0	0	1	1	1
Scharein, ss.	.000	2	0	0	0	1	1	0
a-Levy	.000	1	0	0	0	0	0	0
Bragan, ss.	.000	1	0	0	0	0	0	0
Higbe, p.	.000	4	0	0	0	0	1	0
Totals		36	3	6	3	27	8	2

NEW YORK

	*B.Avg.	Ab.	r.	h.	rbi.	o.	a.	e.
Rucker, cf.	.000	4	0	0	0	1	0	0
Jurges, ss.	.250	4	1	1	0	3	0	1
Demaree, lf.	.250	4	0	1	1	2	0	0
Ott, rf.	.000	2	0	0	0	3	0	0
Danning, c.	.333	3	0	1	0	10	1	0
Young, 1b.	.000	4	0	0	0	7	0	0
Witek, 2b.	.000	3	0	0	0	0	3	1
c-McCarthy	.000	1	0	0	0	0	0	0
Whitehead, 3b.	.000	3	0	0	0	1	1	0
Hubbell, p.	.000	2	0	0	0	0	2	0
d-Moore	.000	0	0	0	0	0	0	0
Brown, p.	.000	0	0	0	0	0	1	0
Totals		30	1	3	1	27	8	2

a-Batted for Scharein in 7th.
b-Ran for Marty in 8th.
c-Batted for Witek in 8th.
d-Batted for Hubbell in 8th.

Phillies	0	0	0	0	0	0	0	3	0	3
New York	0	0	0	1	0	0	0	0	0	1

Two base hit—Danning. Three base hit—Jurges. Home run—Suhr. Sacrifice—Danning. Double play—Warren to Scharein. Left on bases—Phillies, 8; New York, 6. Base on balls—Off Hubbell, 2; Higbe, 3. Struck out—By Hubbell, 5; Higbe, 3. Hits—Off Hubbell, 6 in 8 innings; off Brown, 0 in 1 inning. Wild pitch—Higbe. Losing pitcher—Hubbell. Umpires—Reardon, Pinelli and Goetz. Time of game—2.02.

*1940 batting average.

Chubby Dean Pitches, Bats A's To 2-1 Win Over Yanks in 10th

Long Fly Scores Clinching Run

By JAMES C. ISAMINGER

Continued From First Page

pitcher who made the happy event possible.

A crowd of 20,187 chilled but contented spectators saw Dean climax an afternoon of airtight pitching by driving home Catcher Hayes in the tenth with the winning run. Charley Keller caught Dean's drive to left after a sharp sprint backward but Hayes, who was on third, ran across the pentagon without a play.

FIRST TIME OVER ROUTE

The wonder of it all is that 23-year-old Dean had never before gone farther than seven innings in his Athletic career, which began in 1936. Previously he had been used as a pinch-hitter and relief pitcher, and in the few games he started before, he never went longer than seven innings.

Just one week ago in Atlanta, Dean held the Phillies to one run and six hits, and that is one reason that Connie Mack decided to start him in the opening game yesterday.

Dean would have shut out the Yankees in regulation innings had it not been for an error that made the heavy-hitting Yankees' only run unearned.

BENNY M'COY ERRS

This slip was made by the new Athletic player whose name has appeared in cold type more since last January than any other member of the team.

You guessed it: Benjamin McCoy. Tom Henrich opened the third with a pass. Dahlgren drove a scorcher to short. Bill Lillard came up with it in grand style and zinged the ball straight to McCoy. Benny tried to throw the ball before he squeezed it and it squirted out of his glove. Instead of a simple double play, the Yankees had men on first and second and nobody out.

Ruffing laid down a sacrifice to forward the runners. On Crosetti's fly to Bob Johnson, Henrich carried home the Yankees' lone run of the game. McCoy threw out Rolfe in a smart play to end the half.

Otherwise McCoy played a dashing game, for he accepted seven chances at the keystone, some of them difficult, and grabbed one of the six hits made off Charley Ruffing.

He opened the Athletic third with a virile knock against the ramparts in right for two bases but was never advanced.

YANKEES TAMED

Dean held the Yankees to six hits and issued three passes and was always master of the situation. The Yankees tried hard in closing innings to get one of their big rallies underway but Dean, in most exasperating fashion to them, never lost his head and held them in check.

Even in the tenth the Yankees had a chance to win. Dahlgren opened the inning with a clean single. Ruffing hit rapidly to Al Rubeling, the new third baseman, and the youth contributed another useful play when he made a clean stop and threw to McCoy, who relayed to Siebert for a double killing.

That was the saving play, for Crosetti followed with a single and Rolfe walked, only for Selkirk to raise a boyish fly in front of the plate that Hayes caught.

FANS TAKE HOPE

Spectators took on a lot of hope when the Yankees could not disturb the tie in the 10th and they urged the A's to win in the last half.

After Siebert expired on his pop fly to Gordon, Hayes drew a pass. Then Rubeling raised a short fly near the foul line in right, away from everybody. Selkirk and Gordon made gallant efforts to catch the ball, but could not quite come up to it and the young third sacker had a two-bagger which sent Hayes to third. Selkirk and Gordon collided and Gordon was knocked flat but uninjured and the game was resumed.

Connie Mack, who never made one tactical mistake in the game, nominated Dee Miles to bat for Bill Lillard. A sign from Germantown Joe McCarthy, sitting on the bench, directed Miles being passed purposely. That filled the bases.

DEAN COMES THROUGH

Game little Chubby Dean then carried his bat to the plate. The New York outfield was in close and Dean bashed the ball over Keller's head. Keller ran back for a smart catch, although outfielders in this situation seldom try to catch the ball, knowing it would be futile. Keller caught the ball and kept Chubby from collecting a hit, but there was no play to keep Hayes from pedaling over the rubber with the winning run.

The first Athletic run was a personal contribution from Bob Johnson, who played centre yesterday. Two out in the fourth and nobody on base, Johnson sledged a homer against the architecture in left to tie the score. Had he not done so, the A's would have been beaten in regulation innings. Johnson's first homer of 1940 put the A's in the game and kept them there until they won it themselves in the tenth.

TWO HITS FOR JOHNSON

Bob was the only member of the winning cast to get as many as two hits. He played good ball in centre, too.

The Athletic hit crop would have been larger had it not been for the demoniacal second-base play of Joe Gordon, who accepted 12 chances most of them teasers, without an error.

Gordon threw out McCoy in the eighth while prone on the ground where he capsized after stopping Benny's ripper off balance.

Before yesterday's game there were the usual copyrighted opening day ceremonies.

Connie Delivers

ATHLETICS

	*B.Avg.	Ab.	r.	h.	rbi.	o.	a.	e.
McCoy, 2b.	.250	4	0	1	0	4	3	1
Moses, rf.	.000	4	0	0	0	3	0	0
Simmons, lf.	.250	4	0	1	0	3	0	0
Johnson, cf.	.500	4	1	2	1	4	0	0
Siebert, 1b.	.250	4	0	1	0	10	0	0
Hayes, c.	.000	3	1	0	0	2	1	0
Rubeling, 3b.	.250	4	0	1	0	2	3	0
Lillard, ss.	.000	2	0	0	0	2	2	0
Dean, p.	.000	4	0	0	1	0	4	0
a Miles	.000	0	0	0	0	0	0	0
Totals		33	2	6	2	30	13	1

NEW YORK

	*B.Avg.	Ab.	r.	h.	rbi.	o.	a.	e.
Crosetti, ss.	.200	5	0	1	1	0	0	0
Rolfe, 3b	.000	4	0	0	0	1	0	0
Selkirk, rf	.000	5	0	0	0	4	0	0
Keller, lf.	.250	4	0	1	0	2	0	0
Dickey, c.	.250	4	0	1	0	6	0	0
Gordon, 2b.	.000	4	0	0	0	6	6	0
Henrich, cf.	.667	3	1	2	0	1	0	0
Dahlgren, 1b.	.333	3	0	1	0	9	0	0
Ruffing, p.	.000	3	0	0	0	0	4	0
Totals		35	1	6	1	z29	10	0

a-Batted for Lillard in 10th.
z-Two out when winning run was scored.

New York	0	0	1	0	0	0	0	0	0	0	1
Athletics	0	0	0	1	0	0	0	0	0	1	2

Two base hits—McCoy, Rubeling. Home run—Johnson. Stolen base—Henrich. Sacrifice—Ruffing. Double plays—Ruffing, Gordon to Dahlgren; Rubeling to McCoy to Siebert. Left on bases—Athletics, 5; New York, 8. Base on balls—Off Dean, 3; Ruffing, 2. Struck out—By Dean, 2; Ruffing, 5. Umpires—Summers, Quinn and Pipgras. Time of game—1.58.

*1940 batting average.

20,187 See N. Y. Held to Six Hits

'We'll Beat Yanks,' Predicted Mack, And Dean's Fly Fulfilled Prophecy

By CY PETERMAN

The whole stage was set for melodrama.

Connie Mack had predicted victory as far back as last January. "We'll beat the Yanks on Opening Day," said Mr. Mack.

And now it was the last half of the 10th, the gloaming of as grand a season's opener as Shibe Park ever housed, with the unheralded left-hander from Duke, Chubby Dean, walking grimly toward the plate. The score was 1 to 1.

3 MACKS ON BASE

The New York Yankees, scourge of the American League and fighting as if they didn't have 153 games left to win their fifth flag, had failed to control one of a dozen desperate drives and three Mackmen of 1940 were on base.

One man out, three men on, and anything except a double-play roller would do.

Chubby Dean, redoubtable "pinch-hitter" when not pitching—but in this brilliant mound turn of no value at bat, faced Charley Red Ruffing for the fourth time.

BANGS LONG FLY

And then all the pent-up tension of Opening Day broke loose, for Chubby bashed a long fly into left! Charley Keller, the World Series hero, flashed after it, but with Frank Hayes on third nothing Charley could do could balk the A's. As Keller caught it near the wall, turned and threw futily toward home, Hayes was over the plate with the sweetest Opening Day victory on the home lot since the gay pennant days 10 years back.

That was the finish, but by no means the only high spot of this stirring prelude to another season. A victory over New York's four-time World Champs, 2 to 1—no wonder 20,817 cheered.

Chubby Dean, one of the few pitchers on whom Connie looked with favor this spring, the only one in fact to pitch nine innings previously, had driven in the deciding run. He had limited the powerhouse from New York to six hits and, by all rights, should have owned a 1-0 victory in nine frames. A dropped throw by Benny McCoy allowed the Yanks to score their run without a basehit.

DEAN IS HERO

According to such summary, Dean should be the hero, and among a collection of same, he stands elected. Up to now Chubby has been an

Continued on Page 29, Column 2

Grove Hurls Two-Hit Game

Lefty Blanks Griffs After President Throws Out Ball

Illustrated on Page 30

WASHINGTON, April 16 (A. P.).—Pitching his extra best before President Roosevelt and scores of prominent persons, the veteran Lefty Grove let Washington down with two hits today to give Boston a 1 to 0 victory in the opening game of the 1940 baseball season.

CATCHES BALL

Vice President Garner, accompanied by Will Harridge, president of the American League; Clark Griffith, president of the Senators, and Brigadier General E. M. Watson, of the White House secretariat, led the Army band to centre field for flag raising ceremonies preceding the Presidential pitch from a bunting-draped box on the first base line. The President's toss was wild.

The ball was caught by a policeman after two Washington players fumbled it.

Except for a bit of jitteriness after a teammate's error in the 8th, Grove might have shown the 31,000 fans a no-hit game. He retired the first 21 Washington batters in order, but the 22d, Gerald Walker, reached first on an error by Ted Williams. Walker was thrown out at second on the play, however.

BOSTON	ab.	r.	h.	o.	a.	WASHINGTON	ab.	r.	h.	o.	a.
DiMag'o rf	4	0	0	2	0	Case cf	4	0	0	3	0
Cramer cf	4	0	1	4	0	Wasdell 1b	4	0	0	8	1
Williams lf	4	0	2	3	1	Lewis rf	3	0	0	3	0
Foxx 1b	2	0	1	10	0	Walker lf	3	0	0	4	0
Cronin ss	4	0	0	0	0	Travis 3b	3	0	1	1	1
Doerr 2b	3	1	0	3	2	Blo'rth 2b	3	0	1	0	7
Tabor 3b	4	0	0	0	2	Pofahl ss	3	0	0	3	1
Desautels c	4	0	1	5	0	Ferrell c	3	0	0	5	2
Grove p	3	0	2	0	3	Leonard p	2	0	0	0	1
						a-Welaj	1	0	0	0	0
Totals	32	1	7	27	8	Totals	29	0	2	27	13

a—Batted for Leonard in 9th.

Boston 0 1 0 0 0 0 0 0 0 — 1
Washington 0 0 0 0 0 0 0 0 0 — 0

Errors—Ferrell, Williams. Two base hits—Williams. Left on bases—Boston, 7; Washington, 2. Bases on balls—off Leonard, 3. Struck out—by Grove, 4; by Leonard, 1. Passed balls—Ferrell. Umpires—Hubbard, Moriarty, Rommel and Rue. Time—1:50. Attendance (estimated)—31,000.

Indians' Star Holds Chicago In Opener, 1-0

Parents See Young Cleveland Hurler Muffle Chisox Bats

By EDWARD BURNS

Special to The Inquirer

CHICAGO, April 16.—Bobby Feller, the 21-year-old miracle boy from Van Meter, Ia., pitched a no-hit game today and the Cleveland Indians won the season opener from the Chicago White Sox, 1-0, on a run batted in by his battery pal, Rollie Hemsley. It was a bleak day, but Bobby was sizzling hot all the way, especially after the third inning.

Feller, who put on his great show before his parents, Mr. and Mrs. William Feller, and his sister, Marguerite, retired 15 men in a row from the fourth inning through the eighth. A crowd of 14,000 cheered him on.

It was Feller's first no-hitter, although he has had three one-hit performances in his brilliant major league career. The young star won 24 games last season.

SMITH BRILLIANT

Lefty Edgar Smith, who scored a 1-0 triumph over Feller in an 11-inning night game in Comiskey Park last August, pitched brilliantly and might have been pitching till dark in a scoreless tie with more skillful support by Taft Wright on the hard shot by Hemsley, which went for a triple, to drive Jeff Heath home with two out in the fourth inning.

Smith allowed only six hits in his eight innings of endeavor, and Clint Brown got through the ninth without an Indian reaching first.

Feller struck out eight and walked five. One of the walks and two of the strikeouts came in the first inning; two of the walks and three of the strikeouts came in the second inning, and one of the walks came in the third.

WHITE SOX HELPLESS

From the third inning until two were out in the ninth not a White Sox reached base. Then, with a put-out to go for his no-hitter, Bobby met a stubborn foe in Luke Appling. Appling ran the count to three balls and two strikes, then started his fouling specialty. Luke walked on the 10th pitch.

Wright, next and last up, shot a grounder, to Second Baseman Ray Mack. Ray fumbled, but pursued the ball back to the grass and threw out Wright to end the game.

Feller's supporting cast was forced to snappy fielding only twice to save Bobby his no-hitter. Ben Chapman made a nice catch of Wright's wallop in the fourth, and Mack was pushed to thwart Pinch Batter Larry Rosenthal on a slow bounder at the start of the eighth.

SCORING UNCHALLENGED

There seemed to be no challenges of the official scoring on the one error, tabulated with one out in the second inning when Roy Weatherly misjudged, then dropped Wright's high fly to short centre.

It was the first no-hitter pitched by a Cleveland pitcher since Wes Ferrell handcuffed the Browns on April 29, 1931. The Indians, however, were mixed up in the last prior no-hitter in the American League.

Continued on Page 29, Column 3

Baseball Facts

AMERICAN LEAGUE

Yesterday's Results

Athletics 2, New York 1 (10 innings).
Boston 1, Washington 0.
St. Louis 5, Detroit 1.
Cleveland, 1; Chicago, 0.

HOW THEY STAND

	W.	L.	P.C.
Athletics	1	0	1.000
Boston	1	0	1.000
St. Louis	1	0	1.000
Cleveland	1	0	1.000
Chicago	0	1	.000
Washington	0	1	.000
Detroit	0	1	.000
New York	0	1	.000

Today's Schedule and Pitchers

New York at Philadelphia (Pearson vs. Potter).
St. Louis at Detroit (Auker vs. Bridges).
Boston at Washington (Hash or Bagby vs. Haynes or Hudson).
Cleveland at Chicago (Hudlin or Milnar vs. Rigney).

NATIONAL LEAGUE

Yesterday's Results

Phillies, 3; New York, 1.
Brooklyn, 5; Boston, 0.
Cincinnati, 2; Chicago, 1.
Pittsburgh, 6; St. Louis, 4.

HOW THEY STAND

	W.	L.	Pct.
Phillies	1	0	1.000
Brooklyn	1	0	1.000
Cincinnati	1	0	1.000
Pittsburgh	1	0	1.000
St. Louis	0	1	.000
New York	0	1	.000
Chicago	0	1	.000
Boston	0	1	.000

Today's Schedule and Pitchers

Phillies at New York (Mulcahy vs. Schumacher).
Brooklyn at Boston (Carleton vs. Errickson).
Chicago at Cincinnati (Passeau vs. Walters).
Pittsburgh at St. Louis (Macfayden or M. Brown vs. Cooper).

Continued on Page 30, Column 2

The Philadelphia Inquirer

PUBLIC LEDGER

An Independent Newspaper for All the People

8 A. M. EDITION

CIRCULATION: April Average Daily 411,444, Sunday 1,096,684 abdefgh ★★★ FRIDAY MORNING, MAY 10, 1940 Copyright, 1940, by The Phila. Inquirer Co. VOL. 222, NO. 131 Second Largest 3c Morning Circulation in America THREE CENTS

GERMANY INVADES HOLLAND, BELGIUM AND LUXEMBOURG

Berlin Says Army 'Guards' Lowlands From Allied Drive

By PRESTON GROVER

BERLIN, May 10 (A. P.).—Germany launched military operations today against The Netherlands, Belgium and Luxembourg to "safeguard" their "neutrality."

The official explanation for the sweeping campaign was that the British and French were planning to attack Germany through the territories of the three.

(German Propaganda Minister Dr. Joseph Goebbels confirmed the official explanation in a broadcast today and warned that any resistance would be broken, the United Press reported from Amsterdam.

(Goebbels said Belgium and The Netherlands had plotted against the German Government, and had fostered a German revolution. Therefore, he said, they are enemies.

(Goebbels demanded that the Governments of Belgium and Holland order their troops not to resist, The United Press said.)

SAFEGUARD NEUTRALITY

"In order to ward off the impending (Allied) attack, German troops received orders to safeguard the neutrality of Belgium and The Netherlands," said an announcement by DNB, official German news agency.

"Since the offensive decided upon by France and England shall also include Luxembourg, the Reich's government sees itself forced to expand the military operations under way for staving off attack also to include Luxembourg territory."

SUBMIT MEMORANDA

That was the way DNB concluded the announcement which had been anticipated by Dutch correspondents already listening to their homeland radio broadcasts that German parachute troops had landed and were fighting in numerous places.

At the outset of the brief announcement DNB said that Germany had submitted to the Belgian and Netherlands governments memoranda claiming evidence that the British and French were planning an immediate attack on the Reich through territories of the two neutrals.

'CITES EVIDENCE'

DNB said the evidence "unequivocally proved" that the Allied attack would be toward the Ruhr through Belgium and the Netherlands.

"The Reich's Government therefore ordered German troops to safeguard the neutrality of these countries with all the military means of the Reich."

(A partial text of Goebbels' broadcast, as reported in the United Press dispatch from Amsterdam, follows:

(Almost from the beginning of the outbreak of the war it has been clear that the Western Powers have been

Continued on Page 3, Column 4

INQUIRER AWARDED TYPOGRAPHY PRIZE IN NATIONAL EXHIBIT

Illustrated on Page 2

First honorable mention for excellence in newspaper typography among daily papers of more than 50,000 circulation has been awarded to The Philadelphia Inquirer in the 1940 Newspaper Typography Exhibition conducted by N. W. Ayer & Son, Inc., it was announced yesterday.

Other honorable mentions in the same group were awarded to the Christian Science Monitor and the New York Herald Tribune.

CUP TO N. Y. TIMES

The F. Wayland Ayer Cup, awarded to any daily newspaper in the United States for typographic excellence regardless of circulation or format, was given to the New York Times, which also won the cup in 1933 and 1935.

The Ayer Cup and other awards have been offered each year since 1931 in conjunction with the annual Newspaper Typography Exhibition, held in the Ayer Gallery, Washington Square, the purpose of which is to stimulate consistent improvement in the general appearance and readability of the daily newspaper.

ALL PAGES CONSIDERED

Judgments are made solely on the basis of typography, make-up and presswork, without regard to the editorial content of the publications entered. All inside pages, as well as page one, are considered in the judging.

Honorable mentions were awarded in three other classifications, as follows:

Standard size papers of from 10,-

Continue! on Page 2, Column 4

BLITZKRIEG HITS THREE MORE NATIONS

Germany invaded Holland, Belgium and Luxembourg (arrows) early today. The Reich's planes swarmed over the three countries, dropping bombs on principal airports and floating parachute troops to strategic points. Dutch anti-aircraft gunners and fighter pilots put up a fierce battle against the invaders, and a proclamation said that inundations had been made effective (cross-hatched areas in Holland denote regions prepared for defensive flooding). Belgian officials said the Brussels airport had been bombed. The principal airport of Holland, outside Amsterdam, also were blasted by warplanes. (A detailed map of the lowland countries, showing defense lines, is on Page 22.)

Nazis Pounce by Air; Dutch Fight Fiercely; French Troops on Way

Germany broke the European war wide open at dawn today with lightning air and land attacks which smashed into Holland, Belgium and Luxembourg without warning.

The Allies immediately responded to Dutch and Belgian appeals for military aid.

Hence, there was no doubt this morning that the war had found its battlefield.

The dreaded Nazi air force descended in swarms on dozens of cities, bombed airdromes and landed hundreds of parachute troops heavily armed with automatic weapons.

Holland formally declared war on Germany and pledged never to enter negotiations with the enemy.

The attacks, led by scores of German warplanes and followed by frontier attacks by land troops, apparently came simultaneously, although the news first reached the outside world from Holland when Dutch anti-aircraft batteries and fighter planes engaged the German raiders in fierce battle.

GERMANY EXTENDS 'PROTECTION'

Germany announced it was taking The Netherlands and Belgium under protection and was moving with all its forces to forestall an "immediate" British-French offensive through the Low Countries toward the Reich's rich industrial region of the Ruhr.

Fuehrer Adolf Hitler, following his favorite tactic of striking when his enemy is unprepared, chose a moment when Britain was in the midst of a Cabinet crisis over the failure of its effort to block Germany's invasion of Norway, begun just one month ago yesterday, on April 9.

FRENCH AND BRITISH RESPOND

There were unconfirmed reports of heavy casualties resulting from the first German air raid on Brussels.

The French War Office announced that the previously prepared plan to advance to protect Belgium if it were invaded had been put into operation.

The British Government announced that the invaded nations had asked for British aid and said that "His Majesty's Government will, of course, render all the help they can."

WARPLANES SWARM IN WAVES

The Luxembourg Government reportedly had fled.

Dozens of airdromes, some of them in the immediate vicinity of populous cities, were showered with bombs. German warplanes came from Germany in large formations, wave after wave, some of them dropping high explosives and others landing German troops—some of which were said to be clothed in military uniforms of the invaded countries.

HOLLAND OPENS THE DIKES

Holland authorities said the dikes had been opened and inundation of a large part of the country carried out according to defense plans.

German bombers appeared simultaneously over the Thames estuary, bringing British anti-aircraft guns into action. No bombs were dropped, and it was believed this contingent had been charged with creating a diversion and preventing any quick British air aid to Holland or Belgium, across the narrow English Channel.

The Reich's air force also struck at France, bombing the Bron airport at Lyons—largest in Central France.

FLASH

Lyons Airport Bombed

PARIS, May 10 (Friday) U. P.).—German planes bombed the airport at Lyons this morning. The Bron Airport at Lyons was bombed, the first bombing in France sance the war started. Bron is the largest airfeld in central France and a most important military air base.

Heavy Firing in Channel

LONDON, May 10 (Friday) (8.50 A. M.) (U. P.) — Heavy gunfire and explosions, presumably bombs, were heard for an hour and a half this morning in the English Channel off northern France. It was believed German planes were attacking allied shipping.

Report 400 Casualties

LONDON, May 10 (U. P.).—Exchange Telegraph reported from Zurich, Switzerland, this morning that the first German air raid on Brussels allegedly resulted in 400 casualties, dead and wounded.

Dutch, Belgian Ports Mined

LONDON, May 10 (Friday) (U. P.).—The Berlin Radio announce dtoday that minefields had been laid in front of all Dutch and Belgian ports.

Italians Reported Massing

BUNEOS AIRES, May 10 (Friday) (U. P.).—Unconfirmed reports from Madrid today said the British have closed the Straits of Gibraltar, and that Italy is massing troops on the French frontier.

Allied Planes Over Holland

LONDON, May 10 (A. P.).—French, Belgian and British planes were sighted over Holland this morning, a Reuters (British news agency) dispatch said in quoting The Netherlands radio station at Hilversum, near Amsterdam.

Report U. S. Fleet Sailing

MANILA, May 10 (Friday) (U. P.).—Wholly unconfirmed

Continued on Page 2, Column 6

U. S. ENVOY PHONES WORD OF INVASION

By RICHARD L. HARKNESS

Inquirer Washington Bureau

WASHINGTON, May 10 (Friday).—Fuehrer Adolf Hitler unleached his air and land forces early today in a new blitzkrieg invasion of the little neutral territories of Belgium, Holland and Luxembourg, according to a long-distance telephone report to Secretary of State Cordell Hull from American Ambassador John Cudahy at Brussels.

With President Roosevelt keeping a vigil on Europe's war in his private White House study across the street, Cudahy informed Hull that German airplanes were bombing an airport near Brussels even as he was talking.

CREDITS FROZEN

"German planes continued across the Luxembourg border and are bombing the airport near Brussels," Cudahy said.

"It seems to be a general attack on all three countries (Belgium, Holland and Luxembourg)."

Meanwhile the President ordered all Belgian, Dutch and Luxembourg credits and cash balances in this country "frozen" and summoned chiefs of the State, War and Navy services to conference at 10:30 A. M. (11.30 A. M. E. D. T.) to consider pressing problems on neutrality.

TO WEIGH NEUTRALITY

Hull, Undersecretary Sumner Welles, Gen. George C. Marshall, Army Chief of Staff; Admiral Harold R. Stark, Chief of Naval Operations, and Attorney General Robert H. Jackson were summoned to the

Continued on Page 3, Column 3

Brussels Airport Bombed by Nazis; 100 Planes Attack

BRUSSELS, May 10 (Friday) (A. P.).—Waves of German bombers and troop transports launched the German invasion of Belgium in the dark hours before dawn today.

More than 100 German planes roared over Brussels, the capital. The Brussels airport was subjected to heavy bombing.

LEOPOLD TAKES COMMAND

King Leopold III assumed command of the Belgian army just as his father, King Albert, did when the German army marched into the little kingdom 26 years ago.

General mobilization was proclaimed as the Brussels radio announced that French and British troops were on the way to help.

Parachute troops, said the Brussels radio, dropped from German planes at Nivelles, less than 20 miles directly south of Brussels and at St. Trond, 40 miles due east.

The railway station at Jemelle, in the southeast corner of Belgium, not far from the Luxembourg frontier, was reported in flames.

BOMB ANTWERP AIRPORT

The Antwerp airport also was attacked with bombs.

German troops were landed by parachute at Hasselt, in eastern Belgium, while reports of other troop landings could not be confirmed immediately.

The radio reported parachute troops had landed in the north.

Communications were tied up by a rush of official messages.

Artillery fire was reported on the German-Belgian frontier.

It was reported that after an inter-

Continued on Page 3, Column 4

HOLLAND BATTLES GERMAN INVADERS

By CLIFFORD L. DAY

AMSTERDAM, May 10 (Friday) (U. P.).—Germany invaded Holland early today, land troops being preceded by a Blitzkrieg air attack on Dutch airdromes and the landing of parachute troops at a number of points.

The Dutch resisted to the limit of their strength, anti-aircraft batteries and fighter planes engaging swarms of German aircraft when they appeared simultaneously over a score of Dutch cities.

It was officially announced this morning that Holland was at war with Germany.

An official proclamation said:

Continued on Page 3, Column 6

British Land in Iceland To Forestall Nazi Invasion

LONDON, May 10 (Friday) (A. P.).—Great Britain took protective custody of Iceland today by landing an armed force on the North Atlantic island which is united to German-occupied Denmark by the tie of the throne of King Christian X.

The British Foreign Office announced this action was taken to prevent seizure of Iceland by Germany.

It was not disclosed immediately whether the British force encountered any difficulty with Germans reported to have infiltrated into the island before and since outbreak of the European war.

Iceland has a defense force of her own of only about 70 police.

The Foreign Office said Iceland was given a guarantee that the occupation would be only for the duration of hostilities.

The little northern kingdom is expected to provide the Allies with excellent submarine bases as well as seaplane and airplane bases.

It was disclosed that R. C. Harris, of the British Ministry of Economic Warfare, had arrived in Iceland to-

Continued on Page 2, Column 7

IN TODAY'S INQUIRER

THE WEATHER

Official forecast—Eastern Pennsylvania: Fair today, tomorrow partly cloudy, little change in temperature.

New Jersey and Delaware: Fair today, tomorrow increasing cloudiness, little change in temperature.

(Daylight-saving Time)

Sun rises 5.50 A.M. Sets 8.03 P.M.
Moon rises 8.21 A.M. Sets 11.01 P.M.

Other Weather Reports on Page 2

Picture Parade
SECTION OF
The Philadelphia Inquirer
IN TWO PARTS MAY 12, 1940

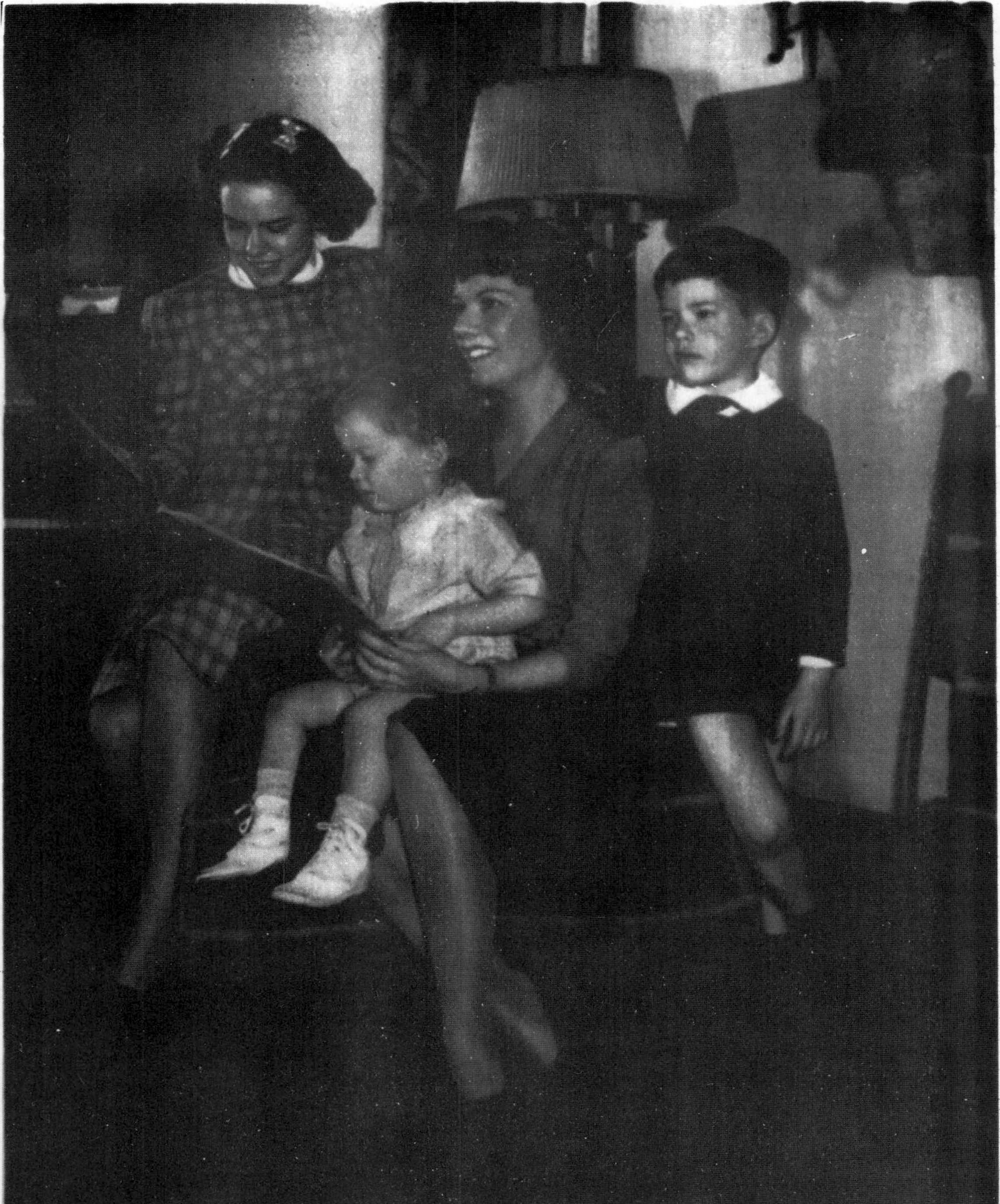

Inquirer Natural Color Photos

The centre of a charming group is Mrs. Frank Paul Kane, of Vallon Tour, Radnor, mother of three. The children are Pauline, aged 12; John Kent, 2nd, aged 5 (named for his grandfather); Peter, the youngest, aged 2.

Mrs. William R. Cross, of Woodland and Rydal roads, Rydal, and daughter, Inez Balena, 4, are caught by the camera in a delightful pose.

Mrs. Gurney P. Sloan, of Woodleave road, Bryn Mawr, has found a plaything which fascinates her young son, Stephen, born last December.

MODERN MOTHER'S DAY BEGAN IN PHILADELPHIA

MOTHERS have been honored since the beginning of time. Rhea, great mother of pagan gods, was worshipped by Greeks and Trojans in Asia Minor centuries before Christ. At the beginning of the Christian era the ceremony became imbued with a new spirit. Later came "Mothering Sunday" in England. In 1873 Julia Ward Howe and a group of her friends set aside a day to be observed annually in the interests of peace and motherhood. Friends of Frank E. Bering, of South Bend, Ind., believe that he was an originator of the day. But Miss Anna Jarvis of Philadelphia, president of the Mother's Day International Association, is commonly recognized as the founder of Mother's Day as it is now observed. Twenty-six years ago she prevailed upon Congress and President Wilson to set aside the second Sunday in May as Mother's Day. The first proclamation was issued in 1914 and the day has been celebrated ever since. The idea spread to many other countries. Tributes to mothers are as old as the ages, but not until late years has a special date been set aside for them.

The Philadelphia Inquirer

PUBLIC LEDGER

An Independent Newspaper for All the People

8 A. M. EDITION

CIRCULATION: May Average Daily 427,485, Sunday 1,065,464 — a b d e f g h★ — FRIDAY MORNING, JUNE 14, 1940 — Second Largest 3c Morning Circulation in America — THREE CENTS

 VOL. 222, No. 166

NAZIS IN PARIS

COUNCIL VOTES TO REJECT ALL HOUSING SITES

Caucus Step, 11-8, May Mean Loss of $19,000,000 Allotted To Phila. by FHA

By CHARLES H. ELLIS, JR.

At a formal and secret caucus held following its meeting yesterday, City Council decided by a majority vote not to approve any further sites for low-cost housing in Philadelphia.

This action, if confirmed by ordinance prior to July 1, automatically would result in Philadelphia's losing $19,000,000 in Federal Housing Administration funds specially earmarked for this purpose.

VOTE REPORTED 11 TO 8

Although there was no discussion or formal statement on the caucus, the vote was said to have been 11 to 8, with three members absent.

The vote was taken after Roland R. Randall, chairman of the Philadelphia Housing Authority, had served notice on Council that the future of low-cost housing in Philadelphia was strictly up to them.

That the caucus had voted disapproval of any further sites was announced by Bernard Samuel, president of Council.

LISTED AS OPPOSED

Those reported to have opposed the housing proposal include the following:

James O. Clark, L. Wallace Egan, Frederic D. Garman, Phineas T. Green, Robert J. Hamilton, Jr., William M. Hollenbach, William A. Kelley, George B. Mansfield, James J. McDevitt, 3d, Joseph J. Milligan and William B. Simons.

For the proposal:

Thomas H. Allen, Eugene J. Haggerty, (both Democrats), Bernard Samuel, Charles E. O'Halloran, John A. Mawhinney, Thomas P. Stokley, Clarence K. Crossan, and James H. Irwin.

3 DO NOT VOTE

Not voting: George Maxman, Charles J. Pommer, Louis Schwartz.

At the end of the caucus, Samuel emerged and said:

"It is the sense of the majority of the caucus that they do not wish to proceed with further low-cost housing for Philadelphia at this time."

He was asked whether he felt there was any likelihood that any of the Councilmanic opponents might reconsider, but replied:

PICKETING THREATENED

Council's action brought a prompt threat last night from Herbert C. Bergstrom, chairman of the Coordinating Housing Council of Philadelphia, that the Republican Na-

Continued on Page 11, Column 4

Hitler Declares He Has No Aims In Americas

By KARL H. VON WIEGAND

Noted foreign correspondent and for 28 years outstanding American political observer in Europe and the Far East.

WITH THE GERMAN ARMIES NEARING PARIS, June 13.—"The Americas to Americans, Europe to the Europeans."

This reciprocal, basic "Monroe Doctrine," mutually observed, Adolf Hitler declared to me today, not only would insure peace for all time between the old and the new worlds, but would be a most ideal foundation for peace throughout the whole world.

He denounced "the lies" that he has or ever had in "dream or thought" played with the faintest idea of interfering in the Western Hemisphere in any way.

He characterized America's fears of him or Germany as most flattering, but "childish and grotesque," and the whole idea of the possibility of the invasion of the United States from Europe by sea, air or the "mythical 'Fifth Column'" as "stupid and fantastic."

WON'T ATTACK 'OPEN' PARIS

With his German war machine, whose perfection of organization, strength, strategical and tactical leadership has startled the world, now on the edge of Paris, Hitler told me he had no intention of attacking the beautiful French capital if it "remains an open city like Brussels."

Vehemently the Fuehrer denied he ever had or even now has as a war aim the "smashing of the British Empire." But with bitter anger he declared:

"I will destroy those men who are destroying that Empire."

The Fuehrer had insisted on formulating his replies to my questions in writing. These in hand, he discussed them for nearly an hour.

'NO INTEREST IN AMERICA'

He began with America's attitude toward Germany and his attitude toward America.

"Germany is one of the few countries which hitherto has refrained from interfering in any way in America," he wanted to remind me.

"At no time has Germany had any territorial or political interest in the American continent," Hitler declared.

Then, with rising voice:

"Nor has Germany any such interest now. Whoever states anything to the contrary is lying deliberately for some purpose.

'NO CONCERN OF MINE'

"How the American continent shapes and leads its life is no concern of mine, and of no interest to Germany.

"And that, let me say, holds good not only for North America, but equally so for South America.

"But let me observe this. I do not believe that a doctrine such as pro-

Continued on Page 6, Column 2

TURKEY AND REICH SIGN TRADE ACCORD AS 'ALLIES APPROVE'

ANKARA, June 13 (A. P.).—Turkey signed a pact with Germany today for the exchange of $14,000,000 worth of tobacco for German machinery parts, but Turkish officials said the treaty had the approval of their allies, Britain and France, and represented no lessening of the alliance.

The Allies, it was said, do not object to Turkish tobacco going to Germany, nor to Turkey getting machines and parts from Germany which she cannot get elsewhere. Most of the parts are for the national railways.

ONLY TWO WEEKS

Officials said the products were ready to be shipped and probably would be entirely moved within the next two weeks.

The deal thus was interpreted as a sign that Turkey thinks it not likely she will be involved in the new Mediterranean war in that time.

REAFFIRMS ALLIANCE

Turkey reaffirmed its purpose to stand by the French-British alliance, and the press punctuated this announcement with scathing attacks upon Italy, although the cabinet has concluded that for the present it is not wise to take an active part in the conflict.

Preparations for any contingency were rushed, including the systematic calling of more men to the colors.

TANKER REPORTED SUNK

American officials of the Socony Vacuum Co. still lacked confirmation of a report one of their tankers, flying a British flag, had been sunk, presumably by an Italian submarine.

How the new treaty with Germany was explained, considerable confusion was caused among Near

Continued on Page 6, Column 6

BRITISH PLEDGE 'UTMOST AID' TO FRENCH ALLIES

Rush Troops From Home Defenses to Fight German Army Encircling Paris

LONDON, June 14 (Friday) (A. P.).—Great Britain, drawing from forces reserved for defense of its own island in the face of an expected German invasion, rushed reinforcements to France today and renewed its pledge "to continue the struggle at all costs in France, in this island, upon the ocean and in the air wherever it may lead us."

PLEDGES 'UTMOST AID'

"Great Britain will continue to give the utmost aid in her power," said the British Government's message to France.

"We shall never turn from the conflict until France stands safe and erect in all of her grandeur, until the wrong and the wronged and enslaved States and peoples have been free from the nightmare of Nazism."

The British said they would share with France the costs of repairing the ravages of war.

BRITISH TROOPS ON SEINE

With every available fighting man, gun and tank pledged to "death or victory" beside the weary French, military sources reported fresh British troops already were there—hurled into the Seine River line.

"Thousands" more, their numbers and route guarded closely, were on the way, as the London press urged that even untrained divisions incompletely equipped be rushed to the Continent.

CHILDREN LEAVE LONDON

With troops pouring out of England, school children were hustled from London to the country, church bells were silenced except to warn of parachute invasion, and a Government spokesman said some "danger areas" might have to be cleared entirely of civilians.

Press and public agreed that home defense must be left to the home guard. The army is needed in the battle around Paris, where, the British said, "if the enemy is thrown back from the gates, he has lost the war."

PUT PRISONERS AT 6000

St. Valery-en-Caux is to be avenged. There German encirclement cut off British and French defense units. British military circles said 6000 Allied soldiers, low on food and ammunition, backed up to the high cliffs of France's English Channel coast, had been captured. Some got away on small ships that came in through a fog. Others fought through to the south and reformed with their comrades to continue the defense of the port city of Le Havre.

Germany claimed 20,000 captured. And of German statements that "incalculable amounts" of war supplies were seized, one British source commented: "Whatever the interpretation of this word, the quantity of material taken was not enormous."

FLIERS KEEP UP ATTACKS

"All available troops and materials," said the Ministry of Information, "are being sent to help the

Continued on Page 2, Column 6

Army Is 'Inside Gates,' U.S. Notified by Bullitt

A half-page detail map of Paris is on Page 22.

By WILLIAM C. MURPHY, JR.

Inquirer Washington Bureau

WASHINGTON, June 14 (Friday)—William C. Bullitt, United States Ambassador to France, early this morning notified the State Department that the German army is "inside the gates of Paris."

Bullitt, who has remained at his post in the beleaguered capital, telephoned his message to Anthony J. Drexel Biddle, Ambassador to the Polish Government now domiciled in Tours, France, at 7 o'clock last night Paris time (3 P. M. Thursday, E. D. T.) "The city was quiet," it said.

Biddle relayed the message to Washington, where it was received just before 2 A. M. (E. D. T.)

The message as relayed gave no indication of what Bullitt meant by "inside the gates." It was not known here how large a German force had entered the city, which the French had decided not to defend from within.

SEVENTH CAPITAL ENTERED BY NAZIS

(A United Press dispatch said Bullitt's message revealed that the Germans entered Paris at 7 P. M. French time.)

It was Bullitt who conveyed to German authorities yesterday the French proclamation of an "open city" status for Paris to save the metropolis from the destruction of bombardment.

Paris was the seventh foreign capital entered by Nazi forces since the European war started last Sept. 1, the Germans previously having taken Warsaw, Copenhagen, Oslo, The Hague, Brussels and Luxembourg.

FRANCE CANCELS MILITARY PRESS PARLEY

TOURS, France, June 14 (Friday) (A. P.).—There will be no military press conference this morning, it was announced early today, and it was not certain whether the customary military communique would be issued.

The Associated Press staff here prepared to leave for Bordeaux during the day.

Coupled with announcement that there would be no military conference and uncertainty regarding is-

Continued on Page 2, Column 1

Reynaud Begs For 'Clouds' of U. S. Planes

By M. S. HANDLER

TOURS, France, June 13 (U. P.).—Premier Paul Reynaud broadcast a "final appeal" tonight to President Roosevelt, imploring the United States to "declare itself against Germany" and send "clouds" of warplanes to smash Fuehrer Adolf Hitler's armies overrunning northern France.

Pleading desperately a few hours after Paris and its priceless beauty had been abandoned to the mercy of the Germans pounding at the city's gates, Reynaud suggested that it would be suicidal to continue the struggle unless hope of ultimate victory appeared.

He indicated clearly the crushing weight of the decision resting upon the shoulders of his Government, which now must ponder all aspects of the situation.

MIGHT INDICATE PEACE MOVE

(This might indicate that, unless France obtained aid, the Government might seek peace on the best possible terms.)

Reynaud spoke of the French as "losing this battle," but declared that "despite our reverses the power of the democra-

Continued on Page 3, Column 1

Summary

The German Army is "inside the gates of Paris," Ambassador William C. Bullitt informed the State Department early today.

German forces pressed toward the rich Loire Valley and the routes leading through the centre of France toward the emergency capital of Tours. The French declared Paris itself an "open city" to save it from bombardment.

In a "final" appeal to President Roosevelt last night, Premier Reynaud, of France, pleaded for "clouds" of planes and urged the United States to "declare itself against Germany." Reynaud hinted it might be useless to continue the struggle unless aid should make ultimate victory appear possible.

"Everything possible is being done to forward supplies to France," White House Secretary Stephen T. Early said immediately after President Roosevelt had received reports of Reynaud's appeal.

Britain drew direly needed reinforcements for France from its own home defenses and its air fighters continued their attacks on the enemy in Norway, France and Africa.

Turkey signed a $14,000,000 trade agreement with Germany, officials claiming the approval of Turkey's allies, Britain and France.

IN TODAY'S INQUIRER

Britain Restricts Trade With Southeast Europe

LONDON, June 13 (A. P.).—The export of all classes of goods from Britain to Bulgaria, Greece, Hungary, Rumania, Switzerland, Jugoslavia and the Black Sea ports of Russia was prohibited by Great Britain today except under a board of trade license.

A Board of Trade announcement said the order was made to "enable necessary control to be exercised over exports to the Mediterranean and adjacent areas."

The announcement said the step was made necessary by Italy's entry into the war and was "not to be regarded in any sense as a decision to discontinue trade with neutral countries" in those areas.

Kennedy Confers With Lord Halifax

LONDON, June 13 (A. P.).—U. S. Ambassador Joseph P. Kennedy conferred with the foreign secretary, Viscount Halifax, today. It was believed their discussion centered on additional United States aid to the Allies.

HOUSE PASSES BILL TO DEPORT BRIDGES

By PAUL W. RAMSEY

Inquirer Washington Bureau

WASHINGTON, June 13.—A bill calling for the immediate arrest and deportation of Harry R. Bridges, West Coast CIO director, was passed by the House late today by the top-heavy vote of 330 to 42.

The measure, a brief document of less than a dozen lines, declares Bridges' presence in this country to be "harmful," and directs the Attorney G neral to send him back to his native Australia.

Final action on the bill, which now goes to the Senate, was preceded by bitter debate in which backers of the deportation move assailed the maritime labor leader as a "trouble-maker," a "disturbing factor" and a "symbol of the 'Fifth Column.'"

LEGALITY QUESTIONED

Opponents of the measure—some of whom even joined in denouncing Bridges—attacked it as an unconstitutional move to invoke judgment upon Bridges without granting him the right of trial. They said it marked the first time that such a bill, aimed at deporting an individual, had ever been passed by the House,

Continued on Page 9, Column 1

WHITE HOUSE GIVES FRANCE ASSURANCE

By WILLIAM C. MURPHY, JR.

Inquirer Washington Bureau

WASHINGTON, June 13.—The White House declared tonight that "everything possible is being done to forward supplies to France."

Stephen T. Early, White House secretary, issued the statement immediately after President Roosevelt had received press and radio reports telling of the "final desperate appeal" made by French Premier Paul Reynaud to the President to aid the hard-pressed Allies before it was too late.

TEXT NOT AWAITED

The statement was issued without waiting for the arrival of the text of Reynaud's appeal and at a time when the State Department said it had no official information that any such message was on the way. Early said:

"The text of Premier Reynaud's statement has not yet been received here. But everything possible is being done to forward supplies to France."

Early did not specify just what was being done, but it was assumed that efforts were being intensified to release "surplus" war material for resale to the Allies and to speed the shipment of such supplies.

The White House reply to the Premier's appeal came toward the end

Continued on Page 3, Column 6

Finland Ready to Pay U. S. Debt Installment

WASHINGTON, June 13 (A. P.)—Battle-scarred little Finland today advised the United States that it would pay its $159,398 semi-annual war debt installment as usual and thus preserve a perfect record of payments.

Hjalmar Procope, Finnish Minister, announced that the check was ready and would be turned over Saturday, when installments will be due from 13 other debtors.

However, proposals are pending in Congress to return to Finland for reconstruction purposes, and as a token of American respect for a little nation's financial honor and military valor, both this week's installment and the $234,693 it paid last December.

250 U. S. Refugees Sail From Genoa

GENOA, Italy, June 13 (A. P.).—The American steamship Exochorda left Genoa for New York tonight with 250 American war refugees aboard, including 50 last-minute arrivals.

Two hundred came from Egypt. The only American ship left in Genoa harbor is the small freighter Prusa, sailing Saturday.

THE WEATHER

Official Forecast—Eastern Pennsylvania: Fair and cooler today and tonight; fair tomorrow, slowly rising temperature.

New Jersey and Delaware: Fair, slightly cooler today; generally fair tomorrow.

(Daylight-saving Time)

Sun rises	5.30 A.M.	Sets 8.30 P.M.
Moon rises	2.49 P.M.	Sets 1.45 A.M.

A MIRACLE OF DELIVERANCE

These soldiers of the crack Lancaster Regiment, typical of the Tommies evacuated from Dunkirk, marched briskly into Belgium at the beginning of the German invasion. They returned to England shattered and torn, but with their morale still at a high level.

French artillery units also moved into Belgium to meet the Blitzkrieg. Then they fought a rear-guard action for nearly 100 miles and made a final stand to cover the embarkation at Dunkirk. The British were forced to abandon nearly 1,000 pieces of artillery.

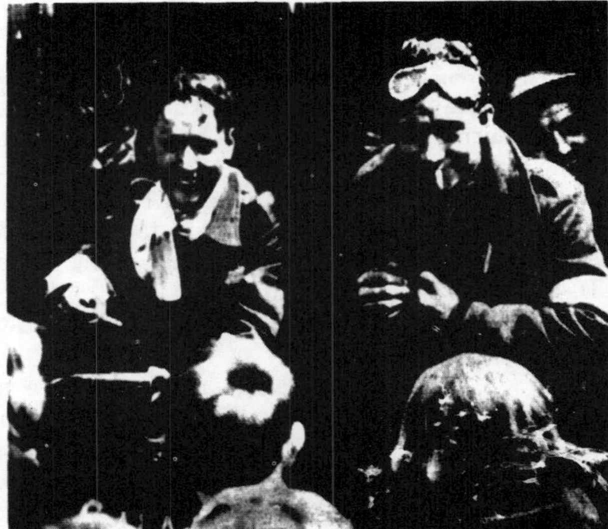

The returning Tommies were greeted with food, cheers and cigarettes at every station in England. British losses in killed, wounded and missing were in excess of 30,000. But there was no hint of anything but a grim determination to continue fighting Hitler.

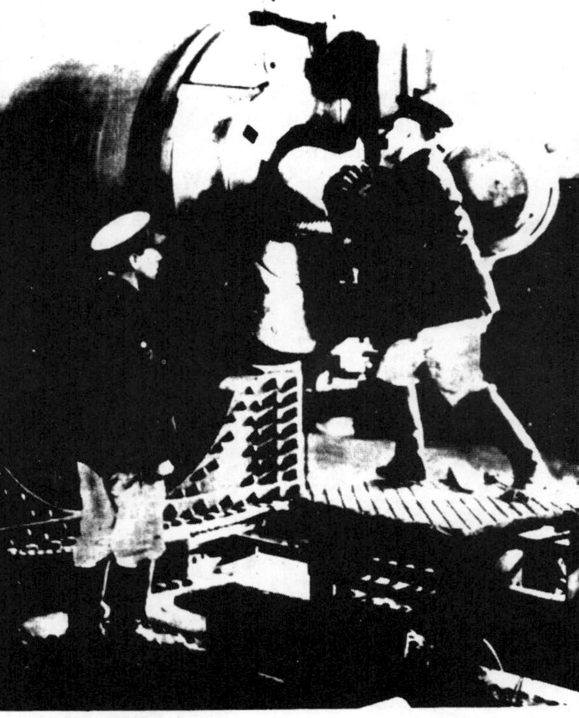

English coast defense guns were readied to repel an invasion that seemed imminent after the debacle in Belgium. These guns also covered the movements of hundreds of vessels shuttling across the channel to rescue the Allied forces.

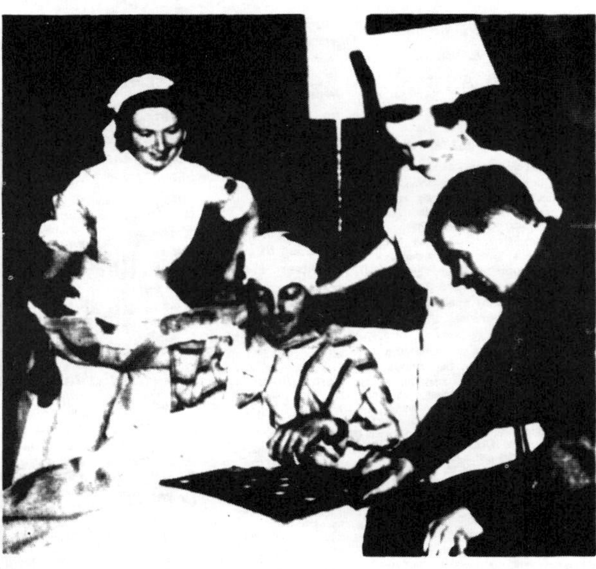

Not all the soldiers of Belgium laid down their arms when King Leopold surrendered and precipitated the disaster in Flanders. Here a Belgian fighter (right), evacuated with the British and French, plays checkers with a Tommy in an English hospital.

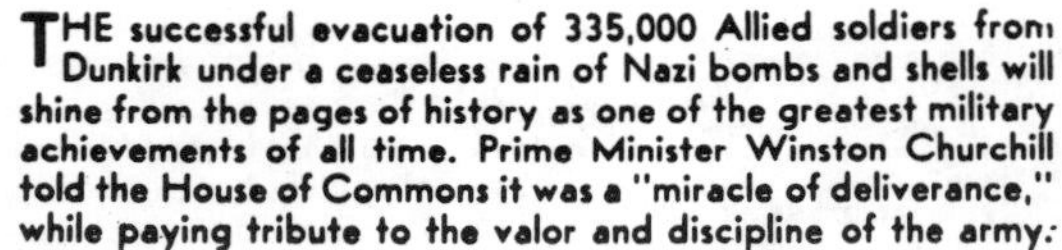

THE successful evacuation of 335,000 Allied soldiers from Dunkirk under a ceaseless rain of Nazi bombs and shells will shine from the pages of history as one of the greatest military achievements of all time. Prime Minister Winston Churchill told the House of Commons it was a "miracle of deliverance," while paying tribute to the valor and discipline of the army.

British anti-aircraft dugouts like this were unable to stop the swarming flights of Nazi bombers which sprayed constant death across the Belgian plains. As the inexorable German advance continued, the dugouts were abandoned. But the rear-guard fighting was not.

An artist's conception of the Battle of the Ports shows Dunkirk flaming into a sky filled with Allied and Nazi planes whirling in combat. A bomb drops from a diving Stuka toward a British warship. Small boats scurry to pick up survivors of a sinking transport.

Rivers which crossed the retreat furnished temporary lines of defense against the German military machine. Rubber boats were used to cross them, then stands were taken upon the opposite shore.

General the Viscount Gort (right), commander of the British Expeditionary Force, was greeted on his return by General Sir John Dill, chief of the Imperial General Staff. King George honored Gort by making him a Knight of the Grand Cross of the Order of Bath.

The Philadelphia Inquirer

PUBLIC LEDGER

An Independent Newspaper for All the People

6 A. M. EDITION

CIRCULATION: July Average 412,087, Sunday 981,964 — a b d e f g h — WEDNESDAY MORNING, SEPTEMBER 4, 1940 — Second Largest 3c Morning Circulation in America — THREE CENTS

Roosevelt Trades 50 U.S. Destroyers To Britain for Air and Naval Bases; House Group Modifies 'Plant Draft'

Today

New Deal Campaign Must Sell Third Term Seems Impossible Job But Not for F. D. R. He Shows Them How

By Paul Mallon

ABOARD PRESIDENT ROOSEVELT'S SPECIAL TRAIN, Sept. 3.

MR. ROOSEVELT can still give them all cards and spades in campaigning. The technique this time was to answer Willkie without conceding that there is such a man.

It was to present the heavy breath of Hitler upon the public neck at just the right temperature, not too hot because that would be disastrous war mongering, not too cold as then such a reason for voting for Roosevelt would be lost.

The great humanitarian accomplishments of the first two terms must be heralded, but not by open campaigning because that would disclose personal initiative for a third term. It had to be [illegible], coyly, graciously.

The necessity for a third term must be presented without seeming to. The picture of a man too busy at great projects to waste time in sordid politics, the photo of a leader drafted against his personal inclinations, had to be perpetuated.

That's a tough job, an impossible one, you might say, unless you had accompanied Mr. Roosevelt on his first stump foray since his acceptance speech, the opening gun of his campaign in the hesitant South.

Ickes tried to do it and messed it up with rhetorical overindulgence. Wallace attempted it, but slopped over into painting swastikas on practically everyone except himself and Roosevelt.

Down here the Old Master showed them how it should be done. He demonstrated conclusively that what the Republicans had deluded themselves into believing was only a magic radio voice, was unquestionably sharpest political wit of the age. This is the picture:

The Chickamauga Dam which was finished last March and could have been dedicated anytime since then, or not dedicated at all, because few dam openings have been potted by Presidential hands was selected for the opening of the President's campaign.

It was chosen because it afforded the desired contrast with Willkie, in the heart of the district where he represented private power, a community which has gotten more out of the New Deal than any other.

Never a word about Willkie was there in the speech, only subtle contrasting pledges for cheap electricity, sorrow that "some people" misunderstood the great purposes of TVA, personal recollections showing F. D. R. had always been against private power, how "practical" the President had been instead of wasteful (mentioning his Dutch and Scotch ancestors), how unlike a dictator he had been in letting State and local Governments, farmers and laborers "co-operate" in building the dam.

Not a word about re-election or third term, only: "We propose not only to retain these dams (Willkie said this, too), but to improve and extend them . . . The progress that we propose to continue to make . . . We must have continuance of your labor . . ."

How better could you say: "Re-elect me?"

Then in the Great Smoky National Park which has been ready for dedicating for a full year (it was finished in June, 1939) Mr. Roosevelt chose the occasion to out-pioneer the Willkie acceptance speech, again without conceding there is such a person.

Our ancestors were paraded in this speech, keeping their rifles near their axes to save themselves

Continued on Page 2, Column 2

LONDON REPELS THREE SWARMS OF NAZI PLANES

Reich Fliers Roam Over Wide Area Of England But Lose 25 Craft

Three times Adolf Hitler's Luftwaffe was hurled in giant waves against London yesterday and last night, and three times the roar of anti-aircraft guns and the spitting machine-gun fire of Britain's air fighters turned the invaders back.

The Germans also struck at the Midlands, heart of industrial England, and at many other points throughout England, Scotland and Wales.

The British air fleet did more than serve as defenders, however, claiming successful raids from German-conquered Norway in the north to Italy in the south, while Royal Air Force bombers flew high over Berlin as air raid sirens shrieked.

Meanwhile, the Germans reported successful attacks on eight British harbors in day and night raids, declaring that huge fires roared skyward at many points after the Nazis struck.

In Bucharest, assassination-bent gunmen invaded the palace grounds of King Carol, whose life was saved by prompt action of the palace guards. An Iron Guard plot to seize power and put Carol's son, Crown Prince Michael, on the Rumanian throne, was blamed for the effort to kill the King.

LONDON, Sept. 4 (Wednesday) (A. P.).—German raiding planes in great waves beat in vain yesterday at a curtain of defensive fire thrown up about London and were driven off a third time late last night after a 14-minute engagement at the city's outskirts.

Other night bombers, however, attacked the industrial Midlands; northwest, northeast, southeast and southwest England and areas in

Continued on Page 8, Column 2

KING CAROL

The ruler of dismembered Rumania escaped assassination yesterday when gunmen of the Pro-Fascist Iron Guard invaded the palace grounds and fired seven shots at a window.

ASSASSINS ATTEMPT TO SLAY KING CAROL

BUCHAREST, Sept. 4 (Wednesday) (A. P.).—Gunmen attempted in vain to assassinate King Carol last night in an alleged Iron Guardist plot to seize power and place Prince Michael on the throne.

While the would-be assassins broke through the palace guard and fired seven shots at a lighted window in Carol's palace, other groups of Iron Guardists attacked the Bucharest radio station and the American-owned telephone company's central office.

OTHER COUPS FAIL

Similar coups were attempted at Brasov and Constanza but were quickly crushed.

One Iron Guardist and one palace

Continued on Page 9, Column 3

LEASE OF FIRM URGED RATHER THAN SEIZURE

'Peace' Lobbyist Ejected for Cry Of 'Fascism' as Debate Is Opened

Inquirer Washington Bureau

WASHINGTON, Sept. 4.—The House Military Affairs Committee modified today the Overton-Russell "conscription of industry" amendment to the Burke-Wadsworth conscription bill so as to authorize President Roosevelt merely to lease private plants unable to agree with the Government over terms of defense contracts.

The committee's vote of 12 to 11 came immediately before the House, beginning two days of general debate on the conscription bill, itself, was thrown into an uproar by a man in the spectators' gallery who stood up and shouted:

"American conscription is American fascism."

600 PROTEST BILL

Taken into custody by Capitol police, the man gave his name as William Kenneally, of New York. He said he was a member of the National Maritime Union who had come to Washington with a group of 600 persons protesting passage of the draft bill. He was released.

Wendell L. Willkie has issued almost a daily statement against the Overton-Russell amendment after its passage by the Senate giving blanket power to Mr. Roosevelt to condemn, take over and operate any private plant or "facility" that might be in disagreement with the Secretary of War or Navy.

BANKHEAD FOR ORIGINAL

Mr. Roosevelt has not stated a position either for or against the proposal. But the original amendment was given at least a semblance of Administration support this morning when House Speaker William B. Bankhead (D., Ala.) announced he favored it as it came from the Senate.

As proposed by Rep. J. Joseph Smith (D., Conn.), the new industrial draft amendment would virtually re-enact authority held over plants by President Woodrow Wilson during the World War.

FORCED TO COMPLY

Private companies would be forced to comply with defense orders, or have their factories leased by the Government at a "fair and just" rate of compensation. The plants would be returned to the owners after the emergency.

Smith's amendment carried heavy penalties—a maximum of three years in prison and a fine of $50,000—for persons violating the law. The Overton-Russell amendment provides no punishment.

Whether the House would accept

Continued on Page 5, Column 3

Jackson Opinion

THE opinion of Attorney General Robert H. Jackson on the transfer of over-age destroyers to Great Britain in exchange for military bases holds in brief:

That the President has authority to make the agreement by his constitutional powers as Commander-in-Chief of the Army and Navy and as director of foreign relations.

That Senate ratification is not required because the agreement involves no "commitments as to the future which would carry an obligation to exercise powers vested in Congress."

THAT an Act of March 3, 1883, confirms in the President the right to make such disposition of naval vessels as he finds necessary in the public interest.

That in applying the Act of June 28, 1940, requiring that before any naval weapon is transferred it must be certified as not essential to defense, the Chief of Naval Operations may properly certify the destroyers as not essential if, in his judgment, the exchange of such craft for naval and air bases will strengthen the total defense of the United States.

That an Act of June 15, 1917, forbidding the transfer from the United States, while a neutral, to a belligerent of "any vessel built, armed or equipped as a vessel of war . . ." is not applicable to the over-age destroyers "which were not built, armed, equipped . . . with the intent that they should enter the service of a belligerent."

All Britain Rejoices Over Destroyer Deal; Nazis Say 'Too Late'

LONDON, Sept. 3 (A. P.).—The British rejoiced tonight wherever they gathered, from Cheapside pubs to the austere and misty corridors of the Foreign Office, over the news that 50 over-age United States destroyers will fill the gaps of the Royal Navy in the total German siege of these islands.

First Lord of the Admiralty A. V. Alexander, in a statement, greeted "with the utmost pleasure and satisfaction" the transfer of the destroyers.

"They come at a time when the strain upon our destroyer fleet has been very great," he said, "and will be of inestimable value to us not only for escorting convoys, but also for protecting our

Continued on Page 2, Column 6

WILLKIE CRITICIZES SECRECY OVER DEAL

By WILLIAM C. MURPHY, JR.

Inquirer Staff Reporter

RUSHVILLE, Ind., Sept. 3.—Wendell L. Willkie, Republican Presidential nominee, today said he felt sure the country would approve the transfer of fifty over-age United States destroyers to Great Britain in exchange of naval and air bases in the Atlantic but criticized President Roosevelt for having kept the Nation uninformed about the proposed transfer until it was an accomplished fact.

Willkie issued the following statement:

"The country will undoubtedly approve of the program to add to our naval and air bases and assistance given to Great Britain.

MUST BE CAREFUL

"It is regrettable, however, that the President did not deem it necessary in connection with this proposal, to secure the approval of Congress or permit public discussion prior to adoption. The people have a right to know of such important commitments prior to and not after made.

"We must be extremely careful in these times when the struggle in the world is between democracy and totalitarianism not to eliminate or destroy the democratic processes while seeking to preserve democracy. It is the contention of the totalitarian rulers that democracy is not effective.

"We must prove that it is effective

Continued on Page 12, Column 1

U. S. Board to View Bermuda Base Sites

WASHINGTON, Sept. 3 (U. P.).—Acting Secretary of the Navy James V. Forrestal announced today that a board of Army and Navy experts was leaving here today for Bermuda to examine sites for American naval and air...

Congress O. K. Not Required, Jackson Rules

Texts of all messages and letters made public in connection with the destroyer trade are on pages 6 and 7.

By RICHARD L. HARKNESS

Inquirer Washington Bureau

WASHINGTON, Sept. 4.—President Roosevelt today announced the transfer of 50 over-age American destroyers to Great Britain.

As pay, the United States received 99-year leases to establish naval and air bases on the British-owned islands of the Bahamas, Jamaica, St. Lucia, Trinidad and Antigua, in the Caribbean Sea, and on British Guiana in South America.

In addition, Great Britain ceded as outright gifts to this Government the right to construct defense bases in Newfoundland and Bermuda—gifts "generously given and gladly received," Mr. Roosevelt said.

As further consideration, Prime Minister Winston Churchill promised Secretary of State Cordell Hull that the English would never surrender or scuttle their fleet even if Adolf Hitler captured the British Isles.

The announcement of Churchill's pledge by the Department of State immediately gave rise to speculation here whether, if the British Navy was driven from its home stronghold, it would not come to the Western Hemisphere to continue the war from American-British bases stretching from Newfoundland to South America.

AUTHORIZED BY JACKSON

Mr. Roosevelt's announcement, contained in a special message to Congress, was accompanied by an opinion from Attorney General Robert H. Jackson asserting that the President held personal authority to enter into such a transaction with a foreign belligerent, and that the sale of warships to England was legal.

No action by Congress was required, Jackson stated, and, obviously, nothing could be done by Congress to halt the transfer. The Attorney General's opinion had been delivered to the White House on Aug. 27.

The destroyer deal itself, and the fact that Congress knew nothing of it, brought immediate criticism from members of the Senate and House isolation blocs, including both Democrats and Republicans.

But, apparently, there was nothing that Congressional critics of the latest turn of Mr. Roosevelt's aid-the-British policy could do—except talk.

NO APPROPRIATION NEEDED

In fact, Rep. Carl Vinson (D., Ga.), chairman of the House Naval Affairs Committee, said late this afternoon that Mr. Roosevelt would not even need an appropriation from Congress to begin construction of the vital defense posts.

Vinson pointed out that Congress already had given the President a national defense "blank check"

Continued on Page 2, Column 1

IN TODAY'S INQUIRER

READERS' BATTLEFRONT

The Inquirer publishes herewith the second of a series of letters reflecting readers' views on why they will vote for one or the other of the two main candidates for President of the United States in November—Wendell L. Willkie and Franklin D. Roosevelt.

As in other similar symposia reflecting reader attitudes on significant questions of the day, conducted by The Inquirer in the past, the opinions contained in these and successive series of letters to be published during the campaign do not necessarily reflect this newspaper's editorial attitude.

Five dollars will be paid for each letter accepted for publication in this column. No letter should exceed 250 words in length, and all should be addressed to "Readers' Battlefront," The Philadelphia Inquirer.

Roosevelt Vision On Trend of World Developments Cited

ROOSEVELT

I AM going to vote for President Roosevelt for the following reasons:

Because of his humanitarianism; his intimate knowledge of, and grasp on, international and national affairs; his fearless and diplomatic handling of the for-

Continued on Page 12, Column 3

Willkie Counted on To End 'Curbature' Of U. S. Business

WILLKIE

BECAUSE business, the backbone of the Nation, is, in the United States, suffering from a bad case of "curbature," I am going to vote for Wendell Willkie who, I am sure, can, with his intimate knowledge of that great structure and his keen insight

Continued on Page 12, Column 4

Son of British Envoy Rejects Army Call

OXFORD, England, Sept. 3 (A. P.).—John Stafford Cripps, son of Sir Stafford Cripps, British labor leader and Ambassador to Russia, appeared before a conscientious objectors' tribunal today and was registered as an objector provided that he does work of national importance.

Cripps argued that war was irreconcilable with the Christian belief in the Fatherhood of God and the brotherhood of man.

19 French Planes Land at Gibraltar

ALGECIRAS, Spain, Sept. 3 (A. P.).—Nineteen French planes and bombers from French Morocco landed at Gibraltar today to join others that flew here rather than return to France.

Previous reports have told of the decision by a number of French pilots to fight with the British against the German...

THE WEATHER

Official forecast: Eastern Pennsylvania, New Jersey and Delaware—Fair today and tomorrow; little change in temperature.

(Daylight-saving Time)

Sun rises 6.30 A. M. Sets 7.27 P. M.

Moon rises 9.22 A. M. Sets 9.01 P. M.

Other Weather Reports on Page 2

'Blood and Sand' Bought for Power

Rudolph Valentino Film Slated For Production; Hedy Lamarr Sought to Play Co-Starring Role

By Louella O. Parsons

HOLLYWOOD, Oct. 3.

THE most interesting movie deal of the week is Darryl Zanuck's purchase of "Blood and Sand" for Tyrone Power. So eager was Darryl to get this Rudolph Valentino vehicle that he paid Paramount $100,000—and that certainly is money well spent.

"Blood and Sand," by Vicente Blasco Ibanez, was easily Rudy's greatest picture. I wonder how many of you remember Rudy and Nita Naldi in this romantic story. It was made shortly after the success of Ibanez's "The Four Horsemen of the Apocalypse" and it was considered the biggest picture of the year.

Zanuck Seeks Hedy Lamarr for Role

I was talking with Darryl about his plans to produce this romantic story. He bought "Blood and Sand" for Tyrone after "The Mark of Zorro," in which Ty plays the adventurous, gay Douglas Fairbanks' role so delightfully.

Darryl has now decided to give the popular Power lad more of this type of characterization and he says he would also like to get Hedy Lamarr for the Naldi role—and wouldn't she be marvelous? It wouldn't do Metro-Goldwyn-Mayer any harm either to lend their glamor girl for this movie.

Eddie Albert Gets New Contract

Warner Brothers, sometimes known as the Bureau of Missing Persons, evidently doesn't mind going on man hunts now and then looking for Errol Flynn or Eddie Albert, because Eddie has just been given a new long term contract with a raise. At the present moment Albert is not doing his disappearing act off the coast of Mexico and will be on hand to start work immediately with Sylvia Sidney in "Carnival."

Later there are plans to team him in a series of three pictures with Priscilla Lane—"Weak Link," "Stuff of Heroes," and an untitled original by Robert Kemp. Eddie, who looks like a farm hand—but who has that certain something for the ladies, is going to get a big chance to click on his home lot.

Miss Sullavan Accepts 'Back Street' Part

There was rejoicing indeed on the Universal lot, for Margaret Sullavan has agreed to play the role in "Back Street" that brought Irene Dunne fame. Both Universal and David Selznick were considerably miffed when Joan Fontaine walked out of her agreement to play this role, but Maggie seems to fill every requirement.

She will go into the picture as soon as she finishes "Flotsam." At this very moment they are hunting for a big name star to play opposite her in the role of the married man for whom the heroine is forced to live on a back street.

Hakim Boys Spur Production Plans

The Hakim boys—Raphael and Roberto—are finally getting busy with their movie plans. They are the lads who brought "The Baker's Wife" to this country. I learned that Julien Duvivier will have a little time before he starts "Manon Lescaut" with Merle Oberon and so he will direct the first Hakim picture to be made in conjunction with Jean Levy-Strauss.

In fact Duvivier will do a repeat on his highly successful "Poil de Carotte"—the translation for you and me is "Redhead." This was one of Duvivier's most successful pictures. Raphael Hakim, by the way, has been laid up ever since he and a polo pony had a misunderstanding.

Alice Faye Praises Betty Grable

Chatter in Hollywood: All the gossips who have been saying that Alice Faye and Betty Grable are feuding, should have seen them after the preview of "Down Argentine Way." Alice rushed up to Betty, threw her arms around her and said, "You're simply swell." Betty returned the embrace and thanked Alice profusely.

Lana Turner came all by her lonesome to take a look at Betty, who was engaged to Artie Shaw when Lana eloped with him. It was certainly the Grable girl's night, for later at Ciro's every one rushed up and congratulated her.

Laughtons to Make Home in Hollywood

A Line or Two: Good news that Elsa Lanchester and Charles Laughton expect to make their home in Hollywood. They bought a gorgeous estate in the Huntington Riviera, formerly owned by Collins, a copper magnate.

Eddie Knopf, an extremely able young man, returns to his first love M-G-M, becoming a full fledged producer. He was formerly head of the story department at the Sam Goldwyn Studio.

Van Nuys had a movie wedding without realizing it. Paul Muni's secretary, Charlotte Harding, married his overseer, Oliver Austin, at the First Presbyterian Church. Paul himself was busy at the studio but Mrs. Muni was there to do the family honors.

Stars Discuss Plans for Chinese Party

Went to a meeting at Norma Shearer's house for the Chinese garden party to be held at Mary Pickford's Sunday. Madame Ling, a most interesting Chinese woman, told us of the raids which she and her family experienced—42 within a couple of months. Dolores Del Rio will assist Mary, and Dorothy Lamour will wear an elaborate Chinese wedding dress.

Sylvia Fairbanks and Hether Thacher, who were working next door for the British war relief refugees, came in to express their interest in the Chinese cause.

Attractively Kay Rohrer, now on the M-G-M lot, was champion first baseman for the Bank of America team that toured Japan last year. John Carroll has had eyes only for her since she became an M-G-Mer.

Margaret Lindsay Talks Wedding Rings

Snapshots of Hollywood Collected at Random: Margaret Lindsay and Bill Lundigan are talking wedding rings. Desi Arnaz, Lucille Ball's big moment, has arrived in town for the preview of "Too Many Girls."

Louis Blau, Wayne Morris' attorney, makes no secret of his admiration for Laraine Day.

Hedy Lamarr say she went to dinner with John Howard once and there is no romance with him or any one else. All her attentions are centered on her adopted boy.

Jack Connolly, who started in the film business as long ago as I did, is here for the Roosevelt campaign. He was at Ciro's with Sid Grauman and I was glad to see him and reminisce about old times.

Party Follows 'Argentine Way ' Opening

Marlene Dietrich posed with Billy Wilkerson for a color picture and his tie matched her gown.

Such fun at Sally Eiler's Ciro party. Virginia and Darryl Zanuck, Joe Schenck, the Jack Bennys, the Pandro Bermans, the Jules Steins, Mike Curtiz and Bess Meredith and Irving Berlin all patted Harry Joe Brown on the back for his part in making "Down Argentine Way" such a swell movie.

Myrna Loy is suffering with a bad sore throat. Luther Adler, well known stage actor, arrives here to join his wife (Sylyia Sidney).

A POLITICIAN AND HIS WIFE

Muriel Angelus starts out as his secretary and then marries Brian Donlevy, who's "The Great McGinty," in the film opening tomorrow at the Stanton.

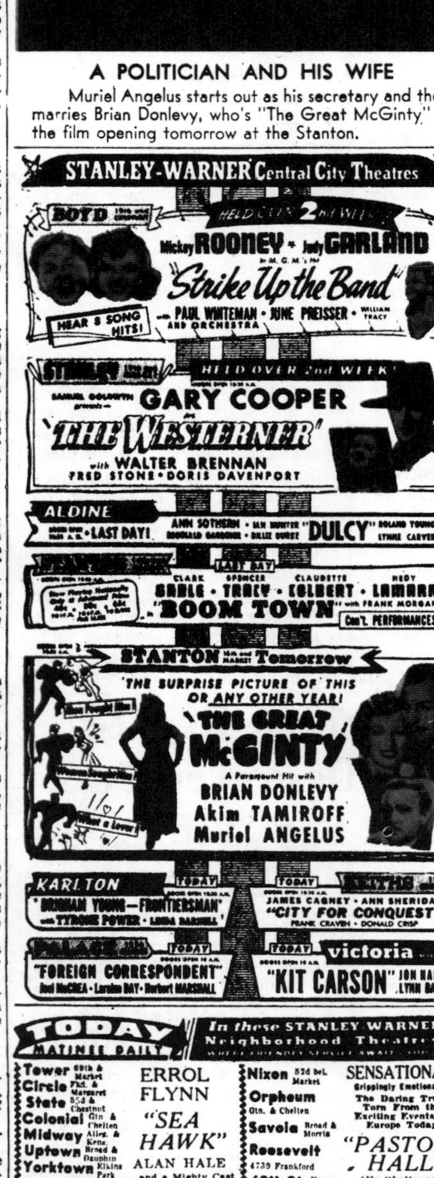

Furred, Feathered Actors Steal Spot As Hollywood Discoveries of 1940

Performances Of Animals Win Wide Acclaim

By Mildred Martin

Elsie the cow, Pepe the monkey, Pard the little dog, Henry the ostrich and Lenchen the pigeon are making it a new kind of movie season.

In place of the beauty contest girls and tall-dark - and - handsome young men who were the "finds" in former years, furred and feathered actors have been stealing the spotlight as 1940's camera discoveries.

ATTRACTED ATTENTION

Few bits of acting attracted greater attention than Pepe's performance as Errol Flynn's monkey in "The Sea Hawk;" while Pepe's tricks during the filming of the picture grew to legendary proportions.

But Pepe was only one of the creatures that stole the spotlight from human actors. Henry the ostrich and Ferdinand the bull walked away with scenes in "Swiss Family Robinson." The towering ostrich and the stunts he performed for Terry Kilburn won open-mouthed amazement. And though he was in the same picture, the black bull from a Hollywood dairy bases his chief claim to frame upon having served as model for Walt Disney's "Ferdinand the Bull."

GIVEN SPECIAL PARTY

Nothing, however, topped the campaign of Elsie, the matronly cow whose privilege it was to be milked by modish Kay Francis in "Little Men." Elsie was given a special party in a Hollywood restaurant, brought her calf into the world attended by the best veterinarians RKO could engage for her, and submitted to the ministrations of make-up men bent upon making her the most glamorized cow in the world.

The crown for canine cleverness is already being claimed on behalf of a perky dog named Pard, who appears with Humphrey Bogart and Ida Lupino in their forthcoming thriller, "High Sierra."

PIGEON SAVED FORTUNE

Part Boston bull, part wire-haired terrier and part guess-who, Pard has a turned up nose, a coat of vari-colored hair and a personality that captivates his fellow players and magnetizes the camera.

The pigeon named Lenchen in "A Dispatch From Reuter's" proved photogenically equal to her task of saving a fortune and a nation for Edward G. Robinson in Warner Brothers' story of the founder of the first world-wide news service.

Ostrich and Bull Share Glory in 'Swiss Family'

CUT FROM FILM

Peter the Python slithered down a tree so stealthily, passed between Carole Landis and Victor Mature so frighteningly in Hal Roach's "One Million, B. C.," that he provided the year's one example of a character actor who was too convincing for his own good. Women fainted when the scene was previewed. So Peter the Python had to be completely cut out of the picture.

Knute Rockne Film at Fox

It was Knute Rockne meeting Knute Rockne when eight-year-old John Sheffield shook hands with Pat O'Brien on a Hollywood movie set.

John had just finished his boyhood portrayal of the famed Notre Dame football coach for Warner Brothers' "Knute Rockne—All American," which opens today at the Fox. O'Brien was just arriving to begin his starring role as the mature Rockne.

"Goodbye, Pat," the youngster said. "He's all yours now." Then added solemnly, "Take care of him."

"Goodbye, Johnny," Pat replied just as seriously. "I'll do my best."

Delay Barrymore Hearing

HOLLYWOOD, Oct. 3 (U. P.)—Elaine Barrie, fourth wife of John Barrymore, didn't have to keep a court engagement with him today. Her attorney and counsel for Barrymore agreed to postpone the preliminary hearing on the "Great Profile's" divorce suit.

Cincinnati Triumphs, 2-1, to Win World Series

The Philadelphia Inquirer

PHILADELPHIA, WEDNESDAY MORNING, OCTOBER 9, 1940 abdefg 25

Two Runs in 7th Decide; Derringer Beats Newsom

Reds Overcome Detroit's 3d-Frame Score And Gain First Title Since 1919

By CY PETERMAN
Inquirer Sports Reporter

CINCINNATI, Oct. 8.—Red fires flamed high in Redland tonight while celebrating burghers went jitterbug-house over Cincinnati's long awaited baseball championship of the world.

Hurling the American League's Detroit Tigers from the rock-like eminence long defended by New York's Yankees, the battling Reds, behind Paul Derringer's brilliant 2-to-1 pitching triumph, not only sealed their first undisputed title in history, but won the first glory for the National League in six years.

FANS GO WILD

Tall Paul, veteran "Duke" of the Reds' staff, outlasted Louis (Bobo) Newsom, twice victorious in previous games, and not only loosed hysteria on the Ohio, but proved it is a long, long worm which has no turning, or which harbors no resentment.

For in beating its tormentors this time, Cincinnati's achievement was two-fold: it squared that affair of 1919 when the crooked White Sox threw the championship to the Reds, and it also emblazoned the Reds into the records as the first team ever to take the world championship after losing four straight to the Yankees the year before.

FOUR WINS TO THREE

Thus by a count of four victories to three, all but one captured on their home Crosley Field, the Reds brought the National League back its pride—and also claimed the $2000-per-man difference as they won the long end of the series' purse.

Derringer, pitching one of the great games of a magnificent career, holding the mighty Bengals to one unearned run and seven well-distributed safeties, just one of which went for extra bases, was Deacon Bill McKechnie's mainstay, just as the heroic Newsom went the distance for Detroit.

BOTH DESERVE VICTORY

Both men deserved to win, just as both teams shared in the glory.

There was so little, indeed, to choose, that when the half-daffy crowd leaped the railings, swarmed crazily on the field, kissing Derringer's be-whiskered countenance and pounding each Red player in jubiliation, the players of both sides struggled together through the exit, all agreeing it was so close they could have tossed a coin, lumped their shares, and called the Series even.

ADOPT FOES' TACTICS

Cincinnati won in the lucky seventh, again following an old tradition.

They won by a revolution in style, too, reverting fiercely to the system of their annual tormentors, abandoning safety-first policies for that up-and-at-'em slugging which for years has beaten their league down. They hooked together two roaring doubles, a sacrifice and walk, and then watched the decisive tally come home on the longest ball of the day, hit by the weakest man in the lineup, Billy Myers.

And on that rally died Detroit's bid for the big money, its try for the sixth straight title for the American League, and Buck Newsom's effort to join those few immortals who hurled three victories in one World Series.

When it came, abruptly as the blast of a powder factory, the Tigers had the lead, 1-0.

REDS' DEFENSE SAGS

The lone marker had come about in the third inning, the result as much of relaxed defense as the two hits by Tiger batters.

Billy Sullivan, who caught every one of Detroit's winning games and was back there with Bobo today, led with a single on which Frank McCormick went butter-fingered. Buck sacrificed and Dick Bartell wilted before Derringer's fast ball, but after one of three walks issued by the big Duke, Charley Gehringer smacked a hot one to Bill Werber.

The fielding ace for the victors and their hitting champ, too, scooped the ball, but was unable to hold it. When he recovered and pegged wide to first, McCormick again relaxed,

Continued on Page 27, Column 2

The Official Score

DETROIT

	Ab.	R.	H.	2b	3b	HR.	TB.	Rbl.	SB.	SH.	O.	A.	E.
Bartell, ss	4	0	0	0	0	0	0	0	0	0	3	2	0
McCosky, cf	3	0	0	0	0	0	0	0	0	0	3	0	0
Gehringer, 2b	4	0	2	0	0	0	2	0	0	0	3	2	0
Greenberg, lf	4	0	2	0	0	0	2	0	0	0	1	0	0
York, 1b	4	0	0	0	0	0	0	0	0	0	5	0	0
Campbell, rf	3	0	0	0	0	0	0	0	0	0	2	0	0
Higgins, 3b	4	0	1	1	0	0	2	0	0	0	0	4	0
Sullivan, c	3	1	1	0	0	0	1	0	0	0	6	0	0
Newsom, p	2	0	1	0	0	0	1	0	0	1	1	0	0
(c) Averill	1	0	0	0	0	0	0	0	0	0	0	0	0
Totals	32	1	7	1	0	0	8	0	0	1	24	8	0

CINCINNATI

	Ab.	R.	H.	2b	3b	HR.	TB.	Rbl.	SB.	SH.	O.	A.	E.
Werber, 3b	4	0	0	0	0	0	0	0	0	0	1	3	1
M. McCormick, cf	4	0	2	1	0	0	3	0	0	0	4	0	0
Goodman, rf	4	0	0	0	0	0	0	0	0	0	3	0	0
F. McCormick, 1b	4	1	1	1	0	0	2	0	0	0	6	1	0
Ripple, lf	3	1	1	1	0	0	2	1	0	0	1	0	0
Wilson, c	2	0	2	0	0	0	2	0	1	1	2	1	0
Joost, 2b	2	0	0	0	0	0	0	0	0	0	5	1	0
(b) Frey, 2b	0	0	0	0	0	0	0	0	0	0	0	0	0
Myers, ss	3	0	1	0	0	0	1	1	0	0	5	1	0
Derringer, p	3	0	0	0	0	0	0	0	0	0	0	1	0
(a) Lombardi	0	0	0	0	0	0	0	0	0	0	0	0	0
Totals	29	2	7	3	0	0	10	2	1	1	27	8	1

a-Batted for Joost in 7th.
b-Ran for Lombardi in 7th.
c-Batted for Newsom in 9th.

DETROIT	0	0	1	0	0	0	0	0	0	—1
CINCINNATI	0	0	0	0	0	0	2	0	x	—2

Earned runs—Cincinnati 2. Double plays—Gehringer to Bartell to York. Left on bases—Detroit, 8; Cincinnati, 5. Base on balls—Off Newsom 1 (Lombardi); off Derringer 3 (McCosky, Sullivan, Campbell). Struck out—By Newsom 6 (M. McCormick 2, Ripple, Goodman 2, Werber); by Derringer 1 (Greenberg). Umpires—Ballanfant (N. L.) at plate; Basil (A. L.), 1b; Klem (N. L.), 2b; Ormsby (A. L.), 3b. Time of game—1:47.

(A. P. Wirephoto)

SPECTACULAR DOUBLE PLAY HOLDS CINCINNATI IN CHECK ON THIS OCCASION

The Reds' threat was stopped in the fifth inning by this speedy double-killing. Eddie Joost, seen racing down the base paths, grounded to Dick Bartell at second, who retired Jimmy Wilson, then heaved to Rudy York at first. York is all set to pull in the ball (indicated by arrow). Meanwhile, Wilson crashed into Bartell in an effort to break up the play to first, but Dick got rid of the ball before somersaulting over Wilson.

Rain Forces Penn Inside For Grid Drill

New Plays Tried To Offset looping Defense of Yale

Forced indoors by the inclement weather and the soggy footing on the River Field gridiron, Penn's varsity football squad yesterday engaged in as intensive and lengthy a workout in Weightman Hall as any held outdoors this fall.

There was no bodily contact work, but for two hours and a half George Munger drove the gridders through a practice that included a lengthy drill on offensive formations to be used against the defensive shifts Yale uses.

The report of the scouts emphasized that the Elis have mastered the art of shifting the defense to meet either a balanced or unbalanced line and were able time and again to stymie the Virginia attack last Saturday, although beaten, 19-14.

DEADLY SERIOUS

This is known as the loop defense, and to offset it Munger and his assistants yesterday installed several new plays in the Penn repetoire. The type of plays naturally cannot be disclosed, but they are such as to give the Red and Blue a better balanced offense against the various defenses the Bulldogs may present.

The Penn coaching staff and the players are deadly serious in their belief that Yale has a strong team. Dispatches from New Haven quoting one of the Bulldog scouts as believing that Yale can defeat the Red and Blue has had an effect on the squad that was reflected in the earnest manner the players participated in yesterday's workout.

The veterans cannot forget last year when the Red and Blue, a decided favorite, was lucky to eke out a 6 to 0 triumph on a Dick Merriwell play with 13 seconds to go in the first half. Yale's dogged resistance is well known to both players and coaches and their respect for it makes them all the more serious about their preparations to meet it.

NO CHANGES IN LINEUP

In addition to running through signals, passing within the confined limits of the gymnasium floor, and dummy scrimmage drills, both offensive and defensive, Munger sent the squad through an offensive drill against a seven-man goal line defense, one of Yale's traditional types of strategy.

There were no changes in the lineup of the first team yesterday. Ed Allen again played the fullback position with Jim Chandler barking the signals from the blocking back position. There is a strong possibility that the two newcomers on the first team will retain their posts the remainder of the week, although Munger again said that he had not definitely decided.

Albert Brechka, injured last Saturday, worked out with the squad but the team physician doubts that he will be able to start. His chest continues sore and unless the soreness disappears before game time he will occupy a seat on the bench while Bob Hunt performs the right guard chores.

Rix Yard was absent from practice

Continued on Page 28, Column 4

Pennock to Direct Boston Farm Clubs

BOSTON Oct. 8 (A. P.).—Billy Evans, director of the Boston Red Sox farm system for the past five years, severed his connection with the organization today, according to an announcement by officials of the club.

He will be succeeded by Herb Pennock, one of the greatest left-handed pitchers in baseball history, who has been serving as assistant director of the farm clubs since the middle of the 1939 season.

Pennock started his major league career with the Red Sox and, during 22 years of service, performed with the New York Yankees and the Philadelphia Athletics before returning to the Sox as relief pitcher in 1934.

His active major league career ended the following year, when he was appointed a Red Sox coach, a post he held until the summer of 1939, when he became assistant farm director.

Mioland Victor In Jamaica Race

Results on Page 30

JAMAICA RACETRACK, N. Y., Oct. 8 (A. P.).—Charles S. Howard's Oregon-bred three-year-old, Mioland, today showed why he is rated one of the best in his division when he spotted four rivals a big advantage at the start, in addition to gobs of weight, then went on to score a sensational victory in the Star Master Handicap.

The 4 to 5 favorite ran over horses in plenty of time and triumphed by three lengths. H. T. Johnson's Gen'l Manager was second by a length and a half, with H. C. McGehee's Ksar of Audley third.

Mioland's stall gate appeared to delay opening and the colt went into the air before settling down to chasing after the field. He seemed hopelessly out of it. Ksar of Audley's stall also was a bit slow to open.

A thin rain was falling as the mile and a sixteenth event was run. A crowd of 6754 saw Mioland carry his 126 pounds, including Jockey Eddie Arcaro, home in 1:45 3-5. The track was little affected at this time.

Dukes Shift Game

PITTSBURGH, Oct. 8 (A. P.).—Duquesne University will play Manhattan Saturday, Oct. 26, at Forbes Field, instead of Friday night under the lights, it was announced today.

Rain Fails to Dampen Temple's Grid Drill

Temple's stiffest practice of the young season was staged yesterday afternoon despite the rain and heavy condition of the ground, and Coach Ray Morrison believes that the two-hour workout was the most productive yet held.

Offense was stressed by the Owl mentor, and the hitches in the attacking plan that showed up in the Georgetown game were straightened. Morrison and his associate coaches viewed movies of the Hoya tilt, uncovering several additional faults that were not seen in the actual game.

STRESS DEFENSE TODAY

The drill on offensive maneuvers was the last heavy practice on this phase of football, for this afternoon plans for an effective defense against Boston College's vaunted attack will be mapped. The same program will be followed tomorrow afternoon.

Temple's squad is in good physical condition; all of the players who suffered the usual bumps and bruises in the Georgetown battle have fully recovered. The Temple gridders, particularly the linemen, had better be prepared for another tough session on Saturday, for Boston College is just as big physically as the Georgetown team, which is listed among the strongest in the East.

PLENTY OF WEIGHT

Chet Gladchuk, Boston College's six foot five inch centre, weights 242; John Yauchoes, the veteran tackle, 253. The rest of the Eagle forward wall averages close to 200 pounds.

Morrison continues to use his backfields in units, so yesterday's practice offered no suggestion as to the probable starting quartet. And the same thing is true of the end posts, where Frank Ford, Max Wharton, Frank Moister and Dick Fox are being given equal consideration.

Today's practice will mean much to members of the Owl spuad, particularly the second and third stringers, for after the drill, Coach Morrison will select the gridders to make the trip to Boston Friday morning.

Boston College, which romped over Centre and Tulane in its first two games, has several scoring threats, one of whom, Lou Montgomery, did not oppose Tulane at New Orleans.

Continued on Page 26, Column 7

Red's Victory 1st Since '34 For Nationals

CINCINNATI, O., Oct. 8.

THE American League's "five year plan" collapsed at Crosley field today.

After five successive World Series triumphs, the American League bowed to the Cincinnati Reds in the vital seventh game, 2-1, to give the senior loop their first triumph since the Cards whipped the same Bengals in 7 games in 1934.

Big Paul Derringer, plus Frank McCormick, plus Jimmy Ripple, equalled the Reds victory. Dicky Bartell helped along with a $100,000 snooze.

It was a glorious game from start to finish—a battle worthy of any World Series—a test that was packed with drama and suspense from the first ball hit by Bartell on a line to Werber until Frey scooped up Averill's grounder for the final out in the ninth.

The highlights in order were:

1. Jimmy Wilson's steal of second in the second inning—a delayed bit of Thievery which caught Detroit sound asleep.

2. Billy Werber's wild throw to Frank McCormick on Gehringer's scratch hit that allowed Sullivan to score from third.

3. Frank McCormick's double to left in the seventh followed by Jimmy Ripple's two bagger off the right field screen which sent Frank McCormick over the plate safely when Bartell held Campbell's return throw to the infield in his hand, with the Red first baseman still 60 feet from home.

4. Billy Myers long fly to centre a moment later which sent Ripple over the plate with the winning run after Jimmy Wilson had sacrificed him to third.

When it was over, Derringer

Continued on Page 27, Column 7

Tiger Boss Will Strengthen Club

DETROIT, Oct. 8 (U. P.).—Walter O. Briggs, owner of the Detroit Tigers, promised today to strengthen the club "so that the Tigers of 1941 may again be a competitor both in the American League pennant race and in the championship Series."

"Far from being disheartened, we will seek to profit by the experience in the Series," he said.

"It was my ambition and hope that the loyal fans of Michigan would be rewarded with a world championship in the Series concluded at Cincinnati this afternoon.

"Fates have decreed otherwise, however, and we accept the result as I know the Tiger supporters will in a spirit of good sportsmanship and with congratulations to Mr. Powell Crosley, Jr., and his associates on the club.

"In the Cincinnati Red: the Tigers met a fine defensive ball club, whose pitching in four of the seven games

Continued on Page 27, Column 1

Detroit Netman Gains in Tourney

HOT SPRINGS, Va., Oct. 8 (A. P.).—George Reindell of Detroit, reached the quarter finals in the annual hot springs tennis tournament today, defeating Earl Backe, Merrick, N. J., 7-5, 6-4 in the fastest match of the tournament so far.

Bunty Lawrence, Los Angeles, defeated Walter Pate, Davis Cup captain, 8-6, 9-7.

Control Big Factor In Derringer's Win

By STAN BAUMGARTNER
Inquirer Sports Reporter

CINCINNATI, O., Oct. 8.—"It isn't what you have—but what you do with it that counts!"

Paul Derringer, pitching hero of the Reds, sat in front of his locker in the Red clubhouse, leisurely pulling off his clothes, tossing first one sock and then another on the shelf.

Crowds of joyful fans still milled about him—some gazed in wide-eyed wonder, others patted him gently on the back, some grasped his hand.

"Boy, you sure had the stuff today," said one.

CONTROL PERFECT

Derringer smiled, turned to the writer and said:

"He's wrong. I didn't have my best stuff today. But I did have control. I felt as if I could have thrown the ball through the eye of a needle. I don't think that one pitch got away from me. I made every batter hit the pitch I wanted.

"I threw low and outside to York—high, inside and on the handle to Greenberg—high and inside to Campbell—high and across the letters to Bartell.

"It seemed as if I could touch the spot I wanted with my finger tips. Big Alex (Grover Cleveland Alexander) gave me my first lessons on control. I never forgot them and I have tried to follow them out.

"Jim (Wilson) gave me a target to shoot at on every pitch and I think I hit it."

WIRES POUR IN

Congratulatory telegrams began to pour in.

"This is the 98th and the game has only been over 35 minutes," said Morris Arnovich, who handed the envelope to Derringer.

Members of the Tigers, Hank Greenberg, Manager Del Baker, Dick Bartell, Pinkey Higgins, Rudy York came in to congratulate Manager McKechnie and the Reds.

Greenberg patted Wilson on the back. "I hope I can steal second base in a World Series when I am as old as you. You did a magnificent job."

Wilson will leave for Chicago to-

Continued on Page 27, Column 6

Enough Catching Sighs Wilson

By CHARLES DUNKLEY

CINCINNATI, Oct. 8 (A. P.).—William (Deacon) McKechnie, kindly, bespectacled 56-year-old manager of the victorious Cincinnati Reds, was the happiest man in baseball tonight.

His triumphant players shared his joy.

Gloom flooded the dressing room of the vanquished Detroit Tigers, but they had no alibis.

SHOUTS AND SHRIEKS

Twenty-one years of accumulated steam blew the safety valve as the victorious Reds clattered past each other up the steel stairs to their clubhouse.

Noise ballooned out of the windows, shouts and shrieks, yipping and songs.

Del Baker, Detroit Tigers' manager, defeated but gallant, came up the stairs with the Reds, was lost in a seething crowd and had to be steered to Manager McKechnie.

PRAISES McKECHNIE

"We lost to a great team, Bill," Baker said, clasping McKechnie's hand.

"We won from a great one, Del," the Deacon smiled.

McKechnie said: "It was the cleanest and hardest World Series I ever saw in my 35 years of baseball. I extend my regards to Owner Briggs of the Tigers, the players and the Detroit fans. It was a pleasure to play the Tigers."

PAUL PATS JIMMY

Paul Derringer, unshaven, worn and wanting only to sit down, trudged up the stairs. As he entered, a tremendous howl cut loose. He sat down beside Catcher Jimmy Wilson, 40 year-old hero of heroes, grabbed Wilson by the hair and gave him a kindly pat on the head and grinned.

Wilson, with tape all over his bruised body and legs, was supremely happy. There was a day's growth of whiskers upon his face, too.

"We gave them h—l, didn't we kid?" he beamed at Derringer. Paul just smiled.

McKechnie came over to shake hands.

"I feel just great," the Deacon said. "I'm ready to go out and play those guys again right now."

"Not for me," yelled the worn-out

Continued on Page 27, Column 1

Byrd-McKittrick Deadlock Kowal-Allman for Crown

Matt Kowal and Dick Allman, of the host club, along with Merion Cricket Club's Sam Byrd and Ralph McKittrick, deadlocked for the title in the fourth annual Phila. District Pro-Greens Chairman golf tournament, held yesterday over Philmont Country Club's rain drenched north course. Each team carded 69.

Allman, who had been putting well most of the round, took three putts on the 18th green to ruin the Philmont team's chances of winning the crown outright. Kowal and Allman scored a 33 going out, and 36 on the home journey.

The Philmont duo's round was featured by the front nine scoring. Allman and Kowal got one birdie and an eagle on the 33 card, two strokes under par. Allman jammed in a 35-foot putt for an eagle on the 9th, while Kowal sank a 20-foot putt for a birdie on the fourth. Kowal also birdied the 10th with another long putt.

Byrd and McKittrick smashed par twice on each nine, made everything else in par but the 14th and 17th where they three putted. Byrd kept the Merion team in front with his fine putting. Sam knocked in putts from 4 to 12 feet.

Richard Hinkle and Dr. J. J. Ryan, Orwigsburg, Pa., tallied a 71 to deadlock Johnny Moyer and N. Fetterolf, Shamokin, Pa., for third place. The Hinkle-Ryan combination went out in 34, registered 37 coming back. Moyer and his partner played the first nine in 36 lowered this to 35 on the last nine.

Al MacDonald and William Adams, Langhorne reeled off a 75 for the fifth position while Marty Lyons and J. N. Wheeler, Llanerch, carded a 76.

Danny MacFayden Released by Bucs

PITTSBURGH, Oct. 8 (A. P.).—The unconditional release of Danny MacFayden, veteran right - hand pitcher from Somerville, Mass., was announced today by Bill Benswanger, president of the Pirates.

The club office commented that being more than 34 years old and with 15 major league seasons behind him, "Danny did not fit in with the policy of Manager Frank Frisch to rebuild the Pittsburgh club with young men."

Delirium Reigns in Cincy As Reds Bring Home Bacon

By HENRY McLEMORE

CINCINNATI, Oct. 8 (U. P.).—This is a city without reason tonight—for a reason.

Its beloved Reds are baseball champions of the world, winners over the Detroit Tigers in the seventh and pay-off game of the series.

The civic madness started at Crosley Field a split-second after the final out and, spreading like chicken-pox in a playground, swept the entire city, from suburb to suburb and city limit to city limit.

Moppets and matriarchs, tots and tycoons, went into the Mid-Western version of the Highland Fling, and if they started stopping now it would take them a week to come to a dead halt.

Fatted calves and fifths of Bourbon were being killed all over town, and every noise-making device known to the devil was in operation. Automobile horns, thousands of them, played their sweet symphonies. Factory whistles screamed as if someone were twisting their wrists, street-car gongs fought to see which one could jar the most eardrums, and thousands of persons just walked around yelling, singing, whistling and clapping hands.

In the mid-town section ladies and

Continued on Page 26, Column 4

Hero at Home

EXPORT, Pa., Oct. 8 (A. P.).—This little Western Pennsylvania town tonight toasted its native son-hero, Jimmy Ripple, of the Cincinnati Reds.

He batted in the tying run and scored the winning tally himself as the Reds beat the Detroit Tigers to win the World Series today.

All over town the sole topic was "Jimmy," who will be 31 years old Oct. 14. A committee got to work to give the Red outfielder a victory dinner Oct. 15 at the Greensburg Country Club.

FAIR AND WARMER

The Philadelphia Inquirer

PUBLIC LEDGER

An Independent Newspaper for All the People

6 A. M. EDITION

CIRCULATION: September Average: Daily 413,725, Sunday 1,044,263 — a b d e f g h ★ — THURSDAY MORNING, OCTOBER 10, 1940 — Copyright, 1940, by The Phila. Inquirer Co. VOL. 223, No. 102 — Second Largest 3c Morning Circulation in America — THREE CENTS

U. S. Orders Full War Fleet in Pacific; Tokio Threatens to Bomb Burma Road; Deaths Mount in Nazi Raids on London

Today

Arm Pacific Outposts
Funds Allotted Quietly
More Steps Planned
Knudsen Is Angered
Threatens to Resign

—By Paul Mallon—

WASHINGTON, Oct. 9.

YOU may never see them—and especially the Japanese will not see them—but steps are being taken to strengthen our weak Pacific outposts, the Philippines and Guam.

Funds which can be used to make the Philippines slightly more formidable have been tucked into recent appropriation bills passed by Congress in such a way that their purpose will not be noticed.

The Navy Admirals simultaneously have gone after the White House for a straight large open appropriation to fortify Guam.

These are coming steps designed to impress Japan with the seriousness of the position she has assumed in the Axis, but there may be others first. Extension of the embargo against shipment of copper has been considered. An investigation of the domestic effects of embargoing cotton and barring silk imports is being conducted.

None of these individual steps would be grave, taken singly, but in progression they would advance nearly the whole distance toward the grave result forecast when Navy Secretary Knox called out the Naval Reserve.

This Government has silently tilted its nose at the British offer to let us use the Singapore naval base. It is not because our Navy likes the British less. It merely likes the Singapore base less.

The naval board of strategy is in full agreement that Singapore is "too far up the creek" for efficient use by American vessels. Its position is too far around from the prospective fighting area in the South China Sea to make its full use desirable.

The Admirals would rather have small storage bases at Mindinao, the southernmost Philippine island, or in British New Guinea. From such storehouses American vessels could operate northward on a shorter line to the scene of probable operations.

The White House has been definitely advised not to take up the British suggestion.

William Knudsen, National Defense Commissioner, has privately threatened to resign his post if the Hillman-Jackson labor quarantine is imposed on the defense program.

Knudsen went to see Mr. Roosevelt at the White House last Friday. No news of their visit got out. What was said was kept private, apparently by both parties involved. But the conversations which both Knudsen and Commissioner Stettinius, the two top business men pushing defense, have held among their associates have left no doubt of what transpired. Both men were deeply upset by the development.

Their positions of responsibility for producing defense would become untenable if the largest and most efficient industries are barred from defense production for political - labor reasons or any others.

The propaganda drive to foster American credits for Britain will have a hard time getting beyond a little-noticed routine Commerce Department report on the present British financial position in this country.

This report disclosed the United Kingdom reduced its cash bank balances in the United States by only about $200,000,000 the first 10 months of war. Only $150,000,000 of American securities were cashed in the same period.

As the United Kingdom had $2,300,000,000 of holdings in this country at the end of 1939, it appears it should now have nearly $2,400,000,000 left. Her position is actually even better because these figures exclude the cash and security holdings of the Canadians, Australians and South Africans.

Britain, therefore, has no need of American credits at this time, nor will it have for a long time to come.

Mme. Chiang Seeks Medical Treatment

CHUNGKING, China, Oct. 9 (A. P.)—Mme. Chiang Kai-shek, wife and chief aide of China's Generalissimo, has gone by plane to Hong Kong for medical treatment and rest, friends disclosed today.

Willkie Pledges Aid to Expand Little Business

Text of Mr. Willkie's New Haven address appears on Page 8.

By WILLIAM C. MURPHY, JR.

Inquirer Staff Reporter

NEW HAVEN, Conn., Oct. 9.—Wendell L. Willkie tonight appealed to "little business" throughout the Nation to rally with him to prevent the third-term election of Mr. Roosevelt and asserted that the economic experiments of the New Deal had actually discriminated in favor of huge corporations and against the interest of the smaller businessman.

He linked his appeal for little business support with a reiteration of his promise to rehabilitate the American economic system as a prerequisite to the creation of a defense system so strong that no totalitarian government would dare to attack the United States.

DON'T PICK FIGHTS

"We don't pick fights," he said, "but once in, we fight until we have won. Ours is not and never shall be a policy of appeasement. We will not appease dictators. An on the other hand, I can promise this for the Republican Party: We will not appease Communists in Washington or anywhere else. We believe in peace and we want peace. But we shall have our kind of peace only by becoming strong."

Willkie asserted that the final products needed for the creation of an adequate national defense rested upon "a world of little industries and little businesses."

GREAT CROWD

Willkie spoke before a crowd, estimated by local officials at 50,000, which jammed New Haven's historic Central Green at the conclusion of a ten-hour motor tour through Connecticut during which he covered approximately 120 miles and made nu-

Continued on Page 6, Column 2

F. D. R.'s Seconder To Support Willkie

TUCSON, Ariz., Oct. 9 (A. P.)—Mrs. Isabella Greenway King, former Democratic Representative from Arizona and an intimate friend of the Roosevelt family, said today she would support Wendell L. Willkie.

In a telegram to the Arizona Daily Star from New York Mrs. King praised the Republican Presidential candidate's "sound and courageous program" and said she was opposed to the principle of a third term.

Mrs. King was a bridesmaid at the wedding of the President and Mrs. Roosevelt. At the 1932 Democratic convention she seconded Mr. Roosevelt's nomination.

13 MILLION PROVIDED TWO CAMDEN FIRMS TO SPEED DEFENSE

U. S. Funds to Help Equip Shipyard And Forge Plant

The New York Shipbuilding Corp., struggling to complete $500,000,000 in Naval orders in record time, yesterday was allocated $10,500,000 in Federal funds to be spent on ways, tools and buildings so that ships might be constructed faster.

The Camden Forge Co., which produces forgings for turrets, propellor shafts, gun housings and similar naval and ordnance work, was given an allocation of $2,873,695 for buildings, machine tools and furnaces at its plant at Mt. Ephraim ave. and the Atlantic City Railroad, Camden.

U. S. TO HOLD TITLE

Allocations to the two Camden plants thus totaled $13,373,695—part of the $96,961,146 which will be spent on similar U. S.-financed expansion of defense plants throughout the Nation, officials in Washington explained.

Title to the new ways, buildings and tools constructed and purchased under the plan will be held by the Government, which hopes thereby to break bottlenecks in the drive for rearmament.

SILENT ON AWARD

Officials at New York Ship would not discuss the award in the absence of Roy S. Campbell, general manager there, who was aboard the 8300-ton, $11,000,000 aircraft tender Curtiss, making her trial run off Boston before delivery to the Navy.

The money, however, is expected to be spent in rehabilitating two of the "Middle Ways" unused since the

Continued on Page 4, Column 6

IN TODAY'S INQUIRER

BENDIX OBTAINS PHILA. PLANT TO AID DEFENSE

Atwater Kent Co. Factory Bought By Aviation Firm; 7000 Jobs Due

Illustrated on Page 16

Further important development of Philadelphia as a centre of national defense industrial preparation was virtually assured yesterday with official announcement that the long-idle plant of the A. Atwater Kent Manufacturing Co., Wissahickon ave. and Abbotsford rd., had been purchased by the Bendix Aviation Corp., an affiliate of the General Motors Corp.

Already possessed of huge national defense contracts for aviation accessories, Bendix will employ between 7000 and 10,000 men when it reaches production, with a pay-roll in excess of $1,000,000 monthly.

Active work will begin as soon as details of the sale are approved by the National Defense Advisory Commission, which is expected to be a matter only of hours.

PHILADELPHIA WINS

Philadelphia won out over a number of out-of-State sites under consideration, it was disclosed, after long negotiations engaged in by Governor James, personally; Richard P. Brown, Secretary of the State Department of Commerce; Frank G. Binswanger, Philadelphia realtor, and officers of the Philadelphia Chamber of Commerce.

Shortly after announcement of the sale was made, simultaneously by Brown in Harrisburg and by Binswanger here, George W. Elliott, general secretary of the Chamber of Commerce and vice president of the Army Ordnance Association, Philadelphia area, disclosed that negotiations for location here of "two or three very big" national industries, now under contract for national defense orders, were in the active stage.

$3,500,000 INVESTMENT

Purchase, renovation and equipment of the huge plant at Wissahickon ave. and Abbotsford rd. represents an investment of $3,500,000, it was stated, and involves an option upon a 45-acre adjoining plot on which additional construction may be started very soon.

"I am confident," Elliott said, "that this is the first step in the acquisition by Philadelphia of a group of outstanding industries associated with the national defense. This breaks the ice.

"Philadelphia has an abundance of skilled labor, superb transportation facilities, and is strategically situated with reference to raw materials. Furthermore, we have a number of

Continued on Page 4, Column 5

BRIDGES ACCUSED OF SABOTAGE PLOT

WASHINGTON, Oct. 9 (U. P.).—Rep. C. Arthur Anderson (D., Mo.) charged in a House speech today that Harry Bridges, West Coast CIO leader, "conspired to commit the crime of murder and plotted sabotage of one of our largest liners in the Panama Canal."

Anderson read what he said was a transcript of evidence that is in the Justice Department's files quoting Walter Carney, former Bridges bodyguard, as saying that two Communists, at a meeting attended by Bridges, agreed to pay Carney $5000 to "eliminate" Joe Ryan, president of the International Longshoremen's Association, so that Communists could control the union.

LINER SABOTAGE PLOT

Anderson quoted another document, which he said also came from Justice Department files, telling of a plot to sabotage the liner Pennsylvania while it was in the Panama Canal in 1936.

Anderson read to the House the following alleged sworn statement of

Continued on Page 10, Column 2

Lindbergh Broadcast Scheduled Monday

NEW YORK, Oct. 9 (A. P.).—Mutual Broadcasting System today announced that Col. Charles A. Lindbergh would discuss "national defense" over its networks Monday from 8.45 to 9 P. M., E. S. T. He will speak from Washington.

FIFTY DISTRICTS OF CAPITAL HIT IN WAVE ATTACK

Churchill Sees Bomber Shot Down; Missiles Blast Famous Locales

LONDON, Oct. 10 (Thursday) (A. P.).—More than 50 districts of London suffered the blasting and burning of high explosive and incendiary bombs last night and early today in one of the worst overnight German air raids yet directed at this capital.

Among the objects struck were a famous church, one of the city's oldest hotels, and a promenade known the world over.

CHURCHILL SEES BATTLE

There were two lulls in the assaults early today, but each ended as fresh waves of Nazis sailed in high over the anti-aircraft barrage to drop new bombs.

One stick of bombs straddled a district which has been persistently attacked since the air war began.

Prime Minister Churchill himself, watching the awesome conflict, saw one raider shot down in his own constituency. (This is the Epping district of Essex, just to the northeast of London.)

CASUALTIES INCREASE

The plane was hit high in the air, and searchlights trailed the three parachuting Nazis fliers to earth.

There was a mounting list of casualties, including many killed.

Simultaneous raids were carried out against Wales and southwestern and northwestern England. They all were heavy, but nothing like the battering London was experiencing.

BRIEF RESPITE

Yesterday London had a brief respite, but the raiders were back again with a concerted effort to pierce the curtain of steel hurled skyward by anti-aircraft batteries.

Great high-explosive bombs and incendiary "breadbaskets" upset buses, struck at rail lines and spread fire and debris from one end of London to the other.

From northern environs to southernmost tip, the Capital trembled with the shock of the exploding bombs and the shuddering crash of an incessant anti-aircraft barrage.

So intense was the din that it was at times almost impossible to tell which noises were those of bombs and which were those of the defense guns.

A few hours after the early start of the raid, eight districts of the city had been hit.

BOMB UPSETS BUS

(Presumably this means such old geographical divisions as Mayfair, Westminster, Elephant and Castle, Bloomsbury and the like. Names and locations of the affected districts are

Continued on Page 2, Column 7

Churchill Is Elected Conservative Leader

LONDON, Oct. 9 (A. P.).—Prime Minister Winston Churchill today was elected unanimously leader of the Conservative Party, succeeding Neville Chamberlain.

His election as head of his party as well as of the Government had been considered certain since Chamberlain last week stepped out of the Cabinet and relinquished his party post.

COL. GEN. WILHELM KEITEL

Chief of the German High Command, who was reported early today to have taken command of the Axis forces in Africa.

LONDON SAYS NAZI IS NEW LEADER OF AXIS AFRICAN ARMY

LONDON, Oct. 10 (Thursday) (A. P.). All the London morning papers today carried Cairo reports saying General Wilhelm Keitel, chief of the German High Command, had taken over the Axis African command, succeeding Italian Marshal Rodolfo Graziani.

The change was said to have been a direct result of the Oct. 4 Brenner Pass conference between Adolf Hitler and Premier Benito Mussolini. General Keitel attended the conference.

The London press described Keitel as "a master of Blitzkrieg strategy."

ENJOYS MATHEMATICS

If Colonel General Wilhelm Keitel follows his great passion, warfare in Africa henceforth will be on a mathematical basis. For the major interest of the 56-year-old, blue-

Continued on Page 2, Column 4

FLASH

DeGaulle Lands In West Africa

DUALA, CAMEROONS, WITH THE DEGAULLE EXPEDITION, Oct. 9 (Delayed) (A. P.).—General Charles DeGaulle landed here today and raised his standard of the "Free French" forces on French soil for the first time since the French-German armistice.

The Cameroons are a former German protectorate in West Africa.

Dr. Grenfell Dead at 75; Noted Labrador Missionary

CHARLOTTE, Vt., Oct. 9 (U. P.).—Sir Wilfred Thomason Grenfell, founder of the Labrador Medical Mission and known throughout the world as "the Labrador Doctor," died of a heart ailment at his home tonight. He was 75.

His secretary, Wyman Shaw, said that Grenfell had been playing croquet and that he laid down on a couch to rest before dinner. He was found dead a few minutes later.

WAS IN RETIREMENT

Grenfell had retired from active missionary work in Labrador several years ago. He had been living at his summer home, Kinlock House, overlooking Lake Champlain, where he spent the last few years, walking in the woods, reading and writing.

Grenfell left England in 1892 to investigate conditions among fishermen of Labrador and Newfoundland. Sent there by the Royal National Mission to Deep Sea Fishermen, Grenfell cared for the natives in a hospital set up on his 90-ton ketch Albert.

TREATED 900 PATIENTS

There never had been a doctor in the country before his arrival and some of his early operations were performed on the beaches by the light of a kerosene lamp. His first summer he treated 900 patients.

The challenge of Labrador was so strong that Grenfell returned the next summer and set up his first cottage hospital. From that small beginning the Grenfell Mission has grown to include five hospitals, six nursing stations, four combined orphanages and boarding schools as well as clothing and food distribution centres.

His work, described as an "inter-

Continued on Page 34, Column 3

Knox Uncertain If Conflict With Japan Is Near

Amid swiftly mounting tension in the United States-Japanese crisis, Secretary of the Navy Frank Knox yesterday announced that the U. S. Fleet based at Hawaii would be built up immediately to its full strength.

In the Far East, the Japanese reserved their verbal ammunition for Great Britain, threatening to bomb the Burma road if Britain persisted in its determination to reopen the route for Chinese military supplies.

Americans in Shanghai stormed shipping offices for passage home.

Reliable sources in London said the Soviet Government had informed both the United States and Great Britain that Moscow's policy toward China remained unchanged despite the adherence of Japan to the Berlin-Rome Axis.

German bombs hurtling from shrapnel-filled skies on 40 different London areas last night and early today caused heavy casualties and blasted a famous church, one of the city's oldest hotels and a world-famous promenade. Censorship forbade mention of the names of the famous places struck by bombs.

The great Krupp works at Essen and oil refineries at Hamburg were fired, 15 tons of bombs were dropped on the Wilhelmshaven naval base and Bremen was raided for an hour and a half, the British Air Ministry declared, when R. A. F. battle planes struck deep into Germany on Tuesday night.

Colonel General Wilhelm Keitel, chief of the German High Command, was reported to have been named leader of the Axis forces in Africa, presumably as a result of the Hitler-Duce conferences at the Brenner Pass last week.

In the Balkans, Britain and Rumania plunged headlong toward what British quarters in Bucharest called an "inevitable" diplomatic rupture over the ascension of German power in the dismembered kingdom once aligned with Britain.

Indo-China Bases Called Aid Against Arms Supply Route

TOKIO, Oct. 9 (A. P.).—Japan will close the Burma road with bombs if Britain persists in its determination to reopen this "back-door" route linking China with vital sources of war materials, the Tokio press intimated today.

Declaring the recent acquisition of airplane bases in French Indo-China had given Japan a tremendous strategical advantage against China, newspapers asserted the Japanese now were ready for direct action.

Further words are unnecessary, the prominent newspaper Nichi Nichi said, because Japan already has explained to third Powers its determination to eliminate the supply routes of Chinese Generalissimo Chiang Kai-shek.

"Japan need no longer conduct any diplomatic negotiations with Britain," said this commentary. "The effect of stationing Japanese forces in Indo-China should now be displayed."

SHIP OFFICES PACKED

SHANGHAI, Oct. 9 (A. P.).—With passenger liners already heavily booked far in advance, travel agencies and steamship offices were besieged today by Americans fearful of the gathering United States-Japanese crisis in the Orient.

Many American business men, accepting the State Department's counsel to get out of the Orient, started liquidation of their holdings and church societies stepped up arrangements to assemble their mis-

Continued on Page 2, Column 2

King Inspects Base Despite Air Raid

LONDON, Oct. 9 (A. P.).—King George VI visited the Aldershot army base during an air raid alarm today and inspected an infantry brigade in training at the "English Plattsburg."

When the air raid sirens wailed the King went on with the inspection.

Paderewski Arrives In Libson After Delay

LISBON, Oct. 9 (U. P.).—Ignace Jan Paderewski, world-famed pianist and former Polish Premier, arrived today and said he would proceed by steamship to the United States.

Paderewski had been delayed for some time in Spain.

Navy Assembles 4200 Recruits to Strengthen Crews

By JOHN C. O'BRIEN

Inquirer Washington Bureau

WASHINGTON, Oct. 9.—Asserting that no one knows whether the United States would become involved in war with Japan, Secretary of the Navy Frank Knox announced today that the United States Fleet based at Hawaii will be built up to full strength.

The present complements, he said, are only 82 percent of authorized strength. The first contingent of recruits to augment the fleet's crews, numbering 4200 men, have been assembled on the Pacific coast and will join the fleet when Admiral J. O. Richardson, who is now in Washington, returns with the portion of the fleet now at San Diego for shore leave.

ASKED TO COMMENT

Knox's remark on the uncertainty of Japanese-American relations was in response to a request for comment on a newspaper story that Washington officials fear the outbreak of war between the two countries 10 days after October 17—the date set by

Continued on Page 2, Column 3

THE WEATHER

Official forecast: Eastern Pennsylvania, New Jersey and Delaware—Fair, with slowly rising temperature today, not quite so cool tonight; tomorrow fair and warmer.

Sun rises 6.05 A.M. Sets 5.29 P.M.
Moon rises 2.36 P.M. Sets 12.43 A.M.

Other Weather Reports on Page 2

2 ROB AUTO DEALER OF $2000 IN TRAP

Bandits Hold Up Camden Man as He Tries to Start Car

Walking into a trap set by two apparently well-informed bandits, a Camden used car dealer was robbed of $2000 shortly before midnight last night as he attempted to start his automobile in front of his home.

Camden detectives later found that the ignition wires of the car had been ripped from their connections.

TWO MEN APPROACH

The victim, John Miller, 39, who lives at 2827 Clinton st., Camden, and operates the M. and M. Motors Co., at 2031 Federal st., was attempting to start the car when the two men masked and armed, approached on both sides, Miller told police

"This is a stickup, hand over your dough," said one of the men. When Miller pulled $300 from his pocket and handed it to them, the speaker took it and then declared:

"We want the dough that's in your wallet too."

TURNS OVER $1700

Miller turned over the remaining $1700.

The dealer told detectives that he left his agency at 10 P. M. and arrived home an hour later after doing some Saturday night shopping for his family. He left the car parked in front of his home, he said, and a short time later went out to put it in a garage.

On information supplied by Miller, detectives asserted they had definite suspects, but refused to divulge how the bandits knew that Miller would return to his car after entering the house.

Anti-Draft Pastor Ousted by Church

AUSTIN, MINN., Oct. 12—(A. P.)—The announced intention of a youthful Methodist minister to refuse to register for the draft brought a prompt demand today for his resignation from one of the two rural pastorates he serves.

Rev. Winslow Wilson, 28, who serves churches at Brownsdale and Dexter, made public his plans yesterday, saying "as a Christian I can take no part in war or preparations for war." Today the seven members of the board of the Brownsdale Methodist Church voted unanimously to demand that he resign.

"We took prompt action," said F. O. Tanner, recording secretary of the board, "because we do not want the public to get the false impression that the community of Brownsdale is in accord with such views."

Air Mail 'Pick-Up' Thwarted by Steer

WEST CHESTER, Pa., Oct. 12—The United States air mail almost picked up a steer late today without obtaining the necessary postage. As the mail plane approached the "pick-up" field just off the Wilmington pike, south of here, a herd of steers, which grazed nearby, wandered over to the apparatus used for aerial mailmen.

The operator of the plane pulled back on his stick in time to avoid the steers and had to circle the field several times before an employee drove the animals away and permitted him to hook the mail bag.

ELECTION EXTRA

The Philadelphia Inquirer

PUBLIC LEDGER

An Independent Newspaper for All the People

8 A. M. EDITION

CIRCULATION: October Average: Daily 415,930, Sunday 1,061,532 a b d e t g h★★ WEDNESDAY MORNING, NOVEMBER 6, 1940 Second Largest 3c Morning Circulation in America THREE CENTS

 VOL. 223, No. 129

ROOSEVELT WINS 3RD TERM WITH 433 ELECTORAL VOTES; WILLKIE LOSES CITY, STATE

NAZI SEA RAIDER SHELLS 2 SHIPS IN N. ATLANTIC

Spee-Class Vessel Attacks British Liner, Freighter 1000 Miles Out

Radio messages intercepted in New York yesterday said that a German war vessel, apparently a pocket battleship, was shelling the British liner Rangitiki, 16,698 tons, and freighter Cornish City, 4952 tons, 1000 miles east of Newfoundland.

Greek troops holding the heights around the Italian invasion base city of Koritza, Albania, were reported to have cut communications between the main Italian Army and a force of 30,000 Italians in the Koritza area. There were unconfirmed reports that the Greeks had occupied Koritza.

Bitolj, Jugoslav city on the border near the northeastern front of the Greek-Italian conflict, was bombed by planes identified as Italian. The missiles killed seven and wounded 35.

Prime Minister Churchill, meanwhile, told the Commons that the increasing U-boat menace, if not stopped, would "touch the life of the State," and disclosed that civilian air-raid dead in England totaled 14,000.

German bombs fell in the London area last night after a day in which the British had beaten off thrusts at the capital.

NEW YORK, Nov. 5 (A. P.).—A running fight in mid-Atlantic between a German raider of the "Graf Spee class" and a British convoy was told in three terse distress messages today, but silence shrouded the fate of the vessels attacked.

Three hours and ten minutes after the 16,698-ton passenger liner Rangitiki wirelessed that she was being shelled by a German raider, Mackay

Continued on Page 3, Column 4

President Carries Penna. by Majority Exceeding 246,000

By JOSEPH H. MILLER

Sweeping Philadelphia by more than 175,000, President Roosevelt carried Pennsylvania and captured its 36 electoral votes in yesterday's election.

The Democratic nominee's State-wide lead over his Republican rival, Wendell L. Willkie, was 246,000, according to tabulations early today.

United States Senator F. Guffey, Democratic candidate, although trailing far behind the President in the voting, was victorious over his Republican opponent, Jay Cooke, along with the rest of the State-wide ticket.

Returns from 7514 of the 8118 divisions in the State, including Philadelphia complete and 872 in Allegheny county, gave:

Roosevelt	2,017,469
Willkie	1,771,016

In Philadelphia, complete unofficial returns gave:

Roosevelt	527,604
Willkie	352,544

The State-wide tabulation in the U. S. Senate race, with 7466 divisions reported, gave:

Guffey	1,906,109
Cooke	1,764,246

Roosevelt Avalanche Leads Ticket to Victory in Phila.

By HERMAN A. LOWE

Another Roosevelt avalanche swept the Philadelphia polls yesterday, giving the President a plurality of more than 175,000 and 40 of the city's 51 wards.

Carried along in the victory parade were Senator Joseph F. Guffey, two Democratic candidates for State-wide office; six of seven New Deal Congressional nominees, all four Democratic State Senators up for re-election, and 36 of the 41 Democrats running for the lower house of the Legislature.

Roosevelt polled 527,604 votes to

Continued on Page 14, Column 6

President Captures Penna. by More Than 246,000 Votes

By WILLIAM F. FEIST

President Roosevelt captured Pennsylvania's 36 electoral votes at yesterday's election and carried with him to victory the entire Democratic State-wide ticket, according to returns from more than three-fourths of the 8118 precincts.

As the President defeated Wendell Willkie, Republican nominee, by more than 246,000 votes in the State-wide balloting, he swept into office with him Senator Joseph F. Guffey, New Deal leader, for another six-year term and State Treasurer F. Clair Ross and G. Harold Wagner, Auditor General and State Treasurer nominees.

COOKE CONCEDES

The Roosevelt victory in the State is also believed to have aided the Democratic Party to win control of the State House of Representatives, although the Republicans appeared to have retained control of the Senate.

Control of the Pennsylvania delegation to Congress was in doubt in spite of the fact the Republicans dropped at least two members, one in Philadelphia, Congressman Fred C. Gartner, and Chester H. Gross, York county, failing to win re-election.

Guffey's election to the Senate for another term was conceded early this morning by his Republican

Continued on Page 14, Column 3

Martin and Fish Win, Barton Defeated

NEW YORK, Nov. 6 (A. P.).—The fate of the triumvirate singled out for criticism by President Roosevelt in two of his campaign speeches—Martin, Barton and Fish—was split two-to-one today.

That of Martin (Rep. Joseph W. Martin, Jr., of Massachusetts, Republican National Chairman) appeared to be successful, for he piled up a heavy lead in first returns of his race for re-election.

That of Barton (Rep. Bruce Barton, of New York, candidate for U. S. Senator from New York) was certain—he conceded defeat.

That of Fish (Rep. Hamilton Fish, Jr., of New York) also was certain—he was re-elected.

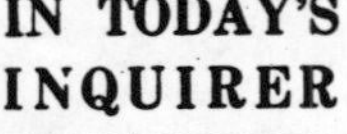

IN TODAY'S INQUIRER

PRESIDENT FRANKLIN DELANO ROOSEVELT

ROOSEVELT ASSERTS HE'LL BE 'THE SAME'

By CHARLES H. ELLIS, JR.
Inquirer Staff Reporter

HYDE PARK, N. Y., Nov. 6—(Wednesday)—President Roosevelt today assured his neighbors that they would find him in the future "just the same Franklin Roosevelt."

Showing very plainly his pleasure at the result of the election, which made him the first three-term President in the history of the United States, the President appeared on the veranda of his ancestral Hyde Park home to greet a torchlight procession of local residents.

'FACE DIFFICULT DAYS'

Standing beside his son, Franklin, Jr., and displaying little evidence of the strain of the campaign, the winning candidate said:

"We, of course, face difficult days, but you will find me in the future just the same Franklin Roosevelt you have always known for a great many years."

That was the only serious remark made by the President in the course of his short, extemporaneous address to the 1000 or more people gathered on the drive and lawn in front of the large white house which is his home.

He joked about himself and his recollection of past torchlight parades, professed surprise at the demonstration, and then returned to the table in the dining room where he had listened to the returns.

President Roosevelt went to bed at 2.35 A. M.

It was just before midnight when the crowd, which had been waiting impatiently outside the grounds, filed in.

They were carrying red torches,

Continued on Page 15, Column 1

City's Biggest Crowd Hails Roosevelt Victory

By JOHN M. McCULLOUGH

Without the slightest evidence of malice or ill-feeling, the largest throng of men and women ever to assemble in central Philadelphia last night and early today raised one mighty, exultant roar of acclaim to President Roosevelt's triumph.

No political victory celebration in the city's history has been like it. Police talked about it. No pedestrian on the street could miss it. It was almost tangible—not merely good-nature, but an evident desire to let bygones be bygones, and to pursue a new unity in the face of outward challenge.

That was the burden of the statement issued by Democratic City Chairman John B. Kelly. U. S. Ambassador to France William Bullitt seconded. But the crowd hadn't heard them. The noise was so terrific no single human voice could have been heard, from Filbert st. south to Spruce along humanity-clogged Broad st.

A union band leading the first Democratic victory parade up Broad st. halted in front of the Union League and played the "Star Spangled Banner," while thousands of celebrants removed their hats, and sudden, spine-tingling silence crept through the massed ranks.

EXCHANGE SALLIES

Union League members exchanged good-natured sallies with Democratic celebrants earlier, and smiled good-naturedly at the many jibes

Continued on Page 15, Column 4

DEMOCRATS BOOST POWER IN CONGRESS

By RICHARD L. HARKNESS

Nation-wide victories scored by Democratic candidates for the Senate and House on the coat-tails of President Roosevelt's landslide defeat of Wendell L. Willkie, assured the New Deal today of control of the next session of Congress.

Republicans not only failed to reduce Mr. Roosevelt's legislative strength in the lower chamber, but actually lost seats in delegations from Pennsylvania, New York, Rhode Island, Connecticut and Delaware on the basis of apparently conclusive returns from yesterday's elections.

In the Senate races, Senator John

Continued on Page 16, Column 1

Biggest U.S. Ballot Sweeps New Deal Back Into Office

By WILLIAM C. MURPHY, JR.

Franklin D. Roosevelt is the first man to be elected President of the United States for a third term.

An avalanche of votes cast in yesterday's election, which broke all previous records for the number of ballots recorded, swept Mr. Roosevelt into office again by a large majority in the Electoral College.

Early this morning Mr. Roosevelt was well ahead in 37 States which have a total of 433 electoral votes.

His Republican opponent, Wendell L. Willkie, at the same hour, was leading in 11 States which have a total of 98 in the Electoral College.

CLOSER MARGIN IN POPULAR VOTE

But the popular vote—the ballots cast by individual citizens—appeared to have been more evenly distributed between the two candidates than the indicated totals in the Electoral College.

With 30,840,282 votes tabulated the count was: Roosevelt, 17,061,280, and Willkie, 13,779,002.

Mr. Willkie retired soon after one o'clock without conceding defeat, but promising a statement at 9 A. M.

Senator Charles L. McNary, of Oregon, the Republican Vice President candidate, however, conceded the election of the Roosevelt-Wallace ticket and wired his congratulations to the victors.

FARLEY CALLS FOR HARMONY

James A. Farley former chairman of the Democratic National Committee, delivered a radio address early this morning calling for harmony in the interests of the Nation. Farley had taken little part in this campaign, presumably because he was opposed to a break in the erstwhile third-term tradition.

Mr. Roosevelt carried Pennsylvania and New York. He had commanding leads in Wisconsin, California, Ohio, Missouri and Illinois.

The third-term candidate swept the Solid South and the Border States, and made devastating inroads into New England, where the Willkie managers counted upon something approaching a clean sweep.

In State after State Mr. Roosevelt's huge majorities in industrial centres overcame the leads piled up by Mr. Willkie in the rural areas and the small towns.

Mr. Willkie carried the traditionally Republican

Continued on Page 14, Column 1

City Vote At a Glance

FOR PRESIDENT	
Roosevelt, D.	527,604
Willkie, R.	352,544
Roosevelt Plurality	**175,060**
FOR U. S. SENATOR	
Guffey, D.	513,752
Cooke, R.	351,428
Guffey Plurality	**162,324**
FOR STATE TREASURER	
Wagner, D.	511,803
Malone, R.	353,480
Wagner Plurality	**158,323**
FOR AUDITOR GENERAL	
Ross, D.	512,634
Gelder, R.	352,826
Ross Plurality	**159,808**

Roosevelt Carries Own District, 376-302

HYDE PARK, N. Y., Nov. 5 (U. P.).—President Roosevelt tonight carried his own home voting district.

The vote: Willkie, 302; Roosevelt, 376.

There were about 20 absentee ballots.

THE WEATHER

Official forecast: Eastern Pennsylvania—Mostly cloudy and much colder, occasional light rain in the mountains today; tomorrow fair.

New Jersey and Delaware—Rain early today, followed by clearing and colder; tomorrow fair and moderately cold.

Sun rises 6.34 A. M. Sets 4.53 P.M.
Moon rises 12.35 P.M. Sets 11.32 P.M.

Other Weather Reports on Page 2

The Philadelphia Inquirer

PUBLIC LEDGER

An Independent Newspaper for All the People

6 A. M. EDITION

CIRCULATION: October Average: Daily 415,939, Sunday 1,081,532   a b d e f g h   THURSDAY MORNING, NOVEMBER 21, 1940   Second Largest 3c Morning Circulation in America   THREE CENTS

VOL. 223, No. 144

Britain to Get 20 Flying Forts, 26 Bombers; Dies Charges Vast Nazi Trade Plot in U. S.; Hungary Signs as Fourth Partner in Axis

Today

Spain Is Wavering
Neutrality at Stake
Unrest Increasing
Franco Desperate
U. S. Should Act

—By Raymond Clapper—

WASHINGTON, Nov. 20.

IT MIGHT almost be said that as Spain goes, so goes the war. If it is not quite that simple there is enough in the idea to warrant the United States and Great Britain trying to hold Spain out of the Axis bloc.

Out of the Axis bloc? Spain is halfway in, and still halfway out. Franco has been holding back. His brother-in-law, Foreign Minister Serrano Suner, is playing with the Axis.

Serrano Suner has again made a pilgrimage to the Axis, this time to Berchtesgaden. He seems to be the leading candidate for the "Fifth Column" job in Spain. If the Axis can go through Spain to Gibraltar then the real trouble for Britain begins. Serrano apparently is ready to co-operate to that end.

Franco is showing reluctance to turn on the green light. One might suspect that the brothers-in-law of Spain are working both sides of the street, playing the Axis against the British in order to shove up the price before opening the door full-wide for Hitler.

Yet there is some reason to question that—enough reason to make it worth the while of London and Washington to canvass the possibility of bolstering up Franco.

That probably would be done in a hurry, principally with American economic aid, if Franco would give convincing assurance that he would keep Spain neutral and not turn it over as a corridor for the Axis forces. If such assurance were forthcoming things might begin to happen.

For some time this Government has had under advisement Spain's request for a large advance of credit. Action has been delayed because of unsatisfactory treatment of American interests in Spain.

Gradually the plight of Spain has become worse, with famine and unbelievable privation ahead and increasing unrest directed at the Franco regime.

The Spanish dictator is desperate and must have aid, if not from the British and the United States then from the Axis. The Axis is in no position to give Franco much help with his food problem. And if he goes over to the Axis, of course, all hope of help from the United States would be ended.

It may be, as has so often been the case in this war, that the United States and Great Britain will be out-traded and miss the bus. The Axis crowd are fast workers and Serrano Suner has gone to see them several times.

Great Britain's interest in heading him off and in holding Franco is immense and immediate. The British, however, are in no position to provide food or other supplies; they could only relax the blockade. The rest probably would be up to us.

Earlier the attitude here toward large credits for Spain was hostile. Now it is much more favorable. But it is not likely that this Government would act, or could gain the support of public opinion, except after a clear demonstration that Franco intended to keep Spain neutral.

Why do we bother with it? Because if the Axis goes through

Continued on Page 2, Column 1

'White Paper' Links Envoys To Propaganda

Special to The Inquirer

WASHINGTON, Nov. 20.—Allegations that the United States is being involved in a web of Nazi post-war business planning are set forth in detail in the 500-page "white paper" of the Dies House Committee, which has been inquiring into Nazi activity in the United States for the last two years.

The "white paper" exposes for the first time an alleged plan entitled "The reorganization of German industry in America after the war."

"The plan outlined," the Dies Committee report notes, "lacks nothing in its effectiveness or in detail for the contemplated organization, not merely of industry and trade, but also proposals to combine these spheres of activity with a great banking institute to underwrite and support the financing of German industry and trade activities.

PATENT AGREEMENTS

"In the proposed industry or trade organization plan there is the obvious intent to draw upon all industrial activities in America that are in any way allied with German industry. Relations would arise out of the extension of patent agreements or cross-licensing of patents.

"The plan further contemplates bringing into the organization representatives from such leading industrial activities in the United States as cotton, cellulose, machine tools, the automotive industry, etc.

"The plan sets forth a very definite link with the industrial life in Germany by providing that all these activities, industry, trade, commerce and academic, shall be directed from a bureau to be established in the German Ministry in Berlin.

GERMAN CONTROL

"There is the very obvious intent to retain control of these activities in the hands of German authorities and not to permit their control to be

Continued on Page 10, Column 1

HILLMAN URGES CIO TO BAN ISMS; BACKS MURRAY AS LEADER

Describing Communists, Nazis and Fascists as a "menace to labor," Defense Commissioner Sidney Hillman called upon the CIO, in convention at Atlantic City, to oust them from membership.

At New Orleans, the AFL heard Sol A. Rosenblatt, general counsel of the Democratic National Committee, declare the recent election gave American publishers their "greatest shock" and predicted many are due for a "great awakening."

By HUGH MORROW
Inquirer Staff Reporter

ATLANTIC CITY, Nov. 20.—Defense Commissioner Sidney Hillman today urged CIO convention delegates to draft Philip Murray for the CIO presidency, called Communists, Nazis, and Fascists "a menace to the labor movement," pleaded for labor unity, and declared the Amalgamated Clothing Workers of America, of which he is president, would stay in the CIO.

In an impassioned speech an hour and 45 minutes long, Hillman answered the challenge of CIO president, John L. Lewis, who yesterday thundered there would be no peace with the AFL except on the CIO's terms, and virtually dared Amalgamated to bolt CIO if it did not like Lewis' opposition to Amalgamated's efforts to achieve labor unity.

DEMAND FOR MURRAY

Hillman made clear there would be no retreat from his position, but emphasized there was "nothing personal" in his differences with Lewis, and expressed "regret" that Lewis

Continued on Page 24, Column 4

House May Move Till Roof Is Fixed

WASHINGTON, Nov. 20 (U. P.).—House Democratic Leader John W. McCormack disclosed tonight that he plans to sponsor a resolution to permit the members to meet outside the Capitol so that badly needed repairs may be made to the 83-year-old House roof.

Both roofs are made up largely of heavy glass squares in order to permit natural lighting of the chambers. Steel supports have so weakened over the years, however, that architects and engineers fear they may collapse under the weight of the glass.

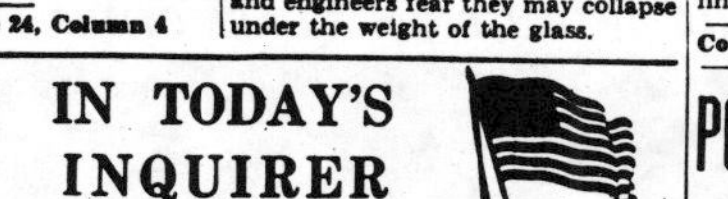

IN TODAY'S INQUIRER

(A. P. Wirephoto)

FLYING FORTRESS WHICH BRITAIN MAY GET

Shown soaring over Mt. Rainier in latest trial flight, this Boeing 4-motored bomber is one of the type which will be released to Great Britain if negotiations now under way are satisfactorily completed. The U. S. Army wants it to have a test in combat.

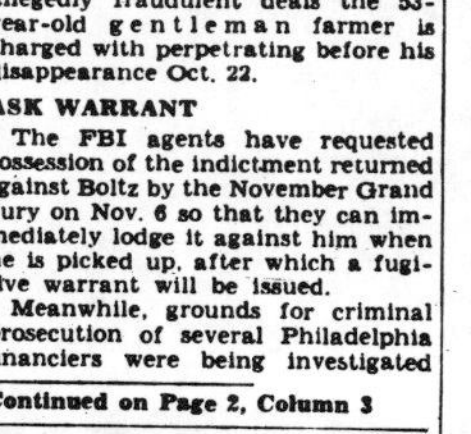

G-MEN JOIN SEARCH FOR BOLTZ; PROBE MAY INVOLVE OTHERS

FBI agents yesterday joined in the Nationwide hunt for Robert J. Boltz, missing investment counsellor who made magic with money, as his financial adventures became even more fantastic in the light of new disclosures by Federal officials.

Sensational repercussions that may shock the city's financial world loomed as a dramatic result of Boltz's fabulous 14-year career, as they joined a small army of investigators working on the $2,500,000 worth of allegedly fraudulent deals the 53-year-old gentleman farmer is charged with perpetrating before his disappearance Oct. 22.

ASK WARRANT

The FBI agents have requested possession of the indictment returned against Boltz by the November Grand Jury on Nov. 6 so that they can immediately lodge it against him when he is picked up, after which a fugitive warrant will be issued.

Meanwhile, grounds for criminal prosecution of several Philadelphia financiers were being investigated

Continued on Page 2, Column 3

POLICEMAN'S BLOOD GIVEN BOY HE SHOT

After he had twice shot and seriously wounded a 17-year-old boy accused of stealing an automobile, a policeman last night gave his blood in a transfusion operation in the hope of saving the youth's life.

The shots were fired by Motorcycle Policeman James Martin at the end of a wild automobile chase in which the boy, Alvan Bussell, of Mount Vernon st. near 15th, sought to escape.

FIGHTING FOR LIFE

With blood from the veins of Martin and another policeman coursing through his body, the wounded boy early this morning was fighting for life in the Lankenau Hospital, where physicians pronounced his condition critical.

Bussell was one of two youths shot last night in police pursuits. The other is Anderson Bullock, 16, Negro, who was struck in the right shoulder by a policeman's bullet near 46th st. and Haverford ave.

The chase which ended with the

Continued on Page 2, Column 5

Zog's Army Reported Battling Italians

LONDON, Nov. 20 (U. P.).—A broadcast by the Turkish radio at Ankara tonight alleged that Albanian troops wearing the uniform of exiled King Zog's army appeared in the rear of Italian troops on the Greek frontier and blew up fuel tanks.

Greeks Report Routing Foe on Central Front; Hungary Joins Axis

Hungary cast its lot yesterday with the Berlin-Rome-Tokio Axis, signing at Vienna a military-political-economic compact pledging itself to joint action against any country which in the future may engage in the European or Japanese-Chinese war. Budapest sources said that Rumania, Bulgaria and Spain might be the next to join.

In the capital of Bulgaria, there was speculation on reports that Germany planned to send troops through Jugoslavia and Bulgaria, and newspapers said that the "day is not far off" when Bulgaria would play a role in the "new order" in Europe.

In the Balkan war, Athens declared that Italian troops were retreating so swiftly along the central Albanian front that the Greeks had difficulty keeping up with them. The Italian flight was called an "utter rout." Contradictorily, Rome asserted that Italian forces on the defensive along the Albanian frontier southeast of Koritza, Albania, had repulsed the foe with heavy Greek losses.

In the Battle for Britain, waves of German bombers again hammered at the war industries of England's Midlands, but early today terrific anti-aircraft fire was reported to have dulled the edge of the attack. The British admitted that the nine-hour attack of Tuesday night and Wednesday morning had strewn wreckage in a dozen towns; the Germans' version was that more than 1,000,000 pounds of bombs had been dropped on Birmingham, knocking that industrial centre out of the war.

The British counter-offensive in the air, London announced, reached to Pilsen, where the Skoda arms plant was fired, and to Berlin.

Budapest Promises Aid Against New Foe In Europe or Orient

By PRESTON GROVER

VIENNA, Nov. 20 (A. P.).—Adolf Hitler annexed Hungary today to the German-Italian-Japanese Axis, which he thus converted into a four-Power alliance dedicated to defeat of Great Britain and to the totalitarian reorganization of Europe, Asia and Africa.

By treaty, Hungary joined its Axis friends in a military, political and economic compact pledging joint action against any country which in the future may engage in the European or Japanese-Chinese wars.

'MORE POWERS WILL FOLLOW'

Conclusion of the accord was followed by a luncheon at which the Fuehrer was host to the top-flight diplomats who participated in the ceremony.

One significant addition to this group was his own military chief, Field Marshal General Wilhelm Keitel.

Hitler and the other conferees left Vienna tonight by train.

Observers noted that, by the signatures of the Foreign Ministers of Germany, Italy and Hungary and

Continued on Page 4, Column 3

Greeks Repulsed In Koritza Sector, Italians Declare

ATHENS, Nov. 20 (A. P.).—A Government spokesman declared tonight that Italian troops were retreating so rapidly along the central Albanian front that it was difficult for the Greeks to keep up with them.

The Italian front, it was said, was broken northwest of Konitza, Greece, some 10 kilometers (about six miles) inside Albania and west of the River Aoos. It was described as an utter rout, and the spokesman said that "very important booty"—including

Continued on Page 4, Column 6

Bullitt Remains As Envoy to France

WASHINGTON, Nov. 20 (A. P.).—William C. Bullitt said after a talk with President Roosevelt today, "I still remain Ambassador to France."

Bullitt announced last week he had resigned, but that the President had declined to accept the resignation.

He said today he intended to attend the Yale-Harvard football game Saturday and then take a several weeks' vacation.

Army Planes In Secret Flight To Canal Zone

By JOHN C. O'BRIEN
Inquirer Washington Bureau

WASHINGTON, Nov. 20.—The United States has released to Great Britain 26 four-engined heavy bombers of the B-24 type and is negotiating for the release of 20 of the latest model "flying fortress," known as the B-17-C.

The Army also has released to the British the Sperry bombsight, more accurate than any now in use by the European combatants, but considered inferior to the Norden sight, which remains the jealously guarded secret of the War and Navy Departments.

The announcement was made today by General George C. Marshall, Army Chief of Staff, who said that in return for the waiving of United States priority on the B-24's, which are manufactured by Consolidated Aircraft Co., Great Britain had released sufficient engines manufactured here on British order to equip 41 "flying fortresses" which would have been accepted for delivery without engines by Jan. 1.

The War Department has neither confirmed nor denied a report, authoritatively circulated here several weeks ago, that 36 of the Army's 59 heavy bombers of the B-17-B type, predecessor of the B-17-C, have been released to the British and already are engaged in trans-Channel bombing raids.

FLIGHT TO CANAL ZONE IS MYSTERY

Likewise unexplained today was the purpose of a mass flight of 21 bombers to the Canal Zone. The squadron landed on Tuesday on a Mexican airfield near Vera Cruz, and their destination reputedly was the Canal Zone. No further report of their progress was received here today.

Twenty of the B-17-B's recently were flown from the West Coast to stage a demonstration for visiting officers of armies of Latin-American countries.

Marshall explained that the principal motive for negotiating the release of the late model "flying fortress"—the B-17-C—was the Army's desire to put this airplane to actual battle test. No comparable plane ever had engaged in battle, he said.

The Army staff chief disclosed that the Army Air Corps has observers in England who go up in British fighting planes

Continued on Page 6, Column 4

British Gunners Blunt Nazi Raid on Midlands

LONDON, Nov. 21 (Thursday) (A. P.).—German planes swarmed out of the night for a second "total" attack on Great Britain's industrial Midlands, but early today it was reported that a terrific anti-aircraft barrage had dulled the edge of the new offensive.

Ground guns, firing with new effectiveness, were said to have dispersed waves of planes attempting a mass raid on an unidentified town in the eastern Midlands after less than two hours of incendiary-bomb-dropping, which is merely the first step in the "Coventry technique."

The bombs were extinguished and little damage was reported.

How the rest of the Midlands fared was not known.

The rapid fire of ground defenses and the rumble of bombs caused observers in the eastern Midlands to say it was the fiercest attack ever made on that area.

OTHER POINTS ATTACKED

Other bombers ranged over London and towns in southwestern England and Wales.

The action, however, did not seem to be as widespread as Tuesday night's, which covered a record area.

The eastern Midlands were show-

Continued on Page 5, Column 6

THE WEATHER

Official forecast: Eastern Pennsylvania—Cloudy, slightly colder in south portion today; occasional rain tonight and tomorrow, slightly warmer tomorrow.

New Jersey—Cloudy and slightly colder today; occasional rain tonight and tomorrow.

Delaware—Cloudy and slightly colder today; tomorrow cloudy, followed by occasional rain.

Sun rises 6.52 A.M. Sets 4.40 P.M.
Moon rises 10.58 P.M. Sets 11.50 A.M.

Other Weather Reports on Page 2

The Philadelphia Inquirer
TUESDAY MORNING, NOVEMBER 26, 1940 adig★ 22

AT INDEPENDENCE HALL DRAFTEES TAKE OATH ADMINISTERED BY LIEUT. COL. FREDERICK SCHOENFELD. AT HIS IMMEDIATE LEFT IS MAYOR LAMBERTON.

RITA GENOVESE OF CAMDEN SAYS GOODBYE TO HER FIANCE JAMES WRIGHT.

They're in the Army Now

The city's first 40 draftees arrived at Fort George G. Meade last night, a year of Army life ahead. They formed the vanguard of 12,500 ultimately to be selected from Philadelphia. They took the oath clustered around the Liberty Bell in Independence Hall after being cheered by thousands during a six-block parade. To Fort Dix went 17 men from Camden.

THE NEW SOLDIERS WAVE TO PHILADELPHIA AT 10TH AND MARKET. THEY WERE IN THE ARMY SOON AFTERWARD.

PHILADELPHIA'S DRAFTEES MARCHING EAST ON MARKET ST. TO INDEPENDENCE HALL FOR THE INDUCTION CEREMONIES.

CAMDEN MEN LEAVE BY BUS FOR FORT DIX IMMEDIATELY AFTER TAKING THE OATH UNDER THE SELECTIVE SERVICE ACT.

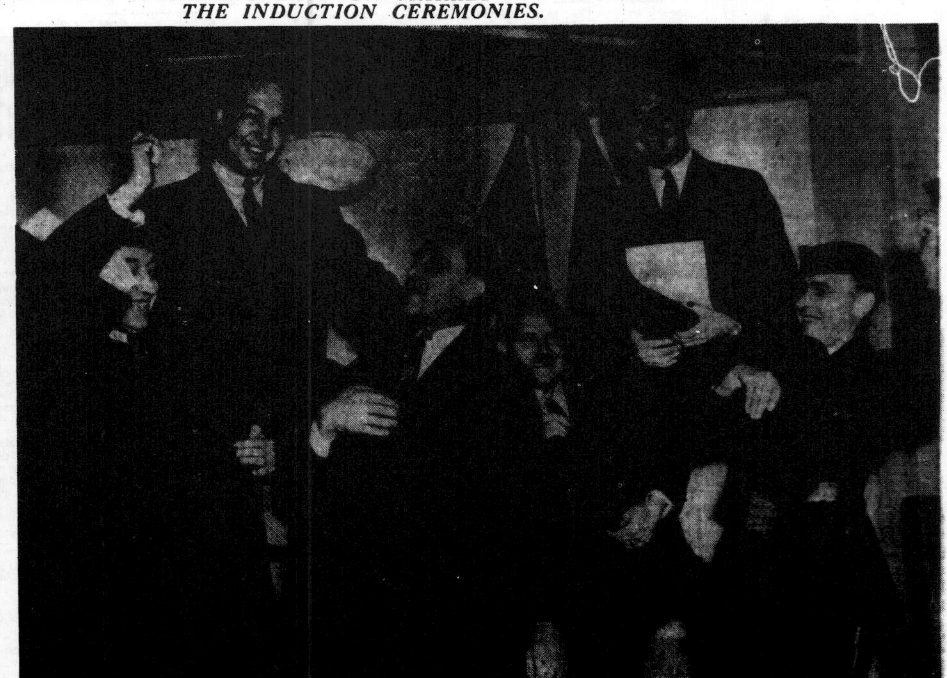

FROM LEFT, STANDING: GEORGE WILLIAMS, DAVID JAMISON, EUGENE ZIEGLER, L. G. McCRACKEN, TOP, WILLIAM FISH (LEFT) AND HENRY HURST, DRAFTEES.

Louis Gains T.K.O. Win Over McCoy in 6th

The Philadelphia Inquirer

PHILADELPHIA, TUESDAY MORNING, DECEMBER 17, 1940 abdefgh 27

(A. P. Wirephoto)

McCOY GOES DOWN UNDER LOUIS' BARRAGE IN FIRST ROUND OF TITLE FIGHT

Al McCoy, Boston heavy, was in trouble as early as the first round in his championship battle with Joe Louis last night at the Boston Garden, Boston, Mass. He's down on one knee after taking a right off the jaw and three rights to the body from Joe Louis, left. Louis retained his heavyweight title by scoring a technical knockout when McCoy failed to come out for the sixth round. Referee is Johnny Martin.

Strictly Sports

So Christmas May Come To a Valley in Scotland

Tale of Tommy Fraser's Funds, And of Those Over There

By CY PETERMAN

THIS may be more a Christmas story than of sports . . . It's been a long time we've intended calling Tommy Fraser, the bra' Scot who builds muscles, restores health and spreads cheer in West School lane, Germantown, and teaches the kids at Mifflin School, East Falls, the proper way to swing a mashie and stroke the ball.

Yes, a long time since he trudged to the press box and introduced himself while John Bromwich slapped the deciding point over the Davis Cup net at Merion that September afternoon—it seems years ago now—Tommy having trained the Aussies for that triumphant tennis effort. We agreed to meet later, for he wanted to talk about golf, an ancient Scottish fancy to which he was natively addicted.

But now, across the luncheon table, there were so many other things to relate and besides Tommy only golfed twice the past summer, so busy has he been with the funds.

"Funds? You're in the money, Tom?"

"Ahh, it's not that," he laughed. "I only gather and pass them on, and truthful lad, they keep me hoppin'. A Scotchman still, you see, looking for a penny here and a shilling there, to put to some worthy use——"

* * *

THE GOLF of which he spoke was so keen that he set 66 as the record over the Loudown Gowf Club in Ayrshire, near the city of Glasgow where the famous Loudown Castle still stands, a monument to the peace signed between England and Scotland. But now Tom's game rusticates as he devotes more time to teaching lassies like Jean Raynor how to play, or coaches John (Bonnie) Fraser, aged 12, who rules all the Mifflin kids at his father's favorite pastime.

You don't have time for 18 holes when treasurer and prime mover of three such charity associations, he explained.

First, there is the Valley Donation Fund, which supplies the needs of the folks in war-ridden Scotland, or at least that nook which contains Tommy's home heath of Galston, and neighboring Newmiln and Darvel. To help them, "exiles" in America, no matter in what city, are tapped for contributions big or little, from individuals to groups like the Scottish Choir here, and have given upwards of $2300 so far.

Tommy mentions the sum with considerable pride, for $2300 in donations to a Scotchman is not petty cash.

"Then there is the Galston District Fund, which is more for the old folks at Christmas," he continued. "We try to assure them one good time that holiday, and last summer I popped over to the World's Fair when our group was attending and believe it, we collected all of $130. "Yes, and they had a merry time on the sum, I was told."

* * *

THIS year the Christmas budget for the old folks reached $200, and we asked Fraser just what it might provide.

"Oh, it's spent a' right," he assured; "they do put on a feast. Everyone gathers in the village hall—the old people, the children, the clergyman and the mayor. They have a bit of prayer and they have a bit of speech, and then they also have a bit of song—if the bombers be not overhead.

"Then there is a jolly feed for everyone, with sociability and a forgettin' of the war and hardship for the moment. Of course, there would be nothing at all, things being what they are in the Valley, if we didn't make for it over here. Our little ones—there are four—have about transferred their whole Christmas over there."

All these charities are co-ordinated through Galston's "wee paper" the 'Supplement,' in which 'Sifter,' the anonymous columnist, records the deeds and travels of Galstonians near and far, and especially Tommy Fraser, who married his golfing partner, Margaret Gallacher, went away to the States, but never forgot the home folks.

* * *

WE FELL to musing on the scene as Tommy talked, and fancied those elder couples, hobbling along the ancient paves, men with knotty canes and quaint caps, womens' cloaks drawn close against the winds which ever punish Scotland. They bobbed into the meeting place—Tommy said it's the Evangelistic hall and every Scottish village has one—where they took their places for the occasion.

The clergyman, now respected more than ever, and other dignitaries present were duly heard, and then, without much cause for Christmas cheer in all of Britain, those old people and the very young, for the able-bodied are mostly in service, would raise their voices in simple carols, with the windows blacked out against terror.

"That sounds like a noble foundation," we said to Tommy, but he was already outlining a third.

"I've been scraping' up silver here and there for a smokes fund for the lads," he said.

By "the lads," of course, he meant the soldiers, explaining how many cigarettes one could ship for $24, and what grateful responses they evoked.

* * *

"HERE, I've a packet of the letters wi' me," he remembered, delving into a veritable sheaf.

The first was from No. 3131643, L. C. Houston.,
Motor Cycle Platoon, H. Q. Co.
6th Batt. Royal Scot. Fusiliers,
Frinton-on-Sea, Essex, Eng.

"Dear Mr. Fraser,

I wish to express my thanks for a generous gift of cigarettes from Galstonians in America, which I assure you is much appreciated in times like these when a soldier's pay is small and cigarettes expensive. A lot of us, though having to make allowances to the folks at home, are only receiving five shillings a week and as cigarettes cost one and three for twenty, you will understand why I appreciate your gift. The food in the Army is good and plentiful and we have another raise of pay coming soon, so I can assure you we are happy and well cared for, and above all, more than a match for the Huns.

A GALSTON BOY."

Another came from Edinburgh under last September's dateline:

"Dear Sir:

As a Galstonian serving in H. M. Forces, I received a parcel containing among many other things cigarettes bought with your kind donation to Sifter, and I now take the privilege of expressing, through you, to all Galstonians in the U. S. A., my humble thanks. Wishing you all the best of luck, I remain,

Till Jerry packs up,
PVT. WM McCARROLL."

We read a couple more and then the waiter brought the bill, but when Tommy put down a tip we pushed it back, reminding it would buy almost two packs for the lads.

13,334 Watch Champ Retain Heavy Crown

Boston Ringman Refuses to Answer Bell After 5th Round

By SID FEDER

BOSTON, Dec. 16 (A. P.).—Joe Louis came back from his six months' vacation to an easy job of work tonight, but he wasn't the devastating Brown Bomber in disposing of Al McCoy, an overgrown Down East light-heavyweight.

It took him five full rounds to cut down a fellow he outweighed by 21½ pounds and who had no more punch than grape juice in his fists. After taking a pummelling for 15 minutes, McCoy, his left eye closed and his ribs red from right hand shots, was unable to come up for the sixth heat. Commissioner George Laplante ruled the bell had rung for the sixth round and that Louis was awarded a technical knockout victory in that round.

2D LARGEST CROWD

The second-largest crowd ever to turn out for a fight in the Boston Garden enjoyed itself thoroughly while it lasted, but didn't like the finish even a little bit, and booed as the public address system announced: McCoy's eye is in bad condition and he refuses to come out for the sixth round."

The attendance was announced as 13,334 customers, with a gross gate of $46,980 and a net of $44,845, of which Louis received between $17,000 and $18,000. The crowd was second in size for the Boston Garden only to that for the Jim Maloney-Tom Heeney tussle 11 years ago.

Although still the most damaging puncher in any league, Joe showed the effects of the long layoff since he disposed of Arturo Godoy, the rugged Chilean, last June. His timing, particularly with his right hand, was off, and for some time he didn't seem to know just what to do about McCoy's circling-away tactics and half-crouching style. As a result, although he floored the Bostonian for no count with three crunching rights to the short ribs in the first heat, Louis failed to put him down once after that.

JOE TAKES PUNCHES

In addition, Joe took some "desperation" right hand pokes to the jaw which he should not have left himself open for. Of course, he could afford to be careless tonight, but he'd better not give away any chances like that to some of the fellows he meets in his "one-a-month" campaign between now and next April.

Immediately after Louis polished off the 26-year-old New Englander tonight, New York promoter Mike Jacobs announced that the champion and Billy Conn would fight it

Continued on Page 29, Column 5

Schmidt Resigns, Ohio State Accepts

Five Other Members of Grid Staff Also Quit Positions

COLUMBUS, O., Dec. 16 (A. P.).—Francis A. Schmidt, the tall, greying Texan who made football a spectacle with his wide-open "razzle-dazzle" style of play, stepped out tonight as head coach at Ohio State University.

The board of athletic control announced it had accepted the resignation of Schmidt and five other members of the coaching staff.

Schmidt submitted his resignation earlier today because, he commented dryly, "the board is dissatisfied." He did not amplify, but an investigation of the "football situation" at Ohio State was launched by the athletic board a week ago tonight following a four-won, four-lost season—the first for the Bucks in 10 years.

FIVE OTHERS RESIGN

The assistant coaches who also resigned were Ernie Godfrey, line coach; Sid Gillman, end coach; Ed Blickle, backfield coach, and Gomer Jones, a scout and assistant line coach.

Frits Mackey resigned as coach of the freshman squad, but will remain as baseball coach. The board said that Blickle also would remain as assistant basketball coach.

The resignations are effective next June 30, when the coaching contracts expire. Ohio State employs its athletic staff on a year-to-year basis.

The board's announcement, which terminated Schmidt's seven-year reign at Ohio State, came after a two and one-half hour session. Rumors were rife earlier that Schmidt had resigned, but he did not confirm this until after the board met in a specially called session.

WON TITLE IN 1939

In his seven years at Columbus, rated as one of the toughest coaching towns in the country, Schmidt's teams won 39 games, lost 16 and tied one. In 1934 the Bucks tied for the Big Ten title, and in 1939 they won it outright—their first since 1920.

Schmidt, who came here from Texas Christian, did not attend the board meeting because "the board doesn't want anything more from me. Mrs. Schmidt and I are going out for the evening."

Athletics Get Pitcher Knott

By STAN BAUMGARTNER

Connie Mack and Jimmie Dykes—total strangers when trades were mentioned at the Major League confab in Chicago—got together yesterday and did more in two minutes than they accomplished in two days in the Windy City.

Mack traded Dario Lodigiani for pitcher Jack Knott. Lodigiani is an infielder who was purchased by the A's from Oakland when the Yankees gave up the coast league city as a farm team. The Italian started out his career with the A's in spectacular fashion then began to miss on all cylinders which including fielding and batting.

He was finally optioned to Toronto and when he failed to start any fires in the International League Connie decided to get rid of him . . . He asked waivers. Dykes refused to waive—and then came the trade with Chicago.

Knott has been around the American League long enough to know all the head waiters in the hotels. He was with the St. Louis Browns until Dykes secured him in trade for Joe Cox, another righthander. With the White Sox last season Knott won 11 and lost 9 which certainly was not bad. He may be a big help to Connie next year—and fill the spot left vacant by Caster's sale to the Browns. He is 34 years old.

Lodigiani batted .281 for Toronto

Continued on Page 29, Column 7

Robert Victor Over Garibaldi

Yvon Robert, 225, of Canada, pinned Gino Garibaldi, 220, St. Louis, in two-out-of-three falls in the feature wrestling bout at the Camden Convention Hall last night.

Garibaldi gained the first fall in 23.12, when he applied an arm lock and forced Robert to concede the fall. Robert retaliated and took the second fall with a body slam and press in 14.12. Then oRbert came back strong after the intermission and subdued Garibaldo in 36 seconds with another body slam and press.

In the semi-windup, Mildred Burke, claimant of the women's mat championship, won a one-fall to the finish match over Carole Starr, Wyoming challenger. Miss Burke gained the fall in 15.10 with a body press.

Donato Beats Nat Litfin

Frankie Fights Off Lates Challenges for 10th Win in Row

By EDWARD J. KLEIN

Frankie Donato, Southwark's left-fisted bantam pride, hung up his 10th straight victory last night when he weathered Nat Litfin's belated fire to cop the decision in the eight-round windup, watched by 1500, at the Broadwood.

Carrying the battle to his opponent, a battle-scarred New Yorker, for five rounds, Donato swept every period and seemed en route to a decisive victory. Then Litfin, a hard hitter with either hand, nearly turned the tide.

NAT TAKES LEAD

Nat, who outweighed the Southwarker by 10 pounds, took the lead as the sixth started, but Donato's deft jabbing and effective counters earned him the period by a slight edge.

Litfin let go with his all in the seventh. Donato gave ground at first, then tossed caution to the winds and started to trade punches. In one of these give-and-take exchanges, Frankie was clipped by a left and dropped to the deck. He was up at one.

For the rest of the heat, Litfin peppered the Southwarker with both mitts and gained the round by a wide margin. Nat kept up his furious firing in the eighth and, despite Donato's game retaliation, this heat was his, too.

CUT OVER EYE

But Litfin's belated rally fell far short of catching Donato's early advantage. Frankie won the unanimous decision of Referee Matt Adgie and Judges Frank Knaresborough and Lou Tress. Adgie gave Donato seven periods, Knarsborough awarded him six, Tress voted for and one even.

Donato suffered a cut over his right eye in the fourth and blood flowed from the wound through the late

Continued on Page 29, Column 7

N.J. Deer Season To Open Today

Thousands of red-clad hunters will start out at dawn today in quest of the reported plentiful deer as New Jersey's five-day hunting season opens. The season closes at sundown, Saturday.

A large majority of the hunters have turned to South Jersey in recent years to meet their demands of large bucks.

The biggest herds have been in the Weymouth forest near Mays Landing in Atlantic county. Many sportsmen who usually hunted bucks in Burlington county, will be forced to seek new stalking grounds, due to a ban issued in the upper part of the county by the Government.

USED FOR ARMY CAMP

The Government has purchased over one-fifth of the land in the Wrightstown and Browns Mills area for use in the enlargement of the Fort Dix military reservation.

Signs have been posted for miles surrounding Fort Dix warning hunters to remain off the reservation. This section has been the best gunning grounds in South Jersey during recent years.

Not all of Burlington county, however, is in the restricted area, but

Continued on Page 28, Column 7

Milnes Wins Verdict In Amateur Thriller

Slugs Way to Victory Over Schiavone In Hard-Fought Duel at Cambria Club

By JOHN WEBSTER

In one of the most hysterical slamming duels ever fought in the old Cambria punch bowl, Wesley Milnes battered Angelo Schiavone to defeat for the major thrill of an Inquirer A. A. elimination program last night.

This bout, a 160-pound open contest, alone was ample reward for the fight fans who braved a black, dripping night to jam the Kensington fight shop to the guards. Yet they had in addition a program packed with colorful, breath-taking battles as 14 bouts were presented under the auspices of the Northeast A. A.

DUNBAR ENTRIES WIN

Tall, dark and possessed of a shattering punch, Milnes smashed Schiavone to the boards for nine seconds in the third period to climax his victory. He took the unanimous decision of Refree Jack Coughlin, a most efficient arbiter, and two judges when a stormy round was finished.

After the two dark-haired huskies had socked each other violently for two rounds, with Milnes landing the harder blows, they touched off high explosives in the final session. Suddenly, the aggressive Wesley moved in, and flattened a right on Angelo's jaw. Down went Angelo.

SCHIAVONE RETALIATES

Schiavone, his wits wandering, sat on the ring floor. He was coming up, however, at nine. Milnes came on the charge from a neutral corner, but Schiavone lashed out with a wild burst of retaliatory punches.

They slugged until the final bell. Yet Schiavone, who counters neatly with a right hand, could never overcome that flooring, or the haymakers he'd sampled in the first two rounds.

Milnes, like Schiavone, is an unattached middleweight of the Greater Northeast district. The two were sub-novices in the 1940 Diamond Belt and Middle Atlantic amateur boxing championships.

Wesley appears to have a fair chance of punching his way into the Tournament of Champions spotlight at Convention Hall on Jan. 27. He has, that is, unless his reckless, give and take style, causes his downfall.

Clem Russo, tall, good-looking youngster from Passon A. A., out-

Continued on Page 29, Column 3

N. J. Raises Limit on Track Investors

TRENTON, N. J., Dec. 16 (A. P.).—The State Racing Commission announced late today it had agreed to increase its limit on investors in any track from 175 to 1000 persons.

Commission Chairman Louis A. Reilly made the announcement after a lengthy meeting with fellow commissioners. He said the action was taken on a request by representatives of the Monmouth Park Racing Association, presently the only State-licensed group. It plans a track at Oceanport, Monmouth county.

Reilly said spokesmen for the Monmouth Association told the commission that economic uncertainty produced by the European war made it difficult for them to raise needed capital with a 175 limit on prospective stock buyers. The commission chairman said the raised limit would apply to any group licensed by the commission.

There would be no relaxed vigilance in commission supervision of financing, Reilly said, in spite of the increased investors' limit.

Reilly said the commission was attempting to work out a compromise between two rival groups seeking a track franchise in Atlantic county—the New Jersey Jockey Club, which has prepared plans for a race oval at the Seaview Country Club, Absecon, and the Atlantic City Jockey Club, which has applied for a track license at Atlantic Pines Golf Club.

The racing chairman said there had been "considerable opposition expressed concerning the granting of a license in Camden county." A group headed by Nicholas S. Ludington, of Philadelphia, had proposed the Camden Airport as a racing site.

NEAR ATLANTIC CITY

Reilly said the proposed site talked of in the suggested compromise was about 22 miles west of Atlantic City, half-way between Elwood and Weymouth, on a road connecting the White and Black Horse pikes.

The chairman expresed hope the two groups might get together on an application for a racing plant on the site which had been offered, he said, by Bennett E. Tousley, Atlantic City hotel operator, as an "alternative" site.

'Lousy Fight,' Admission Of Joe Louis

By BILL KING

BOSTON, Dec. 16 (A. P.).—An apologetic Joe Louis, who appeared slightly worried over the inroads five months of idleness had made in his magnificent fighting machinery, had little to gloat about tonight when he retired to his dressing room after successfully defending his heavyweight title against little Al McCoy.

"It was a lousy fight," Louis said as he beat the newspapermen to the first verbal punch. "I must have looked as bad out there as I did the last time I was here." (On his previous Boston visit, seven years ago, Max Marek, of Chicago, knocked Louis down seven times in a national amateur semi-final.)

GAVE ME TROUBLE

"That McCoy gave me plenty of trouble with his bobbing and weaving. He moved around so much that I had trouble catching him with my right and I had to left-jab him. I know I missed plenty of lefts, but when you've been idle for five months, you're bound to miss a lot of them."

Louis was unable to recall a blow that made any impression on him.

"McCoy can't punch," he explained, "but he sure can make you look bad."

McCOY'S EYE CLOSED

Except for a tightly closed left eye, puffed up when he forgot his handlers' warnings and blew his nose, the much smaller McCoy emerged without another obvious mark.

"I wanted to keep going, and I could have gone the limit, but they wouldn't let me come out for the sixth," McCoy explained.

"Louis hits harder than they say he does," Al continued. "Those rights he landed on my body in the first round almost paralyzed me and I had trouble straightening up.

"I think Billy Conn is a much better boxer than Louis but, of course, he can't punch as hard. If I hadn't been half blinded, I'm sure I could have gone the 15 rounds and I'd be glad to go in with him again if I ever got the opportunity."

Lesnevich K. O.'s Marshall in 4th

NEWARK, N. J., Dec. 16 (A. P.).—Gus Lesnevich, of Cliffside, making his fourth start as a heavyweight, knocked out Jack Marshall, of Dallas, Tex., in 2:43 of the fourth frame of a scheduled 10-round boxing bout at Laurel Garden tonight. Lesnevich weighed 178, Marshall 184.

Lesnevich, leading contender for the 175-pound title, finished off the Texan with a vicious punching attack.

Events of the Week in Philadelphia

TODAY

Foresters of America, Court Nonpareil 183, 42d anniversary banquet, Adelphia Hotel, 1.30 P. M.

Young Men's Christian Association, rededication of Christian St. branch, 1724 Christian st., 3 P. M.

Frankford Friends' Forum, lecture, "The Supreme Court and the Idiom of the Law," by Walton Hale Hamilton, Ph.D., Professor of Law at Yale University, Unity and Wain sts., 3 P. M.

Race Street Forum, lecture, "Freedom and Authority in the National Economy," by Walton Hale Hamilton, Race st. west of 15th, 7.30 P. M.

Pennsylvania State Nurses' Association, District Association 1, annual meeting of Private Duty Section, 311 S. Juniper st., 8.15 P. M.

TOMORROW

Philadelphia County League of Women Voters, lecture, "Legislation to Watch," by Alvin R. Guyler, program director of Public Charities Association of Pennsylvania, Belgravia Hotel, 1811 Chestnut st., 12.30 P. M.

Chamber of Commerce, luncheon, Ritz-Carlton Hotel, 12.30 P. M.

Philadelphia Theatregoers Council, luncheon, Bellevue-Stratford, 12.30 P. M.

Philadelphia Forum, board luncheon, Bellevue-Stratford, 12.30 P. M.

Philadelphia Passenger Association, 25th anniversary dinner, Bellevue-Stratford, 5.30 P. M.

American Society for Metals, Philadelphia chapter, dinner, Engineers Club, 1317 Spruce st., 6.30 P. M.

Saddle Horse Association of Philadelphia, dinner and meeting, Raymond's Restaurant, 41th st. and Parkside ave., 6.45 P. M.

Women's Republican Club of Pennsylvania, meeting, Bellevue-Stratford, 8 P. M.

Grand Lodge Judaic Union, general installation ceremonies, Red Men's Hall, 8.30 P. M.

Izaak Walton League, Philadelphia chapter, meeting, 3313 N. Broad st., 8.30 P. M.

TUESDAY

Presbyterian Board of Christian Education, meeting, 9 A. M.; luncheon, 12.30 P. M., Ritz-Carlton Hotel.

Overbrook Lions Club, luncheon meeting, Overbrook and Lancaster aves., 12.15 P. M.

Kiwanis Club, luncheon, Bellevue-Stratford, 12.30 P. M.

Matinee Musical Club, luncheon, Bellevue-Stratford, 12.30 P. M.

Engineers Club, luncheon, 1317 Spruce st., 12.30 P. M.

Poor Richard Club, luncheon for Mayor Robert E. Lamberton and his Cabinet, 1319 Locust st., 12.30 P. M.

National Association of Cost Accountants, Philadelphia Chapter, meeting, Penn Athletic Club, 6 P. M.

Better Philadelphia Committee, dinner, Warwick, 6.30 P. M.

Germantown Boys' Club, 54th anniversary party, Judge Frank Smith, guest speaker, 25 W. Penn st., 7.30 P. M.

Press Photographers Association, meeting, Bellevue-Stratford, 7.30 P. M.

Philadelphia Psychoanalytical Society, meeting, Bellevue-Stratford, 8 P. M.

Philadelphia Laryngological Society, meeting, College of Physicians, 19 S. 22d st., 8.30 P. M.

West Philadelphia Jewish Community Centre Forum, lecture, "The Turbulent Balkans," by Dr. Michael Dorizas, member of Wharton School faculty, 63d and Ludlow sts., 8.30 P. M.

WEDNESDAY

Daughters of the American Revolution Philadelphia Chapter, meeting, Bellevue-Stratford, 10.30 A. M.

Pennsylvania Society, Daughters of the Revolution, meeting, Bellevue-Stratford, 11 A. M.

Rotary Club, luncheon, Bellevue-Stratford, 12.30 P. M.

South Philadelphia Realty Board, meeting, Adelphia, 12.30 P. M.

Women's Division, Jewish Congress, tea, Warwick, 2 P. M.

United Charities Campaign, dinner, Bellevue-Stratford, 6.30 P. M.

Philadelphia Foremen's Club, dinner-meeting, 5722 Greene st., 6.30 P. M.

American Philatelic Society, meeting, Bellevue-Stratford, 8 P. M.

Geographical Society of Philadelphia, lecture, "The Romance of the Amazon," by Richard C. Gill, Walnut and Juniper sts., 8 P. M.

Philadelphia Art Alliance, lecture, "Line and Color in Decoration for the Theatre," by James Reynolds, stage designer, 251 S. 18th st., 8.30 P. M.

Junior Board of Commerce, host to officers and men from Fort Dix at musical concert, Academy of Music, 8.30 P. M.

THURSDAY

Salvation Army, campaign opening luncheon, Bellevue-Stratford, 12.30 P. M.

Philadelphia Museum of Art, lecture on "Evolution of Furniture Forms," Parkway and 25th st., 3.30 P. M.

Philadelphia Art Alliance, lecture, "The Olympic Games in Ancient Greece," by Walter Woodburn Hyde, 251 S. 18th st., 5 P. M.

Police Chiefs Association of Southeastern Pennsylvania, meeting, Walton Hotel, 6.30 P. M.

Philadelphia Council of Christian Education, conference, "The State, the Child and the Church," Arch Street Methodist Church, Broad and Arch sts., 8 P. M.

Pennsylvania Society of Professional Engineers, Philadelphia chapter, meetnig, Engineers Club, 1317 Spruce st., 8 P. M.

Penn Athletic Club, meeting, 18th and Locust sts., 8.30 P. M.

FRIDAY

Philadelphia Music Club, audition for active membership, Presser Bldg. auditorium, 1714 Chestnut st., 10 A. M. to 12 noon.

English Speaking Union, reception to British Consul, Bellevue-Stratford, 4.30 P. M.

Right Angle Club, annual dinner, Bellevue-Stratford, 6.30 P. M.

Lankenau Hospital Ladies Auxiliary, party and dance, Bellevue-Stratford, 8 P. M.

Veteran Guard, 3d Regiment Infantry, military ball, Bellevue-Stratford, 8 P. M.

Railroad Enthusiasts, Philadelphia division, annual model railroad show, Baltimore and Ohio R. R. city ticket office, Broad and Walnut sts., 8 P. M.

American Foundrymen's Association, Philadelphia Chapter, meeting, Engineers Club, 1317 Spruce st., 8.15 P. M.

SATURDAY

Foreign Policy Association, luncheon, Bellevue-Stratford, 12.30 P. M.

Rosemont College, supper dance, Ritz-Carlton Hotel, 9.30 P. M.

Penny Plus Tax Causes Trouble

RICHFIELD, Utah, Jan. 4 (U. P.). —There's getting to be a tax on everything in Utah—especially the imagination.

Dr. David E. Ostler, Richfield physician, reports a recent incident in which one of his 4-year-old patients was troubled with pains in the throat after swallowing a penny.

While Dr. Ostler was contemplating removal of the coin, the boy coughed and with the penny piece a one-mill Utah tax token was dislodged from his throat.

Conscience Troubled 15 Years

ROCHESTER, N. Y., Jan. 4 (U. P.).—Two checkers, taken 15 years ago from the playground shelter at Rochester Public School No. 12, have been returned to their former place on an unnamed but penitent Los Angeles, Calif., resident.

Baby Exhibits Swimming Form

ST. PETER, Minn., Jan. 4 (U. P.). —Sharon Gabrielsen, 22-month-old daughter of Bramwell Gabrielsen, baseball coach at Gustavus Adolphus College, is a claimant to the world's swimming and diving championship —in her age division.

Sherry, who learned to swim when her father ducked her playfully in a river to overcome her fear of the water, chalked up a distance record of more than 30 feet—which her father claims is the world's record for swimmers under 2 years. She uses a crawl stroke and dives from the regulation board.

Five World Champions to Referee Inquirer Ring Classic, Jan. 27

HE'LL REFEREE: JACK DEMPSEY

BILLY CONN

LEW JENKINS

ANOTHER ARBITER: JIMMY BRADDOCK

Forte Punch Rated Hardest by Salica

That cleft in Lou Salica's chin is not a dent placed there by Tommy Forte's right fist.

Nevertheless, the world's bantam champion admits that the Southwark stripling's rifle shot—a knockdown wallop in their nontitle mill on Oct. 21—was the hardest he ever sampled. He told fight writers here as much on the day when he signed for his 15-round title defense against Little Tom, scheduled for next Monday night at the Arena.

RATES HIM HARDEST HITTER

In this true confession Salica, a Brooklyn citizen, said that Forte hits harder than Sixto Escobar, or any of the punchers he fought in pro or amateur rings. He added that the left hook which the Philadelphian sank into the body earlier was the most telling sock he ever experienced amidships.

"They'd told me to watch Forte's left hook," said Salica, waving his hand toward Hymie Caplin, his manager, and other advisers. "I watched his left hand. He crossed me. He belted me with a right. I found myself on the floor."

YET HE'S CONFIDENT

However, Salica, who arrived here this evening to pitch camp at the Broadwood, bases his confidence in himself on that same knockdown shot. He thinks he's taken the best that Forte has in stock. He believes he will out-fox the younger lad over the longer route—they fought only 10 here in October.

"I took his best shot," observed Salica. "And I got up. I'll do it again. And I'll have 15 rounds this time. I just missed before."

That's the way most fight professionals figure the bout. Forte is extremely dangerous. If he doesn't stretch Salica on the floor he's likely to finish runner-up, however.

DONATO WOULD REPEAT

Frankie Donato will try to repeat tomorrow night in the Broadwood ring, and keep his unbeaten record in pro rings unbroken. The former Inquirer A. A. champion will again face Nat Litfin, New York feather, in the eight-round main event at Joe Wenke's fight shop.

Winner of all his 10 moneyed duels, slim Donato, a downtown lefty, appears one of Philadelphia's finest prospects at this moment. A clever ringman, he stabs with a jarring right hand, picks off punches and mixes furiously, both guns firing, when need be.

ALL-STAR OLYMPIA CARD

Frankie, at 120, spotted 10 pounds to Litfin—and beat him—some weeks ago. However, he was forced to push himself off the floor to win. Tomorrow night's bout calls for 126 pounds at the weigh-in. Litfin, in better trim, might be more redoubtable than before.

Joe Sankey and Wickey Harkins, rival Germantown welters, are to collide in an eight-round co-feature.

Four attractive eight-round pairings comprise Jimmy Toppi's Olympia show for Thursday night. The bouts are Danny Falco vs. Willie Davis, Johnny Forte vs. Nick Spano, Tommy Cross vs. Buck Streator and Billy Mims vs. Andre Jessurun. Every bout could be a small club windup.

Turc Duncan has announced three eight-rounders for the Cambria on Friday night. They are Harvey Massey vs. Johnny Carter, Johnny Myhasuk vs. Vince Kojac and Freddy Damico vs. Charley Burns. Two sixers also are carded.

JOHN WEBSTER

Inquirer Shows Listed This Week

(In Philadelphia)

MONDAY NIGHT—Cambria A. C., Kensington ave. and Somerset st.

TUESDAY NIGHT—Olympia A. C., Broad st., below Bainbridge.

THURSDAY NIGHT—St. Mary's Hall, 60th st. and Elmwood ave.

(Out-of-Town)

THURSDAY NIGHT—at Chester, St. Hedwig's Auditorium; At Harrisburg, the Madrid Palestra; at Tamaqua, Liberty Hall.

FRIDAY NIGHT—at Easton, Moose Hall.

Miss Murphey Tops Seedings

By DORA LURIE

Evelyn Murphey tops the seeded quartet in the fourth annual Philadelphia junior girls' squash racquets tourney which opens tomorrow at 3 P. M. at the Philadelphia Cricket Club, St. Martins.

Miss Murphey, slender Germantown girl, is an all-around athlete. She has been selected on the all-Private School field hockey team for the past three years and is equally as capable in basketball.

Sally Jackson, Baldwin School; Joan Fernley, Shipley School, and Barbara Rossmassler, another Germantown Friends' op-ed, are seeded after Evelyn Murphey in the order named. Miss Jackson, 15, is a member of the Cynwyd Club women's team.

Betty Shellenberger, all-American hockeyist and all-American lacrosse player who won the title last year, is no longer eligible to compete in junior ranks. Betty, however, will act as chairman of the title event.

Top seeded Miss Murphey will meet Betty Dernley, schoolmate, in her opening match. Sally Jackson will oppose Adelaide Craven, another of the many Germantown Friends' entries, while Joan Fernley engages Nancy Scott, Germantown High, and Barbara Rosmassler faces Barbara McDowell, Springside School, in their initial tests.

Miss Fernley, an attractive little blonde, has made quite an athletic name for herself. Joan is a noted equestrienne and also won a post on the all-Private School hockey team to prove her versatility.

The squash draw released yesterday by chairman Betty Shelenberger follows:

FIRST ROUND

Evelyn Murphey, Germantown Friends, vs. Betty Dearnley, Germantown Friends.
Elizabeth Pilling, Springside, vs. Mary Foulkrod, Germantown Friends.
Joan Fernley, Shipley School, vs. Nancy Scott, Germantown High.
Polly Holton, Springside, vs. Sylvia Knowles, Springside.
Sally Jackson, Baldwin School, vs. Adelaide Craven, Germantown Friends.
Betty McLean, Cynwyd, vs. Mary Louise Vanneman, Raven Hill Academy.
Barbara Rosmassler, Germantown Friends, vs. Barbara McDowell, Springside.
Dottie Weeder, Springside, vs. Jean Slaymaker, Shipley School.
Seeded players: Murphey, Jackson, Fernley, Rosmassler.

Today's Sports

BASKETBALL

SCHOOL

CATHOLIC LEAGUE

Roman Catholic vs. La Salle at 20th st. and Olney ave., 2.30 P. M.
St. Thomas More at Salesianum, 2.30 P. M.

INDEPENDENT CATHOLIC LEAGUE

St. Edward's vs. Resurrection at Castor and Shelmire aves., 8.30 P. M.
Xavier vs. St Ambrose at C st. and Roosevelt Blvd., 8.30 P. M.

BRITH SHOLOM LEAGUE

Trenton vs. Haber Lodge, Lewis vs. Emil Zola and Kraus vs. Cardoza at Musical Fund Hall, 810 Locust st., first game 2.30 P. M.

SOCCER

PROFESSIONAL

AMERICAN LEAGUE

Passon-Phillies vs. Brookhattan at Cambria Stadium, Kensington and Torresdale aves., 2.35 P. M.

AMATEUR

PHILADELPHIA LEAGUE

(FIRST DIVISION)

Wissinoming vs. Lighthouse at Frankford ave. and Comly st., 2.35 P. M.
Harrowgate vs. Southwark at I and Tioga sts., 2.35 P. M.
Green Ribbon vs. Loach at Morris - Apsley sts., 2.35 P. M.

(WEST DIVISION)

Lighthouse Men's Club vs. Knight's A. C. at Front st. and Erie ave., 2.35 P. M.
Angora vs. Jewish A. C. at 5820 Baltimore ave., 2.35 P. M.
Cardington vs. Cohocksink at 68th and Catharine sts., 2.35 P. M.

(EAST DIVISION)

Ital-Americans vs. Passon J. V. at League Island Park, 2.35 P. M.
Tyson vs. Lighthouse Blues at Frankford ave. and Tyson st., 2.35 P. M.

Seven Tourney Shows in Week

Seven elimination shows are scheduled this week in The Inquirer A. A. Diamond Belt competition as industrious young boxers move nearer to the Tournament of Champions.

Three of these programs will be staged in Philadelphia. Bouts also are listed in Chester, Harrisburg and Tamaqua; Easton's tournament will be started on Friday night.

In Philadelphia, tournament bouts are carded tomorrow night for the Northeast A. A. show at the Cambria, Kensington ave. and Somerset st. The South Philadelphia A. A. will sponsor a program on Tuesday night at the Olympia, Broad st. below Bainbridge. Completing the week's events locally, the youthful title-seekers will be gunning at St. Mary's Hall, 60th st. and Elmwood ave., under the auspices of the Red Men and Haverford clubs, on Thursday night.

Four shows are on the schedule for Thursday night. Leather is also to fly in Chester, Harrisburg and Tamaqua tourneys.

MILNES FACES GINYARD

Brilliant winners of earlier battles in the tourney are to see action in every one of the Philadelphia shows. Open divisions and subnovice victors will be striving to repeat those triumphs. Several lads, fighting giants of the heavy ranks, will be slugging for the first time.

Outstanding among the many bouts slated for the Cambria is the collision of Wesley Milnes, Southwark, and Earl Ginyard, Eastside, in a 160-pound open contest. Milnes, handsome, reckless and a slugger, defeated Angelo Schiavone in a first-round triller. Ginyard, Negro lefty who was the '40 sub-novice champ, beat Nelson Canty in his march to open honors.

This one shares the spotlight with other prospective thrillers. They are Richard Dabney vs. George Popvic, 112 pounds; Dave Freeman vs. Dave Williams, 126 pounds; Dan Vespa vs. Clem Rosso, Jim Scott vs. Ed Rauch and James Martin vs. James Goodwin, 160 pounds, and Harry Meenan vs. Ted Holland, heavies.

AMBROSANO BOXES

Angelo Ambrosano, national A. A. U. bantam titlist, will mix with Bob Smith, youngster from Crispus-Attucks, in one of the numerous Olympia open features. Ambrosano fights for Pen-Mar.

Another downtown feature will be the meeting of Art Mahon, 48th Ward, and Larry Thomas, Crispus-Attucks, in a feather combat. They are rated as leading threats for the title.

Two lightweight bouts of much promise are Tony Perrone-Charles McGrath and Ed Giosa-Carl Townsend. The latter pair in particular are ranked among the top-liners.

WELTERS TO BATTLE

Of little less interest are these bouts: Harold Solomon vs. Jordan Beamon, heavies; Joe Guarracini vs. Wesley Burden, welters, and Santa Bucca vs. James Tracey, Ontario, 118 pounders.

In all likelihood the fans at St. Mary's Hall will have a peek at the 147-pound open champion on Thursday night. At least it seems very possible they will, since six standout lads are milling that night.

O'HARE MEETS VETTESE

Frank O'Hare, blond Dunbar puncher, is paired with Al Vettese, Haverford boxer; Sig Kobylinski, another Dunbar candidate, faces Ralph Johnson, Crusaders' Negro slugger, and Glenn Smith, another from Crusaders, is to oppose Joe Powers, unattached belter. They're all rated in the top flight.

Each lad has scored two sparkling victories. O'Hare took care of Ernest Frazier and Dennis White; Vettese outfought John Garrity and Herb Black; Kobylinski outpunched Louis Di Stefano and James Maxwell; Johnson defeated John Ciabattoni and William Crudup; Smith whipped Ralph Leslie and Al Paucelli, and Powers beat Jim Harvey and Don Daly.

To Play in Canal Zone

READING, Pa., Jan. 4.—George Kurowski, Rochester third baseman, and former Reading High captain, with several International Leaguers, sailed from New York today for Cristobal, Panama, where they will play in the Canal Zone league team, managed by John Grodzicki, a teammate at Rochester.

Dempsey Tops List Of Famed Ringmen

By JOHN WEBSTER

Continued from First Page

the open and sub-novice groups. A sub-novice is one who had had no more than two bouts when he entered the tournament. Seasoned campaigners mix in the open division. This assures evenly-matched, bang-up contests—with no chance for a lad to be outclassed, or injured. Bouts will be staged in 112-118-126-135-147-160-175-pound and heavyweight classes in each group.

Not only have the elimination bouts met with tremendous success at the local neighborhood clubs, but also at all points in the tournament. The Harrisburg tournament, sponsored by the Harrisburg Telegraph, clicked with a sell-out on the afternoon of its first show. Chester's bouts, conducted by the Chester Times, have become even more popular than last season, the first in The Inquirer tournament.

Tamaqua's tournament was launched last week with an enthusiastic turnout, most gratifying to Tommie Large, director of the event, sponsored by the Knights of Columbus A. A.

The Morning Free Press of Easton, Pa., will start its tournament at Moose Hall in that city on Friday night. Ralph E. Stahlnecker, sports editor of the newspaper, is most optimistic over prospects in Easton.

ROOM FOR EVERYONE

The Inquirer A. A. believes it is fortunate in having secured spacious Convention Hall for its gala event, because there'll be room for everybody who wishes to see a pulse-strumming ring classic. With the vast seating capacity, the prices have been scaled so reasonably that a dollar never stretched so far before.

The tickets, which go on sale tomorow at The Inquirer and advertised agencies, offer the biggest bargain a fight fan ever had. Just $1.14 for choice ringside seat—and 58 cents for many main floor sections, and choice locations in the lower balcony. The remainder of the balcony seats, general admission—sale the night of the fights—will be only 57 cents.

However, don't delay in securing your seats. Of course, Convention Hall will accommodate 14,000 persons—but there's never been a show like this presented to the sports followers in Philadelphia.

MICKEY WALKER

Farm School Five Defeats Bok

DOYLESTOWN, Pa., Jan. 4.—National Farm School opened its 1941 basketball season today with a 31 to 26 victory over Bok Vocational School.

Augie Levitisky, captain, led Farm School in scoring with five baskets for ten points. Jim Charlesworth, a substitute forward, followed with 9 points.

FARM SCHOOL	G.	F.	P.	BOK VOC.	G.	F.	P.
Berger,f	1	0	2	Ernest,f	2	0	4
Gordon,f	1	1	3	Privito,f	1	0	2
Charlesw'h,f	3	3	9	Gildea,c	4	0	8
Groben,c	0	0	0	Orlich,g	0	2	2
Males,g	2	2	6	Nicoola	0	1	1
Levitisky,g	5	0	10	Cohen,g	4	1	9
Totals	12	7	31	Totals	11	4	26

SCORE BY PERIODS

National Farm	10	10	2	9	—31
Bok Vocational	3	5	10	8	—26

Week's Tourney Bouts

NORTHEAST A. A.
(Monday Night)
Cambria A. C.

118-POUND SUB-NOVICE

Dom Riverrose, United Sports; Rube Shelton, Ontario; Ed Schuhl, Nativity; Nat Monroe, Batesville; Charles Grubb, Southside; Russell Regalbuto, Southside; Dom Silvani, Ontario; John Keenan, Lambs; Paul Kubach, Dunbar.

126-POUND SUB-NOVICE

Andy Graham, Eastside; Al Vandiver, Eastside; John Leahy, Dunbar; Patsy Stirti, Lambs; Larry O'Connor, Dunbar; Joe Miller, Eastside; John Walker, Eastside; Harry Johnson, Main Line; Sal Piacente, Batesville; Malcolm King, Main Line; Andy Wason, Dunbar.

147 POUNDS SUB-NOVICE

John Cunnion, Bear's Gym, vs. Frank Mattioni, Lambs.

112 POUNDS OPEN

Richard Dabney, Eastside, vs. George Popovic, Wegletn.

126 POUNDS OPEN

Dave Freeman, John Marquess, vs. Dave Williams, Bear's Gym.

160 POUNDS OPEN

Earl Ginyard, Eastside, vs. Wesley Milnes, Southwark; Dan Vespa, Bear's Gym, vs. Clem Rosso, Passon; Ed Rauch, Seymour, vs. James Scott, Ontario; James Martin, Eastside, vs. James Goodwin, John Marquess.

HEAVYWEIGHT OPEN

Harry Meenan, Bear's Gym, vs. Ted Holland, Eastside.

SOUTH PHILADELPHIA A. A.
(Tuesday Night)
Olympia A. C.

160 POUNDS SUB-NOVICE

Noble Knoche, Eastside; Ralph Lawrence, Pen-Mar; Rocco Paoriello, Pen-Mar; Joe Trainor, J. O'Malley; James Gerdy, Crispus-Attucks; Donald Lafferty, Seymour; James O'Malley; Red Men; William Powell, Red Men; William Powell, Batesville; Sam Diem, Red Men; Art Basile, Batesville.

147 POUNDS SUB-NOVICE

Willis Payton, Bearcat, vs. Wolf Alport, Batesville; Jim Gaspari, Coatesville, vs. Joe Jackson, Crispus-Attucks; Maurice Ferrine, Bear's Gym, vs. Richy Law, 48th Ward; Marty Anfick, Bridesburg, vs. Chas. McNeil, Crusaders; William Barton, Bearcat, vs. Angelo Caruso, Pen-Mar.

118 POUNDS OPEN

Santa Bucca, Pen-Mar, vs. James Tracey, Ontario; Angelo Ambrosano, Pen-Mar, vs. Bob Smith, Crispus-Attucks.

126 POUNDS OPEN

Art Mahon, 48th Ward, vs. Larry Thomas, Crispus-Attucks.

135 POUNDS OPEN

Tony Perrone, Seymour, vs. Charles McGrath, Dunbar; Ed Giosa, Pen-Mar, vs. Carl Townsend, Crispus-Attucks.

147 POUNDS OPEN

Joe Guarracini, Seymour, vs. Wesley Burden, Eastside.

HEAVYWEIGHT OPEN

Harold Solomon, Pen-Mar, vs. Jordan Beamon, Eastside.

RED MEN-HAVERFORD
(Thursday Night)
(St. Mary's Hall)

118 POUNDS SUB-NOVICE

Angelo Capri, Hammonton, vs. Angelo Strisi, Pen-Mar; Charles Lipford, Eastside, vs. Charles White, 29th Century; John Semanyk, Seymour, vs. Wallace Williams, John Gleason, Bear's Gym; Carl Stephens, Bearcat, vs. James Quigley, 48th Ward; Harry Heineman, Seymour, vs. Frank Liney, Dunbar; Reginald Christensen, Eastside, vs. Norman Gibbs, Martin A. C.

118 POUNDS SUB-NOVICE

Leonard Buttignoni, 48th Ward, vs. John Rockins, Haverford.

112 POUNDS SUB-NOVICE

Gerald Galliton, Lambs, vs. Preston Greene, Southside.

135 POUNDS SUB-NOVICE

William Wood, Bearcat, vs. Elmore Castellante, Red Men.

147 POUNDS OPEN

Glenn Smith, Crusaders, vs. Joe Powers, Nabes B. C.; Al Vettese, Haverford, vs. Frank O'Hare, Dunbar; Ralph Johnson, Crispus-Attucks; Sig Kobylinski, Dunbar.

160 POUNDS OPEN

Jacob Gray, Seymour, vs. Artis Williams, Batesville; Rudy Di Ciero, Bear's Gym, vs. Leo Legarde, Bearcat.

175 POUNDS OPEN

Tom Johnson, Bearcat, vs. Herman Reese, Wharton.

Skunk Is Called Bane to Wildlife

By HARRIS G. BRETH

There's no doubt about it—in the past few years the skunk has become a public nuisance. He has left his nomadic paths in the backwoods and farming country and invaded the boroughs and backyards, wending his way unconcernedly under porches, into garages and anywhere within city limits that beckoned his fancy. Morning, noon and night citizens and city taxpayers have had the aroma of his perfumed trails wafted into their nostrils and beyond an irate word or sputtering of condemnation, nothing much has been or can be done about it.

SLOW, LUMBERING

The skunk is a peculiar animal in many ways. A slow, lumbering fellow, he does very much as he pleases of his very effective anatomical apparatus. Neither man nor preying beast cares to purposely disturb the tranquillity of his ways. And, in addition to this protective combination, he has had a "break" in favorable breeding and feeding conditions unequaled in this day and age by any other form of wildlife. To understand that consider the past decade in relation to the skunk's natural needs.

Insects comprise one of the principal items in the skunk's daily menu. That's why he frequents the fence rows, and the open fields, especially when overgrown. In those places he finds beetles, grubworms, crickets, grasshoppers, snails, centipedes—which he eagerly relegates to the custody of his digestive organization. To get these tidbits he lumbers slowly along, using his eyes and his nose to locate their hideaways, in brushroots, under field stones and pebbles, in weed beds and out in pasture and overgrown fields of all kinds.

RABBITS DECREASE

Although the skunk has become a public nuisance, that isn't the sorry part of the situation. It is his activity as a preditator that concerns the sportsman. As the skunks have increased, the rabbits have vastly decreased, and strenuous efforts by sportsmen and the game commission to thwart the trend appear to be making little headway. The fact remains that nature created the rabbit the next door neighbor of the striped, bushytailed, odorsome mammal. They both use the same feeding and forage areas, frequent the same fence rows and take advantage of the same woodchuck burrows.

But, as mentioned, cottontails nest in open fields in small depressions in the ground, and the young are born blind and naked. It takes a week or so before they can leave the next, and until then they are directly in the foraging path of the skunk in its search for food. If the hunter wonders what has become of small game, especially rabbits, if he ruefully contemplates his past season's bag of bunnies he can consider these figures:

The year before last trappers clamped the steel on 230,000 skunks, and last year over 300,000—an increase of over 70,000. The year before last hunters bagged over 3,000,000 cottontail rabbits, and in the 1940 season the total kill will be about 500,000 less.

Ohio State Coach Still Undecided

COLUMBUS, Ohio, Jan. 4 (A. P.).—The Ohio State University football coaching job was discussed but nothing decided, Don Faurot, University of Missouri grid mentor, reported tonight following a conference with Athletic Director L. W. St. John and members of the University Athletic Board.

It was Faurot's second interview and he indicated another might be forthcoming before he leaves tomorrow for Columbia, Mo.

"Any statement concerning the meetings should come from Mr. St. John," Faurot said. St. John said he had no statement to make at present.

Despite attention accorded Faurot, dopesters still regard Paul Brown, Massillon, Ohio, High School coach, as having the "inside track." Others receiving considerable attention are Dr. George Hauser, Minnesota line coach scheduled to come here next week for an interview, and Alan Holman, former Buckeye star and now coach at Franklin and Marshall, Lancaster, Pa.

Barks From Dogdom

Dogs Can Receive 'Lessons' at Matches

By GEORGE BUTZ

How's that Christmas puppy?

In the event the gift is a pure-bred with a pedigree and in good health, the new owner may as well determine the quality of the puppy as a possible show specimen. There is only one method of comparing the dog with others of its particular breed and that is by becoming a novice exhibitor. A comparison can best be made by competition.

Most of the inveterate fanciers, breeders and owners of large kennels once started with exhibiting the first puppy. Usually the first pure-bred dog has been a gift. Interest in the sport of showing dogs has invariably been fostered by the desire of one-dog owners to learn how their canine compares with others.

'WALKING THE DOG'

After the owner has patiently acquainted the frolicsome puppy with a leash, it should be brought into contact with others. The best early training a young dog can receive is to get it accustomed to people and noises. Otherwise, the animal can become nervous and high-strung due to its lack of contact. Puppies are unusually curious, but they should never be allowed to receive an unexpected fright.

Speaking of showing a new dog, especially a puppy, the owner can gain suitable results by entering it at a small match. All-age or all-breed sanctioned matches are being held by kennel clubs to stimulate interest among novice fanciers. At this type of dog match, puppies of any age limit can be shown, whereas the rules of the American Kennel Club stipulate no dog under six months can be exhibited at a point show.

The all-breed or all-age match has proven satisfactory as the training school for a show specimen. At these affairs young dogs become accustomed to people and most important —drawn into close contact with other dogs. They may be stubborn or nervous in this strange environment, but they soon settle down if they are shown with any degree of frequency.

DEBUTS FOR MANY DOGS

Many fanciers in this section will exhibit new puppies at one of these matches this week. Quite a few young dogs of promise should make their debut Wednesday night, when the Quaker City Dog Club holds its first all-breed match of the new year at 2319 N. Front st. in Kensington. Entries at a sanctioned match such as this one, can be made until the start of judging at 8.30 P. M.

Charles Hamilton, professional handler, will lend his services at the Quaker City Club match, Wednesday night, judging a varied number of breeds and also pick the most outstanding dog in the match. Other judges selected, include Fred Mueller, Dachshunds and Boxers; Miss Bessie Livingston, Cocker Spaniels; Mrs. Donald Livingston, Bulldogs; and Mrs. Betty Edwards, Children's class.

Canine Calendar — Winter's first large show is scheduled today and tomorrow in New York, where the American Spaniel Club stages its 24th specialty event in Hotel Roosevelt . . . Ralph Craig, of Albany, will judge American-type Cocker Spaniels, the Cocker Spaniel futurity class and the best-in-show, while Edward D. Knight, of Charleston, W. Va., will judge all other Spaniel breeds. . . . Philadelphia's group of exhibitors will number at least fourteen well-known fanciers and breeders.

BOSTON TERRIER MATCH

Annual meeting involving the election of officers is scheduled by the Bulldog Club of Phila. tomorrow night in the Inquirer Building at 8.30 P. M. The Boston Terrier Club of Phila. also meets tomorrow night at the Stephen Girard Hotel, 2027 Chestnut st. An all-age match is also listed with Mrs. Viola Johnson of this city, doing the judging.

Members of the So. Jersey Field Trial Association gather Tuesday night for their annual election of officers at the Franklin House in Glassboro, N. J. . . . A dinner for members and their wives will follow the election. . . . Camden County Kennel Club meets Tuesday night at the Walt Whitman Hotel in Camden. . . . Trenton Kennel Club holds its January meeting, Thursday night at the Stacy-Trent in Trenton. . . . Jim Mitchell will make a report on the recent match. . . . Guest speaker is Barbara Thayer of New Britain, Pa.

Mrs. Sarah W. Codling of Collingswood, is confident she has a champion or two in a recent litter of six Boston terriers, each a vest-pocket copy of their sire&Zeman's Budget Boy—owned by Mrs. Emma Zeman of North Phila. . . . Betty Whelen of Pocono Kennels (near Norristown) reports Collie and Shetland Sheepdog litters recently. . . . This fancier is especially grooming a "Sheltie" for Westminster's show next month.

'DACHSIE' WINNER

Rickie of Bally Teckel is a wire-hair Dachshund, which is compiling a ring record for its owner, Miss Emilie Bromley of Germantown. . . . Rickie was imported just before the outbreak of the European War and its latest victory was registered last week at Altoona's show. . . . There's a group of nine Cocker Spaniel puppies at Mr. and Mrs. William Hearls' kennel in Germantown. . . . Hearls' Punch was the sire and the dam—Smedley's Peggy—owned by Mrs. M. Smedley of this city.

Before Westminster and the New York whirl of shows, Newark stages its 28th fixture, Jan. 26 and the Maryland Kennel Club's two-day affair holds sway, Jan. 31 and Feb. 1. . . . Baltimore's colorful show will again be held in the Fifth Regiment armory. . . . Philadelphians honored with Baltimore judging assignments include — Mrs. E. H. Dalton, Mrs. William C. Clark, Paul Forbriger, Miss Beth MacHale, Dr. A. A. Mitten, and Cornelius McGlynn.

Eleven clubs have lined up for the Associated Terrier Club's annual conclave in Grand Central Palace, New York—two days before Westminster opens. . . . Speaking of Westminster, the best-in-show award at that classic, has gone to wire-hair Fox Terriers on ten occasions since this prize was first given back in 1907. . . . Smooth Fox Terriers have won the big prize five times; Airedales, four; Sealyhams, 3; Cocker Spaniels and Pointers, each twice.

One of the district's famous shows has been cancelled this year. . . . Ever since 1902, the Wissahickon Kennel Club show has been a feature of the spring season, but due to lack of a site to stage the event this year, officials have deferred the event for 1941. . . . This was the first one-day outdoor show held in this country and has been presided over each year by such jovial hosts as J. Sergeant Price and William Metzger.

However, the spring show in the Philadelphia area will be active with renewed interest in the Bryn Mawr Kennel Club's event. . . . This club is now headed by Dr. M. Ross Taylor, of Wynnewood, prominent Boston terrier breeder and judge. . . . Plans are in the making for a colorful outdoor Bryn Mawr club show this year.

CLOUDY

The Philadelphia Inquirer

PUBLIC LEDGER

An Independent Newspaper for All the People

6 A. M. EDITION

CIRCULATION: December Average: Daily 401,639. Sunday 1,113,391 — a b d e f g h — FRIDAY MORNING, JANUARY 24, 1941 — Second Largest 3c Morning Circulation in America — THREE CENTS

VOL. 224, No. 24

Lindbergh Declares British Can't Win, Urges Peace Now; Rumania 'Crushes' Rebellion

Today

Roosevelt on Aid Bill
Mother Goose Defense
Powers Not Denied
Could Release Navy
But Says He Won't

By Hugh S. Johnson

WASHINGTON, Jan. 23.

THE President says that any suggestion that under the "lease-lend" bill he might transfer part of our Navy to another nation is a "cow-jumped-over-the-moon" idea—meaning, we may suppose, Mother Goose nonsense or a palpable impossibility.

"Hi-diddle-diddle, the cat and the fiddle, the cow jumped over the moon." He also says that he never even considered using the Navy to convoy American shipments to Britain.

A great deal of confusion is creeping into this debate. There is nothing in the "lease-lend" bill about convoying ships. Providing they are not violating the Neutrality Act and the President's own proclamations thereunder, by entering proclaimed war zones, or otherwise, American ships can still sail the sea.

If there is danger of illegal interference with them by another nation while they are in pursuit of their lawful business, the President doesn't need any additional authority to protect them with naval convoys. Therefore the convoy argument is not properly in the debate on the "lease-lend" bill.

But this "cow-over-the-moon" business is something else again. There is no authentic record of any cow jumping over any moon, but there is a very recent and rather startling record of a President transferring a very substantial part of our Navy, to wit, 50 destroyers, to a belligerent nation. It was done without any specific authority.

There is also a considerable record of befuddling public opinion just before election or during debate on hotly contested legislation by promises that were quickly forgotten—for example, the 1932 promise not to violate the gold covenants in our bonds and money.

That was the highest razzle-dazzle in all our economic history. But there was no remedy. All that happened was that "the little dog laughed to see such sport and the dish ran away with the spoon."

If there is no intention to transfer any part of our sorely needed armament, why is it necessary to grant unlimited authority to do so?

With a little paraphrasing and transposition, which does no violence to its intent, the bill authorizes the President "to sell, transfer, lease, lend or otherwise dispose of . . . any weapon, munition, aircraft, vessel or boat . . . any component material . . . any other commodity or article for defense."

This "includes any (such defense) article . . . manufactured or processed . . . or to which the United States . . . has or hereafter acquires title, possession or control.

This transfer may be made to the "Government of any country whose defense the President deems vital to the defense of the United States."

The terms of transfer "shall be those which the President deems satisfactory and the benefit to the United States may be payment or repayment in kind or property, or any other direct or indirect benefit which the President deems satisfactory"—for example, a few kind words.

There is no doubt about it, the bill in its present form includes outright donations to the President of the power of gift of any or all of the defense resources of the United States, the power to wage all-out economic war and a very substantial part of the power to wage undeclared military and naval war for any cause or without cause and for or against any nation anywhere in the world.

There has been no showing of necessity for any such drastic delegation of power, any such abdication of Congress. The argument is not against that assertion—not that such powers are not granted by the bill—but only that such extreme powers will not be used. "Hi-diddle-diddle."

PENNA. SEEKS TO OUST REDS FROM SCHOOLS

Reno Makes Study; Ban on Communists In All Public Jobs Is Urged by Legion

Legal means of barring Communist teachers from the schools is being sought by Pennsylvania's Attorney General Claude T. Reno, he disclosed yesterday.

From other sources came demands that Communists be barred, not only from the schools, but from all public payrolls and from labor unions.

The demands were an outgrowth of the charges that Reds control Philadelphia Local 192 of the American Federation of Teachers—a charge which is to be studied by the Central Labor Union, central body of AFL locals in this city.

GREEN BRINGS CHARGES

At Washington, William Green, president of the AFL, said he had instigated the charges against Local 192's officials at the request of the teachers' union's national administration. Green said the purpose was to oust any Reds and plan anew on a "sound and enduring AFL basis."

Add B. Anderson, secretary of the Board of Education, said he was in favor of barring adherents of subversive doctrines from jobs on all public bodies, and the American Legion announced it was preparing just such legislation for submission to the State Legislature.

WILL REPORT TO JAMES

Reno said he would study the whole matter of possible ways of banning Communists from the school system over the week-end. When he makes a report, he said, it will be to Governor James, who called a few weeks ago for legislation barring all subversive groups from the ballot.

"The question in our minds," Reno said, "is whether Communists can be excluded from the schools under our existing laws, or whether new legislation is needed to do it."

The question of whether Local 192 is controlled by Communists, as has been charged by an opposition group

Continued on Page 5, Column 3

Poison Widow Gets Life For Murder

Mrs. Agnes Mandiuk, 44-year-old "arsenic widow," was found guilty of murder in the first degree, with sentence of life imprisonment, by a jury of four women and eight men in Quarter Sessions Court last night.

The jury returned its verdict to Judge Otto R. Heiligman in Room 653, City Hall, at 9.02 P. M., less than three hours after it had received the case at 6.22 P. M.

DEFENDANT CALM

Mrs. Mandiuk, accused of poisoning her husband, Romaine, a baker, to get his $13,000 insurance, was in the courtroom as Charles Dickinson, of 2930 S. 24th st., the jury foreman, handed up the verdict. She remained calm as it was announced, and seemed scarcely to need the proffered help of two court attendants as she left the room to return to her cell.

An individual poll of the jury by

Continued on Page 2, Column 3

WALKOUT OF 60 IMPERILS WORK AT NAVY YARD

Row Among Unions Reported Cause of Stoppage; 60-Hour Week Is Ordered

Delay in completion of what is to be the world's largest drydock—a vital factor in speeding production of mammoth battleships—was threatened yesterday at the Philadelphia Navy Yard when 60 structural steel workers employed by a private contractor put down their tools and walked off the job.

The walkout, apparently resulting from a jurisdictional dispute with the carpenters' union, came almost simultaneously with an announcement that the Navy Yard's 23,000 civilian employees are to go on a 60-hour week Monday to speed up the defense program.

NEED 700 WORKERS

A shortage of skilled workers has forced the increase from the 48-hour week, it was understood, efforts to find 700 additional workers having failed.

Nominally the force will remain on a 40-hour week, as before, and will get overtime pay at the rate of time and a half for the additional 20 hours.

Only one local of the iron workers—Local 401—walked off the job. Members of other iron workers locals remained at work, as did members of Local 8 of the carpenters. All are American Federation of Labor unions.

UNION HEADS AWAY

The walkout was started at 8.30 A. M., 90 minutes after the day shift had started work, and last night the contractors and Navy Yard officials still had no official explanation of what had prompted the stoppage, because responsible officials of the iron workers union were out of the city.

Dan Young, job manager for Drydock Associates—the corporate title for the three engineering and construction firms which have joined their efforts to finish the huge undertaking as quickly as possible—said:

"I have tried to get in touch with union officials since the men walked off the job, but without success. It seems to be a jurisdictional dispute between the steel workers, members of Structural Steel Workers Union, Local 401 (AFL), and members of the Carpenters and Joiners, Local 8 (AFL), who have been working together on the job.

OFFERS EXPLANATION

"My understanding of the dispute—and this may not necessarily represent the unions' view of it—is as follows:

"The steel workers have assembled the steel frames in which the concrete for the huge basin is to be poured. Members of the Carpenters and Joiners Union have been placing the completed boxes preparatory to the concrete pouring, and the steel workers maintain that this is part of their job.

"Stewards of the union describe

Continued on Page 4, Column 2

Oppenheim Reaches England With Wife

LONDON, Jan. 24 (Friday) (A. P.).—E. Phillips Oppenheim, author of many thrillers, arrived in England yesterday after an adventurous journey from Southern France with his wife and maid.

The 74-year-old author said he had a "rough time" and added that the French were showing a "definite change of feeling" — against the Germans.

IN TODAY'S INQUIRER

British Army Presses Drive Against Derna

The Antonescu Government of Rumania announced yesterday that a rebellion of radical Iron Guardists and Communists had been crushed and that a compromise had been reached with Iron Guard "moderates" led by Vice-Premier Sima. Border dispatches estimated the dead at 2000 throughout the country, with total casualties estimated at 6000, and added that the revolt still was going on outside Bucharest, especially in Transylvania Province.

As the British announced capture of 14,000 Italians, including four generals, at Tobruch, British motorized units were reported to have reached positions in the region of Derna, Italian base 95 miles to the west, which was heavily bombed by the R. A. F.

The Vichy Government announced it had accepted Japan's offer to mediate in the border conflict between Thailand and French Indo-China.

For two and a half hours overnight, British bombers blasted at the steel, oil and munitions industries at Duesseldorf, following an attack by British and Polish fighter planes on German troops and installations along the French coast of the Channel.

For the fourth consecutive night, there was no bombing of London.

In Albania, the Greeks said they had repulsed heavy Italian counter attacks in the Klisura area, while improved weather allowed the Greeks to resume their drive against Valona, last big southern Albanian port in Italian hands.

Antonescu to Revise Regime in Pact With Moderate Guardists

BUDAPEST, Hungary, Jan. 23 (U. P.).—Premier Ion Antonescu of Rumania announced tonight that he had crushed a rebellion of radical Iron Guardists, including Communists, and would completely reorganize his regime under a compromise reached with Iron Guard "moderates" led by Vice-Premier Horia Sima.

Antonescu appealed to the army by radio to "have faith in me and your friends—Italy and Germany."

GERMAN TROOPS INACTIVE

Antonescu and the strongly pro-Nazi Iron Guard will reorganize the government with "reliable and capable men," D. N. B., the official German news agency, said in a Bucharest dispatch.

Germany's armed forces in Rumania, variously estimated at between 100,000 and 200,000 troops, were reported here to have remained in their barracks, for the most part, during the disorders.

A broadcast manifesto by Antonescu said that, with support of the army and an agreement with the

Continued on Page 8, Column 1

OUST REGISTRY UNIT, '70' GROUP DEMANDS

By JOSEPH H. MILLER

The Committee of 70 yesterday demanded the Philadelphia Registration Commission be ousted because of its "major failure" in permitting "wholesale disfranchisement" of voters at the 1940 Presidential election and allowing other "abuses" in the city's registry system.

In a report to the committee named by Governor James to investigate alleged irregularities in the registration system, the civic group, through William B. Lex, its counsel, charged the commission is "unfit to further hold the office."

DEAD STILL ON ROLLS

The charges were made after the Committee of 70 submitted evidence which, it asserted, tended to show that thousands of persons were retained on the registry rolls despite the fact that more than a year prior they had either removed from their districts or died.

Presenting a cross-section of a canvass made in two wards, Lex declared that in the 1st ward 982 persons had moved and 27 died in the spring of 1939, yet when a re-check in the fall of 1940 was made, 341 of those who had removed and 10 who had died remained on the rolls.

A cross-section of the 2d ward for the same period, Lex said, showed

Continued on Page 2, Column 6

14,000 Italian Troops Taken Prisoner by Victors at Tobruch

CAIRO, Egypt, Jan. 23 (A. P.).—Great Britain's army sent patrols farther into Libya today, testing prospects for a continuation of the spectacular desert offensive, and laid claim to more than 14,000 prisoners taken in the capture of the vital Italian base of Tobruch.

The fall of Tobruch was described by the British as a major Italian disaster. The town, with a good natural harbor, now becomes a base to supply the advancing British troops.

Italian military losses at Tobruch were said to be at least 32 times as great as the British losses.

2000 ITALIAN WOUNDED

Aside from the Italian prisoners taken—and in listing these as above 14,000 the British Command used the qualifying term "so far"—2000 Italian wounded were being evacuated during the day, a General Headquarters communique said.

Against these relatively enormous losses—which did not include an undetermined number killed in action—the British put their own total casualties at "under 500."

Among the Italians taken prisoner

Continued on Page 8, Column 5

HAILE IN ETHIOPIA TO REGAIN THRONE

SOMEWHERE IN ETHIOPIA, Jan. 15 (Via Khartoum, Delayed)—(A. P.).—Emperor Haile Selassie, accompanied by Ras Kassa, an Ethiopian chieftain, by the highest dignitary of the Ethiopian Church and by a British liaison officer, left Sudan headquarters today for his great adventure—the effort to regain his throne.

At the airdrome, the low, slanting rays of the early morning sun silhouetted the farewell scene in the shadow of a large Royal Air Force machine, where a group of British officers bade au revoir and wished luck and speedy success for the Emperor's mission.

EMPEROR ENTHUSIASTIC

The enthusiasm of the Emperor was apparent as he caught the first view of the land the Italians wrested from him five years ago. He took keen interest in official papers and

Continued on Page 8, Column 6

Hopkins, Eden Reported in Parley

LONDON, Jan. 23 (U. P.).—Harry L. Hopkins, President Roosevelt's personal envoy, and Anthony Eden, Foreign Secretary, were understood to have made a thorough review of the international situation at a long luncheon conference today.

(A. P. Wirephoto)
COL. CHARLES A. LINDBERGH
Is shown as he testified before the House Foreign Affairs Committee against the aid-to-Britain bill.

LUMBER INDUSTRY DRAFT THREATENED UNLESS PRICE IS CUT

Defense Deliveries Must Be Sped, Henderson Warns

By JOHN C. O'BRIEN
Inquirer Washington Bureau

WASHINGTON, Jan. 23. — Leon Henderson, price watchdog of the National Defense Commission, threatened today to recommend that the Federal Government draft lumber for defense needs at prices fixed by President Roosevelt, if prices are not reduced sharply and deliveries speeded up.

The fiery price co-ordinator, veteran of many a price war with producers in the NRA days, cited the rise in lumber prices as a contributing factor in the excessive cost of Army camps and cantonments, which will cost, according to War Department computations, from two to three times the original estimates.

STORMY SESSION

He declared that $25 a thousand feet was a good price for No. 2 Southern pine used in cantonments, which was last quoted at $31.25.

Asserting that "perhaps this industry is not able to handle its own affairs," Henderson warned, "the Government can get all the lumber it wants by having the Commander-in-Chief of the United States Army fix prices and using the Selective Service Act to draft lumber for the camps."

Henderson's explosive condemnation of the industry climaxed a stormy session with the Lumber and Timber Products Defense Committee, which had invited him to explain his recent criticism of lumber prices and threats of Government price-fixing.

WANTS NO MORE EXCUSES

"I have had all of the arguments, excuses and explanations that I want, and a damned sight more than I

Continued on Page 6, Column 3

Roosevelt to Send Assistant to China

WASHINGTON, Jan. 23 (A. P.).—In a parallel move to Harry L. Hopkins' special mission to England, it was announced today that Laughlin Currie, administrative assistant to President Roosevelt, would visit China soon to make an economic survey.

Apparently he is to help determine what aid that country should receive if the pending lease-lend bill is passed.

Emphasizing the Administration's interest alike in Chinese and British resistance to Germany, Italy and Japan, Currie will go to Chungking at the invitation of the Chinese Government and will bear a special message of greeting to Generalissimo Chiang Kai-shek.

General Johnson Says U. S. Won't Be Invaded

By WILLIAM C. MURPHY, JR.
Inquirer Washington Bureau

WASHINGTON, Jan. 23.—Colonel Charles A. Lindbergh and General Hugh S. Johnson today joined in denouncing the Administration's lend-lease program of aid to Britain, as the House Foreign Affairs Committee prepared to report the measure to the House for action next week.

Both Johnson and Lindbergh declared the proposed delegation to the President of discretionary power to lend or lease or otherwise dispose of any present or future military equipment was dangerous to the maintenance of free government in the United States and would tend to push the United States into war. In the picturesque phrase of the columnist-General, "I don't think God ever made a man heavy enough to carry that responsibility." Lindbergh phrased the same idea more conservatively.

SCOFF AT INVASION OF GERMANY

Lindbergh and Johnson agreed that it was nonsense to think that England, even with the full support of American munitions and men, could invade the continent of Europe and defeat Adolf Hitler. They both told the committee also that it was nonsense to think that Hitler could stage a successful invasion of the United States even if England should fall.

But on other issues related to the lend-lease program—which both opposed in its present form—the two witnesses disagreed.

Lindbergh, for example, asserted that he had opposed the aid-to-England policy in its infancy—the repeal of the embargo section of the Neutrality Act; that he still thought that repeal was a mistake and that it had added to the bloodshed in Europe and would have very little effect upon the ultimate outcome of the war. Future aid, he said, should be restricted to the commitments of policy already made.

LINDBERGH HOPES NEITHER SIDE WINS

He told the committee he hoped neither side in the struggle won decisively, because that would mean a devastated continent which would be disastrous to both Europe and the United States.

He advised that the United States should encourage the idea of a negotiated peace, and that even though such a peace might not conform to American ideas of justice it might well be better than the alternative of war to exhaustion.

To several attempts to pin him down to a flat declaration

Continued on Page 7, Column 1

2 Substitute Bills Ask Gifts, Loans to Britain

By RICHARD L. HARKNESS
Inquirer Washington Bureau

WASHINGTON, Jan. 23.—Two substitute aid-Britain bills, each of which would sharply restrict the lend-lease authority President Roosevelt seeks from Congress, were introduced in the Senate today.

One offered by Senator Edwin C. Johnson (D., Colo), proposed an outright gift of $2,000,000,000 worth of American-made "war machines and munitions" to the English.

The only string on the offer would be the requirement that Great Britain make detailed reports to the War and Navy Departments here on performance of American airplanes, guns and ships in actual warfare.

TAFT BILL ASKS LOANS

The second, presented by Senator Robert H. Taft (R., O.), would authorize the Reconstruction Finance Corporation, upon request of Mr. Roosevelt, to lend $1,000,000,000 to England, $500,000,000 to Canada, and $5,000,000 to Greece to enable them to purchase war munitions in this country.

The Taft proposal empowered the RFC to make the loans only when the three countries had exhausted their dollar exchange. Security would be required unless Federal Loan Administrator Jesse H. Jones found it would not be "practical" for the borrower to give it.

The substitutes offered by the two "isolationists" were regarded as another indication of growing sentiment in the Senate for modifying Mr. Roosevelt's original request for

Continued on Page 7, Column 4

THE WEATHER

Official forecast: Eastern Pennsylvania—Cloudy, followed by snow in north and rain or snow in south portion today and tomorrow; colder today and tonight.

New Jersey and Delaware—Cloudy, followed by rain in south and snow or rain in north portion today and tomorrow; colder today and tomorrow.

Sun rises	7.16 A.M.	Sets 5.09 P.M.
Moon rises	4.34 A.M.	Sets 2.46 P.M.

Other Weather Reports on Page 2

Lives and Homes Blasted in South Philadelphia Fire

FATHER MAURICE J. FOLEY (WEARING STOLE) ADMINISTERS LAST RITES TO JAMES CLARKE

POLICEMAN LEADS NURSE INTO FIRE ZONE

Death and Desolation

In a series of gas explosions that ripped out the walls of several homes and started a roaring inferno in South Philadelphia early yesterday, at least five persons were killed, more than a score injured, and many were made homeless. The houses were on Greenwich st. between Passyunk ave. and Dickinson sts. The dead included a fireman and a policeman. The officer was crushed as he ran to the rescue of a family trapped in a toppling home. More than 30 persons were taken to hospitals, others were treated on the scene. Several investigations were started immediately to determine the cause of the explosions. Gas company officials blamed leaky water pipes which they said undermined gas mains.

HARRY DeLEONARDI, CENTRE: HIS PARENTS WERE INJURED

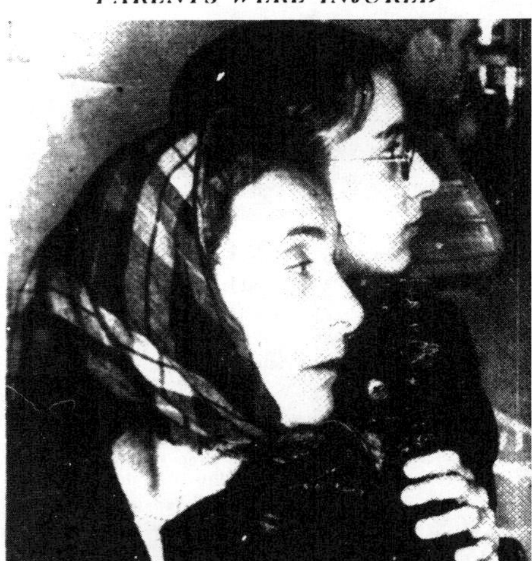

ROUTED: MRS. VEANNA COLLACCHI AND DAUGHTER SIENNA

SEARCHING FOR DEAD: THREE WERE KILLED IN TWO HOUSES AT LEFT

REMOVING BODIES FROM RUINS: SOUTH SIDE OF GREENWICH ST.

Another Full Page Of Blast Pictures On Page 22

Hawaii Seeking Star of Statehood

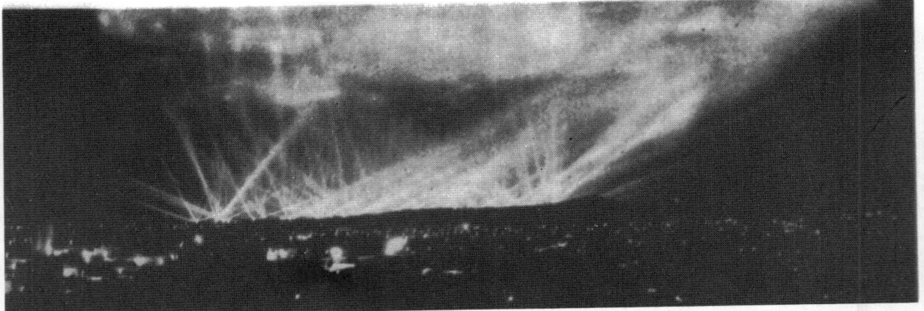

Navy searchlights flood the tropical sky over Honolulu, now the most heavily-defended city in the Pacific.

Seat of the Territorial Government is Iolani Palace. It would become the capitol of the new Hawaiian State.

By Robert Norman Hubner

BEFORE this year is over Hawaiians hope for the promise of a new star in the American Flag. For years the Islanders have striven to have their Pacific home admitted as the 49th State of the Union, and this year a new statehood commission appointed by the Territorial Legislature is expected to press their claim with unprecedented vigor.

What gives fresh hope to the Hawaiians is the fact that Hawaii today is the most important spot in America's whole national defense structure. Statehood for the islands, they say, would be an important step in our defense program.

In the event of a major war in the Pacific, we might conceivably relinquish a Territory to an enemy, but for a State, we would fight to the last American: This was urged in the Territory when its 83,000 voters polled a two-to-one majority favoring statehood in the "feeler" plebiscite of last November, which was calculated to impress Congress favorably with the Territory's ambition. At the same time it was pointed out that strategically, Hawaii is not only in real fact a part of the Union, but its most important military stronghold.

← If Hawaii ever becomes a State, this hula dancer will be able to vote for President.

Hawaii now is actually the Gibraltar of the Pacific—a Gibraltar, moreover, with no potentially hostile mainland at its back door. Pearl Harbor is headquarters of the Commander-in-Chief of the United States Fleet. Oahu is the strongest sea fortress in the world.

Oahu is the main island. On it is located the Territorial capital Honolulu, and the largest U. S. Army Post, Schofield Barracks. There are five other Army forts on this island, and one fort and one air base on each of the five other islands of Maui, Hawaii, Kauai, Molokai and Lanai.

The usual 40,000 soldiers and sailors stationed in the islands have been swelled, in this period of world tension, to more than 100,000. Another 45,000 attend the Battle Fleet, and in addition there is an Hawaiian National Guard of 25,000 men, and two more National Guard units from the Pacific Coast which add another 25,000.

Crucial Position

BUT despite all this strength, the crucial position of American-Japanese relations has strengthened opposition to the Hawaiian hope for statehood. If the islands became a State, it is pointed out, their 156,000 Japanese would become citizens with full rights—and these Japanese constitute more than a third of the Territory's population of 412,000. Likewise these rights would be granted to many Chinese, Koreans and other aliens.

Territorial figures show that among the 83,312 registered voters there are 26,927 Caucasians; 23,777 Japanese; 7,160 Chinese; 3,192 Koreans, besides 22,256 Hawaiians or part Hawaiians. The Caucasian voters thus definitely are outnumbered and opponents of statehood for Hawaii point out that therefore Orientals not only could dominate the islands, but could be elected to Congress as well.

Against this position, supporters of statehood, of all political parties and racial groups, assert that the loyalty of Hawaii's Japanese to the U. S. is unquestionable. Of the 156,000 Japanese, all but 22,000 have registered with the Japanese consulate as Americans by choice.

No single racial group, it is said, has enough numerical strength to dominate an election, and even now, voting does not follow racial lines.

"Racially, there is no valid argument against statehood," Samuel Wilder King, the Territory's delegate to Congress, assured me. "I believe the Japanese people are fundamentally loyal. If they are not, then there is every reason to distrust every minority of foreign racial extraction throughout the nation." To the objection that all Japanese, are considered by Japan to be bound by allegiance to the Emperor, King replies:

"I am sure our Japanese consider themselves American. The Japanese of California also are dual citizens, but California has seen the fallacy of worrying about them."

Rights of Majority

BUT would Hawaii's Japanese support the United States in the event of trouble between America and Japan? The military high command of Oahu made it plain to me that they believe the 118,000 island-born Japanese would be good Americans under whatever circumstances. But what about the 38,000 alien-born? These, frankly, give reason for considerable official concern.

It is urged, however, that they are a small minority, whose existence should not be used as an excuse to deny to the majority certain rights which it believes are being withheld from it.

"Now we have taxation without representation," Mr. King said. "During 1940 Hawaii completed more than $400,000,000 in total business transactions. We send more taxes to Washington than do 14 individual States of the Union. And we don't even have a vote in Congress. Our citizens can't vote for President."

Hawaiian voters now elect territorial legislators and minor territorial and local administrative officials. Their Governor and higher judges are appointed by the President. Their delegate to Congress may speak in the House of Representatives but has no vote.

"Because I have no vote in Congress, I often encounter difficulties," King declared, "especially when I attempt to enlist the support of committee members. Sometimes they frankly explain that they must go against me in some important issue in order to get votes from other members for their own bills. Therefore, the Territory often is left out in the cold when legislation is drafted. Since Hawaii became a Territory 40 years ago, we have paid an average of $5,000,000 a year to the Federal Government and we have received an average of $1,000,000 a year in return. This leaves a tidy profit to Uncle Sam of $160,000,000. This is the only such example of inequitable return in the history of U. S. taxation."

Quick to support Delegate King are the leading sugar growers. They declare that they have lost $30,000,000 worth of business in the past six years because sugar quotas fixed in Washington gave a discriminatory edge to the mainland States. Statehood would "end unfair quotas," they said.

Islanders realize that being 2000 miles distant from the American mainland has retarded Hawaii's drive towards statehood. But distance to the mainland no longer is measured in miles but in time.

It is now possible to reach Honolulu as quickly, comfortably and safely from the mainland as it is to travel from San Francisco to New York or Philadelphia. Giant clippers fly from California cities to Honolulu in 15 hours.

All such arguments are quite as strong, Islanders say, when applied to problems of national defense. For most practical purposes Hawaii is as good as in the Union now, they claim—and Hawaiians want that partnership sealed with a new Pacific star in the constellation of Old Glory.

Statehood for Hawaii would make American citizens of these Territorials. Born in the Islands they are, in ancestry, left to right: Japanese, Korean, American-Hawaiian, Chinese. (Right) An American girl.

Samuel Wilder King, Delegate to U. S. Congress.

Parade of Phenomena in March Skies

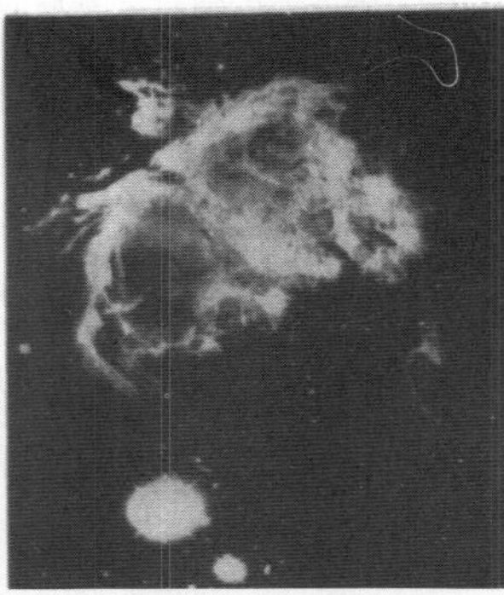

The Great Nebula in Orion, neon sign of skies, can best be studied in a photograph.

By I. M. Levitt
and
Dr. Roy K. Marshall
Astronomers, The Fels Planetarium

SPRING arrives this month, and, in case you should want to time the exact minute when the sun comes northward across the equator it will be March 20, at 7.21 P. M. Eastern Standard Time.

Many astronomical phenomena make March an interesting month. There are four comets in the sky—Cunningham's, another periodic comet and two new ones. If comets continue to swim into our sight from out of space during the remainder of 1941 at the same rate as during the first two months, then this year long will be remembered by astronomers.

During March there will be two eclipses. On March 13, just before the sun rises, there will be an eclipse of the moon, but before much of this can be seen the rising sun will wipe out of the skies our vision of both the moon and the earth's shadow on its face. The Annular eclipse of the sun on March 27 will not be seen at all, north of the equator.

EARLY in March you begin to see the stars that will be prominent in the spring skies. Going down in the west are the constellations that shone so brightly during the winter months. Also disappearing is one of the most interesting sections of the sky — the region around the constellation of Orion.

In the heart of the constellation is found the great Nebula in Orion. This is a beautiful object when seen through a telescope, but strange as it may seem to a layman, it is best observed in a photograph.

Glowing Gases

THE reason for this is that the eye in some ways is a very inefficient optical system. It cannot store the light that falls upon it. A photographic plate can do this, and so the plate can collect light over an extended period, and thereby register objects too faint for the eye to analyse.

Thus, in a small telescope, the great Nebula in Orion appears as a mass of pale greenish light, with four stars shining in the heart of the glow. In a large telescope two more stars are seen. But in a photograph taken through a telescope the size, shape and other characteristics of the Nebula in Orion are made manifest.

This map is your guide to the heavens during March. Each panel of the map shows a different quarter of the sky, as it appears March 2 at 10.00 P. M. Standard Time, March 15 at 9.00 and March 31 at 8.00. To use the map it is necessary only to turn any one of its panels towards the corresponding area of the sky.

LOOKING NORTH
LOOKING EAST
LOOKING WEST
LOOKING SOUTH

It is the neon sign of the heavens. In [illegible]n sign we have gas t[illegible]pped in a tube under very low pressure, and when an electric discharge is passed through, the gas glows. In the nebula there are several familiar gases—hydrogen, oxygen, helium, nitrogen and perhaps some others—and they are all made to glow with their characteristic colors by radiation.

MILLIONS of miles away from us, in space, matter and energy are working together to make a light similar to those we see on restaurants and delicatessen shops. Before man existed that light was glowing in the constellation of Orion.

It glows because, first, the gases in the nebula are under very low pressure. And secondly because the stars in Orion are white hot, emitting vast quantities of short radiations. It is these radiations, taking the place of the electric current in the neon tube, that cause the gases in the nebula to glow. Just how rarefied these gases are we don't know. But we do know that they are so very rare that if we could bring one single ounce of the nebula down to earth (a cubic foot of air weighs about one ounce) it would cover the earth to a depth of one foot.

Watch-Shaped Galaxy

LEAVING the remarkable phenomenon of Orion, we turn to Leo, the Lion, riding high in the southern sky.

A little to the east of Leo is the constellation of Coma Berenices, "Berenice's Hair." Coma Berenices is one of the minor constellations but to the astronomer it is important because it marks the North Galactic Pole, which is the North Pole of our Milky Way system.

To understand what this means, we must realize that we are embedded in the heart of a great system of stars that is shaped somewhat like a watch. In this system of stars, which numbers about 100,000 million, is found almost everything that we see in the sky. All the stars, the clusters, the nebulae and other things in it belong to the same family as our sun.

That sun of ours is located inside the watch-shaped galaxy, some 30,000 light years from the centre. It is, so to speak, inside the face of the watch, underneath the hub of the second hand.

Now—still following our analogy of the watch—when we look straight out along the hub of the second hand, we see the constellation of Coma Berenices. And it is in this direction that we find the North Pole of our galaxy, the Milky Way.

This North Galactic Pole is at right angles to the face of our imaginary watch. It lies at a far greater distance from us than any measure that can be made inside our galaxy, whose diameter is a mere 600,000,000,000,000,000 miles!

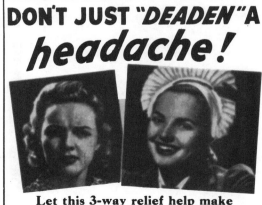

Building debris litters the streets as the 103rd Engineers, of Philadelphia, arrive at Indiantown Gap. Soon, with the aid of efficient top sergeants, it will be a spotless city. Main roads are concrete.

MOBILIZED into the Army, regiment after regiment of the Pennsylvania National Guard has been pouring into the new $10,000,000 wooden city erected for them at Indiantown Gap. By the middle of June 22,000 troops will occupy the 14,000-acre reservation in the shadow of Blue Mountain 15 miles north of Lebanon.

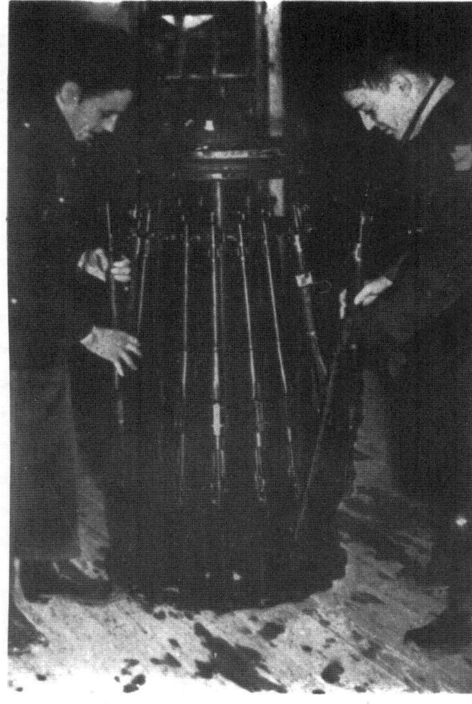

Privates James Jones and Har[illegible]t of Company A, 103rd Engineers, stack their rifles. Major General Edward Martin, commanding the 28th Division, says he is determined "to build as highly trained a fighting division as can be produced in this country."

Inquirer Photos

Men of the 108th Field Artillery, of Philadelphia, uncouple one of their 155mm howitzers. The artillery regiments occupy barracks at the west end of the post. Barracks are two-story and well heated. Mess buildings are provided for each company.

FOOD

FEATURES FOR WOMEN

RECIPES

Spring Calls For Lamb On Menu

Economical Cuts Aid in Saving On Budget

By Virginia Cheney

Spring menu plans naturally turn to lamb. Figures show that a good quality of lamb is available throughout all four seasons but in the spring its popularity hits a new high.

Experiments with lamb, as with other foods, have resulted in new knowledge of its cookery. The practice of removing the "fell," a paper like skin covering, is not necessary for roasts. The roast will cook more quickly and it need not be rubbed with flour when the fell is left on.

QUICK COOKING

The fell will cook tender in the time necessary for roasting but it will not cook in the time allowed for chops. Therefore the old recommendation of removing it still holds for quick cooked cuts.

A roast of lamb should be placed on a rack with the skin side down and the fat side up. This makes it unnecessary to baste it because as the fat melts it runs over and through the meat. If there is not much fat lay several strips of bacon over the top.

Lamb roasts should be cooked uncovered with no water added and at a constant temperature of about 300 degrees. Searing is not necessary because it does not keep in the juices. Average time is 30 to 35 minutes per pound for roasting.

MORE FLAVORFUL

Lamb cooked to medium done will be more juicy and flavorful than that cooked well done. It will probably be more tender too.

A boned roast is ideal for easy carving. It can be cut into attractive servings with few scraps left over. Cuts of lamb that may be boned to advantage are shoulder, breast, loin, and leg. The cavity left after the bone is removed makes an ideal pocket for holding stuffing.

Shoulder is one of the most economical cuts of lamb that can be boned to advantage. It can be stuffed or not as you like. Breast is another of the more inexpensive cuts and it is tender enough to be roasted.

LAMB SHOULDER

To cook a lamb shoulder have your butcher bone and roll it. Sprinkle with salt and pepper and place on a rack in an open roasting pan. Place the roast in a preheated moderate oven, 300 to 350 degrees. Do not cover and do not add water. Allow approximately 35 minutes per pound for roasting.

Lamb is most frequently served with a mint sauce. Make it from the following recipe; dissolve two tablespoons sugar in one cup vinegar and add half cup finely chopped mint leaves. Let stand for one hour, and heat just before serving. If fresh mint is not available dissolve ten to twelve after dinner mints in half cup vinegar and allow a stand overnight. Heat to boiling point and serve.

SCALLOPINE OF LAMB WITH RICE

- 1½ pounds boneless stewing lamb
- Seasoned flour
- 2 onions
- 6 tablespoons fat
- Salt and pepper
- 1 teaspoon sugar
- 1½ cups canned tomatoes
- 1¼ cups hot water

Flatten pieces of lamb until they are thin. Roll them in flour and brown with onions in fat. Add remaining ingredients. Cover and cook in moderate oven, 350 degrees. Keep the heat low and cook for one and a half hours. Serve with a border of rice. Serves six.

My Child Said

The Inquirer will pay $2 for each "bright saying" published. Mail your contribution to "What My Child Said," The Philadelphia Inquirer. Unused manuscripts will not be paid for nor returned.

My son, who is six years old and just learning to read, saw a mail truck going by. He exclaimed, "Mother, that truck says 'Us Mail' and that is very poor English. It should be 'Our Mail!'"—Submitted by Ann Cassell, 3402 Chippendale ave., Philadelphia.

My husband was teasing our daughter by saying that chewing gum was made of horses' hoofs. Turning to me she said, "Oh, no it isn't. It's made of rubber, isn't it, Mother?" — Submitted by Mrs. Charlotte Williamson, 110 W. Champlost, st., Philadelphia.

A simple 50-word letter may win for you a Grand Prize of $100 a Month for Ten Years—or $10,000 in one lump sum. See contest announcement in this issue of The Inquirer.

LAMB IS SPRING MEAT FAVORITE

A boned and rolled shoulder of lamb is one of the economical cuts that is sure to find its way into your spring menu. Boning makes carving easier with no scraps left on the platter. Pickled peach halves, with fresh mint leaves, are the flavor-complimentary garnish.

Mrs. Anna B. Scott's Food Talks

Have you made a recent check on your supply closet? I suggest that you do not delay in doing so if you would avoid waste. Bring to the front those foods which will deteriorate and include them in your menu plans immediately. During warm weather it is advisable to keep prepared pancake flour and packaged cereals in tightly covered containers in your refrigerator if they are to be kept on hand for any length of time.

While canned foods remain good until used, do not carry this year's supply over for the fall season.

All questions pertaining to the following menus and recipes will be cheerfully answered if addressed to me in care of The Inquirer.

CORNMEAL MUFFINS

- 1 cup cornmeal
- 1 cup flour
- 1 cup cold milk
- 1 cup boiling milk
- 1 egg
- 1 teaspoon salt
- 2 tablespoons melted butter or substitute
- 2 tablespoons sugar
- 2 teaspoons baking powder

Put the cornmeal into bowl, add the boiling milk in which the butter has been melted and beat well, then add the cold milk and well-beaten egg, salt and sugar. Sift the baking powder and flour, add slowly and mix lightly. Have muffin pans very hot and well greased; fill half full, put in hot oven and bake 20 minutes.

RHUBARB BETTY MADE WITH CEREAL

- 2 cups cold boiled cereal
- 2 cups chopped rhubarb
- 1 cup brown sugar
- 2 tablespoons butter
- 1 teaspoon cinnamon

Brush earthen or glass bake-dish with butter, spread with one cup of cooked cereal, evenly, cover with the chopped raw rhubarb, half the brown sugar and sprinkle with cinnamon, then cover with the other cup of cereal, the remainder of the sugar and sprinkle with cinnamon. Cover and place in a moderate oven 30 minutes; remove the cover and bake until a nice brown. Serve with fruit syrup.

WHOLEWHEAT GEMS

- 2 cups wholewheat flour
- ½ cup seedless raisins
- 2 teaspoons baking powder
- 1 egg
- 1 cup milk
- 1 teaspoon salt
- 1 teaspoon sugar
- 1 tablespoon melted butter
- 1 teaspoon shortening

Put the wholewheat flour into bowl, add the baking powder, salt and sugar; mix and add the milk slowly, then the well-beaten egg, raisins and melted butter; mix well. Brush gem pans with shortening; put a spoonful of the mixture in each and bake 15 to 20 minutes. This makes about 24 gems.

QUICK DATE AND NUT BREAD

- 1½ cups wholewheat or graham flour
- 1½ cups white flour
- 1½ teaspoons salt
- 4 teaspoons baking powder
- ½ cup brown sugar
- 1 cup chopped pitted dates
- ½ cup chopped nuts
- 1 egg
- 1½ cups milk

Sift the white flour, salt and baking powder together into a large bowl, add the graham or wholewheat flour and the brown sugar. Mix the dates and nuts through the flour, add the beaten egg and milk; stir until mixed. Put the mixture into a loaf pan which has been well greased and floured and bake in a moderate oven (325 to 350 degrees F.) for about one hour. Test for doneness with piece of wire put into centre. Do not slice until it is 24 hours old.

STAPLES FOR THE WEEK

- 5 lbs. sugar
- 1 lb. coffee
- ¼ lb. tea
- 1 lb. rice, ¼ lb. cheese
- 2 lbs. prunes
- Canned fruit and juice
- Canned sweet potatoes
- Canned spaghetti
- 2 packages cereal & pkge. bran
- Canned baked beans
- Canned sardines
- Canned corn
- Pkge. shredded codfish
- Bottle catsup
- Canned tomatoes and juice
- Can sour krout
- 1½ doz. eggs
- 1 lb. butter

VEGETABLES UNTIL TUESDAY

- Potatoes
- Carrots
- Celery, Parsley
- Dandelion
- Lettuce, Onions
- Tomatoes
- Broccoli
- Cabbage

MEAT UNTIL TUESDAY

- Meat special
- ½ lb. bacon
- ½ lb. bologna in one piece

FRUIT UNTIL TUESDAY

- Oranges
- Bananas
- 3 lemons
- Rhubarb

SATURDAY EVENING MEAL

Chow Mein
French Bread
Vanilla Pudding, Rhubarb Sauce
Beverage of Choice

SUNDAY BREAKFAST

Fruit or Juice
Bacon and Eggs
Toast
Coffee Cake
Coffee, Cocoa or Cereal Beverage

SUNDAY DINNER

Vegetable or Tomato Juice
Meat Special
Roast Potatoes
Stewed Celery and Carrots
Bread and Butter
Dandelion Salad
Lemon Pie
Beverage of Choice

SUNDAY EVENING MEAL

Toasted Cheese Sandwich
Peanut Butter and Lettuce Sandwich
Stewed Rhubarb
Beverage of Choice

MONDAY BREAKFAST

Fruit or Juice
Cereal of Choice
Cinnamon Toast
Coffee, Cocoa or Cereal Beverage

MONDAY LUNCH

Sliced Bologna
Baked Bean Salad
Wholewheat Bread
Apple Sauce
Milk or Tea

MONDAY EVENING MEAL

Fried Tomatoes, Cream Gravy
Corn Fritters
Broccoli
Bread and Butter
Coleslaw
Cold Creamy Rice Pudding
Beverage of Choice

TUESDAY BREAKFAST

Fruit or Juice
Cereal of Choice
Poached Eggs on Toast
Coffee, Cocoa or Cereal Beverage

TUESDAY LUNCH

Utilize all Left-Overs
Milk or Tea

Some Points For Parents

Mother (firmly but without anger): "I've given you the reasons for my decision, daughter, and you've presented your case. There is nothing to be gained by going over it again. I must go down town."

Daughter: "But Mother, I still don't see why I can't go."

Mother: "Then sit down here and I'll explain it to you again. This is at least the sixth time I've tried to make you understand."

Parents who are over-anxious to be reasonable are in danger of becoming the type of parent who talks and talks but never gets anywhere.

Glazed Cherry Tarts

- 2 tablespoons cornstarch
- ¼ cup granulated sugar
- ⅛ teaspoon salt
- 1 tablespoon lemon juice
- 1/3 cup cherry juice
- 6 deep baked tart cases
- 2 cups drained, slightly sweetened red cherries

Mix cornstarch with sugar and salt. Add juices and cook until very thick—in double boiler. Cook five minutes and pour over cherries, place in cases. Serve warm or cold.

My Favorite Recipe

The Inquirer will pay $2 for each recipe published in this column. Mail YOUR favorite recipe to "My Favorite Recipe," The Philadelphia Inquirer, Philadelphia. Unpublished recipes will not be paid for nor returned.

TODAY'S WINNER

Mrs. Walter Sechrist, 668 South Main st., Red Lion, York county, Pa.

Corn Cakes, Pennsylvania Dutch Style

- 2 cups cornmeal
- ½ cup white flour
- 1 egg
- salt, a pinch
- 1 tablespoon melted butter
- 1 teaspoon baking soda
- 2 cups buttermilk

Mix the cornmeal, flour, salt and soda together. Break the whole egg into it, add melted butter, then add buttermilk a little at a time while stirring. When the mixture is smooth bake on hot griddle as with any other hot cakes. Serve with butter and hot syrup or honey.

The Inquirer Daily Dinner Menus

By Mrs. Anna B. Scott. The menus are based on table budget for families of four, two adults and two children.

For the $12 to $15 a week table allowance, or the $50 a month budget

Baked Shad
Scalloped Potatoes
Spinach Egg Garnish
Bread and Butter
Gelatine
Beverage of Choice

For the $15 to $20 a week table allowance, or the special or company dinner:

Oyster Cocktail
Radishes Celery
Baked Shad with Roe
Shoestring Potatoes
Asparagus, Hollandaise Sauce
Soft Rolls
Lettuce, French Dressing
Cherry Tarts
Coffee

In The Inquirer on Fridays and Tuesdays Mrs. Scott gives the complete weekly menus and marketing lists for the $50 a month budget.

Fruit Syllabub

- 1 cup whipped cream
- 1/3 cup granulated sugar
- 1 tablespoon lemon juice
- ¼ teaspoon nutmeg
- 1 cup cubed pineapple
- 2/3 cup diced bananas

Mix cream with sugar, juice and nutmeg. Chill, add fruits and chill until serving time. Serve in glass cups.

Hitler, 52, Celebrates At Birthday Party On Balkan Warfront

BERLIN, April 20 (A. P.).—Adolf Hitler celebrated his 52d birthday today in a flower festooned railway dining car surrounded by his military leaders somewhere on the Balkan front behind his victoriously advancing troops.

The Fuehrer spent part of his celebration, described as marked by "soldierly simplicity," studying military maps and receiving felicitations of his Army, Navy and Air Force chieftains. Radio announcers at the scene said he responded to each of the greetings with a word of thanks and a handshake.

His special train was parked on a siding in a valley near a station, the broadcasters said, with German anti-aircraft units visible on nearby mountain tops.

U. S. FLAG DISPLAYED

In Berlin, where in peace times the event is marked by pomp and ceremony, the only outward sign was the presence of thousands of swastikas waving from windows. The United States Embassy participated to the extent of displaying its national colors in keeping with international courtesy.

Leland Morris, United States Charge d'Affairs, called at the Reichs Chancellory and entered his name in the diplomat book of birthday greetings to the Fuehrer.

SUCCESSES HAILED

Hitler's private celebration began last midnight when members of his staff assembled in his dining car.

General Field Marshal Wilhelm Keitel, chief of the High Command of the armed forces, started the round of felicitations. He termed the last year as one of "big and gigantic successes" and added that now under Hitler's leadership "we are chasing the fleeing British from the European continent."

Then Hitler raised his glass "and with the gentlemen of his staff toasted to victory," D. N. B., the German official news agency, reported.

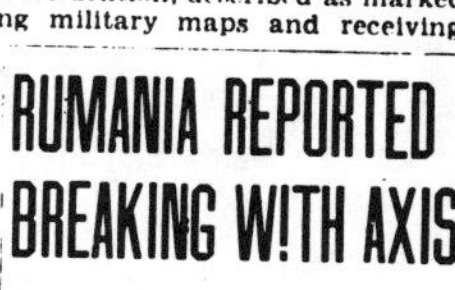

RUMANIA REPORTED BREAKING WITH AXIS

Continued From First Page

his people as indicating a clean break with the Axis.

The Rumanians were reported in a Transylvanian dispatch to have halted traffic along the Bulgarian and Hungarian borders, with shots heard day and night because of guards shooting anyone who attempted to leave the country.

Antonescu, in an Easter message yesterday (today is the Orthodox Easter), spoke of Rumanian reverses and loss of territory, but declared that "justice and God's love will save us and the Rumanian people will rise again from death."

He also said that the Rumanian Army was ready to fight and quoted an order to his army command that "it is the holy duty of the army to wipe out the shameful blot of 1940."

If the Premier's message meant that he had broken with the Axis, some Hungarians asserted that he was running the risk of being crushed between the millstones of the Iron Guard and the Axis Powers.

LEAFLETS DISTRIBUTED

Inflammatory leaflets strongly reminiscent of former Iron Guard writings again are being distributed by the thousands, Hungarian reports said.

Antonescu, who last week threatened immediate execution of terrorists after uncovering a plot to assassinate him during Easter week, published a decree last night requiring all printers to register with police every page printed by them. A five-year prison sentence was threatened for failure to comply.

The Hungarian press answered sharply that Antonescu could not invalidate by armed force the Axis Vienna arbitration of last year which handed part of Transylvania to Hungary.

CONFERENCE PLANNED

Meanwhile, informed Budapest circles said that the Axis Powers already were laying plans for a Vienna conference of southeastern European states after the Balkan war to make final decisions on disposition of disputed territorial questions as well as to promulgate a "new order" for the area.

All war prisoners born on former Jugoslav territory now held by Hungary have been sent home by German military authorities. Between 7000 and 8000 already have gone.

Croat priscners held by the Hungary also are being sent home.

(A. P. Wirephoto)

HITLER CONGRATULATED ON 52D BIRTHDAY

Adolf Hitler, left, congratulated Field Marshal Wilhelm Keitel last month on 40 years' service in the German Army but yesterday the German Army leader started a round of felicitations on the occasion of the Fuehrer's 52d birthday.

ALBANIA RETAKEN, ITALIANS DECLARE

ROME, April 20 (A. P.).—The Italian High Command claimed today a Fascist advance had carried divisions of the Ninth and Eleventh Armies to the Albanian-Greek frontier.

"Numerous fighting, bombing and dive-bombing planes, altogether 450 of them, carried out intense and continuous actions against the retreating Greek Army," the High Command added. It said "hundreds of truck loads of troops and materials" were destroyed.

The communique said the Greek rear guard had put up a stiff fight and that the roads were full of obstacles, but that in spite of these handicaps the Italians moved steadily ahead.

"Numerous prisoners and large quantities of arms and materials were captured," it said.

The communique did not say whether the attacking planes were Italian or German or both, but it declared troop concentrations, barracks and artillery positions were all showered with machine-gun fire and bombs.

Five planes were destroyed in a low-flying attack on Katsike airport near Ioannina, Greece, the communique said, and added that the Preveza naval base was bombed.

German Air Corps squadrons bombed the Micaba airport at Malta, it continued, "and port works were hit and one large steamer damaged."

The High Command also claimed that an Italian submarine torpedoed "an enemy destroyer" in the eastern Mediterranean.

It acknowledged British air raids on Bengasi and Tripoli but said there was no appreciable damage done.

Nazi General Named Minister to Zagreb

BERLIN, April 20 (U. P.).—Adolf Hitler has appointed storm troop Major General Siegfried Kasche as the first German Minister to Zagreb, in newly proclaimed Croatia, the official news agency said today.

Admiralty Chief Denounces 'Armchair Critics' of Greece

LONDON, April 20 (A. P.).—First Lord of the Admiralty A. V. Alexander lashed out at "armchair critics" of Britain's decision to send troops to Greece today, and declared to his London audience that Italian transports destroyed by the Navy run into "six figures."

"There are some who can be wise after events and who criticize strategy and military dispositions," he said. "I ask them to realize the vast change in the situation since last June when France collapsed and the assassin Mussolini entered into the war thinking he was going to get something cheap.

VICTORIES ENUMERATED

"There were many people then who doubted our ability to last many weeks."

Alexander indicated that the 10 Coast Guard cutters received from the United States already have been placed in service.

"Believe me," he said, "they are some ships. Most of them are a little bit bigger than a destroyer. They were built to stop bootleggers' ships and we think they will be ever more usefully employed in protecting our convoys and hunting German Pirates."

Alexander enumerated Britain's African victories and said:

"It seems wrong in the circumstances for an armchair critic to tell us we ought not to have risked our position in Libya to go to the aid of Greece. . . I do not think the Government has any need to apologize for its decision."

BURDEN IN BATTLE 'HEAVY'

He said Britain's burden in the Battle of the Atlantic was "grievous and heavy," but predicted an increasing toll of German submarines and long range planes.

He declared Britain would have to go on struggling "to get back to something like the escort position we had in the last war when we worked not only as a single fleet but had five powerful allied fleets and five times the number of destroyers we have now."

"The amazing thing," he said, "is that the Navy has kept the lifeline open."

The First Lord said one of Germany's best submarine commanders, Schepke, was dead and that Commander Otto Kretschmer, credited last December with having sunk more than 250,000 tons of shipping, was a British prisoner.

Kretschmer, Alexander continued, was "idolized in Germany as the wolf of the Atlantic."

113 Axis Planes Lost In Week, British Say

LONDON, April 20 (U. P.).—Germany and Italy lost 113 planes last week, the second consecutive week in which their losses exceed 100, the authoritative Press Association said today.

Twenty-eight German planes were reported lost over Britain and German-occupied territory, and 85 Axis planes were downed in the Middle East. The two-week toll was placed at 283.

Royal Air Force losses for the same period was 30 over German-occupied territory, 21 in the Middle East and none over Britain, the report said. Figures include Saturday dusk to the following Saturday.

Churchill Foresees Prolonged War

LONDON, April 20 (A. P.).—Prime Minister Winston Churchill told Czech sɑldiers today that Britain is in for an "undoubtedly long and formidable war."

"I do not know what the course of war will be," he said, "and I do not know how it will reach its end, but I am sure Great Britain will never cease from war with all her energy and all the resources of her empire."

Don't miss Jimmy Hatlo's brilliant daily cartoon of fun and humor . . . it's always amusing . . . it's always different.

Tells of 'British Rout'

Wild Confusion of Foe Described by German

BERLIN, April 20 (U. P.)

THE British Army's "glorious retreat from Greece is in full swing" under a terrible aerial bombardment that is turning the enemy route of flight into "an inferno and mass of wild confusion," a German war reporter said tonight.

The reporter of the German Army's propaganda company, flying in a Luftwaffe bomber over the British withdrawal, said in a D.N.B. agency dispatch that the German armored drive down through Greece already had reached a point "far beyond Larisa."

"The fleeing Tommy is in a great hurry to reach the evacuation ports," the reporter said. "The British may speak of the heroic deeds of the B.E.F. but German bombs speak a clearer language and they will so speak until the last Tommy is thrown out of Greece."

• • •

DESCRIBING his trip in the bomber, the reporter said:

"The first DO-17 releases its bombs from 20 iron portions hanging from its belly. The effect is undescribable. The devil breaks loose below. Columns break up and scatter wildly. Enemy anti-aircraft fires ineffectively. Two German pursuiters appear to offer protection to the bomber formation.

"The DO's again zoom down. Motorized units already are on fire from the first load of bombs. As the DO's attack for a third time bomb explosions are accompanied by the music of barking machine guns. Inferno reaches its height. Tanks and motorized units are set afire. Other vehicles on both sides of the road are destroyed.

"The retreating march is changed into a mass of wild confusion. Many of these British will never reach the coast."

Scottish Towns Strafed By Nazis as London Digs Out of Heavy Raid

LONDON, April 20 (A. P.).—German daylight raiders strafed two Scottish towns today, killing a boy and injuring 10 persons, while in London hard-handed rescue squads worked from dawn to dusk lifting out numerous dead and injured left by Saturday night's large-scale assault by the Luftwaffe.

Other high-flying German formations, soaring through cloudless Channel skies also attacked the southeast coast, where the sound of machine-gun fire and cannons of diving planes was heard. One raider headed toward this area was reported intercepted and shot down into the Channel.

R. A. F. STRIKES BACK

The R. A. F. struck back with daylight raids on German shipping in the Channel and against Brest and other targets on the Nazi-held French coast. One German plane was destroyed and another was seen diving out of control, the Air Ministry announced, adding that the foray cost the R. A. F. one plane.

The Government acknowledged many casualties and heavy damage was inflicted here in the overnight raid, which was almost as bad as Wednesday night's worst attack of the war on this capital of Empire. The south and southeast counties also were hit, it added, but nothing like London.

RESCUE WORK GOES ON

Evidence of the death and destruction caused by the raiders was unfolded as rescue squads with cranes and pneumatic drills worked throughout this Sunday and into the night freeing those trapped and clearing away wreckage.

At least 28 persons were killed at one intersection by a bomb, the United Press said, adding that the wreckage was so great that many bodies probably would not be located for days.

The people took stoically this reopening of the Battle of London, and once more there was raised the demand to "Give it back to Berlin."

MARRIED AMID RUINS

Two smiling couples were married in the smoking ruins of a church where firemen still were moving about with their ladders.

From one of the hardest-hit places 80 persons were brought out alive today. Two fire department sub-stations got direct hits and some firemen were buried.

The Air Ministry announced that British bombers in their own offensive yesterday sank a 5000-ton Axis supply ship and damaged another of 7000 tons off The Netherlands coast.

The Philadelphia Inquirer

PUBLIC LEDGER

An Independent Newspaper for All the People

6 A. M. EDITION

CIRCULATION: April Average: Daily 408,650, Sunday 1,121,656 — a b d e f g h — TUESDAY MORNING, MAY 13, 1941 — Second Largest 3c Morning Circulation in America — THREE CENTS

 VOL. 224, No. 133

Hess, Hitler's 2d Heir, Flees Germany In Plane; Lands by 'Chute in Scotland

Nazi Chief Held in Glasgow, Berlin Calls Him Insane

LONDON, May 13 (Tuesday) (A. P.).—Rudolf Hess, head of the German Nazi party and one of the oldest confidantes of Adolf Hitler, has landed by parachute in Britain under circumstances suggesting the most profoundly important desertion in all history.

The British Government announced from the home of Prime Minister Winston Churchill at No. 10 Downing Street that Hess was in a Glasgow hospital under treatment for a broken ankle suffered in floating down from a German Messerschmitt fighter plane near there.

While the British statement did not specifically say that he had deserted, it made three observations of seeming inescapable significance.

That Hess had brought along photographs taken at varying years in his life to establish his identity if it were questioned.

That he arrived in a plane which could not possibly have had enough gasoline for return to Germany—and thus, inferentially, that his trip was clearly not a one-man offensive but a one-way flight.

That the Messerschmitt's guns were empty.

NAZIS SAY HE IS UNBALANCED

(Moreover, the British radio in a broadcast heard in the United States referred to Hess as "the only idealist" in the Nazi hierarchy.)

This most extraordinary flight of this or any other war was disclosed in London a few hours after the Germans in Berlin had announced that Hess—Hitler's No. 2 political heir—was missing, that he presumably had taken a forbidden plane flight and had cracked up; that he appeared to have been suffering "hallucinations" and had "left behind a confused letter."

The Berlin implication was that he was mentally unbalanced and had been deranged for some time; for it was stated that Hitler personally had directed that he not be permitted to use any plane.

NO. 2 SUCCESSOR TO HITLER

(Early today, German informants in Berlin insisted that they knew nothing beyond the Reich's original announcement of Hess' disappearance.)

The 47-year-old Hess from the beginning of National Socialism had stood at Hitler's right hand and in the Reich's councils of war he had held an inner place—the possessor of the deepest of military secrets and one of the most influential of all Nazis.

At the war's outset Hitler publicly gave him an extraordinary accolade by announcing that, should he himself fall, Reichsmarshal Hermann Wilhelm Goering should be considered the new Fuehrer and the dour and earnest Hess heir apparent to Goering.

FLOATED DOWN WITH 'CHUTE

The story of Hess' strange and lonely flight to England, as told in the Government's announcement from Downing Street, showed that he first crossed the Scottish coast last Saturday night (and that was the date given by the Germans for his disappearance).

He flew on in the direction of Glasgow and later—just

Continued on Page 10, Column 1

'THE ONLY NAZI IDEALIST'

Rudolf Hess, No. 3 Nazi who fled the Reich in a warplane Saturday, parachuting to earth in Scotland, was referred to by the British Broadcasting Company in an announcement of his arrival as "the only idealist" in the Nazi hierarchy. He was in line to succeed Hitler.

Today

U. S. Half Awake
Job Underestimated
Army Flatfooted
British May Quit
Yet We Dream On

—By Raymond Clapper—

WASHINGTON, May 12.

THIS country still is only half awake. Telltale signs of that are seen on every hand.

It was a year ago this month that William S. Knudsen was called to Washington and a Government defense organization set up. The first thing that was discovered was that there was a grave shortage of machine tools.

Yet now, a year later, we are just getting around to calling for complete around-the-clock use of machine tool facilities. Furthermore, even at this late date, hundreds of machine tools are not being used as the recent survey of the National Association of Manufacturers shows. That's just one symptom of our sluggishness.

We have underestimated the job straight through. For months Office of Production Management officials insisted we would have no shortage of aluminum. Now they are taking aluminum out of civilian use and still there won't be enough for the airplane program. Months late we realized that an enormous expansion would be necessary.

Last summer some were urging expansion of steel capacity. But we were assured there was plenty of capacity, enough for civilian use as well as defense. Now we have discovered that capacity is inadequate.

We made the mistake of not setting out to do the impossible. We thought to take it in our stride—with business as usual. But we have had to go into price fixing, into rationing, and a year later in some respects—as with automobiles. Bomber assembly plants are nearing completion, but the automobile industry was not put to work in time. So the parts are not coming along for assembly.

The Army was caught flatfooted. A few weeks ago General Marshall, chief of staff, testified before a Congressional committee that the Army had just finished working out the lessons from the German military campaign in France a year ago. We were taken by complete surprise with the new German tank-air team. Didn't know such a thing was in existence.

For more than a year the Government has been trying to accumulate reserves of rubber and some other materials which must be imported. But it has been slow going because civilian manufacture was not cut down. We have succeeded in accumulating only half a year's reserve supply of rubber, although the source can be cut off any time the Japanese move.

You can go on and finish the list yourself. There's that aircraft factory in Baltimore that still stands idle where they left it when the depression hit. There are tobacco people, the soda pop people, the brewers and all kinds of other people trying to talk Congress out of taxing them.

There are the railroads, caught unprepared by the sharp withdrawal of intracoastal ships. There are President Roosevelt and Harry Hopkins, a semi-invalid, trying to write the script, direct the production, paint the scenery, play the leading parts and sit in the box office.

There are the 100 Republican Congressmen who voted against the bill to requisition idle foreign shipping. They haven't learned anything since Munich. There is the whole country working itself up into a lather over the convoy issue when that already has become outmoded. The real question has moved beyond that, and is whether the United States Navy goes into joint general action with the British in many ways.

We are blissfully unaware that a big chunk of the British fleet is in danger of being lost in the Mediterranean, blissfully unaware that unless the British are soon convinced that we are going in with our Navy they will probably give up and leave us on our own.

We're still just about where we were a year ago—when we didn't think Hitler could ever break through into France. We are still dreaming that we have a safe Maginot Line in England.

GUESTS ROUTED BY FLAMES AT RITZ-CARLTON

Thousands Watch Firemen Risk Lives Fighting Stubborn Two-Alarm Blaze

Illustrated on Pages 3 and 18

Thousands of persons, jamming into Broad st. and peering from windows of towering buildings nearby, watched the daring exploits of firemen yesterday as they battled for two hours to control a stubborn blaze in the two top floors of the Ritz-Carlton Hotel, Broad and Walnut sts.

Broad st., from Chestnut to Spruce, was blocked to all traffic except fire apparatus during the blaze, which was checked before it could spread downward from the affected floors, neither of which contains guest rooms. The fire started shortly before 2.45 P. M.

GUESTS LEAVE ROOMS

About 50 guests, occupying suites on the eighth, ninth and 10th floors, were escorted by firemen and hotel employees to the main lobby when tons of water cascaded down stairways and elevator shafts.

Dozens of employees who were at work in the two burned floors, where the storage lofts and accounting department of the hotel are housed, fled before firemen, summoned by two alarms, arrived on the scene.

DAMAGE IS $60,000

Gas masks were used by the firemen when thick clouds of acrid smoke piled up like a wall in the stairways leading to the blazing floors.

Most of the damage, estimated by the management and by firemen as between $50,000 and $60,000, was done by water, soaking valuable furniture and rugs and splashing down shafts into the engine rooms in the basement, forcing a shutdown of hotel utilities.

The fire was discovered when wisps of smoke began curling out from beneath a door of the rug and upholstery room in the loft. Henry Mastro, of 2238 S. Chad-

Continued on Page 3, Column 3

U-Boat Is Reported Landing in Mexico

MEXICO CITY, May 12 (A. P.).—Unconfirmed reports circulated in informed quarters here tonight that a large German submarine three weeks ago landed several passengers—presumably Nazi agents—in Mexico and left after loading a cargo of antimony concentrates.

According to the unconfirmed reports, the submarine landed about April 21 somewhere in the almost deserted 50-mile stretch between Vera Cruz and Alvarado, on the Gulf of Mexico.

Northeast Dry After Water Pump Breaks

Illustrated on Page 2

Bucket brigades of nurses kept 63 patients supplied with water yesterday at Jeanes Memorial Hospital, Fox Chase, when a broken shaft in a 20-year-old city pump at Lardner's Point left wide sections of the Northeast dry all morning and part of the afternoon.

While city shops rushed the casting of a new shaft for the pumping station, the hospital was forced to rely upon buckets and basins filled from bathtubs and a storage tank for its drinking and washing supply.

THREE AREAS HARD HIT

The city water supply to portions of Fox Chase, Burholme and Somerton trickled to a stop at 7:30 A. M., when the extraordinary demands of Monday morning washing cut down the pressure almost to the vanishing point.

Mrs. Eleanor C. Bernhardt, superintendent of the hospital, said that it

Continued on Page 2, Column 3

ROOSEVELT CANCELS SPEECH TOMORROW; GIVES 'CHAT' MAY 27

His Recent Illness Reason for Change; Envoys to Attend

Inquirer Washington Bureau

WASHINGTON, May 12.—President Roosevelt's eagerly awaited address to the world will be delivered in the form of a "fireside chat" on the night of May 27 instead of this Wednesday night, the White House announced tonight.

The engagement to speak Wednesday night at a reception to have been given in honor of the President and Mrs. Roosevelt by the diplomatic representatives of the Latin-American republics was cancelled because of the President's recent indisposition.

HULL BIDS ENVOYS

Today, the President extended an invitation to the Latin American envoys through Secretary of State Cordell Hull to see and hear a fireside chat at the White House the night of May 27. After listening to the broadcast, the diplomats will be served refreshments in the State dining room and will listen to the music of a marimba band sent to the United States by the President of Guatemala.

As in the case of the address that was to have been delivered Wednesday night, the President's remarks on the night of May 27 will be broadcast to the entire world over all do-

Continued on Page 8, Column 6

HERSHEY ASKS U. S. TO DEFER OLDER GROUPS

Urges Congress To Amend Draft Law; Classifying To Be Speeded

By CHARLES H. ELLIS, JR.
Inquirer Washington Bureau

WASHINGTON, May 12.—Brigadier General Lewis B. Hershey, acting director of Selective Service, today asked Congress to amend the draft law to permit wholesale deferments to those in the upper age groups.

Hershey mentioned no ages, but at Selective Service headquarters it was said that the plan was to defer those over 30, "or a little below."

The 6500 local draft boards, meanwhile, were asked to complete the job of classifying all of the men between the ages of 21 and 36 who registered last Oct. 16, it was learned.

TO 200,000 PHILA. MEN

(Selective Service questionnaires will go out shortly to all of the 200,000 Philadelphians who have not yet received them, as a result of the national order yesterday to classify all registrants at once.

(About 20 percent of the 250,000 who registered here have received their questionnaires, draft officials said, and the 200,000 still unclassified will start receiving theirs as quickly as possible.)

Slightly more than 6,000,000 of the 17,000,000 registrants have been classified, and the rest of the job, it was said, is to be done by July 1, or as quickly as the boards can handle it. Draft officials said the classification does not mean that all the men will be given physical examinations, or that any enlargement of the program is contemplated.

YOUNGER MEN BETTER

Hershey's letter to Speaker of the House Sam Rayburn (D., Tex.) was the first official request for power to lower the age limits, but Army officers have stated that the older men generally do not make as good soldiers as those in their early twenties.

Under the amendment proposed by Hershey, President Roosevelt would have power to defer groups according to ages, although all of those within the present age brackets would remain liable for service if the President should find it necessary.

IN RESERVE 10 YEARS

"I am informed," wrote Hershey, "that men in the younger age brackets are best qualified for the training and service contemplated under the act."

He pointed out that, since trainees are to be kept in the reserves for 10 years, "it is desirable that the age of those trained be kept as low as the national interest will permit, so that the reserve forces will be composed of men whose effectiveness will remain at a high level throughout that period."

Members of the House Military Affairs Committee, who have been cold to any suggestion of a change in the draft age limits, appeared surprised by the Hershey letter.

Chairman Andrew J. May (D.,

Continued on Page 6, Column 4

Von Papen Nears Ankara on Flight

BERLIN, May 12 (U. P.).—Franz Von Papen, German Ambassador to Turkey, arrived at Istanbul late today and continued after a short stop to Ankara, traveling by airplane.

COAST MACHINISTS DEAF TO OPM PLEA

SAN FRANCISCO, May 12 (A. P.).—AFL machinists, who joined with CIO unionists in a strike at 11 shipbuilding and repair plants holding contracts for $500,000,000 in warships, freighters and other defense work, today rejected an Office of Production Management request to return to work pending negotiation.

The 11 plants in San Francisco, Oakland and Alameda, employing between 15,000 and 20,000 workmen,

Continued on Page 4, Column 6

BIG NAZI SHIPYARDS WRECKED BY R.A.F.

Today's War Summary appears in conjunction with the War Almanac on Page 12.

LONDON, May 12 (A. P.).—British bombers, apparently still concentrating on efforts to paralyze Germany's sea power at its source, were reported officially today to have left Hamburg and Bremen, two of Germany's great shipbuilding centres, in chaos after devastating new overnight attacks.

The R. A. F. continued "destruction and disorganization of vital parts" of Hamburg, the Air Ministry said, and delivered an equally heavy raid on Bremen with corresponding success in the brightness of a clear, moonlit night.

9 NAZIS DOWNED

Anti-aircraft defenses at home, meanwhile, both planes and guns, were shooting down nine more Nazi raiders during German night attacks

Continued on Page 12, Column 3

Senate Committee Approves Ship Seizure Bill by 11 to 4

By RICHARD L. HARKNESS
Inquirer Washington Bureau

WASHINGTON, May 12.—The Administration scored an important victory for its aid-Britain program today when the Senate Commerce Committee approved President Roosevelt's ship seizure bill by a vote of 11 to 4 after killing an isolationist amendment forbidding the President to transfer any Axis flag vessels to the Union Jack.

The onesided vote upholding the President's plan to use foreign ships now immobilized in American harbors to keep Great Britain afloat, made it virtually certain that the Administration also had the votes to kill the anti-convoy amendment of Senator Charles W. Tobey (R., N. H.) when the measure reaches the Senate floor, probably Wednesday.

The House passed the bill last week on a roll call of 266 to 120. Senate passage and Mr. Roosevelt's signature are all that remain, therefore, before the White House can start replenishing England's merchant marine to offset sinkings by German submarines and bombers.

Eighty-three German, Italian, Danish and other foreign flag vessels aggregating 500,000 tons are under Government jurisdiction in U. S. ports, but Axis crews sabotaged their ships and they must be repaired. In addition, the Government recently boarded 17 Jugoslav merchantmen in American ports to keep them out of German hands.

Apparently fearing the strength of the isolationist bloc in the Senate Commerce Committee, Secretary of

Continued on Page 8, Column 3

Huge U-Boat Toll Claimed by British

LONDON, May 12 (A. P.).—Brassey's Naval Annual, a British publication, appeared today with an estimate that more than 70 percent of the German submarines commissioned in the past 12 months have been sunk.

Commander Harry Pursey, retired naval officer, wrote: "This rate, which should be possible of improvement, is probably greater than that of German replacement . . . and certainly greater than the supply of efficient crews available."

White House Pickets, Service Men Clash

WASHINGTON, May 12 (A. P.).—A clash between what police said was soldiers and Marines off duty and a group picketing the White House occurred tonight.

Police who were called to Pennsylvania ave. in front of the White House brought one soldier and one Marine back to headquarters and said a picket had been sent to a hospital for treatment of minor injuries.

Placards carried by the pickets identified the demonstration as that of the American Peace Mobilization. Earlier in the evening the organization announced it had conducted a "perpetual peace vigil" in front of the White House for 75 hours.

THE WEATHER

Official Forecast: Eastern Pennsylvania, New Jersey, and Delaware Fair and rather cool today, tomorrow partly cloudy and warmer.

(Daylight-Saving Time)

Sun rises 5.47 A. M. Sets 8.06 P. M.
Moon rises 10.54 P. M. Sets 8.09 P. M.

Other Weather Reports on Page 2

IN TODAY'S INQUIRER

Baseball World Shocked by Death of Gehrig

The Philadelphia Inquirer
PHILADELPHIA, TUESDAY MORNING, JUNE 3, 1941

Strictly Sports

Lou Nova Is Worried-- But It's About Louis

Cosmic Puncher Frets Because Joe Might Be Licked Meantime

By CY PETERMAN

IT DOESN'T make a particle of difference, but we thought you might like to know that Lou Nova, the re-conditioned heavyweight who in his own way is worrying in all-out fashion, fights our local mittman, Jim Robinson, this week in Minneapolis.

So far as we know, this is strictly Minneapolis' own fault, and nothing can be done about it. Nova needs the exercise to keep his hand in for Joe Louis in September, and Robinson can use the cash.

What concerns the apostle of Yogi, however, is whether Joe will be wearing a crown when they collide. This is the text of our column.

We got wind of the strange Nova dilemma during a rainy prelude to the Louis-Bud Baer bout in Washington, when Ray Carlin, manager of the cosmic puncher, confided his problems.

* * *

"OUR big gamble is not what Lou can do when he meets Louis, but whether it will be worth our while," Carlin said.

"You mean he might be an ex-champ and all that?"

"Exactly. Take tonight, for example. This Buddy Baer, if he comes in there with that right hand cocked and the left extended, and doesn't try to huddle behind his own shoulders and thus lose all his punching form, well—he might jolt Joe off in a wallop."

We considered this for a full half a second and disagreed. Buddy would probably huddle behind his own bulk and go down to defeat.

As we spoke, we had no idea Baer the Younger could topple Joe through the ropes, that Referee Donovan would suffer a brainstorm, or that a series of comic, not cosmic, events were in store.

We were right in doubting Louis would be jolted, but we had the program badly mixed in our mind's eye.

* * *

"THAT'S the trouble with these heavy bouts," Carlin said. "Anything can happen. Mostly it doesn't, the better battler wins and things go according to plan. But there's always the chance. Especially when you're spotted No. 3 on the list—"

"You consider Billy Conn a definite threat then?"

"We certainly do. We hoped to get the June bout ourselves," Ray declared. "We think Nova is ready now."

Well, Carlin could be wrong as he was once before, we suggested, and he had to smile at that.

"Yes, it was quite a shock that fight with Galento," he agreed. "Funny thing, we did everything according to plan, too, but we'd underestimated Tony's belly.

"During the training period, if you recall, I had Lou practicing a right-hand counter punch to the heart. Seeing Tony swing that overhand left, it occurred that he was wide open for a right smash to the body, and Lou was prepared to pour them in.

* * *

"AS THE fight went on, Galento repeatedly threw the sweeping left and Lou, if you remember, stepped in and drove home the right. But he'd go down under the Galento blow just the same and Tony, partly from momentum and also from the heart punch, always fell on top. It was awful."

To this we nodded profound accord. Awful was the word. Nothing like it before or since. We wondered how Nova had lived, let alone contrived a comeback.

"That fight didn't do either principal any good," Carlin remarked. "Lou, with strep germs in his system, was more than a year regaining health, nursed steadily by his wife in California. When he felt ready to resume training, I noticed he wasn't at all fit, and when he began to lose weight again, sent him to Arizona.

"There he fell in with a party who gave him ideas on this new blow. He calls it the cosmic punch, but you can discount as you will on the name—it's something to call it, anyway.

"Funny thing, though, in his fight with Max Baer last April in New York, Lou was distressed when they stopped it. He was all set to finish Max with his pet blow, he told me, had him properly reduced and teed up as it were—"

* * *

"BUT what's this about the two of you worrying?" we broke in.

"Well, it's about Louis. We're concerned about Joe. Not so good as he used to be, you know. Older, a little slower perhaps. And meeting this Buddy Baer, then Conn before we get our shot—it makes you jittery. Nova is set on winning the title, you know."

Carlin paused as if the statement was mere corroboration of an accepted eventuality.

"He said the same about Galento," we remembered.

"He's greatly changed now. Experienced. Not so fresh but even more confident. He really thinks that punch of his can beat anyone. And you know he's a brute for taking punishment."

In other words, Nova would weather Joe's best assault and, middle of the fight or beyond, go to work and cop the crown via cosmic punching. Carlin nodded.

"Exactly," he said.

"And you're actually worried about Louis rather than Lou," we insisted.

* * *

"EXACTLY," Carlin repeated.

"Does Uncle Mike Jacobs know you're worried?" we pursued.

"He's fed up with us. Told me today, 'For gosh sake, go manage your own fighter and quit fretting about these two.' "

Carlin hesitated, attempted to strike a pose, reconsidered and compromised.

"I'll have Lou do it first time we meet," he promised. "As a matter of fact, it's hard to demonstrate. I think I know what he means, but he'd better explain. Something about perfect balance, plus perfect timing, plus perfect aim—"

"It sounds perfectly perfect," we concluded, and Manager Carlin had to laugh, too.

Frick Finds Danning $150 for Argument

NEW YORK, June 2 (A. P.).—Harry Danning, New York Giants' catcher was fined $150 today by President Ford Frick of the National League for his conduct in yesterday's doubleheader with Cincinnati at the Polo Grounds.

Danning was ejected in the seventh inning of the first game when he registered too strenuous a protest at Umpire Lee Ballanfant's decisions on balls and strikes.

WHEN EX-MATES HONORED BASEBALL'S IRON MAN—The game's great "iron man" bowed out of baseball on July 4, 1939, when "Lou Gehrig Appreciation Day" was observed at the Yankee Stadium in New York before a capacity throng. View above shows Lou, with tears in his eyes, surveying group of trophies he received from admirers. His manager, Joe McCarthy, is on the right.

THE BABE PAYS HIS TRIBUTE TO A COURAGEOUS PAL—Gehrig is shown above with his former teammate, Babe Ruth. The genial Bambino of Swat and Lou were inseparable pals, when both were hitting heroes and known as the homerun twins. Gehrig joined the Yankees five years after the Babe in 1925, but set up a remarkable record of playing 2130 consecutive games at first base for the Yankees.

Lou, Long Ill, Was Game's 'Iron Man'

Continued From First Page

sclerosis," a hardening of the spinal cord which caused muscles to shrivel.

He wasted away sharply in the final weeks and was reported 25 pounds underweight and barely able to speak shortly before he died.

He had served for a year and a half as a member of the New York City Parole Commission and visited his office regularly until about a month ago, when he decided to remain at home to conserve his energy.

FAMOUS FOR LONG RECORD

In his playing days Gehrig was one of baseball's greatest stars, but was most famous for his great physical feat in playing 2130 consecutive regularly scheduled American League games in 14 years.

He twice was chosen the "Most Valuable Player" in the league and over a year ago was voted a place in baseball's "Hall of Fame," joining a score of the game's immortals.

He participated in 34 World Series games and piled up numerous batting records of various kinds.

BELOVED PLAYER

Through all the years Gehrig was known for his clean habits and affable disposition and these factors made him one of baseball's best beloved players.

They also helped him stand off the ravages of his disease after others had given up hope.

Gehrig refused to believe that his disease was incurable and as long as possible maintained a normal routine.

QUIT VOLUNTARY

He had withdrawn voluntarily from the lineup in the spring of 1939 because he was in a slump. At that time no one realized he was ill. But after benching himself while the club was in Detroit, Gehrig went to the Mayo Clinic at Rochester, Minn., where the nature of his trouble was learned.

A treatment of daily injections was prescribed and followed faithfully for two years. Gehrig remained with the ball club for the remainder of the 1939 season, sitting in a far corner of the dugout and occasionally limping out to home plate to present the lineup to the umpires, but never taking part in another game.

SPECTATOR FOR 1ST TIME

The Yankees won their fourth straight world championship that fall, but Gehrig for the first time in his career with the club was a mere spectator.

After the hubbub of the baseball campaign had quieted, Mayor F. H. Laguardia offered Gehrig a 10-year post on the City Parole Board at an annual salary of $5700.

The big, dimple-cheeked star who had earned an estimated $400,000 in his years on the diamond, with a salary that reached $39,000 a year at its peak, accepted immediately.

La Guardia expressed belief that Gehrig would be "an inspiration and a hope to many of the younger boys who have gotten into trouble."

'DEVOTES LIFE TO PUBLIC'

"Surely the misfortune of some of the young men," La Guardia said, "will compare as trivial with what Mr. Gehrig has so cheerful and courageously faced. He expects to devote his life to the public service."

Gehrig took office the next Jan. 2,

Continued on Page 24, Column 1

Yanks Stunned

DETROIT, June 2 (A. P.).—The death in New York City tonight of Lou Gehrig, one of baseball's greatest stars, stunned members of the New York Yankees baseball team on their arrival here from Cleveland for a series with the Detroit Tigers.

"What can I say?" said Manager Joe McCarthy. "I am at a loss for words to express the sincere sympathy that I feel. He was my best personal friend, one of baseball's greatest figures, and a grand fellow."

Catcher Bill Dickey, Gehrig's roommate when the Yankees were on the road, said "I feel that is like one of my family passing."

"Lou was my best friend," he added, "and baseball loses a great friend."

"It is the most painful news I have ever heard," said Art Fletcher, Yankee coach. "I don't know what to say."

The Yankees had arrived at their downtown hotel headquarters here only a few minutes before a reporter told them their former teammate had died.

Baseball Veteran Dies

PALO ALTO, Calif., June 2 (A. P.).—Richard Lloyd "Nick" Williams, 61, former player, scout and manager in the Pacific Coast League and prominent in baseball for more than 30 years, died today. Williams managed the San Francisco Seals from 1926 through 1931.

Kid Cocoa Wins

NEWARK, N. J., June 2 (A. P.).—Louis (Kid) Cocoa, 146, of New Haven, Conn., won a close 10-round decision over Norman Rubio, 145, of Albany, N. Y., at Meadowbrook Bowl.

Gehrig's Record With Yankees

Born, New York City, June 19, 1903.
Batted Left. Threw Left. Height, 6 feet, 1 inch. Weight, 205 pounds.

Year	Club	League	Pos.	G.	AB	R	H	2B	3B	HR	RBI	SB	Avg.
1923	New York a	A. L.	1B	13	26	6	11	4	1	1	9	0	.423
1923	Hartford b	E. L.	1B	59	227	54	69	13	8	24		3	.304
1924	New York c	A. L.	1B	10	12	2	6	1	0	0	6	0	.500
1924	Hartford d	E. L.	1B	134	504	111	186	40	13	37	—	6	.369
1925	New York	A. L.	1B	126	437	73	129	23	9	21	68	6	.295
1926	New York	A. L.	1B	155	572	135	179	47	*20	16	107	6	.313
1927	New York e	A. L.	1B	155	584	149	218	*52	18	47	*175	10	.373
1928	New York	A. L.	1B	154	562	139	210	*47	13	27	*142	4	.374
1929	New York	A. L.	1B	154	553	127	166	33	9	35	126	4	.300
1930	New York	A. L.	1B	154	581	143	220	42	17	41	*174	12	.379
1931	New York	A. L.	1B	155	619	*163	*211	31	15	*46	*184	17	.341
1932	New York	A. L.	1B	155	596	138	208	42	9	34	151	4	.349
1933	New York	A. L.	1B	152	593	*138	198	41	12	32	139	9	.334
1934	New York	A. L.	1B	154	579	128	210	40	6	*49	*165	9	*.363
1935	New York	A. L.	1B	149	535	*125	176	26	10	30	119	8	.329
1936	New York e	A. L.	1B	155	579	*167	205	37	7	*49	152	3	.354
1937	New York	A. L.	1B	157	569	138	200	37	9	37	159	4	.351
1938	New York	A. L.	1B	157	576	115	170	32	6	29	114	6	.295
1939	New York	A. L.	1B	8	28	2	4	0	0	0	1	0	.143
Complete Major League Totals			Yrs. 17	2163	8001	1888	2721	535	161	494	1991	102	.340
World's Series Record													
1926	New York	A. L.	1B	7	23	1	8	2	0	0	4	0	.348
1927	New York	A. L.	1B	4	13	2	4	2	2	0	5	0	.308
1928	New York	A. L.	1B	4	11	5	6	1	0	4	9	0	.545
1932	New York	A. L.	1B	4	17	9	9	1	0	3	8	0	.529
1936	New York	A. L.	1B	6	24	5	7	1	0	2	7	0	.292
1937	New York	A. L.	1B	5	17	4	5	1	1	1	3	0	.294
1938	New York	A. L.	1B	4	14	4	4	0	0	0	0	0	.286
World's Series Totals				34	119	30	43	8	3	10	35	0	.361

* INDICATES LED LEAGUE OR WAS TIED FOR LEAGUE LEADERSHIP

a Optioned to Hartford. b Recalled by New York. c Optioned to Hartford. d Recalled by New York. e Voted the most valuable player in the American League for 1927 and 1936.

Gehrig attended Columbia University at New York.

Farnsworth Stanton Victor

7000 Watch Aged Sprinter Account For Fifth Triumph

By JOHN WEBSTER
Inquirer Sports Reporter

STANTON, Del., June 2.—Bill Farnsworth, stout-hearted veteran from the Tall Trees Stable, roared to a head triumph this afternoon in the Newark, an allowance sprint which featured the Delaware Park racing program.

Runner-up in the photo finish was Busy Morn, flying the silks of Gene Autry, radio, rodeo and movie star. Mrs. Veader Leonard's Happy Lark, two lenths off Busy Morn, was third, with Scotch Trap and Hants completing the field.

Backed confidently into favoritism by the majority of the 7000 spectators, the winner, an eight-year-old Crack Brigade gelding, returned $4.70 for a two-dollar straight bet. He carried 121 pounds, top weight, as did Scotch Trap and Hants, and rolled around the six furlongs of good footing in 1.13 2-5.

FIFTH 1941 TRIUMPH

In victory, Bill Farnsworth gained his fifth triumph in 10 starts this season for his owner Mrs. Frank Navin, widow of the former owner of the Detroit Tigers ball club. Old Bill had won two of his recent three starts at Churchill Downs.

The Tall Trees sprinter broke close behind Busy Morn, first to show as the field got away from the gate over on the turn into the backstretch. However, Hants, a former steeplechaser who races for Brooks Parker, zipped along the inside, and had

Continued on Page 25, Column 8

Litwhiler's Homers Aid Phils; Rain Halts A's; Play Sox Today

Special to The Inquirer

ST. LOUIS, Mo., June 2.—The Athletics will carry their spectacular pennant drive to Chicago for their next series. The closing game of their tussle with the tail end Browns this afternoon was washed off the boards by a June shower, and the fact that only a handful of patrons would have attended the game.

With the Browns in last place, the local populace has turned its attention to other sports, and the club's management was smart enough to realize this fact, announcing the postponement of today's game as early as 10.30 A. M.

A'S IN THICK OF IT

Thus the A's, riding on a winning streak of 13 victories in their last 16 games, will see what can be done toward stopping the red-hot White Sox. Jimmy Dykes, Athletic alumnus, is doing a swell job of managing the Sox, and his old master, none other than the much-admired Connie Mack, would like nothing better than to swat the rotund James thrice in the same place at Comiskey Field, starting tomorrow.

It is recalled that the Indians and Yankees were to fight it out for the American League pennant in this year's pre-season forecasts. Bob Feller would turn the trick, plus the change from Ossie Vitt to Rog Peckinpaugh, said those Clevelanders. The Yanks were to be strengthened by the addition of flashy minor league recruits, argued the boastful New Yorkers. Here the Sox and the A's are right in the thick of the American League pennant.

This spurt by the A's started on May 17. On that date they were battling with the Browns in a tail-end combat, the Macks showing a record of only 10 victories and 18 defeats. Then the grand old warrior, Connie Mack, waved a magic wand and, presto, the A's knocked off the Indians for three in a row at Shibe Park and continued their snappy brand of baseball, until they are within reach of first place.

Baseball Facts

AMERICAN LEAGUE
YESTERDAY'S RESULTS

Cleveland 7, New York 5.
Washington 8, Chicago 3.
Boston 9, Detroit 1.
ATHLETICS at St. Louis (postponed, rain).

HOW THEY STAND

	W.	L.	P.C.	G.B.
Cleveland	30	19	.612	—
Chicago	26	18	.591	1½
New York	25	20	.556	3
Boston	22	19	.537	4
ATHLETICS	23	21	.523	4½
Detroit	23	23	.500	5½
Washington	16	29	.356	12
St. Louis	13	29	.310	13½

G.B.—Games Behind Leader.

Today's Schedule, Probable Pitchers And Their Records

ATHLETICS at Chicago—Knott (2-5) or Beckman (1-3) vs. Lee (6-2).

New York at Detroit—Peek (2-0) vs. Trout (2-1).

Boston at Cleveland (night)—Harris (2-2) vs. Bagby (3-3).

Washington at St. Louis (night)—Leonard (3-6) vs. Auker (3-5).

NATIONAL LEAGUE
YESTERDAY'S RESULTS

PHILLIES, 3; Chicago, 2.
St. Louis, 5; Brooklyn, 4.
Cincinnati, 4; New York, 3.
Boston, 2; Pittsburgh, 0.

HOW THEY STAND

	W.	L.	Pct.	G. B.
St. Louis	32	12	.727	
Brooklyn	31	13	.705	1
New York	21	19	.525	9
Cincinnati	21	24	.467	11½
Chicago	19	22	.463	11½
Pittsburgh	14	22	.389	14
Boston	14	24	.368	15
PHILLIES	13	29	.310	18

G. B.—Games Behind Leader.

Today's Schedule, Probable Pitchers And Their Records

Chicago vs. PHILLIES at Shibe Park (3.15 P. M.)—Lee (5-4) vs. Hughes (2-4).

St. Louis at Brooklyn—M. Cooper (6-1) vs. Wyatt (8-2).

Cincinnati at New York—Derringer (4-6) vs. Carpenter (2-0).

Pittsburgh at Boston—Heintzelman (1-3) vs. Lamanna (2-1).

Continued on Page 25, Column 3

By STAN BAUMGARTNER

Danny Litwhiler, who turned in his school books for a baseball bat, socked two home runs and a single yesterday afternoon at Shibe Park as Johnny Podgajny held the Chicago Cubs to seven hits. The Phillies scored a 3-2 victory, the first of the season against the Chicagoans.

Litwhiler and Podgajny were the whole show. Danny drove in both the second and third runs that made victory possible with circuit clouts into the left field stands. They came in the third and sixth innings.

Podgajny pitched courageously in the pinches to hang up his third triumph of the season. The Chester lad does not look very rugged on the mound, but he has plenty on the ball and he went the full distance yesterday, although he walked six men.

STOPS HANK LEIBER

He was in many tight spots and on four occasions was forced to pitch to the mighty Hank Leiber with the tying or winning runs on the bases. In three instances Leiber did not get the ball out of the infield. That was really a glittering performance by a young fellow who was serving baseballs in the Class D. Canadian League less than a year ago.

The Phillies also had the satisfaction of taking the measure of an old jinx, Larry French. The veteran southpaw pitched good ball all the way and baffled the Phils hitters, but he neglected to inform Litwhiler of the secret.

The Phillies led all the way, although the Cubs kept knocking at the door throughout. Prothro's men took a 1-0 lead in the first inning after two were out when Joe Marty doubled and Nick Etten singled. Litwhiler also hit safely in this frame and Bragan walked loading the bases. Livingston, however, skied out to right.

Litwhiler's boundary belt into the upper deck with no one on gave the Phillies a 2-0 lead in the third. Chicago got one of these back in the sixth on singles by Dallesandro and Novikoff and Cavarretta's fly to Marty.

Litwhiler hammered his second

Continued on Page 25, Column 1

Gus Dorazio Wins From Kapovich

BALTIMORE, June 2 (A. P.).—Gus Dorazio, 189, of Philadelphia, won a unanimous decision over Johnny Kapovich, 180, of Baltimore tonight, coming back strongly in the final two rounds of a 10-round bout with a winning margin.

fierce body attack to capture the Dorazio pounded Kapovich freely in the opening session, but the Baltimorean held his own thereafter, making his best showing in the eighth with the fight about even. Then Dorazio's bull-like boring-in tactics took effect. Just before the final bell, Kapovich went to his knees under a hard drubbing, but got up before count was started.

Jack Beats Speigal

HOLYOKE, Mass., June 2 (A. P.).—In an upset, Beau Jack, 136½, of Springfield gained an unanimous eight-round decision tonight over Tommy Speigal, 136½, of Uniontown, Pa. Jack was awarded every round over the Pennsylvania lightweight.

Back Injury May Keep Snead Out of National Open Golf

FORT WORTH, Tex., June 2 (A. P.).—Samuel Jackson Snead, who had to withdraw from the Goodall round-robin two weeks ago because of a back injury, may not be able to start in the 45th U. S. Open golf championship which gets under way at the Colonial Club on Thursday.

Sam came in from Oklahoma City this morning, but hit no more than a few iron shots. "The first few felt pretty good, but then he tried to whale into a No. 3 iron and the pain almost knocked him down. Snead has suffered from an injured vertebra near the base of his spine for two years, and aggravated the injury several weeks ago when he slipped on a rock while fishing.

"I won't even try to play a practice round till Wednesday," said Sam, "and if it doesn't go right I won't start. For one thing there's no sense taking a chance on hurting myself more seriously, and for another it wouldn't be fair to my friends and others who might bet on me if I went in there knowing I couldn't do my best."

Another "cripple" in the field is Craig Wood, the man who pulled a back muscle because he sneezed at the moment he stooped to pick up a razor blade. The first two days he was here he had his back taped but today he tried wearing a polo belt, and reported better results. Wood shot a 74.

Lloyd Mangrum, one of the home-grown Texas stars, and former amateur champion Willie Turnesa claimed one-under-par 69's in the day's outstanding scoring feats.

The Philadelphia Inquirer

PUBLIC LEDGER

An Independent Newspaper for All the People

FINAL CITY EDITION

CIRCULATION: July Average: Daily 418,268, Sunday 1,081,595 — a b d e f g h — FRIDAY MORNING, AUGUST 15, 1941 — Second Largest 3c Morning Circulation in America — THREE CENTS

Roosevelt and Churchill Vow to Destroy 'Nazi Tyranny,' Proclaim Victory Aims After Meeting Aboard Warships at Sea

Today

Allies' Eight Points Any Promises? Can't Be Lived Up to Past Pledges Violated World War Cited

By Mark Sullivan

WASHINGTON, Aug. 15.

HAD a good angel attended Mr. Roosevelt and Mr. Churchill as they met to write their eight points; had he been really a good angel, with a strain of austerity, no mere comforter or yea-sayer—that angel would have put his final admonition in one sentence: Be sure you make no promises, unless you are absolutely certain they can be lived up to.

The first test to be applied to these eight points is: To what extent are they promises? If they contain promises, is it absolutely certain they can be lived up to?

Of all the causes of the world's present travail, the most devastating is the loss of peoples' faith in the promises of statesmen and government. Over and over during the present generation, peoples have seen governments make contracts, leaders hold out assurances, create hopes. Over and over, peoples have believed, have felt the exaltation of faith. Over and over they have been let down.

Over and over the exaltation of faith has turned to the bitterness and cynicism of disillusion. And that disillusion, that spiritual blight, is the principal cause of the world's disease. The cure will take long. First there must be a generation of statesmen who are careful about promises; then there must be a long experience of seeing all promises kept, until peoples gradually recover their faith.

Consider the somber record, beginning in 1914. Germany signed a treaty to respect the neutrality of Belgium—then called the treaty a "scrap of paper" and invaded Belgium. Wilson was reelected President upon a slogan (put out by his party, not himself) which said "He Kept Us Out of War," with the implication that he would continue to keep us out—and Wilson went to war within five months after he was re-elected.

Wilson said we were going to war to "Make the World Safe for Democracy"—Wilson gave out the Fourteen Points; Germany accepted them, they became part of the Armistice contract—but France and Britain made Wilson violate at least two of them.

Wilson promised the world a League of Nations—but America would not join; the League failed nations and peoples who relied on it, finally faded away.

Those broken promises of the Great War and the peace that ended it were followed by 20 years of treaties sometimes not lived up to—the Nine-Power Pact, the Kellogg-Briand treaties; promises broken or hopes disappointed in the economic field—"new economic era," "new economic plateau" from which prices would never descend; promises of governments to redeem their currency in gold, the promise of our own Government to pay its bonds in gold.

Just now, promises made last year by both party platforms and both Presidential candidates that American soldiers would not be sent to fight outside the Western Hemisphere are an embarrassment to our military efficiency, a contributing cause of our widespread mood of apprehension. It does not matter that most of these promises were made in good faith, nor that in most cases the breach was not wilful. The hurt to peoples' faith has been equally devastating.

Happily the eight points do not to any great degree take the form of promises. The angel of

Continued on Page 6, Column 3

RUSSIA ADMITS YIELDING TWO UKRAINE TOWNS

High Official Denies Troops Are Ringed; Fighting Renewed On Entire Front

War Map on Page 8

Red troops have abandoned two Ukraine towns, each about 100 miles from the strategic Ukrainian Black Sea port of Nikolaev, Moscow acknowledged early today, adding that fierce fighting raged along the entire front.

The Russians officially denied that the Red armies in the Ukraine had been encircled, and asserted that a Nazi tank corps, 11 other divisions and 13 regiments had been annihilated in the savage fighting.

The German High Command claimed that its troops and their Italian, Rumanian and Hungarian allies had completed the encirclement of Odessa and Nikolaev, and had reached the iron centre of Krivoi Rog, only 80 miles southwest of the Great Red industrial centre of Dnepropetrovsk.

On the northern front Russian forces were claimed to be entrapped by the Finns on the northern coast of Lake Ladoga and attempting to escape in transport vessels.

Despite its various claims to success, Berlin reported in possible anticipation of announcements of a slowing down of the Nazi drive—that it had begun to rain again in the Ukraine.

MOSCOW, Aug. 15 (Friday) (A. P.)—Red troops battling to stem German drives into the Ukraine have abandoned Pervomaisk and Kirovograd, each about 100 miles northwest and northeast, respectively, of the strategic Soviet Black Sea port of Nikolaev, the Russians acknowledged early today.

But S. A. Lozovsky, Soviet Vice Commissar for Foreign Affairs, denied the German claim that the Red armies in the Ukraine had been encircled.

NAZIS LOSE HEAVILY

Fierce fighting along the whole front from the White Sea in the far north to the Black Sea was reported in the Soviet Information Bureau's latest communique, and Russian

Continued on Page 8, Column 2

(A. P. Wirephoto)

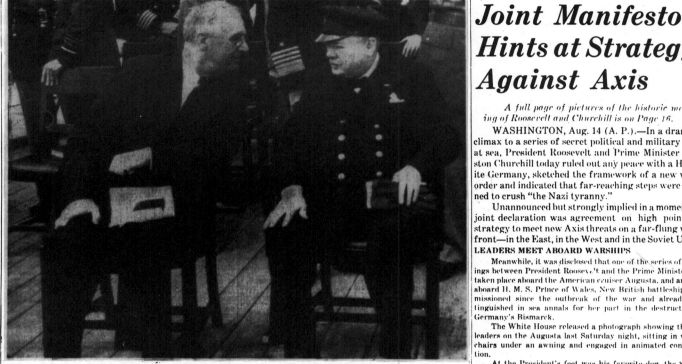

FIRST PICTURE OF ROOSEVELT-CHURCHILL CONFERENCE

This official photograph released by the White House yesterday shows President Roosevelt chatting with British Prime Minister Winston Churchill aboard the British battleship Prince of Wales. The picture of the momentous meeting, first to reach this country, was taken Aug. 10 after church services aboard ship.

Joint Manifesto Hints at Strategy Against Axis

A full page of pictures of the historic meeting of Roosevelt and Churchill is on Page 16.

WASHINGTON, Aug. 14 (A. P.).—In a dramatic climax to a series of secret political and military talks at sea, President Roosevelt and Prime Minister Winston Churchill today ruled out any peace with a Hitlerite Germany, sketched the framework of a new world order and indicated that far-reaching steps were planned to crush "the Nazi tyranny."

Unannounced but strongly implied in a momentous joint declaration was agreement on high points of strategy to meet new Axis threats on a far-flung world front—in the East, in the West and in the Soviet Union.

LEADERS MEET ABOARD WARSHIPS

Meanwhile, it was disclosed that one of the series of meetings between President Roosevelt and the Prime Minister had taken place aboard the American cruiser Augusta, and another aboard H. M. S. Prince of Wales, New British battleship commissioned since the outbreak of the war and already distinguished in sea annals for her part in the destruction of Germany's Bismarck.

The White House released a photograph showing the two leaders on the Augusta last Saturday night, sitting in wicker chairs under an awning and engaged in animated conversation.

At the President's feet was his favorite dog, the Scottie Falla. The President, Churchill and other civilians in the picture wore evening clothes.

ATTEND CHURCH SERVICES TOGETHER

Another photograph showed Churchill in seafaring togs and the President in civvies, talking aboard the Prince of Wales after church services last Sunday, which was the first day that no word was received in Washington from the President, who had been cruising off New England in the Presidential yacht Potomac.

The leaders of the two great Western powers gave no hint that the United States had been assigned any immediate part other than as "the arsenal of democracy" in a stepped-up effort to win the war against the Axis.

STEPS TAKEN FOR SAFETY

But neither was there any indication from their pronouncement that the United States would remain indefinitely on a "short of war" basis in "the steps which their countries

Continued on Page 4, Column 2

MEASURE EXTENDING CONSCRIPTION TERM GOES TO ROOSEVELT

WASHINGTON, Aug. 14 (A. P.).—By a vote of 37 to 19, the Senate today accepted minor House changes in the controversial Army service extension legislation and dispatched the measure to President Roosevelt.

Senate attaches said they assumed the bill would be flown to President Roosevelt at sea in order to go on the books as quickly as possible. General George C. Marshall, the Army Chief of Staff, originally fixed Aug. 1 as the deadline on which the measure could be enacted without inconvenience to the Army.

ONLY 8 MINUTES DEBATE

The final Senate vote, terminating weeks of dispute in both Houses, came after only eight minutes of

Continued on Page 7, Column 1

8 Points for Peace

WASHINGTON, Aug. 14 (A. P.). The eight points on which President Roosevelt and Prime Minister Churchill agreed:

1. Their countries seek no aggrandizement, territorial or other.

2. They desire to see no territorial changes that do not accord with the freely expressed wishes of the peoples concerned.

3. They respect the right of all peoples to choose the form of government under which they will live; and they wish to see sovereign rights and self government restored to those who have been forcibly deprived of them.

4. They will endeavor, with due respect for their existing obligations, to further the enjoyment by all States, great or small, victor or vanquished, of access, on equal terms, to the trade and to the raw materials of the world which are needed for their economic prosperity.

5. They desire to bring about the fullest collaboration between all Nations in the economic field with the object of securing, for all, improved labor standards, economic advancement and social security.

6. After the full destruction of the Nazi tyranny, they hope to see established a peace which will afford to all Nations the means of dwelling in safety within their own boundaries, and which will afford assurance that all the men in the lands may live out their lives in freedom from fear and want.

7. Such a peace should enable all men to traverse the high seas and oceans without hindrance.

8. They believe that all of the Nations of the world, for realistic as well as spiritual reasons, must come to the abandonment of the use of force. Since no future peace can be maintained if land, sea or air armaments continue to be employed by Nations which threaten, or may threaten, aggression outside of their frontiers, they believe, pending the establishment of a wider and permanent system of general security, that the disarmament of such Nations is essential. They will likewise aid and encourage all other practicable measures which will lighten for peace-loving peoples the crushing burden of armaments.

BEAVERBROOK SAYS U. S. AID TO BRITAIN STILL ISN'T ENOUGH

Illustrated on Page 5

By JOHN C. O'BRIEN

Inquirer Washington Bureau

WASHINGTON, Aug. 14.—Lord Beaverbrook, British Minister of Supply, describing himself as "the biggest buyer on the cuff you ever saw," declared tonight, after participating in the secret conference between President Roosevelt and Prime Minister Winston Churchill, on the high seas, that England must have American weapons and food in expanding volume if Britain is to win the war.

The Cabinet Minister, who until May was in charge of Britain's aircraft production, arrived here in an American-built bomber with British markings at 1.45 P. M., landing at Bolling Field where Army authorities had taken elaborate precautions to assure privacy.

SAYS AID ISN'T ENOUGH

He was driven to the British Embassy, arriving while Viscount Halifax, the British Ambassador, and Alfred Duff Cooper, former British Minister of Information, were attending a luncheon at the National Press Club, at which Duff Cooper spoke "off the record."

At a press conference at the Embassy later in the day, Lord Beaverbrook, bluff, gruff-spoken former Canadian, expressed his gratitude for the help thus far received from this country but declared that it was not enough.

"I am here seeking more supplies under the Lend-Lease Act," he said bluntly. "Britain wants more supplies

Continued on Page 5, Column 6

British Battleship, U. S. Cruiser Were Meeting Scenes

WASHINGTON, Aug. 14 (U. P.).—Official pictures released by the White House tonight disclosed that President Roosevelt and British Prime Minister Winston Churchill held at least two of their historic oceanic conferences aboard a British battleship, H. M. S. Prince of Wales, and the U. S. cruiser Augusta.

In addition to lifting the veil of secrecy on where the meeting took place, the photographs confirmed that high ranking British and American officials, including Harry L. Hopkins, the lend-lease administrator; Undersecretary of State Sumner Welles; General George C. Marshall, U. S. Army Chief of Staff, and Admiral Harold R. Stark, Chief of Naval Operations, had participated.

2 GROUPS OF PHOTOS

There were two groups of photographs. One picture, portraying the President and Churchill aboard the British battleship, bore the cap-

Continued on Page 4, Column 6

'Hard to Tell who Looked Happier,' Eyewitness Says

LONDON, Aug. 14 (A. P.).—A constantly moving circle of destroyers, patrol boats and other small warships formed a precautionary defensive ring around the Roosevelt-Churchill conference ship, and American planes droned overhead, the Daily Mail said today in a dispatch from its correspondent "somewhere on the American Atlantic coast."

Correspondent Walter Farr said President Roosevelt and Prime Minister Churchill sat on the sunlit deck of the ship "with seagulls wheeling around."

"Occasionally the drone of a big

Continued on Page 4, Column 6

THE WEATHER

Official Forecast: Eastern Pennsylvania, New Jersey and Delaware: mostly cloudy and somewhat higher temperatures with showers today and tonight; tomorrow showers and local thunderstorms.

(Daylight Saving Time)

Sun rises 6.11 A.M. Sets 7.58 P.M.

Moon rises 12.07 A.M. Sets 2.13 P.M.

Other Weather Reports on Page 2

IN TODAY'S INQUIRER

Purvis, British Buyer, Killed in Plane Crash

MONTREAL, Aug. 14 (A. P.). The Rt. Hon. Arthur Purvis, director-general of the British Purchasing Commission in the United States, has been killed in a flying accident in the United Kingdom, the Ferry Command of the Royal Air Force announced tonight.

It was not announced whether the fatal crash was the one in which 22 persons, including American ferry pilots, were killed Sunday night.

Beaverbrook Plane's Companion Crashed

LONDON, Aug. 14 (A. P.). Lord Beaverbrook, British Minister of Supply who participated in the Roosevelt-Churchill conferences and now is in Washington, flew the Atlantic in a companion plane to that which crashed with a loss of 22 lives Sunday night, it was disclosed tonight.

The Beaverbrook plane flew on, landing him and his staff without incident.

Ex-Theatre Head Is Slain In Germantown Mystery

Illustrated on Page 2

Frank Frey, former manager of the Band Box Theatre, was found fatally beaten in a darkened Germantown street last night under mysterious circumstances.

A mysterious tan sedan, which lingered at the murder scene at Germantown ave. and Penn st. until another car pulled up, led the way to Germantown Hospital and then vanished.

NO DESCRIPTION OBTAINED

Police said the occupants of the sedan, of whom no description was obtained by the other motorists, might have had some connection with the murder.

The victim, who was 27, and lived at 306 E. Bringhurst st., Germantown, was employed at the time of his death as a stock clerk in a Germantown five-and-ten-cent store.

He was found, still alive but with his head badly battered, as if by a lead pipe, in the shadows before an unoccupied mansion at 38 E. Penn st. No marks were on his body or his clothing, indicating that he had not been struck by an automobile, but

Continued on Page 2, Column 5

Cards Defeat Reds, 6-3; Dodgers Win, 13-6

The Philadelphia Inquirer

PHILADELPHIA, MONDAY MORNING, SEPTEMBER 1, 1941 abdefg 19

Strictly Sports

Riggs or Kovacs Likely To Take U. S. Net Crown

Don McNeill, '40 Champion, Must Recover Form If He's to Win

By GRANTLAND RICE

THE leading soothsayers are about evenly split between Bobby Riggs and Frank Kovacs at Forest Hills this week. They give Don McNeill a chance to defend his crown if he can work himself into better form. The 1940 winner needs more tennis and this may spoil his chance to repeat.

So, barring some brand of upset, Riggs and Kovacs should be the surviving pair when the show reaches the final act.

Concerning these two; Riggs is the more dependable—Kovacs the more brilliant. With both at top form, Kovacs should win. But Riggs is more likely to be at his best than Kovacs, who at times is harder to guess than an entry at Saratoga or Aqueduct.

McNeill is the only remaining party who might upset this final selection and McNeill will have to be in a form-recovering hurry through the next few days to get as far as the final frame. In top form he is as good as either. Last year he was better.

• • •

U. S. TENNIS has known a long parade since Bill Larned reigned and Maurice McLoughlin boosted the game with his smashing style. You can look back on Norris Williams, R. L. Murray, Little Bill Johnston, Big Bill Tilden—and the charge of the French with Rene Lacoste and Henri Cochet until Bill Tilden and Ellsworth Vines stopped it.

Then Fred Perry and the British moved in until Don Budge hit the heights.

But the days of international tennis are over for some time. Only the United States is involved at Forest Hills this week as far as any championship might go.

What about an upset—which means the defeat of Riggs or Kovacs before the closing day?

Both have been beaten before during this season and it can happen again. In fact, Julian Myrick, a veteran observer who knows his tennis, figures this tournament a fairly open one, much more so than many believe. There is a better chance for an upset in one of the minor tournaments, however, than there should be in a championship meeting where the leaders have worked themselves into winning form and where the pressure will be harder on the underdog.

• • •

MOVING from Bill Larned through Don McNeill, who is the greatest champion of the lot from this long parade? I put this query up to a number of experts, tennis players and noncombatants, and the verdict went to Tilden with something to spare. They were talking of Tilden in his best years.

"Tilden," one of his old competitors said, "had about everything. I mean speed—power—control—skill—general-ship—cunning—stamina—and whatever else it takes. He had the service, the forehand, the backhand, and court-covering agility. He was a cat on the court, always in position to make his return."

They rank Little Bill Johnston as one of the great competitors of all time. Little Bill, weighing only 118 pounds, fought Tilden to the final stroke more than once.

• • •

THE slender Californian was as determined a battler as anyone can ever hope to see in action. He was especially a form of killing poison for all foreign players.

Strangely enough, the Davis Cup moved to Australia as the first World War started. This was August, 1914, when Brookes and Wilding stopped McLoughlin and Williams. The cup remained in Australia six years before Tilden and Johnston brought it home.

Australia won again as the second World War opened, and how long it will be before another recovery march is launched is beyond anyone's guess.

So, the Forest Hills meeting becomes the lone major spot in modern tennis until the world again becomes worn-out with war. While Riggs, Kovacs and McNeill should be the top trio, there is still enough class left to round out an interesting week and bring out first-class crowds.

Cy Peterman, conductor of this column, is on vacation. He will resume writing the column on Sept. 15.

Miss Betz Forced to Limit By Miss Hart in U. S. Tennis

FOREST HILLS, N. Y., Aug. 31 (U. P.).—Top-seeded Pauline Betz, Los Angeles, had to call on all her shots today to get by plucky, 16-year-old Doris Hart, Miami, 5-7, 6-0, 11-9, in the first round of the National singles tennis tournament at West Side Tennis Club.

Miss Hart, runner-up in the recent National Junior tournament at Philadelphia, came here unseeded, but she gave Miss Betz the battle of her life before the California girl finally broke service in the 20th game of the decisive set.

Miss Hart played smart tennis to stay with the favorite so long. She won the first set with her man-sized service and drives that clipped lime off the sidelines, then took it easy in the second set, losing several games at love. The 4000 fans prepared for a thrilling third set and they got one.

THRILLING BATTLE

Each girl broke service once before the set ran into extra games and then they held, with Miss Hart once overcoming a 40-15 disadvantage to win her serve and stay in the match.

The break came on the first point in the 20th game when Miss Hart, serving, dubbed an easy kill into the net. Then she watched a lob hit the baseline and Miss Betz went on to win the game at love.

Miss Hart's brother, Richard Hart, was easy for Frank Kovacs as the second-seeded Californian moved into the third round of the men's division with a 6-3, 6-2, 6-3 victory.

McNEILL TRIUMPHS

The defending champion, Don McNeill, Oklahoma City, seeded third, and Wayne Sabin, Reno, Nev., ranked sixth, also advanced with little trouble. McNeill trimmed George Toley, Los Angeles, 6-3, 7-5, 6-4, and Sabin won from Gilbert Hunt, Washington, 6-3, 6-2, 6-4. Sabin will have his work cut out for him in the third round against Ladislav Hecht, the

Continued on Page 22, Column 2

Storm Upsets 20 Sailboats

Twenty boats capsized and others had broken masts, ripped sails or minor damage, when a wind and rain storm hit the fleet of 45 small sailboats competing in the annual open regatta of the Red Dragon Canoe Club on the upper Delaware River at Edgewater Park, N. J., yesterday afternoon.

Morning races produced keen competition, as the opening races of the regatta were staged under ideal conditions. Phil Somervell, national comet class champion, won in the comet class, for the Red Dragon Club, sailing his comet yacht No. 1968, to take the feature honors. He sailed a fine race, and won by more than a minute from Bud Farrington, another home club skipper, with Sever's 1226 playing third.

In the crickets, Bob Knipp, of Beverly Y. C., sailed his No. 15 to a handy victory over Jack Denatt, a clubmate, and Austin Haines, another Beverly skipper.

Ed Smith, of Riverton, took the star class event in his boat No. 128, while Bert Shoemaker, another Riverton ace, triumphed in his No. 4 in the duster class over Dean Birch, of Red Dragon, in a well-fought race, with a field of eight competing.

(A. P. Wirephoto)

YOUNG'S SAFE AT THIRD IN GIANTS-DODGERS BATTLE

New York infielder advanced on Joe Moore's single in the first inning. Lavagetto took Reiser's throw; umpire is Pinelli. The Dodgers won, 13-6.

Rallies Defeat Giants

Camilli's 3-Run Homer Wins; Cards in Lead

The pacemakers in the torrid National League race kept up their whirlwind dash down the pennant stretch yesterday. The St. Louis Cards won their fifth straight game by beating the Reds, 6 to 3, while the Dodgers overcame the Giants in a slam, bang, nip-and-tuck tussle by 13 to 6.

There was no relative change in the standing between the two teams. The Cards hold first place by a margin of two points, less than half a game.

They stand as follows:

	W.	L.	Pct.
St. Louis	81	45	.643
Brooklyn	82	46	.641

Both clubs are scheduled for twin bills today, the Dodgers entertaining the Boston Braves in Brooklyn, while the Cards go home to tackle the tough Pittsburgh Pirates.

Brooklyn Loses Early Lead; Late Flares Upset N. Y. Giants

NEW YORK, Aug. 31 (A. P.).—Just about the time you could actually hear Brooklyn hearts busting all over the Polo Grounds today, the Dodgers pulled themselves together and walloped the Giants, 13 to 6, to remain on the heels of St. Louis in the hot National League flag chase.

"Dem bums" piled up four runs in the first inning, blew that lead and were behind 6-4 at the end of six frames before they finally went to work before a crowd of 24,694. Then Dolph Camilli clouted a three-run homer in the seventh to put the game on ice and in the eighth the Brooklyns knocked the roof in on their old enemies with five unearned runs.

PLENTY OF PITCHERS

It was strictly a roll-up-your-sleeves - and - knock - the - other-guy's-ears-off kind of a ball game,

Continued on Page 21, Column 3

Cards Win 5th in Row; Walters Beaten; Reds' Rally in 9th Fails

CINCINNATI, Aug. 31 (A. P.).—The St. Louis Cardinals turned back a ninth-inning bid by the Cincinnati Reds today to win their fifth straight 6 to 3 and keep the National League lead.

Trailing 6-2, the Redlegs loaded the bases in the ninth when Relief Pitcher Harry Gumbert walked Eddie Joost after Bill Werber and Harry Craft had singled. Bill Crouch replaced Gumbert and let Werber score on a balk, but Mike McCormick grounded for the third out.

Morton Cooper of the Cards beat Bucky Walters of the Reds for the third time out of four, although both pitchers gave way to relief hurlers for the last two innings.

Walters allowed only five hits, but gave five walks and had a wild pitch and a wild throw. The wild throw,

Continued on Page 21, Column 6

Hogan Scores 275 to Win

17 Under Par, Sets Record; Mangrum Second With 280

By FRED BYROD

Inquirer Sports Reporter

HERSHEY, Pa., Aug. 31.—Ben Hogan, the little Texan who succeeded Henry Picard as golf professional here last spring, wiped out a record set by Picard in 1937 today when he won the $5000 Hershey Open championship with a breath-taking 72-hole total of 275, 17 under par.

Five shots better than Picard's record and five shots ahead of his closest pursuer, Lloyd Mangrum, of Monterey Park, Calif., was the 138-pound Hogan when he hastily tapped in a birdie deuce on the 18th hole for a 3 under par 70.

MANGRUM TRAILED

This tournament developed into a two-horse race after the first round, when Hogan was involved in a four-way tie at 69, with Mangrum a stroke behind. Lloyd clung gamely to Ben's heels, but regardless of what he did Hogan bettered it, with a 67 against a 68 in the second round, 69 against a 70 in the third and the 70 against Lloyd's 72 for 280 today.

And there was even a wider gap between Mangrum and the next in line, Jack Grout, Pittston, Pa., and Clayton Heafner, Linville, N. C., tied at 286. Heafner scored a 72 today, Grout 74.

FAZIO CARDS 67

George Fazio, of Cedarbrook, who had matched Hogan's opening 69 and then gone into a tailspin, bounced back with the day's best round, a brilliant 67 which hoisted him into a four-way deadlock for fifth place at 287 with Sam Snead, Hot Springs, Va.; Denny Shute, Chicago, and Felix Serafin, Scranton.

Gene Kunes, Holmesburg, at 288; Horton Smith, Pinehurst, N. C., 289; Chandler Harper, Portsmouth, Va., 290; John Bulla, Greensboro, N. C., 291; Brothers Mike Turnesa, Fairview, N. Y., and Joe Turnesa, Rockville, N. Y., both 292, and Sam Byrd, Merion; Reg Kirkwood, Huntingdon Valley; Henry Poe, Reading, and Harry Nettlebladt, Farmingham, Mass., all 293, rounded out the list of money-winners.

BEN WINS $1200

Victory was worth $1200 to Hogan, who hasn't been out of the money in 54 consecutive tournaments, and increased his booty for the year to $13,933. Snead, with $9198, is nearest in this respect to Ben, top money winner in pro golf for two years.

Ben exhibited his usual methodical shot-making perfection from tee to green, but poor approach putting gave him some uneasy moments on the

Continued on Page 22, Column 5

Money Winners

1—Ben Hogan (275)	$1200.00
2—Lloyd Mangrum (280)	750.00
3—Jack Grout (286)	500.00
4—Clayton Heafner (286)	500.00
5—George Fazio (287)	287.50
6—Sam Snead (287)	287.50
7—Denny Shute (287)	287.50
8—Felix Serafin (287)	287.50
9—Gene Kunes (288)	190.00
10—Horton Smith (289)	170.00
11—Chandler Harper (290)	140.00
12—John Bulla (291)	120.00
13—Mike Turnesa (292)	100.00
14—Joe Turnesa (292)	100.00
15—Sam Byrd (293)	20.00
16—Reg Kirkwood (293)	20.00
17—Harry Nettlebladt (293)	20.00
18—Henry Poe (293)	20.00

Art Gallagher Triumphs Twice In Middle States Rowing Event

Art Gallagher, 23-year-old Penn Athletic Club sculler, moved a step nearer the single sculling pinnacle of the United States when he scored two victories in the 50th annual Middle States regatta on the wind-swept Cooper River in Camden yesterday.

Gallagher achieved a long-cherished ambition by defeating Joe Angyal, the lightweight fireman from New York City, in the championship singles race.

Earlier in the day he had won the heavyweight quarter-mile dash, while Angyal took the 145-pound quarter-mile dash rather handily.

Gallagher's victory was especially sweet to the many Penn A. C. rooters in the crowd of 10,000, for in this regatta two years ago at Baltimore, Angyal shattered Joe Burk's record string of 37 consecutive victories. Angyal also won the title last year on the Schuylkill.

Bob Clair, of Worcester, Mass., collapsed after the finish of his race, and it was some time before physicians could revive him after his rescue from the water. He was reported as completely recovered after the regatta. His collapse occurred after his doubles crew, in which he was paired with Albert DeAngelis, finished second in the senior doubles race. It was Clair's second race of the day, and apparently was too much for him. Fairmount won the race when the crew comprising John Kieffer and Charles Kain triumphed by two lengths. Worcester is the national champion. Penn A. C.'s Joe Alessi and Art Gallagher, Canadian champs, were fourth.

FAIRMOUNT LEADER

Fairmount Rowing Association crews topped the field with four victories. In the junior eight-oared shells, the Fairmount crew came from behind in the last 100 yards to win by a bare two feet against a fast field of five prominent Eastern crews.

Bob Coughlin proved an iron man for Fairmount when he stroked two crews to victory, the junior quadruple sculls and the junior doubles, in each of them with Joe O'Keefe. The quad won by seven lengths from the Old Dominions, of Alexandria, Va., and the double by eight lengths from Virginia B. C., Richmond. The fourth victory was an unexpected one in the senior doubles. Three Catholic High School oarsmen were in the Fairmount eight which scored its close victory. They were Harry Moore, stroke; Joe Everly, No. 7, and Jim Lobley, bow. The time of 6.16 was good against the strong head wind.

RETURNS AS COACH

Gallagher's two victories, and a surprising triumph by the Penn A.

Continued on Page 22, Column 3

Motorcycle Title Is Won by Hayes

By PERRY LEWIS

Tom Hayes, from Dallas, Texas, won the 100-mile national motorcycle championship at Langhorne yesterday.

A crowd of 20,000 saw the youth from the Lone Star State get his first call from the announcer at the end of the 50th mile, when he rode into fourth place. From this point onward, Hayes steadily bettered his position. At the end of the 60th mile he had moved into third place, and 10 miles later was second to June McCall, Salisbury, Md.

When McCall had the misfortune to blow his tire on the 76th lap, Hayes went into first place, and stayed in front to the finish. The winner's time was 1.15.46.

Eddie Kretz, from Wilmer, Calif., the defending champion, took second place, finishing about a half mile behind the winner after steadily moving up from third place. Over the last 20 miles, Hayes and Kretz fought a desperate battle of speed and at one time the Californian was only a quarter of a lap behind the leader. But after the 95th mile had been called, Hayes stepped on it and steadily increased his lead.

Third place went to Bill Huber, of Reading, while Andy Drobeck from Reading collected fourth money and John Spiegelhoff, of Milwaukee, was fifth.

Only one serious accident marred the program. It sent John Karpowich, of Bethlehem, to the Mercer Hospital in Trenton with a fractured right leg.

CRASHES INTO RAIL

On the fourth lap of the 100-mile event, Karpowich went into a skid coming out of the north turn and crashed into the rail.

When the ambulance reached the scene, physicians decided it would be necessary to put the injured man in a splint right on the spot and while

Continued on Page 20, Column 3

Spartons, S. E. Phils Score Shutouts

Sparton A. A. and the Southeast Phils scored shutouts in the Philadelphia Amateur League race yesterday afternoon. Sparton blanked the Black Tigers, 4-0, at 26th and Morris sts., while the Southeast Phils were whitewashing Jefferson, 6-0, at Front and Mifflin sts. In the other game in the same circuit, the West Philadelphia Ramblers gained a 13-7 victory over the Cambridge A. A. at 44th st. and Parkside ave.

Harrisburg Wins Twice, Takes Title

HARRISBURG, Aug. 31 (A. P.).—The Harrisburg Senators clinched the Interstate League pennant today by sweeping both ends of a doubleheader with second-place Hagerstown, 4 to 3, and 4 to 2.

The first game went to 11 innings before Danny Taylor supplied the winning blow—a resounding double that scored Bill Luzansky who had walked. By taking this contest, the Senators made sure of the title. They had been three and a half games in front of Hagerstown with four left to play.

BRINSKY HITS HOMER

Officials first announced 5000 persons jammed Island Park for the crucial series, but later revised their figures to 3933.

Emil Brinsky homered in the eighth inning of the first game with two on to account for Hagerstown's three runs as the home club scored in the third, fifth and ninth.

In the second game—seven innings—the Senators accounted for tallies in the first three frames and the fifth as young Charley Miller put on a fine pitching exhibition to halt the visitors. The 20-year-old Harrisburg youngster gave up only four hits, three of them in the first inning.

TWO CIRCUIT CLOUTS

Harvey Johnson homered in the second inning of the nightcap and Luzansky followed suit in the third.

Continued on Page 22, Column 8

Helmer Wins Comet Race

BRETON WOODS, N. J., Aug. 31.—Phil Helmer, of Westmont, held a winning hand on the helm of the Spider today and won the Class B race at the Breton Woods Yacht Club. The yachting events there today were a part of the club's annual water carnival in which swimming events and a decorated boat contest were other features. Second to the ancient Spider was Comet No. 1898, sailed by Robert Browski and another comet, No. 1507, finished third with Bruce Hargan sailing.

In the Class A event, Joseph Crate, of South Orange, won in his Joan, leading Henry Reeves, of Westmont, by 50 seconds. The VI, the Reeves boat, was across the line more than two minutes ahead of the third-place Nixie, sailed by Starley Okell, of Cranford.

Macks Lose, 5-3, Beat Boston, 3-2

Special to The Inquirer

BOSTON, Mass., Aug. 31.—An astonishingly large crowd of 22,570 watched the A's and the Red Sox split even in the east wind-saturated atmosphere of chilly Fenway Park this afternoon. And it was Phil Marchildon who saved the day for the Macks by winning the second game, 3 to 2, called by darkness at the end of the seventh, after the Red Sox had hammered out a 5-3 verdict in the opener.

A'S DROP TO 7TH

The Sox moved into second place by sharing the bill as the Chicago Sox were beaten twice by the St. Louis Browns, 12-8 and 5-4, at St. Louis. The A's, in turn, dropped to seventh place in the standings.

Sam Chapman came very close to being the A's hero of that opener. He made his 23d homer of the season off Heber Newsome in the fourth inning with two pals on base, giving his side a 3 to 1 lead for the time being. Then Ted Williams, Sox league-leading slugger, went to town on a Jack Knott pitch in the sixth with two on and lined it right into the teeth of the sturdy east wind for his 31st homer of the season. That put the Hose ahead, 4 to 3, and they made a fourth run in the same frame before being retired.

MARCHILDON WILD

Marchildon's control was not so hot. He walked 10 men, but three of these strolls were intentional passes to Ted Williams. Phil let Ted swing only once and that was with none out in the fifth, when he sent up such a high, wavering foul that Frank Hayes finally caught it but fell down in a dizzy swoon after making the connection. That gives you a sketchy idea of how high up this sock went.

Marchildon pitched with plenty of courage, however, and he restricted the Sox to three hits in those seven frames, all singles. And to his credit you must write down that he scored

Continued on Page 21, Column 1

McCarthy Soon To Leave Hospital

WASHINGTON, Aug. 31 (A. P.).—The condition of Joe McCarthy, manager of the New York Yankees baseball team, was said by his physician today to be considerably improved.

McCarthy is confined to a hospital with gall bladder trouble. Dr. Hugh H. Hussey, the physician, said he thought he would be released within a few days.

Phils Divide With Braves

Boston Triumphs In 1st Game, 8-3; Quakes Win 2d, 8-5

By STAN BAUMGARTNER

Just when it appeared the Phillies were going to absorb a double shellacking and go down for their fifth set-back, they rallied in magnificent fashion to win the second game of the double-header from Boston yesterday at Shibe Park to split a twin bill before 5661 people.

Boston won the first game, 8 to 3, when they uncorked a five-run rally in the fifth inning to erase a 2-1 lead by the Phils.

Lobert's men won the second game in practically the same fashion when they exploded five runs in the same fifth inning to overcome a 2-1 lead held by the Braves and march on to their ultimate triumph.

THRILLING FINISH

They had a much harder battle to the finish in this encounter, however, for the New Englanders kept pegging away at Relief Pitcher Pearson and had the bases loaded, two out and the score at 8 to 5, when Danny Litwhiler jumped up against the left-field wall to make a sensational catch of Demaree's bid for a home run.

Had the ball gone safe three runs at least would have scored and Demaree would have been in position to score what might have been the winning run on another safety.

The Braves took a 1-0 lead in the second inning, but Joe Marty tied it at 1-1 with a home run into the left field stands in the fourth. Boston took the lead off Starting Pitcher Podgajny with another run in the fifth.

RIZZO COMES THROUGH

The Phillies then went to work. May started the inning by walking, but was forced at second by Bragan.

Continued on Page 21, Column 4

Baseball Facts

AMERICAN LEAGUE

YESTERDAY'S RESULTS

Boston, 5; ATHLETICS, 3 (first game).

ATHLETICS, 3; Boston, 2 (second game, called end 7th, darkness).

New York, 5; Washington, 2.

Detroit, 7; Cleveland, 5 (first game).

Cleveland, 7; Detroit, 4 (second game).

St. Louis, 12; Chicago, 8 (first game).

St. Louis, 5; Chicago, 4 (second game).

HOW THEY STAND

	W.	L.	Pct.	G.B.
New York	88	44	.667	..
Boston	68	63	.519	19½
Chicago	68	64	.515	20
Cleveland	65	63	.508	21
Detroit	62	69	.474	25½
St. Louis	58	71	.450	28½
ATHLETICS	57	72	.442	29½
Washington	53	73	.421	32

G.B.—Games behind leader.

Today's Schedule, Probable Pitchers and Their Records

New York vs. ATHLETICS at Shibe Park (2 games, first starting at 1.30 P. M.)—Chandler (7-4) and Ruffing (14-5) vs. Ferrick (8-8) and Babich (2-7).

Washington at Boston (2)—Carrasquel (5-1) and Chase (5-14) vs. Harris (4-14) and Dobson (8-5).

St. Louis at Detroit (2)—Harris (11-11) and Niggeling (6-7) vs. Benton (9-6) and Newhouse (9-9).

Chicago at Cleveland (2)—Lee (17-9) and Rigney (11-11) vs. Bagby (9-11) and Milnar (10-15) or Gromek (1-1).

NATIONAL LEAGUE

YESTERDAY'S RESULTS

Boston, 8; PHILLIES, 3 (first game).

PHILLIES, 8; Boston, 5 (second game).

St. Louis, 6; Cincinnati, 3.

Brooklyn, 13; New York, 6.

Pittsburgh, 4; Chicago, 3.

HOW THEY STAND

	W.	L.	Pct.	G.B.
St. Louis	81	45	.643	..
Brooklyn	82	46	.641	..
Cincinnati	69	56	.552	11½
Pittsburgh	68	57	.544	12½
New York	60	66	.476	21
Chicago	56	73	.434	26½
Boston	52	74	.413	29
PHILLIES	36	89	.288	44½

G.B.—Games behind leader.

Today's Schedule, Probable Pitchers and Their Records

PHILLIES at New York (2)—Blanton (6-11) and Pearson (4-12) vs. Schumacher (10-10) and Carpenter (7-6).

Cincinnati at Chicago (2)—Vander Meer (13-11) and Derringer (9-13) vs. Mooty (7-5) and Root (7-7).

Pittsburgh at St. Louis (2)—Heintzelman (8-9) and Lanning (8-8) vs. White (16-4) and Pollet (2-1).

Boston at Brooklyn (2)—Javery (8-9) and Johnson (6-10) vs. Davis (10-6) and Fitzsimmons (5-1).

The Philadelphia Inquirer

PUBLIC LEDGER

An Independent Newspaper for All the People

FINAL CITY EDITION

CIRCULATION: August Average: Daily 414,720, Sunday 1,095,343 — a b d e f g h — FRIDAY MORNING, SEPTEMBER 5, 1941 — Second Largest 3c Morning Circulation in America — THREE CENTS

 VOL. 225, No. 67

SUB ATTACKS U. S. DESTROYER; SHIP SAFE, FIRES BACK AT FOE

Today

U. S. Cringes in Crisis
Inflation at Hand
Labor, Farm Demands
Political Dilemma
Roosevelt Should Act

By Paul Mallon

WASHINGTON, Sept. 4.

THIS Government seems to me to be cringing in the face of a crisis. Mr. Roosevelt and Mr. Henderson told us a dangerous inflation was at hand, and they said nothing to make us think it could be avoided.

They have recommended some strong legislation which will enable them to take hold of the price situation they foresee, but the legislation is tied up in Congressional committees where cotton Senators do not like it. The Senators' attitude is that the cotton farmer has suffered for many long years, and now is his time to get his just dues. They don't think a little inflation would hurt the country. But every reasoning man knows that every time you lift the price of cotton you cut a wage.

We are in a condition where a lot of people who have only made $20 a week in all their long lives, are now making $90 and $100 a week. Naturally they want to spend it. If they spend it, as they must, they create a demand for goods of which there is already a shortage due to our defense needs and the demand for British sustenance. So where are we?

We are just in the middle of a stream in which the farm bloc and the labor bloc seem to be pushing us into what they think is the best economy for the country and it is certainly best for them.

High farm prices and high labor wages sound like something we ought to have. There would certainly be nothing greater for the country as a whole than a farm price of 110 percent parity, which is the point at which Congress now is trying to fix it.

There would be nothing better from labor's standpoint than a wage which gave it a similar superior hold on the economic system.

But what about us other people? What about the consumers? You can't fix a farm price at an outstanding degree of prosperity, and a labor wage at what labor thinks it should be, and still have a functioning economic system. That's simple common sense.

In a runaway situation, such as we have now, it is obvious that someone has to step out and exert some measure of control. You just can't let a democracy run away with itself. There are fundamental things that you must correct in their inception.

And as a columnist, writing about what I see and hear, I think the time has come when Mr. Roosevelt should stop asking the farm and labor blocs what he should do and step out and assert the leadership which we know is for the common good of all.

Unless he does, the country is sure to arrive at the destination which he and Mr. Henderson have so gloomily forecast.

Defense expenditures now are running about $1,300,000,000 a month. The Government wants to get them up to $3,000,000,000. They tried a tax bill to siphon some of the superfluous defense spending back.

They are trying to sell bonds, but are not selling very many, because they can't sell bonds against an inflationary situation. They are trying to curtail the availability of credit to effect the same result.

The results so far are nil. They are faced with a predicament that apparently they don't dare to face. They must take steps, which the farm bloc and the labor bloc do not like.

They are being crowded into a political dilemma. But as everyone else knows the answer, it will not be long delayed.

11 BIG OIL FIRMS WILL USE TANK CARS IN CRISIS

Agree to Move to Ease Shortage in East After Railways Accept Rate Slash

By CHARLES H. ELLIS, JR.
Inquirer Washington Bureau

WASHINGTON, Sept. 4.—Representatives of 11 leading oil companies tonight agreed to use all available railway tank cars to relieve the shortage on the East Coast.

The agreement was signed by officials of the companies during a long conference with railway men, at which the latter offered to reduce rates by as much as 50 percent.

HOPE TO MEET NEEDS

While there was no indication that **the agreement would result in an end** to the 10 percent cut in deliveries to dealers on the Atlantic Seaboard or the 7 P. M. to 7 A. M. closing of gas stations, Ralph K. Davies, acting defense oil co-ordinator, announced:

"With the co-operation of the oil companies with the Office of Petroleum Co-ordinator, it remains the hope of this office that more drastic restrictions and curtailments on the use of gasoline may be avoided and that supplies of industrial oils and oil for heating homes can be brought

Continued on Page 5, Column 4

Hit-Run Dies As Victim Of Hit-Run

A young defendant failed to appear in Quarter Sessions Court yesterday to answer charges of hit-run driving because he had died under the wheels of another hit-run driver's car.

In a quiet voice, a detective announced to Judge Edwin O. Lewis when the case of the Commonwealth against Stephen Zobowicki was called:

"The defendant is dead. He died the victim of a hit-run driver."

Detective Sergeant John M. Thistle of the Accident Investigation Squad then explained the circumstances of the strange case.

Zobowicki, who was 18 and had

Continued on Page 2, Column 5

SENATE VOTES CUT IN INCOME TAX EXEMPTION

43-23 Margin Makes $15 a Week Salary Subject to Levy; New Bill Forecast

By RICHARD L. HARKNESS
Inquirer Washington Bureau

WASHINGTON, Sept. 4.—The main feature of the Administration's new $3,679,800,000 defense revenue bill—lowering of personal income exemptions to a point where the Government will collect taxes on salaries of $15 a week—today won approval of the Senate by a formal roll-call vote of 43 to 23.

By almost a two-to-one margin, **the Senators adopted recommendations of President Roosevelt and its own Finance Committee to slash allowable deductions from $2000 to $1500 for married persons and from $800 to $750 for unmarried individuals.**

NEW BILL LIKELY

Then, with Majority Leader Alben W. Barkley (D., Ky.) admitting the Administration may have to offer a second tax bill this year to pay mounting defense costs, the Senate approved excess profits taxes on business below the level passed by the House and refused to increase present levies on gifts and estates.

As result of the six-hour session, the record-breaking tax bill was pushed near the point of passage. Only one hurdle remained — the brewing battle over the Senate Finance Committee amendment outlawing separate income tax returns in the eight States having community property systems for husbands and wives.

FILIBUSTER HINTED

There were reports — they could not be confirmed—that Senators Tom Connally (D., Tex.) and Allen J. Ellender (D., La.), representing two of the eight States, were threatening to filibuster the measure because of the amendment.

The 43-to-23 rollcall vote slashing income tax exemptions came on the proposal of Senator Robert M. La Follette, Jr. (Prog., Wisc.), to maintain exemptions at the present levels of $2000 and $800.

Senator Joseph F. Guffey (D., Pa.) voted for the additional tax. Senator James J. Davis (R., Pa.) was paired against cutting exemptions.

TAX EFFECT ESTIMATED

The Senate's action, if agreed to by the House, meant that a single person with no dependents would

Continued on Page 6, Column 5

(A. P. Wirephoto)

A SAILOR'S PICTURE OF THE GREER

This photograph of the U. S. destroyer Greer, Philadelphia-built vessel which was the target of attack by submarine, was made by a member of the crew.

FIRST U. S. AID SHIP REACHES SIBERIA IN DEFIANCE OF JAPAN

WASHINGTON, Sept. 4 (U. P.).—The American tanker L. P. St. Clair has arrived safely in Vladivostock with a cargo of gasoline for the Soviet Union without molestation by Japan, which had sharply protested the routing of the ship through Japanese waters, the State Department revealed today.

Safe transit of the vessel, one of four American merchantmen carrying war supplies to Russia through the Sea of Japan, had been awaited with some trepidation. In effect it was a showdown test of President Roosevelt's determination to preserve his freedom-of-the-seas policy.

TEST MAY BE DELAYED

Had the tanker been detained, some quarters believed it possible that already tense Japanese-American relations might have exploded. Russia, too, might have become embroiled. Moscow had warned Japan that any interference with the vessel would be considered an unfriendly act.

It was pointed out, however, that

Continued on Page 8, Column 1

FRAUD IS REPORTED IN JOBLESS CLAIMS

Inquirer Harrisburg Bureau

HARRISBURG, Sept. 4.—Because of fraudulent unemployment claims which have been paid, a huge amount of money has been leaking out of the State's $180,000,000 unemployment fund for more than a year.

That was revealed here today when it was made known that a report describing the situation was submitted to Attorney General Claude T. Reno eight months ago.

21 EMPLOYERS CHECKED

How great is the amount which has thus been lost cannot be determined without an exhaustive check-up of compensation cases throughout the State.

However, spot checks made of the records of 21 employers in six counties early this year turned up losses of $33,000 which had been claimed fraudulently in 965 cases.

That check-up was made by employees under David R. Perry, special Deputy Attorney General in charge of the legal division of the Bureau of Unemployment Compensation.

The results of the check-up were contained in a report submitted by him in January to Attorney General Reno, in which a protest was registered against a Federal Social Security Board order that Perry's investigating staff be cut from 10 to two.

The claims which have been paid out, it was learned from competent

Continued on Page 2, Column 6

(A. P. Wirephoto)

LAURENCE H. FROST

Lieutenant Commander in charge of the destroyer Greer attacked by a submarine en route to Iceland.

Nazi-Swiss Wire Link Cut in Air Alarm

BERN, Switzerland, Sept. 5 (Friday) (A. P.).—Communications with Berlin were restored early today after being cut for several hours because of an air raid alarm in the German capital.

The communications were cut about 11 P. M. Swiss time and were restored around 2 A. M. today.

During the period it was impossible to reach Berlin by telephone or telegraph from Bern.

Cario, Suez Canal Raided

CAIRO, Egypt, Sept. 4 (A. P.).—One person was killed and 21 injured in an air raid on the Cairo and Suez Canal areas last night, it was reported today.

NEW NAZI ATTACKS HALTED ON DNIEPER AND AT LENINGRAD

The Soviet Union asserted yesterday that her army before Leningrad was standing firm and repelling assaults by fresh German forces while Russian troops in the Ukraine were turning back German efforts to cross the Dnieper River. Russia also claimed new gains in counter-attacks at the approaches to Kiev, Ukranian capital.

The Germans stressed action along the Black Sea coast, where they reported smashing a Russian attempt to land troops, and also claimed to have destroyed two Red divisions on the central front.

Prime Ministers Churchill of Britain and Mackenzie King of Canada appealed for American support of Britain in every field, the latter suggesting a U. S. guarantee of support for Britain similar to that Churchill made to the U. S. concerning Japan.

Arrival in Vladivostok of an American tanker carrying fuel for Russia, against which Tokio had complained vigorously, was announced officially.

MOSCOW, Sept. 5 (Friday) (A. P.).—The Red Army before Leningrad is standing fast and "consuming" assaults by masses of fresh German troops, while other Soviet troops to the south in the Ukraine are beating back new German attempts to cross the Dnieper, the Russians reported today.

The early-morning communique told of the Dnieper battles and said fighting raged along the entire front

NAZI TRANSPORT SUNK

It also said Russian planes and torpedo boats sank one German transport and two torpedo boats in the Baltic, Leningrad's sea front, but did not disclose whether the transports were attempting any new Baltic landings.

The account of the Leningrad

Continued on Page 11, Column 4

Depth Bombs Loosed, Fate of Raider Unknown

WASHINGTON, Sept. 4 (A. P.).—A submarine of undetermined nationality and a United States destroyer took part in an actual shooting exchange in the North Atlantic today—marking the first hostile action against an American warship since the war began.

The submarine fired a burst of torpedoes at the destroyer Greer, which was carrying mail to Iceland. The Greer, unhit, then counter-attacked with depth bombs.

With the exchange, the first "incident" consequent to the activities of the Navy's Atlantic Patrol and occupation of Iceland had occurred, its results at sea uncertain and in the broader field of international relations a matter of conjecture.

The Navy, announcing the skirmish, **said only:**

"The U. S. S. Greer, en route to Iceland with mail, reported this morning that submarine attacked her by firing torpedoes which missed their mark. The Greer immediately counter-attacked with depth charges.

"Results unknown."

LOCATION OF ATTACK NOT KNOWN

Quickly the long awaited news of any occurrence tending to draw the United States closer to the war spread to the far corners of the world.

The exact time of the short-lived battle was not made known, but a veteran submarine officer was of the opinion that it came after daylight.

"You can't see a torpedo track at night," he commented.

While the position of the encounter was unknown, too, in the light of what is known of the range of submarines and the activities of the Navy, it was assumed that it probably occurred somewhere in the vicinity of Greenland or Iceland.

BERLIN HAS NO KNOWLEDGE OF ATTACK

(In Berlin the German Navy Department and other Berlin authorities available early Friday said they had no knowledge of the reported submarine attack on an American destroyer as announced by the U. S. Navy.)

Immediate reaction in Congress indicated surprise that any submarine would attack a United State destroyer.

Cool heads in Washington urged that the country not be excited, but their apprehension was nevertheless apparent.

The Navy rested on its three-sentence statement and closed its Information Offices for the night, leaving the details of the attack on the Greer to speculation, and investigation elsewhere.

The Greer, built in 1918 in Philadelphia, has a silhouette identical with those of the 50 World War de-

Continued on Page 8, Column 2

IN TODAY'S INQUIRER

THE WEATHER

Official forecast: Eastern Pennsylvania, New Jersey and Delaware—Partly cloudy and warmer today and tomorrow, with a few scattered afternoon showers.

(Daylight Saving Time)

Sun rises	6.31 A.M.	Sets 7.26 P.M.
Moon rises	7.26 P.M.	Sets 6.19 A.M.

Other Weather Reports on Page 2

Lines on the News

There's Real Pathos Here In Story of 'Klondike'

Oldtime Handbook Operator Had Case to Solve—And He Did It!

By BOB FRENCH

PARI-MUTUELS, as we have stated more than once, have taken much of the color out of horse racing. The favorite stories of horse players stem back to the days of the open book, because the problems of the handbook operator at a track were intensely human. And humanity is the best source of humor.

Among the quaint characters who operated the betting rings in the oral wagering days in New York State was one Klondike. Why he was called Klondike no one knew. His accent betrayed his Russian origin and it was suggested that he was called Klondike because he had been thrown out of Alaska shortly after the Seward purchase.

Klondike kept on getting thrown out of places, and was not allowed to make book with the big operators in the club houses of the race tracks. He wasn't too sure of his ability to make prices either. Therefore, he retained two runners, one to observe the odds and action in the clubhouse, the other to check on his fellows in the ring.

ONE day a three-horse race came up. After getting the line from Lob and Ike, Klondike chalked up the odds on the board, and awaited his players.

In a very short time Lob came rushing from the clubhouse, quite out of breath.

"Rub out that top horse, Klondike," he gasped. "The clubhouse is loaded, and they're coming over here."

In a flash, Klondike had "rubbed out" the top horse. He'd take no bets on that one.

Moments later the faithful Ike came on the gallop from nearby books. He was equally excited.

"Klondike, Klondike," he roared. "There's a ton o' money for the bottom horse. Rub him out, quick!"

Klondike rubbed out the bottom horse. Just one horse, the middle one remained on his board to be played. He looked ruefully at the board, shook his head, and then slowly erased the last remaining horse.

"Vell," he sighed. "It should happen to me. I like that one myself."

Censored Again

A [illegible] Bryn Mawr well to do
Writes quips for The Inquirer, too
The censor deletes
Half the good stuff by Skeets
$*&*-?$ to you.*

YOUNG GEORGE

• • •

A Boost for Ches

If it's true that your contributions go all your work, I'd like to put in a good word for Ches Peek of "Covetown." I like his original humor and think he's on a par with the famous Chet Shafer of the Chicago Daily News. K. R. O.

• • •

WEASEL WORDS
What we need is young blood."
W. J. H.

• • •

Philadelphia Story

(From the play by play account of last Friday's game between the Phillies and the Cubs.)

First Inning

Phillies — Murtaugh walked, Benjamin flied to Nicholson. Murtaugh stole second. Marty struck out. Murtaugh went to third on a bad pitch. Etten struck out. No runs, no hits, no errors, one (Murtaugh) left on base. SHEF

• • •

HOMER "and" HANK": Your addresses are lost.

• • •

Hard to Digest

It sounded like the windup of a picnic the way the horses finished in the third race at Aqueduct the other day. Grand Party was first, Blueberry Pie was second and Strawberry finished third. We wonder what would have happened if Ice Cream was in the race.

• • •

FAMOUS ASIDES
Curb Service
LOUIE DE BONBON

• • •

Sound Effects Contest

We've been going mad trying to find a way to spell one of the commonest expressions in everyday speech. Perhaps your contribs can help. It's a cinch to spell

Uh-huh,

meaning yes. But what about those two shorter and more significant grunts which mean no. The best we can do is

UH-uh,

but we've never seen this in print and it looks too much like "Uh-huh" to entirely satisfy us.

PROF & DOC

• • •

With kindest regards:
Goodby, Cards."

DODGER FAN

• • •

Famous Comebacks

Frost

P. O. M.

• • •

we'll get by • • • when others try

Famous Last Words

License revoked.

LITTLE BILL

GOLF IMMORTAL ARRIVES IN CITY OF GREATEST CONQUESTS

Bobby Jones (left), who completed his "double grand slam" at Merion in 1930, reached Philadelphia last night to play exhibition matches prior to the Henry Hurst invitation tourney at the Torresdale-Frankford C.C. He is shown at the 30th St. Station with Ed Dudley, former Country Club pro who will play in the tourney.

Banks Victor In Midget Auto Feature

Michigan Driver Beats Len Duncan; Tappett Forced Out

Henry Banks, of Royal Oak, Michigan, captured the feature race of the midget auto card last night at the Yellowjacket Speedway, winning by a margin of half a wheel over Len Duncan, New York.

Banks trailed Duncan until the last lap, but a last-minute spurt gave him the triumph. His time was 12:14.72. Walt Walker, Philadelphia driver, was third while Johny Ringer, New York, was fourth.

Ted Tappett led the field during the early going. But engine trouble forced him out on the 34th lap. Had Tappet won it would have marked his fifth "main event" victory at the Speedway. He was leading by 50 yards when forced out of the race.

First qualifying heat (12 laps) Six to qualify for semi-finals: 1. Ted Tappett, Detroit; 2. Rex Records, Philadelphia; 3. Lyle Dickey, Los Angeles; 4. Tony Bonadias, New York City; 5. Bob Lang, Philadelphia; 6. Johnny Pearson, Wilmington, Del. Time—2:53.56.

Second qualifying heat (12 laps) Six to qualify for semi-finals: 1. Kid Beebe, Philadelphia; 2. Mike Josephs, Philadelphia; 3. Johnny Ringer, New York City; 4. Henry Steiger, White Plains, N. Y.; 5. Andy De Vercelli, Flourtown, Pa.; 6. Lou Volk, Paterson, N. J. Time—2:56.28.

Third qualifying heat (12 laps) Six to qualify for semi-finals: 1. Len Duncan, New York, N. Y.; 2. Walt Walker, Philadelphia; 3. Henry Banks, Royal Oak, Mich.; 4. Ernie Gessell, Hollis, N. Y.; 5. Len Woofsey, Danbury, Conn.; 6. Bill McConnell, Norristown, Pa. Time—2:56.18.

First semi-final (15 laps) Six to qualify for main event: 1. Ted Tappett, Detroit, Mich.; 2. Kid Beebe, Philadelphia; 3. Lyle Dickey, Los Angeles; 4. Andy De Vercelli, Flourtown, Pa.; 5. Tony Bonadias, New York City; 6. Henry Steiger, White Plains, N. Y. Time—3:37.46.

Second semi-final (15 laps) Six to qualify for main event: 1. Walt Walker, Philadelphia; 2. Johnny Ringer, New York, N. Y.; 3. Len Duncan, New York, N. Y.; 4. Henry Banks, Royal Oak, Mich.; 5. Bob Lang, Philadelphia; 6. Lou Volk, Paterson, N. J. Time—3:40.24.

Consolation race (15 laps) Two to qualify for main event: 1. Frank Beebe, Philadelphia; 2. Len Woofsey, Danbury, Conn. Time—3:16.66.

Feature Event (30 laps) 1. Henry Banks, Royal Oak, Mich.; 2. Len Duncan, New York City; 3. Walt Walker, Philadelphia; 4. Johnny Ringer, New York City. Time—12:14.72.

Mid-Atlantic Body Re-Names Officers

Bonniwell Again Heads Association: Committee Appointed for Convention

The Middle Atlantic Association, of the Amateur Athletic Union, last night elected officers for the 1941-42 term in a meeting held at the Broadwood Hotel. Judge Eugene C. Bonniwell again was named president of the organization without opposition.

Also re-elected unanimously were Ralph M. Marlowe, first vice president, Anthony A. Roeser, second vice president, and Frank N. Percival, secretary and treasurer. James P. McGinley was elected handicapper.

DELEGATES ELECTED

Named as delegates to the National Convention were Judge Bonniwell, Marlowe, Percival, McGinley, Robert Hoffman, Charles O. Roeser and Albert Rosenheck. Tying for the other remaining post as delegate were Arthur Justin and James E. Snyder, who will each have one-half vote at the convention to be held here on Nov. 15, 16 and 17.

Alternate delegates named were Anthony A. Roeser, Frank Palermo, William Peck, Martin Conboy, Charles McKee, John F. Kelly and Ernest Winterbottom. Spencer M. Bennett and Harry Radel finished in a tie for the other position.

Walter H. Annenberg was elected delegate to the United States of America Sports Federation convention in New York on Nov. 19. Marlowe was named alternate delegate. This convention will work out plans for the Pan-American games in 1942.

PLAN FOR CONVENTION

Elected to the Registration Committee were Marlowe, Peck, Percival, Rosenheck, Kelly, James Barr and Charles O. Roeser.

Judge Bonniwell announced that plans for the convention here are progressing smoothly, and that arrangements for the entertainment of the delegates are being completed. He is giving a dinner on Thursday night for the members of the Convention Executive Committee.

Comprising this committee are Ralph M. Marlowe, chairman; Walter H. Annenberg, Daniel C. Crawford, Jr., George Elliott, Nathan F. Folwell, Louis Goldsmith, Charles H. Grakelow, Albert M. Greenfield, Guy Gundaker, Charles B. Helms, Robert Hoffman, Arthur Justin, John B. Kelly, Charles Klein, Albert H. Ladner, Jr., Albert H. Light, Judge Harry S. McDevitt, James P. McGinley, James McKaig, August Myers, Leon L. Rains, Charles O. Roeser, Major Stanley W. Root, Albert Rosenheck, Judge Frank Smith, Nathan Snellenburg and Ernest Winterbottom. The president and secretary-treasurer of the Middle Atlantic Association are ex-officio members of the committee.

On display at the meeting was the gold trophy which will go to the winner of the William Riggs Memorial event, a 10,000 metre handicap walk, scheduled for Sunday, Nov. 16, second day of the convention. This test will be sponsored by the Mitchell A. A. The trophy will be placed in competition annually in memory of the sportsman who was well known in amateur wrestling circles.

Kelly Anxious To Buy Phillies

Continued from First Sports Page

Larry MacPhail, lacking the extensive organization of minor league clubs of St. Louis, having no gum fortune to fall back on as in Chicago, they dropped steadily downward until this summer bottom seemed indeed at hand.

MANY RUMORS

Rumors about the Phillies' condition have flown faster and more often than their players, but they remained rumors. The present ownership declined to give up until every resource and possibility is exhausted.

Dissatisfaction with the situation has long been known throughout the rest of the league, but from the league headquarters down nothing could be done about it. The majority of stockholders have been willing to weather it through, so the Phils staggered along.

One of the liveliest reports had Branch Rickey buying into the club, despite the fact he makes $35,000 cash as general manager of the St. Louis Cardinals chain, and is at present preparing to sell more minor league stars than the Phillies have in their lineup.

Another favorite was that Bill Terry of the Giants would head a group of new owners; syndicates were reported forming all over the East, but the Phillies always remained as is.

Said by Connie Mack to be worth a half-million dollars as a franchise, disregarding player worth, the Phil owners have always held out for more than offered. Once, 'tis told on excellent authority, a transfer was well considered only to have it flop when one of the chief stockholders abruptly rose and walked out of the conference.

PRESIDENT SINCE 1932

The present owners have had Nugent in the president's chair since 1932, succeeding William Ruch who came in after the death in 1930 of the long-time Phillie boss, William F. Baker, after whom the old park was named.

The only definite fact in regard to the club known in Philadelphia is that it is finishing last for the fourth straight time.

Jones Will Play In Exhibition

Continued from First Sports Page

(Jack) Kelly, director of the National Physical Education program, and Ed Dudley in still another feature exhibition Thursday afternoon. The match, originally scheduled for today, was postponed when Hope was delayed.

Dudley, former Philadelphia Country Club, now at Broadmoor, Colo., turned in the best practice performance, a two-under-par 68, yesterday at Torresdale-Frankford as the vanguard of the links luminaries arrived for Philadelphia's bigest week of golf since the National Open two years ago.

Bruce Coltart, who holds the course record, a 67, was one stroke behind Dudley. Others practicing included Harold (Jug) McSpaden, Tony Penna, Henry Ransome, Gene Kunes, George Smith, Leo Diegel, John Scheubel and Jack Sawyer.

A dozen or more of the top-flight pros will visit nearby Holmesburg Country Club for a shot-making demonstration under arclights tomorrow at 8.30 P. M.

Perhaps as a forerunner of what is to be seen later in the week Bill Cleary, Torresdale-Frankford member, holed a No. 7 iron for an ace on the 133-yard ninth hole yesterday.

Brooks Top Reds in 17th, 5-1, As Bickering Marks Contest

By JOHN FRYE

Continued From First Page

his heart out was through, but you couldn't tell for sure in the shadows.

Dolf Camilli whipped out a single to left and Lew Riggs sent one to right. That was all for Derringer, who went out in his 14th defeat amid cheers, and Joe Beggs came in.

About now the funny stuff started. Benny Zientara fumbled Joe Medwick's grounder and let in a run. Dick West made another error. Manager Leo Durocher was yelling from the dugout to Mickey Owen, "strike out, strike out." But Mickey singled to left for two runs and the ball game went on. Somewhere along here Jim Turner relieved Beggs and threw what was believed to be a wild pitch, one more run scoring.

Somehow it got along to two down with Dixie Walker hitting an infield fly to third for an automatic out, there being men on first and second at the time. Billy Herman finally fanned on purpose.

But there was still a good chance for the game to be called and the score revert to the 16th inning. Two walks, prolonged all possible, then a single by Harry Craft and an infield out produced the run that kept the Reds from being shut out shortly after 7 o'clock. Casey at last squeezed Eddie Joost's little popper and tossed to first to end the exhibition.

However, not before Manager Bill McKechnie, of the Reds, had suggested a couple of times to Umpire Larry Goetz that the moon wouldn't be up for hours.

FIRES IN BLEACHERS

About the only light on the field at this time was from the big red illuminated numbers on the score board and the fires in the bleachers, but the umpires saw it to the bitterest of bitter ends.

The farcical ending completely blotted out the magnificent work of Derringer and Allen in the daylight innings. For the normal nine frames Zientara, a rookie just up from Indianapolis, was the only Red to get a hit, a scratcher in the third that Reese couldn't quite handle.

Derringer was giving up many more hits, but when it came to scoring, he couldn't be touched. He made Camilli fan with the bases loaded in the third.

For Derringer it was the second extra inning defeat in a few days. Last week the Boston Braves beat him in 15 innings, and on June 22 the Dodgers beat him, 2 to 1, in 16 in the first game of a double-header.

The big Kentuckian showed all the form that made him a great pitcher until a training camp injury, since operated on, laid him low this summer.

CINCINNATI	ab	r	h	o	a	BROOKLYN	ab	r	h	o	a
Joost, ss	8	0	1	7	3	Walker, rf	9	0	2	1	0
Waner, rf	7	0	0	8	0	Herman, 2b	9	0	4	4	3
Werber, 3b	5	0	1	2	3	Reiser, cf	7	1	2	7	0
F. McC'k, 1b	6	0	0	16	3	Camilli, 1b	5	1	1	22	0
Lombardi, c	1	0	1	2	0	Riggs, 3b	8	1	1	4	5
West, c	2	0	0	3	0	Medwick, lf	8	1	2	3	0
a-Gleeson	1	0	0	0	0	Reese, ss	8	0	2	6	9
M. McC'k, lf	4	1	1	5	0	Owen, c	8	1	1	4	2
Craft, cf	4	0	1	3	0	Allen, p	7	0	0	0	4
Zientara, 2b	6	0	2	3	5	c-Coscarart	0	0	0	0	0
Derringer, p	6	0	0	2	2	Casey, p	1	0	0	0	1
Beggs, p	0	0	0	0	1						
Turner, p	0	0	0	0	1						
b-Koy	1	0	0	0	0						
Totals	54	1	7	51	18	Totals	70	5	15	51	24

a-Batted for West in 17th.
b-Batted for Turner in 17th.
c-Ran for Allen in 16th.

Brooklyn 0 0 0 0 0 0 0 0 0 0 0 0 0 0 0 0 5 — 5
Cincinnati 0 0 0 0 0 0 0 0 0 0 0 0 0 0 0 0 1 — 1

Errors—Herman, Joost, Waner, West, Zientara, 2. Runs batted in—Reiser, Medwick, Owen, 2; Koy. Home runs—Reiser. Stolen base—Coscarart. Sacrifices—F. McCormick, M. McCormick, Craft. Left on bases—Brooklyn, 19; Cincinnati, 12. Bases on balls—Off Allen, 4; off Casey, 3; off Derringer, 4. Struck out—By Allen, 3; by Casey, 1; by Derringer, 3; by Turner, 1. Hits—Off Allen, 6 in 15 innings; off Derringer, 14 in 16 (none out in 17th); off Casey, 1 in [illegible]; off Beggs, 1 in 0 (pitched to 3 batters); off Turner, 0 in 1. Wild pitch—Turner. Winning pitcher—Casey. Losing pitcher—Derringer. Umpires—Goetz, Reardon and Conlan. Time—4:03. Attendance—5061.

Reds' Pilot Won't Protest

CINCINNATI, Sept. 15 (U. P.).—Manager Bill McKechnie, of the Cincinnati Reds, tonight said he would not protest today's Reds-Brooklyn game, which Brooklyn won, 5 to 1 in 17 innings.

McKechnie said his reason for not filing a protest on the contest, which ended in darkness, was because the matter of whether there was sufficient light for baseball came under the head of "umpire's judgment."

"It was a mistake to start the 17th inning and another mistake not to call the game when darkness descended, but there is no appeal from an umpire's judgment," McKechnie said.

New York Yankees Down Indians, 4-2

NEW YORK, Sept. 15 (A. P.).—Lefty Gomez got credit for his 15th victory today as the New York Yankees downed the Cleveland Indians, 4 to 2 although the American League champions were outhit, 9 to 6 and Gomez had to be rescued in the ninth inning.

CLEVELAND	ab	r	h	o	a	NEW YORK	ab	r	h	o	a
B'dreau, ss	5	0	1	2	3	Sturm, 1b	4	0	2	10	0
Walker, cf	5	0	1	3	0	C'setti, ss	4	0	0	4	6
Emerson, rf	3	1	2	1	0	Henrich, rf	4	1	1	0	0
Heath, lf	4	0	0	1	0	DiM'gio, cf	3	0	1	1	0
Keltner, 3b	3	0	0	2	3	Gordon, 2b	3	1	1	2	3
Mack, 2b	4	1	2	3	1	Dickey, c	1	0	0	1	0
Hegan, c	4	0	2	4	1	Rosar, c	2	0	0	5	0
F'burger, 1b	4	0	1	6	3	Selkirk, lf	2	0	0	4	1
Smith, p	2	0	0	2	2	Priddy, 3b	2	1	0	0	3
a-Grimes	1	0	0	0	0	Gomez, p	2	1	1	0	0
Gromek, p	0	0	0	0	0	Branch, p	0	0	0	0	0
b-Bagby	0	0	0	0	0						
c-Lemon	0	0	0	0	0						
Totals	35	2	9	24	13	Totals	27	4	6	27	13

a-Batted for Smith in 8th.
b-Batted for Gromek in 9th.
c-Ran for Bagby in 9th.

Cleveland 0 0 0 1 0 0 0 0 1 — 2
New York 1 0 1 0 0 1 1 0 x — 4

Errors—Crosetti. Runs batted in—Henrich, Sturm, Mack, Priddy, Freiburger. Three base hits—Boudreau. Home run—Henrich. Sacrifice—Gomez. Double plays—Keltner, Mack and Freiburger. Left on bases—New York, 2; Cleveland, 9. Bases on balls—Off Smith, 2; off Gomez, 3. Struck out—By Smith, 1; by Gomez, 4; by Gromek, 3; by Branch, 1. Hits—Off Smith, 6 in 7 innings; off Gromek, 0 in 1; off Gomez, 9 in 8 1-3; off Branch, 0 in 2-3. Winning pitcher—Gomez. Losing pitcher—Smith. Umpires—Quinn, Pipgras and McGowan. Time—1.55. Attendance 2775.

EASTERN SHORE LEAGUE
(Final Playoff)
YESTERDAY'S RESULTS
Easton, 6; Milford, 5 (night).
HOW THEY STAND

	W.	L.	P.C.
Easton	3	3	.500
Milford	3	3	.500

TODAY'S SCHEDULE
Easton at Milford (night).

EASTERN LEAGUE
(Final Play-Off)
YESTERDAY'S RESULTS
Elmira, 3; Williamsport, 1 (night).
HOW THEY STAND

	W.	L.	Pct.
x-Elmira	4	3	.571
Williamsport	3	4	.429

x-Won final play-off series.

Dixie Conference Rookie

George Washington University of Washington, D. C., is a newcomer in the Southern Conference football campaign this fall.

Clift's Single, With Bases Loaded, Beats A's in 10th

By STAN BAUMGARTNER

Continued from First Sports Page

[illegible] bigger than one of Ward [illegible] bases were [illegible]

[illegible] followed with his hit and [illegible]

It was rather a sad ending to a [illegible] interesting and well played game. Fred Caligiuri, on the mound for the Mackmen, pitched very cleverly, tied the Browns in knots most of the time with his sidearm roundhouse curve and when he did get in trouble was given sensational support by his mates, Dee Miles, Eddie Collins and Sam Chapman.

Harris was equally effective for the Browns, and, except for a woozy bit of fielding by Ray Cullenbine, on a drive by Frankie Hayes that went for a double in the sixth, he might have won in regulation innings.

The defeat sunk the A's deeper in the cellar and sent the Browns three and one-half games ahead in the battle for sixth place.

[illegible]

Hawthorne Card

[illegible]

Senators Trounce Detroit Tigers, 8-5

WASHINGTON, Sept. 15 (A. P.).—The Senators combed three Detroit pitchers for 11 hits today and defeated the Tigers, 8 to 5, behind Dutch Leonard's adequate knuckle-balling. It was Leonard's 17th victory.

DETROIT	ab	r	h	o	a	WASHINGTON	ab	r	h	o	a
Radcliff, lf	5	1	2	1	0	Case, rf	[illegible]	[illegible]	1	2	0
Gehr'ger, 2b	5	0	0	3	3	Cramer, cf	5	2	3	4	0
McCosky, cf	2	1	1	1	0	Let'as, 2b	4	0	1	1	5
York, 1b	4	0	1	10	0	Travis, ss	4	0	1	[illegible]	[illegible]
Campbell, rf	4	0	0	0	0	San'd, 1b	4	0	1	11	0
Higgins, 3b	3	1	1	0	2	Ortiz, lf	4	1	2	[illegible]	0
Tebbetts, c	4	1	1	6	2	Bl'd'th, 3b	2	0	0	[illegible]	1
Perry, ss	3	1	1	3	3	Evans, c	3	2	1	4	0
Newhous'r, p	1	0	0	0	0	Leonard, p	[illegible]	0	1	0	3
Trout, p	1	0	0	0	2						
a-Rowe	1	0	0	0	0						
Thomas, p	0	0	0	0	1						
b-Wakefield	1	0	1	0	0						
Totals	34	5	8	24	14	Totals	32	8	11	27	12

a-Batted for Trout in 7th.
b-Batted for Thomas in 9th.

Detroit 0 2 0 0 0 0 0 2 1 — 5
Washington 2 3 0 0 0 0 0 3 x — 8

Errors—Travis, Ortiz. Runs batted in—Letchas, Travis 3, Perry, Newhouser, Cramer 3, McCosky, York, Case, Radcliff. Two-base hits—Higgins, Perry, Cramer. Three base hit—York. Sacrifices—McCosky, Bloodworth, Leonard. Double play—Letchas, Travis and Sanford. Left on bases—Detroit 6, Washington 7. Base on balls—Off Newhouser 2, Trout 1, Thomas 1, Leonard 3. Struck out—By Newhouser 1, by Leonard 3, by Trout 1, by Thomas 2. Hits—Off Newhouser 5 in 1 2-3 innings, off Trout 3 in 4 1-3, off Thomas 3 in 2. Losing pitcher—Newhouser. Umpires—Hubbard, Geisel and Grieve. Time of game—2:11. Attendance (estimated) 5,398.

Chicago Sox Lose To Boston Red Sox

BOSTON, Sept. 15 (A. P.).—The Boston Red Sox closed a season's rivalry with the Chicago White Sox today, by defeating the visitors, 6 to 1.

Boston took 16 of 22 games they played. Ted Williams poled out his 35th homer with two on in the 7th inning. Chicago's only run was Dario Lodigiani's homer in the 9th.

[illegible]

Baseball Facts

Continued From First Page

RUNS FOR THE WEEK

[illegible]

10 LEADING HITTERS
(Five Leaders in Each League)

NATIONAL LEAGUE

	G.	Ab.	R.	H.	P.C.
Reiser, Brooklyn	127	500	106	168	.336
Mize, St. Louis	122	458	67	148	.323
Medwick, Brooklyn	124	489	94	156	.319
Hopp, St. Louis	120	392	74	125	.319
Hack, Chicago	141	552	104	175	.318

AMERICAN LEAGUE

	G.	Ab.	R.	H.	P.C.
Williams, Boston	131	420	124	172	.409
Travis, Washington	139	561	97	200	.357
DiMaggio, New York	130	508	116	181	.356
Heath, Cleveland	140	542	81	184	.339
SIEBERT, A'S	121	467	63	156	.334

HOME RUNS
(Three Leaders in Each League)

AMERICAN LEAGUE

WILLIAMS, BOSTON	35
KELLER, NEW YORK	33
HENRICH, NEW YORK	30

NATIONAL LEAGUE

CAMILLI, BROOKLYN	31
OTT, NEW YORK	27
NICHOLSON, CHICAGO	25

RUNS BATTED IN
(Three Leaders in Each League)

AMERICAN LEAGUE

KELLER, NEW YORK	122
WILLIAMS, BOSTON	116
DI MAGGIO, NEW YORK	116

NATIONAL LEAGUE

CAMILLI, BROOKLYN	111
YOUNG, NEW YORK	101
MIZE, ST. LOUIS	100

STOLEN BASES
(Five Leaders in Each League)

AMERICAN LEAGUE

CASE, WASHINGTON	27
KUHEL, CHICAGO	17
HEATH, CLEVELAND	17
APPLING, CHICAGO	12
TABOR, BOSTON	16

NATIONAL LEAGUE

MURTAUGH, PHILLIES	18
HANDLEY, PITTSBURGH	16
FREY, CINCINNATI	16
BENJAMIN, PHILLIES	15
WERBER, CINCINNATI	15
ROWELL, BOSTON	11

INTERNATIONAL LEAGUE
(Play-Off Series)
YESTERDAY'S RESULTS
Montreal, 11; Buffalo, 3.
HOW THEY STAND

[illegible]

x-Won semi-final play-off.

TODAY'S SCHEDULE
No games scheduled.

Rookies Look Good

CINCINNATI, Sept. 15.—Two youngsters who joined the Cincinnati Reds during the late stages of this 1941 National League schedule, made a very decided impression upon Manager Bill McKechnie. Reference is made to Hank Sauer and Benny Zientara, both of whom have a great opportunity to stay with the Reds in 1942.

INTER-STATE LEAGUE
(Final Playoff)
YESTERDAY'S RESULTS
[illegible]
HOW THEY STAND
[illegible]
TODAY'S SCHEDULE
[illegible] at Harrisburg (night).

Westbrook Pegler

Roosevelt Skips Issue In Articles on Court

Fails to Discuss Purpose of Plan To Centralize Lower Tribunals

Paul Mallon is ill. His column, which appears regularly in this space, will be resumed when he returns to work.

PRESIDENT ROOSEVELT has now dropped that other shoe in his two-part discussion in Collier's of the attempt to pack, or unpack, the Federal courts and I find, on careful study of both pieces, that he has entirely evaded discussion of one of the principal points of the original proposal which was slyly expressed and was denounced as iniquitous.

So fast and confusing has been the rush of events in these years of the New Deal, and so superficial is most of our reading on vital issues, that the court fight left most of us with an impression that only the Supreme Court was to have been packed or, if you insist, unpacked. However, the original bill called for the appointment of additional circuit and district judges as well, who obviously would be chosen for their political bias, and there was a further provision, expressed in just two words, "hereafter appointed," that these new men and these men only might be assigned to duty outside their home districts.

Denounced as Hidden-Ball Trick

John C. Knox, the senior judge of the Southern District of New York, a New Dealer himself, detected and denounced this hidden-ball trick in the hearings held by the Senate Judiciary Committee and he deals with that opposition of his in his memoirs, A Judge Comes of Age, published this year. Quoting from his statement to the Judiciary Committee, Judge Knox's book reads:

"Passing now to a feature of the proposed bill that seems not to have been particularly stressed in the hearings had before your committee and which, in my opinion, is almost as objectionable as that having to do with the Supreme Court, I call attention to provisions of the act dealing with the assignment of judges from one circuit or district to another. If the new circuit and district judges who come to power under the plans of the President are to be selected because of their young blood and forward-looking ideas, the bill now under consideration exhibits a consistency of purpose that is of sinister aspect to every man who upon principle, is opposed to the use of a stacked deck of cards."

Puts Finger on Two Stealthy Words

Judge Knox then puts a finger on the two stealthy words, "hereafter appointed," and asks, "What good reason can be advanced for the exclusion from needed service of men who, for years, have demonstrated ability and impartiality and who are qualified by experience to discharge any judicial task that may come before them? If I were asked to answer the question I should reply that, without further information from the proponents of the bill, there is a possibility that somewhere there is someone who fears that judges heretofore appointed will not be amenable to suggestion as to how particular cases should be decided. So far as the Southern District of New York is concerned, I desire that it should never for any purpose whatsoever be beleaguered by a flying squadron of judges who, perhaps under some conditions, might be classified as privateers."

The report of the Judiciary Committee also addressed in similar vein this now conveniently forgotten attempt to pack the lower courts. The committee also put a finger on those two words "hereafter appointed" and said that such a plan "creates a flying squadron of itinerant judges appointed for districts and circuits where they are not needed, to be transferred to other parts of the country for judicial service."

Committee Cites Obscurity of Purpose

To a greater and greater degree," the committee reported, "under modern conditions, the Government is involved in civil litigation with its citizens. Are we then through the system devised in this bill to make possible the selection of particular judges to try particular cases?"

And in the summary of the adverse report the Judiciary Committee flatly charged that the bill was presented to Congress "in a most intricate form and for reasons that obscured its real purpose."

It contains the germ of a system of centralized administration of law that would enable an executive so minded to send his judges into every judicial district in the land to sit in judgment on controversies between the Government and the citizen. It is a measure that should be so emphatically rejected that its parallel will never again be presented to the free representatives of the free people of America."

Here both a judge Democratic in his politics and sympathetic with the New Deal and the Senate Judiciary Committee expose a subtlety and impugn the good faith of its proponents and the committee flatly charges that the real purpose of the bill was obscured.

This whole issue is ignored, however, in President Roosevelt's triumphant and self-vindicating magazine discussion of the fight.

S. American 5th Columns

Nazi Roundups Indicate Continent-Wide Web

By John Lear

BUENOS AIRES, Sept. 17.

LAST March the German diplomatic chiefs in Argentina, Bolivia, Chile, Peru and Uruguay held a conference in Santiago, Chile.

In July the Argentine committee investigating subversive activities seized, aboard a commercial plane, the radio transmitter being carried from the German Legation in Lima to the German Embassy in Buenos Aires under what the German Government termed "diplomatic immunity."

In La Paz, Bolivia, that month, the German Minister to Bolivia, Ernst Wendler, left his post on demand of the Bolivian Government after it announced discovery of a letter addressed to Wendler, signed by a Bolivian Army officer, Elias Belmont, who was stationed in Berlin, discussing a conspiracy to overthrow Bolivia's president.

It is difficult to trace a connection between such widely differing affairs. But here is what persistent investigators have learned to date:

• • •

ARGENTINA—The committee found an "almost military" organization of 60,000 men formed into "cells" under the guise of welfare work, sworn to support Hitler, watched to make sure of their loyalty, punished for lapses, taxed to maintain a system which forces children Nazi doctrine through fairy tales.

Ambassador von Thermann is accused of collecting money from Berlin through Uruguay, Chile and Peru, distributing it all over Latin America. A definite relationship between Nazis in Argentina and Chile, the Argentine committee declared, was established by membership in German societies in Argentina carrying Chilean addresses.

CHILE—Across the border from the places where those cards were discovered, Chilean Government agents reported caches of guns and ammunition, and battle practices complete with machine guns, under direction of a uniformed, army-like organization of 25,000 men wearing Swastikas on their coat lapels.

• • •

BOLIVIA—While Chile was pursuing a careful thumb on the Nazis, Bolivia was arresting the son of her ambassador to Chile. No explanation has been offered for his continued detention. An inquiry into anti-Bolivian activities is continuing.

BRAZIL—German agitation has been quieter as the result of laws against foreign language schools and centralized control of communications. The heavily concentrated German population has been deemed less dangerous since President Vargas declared himself for the United States and his son-in-law quit a job with the Italian Lati airline which crosses the South Atlantic.

PERU—Peru halted activities of the German-subsidized, so-called news agency, Transocean, and grounded a German airline after Congress voted to protest an unauthorized flight over the Ecuadorian border which precipitated a new outbreak in the border war.

ECUADOR—President Arroyo del Rio, blaming Axis influences for Peru's attitude toward the border dispute, closed Ecuador's German-owned airline which carried army officers free and sought permission to fly to the lonely Galapagos Islands south of the Panama Canal.

• • •

COLOMBIA—Has nationalized the German airline after it was found to be mapping approaches to the Panama Canal. Later President Santos broke up a military plot, seized a group of "scientists" exploring the southeast flatlands which are believed to be rich in undeveloped oil and are called a hot-bed of propaganda brought surreptitiously upstream from Brazil.

The Government announced an investigation of reported Nazi air bases on the Caribbean coast mentioned by President Roosevelt in a recent speech.

URUGUAY—The Transocean investigation in Washington really started in Uruguay, where South America's first decisive Nazi inquiry last year disclosed a bomb depot, broke up a cellular organization and put eight Nazi leaders in jail.

PARAGUAY—Decreed death for "Fifth Columnists" a week after the Bolivian putsch was smashed.

VENEZUELA—German technicians have long since been rooted out of strategic oil fields, but a Nazi agent was seized a few weeks ago on oil fields which specialized in aviation fuel. Secret radios still broadcast anti-American talk.

The Inquirer Reporter Inquires

Do you want to know what answer Mr. and Mrs. Philadelphia would give to some question you want to ask? If you do mail your question to The Inquirer Reporter Column, The Philadelphia Inquirer. To the writer of every question that is published The Inquirer will pay $5. Questions not used in this column will not be returned.

TODAY'S QUESTION

Is it advisable for a girl to help finance her boy friend through college on a promise of marriage?—Submitted by Daisy S. Chase, 230 E. Haines st.

WHERE ASKED

Germantown ave. and Lycoming st.

MISS MABEL MELLOR, 4031 N. Nice st., unemployed: "Sure, she should help him along. It wouldn't hurt her at all if she advanced some money to him to help him complete his college education. After all, he will marry her, won't he? She would be doing some good for him and for herself. With a better education, the boy would probably have a better job and would make more money when they are married. It would give both of them more opportunities in life."

MISS MELLOR

ANTHONY CHARLIN, 3970 Germantown ave., gasoline station attendant: "The girl should be pretty careful before she gives any cash to a man. She should be sure she knows him for a long time. If she's sure that he's going to marry her, then I would say it was all right if she did help to finance him in his college education. If she's not sure he's going to marry her, she would be taking a chance, but maybe in the end it would be worth-while."

A. CHARLIN

MISS HELEN WEBB, 3413 N. 19th st., hosiery knitter: "No. If the man has any ambition at all he'll find a way to pay for his own college education. Besides that, the girl is taking a chance with her money. Four years in college gives young men a lot of new ideas and he may become an entirely different person and decide not to marry her. Don't forget a young man can meet a lot of people by just going to college."

MISS WEBB

MRS. MIRIAM GAVIN, 4013 Nice st., housewife: "I don't think so. A boy just starting out to college wouldn't know his own mind. If the girl was his age or younger, she wouldn't know either. They just couldn't take it for granted that they are going to marry after he finishes college. Let the boy pay his own way. That's the safest course for the girl. Even if they do marry, it's not nice for a girl to pay for the man's college education."

MRS. GAVIN

GEORGE MULLEN, 3918 N. Elser st., painter: "A guy who takes money from a girl to pay for his college education must be lazy. He's not much of a man if he's going to depend on the girl. If she lets him get away with that before they marry, after they're married, he'll depend on her to make the living for the both of them. A fellow who asks a girl for funds to help him get through college can't have very much backbone."

GEORGE MULLEN

FRED SHAPFERT, 3302 N. 18th st., automobile mechanic: "The girl is taking a chance on losing her boy friend and her money. Soon as a man gets a little education his views on life and marriage become different. He might change entirely. By the time he's finished with college, he's liable to have another girl friend. A girl is better off putting the money in the bank and saving it for a rainy day."

FRED SHAPFERT

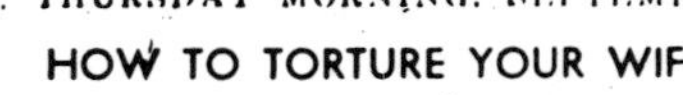

HOW TO TORTURE YOUR WIFE

WELL, I GOT THAT UPSTAIRS PORCH PAINTED—WHAT'S TH' MATTER?
WEBSTER
©1941 N.Y. TRIBUNE INC.

Gen. Hugh S. Johnson

Plan for Survey on Defense Needs And Supplies Is Encouraging, But Late

WASHINGTON, Sept. 16.

IT IS certainly encouraging to know that the new Supply Priorities Allocation Board is now going to try to make a survey of "requirements" of our gigantic war program—what it needs of steel, copper, oil and all other commodities, facilities, power and transportation to supply England, Russia, China and the other "democracies," our own Army and Navy, and, in a small squeaky rump position, our civilian population.

It is encouraging, but it is a hell of a time to be doing it. If it hadn't been written in the book of world war one experience that this was the first step in any industrial mobilization, the common sense that God gave geese should have suggested it.

Prancing in Perfect Orgy of Threats

Instead of that, we pranced up and down in a perfect orgy of priorities, threats of rationing and general disorganization of our economic pattern on cries of "shortage" and famine in supply. The "gasoline shortage" fiasco is a sufficient example without any extended argument on the nature of this blunder.

But a survey of "requirements" is only half of this problem. It is generally conceded that we are or shall be short in some very important items. There are two important things to know. The first is "how many mouths are there to feed?" That should be determined roughly by a survey of "requirements." But the second is equally important. "How much flour is there left in the barrel to feed them?" That needs just as determined an effort as the study of "requirements." It needs a survey of inventories, sources of supply and, above all, a hard-boiled realistic questioning of any of our many customers for this scant supply as to the actual need for what they ask and what they have tucked away in anticipation of shortage.

Directed Against Private Industries

Something of that sort is also going forward, but it is directed principally against private industries. Again referring to the gasoline bungle and to the experience of world war one, experience has proved that the principal hoggers, hoarders and devil-take-the-hindmost boys are government supply departments themselves and their associated agencies or contractors.

As has been repeatedly pointed out in this column, the Government method to date seems to have been an implicit acceptance of anything these grabbers say as to their needs and imperial decrees granting them priorities with almost no regard for what may be a destructive effect on the means of living of our civilian population.

No, there isn't enough flour in the barrel to go all the way round. Some system of rationing and control is necessary. That doesn't necessarily mean ration cards and people standing in queues, but it does mean a studious appraisal of supply and demand—requirements and available materials—and, in defense of our own system, stern denials both to that system and to foreign interests demands that are beyond our reasonable power to produce and deliver.

Delays Indicate Incompetence or Prejudice

It is difficult to write with patience about this subject because the principles are so simple, the experience so well authenticated and so frequently insisted upon, that these delays and woefully belated and half-hearted grasping of these principles indicate an incompetence or a prejudice almost beyond belief.

Months in time and billions in money have been wasted in this error. But the worst may be yet to come. If there is not some prompt and realistic application of them the harm soon to be suffered by labor and small enterprise in this country could surpass anything the depression ever produced.

Sometimes one is reminded of David Harum's sale of a sightless horse to a careless trader. When the horse began butting into brick walls, David's explanation was: "He ain't blind. He just don't give a damn."

Opinions

The signed columns of America's leading writers and commentators appearing each day on this and other pages of The Inquirer are presented so that our readers may have the benefit of a wide variety of viewpoints on important issues of the day.

These viewpoints often contradict one another. They have no connection with the editorial policy of this newspaper and sometimes, in fact, may represent exactly an opposite opinion. The opinions and views expressed belong solely to the writers.

The Inquirer Extends Birthday Congratulations to—

GENERAL EDWARD MARTIN

Commander of the 28th Division, Pennsylvania National Guard, in encampment at Indiantown Gap. When General Martin entered active service in the early part of this year Governor James gave him a leave of absence as State Adjutant General. Born in Greene county, Pa. He attended Waynesburg College and Washington and Jefferson College. He practiced law for several years. A veteran of two wars, his military career dates from 1898 and in the World War he was decorated for distinguished service.

—Photo by Bachrach

WILLIAM B. MARGERUM

Founder and owner of William B. Margerum, victualers, in Reading Terminal Market. Member of the Cheltenham Township Board. A life-long Philadelphian, he was graduated from Old Central High School. He has held the office of president in the Philadelphia Retail Meat Dealers Association, the National Association of Retail Meat Dealers, the Melrose Park Improvement Association and the Board of Trustees of the Tioga Methodist Episcopal Church.

—Photo by Blank & Stoller

S. E. MITTLER

District manager of the Ericsson Line, Inc., the Bull Steamship Line and the Bull-Insular Line. Born and educated on Long Island, Mr. Mittler, who came to this city in 1929, formerly was employed as Port Superintendent for the Bull Lines in New York and has been associated with the Bull Lines for 26 years. During the World War he served with the United States Army as master engineer, senior grade. Member, Philadelphia Traffic Club and the Foreign Traders Association.

—Photo by Phillips

JUDSON C. BURNS

Head of the Judson C. Burns Company, distributors of electrical appliances, which he founded 30 years ago. Born in Clarion, Pa., Mr. Burns, who is a graduate of Muskingum College, is interested in all forms of athletics and takes an active part in Y. M. C. A. and church work. He has been a Bible teacher in this city for more than 30 years and for 13 years has taught a class over the radio. For several years he has been a supporter of the Eighth Street Mission.

Military Expert's Views

War in Ukraine to Give Clue to Russia's Might

Strength of Counter-Attacks Will Shed Light on Air Power

By Major George Fielding Eliot

Formerly Military Intelligence Reserve, U. S. A.

NEW YORK, Sept. 17.

FAR more strategical interest attaches to the reported German advances in the Ukraine than to the slow-moving operations around Leningrad.

The Germans are reported to have established "several" bridgeheads on the eastern bank of the Lower Dnieper River, and to be pushing eastward on a broad front, threatening the communications of the Crimean Peninsula with the interior.

This brings forward the influence of a river line on modern defense. The Dnieper is a broad and deep river, with marshy banks in its lower course; a formidable military obstacle. But modern defense requires great depth, a succession of positions which gradually absorb the shock of the terrifically powerful attack which the weapons of today make possible. A river is a single obstacle, a wet ditch: no more.

Depth Needed to Check Attacker

Extending along the whole of an army's front, as did the Dnieper along the whole of Marshall Budyenny's, it tends, if it is to be everywhere defended, to absorb an undue proportion of troops in a linear defense which is tactically unsound.

It is pretty generally accepted that a determined attack will penetrate any linear defense; unless there are other lines behind (defense in depth) there is little hope of stopping the attacker. There is little hope of defeating him unless there are also mobile counter-attack elements available to hit him hard at the moment when he begins to lose his forward velocity, when he is weakened by defensive fire and has outrun the support of his major artillery.

These counter-attack elements must be both ground and air, for no attacker is without a form of artillery support while his air force is operating overhead.

Depends on Soviet Scheme of Defense

As to the further success of the German operations, a good deal depends on Budyenny's scheme of defense. If the Marshal, depending on the broad "wet ditch" of the Dnieper, has used too many troops in trying to hold that line everywhere, the Germans may gain ground rapidly.

If the Russian commander has, as he did on the Dniester, left the actual defense of the crossings to special outpost elements and local troops, he may be able to launch successful counter-attacks against the German columns.

He has a long front to hold, and probably none too many troops to hold it. He certainly sustained severe losses in the western Ukraine, and had to give up many troops to hold the central front.

The curve of the Dnieper offers opportunity to the Germans to split Budyenny's forces into two parts: one attempting to hold back the German thrust in a northeasterly direction from Kremenchug on Poltava and Kharkov, the other trying to hold back an eastward thrust from the Lower Dnieper against the Crimean communications and perhaps, eventually, the Don Basin.

It is in such a situation, however, that the strategical flexibility of air forces makes them of immense value to the defense. The defense, from well-established bases, can hurl the whole of its air power on the enemy threat which is most dangerous at the moment: the same squadrons can one day assail one enemy force, and on the following day be launched against another enemy force hundreds of miles distant. Much, therefore, depends on the amount of reserve air power which the Russians now have in hand.

Russian Counter-Attacks to Provide Clue

If large scale air operations of this nature do not develop, including concentrated attacks on the German bridgeheads and bridges, we may assume that the Russian air force is at last weakening, finding difficulties in replacing machines and flying personnel, and perhaps difficulties in maintenance and fuel supply.

The same may prove true of Russian armored forces, and the criterion will be the strength and success of the Russian counter-attacks which should now be in progress.

For the immediate future, the eyes of most military observers will be upon the German bridges across the Dnieper, and the very considerable possibilities opened to a vigorous Russian counter-offensive in this area. If it does not develop, there will be ground for believing that the Russian defense is growing weak, and further German successes, even an advance to the Don, may prove possible before the season grows too unfavorable.

Dr. James W. Barton

Active Liver Prevents Symptoms of Allergy

Send today for Dr. Barton's helpful booklet entitled "Eating Your Way to Health" (No. 101.) It gives list of foods rich in calories, in minerals and vitamins and how much you should eat for an all-round diet. Address your request to Dr. Barton, care Philadelphia Inquirer, Postoffice Box 75, Station O, New York, N. Y., enclosing ten cents to cover cost of handling.

FOR many years, many physicians believed that the liver was in some way to blame for migraine—one-side headache. Too much worry or emotion was interfering with the flow of bile and it was the lack of bile that was responsible for the symptoms. When recently, investigators found that allergy—being sensitive to certain substances—was to blame for migraine, I felt that physicians, including myself, were wrong after all in blaming the liver.

That physicians were not altogether wrong in blaming the liver and gall bladder for causing migraine is shown by the number of cases of migraine where draining or removing the gall bladder or giving the patient bile brought a cure of the migraine.

Cured by Draining

Not only migraine but hives, asthma, chronic eczema, intestinal disturbances and hay fever all due to allergy—have been cured by draining or removing the gall bladder.

In the American Journal of Digestive Diseases, Drs. H. Shay, J. Gershon-Cohen, and S. S. Fels, report that they were able to cure a number of cases of the common diseases due to allergy—hay fever, hives, asthma—by simply giving ox bile to stimulate liver and gall bladder and thus more completely filter out the substances causing the symptoms.

What does this mean? This means that if the liver is doing its work of making bile properly, there will be enough bile present to stimulate the liver to be a better filter and to stimulate the gall bladder to empty itself in less time so that more bile will flow down into the intestine to make intestine more active and kill harmful organisms.

Exercise Advised

The best way to keep bile flowing and liver and gall bladder active and so prevent migraine or other allergic symptoms is by bending exercises with knees straight. Bending exercises squeeze the liver and gall bladder.

When vigorous exercise cannot be taken, long deep breaths will push the floor of the chest down against the liver and stimulate liver action.

When little or no exercise can be taken, the use of ox gall or ox bile as prescribed by the physician is used.

Gas-Forming Foods

Q. What causes gas?—L. B.

A. The commonest cause is eating gas forming foods such as cabbage, cauliflower, onions, radishes. A sluggish liver and gall bladder is also a common cause.

Paralysis Symptoms

Q. Please write the early and late symptoms of infantile paralysis.—C. H.

A. Early symptoms of infantile paralysis are about the same as any other children's ailment. Onset is sudden rapid pulse, slight rise in temperature, headache, pain in back, tiredness, restlessness, nose may run, throat, red. Later there is severe stiffness of neck and

DAILY PICTORIAL PAGE

The Philadelphia Inquirer
WEDNESDAY MORNING, OCTOBER 1, 1941 a d e f g 22

"BUBBLE-BATH" COUNTER, WHERE COSMETICS TAX FALLS HEAVILY IS BESIEGED BY WOMEN

Buying Rush Beats New Tax

Yesterday was the last day to buy many varieties of goods before the new Federal Defense taxes go into effect today. "Luxury" items were chiefly affected, and department store counters and specialty shops in down-town Philadelphia were stormed by crowds of women all day. Above: the "bubble-bath" counter in a Chestnut st. store. Below: the perfume counter of a Market st. department store.

LIPSTICKS AND FACE CREAMS ARE QUICKLY SNAPPED UP

SHE WILL BE STATE'S FIRST LADY

Governor Takes a Wife

Governor James will be married today to Mrs. Emily Radcliffe Case, of Doylestown, former house mother at Cornell University, who is shown above. Below, at left, is the home at Doylestown Mrs. Case will forsake for Governor's mansion at Harrisburg. Right, below, is the Presbyterian Church at Doylestown where a simple ceremony will be held at noon.

HOME OF GOVERNOR'S BRIDE

WHERE WEDDING WILL TAKE PLACE

CHILDREN FLEE ROOF FIRE Among the hundreds who fled from Admiral Apartments at 48th and Locust sts., where wooden planks on sun deck burned last night, were Mrs. B. Walton, left, with daughter, Grace, 7; Mrs. K. Behrendt, son Albert, 1.

IT'S JUST RIGHT FOR THE LEATHERNECKS "We'll fight our country's battles, on the land and on the sea," goes the anthem of the United States Marines, and this new amphibian is what they need to help them do it. It's a Roebling amphibian tank, shown hurtling through the waters of the Gulf of Mexico in a test run several miles off the Florida shore, near Hurricane Pass. They'll operate just as easily on land, say the Marines.

Entire Block, Market, 11th to 12th Streets—Store Hours: 9:30 to 5:30 P. M.—Mail and Phone Orders Filled—Call LOCust 5200—Camden WX-1150—Chester or Wilmington Enterprise 1-0160

Fall Snellenburg Week

Philadelphia's Outstanding Store-Wide Sale!

Our Credit Coupon Books Enable you to buy the things you need now and Save during Snellenburg Week

Beautiful Rayon Satin and Crepe

GOWNS

$1.79

Exquisite gowns that you'll be overjoyed to find at such a low price! Soft rayon satin and rayon crepe in lacy and tailored styles; also pretty figured rayon satin in tailored styles. Delicate pastel colors. Sizes 32 to 40.

Lingerie, Second Floor

IT'S FALL SNELLENBURG WEEK!

Men's 55c and 65c New Fall

TIES

39c

Hand-tailored of quality rayons in hand picked patterns and colorings. Hundreds of different styles, all in handsome color blendings to enrich your Fall and Winter attire. Early gift shoppers will anticipate many needs at this low price.

Men's Furnishings, First Floor

IT'S FALL SNELLENBURG WEEK!

$5.95 Pepperell Solid Color

BLANKETS

EACH $4.89

A full double bed size blanket (72x90 inches), woven of a warm, soft mixture containing 50% rayon, 25% wool and 25% cotton. All popular boudoir colors, with wide rayon satin bindings to match. A remarkably fine blanket for under $5.00!

Bed Coverings, Second Floor

IT'S FALL SNELLENBURG WEEK!

Sateen Covered Large Boudoir

CHAIRS

$11.50

A deep, luxurious, extra large chair for boudoir lounging. Well built, with wide seat, tufted back, valance all around the bottom, and fine coverings in a choice of pretty patterns and colorings.

Furniture, Fifth Floor

IT'S FALL SNELLENBURG WEEK!

$3.95 "Classmates" For Youthful

FIGURES

$2.89

Our exclusive designs for young moderns. Stepin girdles in long and short styles, boneless and lightly boned. Several of rayon satin elastic, most of them Talon - zipper fastened. Several all-in-ones included in this important group.

Young Modern Corset Shop, Second Floor

IT'S FALL SNELLENBURG WEEK!

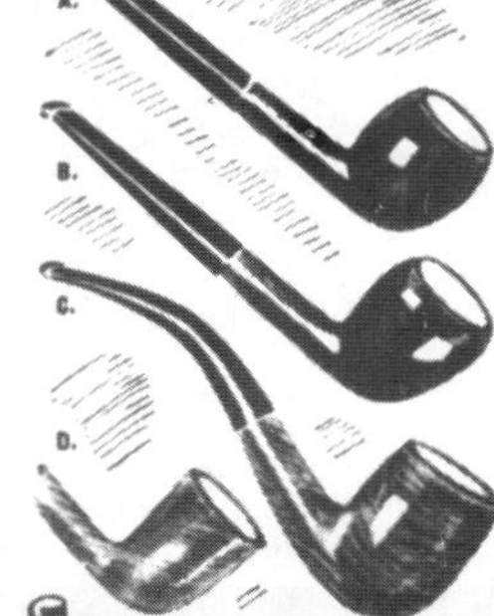

Sale of $2.50 Meerschaum-Lined

PIPES

$1.29

More durable than all-meerschaum pipes, but just the same from the standpoint of smoking pleasure—and pipe smokers say that nothing beats meerschaum for a fine smoke! Lined with genuine imported meerschaum, in 40 different shapes. Gift boxed. Mail and phone orders filled.

Smoke Shop, First Floor

IT'S FALL SNELLENBURG WEEK!

$1.79 Famous Pepperell Duchess

SHEETS

72x108" or 81x99" $1.35

Woven 144 threads to the square inch—which means long, hard wear!

81x108 inches....$1.59
90x108 inches....$1.69

Bedmuslins, Second Floor

IT'S FALL SNELLENBURG WEEK!

Cotton-and-Rayon Damask Dinner

CLOTHS

$1.95

Firmly woven damask cloths of a permanently lustrous cotton-and-rayon mixture in rich solid shades of peach, gold and ivory. Size 57x87 inches. Beautiful pattern.

Matching Napkins, 18c ea.

Linens, Second Floor

IT'S FALL SNELLENBURG WEEK!

Regular $32.00 Fully Equipped

BICYCLES

$25

Two-tone model with white side wall tires. Equipped with electric horn, electric light, streamlined tank, de luxe carrier, New Departure coaster brakes, gothic style mudguards. Red-ivory, blue-ivory, black-ivory. Full sizes for men, women, boys, girls.

Sporting Goods, Third Floor

IT'S FALL SNELLENBURG WEEK!

Women's 35c-50c Hand-Embroidered

HANKIES

29c

Beautifully hand-made handkerchiefs of fine linen in exquisite embroidered styles, mostly of drawn and mosaic types, all imported from abroad.

Men's White Linen Handkerchiefs, 18c

Handkerchiefs, First Floor

IT'S FALL SNELLENBURG WEEK!

$1.19 Knitting or Mending

BAGS

89c

Cretonne and cotton tweed bags of good size, in walnut lacquer finished wooden folding frames. Stand firm when open, with the bottom of bag extended as far as the top. Two pockets for sewing or knitting accessories.

Art Needlework, Fourth Floor

IT'S FALL SNELLENBURG WEEK!

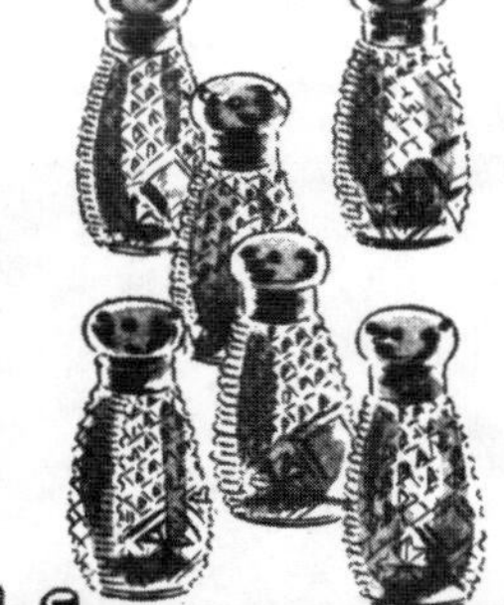

Individual Salt and Pepper

SHAKERS

set of 6 89c

Six sparkling glass individual size salt and pepper shakers all with sterling silver tops. Smartly boxed for gift giving. They'll make welcome additions to anyone's table appointments, and at this modest price are worth buying for future gift giving!

Silverware, First Floor

IT'S FALL SNELLENBURG WEEK!

Women's 50c Soft Rayon

UNDIES

33c

3 for 95c

Fine gauge rayon, long-wearing, smooth textured. Band leg pants, flare leg pants and bodice vests in tearose shade. Well proportioned sizes 36 to 44.

Underwear, First Floor

IT'S FALL SNELLENBURG WEEK!

Samples of New $1.95 and $2.95

COLLARS

94c

Not only collars, but collar and cuff sets, vestees and reveres in this amazing group of beautiful sample neckwear! Dainty lingerie types in crisp tailored styles! White, pink and blue. effects. Styles for every neckline —for business and afternoon frocks! And what values!

Neckwear, First Floor

IT'S FALL SNELLENBURG WEEK!

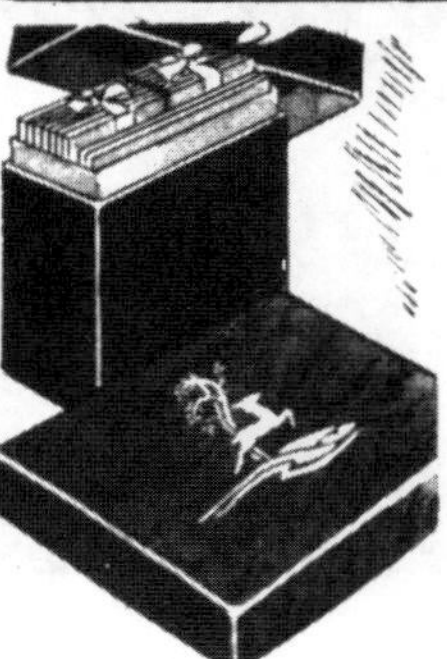

Six Styles of 39c Stationery

BOXES

29c

Handsome gift boxes, covered with paper that looks like leather, all containing fine writing paper and matching envelopes in various sizes and styles. Paper colors are white, ivory and blue.

Stationery, First Floor

IT'S FALL SNELLENBURG WEEK!

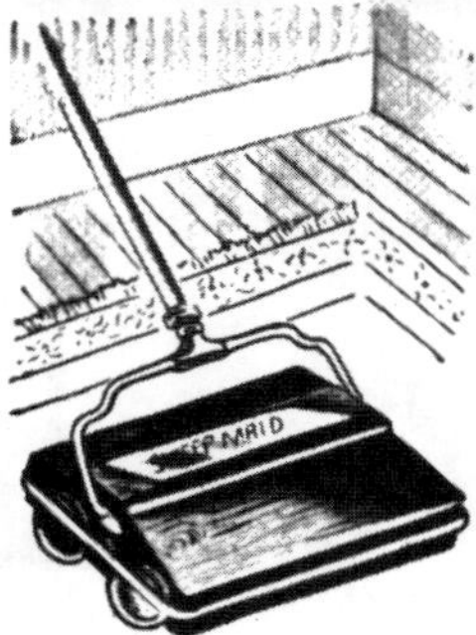

Usual $4.75 Ball-Bearing Carpet

SWEEPER

$2.99

Just 300 at this Special Price! Made with walnut finished wood case, heavy rubber bumper, genuine bristle brush with comb, adjustable wheels for different rug naps, rubber tires on wheels.

Housewares, Third Floor

IT'S FALL SNELLENBURG WEEK!

ECONOMY BASEMENT SUPER SAVINGS FOR FALL SNELLENBURG WEEK

A Saving for Snellenburg Week!

WOMEN'S 59c BOUDOIR SLIPPERS

47c

Simulated alligator with soft padded soles and comfortable Cuban heels. Leather top-lifts. Red, black or blue. Sizes 4 to 8, no half sizes. Serviceable and comfortable.

Snellenburgs Economy Basement

Take Your Choice of a Bargain!

HANDSOME CHAIR OR ROCKER

$6.44 each

As sturdy as they are beautiful! Solid hardwood frames, hand-rubbed to a rich walnut finish. Spring seat and upholstered back. Choose from several wanted colors in smart cotton tapestries.

Snellenburgs Economy Basement

Untrimmed Coats & 2-pc. Suits

$9.85

Smart plaids, herringbones, tweeds and fleeces* Rich new colors. Sizes in coats: 9 to 17, 10 to 20, 38 to 46. Suits, sizes 10 to 18 only. *See label for wool content.

Snellenburgs Economy Basement

NEW SPUN RAYON DRESSES

$2.00

Semi-dress and tailored types. Chic button-down-front coat models. Blue, green, brown and wine. Sizes 14 to 20, 38 to 44.

Snellenburgs Economy Basement

STRONG TRUNKS

$4.44

Made of enameled sheet steel. Steel nickel-plated hardware. Removable tray. Two handles. 30-inch size.

Snellenburgs Economy Basement

NOVELTY PILLOW CASES

25c

"His and Hers" or "Mr and Mrs." cases, charming for gifts. Hemstitched cases, some embroidered. Seconds. Regular size.

Snellenburgs Economy Basement

15c KITCHEN TOWELING

10 yds. 90c

Heavy absorbent toweling for kitchen or hand. Bright colored borders of red, blue, green or gold. Cellophane wrapped.

Snellenburgs Economy Basement

CRINKLED BEDSPREADS

79c

Pretty colorings in this very attractive and serviceable style. Full size.

Snellenburgs Economy Basement

"FENTON" Hand Made GLASSWARE

20c to 90c

Hobnail pattern on white glass with turquoise trim. Vases, bonbon dishes, pin trays, etc. Every piece hand made!

Snellenburgs Economy Basement

36-INCH DRAPERY MATERIAL

25c yd.

Rayon-and-cotton damask in lustrous gold, blue, rust and red. For drapes, pillows, etc. Full pieces.

Snellenburgs Economy Basement

BOYS' CORDUROY KNICKERS

$1.50

Brown or gray ... wonderfully serviceable. Sturdily made and full lined. Knit cuffs. Sizes 8 to 16.

Snellenburgs Economy Basement

"WORTHMORE" CLEANING MOPS

59c

Regularly priced at 79c! Wrings dry without wetting your hands. Efficient and time-saving.

Snellenburgs Economy Basement

CURTAIN STRETCHERS

$1.98

For full-size curtains and doilies. New type folding hinges. Rustless pinchers. Heavy hardware.

Snellenburgs Economy Basement

VELVET RUGS AND A FEW AXMINSTERS

$14

Velvet 6.9x9 ft. in leaf. A few 6x9 Axminsters for first comers. Rich colors.

Snellenburgs Economy Basement

Ready for Winter Men With

BURLY NEW OVERCOATS

$17.95

Extra heavy fabrics ... fleeces, tweeds and herringbones ... that insure you against wintry blasts! Snappy new styles in single and double-breasted models. Raglan or set-in sleeves. Blues, camel hair shades, brown, greens.

Snellenburgs Economy Basement

9x9, 9x12, 9x10.6 Famous

"CRESCENT SEAL" CONGOLEUM-NAIRN RUGS

$3.59 ea.

Seconds of $4.98 to $5.98 Kitchen tile and floral patterns. Every rug bordered and guaranteed for your satisfaction. Packed in individual cartons. Bright, easy-to-clean surfaces.

Snellenburgs Economy Basement

The Philadelphia Inquirer

PUBLIC LEDGER

An Independent Newspaper for All the People

FINAL CITY EDITION

CIRCULATION: September Average: Daily 413,900, Sunday 1,118,287

a b d e f g h FRIDAY MORNING, OCTOBER 17, 1941

VOL. 225, No. 109

Second Largest 3c Morning Circulation in America

THREE CENTS

Soviet Government Fleeing Moscow

Schools Not Concerned With Hungry Pupils

Today

Malnutrition a Blight
But It Can Be Cured
Feed Our Children
Many Go Hungry
In Midst of Plenty

By Fred G. Hyde

PHILADELPHIA'S misfits and outcasts of tomorrow are sitting in its schoolrooms today.

Their older brothers are being called up by the Army for draft service—and being rejected.

As poor in mind as in body, they are the dull, stunted, rickets-ridden products of civic shortsightedness, and their support the price Philadelphia must pay for years to come for letting its under-privileged school children go hungry.

Unless we are to produce still more like them, a drastic cure is in order, Dr. Arthur P. Keegan declared yesterday. He is chairman of the committee on public health and preventive medicine of the Philadelphia County Medical Society.

The cure? Spend money. Lots of it. Put it to work to see that every school child has the proper diet and enough of it. That is the prescription of the man who as chief surgeon of the Bureaus of Police and Fire has examined thousands of candidates for the city's uniformed services, and who has seen what malnutrition in childhood can do to the body of a man.

Today, even in the midst of plenty, many a Philadelphia school child, in the poorer sections of the city, attends class on a diet made up largely of soda crackers, beans and cabbage soup—items that are cheap, have bulk, and go a long way in a big family. Items, too, that supply but a small percentage of the calories, proteins and vitamins needed by growing bodies.

The result is an appallingly large percentage of children who have neither the will nor the capacity to learn. Children suffering from poor teeth, from chronic colds, from all the defects of posture to which inadequate bone structure contributes.

"These conditions can all be traced back to improper feeding of our children," declared Dr. Keegan yesterday. Malnutrition, he asserted, is at the root of the troubles which have caused one out of every two draftees to be turned down by the Army in recent months.

"We didn't take heed of the warning in the past," he said, "but if we take advantage of these lessons, we will not have such a condition in the future.

"If the Board of Education spent twice or four times as much as they do now on buildings, teachers' salaries and textbooks, in building healthy bodies and minds, minds which would be able to absorb the teaching now given the children, it would be worth it.

"If we spent money to feed our undernourished and often unfed children, we could develop a citizenship that could pass any physical test, and not be rejected for Army service when they reached manhood because of physical defects. If we did so all over the United States, we could build an army greater than all the armies in continental Europe."

Delinquency among school children, Dr. Keegan added, can be traced in a great majority of cases to an environment where little if any attention is paid to them during the early days of life. When they attain school age,

Continued on Page 6, Column 2

Of Special Interest Today

Mary Padgett, Woman's Club Editor, reports the speech of Attorney General Biddle before the Women's University Club.

Page 21, Cols. 1-2-3

BOARD OFFICIAL AGAINST ALL ON FREE FOOD PLAN

Business Manager Rejects Survey Showing 160,000 Are Undernourished

Illustrated on Page 6

By ALEXANDER KENDRICK

To 160,000 undernourished Philadelphia school children the paid administrative officials of the Board of Education yesterday said:

"You're no concern of ours."

Given the alternative of feeding the children with free Federal food, or letting their undernourishment become a blot upon a whole generation, the paid officials said, in effect:

"Let 'em starve."

Reminded that they have already had three years in which to adopt some sort of feeding program, the officials said:

"We've got to make some more surveys before we do anything about feeding."

REJECTS MEDICAL SURVEY

The callous attitude was typified by the words of Add B. Anderson, $12,000-a-year secretary and business manager of the board.

He threw out the window a report by Dr. Walter S. Cornell, the director of medical inspection, certifying that 160,000 school children are undernourished in Philadelphia.

He approved, instead, a "survey" made by his non-medical $8100-a-year school cafeteria head, Clarence B. Kugler, showing that only 22,000 children are undernourished.

DIFFERENT STANDARDS

"Dr. Cornell's survey can't be taken into consideration," Anderson declared.

"After all, a doctor's standards of undernourishment might be different from ours.

"We can't judge undernourishment by a doctor's standards."

Anderson himself believes, he said, that the school nutrition problem concerns only 11,000 children—those financially unable to buy food.

In line with his policy of giving food to as few undernourished children as possible—and at the same time preserving the school system's profitable cafeteria system—Anderson then agreed in principle yesterday to a Federal school feeding project here.

138,000 GET NOTHING

But—this project will take care of only 22,000 children, at maximum, and probably only the 11,000 of whom Anderson speaks.

The other 138,000 Philadelphia children who are suffering from undernourishment and the diseases it breeds will get nothing—even though the Federal Government has offered to feed them three times a day.

Further—Anderson's limited project calls for only one meal a day for 22,000 children, instead of three meals for 160,000.

And finally—the feeding project

Continued on Page 6, Column 2

BREAD OR A STONE

Read Editorial "Feed Those Hungry Children!" on Page 14.

TOKIO CABINET QUITS IN SPLIT ON U.S., SOVIET

Stronger Pro-Axis Regime Expected to Succeed Konoye's; Matsuoka Due Back

TOKIO, Oct. 16 (A. P.).—Prince Fumimaro Konoye's third Japanese Government collapsed tonight in the face of a grave impasse on national policy toward the United States and the Soviet Union.

The Cabinet resigned en bloc. Not yet three months old, it had been occupied during most of its tenure with roundabout Washington negotiations and uneasiness caused by the consequences or opportunities to be afforded Japan by Germany's war with Russia.

COULDN'T AGREE

A communique said Premier Konoye and his Ministers had resigned because they could not agree "on the way to pursue national policy."

Most observers considered this to mean that seven weeks of Japanese-American negotiations in Washington had taken a decisive turn unpleasant for Japan.

This was coupled as a major factor in the Cabinet collapse with growing militarist pressure for action against Russia, now that the fate of Moscow itself is in the balance.

Informed sources foresaw the likelihood of more vigorous Japanese foreign policy under a new government, which may take shape Friday. This policy would be characterized, it was believed, as necessary to break the so-called "ABCD" encirclement of Japan—military and economic measures of the United State, Britain, China and the Dutch (Netherlands) from their East Indies bastion.

SENIOR STATESMEN CALLED

(Senior statesmen of Japan were called into conference with Emperor Hirohito at 1 P. M. Friday to recommend a new Premier.

"Those called to confer included Marquis Koichi Kido, Lord Keeper of the Privy Seal; Dr. Yoshimichi Hara, president of the Privy Council; Baron Reijiro Wakatsuki, Koki Hirota, Admiral Keisuke Okada, Admiral Mitsumasa Yonai, General Nobuyuki Abe and Count Keigo Kiyoura.)

The third Konoye Government, formed July 18, after the start of the German-Russian war, saw the eclipse of Foreign Minister Yosuke Matsuoka and of his pro-Axis policies, and might be termed in retrospect an interim regime for a frightened and isolated nation.

MATSUOKA MAY RETURN

Now, Axis-minded Japanese hope the seeming collapse of Moscow and the impasse at Washington will bring a resurgence of Matsuoka's policies of close Axis collaboration, or possibly the return of Matsuoka himself to the Government.

(Competent quarters in London regarded a new pro-Axis Cabinet as a foregone conclusion; in Washington, informed observation was to the effect that Konoye's resignation might mean surrender of the

Continued on Page 10, Column 4

Stalin Reported Staying Behind To Direct Defense

By Associated Press

Officials of the Soviet Government were reported on good authority early today to be evacuating Moscow while three unhalted German offensives directly menaced the capital, and it appeared that Kazan, 450 miles to the east, was becoming the new seat of Soviet authority.

Censorship hid the full extent of the withdrawal, but some informants in London understood in fact that governmental heads had departed, leaving Moscow a capital only in name and in the hands of the Red Army.

(A United Press dispatch from London reported that Premier Stalin and other leaders were remaining behind to direct the defense of Moscow.)

The Soviet Command's communique for this morning indicated no essential change in the critical situation, merely reporting continued fighting on all fronts with particularly heavy losses for both sides west of Moscow.

While the Russian centre apparently was being pushed back toward disaster, the Red far-southwestern anchor was declared to have been smashed. Both the Germans and the allied Rumanians announced that Odessa, on the Black Sea, at last had fallen after 59 days of siege and thus that substantially the whole of the coast from the Rumanian frontier eastward to the approaches to the Crimean peninsula now was in German control. The Moscow radio said that the forces "encircling" Odessa had been "checked and forced to dig in."

The Germans officially claimed that some of their columns were within 60 miles of Moscow from the west. Some Berlin observers suggested that this figure applied to main bodies of troops, and that others probably were considerably more advanced.

Concurrent with all this, Japan went through another political convulsion which informed opinion in both Britain and the United States held likely to produce a more belligerent attitude—conceivably an attack on Russian Siberia or a harder policy toward the United States which might in the end lead to war.

The Japanese Government of Prince Koyone, which to the distaste of the militarists had conducted long negotiations with Washington looking toward a restoration of full amity between the two countries, resigned and probably will be succeeded by a more militant leadership.

Boy Says He Killed Man For 'Advances' to Girl, 15

Illustrated on Page 3

Sobbing and wringing his hands nervously, a frail 16-year-old Alexandria, Va., youth confessed yesterday in Portland, Me., police there said, that he shot and killed a 38-year-old man near Baltimore because the man was "making passes" at a high school girl.

He then took the murdered man's car, his wallet, and his watch, and finally dumped the blood-spattered body in a thicket along the road near the Pennsylvania-Maryland State line, according to the story told police.

REPORTER FINDS BODY

Several hours after the youth, Herbert H. Cox, Jr., who was running away from home with two girls, had allegedly confessed and police of the two States had begun a search for the body, it was discovered five miles south of Conowingo, Md., by a Baltimore News-Post reporter.

The body, lying face down, was covered with blood. The pockets of the suit had been turned out.

HOST TO HITCH-HIKERS

Late in the afternoon the slain man, whom the youth had known only as "Browning," was identified as Grainger G. Browning, an itinerant carpenter, of Mount Olive, N. C., who had given the runaway trio a lift in his car at Alexandria.

With young Cox were a dark-com-

Continued on Page 3, Column 1

BRITAIN WILL GET 2 U. S. SUBMARINES

WASHINGTON, Oct. 16 (A. P.).—Two old Navy submarines considered useful chiefly for coastal patrol and short range operations will be transferred to Britain soon, raising the total of warships thus far released to the British to 78.

Secretary of the Navy Frank Knox announced today that the undersea craft would be turned over to Britain under provisions of the Lend-Lease law and would be manned by British officers and crews before leaving American waters. The date on which the British will take over was not disclosed.

FOLLOWS DESTROYER DEAL

The first war vessels transferred by this country to strengthen the British fleet were 50 old destroyers, traded for a chain of naval and air base sites in Atlantic and Caribbean waters in September, 1940. Last April, Knox announced that 16 high-speed torpedo boats were being transferred under the Lend-Lease program. Ten Coast Guard cutters also were released last spring.

Whether release of the two submarines is a closed deal in itself or indicates a possibility that more may be transferred as new subs join the American fleet was a question on which naval authorities declined comment.

Knox's announcement said that as of Oct. 1 this country had 113 submarines in active service and 73 un-

Continued on Page 8, Column 4

IN TODAY'S INQUIRER

YOUTH SLAIN, 2 SHOT IN WHITE HILL BREAK

Illustrated on Page 5

By GERSON H. LUSH

Inquirer Harrisburg Bureau

HARRISBURG, Oct. 15.—A 19-year-old "bad boy" was shot and killed and two of his three companions were wounded today as they tried to escape from the new White Hill Industrial School for Boys.

Shot in the chest as he tried to crawl over the barbed wire enclosure outside the institution, Paul Selfridge, of Butler, died 20 minutes later in the reform school infirmary.

CUT WITH BARBED WIRE

Those wounded by the guards' gunfire were Clayton Bird, 20, of Williamsport, and George Clark, 19, of Manton st. in South Philadelphia. The third boy, captured after the barbed wire had badly cut his hands and arms, was Earl Ward, 17, of Unruh st., Philadelphia.

It was the fourth attempt at a break since the $3,000,000 correctional institution was opened as a model of its kind. But it was all over in eight minutes—even before the return of Major Henry C. Hill, the superintendent, who had left the institution grounds for a few minutes.

SCRAMBLE OVER FENCE

The four inmates exposed themselves to a fusillade when they tried to scramble over the sharp barbs of

Continued on Page 5, Column 4

AFL Favors Aid to Russia, But Denounces Communism

SEATTLE, Oct. 16 (A. P.).—The AFL adjourned its 61st annual convention tonight after endorsing full aid to Russia but denouncing Communism in caustic terms.

The aid to Russia action highlighted a day which saw suspension of the brewery workers union from the AFL after bitter debate between leaders of the brewery workers and the teamsters union.

WELDERS MAKE THREAT

The suspension was for the union's refusal to abide by the Federation's standing decision that the teamsters have jurisdiction over beer truck drivers.

There also was a threat that AFL welders would bolt their AFL union and form an independent international union.

The Resolutions Committee's proposal, as adopted by the convention, carried even stronger denunciation of Communistic practices than did the Executive Council's report.

POST-WAR HOPES

The adopted resolution said:

"It is the opinion of your committee that a victory by Stalin over other countries in Europe would be as disastrous to free institutions as a victory by Hitler."

"It is the sincere hope of your committee, now that Great Britain and her Allies are actively assisting that

Continued on Page 48, Column 1

Washington Silent On Bergdoll Release

FORT LEAVENWORTH, Kas., Oct. 16 (U. P.).—Colonel Converse R. Lewis, commanding officer of the disciplinary barracks here said today that he had received no word from the War Department concerning the release of Grover Cleveland Bergdoll.

Bergdoll's application for parole was sent to Washington about two weeks ago. He has been employed as a laborer on a prison yard gang.

Red Tanks Battling Desperately to Halt Germans' Onrush

MOSCOW, Oct. 17 (Friday) (A. P.).—The Red Armies, admittedly breached and bleeding on the approaches to imperiled Moscow, fought on today with undiminished ferocity, claiming a heavy toll of the assaulting Germans, even while acknowledging great losses of their own.

The German frontal assault, implemented with everything the Nazi army and arsenal could produce, was being met by Soviet forces still "alive and struggling" with the aid of fresh Russian tank formations, official dispatches declared.

HEAVY LOSS ON BOTH SIDES

A communique early today summed up the situation in this manner:

"In the course of Oct. 16 fighting continued along the whole front. It was especially fierce in the western (central) direction of the front.

"In the course of fighting in the western direction of the front, both sides sustained heavy losses."

ODESSA DRIVE CHECKED

(The British Broadcasting Corp. quoted the Moscow radio early Friday as saying that the forces encircling Odessa—which the Germans earlier had claimed to have

Continued on Page 11, Column 1

Fire Damages Roof Of Mattress Plant

Fire damaged a newly-laid roof at the plant of the Honor Bilt Products Corporation, Venango and Sepviva sts. at 1.30 A. M. today and drove about 20 employees working on the night shift into the street.

The company manufactures mattresses and sparks from the roof set fire to ticking stored on the second floor of the two-story structure. Firemen from Belgrade and Clearfield sts. were able to check any spread of the blaze inside the plant.

British Halt Film Ridiculing Russia

LONDON, Oct. 16 (U. P.).—British bookings for the Hollywood-made movie "Comrade X" have been stopped after protests against its "untimely ridicule of Russia."

U. S. Envoy Leaves Moscow; Kazan Likely To Be New Capital

War Map on Page 10

LONDON, Oct. 17 (Friday) (A. P.).—The leaders of Russia's Government, or at least part of them, were reported early today to have left Moscow to the desperate arms of the Red Army, and it was believed they were setting up a war-time capital at Kazan, 450 miles to the east, to continue the fight.

There was no immediate official confirmation of the reports, which came from reliable sources just as Washington dispatches disclosed that United States Ambassador Laurence A. Steinhardt and his Embassy staff were leaving Moscow in a general diplomatic evacuation for an undisclosed destination in the interior—presumably Kazan.

STALIN STAYS BEHIND

(Premier Josef Stalin and other leaders are staying behind to direct the defense of Moscow, the United Press reported in a dispatch from London. Nowhere was there any indication that Stalin would declare Moscow an open city, this dispatch declared the Premier apparently pre-

Continued on Page 11, Column 4

U. S. WEATHER FORECAST

Philadelphia and Vicinity: Increasing cloudiness and continued cool today. Highest temperature about 62 degrees; generally variable winds.

Eastern Pennsylvania, New Jersey and Delaware: Increasing cloudiness and continued cool today; tomorrow occasional light rain with slowly rising temperature.

Sun rises	6.12 A.M.	Sets 5.18 P.M.
Moon rises	2.36 A.M.	Sets 3.42 P.M.

Other Weather Reports on Page 2

Jean Phillips Wins Lead in Series

Jean Harlow Stand-in to Appear In 'Dr. Broadway' Films; Bob Taylor And Lana Turner Cast in 'Seattle'

By Louella O. Parsons

HOLLYWOOD, Oct. 16.

MARY DEES is the only Jean Harlow stand-in I ever knew, but Paramount assures me that Jean Phillips was a Harlow stand-in long before Mary's time. Jean is in the news because after two years of minor roles she's been handed the feminine lead in the new series Para will produce, "Dr. Broadway." I asked if she looked like the little Harlow and I was told she is a dead ringer for Ginger Rogers.

Some evening I'm going to tour the neighborhood movie theatres, catching up on the series pictures. More people write me about the "Kildares," "The Hardys" and "The Saint" pictures than almost any other movies.

"Dr. Broadway," as the title indicates, is about a young medico whose practice is chiefly made up of Broadway characters, chorus girls, gunmen, playboys, and so forth. MacDonald Carey, who was with Gertie Lawrence in "Lady in the Dark," inherits the role of the M. D.

Taylor Praises Leroy as Director

On my tour of M-G-M sets I stopped to talk with Lana Turner and Robert Taylor, and they were just finishing a highly dramatic scene in "Johnny Eager," for Mervyn Leroy Lana looked fetching in a blue negligee that set off the new blonde hair.

Bob told me that he considered Mervyn one of the very best directors he had ever worked for and that Mervyn wasn't afraid to experiment with original ideas. Later I learned that Bob and Lana are to make another movie for Mervyn, which John Considine, Jr., is to produce. It's called "Seattle," laid in the Alaskan gold rush era and based on Johnny's original idea.

"San Francisco," with Clark Gable, Jeanette MacDonald and Spencer Tracy, was such a record money maker that M-G-M hopes lightning will strike twice in the same place—or near the same place, so they are moving farther north into Washington.

John Rogers to Produce 'Powers Girl'

John Rogers, son of Producer Charles Rogers, is another boy of the second generation who has made good on his own. John for some time was associated with Bill Pine and Bill Thomas in producing movies at Paramount. Now he is setting out on his own with Monty Schaff and he will make three pictures a year.

His first will be "The Powers Girl," a musical. John Powers, whose glamorous models have attracted so much attention, will act as technical adviser. Georgie Hale will arrange the dancing and James McHugh and Frank Loesser have been assigned to write the music and lyrics. There is a deal pending with Columbia to release "The Powers Girl," although another offer was made to the youthful producers that interested them.

Mickey Rooney Prefers Judy's Acting

I stopped on the "Babes on Broadway" set to talk to Mickey Rooney and Judy Garland. Judy, Mickey told me, is the best actress on the screen. "You can have your Bette Davises, your Greta Garbos or your Ginger Rogers," said Mickey. "Admittedly they're all good, but Judy's the best."

It is marvelous the way these two kids have made so many pictures together without a harsh word. They're really a lesson for other teams who get jealous and bicker and fight for footage—but come hot or cold Judy is for Mickey and Mickey is for Judy.

I must say I have an awful soft spot in my heart for Mickey. Whenever I go out on the set he always seems so really glad to see me whether he means it or not. Guess I am like all the girls—I like attention.

Hayden Quit Films Over Romance

Chatter in Hollywood: The real story of why Stirling Hayden walked out of Hollywood at the height of his fame has just been revealed. Stirling was terribly in love with Madeleine Carroll and wanted to marry her, but Madeleine felt the difference in their ages might result in an unhappy marriage, and ruin both of their careers.

She was very fond of Stirling and begged him to forget his love for her. Besides, Madeleine is already engaged to a French aviator, and has been for some time. Stirling said he left Hollywood because he didn't like the paint and powder on his face. He came out to Marsons Farm to see me when he first came to Hollywood, and I was very impressed with him, and I was sorry to hear later that he was not returning to Hollywood.

Preston Fosters Have Adopted Child

There's a human interest story and some real news back of the sequence in "Heliotrope Harry," in which Preston Foster adopts a three-year-old daughter of a condemned criminal (Brian Donlevy). The little girl is actually Preston's little adopted daughter, Stephanie—and to the best of my knowledge this is the first time it has been printed that the Fosters had an adopted child.

Snapshots of Hollywood Collected at Random: Jean Gabin and Michele Morgan rekindling an old flame that started in France. Gabin and Marlene Dietrich are still friends but aren't seeing each other every night.

Mrs. Billy Gilbert parted with her tonsils at the Hollywood Hospital. Kay Francis, on the Warner lot for the first time in four years, was being fitted by Orry Kelly and made up by Perc Westmore. Both of the boys adore her, and are they happy that she is making a movie there.

Robert Coote Leaves to Rejoin Regiment

Phyllis Brooks put Robert Coote on the plane for Canada and kissed him goodbye. He rejoins his regiment.

Martha Raye with Charlie Barnet and a party of friends, having themselves a time at the Palladium.

George Sanders had a spill from his horse on the set of "Son of Fury" and he has a bad gash in his forehead.

Lady Furness and Lady Castleross inviting their friends to a cocktail party.

Doris Nolan and Borrah Minnevitch the harmonica player, and a group of friends at the Seven Seas.

Judy Canova picking up all her Southern accent at Bill Jordan's Bar of Music while she talked to Jimmy Byers a musician who comes from "Way down South."

Joe E Brown is back in town after a terrifically successful tour. I'll say for Joe, he is one of the best ambassadors of good will Hollywood has ever had.

WHAT WON'T THEY THINK UP NEXT?

To show how Janet Blair can keep cool in unusually warm California weather, the photographer posed her on a cake of ice, with a brick of ice cream and an electric fan. Janet's next film is "Three Girls About Town," with Joan Blondell and Binnie Barnes.

Four Varied Sonatas Heard In Second Recital of Series

Four sonatas of musical variety and substance comprised the second of two programs given by Virginia Pleasants, pianist, and George Beimel, violinist, last night at the Barclay. The sonatas were by Handel, Mozart, Tibor Serly and Beethoven.

The Serly sonata, not heard here since it was given on a program of the violist-composer's works nearly six years ago, provided admirable contrast to the classical items. It held interest, though lacking in clarity of form, because of its tonal coloring—sometimes reminiscent of Debussy's, sometimes with a dash of dissonance—and its staccato piano chords effectively employed in the final movement.

But contemporary works gave way once more to the mighty Beethoven when his Sonata No. 10 in G, Opus 96, closed the program. The concert opened with Handel's melodious Sonata No. 4 in D and the two-movement Sonata of Mozart, No. 17 in E minor.

S. L. S.

'Blondie in Society' At Earle Today

Irving Bacon takes all a stunt man's risks and still retains his status as a featured player.

Bacon is the postman in the "Blondie" series. And as that much-battered individual, he has been bruised and beaten in all nine of the comedies. During filming of "Blondie in Society," opening at the Earle today in which he again supports Penny Singleton, Arthur Lake, Larry Simms and Daisy, the dog, Bacon took what he estimates to be his 13th fall for the merry sake of the Bumsteads.

Charlie Barnett and his orchestra head the new stage bill on which Pinky Tomlin also appears.

War Film Opens Today At Aldine

Gary Cooper Heads Cast of 'Sergeant York'

Gary Cooper vouches for this one. The star of "Sergeant York," due at the Aldine today, declares he heard it happen.

They'd been shooting battle scenes all day on Warner Brothers' battlefield setting in the Simi hills. For some shots as many as 90 ground explosions had been fired. Machine guns and rifles had been barking furiously. It was fully as noisy as any real war could possibly be—if not noisier. There hadn't been a quiet moment until the end of the day.

Came quitting time and grimy-faced "powder monkeys" were packing away their explosives.

"My favorite radio program is on tonight," said one.

"I make my kids turn off the radio when I get home," said another. "Can't stand the racket. I'm allergic to noise!"

Featured with Cooper in this dramatization of the life of Tennessee's sharp-shooting soldier-hero are Walter Brennan, Joan Leslie, George Tobias and Margaret Wycherly.

Musical to Open On Screen at Fox

"Winston Churchill" owes the 20th Century-Fox wardrobe department $250. He ruined a costume Alice Faye was scheduled to wear in "Week-End in Havana," musical coming to the Fox today, in which Alice is starred with Carmen Miranda, John Payne and Cesar Romero.

But make no mistake. "Winston Churchill," in this case, is definitely not the Prime Minister of England. He's a six-week-old English bulldog Alice named in Churchill's honor.

She brought the puppy to the "Week-End in Havana" set and made the mistake of leaving him in her dressing room while she was before the camera. When she returned, she found the negligee she was supposed to wear for the afternoon's shooting in shreds and the pesky pup with a guilty expression.

Dr. Joseph Fort Newton's daily inspirational essays on problems of life reflect the wisdom of a distinguished scholar and clergyman.

Shirley Temple Returns to School

HOLLYWOOD, Oct. 16 (A. P.).—Shirley Temple, returning to classes after completing her new picture, discovered Sarah Lynn Marshall, 8, a schoolmate, is the daughter of actor Herbert Marshall.

"That makes us sisters, sort of," Shirley exclaimed.

Marshall, you see, had been Shirley's screen father in "The Girl on the Hill."

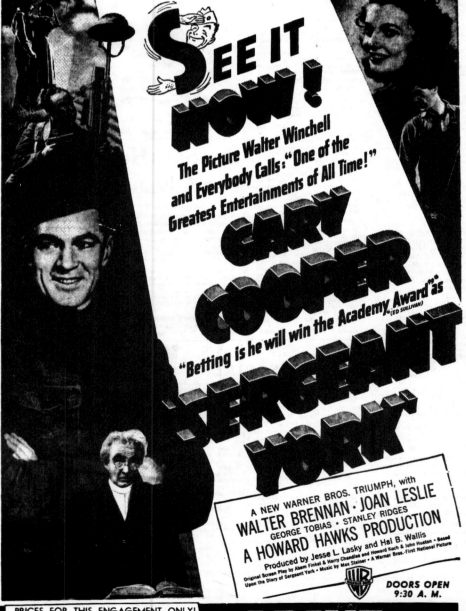

The Philadelphia Inquirer
SATURDAY MORNING, NOVEMBER 1, 1941 adh 14

GENERAL VIEW OF ENTRANCE TO PLANT, SHOWING SOLDIERS ON DUTY AND STRIKERS AWAITING DEVELOPMENTS

THERESA RULLI, SAFE WITH FATHER

Production at Bayonet Point

Carrying machine-guns and bayonets, and wearing trench helmets, 2100 Federal troops from four Army posts yesterday took over the Aircraft Associates plant at Bendix, N. J., where a strike dispute had tied up vital defense production. The soldiers, acting on orders of their commander-in-chief, President Roosevelt, ordered everyone from the plant, pending resumption of production under Army control. The picture above and below illustrate the arrival of the soldiers, what they found at the plant, the buisness-like way in which they set up an encampment, and the emplacement of machine-gun batteries. All the pictures are by William Irving, Inquirer Staff photographer.

THE COOK TENT IS SET UP: THEY PLAN TO SETTLE DOWN

MACHINE-GUN BATTERY FROM FORT HANCOCK DIGS IN

AT NO. 1 CAR HIT ANOTHER, AT NO. 2 THE CHILD, AT NO. 3 MAN AND WOMAN

An Auto Runs Wild

A woman was killed and two other persons injured at 24th st. and Indiana ave. yesterday noon, as an automobile plowed along the 24th st. sidewalk. Mrs. Nora Ryan, 55, of 3029 N. 24th st., died in Temple University Hospital. Injured were four-year-old Theresa Rulli, of 3001 N. Judson st., and her grandfather, Vincent De Amora, 76, of 3019 N. 24th st. shown above and at bottom. At left, a picture diagram showing what happened. Directly below, the woman driver, Mrs. Gertrude Beach, of 583 Abbotsford ave.

MRS. BEACH, DRIVER

VINCENT DE AMORA

Reported on Torpedoed Reuben James

RALPH KLOEPPER ST LOUIS

JOHN KIMBERLY FLORIDA

ENSIGN H. B. WADE GLEN RIDGE, N. J.

LIEUT. J. W. BELDON SYRACUSE

JOSEPH HAJOWAY AKRON, OHIO

JAMES B. CLARK AKRON, OHIO

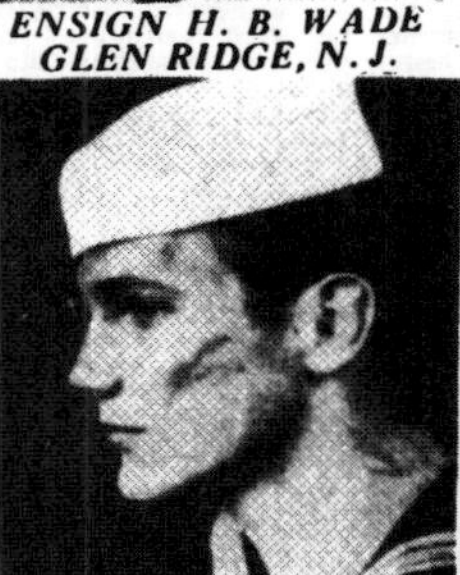

C. C. HAYES AKRON, OHIO

R. F. BOWLES LAKE CITY, FLA.

JAMES DUTY LANCASTER

JAMES BARAT NO ADDRESS

ROBT. FITZGERALD RAVENNA, OHIO

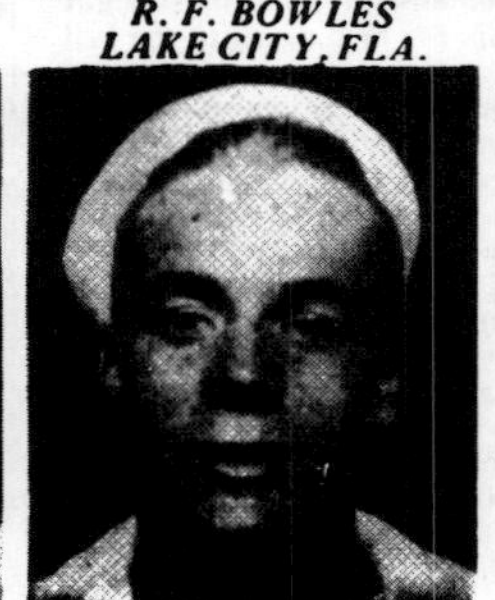

DAN SLAGEL NO ADDRESS

Green Bay Stops Chicago Bears, 16 to 14

Strictly Sports

'Navy Was Better Team,' Sums Penn's First Defeat

Geared for Open Attack, Rain Turned Issue Against Munger's Men

By CY PETERMAN

BEFORE spilling any tears over the defeat of Pennsylvania's fine football team, let us first cast about and see who in this broad realm of friendly gridiron conflict remains with perfect record.

Minnesota, yes, but it required a tricky strategem and two points contributed by Northwestern on top of a great game of ball.

Fordham's power rolled on again, and Texas seems undisturbed by any foe. Duke is rolling through the easy half of its schedule while Notre Dame, like Army and the Navy, has no reason to mourn a scoreless tie.

There may be a few others, but not many. What we prefer to point in Penn's case is this: They played their best and lost to a better squad. More than that you cannot expect.

Yesterday, after he had time to console the kids and check injuries and other details, we talked to George Munger, head coach at the University, who had personal reason to rue that 13-6 reverse in the mud of Franklin Field. It so happens this was the first time Navy had beaten a Munger-coached eleven; in his second year they both went scoreless, but Penn won the other three clashes.

• • •

THE coach wasn't as downcast as you'd suppose.

"Maybe I'm becoming philosophical," he said, "but since we did our best and there were no especial flaws or reasons for the defeat, I think the thing to do is try to win what we can of the remainder.

"All three of the last games are mighty difficult, and we will be happy to win two of them. But we're not going to give way to remorse over Navy's splendid victory—we feel they deserved it and are only glad we don't have to play them next week, too."

No alibis for the squad, no ifs or buts on weather conditions which undeniably militated against both squads. The Penn folks took the licking and while the boys were bitterly disappointed, they also know the other fellow must have his days, too.

For this Navy, remember, was largely the same as came up here last fall, confident of victory only to suffer a 20-0 trimming. Bill Busik, Sammy Boothe, Captain Froude, Chewning, Flathmann, Vitucci and Clark—all had taken it on the chin and were out to square accounts.

Small wonder then they dug in from the outset, and when breaks came their way, seized each in turn.

• • •

THERE was the very first turn of luck, the flip of the referee's coin. Penn lost. Navy took the wind, kicked deep to Penn and kept them pinned to their 20-yard line the whole first half. We asked Munger whether his team might have operated differently had they won first choice.

"I doubt if it had made much difference. We'd have taken the wind, kicked off to them and they'd returned at least to their 25. Then Busik undoubtedly would have punted and—well, you saw how he kicked. We'd still have been shoved deep down the field."

The mud, George also indicated, was not enough of a handicap to swing the scales.

"I think our fellows might have scored a couple of times, but if we made two touchdowns they would probably have scored four, or some of those field goals would have clicked. They were just too good for that game in my estimate."

From a technical standpoint, Navy relied on proven methods to beat Penn. Deploying a six-man line with the backers close up, the Middies smeared Penn's sharp opening plays by the quick rush of their secondary. The two centres, Donaldson and later Fedon, with Fullback Cameron and the defensive halves made plenty of tackles, usually close enough to the line of scrimmage to keep Penn's backs from breaking loose or getting yardage for first downs.

• • •

PENN'S backers, on the other hand, had more trouble holding Navy, largely it seemed because the Middie ball-carriers came bounding through at high speed. Take nothing from Busik, Boothe and Clark on those piledriving runs, and Cameron did his share too.

It was interesting to see the similarity in Clark's long dash and the 34-yard touchdown gallop of Joe Kane. The latter, incidentally, has about cinched that halfback post—he hasn't flopped yet this season. Saturday's run, made on the difficult in-and-out maneuver of the end from right formation, required sure-footed speed and plenty of daring. Clark's play was a carbon copy of Frank Reagan's favorite device last year.

Most of the time Penn had the ball, Navy's guards and tackles wrecked the program, however. Vito Vitucci, one of the country's very best; big Gene Flathmann, Bill Chewning and Art Knox were hard to get out of the way. The Middie guards gave Penn's pivot men a particularly hard afternoon, Don Bitler retiring with a bad ankle which, however, won't keep him furloughed long.

The heavy turf nullified much of the fancy stuff, the darting in and out, quick blocking, mousetrap specialties, well-timed spinners and hipper-dippers. We had to admire the kids who passed that soggy ball; even as early as Boothe's touchdown catch it sailed through the air with the buoyancy of a sashweight.

• • •

IT WAS a day made to order for old-style going on straight power plays, with a premium for holding on to the ball and long kicking.

When up against such a proposition, the imperative need is plenty of men. Navy had them, Penn didn't.

Penn was weary and battered at game's end, tired and discouraged. What they had suspected all week, that Navy was unbeatable on the strength of allowing no touchdowns to five previous opponents, had come true. Penn scored, to be sure, but even then they realized Navy might get it back.

Don't think they quit, for they didn't. You aren't quitting when you hold for downs as many times as those kids did, take the ball repeatedly as placements missed or Navy surges ceased once on Penn's one-foot line. They aren't quitting either when they'll throw passes from the end zone, hoping for a tying touchdown. They merely tired.

Penn's luck ran low and they caught a great squad at peak performance. When the rains came to offset their open attack, the die was cast. In our book, the defeat of the Red and Blue was the one major game which ran, under those conditions, to form.

The Philadelphia Inquirer

PHILADELPHIA, MONDAY MORNING, NOVEMBER 3, 1941 abdefg 23

ROMAN CATHOLIC WORKS AN END-AROUND PLAY FOR EIGHT-YARD GAIN AGAINST W. CATHOLIC

John Conlon is carrying the ball, with John Reilly blocking Burr tackler in game at Municipal Stadium yesterday.

West Catholic Beats Catholic Eleven, 19-6

West Catholic High preserved its undefeated record in defense of the Catholic League crown yesterday by pushing across two touchdowns in the final few minutes for a 19-6 triumph over Roman Catholic before 20,000 fans at the Municipal Stadium.

Leo Dillon and Bob Hatch registered the tallies to give the Burrs their triumph. Dillon went over on a reverse from the three-yard line after his team had marched 55 yards. Hatch scored on a 24-yard gallop, the run climaxing a 48-yard advance. John Willis place-kicked the extra point.

Dillon's touchdown plunge was his second of the contest. It was his efforts at the line that brought the Burrs their first marker in the opening period. This also came after a 55-yard march and Dillon, on this one, crashed over from the one-yard stripe on a reverse.

PASS BRINGS SCORE

Roman Catholic's only score came in the second period. A pass, Jim Friel to John Conlon provided the marker on the first play of the quarter and it culminated a 61-yard drive started near the end of the first quarter.

While West Catholic's powerhouse had the better of the going most of the time, it was checkmated continually by a determined Cahillite forward wall when danger approached. The game might have ended in a scoreless tie had not the Cahill centre, Joe Friel, been injured in halting the ever threatening Burr machine.

This occurred in the fourth period after a pass interception by West's Temple had sparked a drive from the Cahill 44 to the five-yard line. The hard - charging Cahill forwards caused Willis to fumble and Roman took over on the six-yard line. Friel was hurt. On the second play a bad pass from centre was dropped by Joe Rogers in the end zone.

BRADLEY RECOVERS

It bounded out to the one-yard line where Bradley recovered for the Burrs. Three times Willis hit without avail, but on fourth down Dillon circled left end on a reverse. He was tackled on the three, but gave a mighty lunge through the air and carried over. Willis place-kicked the extra point to give West Catholic the lead.

West Catholic opened fire shortly

Continued on Page 26, Column 7

St. Joseph's Tops No. Catholic, 31-0

St. Joseph's High gridders scored in every period yesterday to register an easy 31-0 victory over North Catholic High before 6000 Alumni Day fans at G st. and Erie ave. It was their third Catholic League triumph as against one setback.

Scoring almost at will, the St. Joseph's backs, especially a pair of nimble Johns, McTamney and Welsh, who scored three and two touchdowns, respectively, ran around the North ends and over the tackles until they were almost exhausted.

McTAMNEY REGISTERS

McTamney broke into the scoring column on the second play following the opening kick-off when he raced 69 yards down the far sideline to score. A bad pass from centre erased John Buoy's chance to convert the extra point.

Before the startled crowd could get seated the Hawklets were again in possession of the ball on their own 44 stripe after Dugan fumbled and in three plays, the second of which was a 42-yard off-tackle gallop by Cliff Gardner, who was finally halted from behind on the Falcon 9-yard stripe, pushed over the second six-pointer. John Welsh went over on a

Continued on Page 26, Column 1

Scots Trounce Germans, 3-2

By GEORGE BUTZ

An improvement in goal shooting accuracy in the second half enabled the Scots-Americans, of Kearny, N. J., to turn back the German-Americans, 3-2, yesterday afternoon at the Cambria Stadium, Kensington and Torresdale aves. The local booters rallied late, but could not catch the perennial American League soccer champions, so they fell to their third defeat of the season.

Both teams missed countless scoring chances in the early part of the match. However, they went to work bombarding the nets with a will after the Scots found the range 12 minutes after the intermission.

SCOTS LEAD, 3-0

The Scotsmen broke the scoring ice and rattled off a 3-0 edge before the locals finally crashed into the scoring column. In the goal-getting spree, confined to the last portion of the match, the Scots' goals were netted by Sam Dente, Billy Gonsalves and Frankie Fisher.

In their bold bid to eradicate the count in the final five minutes, Ray Kelly and Andy Ferko tallied for the Philadelphians.

Besides missing fire in at least seven glaring openings, the Philadelphians were handed two penalty tries—one in each half—but missed both. It was Ted Swieconek who toed up the ball on these tries, but one squirted off to the side and the Scots' goalie, Yingling, took the other drive.

GONSALVES GLEAMS

Billy Gonsalves, called soccer's "Babe Ruth" because of his torrid goal shots for the past decade, aided materially in the Scots' victory. He was last seen here in 1936 as a member of the St. Louis Shamrocks. Billy looked slow in the first-half,

Continued on Page 25, Column 4

Brooklyn Dodgers Down Eagles, 15 to 6

By FRANK O'GARA

Inquirer Sports Reporter

BROOKLYN, Nov. 2.—The Philadelphia Eagles, whose specialty is losing games the hard way, varied the procedure today by dropping one in a novel fashion when they allowed the Brooklyn Dodgers to score via every method known to football.

The unique combination—two field goals, a safety, a touchdown and an extra point—gave the Dodgers a 15-6 triumph before 15,899 fans at Ebbets Field.

EAGLES' RALLY FUTILE

Two placement boots, punctuated by the safety, got the victors off to an 8-0 lead, but when the Birds rallied for a spectacular touchdown and a half-time deficit of only 8-6, it was still either team's game. But the Quaker City eleven shot its bolt with a 50-yard drive that stalled on the five-yard stripe early in the third period, and the Dodgers powered 62 yards for a fourth-period touchdown to sew up the decision.

The game was far from a great offensive battle, for both rivals harvested every gilt-edged scoring chance that accrued, with the exception of the Eagles' single failure. First downs favored the Dodgers, 12-11, and the victors also had the edge in total yardage, 253-168. The Birds actually gained about 50 more yards, but holding penalties on the plays cancelled them.

DODGERS SCORE QUICKLY

The Dodgers used the opening kickoff as a springboard to their first score—a 35-yard field goal by Merlyn Condit, who was with the Eagles only long enough to be the means by which the game was played today. As a condition of the sale of Condit to the Dodgers, the Eagles stipulated that the game be staged today instead of the original date of Nov. 23.

Ace Parker, all-league quarterback, whose running didn't trouble the Birds, but whose passing was a constant menace, furnished the big gains

Continued on Page 26, Column 3

Demaret Wins Argentine Golf

BUENOS AIRES, Nov. 2 (A. P.).—Jimmy Demaret, the smiling Texas golf professional, won the Argentine Open championship today over the San Isidro links with a 72-hole total of 279—lowest score ever made in the 37-year history of the meet.

Demaret climbed from fourth place at the start of the day's shooting to a deadlock with Leonardo Nicolosi at the end of 54 holes. In the afternoon he fired a 32-37—69, three below par.

Eduardo Blasi, the Argentine professional champion, and Enrique Bertolino tied for second with totals of 283. Blasi and Bertolino made a tour of the United States last year.

SNEAD HAS 286

Nicolosi slipped to a 74 on his final round and tied for fourth with Ernesto Caserio at 284. Demaret's touring mate, Sam Snead of Virginia, placed sixth with 286 despite a putter that misbehaved constantly.

Demaret's total was three strokes under the former record, set by Paul Runyan, of New York, when he won the title in 1938. The Texan succeeds Mario Gonzales, who did not defend his title.

KRAMER, M'NEILL WIN

BUENOS AIRES, Nov. 2 (A. P.).—United States tennis players, here to compete in the Argentine National championships, were impressive in exhibition matches today despite Katherine Winthrop's defeat by Argentina's Mary Teran, 7-5, 6-4.

Jack Kramer, of California, defeated Heraldo Weiss, 1-6, 7-5, 7-5, and Don McNeill, of Oklahoma City, stopped Alejo Russell, 7-5, 6-1. Later Kramer and Elwood Cooke, of Portland, Ore., overcame Russell and Augusto Zappa, 10-8, 9-7.

In a one-set match Miss Winthrop and Dorothy Bundy defeated Mrs. Sarah Palfrey Cooke and Felisa Piedrola, 6-3.

Good Boxers Are Developed -- They Don't Happen Along

By JOHN WEBSTER

You can't tell us that many young fellows are born brilliant boxers, and not developed in the gymnasiums.

No, indeed, we can't be convinced even if an exceptional case, or two, were advanced in strength of that argument. Nor does the rough-tough youth who learned to fight in the streets have a good chance against the lad who has been schooled and trained by skilled hands in the gyms.

NOVICES BECOME PROFICIENT

We have seen too many unskilled youngsters come into the sub-novice division of The Inquirer A. A. boxing tournaments, and learn to use their fists quite expertly in the course of tourney competition. They have not only the advantage of good instruction but also enjoy the benefit of competition with novice opponents.

The result almost invariably has been that the tyro becomes an astonishingly capable boxer before many weeks have passed. He participates in healthful sports activity, gains new self-confidence and acquires a high standard of sportsmanship.

TWO DIVISIONS IN TOURNEY

This sixth annual Diamond Belt and Middle Atlantic Amateur Boxing Championship competition, conducted by The Inquirer A. A., is, as in former years, divided into two classes. Experienced boxers meet in open division bouts, while the youngsters who've had no more than two

Continued on Page 26, Column 8

Wehrle Captures Mexican Golf Title

MEXICO CITY, Nov. 2 (U. P.).—Wilfred Wehrle of Racine, Wis., won the Mexican amateur golf championship today by beating Verne Stewart of Roswell, N. M., 2 and 1, in the 36-hole final.

Wehrle won from Carlos Belmont, Mexico City, 7 and 6 in the quarter-finals and entered the final round with a 2 and 1 victory over Ed White of Houston.

Stewart defeated Marvin (Bud) Ward, U. S. amateur champion, one up in the quarter-final and then eliminated Richard Nauts, Houston, Tex., 5 and 4 in their semi-final match.

Phoenix Booters Win League Clash

Phoenix won its second soccer game in the E. D. U. League by scoring a 2-1 conquest of German American Vocational yesterday at Feasterville, Pa.

In two other league clashes Reading German Americans blanked the German Americans of Philadelphia, 2-0, at Kensington and Erie aves., and Erzgebirge and Cakebakers battled to a scoreless tie at 8th st. and Tabor rd.

Champs Suffer 1st Loss

46,484 Watch Packers Take Western Lead

By TOM SILER

CHICAGO, Nov. 2 (A. P.).—The mighty Chicago Bears, shackled completely for three periods, bowed to an inspired Green Bay eleven today, 16 to 14, in the most stunning upset of the National Football League season.

A sell-out crowd of 46,484 watched the community-owned Packers from the little Wisconsin city outclass the hitherto undefeated Bears, who had won five straight games by rolling up 209 points in the most crushing offensive the pro game ever had seen.

FUMBLE SEALS DEFEAT

The Bears finally awakened in the fourth period and produced a driving two-touchdown rally, but a fumble in the waning minutes robbed them of a slim chance to overtake the Packers.

The triumph gave the Packers, who have won seven of eight games, the lead in the Western Division race. The champion Bears have won five of six.

The Packers' defense in the first half was amazing, holding the Bears to a total net gain of 25 yards for two periods in which the champions made only three first downs.

PACKERS SCORE QUICKLY

The Packers wasted no time showing where they were going, driving 63 yards to a touchdown the first time they got possession of the ball. Two pass interference penalties cost the Bears 26 yards and Cecil Isbell, brightest of many Packer stars today, sparked the drive to the four where Green Bay got a first down. Clark Hinkle picked up two and Isbell slid off left tackle for the touchdown. Don Hutson's placement was blocked by John Siegal.

The Packers, always threatening with a brilliant ground and air attack, were held away from the goal the rest of the half but got close enough twice for futile field goal efforts by Hinkle.

The Packers started rolling again early in the third period, going from their own 15 to the Bear 34 before Isbell fumbled and Bill Osmanski recovered. On the first play, Hugh Gallarneau fumbled and George Svendsen recovered for the Packers. Isbell's pass to Hutson was knocked down. Then he flipped a 36-yard

Continued on Page 26, Column 2

Rockets Beaten By Washington

Special to The Inquirer

WASHINGTON, D. C., Nov. 2.—The Philadelphia Rockets bowed to the Washington Ulines, 5-3, here tonight before 1500 spectators. It was the first win of the year for Washington, Philadelphia's first defeat.

The Rockets fought bravely in turning back the Green and Gold lines time and time again. Philadelphia's goalie, Alf Moore, took the laurels for the losers with his miraculous saves throughout. He was credited with 38.

George Mantha and Louis Trudel starred for the Washington sextet, each scoring two goals.

ROCKETS ALWAYS THREAT

Philadelphia, undermanned as it was, came from behind twice to knot the game, extending Washington every minute of the game.

Each team tallied a pair of goals in the opening session. The Rockets started the scoring mid-way in the period when Defenseman Rollie Rauleston took the puck from Frank Daley and Ossie Asmundsen and shot it through a maze of players past Washington Goalie Paul Bibeault.

Mantha, a few seconds later, accounted for the Ulines' first goal on

Continued on Page 26, Column 6

Chiefs Smother Kimbrough In Win Over Americans

NEW YORK, Nov. 2 (A. P.).—The New York Americans' lower-priced talent stole the play from John Kimbrough today and the lowly Milwaukee Chiefs stole an American League football game from all of them with a burst of laterals in the third period for a 7-6 triumph at the Yankee Stadium. Kimbrough carried the ball 15 times for a gain of 40 yards.

The upset lifted Milwaukee to third place behind the Americans.

A slumbering crowd of 11,753 snapped to attention abruptly in the third quarter as the Chiefs unloosed the explosives. Jack Maltsch took Bill Hutchinson's kick on his five, and lateraled to Connie Berry, who tossed to Len Akin. Akin pitched the ball back to Jim Trebbin, who was stopped on the Milwaukee 34.

Maltsch then heaved to Berry, and successive laterals to Akin and Trebbin covered 51 yards for a first down on the New York 15. Two plays later, Howie Weiss passed to Berry for the touchdown, and Bob Eckl placekicked the conversion.

Phil Martinovich booted a 20-yard field goal for the Americans in the first period and one of 44 yards in the fourth for the locals' only scores.

Phil Manders, of Milwaukee, suffered a slight brain concussion in the second quarter, but did not need hospital treatment.

Milwaukee	0	0	7	0	— 7
New York	3	0	0	3	— 6

Touchdown—Berry. Point after touchdown—Eckl (placement). Field goals—Martinovich 2 (placements).

PARTLY CLOUDY

The Philadelphia Inquirer

PUBLIC LEDGER

An Independent Newspaper for All the People

FINAL CITY EDITION

CIRCULATION: October Average: Daily 415,982, Sunday 1,185,512 abdefgh MONDAY MORNING, NOVEMBER 10, 1941 Copyright, 1941, by The Philadelphia Inquirer Co. VOL. 225, No. 133 Second Largest 3c Morning Circulation in America THREE CENTS

18 TO 23 KILLED IN P. R. R. WRECK

Today

Hess Mystery Solved? Hitler Let Him Go Anti-Red, Peace Plan It Left Empire Intact Churchill Rejected It

By Paul Mallon

WASHINGTON, Nov. 9.

STALIN talked as if he knew something about the mysterious descent of Herr Hess into England. No doubt he does. That mystery has been cleared in every Chancellery in the world.

The story is that Hitler turned his back and let Hess go to London with a world anti-Communist peace proposal.

The idea was Hess' own, but he was furnished with a double-tanked airplane, complete charts showing the way to England and a full set of navigation instruments (not plentiful in Nazidom).

Hess thought he could contact anti-Communist peers and high-ranking Britishers to force a peace upon the British Government. The plan he submitted would have left the British Empire untouched.

Churchill buried the scheme with the approval of Mr. Roosevelt. They recognized the project for what it was—a compromise with Hitlerism.

The Duke of Hamilton, upon whose estate Hess landed, has suffered from the incident more than Hitler's right-hand man. The Duke was busy fighting in the Royal Air Force at the time, and since has taken a severe ragging from British officials.

Hess was removed some months ago from a London hospital to a comfortable place in the British countryside.

Stalin's speech was designed to incite the British and Americans to open another front in Europe. But the suggestion has fallen on flat ears.

The British claim they have insufficient equipment, although their secret production figures indicate that they have made a sensational progress in that respect since Dunkirk. In any event, we certainly have insufficient power to start anything.

Around here, the idea of an invasion through France or Spain is considered preposterous.

All plans locally are projected toward the possibility of a 1942 campaign.

At a not too widely advertised session of the 156 House Republicans (only nine absent) a resolution was adopted reaffirming the Philadelphia platform.

The reaffirmation pledged the House minority to this following stated party principle:

"The Republican Party is firmly opposed to involving this Nation in foreign war."

Only four votes were cast feebly against this reaffirmation. The result was not sent to Mr. Willkie but he probably will hear about it.

Senator Tydings gave expression to a cloakroom conviction when he suggested that Mr. Roosevelt has not thought out the economic results of his war program.

Of Special Interest Today

CHUCKLETS! A New Puzzle Contest With Cash Prizes **Page 23—Col. 6**

• • •

CITY WAGE INEQUALITIES First of a Series on a Problem Confronting City Council **Page 2—Cols. 4-5**

• • •

THAT PENN SAFETY! Cy Peterman and Bob French Discuss it **Sports Pages**

65 ARE INJURED AS LOCOMOTIVE STRIKES TOWER

'The Pennsylvanian' Is Derailed Near Kenton, O.; Blast On Freight Blamed

KENTON, O., Nov. 9 (A. P.).—Eighteen to 23 persons were reported killed tonight as a speeding Pennsylvania Railroad passenger train hurtled from the tracks at Dunkirk, nine miles north of here.

About 65 persons were injured.

First reports to railroad officials indicated that a cylinder head blown off a freight train passing on an adjacent track may have derailed the speeding passenger train, "The Pennsylvanian," en route from Chicago to New York. The wreck occurred at 10.19 P. M.

POLICE COUNT 23 DEAD

Coroner J. A. Mooney, of Hardin county, said nine bodies had been accounted for and that railroad men told him that at least nine more probably were dead in the wreckage of a coach. It was ripped apart. Several hours later the coroner said he still could account for only nine bodies.

(The United Press said ten were known to be dead and quoted Kenton police as saying that the dead probably numbered between 20 and 30.)

Guy Davis, of Chicago, a passenger, said he was told by a highway patrolman making a list of dead that at least 23 were killed.

PHILADELPHIAN HURT

J. L. Gephart, of Fort Wayne, Ind., fireman on the passenger train, was the first of the dead identified.

Several hours after the wreck, only one other body had been identified. It was that of Ernest Houseknecht, of Freeport, Ill.

The incomplete list of injured included a Philadelphian, Mat Morgan, whose street address was given as 2423 South Third st.

EIGHT-CAR TRAIN

C. S. Willeke, a Dunkirk barber, said that he counted five bodies in the wreckage of the dining car, which was ripped wide open. Seven other bodies were strewn in other wreckage, he reported, adding "at least 12 or 13 more are dead."

Railroad officials in Chicago said that the train was an eight-car combination — passenger - baggage.

Continued on Page 4, Column 4

Freighter Aground In Vineyard Sound

VINEYARD HAVEN, Mass., Nov. 9 (A. P.).—The British freighter Ungava, carrying asphalt from New York to Newfoundland, was aground tonight off Pasque Isle in Vineyard Sound.

The spot where the 1914-ton ship was in difficulty is known among seamen as "ships' graveyard." There have been more wrecks there than any place north of Hatteras.

Several Coast Guard craft, including the cutter General Greene, were alongside the freighter.

Double Life Is Blamed for Love Shooting

Illustrated on Page 3

Special to The Inquirer

READING, Nov. 9.—When Edward J. Brechlin, prosperous New York accountant, fired the shots which ended his life and seriously wounded the girl with whom he was infatuated, he believed that he was taking the only way out of the consequences of a double life.

For 30 months while he courted 24-year-old Anne Myers, of nearby Mohnton, and became engaged to marry her, it was disclosed today, he also lived, in seeming domestic bliss, with a wife in Flushing, L. I.

DUPLICITY DISCOVERED

Only when Miss Myers discovered his duplicity and sought to shut him out of her life, investigators established today, did the emotional storm arise which ended in a blast of bullets.

That tragic moment came yesterday when Brechlin fired one bullet into Miss Myers' chest and another into her jaw in the home of her sister, Mrs. Mary Stamm, and then fired a final shot which wrote finis to his own existence.

EACH IGNORANT OF OTHER

During all the months that the 36-year-old chief accountant for the New York music publishing firm of

Continued on Page 3, Column 5

3 BOYS ARE INJURED AS 2 AUTOS MOUNT CURB IN COLLISION

Unlicensed Driver Held After Car Rams Into Children

Illustrated on Page 2

Three small boys playing on the sidewalk at 26th and Sergeant sts., were injured yesterday afternoon, two of them critically, when an automobile operated by a 15-year-old, unlicensed driver, swerved over the curb after colliding with another car.

A youth riding in one of the automobiles also was seriously hurt. He was thrown to the street when the cars crashed.

LEGS CRUSHED

The three injured boys are Wayne McFadden, 7, of 2529 W. Sergeant st.; Martin Scott, 8, of 2539 W. Sergeant st., and the latter's brother, Joseph, 7.

The McFadden boy's legs were crushed beneath the wheels of an automobile driven by Joseph Kunkle, 15, of Firth st. near 24th. At Woman's College Hospital one of the legs was amputated, and physicians said the boy was in critical condition.

ONE HAS SKULL FRACTURE

Both the Scott boys were taken to Women's Homeopathic Hospital, where Martin was treated for a skull fracture, and his brother for less serious head injuries.

The fourth person injured was

Continued on Page 2, Column 3

RELIEF BOARD FIRES 14 MORE HERE AS REDS

Signing of Petitions For Communists Given as Basis for Hatch Act Dismissal

In a continuing clean-up of the Philadelphia County Board of Assistance, dismissal of 14 additional employees was announced last night by Guy H. Bloom, the board's executive director.

With the announcement of the 14 firings, Bloom specified for the first time that the dismissals were necessitated because the persons involved "are members of the Communist Party or are supporters of its policies."

36 FIRED EARLIER

The new clean-out followed the discharge of 36 employees of the board on Oct. 20, when it was announced that the dismissals were ordered under Federal and State laws barring civil service employees from political activity.

Those among the first group discharged were charged generally with political activity, subversive activity and coercion of fellow employees, but were accused more specifically of "illegal use of their positions to spread the political doctrines of subversive organizations of which they are members."

In announcing the dismissal of the 14 additional employees last night, Bloom said that by signing their names to nominating petitions of the Communist Party they had asserted themselves as sympathizers with the policies of that party.

REASON STATED

Notices of dismissal mailed to each of the 14, it was said, stated that the grounds for the board's action were as follows:

"That each had "furnished just cause for dismissal, under Section 1104 of the regulations, because of affiliation, as a member or otherwise, with a political party or organization which advocates the overthrow of our constitutional form of government, such employment being forbidden by the terms of the Hatch Act, which fact is evidenced in part through your having signed a petition for the nomination of candidates of the Communist Party."

IN ADDITION TO 36

The notice continued:

"It is understood that these dismissals are in addition to the 36 dismissed on Oct. 20.

"It is understood that by signing such petitions, persons dismissed publicly signified that they are members of the Communist Party or are supporters of its policies."

THREE-HOUR STRIKE

The discharge of the first 36 employees brought a violent protest from Local 46, State, County and Municipal Workers Union (CIO) and a three-hour work stoppage of the 246 unionized employees of the board on Oct. 22.

As a result of that brief strike, the board voted to deduct a half-day's pay from each of the striking employees.

ROOSEVELT FACES LABOR SHOWDOWN

WASHINGTON, Nov. 9 (U. P.).—President Roosevelt faces a possible showdown this week with organized labor on the issue of strikes in the Nation's sprawling defense industry.

It may come over the demand of John L. Lewis, head of the United Mine Workers (CIO), for a closed shop—one in which only union members can work—in the steel industry's captive coal mines. The dispute, which precipitated a four-day strike a fortnight ago, is before the National Defense Mediation Board.

WOULD RESUME SATURDAY

Lewis yielded to the President's demands that he call off that walkout, but he set Nov. 15 as the date for the resumption of the strike in the event the Mediation Board does not recommend a satisfactory solution. Chairman William H. Davis said during the week-end that the agency would make its decision before the new deadline.

It is the first time the Board has been compelled to take a definite stand on the explosive closed vs. open shop issue and its task has been complicated by the effect a decision favorable to Lewis might have on other industries, including steel and shipbuilding, which negotiate with unions but which do not have the closed shop.

SAYS HE WON'T YIELD

Local mine leaders say Lewis has assured them that he will not yield on the closed shop. If he doesn't get

Continued on Page 7, Column 3

British Sink 11 Ships Off Italy; Nazis Report New Smash at Moscow

Resume Attack In North

LONDON, Nov. 10 (Monday) (A. P.).—Renewed German offensives against Moscow and Leningrad were reported yesterday.

While the Russians told of the massing of a host of fresh Nazi troops for a final blow at the Red capital, the Berlin radio reported a break-through on the central front before Moscow with the destruction of 80 bunkers.

YALTA CAPTURED

The Moscow radio disclosed that the Germans were bringing up new reserves and said "it is obvious that a new and furious offensive will be launched within the next few days at the approaches to the capital. Our troops are ready."

The German High Command reported the capture of Yalta on the Crimean shore of the Black Sea. This raised a new threat to Sevastopol, big base of the Red fleet 30 miles to the west, German commentators said. They claimed that Sevastopol was now encircled, except for its sea approaches.

Thousands of German troops are striking at Leningrad from the north in a drive to score a major success from Finnish positions before Finland answers the United States demand that she quit the war, Russian quarters said.

VILLAGE RECAPTURED

Moscow dispatches reported gains in the Volokolamsk sector 65 miles northwest of the capital, where charging Red cavalrymen were said to have recaptured the important village of "S."

Both German and Russian broadcasts told of the violent new fighting after weeks of quiet on the Karelian front.

Russian sources said the Germans were aiming their main drive between Lakes Ladoga and Onega, 100 to 150 miles northeast of Leningrad, but also were attempting to press forward on a more direct line of attack down the Karelian Isthmus due north of the city.

The Russian radio said the Germans had been thrown back, leaving 2500 dead on the field, at Kestenga, a small village not shown on maps, but which apparently is in the 75-mile-wide territory between the two lakes.

HOPE TO SEIZE LAKE

The German drive apparently was launched with the hope of completing the encirclement of Leningrad by cutting the remaining eastern railway outlets and gaining full possession of Lake Ladoga's shores. A direct attack on the city over the ice

Continued on Page 10, Column 3

War Summary

The British Admiralty announced last night that two British cruisers and two destroyers had "annihilated" two Mediterranean convoys protected by stronger Italian naval forces.

The outgunned British ships sank ten transport ships and a destroyer and left another destroyer severely damaged.

The R. A. F. kept pace with the navy by hammering both Italy and Germany again Saturday night and yesterday in a stepped-up air offensive.

Renewed German drives against Moscow and Leningrad were reported. The Berlin radio said Nazi forces had broken through defenses before Moscow. Russians said thousands of German reserves were gathering for a final assault on the capital.

A strong Axis force was reported between Lakes Ladoga and Onega in a new thrust at Leningrad.

Germans claimed capture of Yalta, Crimean town on the Black Sea east of Sevastopol.

JAPANESE MASSING CLOSE TO THAILAND, HINT MAJOR ACTION

HANOI, French Indo-China, Nov. 8 (Delayed) (A. P.).—Japan appeared today to be concentrating her main Indo-Chinese forces in territory within reach of Thailand and British-protected Malaya.

Her military arrangements coincided with arrivals of Kenkichi Yoshizawa, one of Japan's South Seas experts, who has been named Ambassador to Indo-China.

EXTRAORDINARY POWERS

Heading a staff of officials, which ultimately will total about 350, his arrival was believed by many Far Eastern observers to presage major military developments in the Southern Pacific.

Yoshizawa himself is invested with extraordinary powers, and a large staff of political, economic and cultural experts gives Japan a greater representation here than in any other country in the world.

WRITER SURVEYS AREAS

Indications that Japan is paying closest attention to Thailand and Malaya, the elongated peninsula leading to Singapore, were seen in the personal inspection by an Associated Press correspondent of the Northern border areas.

No Japanese military activity whatever could be observed in the vicinity of Caobang, Dongdang and Langson adjoining Kwangsi Province of China.

Authoritative sources said the Japanese were constructing no fortifications at all along the Chinese frontier and that there were practically no troops near the borders of Tonkin and Laos, the Indo-China territories facing Yunnan Province of China.

Continued on Page 9, Column 1

4 War Vessels Whip Stronger Enemy Units

Map and Illustrations on Page 10

LONDON, Nov. 9 (A. P.).—Under the guns of a heavier Italian naval force, a British warship patrol struck a crippling blow at the supply of Axis armies in North Africa early today when it "annihilated" two convoys, sinking 10 transport vessels and one destroyer and seriously damaging at least one other, according to an Admiralty announcement.

Despite the presence of two 10,000-ton Italian cruisers with their superior fire power and Italian destroyers at least double the number of the British, the British force of two small cruisers and a pair of destroyers came off without a scratch, the Admiralty said.

The battle was fought south of Taranto, off the instep of the Italian boot.

ESCAPE TORPEDO PLANES

The British likewise escaped unscathed from a subsequent torpedo plane attack.

Captain W. G. Agnew, known as one of the British Navy's outstanding gunnery experts, commanded the British flotilla which appeared on the scene as the two convoys—one of eight supply ships and the other of two—were making a rendezvous, presumably en route to Libya.

By British count, the destroyer sunk was the 13th lost by Italy in this war.

The fact that the 10 Axis ships were given such a strong escort was said by informed sources to show the Germans and Italians were taking desperate measures to maintain the Libyan armies.

CHURCHILL CONGRATULATES MEN

The Admiralty called it a "brilliant and determined action," and Prime Minister Winston Churchill sent his congratulations "upon this most important and timely action which gravely interrupts the enemy's supply lines to Africa and impedes his long-boasted offensive against the Nile Valley."

The Prime Minister asked the Admiralty to "convey my congratulations to all concerned."

The British warships were guided to the scene of action, off Taranto, by the reconnaissance of American-built planes

Continued on Page 10, Column 6

R.A.F. Fleets Intensify Assault on Reich, Italy

LONDON, Nov. 9 (A. P.).—Ignoring heavy plane losses averaging four and a half to one, the Royal Air Force bombarded both Italy and Germany heavily again last night in a stepped-up air offensive regarded in some quarters as Britain's answer to persistent demands for a second front.

Essen, home of the great Krupp munitions works, and other industrial centres of Germany's Ruhr Valley felt the main weight of a strong British bomber force, while an Italian High Command announcement disclosed that British planes pounded Italy for the second successive night, hitting the big port of Naples and other points in southern Italy and Sicily.

In addition the R. A. F. intensified a day and night offensive against Axis strongholds in North Africa, a region frequently mentioned in connection with possibilities of the opening of a second front.

ENGLISH COAST ATTACKED

German planes struck back at England tonight, twice attacking a southeast coast town where houses were damaged and some residents trapped in the wreckage.

(The German news agency, D. N. B., said several waves of German planes bombed an important supply

Continued on Page 10, Column 4

U. S. WEATHER FORECAST

Philadelphia and vicinity: Partly cloudy today and tonight. Highest temperature 50 degrees. Gentle to moderate west winds.

Eastern Pennsylvania, New Jersey and Delaware: Partly cloudy and continued cold today and tomorrow.

Sun rises 6.39 A.M. Sets 4.49 P.M.
Moon rises 10.18 P.M. Sets 11.45 A.M.

Other Weather Reports on Page 2

Oumansky to Head Soviet News Agency

KUIBYSHEV, Russia, Nov. 8 (Delayed) (U. P.).—Constantine A. Oumansky, former Soviet Ambassador to the United States, has been appointed director general of Tass, the official Soviet news agency.

First Snow of Season Falls in New Jersey

SUSSEX, N. J., Nov. 9 (A. P.).—Snow, the first of the season, fell today at High Point State Park near here for two minutes but melted as it reached the ground. The temperature here at 9 P. M. was 30 degrees.

High Point, approximately 1600 feet above sea level, is one of the coldest spots in the State.

Boy Reprimanded by Mother Fires Bullet Into His Head

Piqued over a reprimand from his mother who objected because he remained out until 2 A. M. yesterday morning, Earl Walton, 17, of New st., West Chester, a senior at the West Chester High School, last night attempted to end his life by firing a bullet into his right temple.

He was taken to the Chester County Hospital, where physicians said his condition was critical.

'I'LL BEGIN SHOOTING'

Police who investigated said his mother had complained when he remained out late. They said they discovered that when he went to a friend's house yesterday afternoon his mother followed and ordered him to go home.

A short time later, according to a story his mother told police, he said to her, "If you don't leave me alone, I'll begin shooting."

SISTERS HEAR GUNFIRE

The mother paid no attention to his words at the time, although she later remembered he was in possession of .32 calibre revolver formerly owned by his father, Orne, a paper hanger, who died two years ago.

Early last night, two sisters, Helen, 20, and Dorothy, 22, sitting in a living room on the first floor of the house, heard a shot. They ran upstairs and found their brother unconscious, a bullet imbedded in his skull.

IN TODAY'S INQUIRER

FOOD

FEATURES FOR WOMEN

STORY

SOUP

Lentil Soup Economical As Main Dish on Menu

Vegetables May Be Served as Meat Substitute to Combat Rising Costs

By Anna B. Scott

In these days when so many homemakers are discussing the rising cost of foods, I suggest the use of inexpensive, yet nourishing soups for the main dish in your menus. As the temperature goes lower, food served in this manner is enjoyed more. In order to make variety and at the same time serve low cost foods of high food value, I recommend the use of lentils and dried green peas, as given in recipes appearing below. To balance your meal, serve a salad such as cabbage, lettuce, tomato aspic, broccoli, etc., and a fruit dessert as suggested in menu given for the Tuesday evening meal. Both of the vegetables mentioned should be served as a meat substitute.

For additional soup suggestions, inclose a stamped, addressed envelope with your request.

All questions pertaining to the following menus and recipes will be cheerfully answered if addressed to me in care of The Inquirer.

LENTIL SOUP

1 lb. lentils
4 tablespoons finely cut bacon
2 tablespoons finely cut onion
2 cups diced potatoes
1 tablespoon finely chopped parsley
1 tablespoon salt
¼ teaspoon pepper
1 tablespoon flour

Wash the lentils, cover with cold water and soak overnight. Put on to boil with two quarts of water; boil slowly 3½ hours, or until tender, then add the diced potatoes. Put the bacon and onion into frying pan; fry slowly but do not brown the onion; add to the lentils and potatoes; boil 30 minutes; add the salt, pepper and parsley. Mix the flour with a little cold water and add to the soup; boil three minutes. Finely grated raw carrot sprinkled over each serving makes an attractive garnish.

PUREE OF SPLIT PEA

2 cups split peas
6 cups water
1 tablespoon butter or bacon drippings
1 tablespoon chopped onion
1 tablespoon flour
1 teaspoon salt or to taste
1 tablespoon finely cut parsley
⅛ teaspoon thyme
¼ cup chopped celery top
Paprika

Wash and soak the peas 24 hours and put on with six cups of boiling water; boil slowly or simmer four hours, or until soft. Mash, strain and add the onion which has been fried until tender, but not brown, in the fat, then add the flour which has been mixed until smooth with a little cold water, salt, pepper, parsley, thyme and paprika and serve.

CREAM OF CELERY SOUP

Use the coarse outer stalks, scrub well and cut in one-half inch lengths; put into saucepan, cover with boiling water and boil until tender. Drain and save the water. Mash the celery through a strainer, return to the water and boil a few minutes. To each cup of celery stock add a cup of hot milk; season to taste and thicken with a little butter or substitute creamed with a little flour. Boil a few minutes and serve with a little chopped green on top.

STAPLES FOR THE WEEK

5 lbs. sugar
1 lb. coffee
¼ lb. tea
1 lb. rice
½ lb. cheese
1 lb. prunes
Canned fruit and juice
2 kinds cereal & pkge. bran
Package tapioca
1 lb. dried lima beans
Package gelatine
3 cans evaporated milk
1 lb. lentils or soup beans
Can pumpkin
Syrup
Cornmeal
Canned tomatoes
1 doz. eggs
1 lb. butter

MEAT UNTIL TUESDAY

Spare ribs
¼ lb. dried beef
Meat special
¼ lb. sliced bologna

VEGETABLES UNTIL TUESDAY

Potatoes
Turnips
Onions
Carrots
Cabbage
Pepper
Celery
Spinach

FRUIT UNTIL TUESDAY

Apples
Oranges
Pears

SATURDAY EVENING MEAL

Baked Spare Ribs with Lima Beans
Grated Raw Turnip Salad
Bran Muffins
Creamy Rice Pudding
Beverage of Choice

SUNDAY BREAKFAST

Fruit or Juice
Creamed Dried Beef
Waffles, Syrup
Coffee, Cocoa or Cereal Beverage

SUNDAY DINNER

Tomato Juice
Meat Special with Onion, Potatoes and Carrots
Raw Vegetable Salad
Corn Bread and Butter
Fruited Gelatine, Vanilla Sauce
Beverage of Choice

SUNDAY SUPPER

Sliced Bologna
Potato and Celery Salad
Bread and Butter
Fruit
Milk Tea

MONDAY BREAKFAST

Fruit or Juice
Cereal of Choice
Cinnamon Toast
Coffee, Cocoa or Cereal Beverage

MONDAY LUNCH

Cup Cream of Celery Soup
Toasted Peanut Butter Sandwich
Cream Cheese and Jelly Sandwich
Milk Tea

MONDAY EVENING MEAL

Meat Cakes or Croquettes
Candied Sweet Potatoes
Spinach
Bread and Butter
Coleslaw
Tapioca Pudding
Beverage of Choice

TUESDAY BREAKFAST

Fruit or Juice
Cereal of Choice
Creamed Hard Boiled Eggs on Toast
Coffee, Cocoa or Cereal Beverage

TUESDAY LUNCH

Utilize Left-Overs
Milk Tea

Keeping Cake Fresh

Don't store crackers with cake. It makes them soggy. To keep a layer cake fresh cut it through the middle and take slices from the centre out so that the two halves can be rejoined. Wrapped in waxed paper, the cake will keep moist.

CHING CHOW

IT HAS BEEN SAID—VOWS MADE IN STORMS ARE FORGOTTEN IN CALM.

My Favorite Recipe

The Inquirer will pay $2 for each recipe published in this column. Mail YOUR favorite recipe to "My Favorite Recipe," The Philadelphia Inquirer, Philadelphia. Unpublished recipes will not be paid for nor returned.

TODAY'S WINNER

Mrs. Mildred Estabrook, 6324 Kingsessing ave., Phila., Pa.

Pork Chops With Vegetables

4 lbs. of pork spareribs
8 potatoes cut in strips
8 carrots cut in strips
2 cups of chopped celery
2 tablespoons chopped parsley
2 teaspoons salt
2 cups boiling water
Pepper
Flour

Lay the spareribs over the vegetables which have been placed in a basting pan. Add the boiling water. Dredge with flour, and add the seasoning. Roast 1 to 1½ hours in a moderate oven (350 degrees). Sprinkle with parsley. Serves six.

Buttons and Buckles

They serve two purposes on coats and suits. They provide utility and adornment. Buttons are made of rubber, ivory, plastics, wood, nuts, metals and many other materials.

All buttons except for decorative purposes should be either sewed on with small stay buttons or else taped between lining and outer cloth. This will prevent them from being yanked off and taking a piece of the garment out at the same time. If they are sewn flat, the cloth is strained when the garment is fastened, and eventually will pull out. Such details, though small in themselves, make for durability.

The Inquirer's Daily Short Story

Unwanted Soldier

By Charles McGuirk

Principal Character

BILL, whose very life is centered in the Army. He leaves folks and home behind and reports for recruiting at the Army base. But Bill learns he'll have to wait a while—he's a little too young.

Soldiers had it nice. They slept every morning until the bugle blew and then they got out of bed and hustled around until they were called for setting up exercises. Then they ran a couple miles and then they got called for breakfast. After that, they grabbed their guns and they drilled or they walked.

They went blocks and blocks and they saw a lot of new things. They worked around the camp or did something or other until around 3 o'clock and then they were all through for the day. Bill wished he was a soldier. He was going to be a soldier. He was going to do all the things they did, especially hang around the base and talk. He wouldn't talk about girls all the time like they did because he didn't care for girls. Girls were sissies. He'd like to tell the soldiers that, but he didn't dare. He was lucky to be around the base at all and he had to keep pretty still. Even then, he wasn't always sure of staying. Once in a while one of the soldiers would say a bad word and then another one would look at the swearer. And then he'd look at Bill and he'd say to the swearer:

"Nix. Little pitchers have big ears and your mouth would be like a sewer, if you cleaned it up."

No Sissy

And the swearer would look at Bill, too, and he'd get red around the ears and he'd say,

"Scram kid. Beat it. Why don't you go home where you belong? What's your mother doing all the time to let you hang around? You ought to be in school."

So Bill would have to scram. Often, he felt like crying when they talked that way to him. But if he cried, they'd think he was a sissy. And Bill was no sissy. He was a man. He was five years old.

Bill was, as a census taker would say, one of a family of four. He had a mother and daddy and a sister, Evelyn. Evelyn was sixteen and she was almost as bad as the soldiers only she talked about boys all the time, instead of girls, like the soldiers did. He guessed she was pretty. She had blonde hair and blue eyes and she was always putting stuff on her face to make it look nicer. She wasn't as pretty as Mom, of course, but she was nice enough. So was Pop except that he wasn't home a lot of the time. He was a salesman and he traveled.

First Sounds

Well the way Bill got to know so much about soldiers, he was born just a couple blocks from the base which was on the outskirts of the city. He guessed the first sounds he recognized after his mother's and daddy's voices were the notes of bugles and the roll of drums, the clank of rifles and the hoarse shouted commands of officers putting their companies through drills.

When he could just toddle, his mother took him over to the parade grounds to watch them drilling. So his first memory of movement was soldiers marching in geometric patterns to the strains of martial music. It must have marked him, this experience.

Along about the time he was four years old, he began to hear rumors of wars. It was pretty vague, the picture he got. There was some man named Hitler and he lived in a place called Germany and he and millions and millions of soldiers were walking up and down a place called Europe and diving in planes and firing off cannon and capturing places called France and Holland and Belgium and Norway—Oh, there was a lot of them.

And the soldiers were always saying things that started with, "When we get into it." They talked of things Bill couldn't understand. Tanks and luftwaffe and co-ordination and bridgeheads and where an AEF would land. Some said in a place called Italy, others in Norway, while others held out for a place called "Marsales" because did you ever notice? The RAF never lays any eggs on "Marsales" and I read in a book where it's the place where everything is shipped into Germany from all the Mediterranean ports.

Planning Ahead

Bill startled his family at table one night by saying:

"I'm joining up for the duration when I get big enough. Then I'm putting in for sergeants' school and when I get to be a top kick, I'm putting in for a commission. No lousy buck private for me. I'm gonna be up there where you get the gravy. Hell, if I marry, the Government pays me regular pay and maintenance besides. Then I ain't gonna drop outa the Army when the war's over. I'm gonna stay right in because there'll be draftees coming in every year to be trained and I'll get to be a first looey and then a captain. That's the way you get by in this man's Army."

"Billy!" his mother demanded. "Wherever did you hear such talk?"

"He's hearing it over at the base, Mother," Evelyn informed her indignantly. 'He's over there all the time and you shouldn't allow him there at all. You don't know what he'll pick up. The way those soldiers talk is awful."

"It ain't," Bill denied. "How do you know? You don't go over there do you? You'd like to but you don't dare. They don't want no old girls over there. He knew that was the biggest lie he ever told.) They just want soldiers over there."

"Oh!" gasped the horrified Evelyn, "Mother, you've just got to forbid him to go to the base. You've just got to!"

"Yes," his mother agreed thoughtfully. "Billy, you can't go to the base any more unless I give you permission."

Evelyn attracted quite a bit of attention and got numerous offers of military help.

That was all right with Bill. It was a nuisance brought about by Evelyn who was a girl and his sister, both of which facts he wished weren't so. It meant dropping everything and running to his mother to ask permission but that was all there was to it. She'd give it to him and he could go on his way.

The trouble was, however, that his mother wouldn't give him permission. She told him he had been going over to the base too much and that those grown men didn't want a child hanging around and he'd have to learn to play with other children his age. "No, darling," she wound up the first time, "you can't go today. Maybe some other time but not today. You go and play with Georgie and Mary and Jacky. They are very nice children."

Tried to Obey

You'll have to give this to Bill. He tried to obey his mother. He went and tried to play with Georgie and Mary and Jacky. And he guessed they were nice kids, too. But they didn't know anything about Europe and France and Hitler. They didn't know how to "present," "right shoulder," "right dress," "tenshun!" Jacky, who was bigger than Bill said he wasn't going to play soldier and Bill hit him and Jacky hit back and the end of it was that Jacky's mother told Bill's mother that her child was too rough to play with.

Bill got a licking that evening and the next day the world turned blue. The next day he learned that the only place he could have a good time was at the base and the only people he could have it with were the soldiers. It was the day after that he ran away the first time.

Evelyn proved to be the psychologist of the family. To their frantic mother she said practically:

"There is no sense in worrying, Mother. Billy's over at the base. I just know he is because he's so spoiled by the men over there that he won't be satisfied any place else. I'll go and get him and he should have a good spanking when he gets home. You spoil him to death."

So she went over to the base and she picked him up immediately. He was standing a little apart from a group of soldiers listening with all a small pitcher's big ears. Evelyn reached for him but he protested. In the ensuing argument, Evelyn attracted quite a bit of attention and got numerous offers of military help. In fact, she had to accept the offer of Private John Endison because he had a way with Bill and as nice a pair of shoulders as she ever saw on any man, soldier or civilian.

Bill didn't get a licking for this adventure. His mother didn't think lickings would help and Evelyn didn't insist on discipline. She was too busy thinking about Private Endison to worry about Bill. Bill's mother thought the solution might be to move away from the base. They did that. They moved clear across the city, five miles or more away. And that did seem to be the solution, all right, because Bill never mentioned the base or the soldiers again.

Making Plans

The reason he didn't was because he was thinking. He was thinking that it might be a good idea to run away and enlist in the Army like he had heard one soldier tell the others he had done. He was under age, seventeen, but he'd sworn to the recruiting sergeant that he was twenty-one and the sergeant signed him up.

Bill didn't say anything to anybody. He just waited. For two weeks. Then on one nice autumn day, he slipped away from the house and struck toward the base. He wasn't sure just where it was but he knew it was generally east, though he didn't know east by name. He left a little before noon and he walked and he walked and he walked. Along about 4 o'clock, he was pretty tired and hopelessly lost. He asked a policeman where the base was and policeman after a hard look at him, told him it was about half a mile.

When Bill reached it, it hadn't changed a bit. The men were standing at the base of the monument talking and Bill passed them and went on to headquarters. He went into the office. A private was writing on a typewriter and Bill told him he wanted to talk to the sergeant. The private pointed to the uniformed man at another desk. "That's him," he said and Bill walked over to him.

"Sergeant," he said, "my name's Bill Henry and I want to join up."

"O. K., buddy," the sergeant said, not cracking a smile. He pulled an enlistment form toward him and poised a pen over it. "Name. Age. Position. What branch do you want to join?" he intoned.

"Bill Segard," Bill said. "I'm twenty-one. I help my mother. I'm joining the infantry."

"Right," the sergeant said, "what's your address?"

"Well," Bill hesitated, "do you have to have that?"

"Yeh," the sergeant said, "it's the regulations."

"O. K.," Bill said resignedly, "480 Post road. We just moved there two weeks ago. We just got our telephone."

The sergeant wrote it all down and then told Bill to wait. "At ease," he ordered because Bill was standing pretty stiff. "I'll be back in a minute." He went into another office where John Endison was working at another typewriter and he said, "That classy doll's brother is in again. Wants to join the Army. I expect his mother is nuts by this time. You better take him home."

So John Endison rode home with Bill in a bus. And he got the thanks of both Evelyn and Bill's mother. Because on the way home, he had persuaded Bill that he ought to wait a few years. Bill's now engaged in waiting. It's only a matter of time.

THE END.

Tomorrow, "The Tentacle Forest," by Anthony Rud.

Dr. Joseph Fort Newton's daily inspirational essays on problems of life reflect the wisdom of a distinguished scholar and clergyman.

Inquirer Daily Dinner Menus

By Mrs. Anna B. Scott. The menus are based on table budget for families of four, two adults and two children.

For the $12 to $15 a week table allowance, or the $50 a month budget:

Fish Cutlet
Potato Cakes
Stewed Tomatoes
Bread and Butter
Steamed Carrot Pudding, Vanilla Sauce
Beverage of Choice

For the $15 to $20 a week table allowance, or the special or company dinner:

Cup Mushroom Soup
Escalloped or Deviled Tuna Fish
Baked Potatoes
Broccoli, Hollandaise Sauce
Clover Rolls
Banana Salad, Cranberry Mayonnaise
Sponge Cake
Coffee

In The Inquirer on Fridays and Tuesdays, Mrs. Scott gives the complete weekly menus and marketing lists for the $50 a month budget.

PUZZLE AND PASTIME FEATURES

129 WEEKLY PRIZES! *Payable in Defense Savings Bonds and Stamps or Cash!*

If This Happened to You . . . ?

You make a bet with friends that you can marry a man with money without loving him. A wealthy man proposes and you fall madly in love with him. A jealous person threatens to tell him of the bet. If This Happened to You, would you . . . ?

($10.00 Defense Stamps to Mrs. H. R., West Philadelphia.)

How would you solve this problem? For the best solution of 50 words or less, **The Inquirer will give an $18.75 Defense Savings Bond (10-year maturity value $25.00) for each one printed.**

The Inquirer also is seeking unusual and interesting life problems, which can be presented to its readers for solution. **It will pay $10.00 in Defense Savings Stamps for each one printed.**

Address all entries to IF THIS HAPPENED TO YOU . . . ? P. O. Box 8245, Philadelphia Inquirer. Today's problem answers must be received by midnight Sunday.

Solution for Monday, Dec. 1

You are engaged to be married. Not long before the date set your future husband introduces you to a very dear friend who is visiting him. During the visit the three of you go everywhere together. It isn't long before you find yourself deeply in love with your fiance's friend. He has told you he feels the same way about You. If This Happened to You, would you . . . ?

"In fairness to the three of us my fiance would have to be told immediately of the altered relationship. His disillusionment now would be more considerate than an attempt to hide our feelings, which would only result in a greater disappointment at a later date."

($18.75 Defense Savings Bond to Gilda Victor, Philadelphia)

Defense Savings Slogans

"The Luxury of Freedom Is Worth a Sacrifice Now; Buy Defense Bonds!"

($5.00 Defense Stamps to Polly Yarnell, Philadelphia)

A Vital Contribution To Our National Defense, Defense Bonds and Stamps!"

($2.00 Defense Stamps to Herbert R. Levis, Camden, N. J.)

Keep America Free And Make the World Likewise, Buy Defense Bonds!

($2.00 Defense Stamps to Harris Samonisky, Wilmington, Del.)

For the best Defense Savings Slogan each day, The Inquirer will pay $5.00, and, in addition, will award two prizes of $2.00 each, all prizes to be paid in Defense Savings Stamps.

Address all entries in this contest to DEFENSE SAVINGS SLOGANS, P. O. Box 8245, Philadelphia Inquirer.

MOVIE TITLEGRAMS

"The Old Maid" "Hotel for Women" "The Honeymoon's Over," "My Man Godfrey" "Going Places" "Every Night at Eight."

"Daytime Wife"

$5.00 in Defense Stamps to: Miss L. Peachey, Philadelphia.

Can you write a MOVIE TITLEGRAM?

Either a straight "Wire," night letter or day letter, constructed out of Movie Titles, may win you the daily major prize of $5.00 in cash or Defense Savings Stamps, or you may qualify for one of the other $2.00 prizes, two of which will be awarded each day.

Read over the sample wire above and then get busy.

Entries in this contest should be addressed to MOVIE TITLEGRAMS, P. O. Box 8245, Philadelphia Inquirer.

Brain Twizzlers

By Prof. J. D. Flint

Four automobile dealers found that by placing their orders for new cars from the factory at the same time they could get better shipping rates. As a result they placed some orders as follows: 1. Dealer A ordered one Roller, three Brakers and seven Sporters. These were to cost him fourteen thousand dollars. 2. Dealer B ordered one Roller, four Brakers and ten Sporters. These were to cost him seventeen thousand dollars. 3. Dealer C ordered ten Rollers, fifteen Brakers and twenty-five Sporters. 4. Dealer D ordered one Roller, one Braker and one Sporter. With all of this information at your command, can you figure out how much their orders were to cost Dealer C and Dealer D? (Answer elsewhere on this page)

Save These Pages

When entertaining in your home, you will find these Puzzles and Pastimes provide diversion and amusement for your guests.

— America's New Game Craze —

PHOTOPUN

12-5

A Novel: When this book on the stands appeared The critics raved, the readers cheered.

The picture above is carefully posed to represent a definite subject. Check the clue line above with the picture and get the solution—along with a chuckle.

(Answer elsewhere on this page.)

MINUTE MYSTERIES

by H. A. RIPLEY & ROY POST

Try your wits on this mystery—it takes but ONE MINUTE to read. Every fact and every clue necessary to its solution are in the story itself — and there is only one answer. HOW GOOD A DETECTIVE ARE YOU?

"Infidelity Wears Dark Glasses"

"Listen, Shelby, we're going to have a show-down—now! Don't you think I know what's been going on between you and Myrtle? And you my friend! Get up, you rat!"

George Grange and Shelby Russell fought furiously as Myrtle Grange begged them to stop. A vicious blow knocked Grange to the ground. His head crashed against a rock.

"You've killed him! You've killed him!" Myrtle shrieked.

"No, dear, he isn't dead—yet. But, if you're game . . ."

"You . . . you mean . . . ?"

"Yes,—isn't our love worth it? Well?"

Myrtle nodded her head.

* * *

Fordney looked at the contents of Grange's pockets. Six $5 bills, 90 cents in small change, his car keys, two handkerchiefs, check book, pencil, three smashed cigars, lighter empty of fuel and a compass. At a sign Shelby Russell continued:

"George, Myrtle and I came out here for a picnic—we've been friends for years. We were preparing lunch. I had my arm around Myrtle's waist—as a hundred times before. Suddenly George shouted accusations at me like a wild man; called Myrtle some vile names, ran to his car, started it, ran it over the cliff!"

Myrtle sobbed uncontrollably.

Thinking of Grange's broken body, taken from the twisted, battered car twenty minutes earlier, the criminologist inspected the spot where it had stood. He nodded twice, murmured, "Quite," then asked: "How long after you arrived here did the tragedy occur?"

Russell and Myrtle said it was at least half an hour.

The Professor shook his head, quietly said, "This was no suicide; book them for murder, Sheriff."

What single clue disproved Russell's story; proved Grange had been murdered?

(Answer elsewhere on this page.)

Chucklets!

When I watch Suave William Powell, I find that "Ohs" My most used vowell.

($2.00 Defense Stamps to Mrs. Alice Rhodes, Vineland, N. J.)

If you have hopes You cannot quell, Peruse each day The Wishing Well.

($2.00 Defense Stamps to A. C. Low, Philadelphia.)

Tommy Manville may Get me yet, He's not half way through The alphabet.

($2.00 Defense Stamps to Madeline Napoleon, Philadelphia)

Bing Crosby's race horses Earn turf-wide renown; They beat other ponies In standing their ground.

($2.00 Defense Stamps to Pvt. George E. Washington, Winchester, Va.)

I write Chucklets And always lose, But even so They chase my blues.

($2.00 Defense Stamps to Joseph Laumakis, Philadelphia)

Try your hand at a CHUCKLET rhyme—just write four lines. It must be amusing and must be about some well-known person or on some topical theme. Examples are printed above.

The Inquirer is seeking amusing CHUCKLETS and will pay $2.00 in Defense Savings Stamps for each one printed.

Entries in this contest should be addressed to CHUCKLETS, P. O. Box 8245, Philadelphia Inquirer.

Jumbles

Ten things women like are listed below. How many can you unscramble to read correctly?

1. CLESTOH
2. GOPSIS
3. SSHWO
4. STIONCONFEC
5. EMN
6. SNACDLA
7. BGINTAH
8. BGERID
9. PIESRAT
10. DESNAC

(Solution Elsewhere on this Page)

LAUGHLINES

"He went through the old covered bridge."
($5.00 Defense Stamps to Florence J. Long, Millersburg, Pa.)

"Their bridge game consisted of six rubbers."
($2.00 Defense Stamps to C. M. Wright, Glenside, Pa.)

"The wash woman wasn't efficient because she just slid over the clothes."
($2.00 Defense Stamps to E. J. Varnum, Philadelphia.)

How often have you encountered a line of description in a short story or a book that would lend itself to a "LAUGHLINE" illustration? Above you will find an example.

The Inquirer is seeking amusing "LAUGHLINES" and each day will pay $5.00 in Defense Savings Stamps for the best one and two additional prizes of $2.00 each in Defense Savings Stamps. Just send in your "Laughlines" and one of The Inquirer's artists will do the illustrating.

Entries in this contest should be addressed to LAUGHLINES, P. O. Box 8245, Philadelphia Inquirer.

Test Your Knowledge

By DR. GEORGE W. CRANE

Select the answers which you consider best. The last problem counts five points.

1. A standard bale of hay is fastened with how many wires? 1 2 3 4
2. A gallon of lubricating oil weighs approximately how much? **4½ pounds 5½ pounds 6½ pounds 7½ pounds**
3. Which one of these craftsmen would most likely employ a swage? **Tailor Blacksmith Electrician Bricklayer**
4. "Me and My Shadow" should remind you of a **Book Dog Painting Song**
5. If you were boating on the Yellow River, you would be in **China Mexico Egypt Brazil**
6. Each sport has its own distinctive language. How well do you understand the bowling terms listed below? You are entitled to one point for each correct matching.

(a) Backup. (v) Knocking down all pins with the first ball.
(b) Hook. (w) A ball that curves from right to left on its way to the pins.
(c) Spare. (x) A ball that curls to the right.
(d) Dead apple. (y) Topping all pins with two balls in one frame.
(e) Strike. (z) Delivery of a ball that is without power.

Score yourself as follows: 0-2, poor; 3-6, average; 7-8, superior; 9-10, very superior.

(Answer elsewhere on this page.)

Puzzle Answers

Word Game Answers

Yesterday's Word———PAMPINIFORM

[illegible] norm, farm, [illegible] fain, [illegible] form, [illegible] foam, [illegible] ... foam

Test Your Knowledge Answers

[illegible] ... ball (z), [illegible] A down first ball (v).

Jumbles Answers

[illegible] 6. Scandal 7. Bathing 8. Bridge 9. Parties 10. Dances

Yesterday's Cryptogram

[illegible] we hear, you should de[illegible] and some work [illegible] would help, too

Answer to Today's Twizzler

[illegible] order was to cost him ninety-[illegible] dollars and Dealer D's order [illegible] eight thousand dollars

Photopun Answer

"The Postman Always Rings Twice."

Minute Mysteries Solution

[illegible] keys in Grange's pocket told Fordney [illegible] story was a lie, that Grange [illegible] over the cliff as he [illegible] had the keys would have been in [illegible] Russell and Myrtle put Grange's [illegible] in his car and shoved it [illegible] In their haste and panic they [illegible] the keys were not in the [illegible] realize that, if found in Grange's [illegible] utterly disprove their [illegible] didn't think of the keys [illegible] IS WORSE THAN IGNOR[illegible]

Additional Winners

Movie Titlegrams

[illegible] Defense Stamps to Peggy Mc-[illegible] Philadelphia [illegible] Norma Bess, Maple [illegible]

Mr. Fixit

[illegible] Defense Stamps to Mrs. [illegible] Philadelphia, Mrs. [illegible]erta [illegible]

The Philadelphia Inquirer may be examined free at its offices or Public Libraries. Entrants in any of the competitions or tests offered on this page may if they desire copy or trace any needed item. In case of ties, duplicate awards will be paid to tying contestants.

LITTLE ORPHAN ANNIE

Featured in Colors in The Sunday Inquirer

By Harold Gray

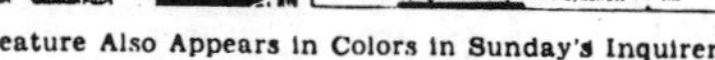

TERRY and the PIRATES

This Feature Also Appears in Colors in Sunday's Inquirer

By Milton Caniff

TILLIE THE TOILER

By Russ Westover

THE WORD GAME

Today's Word———CONCRESCENCE

(CONCRESCENCE: Kon-kres'ens. Growth, increase.)

Average mark—25 words Time limit—25 minutes

At least thirty-two common English words of four or more letters can be found in the letters in CONCRESCENCE. Can you find as many or more? The list will be published tomorrow.

MR. FIXIT!

Mr. Fixit fixes the inconsiderate husband who uses the dish cloth to clean his golf clubs!

($5.00 Defense Stamps to Mrs. James O. Hawkins, Spring Grove, Pa.)

The Inquirer is seeking amusing or constructive suggestions for MR. FIXIT and will pay $5.00 in Defense Savings Stamps for each one printed and two additional prizes of $2.00 in Defense Savings Stamps. Just send in your suggestion and one of The Inquirer's artists will do the illustrating.

Entries in this contest should be addressed to MR. FIXIT, P. O. Box 8245, Philadelphia Inquirer.

The Philadelphia Inquirer

PUBLIC LEDGER

An Independent Newspaper for All the People

Telephone Your WANT ADS TO THE INQUIRER RITtenhouse 5300 Broad 5000

CIRCULATION: November Average: Daily 415,750, Sunday 1,226,225 · a b c d e f g · SUNDAY MORNING, DECEMBER 7, 1941 · A · Second Largest 3c Morning Circulation in America · PRICE TEN CENTS

VOL. 225, No. 160

Roosevelt Sends Personal Note to Emperor In 'Final' Effort to Avert War With Japan; Reds Report Nazi Rout West of Moscow

SENATE MAY DELAY LABOR LAWS DURING STRIKE BILL HEARING

Smith Measure Expected to Reach Floor in Week

WASHINGTON, Dec. 6 (A. P.).—Senate leaders were reported to have reached an informal agreement today to delay action on pending labor legislation until Dec. 15 while the Senate Labor Committee holds hearings on the Smith bill to curb strikes in defense industries.

Members said the committee probably would order limited hearings on the House-approved measure at a meeting Monday morning and would seek to complete its consideration of the bill during the week so it could be called before the Senate the following Monday.

ONLY NEW TESTIMONY

Senator Joseph H. Ball (R., M[illegible]), author of a milder measure [illegible] approved by the committee, [illegible] would suggest that witnesses be asked to testify only on portions of the Smith bill not covered by testimony taken previously on other strike measures.

The House-approved bill, sponsored by Representative Howard W. Smith (D., Va.), would establish a cooling-off period during which the National Defense Mediation Board would attempt to settle labor disputes and avoid strikes. Jurisdictional and sympathy strikes would be banned and no walkout could be called unless sanctioned by a majority of workers in a secret ballot.

MAY SIT IN

Proposals for a conference of Government, labor and industry leaders to [illegible] some system of voluntary settlement of disputes came during the day from two sources. Chairman Elbert D. Thomas (D., Utah), of the Senate Labor Committee, told reporters such a meeting of [illegible] respected persons of all factions [illegible] could be attended by members of Congress.

A conference of C. I. O. officials [illegible] made the proposal in a resolu-

Continued on Page 21, Column 5

KING LEOPOLD III WEDS COMMONER IN BELGIAN RITES

Monarch Married In September, Nazi Broadcast Reveals

LONDON, Dec. 6 (A. P.).—A report broadcast by the German radio that King Leopold III of the Belgians had married Lelia Baels, daughter of a former Belgian Cabinet Minister, was confirmed in Stockholm tonight by the sister-in-law of Leopold's late wife.

The German broadcast said the marriage of the King and Mlle. Baels, a commoner, on Sept. 11 would be announced in Belgian churches tomorrow in a pastoral letter by Bishop van Roey of Belgium.

Stockholm reports said the marriage took place three months ago near Laeken Castle, Brussels, where the King has been living since he ordered capitulation of Belgian armies to the Germans in May, 1940. These accounts added that a civil ceremony would be held Monday.

WEDDING CONFIRMED

The broadcast said the letter would state that children from the King's second marriage will be ineligible to succeed to the throne, that right being reserved for Leopold's two sons and one daughter by his first wife, Queen Astrid, who was killed in an automobile accident in 1935.

In Stockholm, Princess Elsa Bernadotte, wife of Prince Charles, who is the brother of the late Queen Astrid, said Leopold had married a well educated, simple woman named Baels.

Belgians here termed the marriage "incredible" and "strange."

An English acquaintance of Mlle. Baels said she was about 30. "She speaks English perfectly and is well-read in English literature," the acquaintance said., "She, her mother and her sister came to Britain as refugees during the World War.

"The girls were educated in a Lon-

Continued on Page 10, Column 3

Rep. Mary Norton Ill With Severe Cold

WASHINGTON, Dec. 6 (U. P.).—Capital physician George W. Calver today reported that Chairman Mary T. Norton (D., N. J.), of the House Labor Committee, who has been ill with a severe cold, "is making satisfactory progress."

"It is hoped that she will be able to return to her home in New Jersey some time during the coming week," he added.

Batista Asks Power To Rule by Decree

HAVANA, Cuba, Dec. 6 (A. P.).—President Fulgencio Batista today asked Congress to declare a state of emergency and grant the Cabinet extraordinary powers to rule by decree for 45 days.

"The time has come to adopt the extraordinary measures required by national defense," Batista said in his message to Congress.

The message did not name specifically the powers which Batista asked, but he called for a state of emergency as provided in the Constitution.

25,000 in Huge Parade Display Defense Unity

Illustrated on Page 18

A huge parade in which 25,000 Philadelphians of every race, color and creed participated, and a meeting last night at Convention Hall, addressed by Governor James, yesterday concluded the observance of Philadelphia Defense Week.

Marching in a crisply perfect Defense [illegible] scores of organizations [illegible] afternoon helped make Unity Day one of the most vivid celebrations held during the week.

CITY ASKED TO DO BEST

At last night at Convention Hall, Governor James and other speakers, including T. Semmes Walmsley, deputy director of U. S. Civilian Defense, Mrs. Bernard Samuel, Dr. Hubley R. Owen, head of the Philadelphia Defense Council, and the A. P. Myers [illegible] director of the State Council of Defense, called on all Philadelphians to contribute their utmost to the cause of national safety.

Last night's meeting was attended by possibly less than 1000 persons, but Charles H. Grakelow, Director of Purchases and Supplies, and chairman of Philadelphia Defense Week, made this comment on the situation:

"The impossible has been accomplished. We have tired out Philadelphia with a week of intense activity, until its citizens have become too exhausted to attend the meeting tonight."

ASSAILS NEW DEAL

Governor James in his speech criticized the "New Deal Family" and accused it of "whatever disunity may exist in America."

"If," he said, "there is disunity in

Continued on Page 18, Column 3

GERMANS LOSE 2000 SOLDIERS IN BITTER COLD

Soviet Ski Troops And Tanks Halt Invaders After 8-Mile Advance

KUIBYSHEV, Russia, Dec. 6 (A. P.).—The Red Army was reported tonight to have hurled back the Germans pressing on Moscow from the Maloy-Aroslavets sector with a strong counter-attack, routing a large Nazi force and killing 2000 soldiers.

Dispatches from the front said the fighting was taking place in sub-zero weather and that Soviet ski troops armed with automatic rifles were playing a vital role.

The Nazis were said to have broken through Red defenses for eight miles and to have threatened the Soviet forces in the Mozhaisk direction, west of Moscow. But the Red Army braced itself and turned on the Germans with a heavy tank charge, the Russians said.

By HENRY SHAPIRO

KUIBYSHEV, Russia, Dec. 6 (U. P.).—Soviet dispatches today reported that German forces were "retreating in disorder" on two vital sectors of the Moscow front—at Mozhaisk and Volokolamsk—under the blows of terrific Soviet counter-attacks.

Russian forces launched their attacks in fierce cold. A biting wind sent the temperature down to 17 below zero Fahrenheit as the Red Army drove forward with terrific impetus, front-line dispatches reported.

The Soviet attacks sent the Germans reeling backward along the Mozhaisk highway, the reports said, leaving thousands of killed and wounded behind in the bitter cold.

1,500,000 NAZIS IN BATTLE

A co-ordinated thrust was made by the forces of Lieutenant General Konstantin Rokossovsky in the Volokolamsk sector which drove the Germans back, dispatches said. Mozhaisk and Volokolamsk are key sectors about 50 to 60 miles west of Moscow.

(An entirely different picture of the situation at Moscow was presented in an Associated Press dispatch from London, which said Moscow appeared to be in her direst peril.

(The dispatch quoted the Italian radio as saying that 1,500,000 men, 8000 tanks and 1000 guns were being hurled at Moscow by the Axis in "the most terrific offensive of all time," with the temperature at 31 degrees below zero Fahrenheit.

NAZIS CLAIM MOZHAISK

(Berlin claimed Saturday that Mozhaisk had been captured by German troops.)

The front reports said that the Russian forces pounding ahead in the Mozhaisk area smashed a big German wedge along the highway and thus relieved "most dangerous" pressure which had existed since Dec. 1, when the Germans broke through Soviet positions and punctured the Red Army lines as far as the highway.

Meanwhile, along the Sea of Azov, where Marshal Semeon Timoshen-

Continued on Page 2, Column 3

FINNISH SHIP SEIZED BY COAST GUARDSMEN

This is the Advance, one of seven Finnish freighters seized in this country yesterday under the Navy Department's policy of protective custody for Axis or Axis-dominated ships in American ports. It is pictured as it was taken over by Coast Guardsmen last night at Pier 80, at the foot of Snyder ave., in this city. Its crew indicated they expected the seizure. (Story on Page 4.)

GERMANS CAPTURE 5 TOWNS IN DRIVE TO FLANK MOSCOW

BERLIN, Dec. 6 (A. P.).—A strong new Nazi flanking drive mid-way between Moscow and the fiercely contested Donets Basin was reported tonight in military dispatches which pictured the Germans as overrunning five more towns and swinging close to the headwaters of the Don River 200 miles southeast of the Soviet capital.

INTENSE COLD

Intense cold, with temperatures as low as 31 degrees (Fahrenheit) below zero on the Moscow front, hampered all operations, but the Germans declared the severe conditions were temporary and had been anticipated.

Numbing temperatures were reported even on the Donets front, where the Germans acknowledged that the Red Army still was coming on in a spirited offensive which they said disregarded heavy loss of lives.

RED ATTACKS 'SMASHED'

The High Command, giving no details on the fighting there, said only that the Soviet attacks were being repulsed.

(German military quarters claimed that Marshal Semyon Timoshenko's Russian offensive on the southern front had been "brought to a stand still and smashed," the United Press reported.)

Other Russian attempts to break through the German lines at Leningrad and local counter-offensives elsewhere along the front also were reported beaten back with heavy losses.

A spokesman said the massed Ger-

Continued on Page 2, Column 5

Developments

President Roosevelt went over the heads of Japan's military government last night and sent a personal message to Emperor Hirohito in the latest diplomatic maneuver of the stalemated Japanese-American negotiations. There was no hint as to actual contents of the message.

Simultaneously, Washington reported new information of heavy Japanese troop concentrations in French Indo-China, placing the total of Nipponese forces concentrated there now at 125,000.

Two heavily guarded Japanese convoys were reported steaming toward the Gulf of Siam (Thailand).

On Europe's Eastern Front, the Germans appeared still to be getting the worst of it at the hands of the Red armies, despite a new threat to Moscow in which the Nazis were reported using 1,500,000 men and 8000 tanks in "the most terrific offensive of all times."

The Russians, fighting in bitter cold, were reported to have thrown back the Germans "in disorder" on two vital sectors of the Moscow front, at Mozhaisk and Volokolamsk, in a fierce counter-attack which parried the re-invigorated German drive.

U.S. ORDERS SEIZURE OF 7 FINNISH SHIPS IN AMERICAN PORTS

WASHINGTON, Dec. 6 (A. P.).—The United States tonight ordered Finnish ships in American ports put under protective custody—finally taking the view that her one-time close international friend was now part and parcel of the Axis.

Announcement of the action was made through the Navy Department, which said it had instructed the Coast Guard to take over Finnish merchantmen tied up in ports of this country. The order was timed to fit the hour at which Great Britain formally declared herself at war with Finland, Hungary and Rumania—one minute after midnight, British time.

ENVOY HAD CALLED

Hjalmar Procope, the Finnish Minister, had called at the State Department a few hours earlier, and presumably the decision was made known to him at that time.

The Navy announcement listed seven ships known to be in American ports at this time.

The Navy announcement gave this accounting of Finnish ships:

Olivia, known to be at Boston, Dec. 4.

Kuurtanes, Kurikka and the motor

Continued on Page 5, Column 1

Italian King Escapes British Bombing Raid

ROME, Dec. 6 (A. P.).—Narrow escape from British bombs by King Victor Emmanuel III of Italy was disclosed today when the little monarch returned from a nine-day tour of air-pounded Sicilian towns.

The King arrived at Villa San Giovanni, across the Straits of Sicily from Messina on the toe of the Italian boot, Thursday afternoon just after five British planes bombed and machine-gunned the town, injuring nine persons, Fascists said.

VISITING IN SICILY

They said anti-aircraft fire and a formation of Italian fighter planes shot down two of them and chased away the other three, just before the ruler arrived. One of the three, pursued, was finally brought down far out over the Mediterranean.

The King had been visiting the places in Sicily which have suffered most from almost constant Royal Air Force raiding.

Last night the British again bombed Naples. The High Command communique said seven persons were killed and 40 injured and reported "notable damage was caused to civilian dwellings and various fires started."

Continued on Page 3, Column 7

Ingrid Undergoes Operation in Denmark

COPENHAGEN, Denmark, Dec. 6 (A. P.).—Crown Princess Ingrid underwent a minor abdominal operation at a clinic here Thursday. It was expected she would leave the hospital within a few days.

Chilean Ex-President Disarms 'Assassin'

SANTIAGO, Chile, Dec. 6 (U. P.).—Maud Fernandez, 34, attempted to shoot former President Arturo Alessandri, the police announced today.

As Alessandri, who is 73, left his apartment in Calle Central this afternoon, the woman appeared and drew a revolver which she pointed at him.

Police said the woman pressed the trigger three times. Alessandri himself took the revolver from the woman's hands. It was not loaded.

Alessandri said that he would make no accusation against her as "she seemed to be mentally unbalanced."

Lady Domvile Freed From British Prison

LONDON, Dec. 6 (A. P.).—Lady Domvile, wife of Admiral Sir Barry Domvile, was released by British authorities today after 16 months' detention under defense regulations.

Sir Barry and their son, Compton Domvile, who likewise were detained July 8, 1940, remained in custody. Sir Barry was a former director of the British Naval Intelligence Division.

Lady Domvile is of German origin. Her maiden name was Vonderheydt. She was actively interested in the Link, an Anglo-German organization founded in 1937 with Sir Barry as chairman. The Link was dissolved in 1939.

15 Shopping Days Until Christmas

New Tokio Forces Reported Bound For Indo-China

By WILLIAM C. MURPHY, JR.

Inquirer Washington Bureau

WASHINGTON, Dec. 6.—President Roosevelt tonight sent a personal message direct to Emperor Hirohito of Japan, apparently in a last-minute and final effort to avert war between the United States and the Far East partner of the Berlin-Rome-Tokio Axis.

Terms of the message were not disclosed, but an announcement by the State Department was couched in language such as to indicate that the President was appealing to the Emperor over the head of the Japanese Government and apparently was informing the Emperor that the latter's ministers had misrepresented facts to this Nation at least.

ANNOUNCED IN 3 PARAGRAPHS

The department announcement was a three-paragraph affair:

1. A message was being sent by the President to the Emperor of Japan.

2. Reports reaching the State Department show that the Japanese troops being assembled in the Indo-China area are estimated as 82,000 in southern Indo-China; 25,000 in the north, and 18,000 on ships in harbors in Indo-China—a total of 125,000 troops. The 18,000 last mentioned are reported to be on board 21 transports in Camranh Bay.

3. Other reports have reached the Department indicating that two large and heavily escorted Japanese convoys were seen this morning, the 6th of December, to the southeast of Point de Cameau, the southern point of Indo-China, steaming westward toward the Gulf of Siam (Thailand.)

IMPLIES JAPANESE FALSIFIED REPORT

Only last night the White House had made public a note from the Japanese Government declaring that there had been no concentrations of Japanese troops in Indo-China beyond the limits fixed by the agreement last June between Japan and the Vichy Government of France—in other words a total of about 25,000.

Thus the direct implication of the Department's statement tonight was that the Japanese Government had conveyed false information to the United States in response to this Nation's recent request for a statement concerning the

Continued on Page 8, Column 5

Two Japanese Convoys Head for Thailand

NEW YORK, Dec. 6 (A. P.).—The British radio reported tonight, in a broadcast heard here, that "two large and heavily escorted Japanese convoys were seen steaming toward the Gulf of Siam (Thailand) this morning"—Sunday. The broadcast was heard here by CBS.

MANILA, Dec. 7 (Sunday) (U. P.).—The Far East battened down today for the war that appeared imminent.

The Philippines Government ordered immediate evacuation of Manila "danger zones."

All British navy, air and army personnel at Singapore, bastion of South Pacific defense, were suddenly recalled to stations and ordered to stand by on a war footing.

Australian forces stood at their war posts.

A British officer at Singapore, recalled to his ship after being ashore for the first time in weeks, expressed the sentiment that was on almost every tongue in the great Pacific centres of Manila, Singapore, Shanghai, Hong Kong, Batavia and Bangkok.

"Now, I suppose, we are going to fight Japan," he said.

The storm signals were up and

Continued on Page 8, Column 4

U. S. WEATHER FORECAST

Philadelphia and Vicinity, clear and a little colder today and tonight. Highest temperature 45 degrees. Moderate to fresh west and northwest winds.

Eastern Pennsylvania: Partly cloudy, rather cold today; fair, slowly rising temperature tomorrow.

New Jersey and Delaware: Fair, rather cold today; fair, slowly rising temperature tomorrow.

Sun rises 7.08 A. M. Sets 4.35 P. M.
Moon rises 8.12 P. M. Sets 9.46 A. M.

Other Weather Reports on Page 2

The Philadelphia Inquirer
PUBLIC LEDGER
An Independent Newspaper for All the People

LATEST WAR EXTRA

CIRCULATION: November Average: Daily 415,750, Sunday 1,226,225 abdefgh★ MONDAY MORNING, DECEMBER 8, 1941 Second Largest 3c Morning Circulation in America THREE CENTS

VOL. 225, No. 161

JAP AIR TROOPS IN PHILIPPINES

NEW YORK, Dec. 8 (Monday) (A. P.).—Mutual Broadcasting System's correspondent in Manila reported today that Japanese parachute troops had been landed in the Philippines. The National Broadcasting Co. said the U. S. aircraft tender Langley was reported unofficially in Manila to have been damaged in action with Japanese forces. As an aircraft tender, the Langley is a floating base for seaplanes.

Pearl Harbor Raid Kills 104; 300 Wounded

By FRANCIS McCARTHY

HONOLULU, Dec. 7 (U. P.).—War broke with lightning suddenness in the Pacific today, when waves of Japanese bombers assailed Hawaii and the United States Fleet struck back with a thunder of big naval rifles.

Japanese bombers, including four-motored "flying fortresses," dive bombers and torpedo-carrying planes, blasted at Pearl Harbor, the great United States naval base; the city of Honolulu and several outlying American military bases on the Island of Oahu.

U.S.S. WEST VIRGINIA REPORTED SUNK

A tight censorship was imposed on later Honolulu dispatches, but official and unofficial accounts declared that the United States had suffered heavy loss.

The Berlin radio broadcast a report that the United States battleship West Virginia had been sunk and the battleship Oklahoma set afire. The broadcast said that the battle was "still going on" and that altogether three United States ships were hit. The third was not named.

A National Broadcasting Co. report from Honolulu earlier had said the Oklahoma was set afire.

In Washington, the War Department's first official estimate of casualties was: 104 known dead and more than 300 wounded in the Army forces. These figures did not include civilian or possible naval casualties.

There was heavy damage in Honolulu residential districts and the death list among civilians was large but uncounted.

An N. B. C. observer reported from Honolulu that 350 men were killed by a direct bomb hit on Hickam Field, Army bomber base. A bomb was reported to have struck a defense housing project, with many civilian casualties.

Reliable quarters in Washington said anti-

Continued on Page B, Column 1

ROOSEVELT TO GIVE MESSAGE ON WAR TO CONGRESS TODAY

Text of President's final plea to Emperor of Japan on Page 11.

By WM. C. MURPHY, JR.
Inquirer Washington Bureau

WASHINGTON, Dec. 8 (Monday). —President Roosevelt will go before a joint session of Congress at 12.30 o'clock this afternoon to report on Japan's attack upon American possessions in the Pacific and ask for appropriate legislative action—presumably a declaration of war.

This was announced shortly before midnight after the President had conferred for almost three hours with his Cabinet and Congressional leaders of both major parties.

WHITE HOUSE STATEMENT

While the White House and all participants in the conferences declined to be specific as to what the President would recommend to Congress there was no doubt that the net result would be formal recognition of the state of war which began when Japan attacked U. S. bases in the Pacific yesterday.

The following statement was issued by the White House:

"At 8.30 P. M. the Cabinet met with the President in the White House. Shortly after nine legislative leaders from both branches of the Congress and both parties, arrived and participated in a joint meeting with the President and the Cabinet.

HEAVY NAVAL LOSSES

"The President reviewed for them all information received up to that time and gave them also other information not yet verified and which at the time to be classified as rumor. The President told them of doubtless very heavy losses sustained by the Navy and also large losses sustained by the Army in the island of Oahu.

"The legislative leaders approved the request of the President to address a joint session of the House

Continued on Page D, Column 1

JAPAN STARTS WAR ON U. S., DECLARES IT THE NEXT DAY

Text of Emperor Hirohito's proclamation declaring war on Page 11.

TOKIO, Dec. 8 (Monday) (A. P.). —Japan went to war against the United States and Great Britain yesterday with air and sea attacks against Hawaii, followed by a formal declaration of hostilities today.

Japanese Imperial headquarters announced at 6 A. M. (4 P. M. Sunday, E. S. T.) that a state of war existed among these nations in the Western Pacific, as of dawn.

ATTACKS ANNOUNCED

Sudden Japanese attacks on Hawaii and other American military and naval island strongholds in the Pacific and on the British bastion of Singapore were announced by Imperial headquarters.

The Japanese carried out a swift attack on American naval, military and air forces in Hawaii, the announcement said.

Far to the west of that action, the Japanese added, their forces captured the U. S. gunboat Wake and sank the British gunboat Peterel. Both were stationed at Shanghai.

'SUCCESSFUL RAID'

Bombing of military objectives at Singapore, Britain's great Far Eastern naval base, was said to have been executed successfully.

Japanese attacks on the small American islands of Wake and Guam, in the Pacific, also were reported in the announcement.

CONFERS WITH CABINET

Premier-War Minister General Hideki Tojo held a 20-minute Cabinet session at his official residence at 7 A. M., and shortly afterwards it was announced that both the U. S. Ambassador, Joseph C. Grew, and the British Ambassador, Sir Robert Leslie Craigie, had been summoned by Foreign Minister Shigenori Togo.

The Foreign Minister, Domei said, handed to Grew the Japanese Gov-

Continued on Page B, Column 7

By ALEXANDER KENDRICK

(Compiled from dispatches of the Associated Press, United Press, The Inquirer's Washington Bureau and special Inquirer news services.)

The United States and Japan are at war.

Without warning, in yesterday's dawn, a Japanese air fleet struck at America's chief naval base in the Pacific—Pearl Harbor, Hawaii.

Another attack followed shortly, by a deadly wave of dive bombers and flying fortresses.

Simultaneously, the Japanese bombed the islands of Guam and Wake.

Last night (this morning in the Orient) they began the second day of conflict with aerial attacks upon Davao and an Army camp at Baguio, in the Philippine Islands.

Meanwhile, Japan also waged war against Great Britain. She landed forces in Malaya and attacked Singapore, 5000 miles from Hawaii. Other Japanese detachments began an invasion of Thailand.

104 SOLDIERS, SAILORS KILLED

One hundred and four American soldiers and sailors were killed and more than 300 wounded in the attack on Hawaii, the War Department's first report said. Civilian casualties, believed heavy, have not yet been estimated.

President Roosevelt last night indicated that both Navy and Army losses in Hawaii had been heavy. Whether he referred to personnel or ships was not made clear.

He was reported to have said the American base at Guam had been virtually destroyed. The Tokio radio said the island outpost had been surrounded by Japanese warships, and

Continued on Next Page, Column 1

Late Flashes

JAPS AND BRITISH FIGHT IN THAILAND

BERLIN, Dec. 8 (Monday) (A. P.).—DNB quoted Domei, authoritative Japanese news agency, as saying today that Japanese and British armed forces were engaged in fighting in Thailand.

2 U. S. TANKERS REPORTED SUNK

NEW YORK, Dec. 7 (U. P.).—Radio Rome reported tonight that two American tankers were sunk in the Japanese attack on Pearl Harbor.

60 KILLED IN SINGAPORE RAID

LONDON, Dec. 8 (Monday) (U. P.).—The Exchange Telegraph reported from Singapore today that Governor Sir Shenton Thomas said 60 persons were killed and 133 injured in the Japanese bombing of Singapore this morning.

94 JAPANESE SEIZED IN N. Y.

NEW YORK, Dec. 8 (Monday) (A. P.).—Federal agents working with city detectives rounded up 94 Japanese by 4 A. M. (E. S. T.) today, of whom 54 were taken to the U. S. Immigration Station on Ellis Island on charges of violating the Enemy Alien Act.

Japanese Land in Malaya, Thailand; Bomb Singapore

SINGAPORE, Dec. 8 (Monday) (A. P.). — The Japanese landed in northern Malaya, 300 miles north of Singapore, today and bombed this great British naval stronghold, causing small loss of life among civilians and property damage.

Japanese troops also have invaded Thailand, the Tokio radio said. "In order to maintain the independence of Thailand, Japan has entered the southern portion of the tiny country to combat British troops which have entered from the Malayan border," the broadcast said.

REPORT BANGKOK RAID

The broadcast also said informed quarters in Japan believed Germany would declare war on the United States within 24 hours.

The British Broadcasting Corp. broadcast an unconfirmed report that Bangkok, capital of Thailand, had been bombed.

(An Australian broadcast reported that Bangkok also was being shelled by a Japanese naval squadron.)

About 300 Japanese troops landed on the east coast of Malaya and began filtering through jungle-fringed swamps and rice fields toward Kotabahru airdrome, which is 10 miles from the northern terminus of a railroad leading to Singapore.

An official report from the northern front said that all Japanese surface craft fled at high speed under British fire after leaving a few troops on the beaches.

British defenders had repulsed the

Continued on Page B, Column 5

War Pictures
Three Full Pages
18, 19 and 20
Others on Pages
A, B, C, D, 2, 3, 10, 12

BRITISH TO DECLARE WAR ON TOKIO TODAY

LONDON, Dec. 8 (Monday) (A. P.) —The British Parliament was called into special session for 3 P. M. today (9 A. M., E. S. T.) to hear a Government statement which everyone agreed would be a declaration of war against Japan which was expected to coincide with similar action by the United States.

(Canada, the Netherlands East Indies and the Dutch Government in exile last night declared war on Japan.

(Australia followed with its declaration this morning.)

Japan already had declared war on Great Britain and the United States last night as Prime Minister Winston Churchill conferred with U. S. Ambassador John G. Winant and as London awaited fulfillment of Churchill's now unneeded pledge to declare war on Japan "within the

Continued on Page C, Column 1

Man in the Street Confident U. S. Will Conquer Japan

The men and women of Philadelphia, interviewed on the streets last night by Inquirer reporters, gave their reactions to the bombings of Hawaii and Guam Island and the subsequent declaration of war on this country by Japan.

Here are the representative comments:

Frank Killen, 40, 1672 N. Felton st., bartender:

"Just like a fighter, Japan apparently has gained an advantage by getting in the first blow. We allowed them time to plan, but now we should take quicker action."

Herman Einhorn, 31, 731 Porter st., cab driver:

"The United States was slow in acting. Japan got in the first blow. Now we should make every effort to defeat them quickly, even if it slows aid to Britain. We come first."

Harry Gershenson, 27, 2216 McKean st., hat salesman:

"We were attacked and we should fight back until we win. The protection of our families and country come above all else. I was married recently, but I'm willing to go."

Allen Wagner, 29, 649 N. 52d st., machine operator:

"The boys here should go and fight there, to protect the people here."

Miss Rose Costilo, 24, 1440 S. 5th, secretary:

"I stopped thinking, but my heart is beating faster. There should be

Continued on Page 12, Column 1

The four pages following this page of today's Inquirer are lettered A, B, C and D: Page 2 immediately follows Page D. The Inquirer's "In Today's News," usually appearing on this page, today appears on Page A.

U.S. ARMY AIR FLEET HOPS OFF AT MANILA

MANILA, Dec. 8 (Monday).—United States Army bombers and pursuit planes roared into the air and headed northward at dawn today soon after word reached Manila of the outbreak of hostilities between Japan and the United States.

This was the only sign of war here at 5.25 A. M. (4.25 P. M. E. S. T. Sunday).

Upon being advised of the attack on Pearl Harbor, Hawaii, Lieutenant General Douglas MacArthur, commander of the U. S. forces in the Far East, placed his entire command on the alert.

Admiral Thomas C. Hart, commander-in-chief of the U. S. Asiatic Fleet, declared that all steps had been taken to meet the situation.

For the past 10 days Admiral Hart has kept the fleet out of Manila Bay, patrolling the Philippines.

Britain's defense forces at Hong Kong and Singapore and Dutch forces at Batavia also have been at

Continued on Page B, Column 8

U. S. WEATHER FORECAST

Philadelphia and vicinity: Increasing cloudiness and slowly rising temperatures today; highest temperature, 43 degrees. Cloudy and not so cold tonight; moderate to fresh southwest winds.

Eastern Pennsylvania: Mostly cloudy and warmer today, light rain or snow in north portion at night; tomorrow mostly cloudy and somewhat colder with snow flurries in the mountains.

New Jersey and Delaware: Increasing cloudiness with rising temperature today; tomorrow mostly cloudy and somewhat colder.

Sun rises 7.09 A.M. Sets 4.35 P.M.
Moon rises 9.09 P.M. Sets 10.26 A.M.

The Philadelphia Inquirer

PUBLIC LEDGER

An Independent Newspaper for All the People

LATEST WAR EXTRA

CIRCULATION: November Average: Daily 415,750, Sunday 1,226,225 a b d e f g h ★★ | THURSDAY MORNING, DECEMBER 18, 1941 | Second Largest 3c Morning Circulation in America | THREE CENTS

 VOL. 225, No. 171

U. S. COMMANDERS OUSTED FOR DISASTER IN HAWAII

Today

War-Life Warnings
Prices to Increase
Tires on Banned List
Consumer to Suffer
Real Production Gait

—By Paul Mallon—

WASHINGTON, Dec. 17.

ADVANCE warnings to worker and housewife that war-life behind the lines will be different this time are beginning to be realized. You will see the change within 60 days.

It is true those old meatless days, motorless Sundays, one lump of sugar, weaker coffee are not in prospect now. A shortage of ships may cause some eventual deficiencies in sugar and coffee, but not soon. Meats, vegetables, cigarettes will be plentiful, although higher in price. Canned goods will be available (defense regime has already allotted sufficient precious tin for that purpose). Tea, pepper, tapioca and possibly soap will be scarce.

In general you can count on getting sufficient food, clothing and services. Shortages in domestic wool goods will be made up by British importations and by cotton textiles. Synthetic silk goods do not yet seem ready to do the same job as silk at the same price, but they will be available.

As this is a mechanical war, the main privations of the people will be centered in mechanical lines. High-test gas will be denied to motorists, and saved for planes. Plenty of straight gas will be available. New autos will not be manufactured. Used cars will soar in price. (Perhaps one auto concern will be allowed to turn out 3000 cars or so a year.)

We had about a ten months' supply of tin when the war started, and have arranged for more from Bolivia. But the use of tin containers for oil, beer and such consumer goods will be stopped. Wooden, plastic and glass containers will be favored (despite the opposition of big oil companies.

Rubber tires will not be available. Synthetic rubber will eventually be furnished as a substitute. It wears better, but costs much more. Out of our lives will go new radios, typewriters, vacuum cleaners, washing machines, housing facilities. Limited will be the supplies of furniture, fur-

Continued on Page 2, Column 3

ARMY SERVICE FOR MEN 21-45 VOTED IN HOUSE

Registration of All Males 18 to 65 Also Approved Without One 'No'

By CHARLES H. ELLIS, JR.
Inquirer Washington Bureau

WASHINGTON, Dec. 17.—Rejecting appeals from President Roosevelt and the War Department, the House today refused to lower the present draft age limit of 21 years.

After beating down Administration attempts to permit the induction of youths of 19 and 20, the House, without a record vote, passed a bill requiring every male from 18 to 64, inclusive, to register, and making all men from 21 to 44, inclusive, subject to service in the armed forces.

SENATE REVOLT HINTED

In the Senate, which may vote on the bill tomorrow, there were signs of a similar revolt against the War Department's recommendations that the draft age limit be dropped to 19, although the Military Affairs Committee there had approved the lower limit.

Frantic attempts of the Administration leaders to gain at least a compromise on the lowered ages were fruitless as the House first refused to reduce the draft limit to 20, and then overwhelmingly turned back a move to make it 19.

PACKED BY ROOSEVELT

President Roosevelt had written a letter backing the War Department's request for a minimum draft age of 19 years, and Administration leaders at first tried to gain that objective, in the face of strenuous opposition

Continued on Page 2, Column 1

FILIPINOS CHASE JAPS FOR MILES IN NEW BATTLE

Penna. Air Hero Leads Vigan Raid As U. S. Wipes Out Foes' Plane Nest

MANILA, Dec. 18 (Thursday) (A. P.).—The Far Eastern Command announced today the Japanese suffered a number of casualties in a clash south of Vigan Monday afternoon and the invaders were pushed back many miles before darkness halted the fighting.

The U. S. communique praised the morale of the Filipino soldiers involved in the fighting.

Vigan is about 200 miles north of Manila on the west coast of Luzon island. The Japanese landed there soon after the war started.

Earlier today the Army headquarters issued a communique saying "the situation remains unchanged."

Manila went through another night without an air raid alarm.

PLANE NEST DESTROYED

MANILA, Dec. 18 (Thursday) (U. P.).—American fliers led by Lieutenant Boyd M. (Buzz) Wagner, of Johnstown, Pa., No. 1 hero of the Philippines, have blasted out a nest of 26 Japanese airplanes at Vigan, 200 miles northwest of Manila, while submarines of the United States Far Eastern Fleet have made two "successful" attacks at sea.

The air attack wiped out one of the main threats to this Philippines capital, which now has gone 60 hours without an air raid alarm.

FIRST AMERICAN ACE

Credit was given mainly to Lieutenant Wagner, a 25-year-old squadron commander, who already had been cited for heroism and who had

Continued on Next Page, Column 5

HUSBAND E. KIMMEL
Admiral Kimmel, who has been commander of the United States Fleet. He is replaced by Admiral Chester W. Nimitz, shown below.

WALTER C. SHORT
Lieutenant General, who lost his command of the Department of Hawaii to Lieutenant General Delos C. Emmons, below.

FREDERICK L. MARTIN
Major General, who was ousted from command of the air forces in Hawaii. Brigadier General C. L. Tinker, below, succeeds him.

CHESTER W. NIMITZ

DELOS C. EMMONS

C. L. TINKER

Kimmel Loses Post With Fleet; 2 Generals Out

By JOHN M. McCULLOUGH
Inquirer Washington Bureau

WASHINGTON, Dec. 17.—The War and Navy Departments tonight simultaneously announced a clean sweep of their High Commands in the Pacific, as a result of the "unpreparedness of the situation" when Japanese air and naval units launched their savage blow Dec. 7 aimed at shattering the Pacific Fleet and Pearl Harbor's air defenses.

The changes were phrased in terse announcements issued by Secretary of the Navy Frank Knox and Secretary of War Henry L. Stimson at 6.30 o'clock tonight.

'TEMPORARY DUTY' FOR KIMMEL

The Commander-in-Chief of the United States Fleet and also of the Pacific Fleet, 59-year-old Admiral Husband E. Kimmel, is relieved of both commands and assigned to "temporary duty" in the 14th Naval District, Pearl Harbor.

Also relieved of their commands are Lieutenant General Walter C. Short, Commander of the Military District of Hawaii, and Major General Frederick L. Martin, commander of the islands' air forces.

Admiral Kimmel will be replaced by Rear Admiral Chester W. Nimitz, who leaves his office as Chief of the Bureau of Navigation to assume command of the Pacific Fleet and acting command of the United States Fleet.

It is intimated that a new commander for the entire Fleet will be named to take over the administrative duties of that post. Admiral Nimitz will win the rank of a full Admiral with his new post, two grades above that which he now occupies.

FOLLOWS KNOX INSPECTION TRIP

It is evident that the changes were decided upon almost immediately after Secretary of Knox made his personal report to President Roosevelt Monday morning, following his whirlwind 5½-day personal inspection trip to Honolulu.

This is emphasized by disclosure that Lieutenant General Delos C. Emmons, who replaces Lieutenant General Short as commander of the Military Department of Hawaii, already has arrived in Honolulu.

General Emmons becomes the second Air Corps officer to

Continued on Page 8, Column 7

Roosevelt Asks Labor, Industry to Ban Strikes

Text of the President's message is on Page 6.

By WILLIAM C. MURPHY, JR.
Inquirer Washington Bureau

WASHINGTON, Dec. 17.—President Roosevelt today asked the industry-labor conference delegates to reach an agreement to prevent any stoppages of production in war industries—and to do so by Friday night at the latest.

He told the representatives of management and unions that an agreement of that nature was a "must" assignment in view of the nature of the war emergency.

"I have asked you here to help win this war, just as much as if you were in uniform," the President said, explaining why he used the word "must," a word which, he said, nobody likes.

U. S. THINKING CHANGED

"Two weeks ago," the President said, "I suppose the average American felt either that we wouldn't get into the war, or that if we did, we would mop up, if it came to war in the Pacific, in very short order. Rather derogatory remarks were leveled all through this country against any danger from Japan. Of course, as we have begun to realize now and realize more deeply as time goes on, there is very real danger to the whole world, because there is a new philosophy in the world which would end for all time . . . private industry, and . . . trade unionism equally.

WAR TO GO ON 'FOR LONG TIME'

"It is a real danger. We haven't won the war by a long shot. It is going to go on for a long time."

The Administration hopes that out of the conference which opens today there will come some kind of an effective "no strike" agreement which will make unnecessary the enactment of drastic legislation.

Pending the outcome of the con-

Continued on Page 6, Column 3

RED STEAMROLLER GAINS 40 MILES TO MAKE MOSCOW SAFE

By HENRY C. CASSIDY

WITH THE RED ARMY ON THE MOSCOW FRONT, Dec. 17 (A. P.).—Crunching down on the rear of the retreating German Army, the Russian steamroller has rumbled forward more than 40 miles beyond the starting point on the flanks of the Moscow front, pushing the invaders back to a distance that means security for the Soviet capital.

Five Nazi divisions have fallen north of Moscow and several more have been destroyed to the south as the Red Army defeated the Germans in the greatest battle and first major anti-Axis victory in this war in Europe.

NEAR VOLOKOLANSK

Over icy, snow-packed battlefields, the Soviet forces are continuing to rush forward, closing in on Volokolamsk, key to the central front northwest of Moscow. Its fall appeared imminent tonight.

The Russian troops, their steel

Continued on Page 8, Column 2

Auto Tire Rationing to Start Jan. 4

By ROBERT BARRY
Inquirer Washington Bureau

WASHINGTON, Dec. 17.—Americans will get their first taste of wartime rationing on Jan. 4, after which date civilians will have to obtain certificates before they can buy new automobile tires.

The certificates will be available only to "essential" users and they will be issued by rationing boards that might, at some later date, be used to parcel out other materials made scarce by the war.

In order to prevent a wave of new tire buying in the interim, the Office of Production Management has extended its ban on all new tire sales from Dec. 22 to Jan. 4. Controls also will be established over the sale of retreaded tires and the retreading of tires.

OPM TAKES OVER TIN

Meanwhile OPM has taken over the control of all tin supplies in or coming to the United States, and some time late in January it will be decided here whether there will be

Continued on Page 4, Column 2

BORNEO OIL BLASTED AS INVADERS LAND; JAP DESTROYER HIT

SINGAPORE, Dec. 17 (A. P.).—A Japanese Expeditionary Force has invaded the rich Miri oil country of Sarawak, British-protected kingdom of the White Rajahs on the northwest coast of Borneo, but has found the refinery and all oil field equipment utterly destroyed by withdrawing British forces, it was announced officially today.

A Japanese destroyer was hit directly by a bomb from a Dutch plane while supporting the landing, the Netherlands East Indies Command disclosed.

STATUS QUO IN MALAYA

The British Singapore Command announced tonight that there was nothing new to report from Kedah and Kelantan states, Malayan fronts north of Singapore, indicating that the situation there was stabilized.

In the air, the Royal Air Force carried out wide Malayan reconnaissance without meeting the foe, the communique said.

INVASION RECTANGLE

This latest Japanese move completed a vast invasion rectangle in the South China Sea, its corners touching the British crown colony of Hong Kong, the Philippine island of Luzon, Northern Malaya and Sarawak, the last a country of 50,000 square miles which has been ruled for 99 years by Sir James Brooke and his descendants.

In this rectangle the Japanese were trying for quick knockouts of Allied strongholds, establishment of bases, seizure of important resources and control of the West Pacific sea communication lanes to block Allied reinforcement and co-ordination.

"Enemy landings," said a commu-

Continued on Page 8, Column 1

U. S. WEATHER FORECAST

Philadelphia and vicinity: Partly cloudy and warmer. Highest temperature 55 degrees.

Eastern Pennsylvania and New Jersey: Fair and warmer, except for some cloudiness in north portions today.

IN TODAY'S INQUIRER

City Hall Darkened By Power Failure

City Hall had an unscheduled blackout early today—but it was due to trouble in the municipal building's own power plant and lasted only 30 seconds.

Every light in the structure went out at 1.30 A. M., including the circle of powerful bulbs at the base of the William Penn statue, when a technician switching the output of electric current from one dynamo to another in the City Hall sub-cellar missed on the timing. He completed the task in a half minute, however, and all the lights flashed on again.

Samuel Is Defense 'Boss' Of 8 Counties, Marts Says

Mayor Bernard Samuel, as Co-ordinator of Civilian Defense for the Philadelphia metropolitan area, is in complete charge of all defense activities in that eight-county zone.

Acting to clear up possible misunderstanding of the relative roles of Mayor Samuel and Colonel Milton G. Baker, executive director of defense for the area, Dr. Arnaud C. Marts, director of the State Council of Defense, said in Harrisburg yesterday that Samuel "is the boss."

BOTH CLAIMED LEADERSHIP

The Mayor himself defined his position as the "chief commanding officer" of the metropolitan area, while Colonel Baker, in a statement, said the Mayor might be "compared to the Secretary of War and I to the commanding officer of the troops."

Both appointments were made by Mayor F. H. LaGuardia, of New York City, who is Director of Civilian Defense.

CHRISTMAS LIGHTING

Misunderstanding of the situation by a portion of the public first arose when Colonel Baker asked that outdoor Christmas lighting of trees or store and house fronts be ended.

Mayor Samuel declared that the lights on the city's own Christmas decorations, on City Hall Plaza,

Continued on Page 10, Column 6

Late Flashes

REDS NEARING KHARKOV

BERNE, Switzerland, Dec. 18 (Thursday) (A. P.).—Haras reported in a dispatch from Bucharest today that German withdrawals in the Ukraine had brought Kharkov, the "Russian Pittsburgh" in the Donets Basin, again into the battle zone.

AXIS FORCES CUT OFF IN LIBYA

LONDON, Dec. 18 (Thursday) (U. P.).—Reliable informants reported today that British forces in Libya had cut off the German-Italian line of retreat to the west and Axis tank, infantry and artillery forces faced annihilation.

BRITISH RETREAT IN MALAYA

SINGAPORE, Dec. 18 (Thursday) (A. P.).—British headquarters announced today that troops defending Kedah and the Province of Wellesley from Japanese invaders of Malaya had withdrawn to new positions in the night.

R.A.F. BOMBERS ATTACK BREST

LONDON, Dec. 18 (Thursday) (A. P.).—British bombers attacked docks at Brest, German-occupied naval base in France, a British official reported today.

ROME ANNOUNCES SUB LOST

ROME, Dec. 18 (Thursday) (Official Radio Received by A. P.).—An Italian submarine is missing, the Italian High Command said today in its daily communique. (The British yesterday announced the sinking of the Italian submarine Ammiraglio Caraccioio in the central Mediterranean.)

Real Estate for Sale CITY

Real Estate for Sale CITY

WILL YOU BE PREPARED?

An EASIER-TO-OWN HOME is your best protection against possible housing shortages, increased rentals, higher sales prices. And you SAVE MONEY—monthly costs are actually less than current rent. Small down payment—no financing charges. Get complete lists of houses still available.

CONSULT THESE AUTHORIZED AGENTS

For homes in N. W. Phila., Lansdowne, Drexel Hill, Yeadon
WALNUT MANAGEMENT CO.
1528 Walnut St.
SAR. 1818 PEN. 0800

For homes in Overbrook & W. Phila.
WM. H. W. QUICK & BRO.
8 S. 40th St. EVE. 2386

For homes in Germantown, W. Oak Lane
PRIESTMAN-HELMETAG CO.
18 W. Chelten Ave.
VIC. 8000

For homes in the Northeast
HEYER-KEMNER, INC.
7319 Rising Sun Ave.
PIL. 7300

For homes in North Phila.
ASSOCIATE BROKERS CO.
3708 N. Broad St.
RAD. 2050

For homes in Delaware & Montgomery Counties
KERSHAW & RANEY
51 Long Lane Upper Darby
GRAnite 1700 Boulevard 1700
Office Open Sunday After 1 P. M.

SEE CLASSIFIED COLUMNS FOR LISTINGS OF EASIER-TO-OWN HOMES

SUBURBAN

MERION
INVEST IN AMERICA
First: BUY DEFENSE BONDS.
Second: BUY A HOME.
NEAR 54TH STREET & CITY LINE
Semi-detached, 4 bedrooms & 2 baths, enclosed porch, central plant heat, garage. $7,750. 10% cash. Will also consider leasing. $75 per month. Inspection by appointment.

WILLIAM PUGH
Montgomery Avenue & Old Lancaster Rd. GRE. 3300 Merion CYNWYD 3300.

MERION
FOR THE BEST BUYS TODAY
Consider one of these properties
217 Latches La. cor. Old Lancaster rd. $30,000
215 Anthwyn Road — $15,000
For Description and Inspection Consult

F. E. CABALLERO,
Exclusive Agent
Meeting House Lane, Merion
Gre. 1804 Gre. 6701 Cyn. 1804.

MERION. All masonry, corner, single home. In excellent cond. Nicely planted grounds. Attractive 1st floor plan with centre hall. 5 bedrooms, 2 baths, 2-car detached gar. Real bargain at $10,500.
WILLIAM I. MIRKIL CO.
1500 Walnut St. Kin. 1100

MERION
Having purchased larger new home, wish to sell home built to order in 1933. 4 bedrooms, 2 baths, heated by oil. $16,500. Merion P. O. Box 5.

MERION. 380 Merion rd. All-stone Colonial home, slate roof, center hall, 4 bedrooms, 2 baths, servants quarters. Best value.

BIDDLE H. HUNT
Ardmore 4480 Trinity 4480

MERWOOD PARK
ON A HILLTOP
Single home with large living room, real log-burning fireplace, cozy breakfast room, three comfortable bedrooms, tile bath, stairway to attic.
$300 DOWN
FREE FINANCING
"Buy the Clarke way And save on outlay"

W. A. CLARKE CO.
6822 Market St. Blvd. 960 or ALL. 2653

MONTGOMERY COUNTY. Several suburban homes can still be bought with 10% down payment. Price $4500 up. Get list. KELLNER, 400 Bethlehem Pike. Che. 3857.

NORTH HILLS MANOR. Country atmosphere, yet within walking distance of excellent transportation. Stone & clapboard, centre hall, Colonial, 3 baths, 2-car garage. Far below duplication cost at $11,500. Robert K. Clifton, Jenkintown, Ogontz 1212. Evenings phone Germantown 5894.

NORWOOD. 3 stores and 7 other rental units. 3-car garage. Annual rental, $2700. Price $16,000. Terms. 20% cash. SWOPE & SON, Inc. 516 Main Street, Darby.

OLD YORK ROAD SECTION. We Offer a Large List of Attractive, Low Priced Homes for Sale in this Desirable and Convenient Neighborhood. Prices range up to $8000.

T. W. MONTAGUE CO.
Jenkintown, Pa. Open Sun. Ogontz 760.

OVERBROOK
59TH & CITY AVE.
Near Overbrook Station P. R. R.
2 NEW HOMES
All-stone construction, slate roof, centre hall, large living room, dining room, powder room, breakfast room, kitchen, 4 spacious bedrooms, 2 tile baths, two-car garage. Beautiful planted grounds with old shade.
We invite your inspection.

WILLIAM PUGH
Old Lancaster road & Montgomery ave.
Gre. 3300 Merion Cynwyd 3300

OVERBROOK HILLS IN MERION. Harrogate Road. New single Colonial type homes, center hall, 4 bedrooms, 2 baths, automatic heat. Price $11,500 and up. Open daily 1-5 P. M.
CABALLERO — Cyn. 1804. Gre. 1804

PAOLI. 1 blk. from station & school, secluded home sites, one block from Lancaster Pike & busses. 80x150', with paved st., municipal water & elec. in. And new homes being built. Price $700. Will finance. Charles M. Miller, 1217 N. 29th st., Phila. Fre. 1217 or Phoenixville 9976.

PENN VALLEY
FOR THE BEST BUYS TODAY
Consider one of these properties
422 McClenaghans Mill Road — $13,500
Penn Tract, Conshohocken State rd. 15,000
615 Moreno Road — 20,000
Penn Valley Farms — 14,950
For description and Inspection Consult

F. E. CABALLERO,
Exclusive Agent
Meeting House Lane, Merion
Gre. 1804 Gre. 6701 Cyn. 1804

PROSPECT PARK, Pa. 10-rm. house, tile bath, lot 75x150 ft. desirable location. 5 min. to Westinghouse & Baldwins, close to all industrial plants, 1 block to station & stores. Splendid opportunity for boarding or rooming. Call or write Mrs. C. McKay, [illegible] Chester, Pa. Conrdsville 21-R-5.

PROSPECT PARK. 729 15th ave. 3-story, semi-det. bungalow, 6 rs., encl. pch., 2 ba., htwd. fls., 2-car gar. Price & terms just right. Ready for inspect. Peter Lewicki, realtor, 202 Concord ave., Chester, Pa. Ph. Chester 2111.

ST. DAVIDS
INVEST IN AMERICA
First: BUY DEFENSE BONDS.
Second: BUY A HOME.
Inspect this outstanding offering. Near station. 6 bedrooms & 4 baths. Servant's quarters, oil heat, garage. 5 acres of beautiful rolling ground affording long views of surrounding country. The offering price is less than 1/3 its original cost.

WILLIAM PUGH
Montgomery Ave. & Old Lancaster Rd.
GRE. 3300 CYNWYD 3300.

SPRINGFIELD
This is our last new home in this development. Ready to occupy. High on a hill with magnificent view and country-like atmosphere, but only 1 block to train and free school buses.

Lot 72'x100'. 3 bedrooms, 2 tile baths, open fireplace, huge kitchen with all electric appliances. Outside cellar entrance, slate roof and full insulation (including all sidewalls).

146 Scenic rd. Out City Line or State rd., cross Darby Creek, turn left on first road (Rolling rd.) and turn left again on first road (Scenic rd.).
Cash $[illegible], $62 per month.
Open Daily and Sunday

ROACH BROS.
425 McCLATCHY BLDG.
Blvd. 2800 Eves., Gra. 4325

SPRINGFIELD det. Colonial, almost new, 3 lge. bedrms., screens. Beaut. garden. 20% down. $7200. Le Baron, Swarthmore 121.

SWARTHMORE. Near the college, a fine home in a fine neighborhood. Open today. Call WITHAM. Swarthmore 1000.

SWARTHMORE. Attract. roomy home on [illegible]. Oil heat. Porches, shade. Pleasant, [illegible] $9000. Swarthmore 2572.

TORRESDALE. Aubrey ave. and Tulip st. Single 7 rms., all stone house, open fireplace, tile bath and kit., h.-w. ht., water closet in basement, brick garage. Owner on premises. Lot 50x200.

TREVOSE. 6-room frame bungalow, with [illegible] including oil burner, heat, corner [illegible] near train. $3800.

CLINTON M. SMITH
[illegible] Phila. Pa. Somerton 8080

UPPER DARBY. Ashby Road. Please make offer. Owner must sell. See salesman at 7026 Radbourne Rd., Sunday. S. A. Baron, 157 W. Girard ave.

UPPER DARBY. [illegible] Hampden rd., corner. [illegible] See salesman at 7026 Radbourne road Sunday. S. A. Baron, 157 W. Girard avenue.

WE CAN SELL YOUR REAL ESTATE
. . . for all cash within 3 weeks. City or suburban, residential or business property, large or small.
WRITE N-254 INQUIRER

SUBURBAN

VALLEY FORGE vic., 4 blks. from school, roads paved, elec. in., use of lake included; ½ acre home sites at $400. Charles M. Miller, 1217 N. 29th st., Phila. Fre. 1217 or Phoenixville 9976.

WAYNE. 4 Forrest road, attractive, modern home, 1 acre lot beautifully planted, stream, tennis court, 5 bedrooms, 3 baths, oil heat, must be seen to be appreciated. Owner will trade for smaller home. For inspection and price consult
CABALLERO, Gre.: 1804—Cyn. 1804.

WAYNE—Here is real value. 5 bedrooms, 2 baths, 2-car garage. Perfect condition. Lot 60'x225'. Nr. sta. & schools. $7000. C. S. Boles, 214 Walnut ave. Ph. Wayne 2284.

WILLOW GROVE sec. Semi-bungalow, 5 rms. & bath first floor, 2 rms. & bath second floor. Transportation at door. Lot 40x175. Garage. $3700. Freeman Co., 317 N. Easton rd., Willow Grove.

WILLOW GROVE, single 2-sty. house, modern, h.w. ht., 2-car garage; $4250. KELLNER, 400 Bethlehem Pike. Che. Hill 3857.

WYNCOTE—Single cor. home, nr. sta. and schools. Large bedroom, 2 ba. Wm's Oilomatic, s. & w. hookup. Bright sunny expos. Large lot. Big trees. $7500. Gerhard. Han. 1801

WYNNEFIELD. Mod., 8 rms., gar., 1 fare to city. H. M. McClure, ph. Lombard 2121.

WYNNEWOOD
A picturesque Penna. farm house (less than 15 months old) on almost ½ acre ground.
The interior plan is excellent and features a different type centre hall, a large dining room with an immense bay window; a cozy panelled library, 4 very large master rooms, 2 baths and servants' quarters. Among the many extras are random width floors, a large cedar closet, panelled recreation room with built-in bar and General Electric oil furnace.
Very convenient and a very good value at $19,000.

CAMPBELL
Tri. 1410. Cynwyd 4600

WYNNEWOOD
INVEST IN AMERICA
First: BUY DEFENSE BONDS.
Second: BUY A HOME.
Attractive farmhouse Colonial type residence built in 1937 by well-known Main Line builder. 5 bedrooms & 3 baths, centre hall, large library, powder room, recreation room, oil heat & 2-car garage. Immediate occupancy. Will also consider leasing to responsible tenant.

WILLIAM PUGH
Montgomery Ave. & Old Lancaster Road.
GRE. 3300. CYNWYD 3300.

WYNNEWOOD
NEW EXCLUSIVE OFFERING
538 Manor Road
$11,500.
Brick Colonial, 2 years old. Beaut. liv. rm., din. rm., 3 bedrms., 2 tiled baths, large store room. Att. garage. Rec. room in base. Large lot in highly desirable neighborhood.

NASH REALTY CO.
Gre. 2494 Open Sun. 2-5 Tri. 6242

YEADON
NEAR TROLLEY
Enclosed porch, three cheerful bedrooms, tile bath, garage. See it!
$275 DOWN
FREE FINANCING
"Buy the Clarke way And save on outlay"

W. A. CLARKE CO.
6822 Market St. Blvd. 960 or ALL. 2653

YEADON. All-brick house, now vac., 8 lge. rms., bath, gar., encl. pch., near car line & new school. $5500. Manley, 712 Church lane, Yeadon.

69TH ST. SECTION
$3990
Modern—6 Rooms. Tile Bath. Separate Stall Shower. Garage. Short walk to Terminal. Only $34.50 total monthly charges.

HURLEY
Long Lane & Walnut st. Open Sun. Blvd 2500

69TH ST. SECTION. Looking for a modern semi-detached home with 7 rooms, tile bath, garage, beautiful stone front? I have one at 20 Overhill Road. Can give possession by February 15th and will sell very cheaply. See me Sunday at 7026 Radbourne road, near 69th and Market.
S. A. Baron, 157 W. Girard Avenue.

69TH ST. SECTION. Hurry! Hurry! Only 3 left. 7026 Radbourne Road. All modern home completely renovated. 2-story, large terrace, porch, 6 rooms, tile bath, garage. Immediate possession. Only $2975. FHA financed. Monthly payments $24.50 includes everything. Open for inspection. S. A. Baron, 157 W. Girard avenue. Reg. 8191.

69TH ST. SECTION. A beautiful 4-bedroom house within walking distance of 69th St. Terminal; in elegant condition. Enclosed porch, weatherstripping, etc. Immediate possession. ASKING PRICE ONLY $4500. For appointment phone Hilltop 1120-J.

69TH ST. SEC. Completely renovated and ready to move in. A sturdy semi-det. home with elec. kitchen & breakfast room, cheerful living & dining rm., 3 dandy bedrms., tile bath, oil heat and garage, for only $5350. See this home Sunday. Phone Hamilton & Ezekiel, Sunset 8200.

69TH ST. SECT. Completely reconditioned. Now vacant. Modern home with oil heat, summer-winter hookup, garage. Convenient to everything. Int. terminal. $28.34 a mo. with savings of $15. Full price $3500. WM. M. KNATZ, INC., Blvd. 400 or ALL. 8633.

69TH ST. Section. 300 block, Margate road. Priced for quick sale. Beautiful, modern 6-room & tile bath home. FHA financed. See Salesman at 7026 Radbourne road, Sunday.

69TH ST. 7226 Bradford. Renov. 6 rs., semi-det. dwg., h.-w. ht., bkfst. nook, gar., $395 down. Hatch, Collingdale. Sh. Hill 600.

69TH ST. $3500. Near terminal. A-1 condition. Immediate possession. Many extras. 6 rooms, bath. Fox, 6912 Market. Blvd. 2800.

69TH ST. Sect. 3 years old, 5 rms., tile b., gar. H.-w. ht. Nr. terminal. $4300. Sunset 3100.

69TH ST. 6 rms., tile b., stall shower, oil ht. Gar. $4400. Kershaw & Raney. Blvd. 1700.

LESS THAN RENT
EASIER-TO-OWN HOMES
In Southwest Philadelphia, Upper Delaware County, Lansdowne, Drexel Hill, Wynnefield and Yeadon at terms that are actually less than current rent!
Attractive, modern, well-built homes in established residential sections—immediate occupancy.
Small down payment. No financing charges. Protect yourself against rent increases, higher sale prices and scarcity of desirable homes. See our lists of attractive EASIER-TO-OWN homes.

WALNUT MANAGEMENT CO.
1528 Walnut St.
Pen. 0800 Sar. 1818

$230 DOWN
FREE FINANCING
Six VERY LARGE rooms, tile bath, shower, cozy log-burning fireplace. Garage. May we show it to you today?
"Buy the Clarke way And save on outlay"

W. A. CLARKE CO.
6822 Market St. Blvd. 960 or ALL. 2653

$6500—69TH ST. SECTION
4 bedrms., twin, 2 auxiliary rooms on 3d floor. Gar. oil burner. Home completely modernized. Venetian blinds throughout.

W. S. PEACE, INC.
69th & Walnut Sts.
AP. 3800 Blvd. 4800

$2000 FULL PRICE CLEAR!
Colonial home, suitable for remodeling, near Valley Forge on State Highway. Stone & wood built in shape. Water & elec. in 1½ acre tract. Charles M. Miller, 1217 N. 29th st., Phila. Fremont 1217 or Phoenixville 9976.

Real Estate for Sale SUBURBAN

WYNNEWOOD PARK
Lowest Priced Single Homes in LOWER MERION TWP.
$5735
Includes Settlement Charges
$635 CASH — $37.29 MONTHLY
3 Roomy Bedrooms
SAMPLE HOME—Open Daily and Sunday 10 A. M. to 9 P. M.
FURNISHED BY SNOWDEN'S, INC.
111 State St., Media
Due to Lower Merion Township's low tax rate, you will save approximately $900 in taxes alone during the life of your 25-year mortgage.
DIRECTIONS
Lancaster Pike to Wynnewood Road, turn left 1¼ miles to sample.
Haverford Road to Wynnewood Road, turn right ½ mile to sample.
MERION BUILDERS
ARDMORE 9469

OPENING TODAY

In DREXEL HILL
Beautiful
TWIN BRICK HOMES
Featuring six spacious rooms, tile bath, modern all-metal kitchen, oil burner, air conditioned, detached garage. Large lot. See model and schools at your door.
From 63d & Sansom Sts.—out Marshall Rd. to Childs Ave., right to operation. Important—Marshall Rd. turns sharply to right just beyond first R. R. underpass.
$5150 — $550 DOWN
RALPH B. WHITLEY, Builder
DREXEL HILL Boulevard 2879

THE COMMUNITY UNUSUAL
Aronimink Estates
IN DREXEL HILL

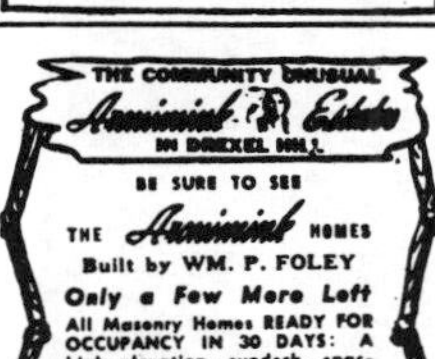

BE SURE TO SEE THE *Aronimink* HOMES
Built by WM. P. FOLEY
Only a Few More Left
All Masonry Homes READY FOR OCCUPANCY IN 30 DAYS: A high elevation, sundeck, spacious rooms, newest G. E. Kitchen, G. E. Oil Furnace with year-round hot water.
—$6550—
DIRECTIONS
Furnished Sample Home Open Every Day to 9 P. M. From 69th St. proceed out West Chester Pike to City Line. Left 2½ miles to Aronimink Estates, right at Treaty Road, 1 block.
ARONIMINK CORP., Developers
WM. P. FOLEY, Builder

WEST OAK LANE

Greenwood Gardens
West Oak Lane
7900 BLOCK MICHENER ST.
$5150
WITH GAS or OIL HEAT
Marple & Clemons, Agts. Vic. 8566

THRIFT HOMES
1500 BLK. PASTORIUS ST.
All-Brick Construction. Three bedrooms, tile bath, garage; Duo-Therm Oil Heat. N. on Stenton Ave. to Walnut Lane, E. ½ blk. to Cornelius St., N. 1 block to Homes.
$4690 — $590 CASH
ERLEN REALTY CO.

SUBURBAN

New Period Home
ONLY 20 MINUTES FROM MAJOR DEFENSE PLANTS
A home built to suit the most exacting taste. On a lot 52'x 100'. Surrounded by towering pine trees. The living and dining rooms are both enhanced by large bay windows which afford a beautiful view and keep rooms bright and cheery. Built of the finest materials to assure long life.

G-E oil furnace with Summer-Winter hot-water hook-up. G-E equipped kitchen. Johns - Manville Building and Insulation materials.

Other features include: 3 bedrooms, concealed radiators, cross ventilation, spacious closet space. See this lovely home before you buy. Compare it and you will be convinced.

Cash, including settlement — $1050
Monthly carrying cost — $41

$6250

Directions: City Line, West of Haverford Ave., next to P. & W. Station. Right on 2 bus lines.

Chatham Village
(Brookline)
A McClatchy Development
or call BLVD. 0696

Keep your cost of living down by buying a home. Are you near transportation? These 5 houses are!!

Bentley ave., Cynwyd	$10,000
Llandrillo rd., Cynwyd	$14,250
Roberts rd., Rosemont	$8500
Llanfair rd., Ardmore	$11,000
Lancaster ave., Haverford	$9200

Call C. L. Wilcox — Sunset 7448-W

2000 blk. S. AIKENS. 6 rms., h.w.ht.	$2200
7300 blk. Elmwood. 6 rms., bath, gar.	$3500
2000 blk. S. Frazier. 6 rms., renov.	$3000
6600 blk. Guyers. 6 rm., gar., renov.	$3200
2639 S. Dewey. 6 rms., end, renov.	$2700
60th & Lindbergh. 6 rms., bath, gar.	$2800
2300 blk. S. 70th. 6 rms., bath, vacant.	$3000
6100 blk. Harley. 6 r., gar., vacant.	$2800

DAVID E. TRIESTER
6622 WOODLAND AVE. SAR. 3200

RENOVATED—VACANT
COLLINGDALE. Semi-det. $2990. $290 down. Collingdale. Single. $3590. $390 down. B. M. Hatch, 61 McDade Blvd. Sharon H. 600

$4000. NEAR Valley Forge. Modern bungalow & 2-acre lake on State Highway. Chas. M. Miller, 1217 N. 29th st., Phila. Fremont 1217 or Phoenixville 9976.

5 LOTS, 60x600' at Bristol, high ground, water, gas and electric, cheap to settle an estate. F. C. King, Bristol, Pa.

BUSINESS PROPERTIES

YEADON. Imm. poss. Excel. loc. for grocery line or drug bus. Can be rented with option to buy. Manley, 712 Church lane, Yeadon.

MISCELLANEOUS

CANADIAN TAX SALE LANDS for a dollar an acre and up. Small monthly payments. Farms, timber, hunting and fishing camps, minerals. Limited number of properties. Write at once for free illustrated booklet. TAX SALE SERVICE, Room 715, 72 Queen st., W., Toronto, Canada.

Real Estate for Sale SUBURBAN

Initial Showing Today
NEW FURNISHED GUEST HOME
In Beautiful
BAEDERWOOD
YORK ROAD, JUST NORTH OF JENKINTOWN
A FOUR-BEDROOM COLONIAL
for only $10,500
Situated on an extremely large lot with a beautiful wooded background, convenient to trains and shopping center. Includes porch, which extends full width of front, beautiful kitchen with an entire 13' wall of cabinets, bath with gray glass walls and disappearing fixtures; first-floor lavatory, overhead garage doors.
ALSO A STONE CENTER HALL Colonial with 2 baths, $11,400.
ON WHARTON ROAD WEST OF YORK ROAD

Personalized Homes
In all probability it will be impossible to build homes of this type at ANY price during the next few years. Our extensive resources and foresight enabled us to purchase materials for these homes at prices far lower than would be possible today. Take advantage of it!
Gethel-Holmes Inc.
BUILDERS OF Quality HOMES FOR OVER 20 YEARS
KUHN & LOWERY, Inc., Agt. Mic. 2638

ENJOY THE SECURITY OF AN OWNED HOME
Present conditions make it more desirable than ever before to own a home of your own. If you "buy the Clarke way and save on outlay" you can enjoy the **security** of home-ownership with a total down payment of only a few hundred dollars. Your **total** monthly outlay will probably be less than rent. Financing is **free**. For a few specific examples of the modern homes now available on these easy terms, read our classified ads. Then—**see it through in '42.**

W. A. CLARKE co.
DISTRICT OFFICES

WEST PHILADELPHIA	111 South 52nd Street	
NORTH PHILADELPHIA	Broad St. & Olney Ave.	
69th STREET & SUBURBS	6822 Market Street	Executive Offices:
CAMDEN & N. J. SUBURBS	521 Cooper Street	1518 Walnut Street

UNPARALLELED HOME VALUES **$6590** UP
Ridgewood Park
WEST CHESTER PIKE, WEST OF EAGLE RD.
Brick, stone, many styles.
TYSON CONSTRUCTION CO.
R. B. Thompson, Agt. All. 7900

Delaware County's Most Beautiful
Woodmere Park
Burlington and Mill Roads, Brookline
SINGLE CORNER HOMES $8500 UP
WITH 2 BATHS
Tyson Constr. Co., Thompson, Agt., All. 7900

Penn Manor **$6090**
LARGE LOTS 65'x120'
20-YEAR-OLD SHADE
UPPER DARBY: From Lansdowne Ave. and Providence Rd. in Lansdowne, drive out Providence Rd. ½ mile to corner of Springfield and Providence Rds.
W. S. PEACE JOS. A. MELONEY
Sales Represent. Builder for 34 Years

LEEDOM ESTATES
RIDLEY PARK
NEW, SINGLE HOMES
$5335 $535 CASH $36.49 Month
6 Rooms, 3 Bedrooms, Bath & Garage
Drive Out Chester Pike to Leedom's Lane, Turn Left
Hinckson Blvd., Turn Left

GREAT BIG SOLID STONE-FRONT AIR-CONDITIONED HOMES
IN
$5990 LONGACRE PARK
Yeadon's Most Beautiful Section
Bailey Rd. & Rose St.
HAROLD S. LOGAN, Agt.

MISCELLANEOUS
FLORIDA

ORLANDO, FLORIDA—HEALTHSEEKER, homeseeker, here's a fairyland in Sunny Florida. 5-acre tracts on highway, $85 per acre; $2 acre cash, $1 acre per month. Booklet free. Interstate Development Co., Orlando, Fla.

MARYLAND

ONE to 10 acres on the Sassafras River. Wooded or clear, price & terms surprisingly low. Route No 213 to Locust Grove then Kentmore Rd to River. See Mr. Mitchell.

BUILDING LOTS
CITY

LOTS. Hillside loc., about ½ acre. Sell for less than half cost. $450. Del. 2511.

REAL ESTATE WANTED

WHEN you list with us you receive the following: 1. free appraisal; 2. free photographs of your home; 3. free advertising; 4. QUICK ACTION. Our Fall Sales drive has sold many of our homes. We need many more to satisfy our numerous prospects. Sun., 1-5. H. G. RINER, 6727 N. Broad. Liv. 2533.

WANTED To Buy, 10% cash, 2 or 3-bedroom house with hot water heat. Prefer convenient to elevated or Broad St. Subway. State pr. & dets. Chas. L. Sacrey, 2170 E. Letterly st.

SELLING very fast, houses in every section (bargains only); also cheap houses in white & colored sections. Rudolph, 6607 Ogontz ave. Wav. 7069.

WILL give cash & small rented city houses for larger dwelling, or store & dwelling, or mortgages in default. L-240 Inquirer.

CASH buyers for houses in this section, 2 or 3 stories. Send full details. Schneider, Realtor, 1827 W. Erie ave.

HAVE buyers for N.E. homes. Give full details. Try us. HOUSE OF SENDERLING, 3900 Frankford ave. Jef. 5500.

WTD. in W. Oak Lane, 6 rms., tile bath, gar. Modern home, oil heat pref. Compl. renovated. Approx. $4000. Ph. Ten. 1879.

CAN sell your house in 30 days for cash. C.F. Schnabel, 1420 W. Allegheny. Sag. 8300

OWNERS! We need homes for sale. Lehman & Snyder, Realtors, 3701 N. Broad. Rad. 1440.

SMALL farm, not less than 1 acre; 4 or 6-room house. B-294 Inquirer.

CLIENT desires 2-story house. Pay cash. Write Mr. Smith, 405 W. Norris St.

WANT to buy small property in Phila. All cash. Carney, R. D. No. 2, Bristol, Pa.

SELL your property to me. Quick action. No commission. H. C. Little, 3139 N. 15th.

A WANT AD INSERTED IN THE CLASSIFIED COLUMNS OF THE INQUIRER WILL BRING QUICK RESULTS.
PHONE AND ASK FOR AD TAKER
BELL: RITTENHOUSE 5000
KEYSTONE: BROAD 5000

Real Estate for Sale SUBURBAN

Ardmore Homes
Morris & Georges Lane
Semi-detached, 3 bedrooms, bath, garage, oil heat with Summer-Winter hook-up. Every modern convenience.
$5690
Including Settlement Charges
From City Line & Haverford Ave. out Haverford Ave. 2½ miles to Georges Lane—2 blocks to Sample House. By trolley from 69th St. Terminal. Take Phila. Suburban transportation trolley to Belmont Station, 2 blocks to Sample House. Or from Ardmore take bus on Morris Ave to homes. Open Daily & Sunday, 9 A. M. to 9 P. M.
Woodcrest Construction Co.
ARDMORE 9430 TRI. 5572

Penn Park **$6090**
Price Includes Oil Burner with Year 'Round Hot Water
KIRKLYN: Drive or take trolley 1½ miles out West Chester Pike from 69th Street Terminal, turn right at sign (Kirklyn Ave.), or drive out City Line to Meadowbrook Ave.
W. S. PEACE JOS. A. MELONEY
Sales Represent. Builder for 34 Years

Now Ready
NEW COLONIAL TYPE 3 BEDROOM HOMES

Overlook Hills
ATOP ABINGTON TOWNSHIP
NEW AMERICAN COL. HOMES
MORELAND ROAD at HARDING AVE.
3 large bedrooms, garage, hot water heat. North on York Rd. beyond Abington Hospital to Moreland Rd., right to Harding Av.
$5790 — $590. DOWN
JACKSON-CROSS CO., Agts. MAJAR CONSTR. CO., Bldrs.

BUSINESS PROPERTIES

CONSHOHOCKEN
BAKERY PROPERTY
Complete with 2 brick ovens or suit small manufacturing. Wonderful opportunity. SACRIFICE PRICE. Small down payment. Balance can be financed on easy terms. Low interest charge.
BRIDGEPORT REALTY CO.
100 DeKalb St. Norristown 2860

MAYFAIR

4700 LANSING ST. AT 7700 BLOCK TORRESDALE AVE.
BERMAN BUILT
VICTORY HOMES
A complete modern brick home, 3 bedrooms, living room, dining room and kitchen, tile bath with shower, and garage.
PRICE $4190
NO DOWN PAYMENT PLAN AVAILABLE
Ask Representative on Premises for Information.
BERMAN BROTHERS, INC. 6032 MARKET STREET
Sample House, 4721 Lansing St. Phone Mayfair 9984
SAMPLE HOUSE OPEN 9 A. M. TO 9 P. M.

Association Plans Fewer Meetings

Alexander Summer, Teaneck, president of the New Jersey Association of Real Estate boards, announces that in order to conserve automobiles and tires, the number of meetings of the association will be reduced during 1942, and all meetings will be held in centres easily accessible by train.

The January meeting will be held in Newark at the Newark Athletic Club, on Friday.

Bartenders to Thirst For Defense Stamps

FALL RIVER, Mass., Jan. 10 (U. P.)—Francis P. Moffitt and his son, who are conducting an individual defense stamp selling campaign in their restaurant, hung up a sign reading: "Instead of buying a drink for the bartender, buy a stamp for democracy."

They almost sold out their entire $250 stamp stock the first day.

Real Estate for Sale SUBURBAN

Real Estate for Sale SUBURBAN

Real Estate for Sale SUBURBAN

A BEAUTIFULLY PLANNED NEW COMMUNITY OF UNSURPASSED CHARM AND LOVELINESS
DREXEL PARK GARDENS
LESS THAN 5 MINUTES FROM 69TH ST. TERMINAL
ONLY $565 CASH—INCLUDING
General Electric Automatic Oil Furnace with Summer - Winter Hookup . . . Venetian Blinds . . . Tile Kitchen . . . Finished Recreation Room . . . Toilet Room in Basement . . . Built-in Mirror Cabinets with Concealed Lighting . . . Overhead Garage Doors . . . Normandy Chimes . . . All-Stone Foyer and other De Luxe Equipment worth $1660.
$37 PER MONTH INCLUDES EVERYTHING
DIRECTIONS
From 69th and Market Streets go straight out West Chester Pk. to State Rd. Turn left out State Rd. to Drexel Park Gardens at State Rd. & Lansdowne Ave.
Beautifully Furnished Sample Homes Open Daily and Sunday from 10 A. M. to 9:30 P. M.
WARNER-WEST CORPORATION
America's Foremost Residential Developers

GREAT NORTHEAST

THE HOME THAT HAS *Everything*
ENGLISH TYPE STONE AND BRICK FRONT
HOT WATER HEAT
RECREATION ROOM
OIL OR GAS HEAT
AUTOMATIC HOT WATER
ROCK WOOL INSULATION
3 FINE BEDROOMS
COLORED TILE BATH
GARAGE, SHADES
UNEQUALLED VALUE AT **$4690**
6800 KINDRED ST.
Go north on Castor Ave. to Knorr St. (6800), turn right to Kindred St.
BENJAMIN DINTENFASS, Inc., Bldr.
Jackson-Cross Company AGENT DAV. 2000

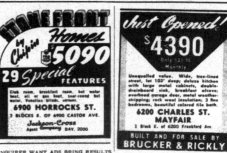

GREAT NORTHEAST

ANOTHER LARGE UNIT READY!
2500 E. VENANGO ST.
FOX SQUARE GARDENS
$3450
PAY ONLY **$49** DOWN AND MOVE IN
FHA TITLE
NO MONEY DOWN
APARTMENT-TYPE HOMES
2 bedrooms. Gas heat. Recreation-room basement. Modern bath & kitchen. Choice 4 Easy Finance Plans. Take No. 15 car to 2600 Richmond Street—Walk West.
Open Sun.—Daily—Eves. Till 9 P. M.
EDWARD A. KERR & CO., BLDRS.

Now Ready
NEW COLONIAL TYPE 3 BEDROOM HOMES
$4390
With DUO-THERM Oil Heat
$32.15 MONTH — $410 TOTAL CARRYING COST
5400 CLARIDGE ST.
1 Block West of Sears-Roebuck Roosevelt Blvd. Store
SYDNEY B. PALLEY • Bldr.

Ideally Located — 3100 Block —
WELLINGTON STREET
1 BLOCK SOUTH OF COTTMAN STREET
2 BLOCKS EAST OF ROOSEVELT BLVD.
NOW OPEN FOR YOUR INSPECTION
HOT WATER HEATING SYSTEM
GENERAL ELECTRIC OIL-FIRED BOILER
ALL YEAR 'ROUND HOT WATER
$4650
$33.24 Total Monthly Pay'ts.
3 Bedrooms, Tile Bath, Overhead Garage Doors, Copper Water Pipes, Venetian Blinds, Shades, Screens.
F. H. A. Inspected and Approved.
Built By BOARDMAN-SMITH Corp.

$490 DOWN
7211 WALKER ST.
Breakfast nook, tile bath, garage, oil or gas heat. Immediate occupancy.
$4290
OPEN 2 TO 9 P. M.
SEGAL-BUILT HOMES
JACKSON-CROSS CO., AGT. DAV. 2000

BUY NOW... BEFORE THE RISE IN PRICE!
4200 BLK. OAKMONT ST.
1 Block East of 7300 Frankford Ave.
Hot Water Heat, Oil Burner
$450 CASH
Ames Co., Inc., Bldrs. MAY. 9946

CUTLER-BUILT Homes
Largest home of its type in this section.
$4890
HOT WATER HEAT
OIL BURNER
7200 COTTAGE ST.
East of 7200 Frankford Ave.
MAY. 9721, DEL. 5443

OCCUPANCY WITHIN 3 WEEKS
$4290 4429 SHELMIRE ST.
2 blocks east of 7300 Frankford Ave.
ZERBEY, BLDR. Prieto, Agt. May. 9703

KORMAN'S
$4295
HOT WATER HEAT
GAS OR OIL BURNER
SHELBOURNE ST. AT WYOMING AVE.
J. Korman's Sons, Bldrs. Jef. 9609

NORTHWOOD

ECONOMY HOMES
IN NORTHWOOD
Only **$31.30** PER MONTH
$4290

Just Opened!
$4390
6200 CHARLES ST.
MAYFAIR
BUILT AND FOR SALE BY
BRUCKER & RICKLY

HAVE YOU A HOUSE FOR RENT? A SMALL AD IN THE CLASSIFIED COLUMNS OF THE INQUIRER WILL QUICKLY BRING YOU A TENANT.
PHONE AND ASK FOR AD TAKER
BELL: RITTENHOUSE 5000
KEYSTONE: BROAD 5000

INQUIRER WANT ADS BRING RESULTS

Roosevelt Gives Baseball 'Go Ahead' Signal

The Philadelphia Inquirer

PHILADELPHIA, SATURDAY MORNING, JANUARY 17, 1942 — adefgh 21

More Arc Games Urged to Landis

Owners Believe Full Schedules Will Be Permitted in 1942

By HAL COOPER

WASHINGTON, Jan. 16 (A. P.).—President Roosevelt cheered the leaders and fans of organized baseball today with a declaration that he thought the war should not be permitted to black out the national pastime.

His statement brought a collective sigh of relief from club owners who have been in an agony of doubt over whether they reasonably could go ahead with plans for the 1942 season.

The President, a great fan himself, made it plain that he expressed only his personal point of view. But leaders of the sport obviously took his remarks to mean that major and minor leagues, although shorn of many stars by calls to the armed services, would be permitted to play out their schedules.

Mr. Roosevelt read a letter he wrote to Judge Kenesaw M. Landis, High Commissioner of baseball.

QUALITY SECONDARY

After disclosing that the Chief Executive favored continuance of the game, the letter went on to say:

"As to the players themselves, I know you agree with me that individual players who are of active military or naval age should go, without question, into the services. Even if the actual quality of the teams is lowered by the greater use of older players, this will not dampen the popularity of the sport. Of course, if any individual has some particular aptitude in a trade or profession, he ought to serve the Government. That, however, is a matter which I know you can handle with complete justice."

"THOROUGHLY WORTHWHILE"

Workers would be putting in longer and harder hours than ever before, the President said, and should have an opportunity for recreation. He calculated that 300 teams would employ 5000 to 6000 players and provide entertainment for twenty million people. And that, he said, was "thoroughly worthwhile."

Mr. Roosevelt's additional suggestion that there be more night games, in order that daylight workers could relax with a bottle of pop, a bag of peanuts and a seat in the stands after their day's toil, met with prompt approval.

Clark Griffith, president of the Washington Baseball Club, said he would suggest at the major league meeting in New York February 2 that the present limit of seven night games per park be doubled.

Donald L. Barnes, head of the financially unsuccessful St. Louis Browns, called it the best news he had heard in a long time. Alva Bradley, president of the Cleveland Indians, said that although he had been a leading proponent of the seven-game rule he might be persuaded to change his mind.

ONTARIO CLUB BOXER GOES DOWN BY TECHNICAL KNOCKOUT ROUTE IN INQUIRER BOUT
Dick Kaszynski hits floor hard from punch by Frank Granata, Haverford, in third round of Olympia battle

Ray Robinson Beats Fritz Zivic in 10th

By JACK CUDDY

NEW YORK, Jan. 16 (U. P.).—Unbeaten Ray Robinson, Harlem's dancing dynamiter, clinched a shot at the world welterweight crown tonight by scoring a technical knockout over former Champion Fritzie Zivic in the 10th round of their return bout before 13,000 fans at Madison Square Garden.

Referee Arthur Donovan stopped the bout at 31 seconds of the 10th when 28-year-old Zivic was on the floor for the second time in the scrap. Fritzie had been battered into virtual helplessness on the ropes before he sank to the canvas.

ZIVIC DOWN FOR NINE

Slender, brown-skinned Robinson readied his man for the end in the previous round when his lightning right fist exploded on Fritzie's chin and sent him to the canvas on his face. Fritzie rose at the count of nine, with his face smeared with resin dust. Robinson was after him immediately, barraging him to body and head, but the bell apparently saved the Pittsburgh veteran.

Until that thundering right in the ninth round, Zivic had made a better showing than in their first scrap on Oct. 31 when Robinson took a 10-round decision. Tonight's return match was slated for 12 rounds, but didn't go the distance as Fritzie suffered the second kayo in his long career. Only once before had he been stopped in more than 150 fights. Milt Aaron registered a technical kayo over him a couple years ago.

27TH STRAIGHT VICTORY

Robinson's 27th straight professional victory and his 21st kayo

Continued on Page 23, Column 5

Nelson Tightens Lead at Oakland

By RUSSELL NEWLAND

OAKLAND, Calif., Jan. 16 (A. P.).—Like a handicap horse stuck in with a bunch of selling platers, Byron Nelson galloped away from the field today in the second round of the 72-hole $5000 Oakland Open golf tournament.

The husky, iron shot master from Toledo, O., clubbed another sub-par round from the Sequoyah course and at the 36-hole mark posted a 136 for a four-stroke advantage over his closest rivals.

SHOOTS 69

Nelson tacked a 69 on to his opening round 67 to draw away from a field that numbers most of the outstanding players in the country. He started weakly and finished like a champion, a distinction he has held in the past.

The former National Open and P. G. A. title holder three-putted the [illegible] for a one over-par five, then [illegible] off even pars for the [illegible] for a 36.

On the incoming stretch he chalked up a birdie three on the 10th from a [illegible] putt and knocked in a [illegible] for a birdie three on the [illegible]. He missed a three-foot try on the 18th for what would have been another birdie but the par gave him a [illegible] 33 and one of the day's [illegible] rounds.

The tournament favorite, until his [illegible] rival, Nelson moved in, was Ben Hogan of Hershey, Pa. They [illegible] together as caddies in Fort Worth, Tex., and the rivalry has continued as they attained starring roles on the links.

Hogan, after a solid 68 yesterday, faltered today and came in with a 72. He lost the edge from his usually [illegible] touch.

Grid Official Dies

BUFFALO, N. Y., Jan. 16 (U. P.).—[illegible] Earle Motzer, 4[illegible], Western New York football official and a former [illegible] athlete at Miami University, Oxford, O., died of a heart attack at his home today.

Dorazio Wins From Gardner

By EDWARD J. KLEIN

Stocky Gus Dorazio slammed and slashed Jimmy Gardner, Lawnside (N. J.) Negro, through 10 rounds last night to easily win the decision in the main event of the four-bout boxing show at Camden Convention Hall.

In a tune-up duel for his fight with Lou Brooks at the Arena Jan. 26, Dorazio took command early and battered Gardner severly about head and body. On Referee Joe Mangold's tally sheet, Gus won nine periods, with the fifth even.

DORAZIO FORCES ACTION

Dorazio, who forced the action all the way, leveled his shots at Gardner's mid-section for two rounds, then let go with two-handed barrages to the head in the third. Through the late sessions he cuffed his lanky foe often and hard, doing his best work at close quarters.

Gardner's light left jabs bothered Dorazio somewhat, but did little damage. The swarthy Southwark heavyweight, at 191, outweighed his victim by 13 pounds.

Tony Paoli, 160, Philadelphia, floored Artis Williams, 162, Berlin (N. J.) Negro for a nine-count in the

Continued on Page 23, Column 6

Mahon Topples Williams In Inquirer A. A. Feature

By JOHN WEBSTER

Battering his way to victory in a rough, punch-shortened engagement, rugged Art Mahon last night began his campaign for The Inquirer A. A. open division feather crown with a technical knockout triumph.

His first battle in the 1942 Diamond Belt and Middle Atlantic A. A. U. eliminations was a winning one when he halted Charley Williams, chubby little Negro, after two rounds of rough-house belting. His right ear cut by a blow, and himself shaken by Mahon's second-round slugging, Williams was unable to answer the bell for the third round in the final contest of The Inquirer A. A. program at the Olympia, Broad st., below Bainbridge.

After an examination of Williams' injury, Dr. Angelo M. Perri, an A. A. U. physician, decided that the John Marquess ringman, should not continue. The referee, Joe Shannon, then elevated Mahon's knuckles in token of third-round triumph.

Since Mahon is the leading candidate of the 48th Ward Boys' Club for tournament honors, his victory was the most popular of the night with the large, enthusiastic crowd which witnessed the bouts sponsored by that downtown organization.

Beginning his fourth Diamond Belt tournament drive, the sturdy Irish lad met with some trouble from Williams in the first period. That youth pecked away with an accurate left hand, and in addition to his jabbing, fought Mahon at a mad pace in shoulder-to-shoulder lashing.

However, Mahon's strength began to tell in the second. He brushed past jabs, bombed Williams with head blows against the ropes, and smashed away to the body when the John Marquess boxer had edged away from the ring rigging.

In a brisk exchange in mid-ring, Williams, no longer able to match

Continued on Page 23, Column 3

L. Merion Passers Conquer Upper Darby by 32-16 Score

Lower Merion High continued its basketball sweep in defense of the Suburban One League title by mowing down Upper Darby High last night, 32-16, on the home floor.

Bill Koehler, former Southern High ace, helped the Ardmorites to victory by tallying 12 points, while Greer Heindel, veteran centre, added 11 points.

In the other Suburban One League tilts, Ray Uccelletti, Abington's sharpshooter, fired from mid-court with 10 seconds to go and the ball cut the cords for Abington's 30-29 victory over Cheltenham at the Abington court. Bob Arnold salvaged a little glory for the Panthers with the scoring honors at 16 points. Norristown invaded Haverford to turn in a 37-32 conquest.

Lansdowne, stopped by Radnor early in the week, came back last night to defeat Darby, 34-25, at Darby with Gunner Wilcox and Fred Welte sharing the honors with 10 points each.

Phoenixville bounced back from the Coatesville reverse to trounce Three League game, Floyd Lilley

Continued on Page 23, Column 6

Fiantini Beaten By Johnny Forte

By FRANK O'GARA

Dom Fiantini, squat little Reading scrapper, fought his final battle last night before enlisting in the U. S. Coast Guard, but he may have to be put in drydock for repairs before being of much use to that organization.

His present condition was induced by the flailing fists of Johnny Forte, former Inquirer A. A. champ, who handed him an unmerciful hiding before 1500 fans at the Cambria.

Fiantini, aiming to reverse a previous decision against him in the same ring a month ago by Forte, never desisted from his role of catching leather. Although he strove gamely, Dom failed even to take one of the eight rounds as Johnny stalked him around, rigorously thumping at every legal portion of his anatomy.

Forte, at 127¼, gave away a pound to his foe.

In the semi-windup, a six-rounder, Eddie Allen, 135¼, South Philadelphia, ran his string of triumphs to 23 straight by gaining a split decision over Jack Sheppard, 133¾, Strawberry Mansion. Matt Adgie,

Continued on Page 23, Column 2

P.M.C. Beaten By Moravian

CHESTER, Pa., Jan. 16.—Moravian College turned back P. M. C. in one of the most spectacular basketball games of recent years at Chester last night. The Bethlehem speedsters outgunned the Cadets to win a 52 to 43 battle.

P. M. C.	G.	F.	P.	MORAVIAN	G.	F.	P.
Smith, f	1	0	2	Wolfram, f	0	0	0
Bartow, f	2	0	4	Majczan, f	8	4	20
Miller, c	9	5	23	Marcincin, c	5	0	10
Klein, g	3	0	6	McMonigle, g	2	0	4
Wood, g	4	0	8	Calvo, g	7	2	16
Lesnow, g	0	0	0	Levy, f	1	0	2
Piff, f	0	0	0	W'niewski, c	0	0	0
Murawski, f	0	0	0				
Button, g	0	0	0				
Totals	19	5	43	Totals	23	6	52

P. M. C.	10	12	15	6	43
Moravian	8	24	13	7	52

Missed fouls—P. M. C., 7 (Smith, Miller, 4; Klein, 2); Moravian, 6 (Marcincin, 2; McMonigle, Calvo, 2; Levy). Personals—P. M. C., 10 (Bartow, 2; Miller, Klein, 3; Wood, 3; Lesnow); Moravian, 9 (Majczan, Marcincin, 3; McMonigle, 2; Calvo, 2; Wiszniewski). Referees—Stackowski and Glascott.

Passon Suffers First League Loss

Passon suffered its first defeat in the South Philadelphia League last night, when it bowed to Regal Owls, 32 to 31 victory at Sixth and Catharine sts. The defeat dropped Passon out of first place in the league race.

DePalma stepped into first place by handing Red Jackets a 83 to 50 defeat at the Dixon House, 1920 S. 20th st.

Don't Look Now, But --

Penn A. C. Plans to Go Through With Its Track Meet

REGARDLESS of what happens to the club house in the current dealings with the Government, the Penn A. C. plans to go through with its annual indoor track meet Feb. 13 at Convention Hall. U. of P. and Olympic Coach Lawson Robertson, who is again serving as director of the Pennac games, disclosed yesterday that a committee of club members is being formed to underwrite expenses. Several big-name athletes from points distant enough to make trainfare a sizeable item have already accepted tentative invitations to compete here.

Triple Threat—George Munger, Penn football coach who is said to be anxious to appoint Gene (Stinky) Davis to the backfield coaching vacancy left by Howard Odell's appointment at Wisconsin, is fond of telling this one on his star captain and quarterback of 1941: "In his three years of college football Stinky intercepted a lot of forward passes; but he never was able to get loose with any of those stray aerials. In the Cornell game, sure enough, he intercepted another, but this time he raced up to the line of scrimmage and managed to get a yard the other side before being downed. Getting up, he turned to the other Penn players: 'There,' he gloated, 'see what a great broken field runner you fellows have been passing up all these years!'"

Local Boys—Nine native Philadelphians are included on the Phils' roster, more hometown players, perhaps, than any other big league club can boast of. The Philadelphia Phils are Frank Hoerst, Tommy Hughes, John Behrenda, Andy Lapihuska, Danny Litwhiler, Harry Marnie, Danny Murtaugh, Bill Peterman and John Podgajny ... And Manager Hans Lobert, born in Wilmington, has been a resident here for 30 years ...

Freezing the Ball—The next time Coach Ernie Messikomer finds his Temple basketball team in a position where stalling for time is imperative, he might call upon Dick Nochimson, substitute forward. He's had experience. One night three years ago Nochimson, working at a Paterson gas station, caught a radio flash that a couple hold-up men were in the neighborhood, to be on the look-out; just then a couple suspicious characters pulled in for fuel. Nochimson, signaling his partner, took over, and not even the best of his customers ever received more service than the bandits: windshield polished, water refilled, oil double checked, rear window wiped. In fact, Nochimson was just starting the whole process a third time when the police finally arrived.

A. R. H. M.

Night Games Now Certain

By STAN BAUMGARTNER

It is practically certain that each major league club—at least the American League—will play 14 night games this season.

Taking a tip from President Roosevelt, who went on record yesterday as urging more night games, the major leagues will meet in extraordinary joint session in New York on Feb. 3, and undoubtedly rescind their rule which prevents more than seven night games.

For the past three years the American League has strongly supported Connie Mack and Clark Griffith as well as Don Barnes in their demand for additional arc light contests and each year the junior circuit has gone into the joint meeting determined to argue the point. But each year the National League has stood on its hind feet and voted against the proposition.

With the two leagues deadlocked, Judge Keneshaw Mountain Landis who was able to cast the deciding vote, always put in his ballot with the National Leaguers.

However — with the President's personal wish before him—the Commissioner will undoubtedly put on the pressure the other way. The American League will be permitted to stage 14 night games—and the National League to protect themselves —will follow suit.

Hallahan Girls Defeat Bethlehem

The Hallahan Catholic Girls' High basketball team opened its season with a 35-13 conquest of Bethlehem Catholic at 19th and Wood sts. yesterday.

It was the fifth consecutive triumph for Hallahan after its long streak was snapped last year by Norristown.

Coach Catherine McPeak used 19 members of her squad against the visiting sextet in the walkaway triumph. Eight of the nine forwards employed scored at least one point. Florence McLoughlin led the victors with 13 markers, while Elizabeth Di Fillipo scored six and Mary Sheehan, Mary Rowan and Margaret McLoughlin, Florence's sister, checked in with four apiece.

HALLAHAN	G.	F.	P.	BETHLEHEM	G.	F.	P.
F. McL'hlin, f	6	1	13	Turbach, f	0	[illegible]	3
M. Sheehan, f	2	0	4	C'ningham, f	0	2	2
Rowan, f	2	0	4	Pvelko, f	2	2	6
DiFillipo, f	3	0	6	King, f	1	0	2
D. Sheehan, f	0	0	0	Ulrich, g	0	0	0
M. M'L'lin, f	2	0	4	Udvardi, g	0	0	0
Peiffer, f	1	0	2	Kalabin, g	0	0	0
Meissler, f	0	1	1				
Brennan, f	0	1	1				
Joyce, g	0	0	0				
Flood, g	0	0	0				
Weyler, g	0	0	0				
Totals	16	3	35	Totals	3	7	13

Sphas Outscore Trenton, 35 to 33

TRENTON, N. J., Jan. 16.—Ossie Schechtman led the Philadelphia Sphas to a 35-33 win over the Trenton Tigers in an American League basketball game here tonight at the Arena.

SPHAS				TRENTON			
Rosan, f	1	3	5	Gershon, f	3	0	6
Gotthoffer, f	2	3	7	Davis, f	0	0	0
Wolfe, f	0	0	0	Paris, f	3	2	8
Torgoff, c	0	1	1	Bloom, c	5	0	10
Schechtman, g	7	1	15	M'zkowski, g	2	5	9
Lautman, g	3	1	7	Boardman, g	0	0	0
Goldman, g	0	0	0				
Totals	13	9	35	Totals	13	7	33

Sphas	9	13	13	35
Trenton	13	12	8	33

Referees—Poliskin and Silverman. Time of periods, 15 minutes.

Phila. Assured Of Title Rowing

This city is virtually assured of the 1942 National Rowing Championships, and the classic regatta will probably be held on the Schuylkill in Fairmount Park next July.

Award of the regatta is scheduled to be made this afternoon at the mid-winter meeting of the Executive Committee of the National Association of Amateur Oarsmen, which will be held at the New York Athletic Club at 3 P. M.

Penn Evening School Rallies to Win, 46-36

Penn Evening School rallied with five field goals in the closing minutes to turn back Lincoln Business College, 46-36, at Weightman Hall last night.

Penn Evening School	G.	F.	P.	Lincoln Bus. Coll.	G.	F.	P.
Hen'sey, f	2	1	5	O'Neill, f	1	0	2
Dawson, f	4	1	9	Baker, f	6	1	13
Brown, c	2	0	4	Snider, c	5	1	11
Bye, g	3	0	6	T. Manning, g	2	2	6
Black, g	1	2	4	Kelly, g	1	1	3
Early, f	1	0	2	J. Manning	0	1	1
Boyle	2	2	6				
Conover, c	1	2	4				
Jacobucci	3	0	6				
Totals	19	8	46	Totals	15	6	36

First half score—Penn Evening, 21; Lincoln Business, [illegible]. Referee—Brewster, Penn State. Time of halves, 16 minutes.

Champs' Tourney Tickets on Sale

Tickets for the Tournament of Champions, the highlight of the Diamond Belt and Middle Atlantic Amateur Boxing Championships, are now on sale. The winter's outstanding sports event is to take place at Convention Hall on Monday night, Feb. 2.

Reserved seats, priced at $1.75 and $1.25, may be obtained at The Inquirer, Broad and Callowhill sts.; Herman Taylor's ticket office (Lew Tendler's Restaurant), Broad and Locust sts.; Gimbels, 9th and Chestnut sts., and Bond's, 16th and Chestnut sts.

General admission will be on sale only at Convention Hall on the night of the show.

In the Tournament of Champions, winners of The Inquirer A. A. eliminations in Philadelphia will face champions from Wilmington, Harrisburg and Tamaqua.

Holman Quits F. & M. Job To Go Into Realty Business

LANCASTER, Pa., Jan. 16 (A. P.).—Alan M. Holman, who gained national prominence in 1940 when his Franklin and Marshall eleven upset Dartmouth, unexpectedly resigned today as football coach of the Diplomats.

Holman arrived here last night for a conference with "Uncle Charley" Mayser, director of athletics. The athletic authorities at F. and M. made the surprise announcement this afternoon.

No reason for Holman's sudden move was given, but a dispatch from Columbus, O., said the F. and M. coach would become associate with the Galbraith Real Estate Co. there.

Holman, whose contract still had a year to run, developed many winning Diplomat teams, several of which won Eastern Pennsylvania collegiate conference titles. He was under consideration to become head coach at Ohio State before the job was given to Paul Brown, famous Massillon (O.) grid mentor. Holman came here from Ohio State 11 years ago.

In 1940 the Diplomats won seven and lost two games and placed several men on the Associated Press All-State and little All-America teams. Last year, with a squad of only 25 men, he turned in a record of five games won in seven played.

MERCHANDISE AND SERVICE FOR YOU, YOUR CAR AND HOME

PARCEL POST BUSINESS

ADDITIONAL PARCEL POST BUSINESS ON OPPOSITE PAGE

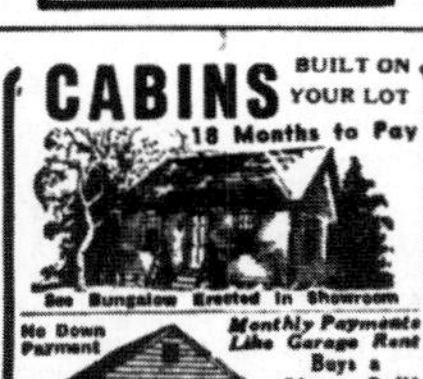

All-Out Indian Effort Is Urged

MADRAS, India, Jan. 17.—Sir Bijoy Prosad Sinch Roy, in a presidential address to the 23d Indian National Liberal Federation, said yesterday that Indians should join all branches of the fighting forces despite grievances against British rule.

"As realists we cannot be indifferent to the need for co-operation in the war effort," he said. "War has already reached our frontiers and to stand by and watch the vandalism of infamous aggressors is to invite disaster."

Suprise Tear Gas Exercise

A tear gas exercise conducted by the Air Raid Precautions Unit at Erith, England, took a wedding party by surprise and as the bride and groom left All Saints' Church tears streamed from their eyes because they had forgotten their gas masks.

Bauxite in U. S. Put at 6-Year Supply

WASHINGTON, Jan. 17.—The Bureau of Mines estimated today that reserves of bauxite, the source of vital aluminum, would be exhausted in the United States within six years if foreign imports are stopped and the present rate of consumption is maintained.

A report placed the commercial bauxite reserves in this country at roughly 18,000,000 tons.

In addition there are reserves of 11,000,000 to 14,000,000 tons of bauxite of a grade too low to recover under present commercial processes.

The report said bauxite requirements would reach almost 3,000,000 tons annually by July, 1942. This is four times the 1940 consumption for all purposes.

Boat Service Started

Panama has inaugurated a boat service from Colon to the primitive San Blas Islands, where the Indians cling to centuries-old customs.

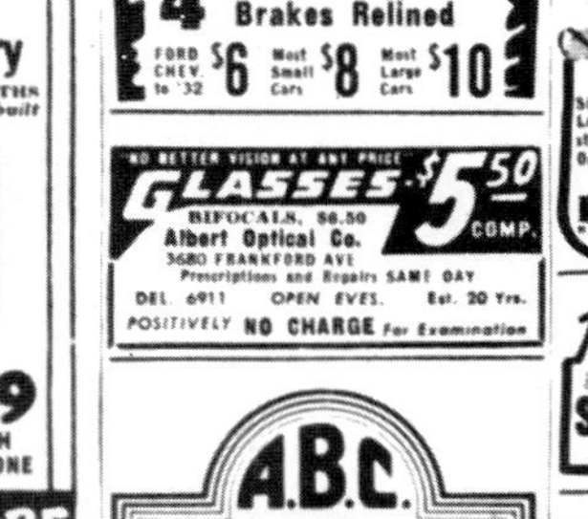

'Cover Girls of '42' Planned by Columbia

Rita Hayworth to Get Starring Role, With Jinx Falkenburg, Janet Blair, Harriet Hilliard Slated for Cast

By Louella O. Parsons

HOLLYWOOD, Jan. 23.

APPROPRIATE that Rita Hayworth, who has won a record as the girl who has been on more magazine covers than any other actress in 1941, is to be starred in "Cover Girls of 1942." This is the first brainchild of that bright boy, Bob Taplinger, since he joined Columbia. With Rita will be 12 of America's most glamorous magazine cover models. These beauties will be submitted by such important publications as Cosmopolitan, Red Book, Saturday Evening Post, Photoplay, Ladies' Home Journal and other magazines that go in for real life models.

JANET BLAIR

"Cover Girls of 1942" includes Jinx Falkenburg, who has been much photographed, Janet Blair and Harriet Hilliard—and it wouldn't be a Taplinger idea if it didn't include a tour of the country. Remember the Navy Blue Sextet? Well, the 12 beauties will be sent out to sell bonds and also to appear at Army camps.

Donald Duck is the first Walt Disney movie favorite to be sent out by Uncle Sam on an income tax mission. He's the star of "The New Spirit," a movie made to show us how to pay our income tax. Donald, of course, is a bachelor, so he doesn't have to pay for a wife, but he has some married friends in his movie. Over 1000 prints have been ordered and it is estimated that the picture will be seen by 85,000,000 to 125,000,000 people. More people will hear and see Donald Duck in his income tax epic than saw "Gone With the Wind."

Damon Dunyon is the world's greatest night owl. He stays up all night and does more work in the late afternoon than most folks do in a week. Well, he would like, more than anything in the world, to borrow Susan Hayward for the girl's role opposite Henry Fonda in "It Comes Up Love," formerly "Little Pinks." If Susie finishes "Forest Ranger" in time she will be the gal chosen for the Runyon movie. Yes, Para has put her into their outdoor epic with Paulette Goddard and Fred MacMurray. Paulette plays the Madeleine Carroll role and Susan inherits the part originally given the vivacious Goddard gal. Again Para promises us our Susie gets a chance. We hope so.

Carole's Last Film Due Feb. 12

"To Be or Not to Be," Carole Lombard's last picture, will be dedicated to her. Ernst Lubitsch has written a beautiful foreword in which he says that because Carole liked to make the world laugh it is fitting that the public should see her in a comedy. She hated sadness. The picture will be released in 100 theatres as near Feb. 12, the original date, as possible. While many posthumous pictures have not been financially successful, "Saratoga," Jean Harlow's last picture, which she made curiously enough with Clark Gable, cleared half a million. "Steamboat Bill," starring Will Rogers, released after his death, was also a money maker. Ernst Lubitsch, Jack Benny and Carole made this movie on a percentage basis.

Jean Gabin, French Star, Sees Ginger Rogers

Chatter in Hollywood: Remember last week we told you that Jean Gabin had asked Ginger Rogers for an "atonement" date? Well, boys and girls, it must have worked for these two are the latest torrid duet in Hollywood. Gabin, long a devoted swain in Marlene Dietrich's entourage, is now calling Ginger steen times a day and sending flowers by the carload. In case you've forgotten the details of the "atonement" date it happened this way: When the French actor first came to Hollywood he asked Ginger to dine with him. But at that time he could speak only such phrases as "thank you" and "steak and salad." "I am sure the lady was very bored," he said. But now Gabin has learned our language and things are different—and how!

A Line or Two: Constance Moore has been in bed over a week with wisdom tooth trouble, but that isn't keeping her from joining Joe E. Brown and Ben Oakland in a tour of some of the eastern camps. Connie, who sings like a bird, will be accompanied by Oakland, and Brown will do one of his famous monologues.

Babe Ruth, who almost killed himself trying to whittle himself down to proper movie size for the Lou Gehrig role, is out of the hospital. He is still a little shaky in the knees but will arrive here in a couple of weeks for his stint in Sam Goldwyn's "Pride of the Yankees."

A telegram from Arizona says that Helen Gahagan will be a principal speaker at the children's welfare conference to be held in Phoenix. Miss Gahagan and her husband, Melvyn Douglas, have been interested in child welfare for a long time and she has given up her acting career to be a Democratic National Committeewoman.

HARRIET HILLIARD

Maxie Rosenbloom, who is staging a fight for the local tuberculosis fund on March 15, is trying to persuade Darryl Zanuck to lend him John Payne for an exhibition match. Can't blame Darryl for considering this offer carefully, for with Slapsie Maxie turned loose heavens knows what would happen to 20th's pet and pride.

Snapshots of Hollywood Collected at Random: Bruce McFarlane, who is in the "My Sister Eileen" show in New York, is a proud papa. His wife presented him with a daughter at Good Samaritan Hospital, Los Angeles.

Hugh Herbert has just had a cyst removed from his head and he looks like the wounded warrior with the bandage he is wearing.

Harry Edington, who has left R. K. O., returns to the agency business. He once handled Garbo.

Virginia O'Brien heads for New York in another two weeks to see her fiance, Kirk Allyn.

Rex St. Cyr, the town's prize party-giver, has ordered a large table for the Mayfair party tomorrow night. The Jack Warners, Norma Shearer, the Danny Dankers are others who are bringing parties to the opening of the club, the proceeds of which go to Ann Lehr's Hollywood Guild.

Donna Reed of M-G-M entertaining Jack Nau, flying cadet from Iowa.

Darryl Zanuck has presented most of his thoroughbred polo ponies to the Army and Chester Lauck (Lum, of Lum 'n' Abner) is doing the same with most of his horses.

Dorothy Lamour will go to Phoenix, for a brief rest after the President's Birthday Ball and her recent bond-selling tour in the East.

"Let's be specific, to win in the Pacific—buy defense bonds," says Eddie Welch, 20th Century-Fox writer. If you have any idea for slogans send them to this column and if we use them we will credit you.

10 Groups to Join Music Festival

Ten groups will participate in an Elementary Music Festival at 2.30 P. M. today in Irvine Auditorium, 34th and Spruce sts.

Sponsored by the Cultural Olympics of the University of Pennsylvania, the festival will give expression to chorus, glee clubs and orchestras of grade schools.

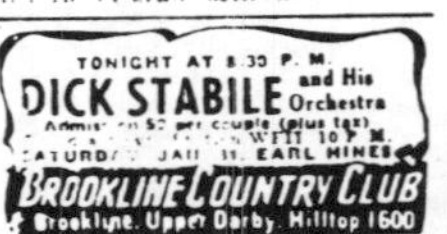

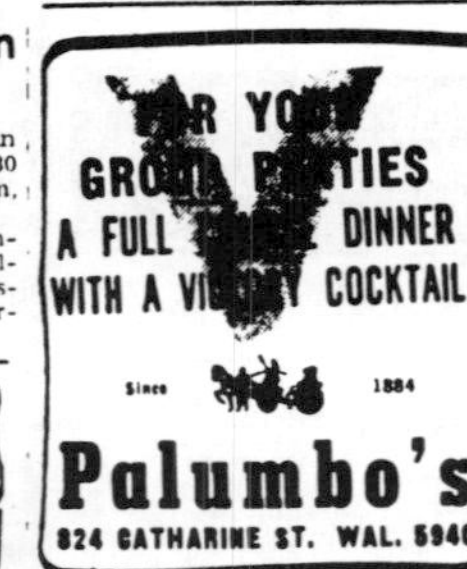

PRINCIPALS IN ROMANTIC COMEDY

George Montgomery and Carole Landis are the lovers in "Cadet Girl," which opened yesterday at the Earle.

Award Is Urged For 'Citizen Kane'

HOLLYWOOD, Jan. 23 (U. P.).—Orson Welles' first movie, "Citizen Kane," was nominated with 10 other films today for the annual Academy Award for black and white art direction.

A committee of art directors from all studios will attend the showings of the pictures and choose one for the award. "Citizen Kane" already has been chosen picture of the year by New York critics.

Others nominated were "Flame of New Orleans," "Hold Back the Dawn," "How Green Was My Valley," "Ladies in Retirement," "The Little Foxes," "Sergeant York," "Sis Hopkins," "Son of Monte Cristo," "Sundown" and "When Ladies Meet."

Arnold Off to Capital

HOLLYWOOD, Jan. 23 (A. P.).—Edward Arnold, screen actor, was en route to Washington today for the President's Diamond Jubilee Birthday Ball on Jan. 30. He was the first of 20 film stars to leave for the celebration of Mr. Roosevelt's 60th birthday anniversary.

Prima's Band Tops New Show at Earle

Rafter-Rattling Music Mixed With Novelties

By Mildred Martin

"CADET GIRL," a 20th Century-Fox picture; original story by Jack Andrews and Richard English; screenplay by Stanley Rauh and H. W. Hanemann; lyrics and music by Leo Robin and Ralph Rainger; directed by Ray McCarey; opened yesterday at the Earle in conjunction with a stage program.

THE CAST

Gene Baxter	Carole Landis
Tex Mallory	George Montgomery
Bob Mallory	John Shepperd
Runt	William Tracy
Mary Moore	Janis Carter
Walton	Robert Lowery
Red	Basil Walker
Jimmy	Charles Tannen
Benny Burns	Chick Chandler
Foo	Otto Han
Trainman	Irving Bacon
Ona	Jane Hazzard
Mona	Edna Mae Jones

Louis Prima, of the expansive personality and sizzling trumpet, gave the Earle one of the best and breeziest bills it has had this season upon his arrival yesterday. Prima, apart from his chores as cornet-tootling maestro, puts on a lively show with his patter and some odd gyrations that might or might not be called dancing. And he has the happy faculty of making the audience part of the entertainment. In fact, yesterday he lured four courageous, if self-conscious, girls up on the stage to assist in "Tika-tee, Tika-ta," rewarding each with a recording of the song.

RAFTER-ROCKING NUMBER

The Prima band really cut loose in "Chant of the Groovers," rafter-rocking number presented yesterday for the first time and with Louis providing the hot trumpet solo. Other numbers warm enough to blister the paint were "Georgia Brown," "You Made Me Love You," sung by the versatile Prima; and "Dark Eyes," played by the band's instrumental sextette with Leon Prima proving that trumpeting runs in the Prima family.

Pretty, brunette Lily Ann Carol sang "He's 1-A in the Army and A-1 in My Heart," "Shrine of St. Cecilia," and, amusingly assisted by Louis, "Daddy." Sol Marcus, "I Don't Want to Set the World on Fire" composer, offered his popular song as a piano solo.

Eddie Bracken, of stage, screen and radio fame, won enthusiastic applause with baseball pitcher and prize fighter pantomimes and a cock-eyed description of how to build up a character for the movies. The Burns Twins and Evelyn offered superior tap routines, Evelyn doing a nimble number in ballet slippers. And Roy Davis virtually stopped the show in hilarious antics sychronized with phonograph records.

'Cadet Girl' Is Feature On Screen

ABOUT THE PICTURE

"Cadet Girl," on the screen, is a soggy, pseudo-patriotic yarn about a West Point cadet who wants to play the piano and get married instead of sticking to the Army. The Army and the Mallory tradition get him in the end, if anybody cares.

Some pretty bad acting and music is scattered through the silly little piece. Ex-Cowboy George Montgomery is the recalcitrant cadet; brassy blonde Carol Landis, the girl; and John Shepperd, the bandleading Mallory who didn't join the Army himself but makes it hot for his brother when he wants to chuck West Point.

Your contribution to the "Buy a Bomber" fund will help blast the way to victory. Don't delay! Send it today.

Remember Pearl Harbor! Help buy a bomber for Uncle Sam. Send a contribution today.

The Philadelphia Inquirer

PUBLIC LEDGER

An Independent Newspaper for All the People

FINAL CITY EDITION

CIRCULATION: February Average: Daily 436,153, Sunday 1,284,022 a b d e f g h ★★ | WEDNESDAY MORNING, MARCH 18, 1942 | Second Largest 3c Morning Circulation in America | THREE CENTS

 VOL. 226, No. 77

441 Tops Phila. List in Third Draft, 3485 Is First in National Lottery; MacArthur Shift Hints Offensive

This Is America, 1942

Mormons Endure Many Sacrifices To Aid U.S. at War

(Eighteenth of a Series)

By IVAN H. "CY" PETERMAN

Inquirer Staff Reporter

(Copyright, 1942, The Philadelphia Inquirer)

SALT LAKE CITY, Utah, March 17.

IT WILL soon be springtime in the Rockies with Utah's fruit trees all in bloom, the mighty snows of a hard winter again trickling down rugged slopes to waiting reservoirs, awakening with murmuring rivulets the season's first wild flowers.

The sun, each day grown more friendly, smiles into the crannies of Cottonwood and Emigration canyons through which so long ago Brigham Young led his Mormon band, pioneering a remote new homeland.

The familiar honk of wildfowl, soaring northward across Great Salt Lake, echoes as ever to the plateau where luxuriant groves and productive ranches attest the industry of those who irrigated the desert "to make it blossom as the rose."

And the Gothic spires of the stately Temple, reflecting a new summer's brilliance, will vie once more as in decades past, with the gleaming crests of the Wasatch.

But the Latter Day Saints will hold no April conference in Salt Lake City.

There will be no convocation of the faithful, the bishops, the presidents, the councillors of the wards and the stakes, or the ruling elders, and there will be no 112th Conference as in those Aprils past. Economy, restrictions on travel, rules against convocation forbid. The constricting hand of war has touched the Mormons.

• • •

IT HAS touched them in a wide, encircling fashion, so profoundly and relentlessly as to threaten from all sides the ordered way of living now established for nearly a century. It was in 1847 they emerged from yonder canyon.

Stoically, with patience and courage and rebukes for nobody, the Church embarks upon its ordeal, the unprecedented experience of sharing this broad valley with the legions of Mars.

This Nation has been hearing a lot about sacrificing to win the war; there is much of economy, buying bonds, giving up tires and autos and sugar and canned goods and travel, new clothing and comforts of all sorts. This is as it should be. This is the only way.

But I have found here in the Salt Lake Valley such an outstanding example of group sacrifice, such a penetrating, perhaps enduring change in the lives of people—of deeply religious, unchanging people who in the beginning trekked painfully across the plains and mountains to be alone unto themselves—that I must write about it to show what true sacrifice can mean.

Whether you know it or not, whether this area wished so or not, the fact is that Utah, especially its great Salt Lake Valley, has become a focal point in the military plans of the West Coast. Not only has this once agrarian paradise been abruptly turned into a mass-producing arsenal and storehouse, but it is bristling with the armed forces.

• • •

IN THE last few weeks General Headquarters of the 9th Corps Area were moved here from San Francisco. General DeWitt remains at

Continued on Page 12, Column 2

IN TODAY'S INQUIRER

U. S. GENERAL MADE SUPREME CHIEF IN PACIFIC

Flies From Bataan To Australia; Brett Named Commander Of Allied Air Forces

Illustrated on Page 2

By JOHN M. McCULLOUGH

Inquirer Washington Bureau

WASHINGTON, March 17.—General Douglas MacArthur, 62-year-old hero of Bataan, arrived by plane at an undisclosed point in Australia today to take over supreme command of all Allied forces in that vital area.

A few hours after the electrifying news, contained in a War Department communique, had awakened echoes of world-wide enthusiasm, President Roosevelt announced at his press conference that the former Chief of Staff would be in supreme command of all Allied forces—land, sea and air—east of Singapore.

BRETT HEADS AIR FORCES

(Lieutenant General George H. Brett, of the U. S. Army, has been appointed commander of the combined air forces of the United Nations in the Western Pacific, Prime Minister John Curtin announced in Canberra, Australia, early Wednesday morning, acording to the United Press.

(President Roosevelt approved Brett's appointment to the command on recommendation of the Australian government, Curtin added.)

EARLY DRIVE INDICATED

There were indications both in the President's comment and in the announcement last night of the arrival of "considerable numbers" of American air and ground reinforcements

Continued on Page 2, Column 1

CCC DESTROYS VITAL TOOLS AT ANOTHER CAMP

New Equipment Found Damaged by Picks and Torch Near Renovo Site

By GERSON H. LUSH

Inquirer Staff Reporter

RENOVO, Pa., March 17.—New evidence of waste and destruction of vital and valuable materials in Federal Civilian Conservation Corps camps in Pennsylvania was uncovered today by investigators for The Inquirer.

NEW TOOLS JUNKED

Investigators visited Twin Valley CCC Camp S-75, 10 miles from this place, and at the camp's Hyner Run storehouse found:

Equipment and tools described by experts as "brand new," piled up on a junk heap to be sold at some future date as scrap metal.

Quantities of other tools, apparently never used, but damaged by picks and acetylene torches so as to be unusable, piled up on the same scrap heap.

N. Y. PROBE SOUGHT

Meanwhile, on the heels of a report that there might be similar waste and destruction in CCC camps in New York State, Representative Joseph Clark Baldwin (R., N. Y.) introduced a resolution in Congress calling for an investigation by the House Labor Committee which was instrumental in forming the CCC. Baldwin acted at the request of Representative W. Sterling Cole (R., N. Y.) who said he had received the reports of conditions in New York State.

Representative Charles I. Faddis (D., Penna.), chairman of the special sub-committee of the House Military Affairs Committee, which investigated The Inquirer's findings at Pine Grove Furnace, Pa., announced in Washington his investigators found "nothing alarming." However, he added that he would continue the probe to determine whether the CCC still held materials needed for the war program.

MATERIALS LISTED

If nothing has happened to the "junk" piles at Twin Valley Camp since they were examined yesterday, here is some of the new material of interest to the House investigators:

Steel files.

Automotive equipment, includ-

Continued on Page 12, Column 6

Phila. Numbers

Draft serial numbers drawn in Washington last night and affecting Philadelphians, in the order in which they were drawn, follow:

(Read left to right)

441	1817	1103	1790	1584	176	1577	1156	2309	2203
606	359	129	968	1337	537	2321	2402	2182	1218
1256	1291	1064	2236	1831	1423	244	1111	636	1092
967	1633	2306	1818	657	131	2391	345	1863	255
2146	1209	1277	1343	1608	937	54	1345	179	2387
69	1843	212	2316	2291	459	369	233	324	750
2286	31	2313	1400	193	518	485	1127	57	573
1958	585	518	186	2453	2265	769	526	1826	530
1334	1170	1140	731	1752	884	55	2290	415	900
1523	476	734	1806	1972	1814	706	1030	2153	2432
1553	997	1899	1586	1429	471	2036	871	1179	1681
1425	2107	1925	890	898	2055	681	1691	1177	1851
1450	1736	1426	338	1221	297	588	1528	1998	88
1742	907	912	251	2263	1920	33	2155	1639	1719
1135	2303	2328	614	1217	1576	1911	1052	1215	1569
67	2011	293	773	1957	1108	628	167	2199	1175
744	2166	2171	2371	1554	605	418	2382	53	138
1341	2414	1973	111	1379	1969	2101	687	89	1315
1289	1255	1651	349	662	2032	1005	1402	2238	239
1293	1455	861	618	1221	2103	630	632	1824	1944
437	939	1131	634	1744	2384	308	2175	1018	2232
452	1472	2060	1286	726	1364	1045	2447	938	1319
2397	700	894	1563	2273	1062	1724	2230	1259	40
442	266	1251	264	272	2017	2279	665	1971	77
1084	2062	1456	1802	1535	2211	542	1828	2031	1446
1861	751	1877	1305	977	595	2119	850	2131	1889
1672	1470	1309	1462	1303	1922	1077	1923	278	1440
2186	1025	1844	213	934	1222	2104	1253	780	1050
2139	2274	1687	430	2144	1942	1454	26	1323	1340
1181	776	1124	1575	2357	1515	743	674	1622	197
1615	689	1027	1123	893	1517	128	2269	1772	1091
2088	1464	2150	1938	929	2123	1180	2217	1055	146
51	504	1469	920	2416	260	1641	1363	25	1994
1063	2256	1612	715	2428	1859	1053	1118	2210	1075
1529	1810	591	106	1000	691	1090	1171	1597	1357
991	821	1175	804	1607	1601	2056	603	1058	2373
1236	2046	1342	1262	863	1668	63	754	204	352
1126	600	1326	1057	1071	177	228	308	39	265

Continued on Page 17, Column 3

U. S. Will Select Some to Work, Others to Fight

Illustrated on Pages 14, 15, 16 and 17

By JOHN C. O'BRIEN

Inquirer Washington Bureau

WASHINGTON, March 17.—In a solemn setting befitting the first war-time Selective Service lottery since the first World War, Secretary of War Henry L. Stimson dipped a groping hand into a bowl of shamrock-green capsules tonight and drew forth the first of a series of numbers that will determine the order in which the Feb. 16 Selective Service registrants will be called for service in the Army.

The number for which 9,000,000 men between the ages of 20 and 44 were waiting throughout the length and breadth of the land was T-3485—too high to affect the registrants of a majority of the local boards of the country whose registration averages around 3000.

FIRST PHILADELPHIA NUMBER IS T-441

The first number to affect Philadelphia's 137,990 draft eligibles was T-441, the fourth to be drawn. It hit registrants in every one of the city's 85 local draft boards. The T before each number simply designated the third draft and is omitted in the various lists.

Other early numbers drawn, which matched the serial numbers of Philadelphia eligibles, were the 19th, 1817; the 21st, 1103; the 23d, 1790; the 24th, 1584; the 26th, 176; the 28th, 1577, and the 29th, 1156.

Philadelphians who registered Feb. 16 and hold these numbers will be among the first to receive Selective Service questionnaires—and the first, if they are otherwise eligible, to be inducted into Army service when the new class is called up early in June.

The highest serial number held by any potential draftee in Philadelphia was 2459, so that numbers higher than that, when drawn here, were disregarded by boards in that city.

SOME MAY BE DRAFTED FOR FACTORIES

In a speech which set the tone for a ceremony stripped of non-essentials, Brigadier General Lewis B. Hershey, National Selective Service director, told assembled Government dignitaries and department clerks that some of the men whose numbers were drawn tonight might be drafted to man factories while their comrades manned guns.

The lottery, he emphasized, was to add "millions to that pool of men who stand ready for selection for the necessary tasks, whatever they may be.

"Modern war, mechanized war, yes, total war, demands a great variety of tasks from the citizens of a Nation," he said. "Men are selected to fly airplanes; they may be selected to build airplanes. Men should be selected to man ships; they should be selected to build ships. Men have been selected to drive tanks—to gain victory on the battlefields. Men should

Continued on Page 16, Column 7

NORWEGIAN PORTS CLOSED BY NAZIS

LONDON, March 17 (A. P.).—All Norway's ports from North Cape to Alesund had been closed by the Germans today, presumably to screen even from the suppressed but restive Norwegians a stealthy marshalling of Nazi military and naval forces which indicated that those far northern waters were about to become a newly active major war theatre.

Speaking just after a disclosure that the mighty German battleship Tirpitz "appears to have avoided" a recent British torpedo-plane attack off Narvik and thus even now is presumably loose upon the high seas, a responsible London informant speculated that the Germans were preparing attempts to isolate Russia's Arctic ports, cut her supply lines from the Allies or even move against American and British-garrisoned Iceland.

FEAR SECOND FRONT

Another informant in constant communication with the Norwegians suggested a second possible interpretation—that the Nazis were worried about Allied response to Russian calls for the opening of a second front. He declared Norway was literally seething against the German conquerors.

Among the day's accumulating in-

Continued on Page 7, Column 2

Vichy Reports Loss Of French Freighter

LONDON, March 17 (U. P.).—The Vichy radio reported tonight that the French merchant ship, St. Marcel, had been torpedoed Saturday night in the Mediterranean by a submarine of unknown nationality. Two members of the crew were reported missing.

DROP DOUBLE TIME, F.D.R. ASKS LABOR

By WILLIAM C. MURPHY, JR.

Inquirer Washington Bureau

WASHINGTON, March 17.—President Roosevelt today called for the voluntary abolition of double time payments for war production work on Sundays and at the same time warned against hasty legislation designed to prevent strikes in war industries.

He declared there was "an amazing state of public misinformation" concerning the labor situation and based his opposition to immediate anti-strike legislation upon the assertion that there was no serious strike problem today.

When things are going well they should be left undisturbed, he said. However, his remarks were carefully limited to the situation existing at

Continued on Page 10, Column 1

WOMEN'S ARMY UNIT IS VOTED BY HOUSE

Inquirer Washington Bureau

WASHINGTON, March 17.—Establishment of a Women's Auxiliary Army Corps, which could be sent anywhere in the world to perform non-combatant services with the armed forces, was approved today by the House.

The legislation, permitting the enrollment of 150,000 women who would relieve men for active duty by working as clerks, dieticians, hostesses, cooks and aircraft spotters, was sent to the Senate by a vote of 249 to 86.

12,500 TO BE SOUGHT

About 12,500 recruits will be sought at once, War Department officials said, to take up posts in the Air Raid Morning Service. Others will be admitted—at a base pay of $21 a month—as the need develops.

Age limits in the bill are from 21 to 45, and an attempt to raise the upper limit to 50 was defeated. Ranks corresponding to those in the Army are established, and the bill also provides for appropriate uniforms.

Representative Joseph P. O'Hara

Continued on Page 12, Column 5

Allied Planes Raid Capital of Timor

CANBERRA, March 18 (Wednesday) (U. P.).—Allied aircraft—presumably including American planes—raided Koepang, capital of the Dutch half of Japanese-occupied Timor, yesterday, Prime Minister John Curtin announced today.

Air raid alarms were sounded in Darwin, northwest Australia, and Port Moresby in New Britain, but no attacks developed, he added.

Strong Earthquake Shakes Bucharest

BERLIN, March 17 (From German Broadcasts) (A. P.).—An earthquake strong enough to wake up residents occurred in Bucharest at 2.35 A. M. today (7.35 P. M., E. W. T., Monday), dispatches reported today.

Let's Buy a Bomber

'Soldier Night' at Rink Will Help Boost Fund

Will the boy friend be home from camp on Monday night?

All right then, girls, here's your chance to show him a good time!

Be bomber-minded and take him to a grand stage show on skates at the Arena! You can do it for a song.

For Monday night is "Soldiers' Night" at the Arena, 45th and Market sts., where the star-studded "Skating Vanities of 1942" opens for a gala week of musical comedy in the Fanchon and Marco manner.

FREE TICKETS FOR SOLDIERS

To every girl who buys a ticket at any price for Monday night's show, the Arena, under the direction of Pete Tyrrell, has agreed to give another ticket free, to bring her boy friend in uniform along.

And so that service men without girl friends won't be disappointed if they have Monday night leave, 300 additional tickets will also be given away to them. Men in uniform may

Continued on Page 17, Column 8

Bomber Honor Roll

The Inquirer acknowledges with thanks the following contributions received for the Bomber-for-Uncle Sam Fund:

Heintz Manufacturing Co., and Heintz Employees' Union — $500.00

Austin Meehan String Band, 35th Ward — 181.54

Lathe Shop (NL) Department, A, B and C Shifts, Instrument Dept., Frankford Ar-

Continued on Page 17, Column 8

Mannerheim Gets Top Swedish Award

HELSINKI, Finland, March 17 (A. P.).—Prince Gustaf Adolf, grandson of the Swedish king, conferred the Knight's Grand Cross of the Order of the Sword today on Field Marshal Baron Karl Gustaf Mannerheim, commander of Finland's armed forces (now Germany's allies).

The decoration is the rarest and highest Sweden can confer and was last given to Napoleon III of France in 1861.

The ceremony took place at headquarters of the Finnish High Command. The Prince, making the award, repeated Mannerheim's motto, "with a clean sword for a clean cause."

U. S. WEATHER FORECAST

Philadelphia and Vicinity: Eastern Pennsylvania and New Jersey: Somewhat colder today.

Sun rises 7.08 A. M. Sets 7.09 P. M.

Moon rises 8.08 A. M. Sets 9.01 P. M

Other Weather Reports on Page 2

Philadelphians Drawn In Draft Lottery

Names of Philadelphians whose numbers were called early in the draft lottery last night are listed below with their draft board numbers:

No. 441

Board No. 1— Joseph Giosa, 827 Fernon.

2—Samuel Tabb, 1214 Montrose.

3—Virgil Edward Cimorelli, 804 S. 6th.

4—Samuel Posternack, 536 South.

5—Harry Abrams, 1435 S. 5th.

6—Joseph Noll, 811 Orianna.

7—James Lewis, 718 Addison.

8—Frank J. Mahoney, 2043 Chestnut.

9—Ernest W. Arthur, 634 Callowhill.

10—Henry D. Fries, 709 N. 17th.

11—Leon J. Leiberman, 2601 Parkway.

12—I. Molnar, 1323 N. 5th.

13—Clinton B. Tucker, 917 S. 19th.

14—John Fred Rubinson, 1226 N. Hollywood.

15—Henry H. Fourtner, 2445 Germantown.

16—Alfred J. Heck, 2044 N. Orianna.

17—John Henry Bunn, 940 N. 13th.

18—Charles R. Metzcher, 1343 E. Columbia.

19—Frank Lewis Ingram, 2115 N. 9th.

20—Charles Egrich, Jr., 4676 Umbria.

21—Louis Makransky, 6500 Wissahickon.

22—Leroy W. Thompson, 4622 Adams.

23—Frank Kuck, 4331 Penn.

24—Benjamin Mogul, 3522 Haverford.

25—Harry J. Wicken, 3620 Fairmount.

26—James Vincent Barone, 1152 S. Clarion.

27—William S. Stein, 331 S. 43d.

28—Peter Paliaga, 1520 Morris.

29—Charles Miller, 229 E. Colorado.

30—Charles J. F. Carlin, Jr., 3117 Belgrade.

31—Joseph M. Michels, 3016 Weikel.

32—Leo F. Flannery, 2521 N. Opal.

33—Seymour Mount, 2465 N. 31st.

34—Joseph Lambert, 2541 Columbia.

35—William J. Yorstan, 2341 E. Dauphin.

36—William C. Nestel, 3036 N. D.

37—Edward Peberdy, 724 E. Madison.

Continued on Page 14, Column 1

The Philadelphia Inquirer

PUBLIC LEDGER

An Independent Newspaper for All the People

FINAL CITY EDITION

CIRCULATION: February Average: Daily 436,153, Sunday 1,284,022 — a b d e f g h — TUESDAY MORNING, MARCH 24, 1942 — Second Largest 3c Morning Circulation in America — THREE CENTS

 VOL. 226, No. 83

Jap Drive on Australia Stalls, Tokio Admits Heavy Losses; British Subs Sink 11 Ships

This Is America, 1942

San Diego Stampede

Mushroom Growth

Base for 4 Services

18 War Industries

Scornful of the Japs

—By Ivan H. Peterman—

Inquirer Staff Reporter

(Twenty-fourth of a Series)

(Copyright, 1942, The Philadelphia Inquirer)

SAN DIEGO, Calif., March 23.

LAST week, as per legendary custom, the swallows flocked back to San Juan Capistrano, 90 miles directly north of this city, and lucky they are to nest there. Not even a bird could find accommodations here.

It is said that a visiting delegate from Washington, D. C., reputedly the most crowded area on this globe, recently was caught in the traffic around one of the 10 bars in Sherman's nightery, eddied upon the dance floor where 5000 jitterbug simultaneously like so many Pratt-Whitney propellers, and before the orchestra was stopped, practically had been trampled into the hardwood polish.

Sight-seers are urged to take out accident policies before they embark upon an evening's frolic at the Paris Inn, while the motoring fool who rushes in where angels fear to chauffeur, quickly wishes he were driving a heavy tank.

• • •

I THOUGHT San Francisco's hills and Oakland's Sunday traffic were something, but Mr. Military Policeman, will you please show me the way out of San Diego?

To begin with, the place has grown from 182,500 in the fall of 1939 to its present population of 305,000. Between May, 1940, and December, 1941, it increased 100,000 souls.

A few left suddenly when the first alert sounded; when the blackout lifted some of the "Okies" and about the same number of "Arkies" silently had packed their jalopies and rolled away. They were working in the bomber plant but preferred the dust bowl's quiet to the disturbing warning of a air-raid siren.

I haven't seen such a stampede since the crowds jammed all North Jersey waiting for the Graf Zeppelin to come in. Nobody's waiting for such a visitor here.

Outside is the Plaza, its fountain the only attraction. Soldiers, sailors and Marines are lined up solidly around it, waiting for something to happen. The lobby of the U. S. Grant Hotel is packed; people have been waiting an hour to have their names called so they can go in to dinner. You stand in line for a shave and haircut. There's no shortage of cabs, however, because there isn't anywhere to go.

• • •

MOST of these lads are clean-cut, fine looking Americans. They're from all over the country. I talked to two from Louisiana, one from

Continued on Page 4, Column 3

War Factory Paid $39,356 in Year to Woman Secretary

Man on Payroll Only 46 Days Got $11,000 Bonus, He Testifies at House Probe Into Profits of Ohio Firm

Illustrated on Page 4

By CHARLES H. ELLIS, JR.

Inquirer Washington Bureau

WASHINGTON, March 23.—Huge bonuses, including one of $33,000 for a woman private secretary who received $39,356 in salary and bonus in 1941, were paid by an Ohio firm working on Army and Navy contracts, and were written into assertedly excessive costs of those contracts, the House Naval Affairs Committee was told today.

The secretary to the president of Jack and Heintz, Inc., Bedford, Ohio, testified that her salary recently had been raised to $25,000 a year. Besides that, she said, she had received bonuses of $33,000 in 1941, and $13,295 so far this year.

An assistant controller of the firm admitted receiving $11,000 in bonuses last December, although at the time he had been with the firm just 46 days.

REFUSED TO CUT PRICE

And the president of the firm, which is manufacturing $58,000,000 worth of airplane starters for the Army and Navy, acknowledged that he had thrice refused Navy requests to reduce the unit costs, although committee investigators' audits indicated the Navy is paying twice what the starters cost.

The "share-the-wealth" aspects of the company's war business—at the expense of the Government—brought from members of the committee sharp questions indicating they thought the motive was to avoid excess profits taxes.

DEFENDS HUGE BONUSES

William S. Jack, president of the company, denied the suggestions just as sharply, and defended the payment of bonuses as building morale and speeding production.

Edmund J. Toland, chief investigator for the committee, said that the total of bonuses paid out in 1941 was $691,079. In the first two months of this year the company bought $900,000 worth of Government bonds, he added, commenting acidly that "they are buying Government bonds with Government money."

CHRISTMAS PRESENTS

Last Christmas, he asserted, the company paid out 144 bonuses of $600, 117 of $550, 95 of $500 and hundreds more in lesser amounts, in addition to the fat bonuses paid the president and other of the higher officials.

As the witnesses completed their tale of war-boom earnings and profits, Chairman Carl Vinson (D., Ga.), with elaborate irony, directed Toland to "be sure that the witnesses today are paid their $2 for testifying."

ONLY ONE DEFENDS IT

Only one of the three minor employees who received bonuses of several times their salaries defended it

Continued on Page 4, Column 2

F.D.R. CALLS ON LABOR TO MEET AXIS CHALLENGE

Cites War Needs As Nelson Urges End of Double Pay For Sunday Work

By JOHN C. O'BRIEN

Inquirer Washington Bureau

WASHINGTON, March 23.—President Roosevelt told organized labor today that "nothing shall interrupt our country's march to victory over the Nazis and Japs."

"Our free workers," the President said, "can give to victory far more than the Axis taskmasters can ever wring from the unwilling muscles of the regimented toilers of Europe and Japan."

READ TO C.I.O. GROUP

The President's message, in the form of a letter, was read at a meeting of 400 delegates of the C.I.O. who heard Donald M. Nelson, chairman of the War Production Board, assure them that the Government is "going to see to it that nobody pushes you around and that labor doesn't push any one around."

"By the freedom they enjoy and the privileges they have won, American workers dare do no less than meet the new challenge of old slavery with courage, with energy and with determination that nothing shall interrupt our country's march to victory over the Nazis and the Japs," the President's letter said.

'MUST EARN FREEDOM'

The President asserted that new privileges gained and old rights reaffirmed in recent years were being tested by fire.

"If we lose this war, they and all the rest of our American liberties will be lost," he said. "Only victory can protect our freedom. If the freedom of any of us is lost, the freedom of all is lost.

"We are learning in the hard days of war what is sometimes overlooked in the easy days of peace; that liberty and freedom belong only to men and women who earn them, and that some of the values which make life in America worth living cannot be retained except by people who will give everything and do everything to keep them.

BIG POINT FOR LABOR

"This has especial point for organized labor—for its leaders and for the men and women in the ranks."

Nelson, who assured Congress last week that there is no need to suspend the 40-hour week, reiterated his belief that in war industries labor

Continued on Page 6, Column 3

STATE LABOR BOARD BARRED IN COURT AS IMPARTIAL AGENCY

'Can't Be Litigant And Judge, Too,' Penna. Bench Says

Pennsylvania's Labor Relations Board was virtually barred as a litigant from the courts of the State in a far-reaching decision by the State Supreme Court yesterday.

The board, according to the ruling handed down in Pittsburgh, does not have the right to "espouse" the cause of either labor or management in the courts because of its own judicial nature.

COMPLETE SURPRISE

The ruling took members of the board and its representatives here completely by surprise.

Through Alex Ratinsky, a board attorney in this city, the board declined to comment pending an opportunity to acquaint itself with the full text of the opinion.

"For the board to become a litigant is repugnant to the traditional common law heritage of judicial detachment and freedom from interest," said the court.

APPEAL DISMISSED

The opinion, written by Chief Justice William I. Schaffer, dismissed the board's appeal from a Common Pleas Court No. 1 decision setting aside its order to Heinel Motors, Inc., to reinstate two members of the C. I. O. United Auto Workers Union in this city.

Justice Schaffer added that the court was willing to review the case at the request of either the union or the motor company, acting directly rather than through the board.

"Such a tribunal as the Labor Relations Board, quasi judicial in character, intended to be impartial, given the power to hear and determine and adjudge, should not be able to convert itself into a litigant and become the partisan advocate of one or the other whose cause it has heard," the opinion continued.

OPPOSED TO TRADITIONS

"This would tend to destroy its quasi judicial character and its impartiality. Furthermore, to convert

Continued on Page 6, Column 4

HOME APPLIANCES PRICE CEILINGS SET

By ROBERT BARRY

Inquirer Washington Bureau

WASHINGTON, March 23.—Maximum retail prices for mechanical refrigerators, vacuum cleaners and attachments, stoves and ranges, washing and ironing machines, radios, phonographs and typewriters were set by the Office of Price Administration today.

With the exception of automobiles and tires, which the average civilian cannot buy anyway, it was the first retail price order issued by OPA in its effort to combat inflation, and it will affect nearly every household and office in the country.

PLANTS MAKE MUNITIONS

Action was taken to prevent runaway prices in those consumer goods which have been sharply curtailed at the manufacturing source by the demands of war production. Plants

Continued on Page 5, Column 4

Attack In Sight Of Italy

LONDON, March 23 (A. P.).—British submarines have destroyed two Italian submarines, one troopship and eight other transports within view of humiliated Fascists on the shores of Italy and Albania, the Admiralty announced today even when Axis forces were striking with indifferent success at a British convoy elsewhere in the Mediterranean.

The largest individual haul for the four British submarines engaged was credited to Commander J. W. Linton, who sank six large schooners—one of them flying the Nazi flag—and a motorship jammed with troops. Disdaining the use of torpedoes, Linton surfaced his submarine and destroyed all seven vessels with gunfire.

CITED FOR 2 SINKINGS

(He was cited last year for sinking two Italian supply ships with his submarine Pandora.)

Another British submarine sank the brand new 1461-ton Italian submarine Ammiraglio Millo off Salo Point, Calabria, southern Italy, under the gaze of persons gathered on shore.

"While His Majesty's submarine was engaged in picking up survivors she was subjected to ineffectual machine-gun fire from land," the Admiralty reported.

IN MESSINA STRAITS

The second Italian submarine, the 778-ton Argonauta class, was torpedoed and sunk in the southern approaches to the Straits of Messina, which separate the Italian mainland from Sicily.

"An attempt to rescue survivors from the U-boat who were struggling in the water was interfered with by enemy aircraft and had to be abandoned," the Admiralty said.

The same British submarine was credited with torpedoing and "almost certainly" sinking a large, strongly-escorted Axis supply ship.

PENETRATES ADRIATIC

The fourth British submarine, penetrating to the Adriatic Sea, used her deck gun to sink a small enemy supply ship, then departed unscathed by the fire of Italian shore batteries in Albania.

(As if to build a backfire to this series of British successes, the Italian command reported a British convoy sailing to Malta had suffered "repeated hits" from Axis torpedo planes and that Italian naval formations had overtaken and en-

Continued on Page 3, Column 5

Darlan Agreement With U. S. Denied

VICHY, March 23 (U. P.).—Authorized sources today denied British radio reports that Vice Premier Jean Francois Darlan had concluded a general agreement with the United States concerning all French colonial possessions.

The only agreement reached, these sources said, concerned Martinique, where it was decided to close the port to all warships, Allied or Axis, after the United States protested the landing there of a wounded officer from a German submarine.

War Summary

Tuesday, March 24, 1942

PACIFIC FRONT

The Japanese were reported to be stalled in their drive toward Australia yesterday but launched a terrific aerial and land offensive in Burma.

Tokio admitted heavy casualties at Rabaul, New Britain had checked the move southward. The enemy's losses were put at 7000 men, 50 ships and 100 planes in the last 59 days. The Allies continued to blast at Japanese invasion bases in the arc north of Australia with considerable success.

Fierce battles were raging in Central Burma as the Allies sought desperately to attain control of the skies over that vital area. The opposing armies were locked in a pitched battle near Toungoo, 125 miles north of Rangoon.

The Navy Department announced U. S. submarines in Jap waters had sunk or damaged five enemy merchant ships and a destroyer or anti-submarine vessel was attacked and probably sunk.

OTHER FRONTS

Four British submarines in an audacious raid sank 11 Italian ships within sight of the shores of Italy and its satellite, Albania. Sent to the bottom were two submarines, a troop ship and eight transports.

German planes gave a southeast English coastal town one of its worst bombardments of the war in what was regarded as the start of a spring offensive against Britain. The raids were the heaviest against England in almost a year.

In a burst of renewed aerial warfare in Russia, the Reds last night announced they had destroyed 278 German planes since March 15. American-made Airacobras played an important role in the Red successes.

U-BOAT SHELLS SHIP TO SAVE TORPEDOES

NEW YORK, March 23 (U. P.).—Survivors of a small United Nations' merchant ship sunk in the South Atlantic March 5 said today that their vessel was shelled and machine-gunned for nearly a half hour by an Axis submarine in an obvious attempt to conserve its precious torpedoes.

Arriving in two groups at different parts of the harbor—one at Brooklyn, the other at Edgewater, N. J.—the survivors differed as to whether the U-boat finally used a torpedo to sink their ship.

NONE OF CREW LOST

The captain told naval authorities none of his crew was lost. His party of 16 was landed at Edgewater. Eleven others were landed in Brooklyn by a second rescue ship, to which they were transferred in mid-ocean. Despite the attack and the 11 days

Continued on Page 3, Column 1

Foe's Toll Is Put At 7000 Soldiers And 50 Vessels

Map on Page 2

By BRYDON TAVES

MELBOURNE, Australia, March 24 (Tuesday) (U. P.).—Japan's drive to the south has been temporarily stalled, in spite of a fierce new offensive, by the loss of 7000 men, 50 ships and 100 airplanes in 59 days of warfare around the islands off North Australia, reports from that sector said today.

Less than 24 hours after Japanese planes had struck the heaviest blow of the war at Port Moresby, a dispatch from that Papuan capital said the Japanese drive in that direction had broken down and that the invaders had reached "a more complete stalemate than they have encountered in any other war zone in the Pacific war."

The reasons given were that the Japanese lost 7000 men, by the admission of their own radio broadcasts from Tokio, in landing an invasion force at Rabaul, capital of New Britain Island, early in January, and that their losses since then had mounted to at least 50 ships and 100 airplanes under the incessant battering of Allied air and naval units.

MANY MORE REPORTED DAMAGED

In addition to the Japanese ships and planes destroyed for certain, many more were reported damaged.

Since landing at Rabaul, the Japanese have captured only one town on New Britain—Gasmata—and they have not been able to extend their hold on New Guinea beyond the beachheads at Lae and Salamaua, except for a slight advance into Markham Valley, the Port Moresby dispatch said.

The Japanese air offensive, however, continued.

Nineteen Japanese heavy bombers and three fighters raided Port Moresby, 350 miles across Torres Strait from Cape York, but a communique said they caused little damage and no casualties.

DROP 60 TO 70 BOMBS ON PORT MORESBY

The communique said the Japanese dropped 60 to 70 bombs on Port Moresby, apparently concentrating on the airdrome in an effort to make it useless as an Allied base. While it said two crack Japanese "Zero" fighters crashed outside the town, a Port Moresby dispatch reported a third was known to have been hit.

The Jap planes losses brought to a probable 27 the number destroyed or damaged by the Allies in two days of the most savage aerial fighting yet waged at the approaches to Australia.

For the first time "unidentified" single planes, presumably

Continued on Page 2, Column 1

U. S. Subs Sink 3 Ships, Hit 3 Others Near Japan

By JOHN M. McCULLOUGH

Inquirer Washington Bureau

WASHINGTON, March 23.—Another series of numbing blows has been struck at Japan's extended supply line by intrepid American submarine commanders, the Navy Department announced in a communique tonight.

Three enemy merchant vessels, totaling 18,000 tons, have been sunk, two 2000-ton freighters damaged and an "anti-submarine" vessel, probably a destroyer, hit and probably sunk.

FIRST REPORT OF ACTIONS

None of these actions has been reported in any other official dispatch from the Far East, the communique asserted.

Most significant, from the point of view of retaliatory blows at the enemy, is the fact that the new submarine actions occurred in "Japanese waters," thousands of miles north of the most advanced theatre of combat in the Timor-New Guinea-New Britain area immediately north and northeast of Australia.

The successes reported in tonight's communique raise to 16 the number of vessels flying the imperial rising sun which have either been sent to the bottom or seriously damaged in the enemy's home waters.

DESTROYER SUNK

Only two weeks ago, a similar communique, carefully refraining from designating the exact area in which the attacks occurred, announced the sinking of a destroyer flotilla leader and a large naval tanker, and direct torpedo hits upon an aircraft carrier and three cruisers.

The vessels involved in the actions reported tonight include one 7000-ton tanker, a 6000-ton ship, probably a merchant vessel, and one 5000-ton freighter sunk, in addition to two

Continued on Page 2, Column 6

Sweden Mobilizing, British Editor Says

LONDON, March 24 (Tuesday) (A. P.).—The military maneuvers in northern Sweden are a screen for complete mobilization of the Swedish army in the face of heavy German concentrations along the Baltic coast, the Daily Express' foreign editor, Charley Foley, wrote today.

The final stage of mobilization is expected by April 9, the second anniversary of the invasion of Norway, he said.

Jap Fleet Reported In Bay of Bengal

LONDON, March 23 (A. P.).—The Rome radio broadcast a Shanghai report tonight saying a strong Japanese fleet had been sighted in the Bay of Bengal.

This roundabout account said a landing in Bengal can be expected "at any moment."

U. S. WEATHER FORECAST

Philadelphia and Vicinity: Rising temperature and not so windy today.

Sun rises 6.58 A. M. Sets 7.16 P. M.

Moon rises 11.49 A. M. Sets 1.40 A. M.

Other Weather Reports on Page 2

IN TODAY'S INQUIRER

Sikorski Arrives To See Roosevelt

WASHINGTON, March 23 (U. P.).—Polish Prime Minister General Wladyslaw Sikorski arrived in Washington today from Montreal for conversations with President Roosevelt and other officials.

Sikorski was met at the station by representatives of most of the United Nations, including the British Ambassador, Viscount Halifax. Sikorski expressed his "profound admiration for America's foremost soldier"—General Douglas MacArthur.

He praised the Russian armies, saying that the fact that Soviet forces were "gradually approaching the eastern boundaries of Poland" created new problems for Poland "which have to be taken into account and discussed here."

MacArthur's Son Gets 'Civilian' Clothes

MELBOURNE, March 23 (U. P.).—Mrs. Douglas MacArthur's plans to get a new wardrobe and visit a beauty salon didn't materialize today because she spent so much time outfitting her four-year-old son, Arthur.

Arthur, who had been wearing a soldier's hat and cutdown uniform since he flew here with his parents from Bataan, got a new outfit and also a haircut.

Mrs. MacArthur purchased items that ranged from woolly underwear to a heavy overcoat for him, and when the wardrobe was complete she discovered it was too late to make her own purchases.

Let's Buy a Bomber

Ukrainians Give $100 To Boost Plane Fund

Illustrated on Pages 8 and 18

By FRED G. HYDE

Philadelphians and their neighbors, eager to make more of the heartening news that is coming out of the Southwest Pacific, trundled their Liberty Bell Bomber closer to her christening berth yesterday.

Their contributions toward the purchase of the speedy big ship reached a total of $136,585.63 during the day as the Ukrainian-Americans of the area led the drive with a $100 gift.

WOMAN HEADED DRIVE

Collected by Mrs. Helen Shtogryn and members of her committee, the money was turned over to Michael Darmopray, president of the Ukrainian-American Citizens Association, who in turn presented it to The Inquirer, sponsor of the Buy-a-Bomber campaign.

Ninety-three defendants brought

Continued on Page 8, Column 5

Bomber Honor Roll

The Inquirer acknowledges with thanks the following contributions received for the Bomber-for-Uncle Sam Fund:

Ukrainian American Citizens Association	$100.00
Contributions in Magistrate N. Edwin Lindell's Court	100.00
Employees of the Bomze	

Continued on Page 8, Column 4

Coast Air 'Object' Silences Broadcasts

SAN FRANCISCO, March 23 (A. P.).—Presence of what the Army described as an "unidentified object" in the Los Angeles area led today to a 20-minute shutdown of radio broadcasting in Southern California.

Stations from San Luis Obispo south to San Diego and eastward to Boulder City, Nev., were ordered off the air at 5.35 A. M. (P.W.T.) and permitted to return at 5.55.

By the latter hour, Fourth Army Headquarters reported, "the object was no longer present but still was unidentified."

There was no general alert.

20 Australian Girls Wed U. S. Soldiers

BRISBANE, Australia, March 24 (Tuesday) (A. P.).—The wedding of more than 20 Australian girls to U. S. service men in the last few weeks has led to talk in some quarters of action to discourage the tendency to marry in haste.

Religious leaders are inclined to deprecate the marriage because of extremely brief courtships.

American authorities, however, recognize soldier allotments for Australian wives.

First Photos of the Heroic Defenders on Bataan

(A. P. Wirephoto)
HOW THE JAPANESE ATTACKERS BATTERED BUILDINGS ON BELEAGURED BATAAN

(A. P. Wirephoto)
COMPASSION FOR ENEMY: GIVING DYING JAP A DRINK

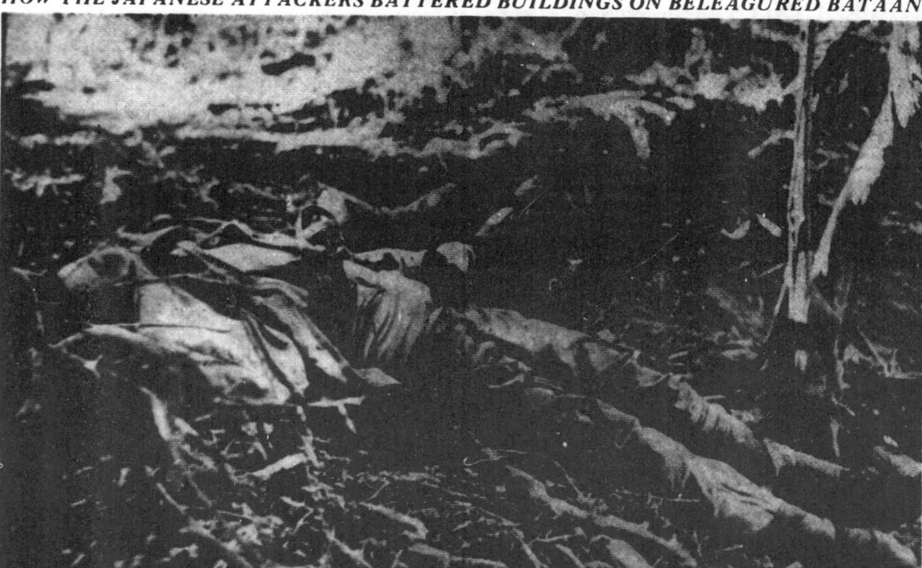

(A. P. Wirephoto)
BODIES OF JAPS SLAIN IN ATTACK

(A. P. Wirephoto)
A BATAAN FIELD HOSPITAL JAMMED WITH WOUNDED

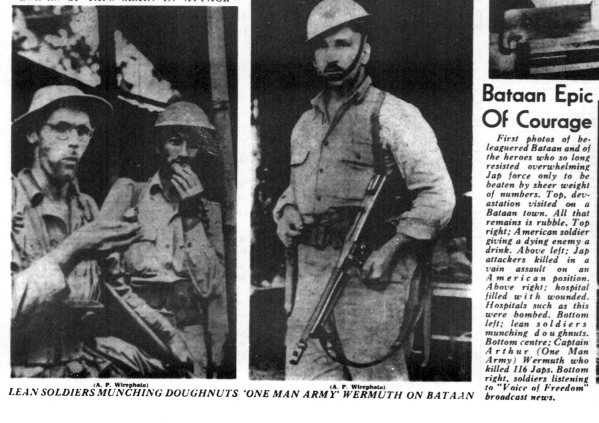

(A. P. Wirephoto)
LEAN SOLDIERS MUNCHING DOUGHNUTS

(A. P. Wirephoto)
'ONE MAN ARMY' WERMUTH ON BATAAN

Bataan Epic Of Courage

First photos of beleaguered Bataan and of the heroes who so long resisted overwhelming Jap force only to be beaten by sheer weight of numbers. Top, devastation visited on a Bataan town. All that remains is rubble. Top right; American soldier giving a dying enemy a drink. Above left; Jap attackers killed in a vain assault on an American position. Above right; hospital filled with wounded. Hospitals such as this were bombed. Bottom left; lean soldiers munching doughnuts. Bottom centre; Captain Arthur (One Man Army) Wermuth who killed 116 Japs. Bottom right, soldiers listening to "Voice of Freedom" broadcast news.

(A. P. Wirephoto)
SOLDIERS LISTENING TO "VOICE OF FREEDOM" IN HUT

The Philadelphia Inquirer

PUBLIC LEDGER

An Independent Newspaper for All the People

FINAL CITY EDITION

CIRCULATION: March Average: Daily 436,541, Sunday 1,303,403 — a b d e f g h ★ — SATURDAY MORNING, APRIL 18, 1942 — Copyright, 1942, by The Philadelphia Inquirer Co. VOL. 226, No. 108 — Second Largest 3c Morning Circulation in America — THREE CENTS

TOKIO BOMBED

Japs Say Planes Struck At Noon, Admit Damage

SAN FRANCISCO, April 17 (A. P.).—Enemy bombers have attacked Tokio, the Tokio radio announced tonight, damaging "schools and hospitals." Casualties are "as yet unknown," the broadcast said.

A communique issued by Imperial Headquarters said that three planes had been shot down in the raids and that the raiders had come from several directions.

"It is confirmed that three enemy aircraft were shot down when hostile planes attacked the Tokio - Tosame region this afternoon for the first time since the war (started)," the communique said.

"The enemy planes approached from several directions."

(The Berlin radio broadcast a D. N. B. news agency report that Yokohama, Tokio's main entry port 18 miles from the capital, had been attacked by the raiders.)

The text of the original Tokio radio announcement said:

"Enemy bombers appeared over Tokio for the first time in the current war, inflicting damage on schools and hospitals. The raid occurred shortly past noon on Saturday, Tokio time (10 P. M. Friday, Philadelphia time.)

CLAIM SCHOOLS, HOSPITALS HIT

"Invading planes failed to cause any damage on military establishments, although casualties in the schools and hospitals were as yet unknown.

"This inhuman attack on these cultural establishments and on residential districts is causing widespread indignation among the populace."

The Tokio radio broke in on a foreign-language program to broadcast the announcement of the Tokio bombing.

NO CONFIRMATION IN WASHINGTON

(There was no hint of where the attacking Allied planes might have been based. Speculation as to the origin of the bombers included a widely held belief that they were based on an aircraft carrier.

(In Washington the War and Navy Departments had no confirmation immediately on the Japanese announcement.

(There was no indication of when a communique might be issued. It was pointed out that if the bombing was a long distance attack, the aircraft would take

Continued on Page 2, Column 1

Today

The War in Asia
Allies Are Hampered
Fail to State Purpose
Natives Indifferent
Heed Jap Propaganda

—By Raymond Clapper—

CAIRO, April 17.

AFTER a month East of Suez, I return here wanting to say some things which I frankly don't know how to say.

No one can go through such an experience and return feeling quite the same. Perhaps it will be some little time before the mass of information and judgments I gathered from scores of key people in India and China can shake down into firm conclusions.

Above all, I return with the feeling that the United Nations have failed thus far to make clear their purpose and aims in Asia. I think the reason is that our cause is not clear to ourselves. It is not enough to beat Japan in Asia. The point is—defeat Japan for what purpose?

Our failure to answer that question clearly is having a strongly adverse effect on the war in Asia. We are short of supplies in Asia, but even shorter in a purpose that will rally the native populations.

The result is that in Malaya and Burma, and now in India, the peoples have been more indifferent to the Allied cause than they should be, considering what they have at stake. We failed to convince them what really is at stake for them.

Before we can do justice to ourselves in Asia, the United Nations must, I think, make a clear and convincing statement of why we are fighting there and what the shape of things will be after the victory.

Until that is done those vast masses of people won't be throwing their full weight into the fight. Japanese propaganda has been playing skillfully on native hatred for Western imperialism. It is fantastic that the Japanese should be regarded as liberators, yet we are letting them get away with it.

Our propaganda job has yet to be done. But it can't be done until our own minds are clear on what the war in Asia is all about, what the status of the native populations is to be after the war, whether to return to previous conditions, or to move into a new stage of more self-government.

A clear, effective statement of the United Nations' purposes, and convincing propaganda to win confidence, seems to me now one of the most important military weapons of the war in Asia.

Until we do that, we are as good as giving Japan extra divisions. It was so in Malaya and Burma. And it looks as if it might soon be so in India.

In Europe the case is clear where the Axis has conquered free peoples. It is totally different in Asia where the Chinese only have been free, and there you see the difference. The Chinese are fighting for themselves.

Elsewhere, the natives see nothing to fight for, if there is to be a continuation of past irksome conditions. Therefore the more ignorant and unthinking of the population see it only as a question of which outsiders are to rule over them.

As to the ultimate might of the United Nations, so far as physical strength goes, there can be no question. Japan can never match the Allies in a long war. But victory in Asia is more than a matter of arms. It can't be won by arms alone so long as we hand the Japanese their propaganda weapon.

Sir Stafford Cripps made an effort to overcome this in India. The fact that he failed was due largely to the bitterness and suspicion generated from the past. This can't be the end, but only a challenge to the United Nations to redouble their efforts for a new deal in Asia that will rally millions to active help on our side.

TEACHER TELLS OF FLOGGING SIX AT NORRISTOWN

Principal Admits He Beat Boys; Victim Says Faculty Men Held Him on Table

While four men teachers forcibly held a 15-year-old struggling and sobbing schoolboy on a table, the principal and two other teachers flogged the boy with an 18-inch, thick black leather strap, a Norristown court was told yesterday.

"They hit me 40 or 50 times," said the boy, Michael Valerio. "Then they asked me questions, and when they didn't like the answers, they put me on the table again, and hit me some more with the strap.

5 OTHERS TELL OF BEATINGS

"My nose started to bleed, and they let me up."

In addition to Michael, five other boys were similarly beaten by the men teachers of Rittenhouse Junior High School, Norristown, they declared to Montgomery county authorities.

As a result of the floggings, which were calmly admitted in a crowded courtroom by Robert B. Taylor, principal of the junior high school, District Attorney Frederick B. Smillie, of Montgomery county, said he believed prosecution of the teachers was warranted.

PLANS POLICE ACTION

He said he would at once put the case in the hands of Chief of Police George Bausewine for action.

The strap, as described in court, was of the type used in factory belt lines. It is 18 inches long, two and a-half inches wide and a half inch thick, and is equipped with a wooden handle.

ASKED BOY BE BARRED

The floggings at the school came to light when Taylor, principal of the school, appeared in Norristown Juvenile Court to ask that the Valerio boy be permanently barred from the school.

Judge Harold G. Knight then asked the boy to tell his story, and he revealed how he had been spread-eagled across the table by four teachers, while the three others whipped him.

"The four of them stretched me out like a bird," he said. "Two held

Continued on Page 7, Column 2

WHITE ASSERTS CITY CAN SLASH PAY TAX SAFELY

Estimates Surplus Of $6,590,000 From All Levies; Figures Hit Council Policy

City Controller Robert C. White yesterday presented figures proving "incontrovertibly" that the Philadelphia wage tax could be reduced safely by one-third.

He said the city would have a tax surplus this year totaling $6,590,000.

He said real estate taxes would bring in $426,000 more than estimated in the 1942 budget.

WATER RENTS HIGHER

He said water rents would be $400,000 higher than expected.

He said there would be a $2,291,000 surplus from other sources such as parking lot levies, taxes on theatre admissions, parking fines and sales of city property.

And from the wage tax itself, he said, receipts would be $4,000,000 higher than budgeted.

ONE DEFICIT LISTED

These surpluses totaled $7,117,000, from which he subtracted $527,000 as his estimate of the amount by which collection of personal property taxes and delinquent real estate taxes would fall short of expectations.

But even the deficit in collection of delinquent real estate taxes, he said, "may be materially reduced if payments of delinquencies continue throughout the year at the rate they are coming in now," while in the case of the surpluses, "the probabilities are" that they will be even bigger than his figures indicated.

RIDDLES ARGUMENT

In short, he knocked into a cocked hat the oft-repeated contentions of City Council's majority that "it isn't safe" to cut the wage tax now because of the possibility of wartime disasters.

He demonstrated, on the basis of conservative estimates, that even if Council cuts the wage tax now, the city would still have a surplus of more than $2,500,000. Further, the city has an emergency borrowing capacity of

Continued on Page 18, Column 2

'V' Army to Sabotage Hitler's Birthday

LONDON, April 17 (A. P.).—Colonel Britton, the B. B. C.'s leader of the secret European "V" army, told the people of occupied countries tonight to observe Adolf Hitler's birthday next Monday—"maybe his last"—in these three ways:

Stay away from work.

Write as many anonymous letters to Quislings and Nazis as possible and mail them on Monday.

Flood telephone exchanges with calls at exactly 5 P. M.

Duke of Gloucester On Middle East Tour

CAIRO, April 17 (U. P.).—A special communique today announced the arrival of the Duke of Gloucester, brother of King George, to visit the Middle East command. He will inspect Navy, Army and air force units.

IN TODAY'S INQUIRER

LEAHY IS RECALLED FOR CONSULTATION IN LAVAL CRISIS

Formal Severance Of Vichy Relations Indicated by Move

By WILLIAM C. MURPHY, JR.

Inquirer Washington Bureau

WASHINGTON, April 17.—President Roosevelt today ordered Admiral William D. Leahy, American Ambassador to Vichy, to return to Washington for "consultation," to the accompaniment of strong indications that this step was preliminary to a formal severance of diplomatic relations.

The President's action was announced by Acting Secretary of State Sumner Welles, who said that Leahy's recall had been ordered because of the events of the last few days and information received by this Government regarding the rise to power of the pro-Axis government of Pierre Laval at Vichy.

'PUPPET' REGIME HIT

(To emphasize the American rejection of Laval, Welles let it be known that this Government views the new Vichy regime as a puppet Government capable of sending puppet communications previously submitted to and approved by German authorities, the Associated Press reported.)

Previously it had been learned that the United States Government was convinced that Laval's accession would be followed by a Vichy attempt to reconquer parts of the French empire now held by Free French forces. Such a move would almost certainly precipitate armed clashes with the United Nations.

NEW STATEMENT POSSIBLE

Welles was asked if a further official statement on relations between the United States and Vichy could be anticipated after Leahy's return. He replied that such a statement might well be forthcoming before Leahy reached Washington—an apparent implication that a formal break might come before Leahy would have time to reach the United States.

It was explained that Leahy's actual departure from Vichy would be delayed for a few days at least, because Mrs. Leahy had been operated on recently and was unable to travel immediately. The Ambassador and Mrs. Leahy will leave for America as soon as Mrs. Leahy's health permits, Welles said.

COUNSELLOR IN CHARGE

When Leahy leaves Vichy, S. Pinkney Tuck, Counsellor of the Embassy, will remain as American charge d'affaires unless there is another change in relationships in the meantime.

The action taken today followed the pattern set when Hugh Wilson, last American Ambassador to Berlin, was recalled—also "for consultation"—in November, 1938. Wilson never returned to Berlin and there was never any expectation that he would return.

An American charge d'affaires remained in charge of the Berlin Embassy until the actual outbreak of hostilities. Meanwhile, shortly after

Continued on Page 3, Column 3

Shore Police Report Blasts, Glare Off N. J.

ATLANTIC CITY, April 17 (U. P.).—Police said tonight that they had received more than 50 calls from Boardwalk strollers reporting explosions and a bright glare "a short distance off the coast."

Coast Guards were reported investigating. The Fourth Naval District public relations office said it knew nothing of the explosions.

Army About To Attack, Stimson Says

By JOHN M. McCULLOUGH

Inquirer Washington Bureau

WASHINGTON, April 17.—Secretary of War Henry L. Stimson today asserted that the United States Army is "getting pretty near to the stage" where it can embark upon the offensive, "however difficult it may be."

"I am now more than ever convinced," he told his press conference today, "that we are going to get on the offensive, and do that at the earliest practicable moment.

'BEGINNING TO MOVE'

"Things are beginning to move—and move in the right direction." In some quarters, the unqualified emphasis with which he spoke is believed to be an outgrowth of the dramatic trip of General George C. Marshall, chief of staff of the Army, and Harry L. Hopkins, chairman of the Munitions Assignment Board, to England for conversations now in progress with British leaders of the war effort.

'NO MISUNDERSTANDING'

The War Secretary also took occasion to settle the controversial issue of General Douglas MacArthur's status by asserting that he is the unchallenged strategic commander of Allied land, sea and air forces in the Southwest Pacific—a status exactly set forth, he said, in a "directive" agreed to April 3 by all Allied nations whose interests and forces are involved in that area.

He emphasized that "there has never been any possible misunder-

Continued on Page 3, Column 2

U. S. JURY TO PROBE COUGHLIN MAGAZINE

By JOHN C. O'BRIEN

Inquirer Washington Bureau

WASHINGTON, April 17.—Attorney General Francis Biddle today ordered a Grand Jury investigation of the magazine Social Justice, recently barred from the mails by Postmaster General Frank C. Walker because of the publication of alleged seditious matter.

The investigation, which will begin next week before the special Grand Jury investigating sedition, will go into all phases of the ownership, distribution, and financial affairs of the magazine and its possible tie-up with Axis propaganda.

DENIES TIE-UP NOW

The magazine was founded by Rev. Charles E. Coughlin, the "Radio Priest," of Royal Oak, Mich., but Father Coughlin now denies that he is directly connected with the publication.

Other developments in Biddle's war on Axis propaganda were:

1. He announced that the Depart-

Continued on Page 5, Column 2

FEVER, HUNGER BEAT BATAAN DEFENDERS, REPORTER DECLARES

20,000 Troops Ill With Malaria for Lack of Quinine

(Frank Hewlett, who was on Bataan when the Japanese overran the peninsula, tells the tragic story of its last days in the following dispatch. He wrote his story in Australia after being rescued this week when General Ralph Royce led an American bombing attack on four Japanese bases in the Philippines and picked up Hewlett, among others, at a secret landing field).

By FRANK HEWLETT

MELBOURNE, Australia, April 17 (U. P.).—In the last desperate showdown, the Battle of Bataan ended because the quinine pills ran out.

I saw the last scenes of the drama and this is the story.

Ten thousand of our troops lay in two field hospitals, most of them ill with malaria. Another 10,000 were confined to camps with lighter cases of malaria.

(There were 36,800 troops in all on Bataan, according to War Department figures. Thus more than half were incapacitated in the final phase of battle.)

AMMUNITION TO SPARE

There was ammunition in plenty to fight off the enemy when I saw American and Filipino soldiers in their last fighting against an overwhelming enemy.

When the end came, a million rounds of .30 calibre ammunition was blown up by our own troops.

There was courage in plenty, too, to pit against the Japanese in those terrible days before Bataan collapsed.

But there was no quinine to fight

Continued on Page 3, Column 6

Ford Gives Lindbergh A Colonel's Salary

DETROIT, April 17 (A. P.).—Charles A. Lindbergh, recently employed as a technical adviser at the Ford bomber plant, is receiving a salary equivalent to that of an Army colonel, a Ford spokesman said tonight. The salary amounts to $3500 a year, plus allowances.

Lindbergh, who resigned his commission as colonel in the Air Corps Reserve before the war, could have written his own ticket when he joined the company, the spokesman said, but told Henry Ford he wanted to work for the same pay he would have received as colonel in the Army.

U. S. WEATHER FORECAST

Philadelphia and vicinity—Cooler today.

Sun rises 6.19 A.M. Sets 7.41 P.M.
Moon rises 8.21 A.M. Sets 10.37 P.M.

Other Weather Reports on Page 2

The Philadelphia Inquirer
SATURDAY MORNING, MAY 2, 1942 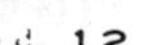

BLAZE Firemen pulling hoses toward a ladder as other fighters direct streams of water on a Chester hardware store. A general alarm called out all Chester's apparatus when blaze spread through three buildings in business district. Firemen battled the flames for two and one-half hours before bringing the blaze under control. Hundreds were routed by smoke from apartments and a hotel nearby.

BRYN MAWR GIRLS WELCOMING MAY DAY WITH TRADITIONAL MAYPOLE DANCE

May Queen Time

May 1 and May Queens arrived simultaneously yesterday in the Philadelphia area. At Bryn Mawr, students marked the traditional spring festival with exercises that began at the first hint of dawn and lasted throughout the day. A highlight of the festivities was the annual dance around the Class Maypoles on Merion Green, pictured above. At the left, Dora Benedict, president of Bryn Mawr's sophomore class, places the crown of flowers on the brow of Jocelyn Fleming, of Washington, senior class president and Queen of the May. Below is Peggy Riley, of Haddonfield, N. J., who was selected Spring Queen to reign over the Spring Prom of the Drexel Institute of Technology at the Bellevue-Stratford hotel last night.

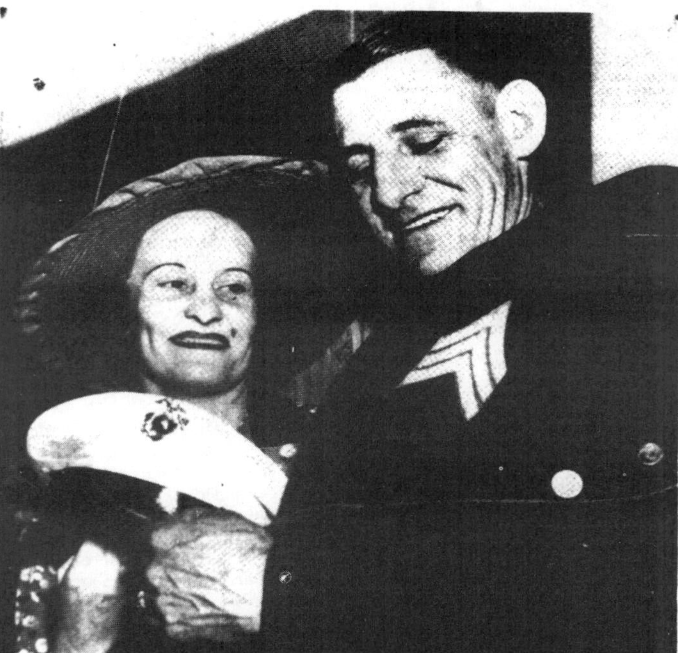

MARINE Mrs. Louis Kauffman admiring the sergeant's stripes on the Marine blouse her husband is holding. He's a Fairmount Park Guard sergeant and has been given the same rank in the Marines where he enlisted yesterday.

SETTING CROWN OF FLOWERS ON MAY QUEEN'S HEAD

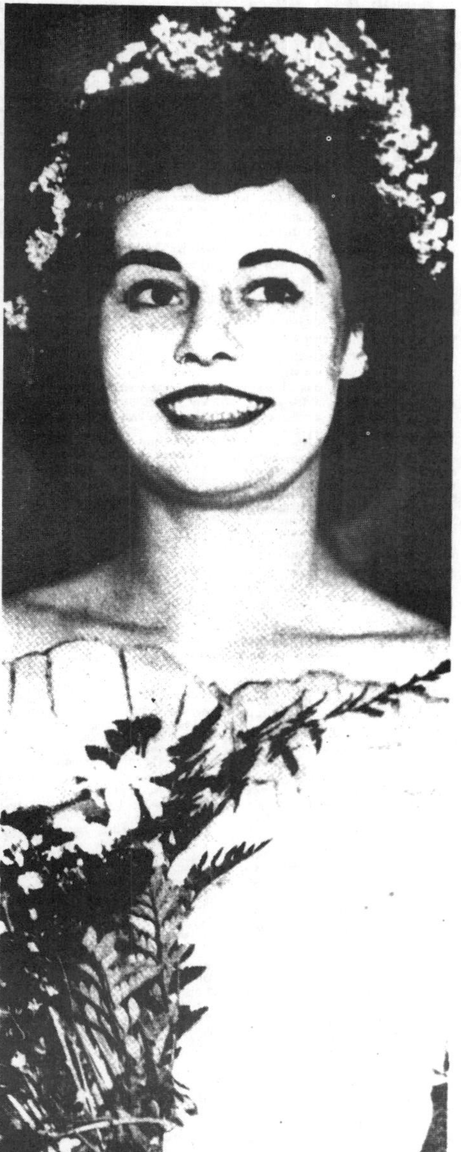

MEET THE SPRING QUEEN OF DREXEL

(A. P. Wirephoto)

GUESTS Stars of Hollywood's Victory Caravan grouped on the south lawn of the White House with their hostess, Mrs. Eleanor Roosevelt. They were guests at a tea given by the First Lady. Tonight these stars will entertain Philadelphians in Convention Hall with the proceeds to go to Army and Navy relief. Seated, left to right, are: Oliver Hardy, Joan Blondell, Charlotte Greenwood, Charles Boyer, Rise Stevens, Desi Arnaz, Frank McHugh, Matt Brooks, James Cagney, Pat O'Brien, Juanita Starke and Alma Carroll. Left to right standing are: Merle Oberon, Eleanor Powell, Arlene Whelan, Marie McDonald, Fay McKenzie, Katharine Booth, Mrs. Roosevelt, Frances Gifford, Frances Langford, Elyse Knox, Cary Grant, Claudette Colbert, Bob Hope, Joan Bennett, Bert Lahr, Jack Rose, Stan Laurel, Jerry Colonna and Groucho Marx. There are 70 film players, many of them among Hollywood's brightest stars, in the Caravan now making a Nation-wide tour.

The Philadelphia Inquirer

PUBLIC LEDGER

An Independent Newspaper for All the People

FINAL CITY EDITION

CIRCULATION: April Average: Daily 437,350, Sunday 1,246,839 abdefgh SATURDAY MORNING, MAY 9, 1942 Second Largest 3c Morning Circulation in America THREE CENTS

 VOL. 226, No. 129

GREAT U. S. SEA VICTORY

Japs Repulsed After Losing 17 Warships

London Hears Enemy Flees After Defeat

LONDON, May 9 (Saturday) (U. P.).—The Japanese fleet has suffered a great defeat in the Battle of the Coral Sea, private advices from Sydney said today.

Big enemy concentrations of shipping were caught by United States dive-bombers which sank two large Japanese aircraft carriers, at least one cruiser and seven destroyers. Many other Japanese ships were badly damaged.

(This would make the toll of Japanese craft sunk at least 16, and the toll of sunk and heavily damaged 22, as Allied communiques thus far listing 11 ships sunk and six damaged have reported only two Japanese destroyers sunk and none damaged.)

The message describing the Imperial Japanese Navy's defeat reported that Japanese ships able to do so were fleeing after their formations had been dispersed.

The advices indicated that the battle virtually was over.

PLANES LEAD ATTACK

The messages indicated that aviation played a leading part in the action. It was believed the Japanese advanced within range of land-based American and Australian planes and were attacked by large formations.

There was noticeable elation in British circles, but officials took the attitude that all information about the action should come from General MacArthur's headquarters in Australia or other American sources.

'AMERICAN SHOW'

The action was described as "mostly an American show."

Describing the aerial attacks, the advices said United Nations planes came over in waves and that American dive-bombers performed "very brilliantly."

One of the Japanese aircraft carriers sunk suffered direct hits from very large bombs and heeled over after the first wave of the attack.

SHIP MASS OF FLAMES

"It sank almost immediately," advices said.

The second Japanese aircraft carrier was attacked simultaneously with bombs and torpedoes. It soon was a mass of flames. It sank within a short time.

After the mass Allied aerial attacks, the Japanese ships scattered quickly and those able to do so fled to the northward pursued by fresh Allied air formations.

R.A.F., DUTCH BLAST 8 MORE NAZI SHIPS; INVASION IS PLEDGED

LONDON, May 8 (A. P.).—The Royal Air Force's Canadian "Demon Squadron" and Dutch pilots plastered bomb hits on eight out of 12 ships in a heavily protected convoy off the Dutch coast during an overnight continuation of the British air offensive which, Air Minister Sir Archibald Sinclair declared today, will lead directly to British invasion of the continent.

The "Demons," who in seven days have damaged at least 19 enemy supply ships and a destroyer, reported hitting seven ships in the convoy and Royal Netherlands naval air service pilots got the eighth.

U. S. FLIER GETS ONE

An American with the Canadians, Pilot Officer G. L. Mosier of Waverley, N. Y., made one of the hits.

Today the German air force made a 20-second reprisal attack on a southeast coast town, hitting a school building with a bomb and killing a number of children. Streets were sprayed with cannon and machine-gun fire.

Wing Commander A. C. Brown, of Winnipeg, the Demons' commander, told the story of the convoy attack

Continued on Page 3, Column 2

IN TODAY'S INQUIRER

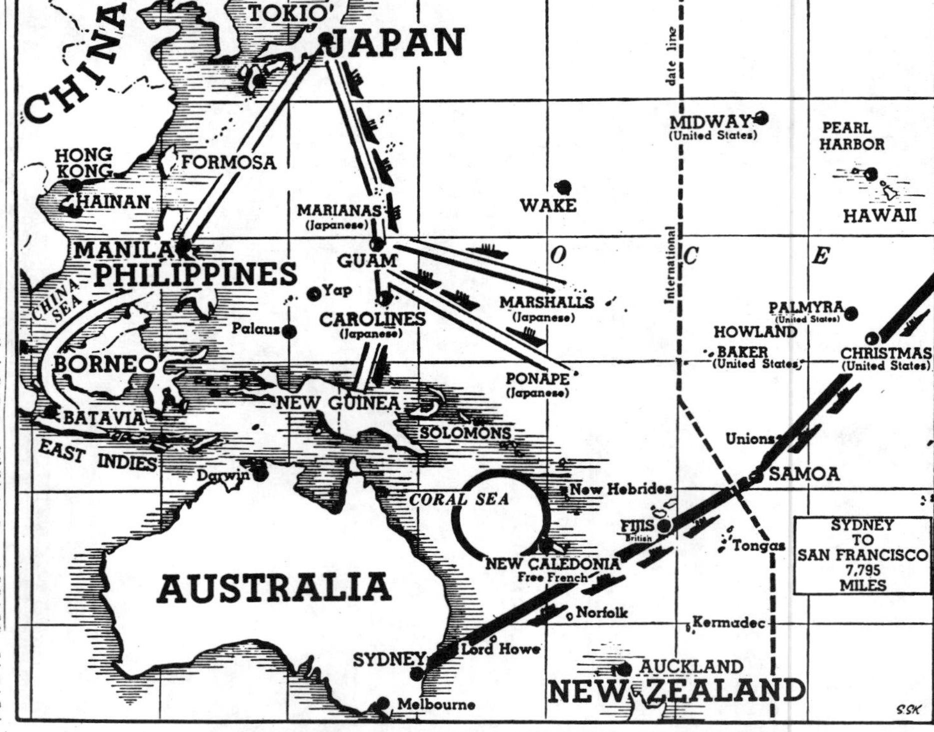

CORAL SEA VICTORY SAVES U. S.-AUSTRALIA SUPPLY LINE

United States victory in the great Battle of Coral Sea (circle), which "temporarily ceased" early today as the Japanese fleet was repulsed, removes for the present the Jap threat to the supply route to Australia (indicated by small ships and heavy line), and puts Allied ships in position to menace Japs communications (lighter lines). The victory also eases immediate peril to Australia, New Caledonia and New Hebrides (detail map on Page 2).

Navy Smashes 2 Air Carriers And 4 Cruisers

By C. YATES McDANIEL

ALLIED HEADQUARTERS, Australia, May 9 (Saturday) (A. P.).—Allied naval and air forces fighting with "marked skill, courage and tenacity" have repulsed a Japanese invasion fleet off northeastern Australia in one of history's most fateful struggles, General Douglas MacArthur's headquarters announced today.

With 11 or more of its warships sunk and six or more damaged, including two aircraft carriers and four cruisers—and presumably thousands of its finest warriors at the bottom of the Coral Sea—the battered Japanese enemy was reported limping northward with United States and British Imperial units in hot pursuit on the sixth day of the epic engagement.

"Our attacks will continue," the Allied communique said in reporting that the battle had ceased "temporarily."

'SKILL, COURAGE, TENACITY'

The repulse of the Japanese occurred after Allied air units discovered the enemy fleet streaming southward six or more days ago, and the communique concluded with these words:

"Our naval forces then attacked in interceptions. They were handled with marked skill, fought with admirable courage and tenacity, and the enemy has been repulsed.".

The latest communique made no claims of additional casualties other than those already reported Friday both here and in Washington. There has been no inkling from Allied sources of their own losses.

Presumably a complete summary of the battle losses on both sides will be forthcoming shortly.

IN SHADOW OF AUSTRALIA

The battle was fought in the shadow of Australia and involved the safety of the continent and control of much of the southern seas.

The headquarters communique said the action represented a "continued effort of the Japanese to extend their aggressive conquests towards the south and southeast."

Many quarters regarded the thwarted Japanese fleet movement as a possible attempt to invade Australia.

The text of the latest communique:

"The great naval and air battle off the northeast coast of Australia has temporarily ceased. This action

Continued on Page 2, Column 1

4 JUDGES CONDEMN BARING OF NAMES IN BAR 'RACKET' PROBE

Members of the Board of Judges and the Committee of Censors of the Philadelphia Bar Association joined yesterday in strongly condemning publication by a Philadelphia newspaper of the names of 47 cited lawyers.

The Inquirer did not publish the names.

The judges declared the names should not have been published until the lawyers in question had been given an opportunity to defend themselves.

NOT AN INDICTMENT

The Committee of Censors, which made the citations, emphasized that its report was not an indictment of the lawyers mentioned therein, but merely a summary of testimony which it had heard.

The judicial disapproval of publication of the names came from the President Judges of four of the seven Common Pleas courts, who also would be members of a disciplinary court set up to hear the charges of unethical practices against the lawyers.

CALLS IT 'OUTRAGE'

President Judge Frank Smith, of Common Pleas Court No. 5, declared: "I consider it an outrage to broadcast the names of the attorneys mentioned in the report, until they have had an opportunity to defend themselves."

President Judge Harry S. McDevitt, of Common Pleas No. 1, said: "I have no personal knowledge of the contents of the committee's report. No man should be condemned without having his day in court. Justice requires us to hear both sides, and time will tell whether it is evidence or vaporings of prejudiced minds that we have before us."

A joint statement was issued by President Judge Thomas D. Fin-

Continued on Page 6, Column 7

War Summary

Saturday, May 9, 1942

PACIFIC FRONT

United States and Allied warships, fighting one of the greatest sea battles of history, have smashed a Japanese invasion armada in the Coral Sea off northeastern Australia after an epic six-day fight on which the fate of Australia may well have hinged.

General MacArthur's Headquarters in Australia officially announced today that the Japanese had been repulsed after 11 or more of their warships and auxiliaries were sunk and six others damaged. Two aircraft carriers and four cruisers were among the Japanese warcraft blasted.

The battle has ceased "temporarily," MacArthur's headquarters said, after the Allies fought with "skill, courage and tenacity."

United States losses were not yet known, although the Navy cautioned against acceptance of Japanese claims.

While Chinese forces routed two Jap columns penetrating into Yunan Province along the Burma road, the British moved rapidly to forestall Jap blows at India by reinforcing Ceylon and mopping up in Madagascar across the Indian Ocean. The western Burma port of Akyab fell to the Japs, who were massing at Rangoon for a sweep on India despite renewed bombings by American raiders.

EUROPEAN FRONT

R.A.F. and Dutch fliers, paced by the Canadian "Demon" squadron, blasted eight Nazi supply ships in a convoy off Holland, bringing their week's total to 20 vessels damaged or sunk.

A three-way German effort to penetrate Soviet Karelia from Finland was smashed by the Red Army. The six-week Nazi air offensive against the Allied northern sea lanes to Russia also was reported to have ended in failure.

No News Good News, Navy Tells Relatives

WASHINGTON, May 8 (U. P.).—The Navy today advised families and friends of Navy men on sea duty not to entertain fear because of delays in receiving letters from them.

Because of the great distances involved in ship operations, the Navy said, it is only natural to expect delays in correspondence.

The Navy said it always notifies the next of kin when serious casualties occur, and therefore, "it is safe to assume that no news is good news."

Japs Disarm French Seeking to Aid China

CHUNGKING, April 8 (U. P.).—French soldiers from Indo-China who attempted to desert their barracks and join Chinese forces were disarmed by Japanese soldiers April 28, the Chinese Central News Agency said today.

The agency said more than 100 French troops were disarmed at the outskirts of Chennankwang.

Leahy Takes Off On Clipper for U. S.

LONDON, May 8 (A. P.).—The Vichy radio said today United States Ambassador William D. Leahy, who is returning home, had left Lisbon by clipper.

2 GALLONS A WEEK SET AS RATION FOR PLEASURE DRIVERS

By ROBERT BARRY

Inquirer Washington Bureau

WASHINGTON, May 8.—The average Eastern seaboard motorist, who uses his car for pleasure only, will be allowed to buy between two and three gallons of gasoline a week after May 15—probably no more than two—Price Administrator Leon Henderson revealed today.

"And in view of the present shortage," Henderson remarked, "that's a damned sight more than he's entitled to."

2 GALLONS STRESSED

In reporting the situation to the House Interstate Commerce Committee, the rationing czar stuck persistently to the two-gallon limit, winding up with an assertion that he had seen no figures to show how the ulti-

Continued on Page 6, Column 4

Bravery of Dutch Hailed by Roosevelt

WASHINGTON, May 8 (A. P.).—Dutch heroism in the face of aggression at home and overseas has stirred the imagination of the American people, President Roosevelt told Queen Wilhelmina in a letter presented to her in London today by Anthony J. Drexel Biddle, Jr., as first United States Ambassador to the Netherlands.

Ambassador Biddle, who functioned as Minister to the Netherlands government in London until the elevation of the respective missions to embassy status, formally presented his credentials to the Queen today.

Masaryk Cautions 2d Front Advocates

NEW YORK, May 8 (A. P.).—Dr. Jan Masaryk, Czechoslovakian Minister of Foreign Affairs, said today that talk of a second front in Europe at this time was premature.

"We should not kid ourselves that we can start a second front as easily as snapping our fingers," he told the second world congress of the International Free World Association. "The failure of a second front would be a great blow to the cause of democracies, and therefore we should not encourage the peoples of occupied countries to expect the impossible at this time."

Churchill Broadcast Set for Tomorrow

Prime Minister Winston Churchill will broadcast an address to the world at 3 P. M. (E. W. T.) tomorrow.

Every station in the Philadelphia area will carry the talk by Churchill, who will speak from London. The subject of his talk has not been announced.

U. S. Weather Forecast

Philadelphia and vicinity: Somewhat higher temperature today.

Sun rises	5.51 A.M.	Sets 8.02 P.M.
Moon rises	3.07 A.M.	Sets 2.42 P.M.

Other Weather Reports on Page 2

War Film Ready For Jane Withers

Republic's 'Johnny Doughboy' Awaits Tomboy Star, on Bond-Selling Tour

By Louella O. Parsons

HOLLYWOOD, May 28.

HERBERT YATES, of Republic, is crazy—like a fox—in signing Jane Withers on a three-year deal and a starring contract. First, Janie is packing them in like sardines on her combination bond-selling and personal-appearance tour. Second, even though her pictures were secondary to Shirley Temple's when they were both on the 20th Century-Fox lot, there was box-office gold in the little tomboy star who can sing and dance and who is such a swell little actress.

So anxious is Republic to get Jane back on the screen after her stint for Uncle Sam that Moe Siegel, producing head, has already lined up her first, "Johnny Doughboy," starting immediately upon her return. If you look over Republic movie titles you will find that many of them carry the names of popular songs whenever possible because of the "ready-made" audience appeal. John H. Auer has been given the directorial assignment.

The old home lot at RKO, where Fred Astaire and Ginger Rogers made their popular dance hits, is getting ready to lay down the red velvet carpet. Yes, Fred is returning to his alma mater, but without Ginger. And I reckon it's the story by James Kern and S. K. Laurens that sold him the deal. Called "Look Out Below," it has a honey of a plot about an inhibited flier on a 10-day furlough who does all the things on his leave that he has wanted to do but has been afraid to do all his life. Dancing is one of these things and, of course, Fred dances. David Hempstead has been assigned the producer's job.

GINGER ROGERS

I am getting dizzy over all of these wartime stories that are being gobbled up by the movies. One of the most interesting is one which Bogart Rogers and Mark Kelly have just sold to M-G-M. It is the first, so far as I know, on the present conflict in Australia, and it has more than just the angle of General Douglas MacArthur's arrival in the Antipodes. Bogart and Mark have brought in World War I and they tell about the soldier who brings two refugees back from Belgium to Australia. Of course they are all grown up and ready to fight in the second World War. Wallace Beery has been handed the story and because of its timeliness it will go into production without delay.

Chatter in Hollywood: Through the old reliable underground I hear that Errol Flynn has just presented Mary Ann Hyde, 19-year-old Beverly Hills girl, with a topaz ring set in emeralds and diamonds. The description given me is that it is as big as a battleship. The Hyde gal has just made a test at Warners' and, according to my operator No. 59, she is a beauty. Errol, by the way, will co-star with Annie Sheridan in "Edge of Darkness." Yes, I know, Humphrey Bogart was announced, but Bogie is tied up on other movies. This is the novel by William Wood, and Warners will get it in before Annie reports at Paramount for "Texas Guinan."

A line or Two: Seeing Virginia Grey and Dick Arlen together leaves no doubt that they have indeed kissed and made up. They were in the same party, including Bill Pine and Bill Thomas, who went to San Francisco for the Paramount convention . . . Ann Sothern isn't going to let a fishing trip in Mexican waters keep her away from Robert Sterling, who leaves soon to join the Army Air Corps. Soon as she learned that Bob would be called any day she sent her regrets to the Ray Millands. Can't say I blame her . . . Eleanor Penner, Joe's widow, staged the revue at the "Louisiana," formerly the Wilshire Bowl. The entire place has been redone and I am wondering if Mrs. Penner, who has theatrical inclinations, hasn't some money in the venture . . . Wonder if Wally Vernon, whose wife and twins were so often in the newspapers during the many times they took their troubles to court, is married again. Someone said that he introduced a girl as his new wife the other eve at the Bandbox . . . According to Mrs. Helen Lloyd, Harold's step-ma, Priscilla Dean, who is now Mrs. Lester Arnold, is living in Tenafly, N. J. Her husband is an air pilot. This will answer Frances Watson.

MYRNA LOY

Snapshots of Hollywood Collected at Random: John Payne's new heart throb is Jane Russell; Myrna Loy gets her divorce decree June 1 and she goes directly to New York. The house she and Arthur Hornblow, Jr., built in Coldwater Canyon has been leased to non-professionals; David Selznick is turning over the first day's proceeds from "G. W. T. W." at the Carthay Circle to A. W. V. S. Vivien Leigh's original tests will be shown for the first time; Arthur Farnsworth and Bette Davis have said adieu for the time being. He has gone back to his job in Minneapolis; What goes on with Mary Beth Hughes and Bob Stack? They were out stepping again at the Palladium; The Arnold Kunodys have dated the stork. He used to be a Hollywood insurance broker; Susan Hayward hosted a cocktail party in honor of Bradshaw Crandall, Cosmopolitan cover artist who was here to paint Susan's portrait; Dan Topping has been called to Washington by the Navy. Sonja Henie joins him after she finishes "Iceland"; Frank Morgan, that enthusiastic old yachtsman, has bought a ranch. Many people are moving to the San Fernando Valley because it's safe from bombs—we hope! Mrs. Lou Gehrig has returned to New York after seeing an uncut version of "Pride of the Yankees"; Paulette Goddard is off again to Phoenix and New York to remain until "The Crystal Ball" starts.

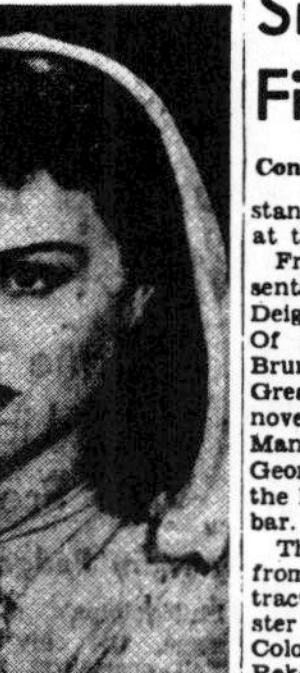

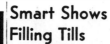

IN SPY FILM
Paulette Goddard has some exciting adventures with spies in "The Lady Has Plans," which opens at the Earle today.

Can't Nibble Movie Beans,

One of the daffiest scenes ever picked up by the camera went into Hollywood's wistful collection of shots that will never be shown. It all happened on the set of 20th Century-Fox's Technicolor musical, "My Gal Sal," co-starring Rita Hayworth and Victor Mature, which opens at the Fox this morning.

As Paul Dresser, composer of "On the Banks of the Wabash" and the title song, Mature was required to lean over a cafe bar. After ordering drinks, he was supposed to reach into a bowl on the counter, pick up some coffee beans and nibble them.

The Klieg lights glared down hotly. The camera started. Mature gave his order to the bartender and then reached for the beans. His hand stopped in mid-air. The next minute he strode over to Director Irving Cummings and yelled:

"They bit me! The coffee beans!!"

The assistant director shouted for the prop man. "What kind of beans did you put in this bowl?" he demanded.

"The best Mexican jumping beans, of course," solemnly explained the prop man. "They look more like coffee beans in Technicolor than the real thing."

For intelligent suggestions on the care and feeding of your child, read Carolyn Randolph's column in The Inquirer.

Smart Shows Filling Tills

Continued From Preceding Page

stand, and continuous entertainment at the Merry-Go-Round Bar.

Frank Murtha, singing emcee, presents a sparkling floor revue at Neil Deighan's, Airport Circle, Camden. Of note are the Four Hollywood Brunettes, dancing beauties; the Great Martinelli; the Le Shonnes, novelty dance team; La Fleur and Manners, in a "human top" act; George Marchetti's orchestra and the Rhythm Maniacs at the cocktail bar.

The Watkins Twins, two dollies from the Follies, are must-see attractions at the Silver Lake Inn, lobster capitol at Clementon, N. J. Colonel George Reed also introduces Rekoma, for acrobatics and comedy combined; the Duchess and Jack Herman, piano twins; comedienne Alice Lucey and Frank Hassel's music.

Continuous whirl of entertainment, too, at the New 20th Century, 15th below Chestnut. Marjorie Hyams and her Stylists are solid senders, while in a more sentimental vein are Harry McKay, his guitar and trio, with Evelyn Kerwin taking the spotlight for clarinet solos. Sally La Marr presides at the mini-piano at cocktail time.

Jack Stamp bows to public demand to retain Arnold and LaMont, socko comedy team now holding hilarious sway at Jack's cafe on the Delaware at Poplar st. Also the "Four Hollywood Blondes," Babe Cummings, baritone; Lanny Vale and the WJZ Orchestra.

Scarey Gavin, at Lou Tomasco's College Inn, 2256 N. Broad st., introduces the Mallery Sisters, nimble dancers; Ruth Templeton, the songbird; Diana "Bumps" Del Rio, a unique dancer; the Thunderbolts, sepia dancers, and the Crescent Quintette.

The Musical Bar in Irvin Wolf's intimate Rendezvous, Hotel Senator, 915 Walnut st., remains tops in continuous entertainment. The Shadrach Boys, a duo of sepia harmonizers, and the Three Internationals, for instrumental and vocal jive, are the big attractions.

Hamid's Pier 'Blacked Out'

Officials of Hamid's Million Dollar Pier in Atlantic City yesterday announced that the pier had been "blacked out" to prevent any escape of light and that entertainment would be provided as usual during the summer season.

The ballroom, Hippodrome Theatre and other pleasure-ways of the pier are all situated well toward the front of the structure, making it necessary only to blackout the windows facing the sun decks. Only show curtailment necessary will be the elimination of the final nighttime circus performance at the end of the pier.

Amusement Guide to Playhouses of Philadelphia

THEATRE

FORREST—"Macbeth," Shakespeare's drama, with Maurice Evans, Judith Anderson. 8.30.

MOTION PICTURES

ALDINE—"Reap the Wild Wind," adventure off Florida, in color; with Paulette Goddard, Ray Milland, John Wayne, Raymond Massey. 11, 1.10, 3.20, 5.35, 7.45, 10.

ARCADIA—"Rings on Her Fingers," comedy, with Henry Fonda and Gene Tierney. 11, 12.50, 2.40, 4.30, 6.20, 8.10, 10.

BOYD—"In This Our Life," Bette Davis as a home-wrecker; with Olivia de Havilland, George Brent, Dennis Morgan, Charles Coburn. 11.30, 1.35, 3.40, 5.45, 7.50, 10.

CAPITOL—"Remember Pearl Harbor," melodrama, with Alan Curtis and Fay McKenzie. 10.30, 12.50, 3.10, 5.30, 7.50, 10.10.

EARLE—"The Lady Has Plans," spy-chase comedy, with Paulette Goddard and Ray Milland. 10.50, 1.50, 4.45, 7.45, 10.25. On stage, Russ Morgan and orchestra. Opens today.

FOX—"My Gal Sal," musical in Technicolor, with Rita Hayworth and Victor Mature. 11.15, 1.25, 3.25, 5.45, 7.55, 10.05. Opens today

KARLTON—"Larceny, Inc.," crook comedy, with Edward G. Robinson, Broderick Crawford, and Jane Wyman. 11, 12.45, 2.35, 4.25, 6.10, 8, 9.50.

KEITH'S—"My Favorite Blonde," comedy, with Bob Hope and Madeleine Carroll. 11.20, 1.05, 2.50, 4.40, 6.25, 8.10, 10.

NEWS—"Souls at Sea," drama, with Gary Cooper and George Raft. 8, 9.45, 11.36, 1.24, 3.12, 5, 6.48, 8.36, 10.24, all night.

STANLEY—"Ship Ahoy," musical comedy, with Eleanor Powell, Red Skelton, Bert Lahr, Tommy Dorsey. 11, 12.50, 2.40, 4.30, 6.20, 8.05, 10.

STANTON—"Dangerously They Live," John Garfield aids Nancy Coleman, British agent, against Raymond Massey, Nazi spy. 11, 12.50, 2.40, 4.30, 6.20, 8.10, 10.05. Last day.

STUDIO—"The Terror," thriller, with Wilfrid Lawson and Linden Travers. 11.05, 1.20, 3.35, 5.50, 8.15, 10.32, and "Mystery of Room 13." Gibb McLaughlin and Peter Murray-Hill hunt counterfeiters. 12.08, 2.23, 4.38, 7.02, 9.20.

Life Under Nazi Rule--The Grim Tragedy of France

FRENCH HOUSEWIVES, LINED UP FOR MEAGRE RATIONS. LOOK AT EMPTY MILK CANS

(A. P. Wirephoto)
INNOCENT FRENCH HOSTAGE EXECUTED BY NAZIS

Smuggled Pictures Tell Tale

Better than a thousand speeches, these pictures smuggled out of German - occupied France and sent to the United States from London tell Americans why they are fighting this war. For the pictures show the hunger, riots, executions, concentration camps and swaggering, steel - helmeted Nazis which a German victory means to conquered peoples.

(A. P. Wirephoto)
HUCKSTERS' CARTS STAND EMPTY IN LES HALLES MARKET, PARIS

PARISIANS READ LIST OF THOSE EXECUTED

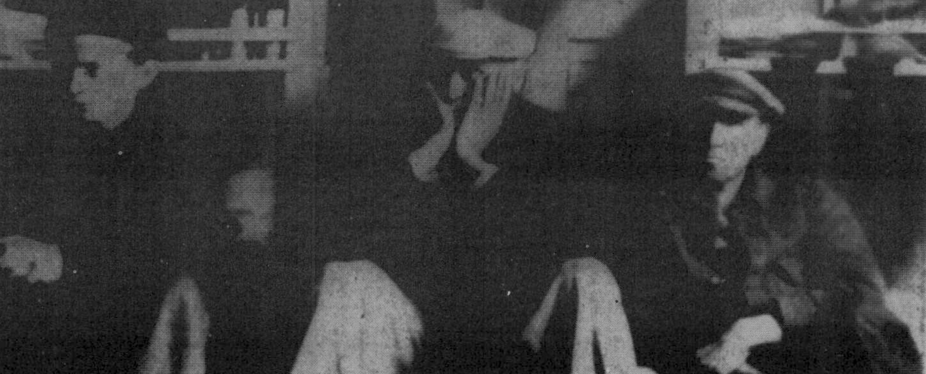

(A. P. Wirephoto)
FRENCHMEN SIT IN SILENCE IN GERMAN CONCENTRATION CAMP

(A. P. Wirephoto)
CLEANING UP WRECKAGE AFTER RIOT AGAINST NAZIS IN PARIS

(A. P. Wirephoto)
GERMAN MILITARY GUARD QUESTIONS MOTORIST AT PARIS INTERSECTION

The Philadelphia Inquirer

PUBLIC LEDGER

An Independent Newspaper for All the People

FINAL CITY EDITION

CIRCULATION: May Average: Daily 444,703, Sunday 1,251,755 abdefgh★ SATURDAY MORNING, JUNE 6, 1942 Copyright, 1942, by The Philadelphia Inquirer Co. VOL. 226, No. 157 Second Largest 3c Morning Circulation in America THREE CENTS

BLASTED JAP FLEET FLEES

Battleships and Carriers Battered; U.S. Continues Attack Off Midway

Foe's Cruisers, Transports Also Smashed

HONOLULU, June 5 (A. P.).—Japanese naval forces attacking Midway Island have suffered "very heavy" damage to carrier, battleship, cruiser and transport classes and appear now to be withdrawing, Admiral Chester W. Nimitz said in a communique tonight.

"As more reports come in," the communique said, "it appears that the enemy damage is very heavy, indeed, involving several ships in each of carrier, battleship, cruiser and transport classes.

"This damage is far out of proportion to that which we have received."

FAIL TO FOLLOW UP FIRST ATTACK

Except for a few ineffectual shots from a submarine last night, the Japanese failed to follow up their initial air attack against the island, Admiral Nimitz added.

"The brunt of the defense to date," the communique continued, "has fallen upon our aviation personnel in which the Army, Navy and Marine Corps all were represented. They have added another shining page to their record of achievements.

"One carrier already damaged by air attack was hit by three torpedoes fired by a submarine.

'U. S. REMAINS IN FIRM CONTROL'

"On every occasion when we have met the enemy, our officers and men have been superlative in their offensive spirit . . .

"There were reported several instances of enemy planes machine-gunning our aviation personnel who bailed out in parachutes or were adrift in rubber boats.

"While it is too early to claim a major Japanese disaster, it may be conservatively stated that the United States remains in firm control of the Midway area.

"The enemy appears to be withdrawing but we are continuing the battle."

BELIEVED ATTEMPTING TO SEIZE ISLAND

Mention in the Admiral's second communique of the presence of transports among the attacking naval forces added support to the belief that the purpose of the invaders was to seize Midway, removing the last island barrier in the Pacific between Japan and Hawaii.

As the fury of the battle rose, with disclosures of the size of the Japanese force at a point so far removed from its bases, there were conjectures that the enemy had first directed a plane raid at Dutch Harbor, Alaska, in a feint to draw United

Continued on Page 2, Column 4

(A. P. Wirephoto)

WHERE JAP FLEET FLEES AFTER BATTERING OFF MIDWAY

Map above shows area in which Japanese fleet was fleeing early today after sustaining heavy losses in great sea and air battle off Midway Island. Midway is keypoint of vital U. S. defenses of the entire Pacific area. Dotted arrows show directions in which Japs could have advanced on Hawaii, Alaska, the U. S. West Coast and Panama Canal.

Today

Isolationists Defended
Liberal Attack Hit
Fake 'Patriotism'
Tax Bill Opposed
Far Short of Needs

By Paul Mallon

WASHINGTON, June 5.

THE ardent liberal campaign to banish all so-called isolationists from public life in the midst of war was started by the New Republic magazine for reasons not clear at the time.

The implication was that they were unpatriotic. But an inspection of their voting records in Congress since Dec. 7 showed they generally supported every war measure and were not talking much. Actually they were no obstacle to the war effort.

When that reason thus fell down, other publications which took up the campaign turned to the point that the isolationists should be exterminated because they opposed getting into the war before we got into the war. The liberals hammered that reason for a while, but it left matters just as much in the dark as ever, because Mr. Roosevelt opposed getting into the war before we got in.

His speeches and statements show this to have been his announced policy in his re-election. If that is the measure of isolationism, then the President was an isolationist and so were most of the people of the country.

Any real reason for the campaign continued to be unexplained until the New Republic's June 8 issue came out this week. Then it offered a good reason.

It said it was not soaking isolationists because they were isolationists, but because most of them were against the New Deal, quote:

"The enemies of the New Deal are the very ones who could keep us from winning the peace. This is an issue which must be fought and won on the domestic front, and it must be won while the war is being waged."

That clarifies the matter. The attack, it now appears, was timed all along for the primaries and the Congressional elections, for domestic political reasons—which are fair enough in themselves. Bust such a clarification certainly requires the liberals to drop that fake mantle of patriotism under which they have been hiding this purely political sword.

The question then is whether the New Republic and associates are going to dictate the peace and future domestic politics after eliminating their political opponents from the discussion during the coming elections.

Mourning about the new tax bill is widespread among those who are making it and who may bring it out in about two weeks. Designed to curb inflation and raise $8,600,000,000, it does neither.

The Government economists are clicking their teeth about it because it will make the Nation's total Federal tax bill about $24,000,000,000 a year, only about one-fourth of our national income and that income may go to $120,000,000,000 by the time the bill becomes effective. They all say it therefore cannot be a guarantee against inflation.

Mr. Morgenthau first asked for a $7,600,000,000 bill and then sent up supplemental requests which would bring it up to $8,600,000,000. As it stands now the bill would raise less than $6,000,000,000.

If a $2,000,000,000 sales tax were

Continued on Page 4, Column 4

BLAST KILLS 21 IN SHELL PLANT; 30 ARE MISSING

41 Injured as Wide Illinois Area Is Jolted by Explosion; Army Plans Probe

JOLIET, Ill., June 5 (A. P.).—An explosion inside the Elwood Ordnance shell loading plant left 51 men dead or missing today, but it halted production in only one of 12 units inside the plant, one of the biggest in the Nation.

One building was destroyed at 2.45 A. M. (Central War Time) as a night crew packed cartons and loaded boxcars with explosives. Army officers said there was no suspicion of sabotage.

21 KNOWN DEAD

Captain David P. Tunstall said 21 persons were known to be dead and 30 others were missing.

Nineteen bodies had been identified 12 hours after the blast. Some had been blown to pieces, and fingerprint experts aided in the identification.

Calls were being made to homes of missing to see if, by their own good luck, they had stayed away from work last night.

Tunstall's original list of dead and missing contained 57 names, but it was shortened as three workmen were located in hospitals and away from the plant.

The ordnance plant's hospital treated 41 injury cases. Five were reported of a serious nature.

The Ordnance Department's policy of scattering buildings over an immense area—the Elwood plant covers 15,000 acres of flat prairie—helped confine to one building the explosion, felt as far away as 100 miles.

With one ear-splitting roar and a flash of flame, the shipping building in Group Two was demolished. Group Two consists of four major buildings,

Continued on Page 9, Column 4

ARMY BASE PAY IS PUT AT $46 IN COMPROMISE

Plan Faces Defeat As House Insists on $50; Rise Would Revert to June 1

By RICHARD L. HARKNESS
Inquirer Washington Bureau

WASHINGTON, June 5.—Senate-House conferees sought today to break the deadlock delaying passage of the Army and Navy pay increase bill by compromising on $46 a month as base pay for buck privates and apprentice seamen.

There were definite indications, however, that Congress would not accept the compromise, insisting on the $50 minimum figure twice approved by the House by roll call votes of 10 to one.

SHOWDOWN DUE MONDAY

The fight in the Senate against $46 will be led by Senator Robert M. LaFollette, Jr., (Prog., Wis.), and in the House by Representative John E. Rankin (D., Miss.). The showdown probably will come on Monday.

The compromise was put forward this afternoon by the three members of the five-man Senate conference committee who have been insisting that the pay raise be limited to $42—Senators Edwin C. Johnson (D., Colo.), Warren R. Austin (R., Vt.), and Chan Gurney (R., S. D.).

The figure was accepted late this afternoon by House conferees, although they had been instructed by a 332-to-28 vote of their colleagues in the lower chamber to insist on $50.

To make the compromise more palatable, the conference committee made the raise retroactive to June 1. Pay of first class privates and seamen would be increased to $52 a month under their agreement.

Army draftees now receive $21 a

Continued on Page 6, Column 7

F. D. R. WARNS JAPAN WE'LL RETALIATE FOR USE OF POISON GAS

By WILLIAM C. MURPHY, JR.
Inquirer Washington Bureau

WASHINGTON, June 5.—The United States will blanket the islands of Japan with poison gas if the Japanese persist in using that type of weapon against the Chinese or any other of the United Nations, President Roosevelt announced today.

The President made that grim announcement at a press conference where he read a formal statement which, he said, had been prepared by the State Department.

His manner was grave and it was obvious that he regarded the declaration he was making as one of the utmost importance.

JAPAN'S RESPONSIBILITY

The statement was:

"Authoritative reports are reaching this Government of the use by Japanese armed forces in various localities of China of poisonous or noxious gases.

"I desire to make it unmistakably clear that, if Japan persists in this inhuman form of warfare against China or against any other of the United Nations, such action will be regarded by this Government as though taken against the United States, and retaliation in kind and in full measure will be meted out. We shall be prepared to enforce complete retribution. Upon Japan will rest the responsibility."

In response to several questions

Continued on Page 2, Column 7

3 War Declarations Signed by Roosevelt

WASHINGTON, June 5 (U. P.).—President Roosevelt today signed declarations of war against Bulgaria, Hungary and Rumania.

U. S. WEATHER

Philadelphia and Vicinity: Not quite so warm today.

Sun rises 5.32 A.M. Sets 8.26 P.M.
Moon rises 1.44 A.M. Sets 1.37 A.M.

Other Weather Reports on Page 2

'Forever Lost'

Papers Depict Cologne Ruin

BERN, Switzerland, June 5 (A. P.).

THE first Cologne newspapers since the monster Royal Air Force raid of last Saturday night reached neutral territory today, carrying the somber statement that the historic Rhineland city, as its people have known it, is "forever lost."

The Koelnische Zeitung, resuming publication on Wednesday of this week, described Cologne as "still smoking ruins," with some fires still alight and "whole quarters of the town empty."

(A German dispatch quoted by the Stockholm newspaper Dagens Nyheter said all the property of 10,000 persons had been destroyed; that the central district of the city was ruined and that the damage had reached deep into the suburbs.)

Said the Koelnische Zeitung:

"The entire aspect of the city is completely changed. Tens of

Continued on Page 3, Column 4

1000 R.A.F. PLANES BLAST 330 MILES OF NAZI-HELD COAST

Illustrated on Page 3

LONDON, June 6 (Saturday) (U. P.).—A thousand Royal Air Force planes, paced by new Whirlwind fighters firing shells from four cannon, swarmed over 330 miles of European coast from dawn to dusk yesterday, blasting German raider lairs, docks and airports in such mighty force that few German fighters dared challenge them.

An early morning Air Ministry communique revealed the Whirlwinds went into action for the first time in simultaneous R. A. F. attacks stretching from the U-boat base at Ostend in Belgium to airdromes on the Breton Peninsula of France.

BOMBERS HIT FIRST

Targets at Osten, Le Havre and Morlaix, Lannion and Abbeville, in France, were battered by American-built Boston (Douglas) bombers, then

Continued on Page 3, Column 3

IN TODAY'S INQUIRER

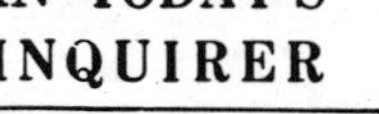

Summary

Saturday, June 6, 1942

PACIFIC FRONT

A victory for United States forces of apparent major proportions in defense of Midway and the whole, vital Allied supply lanes in the Pacific, was indicated today in a new communique from Admiral Chester W. Nimitz.

The U. S. naval commander said the Japanese, with "very heavy" damage to ships of their aircraft carrier, battleship, cruiser and transport classes, seemed to be withdrawing from the original assault on Midway Island.

China is past her worst crisis, Generalissimo Chiang declared as the United States prepared to send swarms of planes to Chungking and the Japs were hurled back again at Chuhsien.

With the Japanese reported only 20 miles from the border, Britain revealed a record convoy had landed troops and equipment in India. U. S. planes blasted Jap shipping at Rangoon.

President Roosevelt confirmed Jap use of poison gas in China and warned Tokio that the United States would "retaliate in kind" unless such attacks ended.

OTHER FRONTS

R. A. F. fighter and bomber planes, 1000 strong, raked 330 miles of the Nazi-held western coast of Europe.

Russian planes hammered the Germans' Arctic bases menacing the Murmansk supply lines.

A gigantic French "Fifth Column" is awaiting establishment of a second front in Europe as a signal to attack the Nazi conquerors, a high source reported in Washington.

Here Are the Last Moments of the U. S. S. Lexington

(A. P. Wirephoto)

ACTUAL PHOTO OF LEXINGTON EXPLODING AS A SKIFF (ARROW) PULLS AWAY

Dramatic Photos of the Death of a Ship

Here are four of the most striking war pictures ever made of the final moments in the life of a man o'war. Pictured is the U. S. S. Lexington, the 33,000-ton aircraft carrier, sunk several hours after the battle of the Coral Sea by a terrific explosion. These photos all were made at close range by "anonymous" enlisted men especially trained to get action shots for their strategic and historic as well as their dramatic value. Telephoto lenses were not used. The men risked their lives for the pictures. Top is the actual blast that tore the carrier apart. Below, billowing smoke almost hides the Lexington. On right, a plane (arrow) is being tossed from the vessel by a blast. At bottom: two destroyers tend the stricken carrier. One, at left, is trying to rescue some of the crew while at right, the other, obscured by smoke, is pouring water into the Lexington.

(A. P. Wirephoto)

THE LEXINGTON BURNING AWAY IN THE LAST STAGES OF HER DESTRUCTION

(A. P. Wirephoto)

TERRIFIC BLAST ROCKS THE CARRIER THROWING PLANE (ARROW) IN AIR

(A. P. Wirephoto)

TWO DESTROYERS TENDING LEXINGTON. ONE IN THE SMOKE AT RIGHT IS PUMPING WATER INTO HER; AT LEFT, ATTEMPTING TO TAKE OFF CREW

ATWILL IS INDICTED IN WILD PARTY QUIZ

Hollywood Actor Accused of Perjury As Case Reopens

HOLLYWOOD, June 30 (U. P.).—A curvaceous Cuban's story of what she called "wild revels on a tiger rug" resulted today in the Grand Jury indicting Lionel Atwill, film star, on charges of perjury.

The jury specifically accused Atwill of exhibiting in his home two lewd films, called "The Plumber's Wife" and "The Daisy Chain" and then denying that he ever heard of them.

OTHER ACCUSATIONS

The 57-year-old Atwill, one of Hollywood's most popular portrayers of British colonels, outraged fathers and Nazi spies, also was accused of serving liquor to 16-year-old Sylvia Hamalaine and of seeing her in what the jury called "a compromising position" with Eugene Frenke, the movie producer husband of Anna Sten, onetime film star.

Atwill posted bond of $1000 and was released until July 2 to enter his plea. He denied the charges through his attorney, Isaac Pacht, who urged that Atwill's friends withhold judgment until the trial.

BRIBE ATTEMPT CHARGED

Pacht charged that his client was the victim of "persecution" because he had refused to be "shaken down" for a $10,000 bribe. Pacht did not name the bribe-seeker.

Atwill's alleged esoteric entertainments in his mansion on the Pacific palisades have been a matter of hush-hush investigation by numerous authorities for more than a year.

WOMAN'S CHARGES

Virginia Lopez, Havana dress designer, brought the matter to judicial attention last year when she charged that the revels on the rug had contributed to the delinquency of plump, blonde Miss Hamalaine, of Hibbing, Minn., who had come to Hollywood in hope of becoming a movie queen.

Miss Lopez, herself, was convicted of contributing to the delinquency of Miss Hamalaine, her room-mate, and paid a $100 fine. Charges against Atwill were held in abeyance until Miss Lopez repeated her accusations to the current grand jury.

SPICY TRIAL INDICATED

She told the jurymen that she had been prosecuted simply because she knew too much about the affairs on the cliff above the Pacific. The indictment which resulted from her story included 30 pages of questions and answers, which indicated Hollywood was in for one of its most lurid trials since the days of Fatty Arbuckle and William Desmond Taylor.

Last year's grand jury tabled the complaints, against Atwill with the announcement that the testimony had taxed its credulity. Both Miss Lopez and Miss Hamalaine claimed they had witnessed lewd acts in the actor's home and named several Hollywood celebrities as having participated.

SAID GUESTS DISROBED

Miss Lopez testified she had attended a party at Atwill's home, where all the guests except herself disrobed and sprawled upon the now famous rug. She said that she sat at the piano watching them, while she played Viennese waltzes.

Miss Hamalaine, an expectant mother, went on to say that she was among those who took off their clothes.

Eventually Miss Lopez was indicted and Miss Hamalaine testified that she lost her virtue in her own apartment, simply because she had become tired of re-buttoning her dress.

'LOST MY STRENGTH'

Miss Hamalaine said that her attacker was Adolph Larue, an automobile salesman, later drafted into the Army. Miss Lopez unbuttoned her dress, she said, while Larue stroked her head.

"I buttoned it up," Miss Hamalaine testified, "and she kept opening it and I kept buttoning it and finally I lost all my strength. I got tired of buttoning it."

Atwill, formerly prominent on the New York stage, was married in 1930 to Mrs. Louise Cromwell MacArthur, daughter of Mrs. E. T. Stotesbury, wife of the Philadelphia financier.

Brokers Describe Check-Cashing at Trial of 'Playboy'

NEW YORK, June 30 (U. P.).—Testimony in Federal Court disclosed today that Samuel H. Feldman, of Petoskey, Mich., who allegedly "kited" checks totaling $890,000 in eight months as a Broadway playboy, was "disappointed" when his check-cashing privileges were withdrawn by a New York brokerage house.

Feldman is on trial before Federal Judge Bascom Deaver, charged with nine counts of mail fraud in connection with his check-raising activities.

METHOD EXPLAINED

According to the Government, Feldman operated for eight months in 1937 by cashing checks drawn on out-of-town banks. His method was to cash a check on one bank and cover it with a check drawn on another bank, depending on clearing delays to provide a safety interval.

Arthur H. Goetz, a broker, testified today that his firm had extended check-cashing privileges to Feldman and when they were taken away, Feldman acted "disappointed." Goetz said Feldman had promised to provide business but had brought in very little, although he cashed checks worth about $16,000.

Paul Forester, manager of another brokerage firm, testified that his organization had given Feldman the same rights on the same promise to provide business. Feldman failed here also, but cashed checks at least four times a week. They were honored until one bounced and then Feldman's privileges were withdrawn, Forester said.

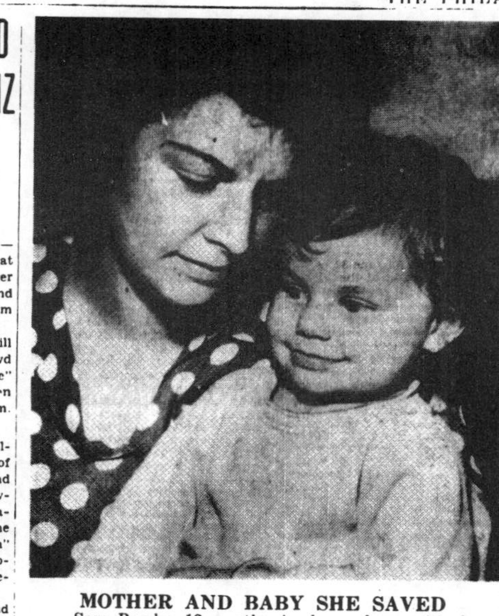

MOTHER AND BABY SHE SAVED

Sara Rambo, 18 months, is shown here with her mother, Mrs. Eleanor Rambo, who revived her by artificial respiration yesterday after the baby was found in a fish pool near their home in Pennsauken, N. J. The child and a young playmate, who went into the water in an attempt to rescue her, had gone wading to "cool off."

NEW HEARING SET TO BALK FARE RISE

By GERSON H. LUSH

Inquirer Harrisburg Bureau

HARRISBURG, June 30. — The Public Utility Commission acted today to stave off an increase in Philadelphia street car fares at least until Oct. 15.

By ordering hearings resumed July 14 on the Philadelphia Transportation Co.'s request for a fare rise, the commission kept alive its power to order the increase held up another three months pending its decision, which may deny the rise altogether.

Had the commission not acted, the company would have been able to put its proposed higher fares into effect on July 15—the expiration of the first six-month suspension ordered last January.

The company had requested that the commission defer action but, instead, resumption of hearings was scheduled for July 14 and will be continued on the 15th, 16th, 17th, 21st, 22d, 23d and 24th.

PROPOSE 10 CENT FARE

The rates proposed by the P.T.C. would boost the fares now two tokens for 15 cents or eight cents a single ride, to ten cents for a single ride, or three rides for 25 cents.

After an executive session of the commission today, Chairman John Siggins, Jr., announced that a new suspension order for three months was being prepared.

Siggins also disclosed that the P. T. C. has made another attempt to forestall final action on the rate case by asking for a conference "for the purpose of discussing a voluntary suspension by the company of its proposed fare increase."

He said the conference had been suggested by Ralph T. Senter, president of the P. T. C., and was rejected by the commission.

"At this time I see no necessity for a conference with the view of further voluntary suspension upon the part of your company," Siggins told Senter.

FURTHER SUSPENSION

"It is my understanding that the first period of suspension expires on July 15, and if the matter is not determined by that time, the commission may further suspend the matter until Oct. 15, 1942."

Several weeks ago Siggins and Commissioners Richard J. Beamish and B. Frank Morgal suggested that the company withdraw its rate petition during the war emergency.

The P. T. C. countered by withdrawing its petition for a temporary increase but declined to drop the case for a permanent rise. Instead, it offered voluntarily to suspend the proceedings until Oct. 15, or later at the discretion of the commission.

PROBE PENDING

This the commission refused to do, pointing out that legally it could only suspend the proposed new rates until Oct. 15.

An investigation by the Office of Price Administration of "possible collusion" between P. T. C. and the P. R. T.'s employees' union to boost fares, is still pending.

A representative of OPA is expected to visit the commission offices here tomorrow.

Commissioner Beamish hurled the "collusion" charges when Frederic L. Ballard, P. T. C. counsel, revealed at a hearing a fortnight ago that the employees had asked for a $4,500,000 annual raise May 18.

State Opens Bids On Road Projects

The State Hnghway Department at Harrisburg, yesterday opened bids on two of the projects in the State-city traffic bottleneck elimination program.

Louis Dolente and Sons, 5122 Master st., was low bidder for .91 of a mile of grading, 110 feet wide, on Essington ave., with a price of $142,-824.50.

Frank R. Curtis, State road and Unruh st., was low bidder for .40 of a mile of divided concrete highway, consisting of two 36-foot lanes on Island ave., between Tinicum and Eastwick aves., with a bid of $120,-291.70.

MOTHER SAVES LIFE OF DROWNING BABY

A young mother, who completed a wartime first-aid course a week ago, called upon her nerve and knowledge yesterday to save the life of her drowning child.

Eighteen-month-old Sara Rambo, 4521 Remington ave., Pennsauken, N. J., and Carl Paul, 2½, of 4518 Remington ave., were playing in the backyard at the home of a neighbor, Ernest O'Nesti, when they decided to go wading in a shallow fish pool. The decision almost cost them their lives.

BOY TRIES TO SAVE BABY

No one was at the O'Nesti house, but Mrs. Bertha Baumbach, 4503 Remington ave., glanced from her kitchen window and saw Carl standing in the water with only his head showing above the surface.

He was futilely attempting to rescue Sara, who was struggling at the bottom of the pool. Mrs. Baumbach shouted to the child's mother, Eleanor Rambo, who waded into the water and carried Sara to the lawn.

WORK OVER BABY

Mrs. Rambo administered artificial respiration—one of the things she learned in a Red Cross first-aid course she completed last week.

As other neighbors gathered, Mrs. Rambo worked over the unconscious child. She grew tired, but found hope in the fact that she was forcing some water from her baby's lungs.

Wallace Bush, 4515 Remington ave., saw that the woman was becoming weary. He offered to take over as Mrs. Rambo ran to call a doctor.

BABY BEGINS TO CRY

Under the fresh efforts of Bush, the breath of life returned to Sara. A few more minutes, and she began to cry—a welcome wail to Mrs. Rambo.

By the time the doctor arrived in an ambulance with an inhalator, Sara was whooping lustily. She was treated for shock and exposure, but required no other medical attention.

Hayden, Miss Carroll Wed 3 Months Ago

NASSAU, Bahamas, June 30 (U. P.).—Stirling Hayden, former Hollywood actor, told the United Press today that he and film star Madeleine Carroll, who arrived here to visit him, were married three months ago in an undisclosed New England town.

The couple will remain at the Hotel Rozelda here while Hayden's schooner is overhauled, a job that will require about two weeks.

Rumors that the pair had been secretly married have been in circulation for several months, but brought only non-commital answers from Hayden and Miss Carroll.

John Garfield Wins Plea to Change Name

LOS ANGELES, June 30 (A. P.).—John Garfield, actor, and Natalie Talmadge went to court today with name-changing petitions, both of which were approved.

Garfield wanted to keep that name. He was christened Jacob Garfinkel. Miss Talmadge, ex-wife of Buster Keaton, comedian, asked that her two sons, James, 20, and Robert, 18, be allowed to drop the name of Keaton and adopt Talmadge. She said neither son had used the name Keaton since 1936.

SLAIN MAN'S BODY FOUND IN DELAWARE

Police Report Bullet Wounds In Head and Chest

Special to The Inquirer

WILMINGTON, Del., June 30.—A semi-clad man, whose body was found yesterday in the woods near Guyencourt, is believed to have been murdered.

Bullet wounds were found in the head and chest, State police reported.

The man's jaw also was fractured. Dr. William N. Fenimore, coroner's physician, said the victim had been dead about two weeks.

Two weeks ago a suit of clothing was found a mile from where the body was discovered. Markings on the suit indicated it was made in Brooklyn, N. Y.

Clad only in underwear, socks and low shoes, the body was discovered by Charles Wolf, of Chadds Ford, and Lee Moore, as they were cutting across the wooded section toward a spring.

Investigators found no clues near the body. The man apparently had been dead for several weeks, and weeds had sprung up around the body to conceal any automobile tracks or markings on the ground.

Boy's Body Found Floating in River; 2d Feared Dead

The body of 10-year-old John Joseph Boyle, Jr., of 1724 N. 29th st., was found floating in the Schuylkill near the Columbia ave. bridge yesterday afternoon, and a second boy was feared to have been drowned there.

The child's father, John J. Boyle, Sr., identified the body at the city morgue last night.

Shortly before 4 P. M. Kenneth Harris, 15, of 1540 N. 26th st., who was sitting on the west bank, was told by two excited youngsters that they had seen a body floating in the river north of the bridge.

SWIMS TO BODY

Taking off his clothes, Harris swam out to the body, which was off Peters' Island, a favorite play spot for young canoeists and swimmers, and dragged it back to shore. Then he notified Park Guards.

After an investigation, clothes belonging to the boy were found. The search also revealed more clothes on the bank of the island, and the Guards were grappling for a second body last night

You will enjoy reading John M. Cummings' timely, intelligent comment on the news of the day.

TEST CASE PLANNED ON TRAILER MEASURE

Operator of Camp Fined $50 After Announcing Appeal

A test case will be made to determine whether the city ordinance requiring permits for trailer camps failed to make provisions for classifying sections where trailer parking lots can be located.

This was decided yesterday as eight operators of such lots appeared before Magistrate N. Edwin Lindell on charges of violation of the sanitation laws. After a conference, the case of William Benner, whose camp is at 6100 N. Broad st., was chosen. He was fined $25.

When Joseph Sharfsin, former city solicitor, representing Benner and two other operators, announced he would appeal, the fine was automatically raised to $50. The test case will clarify the law on Sharfsin's contention that the ordinance failed to make provisions for classification of sections.

Millionaires in Cafe Brawl; Decorum Is Sole Casualty

HOLLYWOOD, June 30 (A. P.).—A couple of millionaires engaged in one of those rousing nightclub engagements early today in which nothing was damaged, as usual, except the decorum of the place.

The scene was the expensive Mocambo, where movie stars usually occupy not only the ringside spotlight, but the "ring" itself.

In one corner, or rather at one table, sat young Alexis Thompson, of about-night clubs and also possessor Philadelphia and New York. Thompson owns the Philadelphia professional football club, a deskful of unpleasant reminders of the recent Bobby Riggs-Don Budge tennis tour and a few million dollars in cash.

His opponent was young Tommy Warner, Jr., Beverly Hills man of much money.

Reports were vague on actual developments, but all agreed no one was hurt and the matter should best be forgotten.

Charles Morrison, Mocambo owner, unwilling witness to several other unscheduled all-star contests, said:

"I'm sorry it happened. You know, I have a pair of boxing gloves in a box in the front entrance of the club. They are in mothballs. Over them I have a sign that reads:

"Out of action for the duration."

Mystic Shrine Order Elects Potentate

CHICAGO, June 30 (A. P.).—Albert H. Fiebach, Cleveland, O., attorney, was elected Imperial Potentate of the Ancient Arabic Order, Nobles of the Mystic Shrine, at the 68th annual session of the order's imperial council today.

Fiebach, a past potentate of the Al Koran Temple, Cleveland, will succeed Thomas H. Law, of Atlanta, Ga.

Picture Parade
SECTION OF
The Philadelphia Inquirer
IN TWO PARTS JULY 12, 1942

Emulating the Wrens, one of whose vital duties is to act as wireless operators, the Nells practice radio receiving under the guidance of Walter R. Faries. They are backed by the Navy League of the U. S.

Nells Operate Behind the Lines In Service for the U. S. Navy

ORGANIZED in Philadelphia last January as the first officially sanctioned women's auxiliary to the Navy, the Navy League Service is carrying on with a variety of activities of help to the Navy. Corresponding to the British Wrens (Women's Royal Naval Service) the Nells now have about 1900 members in Philadelphia and its suburban areas, maintain headquarters at 1429 Chestnut st. with a canteen, officers' clubrooms and lounge, and carry on classes for members in a wide diversity of subjects ranging from parachute packing to victory gardening. All are volunteers and receive no pay.

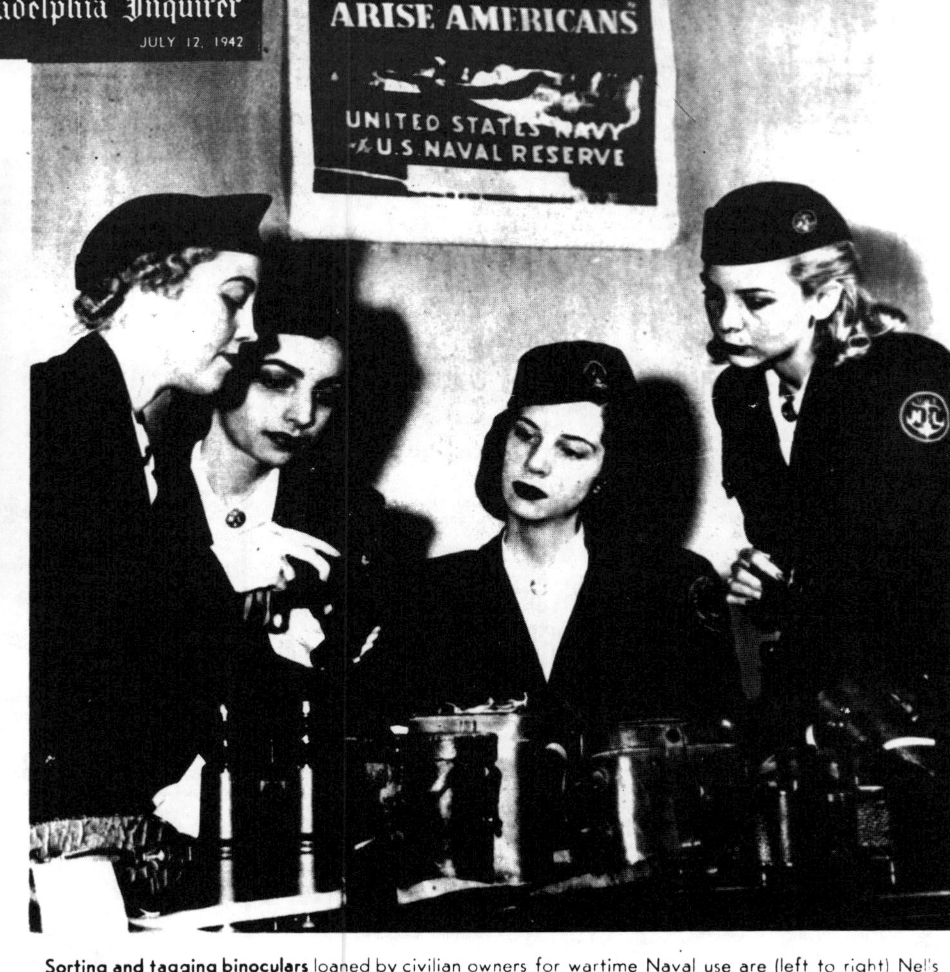

ARISE AMERICANS
UNITED STATES NAVY
U.S. NAVAL RESERVE

Sorting and tagging binoculars loaned by civilian owners for wartime Naval use are (left to right) Nells Ethel M. Turner, Jeanne Robinson, Mrs. Livingston Biddle, Jr. and Bonnie Murphy.

In suburban Philadelphia the Nells have organized a Bicycle Corps for messenger service during air raids or other emergencies. All are fast and expert riders. Here a group starts a practice run at Old Lancaster Rd. and Latches lane.

Naval officers receive instruction in Spanish at headquarters from Mrs. William R. Crawford. The sentence reads: "Oh, the poor Japanese: here come the Marines!"

The Nells Motor Corps is composed of women who furnish transportation to men in the service in their own cars. Among the more than 40 members is Mrs. George U. Pillmore of Paoli.

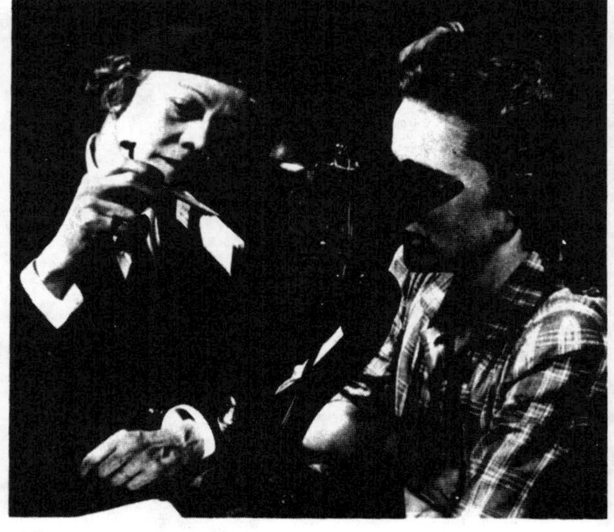
At the trainee acceptance centre on Moore st. Mrs. Raymond Clements Carrick of Ardmore gives an industrial visual safety test. This is one of the many functions which the Nells have taken over.

Inquirer Photos

As part of the Convalescent Service, Mrs. Kenneth S. Lueders (right) of Merion, entertains Private Jacob Pelavin and Seaman Hubert E. Rockey. With them is Mrs. Harold Ingraham.

The Philadelphia Inquirer

PUBLIC LEDGER

An Independent Newspaper for All the People

Telephone Your WANT ADS TO THE INQUIRER RITtenhouse 5000 Broad 5000

CIRCULATION: July Average: Daily 456,534, Sunday 1,238,423 a b c d e f g SUNDAY MORNING, AUGUST 9, 1942 Copyright, 1942, by The Philadelphia Inquirer Co. VOL. 227, No. 40 A Second Largest 3c Morning Circulation in America PRICE, TEN CENTS

6 Nazi Spies Electrocuted; 2 Jailed

U. S. Launches 2 Offensives in Pacific

Gandhi, Nehru Seized After Revolt Call

To All Saboteurs, Traitors, Spies: DEATH!

[EDITORIAL]

Death to saboteurs, spies and traitors!

For such deadly enemies, no lesser punishment can be justified.

They are like rattlesnakes coiled at our feet, ready to strike. We cannot temporize with that breed. We must step on them—or get hurt.

We are not going to win this war wearing kid gloves.

WE HAVE NO RIGHT TO BE SOFT. WE MUST BE TOUGH—OR LOSE ALL THAT WE HAVE.

That is why the execution of six of the eight captured German saboteurs means so much more than just the elimination of a half-dozen Nazis out of many millions.

That is why the death sentence imposed upon the Detroit traitor who connived in the attempted escape of a German aviator has such special significance, beyond the just punishment of one individual who betrayed his American citizenship.

These two cases of justice well served are among the most striking developments since the outbreak of the war. They serve notice that America is wide awake to the menace of organized underground warfare and is DETERMINED TO ANNIHILATE THE ENEMIES WITHIN AS WELL AS THOSE WITHOUT.

The execution of the saboteurs and the death sentence in Detroit are but the prelude, doubtless, to similar treatment of Axis agents and sympathizers found guilty of espionage, of sabotage, or treason.

These actions demonstrate that disloyal elements who work for Hitler in our midst, as well as saboteurs who may be smuggled into the country, face the firing squad or the electric chair.

The conviction and execution of the German agents bring to a fitting climax a spectacular case. It had its beginnings long before we were at war, when Germany was carefully preparing for the day when we would be actively in the war by organizing underground Nazi forces in this country.

The saboteurs were part of that organization. After their return to Germany for sabotage schooling they were brought back here by submarine and landed on remote beaches under the cover of darkness. They were equipped with tools of destruction and maps and orders to guide them on their mission of wreckage and ruin.

Had they escaped capture they might have crippled vital elements in our war program, MIGHT HAVE SENT TO THEIR DEATHS HUNDREDS OF OUR MEN, WOMEN AND CHILDREN.

But they did not succeed in carrying out their orders. They were seized and sent to trial before a military commission, a trial which was interrupted, in a dramatic demonstration of justice under democracy, to permit the prisoners to appeal to the Supreme Court.

Fortunately, these enemies, as well as the traitor in Detroit, WERE UNABLE TO FIND, IN THE CIVIL RIGHTS OF A NATION THEY WOULD DESTROY, AN AVENUE OF ESCAPE. THEY HAVE BEEN GIVEN JUSTICE.

We may be sure that in both the highest of Axis headquarters and the lowest and darkest hole in which Axis agents hide out for ambush attacks upon us here at home the cases of the saboteurs and the traitor have been closely watched.

Had the trials gone the other way, had the invading saboteurs been able to gain lenity for themselves instead of execution, had the pro-Nazi Detroiter been sentenced to a prison cell instead of the gallows, tremendous encouragement would have been given subversive and disloyal organizations working in the interests of the Axis in this country.

The just severity of the treatment accorded the men will act as both a deterrent and a warning. It shows Hitler that if and when he decides the time has come for all-out war on American production, whether by smuggled-in saboteurs or by Nazi "plants," WE WILL BE WAITING FOR HIS AGENTS WITH FIRING SQUADS.

Spies, saboteurs, traitors—the whole ratlike gang is out to destroy us.

We have given them our reply in Washington and Detroit:

FOR EACH ONE OF THEM—DEATH!

The Finger Is On Them

GANDHI, ALL AIDES ARRESTED IN SWIFT ROUNDUP BY BRITISH

BOMBAY, Aug. 9 (Sunday) (U. P.).—Mohandas K. Gandhi, leader of the All-India Congress Party; his lieutenant, Pandit Jawaharlal Nehru, and all members of the party's working committee were arrested today.

Maulana Abdul Azad, president of the vast political group demanding India's independence from Great Britain, was among the Congress leaders arrested.

NATION-WIDE ROUNDUP

A roundup of provincial leaders of the All-India Congress was in progress throughout the country. The president and secretary of the Bombay Provincial Congress were taken into custody.

There were no official details concerning the roundup.

(Among those taken into custody were Gandhi's secretary, Miss Madeline Slade, the Associated Press reported.)

(No warrant was issued for Gandhi's wife, who was told by police that she could accompany her husband. She elected to remain behind.

(Reuters, British news agency,

Continued on Page 5, Column 1

Waldo Frank Leaves Hospital in Argentina

BUENOS AIRES, Argentina, Aug. 8 (A. P.).—Waldo Frank, American author who was beaten by six unidentified men last Sunday, was able to leave the hospital and take a walk today.

He made reservations to fly to Chile next Monday.

Naval Forces Attack Solomons and Kiska; Great Battles Raging

By WALTER B. CLAUSEN

PEARL HARBOR, Hawaii, Aug. 8 (A. P.).—The first American offensive in the Pacific, aimed at rolling back the Japanese invaders and recapturing the bases they seized, is under way.

This was disclosed tonight in a communique issued by Admiral Chester W. Nimitz, Commander-in-Chief of the United States Pacific Fleet and Pacific Ocean Areas.

He said forces of the United States Pacific Fleet, assisted by units of the Southwest Pacific Area, had launched offensive operations yesterday in the Solomon Islands simultaneously with an attack on Japanese-held Kiska in the Aluetians.

Great battles are raging.

'PROGRESSING FAVORABLY'

The Admiral significantly said operations were progressing favorably "in spite of opposition by enemy land-based aircraft and garrisons."

His reference to garrisons and his disclosure of the combined nature of the American forces indicate landing operations and the recapture of enemy-held positions are involved.

Admiral Nimitz's communique said:

"Forces of the United States Pacific Fleet and Pacific Ocean Areas, assisted by units of the Southwest Pacific Area, launched offensive operations in the Tulagi area of the Solomon Islands on Aug. 7, East Longitude Time.

"These operations are progressing favorably in spite of opposition by enemy land-based aircraft and garrisons.

"On Aug. 8, East Longitude Time, a task force of the

Continued on Page 3, Column 2

SOVIET LINES CRACK, TWO NAZI COLUMNS RACE TO MAIKOP OIL

Map on Page 2

By HENRY C. CASSIDY

MOSCOW, Aug. 9 (Sunday) (A.P.).—Two German columns were reported converging on the Maikop oil fields today after cracking Russian defenses in the Krasnodar-Armavir area 60 miles above that prize at the foot of the Caucasian mountains.

The Army organ Red Star announced the German break-through toward Maikop, whose wells supply seven percent of Russia's oil, and the midnight communique gave this version of the reverse at Armavir:

"In one sector after bloody fighting during which 14 enemy tanks were destroyed and 500 Germans killed, our troops withdrew to new positions."

The Red Army defending the

Continued on Page 2, Column 4

Burger Gets Life, Dasch 30 Years; Aid to U. S. Cited

Full page picture story of the spy case on Page 8.

By WILLIAM C. MURPHY, JR.

Inquirer Washington Bureau

WASHINGTON, Aug. 8.—Swift American military justice today snuffed out the lives of six of the eight Nazi saboteurs who landed on the Atlantic Coast late in June to attempt to impede the Nation's war effort.

They were electrocuted in the grim District of Columbia Jail shortly after noon today, following Presidential approval of sentences imposed by a special military commission. The President also had fixed the time and place for the executions.

A seventh member of the Nazi gang—Ernest P. Burger—was given life imprisonment at hard labor and the eighth—George John Dasch, reputed to have "squealed" on his colleagues—drew 30 years, also at hard labor.

NO WORD UNTIL AFTER EXECUTIONS

The men who forfeited their lives today for attempting to serve Hitler in the United States were: Herbert Hans Haupt, Henry Harm Heinck, Edward John Kerling, Herman Otto Neubauer, Richard Quirin and Werner Thiel.

There was no official announcement of the convictions or the sentences imposed until after the executions had been carried out. However, from early morning on, nearly every inhabitant of Washington was aware that the doom of the saboteurs was imminent.

Despite inclement weather crowds attempted to mass around the ancient stone jail—although an overwhelming guard of soldiers with fixed bayonets made it impossible for anyone to draw near.

SECRECY SHROUDS THEIR LAST MOMENTS

Military secrecy shrouded the last moments of the condemned Nazis—how they took the death they had come to deal out to Americans, which of them went first, how long it took each to die, and all the other grim details.

But those near the jail seemed to sense by some mysterious medium that behind its gray walls souls were being torn from bodies and sent to another judgment beyond the grave.

The official story of what happened today was embodied in a brief White House announcement, issued shortly after 1 o'clock.

PRESIDENT COMMUTES SENTENCES OF TWO

It stated:

"The President completed his review of the findings and sentences of the military commission appointed by him on July 2, 1942 which tried the eight Nazi saboteurs.

"The President approved the judgment of the military commission that all of the prisoners were guilty and that they be given the death sentence by electrocution.

"However, there was a unanimous recommendation by the commission, concurred in by the Attorney General and the Judge Advocate General of the Army, that the sentence of two of the prisoners be commuted to life imprisonment because of their assistance to the Government of the United States in the apprehension and conviction of the others.

EXECUTIONS BEGIN AT NOON

"The commutation directed by the President in the case of Burger was to confinement at hard labor for life. In the case of Dasch, the sentence was commuted by the President to confinement at hard labor for 30 years.

"The electrocutions began at noon today. Six of the prisoners were electrocuted. The other two were confined to prison.

"The records in all eight cases will be sealed until the end of the war."

Such was the official record—so barren of details that it did not even specify the charge or charges on which the Nazis

Continued on Page 9, Column 1

75,000 See Eagles Beat All-Stars, 16 to 8

BOB MOSER (98), ALL-STARS BACK, PICKS UP FOUR YARDS OFF TACKLE IN FOURTH PERIOD AS ANDY TOMASIC (17) RUNS INTERFERENCE. NO. 52 IS EAGLES' RAY GRAVES

The Philadelphia Inquirer

PHILADELPHIA. TUESDAY MORNING. SEPTEMBER 1. 1942 adefgh27

Camden Double Pays $2445.60; Favorite Trap, Leo's Brandy Win

Race Chart on Page 26

A former Texas farmhand and a two-year-old thoroughbred that had been sold down the river a few weeks ago, combined to steal the spotlight at Garden State Park yesterday afternoon and bring about a daily double payoff of $2,445.60, the largest of the current meeting.

It was Hubert Trent, 29-year-old apprentice reinsman from the Lone Star State and a former farmhand, astride a maiden juvenile named Favorite Trap, that started the long shot players howling with glee at the South Jersey course.

$166.70 FOR $2

Favorite Trap with Trent in the irons, won the first race, a six-furlong dash for maiden juveniles and returned the handsome payoff of $166.70, $73.45 and $25.80 for the usual $2 investment across the board.

And not to be outdone by the twosome, Leo's Brandy, a two-year-old racing in the silks of Mrs. E. Haughton, which had been sold to her a few weeks ago at Saratoga by a major Eastern stable that had given up on the youngster, streaked around the track in the second stanza to pay off in double figures.

ALATOMO SECOND

Leo's Brandy, outsider in the wagering, covered the six furlongs of the second dash, patterned for two-year-olds, in the smashing time of 1.12 1-5 to defeat a field of seven other runners. Two lengths back of the winner was Alatomo, while able to save third was the 5 to 2 choice, Rocky Craig. Leo's Brandy returned $35.60 to win.

Ten daily double tickets on the

Continued on Page 29, Column 1

Dodgers Defeat Bucs in 11th, 5-4

By HANK SIMMONS

Clark Griffith, the old fox of baseball and owner of the Washington Senators, tossed out the life-line to the faltering Dodgers yesterday by getting Bobo Newsom waived out of the American League and selling him to them for something more than the $7500 waiver price.

The Brooks staggered to an 11-inning, 5-4 victory over Pittsburgh, gaining a half game on the St. Louis Cardinals to lead the league by 3½ games. A wild throw by Elbie Fletcher to Pitcher Hank Gorniski, covering first base let Augie Galan score the winning run from third.

HELPS YANKS, TOO

It was Griffith who, a few years ago, moaned long and loud over the purchase of star players by the Yankees to get them over humps in pennant fights. Griffith worked overtime and had the American League pass a rule forbidding a pennant winner to make trades in the loop the year after winning the flag. Sales were also forbidden near the end of the season. It happened the Yankees lost the pennant the year the rule went into effect.

The measure, unpopular with the other Junior loop club owners, was thrown out after being in force a year and the Yankees came back to win again. Incidentally, C[illegible]f helped the Yanks along by [illegible]ing Roy Cullenbine to them f[illegible]xtra out-

Continued on Pag[illegible]olumn 2

Goldberg Signed By Grid Cardinals

CHICAGO, Aug. 31 (A. P.).—Marshall Goldberg, former University of Pittsburgh star, signed a contract today with the Chicago Cardinals, with whom he played the past three seasons. Goldberg, a left halfback, will continue as an executive of a Chicago machinery company and stipulated in his contract that he would retire from football if the press of business became too great.

Phils Lose 7th In Row by 8 to 1

CINCINNATI, O., Aug. 31.—The Phils absorbed their seventh straight defeat to give them a record of four won and 20 lost for the August dog days when beaten by the Reds here tonight, 8 to 1.

Their downfall was witnessed by a ladies' night crowd of 8228 which was almost equally divided between paying males and guests of the gentler sex. The paid admissions numbered 4108 while there were 4120 ladies in the house.

The Phils stranded 11 more runners on the bases tonight. Elmer Riddle walked eight of them, but allowed only five hits. Two double plays bailed him out of a couple of dangerous spots, if the Phils can be called dangerous.

TIPTON HITS HOMER

Frank McCormick and Eric Tipton settled the issue in the second when McCormick tapped Rube Melton for

Continued on Page 29, Column 1

Baseball Facts

NATIONAL LEAGUE
YESTERDAY'S SCORES

Brooklyn, 5; Pittsburgh, 4 (11 innings.)

New York, 7; Chicago, 6.

Cincinnati, 8; Phils, 1.

HOW THEY STAND

	W.	L.	Pct.	G.B.
Brooklyn	88	40	.688	—
St. Louis	85	44	.659	3½
New York	71	58	.550	17½
Cincinnati	64	64	.500	24
Pittsburgh	58	67	.464	28½
Chicago	60	73	.451	30½
Boston	51	79	.392	37½
PHILS	36	88	.290	50

G.B.—Games behind leader.

Today's Schedule, Probable Pitchers and Their Records

PHILS at Cincinnati—Beck (0-1) vs. Derringer (7-10).

Brooklyn at Pittsburgh—Higbe (13-9) vs. Klinger (8-10).

New York at Chicago—McGee (5-3) vs. Passeau (17-10).

Boston at St. Louis (night)—Javery (12-13) vs. Dickson (5-2) or Gumbert (8-5).

AMERICAN LEAGUE
YESTERDAY'S RESULTS

Chicago, 3; ATHLETICS, 1 (first game).

Chicago, 5; ATHLETICS, 0 (second game).

New York, 8; Detroit, 3.
Boston, 8; St. Louis, 6.

HOW THEY STAND

	W.	L.	Pct.	G.B.
New York	86	44	.662	..
Boston	79	53	.598	8
St. Louis	68	61	.527	17½
Cleveland	67	63	.515	18½
Detroit	64	68	.485	23
Chicago	57	68	.456	26½
Washington	50	75	.400	33
ATHLETICS	49	88	.358	40½

G.B.—Games behind leader.

Today's Schedule, Probable Pitchers and Their Records

Cleveland at Washington—Dean (8-8) and Carrasquel (6-5), (only game scheduled).

Continued on Page 29, Column 7

White Sox Jolt A's, 3-1, 5-0

By STAN BAUMGARTNER

Young Bob Savage—not yet old enough to sit in a barber's chair without blushing—continues to be the Philadelphia Story, from a baseball point of view.

The former Staunton Military Academy pitching ace was the only refreshing moment in a long, dismal afternoon at Shibe Park yesterday, as the A's dropped both ends of a double-header to the White Sox, 3-1 and 5-0.

Savage entered the picture after the Sox had piled up a 4-0 lead off Luman Harris in the first three innings of the second game.

SAVAGE IN FORM

For the next six innings young Bob permitted only one hit and one run. He walked three but had plenty on the ball. The White Sox were trying to make hits, don't make any mistake about that, but they couldn't. He has a fast ball that takes off and he is not afraid to pour it down the middle.

It was Savage's third appearance on the mound and his record is one that any big leaguer would be proud to own. He twirled four innings against the Yanks and didn't allow a hit, although the New Yorkers scored one unearned run. He then pitched two frames against the Red Sox and did not permit a run. He allowed one hit.

Counting yesterday, he has worked 12 innings, given up two hits and had two runs scored against him. One was unearned, the other was the result of a double steal.

A'S BATS FEEBLE

The second game was lost before Savage came to the box. By this time the Sox had spanked Luman

Continued on Page 29, Column 4

Quiniela Returns $4334 to Turf Fan

WACO, Tex., Aug. 31 (A. P.).—Jerome K. Miller of Los Angeles, the only one of 4000 racing fans to pair up Alaskan and Come to Taw in the quiniela betting Sunday, realized $4334.40 on a two dollar ticket, a track record.

Alaskan, a 50 to 1 shot, came up fast on the outside to win by a length and a half and Come to Taw, his other choice was second.

The quiniela betting, which winds up each Sunday program at Caliente, is separate from the regular pari-mutuel betting.

Bob Priestley Catches Two Passes To Lead Pro Team to Triumph

By CY PETERMAN

Air power, that dominant force for victory today, soared to dazzling heights last night in Municipal Stadium as the high-flying Philadelphia Eagles, stopped cold by the College All-Stars fine line, passed twice to touchdowns and triumph in the greatest curtain-raiser local football has yet produced.

By a score of 16 to 8, and thrill-packed to the last desperate sortie, the powerful collegians bowed before 75,000 shouting fans when their own ace in the hole, Bob Moser, of Texas A. and M., was matched by an equally surprise package from Brown.

Young Robert Priestley, so new to the Eagles' roster that his case history is still missing from the dossier, made two running catches in the All-Stars' end zone — pass receptions of the sort even the best professionals would have to ponder—and these, along with a field goal by the veteran Leonard Barnum, were the ball game.

THOMPSON SCORES BULLS-EYES

Two aerials—both thrown by that veteran master of the passing art, Tommy Thompson, the first for 30 yards with Temple's Andy Tomasic vainly trying to claw it down, the second in the final period when the score was still 9-8, this time from the 18-yard line after a drive of 70 yards in nine plays — these, with a 31-yard goal from placement by Quarterback Barnum and his final extra-pointer from touchdown, accounted for the Eagles' total.

But the Stars were not dimmed in this second game in four days.

Displaying even greater prowess in the air than they had at Chicago against the Bears, they made this annual renewal of the Inquirer A. A.'s charity game one to be remembered.

COLLEGIANS SHOW METTLE

While the fans, moving in a steady tide down every street, filling the huge horseshoe to near capacity as they set a new

Continued on Page 28, Column 7

The Lineup

ALL-STARS	POSITIONS	EAGLES
Stanton	Left end	Supulski
Bauman	Left tackle	Sears
Jeffries	Left guard	Gerber
Lindskog	Centre	Graves
Crimmins	Right guard	Conti
Blozis	Right tackle	Eibner
Meyer	Right end	Combs
Hargrave	Quarterback	Thompson
Dudley	Left halfback	Davis
Tomasic	Right halfback	Johnson
Westfall	Fullback	Williams

All Stars	0	6	2	0—8
Eagles	0	6	3	7—16

Eagles scoring: Touchdowns—Priestley (2); Field goal—Barnum; Point after touchdown—Barnum. All Stars—Touchdown—Meyer. Safety—Automatic after blocking of Eagles kick by Bauman (Stars).

Substitutions: Eagles—Leonard, Kaplan, Pate, Brennan, Carter, Sears, Hall, Stackpool, Hrabetin, Priestley, Barnum, Godfrey, Carter, Olsen, Cabrelli. ALL-STARS—Dudley, Ingalls, Graf, Abel, Lillis, Banonis, Hunt, Ebli, Pukema, Farris, Keating, Maddock, Walker.

OFFICIALS

Referee—Samuel Weiss. Umpire—Leo Novak. Field Judge—Eddie Miller. Head Linesman—Larry Conover.

Greasy Thanks Football Dodgers

By FRANK O'GARA

There was a telegram of thanks en route last night—an appreciation from the Eagles to the Brooklyn Dodgers for giving them their victory over the National College All-Stars.

The wire read:

"Bob Priestley, that broken-down end you didn't want in a trade a few weeks ago, caught two long touchdown passes to beat the All-Stars tonight.

"Appreciatively Yours,
"Earle (Greasy) Neale."

Neale couldn't resist laughing every time he thought of the incident in the dressing room after the game—and the mentor was chuckling every other minute.

OH, DEM DOPEY DODGERS

"We needed more backs desperately a few weeks ago before some of our ball-carriers reported," he said, "and we tried to arrange a few trades. A few other clubs turned down Priestley, one of the good men we offered, but they had various reasons for not wanting a trade. The Dodgers, however, were more direct. 'Give a good back for some

Continued on Page 28, Column 1

Stars' Touchdown Biggest Thrill

By LEO RIORDAN

YOU COULD get plenty of votes for plenty of thrills from the 75,000 fans who gave the return of football a roaring welcome as the Eagles defeated the College All-Stars in the charity classic at Municipal Stadium last night, but the press box poll leaned heavily to the Hollywood scenario touchdown in the last three seconds of the first half.

• • •

That play proved the wisdom of the sponsoring Inquirer A. A. authorities' selection of Bob Moser, yippee halfback from Texas A.&M.

• • •

There probably weren't a dozen fans among the 75,000 who thought the play would be anything more than a wistful effort. Even Aunt Minnie must have known that it had to be a forward pass. The Stars were 35 yards from the Eagles' goal line—with three seconds to make it.

• • •

Certainly the Eagles knew it would be a pass, and they swarmed in on Moser like dive bombers. But Bob city-slickered them. He started to run as though he thought he could foot it over. Eluding the first Eagles posse, he "read" his field at a glance, saw Fred Meyer lurking in the coffin-corner and let the ball go without slackening his breakneck stride.

• • •

Meyer, from Stanford's 1940 Rose Bowl-winning team, proved why he had been brought across the Continent by making a crazy catch on the 3-yard line and staggering over the goal line.

• • •

The old movie, "One Minute to Go," featuring Red Grance, the Illinois immortal, was dull stuff alongside this real life thriller-diller.

• • •

Thus The Inquirer A. A. gave the fans a chance to see the storied Southwest passing sensation they had been reading about for three years. But for this game, they would never have seen Moser—and missing Moser was missing the thrill of a football season.

• • •

The old college spirit bubbled when the game ended—after the Eagles had made a grim stand on their six-yard line—the rah-rah boys charged out and splintered the goal posts.

• • •

There was a real Army-Navy game carnival spirit in the stands long before the kickoff. In fact, the crowd had a rigorous throat work-

Continued on Page 26, Column 5

Wisconsin 17	Harvard 19	N. Dame 9	Minnesota 19	Temple 7	W. Virginia 24	Georgia 21	U.C.L.A. 20	Bucknell 13
Ohio State 7	Princeton 14	Navy 0	N'western 7	Mich. St. 7	Penn State 0	Alabama 10	Stanford 7	Lafayette 7

The Philadelphia Inquirer

PUBLIC LEDGER

PHILADELPHIA, SUNDAY MORNING, NOVEMBER 1, 1942 abcdef g S

68,000 See Penn Defeat Army, 19 to 0

POP GOES THE FUMBLE! CAMERA CATCHES ARMY'S DRAMATIC RECOVERY THAT COST PENN A FIRST DOWN IN SECOND PERIOD AT FRANKLIN FIELD

Halfback Bob Odell, at bottom of the pile, had made a 17-yard gain on this play before he was hit by Army's tacklers and sent down so hard that the ball shot straight up into the air. Bob Woods, West Point back, at right in the picture, recovered the ball. A crowd of 68,000 saw Penn win 19-0. It was Army's first defeat of the season and boosted Penn's eastern title hopes.

Football

Georgia Moves Up

Sinkwich's Passes

Wisconsin Prevails

Army Boomerangs

Boston College No. 1

By Herbert W. Barker

Associated Press Sports Editor

THE Bulldogs of Georgia and the Badgers of Wisconsin moved closer to the top of the national football ranking list today as six more major teams fell off the undefeated list in another day of startling surprises.

Georgia, banking on the passing arm of All-America Frankie Sinkwich, rallied for three touchdowns in the fourth quarter to topple Alabama's previously unbeaten Crimson Tide, 21-10, before a crowd of 33,000 at Atlanta.

Wisconsin, undefeated but tied in the early fall by Notre Dame, ruined Ohio State's hitherto perfect record, 17-7, as a crowd of 45,000 looked on at Madison, Wis.

• • •

These two major duels—involving sectional as well as national honors—topped a program marked otherwise by the initial defeats of Army, Syracuse and Penn State in the East, and of Texas Christian in the Southwest.

• • •

Georgia was trailing Alabama, 10-0, as the fourth quarter of their game began, but Sinkwich's rifle passes saved the day for the Bulldogs who now are solidly entrenched as the standout favorite for the Southeastern Conference title with Georgia Tech as the main obstacle still in the way.

Twice Sinkwich's passes went to End George Poschner for touchdowns, while Georgia's remaining fourth-period score was accounted for by Andy Dudish, who picked off a mid-air fumble and ran for a touchdown.

Wisconsin's defeat of Ohio State was in the nature of a real surprise since the Buckeyes have been the No. 1 team in the Associated Press poll for three weeks, and were the betting favorites in this particular test. But the Badgers kept things pretty well under control as Pat Harder scored one touchdown and kicked a field goal, and Dave Schreiner, All-America end, tallied the clinching touchdown on a pass from Elroy Hirsch.

• • •

Army's powerful running game went precisely nowhere against Penn's staunch defense, and the Cadets' passing attempts were boomerangs principally as Penn rolled up a 19-0 count before a crowd of 68,000 on Franklin Field.

In other Philadelphia District football games Michigan State rallied to tie Temple, 7-7; Delaware's uprising defeated P.M.C., 19-14; West Chester Teachers jolted Albright, 6-0; Gettysburg romped over Drexel Tech, 18-0; Haverford triumphed over Wesleyan, 33-21, and Swarthmore surprised Hamilton, 8-0.

Syracuse fell before North Carolina Naval, 9-0, while Penn State was well whipped by West Virginia, 24-0.

Texas Christian, meanwhile, bowed before Baylor, 10-7, as Baylor's Bert Edminson booted a field goal from the 17-yard line. This left Baylor tied with Texas for the Southwest Conference lead as Texas subdued Southern Methodist, 21-7. Texas Aggies ran up a 41-0 count on Arkansas.

The defeat of Illinois by Michigan's Wolverines, 28-14, left Wisconsin unchallenged in first place in the Western Conference race, sole unbeaten team in the group. Herman Frickey, subbing for the injured Bill Daley, scored twice as Minnesota rolled over Northwestern, 19-7. Tommy Farmer's passes gave Iowa a 13-7 verdict over Purdue. Indiana collapsed in the late stages and was soundly whipped by Iowa Pre-Flight, 26-6. A crowd of 65,000 sat in at Cleveland as Notre Dame overcame a stubborn Navy outfit, 9-0, on a touchdown by Angelo Bertelli and a field goal by Tom Creevey.

• • •

Boston College assumed the No. 1 role in the East in a crushing 47-0 defeat of Georgetown. The Eagles, scoring almost at will, are the lone major Eastern team still unbeaten. Yale, showing further signs of improvement, trounced Brown, 27-0, chiefly on passes, while Harvard overcame a two-touchdown deficit and whipped Princeton, 19-14, on a last-minute pass. Columbia nipped Cornell, 14-13, on a late touchdown pass by Paul Governali, and Colgate and Holy Cross played a 6-6 draw. Pitt rolled over Carnegie, 19-6.

Undefeated William and Mary romped at Dartmouth's expense, 35-14, as Bob Longacre scored three touchdowns. Steve Filipowicz scored the only touchdown of the game as Fordham beat St. Mary's of California, 7-0.

Louisiana State's sensational Tigers came a cropper at Knoxville, as Tennessee chalked up a 26-0 victory. Tulane came from behind to nip Vanderbilt, 28-21, in an exciting test. Mississippi State beat Auburn, 6-0, in the remaining Southeastern Conference clash of the day.

Meanwhile, Georgia Tech's Engineers spotted Duke a touchdown and then poured on the power and deception to win, 26-7, first time Tech ever has beaten Duke at Durham. This left Tech, early season victor over

Continued on Page 2, Column 6

Michigan State's Late Score Ties Temple as 10,000 Watch

By STAN BAUMGARTNER

Coach Charley Bachman, who walked across the Red River in East Lansing by way of celebrating his Michigan State team's football victory last Saturday over the Great Lakes Naval Training Station, will wade no rivers tonight.

The Owls held Bachman's highly favored Spartans to a 7-7 tie before 10,000 yesterday at Temple Stadium.

Michigan State was lucky to fare as well as it did. The visitors were trailing, 7-0, as late as the fifth minute of the fourth period. Then the Owls had a momentary lapse, and the Michiganders pushed over a touchdown, scored the extra point and gained a tie. Otherwise, all the honors belonged to Temple.

Presenting a barbed wire defense against one of the outstanding running attacks in the West and spiking the guns of Dick Kieppe, a snake-hipped halfback, for three quarters, the Owls not only held the Spartans scoreless in those first exciting 50 minutes, but took a 7-0 lead three minutes and 45 seconds before the end of the third period.

PAPIANO GOES OVER

Joe Papiano, 193-pound junior from Newfield, N. J., scored the touchdown on a three-yard smash over right tackle after Frank Varga had set the stage for the score by intercepting one of Dick Kieppe's passes on the Michigan State 17.

Papiano then took command and in four tries carried the pigskin into pay dirt and six points for Temple. Sid Beshunsky then entered the game and kicked the extra point to make it 7-0.

As the minutes clicked by and the inspired Owls held their ground, it began to look as if Ray Morrison would have revenge for the 46-0 lacing the Owls received a year ago.

Then the lightning struck—Kieppe began to click. Balked time after time when he attempted to run and often forced to give up six and eight

Continued on Page 3, Column 1

Georgia Rallies To Trip Alabama

By GRANTLAND RICE

Special to The Inquirer

ATLANTA, Ga., Oct. 31.—A desperate Georgia team, facing almost certain defeat, won one of the greatest football battles in Southern history at Grant Field today by beating Alabama, 21 to 10.

At the start of the final period Alabama's famous Crimson Tide, packed with power, was leading Georgia, 10 to 0. Russ Craft had run 47 yards for an Alabama touchdown in the first period and George Hecht had added three more points with a 20-yard field goal.

Meanwhile, Alabama's mighty, fast-charging line had smothered Frank Sinkwich completely and had rolled Georgia's attack into the dust. The 33,000 spectators, wrapped in

Continued on Page 6, Column 6

Football Scores

LOCAL

West Chester, 6; Albright, 0.
Gettysburg, 18; Drexel, 0.
Haverford, 33; Wesleyan, 21.
Penna., 19; Army, 0.
Swarthmore, 8; Hamilton, 0.
Delaware, 19; P. M. C., 14.
Temple, 7; Michigan State, 7.

STATE

Bucknell, 13; Lafayette, 7.
Pitt, 19; Carnegie Tech, 6.
Muhlenburg, 20; Dickinson, 0.
F & M., 14; Western Md., 14.
Juniata, 28; Westminster, 0.
Lehigh, 51; Hampden-Sydney, 6.
Slippery Rock, 12; Grove City, 0.
East Stroudsburg, 12; Mansfield, 6.
Rochester, 41; Allegheny, 0.
Geneva, 6; W. & J., 0.
West Va., 24; Penn State, 0.
Lincoln, 13; Hampton, 13.

EAST

J. C. Smith, 6; Morgan, 0.
Panzer, 47; N. Y. Aggies, 0.
Amherst, 43; Mass. State, 0.
Bowdoin, 13; Bates, 12.
Boston College, 47; Georgetown, 0.
Columbia, 14; Cornell, 13.
W. & M., 35; Dartmouth, 14.
Fordham, 7; St. Mary's, 0.
Harvard, 19; Princeton, 14.
C. C. N. Y., 20; Hobart, 6.
Holy Cross, 6; Colgate, 6.

Continued on Page 7, Column 2

State Crushed By W. Virginia

Special to The Inquirer

MORGANTOWN, W. Va., Oct. 31.—West Virginia University's Mountaineers gave a crowd of 12,016, which included many homecoming visitors, a big treat this afternoon as they toppled the Penn State Nittany Lions from the undefeated ranks and marked up a smashing 24-0 victory by scoring in every period.

It was the Mountaineers' first victory over the boys from State College since 1931, when the Mountain men hung up a 19 to 0 decision—that one also being here at Mountaineer Field. Last year the Lions eked out a close 17-14 victory in a game that was a thriller all the way.

IN COMMAND THROUGHOUT

In handing Coach Bob Higgins' fighting squad its first defeat of the year, the Blue and Gold squad marched to its first touchdown just six minutes after the opening kickoff. Fullback Charlie Schrader started things popping for the home club when he got off a beautiful 65-yard boot which rolled dead on the Penn

Continued on Page 3, Column 7

Badgers Beat Ohio State

By WILLIAM WEEKES

MADISON, Wis., Oct. 31 (A. P.).—Underdog Wisconsin, rising to gridiron heights, blasted Ohio State's Buckeyes from football's number one ranking today.

After 60 minutes of hair-raising football, the Badgers trotted off Camp Randall field to the cheers of most of the 45,000 bulging-eyed spectators with a 17 to 7 triumph. And the score just about tells the story. Wisconsin threatened three times and scored three times. The Buckeyes had one good scoring chance, and cashed it in.

HARDER IS STAR

The headline makers were big Marlin (Pat) Harder, fleet Elroy Hirsch and All-American End Dave Schreiner, but it was a brilliant team victory for Wisconsin. Ohio State's vaunted running attack, which had mauled out triumphs over Fort Knox, Southern California, Indiana, Purdue and Northwestern, piled up a lot of yardage, but when danger threatened, Badger linemen and secondary defenders combined to take charge.

When the Badgers had the ball, fierce charging by the forwards and solid blocking down field gave the backs all the help they needed.

BADGERS UNBEATEN

The triumph, which sent the Badgers to the heights, was Wisconsin's sixth in seven games. After whipping Camp Grant, Wisconsin fought a 7 to 7 tie with Notre Dame, then conquered Marquette, Missouri, Great Lakes and Purdue, to come up to today's all important test undefeated.

The biggest crowd in Camp Ran-

Continued on Page 5, Column 2

Two Pass Interceptions Help Quakers Overpower Cadets

By LEO RIORDAN

Anti-aircraft and interceptor units decided the major battle of Eastern college football yesterday when the University of Pennsylvania knocked vaunted West Point out of the undefeated ranks. Two swift, sure strokes turned a titanic line struggle into a one-sided game and 68,000 Franklin Field spectators looked on unbelievingly as the Quakers glided to a 19-0 triumph that gave no hint of the actual balance of power.

The stubborn, scoreless game was in the fourth minute of the last half when Army, erring on the side of superb daring, set up the springboard of Pennsylvania's incredibly easy victory.

Army was on its own 30-yard line and Quarterback Red Jarrell called upon Hank Mazur, the Cadets' All-America backfield nominee, to flip a short pass across the line of scrimmage to Jim Kelleher, veteran end. Successful, such a play might have disorganized the winner's defense. Failing—well, here in brief is how West Point's bid for an undefeated season turned sour on the pivot of a single play.

PLAY FOREDOOMED BY WELSH

As usual, Mazur passed perfectly. But the play was foredoomed, for the ball was tossed into Jackie Welsh's territory—and this Quaker halfback who led the Nation in interceptions in 1940 happens to be perhaps the most dangerous pass-stealer in the game today. Mazur apparently realized that threat, for the ball was aimed just across the line of scrimmage—too far up for Welsh to cover it normally.

However, Jackie must have sensed the strategy. He deliberately edged up on the play, speared the ball on the Army's 32- yard line and set off at full speed toward the south sideline. Past the 25, the 20 and the 15 sped Welsh, with the Pennsylvania student body roaring ecstatically. Jackie was trying to outrun Jarrell, who covered the play superbly. But the Cadet had Welsh trapped on the sideline at the 12. U-turning suddenly, Welsh cut back toward the middle of the field and raced to the 5, where Jarrell hit him with a jarring tackle. Welsh's impetus carried him to the 4.

Most of the 68,000 spectators—the Ivy's League's largest crowd this war year—must have been on their feet by this time. But there was a sober silence as Army lined up grimly to protect its goal line. Pennsylvania's only first-half drive had been blunted by this trick, tank-trap line. Plainly the game hinged on what happened now.

STIFF SMASHES OVER

Pennsylvania Quarterback Dick Martin received a chorus of volunteer suggestions from the stands and they all ran to one phrase: "Give it to Stiff." Bert, the Quakers' All-America nominee, was definitely on the spot. He now had to rip an

Continued on Page 4, Column 2

Harvard Upsets Princeton, 19-14

By STEVE O'LEA[illegible]

CAMBRIDGE, Mass., Oct. 31 (A. P.).—Harvard's refusal to quit under a two-touchdown handicap was rewarded in the final minute of today's Big Three class with Princeton as Gordon Lyle snatched a touchdown pass from Jack Comeford to give the Crimson a cherished 19-14 triumph.

A throng of 20,000 saw the Crimson perpetrate one of the season's biggest upsets as the previously hapless Harvards finally gained their initial victory after losing four, and tying one of their five previous starts.

It didn't look like Harvard's day at all during the first half and the improved Princeton team seemed to be able to score at will any time the Tiger field general cared to open up his offensive.

Princeton's George Franke and Bill Gallagher accounted for two quick touchdowns early in the second period and the Tigers then settled down to play their cards close to the chest. Harvard's eleven, on the other hand, looked singularly inept and ready victims for further scoring.

But it was a different team in the second half. It was Princeton which cracked and the Tigers bore

Continued on Page 2, Column 2

Notre Dame Blanks Navy Eleven, 9 to 0, Before 65,000 Spectators at Cleveland

CLEVELAND, Oct. 31 (A. P.).—Notre Dame's Fighting Irish, beaten and tied in early-season contests, continued on the comeback trail to the football heights today by defeating a stubborn Navy eleven, 9 to 0, for their fourth straight conquest.

The Notre Dames struck for a touchdown in the first two minutes of the second period, sending their "pitching" quarterback, Angelo Bertelli, over from the one-yard line on a sneak play after a 50-yard march. They clinched it with a 17-yard field goal from placement in the fourth session by Quarterback Tom Creevey.

65,000 SEE CONTEST

Although a few more than 72,000 tickets had been sold for the classic, the actual crowd did not reach that figure. The best guess was that about 65,000 fans were in the huge lakefront stadium.

The Navy, showing surprising strength in the slippery going over a muddy and recently-sodded gridiron, had three good scoring chances in the first half, but failed to capitalize on any of them.

On Notre Dame's second play of the game, the centre's pass eluded the entire T-formation backfield, and Tackle Fred Schnurr of Navy recovered on the Irish 20. Bertelli halted the threat, however, by intercepting a pass in the end zone.

In the second period, after Notre Dame had gone out front, the Middies launched a 35-yard march which finally stalled on the Irish five, Notre Dame taking the ball.

Sub Halfback Harold Hamberg took Bertelli's return punt after the goal line stand and raced 32 yards to the Irish 24, whence he passed to Substitute End Roe Johnston on the goal line — but the wingman dropped the ball and Navy's last chance was gone.

Notre Dame piled up 10 first downs, eight by rushing, one ona pass and one on a penalty, to Navy's seven, five on the ground and two through the air. The Irish aerial first down was the payoff, however, it being a nine-yarder from Bertelli to End Bob Dove on the one-yard line, from which Bertelli sneaked for the game's lone touchdown.

The Notre Dame three-pointer climaxed a drive which started on the Middie 44. Fullback Corwin Clatt plunging six times to reach the 12. The Navy threw the Irish back to the 17. Creevy came in, and with Substitute Back Tom Miller holding the ball, booted the pigskin over for the clincher points.

OUTGAINED VIA AIR

The Irish, who have hit the airways for most of their yardage this year, were outgained via that medium, 23 yards to 16 by the Middies.

Continued on Page 3, Column 3

V. M. I. Misses Muha; Bows to Davidson, 24-6

LEXINGTON, Va., Oct. 31 (U. P.).—The power of the Mighty Muha was proven here today when Davidson's Wildcats took advantage of the McKees Rock, Pa., fullback's absence to knock V. M. I. from Southern Conference unbeaten ranks, 24-6, before a scant 2000 spectators.

V. M. I. opened the scoring during the first period and then had to take a back seat for the rest of the game as Davidson tallied on a fumbled punt, two passes and a field goal.

The V. M. I. cadets severely felt the loss of Joe Muha, all-around potential All-America backfield star. Muha was injured in an inner-squad scrimmage early in the week and was in the ball game for only a few minutes during the third and fourth quarters.

Alsab, Conceding Weight, Runs 3d, Riverland Wins

Illustrated on Page 5

NEW YORK, Oct. 31 (A. P.).—Burdened with 124 pounds and conceding chunks of weight to older stars, Mrs. Al Sabath's Alsab today finished third in the $25,000 added Westchester Handicap at Empire City and lost a chance to pass the retired Shut Out as the year's leading turf money winner.

Riverland, a four-year-old gelding picked up in Chicago by Harold A. Clark for $6000 before developing his current form, took the $19,850 first money, while A. J. Sackett's Tola Rose staved off a mighty but late rush by Alsab to place.

Alsab earned only $2500 for finishing third, making his 1942 total $227,715, or $11,257 short of Shut Out's seasonal mark. The $700 bargain colt now has an all-time total of $338,315.

A crowd of 27,169, which installed Alsab favorite at $1.15 to $1, saw the colt and his rider, Carroll Bierman, make up almost 20 lengths in the mile and three-sixteenths run, yet lose a heart-breaker. He finished a head behind Tola Rose, which was half a length behind Riverland.

Riverland, which finished first eight straight times before winding up third behind Whirlaway and Thumbs Up in the recent Washington Handicap, today returned $10.30 for $2 and was timed in 1:56 2-5

Continued on Page 6, Column 3

The Philadelphia Inquirer

PUBLIC LEDGER

An Independent Newspaper for All the People

CIRCULATION: October Average: Daily 470,018, Sunday 1,340,508 a b c d e f g SUNDAY MORNING, NOVEMBER 8, 1942 A Largest 3c Morning Circulation in America PRICE, TEN CENTS

Vol. 227, No. 131

U. S. Invades French Africa With Land, Sea, Air Forces; Action Opens Second Front

100,000 SEIZED OR TRAPPED IN ROMMEL FLIGHT

British Smash 2d Axis Stand in Egypt, Sweep on Without Letup Toward Libya

CAIRO, Nov. 7 (A. P.).—Approximately 100,000 men of Field Marshal Erwin Rommel's Axis army of 140,000 were reported captured or pinned down in pockets far behind the swiftly moving African front today, as the British Eighth Army swept on toward the Libyan border after smashing the German armor in its second attempted stand.

Disregarding the thousands of foot soldiers left in the dusty backwash of the battlefront, Lieutenant General Bernard L. Montgomery's British and American tanks tore into the disorganized flanks of their main prize—the battered remnants of the German armored divisions—west of Matruh in an effort to eliminate them entirely.

2D HEADLONG RETREAT

They already had caught up with this fleeing force once and sent it into headlong, harassed retreat a second time.

Montgomery spurred his men on to swifter pursuit of the enemy with the admonition that the "battle just won is only the beginning of our task." The British object apparently as to harry Rommel's army constantly so they could not rest or regroup their shattered forces.

ONLY THE BEGINNING

Montgomery's observation was contained in the following order of the day to the Eighth Army:

"I feel sure that the battle we have just won is only the beginning of our task. There is much to be done yet, and it will call for supreme effort and great hardship on the part of every officer and man.

"Forward then to our task of removing the Germans from North Africa. The Germans began this trouble, and they must take the consequences. They asked for it, and now they will get it. Let no officer or man relax, let us drive ahead westward, destroying the enemy wherever he is met."

Today's communique announced

Continued on Page 5, Column 4

A. E. F. Captures Beaches Near 2 Main Objectives

By WES GALLAGHER

ALLIED HEADQUARTERS IN NORTH AFRICA, Nov. 8 (Sunday) (A. P.).—Reports reaching Allied headquarters today disclosed that successful landings had been made by American assault parties on beaches of North Africa near two main objectives outlined in operational plans.

Headquarters stressed the need, however, of caution in evaluating the first reports.

American soldiers, Marines and sailors from one of the greatest naval armadas ever put in to a single military operation swarmed ashore on the Vichy-controlled North Africa shore before dawn, striking to break Hitler's hold on the Mediterranean.

COMMANDER WORKS ALL NIGHT

Tall, decisive Lieutenant General Dwight D. (Ike) Eisenhower, supreme commander of the huge forces involved in the operation, worked throughout the night directing the first great American blow at the Axis.

Included in the forces were crack combat troops, Rangers (air borne units) and the cream of America's airmen.

British naval and air force units supported the American landing forces, who were preceded by a snowstorm of leaflets and a radio barrage promising the French that the United States had no intention of seizing French possessions and only sought to prevent Axis infiltration.

RECORD OVERSEAS MILITARY FEAT

It undoubtedly was the longest overwater military operation ever attempted, with hundreds of ships in great convoys coming thousands of miles under the protection of British and American sea and air might.

I came on one of these big convoys.

Fighting-fit American soldiers and airmen, who did not know their destination until a few hours before scrambling into assault barges, crowded the ships to the very funnels and were guarded by aircraft carriers, cruisers and destroyers.

Our big convoy arrived at its destination with the split-second timing of a subway train, despite storms for many days at sea and danger from planes and submarines.

The entire operation was carried out with the delicate

Continued on Page 8, Column 6

Pictures and stories of the American invasion of North Africa on Pages 8, 9, 10 and 12.

By WILLIAM C. MURPHY, JR.

Inquirer Washington Bureau

WASHINGTON, Nov. 7.—Powerful American forces are landing on the Atlantic and Mediterranean coasts of French North Africa, opening a second front designed to crush German and Italian troops in the Dark Continent and prepare the way for an invasion of Axis-held Europe.

The invasion—greatest single offensive ever undertaken by American forces—was the beginning of the long-heralded United Nations offenfensive designed to carry the war to the Axis Powers in their "home grounds," as President Roosevelt promised several months ago.

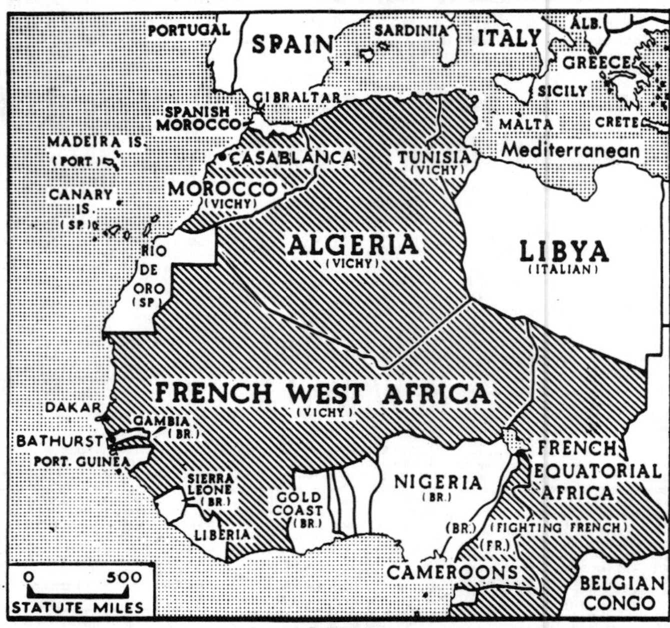

(A. P. Wirephoto)

WHERE U. S. TROOPS BLAST OPEN A SECOND FRONT

Shading indicates French colonies in Northwestern Africa, where a powerful American force was landing last night on both the Atlantic and Mediterranean coasts.

Announcement of the opening of the second front was made tonight by the President, acting as Commander-in-Chief of the Nation's armed forces, who indicated that the objectives of the unprecedented Army-Navy-Air Force operation were:

1. Pave the way for an invasion of Axis-ruled Europe.

2. Create the western arm of a giant pincers to crush the remnants of Marshal Erwin Rommel's African Corps, now reeling westward across the Egyptian desert from blows inflicted by the British Eighth Army.

3. Forestall a Nazi thrust into French Africa, which, if successful, would "constitute a direct threat to America across the comparatively narrow sea from Western Africa."

British naval units and planes of the Royal Air Force co-operated in the gigantic invasion operation and, the President said, American forces in Africa will be reinforced by "a considerable number of divisions of the British Army."

PROBABLY GREATEST ARMADA

The President's statement was issued at exactly 9 P. M. tonight (E. W. T.)—3 A. M. in the French possessions—and the invasion was then in progress, according to White House Secretary Stephen Early.

(London sources declared that probably the greatest armada assembled in Europe since the start of the war undertook the invasion.)

Lieutenant General Dwight D. Eisenhower, commander of American Forces in the European Theatre of War, is in command of the invasion force.

AIR-BORNE U. S. RANGERS LAND

(Parachute troops, Marines and sailors—among them air-borne Ranger shock troops—swarmed ashore in Vichy-controlled French North and West Africa in a pre-dawn foray, according to Associated Press dispatches from the new front.

(Vichy French resistance no doubt was being encountered, these dispatches said, but that initial resistance had been overcome was indicated in a report by Wes Gallagher, Associated Press correspondent, dated "Allied Headquarters, North Africa."

SUCCESSFUL LANDINGS MADE

(Reports reaching Allied headquarters disclosed that successful landings had been made by American assault parties on beaches of North Africa near two main objectives.)

(The American vanguard of amphibious and air-borne troops smashed in to seize control of French airfields and communications centres, to open the way for mass landings, according to Africa dispatches. The Americans went into action under cover of an umbrella of planes from U. S. and British aircraft carriers, these reports said.)

Simultaneously with the launching of the offensive,

Continued on Page 8, Column 1

5188 JAPS KILLED ON GUADALCANAL

By RICHARD L. HARKNESS

Inquirer Washington Bureau

WASHINGTON, Nov. 7.—A total of 5188 Japanese have paid with their lives for their war lords' bloody but vain attempt to hold the southeast Solomon Islands and to drive American Marines and Army troops from the Guadalcanal-Tulagi area, the Navy revealed tonight in a re-

Continued on Page 2, Column 3

Airborne U. S. Troops Join New Guinea Fight

By DEAN SCHEDLER

SOMEWHERE IN NEW GUINEA, Oct. 21 (Delayed) (A. P.).—American infantry soldiers trained to a fighting edge and itching for a scrap have gone into the battle area in the mist-filled jungles of New Guinea in the first United States mass movement of infantry by air.

The 1942 version of the American doughboy, garbed in regulation Army fatigue uniform, camouflaged a motely green, was rushed to New Guinea by airplane ferry and sent into almost immediate combat along with the Australians to drive the Japanese off this embattled island.

The United States Army wrote a

Continued on Page 2, Column 1

War Features

The News Review of the Week and other war features, including columns by Major George Fielding Eliot, Mark Sullivan and Wilfrid Fleisher, appear on Pages 14 and 15 of the sports-news section.

YANKS RAID BREST, R.A.F. RIPS GENOA

LONDON, Nov. 8 (Sunday) (A. P.).—British bombers were over Italy again last night for the second successive night, it was announced today.

LONDON, Nov. 7 (A. P.).—United States heavy bombers smashed at the big German submarine base at Brest in a daylight attack today, as reports from France and Switzerland indicated that the Royal Air Force had its big bombers out tonight for a new attack on Italy following Friday night's raid on the northern Italian supply port of Genoa.

The raid on Brest was made by

Continued on Page 5, Column 1

FLEET OF 125 SHIPS IS SUPPORTING U. S.

LONDON, Nov. 8 (Sunday) (A. P.).—Possibly the greatest invasion armada assembled in Europe since the start of the war undertook the invasion of French North Africa today in the first large-scale action in the European theatre in which the United States has participated.

A force of 24 warships, transports and freighters, followed by the great battleship Rodney and a heavy air escort was reported by the Ger-

Continued on Page 8, Column 5

10 Pct. Cut Indicated In Available Beef

WASHINGTON, Nov. 7 (A. P.).—A reduction in the amount of beef and veal available to the public is in prospect, Government sources who preferred anonymity indicated today.

They said the present 80 percent allotment of beef and veal probably would be reduced to 70 percent, and added the order might be issued next week.

The necessity for the cut was understood to have resulted from heavy buying by the Army and Navy.

Roosevelt's Statement On Landings in Africa

WASHINGTON, Nov. 7 (U. P.).—The text of President Roosevelt's statement follows:

In order to forestall an invasion of Africa by Germany and Italy, which if successful would constitute a direct threat to America across the comparatively narrow sea from Western Africa, a powerful force equipped with adequate weapons of modern warfare and under American command is today landing on the Mediterranean and Atlantic coasts of the French colonies in Africa.

The landing of this American Army is being assisted by the British Navy and Air Forces and it will, in the immediate future, be reinforced by a considerable number of divisions of the British Army.

UNDER U. S. COMMAND

This combined Allied force, under American command, in conjunction with the British campaign in Egypt, is designed to prevent an occupation by the Axis Armies of any part of Northern or Western Africa, and to deny to the aggressor nations a starting point from which to launch an attack against the Atlantic coast of the Americas.

In addition, it provides an ef-

Continued on Page 12, Column 2

ROOSEVELT'S TALK TO FRENCH PEOPLE

WASHINGTON, Nov. 7 (A. P.).—The text of the address broadcast by President Roosevelt, in French, to the French people follows:

My friends, who suffer day and night under the crushing yoke of the Nazis, I speak to you as one who was with your army and navy in France in 1918.

I have held all my life the deepest friendship for the French people—for the entire French people. I retain and cherish the friendship of hundreds of French people in France

Continued on Page 12, Column 1

The Philadelphia Inquirer

FRIDAY MORNING, JANUARY 1, 1943

JOYOUS CROWD THAT GREETED NEW YEAR ON CITY HALL PLAZA

[illegible]ING OUT THE OLD YEAR AT INDEPENDENCE HALL

1943 Arrives

Festive and gay was Philadelphia's welcome to the New Year, despite war time conditions. Brisk weather increased the cheerfulness of mid-city crowds. Above is shown a part of the throng of merrymakers at City Hall Plaza. Horns and noisemakers took the place of the bells and whistles that ushered in other years. A more solemn note was sounded at Independence Hall. There the guards shown at the left, Lara Thomas and William Coull, rang a bell tolling in the New Year and saying farewell to the old. Typical of the gay throng in the streets was the group shown below. They are, from left to right, Marion Aquilla, Russ Pericone, Angela Pericone and Joseph Dipietro.

TH[illegible]Y ADDED TO MERRY UPROAR OF THE MIDTOWN CROWD

4-Story Factory Collapses

A four-story brick factory at Hancock and Jefferson sts. collapsed yesterday, the top floor caving in and showering debris on Jefferson st., as the picture above shows. Firemen are working on the roof of the adjoining building. Fire Chief William Cowden is ordering the children of the family in that building to leave (below). One man was injured.

JINX Richard L. Fenton, Fort Wayne, Ind., bus driver, traveled through snow, sleet, rain storms and drove across many an ice-coated highway without mishap and then, as he came within a few blocks of his destination, his machine was jammed under the Market st. elevated tracks between 30th and 31st sts. This picture shows workmen trying to release the bus. Fenton's accident was attributed to his unfamiliarity with Philadelphia streets and morning's heavy fog.

THE AMERICAN WOMAN OF 1943

An army of young girls will replace men in America's war plants in 1943. At operations requiring swift, deft movement such as assembling machine gun barrel carriers, which this worker does so skilfully, women excel.

LIKE the pioneer women of old, the contribution of women in this war will be a saga in American history. In 1943, several million of them will follow the example of the women of 1942 who left home for factory, who gave up old, non-essential jobs to learn new crafts vitally needed for the war effort. They include women who had never worked before, handicapped women, women burdened with the care of large families, thousands of girls who learned welding and delicate precision work.

There are women who tote guns, too. Typical of the Civil Service women guards who have replaced Marine and civilian guards at the U. S. Naval Air Station, South Weymouth, Mass., and elsewhere, is Grace Walsh.

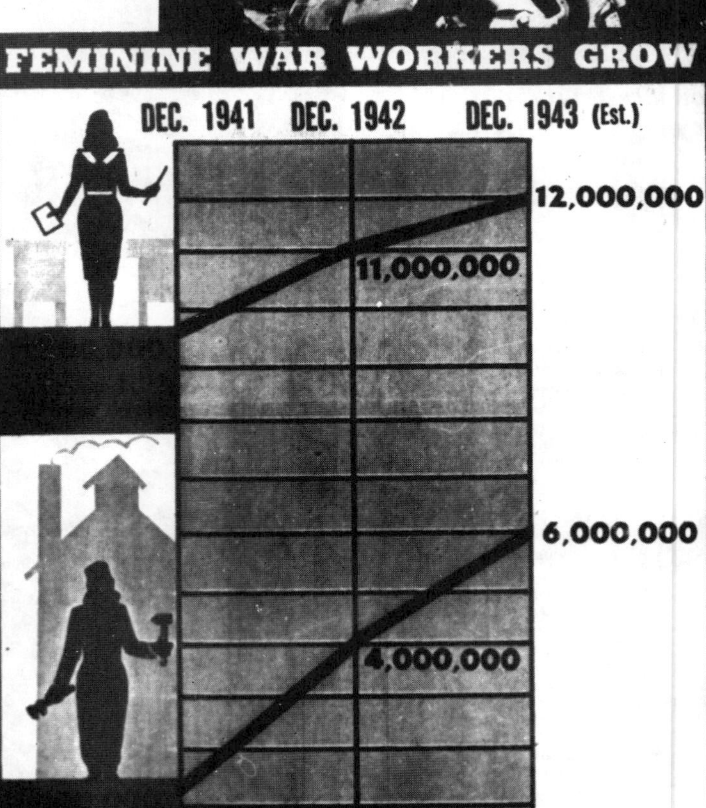

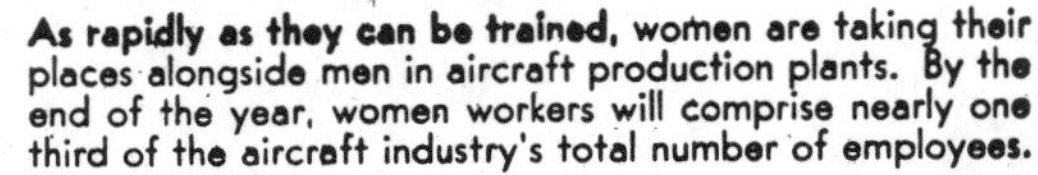

As rapidly as they can be trained, women are taking their places alongside men in aircraft production plants. By the end of the year, women workers will comprise nearly one third of the aircraft industry's total number of employees.

Woman's role in agriculture is symbolized by this farm wife at the wheel of a tractor. Mrs. William Wood of Colona, Mich., manages a 120-acre farm, thereby releasing her husband for war industry. This is only one "chore."

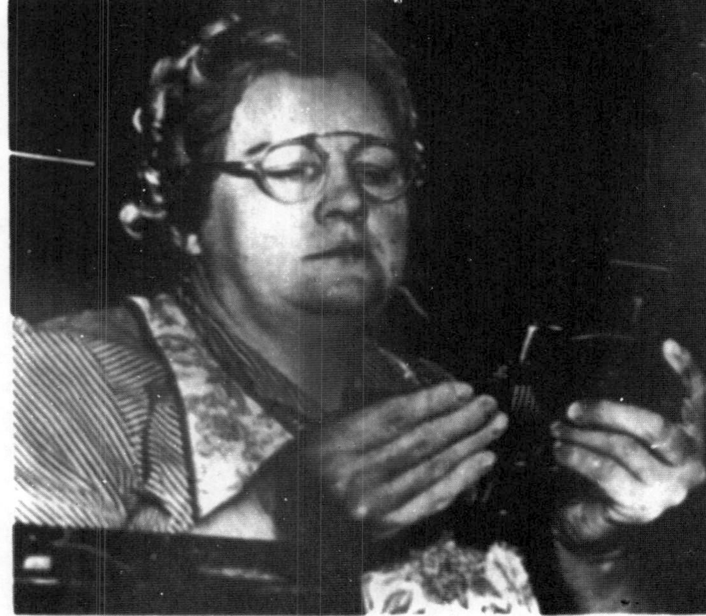

Serious, skilled, reliable, Mrs. Else M. Terry makes an invaluable contribution as a milling machine operator in a midwest plant producing machine-guns. Here she uses a precision snap gauge on a part she has just milled.

At airports as well as in airplane factories, women are contributing to the nation's manpower needs. Mattie Marks, formerly a seamstress in a laundry, now scoots from plane to baggage room in her "gas buggy" transporting passengers' suitcases and overnight bags at the Washington National Airport. This year, women will also be building ships to carry forces to the front.

With the Army's Land and Air Forces

News and Gossip of Phila. Service Men and Women Stationed in U. S. and Throughout the World

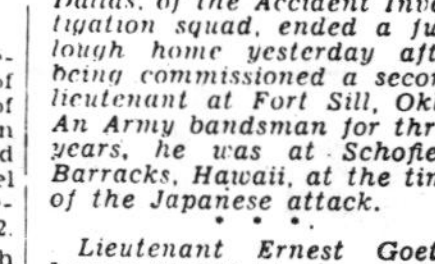

ARMY

Dr. Yale Nathanson, of 1704 Delancey st., former professor of psychology at the University of Pennsylvania and Army captain in the last World War, was promoted from major to lieutenant colonel at Fort Washington, Md. He re-entered the service in March, 1942.

Sergeant Chris Cosfol, 523 S. 9th st., is top man in the War Bond drive among enlisted men at Bolling Field, D. C., having purchased $650 worth of bonds in the last six months.

"War bonds make the best investment possible," Cosfol declared, "and when this war is over, I want something to show for it. We'd like to paper the whole globe with War Bonds to help our buddies on the fighting fronts." Before joining the Army, Cosfol managed a dance band.

SERGEANT COSFOL

Hershel Link, 62 Lewis ave., East Lansdowne, writes that his battalion at Camp Campbell, Ky., was commended by Major General Carlos Brewer for being the first unit of the command to attain 100 percent participation in the purchase of War Bonds at the camp.

Corporal Sidney Krasner, 635 W. Oxford st., "a Yank in the Middle East," is writing poetry to a girl friend, Anne Comer, 5855 Pemberton st.

• • •

David W. Dallas, 7203 Tabor ave., son of Patrolman David Dallas, of the Accident Investigation squad, ended a furlough home yesterday after being commissioned a second lieutenant at Fort Sill, Okla. An Army bandsman for three years, he was at Schofield Barracks, Hawaii, at the time of the Japanese attack.

• • •

Lieutenant Ernest Goetzburger, 5953 N. 3d st., was married last week at Westover Field, Mass., to Miss Mary J. Allo, 339 W. Girard ave.

Harold Cinoman, 4912 Gransback st., was promoted to corporal and transferred from Camp Robinson, Ark., to Camp Atterbury, Ind.

• • •

A mother's prayers were answered at Christmas when a letter from Sergeant Nicholas Falgiatore reached his home at 1335 S. 17th st. from a base in New Guinea. Mrs. Mary Falgiatore said she prayed for two months that a letter would arrive to brighten the family's holiday.

SGT. FALGIATORE

In his letter, Sergeant Falgiatore paid tribute to the bravery of his buddies and expressed the wish that the U. S. O. and American Red Cross would establish canteens in the New Guinea wilds.

James J. Castrogiovanni, 736 Morris st., who had his morning "chow" interrupted Dec. 7, 1941, when the Japs blasted Pearl Harbor, was recently promoted to staff sergeant at his base in the Hawaiian Islands. A younger brother, Corporal Joseph Castrogiovanni, is with the Army Air Forces in California.

Robert Greer, 5930 N. 21st st., is in training as a bombardier cadet at Big Springs, Texas. His father, Russell, is at Camp Campbell, Tenn., and his step-father, Adolph Kurner, is with an Army unit at Clearwater, Fla.

Corporal William Hauenstein, 2124 N. 5th st., was promoted to sergeant at Camp Barkeley, Texas, where he is staff cartoonist and artist for the camp newspaper.

• • •

Staff Sergeant Robert H. Acker, 417 W. Champlost st., former postal employe, was married last week to Miss Norma Albrecht, 4970 Rising Sun ave., a stenographer with the Pennsylvania S. P. C. A. The wedding took place here, while Sergeant Acker was home on furlough from Fort McClellan, Ala. A brother of the bride, Carl Albrecht, is a staff sergeant serving overseas with the Army Pictorial Service.

It's a total war for the Kalman family, of 5214 Diamond st. Acting Corporal James Kalman, Fort Riley, Kan., and his twin brother, Frank, Fort Bliss, Tex., learned last week their mother, Mrs. Belle Kalman, had joined the WAACs. Their father, who died last year, was a sergeant in the last World War.

• • •

Howard J. Hildebrandt, 6108 Nassau road, is scheduled to receive his wings and be commissioned a second lieutenant in the Army Air Forces today at Luke Field, Ariz. His parents, Mr. and Mrs. John H. Hildebrandt, will be on hand for the ceremonies. Hildebrandt, a former junior auditor for the Sun Oil Co., received his pre-flight training in California.

H. J. HILDEBRANDT

John Libhart, 5122 Springfield ave., was advanced to corporal at Kirtland Field, N. M.

Friends are informed that Corporal Anthony Travaglia, 726 Ellsworth st.; Vincent Gogliuzza, 729 Federal st., and Fred Formicola, 1150 S. 7th st., are now in North Africa.

First Lieutenant Gilbert H. Sukin, 4800 Walnut st., former practicing dentist here, is now on duty with the Army Dental Corps at Keesler Field, Miss.

Perry Toombs, 145 Ruby st., has been assigned at Gowen Field, Idaho, to one of the new six-man groups selected on a merit basis from among Negro personnel to service heavy bombers.

First Lieutenant Howard Jones, 1229 S. 61st st., was promoted to captain at Camp Hood, Tex.

• • •

Arthur Bright, 1414 Sparks st., was transferred from New Cumberland, Pa., to the Delaware Ordnance Depot Pedricktown, N. J.

David Bentz, 429 W. Price st., was assigned for training to the Medical Replacement Centre at Camp Robinson, Ark.

• • •

Harold Kempner, 3126 W. Columbia ave., former teacher in Jewish children's schools, is now in the public relations office at Fort Riley, Kan. Originally classified 1-B in the draft because of poor eyesight he tried to enlist, but was turned down because he was not a citizen. A reclassification made him 1-A, but he waited so long for the draft board's call, he got his citizenship papers first, making him eligible to join up.

HAROLD KEMPNER

James Gerety, 4820 Oxford ave., was promoted to technician, fifth grade, and Samuel Fulton, 2311 Watkins st., was raised to technical sergeant at their A.A.F. base in the Caribbean area.

Clayton Thoms, 1244 W. Lehigh ave., was promoted to staff sergeant at Bolling Field, D. C.

Horace Wanamaker, 6291 Large st., was advanced to corporal at Fort Devens, Mass.

Lieutenant Charles Gamper, 2110 Shunk st., was promoted to captain. He is stationed at Camp Lee, Va.

Three men from this area were selected at Fort Bragg, N. C., for transfer to officer candidate school at Fort Sill, Okla. They are Corporals Marvin New, 5433 Sansom st.; Kenneth Bridgen, 7004 Ruskin lane, Upper Darby, and Walter Lowrie, 101 Hathaway lane, Merwood.

• • •

Staff Sergeants Victor Boffa, 2965 Tilton st., and Vincent Gannon, 5230 Columbia ave., completed bombardier-navigation training at the A.A.F. school, Carlsbad, N. M.

Louis Fecca, 1910 S. 11th st., was promoted to staff sergeant at Dale Mabry Field, Fla.

Domenick DiFalco, 865 Wynnewood road, was commissioned a second lieutenant at Camp Davis, N. C.

Corporal Gilbert Rubin, 5766 Colgate st., entered officer candidate school at Gainesville, Fla.

• • •

Winston S. Hutchins, 133 Wayne ave., Collingdale, has returned to duty at Fort Knox, Ky., after spending the holidays at home with his parents, Mr. and Mrs. Leon S. Hutchins. The youth, a private, first class, is a radio operator in the Army.

WINSTON HUTCHINS

Aviation cadet Francis Carney, , 353 Hermitage st., is in basic flight training at the Army Air Field, Greenville, Texas.

Robert Bernstein, 1512 Spruce st., was raised to technician, fifth grade, at the Holabird Ordnance Base, Baltimore.

Elmer Peterman, 3244 N. 6th st., and Thomas Przbytek, 957 N. American st., were promoted to corporals at Key Field, Miss.

Morton Baizer, 2106 S. 6th st., was promoted to private, first class, at Fort Lewis, Wash.

F. Leonard Wagner, 2830 Frankford ave., was advanced to sergeant at Camp Livingston, La.

Aviation Cadet Joseph Smith, 218 Gorgas lane, is in the final phase of his flight training at Lubbock, Tex.

• • •

John Gallagher, 4202 Levick st., was raised to corporal at the Marana Basic Flying School, Tucson, Ariz.

Israel Uram, 5806 Malvern ave., was commissioned a second lieutenant at Fort Mason, Cal., and assigned to duty in the Army Postoffice at San Francisco.

Frank Armstrong, 1640 S. Bailey st., was promoted to sergeant at Fort Mason, Cal., where he is attached to the Army Postoffice.

• • •

Morton Fierman, 6242 N. 11th st., who enlisted in the Army in April, 1941, and was commissioned a second lieutenant last July, has been notified of his promotion to first lieutenant. Stationed in the New Orleans area, Lieutenant Fierman is at present spending a 10-day furlough at home. Prior to his enlistment, he was a junior executive at Stern & Co., 706 Market st.

LT. M. FIERMAN

Corporal James Siegfried, 5040 Osage ave., was advanced to sergeant at Napier Field, Ala. A former member of the Lansdowne Choristers, he frequently appears on the Napier Field radio programs as a baritone soloist.

Nicholas De Santis, 711 N. 3d st., is oh duty with an armored division at Camp Polk, La.

W. H. Lowden, Jr., 620 Miller st., is in basic flight training at Randolph Field, Texas.

Samuel Bayne, 3414 Indian Queen lane, was promoted from corporal to sergeant at the San Angelo, Texas, Army Air Field.

Lieutenant Herbert Serota, 1443 Creston st., who received his commission less than a month ago at Miami Beach, is on duty at the San Antonio Aviation Cadet Centre, Tex.

• • •

Anthony Amorosso, 2406 S. Watt st., was temporarily transferred from Selfridge Field, Mich., to Lincoln, Neb., to take a course in airplane mechanics. Frank Dunn, 522 S. 46th st., was sent from Selfridge Field to Goldsboro, N. C., for a similar course.

Sydney Hirsch, 3024 Page st., and Leonard Landsburg, 5811 Washington ave., completed preflight training courses in navigation at Selman Field, Monroe, La.

James Ryan, 3d, 905 Fox Chase road, Fox Chase, was graduated from an aviation mechanics' course at Seymour Johnson Field, N. C.

• • •

Edward Moffly, 16 W. Bells Mill road; William Pickles, 4143 Paul st., and John Yates, 535 Hansberry st., completed flight training at Shaw Field, S. C.

David Tankle, 3521 Vista st., is now at Sioux Falls, Ia.

Meyer Moscowitz, 2413 S. Fairhill st., was promoted to technician, fifth grade, at Camp Stewart, Ga.

Frank MacKenzie, son of James R. O'Brien, 3303 N. 11th st., was promoted to technician, fourth grade, at Venice, Fla.

Thomas E. Haight, Jr., 3565 N. Warnock st., was advanced to technical sergeant at Walla Walla, Wash.

Second lieutenant commissions were awarded at Fort Washington, Md., to Theodore Gabis, 2302 Delancey st.; Patrick Lynch, 3235 F. Rorer st.; Joseph Moore, 6400 Lincoln drive, and Harold Wolpert, 1600 S. Taney st.

AMARILLO FIELD, TEXAS

Training as aviation mechanics: Milton Green, 6147 N. 17th st., and Louis Agnoni, 1536 McKean st. Graduate aviation mechanics: William McMichael, 3032 N. 8th st.; Stephen Lanush, 963½ N. Lawrence st., and Fred Stamm, 417 W. Hortter st. Assigned to active duty: Second Lieutenants John Birkinbine, Lansdowne, and Norman Strehle, 6141 Dittman st.

FORT BELVOIR, VA.

Newly commissioned second lieutenants: John Bayer, 5647 N. 2d st.; Joseph K. Costello, Jr., Alden Park; Alfred Cruz, 1426 W. Diamond st.; William Diamond, 2628 N. 27th st.; David Dugdale, 2335 N. 18th st.; Walter Farewell, 8114 Germantown ave.; Clinton Fetterman, 55 N. Lindenwood st.; Stephen J. Gifford, Jr., 9230 Germantown ave.; Andrew Griffin, 1433 S. 29th st.; Walter J. Morris, Jr., 5527 Miriam road; William Noblette, 523 Spruce st.; Richard Schilling, 225 E. Meade st.; Ellwood Shallcross, Jr., 111 W. Sharpnack st.; Edward Sklodowski, 2229 Bridge st.

FORT BENNING, GA.

Newly commissioned second lieutenants: William Hamilton, 1224 S. 58th st.; William Nolan, 6059 Irving st.; Edward DeLuca, 5829 Sansom st.; David Fleming, 1315 S. 52d st.; Edwin Willard, son of Mrs. Josephine Willard, 546 W. Clapier st.

CARLISLE BARRACKS, PA.

Graduates of officers' class at the Medical Field Service School: Captains Joseph Belber, 68th ave. and 13th st.; Gerald Fincke, 1345 Grange ave., and Robert Mitterling, 5731 Baltimore ave.; First Lieutenants John Duncan, 2248 S. 22d st.; Norman Sloane, 57th st. and Woodbine ave.; Eugene Thomas, 4856 N. B st.; Jack Lipshutz, 6112 Torresdale ave.; Nicholas DeLeo, 1333 Ellsworth st.; William P. Britsch, Jr., 328 S. 42d st.; Maurice Abramson, 5601 Woodbine ave.; Edward Cuden, 4617 N. Marvine st.; Harold Fine, 5243 Chester ave., and Elmer Feingold, 1301 S. 52d st.

FORT DES MOINES, IA.

Commissioned Third Officers in the WAACs: Jean Wiener, 4912 N. 11th st., and Helen Harwitz, 1117 Ritner st. Completed advanced training in specialist schools: Betty Mandell, 7019 Cedar Park ave.; Mary Wertheim, 4052 Roosevelt boulevard; Mildred Patton, 3150 Tulip st.; Mary O'Neill, 297 Haines st.; Marguerite Naramore, 1214 N. 64th st.; Ida Epstein, 6807 N. Broad st.; Dorothy Bliss, 220 Winona ave.; Esther Martin, 5628 N. 4th st.; Shirley Pepp, Majestic Hotel.

CAMP EDWARDS, MASS.

Recent promotions: Corporals John Miller, 1531 Catharine st., and Gerald West, 152 Fairview st., to sergeants; Alphonso Tuppins, 2230 Fitzwater st., and Henry Watford, 1927 Carpenter st., to corporals; Charles H. Shute, Jr., 2021 Pemberton st., to corporal technician.

CAMP GRANT, ILL.

Graduates of clerical school: John L. Gillies, 3d, 229 E. Highland ave., and Robert Kimmey, 6236 Delancey st., the latter with honors. Picked to attend officer training at Camp Barkeley, Tex.: Paul Quintavalle, 3122 N. 8th st., and Arthur Sabo, 2308 W. Harold st.

KEESLER FIELD, MISS.

Graduates of airplane mechanics' courses: Paul Allen, 6325 Woodland ave.; B. H. Barbakoff, 452 Fitzgerald st.; William Barclay, 2518 Germantown ave.; Anthony Capaldi, 2507 S. Warnock st.; John Carroll, 6026 Cedar ave.; James V. Cossetti, Jr., 1922 Cayuga st.; Charles Crowders, 6217 Buist ave.; Gustav Dannecker, 1006 Belmont ave.; George Davis, 2611 S. 71st st.; J. S. Dobrzynski, 2864 Kensington ave.; Joseph Fantini, Jr., 2534 W. Somerset st.; Bert Goldberg, 5137 Haverford ave.; Leon Haer, 360 Jackson st.; Dominic Loschiano, 3022 N. 21st st.; John Mannella, 5721 Malvern ave.; Herman Marcus, 2427 S. 4th st.; John McDonough, 6139 Walton ave.; L. J. Myer, 2508 S. Adler st.

FORT KNOX, KY.

Graduate radio operators: Christopher Crawford, 1439 N. Felton st.; William Drobness, 738 Ritner st.; Albert Fisher, 543 S. Redfield st.; Malcolm Anderson, 954 Herbert st.; Neil Gallagher, 1931 W. Pacific st. Graduate mechanics: Sergeant Anthony Vacca, 2972 Salmon st.; James Primavera, 1513 N. 6th st.; Victor Giambiasi, 1951 Rowan st. Graduate clerks: Marlin Hummell, 1320 W. Cambria st.; Corporal John Kindon, 249 Lauriston st.; Sergeant Silas White, 1216 S. 46th st. In basic training: Robert Mittleman, 4620 H st.; Alfred Stern, 2527 W. Seybert st.; William Cole, 2773 Coral st.

CAMP LEE, VA.

First Lieutenant Leon Cobaugh, 6083 Regent st., was promoted to captain. He is the officer in charge of the apprentice mechanics' shop in the Quartermaster Corps. Other promotions: Gaeton Anastasi, 1531 S. 8th st.; Joseph DiStanisloa, 2119 Watkins st., and Frank Tosti, 1853 S. Rosewood st., to corporals.

MIAMI BEACH

Graduates of special officers' course: Captain James O'Donnell, 5215 N. Broad st.; First Lieutenants Morris Yermish, 2228 Vine st.; Irvine Williamson, 1512 E. Careza st.; Edward Bloom, 5650 N. Mascher st.; Harry Berlin, 6053 Ogontz ave.; Joseph Bloom, 1538 66th ave.; Herman Medoff, 1735 N. Paxon st.; Ralph Hocker, 6840 Ogontz ave.; Joseph Ballin, 2217 E. Cumberland st.; Nathan Feldsher, 2823 W. Allegheny ave.; Frederick Lauria, 2122 S. 15th st.; Robert Straughn, 1234 W. Hilton st.; Ephraim Rosset, 3107 Diamond st.; Thomas Maye, 2445 W. Cumberland st.; Second Lieutenants Walter S. Falk, Jr., 3457 W. Penn st., and James Clarke, 312 Wellesley rd., Mt. Airy.

FORT MONMOUTH, N. J.

Newly commissioned second lieutenants: Daniel Wallace, 5222 Jefferson st.; Albert O'Kinsky, 8108 Harley ave.; Raymond Daly, Jr., 314 N. 32d st.; Clyde E. Rankin, Jr., 406 Chandler st.; Victor Roma, 273 Tulpehocken st.; Raymond Paradiso, 910 Snyder ave.; Dominic DiGregorio, 3507 N. 22d st.

CAMP MURPHY, FLA.

Enrolled in special courses at the Signal Corps school: Frederick Dye, 1429 E. Oxford st.; Corporal Fred Lichtenberger, 2729 W. Eyre st.; Staff Sergeant Russell Thompson, 375 Lyceum ave.; Technical Corporals Albert Schultz, Jr., 5937 Alma st.; Raymond Lazarian, 5914 Irving st., and Thomas Roth, 2405 S. Percy st.

SEYMOUR, IND.

New arrivals: Francis Wareham, 863 N. 20th st.; Sergeant Hugh Casey, 6956 Ogontz ave.; Staff Sergeant Henry Rambo, 809 N. 5th st.; Corporal Joseph D'Agostine, 619 Tasker st.; Arthur W. Short, 3765 Richmond st.

WILL ROGERS FIELD, OKLA.

Lieutenant George Panisnick, 717 N. 4th st., reported for duty with a service group. Assigned to a bombardment squadron: Sergeants Herman Konchinsky, 1747 N. 7th st., and Howard Rothstein, 6116 Castor ave., and Corporal Nogah Bethlahmy, 6529 N. 13th st.

(A. P. Wirephoto)

OPERA STAR WEDS ARMY PRIVATE

Dorothy Kirsten smiles happily as she leaves the Little Church Around the Corner, in New York City, with her husband, Private Edward Oates, after their wedding. Mrs. Oates is the celebrated diva of Chicago Civic Opera.

2 U. S. Soldiers Cited for Heroism

ALLIED HEADQUARTERS IN AUSTRALIA, Jan. 4 (Monday) (A. P.). A United States soldier who ran a mile to man a machine gun and shoot down an enemy plane, and another who showed he could forget his wounds for the good of the service, received decorations for bravery today.

Staff Sergeant Victory Lorber of San Bernardino, Calif., who hurried the mile to fight a Jap air attack on an airdrome at Malang, Java, Feb. 20, 1942, was given the Oak Leaf Cluster for gallantry by Lieutenant General George C. Kenney, commander of Allied Air Forces in the Southwest Pacific.

General Kenney also presented the Oak Leaf Cluster and the Purple Heart decoration to Staff Sergeant Leroy Penwarden, New Haven, Conn., a side gunner in a Flying Fortress bombing mission against Jap shipping at Milne Bay, New Guinea, Aug. 26.

Battle of Midway Hero Missing

WILMINGTON, Jan. 3 (A. P.).—Staff Sergeant Howard L. Krantz, 23, St. Georges, who was awarded the Army silver star for "meritorious conduct during the Battle of Midway," has been reported missing in action in the South Pacific.

Word was received by Sergeant Krantz' parents, Mr. and Mrs. William Krantz of St. Georges, in a telegram from the War Department. He has been missing since Dec. 28, the telegram said.

Sergeant Krantz was a veteran of several engagements. He was wounded at Pearl Harbor and was confined to a hospital from Dec. 7 to 15 of that year with a chest injury caused by bomb explosions. After his recovery he received his promotion to sergeant and resumed duties with the air patrol in search of submarines.

Sergeant Krantz has three brothers in the armed services.

If you should lose your sugar ration book, oil or gas coupons, advertise in The Inquirer for quick recovery. Phone Miss Allen, Rittenhouse 5000.

With the Sea Forces

News of Phila. Residents At Navy, Marine Bases

NAVY

Aviation Cadet Arthur Evans, 4923 York road, was transferred from Glenview, Ill., to the Naval Air Training Station, Corpus Christi, Texas, for advanced flight training.

Frank Carey, 1510 Womrath st., enlisted in the Navy and is now in training at Bainbridge, Md.

Howard Wallis, Jr., 2756 Airesford st., was graduated from the Naval Training School for machinists at the University of Kansas, Lawrence, Kan.

• • •

The following cadets were graduated from the Pre-Flight School at Chapel Hill, N. C., and transferred to other bases for primary flight instruction: Charles Temkovits, 4653 N. 16th st.; Robert Loughery Ketcham, Jr., 3011 Stenton ave.; Joseph Gawinski, 327 Cedar st.; William J. Debler, Jr., 71 Manheim st.; William Mayer, 1407 E. Duval st.; Harold Bryant, 3526 Sheffield ave.

CADET TEMKOVITS

Charles Elliott, 5221 Wissahickon ave., was commissioned an ensign at Jacksonville, Fla. He is a graduate of Germantown Academy.

Edward Kotz, 6538 Tulip st., was promoted to aviation machinist's mate, third class, at Jacksonville, Fla.

• • •

The following have completed basic training at the Navy Submarine School, New London, Conn.; John Kleinstuber, 1950 Granite st.; William Moore, 804 N. Ringgold st.; Charles Houston, 120 N. Millick st., and George Warren, brother of Mrs. J. J. Burns, 4 Carpenter lane.

• • •

George Higgins, 4408 Locust st., and Charles J. Kraft, Jr., 1534 N. Willington st., won their Navy "Wings of Gold" and were commissioned ensigns in the Naval Reserve at Pensacola, Fla. The new officers are designated as Naval aviators and will go on active duty at an optional training centre before being assigned to a combat zone.

ENSIGN HIGGINS

The following were recently appointed Naval Aviation Cadets and transferred to Pensacola, Fla., for flight training: Clifford Snyder, 4636 N. Camac st.; William Gordon, 400 W. Allen's lane; William Hooven, 1909 E. Letterly st., and Joseph Ferrell, 6420 Fairhill st.

Edward O'Neal, 4122 Taylor ave., Drexel Hill, has been appointed a cadet-midshipman in the U. S. Merchant Marine Cadet Corps and is preparing to become a deck officer at King's Point, L. I.

Graduates of the Hospital Corps School of the U. S. Naval Hospital, Great Lakes, Ill., include Charles Foley, 626 N. 52d st.; Henry Flood, 2046 S. Hemberger st.; Solomon Cohen, 608 Emily st.; Girard Terjan, 6011 Locust st.; Louis Sicilia, 1550 Stevens st.; John Wright, 6815 Chester ave.; David Landsburg, 5811 Washington ave.; Leon Bojanowski, 2613 E. Madison st.; Richard Feeney, 19 S. 55th st.

MARINE CORPS

Lynn M. Brittingham, 3634 N. 15th st., who is serving with the Marines, has been promoted to corporal. Brittingham is only 18, but has had 14 months' service with the Leathernecks. He was a former student at Randolph Macon Military Academy, Front Royal, Va.

CORP. BRITTINGHAM

Lieutenant C. W. Osburn, 4328 Spruce st., was graduated from the officers' indoctrination course at the Fleet Marine Force Training Centre, Camp LeJeune, New River, N. C. The training included the staging of landing operations similar to those made by the Marines at Guadalcanal and other Southwest Pacific islands.

• • •

Corporal Lawrence McDonald, 7108 Keystone st., Frankford, is celebrating his 20th birthday with the U. S. Marine Corps on Guadalcanal Island.

• • •

The following Philadelphians are in basic training at Marine bases: Joseph Wyndal Rice, 4715 Walnut st., Patrick Michael Doyle, 46 W. Seymour st.; Victor N. Cutler, 4111 Leidy ave.; Clifford Thomas Beaver, 38 E. Bringhurst st.; Walter Howard Moore, 2243 N. Broad st.; Albert Brenner, 1616 Wingohocking st.; Arthur Carmen D'Angelo, 2056 Mountain st.; John DeLisi, 1625 S. Jessup st.; Warren H. Birchall, 6530 Tulip st.; Pasquale DiPilla, 1833 S. 22d st.; Curtis Eldredge, 107 N. 34th st.; John Emmet Decker, 1217 Overington st.; John Edward Dieter, 5103 N. 4th st.; Pascal Moraglia, 732 Christian st.; James Joseph Murray, 6161 Harley st.; Frank DiGioia, 3045 N. 23d st.; Charles Priestley, 7228 Charles st.; Emil Ragucci, 5839 Lena st.; Anthony T. Giba, 3949 Alfred st.; Joseph Burns, 3031 Memphis st.; James J. Keenan, Jr., 5538 Linmore ave.; Francis Sullivan, 2013 S. 65th st.; John J. Forester, 1625 S. Conestoga st.; Ernest Hubert, 1821 E. Harold st.; Sydney Axelrod, 606 S. 11th st.; James J. McShane, 423 S. 2d st.; Raymond Joseph McCormick, 239 Gates st., Manayunk; Francis E. Beach, 2007 E. Moyamensing ave.

JOS. WYNDAL RICE

The Philadelphia Inquirer

PUBLIC LEDGER

An Independent Newspaper for All the People

VOL. 228, NO. 38 | 10 Sections—132 Pages | a b c d e f g PHILADELPHIA, SUNDAY MORNING, FEBRUARY 7, 1943 | B | PRICE, TWELVE CENTS

Campaign Launched To Lift Rent Ceilings; Unions Fight Move

ERROL FLYNN ACQUITTED OF ALL CHARGES

Jury Deliberates Almost 24 Hours; Girls Unharmed, 9 Women Decide

Illustrated on Page 2

HOLLYWOOD, Feb. 6 (U. P.).—Nine conscientious housewives acquitted Errol Flynn of statutory rape charges today and left him free to resume his place as one of Hollywood's reigning movie stars.

There were three men on the jury, too, but they didn't count. The ladies, all comfortably married, went into a huddle and considered all the intimate medical testimony concerning the physical condition of Betty Hansen, 17, and Peggy Satterlee, 16, after their evenings with Flynn.

'WE TOLD THE MEN'

"And we decided," said Mrs. Ruby Anderson, the foreman, "that Mr. Flynn could not possibly have harmed these girls. Then we told the men, delicately of course, and they agreed with us."

That was that, and the jubilant Flynn struggled from the courthouse, like a reluctant Pied Piper, with a swarm of his feminine admirers clutching at his pin-striped coat tails, tugging on his lapels and fighting among themselves for the privilege of touching them.

"Wonderful news," sighed Flynn. "Just wonderful."

The jury had deliberated almost 24 hours after it received the case shortly before noon (3 P. M. E.W.T.) yesterday.

TOO NERVOUS TO LEAVE

Flynn had paced the halls of the courthouse nervously for 11 hours yesterday and for three more today, too jittery to go away and wait.

Mrs. Anderson announced the verdict, taking up first the charge preferred by Miss Hansen, who said Flynn attacked her in a Bel Air mansion, and then the two charges of Miss Satterlee, who insisted that the movie hero violated her twice aboard his yacht, Sirocco.

"Not guilty," said Mrs. Anderson. "Not guilty, and not guilty."

'FELT LIKE WHOOPING'

Flynn almost leaped out of his seat when Mrs. Anderson announced her final "not guilty."

"Gosh," he said afterward, "I felt like whooping."

Flynn had sat in court for almost a solid month hearing himself denounced by the State as a violator of young girls, who themselves told lurid tales of how he had undressed and attacked them.

"But this just goes to show," he said "that there is justice in the United States. And am I glad that I am now a citizen of this country."

The court was locked tight while the jury delivered its verdict. When the verdicts were recorded finally by Clerk E. C. Averre, Judge Leslie Still adjourned one of the longest trials of its kind in Los Angeles, and immediately the flash bulbs began to boom and crackle as photographers smashed them on the floor in their hurry to record Flynn's jubilation.

CHEER FOR FLYNN

The press corps dashed from the room as to a three-alarm fire, while the spectators cheered, crowded around the handsome Flynn and thumped his back.

The jury reached its verdict only 15 minutes before it entered the court.

Early yesterday all nine of the housewives and one of the men on the jury agreed that the movie hero was an honest man who told the truth when he said he had had no relations with either of the girls.

TWO JURORS OPPOSED

Two of the elderly men disagreed for hours until even Flynn's attorneys began to wonder whether the case would result in a hung jury. Jerry Giesler, known as one of America's most successful criminal lawyers, said he was "very happy for my client."

"I was convinced of his innocence and the jury's verdict bears out my contention," he said.

Giesler went down the line, shaking hands with each juror and introducing Flynn to every one. The ladies beamed.

The jurors said they tossed out Miss Hansen's charges at once, decided immediately to ignore Miss Satterlee's second accusation of being lured below to view the moon through a porthole, and began to wonder whether she was telling the truth about her first experiences, in which she said Flynn burst into her cabin.

UNDER A STRAIN

"But we finally decided that couldn't be true, either," said one of the feminine jurors.

They all agreed that they had

Continued on Page 2, Column 4

Germantown Man Found Hanged

David Finkelson, 26, hanged himself with his necktie from a closet door in his room at 6320 Norwood st., Germantown, shortly after 6 o'clock last night, according to police at the York road and Champlost ave. police station.

He was pronounced dead at Jewish Hospital. His mother, Mr. Anna Finkelson, told Detective William Arthur that her son had been despondent over illness since last summer.

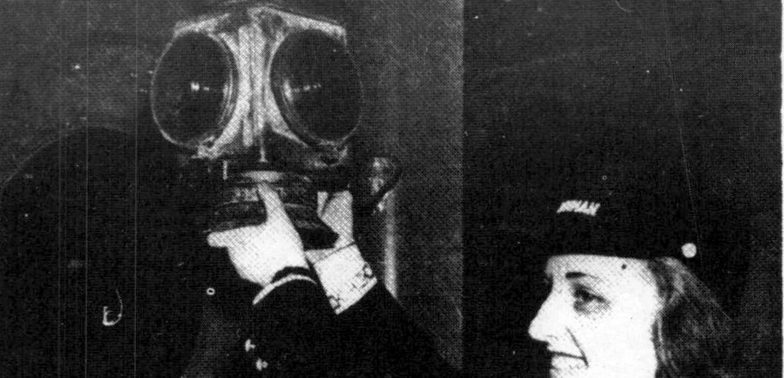

FIRST WOMAN TRAINMAN BEGINS WORK HERE

Miss Elizabeth B. Johns, of 1517 N. 56th st., first of a group of women who will replace passenger trainmen called into the armed forces, brushes up on the technique of hanging a marker lamp before she begins her duties on the Paoli Local out of the Pennsylvania Suburban Station yesterday. Two other women trainmen began work here yesterday, and 27 others are ready to start soon.

FIRST WOMEN START JOBS AS TRAINMEN; PUT ON PAOLI LOCAL

Three Attired In Natty Uniforms; 27 Others Hired

Swinging deftly aboard the 9.45 A. M. Paoli Local out of the Pennsylvania Suburban Station, Miss Elizabeth B. Johns, of 1517 N. 56th st., yesterday became the first woman to replace one of the line's passenger trainmen now in the armed forces.

Two other women, Miss Vera Ruth Demmer, of 306 Cooper st., Camden, and Miss Ethel P. Moore, of 4120 Parrish st., this city, were assigned to similar service on other Paoli Locals during the day.

NATTILY ATTIRED

All were nattily attired in blue coats with the P. R. R. insignia on the lapels, plain blue skirts, white shirts, four-in-hand black ties and blue "trainman's type" hats. A topcoat, quite similar to their male confreres', completed the uniform.

Twenty-seven other women have completed training courses and will be placed on suburban trains and Baltimore and Harrisburg locals as soon as they are equipped with uniforms, the railroad announced.

The women perform the regular trainman's duties of collecting tickets, helping passengers on and off, calling stations and checking signals and switches. "All are over 21," a P. R. R. spokesman said.

Woman Stabbed to Death

An unidentified colored woman, about 30, was found stabbed to death under the ramp of the Pennsylvania Railroad on Washington ave. near 25th st. yesterday afternoon. Authorities at Graduate Hospital said she apparently had been attacked several hours before.

Victory Gardens

The Inquirer Provides Seed-to-Harvest Tips For Urban 'Farmers'

A full page of garden news, hints to amateur growers and other items of interest to garden enthusiasts on Page 11 of the Society Section of The Inquirer today.

By GAY CHURCHILL

Are you a farmer at heart? Have you an empty back yard? Is there a vacant lot near your house? Have you a spade? A trowel? An energetic pair of hands?

Then you're a victory gardener.

The city has set a goal of 30,000 vegetable patches this year but no one will prevent you and your friends tripling that figure.

Every defense and horticultural agency will go out of its way to help you fill the icebox with home-grown edibles.

On the Garden Feature page of today's Society Section of The Inquirer, Jane Leslie Kift, its gardening consultant, offers timely information on the subject. Beginning Feb. 21, in both the daily and Sunday editions of this newspaper, she will explain the A B C's of planting for the unversed enthusiast. Meanwhile, tips on seed-to-harvest cultivation are to be found in her column on the Women's Page.

TENANTS TO GET TRACTS

Lending a hand to the vital wartime project, the Philadelphia Housing Authority announced yesterday that it will place Victory Garden tracts at the disposal of tenants in the city's seven housing projects.

James B. Kelly, the authority's executive director, estimated that about 2500 of the 5500 tenants would signify their intention of growing vegetable gardens. He added that "we are arranging classes on gardening practice to be conducted by specialists from the U. S. and Pennsylvania Departments of Agricul-

Continued on Page 5, Column 2

In Today's Sunday Inquirer

COMPROMISE ASKED ON INCOME LIMIT

By HUGH MORROW
Inquirer Washington Bureau

WASHINGTON, Feb. 6.—Republicans on the House Ways and Means Committee today swung behind a Democrat's proposal to end "confiscation" of net salary earnings above $25,000 a year under an order of President Roosevelt.

The plan would limit at pre-Pearl Harbor levels all salaries which were above the Presidential ceiling before the Japanese attack plunged the Nation into war. It would also provide that salaries below the present ceiling could not be raised above that level.

DEBT ACTION POSTPONED

Representative Wesley E. Disney (D., Okla.) submitted the proposal at a closed meeting of the House Committee, at which action on a bill to raise the national debt limit to $210,000,000,000 was postponed for the second time when it became evident that a bi-partisan coalition was determined to attach a rider repealing the President's salary limitation order.

The ten committee Republicans, at a conference following the meeting, agreed to support the Disney proposal and in effect abandon a plan to lift the high-salary lid entirely. It was pointed out that the latter program would strengthen the hand of John L. Lewis, United Mine Workers' union chief, in his current attempt to wreck the so-called Little Steel formula limiting wage increases.

GEARHART BACKS PLAN

Representative Bertrand W. Gearhart, (R., Calif.), sponsor of an outright repealer of the President's salary limit, agreed to join in support of the Disney plan, which Disney said would impose limitations "by Congressional authority instead of executive confiscation."

Authority which the Treasury now possesses would prevent any excessive salary increases within the ceilings, Disney said.

Supporters of the Disney pro-

Continued on Page 4, Column 5

CURFEW LOOMS IN WAR AGAINST DISEASE, VICE

New Weapon Chosen In Effort to Curb Night Life Evils; Conference Called

A curfew on night life may be imposed in Philadelphia as a public health measure, it was indicated yesterday by Dr. Hubley R. Owen, director of Public Health.

Dr. Owen revealed that plans would be laid this week to wage an "all-out" war against night clubs and bars where conditions affect both industrial workers and military personnel.

The curfew would climax the months-old drive to "clean up" the city, marked by the padlocking of "Barbary Coast" taprooms and the more recent raids on clubs and disorderly houses and would be imposed for these major reasons:

1. To reduce the danger of tuberculosis among industrial workers whose health is endangered by rounds of "night life" after long hours at work.

2. To check a rising rate in juvenile delinquency. Police say many of the night spots are frequented by girls 16 and under.

3. To cut down on absenteeism at war plants, caused by workers who stay out too late at night and are unable to go on the job in the morning.

4. To help Army and Navy officials to maintain their standards for personnel.

In emphasizing that some stringent regulations would have to be put into effect to control the leisure-hour habits of workers and service men, Dr. Owen intimated that the city might consider a curfew such as is now enforced in England.

BRITISH CURFEW AT 10.30

British pubs, the equivalent of taprooms in this country, are closed at 10.30 P. M., he said, and night clubs are closed at an early hour.

During his recent trip to England, Dr. Owen said, he was told by health authorities the curfew was made a law because of an alarming increase of tuberculosis.

"War work wears down the workers' resistance," Dr. Owen declared, "and with additional hours of night life, we fear there can be a great increase in tuberculosis here as in England.

MENACE TO WOMEN

"Women, especially, are affected by the menace."

Dr. Owen said he will meet this week with members of the Philadelphia Hotel Association, Philadelphia Liquor Dealers' Association, Restaurant Association, officials of the State Liquor Control Board, Army and Navy officials, vice squad detectives and representatives of C. I. O. and A. F. L. labor unions.

The time and place of the meeting was not disclosed.

The meeting was suggested by Charles F. Todd, president of the Philadelphia Hotel Association, who wrote to Dr. Owen Friday offering the co-operation of the city's hotel men in improving conditions.

"We feel that perhaps a meeting with the officials, which would include all the hotels, restaurants, retail liquor dealers and all types of bars and clubs, for a frank and open discussion of the situation, might be of assistance in arriving at a means of improving conditions and making the city a safer and more desirable place for men in uniform and others

Continued on Page 3, Column 3.

'Another Work Day' For LaFollette, 48

WASHINGTON, Feb. 6 (A. P.).—Its "just another work day" for Senator Robert M. La Follette, Jr., Wisconsin Progressive, 48 years old today.

La Follette is serving his 18th year in the Senate—exceeded in length of service by only nine Senators, Ellison D. Smith (D., S. C.), Kenneth McKellar (D., Tenn.), Hiram W. Johnson (R., Calif.), Charles L. McNary R., Ore.), Arthur Capper)R., Kan.), Carter Glass (D., Va.), Walter F. George (D., Ga.), Henrik Shipstead (R., Minn.), and Burton K. Wheeler D., Mont.).

Coffee Rush Continues Here Despite Plentiful Stocks

Stores handling coffee were having another of their "ration rushes" yesterday as the deadline for the latest coupon approached.

The No. 28 coupon becomes void at midnight tonight, and the No. 25 becomes effective Monday—good only for a pound for six weeks this time. Previous allowances had been a pound for five weeks, so that the new ration constitutes a one-sixth decrease in the amount allowed to each user.

HAS RESERVE STOCK

One large store in the mid-city section which deals exclusively in coffee, tea and spices reported late in the day that it still was able to supply customers and had some reserve on hand.

This appeared to be typical of the situation at all shops of its kind, but the rush on the reserves became greater hourly. Managers said that the increase in sales since last Thursday was as great as 100 percent.

INCREASES REPORTED

Chain stores reported "some increase," but apparently had experienced a less heavy demand than the coffee houses. Drug stores handling coffee were either completely out of their supply or able to handle only 75 or 80 percent of the demand.

For the time, at least, restaurants were not troubled by the rationing problem, since most of them already had stocked up on their allowance for the period—and were still giving one cup to a customer.

UNITED WAR CHEST LABOR RETURNS		
LABOR GROUP	REPORTED TO DATE	PERCENTAGE OF MEMBERS SUBSCRIBING
UNITED ELEC. RADIO & MACH. WORKERS, CIO LOCAL 107 (WESTINGHOUSE)	$9,318	12%
FEDERAL LABOR UNION, AFL (MIDVALE STEEL EMPLOYEES)	$58,670	94%
UNITED STEEL WORKERS, CIO, LOCALS 2443, 2180, 1278, 2844 (BALDWIN LOCOMOTIVE WORKS)	$61,406	57%
BUILDING TRADES COUNCIL, AFL	$70,000	74%
UNITED AUTO. WORKERS #365, C.I.O. (BREWSTER AERONAUTICS)	$31,000	70%
TEAMSTERS JOINT COUNCIL, AFL	$58,584	55%
UNITED ELEC. RADIO & MACH. WORKERS, CIO LOCAL 105 (INT'L. RESISTANCE CO.)	$7,324	66%
INTL. LADIES' GARMENT WORKERS, AFL	$40,000	100%
UNITED ELEC. RADIO & MACH. WORKERS, CIO BROWN INSTRUMENT CO.	$1,327	50%
TAXI DRIVERS #156, AFL.	$14,400	96%
UNITED RETAIL WHOLESALE & DENTAL SERVICE UNION, C.I.O., LOCAL 349 (350 MEMBERS)	$6,037 FINAL	100%
LAUNDRY WORKERS #10, AFL	$9,227	54%
FURNITURE WORKERS #37, CIO	$2,848	35%
MEMBERS OF FEDERAL LABOR UNION NO. 22254, A. F. L. AND OTHER EMPLOYEES OF HENRY DISSTON & SONS	$22,178	72%
UNITED ELEC. RADIO & MACH. WORKERS, CIO LOCAL 119 (GENERAL ELECTRIC WORKS)	$60,560 FINAL	96%
JOINT BAKERY COUNCIL, A.F.L.	$6,845	30%
UNITED HATTERS, #60, AFL (JOHN B. STETSON CO.)	$10,175	75%

War Chest Volunteers Seek to Reach 80 Pct. Of Goal by Tonight

By JOSEPH F. VAN HART

In the home stretch of their $7,300,000 drive, volunteer workers of the United War Chest are redoubling their efforts this week-end to reach 80 percent of their goal by tonight.

At the last War Chest report luncheon, it was announced that $5,201,599 had been received in cash and pledges, representing 71.3 percent of the goal.

David E. Williams, general chairman of the campaign, warned that 80 percent should be attained by tonight if the full quota is to be reached by Thursday night, when the drive officially ends.

SHARE THE SPOTLIGHT

"Unless this is done, the campaign has little opportunity for success," Williams said. "And failure means that some child will go homeless, some service man unaided, some mother and child in China or Europe unfed."

Meanwhile, executives and "white collar" workers of Philadelphia business and industry shared the spotlight with corporations and organized labor in support of the drive.

K. B. Montgomery, War Chest chairman of the Indemnity Insurance Company of North America, reported incomplete returns of $12,682 from employees there, an average of more than $12 a worker.

FIGURE DOUBLED

"Last year the employees gave just short of $5000 to the United Charities Campaign," Montgomery said. "With returns not yet complete, last year's figure has been more than doubled."

Other groups reporting substantial increases this year include:

McDowell Paper Mills, executives, $70 last year, $140 this year; Pennsylvania Title Insurance Co., executives and employees, $1577 last year, $2317 this year; Roosevelt Bank, executives and employees, from $222 to $710; Haskins & Sells, executives, from $150 to $300.

Frank & Seder, firm, executives and employees, from $1464 to $3176;

Continued on Page 4, Column 3

3 Bills Before Congress

By HERMAN A. LOWE
Inquirer Washington Bureau

WASHINGTON, Feb. 6.—Federal rent control as it exists today is under heavy fire in Congress, with a fair possibility that some of the stabilization strong points may be destroyed by law before many months have passed.

Three bills already have been introduced in the House of Representatives which would have the effect of emasculating to a greater or lesser degree the rent ceilings placed into effect in 355 areas of the country by the Office of Price Administration.

INVESTIGATIONS ASKED

In addition, two Congressmen have called for investigations of the Federal rent regulations—one investigation to look into the problem on a nation-wide basis, the other to study operations in Akron, O.

Real estate interests, led by groups of apartment house owners' associations, are spearheading a pressure drive on Capitol Hill to lift the lid on rents. Already every member of the Senate and House has received a handsome brochure which contends that the rent regulations are doing a grave injustice to property owners.

TENANTS ARE SILENT

Meanwhile, the tenants who were crying out actively for rent ceilings a year ago appear to be either unaware or indifferent to the campaign aimed at their pocketbooks.

The nearest thing to a man on a white horse galloping down the pike to arouse them to the impending fight have been some of the labor unions who have lined up behind Paul A. Porter, Rent Administrator of the OPA.

N. A. M. OPPOSED

And, oddly enough, considerable concern has been expressed by the National Association of Manufacturers. But perhaps this is not so odd, for the manufacturers know better than anyone else that to take the lid off rents would mean tremendous pressure from the working man for increased wages.

OPA, too, is deeply concerned but, being an administrative agency, must mark time and wait its turn to be called to Capitol Hill to give testimony when the House Banking and Currency Committee begins hearings on the bills.

NO DATES SCHEDULED

Chairman Henry B. Steagall (D., Ala.) of the committee said today he had not yet scheduled hearings on the measures but that dates would probably be set within the next week or 10 days.

Most important and far-reaching of the bills is the one introduced by Representative Fred L. Crawford (R., Mich.). The others were dropped in the hopper by Representative Jesse P. Wolcott (R., Mich.) and Representative Harry R. Sheppard (R., Calif.).

ACTIVE IN 2 STATES

The nationwide investigation of OPA rent activities has been asked by Representative Thomas Rolph (R., Calif.).

Apartment house owners' activities against the rent ceilings have centered in Michigan and California.

Perhaps the rent ceiling provision under the heaviest attack is the one which requires landlords to file with OPA district offices their ceiling rents so that no tenant should have any question in his mind about what the legal rent is. This, according to OPA officials, is one of the keystones of the entire rent control program.

Violations of the rent ceilings on file are one of the things that OPA can smash down easily and quickly.

CALLED UNFAIR

Curiously enough, the Congressmen seem to feel this provision is unfair to landlords and should be done away with.

The Wolcott bill would do away with the triple damage section of the

Continued on Page 4, Column 6

Knife Suspect Flees After Arraignment

John Allison, 48, 23d st. near Montgomery ave., escaped from a washroom yesterday a few minutes after he was ordered held in $800 bail for the Grand Jury on a charge of threats to kill with a knife.

Magistrate Joseph H. Rainey, before whom Allison was arraigned at 3120 N. Broad st., said the prisoner had been arrested earlier yesterday on complaint of Ollie Hall, Negro, of the 23d st. address.

Allison, a Negro, crawled out of a washroom window into an alleyway and then vaulted a seven-foot iron fence and disappeared. A constable was waiting outside the washroom door.

Gen. Marshall's Plea For Bigger Army Wins Congressional Backing

WASHINGTON, Feb. 10 (A. P.).—Chairman Andrew J. May (D. Ky.) of the House Military Affairs Committee declared today that General George C. Marshall, Army chief of staff, in a discussion with legislators, "unquestionably" had justified the Army's need for increased manpower.

In a private meeting today with about 50 members of the House and Senate, Marshall was reported to have outlined the progress of American military campaigns and to have explained the need for further increases in personnel which some legislators said would boost the Army's total to 8,200,000 men by the end of this year.

WINS SUPPORT

Several Senators and House members said they were impressed by the clear way in which Marshall outlined the military necessities. Senator A. B. Chandler (D., Ky.) commented:

"It would be a tragic mistake not to give General Marshall all of the men he needs to do the job."

On the other hand, Senator Gerald P. Nye (R., N. D.), who has urged that military personnel not be increased too speedily lest it disrupt the home front war effort, told reporters he thought he read into Marshall's remarks the possibility of some reduction in manpower demands under the goal which would place more than 11,000,000 persons in the armed forces by the year's close.

FOOD SHORTAGE FEARED

Some legislators have been pressing for a reduction in the military manpower goals in order to assure additional workers on the farms.

One of these, Senator Sheridan Downey (D., Calif.), who attended the conference, said he had not changed his opinion that the military forces could not exceed 9,000,000 men without curtailing production of foodstuffs and war materials at home.

7.44 PCT. OF ARMY COMES FROM PENNA.

Inquirer Washington Bureau

WASHINGTON, Feb. 10.—Pennsylvania, with the second largest population in the United States, also has contributed the second highest share of men between the ages of 18 and 45 to armed service, the Office of War Information revealed today.

Pennsylvania accounts for 7.53 percent of the total population, 7.52 percent of total U. S. registrants, and 7.44 percent of all men in the armed services.

NEW YORK IN LEAD

New York leads the list of States with 10.25 percent of the population, 10.48 percent of total registrants, and 10.93 percent of all men in the services.

Enlistments by Pennsylvania men, however, accounted for only 7.01 percent of all enlistments, putting Pennsylvania third on the list of States, with New York first and California second.

JOB DEFERMENTS

Occupational deferments in Pennsylvania were slightly above the national average, which is 4.12 percent of total registrants; in Pennsylvania 4.24 percent were deferred on those grounds.

Pennsylvania is below the national average for deferments for mental, moral, or physical reasons. Nationally, 8.38 of all registrants have been deferred for these reasons and cast into 4-F. In Pennsylvania, 8.20 percent of the registrants are classed as mentally, morally, or physically unfit.

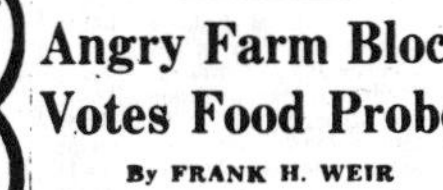

(A. P. Wirephoto)

BRIGADIER GENERAL HOLDING HIS CHIEF'S COAT

General George C. Marshall, Army chief of staff, putting on his scarf after testifying before Congressional committees yesterday while Brigadier General Wilton P. Persons stands by with his chief's coat. General Marshall is reported to have told of the Army's need for further increases in personnel.

Angry Farm Bloc Votes Food Probe

By FRANK H. WEIR

Continued From First Page

mend passage of a bill which would, in effect, increase parity prices by forbidding the Government to deduct any other benefit payments made to farmers in fixing the parity formula. The author of the bill, Senator John H. Bankhead (D., Ala.), predicted the Senate would pass it shortly.

SEEKS FINAL ACTION

(Parity is designed to give the farm population the same relative purchasing power it had in a past favorable period, usually 1909-1914.)

In the House, Representative Stephen Page (D., Ga.), author of a bill to raise parity prices by having them include the increased cost of farm labor since 1909-14, sought approval from the Rules Committee to send his measure to the floor for final action.

COSTS WOULD INCREASE

The committee will probably consider Pace's bill, which has already been approved by the House Agriculture Committee, next Wednesday. Administration experts estimate the bill would increase the cost of food by as much as 10 percent.

Pace and leaders of the Senate farm bloc vigorously assailed Byrnes' attitude on farm prices, as well as his "compulsory back-to-the-farm" plan to force former farm workers to give up jobs in industry under penalty of losing their deferments for military service.

"We face the possibility of a national disaster on food unless farmers obtain adequate labor, equipment and fair prices," Pace declared.

Senator Elmer Thomas (D., Okla.) insisted Byrnes' speech "will have an adverse effect on farm production."

48-HR. WEEK ORDER STUDIED FOR PHILA.

By HERMAN A. LOWE

Continued From First Page

labor committee of both the War Production board and WMC, called for a Nation-wide 48-hour work week in all industries.

GREEN BACKS ORDER

William Green, president of the A.F.L., indorsed the President's 48-hour week proclamation, but asserted he would oppose lengthening the work week beyond 48 hours because it would result in lowering productive efficiency. Philip Murray, president of the C.I.O., and John L. Lewis, president of the United Mine Workers, did not comment.

The Department of Agriculture announced that in the near future it would launch a recruiting program in important counties producing perishable fruits and vegetables for the canning industry. Workers will be recruited locally to aid in harvesting and processing the crops.

FARM LABOR IS PROBLEM

The farm labor program continues the most difficult facing the War Manpower Commission. While a 48-hour work week can step up production substantially in most industrial areas, farmers already work longer than that during their season.

The only answer is more men for the farms. To date, the WMC labor policy is based on the principle of keeping people at work in the areas in which they are located.

To supply farm labor it will be necessary to transport men, women and youths from one area to another. WMC has been side-stepping the issue, but must face it soon. Under discussion is the proposition of returning to farms industrial workers who came from farms, even though this will mean a sharp drop in their earnings.

Also studied is moving non-deferrable men in cities to farms, and recruiting city youths and women for agriculture.

PLANS FACE PRESSURE

While general reaction to the Government's home front program enunciated last night favored the 48-hour week policy, it appeared that the accompanying anti-inflation program faced strong pressure.

Green protested the Administration's determination to permit no wage increases except under the "Little Steel" formula of the War Labor Board, and there was nothing to indicate that other labor leaders were ready to relax their opposition to the formula.

FARM BLOC OPPOSITION

The "Little Steel" formula prevents hourly wage increases, except in extraordinary cases of more than 15 percent above the level of Jan. 1, 1941.

The policy of maintaining price ceilings also faced opposition, especially from the farm bloc and from businesses whose costs might be forced up by overtime pay necessitated by the 48-hour week.

Give to the United War Chest . . . to our less-fortunate neighbors, to our service men and to innocent victims of Axis brutality!

Rep. Scott Asks Army To Accept Interns

Inquirer Washington Bureau

WASHINGTON, Feb. 10.—Although the Pennsylvania Legislature is expected to reduce medical students' internship period in that State from 12 months to nine, the Army has failed to arrange for commissioning such students in the Medical Corps, Representative Hugh D. Scott, Jr. (R.), of Philadelphia, told the House today.

"This is a waste of highly skilled manpower, desperately needed, and is most difficult to understand," Scott said. "Why doesn't the Army adopt a procedure similar to that of the Navy, which will permit the immediate commissioning of interns after nine months and will combine the usual naval indoctrination period with three months of intern training at a naval hospital?"

48-Hour Week Explained

Questions and Answers On Roosevelt Job Order

WASHINGTON, Feb. 10 (U. P.).—The following questions and answers were published by the War Manpower Commission tonight to explain operation of the 48-hour work week ordered by President Roosevelt as a national wartime policy:

Q. Does this order apply to everyone in the country?

A. At the outset, the War Manpower Commission is making it mandatory in 32 designated labor shortage areas. Other industrial areas will be added as labor shortages become acute.

Q. Does it apply to everyone in these areas?

A. To all full-time employment. Part-time workers and self-employed persons, however, have an obligation to their country and themselves to produce as much as they can for the war.

Q. Should firms in other areas today to go on the 48-hour-week?

A. Yes, if by so doing they can reduce their labor requirements and not have to discharge workers now on their payroll.

Q. Must time and one-half be paid for all time over 40?

A. Yes, but no change is made in any collective bargaining agreement as to the rate of overtime pay. The order, of course, abrogates labor contracts restricting the work-week to less than 48 hours in shortage areas.

Q. What about jobs, such as farm workers and domestics, not covered by the Wage-Hour Act?

A. The order does not require overtime pay for these people.

Q. Should a store or office now working employees less than 48 hours go up to 48 at once?

A. Yes, but only if the change results in more effective use of employees or would avert employment of additional persons.

Q. When is the order effective?

A. In shortage areas it is effective immediately and workers should be paid overtime as it is instituted. However, the WMC has asked employers to bring their work-week up to 48 hours by March 31 or to advise how long the changeover will require.

Q. Does the order apply to establishments whose hours are limited by State law?

A. No.

Q. Who handles local problems involving plants, unions and employers?

A. Area or regional officials of the WMC.

Q. If an employer is recalcitrant, how can the order be enforced?

A. All departments and agencies of the Government will require contractors to comply. The U. S. Employment Service will refuse to refer new workers to any employer refusing to comply. Smaller establishments probably will comply for patriotic or economic reasons.

Q. Suppose an employer or worker contends the longer week is impossible in his plant or shop?

A. The WMC will investigate to make possible exemptions.

Q. Does the order apply to coal miners, most of whom have a 35-hour work-week under contract?

A. No coal-mining centres are included in the initially-designated areas.

Q. How much additional productive power will be made available?

A. No statistics are available but a 48-hour week in all industries and areas where it would result in maximum use of labor probably would add the equivalent of 1,000,000 men to the labor force.

Q. Will the longer week be applied to steel mills in shortage areas and not in Pittsburgh, which is not listed?

A. This will be decided after WMC investigation and consultation with the industry.

Q. Will prices be raised to offset increased production costs?

A. That is governed by Office of Price Administration regulations but it is unlikely that more than a small fraction will be added to costs.

Q. Does the order apply to newspapers, laundries and retail stores?

A. Yes, in the critical areas.

Q. What about one-man business and professional people?

A. Self-employed persons are not regarded as employees.

Q. If an employer increases the work-week but declines to raise weekly pay, what can the worker do?

A. Employers governed by the Wage-Hour Act are required to pay overtime. Those not covered are likely to lose workers if they refuse to pay.

Q. Should State and local governments adopt the 48-hour week?

A. Yes, if their employees' hours are not fixed by statute.

Q. Will large pay checks for employees be inflationary?

A. No, because of the great production needs of the war; because the workers will produce more; because the work in any given plant will be spread out among fewer employees; and because price ceilings and wartime limits on luxury goods production will prevent workers from excessive and inflationary spending. In addition, income taxes will recapture part of the added income.

WMC AIDE SAYS CITY WILL GET 48-HR. WK.

Philadelphia will eventually come under the 48-hour work week which at present is affecting much of the rest of the Nation, Louis B. F. Raycroft, regional director of the War Manpower Commission for Pennsylvania, New Jersey and Delaware, said last night.

Speaking at a meeting of the Central Labor Union, Spring Garden st. near 18th, he said, in response to a question from the floor that he "couldn't see how Philadelphia could avoid the situation."

WAR CONTRACTS HEAVY

"When it will happen," he said, "I cannot predict, but it is in point that war contracts are heavy."

Earlier in the day labor leaders here had voiced the opinion that if and when the 48-hour work week is extended to this city the results will be negligible, since many workers are already working beyond the 40-hour week.

In his talk, Raycroft said that by May there will be an additional need in war industries of 71,720 new workers, and by November the number will increase to 109,000.

MOST WORK 45 HOURS

He said there was no need at present to adopt a "controlled hiring plan" here, but that such a need might develop in the future.

The meeting came at the close of a day in which various labor leaders voiced opinions on the situation. George Craig, C.I.O. regional director said that the average work week for C.I.O. members was 45 hours.

"If the President's order were to be extended to Philadelphia," said Thomas Mallon, regional director of the A. F. L. unions, "we would be a couple of steps ahead of him. All A. F. L. unions in this area were geared long ago to the 48-hour week, to expedite war production."

Workers End Strike At Trenton Plant

Special to The Inquirer

TRENTON, Feb. 10.—A walkout of approximately 1000 workers in several departments of the John A. Roebling's Sons Co., cable manufacturers, in protest over inaction by the War Labor Board on the employees' request for a wage increase, was reported "settled" by company officials tonight.

The employees, a spokesman for the company said, stopped work "for a short time" after noon yesterday in a demonstration against several months' delay by the WLB in acting on their request for a five-and-one-half-cent per hour increase. An official of the C.I.O., which represents the workers, said the strike was unauthorized. The company spokesman expressed the belief that everyone would be back to work by tomorrow.

SHORT-WEEK PACTS WITH UNIONS VOID

WMC Says 48-Hour Decree Ends Such Labor Contracts

WASHINGTON, Feb. 10 (A. P.).—The War Manpower Commission announced tonight that the 48-hour minimum work week order abrogates in the areas affected any labor contract provisions which call for a shorter working period.

In a statement clarifying the effect of President Roosevelt's order, which it is charged with enforcing, the WMC also said:

INDUSTRY-WIDE BASIS

Payment of time and one-half overtime compensation for work over 40 hours a week will not be required for some workers. These include farm workers, domestic servants and others for whom such compensation is not provided by wage-hour laws or individual or collective bargaining agreements.

A "few industries" may be put under terms of the order on an industry-wide rather than an area basis where plants in areas not affected by the order would gain a competitive advantage in labor costs over plants in affected areas.

MAY EXEMPT SOME

"Some" hazardous occupations or industry may be exempted.

While the Office of Price Administration will determine if price ceilings should be lifted to cover increase in labor costs resulting from the order, "it is unlikely that increased labor cost will add more than a small fraction to the cost of production."

State and local governments should adopt the 48-hour week unless their hours of work are fixed by State or local laws. The order will not apply to establishments, such as bars in many States, whose hours are limited by State law.

WILL PROBE COMPLAINTS

When employers or workers contend the 48-hour week is "impossible" for them, the WMC "will investigate and make exceptions or exemptions so as to make possible the fullest possible contribution to the war."

In deciding such cases, the WMC will bear in mind that "the purpose of the order is to release workers for war and essential jobs. Mere increase of hours that will not result in this was not intended."

Drug Laboratories Get 'E' Award

Illustrated on Page 14

Employees of the Sharpe and Dohme pharmaceutical laboratories in this city and Glenolden were awarded the Army-Navy "E" at ceremonies here and in the Delaware county community.

The pennant was presented at both ceremonies by Brigadier General Hugh Jackson Morgan, chief consultant in medicine, Office of the Surgeon-General, U. S. Army. The Navy was represented by Commander E. L. Borts, U. S. N. R., of the Naval Hospital here.

In making the presentation to the 2500 employees of the two plants, General Morgan lauded "the pioneer work of this company in developing the methods and equipment necessary for the production of dried human blood plasma" as one of the "outstanding contributions of biological manufacturing . . . which already has saved the lives of many soldiers, sailors and Marines."

Phila. Firm Loses Its Army-Navy 'E'

A falling off in production at the I. T. E. Circuit Breaker Co. plant at 19th and Hamilton sts. has resulted in the firm's being denied a renewal of the Army-Navy's 'E,' it was stated at the Navy Public Relations Office yesterday. The award for excellence was made Aug. 10, and a company official said last night that "we hope to get the award back."

"This flag was awarded for a six-month period on a basis of production," said a Navy spokesman. "The production was not maintained and the award was not renewed. The employees are entitled to retain, but not to wear, the lapel insignia."

Wage-Hour Violations Cost Ribbon Concern $65,000 in Fine, Pay

Denouncing the company's practices as "medieval and disgraceful," Federal Judge J. Cullen Ganey yesterday fined the General Ribbon Mills, Inc., of Catasauqua, Pa., $15,000 for violations of the Federal Wage-Hour Law and ordered it to make restitution of $50,000 to its employees.

The two criminal informations against the company contained 158 counts, the greatest number filed against any defendant since enactment of the law. They also involved the largest number of child labor violations.

EXECUTIVE PAYS $65,000

Joseph W. Stark, vice president of the company, entered a plea of guilty, immediately paid the fine, and deposited a check with the court for $50,000, which will go to 1500 women employees as back pay.

The Government charged that the company forced workers to enter in their handbooks false entries of hours worked. It accused the company of permitting the use of children from 7 to 11 years of age to aid their mothers with piece work at home and of paying many workers 15 cents an hour instead of the regulation 30 cents.

In his sharp criticism of the company, Judge Ganey asserted that "I hope to see the day when the Government will bring the individuals responsible for conditions like these into court as defendants, rather than their corporations."

Navy Yard Plans Mass Launching

Six pre-fabricated steel tank landing ships will be christened today at the Philadelphia Navy Yard in the second mass launching of this type of vessel to be completed here in three months. The ceremonies are to begin at 9 A. M. and the schedule calls for a ship to slide down the ways at half-hour intervals.

Relatives of Navy Yard employees will be sponsors. They were chosen by lot, and each of the women will receive a gold watch from employees' associations. The sponsors are:

Miss Ruth Stout, Ashton and Welsh roads, Holmesburg; Mrs. John Clarke, 2727 S. Mervine st.; Mrs. Arthur Taylor, 107 S. Brown st., Gloucester, N. J.; Miss Mildred E. Kelly, 65 Pitman ave., Pitman, N. J.; Miss Helen B. Higgins, 734 Ashurst road, Upper Darby, and Mrs. Catherine Entwistle, 2929 Wharton st.

Big Nations Must End Exploitation of Weak, Madame Chiang Says

NEW YORK, March 2 (A. P.).—A future in which "this whole world must be thought of as one great state common to gods and men" was held out tonight by Mme. Chiang Kai-shek as the goal of the United Nations.

The wife of China's generalissimo, in an address at a mass meeting in her honor in Madison Square Garden, urged also the necessity of forgiveness for the enemy because "there must be no bitterness in the reconstructed world."

Mme. Chiang was introduced to a cheering crowd of 17,000 by Wendell Willkie as "an avenging angel" seeking the freedom of her people.

STRESSES DIGNITY OF MAN

Asking "what are we going to make of the future?" and "what will the revalescing world, 'recovering from this hideous blood-letting, be like?" Mme. Chiang answered:

"The wisest minds in every corner of the world are pondering over these questions, and the wisest of all reserve their opinion. But, without letting temerity outrun discretion, I venture to say that certain things must be recognized. Never again must the dignity of man be outraged as it has been since the dawn of history.

'EQUAL OPPORTUNITY'

"All nations, great and small, must have equal opportunity of development. Those who are stronger and more advanced should consider their strength as a trust to be used to help the weaker nations to fit themselves for full self-government and not to exploit them. Exploitation is spiritually as degrading to the exploiter as to the exploited.

"Then, too, there must be no bitterness in the reconstructed world. No matter what we have undergone and suffered, we must try to forgive those who injured us and remember only the lesson gained thereby . . .

PLEADS FOR UNITY

"Finally, in order that this war may indeed be the war to end all wars in all ages, and that nations, great and small alike, may be allowed to live and let live in peace, security and freedom in the generations to come, co-operation in the true and highest sense of the word must be practiced.

GEN. ARNOLD SPEAKS

Speakers at the meeting were the Governors of nine New England and Middle Atlantic States, Wendell Willkie, John D. Rockefeller, Jr., Mayor La Guardia of New York, Lieutenant Commander Mildred H. McAfee of the WAVES, David Dubinsky of the International Ladies' Garment Workers Union, Dr. Henry Sloane Coffin and Lieutenant General H. H. Arnold.

General Arnold said wide-scale bombing of Japan "to insure the total destruction of this enemy on his own soil" was the goal of the U. S. Army Air Forces.

PENNA. AID PLEDGED

"Ultimately, our aerial operations in the Pacific must call for—and we must be ready for—wide-scale bombing of Japan itself, bombing of Japanese plane factories, rail centres, shipyards, munitions dumps and docks, bombing day after day and night after night, bombing with complete and utter havoc, bombing to insure the total destruction of this enemy on his own soil," Arnold declared.

Governor Edward Martin of Pennsylvania said: "What China needs, Pennsylvania can and will produce. This is no idle boast. Pennsylvania is among the greatest arsenals of liberty. It produces more than one-fourth of the critical war items used by the United Nations."

If you should lose your sugar ration book, oil or gas coupons, advertise in The Inquirer for quick recovery. Phone Miss Allen, Rittenhouse 5000.

U.S. PILOTS IN CHINA BLAST TROOPS, TUGS

CHUNGKING, China, March 2 (A. P.).—American planes, supporting Chinese troops in their stand on the Salween front in southwestern China, have smashed a number of Japanese tugs, ferry installations, motor convoys and troop concentrations in a series of raids, a communique from Lieutenant General Joseph W. Stilwell's headquarters announced today.

Between Feb. 11 and 17 Warhawk P-40's strafed barges and tugs near Bhamo in Burma, ferry installations and trucks near Lungling along the Burma road, a motor convoy near Wanliakwa and barracks at Laochai, the communique said.

(A. P. Wirephoto)

PHILADELPHIA WAAC INTERVIEWING SPAHI SENTRIES

Sergeant Anne Bradley, of Philadelphia, second from left, and her comrades shown as they learn some African lore from Spahi sentries outside General Henri Giraud's headquarters somewhere in North Africa. The other two WAACs are Auxiliary Joyce Smith, left, of Des Moines, Ia., and Auxiliary Teresa Pike, of Indianapolis. Sergeant Bradley is the daughter of Mr. and Mrs. Joseph Bradley, 4910 N. 12th st. They last heard from her in January.

KNOX VOWS DEATH OF JAPANESE FLEET

By JOHN M. McCULLOUGH
Inquirer Washington Bureau

WASHINGTON, March 2.—The total destruction of the Japanese fleet will be accomplished before the end of the Pacific War, Secretary of the Navy Frank Knox declared before the Senate Foreign Relations Committee today.

Furthermore, he asserted, peace terms probably will be imposed which will spell the doom of Japan as a sea Power.

DOESN'T DESERVE FLEET

Japan "has exhibited that she is not qualified to have a fleet," Knox declared bluntly.

Knox appeared before the committee this morning to urge continuance of the Lease-Lend Act for another year.

The Navy Department this afternoon announced the sinking of five more enemy vessels by United States submarines in the Pacific and in Far Eastern waters, and the damaging of two others.

SUB TOTAL NOW 133

Since December 7, 1941—the date of the Pearl Harbor attack—American submarines have sunk 133 enemy ships, both combat and noncombat; probably sunk 23 and damaged 35.

In the 30-day period ending today, the submarines of the Pacific Fleet have sunk 17 ships, probably sunk one—a cruiser—and damaged four others.

Those ships reported sunk in today's communique include three medium-sized cargo ships, a medium-sized tanker and a small schooner.

Those damaged include a medium-sized transport and a medium-sized tanker.

The war can't be fought on a peacetime budget. Give generously to the Red Cross. Three cents a day will back up a fighting man.

U. S. Communiques

NAVY DEPARTMENT

Communique No. 296
Early Afternoon, March 2

SOUTH PACIFIC (all dates east longitude):

1. On March 1 Dauntless dive bombers (Douglas) with Wildcatt (Gruman 4F4) escort, bombed and started fires in the Japanese-held area at Munda on New Georgia Island. All U. S. planes returned.

Communique No. 297
Late Afternoon, March 2

PACIFIC AND FAR EAST:

1. United States submarines have reported the following results of operations against the enemy in the waters of these areas:

(A) Three medium-sized cargo ships sunk.

(B) One medium-sized tanker sunk.

(C) One small schooner sunk.

(D) One medium-sized transport damaged.

(E) One medium-sized tanker damaged.

2. These actions have not been announced in any previous Navy Department communique.

Do your share for the Red Cross! Help Philadelphia meet its $4,234,000 quota.

GANDHI WILL BREAK 21-DAY FAST TODAY

POONA, India, March 2 (A. P.).—Mohandas K. Gandhi planned tonight to end his 21-day hunger strike on schedule at 9 A. M. tomorrow by drinking a glass of undiluted citrus juice.

No fanfare will accompany the breaking of the fast, for the government ruled out witnesses to the final chapter in the Indian Nationalist leader's self-imposed ordeal.

Only members of Gandhi's family will be permitted to attend the thanksgiving prayer session to be held shortly before the fast ends.

'IN GOOD SPIRITS'

"There is no change in Gandhi's condition and he is in good spirits," said the official government bulletin on the final day of the hunger strike.

In ordering quiet for the windup of the fast, the government took a "back to normalcy" attitude. The British aim was to return the situation to the status it held before Gandhi began his fast in his detention quarters at the guarded palace of the Aga Khan.

Thus Gandhi remains a political prisoner in the palace where he has been held since last Aug. 9 when the All-India Congress Party began a civil disobedience campaign against British rule. No more will he be allowed visitors, as he has been during the past three weeks.

Jap Fleet Dispersed By MacArthur Fliers, Two Transports Sunk

By DON CASWELL

Continued From First Page

several other vessels besides those specifically cited in the communique, and some of these may have been warships.

"The convoy consisted of three cruisers, four destroyers and seven cargo vessels and transports," a headquarters spokesman said. "After the convoy was spotted and shadowed along the north coast of New Britain Monday, the real attack began Tuesday morning, when the Fortresses inflicted most of the damage.

"Tuesday's reports are incomplete, principally because the bombers are shuttling over the targets, not permitting thorough interrogation."

The convoy was trapped north of Cape Gloucester, on the southwest tip of New Britain and 150 air miles northeast of Lae, its apparent destination on the New Guinea north coast, where the Japanese still have a formidable base. Of the 13 planes put out of action, headquarters disclosed, five were destroyed.

6 DOWNED AT DARWIN

In addition, the communique reported, six more Japanese planes were shot out of action yesterday during an enemy raid on Darwin, Australia.

Of the action against the convoy in the Bismarck Sea, the communique said:

"Despite adverse weather conditions, rain, haze and thick clouds, our heavy bombers with fighter escort repeatedly struck a convoy previously reported north of Cape Gloucester in a series of co-ordinated attacks.

"Crippling blows, delivered from a low altitude, were pressed home in the face of heavy anti-aircraft fire and constant interception by enemy fighters.

5 HITS ON TRANSPORT

"A 10,000-ton transport received five direct hits with 1000-pound bombs and was left enveloped in smoke, and later was reported awash and sinking.

"An 8000-ton transport was hit amidships, burst into flames and split in two, sinking within two minutes.

"A direct hit was scored on the bow of a 6000-ton transport and a fourth vessel of medium size was severely damaged near the bow with flames pouring from a forward hatch.

30 TO 40 JAP PLANES

"Other hits or near-hits were scored against warships and cargo vessels, the results of which it so far has been impossible to assess.

"Thirty to 40 enemy fighters acting as convoy cover attacked our formations without cessation, but ineffectually. Thirteen enemy planes were shot out of action and the remnants of the convoy now are scattered and dispersed over a wide area of the sea northeast of Finschhafen, apparently trying to reach their destination at Lae. Our losses were light and the battle continues."

ALLIED PLANE MISSING

Headquarters later said only one Allied bomber was "overdue."

Fifteen Japanese fighters raided an Allied airdrome at Darwin, on the Australian mainland, shortly after noon yesterday and succeeded in causing slight damage. American and Australian fighters took to the air and shot six enemy planes out of action.

The Allied air forces were active in other sectors of the Southwestern Pacific Command.

FOUR AIRFIELDS HIT

A heavy unit flew west of Timor Island and bombed the airdrome at Waingapoe, Soemba (Sandalwood) Island again. Another Japanese air base was attacked near Bima, Soembawa Island.

Allied planes battered a third Japanese airport at Lae in a surprise dawn attack, raking the dispersal areas and anti-aircraft positions "with damaging effect." The enemy airfield at Gasmata was attacked in a dusk raid.

Flying to New Britain Island, a heavy Allied air unit scored a direct hit with a 500-pound bomb on the stern of a medium-sized ammunition ship moored near Brown Island. The vessel exploded and sank, and an adjacent jetty was damaged.

Service Men's Entertainment

Information about events in the city and special affairs being held at the various centres open for service men's comfort and recreation may be obtained at the Philadelphia Hospitality Centre for Service Men, 18 S. 15th st.

This is also the "clearing house," the central point of distribution, for tickets to varied types of entertainment — theatres, sports events, musical concerts and special events.

Tickets to all sorts of entertainment may be obtained also at the Stage Door Canteen, Broad and Locust sts.

5 PHILA. SOLDIERS KILLED IN ACTION

Twenty-three Pennsylvanians, including five from Philadelphia, were among the 435 U. S. soldiers listed yesterday as killed in action.

In a Navy Department casualty list Seaman Harry Leon Poth, father of Miss Jean Poth, 6742 York road, was named among 44 missing. The list also included 11 dead and 16 wounded, none from the Philadelphia area.

The Navy list brings the Navy, Marine and Cost Guard casualties since Dec. 7, 1941, to a total of 6702 dead, 4539 wounded and 12,720 missing.

SEVERAL AREAS COVERED

The War Department announcement listed men killed in the Alaskan, European, North African, South Pacific and Southwest Pacific areas.

The Philadelphia dead:

Private Morril Fifield, son of Mrs. Hazel Fifield, 1747 N. 29th st.

Private First Class Henry F. Denny, son of Mrs. Rachel Denny, 4503 Worth st.

First Lieutenant Robert N. Exton, husband of Mrs. R. N. Exton, 6400 Cobbs Creek Parkway.

Private Michael Fantozzi, husband of Mrs. Annunziata Fantozzi, 827 Alter st.

Private First Class Otto H. Fabry, son of Mrs. Amelia Fabry, 5826 N. Camac st.

WAAC Is U. S. Challenge To Our Brave Women

Have Real Job to Do, and They Are Doing It in Best Possible Way

By Laura A. Tiffany
Third Officer, WAAC

British and Russian women have answered their country's call. The WAAC is America's challenge to our women. Will you accept it?

It must have been about the second week in June, 1942, that my conscience and I decided on the WAAC. I felt that in this project, the Women's Army Auxiliary Corps and my country could make better use of my training, energy and will to work.

LIEUT. TIFFANY

I had an excellent teaching position in a Philadelphia high school and was just testing my fourth class of adults in the Red Cross first aid course. There wasn't much time left over, but I knew that while the war was on there were others who could fill my place.

When I first went to the recruiting station it was with one, and only one thought in mind—if Uncle Sam wanted me, I was willing to go. I didn't expect adventure and glamor. I didn't even expect a good time. I looked for nothing but hard and satisfying work.

During the first week in August I was thrilled to receive a telegram to report for my physical. I arrived as an officer candidate at Fort Des Moines on Aug. 31.

First in my training company, then in my classes, when I was assigned to teaching, and later in the "rookies," I "processed" while platoon commander in the Fourth Receiving Company, I met and became attached to as fine and sincere a group of women as have ever worked together.

Friendships were a help during those first few weeks. It isn't all easy—but it is all worthwhile And strangely, too, it is the hardest assignment you ever had, the regulation you always innocently broke, that, in memory, becomes that which you most enjoyed.

FIRST PARADE

After two weeks' training we marched in our first parade. We won that parade. No degree or honor I have ever received meant more to me than the knowledge that I was one small but necessary part in the honors we took in that, our first parade.

During the parade our captain managed a seat in the stands behind the visiting general, who was judging. As we passed by a very familiar voice rang out, "Boy, just look at those lines! Perfect! Absolutely perfect!" That was our captain. Back at the barracks later we waited for the news.

ON RECRUITING DUTY

All "the old man" would say then was, "You weren't so bad, today—not too bad." Then came the news! New Year's night in Times Square is quiet compared to our barracks that night. Yes, one parade more than makes up for any bumps along the way.

Now, on my third assignment, I am on recruiting service. Now at last I have the chance to spread the good news. Our educational program has no doubt made you conscious of the purpose of the Women's Army Auxiliary Corps — you know that you can actually shorten this war, that you can help someone's son, someone's brother, someone's sweetheart come back from "over there." That is the big thing. That is the reason behind the corps.

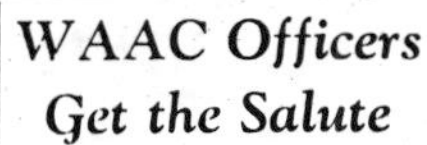

WAAC Officers Get the Salute

Entitled to Same Courtesies as Men

WAAC officers are entitled to the same military courtesies as officers in the men's Army. A recent change in a War Department circular states:

"Those persons entitled to the salute are commissioned officers of the Army, Navy, Marine Corps, Coast Guard, Army Nurse Corps, Women's Army Auxiliary Corps, warrant officers and flight officers, and commissioned officers of Allied Nations in time of war. It is also customary to salute officers of friendly foreign nations when recognized as such."

PHILADELPHIA'S FIRST WAAC
Miss Evelyn Carter, the first Philadelphia woman to become a member of the Women's Army Auxiliary Corps, is shown above at Fort Des Moines greasing an Army truck.

First Phila. WAAC

Silk Hose to Axle Grease Is Record of Miss Carter

SILK stockings to axle grease! That change is part of the war service record of Miss Evelyn R. Carter—Philadelphia's pioneer WAAC.

Miss Carter, whose home is at 4529 North Lee st., was working at the Apex Hosiery Mill here last summer when she heard that recruiting had been started for enlisted members of the Women's Army Auxiliary Corps.

It did not take her long to make up her mind.

So, she won the distinction of being the first Philadelphia woman to be enrolled in the WAAC as an auxiliary.

• • •

HER name was the first to be written on a WAAC service record from this district and her name tops the list of the more than 2500 women from this area who have enlisted at the Philadelphia Recruiting and Induction District since Aug. 12.

When she went to the First WAAC Training Centre at Fort Des Moines, Miss Carter earned another "first." After basic training, she was assigned to one of the first automobile lubrication specialist schools for the WAACS.

Now—Miss Carter is a "grease monkey" and proud of it!

Ask her mother, Mrs. Elizabeth Carter.

• • •

MRS. CARTER said that her daughter writes glowing letters about the interesting job of "grease monkey."

"My daughter's only knowledge of mechanics before she joined the WAACS," said Mrs. Carter, "was obtained by observing the hosiery machines at Apex in action, but in the Army she developed an unusual aptitude.

"Now her mechanical ability is being effectively used in the repair and maintenance of all types of military vehicles from jeeps to those mammoth Army trailer-trucks. She has never regretted joining the colors. In a recent letter, she told me she has applied for Officer's Candidate School."

• • •

AUXILIARY CARTER, according to Mrs. Carter, wants to be an officer in Aircraft Mechanics.

"I'm sure," said Mrs. Carter, "that those gold bars of a third officer in the WAACS are very appealing to my daughter."

Auxiliary Carter represents her family in war service. She has two married sisters, but no brothers.

WAAC to Have 5 Specialist Schools

The first of a group of Administrative Specialist Schools for the Women's Army Auxiliary Corps opened February 12 at the Stephen F. Austin State Teachers College in Nacogdoches, Texas.

Similar schools will be opened the latter part of this month at Arkansas Polytechnical College, Russellville, Arkansas; Arkansas State Teachers College, Conway, Arkansas; Texas State College for Women, Denton, Texas; and East Texas State Teachers College, Commerce, Texas.

Administrative specialist training was previously given at Fort Des Moines and Daytona Beach, but the facilities of these centres are now being used to the fullest extent for basic training because of the rapid expansion of the WAAC.

Answering 10 Queries About The WAAC

21 Is Age Limit; Special Education Not Required

21 Age Limit

Q.—Can an applicant under twenty-one years of age enlist in the WAAC if she has parents' consent?

A.—No. The minimum age limit is 21 with no exceptions.

Education

Q.—What are the education requirements for the WAAC?

A.—There are no specific educational requirements but every WAAC must pass a mental alertness test.

All Can Advance

Q.—Is it possible for a WAAC without a college education to become an officer?

A.—Yes. Every WAAC is given the opportunity to apply for officer candidate school.

Term of Enlistment

Q.—What is the term of enlistment.

A.—WAACS will serve for the duration of the war plus six months.

Training Period

Q.—How long is the training period?

A.—Basic training lasts approximately four weeks. Training in the specialist schools for from six to eight weeks beyond basic. The officer candidates' course occupies six weeks.

Training Schools

Q.—Where are the WAACS sent for training?

A.—At present there are three training centres: Ft. Des Moines, Iowa; Ft. Oglethorpe, Ga., and Daytona Beach, Fla.

All Start Alike

Q.—Do all WAACS enter training as auxiliaries?

A.—Yes. Promotion depends upon a WAACS performance during basic training, upon her leadership and ability, and her length of service.

Allowed to Marry

Q.—Are the wives of service men eligible for enlistment?

A.—Yes, and members of the Corps are privileged to marry during their term of service.

Get All Clothing

Q.—Do auxiliaries and officers buy their own uniforms?

A.—No. All clothing and equipment is issued.

Overseas Service

Q.—Is overseas service voluntary?

A.— A WAAC may express a choice as to where she wishes to serve, but she may be stationed either in the United States or abroad.

Wife of Red Cross Aide Enrolls in WAACS

Mrs. James Snyder, wife of the field supervisor for the American Red Cross in Africa, was a recent enrollee in the Women's Army Auxiliary Corps. Mrs. Snyder enlisted in Reading and left for training at Fort Oglethorpe, Ga.

Walter Winchell On Broadway

Broadway on Toasted Rye

Jane Froman, the lovely thrush, who was injured seriously in the Clipper crash near Lisbon, has had a relapse, her husband just learned . . . A specialist has flown there from London . . . Since the crash, Don Ross, her life partner (he had never been parted from her before), has tried desperately to arrange passage to be with her . . . But he couldn't get the necessary priority . . . Government people were polite and sympathetic, but they couldn't make room on a Lisbon-bound plane . . . Ross went as high as Cabinet officers with whom he has connections, but they were all sorry—no dice . . . Finally, in desperation, he sent a telegram to the President, outlining his plight . . . Within one hour he had a reply from the President, informing Ross that accommodations would be found for him on the very next Clipper, regardless of who had to be put off to make room for him.

• • •

C. Aubrey Smith, the grand old man of Hollywood's British colony of actors, was telling a friend: "Yes, Maude Adams has been laying eggs all over the place." . . . And: "Grace George laid the biggest egg I ever saw!" . . . In the show world "laying an egg" means to fail . . . His listener asked: "Why are you making all those insulting remarks about these actresses?" . . . Mr. Smith explained that he is raising chickens on his Hollywood ranch—and all his best hens are named for his best actress friends.

• • •

Colonel Darry Zanuck, who has seen action in the Aleutians and more recently in Africa, strolled along Broadway the other afternoon . . . He paused to view a restaurant window displaying huge hams and roasts of beef being cooked on grills. Zanuck stared and stared—and then inspected the adjacent window, where fresh fruit was piled high . . . "What's so interesting about that?" his companion asked . . . "There isn't a person in Europe," said Zanuck, "who wouldn't pay a good price for this. Not to eat any of it, mind you—just to look at it—just to look!"

• • •

Lint from a Blue Serge Suit: Bluesinger Mildred Bailey is a pneumonia victim in a Cincy hosp. . . . Ford Harrison, the St. Moritz maestro, nephews for Uncle Sam next week . . . The same five leaders of the Hooper radio survey a year ago are leading today. Fibber McGee and Molly, Bob Hope, C. McCarthy, Aldrich Family and Ben Grauer . . . Best free show in town is watching the novices learn how to roller skate at the Rockefeller rink . . . The midtown clip-joints are begging for trouble "rolling" British seamen. The 54th st. detectives are "casing" them all . . . George Jean Nathan says age is "slowly coming over me like a hurricane."

• • •

Frank Paris, the renowned puppeteer (currently at the Radio City Music Hall), has always had a yen to appear in the movies, and for 10 years he created over 300 puppets in order to be prepared when The Day Came . . . The other day a Paramount executive came backstage and told Paris that Paramount would like to make a screen test of him . . . "That's what I've waited for for nearly 10 years," he ejaculated. "Which puppets shall I bring?" . . . "Oh," said the movie scout, "no puppets—the puppets are out. You look like you might make a new romantic leading man."

• • •

A Broadway bargain: Grace Moore at the Roxy . . . Luckiest gal in town: The one who tried beating her hotel bill. She dropped her scanty wardrobe in a tiny bag from the window and took the elevator down . . . The bag merely hit a cop on the konk, and she was locked up on all sorts of charges . . . That Monte Carlo all-woman brawl started when a gal walked in practically peeled.

BEATRICE KAY
Songstress in the stage show new at the Earle tomorrow.

Horton Here Till April 3

After much long-distance telephoning to Hollywood, Edward Everett Horton has secured permission to remain at the Walnut in "Springtime for Henry" until Saturday night, April 3. Horton will fly to the Coast to start work Monday, April 5, on his new picture, "The Girl He Left Behind Him."

Singer to Stay In Variety Revue

Published reports to the contrary, Luba Malina, featured singer in "Priorities of 1942," variety revue coming Monday to the Locust St., will not leave for a leading role in the film version of "G-String Murders."

Hunt Stromberg, who is producing the Gypsy Rose Lee novel, had approached Miss Malina for a prominent part in the picture, but the singer, who is under personal contract to Lee Shubert, will remain in "Priorities of 1942" until the end of its transcontinental tour.

Next season Shubert plans to star her in a new musical comedy on Broadway.

Amusement Guide in Philadelphia

THEATRES

FORREST—"Ziegfeld Follies," revue, with Milton Berle, Ilona Massey, Arthur Treacher and Sue Ryan. 2.30, 8.30.

WALNUT—"Springtime for Henry," Edward Everett Horton, bachelor, "reformed" by his secretary, Eleanor Lawson. 2.30, 8.30.

MOTION PICTURES

ALDINE—"The Crystal Ball," romantic comedy, with Paulette Goddard and Ray Milland. 11, 12.45, 2.30, 4.35, 6.15, 8.05, 10. Opens today.

ARCADIA—"Random Harvest," romantic drama, with Greer Garson and Ronald Colman. 11, 1.10, 3.20, 5.30, 7.45, 10.

BOYD—"Keeper of the Flame," Katharine Hepburn hides a mystery; with Spencer Tracy. 11.25, 1.30, 3.35, 5.40, 7.45, 10.

CAPITOL—"Power of the Press," melodrama, with Guy Kibbee, Lee Tracy, Gloria Dickson. 11.05, 1.20, 3.30, 5.45, 8, 10. Reviewed today.

EARLE—"The Meanest Man in the World," comedy, with Jack Benny, "Rochester," Priscilla Lane. 11.20, 2.25, 5.30, 8.20, 10.30. Harpo Marx and orchestra on stage.

FAYS—"The Pay-Off," racket melodrama, with Lee Tracy and Tom Brown. 1.15, 3.34, 8.35, 11. Earl Hines and orchestra on stage.

FOX—"Immortal Sergeant," war drama, with Henry Fonda, Maureen O'Hara, Thomas Mitchell. 11, 12.50, 2.40, 4.30, 6.20, 8.10, 10.

KARLTON—"Seven Days' Leave," musical, with Victor Mature and Lucille Ball. 11, 12.45, 2.35, 4.25, 6.15, 8.05, 9.50.

KEITH'S—"In Which We Serve," Noel Coward in his story of a British destroyer's crew. 11, 1.10, 3.20, 5.30, 7.45, 10.

MASTBAUM—"They Got Me Covered," spy comedy, with Bob Hope and Dorothy Lamour. 11, 12.50, 2.40, 4.30, 6.20, 8.10, 10.

NEWS—"Stand-In," Hollywood comedy, with Leslie Howard, Humphrey Bogart and Joan Blondell, 8.15, 10.05, 11.55, 1.45, 3.35, 5.25, 7.15, 9.05, 10.55, and all night.

STANLEY—"Hitler's Children," youth in Nazi Germany; with Bonita Granville and Tim Holt. 11.20, 1.10, 2.55, 4.40, 6.25, 8.15, 10.

STANTON—"Lucky Jordan," Private Alan Ladd foils a spy gang; with Helen Walker. 11, 12.50, 2.40, 4.30, 6.20, 8.10, 10.

STUDIO—"High School Girl," melodrama, with Cecilia Parker. 11, 1, 3, 5, 7.10, 9.10; and "Secrets of a Model," melodrama, with Sharon Lee. 12, 2, 4, 6, 8.10, 10.30.

MERCHANDISE AND SERVICE FOR YOUR CAR YOUR HOME & YOURSELF

PARCEL POST BUSINESS

ADDITIONAL PARCEL POST BUSINESS WILL BE FOUND ON OPPOSITE PAGE

INQUIRER WANT ADS BRING RESULTS

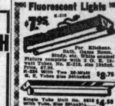

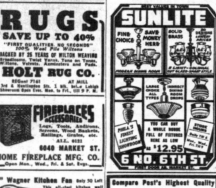

PHILADELPHIA HONORS MARINE HERO TODAY

The Philadelphia Inquirer

PUBLIC LEDGER

An Independent Newspaper for All the People

FINAL CITY EDITION

CIRCULATION: March Average: Daily 460,846; Sunday 1,382,878

SATURDAY MORNING, APRIL 10, 1943

Vol. 228, No. 100

abdefgh

THREE CENTS

Today

Wage, Price Curb Turn for the Better Farm Subsidies Would Aid Rationing And Hit Black Market

—By Walter Lippmann—

SO MANY big statements have been issued about wages and prices that the latest one will be taken at a considerable discount. Nevertheless, Mr. Byrnes is at long last in control of the situation, and we are now very much nearer to a constructive solution than we were 10 days ago.

At that time two opposing forces were threatening to overthrow the whole war-time wage and price structure.

Mr. Lewis was demanding a wage-rate increase which destroyed the "Little Steel" formula, on the ground that retail prices had broken through the ceiling.

If Mr. Lewis were to get his demands, all other trade union leaders would be bound by the law of self-preservation to follow him, or lose their leadership of organized labor.

Parallel with this deadly threat to the wage structure there was the movement of the farm bloc, as expressed through the Bankhead and Pace bills, to knock off the ceiling over farm prices.

The combination of these two converging movements brought the situation to its most acute crisis. A crisis is a point at which things must either become worse or much better. Ten days ago things took a decided turn for the better.

The turn began with the recognition by Messrs. Green and Murray that wage earners could not gain by wage-rate increases because they could never keep up with runaway prices. At the White House conference on Thursday, April 1, therefore, they radically altered labor union strategy by agreeing to demand effective price control rather than higher wage rates.

This action made it possible for Congress to shelve the Pace bill and to wait and see before overriding the President's veto of the Bankhead bill.

The net result of the two actions was to put the influence of labor behind the stabilization of prices, and the influence of the farm bloc behind the stabilization of wages. Thus, instead of converging to destroy the whole price-wage structure, the two great interests were converging to support and enforce the stabilization program which Mr. Byrnes directs. Upon this new situation the President's latest order rests.

This order puts into legal effect the Green - Murray agreement not to ask for general wage-rate increases provided the cost of living is effectively controlled. The rules laid down by Mr. Byrnes for the War Labor Board and other agencies confine wage increases to the "Little Steel" formula, with no general exceptions permitted.

His rulings are likely to be resolutely applied this time because (a) the farm bloc has its big stick available, (b) Messrs.

Continued on Page 13, Column 4

SCHMID TO GET INQUIRER HERO AWARD TODAY

Will Receive Medal, $1000 After Parade To Ceremony at Reyburn Plaza

Parade Route

Starts at 12.30 P. M. from Broad and Spring Garden sts.

South on Broad and around City Hall to Spruce st.

North on Broad and around City Hall to Reyburn Plaza.

Amid the plaudits of a city proud of the record of its fighting men, Sergeant Albert A. Schmid, Philadelphia's famed fighting Marine, will stand before his fellow citizens in Reyburn Plaza at 1.30 o'clock this afternoon to receive the first wartime Inquirer Hero Award.

The man who faced a horde of Japs with a lonely machine gun on Guadalcanal one night last August and mowed 200 of them down, will receive the gold medal and the $1000 check presented by The Inquirer following one of the most heartfelt tributes ever paid a man for extraordinary service to his country.

LEADERS TO ATTEND

Leaders of every major organization and public body in the city and Philadelphians from every walk of life will be present when Major General William G. Price, chairman of The Inquirer Hero Award Committee, presents the check and the specially-engraved Inquirer Award Medal to the gallant fighter.

Anticipating the crowds that will throng streets along the route as Sergeant Schmid makes his way from his home at 1025 Fillmore st. at 11.30 A. M., through his home neighborhood in the Northeast to the beginning of the parade route at Broad and Spring Garden sts., Public Safety Director James H. Malone has ordered heavy details of police on extra duty.

FAMILIAR ROUTE

Sergeant Schmid and his attractive bride will travel a route familiar to him—past the Dodge Steel Co., 6501 Tacony st., where he worked before he began his military duties for his country, past Cramp's Shipyard and the Frankford Arsenal, through Richmond to Broad and Spring Garden sts., where the big military parade will be waiting to begin.

Headed by the Grand Marshal of the parade, Captain John J. Owens, former officer of the 28th Division,

Continued on Page 4, Column 4

PHILADELPHIA'S OWN MARINE HERO: TODAY'S HIS DAY

Marine Sergeant Albert A. Schmid and his bride will leave their Fillmore st. home today to travel, escorted by a guard of honor, along a crowd-packed route to Reyburn Plaza, where the partially blinded Guadalcanal hero, who killed 200 Japs, will receive the first wartime Inquirer Hero Award, a gold medal and a check for $1000.

No Easter Finery For Mrs. Roosevelt

CHICAGO, April 9 (U. P.).—There will be no new Easter finery for the First Lady of the Nation this year.

Mrs. Eleanor Roosevelt confirmed that fact today as she stopped off here aboard a plane en route from San Francisco to Washington.

The First Lady was asked if she had purchased any new Easter garments during her tour of the West Coast.

"Oh, no," she replied. "This year I'm not getting any."

Asked if she thought other women should follow her example, she replied in the negative. "If they need them," she said, "I think they should buy them."

Mussolini Reported Ready to Flee Rome; Key Nazis Quit Africa

4 Ships Sunk By Japs

By JOHN M. McCULLOUGH

Inquirer Washington Bureau

WASHINGTON, April 9.—Four Allied ships, including a destroyer, were sunk in the furious Japanese bombing attack north of Guadalcanal in the southeastern Solomons on Wednesday, the Navy announced today.

A naval spokesman said dispatches have not indicated how heavy casualties might have been.

The nationality of the ships which went down was not revealed.

LOSSES DESCRIBED

Those sunk were:

One destroyer, damaged by bombs and later sunk as it was being towed.

One oil tanker, sunk by bombs.

One corvette—a small escort vessel of 800 or 900 tons—sunk by bombs.

One "small fuel oil boat"—probably a barge or lighter.

JAPS LOSE 34 PLANES

It was announced in a communique issued yesterday that 37 out of 98 Japanese planes which made the attack were shot down. The Navy today revised this estimate downward to 34.

The attack apparently was timed to coincide with the unloading of Allied supply ships in the lanes between Guadalcanal and Florida Islands, where some of the bitterest naval engagements of the Solomons campaigns took place.

BELIEVED U. S. SHIPS

Unofficially, it was assumed that the ships were American, since American combat ships and auxiliaries have played a dominant part in the entire campaign.

The Japanese attack on Allied shipping, which constantly shuttles back and forth to Guadalcanal, bringing supplies to the island garrison, was the first important move in months to halt Allied advance out of the Guadalcanal-Tulagi area.

Judging from the enormous strength of the Japanese attack formation, there was some speculation that the convoy reaching Guadal-

Continued on Page 3, Column 4

Peterman in Tunisia

War Doctors Miracle Men

By Ivan H. (Cy) Peterman

Inquirer War Correspondent

(By Wireless)

WITH THE AMERICAN FORCES IN TUNISIA, April 7 (Delayed).

THIS afternoon I said goodbye to three wounded Yanks who just failed to say "hello" to St. Peter. They only typify Army medical wonders, but since all represent the sort of injury which frequently proved fatal in the last war I must explain.

Jan is the nickname of one infantryman who arrived at a field hospital suffering from an advanced stage of peritonitis after lying two days and nights unattended on the El Guetar battlefield, his stomach punctured by shrapnel. An 88 caught Jan midway in the task of digging a slit trench and he lay there from 7 o'clock one morning until 8 o'clock the next night.

• • •

"SOMEHOW I woke up, and using a rifle as a crutch walked a half mile to a companion," he said. "He helped me another mile to a first-aid station, where I got some sulfa pills before being taken to a collecting station.

"Next I went to a mobile dressing station, where, in a hospital truck, my wounds were re-examined and then I was rushed 15 more miles to the field hospital."

As may be supposed, the punctured colon resulted in serious condition for Jan by the time he reached the operating table at 4 A. M. the following day, but surgeons decided to cut away the infected area of intestine draped outside the abdominal wall.

After a blood transfusion, plenty of sulfa drugs, injection of normal saline and glucose solution into the veins, and the use of Wangensteen tubes, the patient began an amazing rally, although even optimistic doctors failed to hold much hope for him.

• • •

IT SO happened that I watched the next week's improvement of the patient. He was fed nothing at all through the mouth during that time, yet seemed to gain color.

In three days it became apparent that he would live. In four days he was laughing and talking with other patients in the tent. In six he was taking nourishment normally and was ready to be evacuated to a base hospital. Even war-wise nurses became excited over the case.

This case demonstrated that even a wounded man who fails to get immediate attention has still a chance.

During recent battles, the Nazis have made a practice of sweeping the field with machine guns during daylight to prevent the saving

Continued on Page 2, Column 4

Rommel Races For Sfax

LONDON, April 10 (Saturday) (A. P.).—Reuters reported in a Zurich dispatch today that Premier Benito Mussolini was understood to be preparing to evacuate his government from Rome.

The dispatch said Mussolini was reported to have appointed secret commissions to make the necessary arrangements. Florence and Bologna have been mentioned as likely places for the new seat of government, it said.

ROMMEL AIDES MOVE

LONDON, April 10 (Saturday) (A. P.).—Marshal Erwin Rommel has started evacuating some of his key officers and technicians from Tunisia to Messina, Sicily, the Daily Express said today, quoting London sources.

The newspaper said that during the last few days ferry transport planes had been operating between Messina and the Tunis-Bizerte defense ring on a non-stop shuttle schedule.

In addition to Junkers-52's, the Germans were reported using obsolete Junkers-90's and some of their new four-engined transports.

By DANIEL DE LUCE

ALLIED HEADQUARTERS IN NORTH AFRICA, April 9 (A. P.).—Field Marshal Erwin Rommel's Axis forces hastened their retreat today, abandoning Mahares, 50 miles north of Gabes, and leaving nearly 12,000 troops as prisoners of the British and American forces since the Eighth Army's break-through at the Wadi Akarit last Tuesday.

Under the steady hammering of the British at their rear, the Americans, French and British on their inland flank and the great Allied aerial fleet overhead, Rommel's beaten men were fleeing toward the port of Sfax, 22 miles on to the north, and were retreating northeastward from the inland rail point of Mezzouna, it was disclosed here.

KAIROUAN IS TARGET

(Captain Ludwig Sertorius, German military commentator, said there were indications the Allies in the north-central sector were preparing to launch a large-scale "break-through" attack to capture the big German air base at Kairouan and to sweep on 32 miles to the port of Sousse.

(The British Broadcasting Corp. quoted German radio reports that the Axis had evacuated Pichon, on the north-central Tunisian front 22 miles west of Kairouan.)

United States troops, highly praised at a press conference by

Continued on Page 2, Column 6

New Ceilings Promise Relief to Consumer

By WILLIAM C. MURPHY, JR.

Inquirer Washington Bureau

WASHINGTON, April 9.—President Roosevelt and Economic Stabilization Director James F. Byrnes today promised relief to the American consumer in the form of specific dollars-and-cents price ceilings on all commodities affecting the cost of living and held out hope that some prices may actually be reduced.

Byrnes shared Mr. Roosevelt's regular press conference today, which was devoted largely to an amplification of the President's "hold the line" executive order and statement against inflation last night.

SOME DISSATISFACTION

Meanwhile, indicating that some of the special interest groups at least believed the President's action of last night was full of teeth, there were expressions of dissatisfaction from both labor leaders and officials of farm organizations.

The former were enthusiastic about the President's proposed amplification of price controls, but they did not like the idea of no more wage increases. The latter took just the opposite view.

Byrnes took over at the conference at the President's suggestion after Mr. Roosevelt had been asked about the mechanics of carrying out the executive order directive to prevent further price increases.

PLAN IS NEARLY READY

The OES director said that the Office of Price Administration was working on a plan for specific price

Continued on Page 6, Column 4

HOUSE G.O.P. ISSUES PAY-GO ULTIMATUM

By JOHN C. O'BRIEN

Inquirer Washington Bureau

WASHINGTON, April 9.—House Minority Leader Joseph W. Martin, Jr. (R., Mass.), issued an ultimatum today in an attempt to break the impasse on tax legislation.

It was: "No pay-as-you-go tax bill no Easter recess."

Majority Leader John W. McCormack (D., Mass.), readily agreed that plans for adjourning the House April 17 for a two-week vacation would be wrecked if Martin stuck to his guns.

INSISTS ON ACTION

The Republican leader said he was willing to see "any kind of a tax bill" reported by the Ways and Means Committee, but he insisted along with 65 Democrats—that the committee produce a bill at once and abandon its plan to stall tax legislation for months.

Administration Democrats, however, frankly expressed the fear that any tax bill which reached the House floor now would be amended so as to embrace the Ruml plan, which most of the Republicans in the House are supporting.

MAY NOT SHOW LETTER

Chairman Robert L. Doughton (D., N. C.), of the Ways and Means

Continued on Page 6, Column 2

LABOR RACKET CURB ADOPTED BY HOUSE

By HUGH MORROW

Inquirer Washington Bureau

WASHINGTON, April 9.—Organized labor suffered its first setback in the present session of Congress this afternoon when the House passed the Hobbs bills by a roll-call vote of 270-107 and sent it to the Senate.

Labor unions had opposed the measure, which would amend the 1934 Anti-Racketeering Act by providing penalties up to 20 years in prison for robbery and extortion, under greatly broadened definitions, when such activities interfered with interstate commerce.

AMENDMENT REJECTED

An amendment offered by Representative Emanuel Celler (D., N. Y.), which union spokesmen said would make the bill acceptable to labor, was rejected by a teller vote of 126 to 167.

Celler's amendment would have prevented prosecutions under the Hobbs bill of activities defined as legal under the four major pieces of labor legislation now on the books—the Clayton, Norris-La Guardia, Railway, Labor and National Labor Relations Acts.

FEAR NULLIFICATION

Celler argued that his amendment was necessary to protect labor from the "anti-labor" provisions of the bill, but proponents of the bill argued that the effect of the amendment would be to nullify the bill.

However, the House did accept by an overwhelming voice vote an amendment approved by the Judi-

Continued on Page 5, Column 2

Confused Stukas Batter Own Tanks

ALLIED HEADQUARTERS IN NORTH AFRICA, April 9 (U. P.).—Front dispatches said that a considerable formation of German Stuka planes by mistake delivered a "particularly hard attack" against their own tanks on the north Tunisian front yesterday.

British troops who watched the spectacle said they hoped the results were good.

MAIN BREAK PERILS WEST PHILA. WATER

The water supply of a large section of West Philadelphia was temporarily threatened last night by a break in a 36-inch main which feeds 80,000,000 gallons of water a day to the Belmont Reservoir in Fairmount Park.

However, after an inspection of the scene of the break, Martin J. McLaughlin, chief of the Water Bureau, estimated that the damage could be repaired within 24 hours and that during that period West Philadelphia would receive an adequate water supply from the George's Hill and East Park reservoir.

BREAK FOUND QUICKLY

The break sent a geyser up through the earth and flooded the area about the Belmont Pumping Station, located on the West River drive just below the Columbia ave. bridge. Loss of hundreds of thousands of gallons of water was prevented by immediate discovery of the break.

The car barn of the Fairmount Park Transit Co. was flooded, but according to Norman S. Alexander, president of the company, the flood will not interfere with the normal operation of park trolleys. A number of houses in "Brick Row," near

Continued on Page 14, Column 1

IN TODAY'S INQUIRER

130 ARE SUBPENAED IN POULTRY PROBE

Tightening its drive against the poultry black market in this area, the Government yesterday served 130 subpenas on witnesses who will appear before the March Federal Grand Jury when that body resumes its probe into the food situation here next week.

It was learned that many of the witnesses will relate their dealings with a "leading poultry distributor" whose business runs well over $1,000,000 a year and who supplies a sizable percentage of the retailers in this region.

'UP-GRADING' CHARGED

It was believed that the principal complaint against the distributor will be that he has consistently "upgraded" poultry in violation of the Emergency Price Control Act in order to obtain above-ceiling prices.

Other developments on the Philadelphia food front yesterday:

1. George A. Casey, president of the National Association of Independent Meat Packers, stated that Washington's effort to place ceilings on livestock "will not alleviate the meat situation as long as farmers continue to gain special concessions," and added the charge that the present system of point rationing on meats

Continued on Page 6, Column 6

W. C. Fields Found Guilty of Plagiarism

HOLLYWOOD, April 9 (U. P.).—A Superior Court jury tonight found comedian W. C. Fields guilty of stealing a snake story from amateur writer Harry Yadkoe, and awarded Yadkoe $8000.

Fields declared the verdict was "outrageous and ridiculous," and, ignoring Yadkoe's offer to shake hands, tapped the red rubber cask he had brought to court for use "in case the decision goes against me."

2500 Hawaii Japs To Join Army

SAN FRANCISCO, April 9 (A. P.)—The arrival of 2500 Japanese-American soldiers from Hawaii on their way to Mississippi to join the Army's recently organized Japanese-American combat team was announced tonight by the War Department.

The contingent immediately boarded special trains for Mississippi, where they will receive initial training. For many it was their first train trip.

The group is composed entirely of volunteers carefully selected out of over 10,000 applicants.

7-POWER PARLEYS ON RELIEF SLATED

By ALEXANDER KENDRICK

Inquirer Washington Bureau

WASHINGTON, April 9.—Plans for the most important United Nations economic conference of the war—devoted to the relief and rehabilitation of the post-war world—are near completion, The Inquirer learned exclusively today.

No official announcement of the conference has yet been made, but it was learned that the United States took the initiative in proposing it and would ask six other countries to join in formulating its program. The conference is expected to be held at the end of May.

The six countries are Great Britain, Russia, China, Canada, Australia and Brazil.

TREATY DRAFT READY

Formal announcement may be made after the arrival of Dr. Herbert V. Evatt, Australian Minister of External Affairs, who is expected in Washington tomorrow.

The United States has drawn up a draft convention for the conference and is ready to circulate it among the other United Nations, it was learned. Russia, whose territories have been more ravaged by the war than any other belligerent, is understood to have embraced the conference plan enthusiastically.

The draft convention is believed to

Continued on Page 3, Column 6

War Summary

Saturday, April 10, 1943

EUROPE-AFRICA

Swiss reports said last night that Premier Mussolini was preparing to evacuate his Government from Rome, with Florence or Bologna as likely places of transfer. London reports said Marshal Rommel had been evacuating some of his key officers from Tunisia to Messina, Sicily.

On the Tunisian battlefront, Rommel's battered forces were speeding towards the port of Sfax after abandoning Mahares, 50 miles north of Gabes. The Axis also gave up the rail town of Mezzouna and a German report indicated withdrawal from Pichon in the centre. The British Eighth Army and an advancing American column captured 12,000 more prisoners.

Russian troops killed 1200 Germans in hand-to-hand fighting near Balakleya, 35 miles southeast of Kharkov, along the Izyum sector of the Donets front the Reds hurled back the enemy and improved their positions.

R. A. F. raiders blasted Germany anew last night after Mosquito bombers had pounded the Cologne area in a dusk attack following daylight sweeps in which German supply trains in France were shot up. Four Nazi planes were downed over the Channel.

A Fighting French corvette avenged the loss of the torpedoed British destroyer Harvester by ramming and sinking two U-boats in a 12-hour convoy battle in the Atlantic, the Admiralty disclosed.

OTHER FRONTS

At the cost of 34 planes, the Jap air armada which raided shipping north of Guadalcanal on Wednesday sank an Allied destroyer, a corvette, a tanker and a small fuel boat, the Navy announced yesterday. Tokio claimed the sinking of two warships and 10 transports.

The Jap base of Madang, 300 miles northwest of Buna, received its heaviest pounding of the war on Friday when Allied bombers and fighters set supplies afire and destroyed six planes. The Allies strafed other bases and attacked small craft.

Secretary of the Navy Knox asserted yesterday that the American Fleet would be more than double its size by the end of this year, but warned that the "worst of the war still lies ahead."

U. S. WEATHER FORECAST

Philadelphia and Vicinity—Scattered showers, not much change in temperature.

Eastern Pennsylvania and New Jersey—Occasional light rain and not so warm today and this evening.

Sun rises 6.32 A.M. Sets 7.32 P.M.

Moon rises 11.32 A.M. Sets———

The Philadelphia Inquirer

PUBLIC LEDGER

An Independent Newspaper for All the People

FINAL CITY EDITION

CIRCULATION: March Average: Daily 460,846; Sunday 1,382,878

SATURDAY MORNING, APRIL 17, 1943

Copyright, 1943, by The Philadelphia Inquirer Co. Vol. 228, No. 107

abdefgh

THREE CENTS

Allies Gain on Tunisia Hills Despite Fierce Nazi Attacks; 7 U. S. Fleets in Operation

Today

OWI Writers' Revolt

Agency Tells All

Temperament Blamed

May Recall Standley

Cosmic Rays in War

Washington Background

Inquirer Washington Bureau

NOW that the row between Gardner Cowles, deputy director of the Office of War Information, and the 15 writers of the Pamplet Division who recently resigned, has developed into a no-holds-barred brawl, OWI officials have decided to tell all.

Chief cause of dissension, say the OWI spokesmen, was an "acute case of temperament" within the pamphlet writing group. The writers, standing on their rights as "creative artists," it seems, refused to be hurried. In a year's time the Pamphlet Division, which had a staff of 46, turned out a total of 17 pamphlets. These cost the taxpayers $158,900 in salaries of the writers (which ranged from $3200 to $8000), and $212,753 for printing.

The writers, moreover, insisted that their efforts must appear in pamphlet form. About three weeks ago the Division completed a survey of the impact of the war on the medical profession for the enlightenment of doctors. Although the survey was printed in full in the Journal of the American Medical Association (to which most doctors subscribe) the Pamphlet Division writers kicked up a row because OWI refused to print the survey in pamphlet form.

Again, after the newspapers of the country gave wide distribution to the Division's report, "Tale of a City," (one of its best productions) the pamphleteers insisted on having 2,000,000 copies printed.

A group of pamphleteers assigned to investigate drinking in Army camps journeyed 38,000 miles before they felt they had the subject well enough in hand to reduce their report to writing.

Although Elmer Davis, OWI administrator, urged most of the writers who resigned to reconsider, they offered to do so only on their own conditions. A delegation called upon George Lyon, head of OWI's News Bureau, and offered to stay long enough to complete projects they were working on—but they demanded a promise that the material would appear in pamphlet form.

Lyon, a newspaperman for many years, told the group that he never heard of a newspaper reporter imposing the condition that his stories should appear on page one.

Inclined at first to appease the rebel writers, Davis is now definitely through with them.

Herbert V. Evatt, Minister for External Affairs of Australia, detests the Japs. At a recent press conference, opening a passionate tirade, he began: "Why, those yellow ———s." Then he paused.

"Better keep that '———s' off the record."

He was about to proceed when his eye lighted on a Chinese

Continued on Page 17, Column 4

TAX DEADLOCK ENDED, PAY-GO ACTION RUSHED

Rayburn Lays Down Law, Compromise Bill May Reach Floor by Tuesday

By HUGH MORROW

Inquirer Washington Bureau

WASHINGTON, April 16.—Speaker Sam Rayburn (D., Tex.) broke a seemingly hopeless impasse on pay-as-you-go tax legislation today with the result that a compromise bill may reach the House floor next Tuesday.

The presiding officer of the House touched off a series of conferences expected to clear up the tax muddle by summoning leading members of the Ways and Means Committee to his office and "laying down the law."

NIGHT SESSION HELD

As a result, the Republicans on the committee went into a huddle, the Democrats on the committee followed suit a short time later and the ranking Republicans and Democrats held a conference tonight at which they discussed five different plans—all involving at least partial cancellation of the 1942 tax debt—and planned another conference tomorrow morning.

The day's events had two apparent results:

1. **Chairman Robert L. Doughton's plans to delay the tax issue until the committee had completed action on extension of the Reciprocal Trade Agreements Act were blasted.**

2. **House Republicans were ready to give up the fight for the Ruml plan temporarily, agreeing to a compromise so House action could be speeded, because there was an excellent chance that the Senate would substitute the Ruml plan for the House compromise.**

Majority Leader John W. McCormack, (D., Mass.), Minority Leader Joseph W. Martin, Jr., (R., Mass.) and six members of the committee attended the conference in Rayburn's office this morning.

"Will you please see if you can't

Continued on Page 6, Column 6

Bond Sales Soar Despite Bank Refund

Illustrated on Page 6

Total sales of the second War Loan Drive rose to $252,269,200 in Philadelphia yesterday, officials of the Federal Reserve Bank announced.

This total was reached despite the fact that $160,000,000 of the $210,000,000 subscribed to by banks in the previous four days of the drive had to be turned back because the banks had over-subscribed their $50,000,000 allotment.

INCREASE SHOWN

Despite this dent, yesterday's sales netted an increase of $3,000,000 over the first four days, when the oversubscription by the banks was included in the totals.

Of the $252,269,200 in securities purchased here through yesterday, $117,000,000 were subscribed for by mutual savings societies and insur-

Continued on Page 6, Column 7

F. D. R. LOSES POWER TO CUT DOLLAR VALUE

Authority Clipped As Senate Approves Bill to Extend Stabilization Fund

By FRANK H. WEIR

Inquirer Washington Bureau

WASHINGTON, April 16.—President Roosevelt's power to devalue the dollar, one of the oldest and most hotly contested features of the New Deal, was killed by the Senate today after its Banking and Currency Committee refused to extend the authority for two more years.

The Senate did extend the President's control of a $2,000,000,000 currency stabilization fund in a bill which must now go to the House. The dollar-devaluation power, which had been twinned with the stabilization fund since the measures were first enacted in January, 1934, was dropped from the bill.

MORGENTHAU PLEA VAIN

Secretary of the Treasury Henry Morgenthau, Jr., pleaded with the Banking and Currency Committee this morning to give the President the power to devalue the dollar as a "defensive weapon" to be used if other nations attempt to devalue their currency.

President Roosevelt has not used his authority since he devalued the dollar for the first time in 1934. Renewal of his authority, Morgenthau admitted, "is not a matter of life and death, but it would be useful."

TAFT LEADS OPPOSITION

Senator Robert A. Taft (R., O.) led the fight against renewal at a time when the Treasury is conducting its $13,000,000,000 War Bond drive. Morgenthau protested that Taft's remarks would provoke scare "headlines" which would endanger the success of the campaign.

"You're asking the American people to buy $13,000,000,000 worth of bonds and you're asking us to give the President the power to devalue them," Taft charged. "This seems to me to be a peculiarly bad time to ask this power. I can't think of any better advertising for your drive than to tell the American people these bonds cannot be devalued."

FEAR HOT ARGUMENT

President Roosevelt has no intention of using his power, under which he could devalue the dollar by as much as 19 percent, Morgenthau said, but a heated discussion in Congress would "hurt the Treasury" by depressing bond sales.

"Of course there would be a heated discussion," Taft retorted. "If the President can devalue the dollar it is an argument against buying American bonds."

Senator Robert F. Wagner (D., N. Y.), chairman of the committee,

Continued on Page 6, Column 7

Slate Gray Uniforms For Navy Officers

WASHINGTON, April 16 (A. P.).—A new summer uniform for Navy officers designed to make them less conspicuous on shipboard during air attacks was announced today by Secretary of the Navy Frank Knox.

The camouflage effect comes from the slate gray color of the uniform which will replace, as rapidly as the change can be made, the khaki uniform used for summer dress heretofore. The new color blends into the camouflage colors of the ships.

Knox said that the color probably would be adopted for enlisted personnel uniforms also.

Knox Reveals Increase

By JOHN M. McCULLOUGH

Inquirer Washington Bureau

WASHINGTON, April 16.—The United States Navy now has seven fleets in actual existence as compared with the three traditional fleets into which the Naval establishment was organized at the outbreak of war, Secretary of the Navy Frank Knox revealed at his press conference this afternoon.

He declined to reveal either their designations or the general area in which each operates.

FULLY BALANCED UNITS

His use of the world "fleet" rather than "force," however, led observers to suppose that each is a fully balanced combat organization, or at least is in process of being built up to such independent operating strength.

If such is the case, it seems to be one of the most significant disclosures regarding increase in American naval strength in many months. Less than one year ago, the Pacific Fleet with its far-flung components was so weak that its main strength had to be rushed from the victory in the Coral Sea in early May to meet the Japanese thrust at Midway just one month later.

RECALLS PREDICTION

Added significance was given to the announcement when, under further questioning, Knox advised newspapermen to re-read his Indianapolis speech, delivered last Friday, in which he reported that more combatant vessels would be completed this year than were in service in the entire United States fleet at the close of 1942.

He said that he had "nothing at all" to say concerning the situation in the Southwest Pacific, and refused to be drawn into any discussion of the controversy over existing Allied strength in that theatre or its reinforcement.

3 OTHERS NAMED

Official announcement has been made heretofore of the existence of three naval forces in the Pacific, independent of those units based on Pearl Harbor. They are the Southwest Pacific Force, formerly the Anzac Force, under Vice Admiral Arthur S. Carpender; the South Pacific, under Admiral William F. Halsey, Jr., and the Southeast, under Rear Admiral John F. Shafroth, Jr.

Discussion of the fleet dispositions came after Knox announced the sea commands of the four newly created commodores: Oscar Smith, who will command Special Task Force I, U. S. Fleet; L. P. Johnson, who will command the Rear Echelon of the Atlantic Fleet's Amphibious Force; R. G. Coman, commanding Service Force, 7th (Southwest Pacific) Fleet, and L. F. Reifsnider, commanding transports, Amphibious Force, 3d (South Pacific) Fleet.

JAPS BUILDING ON KISKA

On the North Pacific theatre, Knox was considerably more expansive. He asserted that the Japa-

Continued on Page 3, Column 1

(A. P. Wirephoto)

A FIGHTING THREE-STAR GENERAL

This unusual study of Lieutenant George S. Patton, Jr., commander of American troops in Tunisia, was made with a movie camera on the battlefront. The photo gives visual evidence of Patton's character as a combat leader.

British Navy Ready to Smash Axis 'Dunkirk'

Saturday, April 17, 1943

EUROPE-AFRICA

General Anderson's British First Army, hurling back savage Nazi counter-attacks, scored **gains on the heights overlooking Tunis and Bizerte**, it was announced yesterday. Maintaining their hold on the 10 strategic hills they had captured in a week, the British took Djebel Ang, a peak within sight of the Tunisian capital and the naval base to the north.

The British Navy is ready to smash any Axis attempt to stage a "Dunkirk" from Tunisia, Admiral of the Fleet Cunningham declared. He disclosed the sinking of two Italian destroyers in a surprise engagement with British destroyers off Sicily Thursday night.

United States heavy bombers pounded the U-boat base of Lorient and the harbor of Brest by daylight, and the round-the-clock Allied bombing of targets in Nazi Europe swept into its second day.

In Russia, Soviet troops staved off heavy German assaults on a strategic Kuban Valley height in a day-long, see-saw battle.

OTHER FRONTS

In a significant disclosure of the increase in U. S. naval strength, Secretary Knox revealed that the **American Navy has seven fleets in existence**, compared with the three into which it was organized at the outbreak of the war.

As Knox reported that the Japanese were continuing to construct a landing field on Kiska in the north Pacific, a U. S. Navy communique described eight raids in a day on the Jap base in the Aleutians.

In the Southwest Pacific, General MacArthur's headquarters reported today that the Jap convoy of nine ships which had attempted to reach Wewak in New Guinea had fled beyond Allied bomber range after two merchantmen were sunk and two others crippled.

NELSON URGES END OF TOO RIGID TESTS TO SPEED UP STEEL

By JOHN C. O'BRIEN

Inquirer Washington Bureau

WASHINGTON, April 16.—Alarmed by a sharp slump in the delivery of steel plate attributed to "over-rigid" inspection since the Truman Committee's disclosure that one steel mill was "faking" strength tests, Donald M. Nelson, chairman of the War Production Board, called on all steel plate producers today to maintain production at the highest possible level.

Implementing Nelson's action, H. G. Batcheller, director of the WPB steel division, called a conference of steel company executives and officials of the War and Navy Departments and the Maritime Commission and American Bureau of Shipping to consider revision of steel plate specifications. The conference will be held tomorrow.

PRODUCERS 'CAUTIOUS'

Fearful of criticism by the Truman Committee, all producers of steel plate, it was learned, have grown exceedingly cautious, with the result of hundreds of carloads of steel plate, urgently needed in the Navy and Maritime Commission's ship construction program, are immobilized on plant railroad sidings awaiting inspection.

Since the Truman Committee publicly excoriated Carnegie-Illinois Steel Co., charging the steel plates turned out by its Irvin, Pa., plant (located near Pittsburgh) were below specification strength tests, the steel producers have been subjecting their output to the closest scrutiny.

REPORT 35 PCT. DROP

Although WPB officials refused to disclose the extent of the slump, it

Continued on Page 6, Column 3

SPAIN OPENS DRIVE FOR AN EARLY PEACE, AXIS HAILS APPEAL

BARCELONA, Spain, April 16 (A. P.).—Count Francisco Gomez Jordana, Spain's Foreign Minister, launched an appeal today for peace "before the war is prolonged longer than is necessary" and said the nations engaged were too powerful for either a total victory or complete annihilation of the other.

Addressing the Hispanidad Council and South American diplomats, he said Spain hoped that "men of all nations" would support Spain's proposal for peace and added that the Vatican and other neutral nations might also "facilitate the coming of peace and collaborate in a post-war organization."

GERMANY HAILS PLEA

(Whether Gomez Jordana might be extending peace feelers on behalf of the Axis was not immediately clear, but the Berlin radio, in a broadcast of a dispatch intended for use within Germany and recorded by the Federal Communications Commission, promptly hailed the address as "a great political speech.")

(When asked about reports of a Spanish peace effort at his Washington press conference today, Secretary of State Cordell Hull replied that the United States had made it clear that its objective was an absolute, unconditional surrender of the Axis).

'THE NOBLEST INTENTIONS'

He spoke in a public session marking the 450th anniversary of Christopher Columbus' return from his first voyage.

"We understand perfectly," Gomez Jordana said, "that each belligerent . . . patriotically desires a total victory and complete annihilation of its adversary, but . . . this is a state of spirit . . . which does not correspond to the well-being of the family of nations. . . ."

Spain, the Foreign Minister said,

Continued on Page 2, Column 7

2 Italian Destroyers Sent Down in Night Clash Off Sicily

ALLIED HEADQUARTERS IN NORTH AFRICA, April 16 (A. P.).—The British Navy is ready to smash any Axis attempt to stage a "Dunkirk" from Tunisia, Admiral of the Fleet Sir Andrew B. Cunningham declared today while announcing the sinking of two Italian destroyers in a surprise engagement off Sicily last night.

He asserted there was no information available as to whether the Axis was gathering an evacuation fleet for Marshal Erwin Rommel, but said air reconnaissance had revealed many boats in the ports of Sicily and southern Italy.

BOATS ALREADY THERE

"It wouldn't be a question of gathering boats—they're already there," he added.

"Nearly every night there is brisk

Continued on Page 2, Column 6

Infantry Captures Peak Within Sight Of Tunisia Capital

Map on Page 2

By WES GALLAGHER

ALLIED HEADQUARTERS IN NORTH AFRICA, April 16 (A. P.).—Infantry units of Lieutenant General K. A. N. Anderson's British First Army, holding the 10 strategic hills they captured in the Medjez el Bab sector in less than a week, hurled back savage German counter-attacks today and improved their positions on those heights overlooking Tunis and Bizerte.

Supported by artillery, the infantry has pushed steadily eastward in the area north of Medjez el Bab and now holds Djebel Ang, a 2000-foot peak from which both the capital and the naval base to the north can be seen.

British and American artillery

Continued on Page 2, Column 5

FELON CLIMBS BACK INTO ALCATRAZ JAIL

SAN FRANCISCO, April 16 (U. P.).—Floyd G. Hamilton, 36-year-old Texas badman, surrendered to sickness and hunger today after hiding in an Alcatraz Island cave for three days and voluntarily climbed back into the Federal prison from which he escaped Tuesday with three other desperadoes.

Once given up for dead, Hamilton today used his remaining strength to crawl up the steep, rocky slope of the island and through the same window of the model shop building through which he fled three days ago.

GUARDS MISSED HIM

He revealed to Warden James A. Johnston that he had been hiding in the same cave and within a few feet of Fred Hunter, 43, a fellow escapee, who was found under a pile of debris by guards several hours after the escape.

Hamilton, one-time member of the notorious Bonnie Parker gang of Texas, told of the miscarriage of his carefully-planned attempt to win freedom from "escape-proof" Alcatraz. He was emaciated, ill, half-starved, covered with debris and suffering from many cuts and bruises.

LAY IN COLD WATER

The tide of San Francisco Bay had sent chill, salt water around him as he lay covered by old rubber mats.

Continued on Page 9, Column 4

IN TODAY'S INQUIRER

GAS RUSH CAUSED BY FAMINE SCARE

A rush for gasoline reminiscent of the days of the famine last fall struck Philadelphia's filling stations yesterday on the heels of widespread rumors that sales of automobile fuel were to be frozen in the near future.

Motorists, some of them with room for only a gallon or two in their tanks, besieged retailers throughout the metropolitan area, promising to drain quickly the city supply which was admittedly short.

Existence of a definite shortage here was confirmed yesterday by John R. Richards, chief of the gasoline rationing section of the Office of Price Administration in Washington, who said:

"I know that gasoline is short in Philadelphia. Military demands have been very heavy. But there is no freeze of sales scheduled for today, and I hope that there will be none in the future."

THREE FACTORS NOTED

The office of the Petroleum Administrator for War said the shortage is caused by three factors: continued cold weather, increased pleasure driving, and military demands. With normal weather, thousands of tank cars now hauling fuel oil, he pointed out, would be free to haul gasoline.

A spokesman for one major oil company here termed the available

Continued on Page 7, Column 3

OWI Can't Yet Tell Details of Tokio Raid

WASHINGTON, April 16 (U. P.).—War Information Director Elmer Davis said today that after consultation with the War Department the OWI "finds that clearance of the Tokio raid story has not been completed."

Davis announced at his press conference Wednesday that the OWI expected to release this week some of the details of the April 18, 1942, raid on Tokio and other Japanese cities.

"It is impossible at this date to predict when this story will be cleared," Davis said today.

Hitler Gives Keitel Command of Army

By United Press

German broadcasts have indirectly confirmed persistent reports that Adolf Hitler has turned over supreme command of the German armed forces to Field Marshal Wilhelm Keitel.

The U. S. Foreign Broadcast Intelligence Service reported that the German news agency D. N. B., in a Morse code broadcast to German newspapers and radio stations, ordered Nazi editors to delete a reference to Hitler as "supreme commander of the armed forces" from a previously-sent dispatch.

Lorient, Brest Bombed In Non-Stop Air Attack

LONDON, April 17 (Saturday) (A. P.).—American heavy bombers pounded U-boat bases and harbor installations at Lorient and Brest by daylight yesterday, and the steady round-the-clock Allied bombardment of strategic targets continued early today with another Royal Air Force thrust across the Channel.

By moonlight, British heavy bombers took off for the continent last night after their American comrades had completed their smashes.

AXIS STATIONS OFF AIR

For a full hour the roar of the British planes could be heard crossing toward Europe, and Axis radio stations abruptly went off the air.

Four of the big American bombers and two of their Spitfire fighter escorts failed to return from Friday's blow against the Axis-held French ports.

A communique issued jointly by the Air Ministry and the U. S. Army's European Theatre Headquarters said bomb bursts were observed in the target areas.

3D RAID THIS MONTH

The attackers encountered some fighter opposition, the communique said, and the bombers' gunners shot down several enemy planes.

It was the first heavy bomber action by the 8th U. S. Army Air Force in 12 days and, because of bad weather, only the third American raid in the European theatre this month.

BATTLE LASTS HOUR

Fliers returning from the sixth American bombing attack of the war on Lorient reported that the fighter opposition was not as intense as in the previous raids on that port and that the anti-aircraft fire was relatively light.

The running battle with enemy fighters lasted over an hour. The Germans picked up the bombers as they crossed the coast and stuck with them to the target—even plowing through their own flak—and on the

Continued on Page 2, Column 7

U. S. WEATHER FORECAST

Philadelphia and Vicinity—Warmer, showers, becoming colder at night, fresh to strong winds.

Eastern Pennsylvania—Showers east and south portions this morning followed by cooler this afternoon and tonight.

New Jersey—Showers and scattered thunderstorms, somewhat warmer followed by cooler in late afternoon and evening; fresh wind.

Sun rises 6.21 A. M. Sets 7.39 P. M.

Moon rises 5.53 P. M. Sets 5.05 A. M.

With the Armed Forces

News and Gossip About Philadelphians Stationed at Service Camps

FAMILIES in the Philadelphia area are chalking up some sort of a record among Uncle Sam's warriors with a number having four or five of their members in the armed services.

Among them are the five Penfield brothers, who are fighting the enemy on land, sea and in the air.

The boys, sons of Mr. and Mrs. Mason L. Penfield, 219 Crawford ave., are Samuel, 20, first to enlist, who is now receiving gunnery instruction at the Army Air School, Tyndall Field, Fla.; John, 19, stationed at the New Cumberland, Pa., Army Reception Centre; Henry, 27, who studied chemical engineering, with the Medical Corps at Temple, Tex.; L. Mason, who enlisted in the Navy a year ago, is at the Naval Training School of the Ordnance Department in Chicago, and Alvin W., 23, is in the Aviation Corps stationed near Monroe, La.

The father is employed as an inspector at the RCA-Victor plant in Camden.

Three sons and one daughter of Mrs. Felecya Nogar, 463 Gerhard st., and the late Augustus Nogar, clothing manufacturer, are serving in various capacities with the Army.

LT. NOGAR

They are First Lieutenant Emond J. Nogar, in the Intelligence Department of the Army Ordnance, stationed at Camp Forrest, Miss.; Second Lieutenants Veneta A. Nogar, officer in the WAAC, at Camp Monticello, Ark., and Eugene T. Nogar, 21, Air Corps pilot officer, stationed at Camp Monticello, and Private First Class Theodore T. Nogar, 18, stationed at Truax Field, Madison, Wis., a radio technician, who has been selected for Officers' Training.

Lieutenant Jane A. Stretch, former employe of The Philadelphia Inquirer, has been promoted to Captain in the Women's Army Auxiliary Corps, it was announced yesterday.

CAPT. STRETCH

Commanding Officer of the WAAC company now stationed at Fort Dix, 1st Officer Stretch is a resident of Newtown, Pa. She entered the armed forces last July, receiving her basic training at Fort Des Moines, Iowa.

Word of her promotion was received here by her parents, Mr. and Mrs. Harold Stretch.

Private John F. Branigan, 1442 E. Orange st., who was graduated as a radio operator from the Army Signal Corps school at Fort Monmouth, N. J., is now serving with the Army Air Corps in the Alaska area. He is 18 years old.

Lionel Hansen, 2223 N. Carlisle st., a former composing room employe of The Inquirer, has been promoted to corporal at the Army Air Base, Abilene, Tex. He is now a cook in the Officer's Mess Hall at the base.

CORP. HANSEN

H. John Gold, 6412 N. Fairhill st., former newspaper representative and graduate of the Olney High School, the School of Industrial Arts and the Charles Morris Price School of Advertising, has been promoted to sergeant at the Army Base, Fort Dix, N. J., where he is serving in the personnel section of an Air Force unit.

Private First Class William J. Bings, 4238 N. 7th st., graduated as honor man in his class of skilled aircraft mechanics at Seymour Johnson Field, N. C., last week. He is a graduate of Olney High School.

Seventeen-year-old Walter Powell Rahn, 1405 Unruh st., a recent graduate of Girard College, has been enrolled as a Naval Aviation Cadet. He has a brother, William C. Rahn, with the Army Air Corps.

First Lieutenant Richard A. Horstmann, Q. M. C., son of Ignatius J. Horstmann, Church road and City Line, is now stationed at the Boston Quartermaster Depot. Prior to being commissioned in the Quartermaster Corps last September, Lieutenant Horstmann was associated with I. J. Horstmann and Sons, Philadelphia wool merchants. He is a graduate of St. Joseph's Prep and Georgetown University.

Margaret Florette Spaeth, daughter of Mr. and Mrs. A. John Spaeth, of Lansdale, was married yesterday in the Reformed Church, Lansdale, to Sergeant George Bosler, U. S. Army, of Carlisle, Pa. Miss Spaeth, a graduate of Lansdale High School, attended Ohio Wesleyan University, and is now studying at Drexel Institute of Technology. Sergeant Bosler attended Mercersburg Academy and Franklin and Marshall College.

First Lieutenant Charles Cusworth, 3602 Fisk st., pilot of a North American Mitchell bomber somewhere in New Guinea, has carried out 24 missions against Japanese aircraft. The crew of the plane carried out 29 missions, during which two enemy bombers were destroyed and two damaged. In the March battle of the Bismarck Sea, in which Lieutenant Cusworth participated, the Mitchell aided in the complete destruction of a Japanese convoy, and the group's two squadrons in New Guinea scored 16 direct hits and 25 near misses on 10 separate vessels.

LT. CUSSWORTH

Ensign Ted Helmetag, U. S. N. secretary of the Priestman-Helmetag Co., 18 W. Chelten ave., left Philadelphia last Thursday to go on active duty. He has been associated with the Priestman-Helmetag firm since 1936 and has been secretary since 1941.

• • •

Lieutenant Sidney Glazier, 3013 W. Fontaine st., stationed at McChord Field, Washington, recently married Miss Sheila Kohlenbrner, of San Antonio, Tex., in the McChord Field Chapel.

• • •

Thomas T. Holme, 914 Fillmore st., serving with the Army Services of Supply somewhere in England, has been promoted to major. A graduate of Lehigh University where he received a B. S. and Master's degree in science, he entered the Army in September, 1941, as a second lieutenant. He has a brother, Lieutenant (j. g.) Justus M. Holme, U. S. N. R., who is an instructor at Annapolis. Major Holme is the father of two children, Judith, 5, and Thomas, Jr., 19 months old, who reside at the Fillmore st. address with Mrs. Holme.

First Lieutenant Donald C. Phelps, 123 Ellis road, Upper Darby, who served 18 months overseas in World War I, is now attending the Coast Artillery school at Fort Monroe, Va. He formerly was employed in the Claims Department of the Philadelphia Electric Co.

LT. PHELPS

Reuben Fleischman, 829 Ritner st., stationed with the Air Task force somewhere in the Caribbean area, has been promoted to sergeant. He is a radio operator. Also promoted to sergeant and serving in the same area is James Bruner Hoffner, 2615 S. Rosewood st.

• • •

Eric Holliday, 231 W. Johnson st., a commercial artist and former engraver with the Evening Public Ledger, is training to become a medical soldier at the Medical Replacement Centre, Camp Pickett, Va. He is a graduate of the Academy of the Fine Arts.

• • •

Selected for aviation cadet training with the Seventh Air Force in the Pacific are: James C. Willis, 5248 Castor road, who enlisted in the Air Force in September 1941, and prior to his appointment served 11 months in the Hawaiian Islands; and Richard A. Bosch, 3241 Potter st., who enlisted in the Infantry in May 1940. He was a bandsman, prior to his appointment.

Lieutenant George Wichteman, 3230 Rawle st., who was graduated from the Officer Candidate School at Fort Warren, Wyoming, is now serving in North Africa. He is a graduate of Northeast High School and Temple University and was employed with the du Pont Company, Wilmington, before entering the service.

Recent graduates from the Army Air Force Antisubmarine Command School at Langley Field, Va., are Sergeant Patsy Mascio, 422 N. Robinson st., and Corporals Anthony Sadonis, 131 Dudley st., and Wesley V. Golcher, 3550 Sheffield ave.

• • •

Five sons of Mrs. Julia Donnon, of Paoli, who enlisted in the Army and Navy are: Private Andrew Donnon, Jr., with the paratroops at Camp Butner, N. C.; Third Class Petty Officer Charles A. Donnon, a veteran of the African campaign, stationed at Brooklyn, N. Y.; Private Albert Donnon, with a Cavalry unit at Los Angeles, Calif.; Private Edgar W. Donnon, stationed at the Army Reception Centre, New Cumberland, and Seaman Second Class Frank P. Donnon, stationed with the Navy at Williamsburg, Va.

• • •

Private Edwin Mawhinney, 5651 Arch st., a graduate of West Catholic High School, has successfully completed the radio operators' course at Scott Field, Ill.

Private, First Class, Harry W. Muhlberger, 307 E. Levick st., who recently completed the Army clerical course at Woodbury College, Los Angeles, is now stationed at Tinker Field, Okla. He is a graduate of Olney High School.

Commissioned second lieutenants in the Army Air Forces and awarded silver wings of pilots at Turner Field, Albany, Ga., are: George Wright Ferguson, 6242 Wissahickon ave.; Albert Joseph Kernagis, 243 Dickinson st.; Julian Allen Benson, Jr., 7 S. Harwood ave., Upper Darby, and Edward John Adams, 3214 Fanshawe st.

First Lieutenant Richard E. Ricks, 6327 Buist ave., has been transferred to Fort Sill, Okla., for advanced officer's training.

Three soldiers from this city who were graduated from the Army Air Force airplane mechanics school at Roosevelt Field, N. Y., are Ernest C. Prinz, son of Mr. and Mrs. Ernest Prinz, 208 E. Levick st.; Harry E. Mankonen, 2743 S. Beulah st., and Joseph Petty, 22 E. Seymour st. Prinz attended Gratz High School and formerly was employed at the Brewster Aircraft plant near here. For years he was a newspaper carrier in the Tioga section of Philadelphia.

PVT. PRINZ

Private, First Class, Petty's brother, John, is serving in the British Army. His wife, Catherine, lives at the Philadelphia address.

Jacob T. Finger, 135 W. Lippincott st., stationed with the armed forces in the Panama Canal Department, has been promoted to corporal. He entered the Army in July, 1941.

Private Anthony D'Angiolini, 1901 N. Howard st., who has completed his "jumps" at Fort Benning, Ga., is now a full-fledged "Paratrooper." He is now going to communications school at the same base.

Henry A. Weiss, son of Mr. and Mrs. William Weiss, 6518 N. 13th st., has been commissioned a second lieutenant in the Army following his graduation from the Officer's Candidate School, Fort Benning, Ga. A graduate of Northeast High School and Temple University Law School, where he was active in fraternity life and sports, Lieutenant Weiss, before entering the service, was a member of the law firm of Weiss, Bylk and Biron. He is past president and organizer of the Kensington Synagogue and Community Centre and past president of Kraus Lodge, Brith Sholom.

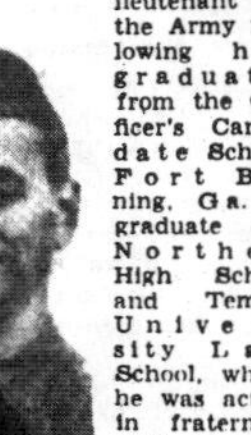

LT. WEISS

• • •

Captain D. Stanley Ross, 1828 E. Lansing st., who served with the A. E. F. in France in the last war, Control Officer in Headquarters Company, New Cumberland Army Reception Centre, has been transferred to the Executive Staff at Camp Lee, Va. He is the father of Corporal Robert S. Ross, now serving with U. S. forces in Africa.

NAVY

Naval Aviation Cadet Charles Robert Mills, 22, son of Mrs. Frank Mills, of Essington, is following in the footsteps of his father, the late Frank Mills, who was one of the first Army aviation instructors in World War I, and founder of the Essington School of Aviation.

Cadet Mills, who was taught to fly seaplanes by his father, recently completed his primary flight training at the Naval Air Base, Anacostia, D. C. He will receive his advanced flight training at the Naval Training Centre, Pensacola, Fla.

A graduate of Ridley Park High School, he was employed at the Naval Aircraft Factory here prior to entering the Navy.

Alexander J. Carota, 5117 Girard ave., is now receiving his recruit training at the Bainbridge (Md.) Naval Training Station.

John Coffey, 2313 W. Tioga st., serving with the Navy in Alaska, has been promoted from seaman, second class, to petty officer, third class.

Dorothy Kauffman Brown, 618 Linwood ave., Collingswood, has been commissioned an ensign in the U. S. N. R. and has been assigned to active duty. She is a graduate of Drexel Institute of Technology. Another WAVE commissioned an ensign in the U. S. N. R. is Miriam B. Jamison, a graduate of the University of Pennsylvania.

ENSIGN BROWN

The following bluejackets are now in training at the Naval Training School for signalmen on the campus of the University of Chicago: Albert Boghosian, 3335 N. Hope st.; Emil R. Geiger, 2818 Overington st.; Andrew J. Galbraith, 2643 Reed st.; Joseph J. Brownlee, 17, 2633 Webster st.; William J. Wendell, 2658 S. 73d st., and John J. Rubison, 712 S. Ithan st.

• • •

Receiving specialized training in anti-submarine warfare at the Submarine Chaser Training Centre, Miami, Fla., are: Electrician's Mate, Second Class, John J. Devine, 1730 N. 27th st.; Fireman, Second Class, Phillip L. Hallworth, 7710 Loretta ave.; Electrician's Mate, Third Class, John F. Campbell, 2754 Gratz st., and Quartermaster, Third Class, William D. Whittby.

• • •

Enrolled in the U. S. N. R. Midshipmen's School at Notre Dame University is William R. Watson, Jr., 4 Griffin lane, Haverford, Pa.

Seaman, second class, Mario Rossi, 2814 Van Pelt st., has completed his basic training at the Naval Training Station, Sampson, N. Y.

Fireman Hallworth, a graduate of Frankford High School, participated in the operations at Casablanca.

Harry A. Oakes, Jr., 19, 2614 S. Rosewood st., serving in a Naval base hospital in North Africa, has been promoted to Pharmacist, first class.

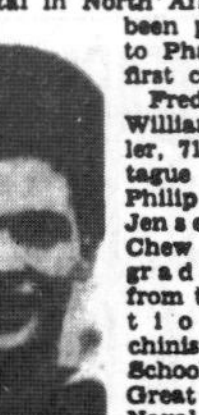

PH.-M. OAKES

Frederick William Dassler, 7180 Montague st., and Philip Joseph Jensen, 5539 Chew st., who graduated from the Aviation Machinist's Mate School at the Great Lakes Naval Training Station, have been advanced to third class petty officer ratings.

Cadet Nelson Bailey Phillips, Jr., 7839 Bayard st., has completed his primary flight training at the Naval Air Station, Hutchinson, Kas. He is a graduate of Germantown High School and attended Drexel Institute of Technology.

• • •

Thomas F. Greany, 2491 N. 50th st., and Paul F. Kyack, 5822 Hadfield st., who completed their preflight training at Chapel Hill, N. C., are now learning to fly airships at the Lakehurst Air Naval Station.

MARINES

John F. Burns, 228 Lincoln ave., Manoa, serving with the Marines in Ireland, has been promoted to sergeant. He enlisted in the Marines in 1938.

Sergeant Thomas J. Stanton, Pennsgrove, N. J., serving with the Marines in the British West Indies, has been promoted to platoon sergeant. With seven years of former service, he re-enlisted in the Marines in May, 1942.

Private Walter J. Kollock, 2616 S. Rosewood st., now serving with the Marines somewhere in the South Pacific, celebrated his 19th birthday yesterday. He is a next-door neighbor of Pharmacist's Mate Harry A. Oakes, Jr., mentioned under the Navy heading.

PVT. KOLLOCK

Charles E. Wardell, 1443 S. Vodges st., attached to Headquarters and Service Company of Headquarters Battalion at the New River, N. C., base has been promoted to corporal.

Private Robert Hecht, 2818 W. Columbia ave., has been accepted for training as a Paramarine at the New River base.

Privates first class Francis J. Spence, Jr., 5834 Dickens st., and Vincent Procopio, 3947 Haverford ave., and Privates John A. M. Kruzinski, 2628 Tilton st., and Frank R. Orant, 1924 N. 2d st., have completed the Field Telephone Operators' course at the New River base.

John William Muldoon, Jr., 209 Third ave., Haddon Heights, N. J., has been commissioned a second lieutenant in the Marines, following his graduation from the Naval Air Training school, Pensacola, Fla.

Garbo May Star In Shaw's 'St. Joan'

Bob Alda Brought to Hollywood To Make Test for Gershwin Role

By Louella O. Parsons

HOLLYWOOD, April 21.

A VERY hot tip just received is that Greta Garbo will in all probability star in George Bernard Shaw's "St. Joan." The Garbo has always been eager to play Joan of Arc and the offer has come to her from Gabriel Pascal, who will make the picture in England and release it through Metro-Goldwyn-Mayer. A deal has been pending for several weeks and is due to be signed any minute.

Very quietly and without one word from the studio, Bob Alda has been brought to Hollywood by Warner Brothers to make a test for the role of George Gershwin. Alda, who formerly worked in burlesque and more recently in night clubs, looks a little like Cary Grant and a great deal like the late composer. I had thought John Garfield was all but set for this role, but apparently Warners are still looking and if this boy's test is all right, he'll get the job.

When Ann Rutherford married the good-looking young merchant, David May, a lot of people said: "Bet he talks her out of a career." But knowing Annie herself, I thought otherwise. And just by way of proving that even a movie columnist can be right part of the time, Mrs. May has not only remained in the movies but 20th has just handed her a new contract. Her first picture on the new deal will be Helen Deutch's "Goodbye, My Lover, Goodbye." 'Tis a sentimental little yarn about a boy rejected by the Army—and his gal.

Chatter in Hollywood: What looked like storm clouds brewing over Linda Darnell's honeymoon in the form of a suspension from 20th Century-Fox is now officially explained as "just a leave of absence" for the bride. Maybe so, but the fact remains that Linda is out of "The Girls He Left Behind" and that someone else will be recruited to take her place in the cast with Alice Faye and Carmen Miranda. As usual in these cases, there are two schools of thought: Linda claims she hurt her leg while dancing with Tony de Marco for a sequence in the movie and asked for a leave, which was granted. But there are persistent rumors that 19-year-old Linda's elopement with 42-year-old cameraman Pev Marley may have had something to do with upsetting the applecart.

ANN RUTHERFORD

A Line or Two: Terrific strain Eddie Polo, former star of the silent screen, has been under. His wife, living in Vienna at the time of the Nazi blitz, seems to have completely disappeared. At least Eddie, staging a comeback in Deanna Durbin's "Hers to Hold," has had no word from her since the Germans marched in . . . Remember Baby Marie Osborne? She has grown into a lovely girl with such a charming singing voice that "U" is looking for a role in a musical for her.

The most original gift of all was the card sent Ouida and Basil Rathbone on their 17th wedding anniversary by David Bacon. He took his No. 17 shoe ration coupon and printed April above it so it looked like April 17. "Now you and Ouida toss a coin for it," he said. The anniversary party was very nice and everyone was there. Dame May Whitty introduced me to her attractive daughter, Market, who is visiting her mother. She has been appearing in Shakespearian sketches. Many guests stayed on to see "Desert Victory" . . . On my way to the Rathbones, stopped at the home of Mr. and Mrs. William Schuchardt to a cocktail party given for Captain Gene Raymond. He looks so well and brought many messages from Bebe Daniels and Ben Lyon. He planed out that night to join Jeanette MacDonald in New York . . . Sabu, minus his turban, which always looks as if it grew on his head, made his first night club appearance at the Florentine Gardens. He is now 18 and will soon join Uncle Sam's Army . . . The New Trocadero opens tonight and it will be a highly important evening to the Naval Aid Auxiliary, for a large part of the proceeds will go to swell their coffers.

Snapshots of Hollywood Collected at Random: The newest dinner duet in town is Errol Flynn and his new leading lady, red-haired Julie Bishop . . . Eleanor Roberts presented her editor husband, Franklin Phillips, with a daughter . . . Joan Fontaine and Brian Aherne gave the boys at the Hollywood Canteen a treat when they appeared there Sunday night. The night before Joan danced every dance with the boys at the Officers Club at the Beverly Wilshire . . . Eva Gabor and Alan Curtis are ablaze . . . Betty Grable has left the hospital but will have to rest for a few weeks before she returns to the studio . . . Helene Reynolds is devoting her evenings to Rodney Soher, rich Englishman.

Veronica Lake's baby, who does as much traveling as Mrs. F. D. R., is coming here to spend Easter with her grandmother . . . Betty Field, who has finished her stint in Charles Boyer's movie, has returned to her husband and baby at their Connecticut farm . . . Ed Wynn directed his whole show the other eve to Jack Benny and had the audience in stitches.

Amusement Guide in Philadelphia

PAGEANT

CONVENTION HALL—"We Will Never Die," memorial for Jews murdered by Hitler. 8.30.

MOTION PICTURES

ALDINE—"Saludos Amigos," Disney's characters tour South America. 11, 12.45, 2.25, 4.25, 6.15, 8.05, 9.55; "Desert Victory," the British chase Rommel in Africa. 11.45, 1.35, 3.25, 5.15, 7.05, 8.55, 10.45.

ARCADIA—"Keeper of the Flame," Spencer Tracy discovers Katharine Hepburn's secret. 11.35, 1.50, 3.35, 6, 8.05, 10.

BOYD—"Slightly Dangerous," comedy-romance, with Lana Turner, Robert Young and Alan Mowbray. 11, 12.45, 2.25, 4.25, 6.15, 8.05, 10.

CAPITOL—"The Mysterious Doctor," melodrama, with John Loder. 11.40, 1.50, 3.55, 6.05, 8.10, 10.15. Reviewed today.

EARLE—"Journey Into Fear," Nazi agents pursue Joseph Cotten on shipboard with Orson Welles and Jack Moss. 11.10, 2.05, 5.05, 8.05, 10.25. Hal McIntyre and orchestra, Alan Mowbray on stage.

FAYS—"Dixie Dugan," Lois Andrews as the comic-strip girl; with James Ellison. 1.10, 3.35, 6.10, 8.40, 11. Dooley Wilson heads stage bill.

FOX—"Something to Shout About," musical, with Janet Blair, Don Ameche, Jack Oakie, William Gaxton. 11.15, 1, 2.50, 4.35, 6.25, 8.10, 10.

KARLTON—"The Powers Girl," musical, with Carole Landis, George Murphy and Anne Shirley. 11.10, 1, 2.45, 4.30, 6.30, 8, 9.55.

KEITH'S—"Hello, Frisco, Hello," musical drama in color; with Alice Faye and John Payne. 11, 12.45, 2.35, 4.25, 6.15, 8.10, 10.

MASTBAUM—"Air Force," a U. S. bomber in Pacific action; with John Ridgely, Gig Young, Harry Carey. 11, 1.15, 3.25, 5.35, 7.45, 10.

NEWS—"The Mad Miss Manton," mystery comedy, with Barbara Stanwyck and Henry Fonda. 8, 9.30, 11.05, 12.45, 2.20, 3.55, 5.30, 7.05, 8.45, 10.20, and all night.

STANLEY—"Star-Spangled Rhythm," musical, with Bing Crosby, Bob Hope, Dorothy Lamour and all-star cast. 11.35, 1.40, 3.45, 5.50, 7.55, 10. Reviewed today.

STANTON—"Frankenstein Meets the Wolf Man," Bela Lugosi vs. Lon Chaney; with Ilona Massey. 11, 12.50, 2.40, 4.30, 6.20, 8.10, 10.

STUDIO—"Diary of a Nazi," German soldiers loose in Europe. 12.16, 2.42, 5.23, 7.50, 10.20; "Spring Song," Soviet musical, added.

EVELYN
Plays her violin with Phil Spitalny and his girl orchestra in the stage show at the Earle tomorrow.

Ghost Film Makes Debut At Capitol

"THE MYSTERIOUS DOCTOR," a Warner Brothers picture; from an original screen play by Richard Weil; directed by Ben Stoloff; opened yesterday at the Capitol.

THE CAST

Harry Leland	John Loder
Letty	Eleanor Parker
Lieutenant Christopher Hilton	Bruce Lester
Dr. Holmes	Lester Matthews
Hugh	Forrester Harvey
Bart Redmond	Matt Willis
Saul Bevans	Art Foster
Herbert	Clyde Cooke
Ruby	Phyllis Barry

All's fair in love or war, so now it's a headless ghost the Nazi agent has cooked up to prevent the British villagers from working that tin mine in rural England and thus help beat Hitler. This is the theme of "The Mysterious Doctor," which opened yesterday at the Capitol.

There's not much to the story. Matt Willis plays the village halfwit, who has sense enough to ferret out the mystery, encouraged by Eleanor Parker, who's pretty and sympathetic. John Loder, Bruce Lester and Lester Matthews have the male leads.

S. L. S.

'Star Spangled Rhythm' Opens on Stanley Screen

Gaiety, Glamor and Goofiness Make This Revue a Bargain

"STAR SPANGLED RHYTHM," a Paramount picture; original screen play by Harry Tugend; sketches by George S. Kaufman, Arthur Ross, Melvin Frank and Norman Panama; lyrics by Johnny Mercer; music by Harold Arlen; directed by George Marshall; opened yesterday at the Stanley.

THE CAST

Pop Webster	Victor Moore
Polly Judson	Betty Hutton
Jimmy Webster	Eddie Bracken
B. G. DeSoto	Walter Abel
Sarah	Anne Revere
Mimi	Cass Daley
Hi-Pockets	Gil Lamb
Mr. Fremont	Edward Fielding
Mac	Edgar Dearing
Duffy	William Haade

With Bing Crosby, Bob Hope, Fred MacMurray, Franchot Tone, Ray Milland, Dorothy Lamour, Paulette Goddard, Vera Zorina, Mary Martin, Dick Powell, Veronica Lake, Alan Ladd, Eddie (Rochester) Anderson, William Bendix, MacDonald Carey, Susan Hayward, Marjorie Reynolds, Betty Rhodes, Dona Drake, Lynne Overman, Gary Crosby, Albert Dekker, Johnnie Johnston, Ernest Truex, Mabel Paige, Cecil Kellaway, Katherine Dunham, Arthur Treacher, Walter Catlett, Sterling Holloway, Golden Gate Quartette, Barbara Britton, Walter Dare Wahl and Company, Slim and Sam, Cecil B. DeMille, Preston Sturges and Ralph Murphy.

By Mildred Martin

Paramount reaffirms its faith in stars—or, rather, star-packed screen revue—with "Star Spangled Rhythm," which opened at the Stanley yesterday. Having gotten its hand in with "The Big Broadcast" series in years past, the studio applies the same method to its latest fancy, vastly entertaining super-duper effort.

Virtually every star, feature and contract player on the lot, plus Cecil B. DeMille and Preston Sturges, have been rounded up for the occasion. And it is an occasion. Most of the skits and individual acts are hilarious. So is the yarn upon which they are strung, which finds Victor Moore, former Western star now gateman at Paramount, posing as executive vice president in charge of production for the benefit of his sailor son.

STARS TO THE RESCUE

Energetically assisted by Betty Hutton, Moore's wistful little Mr. Milquetoast carries off the masquerade in characteristically endearing fashion. Of course, he nearly drives Walter Abel, the real executive, mad. But Son Eddie Bracken and his Navy pals have the time of their lives; and when fate seems about to close in, the stars, to a man or a glamor girl, come to the rescue, put on a whopping show for Bracken's shipmates.

Among the high spots are Paulette Goddard, Dorothy Lamour and Veronica Lake kidding themselves and Hollywood in their "Sweater, Sarong and Peek-a-boo Bang" number; Vera Zorina's lovely "That Old Black Magic" ballet; and the "If Men Played Cards as Women Do" skit featuring Franchot Tone, Fred MacMurray, Ray Milland and Lynne Overman. Bob Hope romps off with the film whenever he appears, particularly when he shares a shower with William Bendix.

BING INTRODUCES GARY

Bing Crosby takes care of the pretentious patriotic finale and, for good measure, introduces Gary, a chip off the Crosby block, to screen audiences. Alan Ladd garners laughs by committing murder with bow and arrow instead of gun; Mary Martin and Dick Powell are charming in a musical sequence; and Rochester, assisted by Katherine Dunham, has a swingy zoot suit song-and-dance. Loudest and longest laughs of all went to Betty Hutton whose frantic attempts to scale a wall are made more frantic by the "assistance" of Walter Dare Wahl and his partner.

This only skims the surface of all Director George Marshall has crowded into "Star Spangled Rhythm," a movie bargain if ever there was one, considering the gaiety, glamor, goofiness and good-nature that have been wrapped up and delivered for the price of a single admission.

Send your original menus using only non-rationed foods—to the Non-Ration Recipe Editor. Win cash prizes for planning ration-saving meals.

Dell Lists Contest For Young Artists

Robin Hood Dell announces a National Young American Artists Competition, open to vocalists, pianists, violinists and 'cellists between 18 and 30 who have previously been unheard as soloist with a major symphony orchestra. The winner will receive $250 and appear in this summer's Dell "Young American Artists" series.

Application forms for auditions may be obtained from the Young American Artists Competition Committee, Bankers Securities Bldg., Juniper and Walnut sts., and must be returned by May 28. Auditions will be held early in June.

Real Estate for Sale
GERMANTOWN

● NEW SINGLE HOMES

Sedgwick Farms

MT. AIRY

$12,500

ARDLEIGH STREET AT MT. PLEASANT AVE.

A. P. ORLEANS & CO., Builders
C. A. PAYTON Agent
Wis. 3433

SUBURBAN

DREXEL HILL

4 Bedroom Single Home

Exceptional value. Vacant. Lot 60'x100'.

$6500

FRANK McCLATCHY
69TH AND WALNUT STREETS
Boulevard 0696 or ALL. 8989

DREXEL HILL. Only 1 remaining. NEW STONE HOME, in finest location. Center hall, den & powder rm., 3 bedrms., 2 baths. All large rooms & closets, latest equipment & improvements. Attractive financing. ½ block to bus. $11,850.
CHAS. SHELDRAKE
Mason & Township Line Sunset 1767.

DREXEL HILL. 904 ALEXANDER AVE. IMMEDIATE POSSESSION! Reconditioned single home with tile bath, unfin. attic, garage & auto. heat. Near transportation, schools, stores, etc. $7550. A REAL BUY! Wm M KNATZ, INC., Boulevard 0400-ALL 8633. OFFICE OPEN TODAY 1 to 5 P M

DREXEL HILL. Here's a fine roomy house for the family man. Colonial center hall, 1st fl. brick, balance clapboard; lge. living rm., dining rm., breakfast rm., kitchen, 5 bedrms., 3 baths, sun parlor, 2-car gar.; lge. lot, best section. With bus or trolley service most conv. Only $9500.
W. J. VOGT. SUNSET 2789

DREXEL PARK

American Colonial Brick and Clapboard home of distinction, with slate roof, is offered at $15,000 for first time today in this choice residential section of Delaware county. An open flagged patio leads from a large living room, 3 fireplaces, 3 tile baths 4 bedrooms, all brick recreation room, weather-stripped, insulated, metal screens, storm doors, 2-car heated attached garage.

DREXEL HILL

Well built stone & cement twin house, 5 bdrms., 3 baths, 2-car gar., lot 200 ft. deep, good section, close to transp. $7500.

New all-brick, coal heat, 3 bedroms, basement laundry, overhead garage doors, immediate possession, $5670.

Many Other Good Properties For Sale

SIDDALL

2269 Garrett Road, Drexel Park
Clearbrook 0173
Open Sunday 1 to 5 P. M.

DREXEL PLAZA. 4000 block Vernon road. 6 rooms, tile bath, garage. Modern. Price $4970. B. and L. clean-up opportunity. WILLIAM PUGH, 5713 Market. Gra. 3300.

EAST LANSDOWNE, Pa. Single house, 7 rooms & bath, attic, steam heat, oil burner, 2-car garage, lot 75 ft. x 180 ft., fruit trees. F. Iles, 38 Hirst ave.

ELKINS PARK

INVESTORS

The finest income-producing

APARTMENT HOUSE

anywhere in this vicinity

7845 MONTGOMERY AVE.

Pressure of other business makes it necessary for owner to sell. Rare opportunity. Brings in $6390 yearly. Never a vacancy. Located only ½ block from R. R. station, shopping center and schools. Olney ave. bus passes door. Includes 11 large, bright, completely modern apartments, in perfect condition, large garage building. Valuable lot 143'x220'. If you recognize a real opportunity, investigate this property at once.

GEORGE W. RICHARDS, JR.
16 S. Broad St. Loc. 7337

ELKINS PARK

8214 Marion Rd. Attractive single home, center hall, library, large lot, 2-car gar. Sacrifice.

GETZ & CO.

6722 York Rd. Open Sun. 2 to 5 P. M.
"Have No Regrets—Deal With Getz"

ELKINS PARK—¾ of an acre, one minute to trains, schools, shopping; 2-story Dutch Colonial, 4 bedrooms, 3 baths, maid's room; 2-car garage, chauffeur's quarters. Exceptional value at $21,000.

JACK M. LANGSDORF
6728 YORK RD. OPEN SUN. HAN. 6500.

ELKINS PARK—$7000. Easier terms. Single 6 rms. & bath, enclos. porch. Fireplace, storm sash, screens. Insulated. 2-car garage, lot 50x150. Immed. poss. HOLLOWAY 6822 York Rd. Han. 1550. Open Sunday 11 to 5. Ask for Mr. Hope.

ELKINS PARK. 2½-sty. det. home near Cheltenham High School. 7 rms., tile bath, open porch, gar. Vacant. $8000. Kuhn & Lowery, Inc. 5th & Rockland sts. Mic. 2638

EVERGREEN ESTATES (Haverford Twp.). Nearly new, brick Colonial single. Large living room; ultra-modern kitchen; cozy breakfast alcove finished in knotty pine. 4 splendid bedrms.; colorful tile bath, garage, insulation & many other extras. Only $7900. Closed Sunday. SLOAN & LYNCH, Llanerch. Hilltop 50-50.

FLOURTOWN, located in open section, with grand view of Whitemarsh Valley, modern single stone & brick house, 2 years old...

GLENSIDE

FENNINGER & RENNINGER

GREENHILL FARMS

WILLIAM PUGH

Real Estate for Sale
GREAT NORTHEAST

Formal Opening Today!

AN ENTIRE COMMUNITY OF NEW HOMES . . .

Pre-Viewing "AMERICA of TOMORROW"

Wissinoming Park Homes . . . in LOWER MAYFAIR

Phila.'s Greatest value, priced at only

$4650

TOTAL MONTHLY $34.10
MONTHLY SAVING 13.33
NET MONTHLY $20.83

Don't miss seeing these new homes embodying ALL the features of beauty, comfort and convenience which are the AMERICAN WAY OF LIVING. Only 3 minutes to Frankford Elevated Terminal, within a block of beautiful 43-acre Wissinoming Park . . . THE PERFECT HOME LOCATION. Automatic gas heat, automatic domestic hot water, 3 bedrooms, garage, rock wool insulation, breakfast nook, recreation space, tile bath with shower . . . every convenience. Furnished guest home open 11 A. M. until 9 P. M. every day.

S. & S. CONSTRUCTION CO.
A. SINGER and JOHN SCHULKE, Bldrs.
MAHLON RANCK, Agt.
Longshore & Rowland Aves.
Jef. 9604 MAY. 1344

LARDNER STREET
1 BLOCK WEST OF
6100 FRANKFORD AVE.

★ WAR WORKERS ★ Here Are the Homes You're Looking For!

ANOTHER SINGER OPERATION—YOUR ASSURANCE OF "QUALITY"

New Colonial Homes
$4600
INCLUDING AUTOMATIC GAS HEAT
Preference Given War Workers
4300 BLK. OAKMONT ST.
ESAN CO., Inc., Builders
ONLY $7.70 WEEKLY OUTLAY

ATTENTION War Workers
THESE NEW HOMES ARE Selling Fast!
3 Bedrooms, Brant gas heat, Garage. Fully Insulated. Large Lot.
$34.28 Monthly Charges
13.66 Monthly Saving
$20.62 Actual Mo. Cost
6300 BLK. GLENLOCH ST.

HARRY W. RAFF
67th & Ogontz Ave. Han. 5533

NORTH PHILADELPHIA

1800 Blk. Eleanor St.
4800 N. (Bet. 18th & 19th Sts.)
$4750
BEAUTIFUL NEW HOMES—IMMEDIATE POSSESSION
6 Rooms, Tile Bath, Hardwood Floors, Garage
These Homes Can Be Purchased by War Workers With a Small Down Payment
BOARDMAN-SMITH CORP.
AGENT ON PREMISES

Half Sold in Two Weeks!
3 BEDROOM HOMES
Only $4490
$490 DN. $33.27 Mo.
Near to Fast Transportation
2 Blocks to #56 Trolley on Erie Ave.
P. Bus Stops at Corner
CLARIDGE STREET
Between Luzerne & Lycoming Sts.
Conrad J. Gettler, BUILDER — John P. Henrie, REALTOR

SUBURBAN

HAVERFORD

$12,500.
This mellowed stone Colonial is outstanding for its charm and individuality. Beautiful lot with dogwood & evergreens. Center hall plan with 4 bedrms. & 2 baths. Easily financed.

WYNNEWOOD

$13,500.
Lovely all-stone Colonial in a select section. Walking distance to transportation & schools. Cen. hall plan with 4 bedrms. & 2 baths; also maid's room & bath.

OVERBROOK HILLS

$10,500.
$1000 down and the balance on mortgage will buy this attractive Colonial residence. Gross monthly chgs. of $85 and an average monthly saving of $47 possible. Unusual 1st fl., with 4 bedrms. & 2 baths on 2d fl., also maid's room & bath. 2-car garage.

NARBERTH

$8000.
Unusual opportunity in a bungalow-type property. Large cor. lot in a fine residential community. 1st fl. contains unusual living quarters with 2 bedrms. & bath plus extra utility rm. 2d fl. has 3 bedrms. & bath. Ideal for professional use. Definitely a bargain price.

NASH REALTY CO.
Main Line Real Estate
Ard. 2400. Nar. 4010.
Gre. 2494. Tri. 6242.

HIGHLAND PARK

NEW ALL-MASONRY HOMES IN "West Overbrook Park"

Close to Transportation, Stores and Schools

$5565—$565 Cash
$39.43 Month

Brand-new, all-stone and brick homes with garage. Featuring Gar Wood heat, 3 bedrooms, modern tile bath with shower, vestibule entrance with coat closet, fireproof slate roof, ¾" oak floors throughout. Rock wool insulation. Immediate contact with several bus lines and high-speed trolley (only 5 min. to 69th st.). Surrounded by 3 golf courses, yet near stores, public and parochial schools, etc. Sample open daily and Sunday. 10 A. M. to 9 P. M. Directions—From 69th and Market drive out West Chester pike to 2d traffic light (N. Lynn blvd.), turn right 1 square to sample or Brookline or Ardmore bus from 69th st. to N. Lynn blvd. and City Line.
COUNTY BUILDERS. Phone Sunset 9939

HIGHLAND PARK

Four bedrooms! You will really enjoy living in this single home. There's a log-burning fireplace...

W. A. CLARKE CO.
6822 Market St. Blvd. 960 or ALL. 2635

HOLMECREST SINGLE STONE HOME
211 HOLMECREST ROAD
KUHN & LOWERY, INC.

JENKINTOWN
Beautiful Single Home
Cor. Cloverly & Rodman Ave.
KUHN & LOWERY, INC.

JENKINTOWN
ALFRED H. TRANK

SUBURBAN

LANGHORNE, single (8) r., 2 bths. 2 kitchens. Can rent portion as apt. $50 per mo. 2-car gar. 3 acres. Beautiful location. $14,500. Inf. C. Harry Heinz, 4413 Frkd.

LANSDOWNE

This home is complete—complete in every detail. Solarium, first floor library and powder room, four bedrooms, two tile baths, two-car garage. $10,000—and well worth it!

W. A. CLARKE CO.
6822 Market St. Blvd. 960 or ALL. 2635

LANSDOWNE—Attractive corner property on lot 110x165. Center hall, lg. living rm.; open fireplace, 4 bedrms., bath & sunporch on 2d fl. 3 bedrms. & bath on 3d fl. (With kitchen added would rent for $40.) Oil burner, h.w. heat. Near Penna. R. R. Station. $6750. Open for inspection today from 3 to 5 P. M. Charles Noll, Marshall road & Windermere ave. All. 4646 or Mad. 3600.

LANSDOWNE—Modern twin with enclosed porch. Library off living rm., 3 bedrms., tile bath, attic, detached garage. Excel. cond. No money needed to be spent to put this property into cond. IMMEDIATE POSSESSION. 2 blocks to Penna. R. R. Asking price $6250. Charles Noll, Marshall road & Windermere ave. All. 4646 or Mad. 3600.

LANSDOWNE—Very attractive 3 bedroom home, almost new, tile bath, weather-stripped, insulated, copper screens, venetian blinds, garage. See it today. $4,850.
Kershaw & Raney, 51 Long Lane
Upper Darby. Gra. or Boulevard 1700.
Office Open After 1 P. M. Today

LANSDOWNE. Semi-detached, 6 rooms, tile bath, hot-water heat. Good condition. Only $37.05 month. Small down payment. WALNUT MANAGEMENT CO., PEN. 0800 or SAR. 1818.

LANSDOWNE, 282 W. Greenwood—Mod. twin, immediate possession, must be seen to be appreciated. Price only $4975. Minimum down payment, balance less than rent. See it today, open 2 to 5 P. M.

LANSDOWNE—Gladstone Manor, 14 Gladstone rd. 7 rms. & 2 baths, enc. porch, ideal loca. 2 minutes to elec. line sta. Price $8,000. Bonneville. Gra. 2223.

LANSDOWNE, 212 Chapman av. Semi-det., 6 rms. & b., det. gar. Immed. poss., $4190. Stapleton, 6539 Elmwood av. Sar. 3959.

LARCHMONT—Bungalow, 6 room & bath, ¼ acre, only $5500. Chas. W. Russell, Newtown Square, Pa.

LLANERCH—Single well built, lge. living rm., fireplace; 3 bedrms. T. bth., encl. sun rm. on 2d floor; lge. attic. Gar. Sunset 2635.

MANOA, 428 Virginia Avenue, one of Today's Outstanding Values, under $8500. Modern used single home on large corner lot, 6 rooms and bath, equipped with combination storm and screen sash, Venetian blinds, insulated, for Inspection Sunday 1-5 P. M. Consult
CABALLERO, EXCLUSIVE AGENT, Gre. 1804- Cyn. 1804.

MARBLE HALL—Gas station & refreshment stand on Ridge Pike. Zoning prevents nearby competition. Estab. business with living quarters. Lot 100x149. Single house, 6 rms., b., encl. pch., 2 car gar. $8750. KELLNER, 400 Bethlehem Pk. Che. 6700.

MEDIA Vicinity $7000 Country Home, good cond., 7 rms. & bath. Modern conv. Hot water heat, coal fired, over 2 acres of level fertile land, 1 acre all ready planted, 15 apple trees, peach, cherry & old shade...

MELROSE PARK
918 MELROSE AVE.
Open for inspection today

MELROSE PARK
1211 STRATFORD AVE.

HAGEDORN
6718 York Road Waverly 1700.

MERION

HOOVER & POLLOCK

HARRIS & BUNTING

MERION

BIDDLE N. HUNT

H. P. MacFARLAND

OXFORD CIRCLE
LARGEST AND BEST BUILT HOME IN TOWN FOR ONLY $4850 EASIEST TERMS
800 BLOCK CARVER ST.
FINESTONE & SONS, INC., Builders
Jackson-Cross Company

(OXFORD CIRCLE) HERE IS VALUE! IMMEDIATE POSSESSION GOOD TRANSPORTATION
$390 DOWN
1300 Blk. Gilham St.
At Magee & Castor Ave.
E. D'AMBROSIO

SUBURBAN

MERION
Northeast Corner
WYNNEWOOD ROAD and LATCHES LANE
Wm. H. W. Quick & Bro., Inc.

MERION
501 Wynnewood Road
Wm. H. W. Quick & Bro., Inc.

OAK LANE

LANGSDORF

OAK LANE

GETZ & CO.

OAK LANE 1008 70TH AVE.

Real Estate for Sale
SUBURBAN

Green Ridge Homes

ASTON TOWNSHIP, DELAWARE COUNTY
Near Chester

ATTENTION, WAR WORKERS!
These Homes Are Ready for Immediate Occupancy

Single homes, modern kitchen, large rooms, large lawns, Victory gardens. Only a 15-minute drive to all defense plants in the Chester area or by short line bus to Chester.
Call Chester 2-9735 for directions to sample home.

$4565 to $4765 ● SMALL DOWN PAYMENT
NET CARRYING CHARGES $30 PER MONTH

F. A. COLLINS, Builder. Chester 2-9735

Every Home-Seeker Should See These Beautiful Modern

"Greenway Ave. Homes"

$3290
20% DOWN

CARRYING CHARGES LESS THAN RENT!

IN ONE OF THE MOST CONVENIENT LOCATIONS ADJOINING WEST PHILADELPHIA

FURNISHED SAMPLE HOUSE OPEN TODAY 1 to 6 P. M.
300 BLOCK GREENWAY AVE.
ONE BLOCK NORTH OF 300 MAIN ST., DARBY

DAVID E. TRIESTER, Agent, 6622 WOODLAND AVE. SAR. 3200

West Overbrook Park

$565 DOWN
$39.43 MONTH

69th SECTION MODERN HOMES $3500
SMALL MONTHLY PAYMENTS / LONG TERM MORTGAGES
ONLY 10% DOWN
For Information Apply to
W. S. PEACE, Inc.
69th & Walnut Sts., Upper Darby
BLVD. 4800 ALL. 3800

Better HURRY! These new COLONIAL HOMES Selling Fast! $7.56 PER WEEK APPROX.
York Garden Homes, Inc.
BUILDERS

DREXEL HILL
$5670 $570 CASH
TWIN BRICK HOMES BRAND NEW
RALPH B. WHITLEY, BLDR.

SPRINGFIELD
16 WINDSOR CIRCLE
OPEN TODAY 2 TO 6 P. M.
TAULANE-SPIESS—Wal. 1860

CITY

ABSOLUTE AUCTION
Clear of Mortgages Without Reserve
BEAUTIFUL CHESTNUT HILL RESIDENCE
203 W. CHESTNUT AVE.
SAMUEL T. FREEMAN & CO.
Auctioneers—1808-10 Chestnut Street

AUCTION
CLEAR OF MORTGAGES
TRUSTEES SALE IN BANKRUPTCY
REAL ESTATE & CREAMERY EQUIPMENT
THOMAS DAIRIES
Wed., May 26, 1943, at 11 A. M.
SAMUEL T. FREEMAN & CO.

ONLY 5 AVAILABLE
Better Decide TODAY!
$3490
$250 DOWN
2-STORY APARTMENT TYPE HOMES . . .
WITH RECREATION-ROOM BASEMENT
3700 BLK. RICHMOND ST.
EDWARD A. KERR & CO., Builders

SUBURBAN

OAK LANE

OVERBROOK

CABALLERO

OVERBROOK HILLS IN MERION

PAOLI

W. A. CLARKE CO.
6822 Market St. Blvd. 960 or ALL. 2635.

PENN VALLEY
EXCLUSIVE

WILLIAM PUGH

PENN VALLEY

BIDDLE N. HUNT

OVERBROOK HILLS

WILLIAM PUGH

Real Estate for Sale
SUBURBAN

UNIQUE in the MAIN LINE SUBURBS ★ 5 SOLD LAST WEEK

NEW MERION HOMES
EDGEHILL ROAD . . . 1 square north 54th & City Line

Stone and brick construction—only new homes of this type available in this exclusive, convenient location. Handy to schools, shopping center, transportation. 4 bedrooms, 3 baths.

PRICE $12,750

CENTRAL PLANT HEAT

J. FRANKLIN MOSS & CO. . . . Builders

27½ ACRES WITH 3 ROAD FRONTS
At intersection of Limekiln Pike, Welsh Rd. & Butler Pike
ABSOLUTE AUCTION
WED., JUNE 2, AT 7:15 P. M.
Louis Traiman AUCTION CO. OF PA.

LIQUIDATION SALE
7 VALUABLE PROPERTIES IN MEDIA, PA.
APARTMENT HOUSE
2 DWELLINGS
4 VALUABLE LOTS
ABSOLUTE AUCTION
SAT., MAY 29

CITY

VALUABLE CORNER HOME
811 W. ERIE AVE.
ABSOLUTE AUCTION
WED., MAY 26, AT 7:15 P. M.
Louis Traiman AUCTION CO. OF PA.

TRUSTEE'S SALE
2 VALUABLE LOTS
ABSOLUTE AUCTION
Wed., May 26, at 3 P. M.
Louis Traiman AUCTION CO. OF PA.

726 N. 19th ST.
ABSOLUTE AUCTION
WED., MAY 26, AT 2 P. M.
Louis Traiman AUCTION CO. OF PA.

NEW JERSEY

MAGNIFICENT RESIDENCE, LOT 100'x200', IN THE VERY FINEST LOCATION ANYWHERE IN CAMDEN'S SUBURBS
259 KINGS HIGHWAY, East
Adjoining HADDONFIELD, N. J.
AUCTION
CLEAR OF MORTGAGES

OPEN TODAY 2 TO 5 P. M.
FRI., MAY 28, 7:15 P. M.
Louis Traiman AUCTION CO. OF PA.

SUBURBAN

HARRIS & BUNTING

SUBURBAN

ROSLYN
NOT A DIME

$6850
BENNEWITT

Continued on Next Page

20,820 Fans Watch Phillies Defeat Cubs, 5-4

The Philadelphia Inquirer

PHILADELPHIA, WEDNESDAY MORNING, MAY 19, 1943

On the Spot

Talking Is Tougher

Ross Prefers Fighting to Speeches

By JOHN WEBSTER

"TALKING," remarked the round-faced young man with the silver streaks in his hair and the three chevrons on his sleeve, "takes more out of men than fighting ever did."

Figuratively, Sergeant Barney Ross, of the Marines, is in there punching every minute when he talks to the workers in the war plants. His intense, straight-from-the-heart words are spoken for his pals out there in the Pacific . . . wherever our armed forces may be, and may require the weapons these home-front soldiers can produce.

TALKS FROM HIS HEART

"I tell them that I've seen lots of blood spilled. My heart's blood is in those talks. I give them a ringside description of this fight," related this Marine hero of Guadalcanal. "To them I explain how vital they are to our fighters. How tremendously important are their jobs. They must keep production moving on time. I make them realize they're on a battlefield, too!"

Sitting in the cool of the lounge in a mid-city hotel, the former lightweight and welter champion explained to his friend, Herman Taylor, how desperately he'd tried to get here from Pittsburgh on Monday night—to attend the Arena fights, as scheduled. "I tried to hire a private plane . . . They told me 'Barney, we'd fly you for nothing if we could' . . . But all planes were grounded."

BOXING HIS FIRST LOVE

Nothing would delight this heroic youth more than to witness the Beau Jack-Bob Montgomery title bout at the Garden on Friday night . . . and the Henry Armstrong-Maxie Shapiro 10-rounder here next Monday night at Convention Hall. . . . He can't make it, however.

"Boxing's my first love," said Barney over and over again as he ate his lunch. He likes ball games, too, and following a banquet last night in Chester, he hurried to Philadelphia to watch the Phils-Cubs night game. "I hardly ever get to see a ball game," he said, ruefully.

IN GOOD TRIM

Ross, who came home suffering from malaria, appeared in good trim. His left arm, he confesses, isn't what it used to be. The elbow was chipped by bullets. "There's nothing wrong with my right arm—or fist, however, I still can take care of any belligerents at his Loop cocktail lounge in Chicago.

"I never lost a fight there," grins the Sarge.

Cathy was out shopping yesterday as Barney sat with the boxing promoter. The Missus, he admitted, takes care of the tough part of traveling. Packing, unpacking and all detail work. They changed hotels here yesterday, due to Barney's whim to be unpacked twice.

CATHY MINDS PURSE-STRINGS

"She asked me if she could go shopping," chuckled the champion. "I said 'Why do you ask me, honey? You've got all our money.'" So Mrs. Ross shopped for a "few dresses 'n' things," but it was Barney who had to buy her robe. "She says I've got marvelous taste!"

Barney has a new idea to submit to his bosses in Washington one of these days. A plan by which he believes he and Cathy can aid materially in the war effort. To date, it's strictly off the record, however.

One of Ross' first moves on reaching Philadelphia yesterday morning was to phone the mother of a chaplain he had met "out in the Pacific." In every city, he has phone calls to make and questions to answer . . . for relatives of our fighting men.

BULLETS PLAY NO FAVORITE

Did I ever see Jimmy Tygh at Guadalcanal? Sure, I knew him . . . and Billy Beauhuld, the lightweight fighter . . . and Indian Johnny Rivers . . . Sure, I knew all those fellows."

Rivers, we told him, had fought in the A. A. Tourneys, was a valiant, distinguished ringman in Philadelphia. He was always in there, punching. Just as he was when a Jap bullet found him.

It doesn't matter whether you were a preliminary fighter or a champion," observed the gray-haired young man. "A bullet plays no favorites."

Soldiers May Compete for Football Title

WASHINGTON, May 18 (A. P.).—Rep. Monroney (D., Okla.) today proposed a National Service teams' football championship for the 1943 season.

"If the War Department would . . . it and select the men to . . . the schedules and so forth, it . . . be handled nicely," Monroney . . . a reporter. "Most of the . . . brains in the country are in . . . schools now; there would be . . . difficulty in outfitting the teams. . . . the games could be played in . . . college fields.

MORALE-BUILDER

"There would be approximately 200 . . . available for eliminations, . . . on a regional arrangement, . . . the regional winners going into . . . final rounds during November.

. . . large colleges and universities . . . already announced that . . . ball would be dropped next fall . . . of a shortage of players. . . of these players now are in . . . branch of service.

. . . hate to see football disappear . . . from the scene in any part of . . . country," Monroney said. "It's . . . fine a morale-builder for the . . . men."

Governali Honored

NEW YORK, May 18 (U. P.).—Paul Governali, Columbia University's great passer, will be awarded the Charles M. Rocker, Jr., Prize . . . at the Columbia senior who . . . himself most worthy of . . . distinction. . . . It was announced today.

Kelly May Be Sports Head

F. D. R. May Appoint 3-Man Committee To Decide Problems

WASHINGTON, May 18 (A. P.).—President Roosevelt said today he probably will appoint a committee of three to consider problems of carrying on organized sports in wartime and make recommendations to him.

The President has been getting a lot of letters, he explained at a press conference, from proponents of various sports asking such questions as whether night baseball should be played and whether this or that sport should go on in view of transportation congestion.

CONSIDERS COMMITTEE

As a result, he said, he is seriously considering naming a small committee which could look into such matters and which would provide the sports world with an official body to which it could take its wartime problems. He added that he thought it would be composed of three persons and would have no power except to make recommendations.

There has been agitation both in sports circles and in Congress for establishment of an agency of that nature, with some urging that a sports co-ordinator or "czar" be named.

VARIOUS REPORTS

Mr. Roosevelt said he was not ready to mention any names. There have been reports in Congress, however, that John B. Kelly, of Philadelphia, might head such a committee. Other names mentioned have included Senator Mead (D., N. Y.) and Herbert Bayard Swope, of New York.

In a speech in the House today, Rep. Dilweg (D., Wis.) urged that sports, including the spectator variety, be encouraged rather than curtailed.

CONTRIBUTE TO VICTORY

"Sports are contributing to American victory," declared Dilweg, an end at Marquette University in his undergraduate days and later wing-man with the Green Bay Packers of the national professional football league. "They are giving our youngsters basic training that makes them the greatest fighting men in the world.

"The strongest argument for sports on the home front," he continued, "is that the men in our fighting forces . . . want spectator sports to continue at home and hungrily await news of sports results.

"Major league baseball, I contend, is an essential industry. So are professional football and other spectator sports, which provide for the relaxation of spectators and offer refreshing news reading for millions of war workers."

FITNESS DIRECTOR

Kelly, former Olympic rowing champion, could not be reached at his home last night. After directing the Hale America movement, he became director of the Nation-wide physical fitness program, a post he still holds.

Apostoli Gets Real Chance At Jap Planes

AN ADVANCED SOUTH PACIFIC NAVAL BASE, May 18 (U. P.).—Freddie Apostoli, the San Francisco bell-hop, who fought his way to the world middleweight championship, is serving as gun captain of an exposed 40-millimeter gun mount in the Pacific Theater, it was disclosed today.

The 30-year-old boxer revealed that he had applied for the post after two Japanese raids in which the turret where he served as "shellman" was not brought to bear on the attackers.

WAITING FOR JAPS

"It made me feel madder than if I were in the ring with my hand tied," Apostoli, veteran of two years in the Navy, said. "I'm ready for those Jap planes to come back again now."

The one-time champion has given over 30 boxing exhibitions on ship and shore in the war zone—at Marine encampments and on board cruisers, carriers and battleships.

Don't Look Now, But---

Gymnastics at Girard

GIRARD COLLEGE will not lack for gymnastic action this summer. Dora Lurie reports, because G. H. Heineman will teach tumbling there. Heineman, a member of Temple's physical education faculty and veteran coach of the Philadelphia Turners, is credited with developing such stars as Annapolis Coach Chet Phillips, Mrs. Eugene C. (Bobbie Ranck) Bonniwell and Pearl Perkins Nightingale. His Turners took 16 of 18 medals in the National A. A. U. gymnastics at New York this winter.

SERVICE MEN—Tom Nelson, the tackle, is in the Signal Corps at Camp Crowder, Mo.; Walter Gregonis, the end, in the Medical Corps at Camp Robinson, Ark.; Walter Monroe, a quarterback, at the Atlantic Ordnance Depot, and Tackle John Donaldson in the Air Corps at Buckley Field, Denver. Col. according to Penn Football Coach George Munger. . . . "A guy who speaks as little French as I do is lost in North Africa," Lieutenant Tom Parrell, ex-Cornell gridder and trackman, writes Leo Riordan, "but I am fast becoming master in the art of sign language." . . . Fred Sweet, Brown U. fullback of a decade ago, is an Army lieutenant teaching illiterates their ABC's at Camp McClellan, Ala. . . George Butz informs.

AROUND AND ABOUT—A.A.U. officials have scheduled the senior mile championship along with the junior national events at New York on Saturday, June 18, instead of on Sunday, June 19, with the other senior events. This is in deference to Miler Gil Dodds, the former Boston divinity student. . . Gene Perrone, Woodrow Wilson High outfielder, got 10 hits in 20 tries for a .500 percentage in his first five games. Charley Smerin relates . . . Cy Twombly, the old big leaguer, recently pitched three innings for his Washington and Lee '03 baseball team against the Army's Special Service batsmen, Lieutenant Dave Zinkoff pens from Lexington, Va.

—ART MORROW

(A. P. Wirephoto)

PHOTO WAS NEEDED TO DECIDE THE PLACE WINNER IN THIS RACE

Pig Tails, Woolford Farms entry, won without question in the sixth race at Lincoln Field track yesterday with N. James in the saddle. But Real Sad (left) and Joan T (No. 2) needed a photo to determine the place victory, with Real Sad being successful. Distant Isle (on the rail) was fourth.

Smith Winner In Big Ten Golf

By DAVE HOFF

CHICAGO, May 18 (A. P.).—Flooded out of its original site and forced to operate for two days under difficult playing conditions at the substitute course, the Big Ten golf tournament came to a novel close today when Ben Smith of Michigan and Jim Teale of Minnesota tied for the championship. It was the first time in the meet's 22-year history this had occurred.

Conference coaches decided that the tie should stand, with both Smith and Teale receiving duplicate championship medals.

MICHIGAN RETAINS TITLE

Michigan successfully defended its team title, but the 1289 total score of its low four men for the 72-hole distance was a record high. Northwestern's team was second, three strokes back at 1292.

Smith and Teale each shot a 72-hole 311, 27 strokes over the Westmoreland Country Club's par. Jim McCarthy of Illinois, the defending individual champion, wound up ninth with a 323 after leading the field the first day.

Ben Smith, Michigan	156	74	81	311
Jim Teale, Minnesota	152	79	80	311
Dick Peterson, O. State	[illegible]	[illegible]	[illegible]	[illegible]
John Stoltz, Northwestern	[illegible]	[illegible]	[illegible]	[illegible]
Jim Stewart, Northwestern	[illegible]	[illegible]	[illegible]	[illegible]
Robert Fife, Michigan	[illegible]	[illegible]	[illegible]	[illegible]
Douglas Oldenburg, Wis.	[illegible]	[illegible]	[illegible]	[illegible]
John Lorms, Ohio State	[illegible]	[illegible]	[illegible]	[illegible]
James McCarthy, Illinois	[illegible]	[illegible]	[illegible]	323
John Campbell, Chicago	[illegible]	[illegible]	[illegible]	[illegible]
Herbert Matter, Illinois	[illegible]	[illegible]	[illegible]	[illegible]
Philip Marcellus, Mich.	[illegible]	[illegible]	[illegible]	[illegible]
Arnold Hennig, Wisconsin	[illegible]	[illegible]	[illegible]	[illegible]
Eugene Modjeska, Ill.	[illegible]	[illegible]	[illegible]	[illegible]
Robert Love, Ohio State	[illegible]	[illegible]	[illegible]	[illegible]
Warren Williamson, NW	[illegible]	[illegible]	[illegible]	[illegible]
Louis Lick, Minnesota	[illegible]	[illegible]	[illegible]	[illegible]
Robert Kogh, Minnesota	[illegible]	[illegible]	[illegible]	[illegible]
Jack Duers, Northwestern	[illegible]	[illegible]	[illegible]	[illegible]
Robert Tapscott, Illinois	[illegible]	[illegible]	[illegible]	[illegible]
Andrew Ladd, Wisconsin	[illegible]	[illegible]	[illegible]	[illegible]
William Ludolph, Mich.	[illegible]	[illegible]	[illegible]	[illegible]
Robert Kampfer, Ohio State	[illegible]	[illegible]	[illegible]	[illegible]
Lyle Robertson, Minnesota	[illegible]	[illegible]	[illegible]	[illegible]
Dick Turnbow, Illinois	[illegible]	[illegible]	[illegible]	[illegible]
Preston Crabill, Ohio State	[illegible]	[illegible]	[illegible]	[illegible]
William Evans, Wisconsin	[illegible]	[illegible]	[illegible]	[illegible]
Jack Peters, Wisconsin	[illegible]	[illegible]	[illegible]	[illegible]
Roscoe Bonisteel, Michigan	[illegible]	[illegible]	[illegible]	[illegible]
Burt Abrahams, Northwestern	[illegible]	[illegible]	[illegible]	[illegible]
Luke Pascale, Chicago	[illegible]	[illegible]	[illegible]	[illegible]
Vytold Yasus, Chicago	[illegible]	[illegible]	[illegible]	[illegible]
Harry Goldstein, Chicago	[illegible]	[illegible]	[illegible]	[illegible]
John Williams, Minnesota	[illegible]	[illegible]	[illegible]	[illegible]
Robert Wilson, Indiana	[illegible]	[illegible]	[illegible]	[illegible]
Walter Zuhl, Indiana	[illegible]	[illegible]	[illegible]	[illegible]
Bill Ritchie, Indiana	[illegible]	[illegible]	[illegible]	[illegible]

Appleton Chase Won By Rouge Dragon

BELMONT PARK, NEW YORK, May 18 (A. P.).—Fresh from two triumphs at Pimlico, M. A. Cushman's Rouge Dragon continued his winning streak this afternoon when he took the $2870 first money in the 22d Charles L. Appleton Steeplechase of about two miles. The Gelded son of Annapolis, well handled by Mr. J. S. (Johnny) Harrison, scored by three lengths over Bayard Sharp's Knight's Quest, the favorite.

Rokeby Stables' Redlands, winner of the stake last year, came from far back to be third. Kent Miller's 1942 jumping champ, Elkridge, again failed to impress, finishing a poor fourth under his heavy burden of 161 pounds. Isidore Bieber's Frederic 2nd was fifth, with G. H. Bostwick's Sussex bringing up the rear.

RIDER SHAKEN UP

The Beak led to the eighth hedge, then fell with J. Jordan, who has a 10 pounds rider allowance. Jordan was removed for first aid. Lechlade lost his rider at the 10th of the dozen obstacles.

A crowd of 13,423 saw Rouge Dragon, the second choice at $8.70 for two, finish in 3:49 4-5.

Jordan was reported merely shaken up.

PIG TAILS TRIUMPHS

CHICAGO, May 18 (A. P.).—Pig Tails, 3-5 choice, carrying the colors of the Woolford Farm Stable, won the Colleens Purse at Hawthorne today.

The four-year-old filly, an eligible for Saturday's $5000 Crete Handicap, took the lead after being given an early tussle by Distant Isle and led the rest of the way under hard urging by Nick Jemas. A length and a half behind, James Emery's Real Sad headed W. U. Ridenour's Joan T. for second. Pig Tails returned $3.20 and the time for the six muddy furlongs was 1.17 1-5.

ABBE PIERRE WINNER

BOSTON, May 18 (A. P.).—One length separated the first three finishers in the $1500 Roslindale, allowance feature over a mile and 70 yards, at Suffolk Downs today, with H. M. Babylon's Abbe Pierre, imported six-year-old, the winner. L. B. Sheppard's Kan as ran second with Charlie Rufi's Dense Path third. Four lengths further back was B. B. Jones' Ksar of Audley.

The field of seven was reduced by one at the gate when B. S. Campbell's Barbara Childs reared and fell in her stall, and so injured herself that the stewards ordered her scratched.

MURPHY DETROIT STEWARD

DETROIT, May 18 (A. P.).—State Racing Commissioner William J. Dowling announced today the appointment of Joseph A. Murphy, veteran turfman from St. Louis, as steward at the Detroit Fairgrounds track for the 73-day meeting starting Saturday.

Murphy is coming out of retirement to accept the new post, Dowling said.

Schoolboy Race To Be Upstream

For the first time in recent history of rowing in this city the annual National Scholastic Championships will be held upstream on the Schuylkill next Saturday.

Officials of the Schoolboy Rowing Association of America, which is sponsoring the titular regatta, decided last night that all of the races will be started south of the Columbia ave. bridge, and the boys will row against the current, upstream, over a one-mile course, with the finish at the Public Canoe House, just south of the Dauphin st. trolley bridge.

REASONS GIVEN

Muddy condition of the river, with shallow spots under the trolley bridge, caused the officials to make the unexpected shift in the regatta plans. W. E. Garrett Gilmore, former national sculling champion, and chairman of the Schuylkill Navy's schoolboy committee, explained last night.

"There was a conference with Fairmount Park officials," Gilmore explained, "and we decided to make the change. We think it will eliminate the shallow spots and produce a fairer course for four crews to row, if that many may appear on the starting line."

AWAIT ENTRIES

Eight-oared crews from the Shrewsbury, Mass., High School, and the St. Andrew's School of Middletown, Del., will compete against Roman Catholic High of this city, in the eight-oared championship, with Lafayette High, of Buffalo, still a possible entry, Gilmore stated.

Moroz Knocks Out Rival in First

NEW YORK, May 18 (A. P.).—Big Ben Moroz, 295-pound slugger from Philadelphia, knocked out Gilbert Stromquist, 256½, Austin, Tex., in the first round of their scheduled 10-round main event at the Broadway Arena.

Moroz flattened Stromquist for a six-count as the bout opened and when the Texan regained his feet the Philadelphian crashed through with a vicious right hook to the jaw. Stromquist toppled once more and Referee Jed Gahan didn't even bother to count to 10.

Green Kayoes Ross

BUFFALO, N. Y., May 18 (A. P.).—Johnny Green, 146½, Buffalo, scored a technical knockout over Joey Ross, 148, Toronto, in one minute and 55 seconds of the fifth in their scheduled eight-rounder tonight.

McLarin Stops Rozo

NEW BEDFORD, Mass., May 18 (U. P.).—Jimmy McLarin, 132, of New Bedford, scored a knockout over Jose Domingo Rozo, 130, of Colombia, in 2:41 of the first round of a scheduled 10-round feature tonight.

Haverford Keeps Interac Title

Haverford School retained the Interacademic League baseball title by defeating Friends Central, 12-0, yesterday at Haverford.

In the other league game, Penn Charter crushed Episcopal, 20-0, at City Line and Berwick road.

Craig Heberton was Haverford's winning pitcher, yielding four hits. Pemm Minster and Bob Russ shared the Friends' hurling, with the latter taking over in the fifth.

PENN CHARTER	r	h	o	a	e	EPISCOPAL	r	h	o	a	e
Dav'son,3b	3	1	0	1	0	Harris, 3b	0	0	1	1	1
Morrow,2b	4	3	1	0	0	B'p'm, 3b	0	0	[illegible]	0	0
G'achall,ss	2	1	0	3	1	Stanley, cf	0	0	1	0	0
Burpee,rf	3	1	0	0	0	Smith, c	0	0	3	3	1
Caldwell,rf	0	1	0	0	0	B'ley, rf	0	0	1	0	1
H'f'rer,1b	2	0	1	0	0	Ryan, lf	0	1	2	0	0
Aiken,1b	1	0	7	0	0	Potter, 3b	0	0	1	0	0
M'F'land,cf	1	0	0	0	1	Kent, 1b	0	0	2	1	3
Meyer,lf	2	2	0	0	0	D'c'sey, 1b	0	0	3	0	0
Hoober,c	1	0	1	0	0	Stone, 2b	0	0	3	0	0
Evans,c	0	0	5	2	0	Pugh, p	0	0	1	1	1
Raleigh,p	1	0	0	1	0	W'rill, p	0	0	0	0	0
Stawn,2b	0	0	0	1	0	Joline, p	0	0	0	0	0
						Ivory, p	0	1	0	1	0
Totals	20	9	15	8	2	Totals	0	2	18	7	7

Penn Charter — 11 5 0 2 2 0 —20
Episcopal — 0 0 0 0 0 x — 0

HAVERFORD S.	r	h	o	a	e	FRIENDS CEN.	r	h	o	a	e
Hunter,2b	1	2	3	1	2	D. F'est, lf	0	2	0	0	0
Baird,ss	2	1	3	0	0	W. F'est, 2b	0	0	3	1	0
L'leton,cf	3	2	0	0	0	Russ,1b-p	0	0	10	0	1
Curtis,c	1	1	5	0	0	Thomas,cf	0	0	0	0	2
Mauck,3b	1	1	0	1	0	Piefer, 3b	0	0	0	1	0
Yarrow,rf	1	0	0	0	0	A'strong,ss	0	2	0	8	1
Stahler,1b	1	0	2	0	0	H'singer,rf	0	0	0	0	0
Bowen,lf	0	0	0	0	0	Ogden, c	0	0	4	0	0
Heb'ton,p	1	1	3	0	0	Minster, p	0	0	4	3	1
Dillon,c	1	0	5	0	0						
Moore,lf	0	0	0	0	0						
Cozens,lf	0	1	0	0	0						
Tls.	12	9	21	2	2	Tls.	0	4	21	13	5

Haverford S. — 2 0 2 5 0 3 0 —12
Friends Central — 0 0 0 0 0 0 0 — 0

Zuppke Paints Grange Portrait

CHAMPAIGN, Ill., May 18 (A. P.).—Resplendent in a gleaming orange helmet and a bright blue jersey, Red Grange is running again—in a portrait painted by Bob Zuppke, the man who coached him to football immortality two decades ago.

After spending 29 seasons at the University of Illinois, Zuppke retired a year and a half ago. He now spends most of his time raising prize pigs (he started out with four and now has 250) down on his farm at Mahomet, Ill., writing V-mail to scores of football men in the service, or puttering around with his paintings.

Frankford Beats Germantown, 3-2

Behind the four-hit pitching of Ed Lyons, Frankford High beat Germantown Academy, 3-2, yesterday at Large and Dyre sts. The winning run was scored on singles by Jackson, Dilkes and Roddy.

GERMANTOWN A.	r	h	o	a	e	FRANKFORD H.	r	h	o	a	e
Garner,2b	[illegible]					Ruoff,3b	1	1	1	1	0
Hickes,3b	[illegible]					Proce,cf	1	1	1	1	0
Rohrer,p	[illegible]					Reid,lf	0	0	0	0	0
Kline,1b	[illegible]					Gitlin,c	0	3	0	0	0
Fluck,cf	[illegible]					Rocco,2b	[illegible]				
Holt,c	[illegible]					Add'son,2b	[illegible]				
Hahn,ss	[illegible]					Wilk'son,rf	[illegible]				
Armst'g,rf	[illegible]					M'C'ey,ss	[illegible]				
Shehle,rf	[illegible]					Ferenzi,lf	[illegible]				
Bechler,lf	[illegible]					Lyons,p	[illegible]				
						Jackson,2b	[illegible]				
						Dilkes,rf	[illegible]				
						Roddy,1b	[illegible]				
						Landell,1b	[illegible]				
Totals	2	4	18	7	1	Totals	3	5	21	9	1

Germantown — 0 0 0 0 2 0 0 — 2
Frankford — 1 0 1 0 0 1 x — 3

3-Run Rally in 5th Decides Night Game

Harrismen Go Into Fourth Place Tie; Northey Hits Homer, Then Is Injured

By STAN BAUMGARTNER

The largest crowd in the history of night baseball in the National League in this city—20,820—saw the Phillies whip the Chicago Cubs, 5-4, for the second successive time at Shibe Park last night.

A dramatic three-run rally in the fifth inning after two were out which erased a 3-2 lead held by the Bruins sent the Phillies on to their triumph in their first arc light battle of the 1943 season.

RON NORTHEY HURT

By their victory the Harrismen moved into a tie for fourth place with the Cincinnati Reds and reached the .500 percentage with 11 victories and a like number of defeats.

The conquest was a bit costly because Ronald Northey, whose thrilling home run started the locals on to their win, spiked himself on the right knee an inning later. He was carried off the field. The wound necessitated five stitches and the outfielder will be out of action at

The big fifth inning started inauspiciously. With the Cubs leading, 3-2, Si Johnson, whose fine pitching earned him his third victory against one defeat, rolled out to Stan Hack and Danny Murtaugh bounced out to Len Merullo at short.

FIREWORKS START

Then the fireworks started. Ronald Northey walloped one of Hiram Bithorn's pitches over the right-field fence for his first home run of the year, and the Phillies' tenth circuit clout of the season, to tie the score.

The huge crowd went wild, and when Danny Litwhiler smashed the next pitch against the left field wall for a two-bagger they almost tore the stands down. Jimmy Wasdell followed with a single at Ival Goodman's feet in right and Litwhiler scampered over with the run that sent the Harrismen ahead.

JOHNSON CHECKS CUBS

The din was terrific as Babe Dahlgren stepped to the dish and smashed a two-bagger to left center that sent Wasdell over the plate.

After that it was just a matter of keeping the Cubs in check and Johnson did this in fine style although the Bruins managed to push over a run in the sixth when Northey spiked himself chasing Bithorn's double and Ed Stanky sent the Cub pitcher home with a single.

STANKY MAKES 4 HITS

Stanky, the stocky little second baseman of the Cubs from our own Nicetown, was the star for the Bruins who, incidentally, lost their seventh consecutive game.

Before the contest Stanky was called to the plate, presented with a huge bouquet of flowers and an onyx clock sent by his Nicetown admirers. He then proceeded to make four successive hits, his first four trips to the plate, and drove in two runs. He was finally stopped on his last appearance in the ninth.

DAHLGREN CALLED

It was the 10th successive game in which he has hit, and he is now batting .350.

Manager Jimmy Wilson was ejected from the game for arguing with Umpire Dunn in the eigth inning.

The third game of the series will be played today with Charley Fuchs due to oppose Paul Derringer on the mound.

Babe Dahlgren, the Phils' shortstop, was notified yesterday to appear before Draft Board No. 52 today at noon, to undergo his physical examination for the Army. He will be given his test at 2601 North Broad st.

CHICAGO	*b.av.	ab.	r.	h.	rbi.	o.	a.	e.
Hack, 3b	.333	4	0	0	0	0	1	0
Stanky, 2b	.351	5	0	4	2	1	3	0
Cavarretta, 1b	.230	5	0	0	0	11	0	1
Nicholson, rf	.276	4	0	0	0	3	0	0
Goodman, lf	.143	4	1	1	0	3	0	0
Lowrey, cf	.296	4	0	1	1	3	0	0
Hernandez, c	.242	3	1	1	0	2	0	0
a-Martin	.270	1	0	0	0	0	0	0
Todd, c	.125	0	0	0	0	0	0	0
Merullo, ss	.222	4	1	2	0	1	3	1
Bithorn, p —W.3-L.4		3	1	2	1	0	1	0
b-D'lessandro	.215	1	0	0	0	0	0	0
Passeau, p —W.1-L.2		0	0	0	0	0	0	0
Totals		38	4	11	4	24	8	2

PHILLIES	*b.av.	ab.	r.	h.	rbi.	o.	a.	e.
Murtaugh, 2b	.313	3	1	0	0	0	2	0
Northey, rf	.275	3	1	1	1	2	0	0
Busby, rf	.000	1	0	0	0	1	0	0
Litwhiler, lf	.268	3	1	1	0	2	0	0
Wasdell, 1b	.288	4	2	1	1	8	1	0
Dahlgren, ss	.357	3	0	2	3	3	1	0
Naylor, cf	.176	4	0	0	0	0	0	0
May, 3b	.280	3	0	0	0	0	4	0
Livingston, c	.232	4	0	0	0	8	0	1
Johnson, p —W.3-L.1		3	0	1	0	1	1	0
Totals		31	5	6	5	27	9	1

a-Batted for Hernandez in 8th.
b-Batted for Bithorn in 1th.
b-Batted for Bithorn in 8th.

Chicago — 0 2 0 1 0 1 0 0 0—4
Phillies — 2 0 0 0 3 0 0 0 x—5

Two-base hits—Bithorn, 2; Litwhiler, Dahlgren. Three-base hit—Goodman. Home run—Northey. Left on bases—Chicago, 8; Phillies, 6. Base on balls—Off Bithorn, 4; Johnson, 1. Struck out—By Johnson, 5; Bithorn, 1. Hits—Off Bithorn, 6 in 7 innings; off Passeau, 0 in 2. Passed balls—Hernandez. Losing pitcher—Bithorn. Umpires—Dunn, Magerkurth and Stewart. Time of game—2.16. Attendance—20,820.

*Batting average 1943.

Norristown Winner

LANSDALE, Pa., May 18.—Norristown High baseball team piled up an early lead to defeat Lansdale High, 8 to 5, at Memorial Park, today. Piazza's three hits paced the County Seaters' attack.

Cardinals Defeat Brooklyn, 7 to 1

11,214 Fans See White and Brecheen Stop Dodgers

BROOKLYN, May 18 (A. P.).—Ernie White and Harry Brecheen, a pair of cagey southpaws, put the old silencer on the Brooklyn Dodger bats today and the St. Louis Cardinals evened their series with the Brooklyns, 7 to 1.

A crowd of 11,214 paying customers watched the Red Birds pound the offerings of the veteran Whitlow Wyatt industriously until they had five runs in less than five innings while White, the Card starter, was taking care of the Dodger batters nicely. In fact, when Billy Herman doubled to left in the fifth he was the first Brooklyn player to reach first base.

BROOKLYN	ab	r	h	o	a	ST. LOUIS	ab	r	h	o	a
Bordag'y,cf	4	0	0	0	0	Klein, 2b	4	1	1	2	2
Vaughan,ss	4	1	1	2	5	H.W'r,cf	5	1	2	3	0
Medwick,lf	4	0	1	0	0	Musial,lf	5	2	3	4	0
Camilli,1b	4	0	0	16	2	W.Co'r,c	5	1	3	2	0
Herman, 3b	2	0	1	2	3	Sand's,1b	3	0	1	6	0
F.Walker,rf	3	0	0	3	0	Brown,3b	4	0	0	3	1
Owen, c	3	0	0	0	0	Garms,rf	4	0	0	4	0
Kamp'is, 2b	2	0	0	3	2	Mar'n,ss	4	0	0	3	2
a-Cooney	1	0	0	0	0	White, p	2	1	0	0	1
Glossop,2b	0	0	0	0	0	Brec'n,p	1	1	1	0	0
Wyatt, p	1	0	0	0	1						
Allen, p	1	0	0	1	1						
b-Moore	0	0	0	0	0						
Webber, p	0	0	0	0	1						
Totals	29	1	3	27	15	Totals	37	7	11	27	6

a Batted for Kampouris in 8th.
b—Batted for Allen in 8th.

St. Louis — 0 1 2 0 2 0 0 0 2—7
Brooklyn — 0 0 0 0 0 0 1 0 0—1

Errors—None. Runs batted in—Brown, Musial 2, W. Cooper 2, Medwick, Klein, H. Walker. Two-base hits—W. Cooper, Herman, Medwick, Brecheen. Three-base hits—Musial, Klein. Sacrifice—Klein. Double play—Klein, Marion and Sanders. Left on bases—St. Louis 6, Brooklyn 3. Bases on balls—Brencheen 2, Wyatt 1, Allen 1. Strikeouts—White 1, Brecheen 1. Hits—Off White, 3 in 6 innings (none out in 7th); Brecheen, 0 in 3, Wyatt, 7 in 4 2-3, Allen, 0 in 3 1-3; Webber, 4 in 1. Winning pitcher—White. Losing pitcher—Wyatt. Umpires—Barlick and Pinelli. Time—1.58. Attendance—11,214.

Braves Blank Pirates, 4-0

BOSTON, May 18 (A. P.).—Home runs by Chuck Workman and Johnny McCarthy, each with a man on base, gave the Boston Braves a 4-0 victory over the Pittsburgh Pirates. It was the fifth straight win for the Braves.

The victory enabled the Braves to hold their second place lead over the St. Louis Cardinals and also to pick up a full game on the league-leading Brooklyn Dodgers, who were trounced, 7-1, by the world champions.

PITTSBURGH	ab	r	h	o	a	BOSTON	ab	r	h	o	a
Russell lf	4	0	0	1	0	Hol's cf	4	0	1	6	0
Barrett rf	4	0	1	3	0	Joost 3b	4	1	1	1	2
Fletcher 1b	4	0	0	9	1	Work'n rf	4	1	1	1	0
Elliott 3b	2	0	0	1	1	Ross lf	2	1	0	2	0
DiMaggio cf	4	0	1	2	0	McC'y 1b	3	1	1	12	0
Gustine ss	4	0	1	2	3	Poland c	3	0	0	1	1
Cos'art 2b	3	0	0	1	3	Ryan 2b	3	0	1	2	4
Lopez c	3	0	1	5	0	Wiet'n ss	3	0	0	2	3
Sewell p	2	0	1	0	2	Javery p	3	0	0	0	2
aWyrostek	1	0	0	0	0						
Herbert p	0	0	0	0	1						
Totals	31	0	5	24	11	Totals	29	4	5	27	13

a-Batted for Sewell in 8th.

Pittsburgh — 0 0 0 0 0 0 0 0 0—0
Boston — 0 0 0 4 0 0 0 0 x—4

Errors—Gustine. Runs batted in—Workman 2, McCarthy 2. Two-base hits—DiMaggio. Home runs—Workman, McCarthy. Stolen bases—Sewell. Double plays—Fletcher to Gustine to Fletcher, Wietelmann to Ryan to McCarthy. Left on bases—Pittsburgh 6, Boson 2. Bases on balls—Off Sewell 1, Javery 2. Strike-outs—By Sewell 5, Javery 2. Hits—Off Sewell 5 in 7 innings; Herbert 0 in 1. Losing pitcher—Sewell. Umpires—Conlan, Barr, Jorda. Time—1.28. Attendance—1026.

Errors Help Reds To Beat Giants

NEW YORK, May 18 (A. P.).—Two errors aided the Cincinnati Reds to score twice in the tenth inning today for a 3 to 1 victory over the New York Giants.

The winning rally started with a pass to Max Marshall after two were out. Gee Walker singled and Marshall came all the way home when Manager Mel Ott threw wild past first. Walker went to second on the play and when Frank McCormick singled to left, Walker scored on an error by Dick Bartell, who deflected Babe Barna's throw.

NEW YORK	ab	r	h	o	a	CINCINNATI	ab	r	h	o	a
Bartell,3b	4	1	1	3	5	B'ster,2b	5	0	0	3	1
Jurges,ss	4	0	1	1	3	Marsh'l,rf	4	1	0	2	0
Mayn'd,cf	5	0	1	6	1	Walker,cf	5	1	1	4	1
Ott,rf	3	0	1	3	0	McCor.,1b	4	0	1	10	1
Lombardi,c	4	0	1	6	0	Tipton,lf	5	0	0	1	0
Barna,lf	2	0	0	2	0	Mesner,3b	4	1	3	2	1
Gordon,2b	4	0	0	1	1	Miller,ss	4	0	1	1	3
Orengo,1b	4	0	0	8	0	Mueller,c	3	0	1	6	0
Sayles,p	2	0	0	0	0	Riddle,p	3	0	2	0	2
a-Mancuso	1	0	0	0	0	Beggs,p	1	0	0	1	1
Adams,p	1	0	0	0	0						
Totals	34	1	5	30	10	Totals	38	3	9	30	10

a-Batted for Sayles in 7th.

Cincinnati — 0 0 0 0 1 0 0 0 0 2—3
New York — 0 0 0 0 0 0 1 0 0 0—1

Errors—Ott, Bartell. Runs batted in—Mueller, Lombardi, McCormick. Two-base hits—Maynard, Bartell. Stolen bases—Barna, Ott. Double play—Walker and Brewster. Left on bases—New York, 8, Cincinnati 8. Bases on balls—Sayles 2, Riddle 5, Adams 1. Strike outs—Sayles 4, Riddle 4, Beggs 1. Hits—Off Sayles 5 in 7 innings; Adams, 4 in 3; Riddle, 5 in 7 2-3, Beggs, 0 in 2 1-3. Passed ball—Lombardi. Winning pitcher—Beggs. Losing pitcher—Adams. Umpires—Reardon, Ballanfant and Goetz. Time—2.24. Attendance—2813.

YANKEES CUT SQUAD

DETROIT, May 18 (U. P.).—New York Yankees pared their squad down to the 25-player limit today by releasing Catcher Aaron Robinson to Newark in the International League on option. Robinson hit 285 with the Bears last year. Robinson recently was reclassified 1-A.

Baseball Facts

NATIONAL LEAGUE

YESTERDAY'S RESULTS

PHILLIES, 5; Chicago, 4.
Boston, 4; Pittsburgh, 0.
St. Louis, 7; Brooklyn, 1.
Cincinnati, 3; New York, 1, 10 innings.

STANDING OF THE TEAMS

	W.	L.	P.C.
Brooklyn	17	8	.680
Boston	12	8	.600
St. Louis	12	9	.571
PHILLIES	11	11	.500
Cincinnati	12	12	.500
Pittsburgh	9	11	.450
New York	10	14	.417
Chicago	7	17	.292

Today's Schedule, Probable Pitchers And Their Records

Chicago vs. PHILLIES, at Shibe Park (3.15 P. M.)—Derringer (1-3) vs. Fuchs (0-3).

St. Louis at Brooklyn—Lanier (0-2) vs. Macon (3-0).

Cincinnati at New York—Vander Meer (4-2) vs. Lohrman (2-2).

Pittsburgh at Boston (2)—Gornicki (1-1) and Rescigno (1-1) vs. Andrews (3-1) and Jeffcoat (0-1).

AMERICAN LEAGUE

YESTERDAY'S RESULTS

ATHLETICS at Chicago, postponed.
Washington at St. Louis, postponed.
New York at Detroit, postponed.
Boston at Cleveland, postponed.

STANDING OF THE TEAMS

	W.	L.	P.C.
New York	14	8	.636
Cleveland	13	9	.591
Washington	14	11	.560
St. Louis	9	9	.500
Detroit	10	11	.476
ATHLETICS	11	14	.440
Chicago	8	11	.421
Boston	8	14	.364

Today's Schedule, Probable Pitchers And Their Records

ATHLETICS at Chicago—Christopher (2-3) vs. Smith (1-2).

New York at Detroit (twilight)—Borowy (1-3) vs. Newhouser (0-1).

Washington at St. Louis (2)—Pyle (3-2) and Leonard (3-1) vs. Galehouse (1-1) and Sundra (2-1).

Boston at Cleveland (night)—Hughson (2-1) vs. Bagby (4-1).

Continued on Page 35, Column 5

Photos by Weegee

Teen age hepcats formed lines at dawn, fought their way into the temple of jive.

When the orchestra began to "send," this couple leaped to the stage, went into their curious contortions.

Daughter of the Regiment

By Penelope Armstrong

JOAN ROBERTS has been called the girl who has everything. She is young, blonde, pretty, with a smile you don't forget and a golden lyric soprano voice. She is the hit of "Oklahoma!" itself the hit of the season on Broadway. (You can catch the end of the box-office line up around New Rochelle somewhere but you'll have to hurry.) She is seen, in fact, as perhaps the most outstanding success of the decade.

But there are two editions of Joan Roberts. The one you're not likely to see is a quiet, thoughtful, serious-minded and deeply religious young woman. One who regards her varied talents as something of a sacred trust; and who is devoted to honoring the memory of a hero father.

Despite late hours and days filled with hard work, Joan arises early each morning to go to church. No matter how busy she may be she manages to set aside some time to answer mail from boys in uniform. And not just because interest in the armed forces is popular at this time.

Joan Roberts, talented daughter of a hero.

AT THE Battle of Chateau Thierry during the First World War a gas alarm was sounded. A youthful sergeant, hurrying on his gas mask, caught sight of the chaplain lying wounded with his mask torn. The soldier tore off his own mask, fitted it on the priest, rushed away to find another for himself. But he was too late. He died that day on the battlefield.

The hero was Sergeant Julius Siegrist, Joan's father. When the remnant of his contingent returned home they looked up Siegrist's widow. They found his little daughter whose birthday is celebrated each year on the fifteenth of July, a date made immortal by the heroic stand of the Fighting Third in France.

The Chateau Thierry division called her 'Purple Heart,' and "Miss Thierry Dawn," presented her in its national convention as "The Third Division Girl," made her honorary colonel of New York's Third Division.

It probably is no exaggeration to say that Joan is even more proud of these honors than she is of the applause which rolls over St. James Theatre when she sings "Many a New Day" and "Out of My Dreams" in the musical "Oklahoma!"

UNLIKE most Broadway celebrities, Joan was born right in New York and now lives in a private house in Bedford Park only slightly removed from Times Square. She began to sing about the time she learned to talk but her voice those days was oddly low-pitched. "My brother, who really sang well, said it sounded like a foghorn," she remembers. Apparently the family agreed, for her warbling left them unimpressed. Then one day she boldly entered an amateur contest at the neighborhood movie theatre, sang "The Prisoner's Song," won first prize. Joan's mother took notice to the extent of giving the girl music lessons. Grandpa David Roberts, one-time top Irish dancer on the stage, began to train her in jigs, hornpipes, tap and ballet dancing.

The next thing that happened was when Joan, at the age of ten, found herself on a regular Saturday afternoon program on the radio. It was called the Sunbeam Hour and she was rigged out in a yellow dress and yellow bows to conform with the title.

Then a professor in high school wrote an operetta, "Heather Glenn" for Joan. He was so interested in her voice that he gave her special training after school, got her to believing she had real talent, awakened in her a first desire to go on the stage. She took part in singing and dancing competitions, won various prizes.

BUT once she had left school Joan got down to a career in earnest. She studied with Rafaelo della Marca and Estelle Leibling, broadcast on the Consolidated Edison hour. MGM became interested, offered her a chance at pictures. "But I wanted to make a name here first," she says.

Her whole idea was to sing at the Metropolitan. "I am a lyric soprano," she says, "and my design was and still is to sing in grand opera. All my studies have been classical. But even a singer has to eat. I was auditioned and got a role with the Municipal Opera in St. Louis in a preview of Oscar Hammerstein's 'New Orleans' in the summer of 1940. It was renamed 'Sunny River' for its New York run.

"I was cast as Madeleine. The critics were kind to me. Mr. Hammerstein liked my voice too. So when they started casting for 'Oklahoma!' well, here I am.

"BUT to take it chronologically. After 'Sunny River' I went to Dallas as the lead in 'The Student Prince,' 'Too Many Girls,' 'Irene,' and 'The Chocolate Soldier.' Then I was auditioned by the head of the Los Angeles Civic Opera and he engaged me for the lead in 'Hit the Deck.' That was in 1941.

"There I worked with Frank Albertson, Eddie Foy, Jr., Jack Durant and June Preisser. The production was given in the Philharmonic Auditorium in Los Angeles."

Then Miss Roberts went back to the St. Louis Municipal Opera, in the summer of 1942, and appeared in "Girl Crazy" and "No, No, Nanette."

Later there was an engagement with the Louisville Light Opera Company in "Naughty Marietta."

"And then," Miss Roberts added, "I came home and worked at Scarsdale, New York, in 'Heels Together.' That is the title of the new musical version of 'Little Jesse James' and it now is being revamped for a fling at Broadway."

"OKLAHOMA!" a musical adaptation of the play, "Green Grow the Lilacs," is a period show, of fifty years ago, done with such tenderness that audiences manage to forget the war briefly. "One night in Boston a kindly old lady came to me and said she couldn't thank me enough," says Joan. "She said, 'I have three sons in the service. I don't know where they are or even if they are alive. So tonight I thought I'd just try to stop worrying and see the play. It just took me out of myself. For two solid hours I was able to forget.'"

And now what may be an even greater triumph has come to the "girl who has everything." After only four weeks on Broadway she was offered a seven-year film contract at $1,000 per week! Whether pretty Joan Roberts will accept hasn't been decided.

But even if she doesn't the offer is an achievement not only for the hit singer of "Oklahoma!" but for that quiet, serious-minded Joan who gets up early each morning to go to church.

Jive Bombers

Youth's Craze for Swing Bands Called an Emotional Tension-Breaker During Critical Period

By Winifred Van Duzer

ABOUT the time dawn silvered the Chrysler spire, not long ago, lines began to converge upon Broadway's Paramount Theater. The lines were composed of youngsters, mostly in their teens, who looked oddly alike.

The boys wore pork-pie hats, trousers shaped like up-ended parachutes, overhanging coats plus dog chains some three feet long. The girls wore sweaters, saddle oxfords, scarves tied over their hair. Their expressions were alike, too; eager, ardent, blissful.

The kids not only looked alike; they were alike. For all were jitterbugs, gathered from New Jersey, up-State New York, Brooklyn, Long Island, to converge on the temple of swing. The sign over the theater marquee said "Harry James in person." And the hepcats had come to pay homage. Some had set their alarms for four o'clock to be on hand when the doors opened. Some had brought their lunches with a day's stay in view.

By seven o'clock long shuffling queues straggled along the block, around the corner, down the next block. At eight o'clock, hour of the first performance, the queue had spilled 7,000 into the theater, the lobby, on the street, around the stage door. Three dozen cops fought to keep order. One retired with smashed ribs. Another called for reinforcements when a plate glass window was shattered.

In the groove. One of 165,000 jitterbugs who helped Paramount gross $105,000 in a week of boogie-woogie.

JAMES is a slender, dark-haired young man, practically a replica of most slender, dark-haired young men. Yet when he stepped into the softened violet spot, raised the trumpet to his lips, blew a long note, his audience lapsed into something like a cataleptic trance.

Only for a moment, however. Then James began to give. "That sends you!" moaned a voice on the center aisle. A girl, probably sixteen, sprang to the stage, began to whirl with a partner. Her arms flailed like a windmill in a gale.

Boys and girls paired off, went through curious contortions up and down the aisles. Others swayed in their seats, clapped their hands, stamped their feet. They were in the groove. They were principals in a scene of mob frenzy.

The scene was repeated seven times daily during the time James and his orchestra played at the Paramount. Audiences for a single day numbered 20,000, mostly swing-crazy kids. When one of the players threw a handful of pictures into their midst they cheered and fought like tigers. A life-size photograph of James in the lobby was covered with lip-stick smears. They jammed the stage door to a point where he was unable to leave the theater.

THE sprinkling of adults who attended the fabulous saturnalia and who watched the hepcats jiggle, writhe, gasp, groan, jump up and scream toward the end of each song, couldn't understand it. A distinguished music critic went to investigate, announced that "Mr. James is a very good player, no better than a round dozen of his highly publicized colleagues of the same calling," confessed himself at a loss.

Then various psychologists, psychiatrists, behaviorists, gave the phenomenon consideration; and nearly all agreed that in times of crisis such as the war has set up with their pervading sense of insecurity, tension, heightened emotions, youth must find ways of working off steam.

"There is an element of mob hysteria in it," says a renowned neurologist. "Certainly no solitary hepcat would gyrate. Surrender to forms of music has run in cycles from primitive times. Musical intoxication is rhythm or the beat.

"All of life—the cosmos itself—is built upon the beat principle. It is the pulse—in this case primitive pulse—and it appeals to the primitive. Its appeal is closely connected with mob hysteria for you see the same responses in Germany, in the Nuremberg meetings, for example, where the multitudes are swung together under control. One of the secrets of Hitler's power as an orator is in his reiteration, in the beat, the rhythm of his speech. What he says doesn't matter!"

Orchestra leader Harry James with his silver trumpet.

OTHERS see a parallel between the jitterbug craze and the Children's Crusade away back in the year 1212. Swept by the induced fervor of the Crusaders, more than 50,000 children from all over Europe formed juvenile armies, followed their adolescent leaders toward the East. Thousands were captured, sold as slaves; thousands died of plague; few returned home.

Not many years later, hundreds of children left their homes in Central Europe to join mobs who gyrated from town to town in the frightful "Dancing Mania." "In Germany in 1237 more than 100 children of Erfurt were suddenly and irresistibly impelled by some morbid hallucination," one authority writes. "Many died of exhaustion; others were afflicted with palsy for the rest of their lives. From this it was but a step to the story of the Pied Piper of Hamelin who lured children into the mountains with the music of his pipes."

Then in the fourteenth century a dance mania called "chorea major" broke out in the Rhine Valley. Hosts of distracted people singly or hand in hand circled and jumped until they collapsed.

IN HIS monograph on "The Organic Background of the Mind," Dr. Foster Kennedy, neurologist of Cornell University, declares that dancing "is a body satisfaction, implicit in structure, not a matter of mind disembodied. Indeed the more primitive a people the more is the beat stressed in their music."

One psychiatrist, Dr. Marion E. Kenworthy, offers the opinion that while swing is not a bad means of working off adolescent tensions, a wise thing to do would be to organize wholesale after-school activities for war-tensed kids. "The emotional impact of war hits children hard," says Dr. Kenworthy. "It heightens existing tensions while reducing the areas of release children enjoy in normal times. Most of them badly want to get into the war somehow. They should be given an active role on the home front, not forgotten as they are."

On the downbeat. Psychologists say mob hysteria makes the fans writhe, sway and scream.

But a distinguished dance critic maintains that the nervousness of aging adults over the "perfectly healthy" desire of boys and girls to dance "in the groove" is itself a subject for psychiatric study. "When the waltz and the polka came they were said to be disrupting good behavior and decent society," argues the critic. "These kids dance, like anyone else, because they are high spirited."

When swing is king. Fans make idols of orchestra players, scramble for their pictures.

Meanwhile the Paramount box-office tabulation showed an attendance of 165,000 during the first week's engagement of Harry James and his orchestra. James bandsmen lost an average of six pounds, policemen stationed around the theater four pounds. Hepcats went so far out of this world that they left behind 93 pork-pie hats, 84 pairs of rubbers, 24 raincoats, 65 fountain pens and 18 wrist watches.

Entire Block, Market, 11th to 12th Streets (Zone 5—) Store Hours Today 12 Noon to 9 P. M.

It Starts TODAY—12 NOON to 9 P. M.

Mail and Phone Orders Filled —Call LOCust 5200—Camden WX-1150—Chester or Wilmington, Enterprise 1-0160.

Men's 2-Piece $22.50 Suits

Special **$19.95**

Porous fabrics that behave beautifully when the temperature tries for a new high record. They refuse to wilt, so keep their shape perfectly. They let in the breeze to keep you cool and calm. They come in serviceable color tones and nifty new patterns. They're tailored to perfection—so what else is there? Come in . . . we have your size.

MEN'S $2.95 Sports Slacks, $2.65

Just what you need for tennis, golf or other active sports—or cool lounging around the house. Some pleated fronts, some plain. Smartly patterned in popular colors.

$3.45 to $3.95 Panama Hats

$2.99

South American Panamas in two types of pinch fronts with choice of plain or fancy Puggree bands or solid color rayon grosgrain ribbons. Suntone or Natural. Included are soft-brim straw hats.

Snellenburgs Men's Clothing and Hats, Third Floor

350,000 Circulars Have Been Distributed to Homes in Philadelphia and Vicinity

. . . telling of this great Sale Event. If you did not receive your copy, kindly stop at the Service Desk on our First Floor where you can obtain one.

Hollander-Blended $249 Northern Back Muskrat Coats

$200 Plus 10% U. S. Tax

Nine out of ten women choose Northern Muskrat, if they have but one fur coat and expect to give it hard wear. These are superb skins, selected for their beauty, depth of fur and silky lustre. Sizes 9 to 42. Sensational Snellenburg Week Values!

Other Muskrat Coats $148 to $445

Plus 10% U. S. Tax

10% Down on Our Lay-Away Plan; Balance in Monthly Payments; Stored Free of Charge Until Fall

Snellenburgs Fur Salon, Second Floor

$42.95 DeLuxe Chaise Cot

You can have just as much fun relaxing in your own backyard as at a resort . . . if you've the proper equipment such as this Innerspring chaise cot with its button-tufted pad.

This very comfortable pad rests firmly on an all-wood frame. The cot can be wheeled around the garden to catch the sun . . . or shade, as you desire. It's an investment in outdoor pleasure.

$38.65

A Summer Snellenburg Week Bargain For Those Who Will Spend Their Vacation Home This Year!

Snellenburgs Outdoor Furniture, Fourth Floor

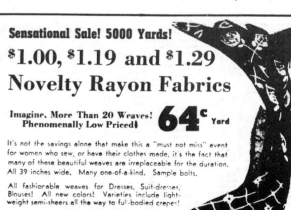

$1.00 Cottage Set Curtains

88c

Charming curtain sets to adorn your kitchen. Clover and dot flocked on scrim. Red, blue or green to add that cheerful touch. They're such a bargain you'll want to buy several pair to keep on ever crisp and neat appearance.

$3.95 Monks Cloth Draperies

$3.49

Replace winter draperies with these natural color monks cloth ones. Softly draped and trimmed with moss fringe in blue, dusty rose, wine or brown. Pinch-pleated and tie-backs . . . ready to hang. 70 inches wide to the pair; 2½ yards long.

Snellenburgs Upholsteries, Fourth Floor

10,000 Sport Shirts

Entire Floor Stock of Samples and Irregulars of $1.65 and $1.95 Grades

$1.29

Sport shirts that bring top satisfaction in Style, Service and Savings! Fabrics and colors such as is seldom seen . . . it's your chance to buy half-sleeved shirts with convertible collars and big pockets. Cool meshes, slub broadcloths and other novelty fabrics. Small, medium, large.

Samples! Irregulars of $2.25, $2.75 Sport Shirts

$1.65

Shirts advertised in Esquire . . . long- and short-sleeved models with convertible collars, action backs and big pockets. Cool, washable cotton meshes, spun rayons and slub broadcloth. Small, medium, large.

Snellenburgs Men's Furnishings, First Floor

A "Topper" in Value! $16.95 Swank Shortie Coat for Misses

$14.00

So young and gay you'll sling it over everything you wear. The new finger-tip length, double-breasted, flap pocketed and rayon lined. Fabric labeled for fiber content. Blue, red, aqua and navy in misses' sizes 12 to 18. A Bargain Highlight of Summer Snellenburg Week!

Snellenburgs Sports Coats, Second Floor

Sensational Sale! 5000 Yards!

$1.00, $1.19 and $1.29 Novelty Rayon Fabrics

Imagine, More Than 20 Weaves! Phenomenally Low Priced! **64c** Yard

It's not the savings alone that make this a "must not miss" event for women who sew, or have their clothes made, it's the fact that many of these beautiful weaves are irreplaceable for the duration. All 39 inches wide. Many one-of-a-kind. Sample bolts.

All fashionable weaves for Dresses, Suit-dresses, Blouses! All new colors! Varieties include light-weight semi-sheers all the way to full-bodied crepes!

Snellenburgs Silks and Rayons, Second Floor

Men's First Quality

$7.45 to $8.95 Slack Suits

$5.88

The cool high-grade fabrics are so handsome and serviceable—the tailoring so finely detailed—the shades so attractive in tone they're practically irresistible. Summer's favorite shades of blue, tan, brown and green. Slacks are smartly pleated, with self belts and zipper fly-front. In or out Coat style shirts, with short sleeves for coolness and freedom of action. Two roomy pockets. The most useful, most comfortable outfit a man could ask for. 28 to 40 waist.

Men's $1.50 Knit Basque Shirts, $1.10

They're comfortable, easily washed and need no ironing. Collarless neckline, short sleeves. Snappy stripes with red, blue, green or navy predominating. Sizes small, medium and large.

Men's $2.95 to $3.95 Sweaters, $2.63

Famous brands in V or crew necks, pullovers, button coat and zipper models. All labeled for fibre content. Plain shades, heathers, two-tones and novelties in blue, brown, tan, green and maroon. Sizes 36 to 46.

Snellenburgs Sporting Goods, Third Floor

Teen Girls' $3.95 Dresses

At a Snellenburg Week Price

$3.54

Dresses in the current fashion . . . cool, comfortable cottons. Pet fabrics and styles in one-piece models plus some adorable pinafores. Beloved for their launderability . . . and now, their low price. Sizes 10 to 16.

Teen Girls' $5.95 Rayon Dresses

$5.00

Cool rayon. Both one- and two-piecers. Also some easy-to-wash cotton seersuckers in cute two-piece styling. Sizes 10 to 16.

$1.10 Arbest Chiffon Hose

Of Famous Quality Rayon **99c** pair

A splendid opportunity to buy really good hosiery at a substantial saving. Superior 51-gauge of beautiful fine sheer texture. Reinforced lisle lined soles. Skyglo, Sungay, Victorious shades for summer wear.

Students' $10.95 to $13.45 Sport Coats

Glen Plaids and Checks that are considered "keen" by fellows wearing sizes 14 to 20. A snappy single breasted model that makes them hold their shoulders back to show the splendid fit.

$9.85

$3.95 Contrasting Slacks ______ $3.55

Perfect for sport coats. Fine rayon gabardine in brown, blue or tan. 14 to 22's will want several pair at this low price.

Snellenburgs Students' and Boys' Clothing.

A'S DEFEAT INDIANS, 6-5; PHILS LOSE THIRD IN ROW, 1-0

Sports--Bridge
Financial--Business

The Philadelphia Inquirer

PUBLIC LEDGER

School News
Puzzles—Pastimes

PHILADELPHIA, SUNDAY MORNING, JUNE 6, 1943

a b c d e f g S

Valo's Home Run Wins for Macks

Revamped Outfield Has Big Role In 6-5 Victory Over Cleveland

By STAN BAUMGARTNER

Connie Mack shuffled his outfield, drew two aces and beat the Cleveland Indians at Shibe Park yesterday, 6-5.

Mack benched Roberto Estalella, put Elmer Valo in left field and Jim Tyack in right. The new alignment accounted for four of the six runs and Valo hit a home run which provided the margin of victory in the seventh when he lifted the ball over the right field fence.

TYACK LEADS ATTACK

Jimmy Tyack drove in three runs with a double and a single and justified his insertion in the lineup as a cleanup hitter.

Oris Arntzen pitched the A's to their victory for his second triumph of the year against two defeats. The big righthander with the folding legs permitted 12 hits and was constantly in hot water but always managed to stay in front by a run or two.

A'S RAP BAGBY

The Athletics jumped off to a lead in the first inning when they larruped veteran Jim Bagby for two hits and two bases on balls. They hiked this to 5-1 with a pair in the fifth and Elmer Valo personally accounted for the sixth.

The Indians kept pecking away at Arntzen in the final frames but never could quite catch up.

WIN—BUT DROP TO FIFTH

By a peculiar quirk of the percentage table the Athletics dropped a notch in the standings—to fifth—although they won. The White Sox, by winning 17 and losing 16, while the A's won 21 and lost 20, have an advantage of a few percentage points although both stood at .500 yesterday morning.

Arntzen might have had an easy time of it except for Oris Hockett and Lou Boudreau. Each made four hits and the Indian manager had a perfect day, 4 for 4. Mickey Rocco, first baseman secured by Cleveland from Buffalo, made an excellent debut with a triple and double. He also handled himself well in the field.

Today, the teams will meet in a double header with Russ Christopher

Continued on Page 2, Column 3

Cards Beat Phils, Take First Place

Game Is Halted In Eighth Inning; Phils Will Protest

Special to The Inquirer

ST. LOUIS, Mo., June 5.—Jack Kraus and Howard Krist squared off in a good, old-fashioned pitcher's battle today before the weather stepped in to halt the proceedings after seven and one-half innings with the St. Louis Cards leading 1-0.

Kraus was nearly the equal of Krist except for a momentary let-up in the sixth inning when the Redbirds put together a single by Lou Klein, Harry Walker's sacrifice and a single by Stan Musial for the only run of the contest.

ADVANCE TO TOP

The victory boosted the Cards into the National League lead by a half game over the Dodgers, who lost to the Cubs, 3-2.

Bucky Harris, Phils' manager, said after the game he was going to protest the umpire's decision to call the contest, inasmuch as the Cardinals made no attempt to cover the field. Harris cited rule 24 to back his protest.

10TH LOSS IN 13 GAMES

Six hits were registered against Kraus, two of them by Frank Demaree and the young southpaw went down to his third defeat of the season. It was Krist's third victory without a loss.

The Phillies thus dropped their third straight decision to the World's Champions, and their tenth loss in 13 games of the current trip.

DAHLGREN SINGLED

The Phillies didn't have a base runner until the third inning when Merrill May rapped a single to left field and after Mickey Livingston popped to Klein, Kraus bunted. Both runners were safe when Ray Sanders threw late to Martin Marion at second base, attempting a force play, but Danny Murtaugh and Ronald Northey failed in the pinch.

Babe Dahlgren singled in the

Continued on Page 2, Column 6

Baseball Facts

AMERICAN LEAGUE

YESTERDAY'S RESULTS

ATHLETICS, 6; Cleveland, 5.
St. Louis, 3; New York, 2 (10 innings).
Chicago, 4; Boston, 1.
Washington, 6; Detroit, 3.

STANDING OF THE TEAMS

	W	L	P.C.	G.B.
New York	21	15	.583	...
Washington	22	18	.550	1
Detroit	20	17	.541	1½
Chicago	17	16	.515	2½
ATHLETICS	21	20	.512	2½
Cleveland	19	21	.475	4
Boston	18	23	.439	5½
St. Louis	13	21	.382	7

G.B.—Games behind.

Today's Games

AMERICAN LEAGUE

Probable Pitchers, Their Records

ATHLETICS vs. Cleveland at Shibe Park (1.30 P. M.)—Reynolds (0-3) and Salveson (2-1) vs. Christopher (4-3) and Wolff (5-2).

Detroit at Washington—Trout (5-2) and Overmire (3-1) vs. Candini (3-0) and Pyle (3-4).

St. Louis at New York—Sundra (3-3) and Hollingsworth (1-5) vs. Donald (0-2) and Borowy (2-4).

Chicago at Boston—Wade (1-1) and Grove (1-0) vs. Judd (4-1) and Terry (1-1).

(All double-headers).

NATIONAL LEAGUE

YESTERDAY'S RESULTS

St. Louis, 1; PHILLIES, 0 (7½ innings, called).
New York, 5; Pittsburgh, 1.
Chicago, 3; Brooklyn, 2.
Boston, 7; Cincinnati, 5.

STANDING OF THE TEAMS

	W	L	P.C.	G.B.
St. Louis	26	14	.650	...
Brooklyn	27	16	.628	½
Pittsburgh	20	18	.526	5
Cincinnati	20	19	.513	5½
Boston	17	18	.486	6½
PHILLIES	18	22	.450	8
New York	16	25	.390	10½
Chicago	14	26	.350	12

G.B.—Games behind.

Today's Games

NATIONAL LEAGUE

Probable Pitchers, Their Records

PHILLIES at St. Louis—Johnson (4-2) and Rowe (3-3) vs. Gumbert (2-4) and Brecheen (2-0).

Brooklyn at Chicago—Wyatt (3-2) and Melton (2-4) od Davis (1-1) vs. Passeau (3-3) and Bithorne (4-6).

New York at Pittsburgh—Wittg (3-4) and Melton (2-2) vs. Klinger (3-1) and Hallett (0-1).

Boston at Cincinnati—Barrett (2-5) and Andrews (4-3) vs. Starr (3-4) and Riddle (4-3).

(All double-headers).

Continued on Page 2, Column 3

Heading for Triple Crown

Count Fleet Wins Belmont

(Acme Telephoto)

START OF BELMONT STAKES: COUNT FLEET (2) BREAKS ON TOP, EN ROUTE TO VICTORY AND TRIPLE CROWN

Derby, Preakness-winning Count was sent to the front by Jockey Longden, obscuring Fairy Manhurst (who ran second); Deseronto, nearest camera, finished third as Count won by 25 lengths. The time of 2:28 1-5 for the mile and a half broke War Admiral's mark.

Shatters Record For Race

Completes Triple Crown By 25 Lengths

By SID FEDER

NEW YORK, June 5 (A. P.).—Count Fleet won the Belmont Stakes and the triple crown today, but you'll never prove it by the other two horses in the race—they wer practically out of sight when it happened.

Topping off his Kentucky Derby and Preakness romps, Mrs. John D. Hertz's rangy brown lightning bolt just waltzed to a 25-length victory this time in the 75th running of Belmont's ancient classic for three year olds to become the sixth triple crown winner. And, as he laughed his way home, he carried two new records with him.

HIS RIVALS IGNORED

One of these was his time of 2:28 1-5 for the mile and a half gallop, which wiped out War Admiral's record of 2:28 3-5 for the Belmont Stakes although falling three-fifths of a second short of the track and North American mark Bolingbroke set for the distance last fall.

The other standard concerned the amount bet on one horse in one race in New York State. Today a comparatively scanty turnout of 19,190 cash customers sent $249,516 into the mutuels on him, thereby smashing the previous high of $196,192 tossed into the iron men on the Count in the Wood Memorial at Jamaica in April.

Today's betting resulted in a "minus pool" on the race and the track had to shell out $15,912.02 from its own pocket in order to pay off the winners at the legal minimum of $2.10 for $2.

WHIRLY WITHDRAWN

The Count was to have been one of the turf's two glamor boys to see action in this "getaway day" program of Belmont's spring meeting, but he finally had to take care of the honors alone. Whirlaway was to have made his 1943 debut in the Henry of Navarre Handicap on the card, but he came up with a tummy-ache early today and was scratched.

Mrs. T. D. Grimes' With Regards won this one at $14 for $2, and in the third part of the tripleheader program, the National Stallion stakes for two-year-olds, Henry Lustig's $2300 yearling bargain, Mrs. Ames, squeaked through to a victory worth $12,320.

WINNINGS AT $250,300

With today's triumph the Count picked up a pay-check of $35,340, thereby boosting his bank roll to $250,300. Naturally, neither Fairy Manhurst, who grabbed the $5000 second money in the Belmont, nor Deseronto, who made $2500 for finishing third, knew anything about all this at the finish of the third, knew anything about all this at

Continued on Page 4, Column 1

Hubbell Wins 250th; Yanks, Dodgers Bow

By HANK SIMMONS

It's a long, long trail that winds along to the 250 mark in victories scored by a major league pitcher, but Carl Hubbell, the 39-year-old veteran of the Giants, reached that milestone yesterday when he turned in one of the most remarkable feats of his lengthy and brilliant career, a one-hit, 5-1 decision over the Pirates.

One of his most remarkable feats is right, for its was against the Pirates that he reached the zenith of all pitchers, a no-hitter fourteen years ago.

HOMER ONLY HIT

The only hit made off the aging lefthander yesterday was impressive enough, a home run clouted by first baseman Elbie Fletcher into the right field stands after two out in the seventh inning.

But King Carl has no regrets about that blow. The Giants won his 250th victory, it stopped his team's losing streak that had reached six defeats in the last seven games (the other was a tie), it halted the Pirates' string of five straight triumphs and it marked old "Long Pants" as the only active hurler with a string of that many decisions to his credit.

ROOKIE AIDS REDS

The Giants blasted young Xavier Rescigno off the mound with three ringing two-baggers in a row in the first inning and continued their assault against Johnny Lanning for three more runs.

A rookie, Butch Nieman, former halfback for the University of Kansas provided the Braves with a 7-5 victory over the Reds. The Cubs, smarting under an 18-5 beating at the hands of the Dodgers on Friday, rebounded and prevailed over the Bums, 3-2, knocking them from first place.

BROWNS BEAT YANKS

In the American League the Yankees maintained their perch atop the standings by a few points after absorbing a 3-2 defeat by the Browns as the Senators charged into second place by turning back the Tigers, 6-3. In Boston the White Sox prevailed over the Red Sox, 4-1.

Nieman set up the Braves' triumph with a triple in the ninth after Lonny Frey, of the Reds, had fumbled a double play ball. Tommy Holmes singled with one away and Johnny McCarthy followed with a grounder to Frey and the inning should have been over. But Lonny fumbled it and set the stage for Nieman's blow.

CUBS GET REVENGE

Hard hitting Manager Leo Durocher used four hurlers in an attempt to stave of the Dodgers' tumble into

Continued on Page 2, Column 7

No Challenger For Willie Pep

NEW YORK, June 5 (A. P.).—As far as the New York State Boxing Commission is concerned there is no leading contender for Willie Pep's featherweight boxing championship.

Chalky Wright, who knocked out Phil Terranova in the fifth round at the Garden last night, was supposed to be "it" but when his manager, Eddie Walker, failed to show up today to sign for a fight with Pep the commission said it had no other contender. Lou Viscusi, Pep's manager, was present with a pen in hand ready to put his "John Henry" on the dotted line.

Pep meets Sal Bartolo in Boston Tuesday night in a fight designated by the Massachusetts Commission as a title affair, but regardless of the outcome Pep still will be the champion in New York State.

Move Started For Service Game

In spite of the many obstacles imposed by war time restrictions, a movement was launched yesterday to bring the 1943 Army-Navy football game back to Philadelphia—in the event the two service academies meet on the gridiron this fall.

John B. Kelly, national director of physical fitness under the Federal Security Agency, suggested the move. He said the teams might play here for the benefit of a war charity, perhaps the USO or the Red Cross.

KELLY CITES FACTORS

While Kelly admitted that it probably seemed "rather ridiculous" to talk about a football game during a heat wave, he thought there was much to be said in favor of the plan. He said the staging of the game here would involve the transportation of only about 100 men from West Point, and as many more from the Naval Academy at Annapolis.

The suggestion met with immediate approval from city officials and football followers here. It was proposed by some that the service classic be staged on a Sunday, so as to interfere as little as possible with the war effort.

BASEBALL CROWDS

Moreover, it was said in some quarters that the burden placed up-

Continued on Page 4, Column 3

Cannon Breaks World Record In Discus at 174 Ft., 10⅛ Ins.

NEW YORK, June 5 (A. P.).—Giving all the credit to the "food you get to eat in the Navy," Ensign Hugh S. Cannon, Staten Island Naval base, today shattered the world's discus record with a toss of 174 ft., 10⅛ in. in the Metropolitan A. A. U. Track and Field Championships.

Performing in front of only a few judges and his fellow competitors in a lot outside the Randall Island Stadium, the 29-year-old former Brigham Young athlete got off the toss that wiped out the 174-foot, 2½-inch record set by Willie Schroeder, Germany, in 1935, and also eclipsed the meet record of 166 feet, 5 inches, set by Al Blozis, former Georgetown ace, last year.

CONSISTENTLY NEAR TOP

(Cannon has been consistently near the top of world discus throwers since 1936 when, with a spin of 157 ft. 2¼ ins., he won the U. S. junior championship as a student at Brigham Young University. Becoming a teacher at Connecticut State, he subsequently represented the New England Harriers in A. A. U. competition, placing fourth in the 1939 national senior championships and fifth in 1942.

(Victor in this year's University of Pennsylvania Relay Carnival with a throw of 160 feet 2 ins., the Staten Island Naval Base ensign is rated as the outstanding favorite to succeed Minnesota's Bob Fitch in the national championships at New York Randall's Island two weeks from today. Fitch won the discus throw title last year with a mark of 166 ft. 10 ins.)

Cannon weighed only 160 pounds while competing for Brigham Young, but has pushed his weight to 187 since joining the Navy.

He now is the assistant supply officer at the Navy section base, Staten Island.

HARRIS HOLDS RECORD

The recognized American record, which has not yet won approval as the world standard, is 174 feet, 8¾ inches by Archie Harris, Indiana, at Palo Alto, Calif., in 1941.

Although Cannon's effort surpasses the listed world mark, Ernst Lampert, Germany, has sought recognition for a throw of 175 feet, 5¼ inches, made last year.

Turning in a sparkling 4:15.9 clocking, Bill Hulse, New York A. C. won the mile title. Hulse took the lead and held it until the middle of

Continued on Page 3, Column 2

Haegg Arrives; Off to New York

NEW ORLEANS, June 5 (A. P.).—Gunder Haegg, Swedish distance runner, landed here today and immediately worked 2000 meters over the Municipal Stadium's cinder path to limber up his legs. He left by plane at midnight for New York.

He arrived on a safe-conduct tanker, the Saturnus.

DUE IN NEW YORK

The runner, who holds or has bettered seven world records at distances from 1500 to 5000 meters, started on his long journey from Stockholm on May 10 and came to the United States at the invitation of the National A. A. U., whose championship track meet will be held at New York on June 19 and 20.

Haegg is expected to arrive in New

Continued on Page 3, Column 2

Honor Athletes At Annapolis

ANNAPOLIS, Md., June 5 (A. P.).—June week at the United States Naval Academy got off to a colorful start today with the presentation of athletic and extra-curricular awards to approximately 400 Midshipmen.

The 20 companies composing the Midshipmen's regiment gathered in "Tecumseh Court," the expansive brick-paved quadrangle in front of Bancroft hall, the Midshipmen's dormitory, and facing the statue of the famous Indian warrior.

AWARDS PRESENTED

The regiment stood in formation as Captain H. E. Overesch, commandant of Midshipmen, and Captain John E. Whelchel, director of athletics, spoke briefly and presented the awards.

Captain Overesch made the presentation of the extra-curricular activities awards to the various chairmen and secretaries of clubs and societies at the Naval Academy.

COURAGE NEEDED

Captain Whelchel told the 255 athletic award winners who were recipients of the coveted Navy "N" prize for athletic ability and leadership, that "it isn't necessary just to have a strong body to be a fighting man. But the body must be attended with something else other than endurance. That other thing is courage. It is absolutely essential.

"It is my hope," Captain Whelchel said, "that in the next year we will go further in intramural and, if possible, in intercollegiate competition."

The presentation of awards was the opening event of the annual June Week ceremonies which are tempered in gaiety this year by the seriousness of the war.

Hamilton, Pre-Flight Head, Gets Sea Duty; Assistant Wickhorst Moves Up to Berth

CMDR. HAMILTON

WASHINGTON, June 5 (A. P.).—Commander Thomas J. Hamilton, who organized the Navy's toughening program for aviators, has been put on duty at sea, it was officially announced today, and associates said the action was in accord with Hamilton's own desires.

He was succeeded as director of the Naval Aviation physical training program by Lieutenant Commander Frank H. Wickhorst, one of the Navy's all-time athletic stars who, for the 10 years ending in 1941, served as line coach and director of intramural sports at the University of California.

In March, 1941, Wickhorst, who was a graduate of the Naval Academy but was actually in reserve status, went on active duty to teach navigation to young reserve officers at California. A year later he was assigned here to assist Hamilton in formation of the physical training program.

NO MODIFICATION

Since the program will be carried on by Hamilton's No. 1 assistant, no change of policy or modification of method is expected in the program to produce aviation cadets capable of becoming the world's toughest combat pilots. The program func-

Continued on Page 4, Column 1

CMDR. WICKHORST

Purdue Wins Two From Bunker Hill

LAFAYETTE, Ind., June 5 (A. P.).—Purdue's baseball team, tuning up for its Big Ten finale with Ohio State next week, drubbed the Bunker Hill, Ind., Naval Air Station today in a doubleheader, 5-4 and 9-7. Both games were to have been seven innings, but the first went eight.

The two games gave the Boilermakers nine victories in twelve starts this season.

Colgate Takes Adirondack Meet

SCHENECTADY, N. Y., June 5 (U. P.).—Colgate University scored 90 points to thoroughly outclass its nearest rivals in the Adirondack A. A. U. track and field championships today. Navy Pre-Flight of Rensselaer Polytechnic Institute finished second with 42 and the Pioneer Athletic Clubs of Schenectady third with 12.

Dick Schnacke, former University of Iowa athlete, who competed unattached, was the high individual scorer. He won the 120-yard high hurdles, broad jump and high jump. There were no records shattered in the 14-event meet.

Bill Watson Wins Four Field Events

YPSILANTI, Mich., June 5 (A. P.).—Big Bill Watson, former University of Michigan one-man track team, won four events and gathered 58 points today in the Michigan A. A. U. outdoor championships. Michigan State College took the team title with 207 points.

Watson, National decathlon champion in 1940, won the shotput, discus, broad jump and hop-step-and-jump. He placed in two other events. His team, the Detroit Police, finished second with 160 points.

Army Refuses Comment on Zamperini

HONOLULU, June 5 (U. P.).—Army headquarters refused to comment today on reports that Lieutenant Lou Zamperini, American Olympic distance-runner assigned to the Seventh U. S. Air Force, was missing in the South Pacific.

(Zamperini's mother, Mrs. Anthony Zamperini, said at Torrance, Cal., that Washington had informed her he had been missing since May 27.)

DECORATED TWICE

It was recalled that Zamperini, who set the N.C.A.A. mile record of 4:08.3 for the University of Southern California in 1938, participated in the Christmas Eve raid on Wake Island and the attack on Nauru Island April 21.

Zamperini was decorated twice for his part in the Wake and Nauru raids. He and the co-pilot of his plane administered first aid to five crew-members wounded in a five-minute running battle during the Nauru attack.

Zamperini had expressed a desire to return to track competition after the war.

M'Arthur, Curtin Plan 'Important Statement'

ALLIED HEADQUARTERS IN AUSTRALIA, June 10 (Thursday). (U. P.)—General Douglas MacArthur flew to Sydney Tuesday and conferred twice with Prime Minister John Curtin, it was announced officially today.

An important statement will be issued later today, it was announced here and at Canberra.

MacArthur also visited Lord Gowrie, Governor-General of Australia, and Lord Wakehurst, Governor of New South Wales. He inspected military installations in the Sydney area.

OFFENSIVE EXPECTED

There is strong reason to believe the information given by General MacArthur to Curtin showed that the holding-war phase of the global strategy affecting the South Pacific and the Southwest Pacific is ending.

The next stage, when it comes, will find Japan on the defensive and threatened by a concentration of forces the like of which she never expected could be arrayed against her from Australian bases.

BIG PINCERS PLANNED

The next phase of Allied strategy following the holding-war period likely will be the building up by the Allies of new air bases for offensive operations.

Thus, Japan will be caught within a gigantic pincers, one jaw extending southward from the Aleutians, the other covering the Netherlands East Indies and the Philippines. This would be vaster in scope and swifter in operation than an island by island infantry advance.

NIMITZ PARLEY RECALLED

(It was recalled that Admiral Chester W. Nimitz, commander-in-chief of the U. S. Fleet in the Pacific, returned to Honolulu this week after a week-end conference on the mainland, which Secretary of the Navy Frank Knox said was with Admiral Ernest J. King, commander of the U. S. Fleet.

(Nimitz announced in an address at Berkeley, Calif., that he had been planning a "headache" for the Japanese, and that Allied strength in the Pacific was growing rapidly.

FORECAST BY CURTIN

(Curtin, in an address at Sydney Sunday, said that American air forces in the Southwest Pacific would be "greatly increased in the near future" as a result of representations to Washington by his government and MacArthur's military associates.)

Meanwhile, a communique from MacArthur's headquarters announced that an Allied heavy bomber had blasted Nabire, Dutch New Guinea, starting great fires visible for 75 miles.

Nabire is on Geelvink Bay, 700 miles north-northwest of Darwin.

The communique, indicating that the bomb had fallen into a munitions warehouse, said that one great explosion which followed jarred the bomber at a 12,000 foot altitude.

Dr. Jane Leslie Kift, nationally famous horticulturist, tells you all you need to know to have a successful, thriving Victory Garden.

NAZI SUBS CALLED 'HORRIBLY BEATEN'

LONDON, June 9 (U. P.)—Lieutenant Commander Richard D. Stannard of the Royal Navy, commanding a destroyer on North Atlantic convoy duty, said today that the U-boat menace was "beaten horribly" by means of new submarine detection devices.

Once we've located a U-boat it hasn't a chance for survival," he told reporters. "They're afraid to come up when there's an escort vessel around."

Stannard, 40, who formerly commanded the ex-U. S. destroyer Ramsay, said commanders of escort ships had full confidence in their ability to whip the undersea raiders and stressed that success thus far had been attained through the "marvelous co-operation" of American forces and Coastal Command Aircraft of the Royal Air Force.

25 SUNK IN MAY

Other competent sources estimated that 25 to 30 German submarines were sunk by Allied forces during May and that many of these were sent to the bottom by planes, including the V.L.R.—very long range aircraft—mentioned yesterday by Prime Minister Winston Churchill in his speech to the House of Commons.

The Air Ministry news service disclosed that the V.L.R. planes are American-built Liberators (Consolidated B-24) with a range of some 2000 miles. It said the Coastal Command and several squadrons of these planes in operation, equipped with long range fuel tanks.

U. S. MASSES FLEET FOR PACIFIC ACTION

ANNAPOLIS, Md., June 9 (U. P.)—One of the mightiest U. S. fleets ever assembled is preparing for new action in the South Pacific, Secretary of the Navy Frank Knox revealed today.

He made the significant disclosure in a surprise and liberal departure from his prepared commencement address before the largest class ever to graduate from the Naval Academy—765 midshipmen.

Extemporaneously summarizing the eight world battlefronts now engaging the United States and her allies, he said:

'STRONGEST EVER ASSEMBLED'

"And then there's the South Pacific front where one of the strongest American fleets ever assembled keeps watch and prepares for fresh activity."

He did not elaborate, but the disclosure was considered highly significant in that it followed by less than a fortnight Roosevelt-Churchill strategy decisions hinting momentous action in the Pacific, and by one week a West Coast conference between Admiral Ernest J. King, commander-in-chief of the U. S. Fleet, and Pacific Fleet Commander Chester W. Nimitz, who said they plotted "more trouble for the Japs in the near future."

He listed the eight war fronts as the Western Mediterranean, the Eastern Mediterranean, the Atlantic, the South Atlantic, the South Pacific, the North Pacific, the Russo-German and the Chinese fronts.

(A. P. Wirephoto)

GENERAL BIDS FAREWELL TO CREW OF 'MEMPHIS BELLE'

The crew of the Flying Fortress Memphis Belle, which was retired from action after completing 25 bombing missions over Europe, is shown at an American bomber station in England yesterday, watching Lieutenant General Jacob L. Devers, commanding general of U. S. forces in the European theater, bid farewell to Captain Robert B. Morgan (back to camera). At right is Major General Ira C. Eaker. The bomber and crew will return to America.

'Memphis Belle' Coming Home

Fortress and Heroic Crew to Get Rest

By PAUL W. RAMSEY

Continued From First Page

looking 50-calibre guns sticking out in all directions.

• • •

PAINTED on the nose by an artist is a long-legged siren in a red bathing suit, and back along the fuselage are painted 25 yellow bombs—one for each raid; eight swastikas for eight German planes shot down for certain; eight yellow stars representing the number of times the ship led a squadron, and seven red stars for the number of times she led the whole group. Try shooting at that record.

Suddenly someone came with word that the generals were arriving. Ten young men in their khaki flying clothes and fleece-lined boots formed a line just in front of and parallel with the right wing.

At the command of their skipper, 24-year-old Captain Robert B. Morgan, of Asheville, N. C., they snapped to rigid attention. They looked strong and young and fine, standing there in the morning sun.

• • •

THE guard of honor also stood at attention to one side as Lieutenant General Jacob L. Devers, commanding general of the European theatre, and Major General Ira C. Eaker, commanding general of the Eighth Air Force, walked briskly toward the plane.

They shook hands with Captain Morgan, inspected the plane and then returned to congratulate each boy individually. And then the two generals addressed them.

General Devers told them they were going on the most important trip they have flown; not carrying bombs, but carrying a message to 130,000,000 people.

"I want you to tell them," he said, "that all of us over here realize that into this plane have gone the work, the thought and determined courage of countless Americans. They mined the material from the earth, spun the fabric, labored in forests, mills, factories and offices to create it. Americans built it.

• • •

"TELL America to send us crews with the knowledge, the training, the determination and courage which I have found with no exception in the Eighth Air Force. Pilots like Captain Morgan, co-pilots like Captain Verinus, navigators like Captain Leighton. . . ."

He went down the list naming each young man standing there at rigid attention. Each one listened for his name, and each seemed to stand just a little straighter when he heard it.

General Devers did not overlook the ground crew—"a most important part of your team." He had the warmest praise for them. They must stay behind in England to service other Fortresses.

General Eaker told the boys they were going home to instruct new crews and to pass on knowledge gained in combat. Other high-ranking officers present were Brigadier General Newton Longfellow, commanding general of the Eighth Air Force Bomber Command, and Brigadier General Haywood S. Hansell.

• • •

THE whole ceremony was viewed from the bomber's plexiglass nose by Stuka, the four-month-old Scotty of Captain James H. Verinus, 25, of New Haven, Conn., co-pilot of the bomber. Stuka has flown several times and went on one raid in a high pressure box so she could breathe at high altitude. She didn't like it.

One Pennsylvanian was among the 10 young men getting ready to go home. He is Cecil H. Scott, RFD 3, Altoona, who is the shortest, lightest and oldest member of the crew. He is 27. The average age is 23.

Captain Morgan said Scott was the best ball turret gunner in the European theater.

"Scott," said Morgan, "has accomplished what armor men say just can't be done. He found one gun not working on our first raid and proceeded to change guns in midair. He had to break the plexiglass in the turret down there underneath the plane to do it. And he rode down there fighting with his guns while the wind whistled in on him. It gets pretty cold at the height we fly."

• • •

SCOTT has one enemy plane to his credit for certain, and has many probables. He has damaged a great number, but is a modest little guy who won't put in a claim unless he sees his victim hit the ground.

If you wonder what he is going to do when he gets home, he is going to fill up on hamburgers and steak and ice cream.

Captain Morgan, whose skill brought the Fortress through many tight spots, is going back to marry Miss Margaret Polk, of Memphis. She is the belle for whom the ship is named.

Master Sergeant Joseph H. Giambrone, of 245 E. Main st., Norristown, was chief of the crew mechanics who kept the Memphis Belle in fighting trim. His engine mechanic was Sergeant Charles P. Blauser, of 613 Ridge ave., York. Duty elsewhere kept them from attending the ceremony.

The combat crew has fought with the ship through many battles when it seemed certain they would be downed by fire from enemy fighter planes. They have been attacked by as many as 50 during a single engagement.

But they always got back. A true combat team, as General Eaker said, "that has met and outfought the best the enemy can offer."

CHINESE ADVANCE ANEW IN RICE AREA

CHUNGKING, China, June 9 (A. P.)—Chinese dispatches reported today that Generalissimo Chiang Kai-shek's forces had smashed the Japanese defense line southeast of Hwajung, the key to the Chinese rice-producing region around Lake Tungtin in northern Hunan province.

In a sudden attack on the defenses of the town north of the lake, the Chinese inflicted more than 200 casualties and captured quantities of equipment, the dispatches said.

Other dispatches reported the recapture of three important points, including Shihlipu, 50 miles east of Ichang and on the highway to Hankow, in the northern sector of the Upper Yangtze front.

Today's Chinese communique said further heavy casualties had been inflicted on Japanese troops fleeing Itu, 18 miles below Ichang on the Yangtze. The port was fully occupied by the Chinese Tuesday.

The High Command said the annihilation of enemy forces south of Sungtze, another Yangtze port between Shasi and Ichang, was expected soon.

Americans Damage Jap Indo-China Base

CHUNGKING, China, June 9 (A. P.)—American bombers attacked Hongay, 30 miles northeast of Haiphong in French Indo-China yesterday, heavily damaging coaling docks, warehouses, railroad yards and power transmission lines, a communique from Lieutenant General Joseph W. Stilwell's headquarters announced today.

Jap Funeral March Honors Yamamoto

By United Press

The Tokio radio said yesterday that a new song—"Funeral March of the Fallen Japanese"—has been written in honor of the late Admiral Isoroku Yamamoto and would be published throughout Japan.

Nazis Report Channel Battle

LONDON, June 9 (A. P.)—The Berlin radio reported today that several British torpedo boats were damaged last night while attempting to attack a German convoy in the English Channel between Dunkirk and Calais.

The Philadelphia Inquirer

PUBLIC LEDGER

An Independent Newspaper for All the People

FINAL CITY EDITION

CIRCULATION: May Average: Daily 472,084; Sunday 1,366,229

MONDAY MORNING, JUNE 14, 1943

Copyright, 1943, by The Philadelphia Inquirer Co. Vol. 228, No. 165

a b d e f g h

THREE CENTS

U. S. Bombers Pound Bremen And Kiel, 26 Lost in Battles; 3d Italian Island Surrenders

While Millions Starve

German-Made Famine Sweeping Occupied Countries of Europe

(Herewith is the first installment of "While Millions Starve," the story of famine-stricken Europe. Written by Alexander Kendrick, of The Inquirer Washington Bureau, it is the result of a series of interviews at the recent United Nations Food Conference with officials of the eight German occupied countries. It reveals for the first time a complete picture of this grim chapter of history in the making.)

By Alexander Kendrick

Inquirer Washington Bureau

(Copyright, 1943, by The Philadelphia Inquirer)

Installment I

THE greatest famine in history is sweeping Europe.

It is not like other famines, caused by nature. This famine is man-made, a deliberate weapon of war used by the Germans to keep the occupied countries in subjugation, and prevent them from rising in revolt when the hour of their liberation arrives.

Widespread starvation grips Europe today, after nearly four years of war. The populations of the occupied countries have been reduced to the role of beggars. The effects of enforced privation will be felt for generations.

Disease, following in the wake of hunger, has helped to sap the resistance of the occupied countries. Tuberculosis is ravaging whole sections of the continent. The death rate, particularly among children, has soared.

This is the grim picture of what the German occupation has done to Europe in the spring and summer of 1943.

It is a picture pieced together by officials and health experts of eight occupied countries—France, Belgium, Denmark, the Netherlands, Luxembourg, Czechoslovakia, Poland and Greece.

It is a picture of Germans stripping the land, killing the cows and pigs, shipping off the machinery, sending farm workers into the Reich for enforced labor, and seizing what small quantities of foodstuffs are produced.

The deliberate Nazi policy of starvation has had its inevitable effect upon people of the occupied countries. It has brought them the lowest standard of living they have ever had, and the greatest measure of poor health. It has taken their strength and reduced many of them to listlessness.

J. V. HYKA

• • •

YET it has not broken their will to resist. Despite all that has been done to them, their morale is still good. They are waiting for the day when they will be able to join the Allied armies of liberation in driving the Germans from their land.

For the German policy of starvation, disastrous though it has been, has failed in its ultimate purpose. One by one, on the basis of the latest reports received through the underground directly from their countries, the eight men who have made this story possible present the evidence to show that Europe still fights.

There is Czechoslovakia, for instance. This is the country which first winced beneath the tread of the aggressor. It is the country which symbolizes European democracy. It is the country which proved to be the grave of Reinhard Heydrich, the hangman.

Czechoslovakia still fights. J. V. Hyka, tall and grey-haired scholar—all the Czech statesmen seem to be scholars—who is on an economic mission to this country and who headed his country's delegation to the United Nations Food Conference, gives the details of Nazi occupation.

• • •

"THE German food rationing gives the Czech population in Bohemia and Moravia a little better ration of bread, potatoes and meat than in 1917.

But very often there is nothing in the shops, and the ration cards bear the note 'if available.' There is a complete lack of edible fats. Butter is practically non-existent. The usual procedure is for the German occupying authorities to seize all production of butter at the dairies and to ship it to Germany.

The same applies to all food products, but in the case of all war industries, the Germans give the working population just enough to eat in order to keep up the production. The slaves must be fed in order to work.

In normal times, Czechoslovakia produced high-quality foodstuffs in great quantities. This production has been reduced as a result of various factors—lack of manpower mobilized for war industries, lack of fertilizers, and draft animals and agricultural machinery.

• • •

"IN ADDITION, a great proportion of all foodstuffs is confiscated for the Germans, so that the Czech population gets only a fraction of its normal needs.

Lack of fodder brought about a reduction in the animal population. This was further aggravated by slaughtering on a large scale, so that now the livestock population is only a portion of what it was before the Germans came. As a result, the meat and fat production has been lowered, but even from this lowered production the Germans take a lion's share.

As a result of the German occupation, the general health of the Czechoslovak population has been seriously undermined.

Continued on Page 2, Column 1

POPE ASSAILS ACCUSATION HE WANTED WAR

Blames Propaganda On 'Enemies of God'; Warns Workers Of 'False Prophets'

By United Press

Pope Pius XII, addressing 20,000 Italian workers whom he received in audience at Vatican City, said yesterday that propaganda was being circulated, especially among workers, alleging that he wanted the war, supported it and supplied money for its continuance.

Asserting that never, perhaps, had a calumny more monstrous or more absurd been launched, the Pope told his hearers:

"When the circumstances of the times and human passions will permit or call for the publication of documents not yet published concerning the constant activity pursued during this terrible war in favor of peace by the Holy See, which feared neither rebuffs nor opposition, there will appear in more than mid-day light the stupidity of such accusations."

BLAMES 'FOES OF GOD'

The Pope did not give the source of the accusations except to say they were of "anti-religious inspiration" and were disseminated by "enemies of God" to disturb workers and turn them against the Church.

"Who does not know, who does not see, who is there that can not ascertain for himself that no one more insistently opposed the outbreak, the advance and the spread of the war that we have in every manner allowed us?" the Pope said in his speech, the official English language text of which was received in Washington by cable.

The Pope said that he had done everything he could to lessen the horrors of the war, and that money donated by the faithful had been used to console war sufferers.

ADMITS WORKERS' BURDEN

He said that the allegations he mentioned sprang not so much from ignorance as from "irreligious spirit and contempt of the Church."

(Though the Pope did not mention that the source of the charges, the German official news agency D. N. B., in a Vatican City dispatch, was heard by London to broadcast that the Pope blamed "Communist propaganda.")

NAZI RADIO CHARGES

(On May 25 the Nazi-controlled Paris radio broadcast a talk by a Dr. Friedrich accusing the Catholic Church of "a crushing responsibility in unleashing the present war." Friedrich charged the Vatican with hostility to Adolf Hitler since 1933 and encouraging German Catholics in an open fight against the Nazis.

Continued on Page 2, Column 7

Planes Batter Sicily

Map on Page 2; Picture Story on Page 14

By REYNOLDS PACKARD

ALLIED HEADQUARTERS IN NORTH AFRICA, June 13 (U. P.).—The islet of Linosa fell today to the Allies' air-powered sweep across the Mediterranean which destroyed at least 150 more enemy planes caught sitting on Sicilian airdromes Saturday by Allied fleets.

The British destroyer Nubian hove off Linosa at sunrise and saw the now familiar white flag of surrender displayed on the island.

GARRISON EVACUATED

The Italian garrison commander had sought to spare his men the terrific bombing which beat down Pantelleria and Lampedusa and a landing party from the destroyer accommodated him, occupying the island and evacuating the entire enemy personnel of 140 men in the matter of a few hours, official dispatches said.

(A delayed dispatch from Lampedusa said from 4000 to 5000 Italians surrendered there Saturday, as compared with the more than 10,000 taken on Pantelleria. The dispatch said 120 British soldiers were moving onto the island as an initial Allied garrison.)

ONLY LAMPIONE LEFT

Linosa, 28 miles north of Lampedusa and with an area of only 16 square miles, had no major fortifications. Its fall left Lampione, 40 miles to the southwest, as the last Axis island in the Sicilian narrows, and Lampione has no military value whatever.

With the Sicilian passage thus swept of Axis outposts at the rate of an island a day, the big arsenal of Sicily itself came more sharply than ever into the Allied offensive focus and American bombers from North Africa were laying a deadly and systematic groundwork.

Three of the biggest air bases in

Continued on Page 2, Column 4

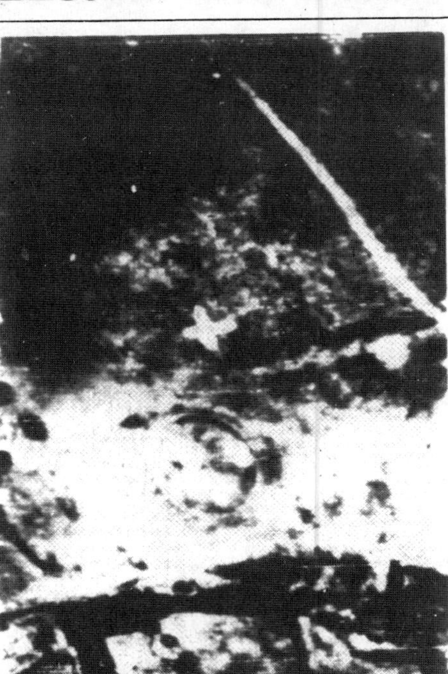

(A. P. Wirephoto From U. S. Army Signal Corps)

PANTELLERIA'S SIGNAL OF SURRENDER

A white cross in the center of the landing field on the Italian island fortress of Pantelleria signals the Allied air forces that their onslaught was a success.

Sky Fleet Fights Swarms of Nazis Above Sub Bases

Map on Page 3

By LEWIS HAWKINS

LONDON, June 13 (A. P.).—Two large formations of American heavy bombers smashed down many German fighters and blasted the U-boat bases at Bremen and Kiel today in the greatest air battle ever waged by the Eighth U. S. Air Force.

The two sky fleets flew unescorted to the heavily defended North German bases for the double-barreled daylight attack. The cost was 26 four-engined bombers, the most severe loss ever suffered by the Eighth Air Force in a single day's operations.

"The attack occasioned the greatest air battle in which Eighth Air Force heavy bombers have yet participated and against the largest concentration of enemy fighters," said the U. S. communique.

BASES ARE 'BOMBED EFFECTIVELY'

Bremen and Kiel, which account for a considerable percentage of the Nazi war machine's U-boat production and servicing, "were bombed effectively and many enemy fighters were destroyed," the bulletin said.

Royal Air Force heavyweights again struck Germany's Ruhr Valley last night, and a big force of British planes was heard roaring back toward the continent tonight a short time after the American airmen returned.

The largest loss ever suffered before by American heavy bombers in a single raid was the 16 downed during the last previous attack on Bremen, April 17. On that occasion 63 German fighters were destroyed.

While deploring the heavy loss of men and equipment in the run to Kiel, Brigadier General Frederick L. Anderson, commander of a Flying Fortress wing, said the "price was not too high for the results achieved."

"Not only did we hit important submarine installations at Kiel but we also drew off practically all enemy aircraft in the area so that the other formation was able to do a splendid job at Bremen with little opposition."

1000-MILE ROUND TRIP TO KIEL

Kiel is about 100 miles north of Bremen, and to get to it the huge squadrons had to fly a round trip of approximately 1000 miles.

The two-way assault increased the moment of the newest aerial offensive against Adolf Hitler's war plants, following by only a few hours the heavy attack by the R.A.F. on Bochum and other key points in Germany's industrial Ruhr Valley. The night raid cost the R.A.F. 24 bombers but the Germans themselves conceded that it caused heavy damage.

New blows also were rained on other enemy targets throughout France and the Low Countries by daylight today. American and British fighters and British medium bombers shuttled over the Channel in a seemingly endless stream to hammer enemy installations in operations which went on virtually all day.

KIEL RAIDERS FACE HEAVY FIGHT

The U. S. communique telling of today's dual bombing assault said "very strong enemy fighter opposition" was "concentrated largely against the formation attacking Kiel."

Pilots participating in the Bremen attack said enemy

Continued on Page 3, Column 1

U. S. Fighters Blast 33 Zeros in Russells

By JOHN M. McCULLOUGH

Inquirer Washington Bureau

WASHINGTON, June 13.—Twenty-five Japanese Zero fighters were shot down and eight others probably destroyed in another of the furious dog-fights which have featured air action in the Solomons in the past week, the Navy Department announced today.

The battle, which took place Saturday, East longitude time, resulted when Army, Navy and Marine fighters slashed with blazing guns at between 40 and 50 Zero fighters in the vicinity of the Russell Islands northwest of Guadalcanal.

6 U. S. PLANES LOST

Six United States planes were lost, but all but two of the pilots were saved.

On the same day, two huge four-engined Liberator bombers, evidently on reconnaissance patrol, shot down a twin-engined Mitsubishi bomber 20 miles west of Buka Island in the extreme northwestern Solomons, at a point less than 150 miles

Continued on Page 3, Column 5

548 PLANES DOWNED BY RUSSIA IN WEEK

LONDON, June 14 (Monday) (U. P.).—Russian airplanes and anti-aircraft guns destroyed 548 German planes during the week ended Saturday to bring a six-week total of enemy craft knocked out to 3369, the Soviet Union reported today.

In addition to the 548 planes officially claimed during the week, many more were damaged or destroyed in four nights of massed attacks on enemy airdromes, the Red Army Sunday midnight communique reported as recorded here.

153 LOST IN WEEK

Russian losses during the week totalled 153, to bring the total of Red Air Force planes lost in six weeks to 893.

Rounding out the week of grim battling for aerial supremacy on the Eastern Front, the Russian Air Force bombed enemy airdromes and the railroad cities of Gomel, Bryansk and Karachev Saturday night, a special communique said.

More than 100 fires, many of them accompanied by fierce explosions, were observed by crews of the long-range Russian bombers among railroad trains and ammunition dumps. Loss of two Russian planes was admitted.

PLANES WRECK TRAINS

The Moscow radio reported that Stormovik dive bombers had wrecked a German train and destroyed 10 freight cars loaded with guns.

Moscow dispatches reported that the huge air toll by the Russians

Continued on Page 2, Column 1

ROBERTS ASKS UNION OF ALLIES IN PEACE

WASHINGTON, June 13 (U. P.).—Associate Justice Owen J. Roberts of the Supreme Court tonight proposed a Federal union of all the United Nations for a powerful organization with authority and jurisdiction over international affairs to maintain peace in the post-war world.

He called on U. S. citizens to display the same "vision and daring" exhibited by the founding fathers 150 years ago and demand of their present leaders that United Nations co-operation for defeat of the Axis be perpetuated through a "fundamental compact" for post-war government.

RADIO FORUM STAGED

He participated in an American Forum-of-the-Air round-table discussion on the question: "Can We Organize Peace on Federal Union Lines?" Supporting him was Clarence K. Street, author of "Union Now." Senator Guy M. Gillette (D., Ia.) and Representative Bartel J. Jonkman (R., Mich.) favored steps to maintain peace but opposed a Federal union.

Gillette said that political, commercial, financial and sociological co-operation, with the United States taking the lead, must be provided but that Federal union was neither feasible nor practicable. A better solution might be provided along the lines of the Monroe Doctrine and Pan-American friendship "which have given the world a cogent example of the possibility of securing peace by international co-operation in the Western Hemisphere," he said.

Rommel Reported Established in France

LONDON, June 13 (A. P.).—Field Marshal Erwin Rommel has established headquarters at Perpignan, France, and is reorganizing French coastal defenses, the Algiers radio said in a broadcast today.

The broadcast said the former commander of Hitler's defeated African Corps had recently inspected the defenses of Corsica, Sardinia and Sicily.

Perpignan is on the Gulf of Lion, just north of the Spanish border.

Eisenhower Hails Allied Unity in Africa

ALLIED HEADQUARTERS IN NORTH AFRICA, June 13 (U. P.).—General Dwight D. Eisenhower, Allied commander, said today that the North African victory stood as a monument to the perfection of Allied unity and that the Axis dictators had suffered a devastating defeat.

Eisenhower gave his statement in a special message to mark United Nations Day tomorrow.

The Fall of Lampedusa

120 Britons Take Over As 4000 Italians Yield

By Paul Kern Lee

LAMPEDUSA, June 12 (Delayed) (A. P.)

A HANDFUL of 120 men are now taking over this island from Italian military, naval and marine personnel numbering from 4000 to 5000 who surrendered a half-hour ago. They are now filing out from their shore-side pillboxes and guns.

It took only two minutes—as quickly as the terms could be understood—for the Italian garrison to agree to unconditional surrender.

Lieutenant Hugh A. Corbett, of the Royal Navy, and I leaped ashore from the destroyer Lookout's launch and after the rapid parley the lieutenant signaled to the sea. He then went out and escorted in a company of the famous Coldstream Guards in landing craft that had hovered offshore all day.

HARDLY had the total success of Pantelleria's capture been clinched than naval forces sped to Lampedusa and inflicted a night shelling between aerial bombings. Twice during the night and again at dawn the ships hurled explosives ashore.

Lampedusa's shore guns, in contrast with those of Pantelleria, replied spiritedly and with danger-ous accuracy. Oil fires ashore, star shells from ships, and the splash of Italian projectiles into the sea made a theatrical spectacle with booming guns and screaming shells as an accompaniment.

The aerial attack continued all day today and in the evening the warships bombarded a fourth time. The last bombers reported what appeared to be a white cross formed at the Lampedusa airfield and said it was believed there were

Continued on Page 2, Column 4

Quezon Enters Hospital

NEW YORK, June 13 (A. P.).—President Manuel L. Quezon of the Philippines entered Doctors Hospital here Saturday for treatment of an undisclosed ailment. An attache today described Quezon's condition as very good.

Nazi-Italian Clash On Rhodes Reported

LONDON, June 14 (Monday) (U. P.).—The Italian garrison on the island of Rhodes has opened fire on German troops attempting to land there, a Tass (Russian news agency) dispatch from Istanbul said today.

The Italians, Tass said, opened up with their big coastal guns and scored two hits on a German transport, killing several men aboard.

The dispatch did not state when the incident occurred. Rhodes is Italy's major base in the Dodecanese Islands in the eastern Mediterranean.

Auto Traffic Is Light; Few Violators Found

Office of Price Administration officials described the volume of automobile traffic in this area as "exceedingly light" yesterday as OPA agents and police reported that only seven percent of 434 motorists stopped in a pleasure-driving check in the afternoon were listed as suspected violators.

"The seven percent figure is just about the lowest reported in any OPA check in this district, and indicates the ban on non-essential motoring is having the desired effect," a spokesman said.

CHECK AT BRIDGES

In a morning-hour check at the Delaware River and Tacony-Palmyra bridges and at the Market st. ferry, 110 drivers were questioned and the names of 50 were turned in to their local ration boards for possible action.

While the percentage of suspected violators was higher in the morning, the spokesman pointed out that those checked represented, in the main, "drivers who thought they could sneak to shore points early without being caught."

RESULTS LISTED

Intersections checked in the afternoon, with the number of motorists interviewed and cited at each, were: Frankford ave. and Margaret st., 51 and 3; Castor ave. and Benner st., 104 and 5; Frankford ave. and Cottman st., 110 and 7; Richmond

Continued on Page 7, Column 3

War Summary

Monday, June 14, 1943

Two large formations of heavy United States bombers yesterday hammered the heavily defended U-boat bases at Kiel and Bremen in the greatest air battle ever waged by Britain-based American air forces. Many Nazi fighters were shot down but the Americans lost 26 four-engined bombers, the largest loss yet suffered in the daylight precision raids on Germany.

The U. S. assaults, increasing the momentum of the Allied air offensive against the Nazi war machine, followed a night attack by R.A.F. heavy bombers on Bochum and the industrial Ruhr Valley. Twenty-four planes were lost, but Germany conceded severe damage had been inflicted.

In the Mediterranean, the Italian islet of Linosa surrendered to the Allies without a fight, the third stepping stone to the Italian mainland to be taken in three days. The island's garrison of 140 men was evacuated by a British destroyer. Meanwhile, Allied planes turned their attention to Sicily, destroying at least 150 enemy aircraft parked on Sicilian airfields.

On the Eastern Front, Moscow announced that Russian planes and anti-aircraft guns had destroyed 548 Nazi planes last week, against a Soviet loss of 153.

In the South Pacific, a mixed U. S. group of Army, Navy and Marine fliers shot down at least 25 Zeros, probably 33, in an air battle near the Russell Islands in the Solomons. Six American planes were lost, but the pilots of four were rescued.

Four-engined bombers under General MacArthur's command dropped almost 30 tons of bombs on the important Jap base of Rabaul, New Britain.

In the North Pacific, Army planes carried out five attacks on the Japs at Kiska Island in the Aleutians.

In central China, Chinese troops stormed and captured the Yangtze River port of Sungtze.

A demand that Generals de Gaulle and Giraud settle their differences was voiced in British newspapers, while in Algiers, French Communist deputies called for a purge of pro-Vichy elements.

U. S. WEATHER FORECAST

Philadelphia and vicinity: Cooler today.

Eastern Pennsylvania and New Jersey: Cooler.

Sun rises 5.30 A.M. Sets 8.30 P.M.
Moon rises 3.28 P.M. Sets 3.07 A.M.

Other Weather Reports on Page 2

JOHN STEINBECK'S WAR STORIES BEGIN TODAY

The Philadelphia Inquirer

PUBLIC LEDGER

An Independent Newspaper for All the People

FINAL CITY EDITION

CIRCULATION: May Average: Daily 472,084; Sunday 1,366,229

MONDAY MORNING, JUNE 21, 1943

Vol. 228, No. 172

abdefgh

THREE CENTS

Miners Out on Third General Strike, Offer to Go Back to Work for U. S.

John Steinbeck

Brown Helmets Make Men Look Like Long Rows of Mushrooms

(With a graphic description of life aboard a crowded troop transport, which is presented herewith, John Steinbeck begins his assignment as a war correspondent. The famous author of "Grapes of Wrath" and "The Moon Is Down" has just arrived in England and will send regular dispatches which will be printed in The Inquirer.)

By John Steinbeck

SOMEWHERE IN ENGLAND, June 20 (By Wireless).

THE troops in their thousands sit on their equipment on the dock. It is evening, and the first of the dimout lights come on. The men wear their helmets, which make them all look alike, make them look like long rows of mushrooms. Their rifles are leaning against their knees. They have no identity, no personality. The men are units in an army. The numbers chalked on their helmets are almost like the license numbers on robots.

Equipment is piled neatly—bedding rolls and half shelters and barrack bags. Some of the men are armed with Springfield or Enfield rifles from the first world war, some with M-1's or Garands, and some with the neat, light clever little carbines every one wants to have after the war for hunting rifles.

Above the pier the troopship rears high and thick as an office building. You have to crane your neck upward to see where the portholes stop and the open decks begin. She is a nameless ship and will be while the war lasts.

Her destination is known to very few men and her route to even fewer, and the burden of the men who command her must be almost unendurable, for the master who loses her and her cargo will never sleep comfortably again. He probably doesn't sleep at all now. The cargo holds are loaded and the ship waits to take her tonnage of men.

JOHN STEINBECK

• • •

ON the dock the soldiers are quiet. There is little talking, no singing, and as dusk settles to dark you can not tell one man from another. The heads bend forward with weariness. Some of these men have been all day, some many days, getting to this starting point.

There are several ways of wearing a hat or a cap. A man may express himself in the pitch or tilt of his hat, but not with a helmet. There is only one way to wear a helmet. It won't go on any other way. It sits level on the head, low over the eyes and ears, low on the back of the neck. With your helmet on you're a mushroom in a bed of mushrooms.

Four gangways are open now and the units get wearily to their feet and shuffle along in line. The men lean forward against the weight of their equipment. Feet drag against the incline of the gangways. The soldiers disappear one by one into the great doors in the side of the troopship.

• • •

INSIDE the checkers tabulate them. The numbers chalked on the helmets are checked again against a list. Places have been assigned. Half of the men will sleep on the decks and the other half inside in ballrooms, in dining rooms where once a very different kind of people sat and found very important things that have disappeared. Some of the men will sleep in bunks, in hammocks, on the floor, in passages, tomorrow they will shift. The men from the deck will come in to sleep and those from inside will go out. They will change every night until they land. They will not take off their clothes until they land. This is no cruise ship.

On the decks, dimmed to a faint blue dusk by the blackout lights, the men sink down and fall asleep. They are asleep almost as soon as they are settled. Many of them do not even take off their helmets. It has been a weary day. The rifles are beside them, held in their hands.

On the gangways the lines still feed into the troopship—a regiment of colored troops, a hundred army nurses, neat in their dark blue and strange in their helmets and field packs. The nurses at least will have staterooms, however crowded they may be in them. Up No. 1 gangway comes the headquarters complement of a bombardment wing and a company of military police. All are equally tired. They find their places and go to sleep.

EMBARKATION is in progress. No smoking is allowed anywhere. Every one entering the ship is triply checked, to make sure he belongs there, and the loading is very quiet. There is only the

Continued on Page 2, Column 1

4-TON BOMBS POUND FRENCH ARMS FACTORY

British Planes Fly 700 Miles to Raid Giant Schneider Plant at Le Creusot

LONDON, June 20 (A. P.).—Heavy British bombers struck another "concentrated and effective" blow at Hitler's war potential last night when they roared more than halfway across France to rain two- and four-ton blockbuster bombs on the huge Schneider armament works at Le Creusot, 170 miles southeast of Paris, it was announced today.

The Air Ministry reported that visibility over the sprawling 750-acre iron and steel works was good and that the bombers, which made a round trip of at least 700 miles, wrought maximum destruction on the plant which has been pouring heavy guns, armor plate and locomotives into the German war machine.

BIGGEST FRENCH PLANT

The Le Creusot plant of Schneider and Co., more than a square mile in area, is the largest arms factory in France and is comparable to the great Krupp works at Essen in its value to German war production. It is the largest and most important of all the plants of the Schneider cartel.

The Vichy radio reported Le Creusot was "heavily attacked" and that "important damage to buildings and casualties were reported." A Paris broadcast said 101 were known to have been killed and 250 injured in the blasting and "many more are buried under the ruins."

FOE DENIES DAMAGE

Both Berlin and Vichy declared, without confirmation from Allied quarters, that American bombers also participated in the attack. A Nazi broadcast said bombs were dropped "haphazardly" and asserted, as usual, that damage was limited mainly to residential sections and hospitals.

Le Creusot, situated just off the main line railway between Paris and Lyons, was bombed only once be-

Continued on Page 2, Column 2

MAP BY INQUIRER STAFF

R.A.F. RAIDS 'KRUPP OF FRANCE'

While British bombers (top arrow) continued to smash targets in the Ruhr and Rhineland, another heavyweight formation (bottom arrow) rained blockbuster bombs on the huge Schneider armament works at Le Creusot, 170 miles southeast of Paris. A power station at Mount Chanin, also was attacked.

DEWEY URGES G.O.P. TO BACK POST-WAR AID

Asks 'Constructive' Program in 1944 As Governors Open Conference in Ohio

By WILLIAM C. MURPHY, JR.

Inquirer Staff Reporter

COLUMBUS, O., June 20.—Governor Thomas E. Dewey of New York, the man who says he is not a candidate for the 1944 Republican Presidential nomination, blew into this capital of the Buckeye State today and immediately took the spotlight away from Ohio's own Governor, John W. Bricker, who is a candidate in every respect except for a formal announcement.

Dewey came here to attend the annual Conference of Governors, to which Bricker is the host this year. There are more than 35 other Governors here also—about half of them Republicans—but the contrast between the New Yorker and the Ohioan was what attracted attention of the politically minded today.

AGAINST ISOLATIONISTS

Dewey's first statement was a declaration that the Republicans must have a "constructive" program of post-war collaboration to offer to the voters in 1944—and he made it clear that he meant a program which would offer no consolation to the isolationist elements within his own party.

However, at the same time, Dewey also said he was hopeful that there would be a meeting in the near future of the Republican post-war advisory council recently appointed by Republican National Chairman Harrison Spangler, which, whatever may be its views with respect to post-war problems, has been generally regarded as composed predominantly of members who have not been enthusiastic about a repeat performance for Wendell L. Willkie as the Republican Presidential candidate in 1944.

WANTS PROGRAM SOON

Dewey said he thought that the council should meet soon and frame a post-war program for the Republican Party to advocate.

"I believe it will do a good job," said Dewey, referring to the post-war council. "I think it will take a very constructive view; you won't find any sentiment for isolationism in that group. It is a good one."

Dewey indorsed the resolution recently introduced in the House by Representative William J. Fulbright (D., Ark.), and approved by the House Committee on Foreign Affairs, which would put Congress on record as favoring American participation in the creation of international machinery to insure a "just and lasting peace." That resolution, Dewey said, would be "a good start."

The net result of Dewey's statements today appeared to be to leave

Continued on Page 3, Column 7

Lewis Denounces WLB Proposal as 'Yellow Dog' Pact

Illustrated on Page 14

By HERMAN A. LOWE

Inquirer Washington Bureau

WASHINGTON, June 21 (Monday).—The Nation's third general coal strike since April 1 began at 12.01 A. M. today after the United Mine Workers repudiated as a "yellow dog" contract the War Labor Board's proposed agreement for settlement of differences between the miners and soft coal operators.

With the expiration at midnight of a two-weeks truce declared by the U. M. W. Policy Committee when the last walkout was ended, the miners generally followed their custom of "no contract, no work," and there was no doubt that most if not all of the half million miners in the anthracite and bituminous fields would be idle today.

WILLING TO WORK FOR GOVERNMENT

The miners, through their Policy Committee, last night declared they were willing to "continue the production of coal for the Government, itself," and preliminary maneuvering began to reach some sort of settlement and make the walkout of short duration.

The U. M. W. statement expressed willingness "to make any necessary sacrifice for the Government" and to work for the Government under the direction of Secretary of the Interior Harold L. Ickes as custodian of the Federally-seized mines.

The statement, which bitterly assailed the War Labor Board, in effect invited Ickes to send the miners back to work as employes of the United States, working out an agreement which would give the miners something and at the same time save face all around.

ISSUED AFTER FRUITLESS NEGOTIATIONS

It was issued after a morning of final fruitless negotiations between the operators and miners, who adjourned their conferences sine die.

Ickes, who had been scheduled to leave for Columbus, O., to address the Conference of Governors, abruptly cancelled his trip. It is not believed that Ickes and John L. Lewis, U. M. W. president, were in communication last night. It was pointed out that even if it had been possible to work out an arrangement to direct the miners to work today, it would have been impossible to get word to many of the men in time.

Another point was that Ickes would probably require an approving nod from someone higher up before he could sit down to do any negotiating, even if he were to seek a formula within the bounds of the WLB directive.

MAY REFER CASE TO ROOSEVELT

Since the strike is in defiance of the WLB directive of Friday, it was expected that the board would meet today and probably refer the case to the White House for action by President Roosevelt.

The only comment from William H. Davis, WLB chairman, on last night's U. M. W. proposal to Ickes, was:

"We have no power or desire to keep anyone from making an agreement. But under the wage stabilization program,

Continued on Page 6, Column 2

Messina Strait Rocked On Both Sides by Allies

Map on Page 2

ALLIED HEADQUARTERS IN NORTH AFRICA, June 20 (A. P.).—Docks and other supply apparatus on both sides of the strategic Messina Strait separating Sicily and the Italian mainland were blown to bits in new concentrated Allied aerial assaults in the 24-hour cycle ended yesterday as the Fascist regime appeared committed more than ever to a last-ditch fight in the Mediterranean.

Reliable Allied quarters flatly denied rumors that Italian envoys were in Algiers or elsewhere in North Africa to sue for a separate peace.

LINKED TO BADOGLIO

The rumors, which apparently originated among the French civil population, named Marshal Pietro Badoglio, former chief-of-staff of all Italian armed forces, Crown Prince Umberto and even King Victor Emmanuel as emissaries.

Allied military censorship, which confines itself to questions of military security, permitted the rumors to be reported abroad but undertook

Continued on Page 2, Column 4

War Summary

Monday, June 21, 1943

British planes flew 700 miles Saturday night to hurl blockbuster bombs on the biggest armament plant in France—the Schneider works at Le Creusot, 170 miles southeast of Paris. Vichy reported heavy damage and casualties.

Allied planes in the Mediterranean continued to blast docks and supply depots on both sides of Messina Strait, separating Sicily and the Italian mainland. Reggio Calabria and San Giovanni in the toes of Italy received most of the punishment.

Eyewitness reports, meanwhile, indicated that Italy was already a beaten nation, with weary civilians eager for an Allied invasion and the end of the war. Mussolini, however, was reported mustering all his military sources for a bitter-end stand.

In the Battle of the Atlantic, British air and naval units sank two U-boats and probably destroyed three others in protecting a convoy last month, it was revealed.

On the political front, General de Gaulle indicated he would leave North Africa unless the French Liberation Committee agreed to his military reform program.

On the Russian front, Red bombers blasted parked planes and supply depots at Bryansk and Karachev, behind Orel.

Smashing a Jap attempt to raid the Darwin area in Australia, Spitfire fighters intercepted 48 enemy planes and destroyed or damaged 22.

Safety Award Won By Army Air Forces

WASHINGTON, June 20 (A. P.).—The National Safety Council's special wartime award was presented to the Army Air Forces today for "distinguished service to safety."

The award was based on the air forces' record of an average of only five injuries for each 100 men in its aviation cadet program.

Presented on the Army Hour radio program, the award was accepted by General Henry H. Arnold, commander of the air forces.

OPA SLEUTHS STALK SHIBE PARK DRIVERS

As automobile traffic remained at a near-minimum level in this area for the fifth successive Sunday, Office of Price Administration agents yesterday conducted a vigorous check on pleasure driving in the area of Shibe Park.

The agents reported, however, that less than six percent of 350 motorists who were questioned before and during the A's-Boston doubleheader were suspected violators.

20 NUMBERS TURNED IN

The agents, who were aided by police, turned in the license numbers of 20 drivers for local ration board action. Two of the 20, accused of "flagrant violations," were required to surrender their gas-ration books on the spot.

Other OPA surveys were made on Saturday night and yesterday at bridges, ferries, country clubs, Fairmount Park, downtown Broad st. and at Beach Haven and Atlantic City.

64 DRIVERS CITED

At the latter resort, 214 drivers were queried. Sixty-four were cited, including five whose books were lifted.

About 1200 cars were halted in

Continued on Page 5, Column 3

Five U-Boats Blasted In 5-Day Convoy Battle

LONDON, June 20 (A. P.).—British air and naval units, protecting Atlantic convoys with counter-attacks against "one of the fiercest and most sustained offensives ever mounted by U-boats," have sunk from two to five of Hitler's submarines and probably damaged several others in a five-day running battle, it was announced tonight.

The newest successes in the Allied drive to clear the Atlantic of enemy submarines were disclosed in an Admiralty-Air Ministry communique. It said the action occurred last month, but gave no specific dates.

FIVE-DAY BATTLE

"During these actions two U-boats were destroyed, three probably were destroyed and others may have been damaged," the communique declared.

Land-based planes, including four-engined Liberators and Flying Fortresses, teamed with warships and aircraft from one of the new escort carriers to defend the convoys from the U-boat packs.

For five days and five nights the battles ranged over hundreds of miles of the Atlantic, but the British

Continued on Page 2, Column 1

IN TODAY'S INQUIRER

SPECIAL DEPARTMENTS

COLUMNS AND FEATURES

ITALY LICKED NOW, WITNESSES REPORT

STOCKHOLM, June 20 (A. P.).—The Allied air offensive is rapidly blasting Italy into a pre-invasion stage by disrupting the normal life of its inhabitants, reliable eyewitnesses who have returned recently from that country said today.

They pictured the Italians as broken in spirit, sick of the aerial bombardments, and longing for an Allied invasion which they know will hasten the end of the war.

KNOW THEY'RE LICKED

"There is a lack of the war discipline characteristic of the Germans," said one informant. "The average Italian is making no bones about it. He feels that the war is lost, that Italy in reality is already knocked out and that the sooner invasion comes the better.

"Everyone is talking invasion. Nobody knows when or where it will come or what will happen when it does come. But persons who know Italian character well predict that morale and discipline now are at a point where, if the Allies strike, it will be 'every Italian for himself.'"

With bombings everywhere, evacuees are constantly on the move, bags in hand, looking for a safe place

Continued on Page 2, Column 6

Planes Over Zurich Cause Raid Alarm

ZURICH, Switzerland, June 21 (Monday) (U. P.).—A large force of unidentified planes flew over Zurich early today, causing an air raid alarm in the city.

Warning sirens also sounded in several other localities in western Switzerland.

The Zurich alarm came shortly after 1 A. M. and observers reported that the formation took 20 minutes to cross the city.

SENATORS FIGHT SHY OF OPA SUBSIDY BAN

WASHINGTON, June 20 (A. P.).—Senators hesitated today to squeeze the trigger of the death gun which their colleagues in the House have aimed at the Office of Price Administration food subsidy program.

They are expected to make their decision this week as the OPA puts into effect its second subsidy to bring a retail price rollback for meat. Meanwhile, some Senators criticized the drastic nature of restrictions which the House voted Friday on the OPA when considering its budget in the $2,898,000,000 war agencies appropriation bill.

MANY DISAPPROVE

Most of those who expressed opinions decried the move to strip OPA of its power to use any of its funds for subsidy administration, and many disapproved the $35,000,000 slash in the agency's operating funds for the coming fiscal year.

Senator John H. Bankhead (D., Ala.) said:

"I think they've gone entirely too far. If the Senate followed the House action, it would cripple the OPA so seriously as to be almost a fatal blow."

Senator Richard B. Russell (D.,

Continued on Page 5, Column 6

All Anthracite Miners Expected to Join Strike

Special to The Inquirer

WILKES-BARRE, June 20.—Pennsylvania's hard coal mines were expected to lie idle tomorrow as the State's 80,000 anthracite miners indicated they would join the Nation's third general coal strike in as many months.

Both Luzerne county mine union leaders and Major W. W. Inglis, of Scranton, chairman of the contract negotiating committee of the hard coal operators and the United Mine Workers, agreed that a work stoppage "appeared inevitable."

The two-week truce under which

Continued on Page 6, Column 4

U. S. WEATHER FORECAST

Philadelphia and Vicinity: Continued warm with thundershowers in late afternoon.

Eastern Pennsylvania: Continued warm and humid with a few scattered thundershowers this afternoon and evening.

New Jersey: A few scattered thundershowers late this afternoon or evening, warmer on the coast; continued warm and humid in the interior.

Sun rises 5.32 A. M. Sets 8.32 P. M.
Moon rises 11.40 P. M. Sets 9.23 A. M.

FORD PRODUCTION HALVED BY WALKOUT

DETROIT, June 20 (U. P.).—A strike of 9000 hourly-rated foremen at four large Detroit area plants of the Ford Motor Co. has cut production at the plants almost in half and threatens to curtail even further output of war materials, a Ford spokesman said tonight.

The company spokesman added it would take "several hours" to determine the strike's effect on tonight's incoming midnight shift.

Union officials said, however, that in any case where absence of a foreman would definitely result in harm to equipment, foremen would remain on the job to protect property.

The River Rouge, Highland Park,

Continued on Page 6, Column 6

Combined Operations: The Story of the COMMANDOS — based on the Book-of-the-Month

FROM THE OFFICIAL RECORDS
ILLUSTRATIONS BY WILLIAM SHARP

In the evening the submarine left port.

"It's your baby," said Clark.

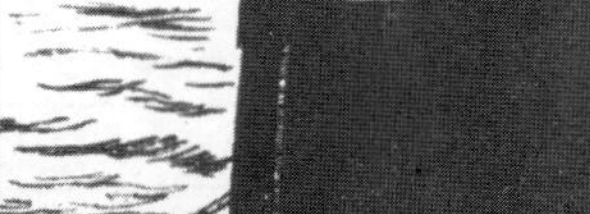
A bright light burned.

Installment XXVII

ONE night in October, 1942, Lieutenant General Mark W. Clark, Brigadier General L. L. Lemnitzer, Colonel A. L. Hamblen and Colonel C. C. Holmes, all of the United States Army, and Captain Jerauld Wright, of the U. S. Navy, were put aboard a British submarine. Three Commando officers, Captain C. B. Courtney, Lieutenant R. P. Livingstone and Lieutenant J. P. Foote, went along. Shortly after the party boarded it the sub put out to sea. The mission on which these men went was at that time of the greatest secrecy and of the utmost importance to the Allied cause. The world now knows that from the moment the submarine got under way, the doom of Rommel and his Afrika Korps was sealed. Clark had orders to get in touch, in French North Africa, with French officers and civilians who were devoted to the cause of the Allies. Information vital to a mass invasion of North Africa, a Commando effort on a far greater scale than ever had been tried before, would be given the Americans.

It was 10 in the evening when the sub left port. She continued on the surface all next day at a speed of 12 knots. This risk of discovery was taken because the element of time was of the utmost importance. The men had a long way to go and not much time to get there. Clark told Courtney, ranking Commando on the trip, something of the problems facing them. He said that certain persons in North Africa desired high-ranking American officers to go there in secret, so that plans for an invasion might be worked out. After warning the ruddy-faced young Commando that he was not at all certain how the visit was going to go or what the results would be, Clark said he would leave entirely in the Commando's hands how the landing was to be made. "It's your baby," the American told him. "You're the people making the landing and we'll do exactly what you say."

During the voyage they played bridge and a game called "Cameroon," which young Wright taught the Yanks and in which he had an amazing run of luck. Shore was reached at 9 in the night, at a point where a bright light was burning. The Americans, carrying their uniforms in haversacks, were wearing a strange collection of civilian clothing. Then the boat in which Courtney and Hamblen were paddling struck the fore plane of the sub and dumped them into the sea.

(Tomorrow: The general hides in a cellar)

Inquirer's News Quiz

How carefully do you read your newspaper? Do you remember what you read? Below are five questions based on news stories and features which appeared in The Inquirer during the past week.

1. The famous author at the right has started a series of graphic war stories in The Inquirer. Who is he?

2. General Sir Claude Auchinleck has assumed the post of commander-in-chief in India. Whom does he succeed?

3. Who is the new chief of the domestic branch of the OWI?

4. The Schneider armaments works, the biggest plant in France supplying the Nazis, has been blasted by heavy British bombers. Where is the plant located?

5. Gunder Haegg, the wonderful Swede, won his first race in America on Sunday. (a) Whom did he beat and (b) at what distance?

(Answers Elsewhere on This Page)

LITTLE ORPHAN ANNIE — By Harold Gray

TERRY AND THE PIRATES — By Milton Caniff

DONALD DUCK — By Walt Disney

BARNEY GOOGLE AND SNUFFY SMITH — By Fred Lasswell

THEY'LL DO IT EVERY TIME — By Jimmy Hatlo

Twistagram

You can start anywhere above to work a TWISTOGRAM, though it's more fun and harder to work from the top down. The trick is to add one letter to each word until you reach the bottom.

2. North Central State.
3. Just a racket.
4. A lot of air.
5. Enlarge.
6. Equipped for flight.
7. Joining with heat.
8. Residence.

(Answer Tomorrow)

Yesterday's Twistagram

R G
P A G
G E A R
R A N G E
G R A V E N
V I N E G A R
A V E R R I N G

Cryptogram

OUTDATED

BF BK VIAAC JPD KPOR NBFRSEFISR GEA KIHHRANC MRGPOR PMKPNRFR. FEQR VPS BAKFEAGR, PIS GPPQMPPQ VSPO NEKF CRES.

Solution Tomorrow

HENRY — By Anderson

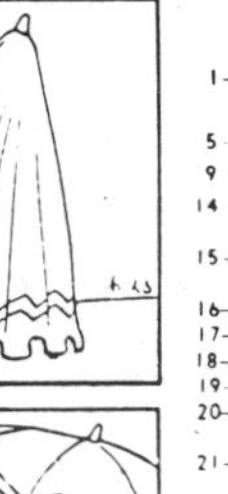
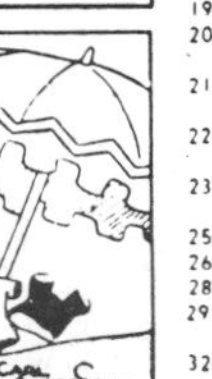

Your Bridge Problems

By Ely Culbertson

With all the misfortunes that can befall a declarer bad suit breaks, unfortunate position of honors, adverse ruffs, and so forth ad infinitum—it is not surprising that a large proportion of contracts that look "cold" fall somewhere by the wayside. It is surprising, however, that so many other contracts which are far easier to fulfill than to lose, meet the same fate.

South, dealer.
East-West vulnerable.

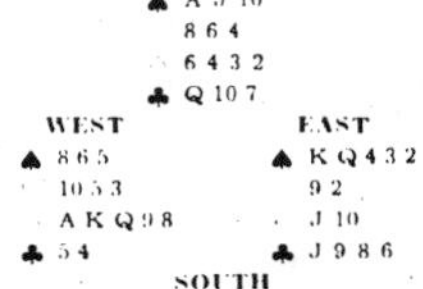
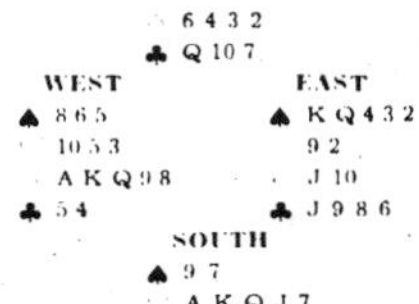

NORTH
♠ A J 10
♥ 8 6 4
♦ 6 4 3 2
♣ Q 10 7

WEST
♠ 8 6 5
♥ 10 5 3
♦ A K Q 9 8
♣ 5 4

EAST
♠ K Q 4 3 2
♥ 9 2
♦ J 10
♣ J 9 8 6

SOUTH
♠ 9 7
♥ A K Q J 7
♦ 7 5
♣ A K 3 2

The bidding:

South	West	North	East
1 ♥	Pass	1NT.	Pass
3 ♥	Pass	4 ♥	Pass
Pass	Pass		

West opened with the diamond king, and when he saw the 10 drop from East's hand, continued with the ace and queen. This sequence of plays should have made matters absurdly simple for declarer, but apparently he was not aware of his good fortune. East tried to strike a blow for his team by ruffing the third diamond with the heart nine, but declarer, of course, over-ruffed and had no trouble drawing all the outstanding trumps in three leads.

HIDES STRENGTH

East, carefully refraining from announcing his spade strength, discarded two low spades. Now declarer led a low club to the queen and then cashed his ace and king of clubs, looking expectantly for a 3-3 break of the suit. To his great disgust, this break failed to materialize and the contract was now irrevocably doomed. Whatever declarer did, East was sure to win a spade and a club.

If West, after cashing only one diamond, had shifted to a spade, declarer would have had a real problem on his hands, but as the play actually went, 10 tricks scarcely could have been colder. After drawing trumps, how could declarer possibly lose by leading a spade and putting in dummy's 10 spot? East had been shown to have no more diamonds and no more hearts. If he won the spade lead, what could he return that would fail to give declarer the rest of the tricks? A spade return would build two spade tricks for declarer and permit him to discard a club; a club return would be up to dummy's Q-10 and assure declarer of four solid club tricks.

Letter Links

Transform the top word to the bottom one by changing but one letter (stroke) at a time. Keep the order of letters constant.

Tent

______
______
______
______
______
______

Arab

(Answer elsewhere on this page)

LETTER OUT

SHRIVEL		Letter Out for a chip off the old block.
GAITERS		Letter Out and it's "for free."
PARENTAL		Letter Out and he's Way Down South.
ALERTS		Letter Out for the smallest one.
TALIAMAN		Letter Out for what we all are after all.

Remove one letter from each word and re-arrange to spell the word called for in the last column. Print the letter in the center column opposite to the word from which you have removed it. If you have "Lettered Out" correctly IT TAKES A BRAVE ONE TO MAKE A HERO.

Answers Elsewhere on This Page

Cross-Word Puzzle

HORIZONTAL

1—Athletic marker
5—Amphibian
9—Blacksnake
14—Porous earthen jar
15—Buddhist priest
16—Gum resin
17—Jetty
18—Death notice
19—A drop
20—Arabian garment
21—Accommodate
22—Medieval stronghold
23—Musical instrument
25—Leave
26—Part of eye
28—Vase
29—A kind of hat
32—Travesty
36—Game of chance
37—Dye indigo
38—Husks
40—Card game
41—Municipality
42—Strong
44—To cultivate
45—To damage
47—Portico
48—Affection
49—Disburden
53—Desire
56—Weed
58—Creek
59—Smallest
60—Title
61—Wide stretching
62—Roman garment
63—The olives
64—Genus of auks
65—Guide
66—Industrious
67—Exigency

VERTICAL

1—So. Am. humming-bird
2—Excuse
3—Fold
4—Attention
5—Fanfare
6—Spring harvest in India
7—Skip
8—Ship channel
9—Cont[illegible]ue
10—Canting
11—Copper
12—Man's name
13—Frost
21—To scorch
22—Mongrel
24—Steep
25—Subdues
27—Plaza
29—Insipid
30—A song
31—Daybreak
32—Composer
33—River mussel
34—Ceremony
35—In the month preceding
36—Deadly
39—Day of week
43—Zero quantity
45—Building material
46—Salutation
48—Kind of stocking
50—[illegible]
51—Passageway
52—Marked with [illegible]
53—Mountains
54—To station
55—Ashen
56—[illegible]
57—[illegible]
60—[illegible] stroke
61—Moving wagon

Solution Tomorrow

Puzzle Answers

Word Game Answers

Yesterday's Word — DEFERVESCE

deer	verse
deter	screed
deserve	sere
ever	seer
fester	seed
fever	sever
freed	severe
reeds	secede
recede	served
reeve	sere
reef	cede
vered	creed

Test Your Knowledge Answers

1. Mottled.
2. Made no will.
3. Redundancy.
4. Building fires.
5. Anthracite.

Tooth Picks

XXXIX

News Quiz Answers

1. John Steinbeck.
2. Field Marshal Sir Archibald P. Wavell.
3. Palmer Hoyt, publisher of the Portland Oregonian.
4. LeCreusot, 170 miles southeast of Paris.
5. (a) Gregory Rice (b) 5000 meters.

Letter Out Answers

SHRIVEL (H) Letter Out for a chip off the old block SLIVER. GAITERS (E) Letter Out and it's "for free" GRATIS. PARENTAL (A) Letter Out and he's way down South PLANTER. ALERTS (R) Letter Out for the smallest one LEAST. TALIAMAN (O) Letter Out for what we all are after all ANIMALS.

Yesterday's Cryptogram

With curtailment of baby carriage manufacturing for the duration, we imagine infants will soon get up in arms.

Who Is It Answer

William Allen White

Letter Links

TENT, tens, teas, team, tram, cram, crab, ARAB.

Party Pages

When entertaining in your home, you will find these Puzzles and Pastimes will provide diversion and amusement for your guests.

The Word Detective

Glimpses of little-known bits of history, often replete with adventure and romance, are to be found in the origin of many words we use every day. THE WORD DETECTIVE is on the trail of those words for Inquirer readers and today reveals the origin of:

Uncle Sam

The abbreviation "U. S." might naturally have suggested the extension "Uncle Sam." There is, however, an often-told story that would seem to fix the date and the circumstances of the origin of the national nickname.

It seems that in 1812 at the outbreak of the war with England a New York contractor by the name of Elbert Anderson journeyed to Troy, N. Y., to purchase a quantity of provisions. His dealings were with one, Samuel Wilson.

Now Samuel Wilson had charge of a large number of workmen, who were handling the provisions purchased by Anderson. When the casks were inspected they were marked "U. S."

Samuel Wilson also had a nickname. He was called Uncle Sam. So when one of the inspectors was asked what the initials "U. S." stood for he answered jokingly, "Uncle Sam."

The Word Detective is not sure whether or not Mr. Wilson had a beard. At any rate, it's a good story.

Toothpick Trick

Place nine toothpicks in a row on the table and then, without splitting or breaking any of them, see if you can re-arrange the nine in such a way that you actually have added 30 to the original number.

(Answer elsewhere on this page)

Test Your Knowledge

By Dr. George W. Crane

Select the answer which you consider best.

1. [illegible] terms would [illegible] a roan horse?
Dark brown White Mottled Tan

2. [illegible] intestate, it would [illegible] he had
Committed suicide Gone bankrupt Made no will Been poisoned.

3. What kind of grammatical error is illustrated by the sentence, "The azure sky was blue?"
Solecism Split infinitive Anachronism Redundancy.

4. In the early days the plainsmen used buffalo chips for
Playing poker Building fires Panning gold Building houses.

5. Which one of these types of fuel is called "hard coal?"
Lignite Anthracite Bituminous Peat.

(Answers elsewhere on this page)

Yesterday's Puzzle Solved

The Philadelphia Inquirer
WEDNESDAY MORNING, JUNE 23, 1943 22

(A. P. Wirephoto)

A DIVE By a dive bomber. A Douglas "Dauntless" dive bomber nosed over on the deck of one of America's newest aircraft carriers, a converted cruiser, after the pilot had attempted a landing. Neither the pilot nor his gunner was injured in the accident which occurred during ship's "shakedown" cruise.

(A. P. Wirephoto)

WOMAN CLIMBING OUT OF STREET CAR TO ESCAPE RIOTING

Detroit Taken Over by Troops

Order was restored yesterday in riot-torn Detroit by steel-helmeted Federal troops. The mob rule, which claimed more than a score of lives and resulted in military rule, is typified in the photo above of a trolley being stopped in heart of the city. Note the woman climbing through the window to avoid the rioters. Below: Troops patroling a riot-ridden area. Note the smashed store fronts and the debris strewn on the street. Bottom: Men and women overturn a smashed auto.

(Official U. S. Army Photo from A. P. Wirephoto)

BOMBS HEADED FOR AN ITALIAN OIL REFINERY (CIRCLED)

Wiping Out Oil Center

Photographic evidence of the accuracy of U. S. bombers. The bombs fall (above) toward an oil refinery and oil storage area at Leghorn, Italy. They strike (below) squarely on the target, destroying the refining plant and exploding the surrounding oil and gas storage tanks.

HUNTER Boarding his plane at a U. S. air base in New Guinea is Lieutenant William C. Day, Jr., of Red Lion, Pa., pictured as he sets out to hunt more Jap planes. Up until June 1, he had been credited with five enemy aircraft, thus making him an ace and one of the leaders at air base.

(A. P. Wirephoto)

TROOPS MOVING ALONG DEBRIS-STREWN DETROIT STREETS

(Official U. S. Army Photo from A. P. Wirephoto)

WHAT HAPPENED WHEN THE BOMBS HIT: THE WHITE BURST IS AN OIL TANK EXPLODING

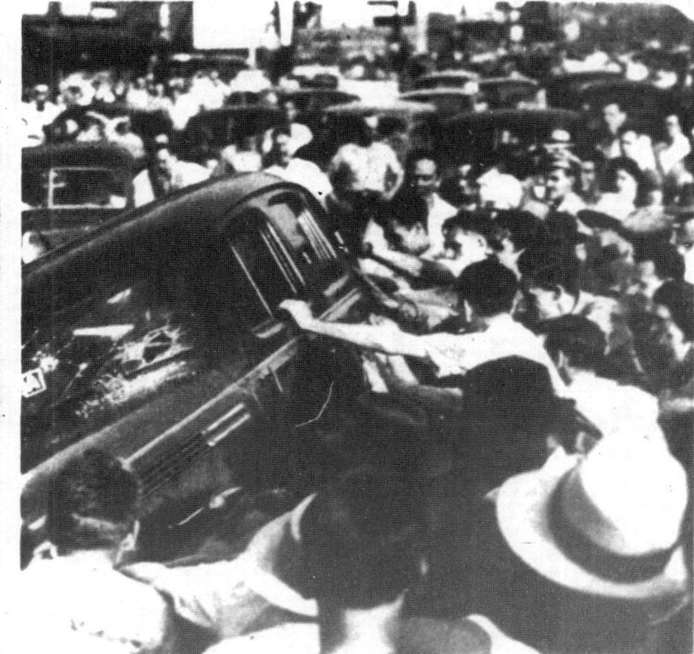

(A. P. Wirephoto)

DETROIT MOB OVERTURNING A BATTERED AUTOMOBILE

Hagerstown Beats Wilmington; Cards, Senators Win; Yanks Lose Two

Interstate League Leaders Down Rocks, 6-1; Allentown, Lancaster Also Triumph

WILMINGTON, Del., July 3 (A. P.).—The Hagerstown Owls dropped the Wilmington Blue Rocks three games behind first place by handing the locals a 6-1 setback before 1289 fans in a ladies night attraction here tonight.

The victory was the second in a row for the Owls over the faltering Rocks in the four-game series which will be concluded here tomorrow afternoon with a double bill.

Gene Enright on the hill for the Owls held the Rocks to four hits and had little trouble winning despite the fact he walked 10 and hit two Wilmington batsmen.

HAGERSTOWN	ab.	r.	h.	o.	a.	WILMINGTON	ab.	r.	h.	o.	a.
Mays.3b	5	1	3	2	2	Sloboda.ss	3	0	0	4	2
Riley.rf	2	1	0	2	1	Antolick.lf	4	0	0	0	0
D'dario.2b	4	0	1	3	6	Cal'han.rf	4	1	0	2	0
Davis.lf	5	1	2	3	1	Burgo.3b	2	0	0	1	0
Maier.cf	4	1	1	3	0	W'lliams.1b	2	0	1	10	0
Watson.1b	5	0	1	8	1	Rullo.2b	3	0	1	1	2
Sabena.ss	5	1	2	4	2	Parisse.c	3	0	1	5	1
Chew.c	4	1	1	2	0	Lowry.cf	4	0	1	3	0
Enright.p	4	0	0	0	1	Koch.p	2	0	0	1	6
						aMoore	1	0	0	0	0
Totals	38	6	11	27	14	Totals	28	1	4	27	11

a—Batted for Koch in 9th.

Hagerstown .... 0 0 0 2 0 2 0 2 0—6
Wilmington .... 0 0 0 0 0 0 0 1 0—1

Errors: Antolick, Callahan. Runs batted in: Maier, Sabena, Mays 2, Davis, Rullo. Three-base hits: Maier, Mays. Double plays: Koch, Parisse and Williams; Davis, Daddario and Watson. Left on base, Hagerstown 13, Wilmington 12. Base on ball: off Koch 6, Enright 10. Struck out: by Koch 5, Enright 2. Hit by pitcher: by Enright (Parisse), by Koch (Riley), by Enright (Sloboda), by Koch (Daddario). Umpires: Dobos, Gillespie. Time, 2:16.

ALLENTOWN, Pa., July 3 (A. P.).—Reaching Johnny Holowka for 14 solid hits, the Allentown Wings tonight defeated the York White Roses, 7 to 6, to square their Inter-State series at one game each.

ALLENTOWN	ab.	r.	h.	o.	a.	YORK	ab.	r.	h.	o.	a.
Sp'r'nza.3b	4	0	0	1	3	C'pbell.2b	5	2	2	3	4
Overman.cf	5	2	2	2	0	Shoff.3b	5	2	3	2	1
Liles.1b	4	1	1	14	1	Sch'ler.1b	5	0	1	10	0
Astbury.lf	3	2	3	1	0	Sweeny.rf	4	0	2	1	0
Kressley.rf	3	1	1	0	0	Sites.lf	4	0	1	4	0
Marcks.ss	5	1	1	1	4	Biros.cf	4	0	1	1	1
Ginley.2b	4	0	2	2	1	Gr'ff'hs.ss	4	0	0	1	2
Cr'm'ling.c	4	0	2	4	2	Daniels.c	3	1	0	2	0
Held.p	4	0	2	2	5	H'lowka.p	4	1	0	0	5
Totals	36	7	14	27	16	Ttls.	38	6	10	24	13

York .... 1 0 1 0 1 2 0 0 1—6
Allentown .... 1 0 4 1 0 1 0 0 x—7

Errors—Marcks, Daniels, Ginley. Runs batted in—Marcks 3, Ginley 2, Astbury 2, Campbell 2, Shoff 2, Sweeny, Schaedler. Sacrifice hits—Astbury. Home runs—Shoff, Astbury. Three-base hits—Sweeny, Biros. Two-base hits—Overman, Schaedler, Marcks. Left on base—York 11; Allentown 7. Stolen bases—Astbury 2. Hit by pitcher—By Held, Daniels. Struck out—By Holowka 2, by Held 6. Bases on balls—off Holowka 5, Passed ball—Daniels. Umpires—Pattie and Heller. Time of game—2:15.

White Sox Beat A's in First, 6-4

Continued From First Page

open...g frame. He gave up four walks, one with the bases loaded, to move across the first Philadelphia run, and Hall bounced a single off Ross' knees to score the other.

CURTRIGHT HITS HOMER

The White Sox, however, rushed back with their secret weapon—Outfielder Curtright. The Sox rookie, who Friday ended a 26-game hitting streak, blasted a home run into the left field stands with Wally Moses aboard to tie the count at 2-all.

The big Sox doings came later in the fourth, when Grant, Kolloway, and Kuhel opened with successive singles. Errors by Hall and White piled up the Athletics' woes, which finally developed into four runs when Tucker collected the fourth hit of the Sox big frame.

DOUBLE PLAY STOPS A'S

The Athletics narrowed the Chicago lead to 6-4 with a brace of runs in the fifth, the result of a walk, two hits and an error. The inning might have budded into quite a rally had the Sox not pulled a double play on Hall's roller to halt the uprising.

FIRST GAME

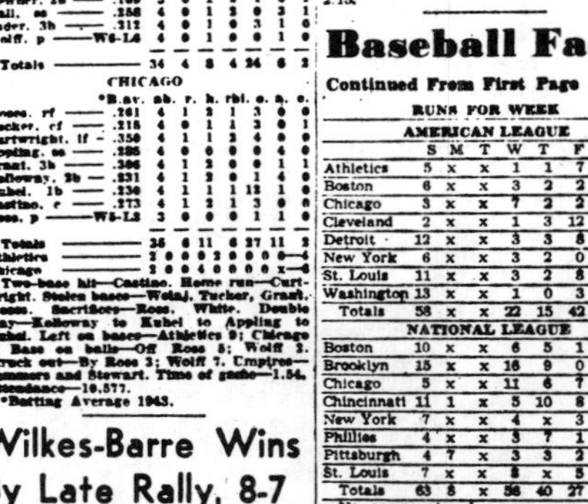

Two-base hit—Castino. Home run—Curtwright. Stolen bases—Weiaj, Tucker, Grant, Moses. Sacrifices—Ross, White. Double play—Kolloway to Kuhel to Appling to Kuhel. Left on bases—Athletics 9; Chicago 8. Base on balls—Off Ross 5; Wolff 2. Struck out—By Ross 3; Wolff 7. Umpires—Summers and Stewart. Time of game—1.54. Attendance—10,577.

*Batting Average 1943.

Wilkes-Barre Wins By Late Rally, 8-7

WILKES-BARRE, Pa., July 3 (A. P.).—The Barons rallied for three runs in the eighth to nip the Binghamton Triplets 8 to 7 today for their third straight triumph.

Alex D. Nelishen, relieving Wink Stroupe in the seventh when the victors went out in front with three markers, was credited with his seventh conquest.

Johnny Rager, second of three trip flingers was the loser, suffering this third loss.

WILKES-BARRE	ab	r	h	o	a	BINGHAMTON	ab.	r.	h.	o.	a.
C Pf'fer.ss	4	2	1	2	2	Baker.cf	4	1	2	0	0
W'dling.rf	3	2	2	2	1	Platek.rf	4	1	2	3	1
Maples.lf	5	0	2	2	0	Nav'cki.1b	4	1	2	8	0
Sudol.1b	5	2	2	8	0	Bartola.c	4	1	1	4	0
Lazzeri.3b	5	2	4	2	2	Dunlap.lf	4	0	1	2	0
Seghi.2b	4	0	2	3	5	Portner.ss	4	0	1	1	4
Koerner.cf	4	0	1	1	0	Patran.2b	4	0	0	5	1
a-Kelinze	1	0	0	0	0	White.3b	4	2	1	0	5
Smith.cf	0	0	0	0	0	Crowe.p	0	0	0	0	0
Devlin.c	1	0	0	7	1	Rager.p	3	1	1	0	0
Stroupe.p	3	0	0	0	0	Davis.p		0	0	0	0
Den'shen.p	1	0	1	0	0						
Totals	36	8	15	27	11	Totals	35	7	11	24	11

a—Batted for Koerner in 8th.

Binghamton .... 1 1 0 0 0 0 3 2 0—7
Wilkes-Barre .... 4 0 0 0 0 0 1 3 x—8

Errors—None. Runs batted in—Platek, Bartola, Porter 2, Rager, Maples, Lazzeri 3, Seghi 3, Navrocki. Two-base hits—Lazzeri 2, Baker, Rager. Sacrifice—Seghi. Double plays—Woodling and Sudol; Lazzeri, Seghi and Sudol; Patrow, Portner and Navrocki; Pfeifer, Seghi and Sudol. Left on base—Stroupe, Crowe 2, Jaeger 4, Danelishen 3. Struck out—Stroupe 6, Rager 3, Danelishen 1. Hits—Off Crowe, 3 in 1-3 inning; Rager, 22 in 7; Davis, 6 in 2-3; Stroupe, 9 in 6 1-3; Danelishen, 2 in 2 2-3. Wild pitches—Stroupe, Rager. Winning pitcher—Danelishen. Losing pitcher—Rager. Umpires—Padden and Winters. Time—2.25.

Johnson Spurns All-Star Berth

Si Johnson, veteran right-handed pitcher of the Phillies, has declined his selection as batting practice pitcher for the National League in the July 13 All-Star game.

Net receipts from the game will be used to purchase balls, bats and other baseball equipment for the U. S. armed services here and abroad.

William D. Cox, president of the Phillies, said the following telegram had been sent to Ford Frick, National League president, and Billy Southworth, manager of the team:

"Mr. Silas K. Johnson regrets that he will be unable to attend your bunting and throwing party on July 13th."

ONE TIME CUBS' PHIL CAVARRETTA DIDN'T BOTHER PHILS WITH HIS POTENT BAT
Chicago's first baseman made two timely hits, but in the sixth inning, he flied out. Catcher Tommy Livington.

Errors Aid Cubs; Beat Phils, 6-1

By STAN BAUMGARTNER

Continued From First Page

in the third. Tommy Livingston drilled a single to left and went to third when Kimball pushed a safety to right. Danny Murtaugh hit sharply to Stanky, and when the latter turned it into a double play Livingston scored.

Chicago added a final duo of tallies in the eighth on hits by Stan Hack, Ed Stanky, Phil Cavarretta and Bill Nicholson.

In the double-header today Si Johnson and Charley Fuchs will oppose Hiram Bithorn and Big Bill Lee.

CHICAGO

	*B.Av.	ab.	r.	h.	rbi.	o.	a.	e.
Hack, 3b	.315	3	0	1	0	1	1	0
Stanky, 2b	.253	4	1	1	0	2	3	0
Cavarretta, 1b	.307	4	3	2	1	11	0	0
Nicholson, rf	.294	4	1	2	1	4	0	0
Goodman, lf	.280	3	0	0	0	3	0	0
Lowrey, cf	.299	3	0	0	0	3	0	0
McCullough, c	.183	4	1	0	1	2	0	0
Merullo, ss	.265	3	1	1	0	1	3	0
Wyse, p —W-1—L-3		3	0	0	0	0	3	0
Totals		31	6	6	4	27	11	1

PHILLIES

	*B.Av.	ab.	r.	h.	rbi.	o.	a.	e.
Murtaugh, 2b	.283	4	0	0	0	1	5	0
Northey, rf	.286	4	0	1	0	3	1	0
Adams, cf	.263	4	0	1	0	1	0	0
Wasdell, 1b	.282	4	0	2	0	11	0	0
Dahlgren, 3b	.341	4	0	0	0	3	2	0
Triplett, lf	.211	4	0	0	0	5	0	0
Brewster, ss	.238	3	0	0	0	0	3	1
Livingston, c	.237	3	1	1	0	2	2	1
Kimball, p —W3-L3		2	0	1	0	0	2	2
aMay	.253	1	0	0	0	0	0	0
Mathewson, p W0-L0		0	0	0	0	0	0	0
Totals		32	1	6	0	27	13	4

a—Batted for Kimball in 8th.

Chicago .... 2 3 0 0 0 0 0 2 0—6
Phillies .... 0 0 1 0 0 0 0 0 0—1

Three-base hits—Cavarretta, Nicholson. Double plays—Stanky to Cavarretta; Brewster to Murtaugh to Wasdell. Sacrifice hit—Hack. Left on bases—Chicago 2, Phillies 5. Base on balls—off Kimball 1, Wyse 1, Mathewson 2. Struck out—By Wyse 2, Kimball 1. Hits—Off Kimball, 6 in 8 innings; off Matthewson, 0 in 1 inning. Passed balls—Livingston. Losing pitcher—Kimball. Umpires—Barlick, Sears and Pinelli. Time of game—1.35. Attendance—3984. * Batting average 1943.

Major Bowles Gives Packers 8 Hits

TRENTON, N. J., July 3 (A. P.).—The Lancaster Red Roses squared their series with the Trenton Packers by taking a 3 to 1 decision here tonight.

Major Bowles, on the mound for the Roses, spaced out eight hits over the route while his teammates were collecting 10 off Hennessey.

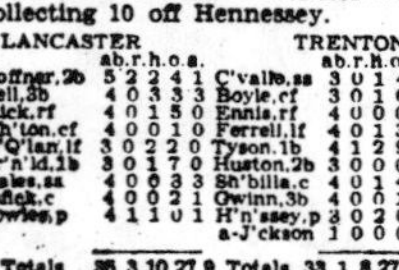

LANCASTER	ab.	r.	h.	o.	a.	TRENTON	ab.	r.	h.	o.	a.
Hoffner.2b	5	2	2	4	1	C'valle.ss	3	0	1	4	7
Kell.3b	4	0	3	3	3	Boyle.cf	4	0	0	3	0
Flick.rf	4	0	1	5	0	Ennis.rf	4	0	0	0	0
Wh'ton.cf	4	0	0	1	0	Ferrell.lf	4	0	1	3	0
M'Q'lan.lf	3	0	2	2	0	Tyson.1b	4	1	2	9	0
Gr'n'ld.1b	3	0	1	7	0	Huston.2b	3	0	0	0	1
Males.ss	4	0	0	3	3	Sh'billa.c	4	0	1	4	1
Sefick.c	4	0	0	2	1	Gwinn.3b	4	0	0	1	1
Bowles.p	4	1	1	0	1	H'n'ssey.p	3	0	2	0	5
						a-J'ckson	1	0	0	0	0
Totals	35	3	10	27	9	Totals	33	1	8	27	15

A—Batted for Hennessey in 9th.

Lancaster .... 0 0 0 1 0 1 0 1 0—3
Trenton .... 0 1 0 0 0 0 0 0 0—1

Hartford Again Beats Utica, 5-1

HARTFORD, July 3 (A. P.).—The Hartford Senators continued their domination over the Utica Braves by beating the Eastern League cellar dwellers for the second straight day at Bulkeley Stadium this afternoon, 5-1. In eight meetings between the two teams this season the Senators have returned the victors in seven.

Baseball Facts

Continued From First Page

INTERSTATE LEAGUE
YESTERDAY'S RESULTS

Allentown 7, York 6.
Hagerstown 6, Wilmington 1.
Lancaster 3, Trenton 1.

STANDING OF THE TEAMS

	W.	L.	P.C.		W.	L.	P.C.
Hagerstn.	37	20	.649	York	28	28	.500
Wilm'gton	33	22	.600	Trenton	23	33	.411
Lancaster	29	25	.537	Allentown	16	38	.296

Today's schedule: York at Allentown, 2 games; Hagerstown at Wilmington, 2 games; Lancaster at Trenton (night).

Batting Averages

Cox, Phils, Hits Frick's Rulings

Continued From First Page

The crowning decision was the halting of the Pittsburgh-Phillies game Wednesday night, June 30, at 11.30 o'clock (under 1940 rules) when under the 1943 rules the game could have proceeded until 12.50 (war time)."

PRAISES LANDIS

After praising Judge K. M. Landis, baseball commissioner, for refusing to issue "an elastic interpretation" in the case of Babe Phelps, the statement says:

"In the St. Louis protest (June 5 game) Mr. Frick believes that he has the right to interpret Rule 26, part of which is 'putting the ground in proper condition for play under penalty of forfeiture of the game by the home team.'

"Here there is no ground for elasticity. The rule is clear, the penalty is clear and in his written opinion Mr. Frick recalls that 'a couple of seasons ago we had this same difficulty with the groundkeeper in St. Louis, and that in this other instance also the groundkeeper delayed with the result that the playing field had become waterlogged so that play could not be continued even though the storm cleared and the rain ceased.'

BAD, BAD BOY

"Just think of this decision against us in line with this statement. It is tantamount to saying to Mr. Breadon you can be a bad, bad boy for quite a few times and papa won't spank nor will I tell you when I am going to spank you, but some day unless you get some sense I may slap you on the wrist.

"In this decision Mr. Frick does not use the proverbial ruler to make the slap. He has used a feather with the result that the rule book, the bible of baseball club presidents, compliments of Mr. Frick, should read complacency of Mr. Frick."

PROTEST SITUATIONS

The protest situations:

On June 5 the Phils' game in St. Louis was stopped because of weather in the last half of the eighth with the Cards leading, 1-0. The rules specify that the home team is responsible for the condition of the field. The groundskeeper was ordered by the umpire in charge to place tarpaulins over the field, pitching mound and home plate. This was not done.

Failure of the home club to use weather-proofing devices when ordered to do so by the umpire in chief is supposed to forfeit the game to the visiting team, 9-0, according to the rules. When play was ordered resumed the infield was a mire and the game was called. The Phillies protested, and Frick ordered the game replayed from the point at which it was halted.

DAHLGREN HIT

In the Giants game at New York, the score was tied with the bases loaded and Babe Dahlgren, Phils first baseman at bat. Dahlgren, irked over the pitcher's delay in throwing, stepped out of the box. The plate umpire ordered the pitcher to deliver the ball, and Dahlgren, watching all this, hopped back into the batter's box and was hit by the ball.

The Giants protested that he had deliberately run in front of the ball, and so would be out. The umpire ordered Dahlgren to bat again. The Babe doubled, cleared the bases, and the Phillies won. The Giants protested and Frick ordered the game played from the point where Dahlgren was batting.

Dixie Walker Christens Ship

NEW YORK, July 3 (U. P.).—Dixie Walker, Brooklyn Dodgers star outfielder, swung a bottle of champagne at a launching today and "got more kick out of sending this ship down the ways than from any home run I ever made."

The occasion was the launching of a submarine chaser at the Brooklyn Yards of the Sullivan Drydock and Repair Corporation.

St. Louis Boosts National Lead By Beating Dodgers; Browns Lose Out to Washington

By HANK SIMMONS

Continued From First Page

Dean and towering Mike Naymick. Cleveland took the lead by scoring one in the third and another in the fourth.

ROOF CAVES IN

Boston tied it up in the sixth by scoring a pair and the roof began caving in in the eighth when they pushed three markers across. Not satisfied with that advantage they added seven more in the ninth against a puny two pushed over by the Tribe. In justice to the Indians its must be noted that they were without the services of Roy Cullenbine, Hank Edwards and Jeff Heath.

As a result of the day's battles the American League race is the closest in years, with the last place Athletics 6½ games from the top. Detroit is third, 2½ games behind the leader, Boston is fourth, three games in arrears, Cleveland and Chicago are fifth, 3½ games behind, St. Louis is seventh.

LITWHILER STARS

Danny Litwhiler's trusty bat aided the Cards in their 5-3 verdict over the Dodgers. He fanned the first two times up but drove Lou Klein home with the winning run in the seventh. The fleet Danny then came all the way home on Walker Cooper's third hit, a double.

Mort Cooper racked up his tenth victory of the season, and except for Augie Galan's homer in the eight, the big hurler had the situation well in hand. It was the Dodgers' third straight loss and they now trail the Cards by two games. Rube Melton was the victim. He gave up two runs in the second on Walter Cooper's single, passes to Whitey Kurowski and Ray Sanders, and Mort Cooper's hit.

OTT HELPS ASSAULT

Home runs by Manager Mel Ott and Sid Gordon gave the Giants a flying start in their first victory. It was Ott's tenth four-master of the year. Johnny Wittig was the winning pitcher although he had to have help from Ace Adams.

Dick Bartell's single with the bases loaded proved the winning blow in the second game although the Giants were held to four hits by Bucky Walters. A single and two walks set the stage for Dick's blow.

JAVERY DRIVEN OUT

The Pirates collected 17 hits in their victory over the Braves. In fact starting pitcher Al Javery gave three doubles and a single before a man was retired in the first inning. The Pirates went on to score 4 of their runs, driving Javery from the mound.

Rudy York's ninth homer of the year in the eleventh inning of the first game sent the Yanks reeling after they had gotten away to a three-run lead. And in the afterpiece they blew a six-run lead as late as the eighth stanza, but it also vanished as the Tigers made three in their half and came back to score four in the ninth and win the game.

Manager Joe McCarthy protested the second victory, advancing the claim that Joe Wood interfered with Joe Gordon on an infield hit by Ned Harris in the ninth.

Box Scores

Pittsburgh .... 4 0 1 0 0 0 0 4 1—10
Boston .... 0 0 0 0 0 0 0 0 1—1

Errors—Ross, Ryan, Farrell. Runs batted in—Di Maggio 2, Russell 2, Elliott 2; Geary, Barrett, Fletcher, Cuccinello. Two-base hits—Elliott 2, Geary, Russell, Holmes. Three-base hit—Barrett. Home run—Di Maggio. Double plays—Elliott, Gustine and Fletcher; Workman and Ryan; Wietelmann, Ryan and McCarthy. Left on bases—Pittsburgh 7, Boston 10. Bases on balls—Gee 3, Rescigno 2, Farrell 2. Strikeouts—Rescigno 1, Farrell 2, Salvo 1. Hits—Off Gee, 1 in 2 2-3 innings; Rescigno, 6 in 6⅓; Javery, 4 in 0 (pitched to 4 men); Farrell, 11 in 7 2-3; Salvo, 2 in 1 1-3. Wild pitch—Farrell. Winning pitcher—Rescigno. Losing pitcher—Javery. Umpires—Stewart, Magerkurth, Dunn. Time—1 56. Attendance—2559.

Phila. Stars Beat Baltimore, 9-3

Barney Brown was in good form last night as the Philadelphia Stars beat Baltimore Elite Giants, 9-3, at 44th st. and Parkside ave., in a Negro National League game.

BALTO EL GIANTS	r	h	o	a	e	PHILA STARS	r	h	o	a	e
Kimbro.cf	1	1	0	0	0	Morton ss	1	0	3	6	1
Russo.2b	0	2	3	6	0	Curry rf	1	1	1	0	0
Snow ss	0	1	3	3	0	West 1b	0	0	15	0	0
Barbee 1b	1	2	14	0	1	Sp'man 3b	2	2	1	1	0
Scales.3b	0	0	0	2	0	Benson.cf	0	2	5	0	0
Hoskins.lf	0	2	1	0	0	Cash c	1	1	2	0	0
Byrd.rf	0	0	1	0	0	Barbage lf	1	1	0	0	0
Clark c	0	0	1	0	0	Tunket 2b	2	3	0	3	1
Burns.p	1	1	0	0	0	Brown p	1	1	0	3	0
x Robins'n	0	0	0	0	0						
Totals	3	9	24	11	1	Totals	9	11	27	13	2

x Batted for Grover in 9th.

Balti. Elite Giants .... 0 1 1 0 0 0 1 0 0—3
Philadelphia Stars .... 0 0 4 0 4 1 0 0 x—9

Greeby Nine Beats Port Richmond, 11-2

Greeby had one big frame, scoring seven runs in the second inning, to set down the Port Richmond Coast Guards, 11-2, yesterday afternoon at D and Tioga sts.

Eagles Plan to Sign Prison Star

NATIONAL Football League rules prohibit a club from signing any player still in college, and the Eagles, according to word from Philadelphia-Pittsburgh pro grid headquarters yesterday, can hardly wait until Tuesday.

On Tuesday one Don MacGregor, a 192-pound halfback, receives his diploma from the Iowa State Penitentiary, and the Eagles plan to sign him up.

MacGregor, who stands six-one, will come to the Eagles with the highest recommendation his classmates could give him. In the first place, they say, he'll fit perfectly into Coach Greasy Neale's scheme of things, for he has been playing T-formation football for the past five years with Iowa State P.'s Bulldogs. In that time, Fort Madison (Ia.) informants continue, MacGregor has averaged almost nine years each time he's carried the ball, and 43 yards per punt. He is also reported to be an excellent short passer, an alert defensive back and a deadly tackler.

"As sports editor," writes Don Thomas, of Iowa State P.'s paper, The Presidio, "I have no hesitancy in saying that I think him as good a back as any in the pro league today. It was MacGregor's 40-yard field goal which brought the Bulldogs the 1941 pro championship of Iowa."

Taking these recommendations at their face value, General Manager Harry Thayer has written MacGregor that the Eagles will give him every consideration as a football prospect. A two-time loser to the Iowa Motor Vehicle Theft Act, MacGregor hopes now to get back at his old trade, welding, with the idea of landing a job in a Philadelphia war industry. That's all right with the Eagles; in fact, they're trying to get the job for him.

Before he can come here, MacGregor must get himself a position Hawkeye penal authorities can approve for so distinguished an alumnus of Iowa State P.

The Philadelphia Inquirer

PUBLIC LEDGER

An Independent Newspaper for All the People

FINAL CITY EDITION

CIRCULATION: June Average: Daily 468,529; Sunday 1,343,788

SATURDAY MORNING, JULY 10, 1943

Copyright, 1943, by The Philadelphia Inquirer Co. Vol. 229. No. 10

a b d e f g h

THREE CENTS

SICILY INVADED

Allies Storm Italian Isle by Land, Sea and Air

ALLIED HEADQUARTERS IN NORTH AFRICA, July 10 (Saturday) (A. P.).—Allied forces stormed the rocky shores of Sicily today to open the second European front. Allied warplanes bombarded Sicily's coastal defenses preceding the landing of General Dwight D. Eisenhower's Allied troops. Warships pounded the enemy from offshore as the first landing craft sped up to the island's beaches.

WHERE 'THE INVASION' HAS STARTED

General map of Sicily, big island off the tip of the Italian "boot" and strategic anchor of Italy's system of defense, where Allied forces today launched their invasion of Europe's outposts with a land, sea and air assault.

(Another map and Page 2; Sicilian pictures on Page 10)

A special communique from advance Allied headquarters announced in terse terms that forces under General Dwight D. Eisenhower's seasoned command had begun a landing operation on Sicily early this morning, adding:

"The landings were preceded by an air attack. Naval forces escorted the assault forces and bombarded the coast defenses during the assault."

U. S., BRITISH, CANADIAN TROOPS

Americans, British and Canadians comprised the invasion force.

The action came on the heels of six days of almost constant bombing of the island, which rocked under the powerful air blows by day and night.

(The Algiers radio, in a broadcast to North America recorded by U. S Government monitors, said the Allied forces had landed on the rock-studded western tip of Sicily, 260 miles from Rome.)

BITTER RESISTANCE EXPECTED

The lightning-quick invasion was launched in good weather by a light moon as troopships, escorted by warcraft, defied minefields and strongly placed enemy guns to reach the objective.

Italians, bulwarked by elite German troops, were expected to offer bitter resistance despite widespread discontent among the Italian population on the island with the course of the war.

The Italians already had engaged in a scorched earth program, destroying harbor installations at Trapani, which is the closest important Sicilian port to Africa.

There was no immediate official report of the scale of the Allied success.

First announcement of the offensive was made in the following communique issued by Eisenhower's "Advance Headquarters:"

"Anglo-American-Canadian forces, under command of General Eisenhower, began landing operations in Sicily early this morning (North African Time). Landings were preceded by an air attack. Naval forces escorted the assault forces and bombarded the coast defenses during the assault."

In another announcement Eisenhower told the people of Axis-dominated France that their turn was coming. He said

Continued on Page 2, Column 1

Adventure in the Sky

'May Day, I've Been Hit, I Think I'm Falling, Come Down to Help Me'

Paul W. Ramsey, Inquirer War Correspondent, was allowed to listen by Army radio to the conversation of pilots of two squadrons throughout their most furious battle. This is the second of a series telling what American fighter pilots say and do in the thick of battle.

By Paul W. Ramsey

Inquirer War Correspondent

By Wireless

AMERICAN FIGHTER BASE SOMEWHERE IN ENGLAND July 9

YOUNG pilots who were flying the Thunderbolts across the North Sea observed radio silence until the enemy was sighted over the coast—one of the most heavily defended areas over western Europe.

Pilots left behind, ground officers and enlisted maintenance men were waiting at flight headquarters for first reports of the battle.

Officers sitting in the ground floor room where the radio loud-speakers was installed leaned forward in their chairs. Enlisted men standing outside crowded each window and others pressed from behind.

The radio squawked and hummed as a tractor motor started up in a nearby hangar. Listeners missed the first words, which I obtained later from pilots in the action. As the planes roared along at 28,000 feet, one of the pilots sighted unidentified planes below and off to the right.

• • •

THERE was no talk while the fliers studied the shapes of the distant planes—18 or more. By this time the strangers were below and several miles off at a right angle to the Americans' course.

Then over the radio to the men in the room came the voice of Colonel Armand Peterson, commanding officer of the fighter base, who was leading the Thunderbolt sweep.

"Our friends should not be there. I am making a 90-degree turn and going down."

And then he called out to pilots:

"They are Huns, lads! Give them hell! Here we go; Tallyho!"

His voice was exultant as he sang out "Tallyho!" And everybody in the room knew battle was about to be joined.

• • •

ENLISTED men in windows passed word back to those behind them outside. "They are attacking," they whispered.

There was a brief silence but every man knew that the Thunderbolts were roaring down at German planes. There was a pause and then:

Colonel Peterson (very calm now): "Okay, lads, retain your altitude. (A pause) "Give them hell! Okay, lads, stay in pairs now."

Voices of other pilots joined in.

Major Roberts: "This is Roberts, you still with me?"

Fleming: "I am still with you."

Roberts: "Atta baby."

Brown: "How we doin', chief?"

Roberts: "Not so bad."

• • •

AND then, somebody else, a little angrily: "Where are the so and sos?"

A long pause followed.

Colonel Peterson: "There are two over there right under you. Now get 'em. That's right. Now somebody else is coming in on his tail."

Captain London: "There are some bandits (enemy planes) at three o'clock, a little above us."

Everybody listening to the radio knew now that the Thunderbolt formations had separated and that some were broken up as dog fights began all over the sky.

Then——

Cooper: "Are you still with me, Put?"

Putnam: "Right behind you."

Colonel Peterson: "Are any of you down here with me?"

Continued on Page 4, Column 2

MUNDA ROCKED BY U. S. FLEET, PLANES, GUNS

100 Bombers Blast New Georgia as Ground Forces Near Enemy Base

Illustrated on Page 10

By MURLIN SPENCER

ALLIED HEADQUARTERS IN THE SOUTHWEST PACIFIC, July 10 (Saturday) (A. P.).—Over 100 American bombers teamed with destroyers and artillery Friday in giving the Japanese air base of Munda on New Georgia Island a three-way pounding.

The heavy attacks were intended to soften up that key base in the Central Solomons for our ground forces, which already have landed on New Georgia on two sides and now are consolidating positions prior to applying a pincers.

Avenger torpedo bombers and Dauntless dive bombers in great force loosed over 700 tons of bombs, ranging up to 2000-pounders on Japanese bivouacs and supply dumps.

WATERS TREACHEROUS

The destroyers maneuvered in treacherous waters, just off the Munda base before dawn yesterday, subjecting the Japanese to an intensive shelling.

On the ground our patrols filtering through the jungles frequently contacted the Japanese, both on the Munda side of the island and to the north, near Rice Anchorage, where one of our two most recent landings was made.

Rout of 45 Zeros seeking to raid our positions below Munda on Rendova Island, Allied aerial pounding of bases above Munda which might supply it air support, and continuous bombing of Japanese jungle positions before Salamaua, New Guinea, were other highlights of today's reports from the far-ranging battlefronts.

SWARMS OF BOMBERS

The softening-up process against the Munda area started shortly after dawn yesterday. Flight after flight of Avengers and dive bombers swept over jungle positions to drop all types of bombs.

General Douglas MacArthur's spokesman termed it the heaviest bombing made thus far against Munda—a base which has been pounded so repeatedly from the air that it has been of little service to the enemy in recent weeks.

The raiders encountered opposition from the anti-aircraft artillery positions they pounded, but received

Continued on Page 3, Column 7

NAZI DRIVE HALTED ON ENTIRE FRONT

By LYNN HEINZERLING

LONDON, July 10 (Saturday) (A. P.).—The Russian armies of the center bloodily beat off savage German attacks all along the Orel and Kursk fronts yesterday, held their own in the Belgorod sector to the south, and destroyed 193 Nazi tanks and 94 planes in the great battle of attrition, the Soviet Command announced early today.

The German dead, in two battle areas specifically mentioned, were nearly 5000 for the day. Moscow declared in the regular midnight communique recorded here by the Soviet monitor, thus bringing to about 40,000 the total German casualties for five days of violent action.

FOE SHIFTS FORCES

German losses in materiel also were rising to tremendous proportions: yesterday's destruction raised

Continued on Page 3, Column 6

'It's the Real Thing,' Algiers Reports

NEW YORK, July 10 (Saturday) (A. P.). — "The invasion of Europe has begun," Robert Bennett, of the British Broadcasting Corp., asserted tonight in a broadcast from Allied headquarters in Algiers. The broadcast was recorded by station WOR in New York.

"This is no hit and run affair," Bennett continued.

"Fighting is going on now. The most difficult military operation of this war has begun."

U. S. WEATHER FORECAST

Philadelphia and Vicinity—Continued moderately warm today.

Eastern Pennsylvania: Continued warm, scattered showers and a few thunderstorms this afternoon and evening.

New Jersey: Moderate temperature on the coast, continued warm in the interior; scattered showers and thunderstorms this afternoon and evening.

Sun rises 5.40 A.M. Sets 8.31 P.M.
Moon rises 1.13 P.M. Sets——

U-Boats' Toll Lowest Since U.S. Entered War

By WILLIAM C. MURPHY, JR.

Inquirer Washington Bureau

WASHINGTON, July 9.—Marked progress toward the extermination of the Axis submarine menace was announced tonight in a joint British-American statement issued here through the Office of War Information.

Merchant shipping losses of Allied and neutral nations in June were reported as the lowest during any month since Pearl Harbor and the second lowest since the war began in September, 1939.

Simultaneously, it was reported there was a decrease in the number of submarine "targets" for United Nations anti-submarine surface and aircraft—presumably reflecting the heavy toll of subs exacted during the previous month.

(In London a new procedure whereby only approved statements on the U-boat war would be issued on the 10th of each month was outlined.

(A statement issued at No. 10

Continued on Page 4, Column 5

Invasion Announced By German Radio

LONDON, July 10 (Saturday) (A. P).—The German overseas radio announced this morning's Allied invasion of Sicily at 7:30 A. M. (1:30 A. M. Philadelphia time).

The Nazi broadcaster, heard by the Ministry of Information, said:

"It has just been officially announced in London that Allied forces began landing operations in Sicily this morning."

A few minutes later the Germans broadcast a second bulletin under a Washington dateline. It said simply:

"British, American and Canadian troops have landed in Sicily."

Special Features

The sixth installment of Ramon Lavalle's "I've Just Come From Tokio," and the latest dispatch from John Steinbeck in Britain appear

Today on Page 11

War Summary

Saturday, July 10, 1943

American, British and Canadian troops under General Dwight D. Eisenhower swarmed ashore on the rocky coast of Sicily, springboard island off the toe of the Italian boot, early today, in the long-awaited Allied invasion.

Under cover of naval and air bombardment, troopships escorted by warcraft threaded their way through minefields and landed the Allied troops on the western coast of the island

Meanwhile in the Pacific, American destroyers, planes and land guns opened up in a concerted three - way assault on the Jap base of Munda, on New Georgia island. The island was pounded by 100 U. S. bombers as ground forces consolidated their positions

In the Battle of the Atlantic, the U. S. and Britain revealed in a joint statement that sinkings by U-boats had fallen to the lowest point since Pearl Harbor,

Unyielding Russian troops flung back every German assault all along the Orel, Kursk and Belgorod fronts in bitter fighting in which the Nazis lost 193 more tanks, 94 more planes and at least 5000 more men.

The R. A. F. was back over Germany again last night after a massive 1000-ton raid on Cologne. A Luftwaffe bomb killed at least 12 children watching a movie in a Southeast England town. London had an alarm and several bombs were dropped.

GEORGE DE B. KEIM, 58 DIES, SUDDENLY

George deBenneville Keim, Jr., former secretary of the Republican National Committee and retired Philadelphia banker, died suddenly last night at Temple University Hospital. He was 58.

A friend of the family said the cause of death was not immediately determined. Mr. Keim lived at Gable Hall in Edgewater Park, N. J.

FATHER WAS SHERIFF

Mr. Keim, whose father was sheriff of Philadelphia county, served as secretary of the National Republican Committee from 1929 to 1932. He was active in politics in New Jersey and was chairman of the New Jersey Commission on Historical Sites.

Prior to his retirement on Jan. 6, 1930, he was vice president of Chandler & Co., investment bankers here. His father operated the now extinct Keim Saddlery Co. in Philadelphia.

N. Y. PORT AUTHORITY MEMBER

Mr. Keim was a member from April, 1930, to July, 31, 1941, of the New York Port Authority.

Mr. Keim, a descendant of a Colonial Pennsylvania family, was born in Philadelphia, Oct. 27, 1884. He was educated at Peirce Business

Continued on Page 12, Column 7

Son-in-Law Arrested In Slaying of Baronet

Illustrated on Page 12

NASSAU, Bahamas, July 9 (U. P.).—A sensational climax in the mysterious death of Sir Harry Oakes, one of the world's wealthiest men, was reached tonight with the arrest of his son-in-law, Count Alfred de Marigny, on a charge of murder.

De Marigny was accused of clubbing the sleeping British baronet to death and then setting fire to the bed clothing.

SERIES OF QUARRELS

Belief was expressed that the slaying was the culmination of a series of quarrels between the two men.

(In the United States, it was reported that Sir Harry had objected to the French Count's marriage to his daughter, Nancy, and had disowned her, later agreeing to a reconciliation. The feud flared up again, however, and Sir Harry reportedly agreed to another reconciliation only if his daughter promised never again to see the Count. She came to the U. S. and entered a girl's school at Bennington, Vt., as Nancy Oakes. The Count remained in Nassau.)

BODY BADLY BATTERED

Announcement of de Marigny's arrest was made by Police Commission-

Continued on Page 12, Column 3

IN TODAY'S INQUIRER

SPECIAL DEPARTMENTS

COLUMNS AND FEATURES

Real Estate for Sale GREAT NORTHEAST

OPENING TODAY!
HERE IS THE HOME
You must See!
$4690

A LARGER HOME ON AN 80-FT. STREET

3 BEDROOMS • TILE BATH

$34.69 TOTAL MONTHLY

PREFERENCE GIVEN TO WAR WORKERS

COME OUT TODAY AND SEE THE FURNISHED SAMPLE

4000 BLK "K" STREET

2 Blocks Above Erie Ave. — On the "P" Bus Line

JOHN P. HENRIE, REALTOR — CONRAD J. GETTLER, BUILDER

Real Estate for Sale GREAT NORTHEAST

ONLY A FEW LEFT — BETTER HURRY!

New Colonial Homes **$4650**

INCLUDING AUTOMATIC GAS HEAT. Preference Given War Workers

6 rooms, colored tile bath, garage. Agent at 4400 Oakmont St.

4400 BLK. OAKMONT ST. — 3 Squares E. of 7300 Frankford Ave. Dewey 1944, Mayfair 9944 — ONLY $7.70 WEEKLY OUTLAY

ESAN CO., Inc., Builders

ONLY **$4690** $590 Down. $34.26 Monthly Carrying Charges, Includes Saving of $12.66 Month.

NEW 3-BEDROOM HOMES. Bryant gas heat, garage. Large lots. A great value you simply must see and it costs so little to carry.

6300 Blk. GLENLOCH ST. 1½ Blocks W. of Torresdale Ave. at Levick St. (6400 N.) Open Sunday. Sample House. Phone Mayfair 5736

HARRY W. RAFF, 67th and OGONTZ AVE. HAN. 0633

ANNOUNCING NEW UNIT OF 60 HOMES

FIRST UNIT SOLD OUT QUICKLY! COME TODAY!

Pre-Viewing "AMERICA of TOMORROW" **Wissinoming Park Homes**... in Lower Mayfair

Only 3 minutes to Frankford "L", gas heat, automatic hot water

$4650 Total monthly cost on FHA plan, only $34.16

LARDNER ST., 1 BLOCK WEST OF 6100 FRANKFORD AVE.

S. & S. Constr. Co.; A. Singer & John Scholis, Bldrs. Mobile Realty, Agt., May. 3344

MAYFAIR—NEW CORNER—$6290. Six large rooms, tile bath, big basement with Colonial entrance and windows for professional use, hairdresser, etc. **4344 OAKMONT ST.** Get our selected list of homes and apartments. Consult us about real estate investments. Jackson-Cross Company, AGENT, DAV. 2000

NORTH PHILADELPHIA

1800 BLK. ELEANOR ST. 4800 N. (Bet. 18th & 19th Sts.) 1 SQUARE SOUTH OF 18TH & BELFIELD AVE. ONLY **$4750** 6 ROOMS. Tile Bath, Hardwood Floors, Garage. These Homes Can Be Purchased by War Workers With a Small Down Payment. **BOARDMAN-SMITH CORP.** Agent on Premises

Selling Fast! Before You Buy Be Sure to See the **LARGEST** HOMES IN TOWN FOR ONLY **$4490** $490 DOWN

"GOLF VIEW HOMES" OVERLOOKING JUNIATA PARK GOLF COURSE

★ Wide Street ★ Exceptionally Deep Set-back ★ Large Kitchen and Breakfast Room ★ 3 Big Bedrooms ★ Garage ★ Unusually Large Tile Bath with Shower ★ Right at "P" Bus to Frankford "L" ★ Public and Parochial Schools, and Churches Just Around the Corner

4300 GLENDALE ST. FIRST STREET WEST OF "M" ST. (Between Bristol and Cayuga Sts.)

LIVE RENT-FREE! Large corner Duplex apartment homes with hot water heat & 2-car garage—$6990.

H. S. BUILDING CORP. JOS. R. McKEON, Agt. Jef. 9836—Pil. 9435. War Workers Given Preference

Real Estate for Sale SUBURBAN

ATTENTION WAR WORKERS IN CHESTER AREA ASTON TOWNSHIP

Green Ridge Homes $50 PER MONTH RENT — $4565 SALE PRICE — SMALL DOWN PAYMENT

Extra Features: • Immediate Occupancy • Single Homes • Modern Kitchen • Two Bedrooms • Only 15 minutes to All Defense Plants

F. A. COLLINS, Builder, Chester 2-9735

ON RETURNING FROM YOUR VACATION WHY NOT MOVE INTO A NEW HOME? BUY YOURS TODAY!

Garages ★ Gar Wood Heat ★ 3 Large Bedrooms ★ Modern Colored Tile Bath with Shower ★ Vestibule Entrance with Large Coat Closet ★ Entire Roof Insulated Against Heat and Cold ★ ¾" Oak Flooring Throughout ★ Overhead Garage Doors ★ Sodded Lawns Well Planted ★ Overlooking 3 Golf Courses ★ Public and Parochial Schools. 2 Bus Lines Pass Within 1 Block of These Homes. Also Convenient to Trolleys.

$565 DOWN — **$39.43** MONTH

UPPER DARBY 69th SECTION MODERN HOMES **$3650** SMALL MONTHLY PAYMENTS LONG TERM MORTGAGES ONLY 10% DOWN. For Information Apply to W. S. PEACE, Inc. 69th & Walnut Sts., Upper Darby. BLVD. 4800 ALL. 3800

$7.56 PER WEEK (APPROXIMATE) Includes all carrying charges. AS LITTLE AS **$300** DOWN! PRICE $4650. ALSO RENTALS AT $50 MONTH. IMMEDIATE OCCUPANCY. 4½ room homes on large lots, 50'x100' to 70'x125'. Near shops, schools, churches, amusements. 17 miles from Philadelphia. DIRECTIONS: BY TRAIN: Reading Railroad to Hatboro Station. Bus Car Meets Trains. BY BUS: No. 55 bus to Willow Grove, then Motor out York Rd. to Hatboro. Sample Home Now Open Daily and Sunday 11 A. M. to 9 P. M. Agent on Premises. York Garden Homes, Inc. BUILDERS, York Rd. & County Line, Hatboro 0177

SINGLE **English Colonial STONE HOME** Overlooking Beautiful Huntingdon Valley. Welsh Rd. and Stahl Rd., Bethayres. Close to Train and Bus. PHONE FOR APPOINTMENT OUR CAR WILL TAKE YOU TO LOCATION. E. STAHL & SON, BUSTLETON 0532

YEADON Twin Brick Homes **$5990** Immediate Possession. Six rooms, Tile bath, garage, large porch. Sample open until 10 P. M. **507 Bonsall Ave.** Baltimore Pike to Church Lane, South 3 Squares to Myra Ave., Turn Right to Sample. RALPH BODEK, Builder

Real Estate for Sale SUBURBAN

BY ORDER OF FIRST NATIONAL BANK OF MEDIA — 8 VALUABLE PROPERTIES Will be sold separately at **ABSOLUTE AUCTION** Without Reserve! Clear of Mortgages!

6 HOMES AND 1 STORE & APARTMENT PROPERTY IN MEDIA and a 202-ACRE FARM NEAR WEST CHESTER

407 E. BALTIMORE AVE., Media. FRI., JULY 23, at 2 P.M. on Premises.

407 W. STATE ST., Media. FRI., JULY 23, at 2 P.M. on Premises.

409 W. STATE ST., Media. FRI., JULY 23, at 2:30 P.M. on Premises.

ONE OF VERY FINEST INCOME-PRODUCING PROPERTIES IN MEDIA. S. W. COR. STATE & JACKSON STS., MEDIA. FRI., JULY 23, 3:15 P.M. on Premises.

N. W. COR. JACKSON AND BAKER STS., Media. FRI., JULY 23, 3:15 P.M. on Premises.

446 E. STATE ST., Media. FRI., JULY 23, 4 P. M. on Premises.

49 N. PROVIDENCE RD., Media. FRI., JULY 23, at 4:30 P.M. on Premises.

202-ACRE FARM NEAR WEST CHESTER ON BRANDYWINE CREEK. SAT., JULY 24, 3 P. M. on Premises. Sales on the premises, rain or shine. Illustrated Circular Sent Upon Request. Louis Traiman AUCTION CO. OF PA. BROKERS 1528 Walnut St. AUCTIONEERS Kin. 2238—Race 6528

CITY

AUCTION CLEAR OF MORTGAGES. TUES., AUG. 3, 1943 on the respective premises. AT 2:00 P. M. INDUSTRIAL SITE N. E. Cor. Milnor & Cottman Sts. AT 4:00 P. M. BUILDING OPERATION SITE S. W. COR. Marshall & Heather Rds. Upper Darby, 69th St. Section. Write for Circular. SAMUEL T. FREEMAN & CO. Auctioneers, 1808-10 CHESTNUT ST.

AUCTION CLEAR OF MORTGAGES. **5819 MARKET ST.** 100-CAR GARAGE & APARTMENT. WITH SEPARATE ENTRANCE. Lot 18x83 and 64x175'. TO BE SOLD WED., JULY 28, 1943, AT 3 P. M. ON THE PREMISES. Deposit 15% at Sale. Write for Circular. SAMUEL T. FREEMAN & CO. Auctioneers, 1808-10 Chestnut St.

CITY

2 Modern, 2-Story Homes 909-11 E. Stafford St. WILL BE SOLD SEPARATELY AT **ABSOLUTE AUCTION** Without Reserve. Clear of Mortgages. Sale on the Premises, Rain or Shine. Wed., July 28, at 7.15 P. M. 

EXCELLENT STORE & DWELLING 408 E. GIRARD AVE. **ABSOLUTE AUCTION** Without Reserve! Clear of Mortgages. Sale on the Premises, Rain or Shine. WED., AUGUST 25, AT 3 P. M. Louis Traiman AUCTION CO. OF PA. 1528 Walnut St. Kin. 2238—Race 6528

AUCTION By Order Board of Public Education. Clear of Mortgages. FARRAGUT SCHOOL PROPERTY S. W. COR. Cumberland & Hancock. Wed., Aug. 11, 1943, at 2 P. M. Write for Circular. SAMUEL T. FREEMAN & CO. Auctioneers 1808-10 Chestnut St.

SUBURBAN

ABINGTON $9000 Brick Colonial built in 1942. Screened porch, living room with fireplace, dining room, kitchen, powder room, 4 bedrooms and tiled bath. Attached garage. Fenced lot of 50'x118'. Air-conditioned oil heat. Prompt possession.

NOBLE $6500 Semi-detached stone and shingle house in a convenient location. 3 rooms and bath on 2d floor. 2 rooms on 3d. Oil burner. Lot 30'x175'.

ROSLYN $5500 Attractive bungalow on shaded lot of 50'x175'. Living room, dining room, kitchen, breakfast nook, 2 bedrooms, 1 bath, basement laundry. Hot water heat—coal. 1-car garage.

JACKSON-CROSS CO. Ogontz 7000 Jenkintown Majestic 0700

ABINGTON TOWNSHIP. Frame Colonial, well planned, powder rm., breakfast rm., gardens, trees, pool & stream. Very attractive & only $11,000.

JENKINTOWN. Hard to find. Modern 4-bedroom home, good coal heat, breakfast room, only $7500.

ELKINS PARK. Luxurious English stone home, 3 baths, powder room, breakfast room. A gorgeous setting. Choice section. $18,500.

MEADOWBROOK. HILLTOP—Acre, fine view. Unusual custom-built English home. Modern baths, stoker heat, breakfast room. Only $20,000.

HUNTINGDON VALLEY. New Cape Cod Colonial. Unique plan. ½ acre, wonderful view. $9750. Byberry rd. off Second st. pike. Open Sunday P. M.

BALL & COFFIN Jenkintown West Ave. Ogontz 0760

ABINGTON TWP.—Rydal. A country place with more than usual charm, fine surroundings & conv. to train & bus. Over ½ acre with 150' frontage, beautifully landscaped with terraces, hedges, shade trees & a formal garden with wall front. The pointed stone slate roof dwlg. has a center hall with Col. stairway, powder rm., large liv. rm., fireplace, heated sun porch, din. rm., brkfst. rm., pantry, tile kit., 5 large bedrms., library with book shelves, 3 baths, 2 tiled, 1 tub & stall shower, 1 shower over tub. Panelled game rm. in basement. H. w. coal heat with elec. Furnaceman automatic stoker. Heat costs less than $200 per yr. Fully equip. with shades, storm sash & elec. refrig. Det. 2-car gar. with gas heat. A fine offering for $25,000.

SHEBLE, DAGER, INC. Ogontz 2000 Jenkintown, Pa.

ABINGTON. Cor. property, 2 sqs. York Rd. bus. 7 rms., bath, lav. Lot 51x150 nicely planted. 2-car gar. $6000.

ABINGTON TWP. Jenkintown Manor. Desirable location, good surroundings. Brick & clapboard dwlg., center hall, 8 rms., 3 baths, enc. porch. H.W. oil heat, f.p. Attached 2-car gar. Lot 60x150 nicely planted. $12,500.

MELROSE PARK. Conv. station, bus & school. Lot 100x150, nicely planted. Pointed stone & shingle dwlg., ent. hall, 12 rms., 3 baths, 1 with shower, hardwood flrs., H.W. heat, f.p., elect. range, storm sash, screens, awnings. Good cond. Det. 2-car gar. Owner occupied, quick possession. $12,500.

SHEBLE, DAGER, INC. Ogontz 3000 Jenkintown, Pa.

ABINGTON. ENGLISH home, 4 bdrms., 3 baths, oil ht., 2-car gar., large well planted lot, conv. to transp. & shopping. Priced $11,500.

RYDAL. Colonial farm hse., 3 bths., coal stoker, 4 ac. ground, within 3 sq. of Jenkintown. Must be seen to be appreciated.

WYNCOTE. An excellent buy in a desirable residential sect. All masonry home 3 yrs. old, 3 bedrms., bath, storm sash, screens. Insulated. Offered at [illegible].

T. W. MONTAGUE CO. Jenkintown Open Sunday Ogontz 0760.

AMBLER. Attrac. single brick & asbestos dwlg. built 1940, lot 100x150, 2-car gar., h. w. ht., coal, oil avail., porch, firepl., 3 lge. bedrms., tile b. Early poss. $9000. Kellner, 400 Bethlehem Pike, Che. 6700.

ANDALUSIA, nr. troll., train, etc. cor. bungalow, 5 rms., bath, heat, lot 75x100; garage. $3950. SENDERLING, 3900 Frankford.

ANDALUSIA, Whittier ave., bung., 5 rms., b. $2750. Lot 80x100 $2750 Clarke, May. 0800.

ARDMORE. Two acres with woods and stream! And within easy walking distance of Ardmore Station, stores, etc. Home originally cost $87,000. Now offered for quick sale at $22,000. Unusual property.

WILLIAM PUGH, Montgomery Ave. at Old Lancaster Road. GRE 3300 Merion Cynwyd 3300

ARDMORE. $4500. Semi-detached, brick, 8 rms., bath. Immediate possession. Good condition. EDWARD DAVIS, Ardmore 2200.

GERMANTOWN

NEW SINGLE HOMES SEDGWICK FARMS, MT. AIRY **$12,500** Ardleigh St. at Mt. Pleasant Ave. 3 blocks E. of 7100 Stenton Ave. A. P. ORLEANS & CO., BUILDER. C. A. PAYTON, Agt., WIS. 3433

SUBURBAN

ARDMORE $7500. Single home in a fine residential neighborhood. Tree lined street. Large lot 100x150. Short distance to shopping and transp. Ideal for a family with children.

NARBERTH $9750. Very attractive red brick colonial only 5 yrs. old. Large lot with lovely old beech and oak, center hall plan with breakfast rm., 2 bedrms. & 2 baths. Air cond. heat. Prompt possession.

HAVERFORD $12,500. A discriminating buyer will appreciate the charm offered in this lovely stone colonial. Tastefully redecorated and ready for immediate occupancy. C. H. plan with circular staircase. 4 bedrms. and 2 baths on 2d floor, 2 bedrooms and bath above.

NASH REALTY CO. Main Line Real Estate. Gre. 2494. Tri. 6242.

ARDMORE—Attractive cor. home. Beaut. landscaped lot, fireplace, breakfast rm., gar., excel. cond. Remington, Blvd. 0320.

ARDSLEY BUNGALOW 556 JACKSON AVE. 5 rooms, tile bath, h. w. heat, detached garage, lot 40x125. Owner occupied.

ROSLYN—BUNGALOW N. E. COR. RADCLIFFE & COLONIAL AVE. 7 rooms, tile bath, hot water heat (gas), hardwood floors, detached garage, lot 70x130, owner occupied.

BENNEWITT 5705 N. 5TH ST. LIV. 4200. CLOSED SUNDAY. CALL MONDAY.

BALA-CYNWYD MAIN LINE and DELAWARE COUNTY. For the Best Buys Today and Everyday Consult **F. E. CABALLERO** Realtor

You are PERMITTED TO DRIVE YOUR CAR to inspect these houses if it is necessary for you to move from your present home. All appointments to inspect the following properties must be made by calling our office. Exclusive Agents. Gre: 1804 Cyn: 1804 Gre: 1804. Residence: Cynwyd 3576

CYNWYD: [illegible] ... PHILADELPHIA: [illegible] ... OVERBROOK HILLS IN MERION: [illegible] ... MANOA: [illegible] ... MERION GOLF MANOR: [illegible] ... LLANERCH: [illegible] ... BROOKLINE: [illegible] ... MERION: [illegible] ... WYNNEWOOD: [illegible] ... ARDMORE: [illegible]

F. E. CABALLERO. Open daily 9-5 P. M. Sundays and evenings by appointment only. Meeting House Lane at Lafayette Road, Merion, Pa.

Farms For Sale VIRGINIA

FOR SALE "WHITE MARSH" Magnificent Colonial Virginia PLANTATION

Front View of White Marsh Mansion

Royal Crown grant to Major Lewis Burwell, 1680, of 3400 acres, 3¼ miles from Gloucester Courthouse, 1 hour from Jamestown, Yorktown, Williamsburg. 20-acre lawn. Private yacht landing. Century-old gardens with ancient boxwood and crepe myrtles. Mansion of 12 rooms, 3 baths. Solarium. 800 acres in meadow and cultivation. Replete with all the history, romance and charm of the original Virginia estates. Rarely do such plantations come on the market. For history, complete description and recently taken photographs write, telephone or wire:

POLLARD & BAGBY, Inc. RICHMOND, VIRGINIA

Real Estate for Sale SUBURBAN

BALA-MERION (54th & City Line) $7500 to $9950. Edgehill Road-Stoneway Lane, Upland Road. All with garages & automatic heat. Close to route 70 and P. R. R. Station. Finest stores-Lowest taxes. Famous Lower Merion Schools. J. FRANKLIN MOSS & CO. Merion 0780

BALA-CYNWYD—Gas rationing does not seriously interfere with life at 111 Edgehill rd. The house sets high, on a ¾ acre lot. It is beautifully landscaped with fruit & ornamental trees. An English stone residence with detached garage. The living room is 15x24 & the dining room 15x17, each of the 4, 2nd fl. rooms will take twin beds & each has cross ventilation. It is air-conditioned. The price invites you. H. P. MacFARLAND 329 Montgomery Av. Merion 3535; Tri. 3939

BALA-CYNWYD—Beaut. home, 16 rs. 4 bs., excel. surround. Conv. transp. Cynwyd 5030

BERWYN, Pa. Pre-Priority House, completed Sept., 1941, all insulated, 3 large bedrooms, tile bath, Venetian blinds, oil heat, summer & winter hook-up, large lot. Only few minutes from Station. Prompt possession. Berwyn 0132-W.

BLUE BELL. Recently renovated, single home, on Skippack Pike, acre lot, 2½-sty. house, all modern equipment. Large poultry house, garage. $8500. KELLNER, 400 Bethlehem Pike. Che. 6700. Open Sunday.

BROOKLINE, $5900. Single, 3 bedrooms, garage. Now vacant. Excellent location. WM. J. OTT, INC. Hilltop 5500.

BRYN MAWR HOMES ONLY 2 LEFT! Old shade, excel. neighborhood, good transportation. When these 2 are gone there will be no more new houses for $12,500. H. P. MacFARLAND 329 Montgomery av. Merion 3535. Tri. 3939.

BYWOOD—One of the finest and most completely modernized homes in this nearby suburb. The owner spared no expense only 2 yrs. ago. Half stone Colonial on deep lot and shaded street; all-electric kitchen; 4 large bedrooms and beautiful colored tile bath on the second floor, finished third floor, garage. New Esso oil unit, electric hot water heater, all new copper piping, new electric lighting fixtures and expensive washable wall paper, Venetian blinds, etc. Inspection only by appointment. KERSHAW & RANEY, 51 Long Lane, Upper Darby, Granite 1700 or Blvd. 1700.

CHATHAM VILLAGE, 515 Cumberland rd. Brick & asbestos shingle, 6 rms. & b., G. E. oil burner & range. Lot 55x110. $7700. Owner or T. R. Bailey, 1505 Race st., Phila.

CHATHAN VILLAGE, 515 Cumberland rd., single home, 1 yr. old, 6 rms. & b., gar., all GE equipment, plot 55x110, price $7700.

CHELTENHAM—5 r., b., h. w. h., excel. cond., $3700; Twin 6 r. & b., lot 28x183, $5500. MYERS, Cheltenham 2859 or Dev. 0281

CHESTNUT HILL—$17,500. 203 W. Chestnut ave. 3 blocks to P. R. R. station. 1 acre, dozens of beautiful big trees, terraced garden surrounded by stone wall, pond, flagstone walks, magnificent shrubbery. Detached residence built to order by former owner. Stone construction, cement plastered, excellent workmanship and materials. Fine hardwood floors, hot water heat. Heavy slate roof, copper spouting. Large living room & library each with fireplace, opening onto terraces, all facing southwest, overlooking exquisite grounds. 4 master bedrms., 1 with fireplace, 2 dressing rooms, 3 tile baths & servants' wing all on 2d floor. Log cabin on rear of lot. 3-car garage with quarters upstairs. Screened from garden by cement plastered stone wall. Surrounded by large estates and within 1 square of Fairmount Park (Wissahickon Valley). This property sold for over $80,000 in 1935 & is one of the greatest sacrifices in suburban Phila. Vacant. Immed. posses. Caretaker on prem. Richard J. Seltzer, 225 S. 15th st. Pen. 8800, evenings & Sundays call Mr. Ashby, Che. 5607.

CHESTNUT HILL, N. E. cor. Gtn. & Moreland aves. 3-sty. single stone & brick dwlg. 1st fl. center hall, liv. rm., fireplace, dining rm., breakfast rm., firepl., kitchen, lavatory, 2d fl., 3 bedrms., tile b., 3d fl., 3 rms. & bath, slate roof, h. w. ht., oil, $6,600. Kellner, 400 Bethlehem pk. Che. 6700.

CHESTNUT HILL, 49 Northwestern ave. Des. res. sec., facing Fairmount Park, well built 3-story, brick, single, lge. rooms, comp. apt. 3d fl., coal stoker, old shade, ½ ac., 2-story 4-car gar., nr. trans., $12,500. Ph. Whitemarsh 3564.

SUBURBAN

CHE. HILL—236 Evergreen Ave. 2½ sty. stone & brick, semi-det. dwell. 5 bedrms., h. w. ht., 1st flr. laundry & open porch, good cond., early possession. $5750. KELLNER, 400 Bethlehem Pk. Che. 6700. Op. Sun.

COLLEGEVILLE bungalow, 3 rms., furn., $1100. Edw. Schlesser, Willow Gr. 1423.

COLLINGDALE. Six delightful rooms, open porch, and garage. $800 cash; $27.91 monthly, including taxes! W. A. CLARKE CO. 6822 Market St. Blvd. 0960 or ALL. 2655

COLLINGDALE—If possession, 1/3 cash req. Semi-detached brick home, lot 19½x100. Price ONLY $3500. Consult: Swope & Son, Inc., 516 Main st., Darby.

CROYDON—8 rm. house, all convs., 2 lots, gar. $3800, $1000 dn. Tryon Agency, Cedar & New York av. Bucks Co., Croydon, Pa.

CYNWYD $10,000. All-stone home, 4 bedrooms, 2 baths, 3 blocks from station, excellent condition. HOOVER & POLLOCK. GREENWOOD 6200 CYNWYD 3400

CYNWYD. Single center hall Colonial residence, 4 bdrms., 2 baths, gar., old shade, near PRR Sta. Owner occupied and reasonably priced. EDWARD DAVIS, Ard. 2200.

DARBY. One block to trolley! Enclosed porch, tile bath, Timken oil burner, summer and winter hook-up; garage. $3600. W. A. CLARKE CO. 6822 Market St. Blvd. 0960 or ALL. 2655

DARBY—GET SETTLED in a HOME OF YOUR OWN! MAY WE HELP YOU? CONSULT: SWOPE & SON, INC., 516 Main st., Darby.

DARBY, 6th & Chestnut sts. Duplex. 3 rms. & bth. each, inc. $70 mo. Sale price $5000. DAVID F. TRIESTER 6622 WOODLAND AVE. SAR. 3200

DARBY. 6 rms., bath, h. w. ht., hardwd. fl. Conv. to War Plants. $2600. SHAW, 858 Main st., Darby, Pa. Phone 0544.

SUBURBAN

DREXEL HILL. For the family who wants country atmosphere with Hi-Speed Electric trans. and a thoroughly Modern Home. Center Hall Living Rm. — Music Rm. — Sun Rm. with south exposure. 5 Bedrms., 3 Baths, Sleeping Porch, 2-Car Gar. Nearly ½ acre. Tennis Court, Fruit. Owner leaving city. $10,750.

Immediate possession, 2-story semi, part stone, enclosed porch, living room with fireplace; garage. Coal Heat. Close to schools, stores and transportation. $4750.

LANSDOWNE. Single corner, slate roof, on Lot 100x125, owner will give immediate possession. Den and Powder Rm. on 1st floor, 3 Bedrms. on 2nd, 3 finished rms. on 3rd. Automatic Heat. Gar. Fine condition. $8750.

MANY OTHER GOOD LISTINGS. SIDDALL 2269 Garrett Road, Drexel Park. Clearbrook 0173. OPEN SUNDAYS 1 TO 5 P. M.

DREXEL HILL 314 SHADELAND AVENUE. Single, stone residence; center hall, 7 bedrooms, 3 baths; gas heat (no rationing). Excellent condition. Lot 70'x180', beautiful landscaping. $17,500. Possession. ALBERT M. GREENFIELD & CO. Walnut & Juniper Sts. KINgsley 1400

DREXEL HILL. Aronimink Park section. Beautiful mod. single stone home, 4 bedrooms, 2 baths, maid quarters, 3d flr.; lge. 2-car gar., cent. plant heat. Many unusual spec. Priced settle est. Immed. poss. Sun. 11-5 P. M., 1128 Belfield ave. Swarth 0333.

DREXEL HILL, 2449 Marshall rd. Small down payment, $42.84 monthly. Mod. semi-det. 6 rs., open porch, garage. Good cond. Vacant. Immediate poss. Open Sun. 2-6 or Walnut Management Co. Pen. 0800. Sar. 1818.

DREXEL PLAZA—4000 Block Vernon Road. Twin 6 & Bath, Garage, $3950. WILLIAM PUGH, 5713 Market st. Gra. 3300.

E. OAK LANE. Desirable semi-det. center hall home, 3 bedrms., sleeping porch, bth., on 2d flr., one rm. & bth. on 3d; 1-car garage. Just redecorated. $7600 for quick sale. Ph. HAGEDORN, Waverly 1700 for appt.

EDDINGTON GARDENS. 6 lots, small house, garden planted. Sacrifice. Han. 6173.

ELKINS PARK, 7815 Mill rd., 10 rms. & b., sgle. home, 70-ft. front. Reas. Melrose 4641 J. Eves. Sat. P. M. and all day Sun.

SUBURBAN

ELKINS PARK. Beautiful single English type home, custom built. [illegible]

GETZ & CO. 6722 York Rd. [illegible]

ENFIELD—[illegible]

FOLCROFT. [illegible]

FORT WASHINGTON. [illegible]

GLENSIDE. [illegible]

W. T. B. ROBERTS & SON, Glenside, Ogontz 1682

GLENSIDE—206 N. Easton Rd. [illegible]

KUHN & LOWERY, INC.

HAVERFORD TOWNSHIP. Seldom these days is one of these SINGLE HOMES available in the fascinating CHATHAM VILLAGE. [illegible] $7250. FRANK McCLATCHY, 69th and Walnut Streets

HATBORO. [illegible] Pennington & Pennington

MILLER & CORNELL Inc. Hatboro, Pa. Ph. Hatboro 1628

SUBURBAN

HATBORO. 6-room bungalow, good condition. [illegible] MILLER & CORNELL, Inc. Hatboro, Pa. Ph. Hatboro 1628

HATBORO. [illegible]

HIGHLAND PARK. [illegible]

JENKINTOWN. NOBLE VISTA. ALL-STONE COLONIAL. [illegible]

KUHN & LOWERY, INC.

JENKINTOWN. [illegible]

LANSDALE. [illegible]

LANSDOWNE. Ideally located home. [illegible] W. A. CLARKE CO. 6822 Market St. Blvd. 0960 or ALL. 2655

LANSDOWNE. [illegible]

LOWER Merion Township. [illegible] BIDDLE N. HUNT

New Jersey REAL ESTATE DIRECTORY

Real Estate for Sale

ATLANTIC CITY (Chelsea). Cor. stores & apts., great speculative possibilities for sale, may accept part exchange. Charles E. Fell Co., 1207 Atlantic ave.

BLACK HORSE PIKE—7 rm. house, elec., h. w. ht., gar., 2 ac. ground, $3500. E. B. Horner, E. Church Rd., Blackwood, N. J.

BLACKWOOD. Bungalow, 4 rms. & bath, interor unfinished. Gar. $1200. Lot 80x90. K-235 Inquirer.

CARDIFF, N. J.—Granite blk. house, gar., 12 rms., 12½ acres, near Govt. airport. $4000 cash. D-278 Inquirer.

CLEMENTON. 4-room bungalow & chicken house, lot 80x100 ft., electric and running water, house needs repairs, $400 cash. J. McSparrin, 31 Smith ter., Clementon, N.J.

COLLINGSWOOD, 6 rms., bth., only $3800. R. R. Harden, Haddonfield 0039.

HADDONFIELD, 549 Chews Landing rd., 12 rms., h. w. heat, slate roof, exclusive section. Over 1 acre. Old shade. Garage. Adaptable to apt. conversion or large family. Make offer. LEEDS, 684 Haddon ave., Collingswood, N. J. Phone 1573.

HADDON HTS., fine 2-fam. apt. hs., lge. lot, 2-car gar.; only $6600. Lamoreaux, 511 White Horse Pk., Haddon Hts.

MAPLE AVE., Lindenwold, N. J., 6 rms. & bath. Finished attic. Hot air heat. 1 blk. from White Horse pike. 1 acre of land. Ideal for farming & chickens. Bus & train service within walking distance. Apply George Golley, No. 5 Chews Landing Road, Clementon, N. J. Ph. Laurel Springs 947-W.

MAPLE SHADE. 19 S. Boulevard ave. 5-rm. bungalow & gar., garden, lot 50x170. Nr. trp.

MEDFORD LAKES. Chipewa Trail. All year round cabin. Beautifully landscaped. Ziegler. Medford 4327 or Ardmore 5420.

Real Estate for Sale

WOODBURY, N. J. Lots $35. Tms. Nr. bus. High, dry, level. Free insp. R-237 Inquirer.

8-RM. HOUSE, approximately 3 acres of land, on Old White Horse Pike. 3 min. walk to R.R., 6 min. to bus stop. Running water. Bath, steam ht. & barn good for garage & chicken house. $3700. R. PIERI, Atco, N. J., Berlin 659R2.

APARTMENT HOUSE, 4 units, 5 rms. & b. each. Brick, modern. 123-125 Melrose ave., Atlantic City, N. J. Good buy. Mortgage to suit. Write Juniper Investment Corp., 250 N. Juniper st., Phila.

6-ROOM frame house, 10 miles from Atlantic City, good condition, lot 150'x250'. Barn 30x60, garage and shed. $2500. Federal Land Bank of Springfield. A. Hulse Mooney, District Office, Somerville, N. J.

SUBURBAN Home, 7 rms., bath & garage, fine shrubbery & garden, ½ block from school. Very convt. transp. Call Maple Shade 3220.

5 ROOMS, bth., gar., lot 50x150, city water & elect., $750 cash, full price $2200. Renwick, 130 E. Main st., Maple Shade 1648.

LAKE property, 5 rms., elec., running water, gar. Vacant. $800 cash. E. B. Horner, E. Church Rd., Blackwood, N. J.

Real Estate for Rent

NORTHFIELD, N. J. Bung., 5 rms. & b., h. a. ht. DAMERAU, Rit. 3752 or Rec [illegible]

HOUSE, 5 bedrms., 3 b. Good lot. Res. Neighborhood. Gtn. area, Elkins Park or Jenkintown. Nr. trans. Willing to buy. Ten. 1212

LAUREL SPRINGS, 211 Madison, 5 rooms, bath, all conveniences on bus line. $37.50 lease.

Continued on Next Page

The Philadelphia Inquirer

PUBLIC LEDGER

An Independent Newspaper for All the People

FINAL CITY EDITION

CIRCULATION: June Average: Daily 468,529; Sunday 1,343,788

MONDAY MORNING, JULY 26, 1943

Copyright, 1943, by The Philadelphia Inquirer Co. Vol. 229 No. 26

a b d e f g h

THREE CENTS

MUSSOLINI OUSTED

King Takes Command, Names Badoglio Premier; Peace Move Hinted; Fascist Party Believed Dead

U. S. Planes Rip Hamburg After Vast R.A.F. Raid

Premier Benito Mussolini, Italy's ruler for 21 years, resigned yesterday under the pressure of inglorious defeat. King Victor Emmanuel replaced the posturing dictator with Marshal Pietro Badoglio as prime minister with "full powers."

London circles indicated the choice of Badoglio as a possible prelude to peace negotiations. The Fascist party apparently had been ruled out of existence and a severe blow had been dealt to the Axis partners of Germany and Japan.

In Sicily, crumbling outpost of Italy, Allied armies were closing in from three directions toward the last core of Axis resistance on the Catania-Mount Etna line.

In Western Europe, American bombers followed the greatest assault ever made by the R.A.F.; a 2300-ton raid on Hamburg, with day attacks on that port and three other points in Germany and one in Belgium. In the Mediterranean, Allied planes smashed Bologna and other Italian railroad centers.

In Russia, the Red Army captured Glazunovka, cracking the southeast corner of the Orel salient.

In the South Pacific, Allied bombers delivered the heaviest attack of the Pacific war on the Jap base at Munda.

Forts Also Smash Kiel and 2 Other Areas in Germany

Map on Page 6

By LYNN HEINZERLING

LONDON, July 26 (Monday) (A. P.).—American bombers battered four places in Germany and struck a target in Belgium by daylight Sunday in the mightiest single day's onslaught of the war, following up the Royal Air Force's record-breaking 2300-ton raid on Hamburg Saturday night.

(It was reported authoritatively that R. A. F. had again attacked Germany last night.)

19 BOMBERS LOST

Nineteen American bombers—all heavyweights—were lost as the United States airmen made their deepest penetration into Germany, attacking Hamburg; aircraft factories at Warnemunde, near the Baltic seaport of Rostock; the seaplane base at Wustrow, and the shipyards at Kiel.

R. A. F. Mitchells attacked the Fokker aircraft factory at Amsterdam in occupied Holland this afternoon also, scoring bomb hits

Continued on Page 6, Column 2

Flying Forts Cover 1500 Miles to Blast Bologna Rail Area

By DANIEL DE LUCE

ALLIED HEADQUARTERS IN NORTH AFRICA, July 25 (A. P.).—U. S. Flying Fortresses, staging their longest hop of the Mediterranean war, blasted the railroad bottleneck of Bologna yesterday in one of a series of crippling blows upon vital Italian rail transport arteries.

The unescorted Fortresses, winging 1500-miles round-trip, exploded an ammunition train and blanketed the crowded freight yards at Bologna with bombs, Allied headquarters announced today, and met no opposition from either fighter planes or anti-aircraft guns.

BATTER RAIL TAGETS

Other Allied bombers lashed out over southern Italy, concentrating on railroad targets to weaken Mussolini's defenses.

Royal Air Force Lancasters pounded Leghorn on the northwest coast of Italy last night in another shuttle-bombing run from North Africa back to Britain, it was announced in London. None of the Lancasters were lost, the Air Ministry said.

R.A.F. Liberators and Halifaxes

Continued on Page 6, Column 1

Column by Clare Luce Banned in Army Paper

NEW DELHI, India, July 25 (U. P.).—Representative Clare Boothe Luce (R., Conn.), describing price fixing efforts on the home front for American troops at the battle front, said those efforts left "consumer and producer alike with tongues hanging out, eyes rolling dizzily and the larder, pocketbook and gas tank empty," it was learned today.

Mrs. Luce has been a columnist for China-Burma-India Roundup, a weekly soldier publication here, but will write no more columns because the War Department considers her views "politically controversial," and has banned them from the paper.

PAPER THRIVES ON IT

Editors of Roundup admitted their tabloid thrives on controversial matter and that the lady from Connecticut "supplied plenty" in her column, "Here the Gavel Fell," furnished free and exclusively to Roundup.

The War Department's action was based on a regulation against "politically controversial" matter in Army publications, but has nothing to do with fights on other subjects.

Roundup editors said they would

Continued on Page 8, Column 6

MUSSOLINI AND HIS SUCCESSOR IN PALMIER DAYS

Benito Mussolini and Marshal Pietro Badoglio as they reviewed some of the troops sent against the Allies in 1940, after the notorious "stab in the back" of prostrate France. (Map of Il Duce's lost empire in Page 2; other pictures on Page 3.)

ALL ALLIED ARMIES BEAR DOWN ON AXIS FORCES AT CATANIA

By REYNOLDS PACKARD

ALLIED HEADQUARTERS IN NORTH AFRICA, July 25 (U. P.).—Canadian troops drove a wedge into the center of the last Axis lines in Sicily today despite fierce resistance, while the British Eighth Army launched a new attack on the ramparts of Catania.

In a simultaneous thrust, American forces swept eastward to attack the enemy's right wing.

The full power of Allied land, air and sea might was being marshaled against the 2000 square miles of northeast Sicily which still barred the doorway to Europe.

TAORMINA SHELLED

Light British naval forces bombarded Taormina, 20 miles above Catania, where they found coastal guns firing inland in possible indication that the Allies had flanked Mt. Etna on the north.

Royal Air Force fighters and American A-36 invaders kept the ports of Messina and Milazzo under almost constant attack, and naval units were roving the Messina Straits without encountering enemy surface opposition.

The American Seventh Army, swelling its prisoner list to more than 200 guns, was moving east

Continued on Page 4, Column 2

Special Features

A page of pictures, showing soldiers from Philadelphia and nearby cities at an Eighth Air Force base "Somewhere in England" will be found on

Page 16

The first installment of "Invasion Armada," Ivan H. (Cy) Peterman's story of the Navy's part in the invasion of Sicily appears on

Page 5

Stage Set for Collapse Of Italy, London Says

British Believe Nation May Rally, Then Sue for Peace

LONDON, July 25 (U. P.).—The Axis front cracked tonight with the ouster of Benito Mussolini, and while there was no indication in London that Italy would fold up immediately, the emergence of King Victor Emmanuel was regarded as a notural and necessary preliminary to that end.

Little more than 15 days after the Allied landings in Sicily, Italy appeared driven toward the next to the last step in getting out of the war.

Mussolini was ousted—overthrown

Continued on Page 2, Column 5

Washington Hails Duce's Ouster, But Maintains Reserve

WASHINGTON, July 25 (U. P.).—The resignation of Benito Mussolini and the accompanying political turmoil within Italy were interpreted optimistically here tonight, but not necssarily as foreshadowing an easy Allied conquest of Italy.

The White House and State Department declined comment pending official confirmation that Mussolini, mentor of Adolf Hitler in the art of Fascism, had quit.

"We, as yet, have no confirma-

Continued on Page 2, Column 6

BIGGEST AIR RAID SMASHES MUNDA

By MURLIN SPENCER

ALLIED HEADQUARTERS IN THE SOUTHWEST PACIFIC, July 26 (Monday) (A. P.).—Allied bombers, attacking Japanese positions in the Southwest Pacific with ever-increasing intensity, yesterday delivered the heaviest raids of the Pacific war against two of the enemy's most important bases.

More than 200 American planes swarmed over the key airbase at Munda, New Georgia, raining 186 tons of bombs upon the Japanese pinned within the air base by American troops who control the surrounding jungle.

AIRDROME BATTERED

At the same time, medium bombers and long-range fighters, manned by Australians, swept up the coast of New Britain for a co-ordinated dawn attack on the Gasmata airdrome. The radio station was destroyed and grounded aircraft, the runway, supply dump areas and enemy personnel "thoroughly strafed," the communique from General Douglas MacArthur's headquarters said.

Strong forces of our aircraft "in

Continued on Page 6, Column 6

RUSSIANS CAPTURE NEW OREL BASTION

By ROBERT MUSEL

LONDON, July 26 (Monday) (U. P.).—Russian troops captured Glazunovka, cracking the southeast corner of the Orel salient, broke across the Oka River northeast of Orel and scored gains of two and a half to five and a half miles in a general advance Sunday against desperate German resistance, Moscow announced today.

Driving through mud and heavy rains, the Russians swept forward to gain 30 villages in a single day in the heart of one of the greatest of German defense zones, according to a Russian special communique and the regular midnight communique, recorded here.

FIERCE COUNTER-ATTACKS

German troops counter-attacked wave by wave in many sectors of the salient where the Russians were driving in from north, east and south.

Eight hundred Germans were killed in one vain counter-attack north of Orel. More than 1500 died east of Orel in another counter-attack, and, in indication that the

Continued on Page 6, Column 4

Axis Suffers Hard Blow; Rome Raid, Sicily Invasion Speed End of Duce's Rule

LONDON, July 25 (A. P.).—Dictator Benito Mussolini resigned tonight as Premier of Italy and King Victor Emmanuel, in a possible bid for peace with onrushing Allied armies, assumed command of Italian forces for "a stand against those who have wounded the sacred soil of Italy."

Marshal Pietro Badoglio, former chief-of-staff and never an admirer of Fascism, came out of retirement to succeed Mussolini as head of a military government accorded "full power" by the King to do what is best for a war-shattered and weary country.

The broken Mussolini went in to the shadows after 21 years of dictatorship in which he had tried to recreate the ancient glories of Rome on a basis of Fascism and military alliances with Germany and Japan.

Military circles took it for granted that the "resignation" was forced.

This dramatic turn in Italy's fortunes was a shattering blow to Germany and Japan, Mussolini's Axis partners.

Badoglio, the 71-year-old new premier, had been dismissed as chief of staff by Mussolini Dec. 6, 1940.

URGES ITALIANS TO BACK KING

He issued a proclamation tonight telling Italians:

"On orders of His Majesty the King, I am taking over the military government of the country with full powers."

He called on all Italians to rally around the King.

"The war continues," he added. "Italy, grievously stricken in her invaded provinces and in her ruined towns maintains her faith in he given word, jealous of her ancient traditions."

The King in his proclamation said Italy, "by the valor of its armed forces and the determination of all its citizens, will find again a way of recovery."

These sensational announcements may be the opening Italian peace moves.

They came as Allied troops were sweeping across Sicily off the southern Italian mainland, less than a week after the 500-plane American air attack on the Fascist capital of Rome, and amid reports that widespread peace demonstrations had occurred in Italy's main cities.

POPE REPORTED URGING PEACE NOW

(French reports, quoted by the United Press, said that Pope Pius desired that Italy make peace now, before an invasion of the mainland opens.

(These reports said the Pope also was understood to have made an urgent new appeal to the King to have Rome declared an open city.)

"No consideration must stand in our way and no recrimination must be made," said the King's proclamation. "We must stand against those who have wounded the sacred soil of Italy."

The "resignation" of the bald, squat, boastful Mussolini ended a career that began with the Fascist march on Rome in 1922. The international and domestic standing of Mussolini, however, has steadily deteriorated since he led his country into war in the summer of 1940.

Mussolini was conferring with Adolf Hitler last Monday when the huge American air attack was delivered on rail and airport installations at Rome.

FUTILE APPEAL TO HITLER

He apparently appealed to Hitler for aid in resisting the Allied onslaughts which clearly are aimed at knocking Italy out of the war as quickly as possible.

If that was his plea he undoubtedly failed in his mission. The King's proclamation, which in effect dismissed the originator of Fascism, followed.

Badoglio, long out of favor with the Fascists, had been reported a likely successor to Mussolini once the country decided to sue for peace.

The resignation of Mussolini, whose empire vanished

Continued on Page 2, Column 1

Duce's Fate Uncertain

By Associated Press

There was nothing from Rome last night to indicate what fate awaits Benito Mussolini, ousted dictator of Italy.

It was announced merely that King Victor Emmanuel had accepted Mussolini's resignation. There apparently were no words from Mussolini in farewell to those who for 21 years shouted "Duce, Duce," when he appeared, arms akimbo, on his famous balcony.

Reports from Bern, Switzerland, that Mussolini and his Cabinet members had been arrested found no confirmation.

Should Mussolini decide to flee Italy, the fallen dictator was handy to the neutral soil of Switzerland. It was either that, or appeal to his friend Adolf Hitler for sanctuary in Germany.

NAZIS SAY ILLNESS FORCED DUCE OUT

LONDON, July 26 (Monday) (U. P.).—The Berlin radio, in its first comment on the resignation of Benito Mussolini, said today that "it was assumed the change in the (Italian) Government was caused by the state of health of Il Duce, who had fallen ill recently."

Berlin made its announcement in a D. N. B. dispatch under a Rome dateline. It came at 3:35 A. M. (9:35 P. M. Sunday E. W. T.)

(A Transocean news agency

Continued on Page 2, Column 4

12 U.S. Fliers Killed In Havana Collision

HAVANA, July 25 (A. P.).—Two American B-25 bombers, starting on a patrol, today collided in midair 2000 feet above Cuban Army Headquarters, killing 12 American airmen.

The planes were loaded with bombs and some of the crewmen might have saved their lives by jettisoning the high explosives on the crowded beaches or Army headquarters, but they tried to make crash landings at sea and the planes blew up. Only one of the 12 bodies had been recovered several hours after the accident.

U. S. WEATHER FORECAST

Philadelphia and vicinity: Continued warm with scattered showers.

Eastern Pennsylvania and New Jersey: Scattered thundershowers today.

Sun rises 5:53 A. M. Sets 8:21 P. M.
Moon rises 1:45 A. M. Sets 3:54 P. M.

Three Phila. Soldiers Wounded in Action

Three Philadelphia soldiers are reported wounded in action in a War Department announcement released last night.

In addition, two men from Allentown are included in the list of 243 soldiers wounded in five battle zones.

The Philadelphians are:

Second Lieutenant Leonard W. Herman; wounded in the European area, son of Mrs. Lena Herman, of 4294 Parkside ave.

Private First Class Joseph J. Zack; wounded in the North African area, son of Mrs. Caroline Zack, of 1319 Wallace st.

Private First Class William B. Knight; wounded in the Southwest Pacific area, son of Mrs. Ethel Ellinger, of 630 Naomi st., Blue Berry Hill.

Among other Pennsylvanians wounded are: Corporal John A. Holzman, of Johnstown, and Corporal John C. Timmins, of Allentown, wounded in the Pacific area. Private First Class Albert J. Cook, of Shippinsburg, was wounded in the Southwest Pacific area, and Private First Class Charles L. Miller, of Allentown, was wounded in the North African area.

PFC. ZACK

Private Zack, 28, was wounded in the North African area July 3, according to a telegram from the War Department to his parents, Ignastius and Caroline Zack. Inducted Thanksgiving Day, 1941, Zack, who has been overseas for eight months, formerly was employed on a construction job in the Navy Yard. A brother, Private First Class Albert J. Zack, 26, entered the Army last Thanksgiving Day.

The Navy Department last night reported a Philadelphian killed in action and another missing in action.

James Morgan, of Plymouth, reported missing, is also included in the Navy list of 22 dead, 13 wounded and 17 missing. This brings the grand total of Navy, Marine Corps and Coast Guard casualties to 9789 dead, 5025 wounded, 9626 missing and 4151 prisoners of war since Pearl Harbor.

The Philadelphians are:

Frederick F. Decker; dead, son of Frederick F. Decker, of 122 Wolf st.

Joseph E. Morris; missing, son of Mrs. Frances Morris, of 2954 Rutledge ave.

F. F. DECKER

Decker, 22, machinist's mate, second class, enlisted in the Navy March 30, 1942. He was a graduate from South Philadelphia High School and formerly was a brakeman for the Pennsylvania Railroad.

His parents, Frederick, Sr., a conductor for the Pennsylvania Railroad, and Anna, received a telegram July 30 from the Navy Department reporting him killed in action. He has a brother, Raymond, 17, and two sisters, Caroline and Catherine.

FORMER ATHLETE KILLED IN ACTION

A former well-known Delaware county high school athlete was killed in action in North Africa July 22, according to word received by his wife from the War Department yesterday.

He is Private Stanley L. Hershey, 514 Clifton ave., Collingdale, who was attached to the Armored Command. A graduate of Collingdale High School in 1941, Hershey was co-captain of the football, basketball and baseball teams. He enlisted in September, 1942.

Before he left for training he married Lenna Mae Adams of Collingdale. Two brothers, William R. and Raymond, are in the Army. Hershey's parents are William E. Hershey, veteran of the last war, and Mrs. Elizabeth Hershey.

Frank P. Grieco, 30, of 216 Denny ave., Pennsgrove, N. J., fireman second class, was killed in action while helping man an invasion barge during the first phase of the landing in Sicily.

His wife, Frances, was notified of his death yesterday in a Navy Department telegram to her home.

Grieco, a graduate of Salem High School and a former employee at the du Pont plant here, enlisted last September.

PENNA. LIEUTENANT DESCRIBES BATTLE

Special to The Inquirer

ATLANTIC CITY, Aug. 17.—A second lieutenant of an airborne division which landed behind the Italian lines in Sicily today told here how a group of paratroopers he commanded held off Italian reinforcements at a road junction until the invasion army arrived.

He is Lieutenant William R. Naugle, 23, of 242 N. 17th st., Camp Hill, near Harrisburg, Pa., who is in Army General Hospital under treatment for gunshot wounds of both legs.

Lieutenant Naugle brought here yesterday with 235 wounded and sick soldiers from various battlefronts, said his group landed at night by parachute in an orchard, near an important road intersection in Sicily.

He and his first sergeant wiped out four Italian soldiers with hand grenades, but the Italians quickly brought up reinforcements. His unit, he said, held the road until morning when the invasion army caught up with them. Lieutenant Naugle was wounded early in the action.

Also among the soldiers hospitalized here are Private First Class Robert E. Hasty, 25, 1849 Welsh road, Bustleton, who contracted malaria in India, and Private John O'Malley, 23, of 7637 Parkview road, Highland Park, Delaware county, Pa., who had been stationed in England.

Phila. Flier Killed In Idaho Plane Crash

Sergeant Nicholas J. Gargano, of 234 N. Edgewood st., was killed when a four-engine Army plane crashed in an attempted landing at the Pocatello (Idaho) base Saturday, it was disclosed yesterday by the War Department.

He was one of three Pennsylvanians involved in the crash. Another man killed was Sergeant Lewis M. Getty, of Indiana, Pa., and among the seriously injured was Second Lieutenant Edward J. Comstock, of Ingram, near Pittsburgh.

Eve Curie to Enlist

NEW YORK, Aug. 17 (A. P.)—Eve Curie, daughter and biographer of her mother, Marie Curie, co-discover of radium, has left for England to become a private in the Corps Fes Volontairles Francaises, an organization corresponding to the American Women's Army Corps.

The Philadelphia Inquirer

PUBLIC LEDGER

An Independent Newspaper for All the People

FINAL CITY EDITION

CIRCULATION: July Average: Daily 481,938; Sunday 1,329,714

FRIDAY MORNING, SEPTEMBER 3, 1943

Copyright, 1943, by The Philadelphia Inquirer Co. Vol. 229, No. 65

a b d e f g h ★

THREE CENTS

ITALY INVADED

British 8th Army Storms Over Messina Strait, Lands at Dawn and Advances Into Peninsula

ALLIED HEADQUARTERS IN NORTH AFRICA, Sept. 3 (Friday) (A. P.).—British and Canadian forces under the command of General Dwight D. Eisenhower swept across the Strait of Messina in today's dawning light and landed on the beaches of Italy. Thus, the Allies had made good their promise to invade the European mainland. The long-awaited and historic assault came on the fourth anniversary of the day that Great Britain declared war on Germany.

The invading forces of the American commander less than three weeks ago brought to a conclusion the victorious Sicilian campaign.

It was from footholds won in that 38-day campaign, from the eastern shore of Sicily, that the mainland invaders sprung.

From there, it was only a brief boat ride, 20 minutes or a half hour, to the mainland—and possibly another good step toward Berlin.

BRITISH 8TH ARMY LEADS DRIVE

British and Canadian troops of the Eighth Army, famed for its fighting in North Africa and Sicily, made up the attacking force.

Allied naval units escorted the landing barges. Overhead, American and British airmen swept away the enemy.

The vanguard of the main invading army swept ashore in the pre-dawn darkness and fragmentary reports indicated they had fanned out immediately into the Calabrian hills to establish their bridgehead firmly so that the real power of Eisenhower's forces in Sicily—the heavy tanks and giant field guns—could be ferried across the Messina Straits in safety.

(The American Seventh Army, which mopped up the greater part of the western half of

Continued on Page 2, Column 1

WHERE ALLIES INVADED ITALIAN MAINLAND

Striking across the narrowest point between Sicily and the Italian mainland, Allied forces spearheaded by the British Eighth Army, have landed in the southern region after crossing the Messina Straits (arrows). Another map is on Page 2.

Today

Parley With Russia
Varied Ideologies
Polish Border Problem
Future of Baltic States
Japan Also a Factor

—By Mark Sullivan—

THIS column aims to make a small number of elementary points which it is desirable the public should bear in mind, about a delicate and serious situation.

President Roosevelt and Prime Minister Winston Churchill, now together in Washington, are approaching negotiations with Premier Josef Stalin of Russia.

The purpose is to arrive at agreement about an extremely wide and complex group of intricately related matters—including conduct of the war from now on, policy about Germany when the war ends, and about post-war arrangements for world peace. That the negotiations should succeed is vitally desirable.

There is every reason to have confidence that Messrs. Roosevelt and Churchill will conduct the negotiations with skill and wisdom, including consideration for Russia.

There is proof, among other evidences, in the extraordinarily able speech of Mr. Churchill this week. That Messrs. Roosevelt and Churchill should have the confidence of their countries is essential to success. If in their conclusions there is anything unacceptable to America, the country has a check, for any conclusions involving international agreement must be laid before the Senate for ratification.

The differences necessary to be bridged are many and deep. A few are:

Russia wishes to hold onto three small countries along her border which she seized in 1939-40—Lativia, Estonia and Lithuania. Russia says she needs these countries for safety against attack. The United States regards these countries as independent, and recognizes exiled governments representing them.

The possibility of compromise here lies in arriving at a program for international peace satisfactory to Russia, so that she would feel safe in permitting these countries to be independent.

The United States and Britain are waging war against both Germany and Japan (with Italy and other Axis satellites). Russia is fighting only against Germany—with Japan she has a pact of non-aggression.

This bears on the problem of the United States and Britain setting up a second front in Europe. They are obliged to use some of their forces against Japan, and to remember, that after Germany is defeated, they will still have the task of defeating Japan.

There is a broad difference between the circumstances in which Britain went to war, and those in which Russia became involved. Britain, although not attacked, went to war immediately after Hitler set out on his career of conquest in September, 1939, for the purpose of stopping Hitler.

Russia did not go to war at that time—on the contrary, she had recently made a treaty of non-aggression with Hitler. Russia went to war only after, and because Hitler, breaking his treaty with her, invaded her ter-

Continued on Page 23, Column 8

Nazis Abandon Donets Line as Reds Push On

Map on Page 3

By JAMES M. LONG

LONDON, Sept. 3 (Friday) (A. P.).—Russia announced early today that five Red armies plunging westward had cut the Bryansk-Kiev railway 150 miles from Kiev, smashed German reinforcements in a six-mile gain on Smolensk, and rolled up Axis lines in a new 45-mile-wide spurt in the Donets Basin.

Premier Josef Stalin's Thursday order of the day said that the Ukraine citadel of Sumy, 90 miles northwest of Kharkov, had fallen to General Nikolai Vatutin's army, and a communique announced the capture of Krolevets and Yampol, two points on the vital Bryansk-Kiev railway linking the enemy's central and southern fronts.

DONETS BASIN CITIES SEIZED

Lisichansk, Voroshilovsk, Slavyanoserbsk, and other cities were seized in the Donets Basin, while Budenovka, 20 miles from Mariupol, was taken in the push along the rim of the Sea of Azov, said the communique recorded by the Soviet monitor.

The swiftness of the Russian advances and the tone of the communique indicated that the Germans were engaged in a large-scale retreat toward the Dnieper River, particularly in the huge Donets Basin. The bulletin, however, emphasized that the Germans were fighting stubbornly all along the 600-mile front.

9000 GERMANS KILLED

More than 9000 Germans were killed yesterday as the Red armies overran nearly 250 cities and villages, many of them strategic prizes, for a two-day bag of nearly 550 localities.

The capture of Krolevets, 25 miles north of the rail junction of Konotop, put the Red Army 150 miles from Kiev after a 130-mile summer lunge from Kursk. Moreover, its fall further flanked Bryansk from the south and may force Germany's south-central armies to fall back on Kiev. Captured Yampol lies 32 miles northeast of Krolevets.

NO CHANCE TO REORGANIZE

"Soviet units are inflicting unceasing blows on the mauled divisions of the enemy, not giving them the possibility of disengaging from pursuit and organizing their defenses," said a communique supplement telling of the fighting

Continued on Page 3, Column 1

GAMBLING VICTIMS ON PIERS PLEDGE WAGES TO USURERS

By RALPH CROPPER

Longshoremen, ship repair workers and seamen "cleaned" of heavy sums by professional gamblers in games going on under the noses of Federal port authorities have fallen prey in recent weeks to unlicensed money lenders, The Inquirer found yesterday in continuing its investigation of wide-open conditions along the Delaware waterfront.

Workmen who are earning wages as high as $20 a day for the first time in their lives have pledged their pay checks to itinerant loan sharks for weeks in advance, it was learned on good authority.

SEEK TO RECOUP LOSSES

The victims, for the most part, have borrowed to finance further "plunges" in games of three-card monte, poker and dice, in the hope of recouping previous losses—and now find themselves committed to pay back with exorbitant interest money for which they have nothing to show.

Both loan sharks and the professional gamblers who had frequented the entrances to piers in the vicinity of Delaware and Oregon aves. were noticeable by their absence yesterday following an Inquirer expose of their activities.

PATROLS ON GUARD

At the gates were strong patrols of Military Police and members of the Port Protection Service of the Coast Guard. City police who formerly occupied sentry boxes just outside the high wire fence of the Government-restricted wharf area were walking beats instead.

Director of Public Safety James H. Malone said yesterday he had received no appeals from the Army or other Government agencies for assistance in policing the wharf area along the southern reaches of Delaware ave.

"The area referred to is a restricted military area, which city police are forbidden to enter unless sent for

Continued on Page 12, Column 5

AIR FORTS, R. A. F. ROCK FRENCH BASES

LONDON, Sept. 3 (Friday) (A. P.).—U. S. Flying Fortresses bombed airfields at Mardyck and Denain late yesterday and other battle planes ushered in the fifth year of the war with further attacks on French targets under the largest fighter cover used in air operations so far in 1943, it was announced today.

'GOOD BOMBING RESULTS'

"Good bombing results were observed on all targets," said a communique issued jointly by U. S. Army headquarters and the Air Ministry.

Squadrons of P-47 Thunderbolts escorted and covered the Flying Fortresses.

"Marauders (B-26s) and R.A.F. Bostons, Mitchells and Venturas bombed targets in Pas de Calais," the communique said. "Other Marauders attacked the power station at Mazingarbe and Bostons attacked the freight yards at Serqueux."

R.A.F., Dominion and Allied Spitfires escorted and supported the light and medium bombers.

Four enemy aircraft were report-

Continued on Page 2, Column 7

206-Ton Raid Rakes Jap New Guinea Base

By C. YATES McDANIEL

ALLIED HEADQUARTERS IN THE SOUTHWEST PACIFIC, Sept. 3 (Friday) (A. P.).—Japanese army headquarters, fuel and ammunition stores have been blown up in the Madang, New Guinea, sector above ground-menaced Salamaua by more than 206 tons of bombs dropped from fighter-escorted bombers, General Douglas MacArthur announced today.

Fires which erased warehouses and buildings sent their flames up for 1500 feet as the heavy and medium bombers spread ruin after the fashion of raids in early August which virtually levelled Salamaua.

STRAFE INSTALLATIONS

The raiders, which added to the havoc by sweeping down to tree-top height to pour 90,000 rounds of machine-gun and cannon fire on enemy installations, struck at Madang, Amron Mission and Alexishafen.

"Widespread havoc and destruction wrought in all three target area

Continued on Page 2, Column 4

Rome Radio Fails To Mention Invasion

LONDON, Sept. 3 (Friday) (U. P.).—The Rome radio broadcast its regular 7 A. M. newscast today without mentioning the landing of Allied troops in southern Italy two and one-half hours earlier.

Special Feature

Walter Winchell's column, "On Broadway," appears

Today on Page 27

HISTORY OF ITALIANS IN WORLD WAR II

By Associated Press

June 10, 1940—Italy declared war on Great Britain and France.

June 23—British Somaliland irregulars carry the war into Italian East Africa.

Aug. 7—Italians enter British Somaliland which the British forces evacuated 12 days later.

Sept. 14—Italians drive to Sidi Barrani in Egypt.

Oct. 27—They invade Greece from Albania, which they had conquered the preceding year.

Dec. 12—The British launch their first offensive to drive the invader from Egypt, capturing Sidi Barrani.

Jan. 5 to Feb. 9—The advancing British take Tobruch, Bengasi and El Agheila, in Libya, where their offensive stalled.

Jan. 15, 1941—Haile Selassie raises his flag again in Ethiopia with the help of British forces.

Feb. 25 to April 12—Axis forces drive British back successively from El Agheila, Bengasi and encircle Tobruch.

Feb. 26—The fall of Mogadiscio.

Continued on Page 2, Column 4

Battle-Seasoned Army Spearheads Invasion

By Associated Press

The invasion spearhead ramming into Southern Italy is forged with planes, tanks, ships and tough, battle-seasoned men half a million to a million strong.

Their invasion springboard is one wrested from the enemy in one of the brilliant victories of the war, climaxed by a triumph in Tunisia that bled the enemy of ground and air strength.

FRENCH PREPARING

In North Africa at the end of the Tunisian campaign, the Allies had at least 500,000 men—Americans and British—and thousands upon thousands more of Frenchmen rapidly being trained and equipped with the best modern armaments of war.

Among the forces at General Dwight D. Eisenhower's disposal are hardened, battle-tested and victory-confident units: the U. S. Second Army Corps, the British First Army, the British Eighth Army, and the Fighting French.

CONQUERED IN AFRICA

These were the men who pushed the Axis out of Africa, who met and bested some of the finest German troops and shattered — in all the African warfare — 36 divisions of enemy troops.

In reserve during the Tunisia warfare, and now possibly destined to carry much of the weight of the

Continued on Page 2, Column 4

First Lady Arrives In Canberra by Plane

CANBERRA, Australia, Sept. 3 (Friday) (A. P.).—Mrs. Franklin D. Roosevelt, wife of the President, arrived today by plane.

The dispatch did not state from where the plane came, but she previously had been in New Zealand.

U. S. WEATHER FORECAST

Philadelphia and vicinity: Cooler today.

Sun rises 6:28 A.M. Sets 7:32 P.M.
Moon rises 9:59 A.M. Sets 9:43 P.M.

Radio Features Today

Subject to Last-Minute Changes by Stations
(All Schedules in Eastern War Time—Friday, September 3, 1943)
(Copyright 1943, The Philadelphia Inquirer)

WFIL 560 WIBG 990
WIP 610 KYW 1060
WEAF 660 WCAU 1210
WOR 710 WCAM 1310
WJZ 770 WHAT 1310
WABC 880 WTEL 1340
WPEN 950 WDAS 1400

9 A. M.
WCAU-Sonny Kendis
KYW, WABC—News
WEAF-Everything Goes
WIP-News; Consumer Reports
WFIL-Breakfast Club
WPEN-Songs
WOR-Quiz Wizard
WDAS-Merry-Go-Round
WIBG-For Women
9.15—WCAU-Women's Program
WIP-Serenaders
KYW-Betty Jordan
WABC-Chapel Singers
WOR-Jam for Breakfast
9.30—KYW-Ruth Welles
WEAF-Women's Program
WOR-News (WCAU at 9.40)
WABC-This Life Is Mine
WIP-Evangelist
WIBG-Mastersingers
9.45—WCAU-Music
WEAF-Robert St. John
WOR-Lorraine Sherwood

10 A. M.
WOR-Pure Food Talk
WFIL-Isabel Hewson
WIBG-News; Variety
WDAS-News; Variety
KYW-Lora Lawton
WPEN-News; Variety
WCAU-Valiant Lady
WIP-Easy Does It
10.15—WIP-News
KYW-The Open Door
WCAU-Stories
WFIL-Novelty
10.30—WFIL-Baby Institute
KYW-Helpmate
WCAU-Amanda
WOR-Loretta
WIP-Dialing
WIBG-Dance Music
10.45—KYW-Drama
WABC-Bachelor's Children
WIP-Hits
WCAU-News for Women
WFIL-Anne Ives
WJZ-Love Problems
10.55—WJZ, WOR-Neighbors

11 A. M.
WCAU-Bob Chester
WIP-Melodies
WOR-News
WABC-Golden Gate Quartet
KYW-Road of Life
WIBG-News
WPEN-Pedi Orch.
WFIL-At Sardi's
WDAS-News; Music
11.15—WOR-For Women
KYW-Vic and Sade
WCAU-Second Husband
WIBG-Dance Music
11.30—KYW-Snow Village
WCAU-Bright Horizon
WFIL-News
11.45—WFIL-Women's Program
KYW-David Harum
WCAU-Aunt Jennie
WJZ-Nutrition Talk
11.50—WIP-What's Your Idea?
11.55—WOR-Neighbors

12 Noon
WCAU-Kate Smith
KYW-News; Songs
WFIL-News; Music
WDAS-News; Band
WPEN-Foreign News
WJZ-Supreme Stewardship
WIP-Commentator
WIBG-News; Dance Music
12.15—WCAU-Big Sister
WIP-Treasury Stars
WJZ-Quiz
WPEN-Foreign Melodies
WOR-Musical Appetizer
12.25—WJZ-News
12.30—WCAU-Helen Trent
WIBG-Rev. G. A. Palmer
WEAF-Variety
WPEN-Drama
WFIL-Music
WJZ-Farm and Home Hour
WIP, WOR-News
12.45—WIP-Guess the Tune
WCAU-Gal Sunday
KYW-News and Comments
WOR-Handy Man

1 P. M.
WFIL-Backstage
WPEN-News
WEAF-Mary McBride
WOR-Commentator
WIBG-News
WCAU-Drama
WIP-Variety
KYW-Music
WDAS-News; Music
1.15—WFIL-Dance
WPEN-Latin Tunes
WCAU-Ma Perkins
WIBG-Music
WOR-Larry and Ginger
WJZ-Woman's Exchange
1.30—WFIL-Novelty
WOR-Lopez Orch.
WDAS-Band Hotel
WIP-News; Variety
WPEN-Theater of the Air
WCAU-Vic and Sade
WIBG-Love Songs
KYW-Dinning Sisters
1.45—WFIL-Woman in Black
WCAU-The Goldbergs
WJZ-Organist
WIBG-Organ
KYW-News

2 P. M.
WIP-News; Variety
KYW-Guiding Light
WJZ-Lavalle's Orch.
WFIL-Melodies
WPEN-News; Variety
WDAS-News; Recordings
WIBG-Round the Town
WCAU-Dr. Malone
WOR-Martha Deane
2.15—WJZ-Mystery Chef
KYW-Lonely Women
WCAU-Joyce Jordan
WPEN-950 Club
2.30—WFIL-Sweet Music
KYW-Light of the World
WJZ-Variety
WIP-Brevities
WCAU-Love and Learn
WIBG-News; Orch.
WOR-News
2.45—KYW-Betty Crocker
WOR-Variety
WCAU-Pepper Young

3 P. M.
WFIL-Morton Downey
WCAU-News; Melodies
KYW-Mary Marlin
WOR-Mary Foster
WPEN-News; Music
WDAS-News; Music
WIBG-Sports; Boston vs. Athletics
3.15—KYW-Ma Perkins
WABC-Joe and Ethel
WCAU-Open House
WJZ-My True Story
WFIL-Dance Music
WOR-Drama
3.30—WFIL-Music
KYW-Pepper Young
WOR-Food Forum
WIP-News; Variety
WABC-Johnny Gart Trio
3.45—KYW-Drama
WJZ-Ted Malone
WABC-Green Valley
WIBG-Harry James

4 P. M.
KYW-Backstage Wife
WJZ-Frolics
WCAU-Home Front Reporter
WFIL-Melodies
WOR-News; Variety
WIP-Variety
WPEN-News; Varieties
WDAS-News; Music
4.15—KYW-Drama
4.25—WCAU-News
4.30—WCAU-Rhona Lloyd
WJZ-News
WFIL-Rhythm
WABC-Perry Como, songs
WDAS-Melodies
KYW-Lorenzo Jones
WOR-Stanley's Orch.
4.45—WCAU-Dolores O'Neil
WABC-Off the Record
WJZ-The Sea Hound
WDAS-Melody Time
WIP-Memory Lane
KYW-Widder Brown

5 P. M.
WCAU-Variety
WABC-Judith Evelyn
WDAS-News; Concert
WJZ-Hop Harrigan
WPEN-News
WFIL-Pinocchio
KYW-Drama
WOR-News; Music
WIP-News; Scores
5.15—WFIL-Dick Tracy
KYW-Portia Faces Life
WIP-Black Hood
WABC-Mother and Dad
5.30—WIP-Novelty
WFIL-Jack Armstrong
WCAU-Katherine Clark
WABC-Are You a Genius?
WIBG-Sports
WDAS-Varieties
KYW-Plain Bill
WPEN-Melodies
WOR-Chick Carter
5.45—WCAU-American Women
WFIL-Archie Andrews
KYW-Front Page Farrell
WIP-Superman
WIBG-News
WDAS-Sports

6 P. M.
WFIL-Terry and the Pirates
WEAF-Jack Arthur, songs
WIP, WJZ-News
WCAU, WABC-News
WIBG-Dance Music
WDAS-News; Hits
WOR-Prayer; Uncle Don
KYW-News; Scores; Music
WPEN-Novelty
6.15—WEAF-News
WFIL-Wayne King
WJZ-Terry and the Pirtes
WCAU-Warrington
WPEN-News Comments
WIP-Johnson Family
WABC-Music
6.30—WCAU-News; Classics
WFIL-Tom Moorehead
WIP-War Needs Wires; Sports
WEAF-Sports
WOR-News
WJZ-Welcome Lewis
KYW-News; Music
WPEN-Waltz Time
6.45—WFIL-Lowell Thomas
WCAU-World News; Comments
WIP-Uncle Wip
KYW-Show Tunes
WOR-Sports (WPEN at 6.55)

7 P. M.
WFIL-War Needs Wires
WOR-Fulton Lewis, Jr. (WPEN at 8.15)
WDAS-Irish Hour
WIP-Domestic Problems
WCAU-Mystery
WJZ-Korn Kobblers
WPEN-News
KYW-Fred Waring
7.05—WJZ-Musical
WFIL-Hot Spot on Map
7.15—WCAU-Secret Weapon
KYW, WIP, WOR-News
WPEN-Serenade
7.30—WFIL-Lone Ranger
KYW-Fred Brady
WEAF-John Q. Public
WIBG-Sports
WCAU-Easy Aces
WOR-Variety Show
WIP-Fashion Review
WPEN-Commentator
7.45—WCAU-Mr. Keen
WIP-Novelty
WPEN-Music
WEAF-H. V. Kaltenborn
WIBG-Music

8 P. M.
WDAS-Italian Hour
WCAU-Corliss Archer
WIP-Commentator
WIBG-Dance Music
KYW-Lucille Manners
WFIL-Watch the World
8.15—WIP-Swing
WDAS-Italian Music
WFIL-Parker Family
WOR-Jimmy Walker
8.30—WIP-Sherlock Holmes
KYW-Hit Parade
WFIL-Meet Your Navy
WIBG-News
WJZ-Ted Malone Quiz
WCAU-Thin Man
WPEN-News Comment
8.45—WPEN-Drama
WIBG-Leathernecks
8.55—WIP-Sports
WCAU-Cecil Brown
WOR-Lorraine Sherwood

9 P. M.
WPEN-Music
WCAU-Raymond Massey in "Casablanca"
WFIL-Gang Busters
WIP-News
WDAS-Commentator
KYW-Waltz Time
WIBG-Classical Music
9.15—WIP, WOR-News
9.30—WFIL-Vincent Lopez
WIP-Double or Nothing
WCAU-Brewster Boy
KYW-Quiz Program
9.55—WFIL-Sports
WIP-Sports

10 P. M.
WFIL-From Cairo, Egypt
KYW-Tommy Riggs
WCAU-The Yanks
WIP-Comments
WPEN-News; Dance Music
WDAS-News; Classics
10.15—WFIL-Treasury Stars
WIP-Swing
WJZ-Tennis Championship Resume
WOR-Skylark
10.30—WJZ-Men's News
WCAU-Show Time
WABC-Talk, "A New Approach to the Making of Lasting Peace," former President Herbert Hoover
KYW-Sports
WPEN-Uncle Sam
WFIL-Corcoran
10.45—WCAU, WIBG-News
WJZ-Income Tax Talk
WDAS-Elmer Davis
WPEN-Of Human Interest

11 P. M.
WCAU, WEAF-News and Comments
WFIL, KYW, WOR-News; Music
WIP-Dance Music
WDAS-News; Music
WPEN-Night Club
WIBG-Dance Music
11.15—WABC-Joan Brooks
WFIL-Hits
WCAU-Powers Gouraud; Movie News
WJZ-Sports; Music
11.30—WOR-Music
WCAU-Eileen Farrell
WJZ-Korn Kobblers
WEAF-Drama
11.55—WJZ-Jack Smith

12 M.
WJZ-News; Music
WFIL-Mosaic
WIP-Griff Williams
WCAU-News; Shep Fields
WEAF-News; Music
WOR-Don McGrane
12.05—KYW-News; Music

Shade Coverings Out

Transparent lampshade coverings that kept your shades clean are a war casualty. A recent order prohibits the use of transparent wrappings for non-essential uses. This is expected to save 10,000 tons of paper each year.

Keep Coffee Cold

If you like coffee fresh and full of its original flavor and aroma, keep the ground or unground coffee beans in a refrigerator.

Baked Eggs Royale

6 large potatoes, baked
2 tablespoons margarine
½ teaspoon salt
Dash of pepper
6 slices American cheese
6 eggs

Choose nice large potatoes that will stand up well and bake soft, cut off caps and scoop out. Use two-thirds of the potato and keep the other third for soup or other dishes. Mix 1 tablespoon fat and salt and pepper with potatoes and return to baked shell. Put a thin slice of cheese into each stuffed potato and break an egg over this. Dot with a bit of table fat and return to oven and bake for 15 to 20 minutes in moderate hot oven (400 degrees F.). Serves 4 to 6.

PATTERN

2089
SIZES 12 TO 46

Jumper Style Holds Favor

Schoolgirl, college girl, career girl, home girl—they all want the jumper. This one has that striking simplicity of line that makes it right for Fall, and right for the duration. It's easy to make, and adapted to the fabric of your choice.

Style No. 2089 is designed for sizes 12 to 46. Size 36 requires 2¾ yds. 35-in. fabric or 1⅝ yds. 54-in. fabric for the jumper; 1⅜ yds. 39-in. fabric for the blouse.

Pattern is hand-cut to United States Standard Measurements and includes chart with step-by-step instructions.

Send 16c for pattern. Write plainly, your name, address and style number. Be sure to state size.

Address orders: Pattern Department, The Philadelphia Inquirer, 111 West 19th street, New York, N. Y. If not delivered within two weeks, telephone Ruth Martin, Rittenhouse 1600, or write her care of The Philadelphia Inquirer.

NOW READY—A completely new FASHION BOOK, the summer issue, filled with smart pattern fashions for all sizes, ages and occasions. Whether sewing for the larger figure, the mature woman, the glamorous miss or even a year-tot, you'll find styles to please you.

FIGURE

How to Cut Inches From Waistline

Three Exercises Suggested for Streamlining

By Ida Jean Kain

You can't have any snap if you are in a slump. That settled waistline means you have let down. The heat and harder work are what got you—along with everybody else. But the cooler weather isn't going to be enough to pull you out of it.

What you need is a few waistliners. They are all to the good at any time, but right now they are indispensable. Just a little of this kind of exercise, done right, will get results that astonish you.

There are three ways of shearing off the waistline inches. First there's stretching. It makes you marvelously supple. The idea is to stretch through the midriff, but not to hunch the shoulders. Rather, keep them down and relaxed. Then, twist to pare off inches. But you must center the twist smack at the waist. Don't let the hips move and don't let up on the up-stretch when you add the twist. Finally, to clinch your waist-trimming, do a side-bend. Don't let the hips bow out to the side or back. Make the waistline muscles come across with action.

DAILY PROGRAM

Those three movements, put into an exercise program, will make short work of slimming you through the waist. If you will do a set of these every day, you can look inches slimmer and feel years younger. Here's a program to start you off.

1. Position: Stand erect with feet fairly wide apart and parallel, hands down at sides.

Movement: Pull up through the midriff and fling the right arm straight out in front, left arm straight up in back, and bend forward to touch right hand to left toes. Come back to starting position and bend to touch left hand to right toes. Continue for five counts.

2. Position: Stand erect with feet parallel and apart, arms stretched overhead by stretching through midriff, not hunching shoulders.

Movement: Hold your hips still and squarely to front, and circle trunk sideward, down in front, up to other side, and come erect. Continue for five circles. As you bring your trunk forward, be careful to keep pulling up and in with lower abdominal muscles.

Classic-Tailored Jacket

A classic-tailored jacket is more fashionable this year than a boxy jacket, and will stay in style longer. A skirt with not more than two box plaits in front and two in the back would be smart.

The all-around boy plaited skirt is not allowed by Government regulations.

Your Figure Query Box

Ida Jean Kain, nationally famous dietitian and figure authority, will answer your questions on Diet, Figure and Nutrition through the columns of this newspaper. Address queries to Ida Jean Kain, The Philadelphia Inquirer.

Gaining Steadily

Q.—For the past year or so I have had perfect weight but in the last few months I have been gaining steadily, with most of the weight at the thighs. Can you help me? JO.

A.—I think you should see a doctor specializing in the treatment of glands. Anyone who suddenly starts to gain weight without an apparent cause and without a change in eating habits should investigate the cause. It may be due to disfunctioning of the glands. The glandular extract you need, plus thigh exercises and for a time a low calorie diet will solve your problem.

Hair on Upper Lip

Q.—I have hair on my upper lip and it is quite noticeable. Is there any remedy that will remove it permanently? K.F.M.

A.—Most remedies are temporary but electrolysis should be permanent. It is extremely important that the work be done by a competent person. Ask your doctor to recommend someone qualified to do this work. If it is making you unhappy, by all means have something done about it.

Answers On Beauty

Patricia Lindsay, nationally famous beauty expert, whose authoritative articles are a regular feature in The Inquirer, will answer your personal beauty questions through the columns of this newspaper.

Address your beauty questions to Patricia Lindsay, in care of The Philadelphia Inquirer.

Hair in Nose

Can you recommend a bleach for hair in the nose which makes nostrils look dark all of the time—B. H.

Yours is a problem for a doctor or skin specialist. Many strong bleaches would harm you. You could try peroxide.—P. L.

Large Hips

I am 15 with large hips. What exercises can I do?—P. W. S.

Write me asking for spot reducing leaflet. Enclose a self-addressed stamped envelope.—P. L.

The Philadelphia Inquirer
MONDAY MORNING, SEPTEMBER 6, 1943 ★ 12

AIR RAID WARDENS DEDICATE SERVICE PLAQUE

Labor Day Celebrations

Philadelphia began its celebration of Labor Day yesterday, when Air Raid Wardens of Post 2, Zone 21 (above) marched with the 25th Ward Color Guard to 2775 N. Helen st., where a service flag was dedicated. Below, Damiano Sassi, national commander of the Italian-American War Veterans, and Mrs. Anthony Cardamone, president of the auxiliary, place a wreath at the statue of Washington in Independence Hall.

SOLDIERS OF THE BRITISH EIGHTH ARMY BOARD INVASION BOATS FOR ITALY

First Pictures of Invasion of Italy

In these pictures, first of the invasion of Italy to be received in the United States, British and Canadian forces composing the British Eighth Army are shown in three stages of the mighty thrust. The photo above shows boats being loaded with soldiers for the invasion. In the center picture amphibious invasion craft enter the water for the trip to the beaches of the Italian peninsula. At the bottom, British soldiers are shown moving inland north of Reggio Calabria, on the toe of the peninsula. (AP Wirephotos)

ITALIAN-AMERICAN WAR VETERANS PAY TRIBUTE TO WASHINGTON

MEN WHO SPEARHEADED THE INVASION OF ITALY GET UNDER WAY

REUNION Carole Landis, of Hollywood, and Captain Tom Wallace, of the Army Air Forces Fighter Command, who were married in England when Carole toured overseas with an entertainment unit, are shown in a New York night club as they celebrated their first reunion in this country. They now are returning to their respective duties for the duration.

BRITISH TOMMIES MOVE FORWARD IN AMPHIBIOUS 'DUCKS' AFTER LANDING ON MAINLAND

The Philadelphia Inquirer

PUBLIC LEDGER

An Independent Newspaper for All the People

FINAL CITY EDITION

CIRCULATION: August Average: Daily 486,207; Sunday 1,271,222

TUESDAY MORNING, SEPTEMBER 7, 1943

Vol. 229, No. 69

a b d e f g h ★

THREE CENTS

75 Killed, 120 Injured in Wreck Of Congressional Limited Here

Today

Refreshing Churchill
A Truly Great Man
Fundamentally Moral
Radiates Nobleness
Gives Meaning to War

By Walter Lippmann

MR. CHURCHILL lunched with the Washington correspondents last week. At the end there were few among us who would not have agreed with the Lord Mayor of the English city when he said in the dark days of 1940 that a speech by the Prime Minister is like a week-end in the fresh air.

I do not remember a time when Washington so badly needed fresh air. In fact, it needs a gale of wind out of heaven to blow away the dust, the cobwebs and the smells of intrigue, vanity, jealousy and vindictiveness.

Mr. Churchill's remarks, which were given as answers to questions from the correspondents, cannot be quoted. In fact, he revealed no secrets and said nothing that is not already known to the attentive reader of the newspapers. Yet, somehow, he restored and refreshed the faith and confidence of a corps of men whose duty it is to report and interpret the conduct of the war.

We may well ask why and we may ask how. For Mr. Churchill is not only the Prime Minister of Great Britain; he is also the one authentic example of greatness in a public man who moves among us. In these times which try men's souls, we are not equal, but we have to learn to be equal to them. We may then remember the profound saying of Whitehead that "moral education is impossible without the habitual vision of greatness." For Churchill's special gift, which enhances all the others, is his moral quality: he draws men out of their meaner selves and fascinates them with greatness.

The fascination of Churchill is not merely in his wit, or even in his humor, which keeps him so near to his fellowmen, or in his genius for war. We may find it is his eloquence provided we do not, as Cardinal Newman said, "consider fine writing to be . . a sort of ornament superinduced, or a luxury indulged in, by those who have time and inclination for such vanities."

Churchill's eloquence is the man himself, and the secret of

Continued on Page 19, Column 3

Allies Push Wedge 10 Miles Into Italy; Reds Win Konotop

Tuesday, Sept. 7, 1943

British and Canadian troops yesterday drove a wedge 10 miles inland in Italy, capturing the town of Santo Stefano on the slopes of Aspromonte in their deepest penetration to date. The Axis meanwhile declared Southern Calabria Province, which occupies the toe, had been evacuated.

Reports from Madrid said the American Seventh Army, under General Patton, had set sail from North Africa, apparently to strike a new blow at some other point of Axis-held territory.

The Germans were rushing defenses in Southern France, in anticipation of an invasion there, and evacuated the public from a lengthy coastal sector near Marseilles.

Russian troops surging ahead in the Ukraine captured Konotop, regarded as the key to the defenses of the great German base at Kiev, and headed for Bakhmach, major rail center 15 miles beyond. The fall of Stalino was imminent. Three hundred more towns fell to the Reds during the day.

British bombers roared back over Germany last night after a savage assault by American planes on Stuttgart, 60 miles southeast of the twin cities of Mannheim and Ludwigshaven, Rhine chemical center battered 12 hours earlier by the R. A. F. The Americans downed 70 Nazi fighter planes while losing 35.

In the Pacific theater, General MacArthur looked on from a bomber overhead as American paratroops landed behind the Japanese at Lae, New Guinea, cutting off the enemy's escape route via the Markham Valley and completing the entrapment of four divisions of 20,000 men in the Lae-Salamaua sector. The chutists met virtually no resistance. The main land drive gained 10 miles.

Patton's 7th Army Reported on Move; Naples Heavily Raided

Map on Page 2

By NOLAND NORGAARD

ALLIED HEADQUARTERS IN NORTH AFRICA, Sept. 6 (A. P.).—British and Canadian troops drove 10 miles inland from their 40-mile beachhead on the Italian toe through extensive demolitions and stood tonight on the forbidding slopes of Aspromonte, a 6000-foot mountain nearly halfway across the Calabrian Peninsula.

(A Berlin radio account quoting D. N. B. said the Axis had evacuated southern Calabria, the Italian province cradled in the toe.)

10 TOWNS FALL

Ten more towns fell and the total of prisoners swelled to 3000. Columns invading the European mainland were nearing Palmi in their drive north, while others curling around the south tip of the Italian toe ex-

Continued on Page 2, Column 4

Key to Kiev Taken, Stalino Capture Near; 300 More Towns Fall

Map on Page 2

By JAMES M. LONG

LONDON, Sept. 7 (Tuesday) (A. P.).—The Red Army captured the stronghold of Konotop yesterday in a broad sweep that put Soviet forces only 115 miles from the Ukrainian capital of Kiev, Moscow announced early today.

The fall of Stalino in the Donets Basin was expected momentarily.

A communique announced the seizure of Konotop and also Novye Mlyny, 25 miles to the northwest near the junction of the Desna and Seim Rivers, whose waters flow southwestward to empty into the Dnieper at Kiev, 115 miles from Novye Mlyny.

DRIVE FOR RAIL HUB

The Russians now are pursuing broken German troops west of Konotop, regarded as the key to the defenses of Kiev, toward Bakhmach,

Continued on Page 2, Column 1

PASSENGER ESCAPING FROM WRECKAGE OF THE LIMITED

A passenger emerging from one of the cars torn open in the wreck of the Congressional Limited, the crack Pennsylvania Railroad train, near Frankford Junction station yesterday. At least 75 were killed and more than 120 were injured in the disaster. The tragedy occurred when a journal box broke.

NAZIS FEAR INVASION OF SOUTH FRANCE

By WILLIAM SMITH WHITE

LONDON, Sept. 6 (A. P.).—The Germans, apparently suffering from a severe case of invasion nerves, were reported today rushing possible measures for the defense of the southern coast of France and other vulnerable spots along Europe's Mediterranean coastline.

German rumors of Allied intentions for the invasion of Adolf Hitler's "Fortress of Europe" flew so thick and fast that the British Broadcasting Corp. sent a warning

Continued on Page 2, Column 7

Girl With Legs Trapped Refuses to Give Up

By JAMES T. GILSON

This is the story of courage . . . the courage of Miss Christiana Nix, of Long Island City, a young woman passenger on the Congressional Limited.

For five long hours of agony, Miss Nix stood with her legs crushed in the mass of twisted steel that was once a smart, modern day coach of the train.

FREED AT 11 P. M.

She was finally freed at 11 P. M.—the last person known to be alive in the wreckage.

During that five hours her courage never faltered. She was given a blood transfusion and frequent doses of morphine, and at one time, while emergency squads were frantically applying acetelyne torches to the metal that held her in its clutches and firemen sprayed water on her body, she managed a grim smile and whispered:

"I'm Irish; I can take it."

Despite the agonizing pain, Miss Nix wouldn't give up. She remained

Continued on Page 7, Column 2

Six Cars Derailed In One of Nation's Worst Disasters

Full page of pictures on Page 18. Other stories of the wreck on Pages 7, 8, 9 and 10.

By FRED G. HYDE

Seventy-five persons were killed and more than 120 injured here last night when the Pennsylvania Railroad's crack Congressional Limited, bound from Washington to New York, left the rails near Frankford Junction in one of the Nation's worst rail disasters of recent years.

The flyer, which had not stopped in Philadelphia and was traveling at high speed, was derailed at 6.08 P. M., about 100 yards southwest of the junction station, by a burned-out journal box.

Six of its 16 cars, jammed to capacity with furlough-bound service men, Government officials and parents on their way home from holiday visits to service camps, piled up like match sticks at a point almost directly above Glenwood and Frankford aves., where the Pennsylvania's cut-off to the shore leaves the main line.

THIRD MAJOR WRECK IN FOUR MONTHS

The wreck, one of the most serious in the road's history, was the third major rail pile-up to occur in the East within the past four months. It blocked all through traffic in both directions, forcing the road to re-route both its north-south and east-west trains for more than four hours.

Many of the dead and injured were burned when one of the two coaches derailed caught fire after contact with live wires dangling from the wrecked overhead power system of the road.

The middle six cars of the express were hurled from the tracks after the engine and the first six cars had safely passed the cut-off.

The derailment occurred when a journal box—the housing for the tip of an axle—burned out in the forward truck of the seventh car, a crowded coach. The overheated axle broke and threw the entire car vertically into the air. Five other cars, including another coach, two diners, and two Pullmans, followed the coach from the tracks.

30 TO 40 DEAD REPORTED IN COACH

Five hours after the wreck, Dr. Saverio Brunetti, a police surgeon, went through the second of the coaches, and upon emerging estimated that 30 to 40 dead remained within.

At 3 A. M. this morning workmen, using acetylene torches and large derricks, were removing the last of the dead from the wreckage.

One victim, still alive, was Miss Christiana Nix, of Long Island City, N. Y., who was pinned from the waist down in the wreckage of the same car. She was given hypodermics to ease her pain while rescue workers began the slow task of cutting her loose with acetylene torches.

After she had been removed at 11 P. M., the coach,

Continued on Page 8, Column 1

U.S. Paratroops Cut Off 20,000 Japs at Lae

By C. YATES McDANIEL

ALLIED HEADQUARTERS IN THE SOUTHWEST PACIFIC, Sept. 7 (Tuesday) (A. P.).—American paratroops, watched from a Flying Fortress by General Douglas MacArthur as they floated down to the Markham Valley, have landed behind Lae, New Guinea, to complete the encirclement of 20,000 Japanese in the Lae-Salamaua sector.

These landings, achieved in considerable force Sunday, caught the Japanese completely by surprise even as a strong force of Australians, veterans of African battles, had done the day before by storming ashore above Lae while warships laid down a smokescreen.

TRAP 4 DIVISIONS

General MacArthur was in a bomber which was part of a huge formation that cruised over the new landing point. He saw the men seize strong positions without en-

Continued on Page 3, Column 4

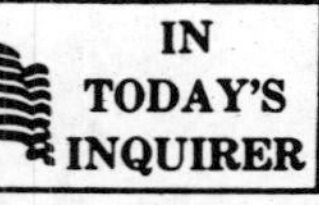

SPECIAL DEPARTMENTS

COLUMNS AND FEATURES

CHURCHILL URGES POST-WAR U.S. TIE

Illustrated on Page 4

CAMBRIDGE, Mass., Sept. 6 (U. P.). — Prime Minister Winston Churchill made a frank plea today for post-war British-American cooperation, military as well as political, as absolutely essential to the safety of the two nations and to world security.

Speaking in Harvard's Memorial Hall, where President James B. Conant awarded him the honorary degree of Doctor of Laws, Churchill said that the United States, "in many ways the leading community in the civilized world," could not hope to escape the responsibility which went with its power.

FIGHTING AS ONE NATION

At present, Churchill said, the United States and Britain were fighting as one nation with the British and American combined chiefs of staff committee under the leadership of himself and President Roosevelt and with General Dwight D.

Continued on Page 4, Column 4

Yanks Rip Stuttgart, Down 70 Nazi Planes

By WILLIAM B. DICKINSON

LONDON, Sept. 7 (Tuesday) (U. P.).—A large formation of United States heavy bombers yesterday attacked Stuttgart, Germany, 60 miles southeast of Mannheim-Ludwigoshaven, which the Royal Air Force had bombed Sunday night, while Allied medium and fighter-bombers attacked railway yards, airfields and docks in northern France, a communique revealed today.

In the wake of the Stuttgart attack, R.A.F. heavy bombers roared over Germany again last night.

The big American bombers shot down 70 enemy fighters in the raid on Stuttgart, it was revealed. In the attacks on industrial centers of southwestern Germany and in northern France, 35 U. S. planes and four Spitfire fighters were lost.

HUGE NIGHT ARMADA

Observers described the streams of R.A.F. night bombers, which had headed for the continent shortly after dark, as one of the largest night bomber forces ever to leave Britain.

Exact location of the night R.A.F. target was not disclosed immediately, but there were indications from Swiss sources that Southwest

Continued on Page 3, Column 3

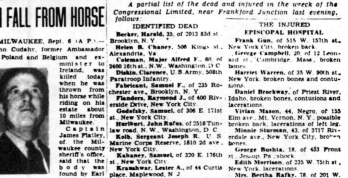

Eastman Asks Parties To Meet in Chicago

DENVER, Sept. 6 (A. P.).—Postmaster General Frank C. Walker said in an interview today that the Office of Defense Transportation has requested that both the Democratic and Republican national conventions be held in Chicago next year because of its central location.

Walker, who is also Democratic national chairman, disclosed that Joseph B. Eastman, director of ODT, had written him and Harrison E. Spangler, Republican national chairman, about the matter.

WEATHER FORECAST

Philadelphia and Vicinity: Continued warm this morning, followed by showers and possible thundershowers this afternoon, cooler by evening.

Sun rises 6.32 A.M. Sets 7.26 P.M.
Moon rises 2.09 P.M. Sets 12.18 A.M.

JOHN CUDAHY KILLED IN FALL FROM HORSE

MILWAUKEE, Sept. 6 (A. P.).—John Cudahy, former Ambassador to Poland and Belgium and ex-minister to Ireland, was killed today when he was thrown from his horse while riding on his estate about 10 miles from Milwaukee.

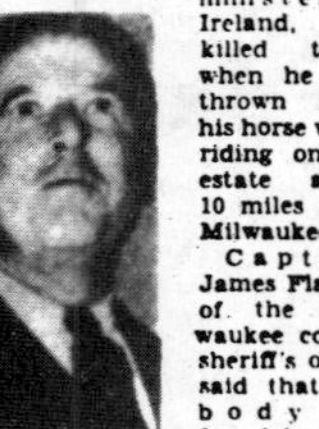

JOHN CUDAHY

Captain James Flatley, of the Milwaukee county sheriff's office, said that the body was found by Earl L. Kramer, of Racine, Wis., who was visiting the estate caretaker. He said Kramer related that he saw a riderless horse and hurried to the spot and found Cudahy's body.

PRONOUNCED DEAD

Dr. T. R. Murphy, of the County General Hospital staff, who sped to the estate, pronounced the former diplomat dead of a broken neck. The

Continued on Page 28, Column 1

List of Dead, Injured

A partial list of the dead and injured in the wreck of the Congressional Limited, near Frankford Junction last evening, follows:

IDENTIFIED DEAD

Becker, Harold, 35, of 2013 83d st., Brooklyn, N. Y.
Helen B. Chaney, 506 Kings st., Alexandria, Va.
Coleman, Major Alfred F., 60, of 2400 16th st., N.W., Washington, D. C.
Diskin, Clarence, U. S. Army, 508th Paratroop Infantry.
Fabricant, Samuel F., of 235 Rochester ave., Brooklyn, N. Y.
Flanders, Raymond J., of 400 Riverside Drive, New York City.
Godofsky, Samuel, of 306 E. 171st st., New York City.
Hurlburt, John Rufus, of 2518 Tunlaw road, N. W., Washington, D. C.
Kolb, Sergeant Joseph R. U. S. Marine Corps Reserve, 1810 2d ave., New York City.
Kahaney, Samuel, of 320 E. 176th st., New York City.
Krauwhar, Lester A., of 44 Curtis place, Maplewood, N. J.
Kusher, Henry, soldier from Camp Pickett, Va.
Oberdorf, Calvin, of 1301 15th st., N. W., Washington, D. C.
Parkin, Private John, of Rockaway, Jamaica, N. Y.
Robinson, Alonzo, Brooklyn, N. Y.
Ryan, Private George, of Rochester, N. Y.
Sugarman, Isadore R., of 169 198th st., St. Albans, N. Y.
Ward, Grace, of 527 Kingston st., Brooklyn.
Wechsler, Harry, of 4574 Bedford ave., Brooklyn, N. Y.

THE INJURED
EPISCOPAL HOSPITAL

Frank Gun, of 515 W. 157th st., New York City, broken back.
George Campbell, 20, of 12 Leonard st., Cambridge, Mass., broken bones.
Harriet Warren, 35 W. 90th st., New York, broken bones and contusions.
Daniel Brockway, of Priest River, Idaho, broken bones, contusions and lacerations.
Vivian Mason, 44, Negro, of 155 Elm ave., Mt. Vernon, N. Y., shock.
Minnie Sturman, 43, of 3717 Riverdale ave., New York City, broken bones.
George Bushta, 18, of 433 Front st., Jessup, Pa., shock.
Edith Morrison, of 235 W. 75th st., New York, lacerations.
Mrs. Bertha Rafky, 78, of 201 W. 89th st., New York City, shock.
Miss Hilda Rafky, 28, daughter of Bertha, shock.
Rose Haken, 47, of 815 E. 14th st., Brooklyn, N. Y., shock.
Joseph Haken, 54, husband of Rose, shock.
Frank Levy, of 2265 E. 23d st., Brooklyn, N. Y., fractured spine.
Marie Reeves, 29, of 414 7th ave., New York City, shock.
Barbara Petersen, of 129 Derby st., Valley Stream, N. Y., leg injuries.

Continued on Page 9, Column 3

BRIDGE

Attendance Marks Broken At Bridge Tourney Here

By Bennett L. Disbrow

Attendance records were shattered last week-end when the Atlantic City tournament was held at the Ritz-Carlton Hotel. This tournament has been transferred to Philadelphia for the duration of the emergency.

Walter N. Connors and Henry A. Smith and Mrs. Ralph C. Young and Edward Cohn scored victories for Philadelphia in the open and mixed pair events, but the two other events were won by players from other localities. Mrs. Bertine Teichman, Roselle Park, N. J., and Mrs. Mabel Ulbrich, Rahway, N. J., who won the women's pairs, were the women's national champions in 1935.

RESULTS

WOMEN'S PAIRS: 1. Mrs. Bertine Teichman-Mrs. Mabel Ulbrich; 2. Mrs. A. M. Sobel-Mrs. Paula Bacher; 3. (Tie) Mrs. Dorothy Slaughenhaupt-Mrs. Georgene Vancourt; Mrs. Olive Peterson-Mrs. Benjamin Golder; 5. Mrs. I. M. Hawley-Mrs. J. O. Gaynor; 6. Mrs. L. C. Robinson-Mrs. Albert Schmuckler; 7. Mrs. H. R. Grove-Mrs. Galoway Morris; 8. Mrs. G. H. Nagle-Miss Louise VanZandt; 9. Mrs. Mark Godfrey-Mrs. R. N. Ligget; 10. Mrs. Samuel Marshall-Mrs. P. M. Hart.

MIXED PAIRS: 1. Mrs. Ralph C. Young-Edward Cohn; 2. Mrs. C. M. Dinker-Michael Levinton; 3. Mrs. Olga Hilliard-C. B. Hawley; 4. Mr. and Mrs. George Kessler, Jr.; 5. (Tie) Mrs. Henry Sabott-Samuel Wessel; 6. Mr. and Mrs. Albert Schmukler; 7. (Tie) Mrs. W. S. Patton-E. C. Brown; 8. Miss Helen Costello-Mr. David Bayless; 9. Mr. and Mrs. C. C. Wallace; 10. (Tie) Mrs. Marie Basher-David Warner; 11. Miss Isabel Reilly-R. A. Miller.

OPEN PAIRS: 1. Walter N. Connors-Henry A. Smith; 2. Sidney Silodor-Harold Frank; 3. Mrs. A. M. Sobel-C. H. Goren; 4. J. J. Buckley-Henry Greer; 5. Bertram Lebhar-Peter Leventritt; 6. S. L. Harris-E. Smith; 7. E. G. Scheck-E. Thiemer; 8. Alvin Goodman-Simon Becker; 9. S. O. Fenkel-Samuel Wessel; 10. Mrs. Albert Schmukler-Mrs. L. C. Robinson.

TEAM-OF-FOUR: 1. H. Karp, J. Sanford, W. Samson, E. Rosemerin; 2. Mr. and Mrs. Ralph Wooley, Mrs. Paul Bacher, M. Levin; 3. Mrs. B. M. Golder, C. J. Solomon, Mrs. A. M. Sobel, C. H. Goren; 4. (Tie) John Crawford, L. J. Golder, Sidney Silodor, E. G. Ellenbogen; Mrs. Nathan Agran, S. O. Fenkel, Simon Becker, Alvin Goodman.

BACKFIRE

One of the deals played in the team-of-four tournament at the Ritz-Carlton on Sunday offered both a tragic and a comedy aspect to one of the competing teams. The unusual situation was created when the East player made a bid out of turn while slightly drowsy.

Both sides vulnerable.
South dealer.

NORTH
♠ 8
♡ 7
◇ Q 4
♣ A Q J 10 9 6 4 3 2

WEST	EAST
♠ A 10 7 3	♠ K J 9 4 2
♡ 10 5 2	♡ K J 9 6 3
◇ A K J 9 8	◇ 10 6 3
♣ K	♣ none

SOUTH
♠ Q 6 5
♡ A J 8 4
◇ 7 5 2
♣ 8 7 5

South opened the bidding with a pass, and East, although it was West's turn to bid, stirred in his slumber and bid a spade.

The tournament director, called to adjust the irregularity, ruled that the bidding should revert to the proper player and that East and West were barred from further bidding, with the additional stipulation that should North or South secure the contract, the declarer could call the lead of any suit.

With West forced out of the auction, it was now North's turn to call and, after a little thought, he decided that his nine clubs would produce a game in no-trump if he could secure the lead. So North brilliantly bid three no-trump and exercised his privilege to call the lead by directing East to lead a club! But East had no clubs to lead and the penalty was cancelled!

Now with the right to lead any suit that he desired, East aroused from his lethargy and pushed out a small spade. West played the 10, cashed his ace and returned the suit, and five spade tricks were won. Then a diamond lead produced five more tricks to make a total of 10. Slow curtain.

THE JUNTO RESUMES

The Junto, Philadelphia's non-profit Adult School, will reopen with a fifth semester next week. The school, under the active direction of Dr. Albert A. Owens, president; George F. Kearney, treasurer, and Philip Klein, secretary and business manager, will offer a schedule of 24 popular subjects, ranging from psychology and Spanish to dancing and contract bridge.

The bridge classes, in two divisions, will be conducted by B. L. Disbrow, bridge editor of The Inquirer, on Monday and Wednesday evenings, 8 to 10 o'clock, at the Mercantile Library, 16 S. 10th st. A course for intermediate players will begin on Sept. 27 and will continue for 10 Mondays, starting Sept. 29. Attractive to the members will be the opportunity to play while learning. Registrations may be presented in person at the library, or be mailed to the Junto at that address.

TOURNAMENTS

LOCUST TROPHY (2 sessions): 1. Robson-Short, 450; 2. Mrs. Golder-Solomon, 446; 3. Fenkel-Kaufmann, 423; 4. Becker-Warner, 422½; 5. Mrs. Sabott-Mrs. Shmukler, 411; 6. Brown-Smedley, 394; 7. Mrs. Robson-Mrs. Taylor, 391½; 8. Mrs. Sondheim-Wessel, 371½; 9. Mrs. Groves-Lang, 370; 10. Mrs. Lull, 367. Average, 351.

DUPLICATE WINNERS
Thursday, September 9

GERMANTOWN Y.M.C.A.—Dr. H. C. Hary-R. B. Schulz; Mrs. R. A. McGuigan-Mrs. E. B. Smedley.

VANCOURT—Mrs. Lee Banville-Mrs. Georgene VanCourt; Mrs. Juanita Eagle-R. R. Rodewald.

VICTORY—Mrs. J. C. Kendall-Mrs. F.

(Continued on Page 12, Col. 7)

ENGAGEMENTS

Miss Lovatt Engaged to R. O. Bracken

Nancy Rohner To Become Bride Of John Ludwig

Bracken-Lovatt

Mr. and Mrs. John J. Lovatt, of Cynwyd, announce the engagement of their daughter, Miss Eleanor G. Lovatt, to Lieutenant Robert O. Bracken, U. S. N. R., son of Mr. and Mrs. Myron T. Bracken, of Piedmont, Calif.

Ludwig-Rohner

Mr. and Mrs. Henry J. Rohner, of Wyndmoor, announce the engagement of their daughter, Miss Nancy Jane Rohner, to Mr. John McEntyre Ludwig, U. S. N. R., son of Mr. and Mrs. Norman S. Ludwig, of Rhawnhurst.

Houston-Rabe

Mr. and Mrs. Louise W. Rabe, of Llanerch, announce the engagement of their daughter, Miss Mary Elaine Rabe, to Mr. Stanley Lyon Houston, son of Mr. and Mrs. Paul Houston, of Longmeadow, Mass.

Clague-McIlvaine

Mr. and Mrs. Reuben Watson McIlvaine, of Baederwood, announce the engagement of their daughter, Miss Eleanor Virginia McIlvaine, to Corporal Donald Herbert Clague, son of Mr. and Mrs. Asa Clague, of Glens Falls, N. Y.

Weighell-Coyne

Mr. and Mrs. Thomas P. Coyne, of Chestnut Hill, announce the engagement of Mr. Coyne's daughter, Miss Agnes R. M. Coyne, of "Merrill Farms," Ambler, to Surgeon Lieutenant Walter K. Weighell, R. N. V. R., son of Mrs. Henry Weighell, of "Mayville," Okehampton, Devon, England.

Gillispie-Vanderbreggen

Mr. and Mrs. C. Vanderbreggen, of Norwood, announce the engagement of their daughter, Miss Dorothy Vanderbreggen, to Mr. Clarence Gillispie, son of Mr. and Mrs. Harry Gillispie, of Roxborough. No date has been set for the wedding.

Duryea-Beck

Mr. and Mrs. Archibald E. Beck, of Hopedale, Mass., announce the engagement of their daughter, Roberta Ellen Beck, to Private Howard E. Duryea, Jr., son of Mr. and Mrs. Howard E. Duryea, of this city

Duker-Weatherly

Mr. and Mrs. J. Lawson Weatherly, of Ardmore, have announced the engagement of their daughter, Miss Barbara Macpherson Weatherly, to Captain John Edward Duker, Jr., U. S. A., son of Mrs. John Edward Duker, of Baltimore, and the late Mr. Duker. The wedding will take place on Saturday, Sept. 25.

Rullman-Gieg

Mr. and Mrs. L. Frederick Gieg, of Rosemont, announce the engagement of their daughter, Miss Margaret E. Gieg, to Lieutenant (j.g.) William H. Rullman, U.S.N.R., son of Mr. and Mrs. Harry G. Rullman, of Annapolis, Md.

Miss Gieg is a graduate of Connecticut College for Women. Lieutenant Rullman is a graduate of Rensselaer Polytechnic Institute.

Mackinney-Wilson

Dr. and Mrs. G. Lloyd Wilson, of Roxborough, announce the engagement of their daughter, Miss Marjorie Eleanor Wilson, to Charles Cyrus Mackinney, Private First Class, Medical Corps, U.S.A., son of Mrs. William H. Mackinney, of Roxborough, and the late Dr. Mackinney.

Miss Wilson is a graduate of the University of Pennsylvania. Private Mackinney, who is a graduate of Dartmouth College, is attending Medical School at Northwestern University, Chicago.

Singer-Lockhart

Mr. and Mrs. Herbert Garrison Lockhart, of Linwood, N. J., formerly of this city, announce the engagement of their daughter, Miss Janey Doris Lockhart, to Dr. Arthur Gregg Singer, Jr., son of Mrs. Arthur Gregg Singer, of Frankford, and the late Mr. Singer.

Mulford-Sears

Mrs. Cecilia D. Sears, of 6201 Wayne ave., announces the engagement of her daughter, Miss Dorothy J. Sears, to Mr. Frank B. Mulford, Jr., of this city and New York. The wedding will take place in November.

Reasor-Benjamin

Rev. and Mrs. Charles Dow Benjamin, of Media, announce the engagement of their daughter, Miss Janet Elizabeth Benjamin, to Ensign Orian Samuel Reasor, U.S.N.R., son of Mr. and Mrs. Orian Samuel Reasor, of Manoa.

Miss Benjamin enters law school at the University of Pennsylvania in November, after completing her prelaw work at Temple University. Mr. Reasor attended the Drexel Institute of Technology.

Mrs. Rader at Home

Mrs. Archibald Fleming Rader returned early in the week to "Alarden," her home in Haverford, after spending two months at North Conway, N. H.

Word Game

Today's Test—Glossopathy

(Glossopathy: Glo sop a thi. Any disease of the tongue.)

Average mark — 80 words
Time limit — 40 minutes

At least 87 common English words of four or more letters can be found in the letters in GLOSSOPATHY. Can you find as many or more?

(Answer elsewhere on this page)

Word Game Answer

Yanks Lose Two; 26,615 See Detroit Lions Win, 35-17

Senators Capture Pair; Streak Reaches Nine

Indians, Cubs, Giants, Pirates Also Win Two; White Sox, Browns Split

By GEORGE BUTZ

Just when the Yankees were figuring they would clinch the American League pennant about Wednesday, they had their plans altered yesterday by Washington's Senators. Before a howling hometown throng of 30,851, the Senators stretched their victory streak to nine straight, by sweeping a double header from the Yanks, 3-2, in the 10-inning opener and 5-1 in the nightcap.

With 14 games to be played, the Yankees are leading the Senators in the unfinished American League race by nine games. However, they need five more victories before they can start grooming to meet the Cardinals in the "one-trip" World Series, starting Oct. 5.

CARDS DROP PAIR

In other American League games, Cleveland won both games from Detroit, 6-2 and 1-0, while St. Louis and Chicago divided, the Browns taking the first, 7-4, and the White Sox, the final, 6-1.

Despite the fact they're the National League kingpins, the Cards were clawed twice by the Chicago Cubs, 6-0 and 10-9; the Giants thrashed the Dodgers in both games, 3-1 and 7-4, while the Pirates grabbed a pair from Cincinnati, 10-3 and 2-1.

MUST WIN 12 GAMES

Through their twin triumph, the Nats earned a split, 11-11, with the Yanks in the season's series.

Of course, the Senators only have a mathematical chance at the pennant, facing the assignment of winning all twelve of their remaining games. Early Wynn, the Nats' right hander, was in rare form in the opener, allowing the Yanks five hits for his 17th victory and besting Spud Chandler in the duel. In the second game, Haefner was real stingy, giving up a single and a triple.

POWELL'S HIT DECIDES

Going into overtime, thanks to Bob Johnson's triple and Jake Early's single to first in the ninth, the Nats clinched the verdict in the tenth frame of the opener on Jake Powell's ringing single, which admitted George Case. In the final, Washington took the lead at the start with a cluster of three runs. The Yanks' lone marker was made by Frank Crosetti's single and Charley Keller's three-baser.

Jim Bagby turned in a two-hit job to win Cleveland's first game, while the Indians went on the warpath for a rally in the fifth to land the second and concluding game at Cleveland this year. Lefty Al Smith pitched the nightcap and shared

Continued on Page 22, Column 2

A's Victors, 6-1, After 14-0 Loss

Mackmen 'Clinch' Last Place by Dropping Opener

By STAN BAUMGARTNER

The Athletics clinched last place in the American League yesterday, losing the first game of a double-header to the Red Sox at Shibe Park 14-0. The Mackmen made it mathematically impossible for the New Englanders to usurp that position.

The A's, however, came back to win the second game, 6-1, and give them an even break in the season's series, 11-11.

ROOKIE STALLER STARS

Fine work by Rookie George Staller, both afield and at bat, marked the even split. In the first game Staller made three hits in four times at bat, while in the second he collected one safety in three trips to the plate, raising his batting average to .391. He also scored two runs and drove in another.

The first game was a walkaway for the Red Sox. Boston hammered Roger Wolff, Orrie Arntzen and Louis Ciola for 21 hits, including six doubles and a triple to break an eight-game losing streak. The Red Sox scored four runs in the first inning and Joe Dobson, their right-hand flinger, was never pressed the rest of the way.

It was Dobson's seventh victory and Wolff's 13th defeat.

The second game was closer, but the A's finished in front with plenty to spare. Jesse Flores pitched splendid eight-hit ball to gain his 11th victory against 14 defeats.

FIRST GAME

BOSTON

	*Bat. Av.	Ab.	r.	h.	rbi.	o.	a.	e.
Newsome, ss	[illegible]							
Metkovich, cf	[illegible]							
Garrison, rf	[illegible]							
Doerr, 2b	[illegible]							
Tabor, 3b	[illegible]							
McBride, rf	[illegible]							
Lupien, 1b	[illegible]							
Partee, c	[illegible]							
Dobson, p	[illegible]							
Totals		45	14	21	12	27	11	0

ATHLETICS

	*Bat. Av.	Ab.	r.	h.	rbi.	o.	a.	e.
Mayo, 3b	[illegible]							
White, cf	[illegible]							
Welaj, rf	[illegible]							
Estalella, lf	[illegible]							
Siebert, 1b	[illegible]							
Staller, lf	[illegible]							
Wagner, c	[illegible]							
Hall, 2b	[illegible]							
Suder, 2b	[illegible]							
Wolff, p	[illegible]							
Arntzen, p	[illegible]							
A-Blackburn	[illegible]							
Ciola, p	[illegible]							
Totals		31	0	5	0	27	10	2

A-Batted for Arntzen in sixth.

Boston — [illegible] —14
Athletics — [illegible] — 0

[illegible]

*-Batting average, 1943.

SECOND GAME

BOSTON

	*Bat. Av.	Ab.	r.	h.	rbi.	o.	a.	e.
Newsome, ss	[illegible]							
Metkovich, cf	[illegible]							
Garrison, rf	[illegible]							
Doerr, 2b	[illegible]							
Tabor, 3b	[illegible]							
McBride, rf	[illegible]							
Lupien, 1b	[illegible]							
Doyle	[illegible]							
Partee, c	[illegible]							
Woods, p	[illegible]							
Ryba, p	[illegible]							
A-Partee	[illegible]							
B-Lazor	[illegible]							
Brown, p	[illegible]							
C-Fox	[illegible]							
Totals		35	1	8		24	13	2

ATHLETICS

	*Bat. Av.	Ab.	r.	h.	rbi.	o.	a.	e.
Mayo, 3b	[illegible]							
White, cf	[illegible]							
Welaj, rf	[illegible]							
Estalella, lf	[illegible]							
Siebert, 1b	[illegible]							
Staller, lf	[illegible]							
Hall, 2b	[illegible]							
Swift, c	[illegible]							
Flores, p	[illegible]							
Totals			6			27	11	3

A-Batted for Woods in sixth.
B-Batted for Ryba in seventh.
C-Batted for Brown in ninth.

Boston — 0 0 0 1 0 0 0 0 0 — 1
Athletics — 0 0 0 2 0 3 1 0 x — 6

Two-base hit: McBride. Three-base hit: White. Stolen base: Hall. Sacrifice: Estalella. Double plays: Doerr to Lupien; Brown to Newsome to Lupien. Left on bases: Boston, 9; Athletics, 6. Base on balls: Off Woods, 4; Flores, 2; Ryba, 2. Struck out: By Flores, 6; Woods, 1; Brown, 1. Hits: Off Woods, 1 in 5 innings; Ryba, 3 in 1. Wild pitch: Flores. Losing pitcher: Woods. Umpires: Grieve and McGowan. Time of game, 2.01. Attendance, 8655.

*-Batting average, 1943.

SOUTHEAST CATHOLIC PASS FAILS—AL CAPPER, ST. THOMAS MORE, BATS DOWN AERIAL
Alert back grounded pass intended for Ray Henry's outstretched hands at Municipal Stadium yesterday; McCaney, South Catholic, is shown at right.

Phils Lose, 3-2, 6-5; Drop Final in 14th

Special to The Inquirer

BOSTON, Sept. 19.—Elmer "Butch" Nieman's homer in the 14th inning of the second game, with Kirby Farrell on base, gave the Boston Braves a 6-5 victory, after they had won the first, 3-2, for their fifth straight over the Phillies. The tragic part of it, from the Phillies' standpoint, was Ron Northey's 15th homer of the season in the same inning had given the Phillies a 5-4 lead, breaking a tie which had obtained from the ninth inning.

Newt Kimball, who had replaced Al Gerheauser in the 10th, was the victim.

AL JAVERY VICTOR

It was the National League finale in Boston. Six thousand and fifty-four die-hard fans sat in on the obsequies and felt well repaid for the four hour and 59 minutes of good and bad baseball.

Al Javery, who defeated the Phillies several days ago with a one-hit performance, rang up his 16th victory of the campaign.

The North Oxford boy would have won the game in regulation innings but for some loose playing on the part of his mates who had five boots for their contribution to his troubles.

By taking today's double-header, the Braves broke even over the season with the Phillies, each club having won 11 games.

Box-Scores

FIRST GAME

PHILLIES

	*Bat. Av.	Ab.	r.	h.	rbi.	o.	a.	e.
Triplett, lf	.282	[illegible]						
May, 3b	.262	[illegible]						
Wasdell, 1b	.264	[illegible]						
Adams, cf	.251	[illegible]						
Northey, rf	.276	[illegible]						
Stewart, ss	.218	[illegible]						
Seminick, c	.216	[illegible]						
Hamrick, 2b	.219	[illegible]						
Kraus, p	W10-L13	[illegible]						
Totals		31	2	5	2	26	9	2

BOSTON

	*Bat. Av.	Ab.	r.	h.	rbi.	o.	a.	e.
Burns, 3b	[illegible]							
Holmes, cf	[illegible]							
Workman, rf	[illegible]							
Farrell, 1b	[illegible]							
Masi, c	[illegible]							
Ross, lf	[illegible]							
Wietelmann, ss	[illegible]							
Rayan, p	[illegible]							
Tobin, p	[illegible]							
Totals		37	3	12	2	27	13	0

xTwo out when winning run scored.

Phillies — [illegible] — 2
Boston — [illegible] — 3

Two-base hit: Tobin. Home runs: Northey and Seminick. Stolen bases: Masi, Workman. Sacrifices: Workman. Double plays: Wasdell, unassisted; May to Hamrick to Wasdell. Left on bases: Boston, 12; Phillies, 4. Base on balls: Off Tobin, 1; Kraus, 5. Struck out: By Tobin, 9; Kraus, 5. Umpires: Conlan, Barr and Jorda. Time of game, 1.52.

*-Batting average, 1943.

SECOND GAME

PHILLIES

	*Bat. Av.	Ab.	r.	h.	rbi.	o.	a.	e.
Triplett, lf	[illegible]							
May, 3b	[illegible]							
Wasdell, 1b	[illegible]							
Adams, cf	[illegible]							
Northey, rf	[illegible]							
Stewart, ss	[illegible]							
Seminick, c	[illegible]							
Hamrick, 2b	[illegible]							
Lee, p	[illegible]							
A-Rowe	[illegible]							
Gerheauser, p	[illegible]							
B-Klein	[illegible]							
Kimball, p	[illegible]							
Totals		52	5	[illegible]		40	18	3

BOSTON

	*Bat. Av.	Ab.	r.	h.	rbi.	o.	a.	e.
Burns, 3b	[illegible]							
Holmes, cf	[illegible]							
Workman, rf	[illegible]							
Farrell, 1b	[illegible]							
Poland, c	[illegible]							
Ross, lf	[illegible]							
Nieman, lf	[illegible]							
B-Masi	[illegible]							
Wietelmann, ss	[illegible]							
Ryan, 2b	[illegible]							
Javery, p	[illegible]							
Totals		[illegible]	6	12		42	9	5

r-One out when winning run scored.
A-Batted for Lee in ninth.
B-Batted for Ross in ninth.
C-Batted for Gerheauser in tenth.

Phillies — [illegible] — 5
Boston — [illegible] — 6

Two-base hits: Ross, Northey. Home runs: Northey, Nieman. Stolen bases: Wasdell, Adams, Wietelmann. Sacrifices: Javery, Seminick, Poland. Double plays: Holmes to Poland; May to Stewart to Wasdell. Left on bases: Phillies, 11; Boston, 13. Base on balls: Off Lee, 1; Javery, 6; Kimball, 1. Struck out: By Javery, 13; Lee, 6. Hits: Off Lee, 6 in 8 innings; Gerheauser, 3 in 1; Kimball, 3 in 4 1-3. Losing pitcher: Kimball. Umpires: Barr, Jorda and Conlan. Time of game, 3.07. Attendance, 6054.

*-Batting average, 1943.

Toronto Reaches Final Playoff

By United Press

The Syracuse Chiefs blanked Newark, 4-0, at Newark yesterday to take a 3-2 lead in the first round of the International League playoffs and now need only one victory to win the series and play the Toronto Maple Leafs in the final round. Toronto went into the finals by winning four straight from Montreal, the last yesterday at Montreal, 5-1.

Tomas de la Cruz turned in a masterful 3-hit game for Syracuse and Dutch Mele hit two homers to pace the Chiefs. Jim Hopper only allowed Montreal four hits as Toronto won easily.

Baseball Facts

NATIONAL LEAGUE

YESTERDAY'S RESULTS

Boston 3, PHILLIES 2, (1st).
Boston 6, PHILLIES 5, (2d, 14 innings).
Chicago 6, St. Louis 0, (1st).
Chicago 10, St. Louis 9, (2d).
New York 3, Brooklyn 1, (1st).
New York 7, Brooklyn 4, (2d).
Pittsburgh 10, Cincinnati 3, (1st).
Pittsburgh 2, Cincinnati 1, (2d).

STANDING OF THE TEAMS

	W.	L.	P.C.	G.B.	T.P.
St. Louis	94	46	.671	--	14
Brooklyn	76	64	.543	18	14
Cincinnati	74	64	.536	19	16
Pittsburgh	76	68	.528	20	20
Chicago	63	75	.457	30	16
Boston	63	75	.457	30	16
PHILLIES	60	81	.426	34	13
New York	53	86	.381	40	15

G.B.—Games behind leader.
T.P.—To play.

Today's Schedule

No games scheduled.

AMERICAN LEAGUE

YESTERDAY'S RESULTS

Boston 14, ATHLETICS 0 (1st).
ATHLETICS 6, Boston 1 (2d).
Washington 3, New York 2 (1st, 10 innings).
Washington 5, New York 1 (2d).
Cleveland 1, Detroit 0 (1st).
Cleveland 6, Detroit 2 (2d).
St. Louis 7, Chicago 4 (1st).
Chicago 6, St. Louis 1 (2d).

STANDING OF THE TEAMS

	W.	L.	P.C.	G.B.	T.P.
New York	88	52	.629		14
Washington	80	62	.563	9	12
Cleveland	76	64	.543	12	14
Detroit	72	69	.511	16½	13
Chicago	70	70	.500	18	14
St. Louis	66	74	.471	22	14
Boston	63	78	.447	25½	13
ATHLETICS	46	92	.333	41	16

G.B.—Games behind leader.
T.P.—To play.

Today's Schedule

No games scheduled.

Continued on Page 22, Column 2

Dunn, Partner Deadlock in Golf

Bob Dunn and Walter Huntzinger tied with Bill Medford and Bud Miller for the low net prize in the 36-hole Springhaven Country Club invitation best ball of partners handicap golf tournament yesterday.

Dunn, Springhaven and Huntzinger, Bala, former University of Pennsylvania and New York Giants pitcher, posted a net score of 65-60—125 for the two-day competition. Medford, Springhaven, and Miller unattached, had led on opening day with a 59 but fell back to a net 66 yesterday for 125.

FIVE UNDER PAR

Dunn and Huntzinger had a round yesterday of 34-31—65, five strokes under par, the best of the day. Their handicap of five strokes gave them a net of 60.

Medford and Miller were around the course in 43-39—82. A handicap of 16 strokes earned them a net score of 66.

PLATT-McCULLOUGH WIN

The 36-hole low gross prize was captured by J. Wood Platt, Springhaven, Philadelphia Amateur champion, and W. B. "Duff" McCullough, Huntington Valley, former runner-up for the National Amateur crown, with 67-66—133, seven strokes under par. Their net score was the same as their handicap was zero. They beat Dunn and Huntzinger by two strokes.

McCullough was the star of the team on Saturday, but yesterday Platt came in o his own and played a fine round of 36-32—68, two strokes under par, while McCullough had 36-38—74.

HERMAN-HOUDRY SECOND

The second low net prize for the 36-hole route went to Norman Herman, Springhaven, and Jack Houdry, Merion, with 64-65—129. The Saturday low net prize winners were Walter Reus, of Springhaven, and Vance Boyd, Llanerch, 63; C. L. Morris, Springhaven, and Joseph A. DeBerardinis, Tully-Secane, 63, and Larry McIntyre and Joe Gallagher, Springhaven, 64.

Sunday's low net winners were A. Brown and Chris Hanway, both of Springhaven, 64; Will Gunn and Allen McCone, both Springhaven, 65; John McCurdy, Springhaven, and Art Cardwell, McCall Field, 65, and George Zahn, of Springhaven, and Hillman Zahn, Charlotte N. C., 65.

Continued on Page 23, Column 5

Gaeta Captures Westinghouse Golf

Joe Gaeta, former South Philadelphia champion, won the Westinghouse A. A. golf tournament yesterday with a 34-36-70, at the Tully-Secane Country Club. He scored three birds.

Joseph A. DeBerardinis was next with 37-36-73. Steve Daly, former pro at the Berkshire C. C. in Reading, was next, 39-39-78. DeBerardinis was low net, 73-6-69.

Shamrocks Split

Shamrocks captured the first game of the twin bill from the Black Meteors yesterday, 5-2, and lost the second, 6-4, at 26th st. and Snyder ave.

Answer to Critics

Princeton Convinced Football Also Serves

By ART MORROW
Inquirer Sports Reporter

PRINCETON, Sept. 19.

THAT natural phenomenon which Arnold Bennett, among others, has called the Solar System had caused the warmth of day to be subsiding even before the sooth-sayer spoke:

"You know," he said, "we had a canvass of our Philadelphia alumni, and one of them said that we had made a mistake even trying to put on a football program."

It seemed like a mistake, too. Shadows were lengthening and the breezes were quite penetrating across University Field. It was no pleasure watching, much less playing, football on a day like this. But there were over 100 undergraduates, mostly Naval and Marine trainees, out there battering each other with a will that would lead one Adolf Hitler to envy. More than 100 young men were battering each other, not merely from a mere sense of duty to harden themselves for more crucial battles to come, but from a simple love of sport.

WAR COMES FIRST

A baseball cap hid the thinning hair of the director, but the sooth-sayer spoke again: "Naturally," he remarked with a dignity only bank presidents or bookmakers can hope to assume, "we paid no attention to the disgruntled Philadelphia alumnus."

One hardly needed the sooth-sayer's word for it. One hardly needed Coach Harry Mahnken's word for it. But the director spoke:

"Naturally," he said, "we can hardly hope to have our old teams back again. This is war—and that comes first. But we feel there is a definite place for football in war, and so we determined to have a team. The team may not be so good as some we have had in the past—but it will be a team, and a fighting one, at that.

IT'S SHORT ANYWAY

"We had few of our 1942 veterans back; as far as Princeton itself was concerned, there seemed little reason for our continuing in football. But most of us were convinced that there is no better athletic training than football for either war or just general conditioning. So we elected to continue. We may not play our old brand of the sport; we may be far inferior; but I am not worrying. I feel that in fielding a team, we will have done our best—and if you could notice the spirit of our players, you would agree with me.

"That is what makes me think we have followed the right course—the spirit of the players."

Even as he spoke, Mahnken—his 150-pound football teams won five Eastern Intercollegiate League championships in six years—was watching a group of 40 Navy V-12 freshmen go through maneuvers on a far side of the gridiron. The V-12 freshmen, just out of high schools, are ineligible for intercollegiate sports until Oct. 23, which

Continued on Page 23, Column 6

Odell to Captain Penn Saturday

Robert H. Odell, veteran back who is awaiting his call for active service as a naval aviation cadet, has been named captain of the Pennsylvania footbll team for the game with Princeton on Saturday afternoon. George Munger, head coach of the Red and Blue, announced this yesterday.

Odell will act in place of Cleo Calcagni, who was elected captain of the team at the conclusion of the 1942 season but who is now in the Marine unit at Cornell. There is a possibility that Calcagni may play against his old teammate, Thanksgiving Day.

FIRST SINCE 1936

In 1918 the late Bob Folwell appointed a captain for each game played during that wartime season. The only other season in which a captain was selected for each game occurred in 1936. At the conclusion of that season, Lew Elverson, the halfback who scored the touchdown that defeated Princeton in one of the great games of that season, was elected permanent Captain.

Odell, the brother of Yale's head coach, will call the signals against the Tigers from the tailback position if Dudley Brundage, injured last week, is unable to start. If the latter is ready, Odell may return to the blocking back position, which he occupied from the time practice started in late July, until last week.

Wilmington, York Win in Playoffs

By Associated Press

Wilmington jumped back into the fight for the Interstate League championship yesterday, winning from Lancaster, 3-1, before 3260 spectators and evening the playoff series at two-all. The same clubs clash in the fifth and deciding game tonight at Lancaster.

Ken Woods' 2-run homer in the 11th climaxed the thrilling game on the winners' field. Another team, York, reached the final of the playoffs, by defeating Hagerstown, 8-2, and eliminating their rivals from the title series.

Football's Cards Fall In Opener

Sinkwich Passes For Score; Hopp Tallies 3 Times

DETROIT, Sept. 19 (A. P.).—The Detroit Lions, with Frankie Sinkwich tossing a touchdown pass in his pro debut, defeated the Chicago Cardinals, 35-17, in the National Football League opener today before 26,615. Fullback Harry Hopp scored three touchdowns for Detroit.

Making their debut under Coach Gus Dorais, who moved from the University of Detroit, the Lions scored as many touchdowns—five—in 39 minutes as they produced while losing all 11 starts last season.

FENEBROCK STARS

Hopp, fullback from Nebraska, and Sinkwich, just up from Georgia via the Marine Corps, did plenty of damage, but the boy who caught the attention of the largest pro turnout here since 1941 was Halfback Chuck Fenebrock, from U. C. L. A. via the Los Angeles Bulldogs. He fired three touchdown passes.

The Cardinals, with a new coach in Phil Handler, seized a first period lead when Lee Stokes booted a 20-yard field goal. After the following kickoff the Lions went 76 yards in three plays for a touchdown, Fenebrock sparking the drive.

CURRIVAN BLOCKS PUNT

The Cards went ahead in the second period when Don Currivan blocked Hopp's punt and ran the ball eight yards to pay dirt, but the Lions came back with a 67-yard march in nine plays, topped by Fenebrock's eight-yard scoring pass to Hopp.

Sinkwich made his first appearance in the second period. Just before the intermission he tossed a 17-yard touchdown pass to Bill Callihan that ultimately provided the winning margin.

GOLDBERG SCORES

Detroit got two more touchdowns in the third period. Fenebrock passed two yards to Hopp for one and Ned Mathews sprinted five yards around end for the other. The Cardinals got one in the fourth period on a nine-yard pass from Joe Bukant to Marshall Goldberg.

Chicago Cardinals (17) Pos. Detroit (35)

[illegible]

STATISTICS

	Ch.	Det.
First downs	9	14
Yards gained rushing (net)	0	168
Forward passes attempted	35	14
Forward passes completed	16	9
Yards by forward passing	137	129
Forward passes intercepted by	4	4
Yards gain runback on int. passes	43	42
Punting average (from scrim.)	41	27
Total yards all kicks returned	104	141
Opponent fumbles recovered	0	1
Yards lost by penalties	40	75

St. Thomas Beats South Catholic

By KEN HAY

Bob Dallas' debut as St. Thomas More High football coach was signalized yesterday with the Golden Bears first league victory since 1940 as a blocked kick for an automatic safety was the lone score in a 2-0 triumph over Southeast Catholic in the first Catholic League game of the season, before 6000 at Municipal Stadium.

Only two minutes remained when three linemen broke through to block an attempted punt from his own end zone by Southeast Catholic's Bill Kerins. Leading the trio was Center Joe Quigley and it was from his chest that the ball bounded, finally coming to rest beyond the end line.

RECOVER FUMBLE

In the second period the Bears marched to the four-yard line only to have the whistle halt play. Just before the blocked kick the Pirates' line held on the two-yard line while the backs spoiled an attempted pass by John Dermigny.

The Pirates threatened in the first period when a kick by Kerins touched Charles Dupell in its progress. Three Pirates fell on the ball and Southeast Catholic got possession on its opponents' 22. Kerins ran 14 yards to the 8 but the Bears held for eight downs during which an intercepted pass was in turn fumbled by the Bears' interceptor.

The drive that led to the safety was engineered from the victors 45. Al Capper sparked a march that carried 53 yards until stopped at the two-yard line. Capper gained 24 yards on an end run and two plunges. He passed a 22-yarder to Substitute George Hoffmaster for a first down on the Pirate 9 but the Bears gained only 7 yards in four plays.

CAPPER GET LOOSE

Later in the first half the Bears marched from their own 42 to the Pirate 4 where the whistle halted action. Capper was again the spearhead but was aided by Dermigny, Dupell and Bob Welde. Capper gained 14 yards and two passes by Dermigny to Dupell and Welde earned 14. Welde cut through left tackle for 10 and Capper reached the four to close the march.

[illegible]

Lange May Call Plays For Temple

Ray Morrison has four days in which to polish off the rough edges of the Temple University football squad as the athletes, resuming practice at the Temple Stadium today after three weeks at Oak Lane, prime for the 1943 opener on Friday night against Virginia Military Institute.

The change in practice sites also means a switch in workout plans, for starting today the Owl aspirants will go through only an afternoon drill of two hours' duration. At the Oak Lane camp, both morning and afternoon drills were scheduled by the coaches.

WOOD EXPECTED BACK

With the probable return to uniform of Pinky Wood, 140-pound wingback, and Len Lasavage, tailback, Morrison and his backfield coach, Hal Williams, will endeavor to finish the job of moulding a first-team backfield for Friday night's encounter. Both Wood and Lasavage figure heavily in Temple's ball-carrying plans. The pair of backs have been sidelined for nearly a week with sprained ankle.

Bob Lange, former St. Joseph's High star, is rated the best chance of starting at blocking back and also calling the team's plays. Lasavage and Tony Hubka loom as the tailback Morrison will select between for the V. M. I. games. The wingback post is in quite a muddle but Wood may get the call. Sid Roche, 190-pounder from Baltimore, is favored to take over the fullback chores even though he has been in camp only a week. Roche not only is a good punter, but he is developing into a good passer.

Beaver Captures Honors at Shoot

Walter S. Beaver, Conshohocken target star, turned in a perfect score of 50 breaks to win the high gun prize at the monthly shoot of the Pine Valley Gun Club yesterday at Clementon.

Harry Rutherford and Howard Nice broke 24 and 25 to win second and third prizes in Class A. Eight shooters, Paul Davis, Eugene Springer, Paul Holloway, Charles Hemsher, R. P. Willis, A. M. Reeves, Louis Paglialighi and Robert Arnell, registered 48s.

FINANCIAL
COMICS
PUZZLES

The Philadelphia Inquirer

PUBLIC LEDGER

NEWS
SPORTS
CLASSIFIED

PHILADELPHIA, TUESDAY MORNING, SEPTEMBER 21, 1943

adefgh 21

Strictly Politics

Complications Hinder Voting by Service Men

But Congressmen May Campaign To Round Up Soldier Ballots

By John M. Cummings

UNDER our Federal setup each State makes its own election laws. To a greater or lesser degree they vary between States not only in basic qualifications for the ballot but in some incidental features. Take, for example, absentee voting.

In normal times absentee voting is only a minor headache. But in these days, with millions of men in the armed forces, it is a major problem, one that is likely to receive some attention in Congress.

Comparatively few applications for an absentee ballot were received in Pennsylvania this year. The primary elections last week were local in character. They aroused little interest and voting was light even by citizens who could have exercised the franchise by simply walking around the corner to a polling booth.

Interest will pick up as we approach the November election, but even so it isn't anticipated there will be a heavy turnout.

Next year will be different. In 1944 we will have a Presidential election. Citizens who never think of voting in local or State elections try to be on deck for the Presidential balloting.

• • •

SOME time ago Representative Sabath or some other statesman suggested Federal legislation covering the men in the armed services. Under the absentees voting laws each elector unable to present himself at his home polling place is required to file application in Pennsylvania to the Secretary of the Commonwealth for an absentee ballot. On receipt of it the citizen fills it out and returns it to the Secretary of the Commonwealth who sees that it is properly credited.

The suggestion which emanated from Washington contemplated the setting up of polling places in all camps, on board ship, or wherever men in uniform were stationed, and would permit them to vote just as they would if they were home.

While the desirability of providing the service men with an

opportunity to vote is generally conceded, complications are bound to ensue. To begin with it is argued that if Congress sets up election laws covering a special case it might conceivably be the first step in depriving the States of a right that has been theirs from the beginning of the country, namely the right to conduct their own elections.

There is, too, the problem of time and space, although the airplane has accomplished wonders in removing this handicap.

Not until next July will the identity of the Republican and Democratic candidates be known for a certainty. It is quite generally assumed, of course, that President Roosevelt will seek a fourth term, but the Republican race is wide open.

• • •

UNFORTUNATELY for any scheme looking to the simplification of voting by service men, under our Constitution we don't vote directly for candidates for President. We vote for Presidential electors and these in turn choose the President.

The votes for Presidential electors would have to be assembled in camps all over the world, on ships sailing the seven seas, and returned to a specific authority in each of the 48 States. Our Presidents, as we know, are not elected by Nation-wide popular vote. In fact it is possible for a candidate to have a majority of the popular vote and still lose out in the electoral college.

Because of our system the votes of the service men cannot be thrown into a common pool. The ballots of Pennsylvania soldiers, for example, must be returned to the Secretary of the Commonwealth at Harrisburg and credited to the election precinct of each individual voter.

• • •

NEXT year, too, we will elect one-third of the Senate and an entire House. It is this phase of the election, perhaps more than the Presidential phase, that has prompted some of our statesmen to suggest methods of rounding up the soldier, sailor and Marine vote.

Experience has demonstrated that men far from home are inclined to overlook the voting opportunity. Too many papers to be filled out. Too much detail work. So they pass it up.

It may be that the spellbinders will invade the camps next summer and fall. To the long list of bugle calls they'll add one assembling the personnel for a political meeting. Under certain circumstances they might wake a camp before reveille. That would be something!

High School Fires Alaska Jeep Tourist

Herbert C. Lanks, meandering history teacher at Jenkintown High School, was "fired" from his educational position last night by the Jenkintown Board of Education.

Lanks' position as teacher of American history and "problems of democracy" was declared vacant by the Board due to his failure to return from an Alaskan expedition in time for the opening of school on Sept. 8.

AWAY TOO MUCH

The board, meeting last night in the high school building, adopted the position that Lanks had "taken entirely too much time off from his educational duties" and therefore should no longer be considered a member of the faculty.

Edgar A. Wambold, chairman of the board, said he had received no word from the teacher-author since he left for the Alaskan highway trip when school closed for the summer.

HAD GAS DIFFICULTIES

Lanks' expedition to the northwestern extremities of the continent ran into difficulty at the start when his right to large quantities of gasoline for a jeep was questioned by OPA authorities.

The matter was settled satisfactorily, however, and the expedition—a commercial trip under the sponsorship of companies producing equipment used to construct the Alcan highway—continued. Two years ago Lanks was given a leave of absence from his school duties to make a trip across South America on the Pan-American highway. From his experiences he wrote a book.

Events of the Day

Overbrook Lions Club, luncheon, Lincoln Court Dining Room, Overbrook and Lancaster ave., 12.15 P. M.

Germantown Lions Club, luncheon, Y. M. C. A., 5722 Greene st., 12.15 P. M.

Allied Jewish Appeal, luncheon, The Warwick, 12.15 P. M.

Exchange Club of Philadelphia, luncheon, Kugler's Chestnut St. Restaurant, 12.29 P. M.

Logan-North City Lions Club, luncheon, Fried's Restaurant, 5822 Old York Road, 12.30 P. M.

Philadelphia Merchants, luncheon, Benjamin Franklin, 12.30 P. M.

Central Lions Club, luncheon, Benjamin Franklin, 12.30 P. M.

Frankford Lions Club, luncheon, Verdi's Restaurant, 4629 Frankford ave., 12.30 P. M.

Kiwanis Club luncheon, Bellevue-Stratford, 12.30 P. M.

American Red Cross, luncheon, Bellevue-Stratford, 12.30 P. M.

Poor Richard's Club, luncheon, 1319 Locust st., 12.30 P. M.

Optimist Club, luncheon, Kugler's Chestnut St. Restaurant, 12.30 P. M.

Optimist Club of Jenkintown, meeting, Sunken Gardens Restaurant, Cheltenham ave. and Limekiln pike, 6.30 P. M.

Rotary Club, Assimilation Committee, dinner, The Warwick, 6 P. M.

Crime Patrols Guard W. Phila.

Extra Police On Guard in Attack Area

Plans to press every available policeman and detective into service for special patrols in the West Philadelphia neighborhood where Grace Loftus, 20, of 923 N. 50th st., was brutally attacked Saturday morning, were announced yesterday by Director of Public Safety James H. Malone.

Following a conference in the director's office with Captain Frank Sadowski, of the 50th st. and Lancaster ave. station, and Inspector Michael Hardiman, Malone said he had ordered plainclothesmen to tour the area in addition to special details of uniformed police.

SEEKS 50 MORE POLICE

Arrangements for the detective detail have been completed with Inspector of Detectives George Richardson, Malone said.

Malone also announced that he expects to swear in 50 more police, if there are enough available on the Civil Service eligibility list. He said he doubted that he would be able to get that many, but he added that the proportionate number of the men he did get would be assigned to special details in West Philadelphia.

PATROLMEN SHIFTED

The Director said he already has ordered the withdrawal of patrolmen from other sections of the city and has assigned them to the district where the attack occurred.

Malone also expressed complete confidence in Lieutenant of Detectives Ervin Mock, of the 5th Detective Division, 32d st. and Woodland ave., to cope with any police problem which arises in his territory.

SEARCH FOR ATTACKERS

The detective head is conducting a city-wide search of cleaning and dyeing establishments for a blood-stained sailor's suit, after it was reported that one of the attackers was wearing a Navy uniform.

At Presbyterian Hospital yesterday the condition of Miss Loftus, who is suffering a fractured skull and other injuries, was reported as serious.

Convict Aids Girl

Skin Grafting to Speed Recovery

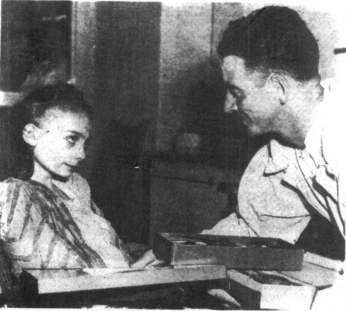

Ten-year-old Judy Rosen, of 547 Fernon st., a patient at Mt. Sinai Hospital since she was seriously burned in an accident last May, is shown with Thomas J. Caulfield, a life-term convict at Eastern Penitentiary, who volunteered skin for an operation yesterday in which grafts were taken for the little girl's badly-seared chest. The successful transfer is expected to speed her recovery.

Ex-Teller Pleads Guilty In $63,449 Bank Thefts

Judge Defers Sentence Pending Result of Parallel Case in Federal Court

John F. Neville, 52, former acting teller of the Olney branch of the Liberty Title & Trust Co., pleaded guilty yesterday to 39 bills of indictment covering bank peculations amounting to $63,449.

Judge Harry S. McDevitt, in Quarter Sessions Court, deferred sentence and committed Neville to County Prison to await the outcome of similar charges in Federal Court when the defendant's attorney, Thomas D. McBride, said a Federal Jury was about to indict his client.

Asserting that Neville could hardly be sentenced twice for the crime by both the Federal and county courts, Judge McDevitt declared that "maybe the two agencies of Government can get together on the sentence."

MAKES NO STATEMENT

Neville, who rose from handyman and guard to acting assistant teller in the trust company's branch office, made no statement in pleading guilty, but his attorney said the defendant had not profited substantially. McBride said a large part of the money was spent in advancing the interests of the Olney Business Men's Association, of which Neville was a former president. Neville also was a member of Draft Board 66, 5428 N. 5th st.

William J. McCuen, a State Banking Department examiner, testified that the 39 true bills, on three charges of embezzlement, misapplication of funds and fraudulent conversion, covered $63,449 in defalcations, but that the net loss to the bank was $70,153. However, he said, the bank and depositors are protected by a $500,000 blanket bond.

BANK A MEMBER OF FDIC

Neville faces Federal indictment, he added, because the bank is a member of the Federal Deposit Insurance Corp.

McCuen testified that Neville on "many occasions" accepted money from depositors, receipted their pass books, but did not credit the sums on the bank's books.

Charles Krumrine, president of the bank, testified that Neville, who lives on Fairhill st. near Olney ave., had been employed since April, 1934, first as a handyman and guard at $1000 a year.

BRINGS PROMOTION

Neville's "nice personality" and ability to make friends led to his promotion to contact man, and he brought in many new accounts, Krumrine said, adding that at the time of his arrest, Neville was being paid $2280 a year, with a six percent bonus.

The bank president told Judge McDevitt that while the defendant was never in charge of the branch bank, he did act as an assistant teller for a short time, during which he took the money.

Toy Maker Gets Respite To Save Jobs

The immediate economic welfare of 25 Philadelphia toy makers temporarily saved Frank Plotnick, manufacturer, from a six-month jail sentence and a $2500 fine yesterday in the U. S. District Court.

Plotnick, 49, of Ninth st. near Lycoming ave., pleaded nolle contendere to Government charges that he attempted to evade payment of $5714.29 taxes on his company's 1938-39-40 income.

ORDER HELD UP

Judge Harry E. Kolodner, who imposed the sentence and fine, directed Plotnick to pay the taxes in full plus approximately $2600 in interest but countermanded his sentence when informed that Plotnick's immediate incarceration might mean that 25 employes of his plant, at Howard st. and Susquehanna ave., would be thrown out of work.

Judge Kalodner postponed imposition of the sentence until Oct. 4 and directed Plotnick to make arrangements for continuation of his plant, the American Toy and Novelty Manufacturing Co.

JUGGLING CHARGED

Assistant U. S. Attorney Thomas J. Curtin charged that Plotnick juggled the sales accounts of his firm and opened multiple small bank accounts to hide his income.

Harry Rosenbloom, counsel for Plotnick, who is the father of four children, ranging in age from 8 to 24, maintained that the manufacturer became confused in his accounts of wages paid homeworkers prior to the 1938 State law prohibiting the use of such labor.

Rosenbloom said that Plotnick, once apprised of his shortage, sent a check for full payment to the Bureau of Internal Revenue but it was returned because the case had reached the stage for "criminal prosecution."

Convict Aids Girl, 10, And Finds Happiness

In the Eastern Penitentiary's infirmary yesterday, a life-term convict grinned from his cot despite his bandages and said again, "Gee, she's a swell kid!"

And across the city, in Mt. Sinai Hospital, "she" dreamed sleepily of the day, perhaps soon to come, when she will be able to play again with other little girls in her neighborhood, because of a "lifer's" generosity.

The little girl is 10-year-old Judy Rosen, of 547 Fernon st., who was critically burned about the arms and chest, when her dress caught fire in her home 19 weeks ago. To complete her recovery, she required an extensive skin graft, and late last week a call went out for volunteer donors at Eastern Penitentiary.

30 CONVICTS VOLUNTEERED

Selected from a group of 30 convict volunteers after his blood had been typed and found to match Judy's, 33-year-old Thomas J. Caulfield, serving a life term for the murder of a policeman in an attempted cigar store holdup in 1929, was taken to the hospital yesterday morning, and the two underwent the operation at 1 P. M.

"She's a swell kid," commented Caulfield after talking with Judy just prior to entering the operating room. "Any little girl that has her grit and determination is all right with me.

HOPES SHE'LL GET WELL

"I'm very happy to be able to do something like this, and I only hope it will help her to get well."

Mindful of the long and tiresome convalescence that still lies ahead of his new friend, Caulfield sent out a hospital aide while he and Judy talked, to purchase her a book of comics and a clay modeling set.

Arsenal Workers To Get Health Test

X-ray examination of civilian workers to prevent the spread of tuberculosis through wartime strain and overwork will begin at the Frankford Arsenal today. Similar examinations were completed at the Philadelphia Navy Yard last week.

The project is sponsored jointly by the Philadelphia Tuberculosis and Health Association and the tuberculosis division of the Department of Health.

2 War Workers Held in $2000 Bail

Charged with stealing Government property, two employes of Baldwin Locomotive works were held in court under $1000 bail each yesterday by Norman H. Griffin, U. S. commissioner.

They were Gaetano John Perry, 1212 N. 55th st., and Ralph C. Pasio, Jr., 927 Segal st., who are charged with taking 85 feet of copper tubing used in the manufacture of tanks. Both were employed in the machine shop.

Dealer Acquitted In Poultry Charge

Albert J. Levit, Lebanon ave. near 53d st., was acquitted of charges of having violated OPA price ceilings in the sale of poultry yesterday by orders of Federal Judge Harry E. Kalodner.

Levit, who was indicted with a cousin, Abe Levit, a member of the firm of A. Levit & Co., 343 S. Front st., was ordered freed after U. S. Attorney Gerald A. Gleeson said the Government could not prove its case. Abe Levit was fined $5000 in Federal Court in June on a plea of nolo contendere.

Messenger Gets 3-Month Term

Walter Dzietczyk, 29, of Albert st. near Almond, was sentenced to serve three months in prison yesterday by Federal Judge Harry E. Kalodner. Dzietczyk had pleaded guilty on U. S. District Court to stealing approximately $200 from the mails.

The defendant was employed as a special delivery messenger for 12 years. He told the jurist that he began taking money last fall. He also pleaded guilty to destroying "dunning letters," missives sent by collection agencies. He said other messengers made a "common practice" of destroying such letters, and collecting the fee for delivery.

Silt Hit By Park Commission

Reporting three floods during the past year caused damage "and considerable expense to correct," the Fairmount Park Commission yesterday declared in its annual report that the silt problem "must be dealt with far up the river near the mines."

The commissioners' report is highlighted by the statement of its president, Joseph Carson, on the silt situation. Carson pointed out that the Schuylkill always has been a flood river, but early floods deposited sand alone.

'COAL DUST A MENACE'

"Today the coal dust is an increased menace not only to the stream as a place of beauty and pleasure, but as to the destruction it carries with it along the banks," the report reads.

The commissioners, Carson says, have opened an auxiliary road parallel with the East River drive, near Midvale ave., in an effort to aid park traffic during flood seasons. Dredging of the river is now confined to clearing a channel for pleasure boats, but placing the dredged material "has now become more than a serious problem."

GUARDS JOIN SERVICE

The report for the year 1942 was submitted to City Council. It cites the difficulty of obtaining labor for regular park employment, and replacements for guards entering the service. At the end of 1942 there were 22 guards and 21 civilian employes in the armed forces.

Couples Celebrate 50th Wedding Fete

Mr. and Mrs. Walter S. Wood, 6017 Wharton st., celebrated their 50th wedding anniversary yesterday when they entertained their family and friends at the Pennsylvania Hotel.

Mr. and Mrs. Henry Wieser, of 4433 N. 18th st., were honored on their 50th wedding anniversary last night at a dinner in the Philadelphia Rifle Club, 7th st. and Tabor road. They were married Sept. 20, 1893, in St. Vincent's Church, Germantown.

$2500 Bail Is Set In Theft of Bus

James St. John, 21, of Sartain st. near Ritner, accused by police of stealing a P. T. C. bus in South Philadelphia Saturday night, was sent to Moyamensing Prison yesterday by Magistrate Nathan A. Beifel in default of $2500 bail. St. John was released from Fitzgerald-Mercy Hospital, Darby, yesterday after treatment for injuries received when the bus crashed into a building in Yeadon.

Police said the bus was stolen from Broad and Pollock sts. while the driver was in a restaurant. The bus crashed during a police chase near the Lansdowne Country Club. St. John told the police he had been discharged recently from the Army.

Nurses Receive Caps

Nineteen students of the class of 1946 of the Abington Memorial Hospital School of Nursing received their caps from Mrs. Ruth L. Hawkins, director of nursing, yesterday, at services in the Abington Presbyterian Church.

Wife Freed, 2 Men Jailed In Holdup

Sentences of four to 14 years were meted out to two Philadelphia holdup men in Montgomery County Court yesterday after they had pleaded guilty to a series of robberies in the vicinity of Elkins Park.

At the same time the wife of one, who attempted suicide in her cell after her arrest, was freed by Judge William F. Dannehower on the assumption that she was acting under duress when she served as a lookout for her husband and his accomplice during the hold-ups.

THOSE SENT TO JAIL

Those sentenced were Frank Maleskie, 30, of Ruffner st. near 22d, seven to 14 years in Eastern Penitentiary, and Edward Simons, 24, of 15th st. near Columbia ave., four to eight years in the same institution. The latter's wife, Sophia, 23, mother of three small children, who had been under arrest on the same charges of burglary and larceny, was released.

Following the capture of the trio last Aug. 7, Mrs. Simons attempted to hang herself in her cell in Cheltenham Township police station, but was cut down by a turnkey who was warned by her husband's shouts.

Maleski, the court ruled, must serve his new sentence concurrently with another of 35 years for violating his parole.

Two Children Injured by Auto

Two school children were injured yesterday when an allegedly stolen automobile was driven along the sidewalk of a Wilmington street.

Beatrice Burke, 13, of 300 E. 2d st., suffered a concussion and bruises, and Esther Brinton, 6, suffered a fracture of the right arm. Both are in Delaware Hospital. Benjamin Warner, of 2d st. near Poplar, Wilmington, was arrested as the driver after a chase.

Electrician Held In Janitor's Death

A Navy Yard electrician was held without bail by Magistrate E. David Keiser at the 55th and Pine sts. police station yesterday pending the coroner's investigation into the death of James Hale, 58, janitor of an apartment house on 49th st. near Pine.

Hale was dead on arrival Sunday night at Misericordia Hospital after he fell ill, police said, following a skirmish with the electrician, Martin Cahill, 27, who lives in the apartment house.

Women Helps Capture Bandit

One of two young bandits who held up the office of the U. S. Office Equipment Co., at 3724 N. Broad st., was captured yesterday with the help of a woman partner in the firm.

The youth, whose accomplice fled with a number of fountain pen sets, entered the store about 2 P. M. While he talked with Mrs. Margaret Tregear, 55, of 3717 N. Carlisle st., his companion leaned over the counter, scooped up the pens, and ran.

Mrs. Tregear screamed for help and three employes came to her assistance. They chased the robbers to Broad and Butler sts., where one was seized by Post Traffic Patrolman Peter Reilley. The prisoner was not immediately identified.

Youth Sentenced As Draft Dodger

While his 18-year-old fiance, Mary Chirdo, of Birdsboro, looked on, Daniel B. Peffley, 20, also of Birdsboro, was sentenced to five years in Federal prison yesterday on charges of Selective Service violations by Judge Harry E. Kalodner, who called the youth a "deliberate draft dodger."

It was testified that the court had given Peffley four opportunities to obey induction orders of his draft board, but he refused each time. Peffley requested duty in a work camp because religious beliefs would not permit him to bear arms. It was testified that he belonged to no organized sect whose members are granted immunity.

Mancuso Trial Set for Monday

U. S. Attorney Gerald A. Gleeson announced yesterday that, barring "any further unforeseen circumstances," Frank Philip Mancuso, of Dickinson st. near 18th, who has blocked his induction into the Army since last March, will go on trial in the Federal Court next Monday.

Mancuso, radio repairman and father of twins, gained his latest delay when Guido DeMasi, chairman of the defendant's local draft board, left Philadelphia last week to attend the wedding of a relative in the Mid-West. Gleeson said yesterday that he is now ready to take the case into court.

Broad St. Station Service Restored

Train service to Broad Street Station has been completely restored, R. C. Morse, vice president of the Pennsylvania Railroad in charge of the Eastern Region, announced yesterday, eight days after the $250,000 fire gutted a block-square track and platform area adjacent to the station building.

All trains ordinarily using Broad Street Station were returned there from the 30th st. and suburban stations Sunday night. Nearly 2500 men have been employed on the repair job. Tracks and platforms have been laid on new supporting structures and overhead electric power wires have been renewed.

Soldier's Allotment Costs Girl $250 Fine

A dark-haired girl street-car operator who pleaded guilty to unlawfully receiving Government allotment checks sent her as the wife of a soldier serving overseas was fined $250 and given a three-month suspended sentence in Federal Court yesterday.

She is Rita Patricia Visco, 24, of 3427 N. 11th st., one of several unmarried women under Federal indictment for receiving the $50 a month allotments granted the wives of service men.

In addition to the fine Miss Visco was placed on probation for a year and directed to return the $400 received from Private Joseph Boeta of Baton Rouge, La., whom she said she intends to marry after the war. Judge Harry Kalodner allowed her six months to pay the fine.

Miss Visco, whose case was described by U. S. Attorney Walter A. Gay as "not flagrant," told the court she did not know her fiance had applied for an allotment and notified by the Government that her checks would be ... to her.

BENNY

by J. Carver Pusey

PHILA. SLUMPS IN WAR BOND DRIVE
1/4 lb. BUTTER WITH EVERY WAR BOND.

WCAU · 1210

CBS Programs—Radio's Finest!

Our station brings you every day the finest in radio: the best in news, comedy, music, drama, war programs, public affairs programs, religious programs... presented over the world's foremost radio network (Columbia) for your entertainment and information. Keep this page near your radio and use it every day for radio's finest programs.

3:00 PM NEW YORK PHILHARMONIC Music of the masters, played by the famed New York Philharmonic-Symphony from Carnegie Hall.

4:30 PM THE PAUSE THAT REFRESHES Music by André Kostelanetz, with famous guests.

5:00 PM THE FAMILY HOUR Gladys Swarthout, Deems Taylor, chorus.

6:00 PM SILVER THEATRE The best of Hollywood, in plays and players.

8:30 PM CRIME DOCTOR Tense, dramatic stories of the rehabilitation of criminals.

9:00 PM RADIO READER'S DIGEST Conrad Nagel brings articles from America's most popular magazine.

9:30 PM TEXACO STAR THEATRE with James Melton, Joan Roberts, Al Goodman's Orchestra, and Jimmy Wallington.

10:00 PM TAKE IT OR LEAVE IT Phil Baker swaps money for information.

12:00 NOON KATE SMITH SPEAKS Radio's First Lady in an intimate program of news and comments.

6:45 PM WORLD TODAY CBS foreign correspondents report, CBS experts analyze world news. Six times weekly.

7:00 PM I LOVE A MYSTERY Two smart detectives, a smart secretary, and a clever plot. Five times every week.

7:30 PM BLONDIE Try as they may, the Bumstead family can't stay out of hilarious trouble.

8:00 PM VOX POP Parks Johnson and Warren Hull travel over the continent.

9:00 PM LUX RADIO THEATRE Cecil B. DeMille directs Hollywood's stars in Hollywood's greatest stories.

10:00 PM SCREEN GUILD PLAYERS Screen stars and stories on "The Stars' Own Theatre".

6:15 PM EDWIN C. HILL An able reporter discusses the Human Side of the News.

7:15 PM HARRY JAMES Favorite of millions, voted best swing band, he swings out in a program of popular music. Three times weekly.

7:30 PM AMERICAN MELODY HOUR Familiar and beloved music with Eileen Farrell, Bob Hannon and other stars.

8:00 PM BIG TOWN...the exciting story of editor Steve Wilson and Lorelei, his lovely girl assistant.

8:30 PM THE JUDY CANOVA SHOW where the funniest things can happen... and do!

9:00 PM BURNS AND ALLEN Gracie's up to her old tricks. George is long-suffering! You'll howl as millions do!

9:30 PM REPORT TO THE NATION A dramatized history of the week, directed by Paul White.

6:55 PM JOSEPH C. HARSCH The man who is always there when the news is happening! Five times every week.

8:00 PM SAMMY KAYE with music that makes you "swing and sway" whenever you hear it.

8:30 PM DOCTOR CHRISTIAN A country doctor in a typical American town, Jean Hersholt.

9:00 PM LIONEL BARRYMORE as Mayor of the Town, a brilliant portrait of a kindly man.

9:30 PM JACK CARSON Something new in comics, in something new in comedy programs!

10:00 PM GREAT MOMENTS IN MUSIC presents the rich voice of lovely Jean Tennyson.

10:30 PM CRESTA BLANCA CARNIVAL Morton Gould's music and the piano of Alec Templeton.

2:00 PM YOUNG DOCTOR MALONE A story of a doctor and his nurse-wife...dedicated to all doctors and nurses.

2:15 PM JOYCE JORDAN, M.D. The private and professional life of a beautiful young girl physician.

7:45 PM MR. KEEN Tracer of lost persons, Mr. Keen dramatically reunites loved ones. Three times weekly.

8:00 PM CHARLIE RUGGLES, MARY ASTOR, MISCHA AUER, in comedy... with music.

8:30 PM DEATH VALLEY DAYS True stories of the West, old and new, with Jack McBride as narrator.

9:00 PM MAJOR BOWES Undiscovered talent comes to life as Major gives amateurs their chance.

10:00 PM THE FIRST LINE Meet the officers and men of our first line of attack... the United States Navy!

12:45 PM OUR GAL SUNDAY The moving story of an American girl married to a wealthy and titled Englishman.

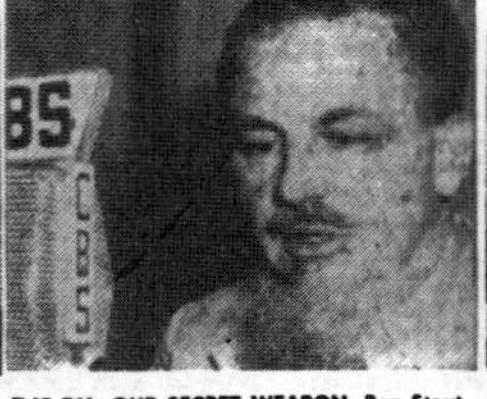
7:15 PM OUR SECRET WEAPON Rex Stout hurls the Axis' lies back in their teeth by using democracy's secret weapon—TRUTH!

8:00 PM KATE SMITH HOUR Radio's beloved Kate, sweet singer with Ted Collins.

8:55 PM BILL HENRY analyzes important foreign and domestic news—five days a week.

9:30 PM THAT BREWSTER BOY Peck's Bad Boy had nothing on Joey. He's a laugh-riot!

10:00 PM THANKS TO THE YANKS Bob Hawk plays Santa Claus to our armed forces.

10:30 PM STAGE DOOR CANTEEN brings you stars of radio, stage and screen from New York.

11:00 AM NEWS WITH WARREN SWEENEY The latest world-wide news from the CBS news room.

11:05 AM LET'S PRETEND with Nila Mack and her talented crew of young stars.

12:00 NOON THEATRE OF TODAY Drama built around the news... with Hollywood favorites as stars.

1:00 PM DICK POWELL in a new and breezy daytime musical show, with band and guest stars.

8:00 PM BLUE RIBBON TOWN Groucho Marx entertains coast-to-coast in a hilarious fun-fest.

8:30 PM INNER SANCTUM opens its squeaking door upon a series of thrills and chills.

8:55 PM NED CALMER in a five-minute, last-minute news round-up. Every Saturday and Sunday

9:00 PM YOUR HIT PARADE with Frank Sinatra, Mark Warnow's Orchestra and the 10 top tunes.

The Philadelphia Inquirer
WEDNESDAY MORNING, OCTOBER 6, 1943

(A. P. Wirephoto)

NEW TURRET The newest weapon to give Flying Fortresses greater protection against enemy fighter planes is this power-operated "chin" turret equipped with two .50-caliber machine guns. It provides the nose gunner for the first time with a powerful weapon.

(A. P. Wirephoto)

HAVOC CAUSED BY BOMBS AT THE FOGGIA RAIL JUNCTION

Accuracy of Allied Bombers

These photos give an idea of the deadly accuracy of the Allied bombing planes which have given the ground troops vital support in all phases of the Italian campaign. Above is the repeatedly bombed Foggia rail junction. Twisted rails and battered buildings are all that remain. Below is a Nazi gun position at Pompeii after a blasting by Allied bombers.

(Inquirer Photo)

PRIVATE EDWARD ORAVEC, STARFORD, PRACTICING FIRST AID ON PRIVATE DANIEL OSIER, SYRACUSE.

Learning First Aid

Pennsylvania soldiers, attached to a medical unit in England, brushing up on their first-aid lessons during field maneuvers. Above: applying a bandage to a "wounded" buddy. Below: demonstrating the proper technique of carrying an injured soldier across a ditch.

CELEBRATION
Mrs. Frances I. Fasy, chairman of the Catholic Church Group, Women's Division of the War Finance Committee and some of the soldier guests from Valley Forge Hospital at the luncheon yesterday marking the group's first anniversary.

(A. P. Wirephoto)

NAZI GUN POSITION AT POMPEII BLASTED BY BOMBERS

(Inquirer Photo)

PENNSYLVANIANS CARRYING A "WOUNDED" SOLDIER ACROSS A DITCH. THEY ARE (LEFT TO RIGHT) PRIVATE R. A. PAUL, SHAMOKIN; PRIVATE MIKE JACOBS, WILKES-BARRE; PRIVATE MITCHELL PERSIN, EXPORT, AND PRIVATE CHARLES NOWAK, SWOYERSVILLE.

(Official U. S. Navy Photo from A. P. Wirephoto)

LANDMARK Pushing its snow-blanketed peak above the clouds, this volcano on Gareloi Island in the Aleutians, west of the Adak base, is a landmark for fliers. Here, a Naval Air Transport Service plane wings past on its way to Attu, with a cargo for U. S. forces on the recaptured island outpost.

The Philadelphia Inquirer

PUBLIC LEDGER

An Independent Newspaper for All the People

FINAL CITY EDITION

CIRCULATION: September Average: Daily 501,034; Sunday 1,250,247

TUESDAY MORNING, NOVEMBER 2, 1943

Copyright, 1943, by The Philadelphia Inquirer Co. Vol. 229, No. 125

abdefgh

THREE CENTS

4 Powers at Moscow Pledge Unity In War and Peace; Reds Seal Crimea

F.D.R. Seizes Mines, Orders Strikers Back

Today

Election Day
Citizen Is Supreme
Council Important
Federal Interference
Samuel for Mayor

By John M. Cummings

ON ELECTION day the citizen is supreme. His role may be compared to that of a juror in the box. It is his business to sift the evidence carefully. He should relegate to a remote recess of his brain the idle blatherings of the professional politicians. He should render a verdict strictly on the basis of legitimate evidence at hand.

In the election today the John Does and Mary Roes of Philadelphia will fill a number of important city and county offices. Topping the list is the office of mayor. While there are three candidates in the field, one has only a nuisance value.

Some time tonight we shall know whether Acting Mayor Bernard Samuel, the Republican candidate, or William C. Bullitt, the Democratic nominee, is the choice of the electorate to head the city government for the next four years.

Councilmen will be elected in every senatorial district. These are important offices. A Council in full sympathy with the policies of the mayor can work wonders for the welfare of the municipality. A Council not in harmony with the mayor would be a distinct handicap to the administration.

In the event of Mr. Samuel's election, therefore, it is highly important that he have the cooperation of Council. This detail, of course, the thoughtful voter will look after while marking his ballot.

On the other hand, it would be only fair and reasonable to give Mr. Bullitt the comfort of a friendly Council if chance, a fickle jade, should elevate him to the mayoralty.

As a matter of fact, in the case of Mr. Bullitt a friendly Council would be an absolute essential. During the campaign Mr. Bullitt demonstrated an uncommon ignorance of municipal affairs and there is reason to doubt he could find his way to the mayor's office without the help of an experienced guide, such as John B. Kelly or James P. Clark.

Mr. Kelly, a bold and venturesome personality, discovered the mayor's office in the administration of the late S. Davis Wilson.

In the matter of qualifications for the office, unbiased judges with whom we have discussed the matter are of the opinion Mr.

Continued on Page 17, Column 3

VOTERS DECIDE BITTER MAYOR BATTLE TODAY

Samuel and Bullitt Forces Hurl New Charges; Control of Council at Stake

By JOSEPH H. MILLER

Philadelphians today will select public officials to run the affairs of the city government during the next four years.

As the heated municipal election campaign ended last night with final appeals for support by candidates and political leaders, interest in the balloting centered principally around the contests for Mayor and 22 member of City Council, the law-making and fiscal policy-determining officials of the city.

NAME CALLING UNABATED

The caustic, name-calling tactics which featured the early days of the campaign continued unabated in the last-minute bids for voter support.

Indications were that when the city's 1335 polling places open at 7 A. M. today for a 13-hour period, the bitterness which existed among rival political leaders might extend to the opposing division committeemen, in a heated bid for votes, until the last ballot is cast.

Bidding for the aid of voters as the actual campaigning ended were Acting Mayor Samuel, Republican nominee for a full term; William C. Bullitt, his Democratic rival; Republican City Chairman David W. Harris; James P. Clark, head of the Democratic organization, and John B. Kelly, Bullitt's campaign manager.

ROW OFFICES AT STAKE

Besides a Mayor and Council members, others to be elected include a District Attorney, Sheriff, Receiver of Taxes, Clerk of the Courts, Recorder of Deeds, three County Commissioners and seven Magistrates. Ten Common Pleas, Orphans and Municipal Court judges will be elected without opposition. A third candidate for Mayor is Jules C. Abercauph, supported by the Independent Voters League.

Only one office will be filled in the

Continued on Page 17, Column 1

ICKES IS TOLD TO SIGN PACT WITH U. M. W.

Men Must Return Tomorrow Morning, President Says; Union Acts Today

By DOROTHY ROCKWELL
Inquirer Washington Bureau

WASHINGTON, Nov. 1. — As a fourth general strike paralyzed the Nation's coal fields, President Roosevelt tonight ordered Secretary of the Interior Harold L. Ickes to resume possession of the struck mines, and directed the miners to be back in the pits by Wednesday morning.

The President instructed Ickes to sign a contract with the United Mine Workers, in the name of the Government and for the duration of Government possession of the mines, embodying the War Labor Board's recommendation in the Illinois soft coal case.

UNION ACTS TODAY

The U.M.W. Policy Committee will meet tomorrow to frame final reaction to the WLB's unfavorable decisions on both the hard and soft coal miners' demands, and is expected to order its members back to work under protest.

Ickes moved immediately to carry out the President's executive order. He signed an order formally seizing all pits of 50 tons capacity or more, ordered the American Flag flown over all the mine properties, and for the time being designated the presidents of the affected mine companies as operating managers.

'NO RIGHT TO STRIKE'

"The grievances of the miners have been heard," the President said in a statement accompanying the

Continued on Page 10, Column 6

RUSSIA
Cherkassy
Kremenchug
UKRAINE
Battle Front Oct. 24th
Dnieper R.
Kirovograd
Dniepero-petrovsk
Marianovka
Alexandrovka
Bug River
Voznesensk
KRIVOI ROG
Zaporozhe
NIKOPOL
Balki
Kairi Zapadnya
Nikolaev
Kakhovka
Melitopol
Kherson
Chaplinka
Novo-Troitskoe
PEREKOP
Novo Alexeyevka
Armyansk Bazar
Sea of Azov
CRIMEA
Black Sea
Feodosiya
Sevastopol
STATUTE MILES

ENTRANCE TO CRIMEA TAKEN BY REDS

Russian forces yesterday took Perekop and Armyanski Bazar (1), sealing thousands of Germans in the Crimea as other Red troops surged down the narrow corridor to the east (2). The Soviets also converged on Kakhovka and Nikopol (3). The Crimea was taken by the Germans after the historic 245-day siege of Sevastopol (A) which ended in July, 1942.

RUSSIANS TAKE PEREKOP, TRAP 90,000 NAZIS

Smash 10 Miles Into Isthmus, Cutting Last Escape Route; Foe Faces Disaster

By JUDSON O'QUINN

LONDON, Nov. 2 (Tuesday) (A. P.).—The Red Army trapped tens of thousands of Germans in the Crimea yesterday by cutting the Perekop Isthmus, and Moscow announced early today that one fleeing enemy group above the peninsula had been surrounded, losing 2000 killed and 6000 captured in a continuing battle of annihilation.

Nearly 5000 Germans also were killed and scores of tanks, guns and trucks were captured or destroyed in fresh Russian gains inside the Dnieper River bend, Moscow said, as the Red Army reached the lower Dnieper 15 miles above the Kakhovka crossing in its pursuit of demoralized German troops, thousands of whom have perished on the Nogaisk steppe.

CAPTURE PEREKOP

In sealing off the Crimea the Russians stormed and captured Perekop, on the isthmus of that name, and smashed five miles beyond across the narrow land bridge toward the Crimea.

The Germans faced one of their greatest disasters since Stalingrad, where Field Marshal General Friedrich von Paulus's Sixth Army of 350,000 was lost. The Nazi Crimean forces are believed to number less than that—possibly 90,000—since some have been evacuated, Berlin says, and the Russians themselves were declared to have had only 200,000 in the area when they lost it during the 1941-42 fighting.

GAIN IN 2 CORRIDORS

General Feodor Tolbukhin's victorious Fourth Ukraine Army drove five miles ahead into both narrow

Continued on Page 2, Column 1

2d Front Details Settled, Austrian Revolution Sought

The texts of the joint communique and other documents issued yesterday from the historic Moscow conference appear on Page 6. Other stories on Pages 4, 5, 6 and 7.

By ALEXANDER KENDRICK
Inquirer Washington Bureau

WASHINGTON, Nov. 1.—The four great Allies—the United States, Great Britain, Soviet Russia and China—today stood bound in the most far-reaching pact of all time to prosecute the war to "unconditional surrender" and to continue united action after the war for "the organization and maintenance of peace and security."

The common policy toward the Axis and toward the titanic problems of post-war reconstruction was agreed upon at the historic two-week Moscow conference of the three Foreign Ministers of the United States, Britain and Russia, it was announced simultaneously by all three countries.

A "second front" in Western Europe, it was disclosed, was covered at Moscow by "frank and exhaustive discussions of the measures to be taken to shorten the war against Germany and her satellites."

'DEFINITE MILITARY OPERATIONS'

In this respect, the Moscow conferees revealed, they discussed "definite military operations with regard to which decisions had been taken and which are already being prepared."

At the same time provision was made to see to it that Germans responsible for war atrocities would be delivered to their accusers for "on the spot" judgment and punishment.

China, it was revealed, also joined in the Moscow meeting through her Ambassador to the Soviet capital, but limited her participation to the joint declaration of policy and was not represented in the talks concerning Europe.

FUTURE OF WORLD ENVISAGED

The future of the world, as it will be underwritten by the four big Powers, envisages:

"A general international organization"—presumably patterned on the League of Nations—"based on the principle of the sovereign equality of all peace-loving States."

Regional federations to implement the decisions of the parent organization, and to solve the political and economic problems of each particular area.

Democratic regimes, with every vestige of Fascism stamped out, and with constitutional freedoms as a basis.

Continuing consultation among the "Big Four" and with other United Nations "with a view to joint action on behalf of the community of nations."

A "practicable general agreement," on the regulation of armaments in the post-war period.

These intentions, the fruits of the Moscow conference, are embodied in a series of five documents, made public si-

Continued on Page 6, Column 1

Bougainville Invaded By MacArthur's Troops

Map on Page 3

By C. YATES McDANIEL

ALLIED HEADQUARTERS IN THE SOUTHWEST PACIFIC, Nov. 2 (Tuesday) (A. P.).—American ground forces captured Empress Augusta Bay at dawn Monday, in a bold invasion of west-central Bougainville Island, 260 miles away from Japan's big key base of Rabaul.

Cognizant that this big move threatened to unhinge the entire Japanese position in the Southwest Pacific and that the enemy must consider strong counter measures, General Douglas MacArthur challenged the Japanese Navy to come out and fight.

LITTLE OPPOSITION

"If the Jap fleet comes out, I will welcome it. I will throw everything we have against it," MacArthur said.

This invasion of Bougainville, translating into air, naval and amphibious action strategy planned by MacArthur, Admiral William F. Halsey and other high officials, moved the Allies 200 miles from the scene of their recent victories in the Central Solomons.

The attacking force, which achieved its initial landings with such surprise that little opposition was encountered from the many thousand Japs who garrison the island, thus by-passed Japanese positions on southern Bougainville and

Continued on Page 3, Column 3

ROOSEVELT INSISTS ON FOOD SUBSIDIES

By WILLIAM C. MURPHY, JR.
Inquirer Washington Bureau

WASHINGTON, Nov. 1.—President Roosevelt today demanded Congressional authorization for a continued and expanded program of food subsidies to hold down prices, stimulate production and minimize the dangers of disastrous inflation.

His proposal, embodied in a 10,000-word message — the longest he has ever sent to Congress—constituted a direct challenge for a showdown with the Congressional farm bloc and

Continued on Page 8, Column 1

FIFTH ARMY TAKES VITAL ROAD CENTER

Map on Page 2

By EDWARD KENNEDY

ALLIED HEADQUARTERS, ALGIERS, Nov. 1 (A. P.).—The Allied Fifth and Eighth Armies, laboring forward in mud and rain, have captured 21 more Italian towns and villages, including Teano, in grim fighting at the approaches to the Germans' massive new trans-peninsula defense barrier.

Teano, important road junction 10 miles northeast of the enemy's towering Mount Massico stronghold, fell to Lieutenant General Mark W. Clark's American Fifth Army after a one-mile uphill fight against elements of the crack Hermann Goering Division, a headquarters communique announced today.

FIVE-MILE THRUST

In another spectacular thrust, American troops advanced five miles through downpours and up dizzy mountain slopes to take Valleagricola, perched on a 2000-foot hill four miles north of Raviscanina. In the two advances Clark's men also enveloped the villages of Anfitica, Otello, Mancanello and Neviere.

General Sir Bernard L. Montgomery's British Eighth Army was pinned down by heavy rain and stiff Nazi resistance along the Trigno River near the Adriatic end of the battle line, but in the mountainous

Continued on Page 2, Column 6

Report U.S. Will Use Russian Air Bases

MADRID, Nov. 1 (A. P.).—A report that Russian front air bases are to be made available to United States bombers for daylight attacks against Eastern Germany were current in Berlin tonight.

Spanish correspondents in Berlin, who have repeatedly said that what worried the average Germans more than any battle front was the bombing from the west, now report the same Germans fear the Moscow conference may bring the same type raids from the east, too.

Morgenthau Back From Mediterranean

WASHINGTON, Nov. 1 (A. P.).—Secretary of the Treasury Henry Morgenthau, Jr., returned to the Treasury today after a three-week tour of Mediterranean battle fronts to discuss fiscal problems with Allied military leaders.

He was accompanied by Harry D. White, Treasury monetary expert, and his confidential assistant, Fred Smith.

EXPERT IDENTIFIES PRINT OF MARIGNY

Illustrated on Pages 16 and 18.

By E. V. W. JONES

NASSAU, BAHAMAS, Nov. 1 (A. P.).—A scholarly New York police expert testified today that a fingerprint reported by the Crown to have been found in the room where Sir Harry Oakes was slain is the impression of Count Alfred de Marigny's little right finger.

Frank Conway, of the New York Bureau of Identification, the first witness of the third week of de Marigny's trial on a charge of murder in connection with the bludgeoning and burning of his millionaire father-in-law, said he studied the fingerprint on exhibit and the impression made by de Marigny when he was fingerprinted after his arrest.

'THEY ARE IDENTICAL'

"My conclusion is that they are identical, and were made by the same person," he swore.

Conway sought to impress the jury with the value of fingerprints

Continued on Page 16, Column 1

NEWS FROM ITALY—and DIRECT from European, Asiatic and South Pacific fronts—with John W. Vandercook and NBC foreign correspondents, 7:15 P. M., and KYW "Dispatch from Reuters" at 12:05 A. M. Advt.

New Postal Rate Boost Voted by House Group

By HUGH MORROW
Inquirer Washington Bureau

WASHINGTON, Nov. 1.—The House Ways and Means Committee ended its tax deliberations today by voting an indirect income of $140,000,000 in income taxes, and a one-cent increase in the postage required on an ordinary letter.

The income tax increase was accomplished by forbidding deduction of Federal excise taxes paid in computing income levies. The action reversed the committee's previous decision against increasing the burden on individuals aside from an incidental $12,000,000 picked up in the formula for integrating the victory tax with the normal income tax rate.

AVERAGES $3.45 EACH

However, the total income tax increase of $152,000,000 would be only a little more than 2.3 percent of the increase in income levies asked by

Continued on Page 7, Column 4

IN TODAY'S INQUIRER

Austrians Refuse To Fight Italians

PORT BOU, Spain, Nov. 1 (A. P.).—A division of Austrian Alpinists ordered to rout about 10,000 Italian troops loyal to Premier Marshal Pietro Badoglio from the French Maritime Alps, fraternized with them instead and even supplied them munitions, a border dispatch said today.

This state of affairs was reported finally to have forced withdrawal of the Austrians from the region between Nice and Menton and their replacement by an S.S. division, neither trained nor equipped for mountain work but politically dependable, and a regiment of Nazi mountaineers.

Algiers a Year Later

Ivan H. (Cy) Peterman, Inquirer war correspondent with General Eisenhower's forces, etches the famed African headquarters city in the second of two articles

Today on Page 19

3 Huge Nazi Planes Wrecked in Corsica

ALLIED HEADQUARTERS, ALGIERS, Nov. 1 (A. P.).—The wreckage of three huge six-motored Merseburg-323 transport planes, in one of which 112 German soldiers apparently perished, has been found near Bastia airfield in Corsica as well as many JU-52 troop carriers blown up by the Germans because escape appeared impossible.

BADOGLIO INDICATES KING SHOULD QUIT

By WES GALLAGHER

SOMEWHERE IN SOUTHERN ITALY, Nov. 1 (A. P.).—Premier Pietro Badoglio told aged King Victor Emmanuel today he could not form a representative government while the King remained in power.

Thus Badoglio, who had just returned after an air tour of Southern Italy, including Naples where he conferred with political leaders, handed the King his toughest problem in the 43 years of his reign—whether to abdicate or allow Italy to tear herself apart by political strife.

SAW SFORZA, CROCE

In Naples, Badoglio had conferred with Count Carlo Sforza and Benedetto Croce, the Italian philosopher, among others.

Sforza, anti-Fascist leader who is outstanding among Italian political figures, is said to have told Badoglio he never would join the government so long as the King retained the throne. He was reported to be backed by Croce and the entire National Liberation Front, which includes Italy's six political parties.

ALLIED HANDS OFF

Badoglio was accompanied by representatives of the Allied military mission, including its chief, Lieuten-

Continued on Page 2, Column 7

War Summary

Tuesday, Nov. 2, 1943

Ending the historic Moscow conference on a ringing note of victory and lasting world peace to follow, the United States, Great Britain, Soviet Russia and China yesterday stood pledged to beat the Axis into unconditional surrender and to collaborate in a "general international organization" to maintain peace and security.

The U. S., Britain and Russia also agreed upon plans for a second front in Western Europe and made provisions that the Germans responsible for war atrocities would be delivered to their accusers for "on the spot" judgment and punishment.

They further pledged the liberation of Italy and Austria, in what was regarded both as a bid for the latter nation to rise in revolt against Hitler and as paving the way for a Danubian Federation. The report aroused acclaim both in Washington and London.

Meanwhile, on the Russian battlefront, the Red Army sealed off the Crimea, trapping an estimated 90,000 Germans, as they captured Perekop, the last escape gate, in a 10-mile drive into the isthmus. The Nazis were facing their greatest dis-aster since Stalingrad, and their forces in the lower Ukraine were streaming in wild disorder toward the Dnieper River.

In Italy, the Allied Fifth Army seized Teano, an important road center in the Mount Massico line and gained one to five miles in other sectors; the Eighth Army also moved ahead. In all, 21 towns fell to the two Allied forces.

Premier Badoglio informed King Victor Emmanuel he would be unable to form a government while the King remained in power, as a result of stands taken by Count Sforza and other leaders.

The mounting Allied offensive in the Southwest Pacific reached a new peak as American forces invaded Bougainville Island, last Japanese base in the Solomons and key to the big enemy citadel at Rabaul.

U. S. WEATHER FORECAST

Philadelphia and Vicinity—Warmer and occasional light showers.

Sun rises 7.29 A M Sets 5 59 P M
Moon rises 12 01 P M Sets 9 57 P M

Other Weather Reports on Page 3

The Philadelphia Inquirer

PUBLIC LEDGER

An Independent Newspaper for All the People

FINAL CITY EDITION

CIRCULATION: September Average: Daily 501,034; Sunday 1,250,247

WEDNESDAY MORNING, NOVEMBER 3, 1943

Copyright, 1943, by The Philadelphia Inquirer Co. Vol. 229. No. 126

abdefgh★

THREE CENTS

SAMUEL IS ELECTED

Transit Dispute Settled as Union Yields on Buttons

Plant Near Vienna Pounded by New U.S. Bomber Force

Wednesday, Nov. 3, 1943

Bombs bursting on the Messerschmitt assembly plant near Vienna marked the inauguration yesterday of the U. S. 15th Air Force, which will concentrate on long-range raids on German territory from Africa and Italy. The new air force is in charge of Lieutenant General Carl A. Spaatz, who has been appointed commander of all American air forces in the Mediterranean.

Troops of the Allied Fifth Army fought their way to important heights on Massico Ridge and Mount Matese at the core of the new German line in Italy. American forces won a good part of Matese, while British units gained four miles to seize a town high on Massico Ridge.

Russia's Fourth Ukraine Army captured the city of Kakhovka on the Dnieper as thousands of Germans, attempting to flee to the west bank, either were drowned or mowed down by Soviet guns. Another Red column seized the Black Sea city of Skadovsk, while inside the Dnieper bend the battle for Krivoi Rog raged unabated.

In the Pacific, Allied warships repelled an attempt by Jap fleet units to interfere with landing operations on Bougainville in the Solomons on Monday night.

Spaatz Commands All Air Operations In Mediterranean

By NOLAND NORGAARD

ALLIED HEADQUARTERS, Algiers, Nov. 2 (A. P.).—Creation of a new U. S. 15th Army Air Force, teamed with the veteran 12th in an all-American Mediterranean aerial fleet under Lieutenant General Carl A. Spaatz, was announced tonight a few hours after its heavy bombers had battered the Messerschmitt assembly plant at Wiener Neustadt.

Aimed to "increase greatly air power in this theater," the announcement from Allied headquarters said the 15th Air Force "will concentrate on long-range, strategic bombing against Germany and military targets in occupied and satellite countries."

Wiener Neustadt, 27 miles south of Vienna, falls well within that definition of targets.

SUCCESSFUL ATTACK

A large number of Flying Fortresses and Liberators plastered the Wiener Neustadt aircraft factory for the third time in an attack which returning pilots described as highly successful.

"They encountered clear weather over the target and the bombs were seen to explode on the target," a communique said. "Preliminary re-

Continued on Page 2, Column 1

Allies Pierce Core Of Rommel's Line; Gain Vital Heights

Map on Page 2

By EDWARD KENNEDY

ALLIED HEADQUARTERS, ALGIERS, Nov. 2 (A. P.).—Launching a heavy attack on the core of the German defense line across Italy, the Fifth Army has captured "important positions" on towering Massico Ridge and Matese Mountain in the face of fierce enemy resistance, the Allied Command announced today, and a spokesman described the Nazi wall before Rome as "severely shaken."

American troops of Lieutenant General Mark W. Clark's Salerno army, fighting forward through rugged, rain-soaked terrain, won a good part of Matese, the lofty peak that dominates the upper Volturno Valley, while British units advanced four miles in the Mediterranean coastal area to seize the town of Casanova, high on the steep slopes of Massico Ridge.

'VERY ENCOURAGING'

Reports from the front did not indicate exactly how much of Matese Mountain which sprawls over an extensive area, had been occupied by the Americans, but they said a good part of the whole ridge and some of its highest points were cleared of Germans. An Allied of-

Continued on Page 2, Column 3

ACTION BY U. S. PREVENTS WIDE TIEUP IN CITY

6-Hour Parley Held; Workers Returning 'Immediately;' WLB To Decide Issue

Illustrated on Page 28

The threat of a city-wide tie-up of the Philadelphia Transportation Co.'s trolley, bus and subway-elevated services was averted late last night as members of the C. I. O. Transport Workers Union, after a six-hour conference with Government conciliators, yielded in their dispute over the right to wear union buttons on duty.

The dispute, beginning early yesterday, had flared suddenly to disrupt service on a number of trolley and bus lines throughout the day and, when the conference ended successfully at midnight, was threatening to spread to other branches of the P. T. C. system.

RETURN 'IMMEDIATELY'

Dr. Alexander H. Frey, vice chairman of the regional War Labor Board here, emerged from a session with representatives of the company and the union to announce that the transport workers had decided to return to work "immediately."

They had agreed further, he said, to refrain from wearing their union buttons while on duty. The work stoppage yesterday, termed a strike by the company and a lock-out by the union, was caused when the company ruled that operators wearing union buttons could not operate its vehicles.

ISSUE NOT DECIDED

No conclusion as to the dispute itself was reached, Dr. Frey explained, but both parties have requested the WLB to exercise jurisdiction over all phases of the controversy. Each has indicated its willingness, he said, to have the case heard by a hearing officer to be designated by the regional WLB.

"I have requested the union members to refrain from wearing their union buttons while at work, until there has been an opportunity for the WLB to determine all matters relating to the validity, application and enforcement of the company's orders concerning the wearing of badges, etc., and including the matter of payment to employes who did not work runs on Nov. 2," said Dr. Frey.

LEADER TO TOUR BARNS

"I am confident that in the interests of the war effort, the work-

Continued on Page 13, Column 1

U.M.W. CHIEFS IGNORE F.D.R. WORK APPEAL

Policy Committee Abandons Meeting As Lewis Holds Parleys With Ickes

By DOROTHY ROCKWELL
Inquirer Washington Bureau

WASHINGTON, Nov. 2.—The leadership of the United Mine Workers today ignored President Roosevelt's appeal for the resumption of work at the strike-bound coal pits tomorrow, and the strike, presumably, will continue unabated for at least two more days.

John L. Lewis conferred twice during the day with Secretary of the Interior Harold L. Ickes, who this morning took over the coal mines at the President's direction.

ABANDON MEETING

The U.M.W. Policy Committee, which was to have met at 4 P. M. today to issue a back-to-work order, first postponed and then abandoned its meeting, apparently in deference to the Lewis-Ickes conferences. Lewis met briefly late this afternoon with the U.M.W. district presidents. The Policy Committee "may" meet tomorrow.

"No coal will be mined tomorrow, that's sure," said a U.M.W. spokesman.

As the mine crisis dragged on, it became obvious that even with complete co-operation of U.M.W. leadership, full production at the mines could not be expected until next Monday.

It was presumed, in the absence of official statements, that Lewis and Ickes had been discussing terms of a contract which Mr. Roosevelt instructed Ickes to offer the U.M.W., embodying the recommendations made by the War Labor Board in

Continued on Page 12, Column 4

Bowles Says Butter Stays at 16 Points

MADISON, Wis., Nov. 2 (U. P.).—Acting Price Administrator Chester Bowles said today that butter ration points cannot be reduced, despite huge supplies stored for the armed forces.

In a letter to Acting Governor Walter S. Goodland, Bowles said there was enough butter stored to meet the needs of the armed forces until next spring. But, he said, production will drop during the winter, and civilian demands will surpass the supply.

ELECTED FOR FULL TERM
Acting Mayor Bernard Samuel shown in his office at City Hall last night after his victory over his Democratic opponent, William C. Bullitt, by approximately 65,000.

Lead Over Bullitt Passes 65,000 in Sweep for G. O. P.

By JOSEPH H. MILLER

The Republican municipal ticket, headed by Acting Mayor Bernard Samuel, candidate for a full term, scored a smashing victory at yesterday's election.

With only a few of the city's 1335 divisions missing, Samuel defeated William C. Bullitt, his Democratic opponent, by approximately 65,000 votes.

Although Samuel's election was evident within an hour after the polls closed at 8 P. M. last night, as a result of an ever-increasing trend toward the Republicans, it was not until 12.15 o'clock this morning that Bullitt admitted his defeat.

Unofficial returns from 1312 divisions collected by The Inquirer at 2 A. M. today showed these results in the Mayoralty race:

Samuel —— 339,611
Bullitt —— 274,575

In another tabulation, collected by the police, returns from all of the 52 wards, showed the following vote:

Samuel —— 342,288
Bullitt —— 279,026

Jules C. Abercauph, Mayoralty candidate of the Independent Voters League party, who was backed mainly by members of the Communist Party, polled approximately 4000 votes.

TOTAL OF 625,000 VOTES CAST

The results of the Mayoralty race indicated that approximately 625,000 of the city's 978,771 registered voters participated in the balloting.

Besides winning the Mayor's office and the other municipal posts, the returns showed the Republicans had retained control of City Council by at least a 19 to 3 margin. Also captured by the Republicans were four of the seven Magistrate's posts. However the Council contests in the 4th (West Philadelphia) district were so close that the results may not be ascertained until the official count is completed.

REPUBLICANS ELECTED TO ROW OFFICES

Elected with Samuel to other municipal offices were:

District Attorney—John H. Maurer, court-appointed incumbent, who defeated Todd Daniel.

Sheriff—Austin Meehan, 35th ward Republican leader, who defeated Elmer Kilroy, former Speaker of the State House of Representatives.

Receiver of Taxes—W. Frank Marshall, City Council-appointed incumbent, who won over Joseph A. Wilson, former chief of the income tax division, U. S. Bureau of Internal Revenue.

Recorder of Deeds—Charles J. Pommer, incumbent ap-

Continued on Page 16, Column 1

REPUBLICAN WINS IN NEW YORK STATE

NEW YORK, Nov. 2 (A. P.).—Joe R. Hanley, 67-year-old Republican State Senator, was elected Lieutenant Governor of New York today, assuring the Republicans of control of the State administration in the event that Governor Thomas E. Dewey should seek and win election to the Presidency.

Lieutenant General William N. Haskell, 65, Democrat, who had campaigned for the office with the support of all party leaders and with the backing of the American Labor Party, conceded Hanley's election at 10 P. M. (E. W. T.).

HAD CLAIMED VICTORY

Shortly before that time, Hanley had claimed his election, saying that the only issue of the campaign had been continuance of "the sound government" of the Dewey Administration which took office last Jan. 1. The election was to fill the vacancy caused by the death of Thomas W. Wallace.

With 8907 of New York's 8987 dis-

Continued on Page 18, Column 3

EDGE WINS JERSEY BY 100,000 VOTES

Walter E. Edge, Governor of New Jersey during the First World War, early today was returned to that post by a majority approximating 100,000 votes.

The Republican candidate's victory was assured shortly after 1 A. M. when his Democratic opponent, Mayor Vincent J. Murphy, of Newark, conceded the election.

Unofficial returns from 3073 of the State's 3647 election districts gave this vote:

Edge —— 537,214
Murphy —— 420,912

Tabulations from 11 of the State's 21 counties were complete at 3 A. M. Of these, Edge carried all but one and was leading in eight of those remaining incomplete.

MURPHY STRONGHOLD

Murphy won Middlesex county by a margin of less than 3000 votes and was leading in Camden and Hudson counties. He carried his own home of Newark but was trailing by a large margin in Essex county.

Less than an hour before Mayor Murphy admitted defeat, Lloyd B. Marsh, Passaic county clerk and Edge's campaign manager, claimed the election.

In a telegram to the 70-year-old victor, Murphy congratulated Edge

Continued on Page 17, Column 6

JAP SHIPS ROUTED FROM BOUGAINVILLE

By C. YATES McDANIEL

ALLIED HEADQUARTERS IN THE SOUTHWEST PACIFIC, Nov. 3 (Wednesday) (A. P.).—General Douglas MacArthur's headquarters said today that Japanese and American warships had clashed in a battle which have an important effect on the ability of United States Marines to control their new invasion positions on the west-central coast of Bougainville in the Northern Solomons.

Headquarters awaited complete reports, saying preliminary advices from Admiral William F. Halsey, Jr., were that Japanese cruisers and destroyers were intercepted in the Solomons Sea and were forced to withdraw after clashing Monday night and early Tuesday.

AFTER U. S. LANDINGS

(This action probably is the same one reported previously by Admiral Halsey's spokesman in the South

Continued on Page 5, Column 1

Reds Win Dnieper City, Nazi Hordes Drowned

Map on Page 2

By ROBERT S. MUSEL

LONDON, Nov. 3 (Wednesday) (U. P.).—General Feodor I. Tolbukhin's Fourth Ukraine Army yesterday captured the historic city of Kakhovka, where thousands of Germans drowned in the swirling Dnieper or died under murderous Russian fire as they attempted to flee to the west bank of the river.

Another German force, encircled Monday and Tuesday in the south of the Nagaisk steppe, was driven back to the shores of the Sivash lagoon and "completely annihilated," communiques broadcast by Moscow announced. A large number of prisoners was taken.

PRESS FLANK DRIVE

War Bulletins issued by the Soviet command gave no new details of the fighting within the Perekop isthmus, where the Red Army had smashed into the Gateway of the Crimea. But they disclosed that Soviet columns had raced 36 miles west of the isthmus to take the town of Skadovsk on the Black Sea coast in a direct threat to flank the im-

Continued on Page 2, Column 6

IN TODAY'S INQUIRER

SPECIAL DEPARTMENTS

COLUMNS AND FEATURES

MARIGNY EX-WIFE GAVE HIM $100,000

Illustrated on Page 24

By E. V. W. JONES

NASSAU, Bahamas, Nov. 2 (A. P.).—A statement that Count Alfred de Marigny spent more than $100,000 of his second wife's money was introduced today at his trial for the murder of Sir Harry Oakes after an earlier Crown witness drew a severe reprimand for changing his testimony.

In a Bahamas Supreme Court session which started on a calm note but soon developed into one of the most heated exchanges of the trial, John H. Anderson, banker, brought out de Marigny's financial dealings with his former wife, Ruth, from whom he was divorced shortly before he wooed and won the slain millionaire's eldest daughter Nancy.

REPORTED ON FINANCES

Anderson, manager o the Bahamas General Trust Company, said de Marigny laid before him last June—about a month before Oakes' beaten and burned body was found at his estate Westbourne—a financial statement showing his dealings with Ruth.

The statement showed, Anderson said, that the defendant had re-

Continued on Page 24, Column 2

French Assembly To Convene Today

ALGIERS, Nov. 2 (U. P.).—The French Consultative Assembly will convene tomorrow for the first time amid an atmosphere of bitter disappointment that France was not invited to participate in the newly-created European Commission in London.

General Charles de Gaulle, co-chairman of the French Committee of National Liberation, was expected to voice French dissatisfaction in an inaugural address before the assembly, a limited parliamentary body to serve until a general election can be held in France.

Emergency Decreed In Berlin, 40 Cities

LONDON, Nov. 2 (A. P.).—The Reuters news agency, quoting the Malmoe correspondent of the Stockholf Svenska Dagbladet, said tonight that a state of emergency had been decreed in Berlin and 40 other German cities.

The report was confirmed by travelers, arriving from Germany by way of Denmark, it was said. Among the cities declared affected was Flensburg, on the German-Danish border.

(This dispatch did not bring out the provisions of the "state of emergency," but presumably it brought further tightening of restrictions imposed by Heinrich Himmler's interior functionaries.)

RENO SWAMPS BOK FOR SUPERIOR COURT

By GERSON H. LUSH

Superior Court Judge Claude Trexler Reno snowed under his Democratic opponent, Judge Curtis Bok, of Philadelphia, in yesterday's only State-wide election, winning a 10-year term on the Appellate Court bench.

Republican State leaders viewed Reno's clear-cut victory as an indication of the party's strength in next year's Presidential election.

As returns were being tabulated early this morning, the former State Attorney General's lead was mounting hourly.

PROHIBITIONIST SWAMPED

Unofficial results from 3014 of the Commonwealth's 8192 election precincts gave Reno a lead of more than 121,421 over Bok. He apparently was assured of an additional majority of 60,000 in Philadelphia.

The Republican jurist, on the basis of the early returns, was running ahead of Bok in 61 of the State's 67 counties. In the Democratic column were Greene, Elk, Westmoreland, Fayette, Washington and Allegheny counties.

Charles Palmer, of Ridley township, Delaware county, aspirant of

Continued on Page 17, Column 7

19 COUNCIL SEATS SWEPT BY G. O. P.

By J. TAYLOR BUCKLEY

Exceeding the most optimistic expectations, the Republicans appeared the winner of at least 19 seats in City Council in yesterday's election, with the remaining three in doubt early this morning.

The unofficial tabulations for the three posts in question, one in the Strawberry Mansion - Brewerytown 7th, and two in West Philadelphia's 4th, were so close that the winners probably will not be known until the official count is completed.

COMPLETE CONTROL

However, the Councilmanic sweep assured the G. O. P. of a heavy majority in the chamber next year and gave complete control of the city

Continued on Page 17, Column 5

U. S. WEATHER FORECAST

Philadelphia and Vicinity: Fair and cooler with light rain today.

Sun rises 7.32 A. M. Sets 5.56 P. M.
Moon rises 12.56 P. M. Sets 10.59 P. M.

Other Weather Reports on Page 7

4-Year Age Difference Not Bar to Marriage

By Martha Foster

Your Port in a Storm

When he was a young man, Ben Franklin laid down a wonderous set of rules by which to live. But he admitted later that they weren't kept too well. I think that holds true for all of us. Hard and fast rules for living would hobble rather than help us. For instance, I don't feel it's generally wise for a woman to marry a man much younger than herself, but that needn't be a bar to "K. N." who writes:

• • •

Not Too Much Difference

"Dear Martha Foster:

"About a month ago I gave up a boy I love very dearly, because of his age. I am four years older than he, but his appearance and speech make him appear older than his years. He couldn't understand why I should break up such a lovely friendship for a matter of a few years.

"I told him he should be going out with younger girls, and shouldn't be tying himself down at such an early age. He has told me he loves me and that I would be his wife. When he got older, don't you think he would feel that perhaps he had made a mistake in marrying me?

"I was really thinking of his and my future. I'm not the type of girl to plunge into marriage and not care whether we would be happy later. Now, though, I've left this boy broken hearted how can I make it up to him? Shall I call him up and seek a reconciliation, or just assume it happened that way for the best? "K. N."

ANSWER—A boy as devoted to you as he is deserves better treatment. There is certainly no reason why you shouldn't be friends, or, for that matter, consider marriage. The difference in your ages would hardly be significant. So let him know you think perhaps you're the one, after all, who made the mistake! I'm quite sure this four-year difference would lead to no regrets.

Advice to 'S. B.'

This letter from "Experience" is addressed to "S. B.," whose stepmother claims she is wayward and who in turn wrote to explain her unfortunate home life:

"Dear Martha Foster:

"S. B." is more sinned against than sinning. May I have a word with her? S. B., do not for a second accept physical abuse. Go to the nearest welfare agency, and there you will find friends. Attend your little parties, make nice friends, try not to offend. Do not stay in your room and brood. Your whole outlook on life will become warped. The world is full of splendid people: kind fathers, and even devoted stepmothers. Do not feel degraded because you are ill-used. The fault is not yours.

"It is truly amazing that a woman with children should advocate added brutality in your case. Such advice is a sad commentary on her ability to raise a family. Every parent knows that firmness, not severity, counts. The modern mother, even when forced to drastic measures, has something better to offer a 16-year-old than beatings with a razor strap . . . You have my sincere sympathy.

"EXPERIENCE"

Note to 'H. G.'

To "H. G."—Since your question is of a legal nature, I have referred it to "The People's Friend," the column of legal advice appearing daily on The Inquirer's editorial page. Watch for your answer there.

Note to 'Fair Widow'

To "A Fair Widow"—I see no objection to your asking this man to your home. He seems quite suitable, and after an adequate period of mourning, you should feel perfectly free to make new friends.

• • •

Tell your troubles to Martha Foster. Her thoughtful and kindly counsel can help you as it has helped others. Write to her at The Inquirer and watch this column each day for your answer.

Old-Fashioned Embroidery

Old fashioned figures in cross stitch are favorite embroidery for tea towels, luncheon sets, curtains, etc. Hot iron transfer pattern No. 504 contains 11 motifs measuring from 1½ by 1½ to 3 by 4½ inches each with complete instructions.

To order pattern: Write, or send above picture with your name and address with 16 cents in coin or stamps plus 3 cents for postage to cover mailing costs to NEEDLEWORK BUREAU, Philadelphia Inquirer, 229 Fifth Avenue, New York, New York.

Point Ration Budget Menu

By Mrs. Alexander George

Dinner With Advance Preparations

(Point-Rationed Items Are Starred)

Shepherd's Pie
Buttered Green Beans
Hot rolls — Apple Jelly
Vegetable Relish — Jellied Salad
Chocolate Cream Pudding
Cream
Hot Coffee

(Recipes Serve Four)

Shepherd's Pie

- *1 pound lamb shoulder
- *3 tablespoons bacon fat (or other kind)
- 2 tablespoons minced onions
- 1-3 cup diced celery
- 2 cups water
- Pinch of thyme or marjoram
- ½ teaspoon salt
- ¼ teaspoon pepper

Cut lamb into inch pieces, and brown well in fat, heated in frying pan. Add rest of ingredients and simmer, covered, about an hour. Add sauce.

Sau

- 3 tablespoons flour
- *3 tablespoons margarine, butter or chicken fat
- 1 cup milk
- ½ cup carrot stock
- 1 cup cubed cooked carrots
- 1 cup cubed turnips
- 1-3 teaspoon salt
- ⅛ teaspoon pepper

Mix flour with margarine and add milk. Pour into cooked meat blend and simmer 5 minutes. Add rest of ingredients and pour into greased shallow baking pan. Cover with 2 cups mashed, seasoned potatoes—white or sweet—and bake 25 minutes in moderate oven.

Hot Tamale Pie

- ½ cup corn meal
- 1½ cups water
- ½ teaspoon salt
- 1½ cups irradiated evaporated milk
- 1 tablespoon fat
- ½ cup onion, chopped
- 1 cup (½ pound) ground raw beef
- 1 cup tomatoes, canned or raw
- 1 pimiento, if desired
- Dash of cayenne pepper
- ¾ teaspoon salt

Measure meal into top of double boiler. Add water and one-half teaspoon salt. Boil until mixture begins to thicken. Add milk, bring to a boil, stirring constantly. Then set over boiling water to finish cooking, stirring occasionally. Cook onion slowly in fat until yellow. Stir in meat and continue cooking until the red color disappears. Add tomatoes, diced pimiento and seasoning. Pour into greased baking dish which has been lined with three-fourths of the corn meal mush. Cover with remainder of mush and bake in a moderate oven (375 degrees F.) until delicately browned (about 45 minutes).

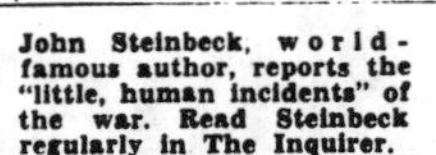

STEPFATHER ADMITS SLAYING OF CHILD, 4

CHICAGO, Nov. 11 (U. P.).—John Schaffer, 28, a railroad brakeman held in the slaying of his four-year-old stepdaughter, confessed today that he beat the child with a heavy leather strap, bound and gagged her, dipped her in a tub of water and locked her in a closet.

"I guess I shouldn't have done it," Schaffer told police. "But she annoyed me — she made noise so I couldn't sleep."

'I HATE HIM,' WIFE SAYS

The child's mother, who said she was present during the beating, was arrested and held on an open charge. She told police her husband frequently beat their children, and herself as well.

"I hate him," she said. "He always hated my children from my first marriage and told me they were like animals."

The Schaffers have three other children — Dorothy Weir, 7, Tommy Weir, 3, and Ida Schaffer, 19 months.

Ex-Wife of 'Yahweh' Gets $1432 Alimony

LOS AN ELES, Nov. 11 (U. P.).—Superior Court Judge Emmet H. Wilson scored a cleancut knockout over "The Great Spirit Yahweh" by returning a judgment of $1432 in alimony to Mrs. Joy Jeffers, ex-wife of Rev. Joe Jeffers, pastor of Kingdom Temple.

Jeffers vanished from Los Angeles two months ago shortly after the alimony money was in a bank account in the name of the temple. The pastor's flock vigorously opposed paying Mrs. Jeffers' alimony out of the church funds.

"I am not sure who this Yahweh person is," commented Judge Wilson, "but I think the Kingdom Temple people should pay Mrs. Jeffers' alimony."

Crane Operator Killed

READING, Pa., Nov. 11 (A. P.).—Guy L. Bierman, 53, a crane operator, was fatally injured today in a 40-foot fall from his machine in the Reading Co. yards. He landed on his head on a concrete driveway at the base of the crane, and died two hours later.

STARS PERFORMING IN NIGHT CLUB SHOWS

Deane Carroll (upper left), Palumbo's Cabaret; Joan Coraz (center left), Sam's Cafe; Ann Rubert (lower left), Tahiti Bar; Hal Sidare (upper left center), Weber's Hof Brau, Central Airport, Camden; Al Stevens (upper right center), Rathskeller; Johnny Cahill (center left), Sciolla's Cafe; Kate Ellen Murtah (center right), Jack Lynch's Walton Roof; James Barton (lower center), Shangri-La; Marcelle (upper right), Latimer Club; one of the Owen Sisters (center right), The Cove, and Betty Wharton (lower right), Benjamin Franklin Hotel.

4 MISSING IN BLAZE AT CHEMICAL PLANT

CLEVELAND, Nov. 11 (U. P.).—Officials of the Warren Refining and Chemical Co. said tonight that all employes except four women whose names were not available had been accounted for after fire destroyed the plant here today.

Eyewitnesses said they saw one woman fall back from a window on the third floor into the flames. Others told of seeing three women caught on the roof. Search of the ruins was postponed until they cooled off.

Fire flashed through the oil and grease-soaked floors of the plant shortly before noon and almost trapped approximately 60 employes working in the building. Many of them escaped by diving through windows as a series of explosions sent flames shooting 400 feet into the sky.

Youth So Startled He Leaped 3 Floors

WILMINGTON, Del., Nov. 11.—It's a question who was more startled—the two city detectives who entered a third-floor room in a W. Front st. dwelling by mistake today, or 18-year-old James J. Tardy, who jumped out the window when they entered.

Detectives Frank Miller and Edwin Rich were unable to find any reason for the youth's leap to an alley, in which he hurt his right foot. The only explanation they could get was that their entrance made him nervous. Despite the injury, they had to chase him 10 blocks to overtake him and send him to Delaware Hospital, where he was treated.

Serious trouble has broken out in Lebanon, and a British report said martial law has been proclaimed by the French in the little republic at the eastern end of the Mediter-ranean.

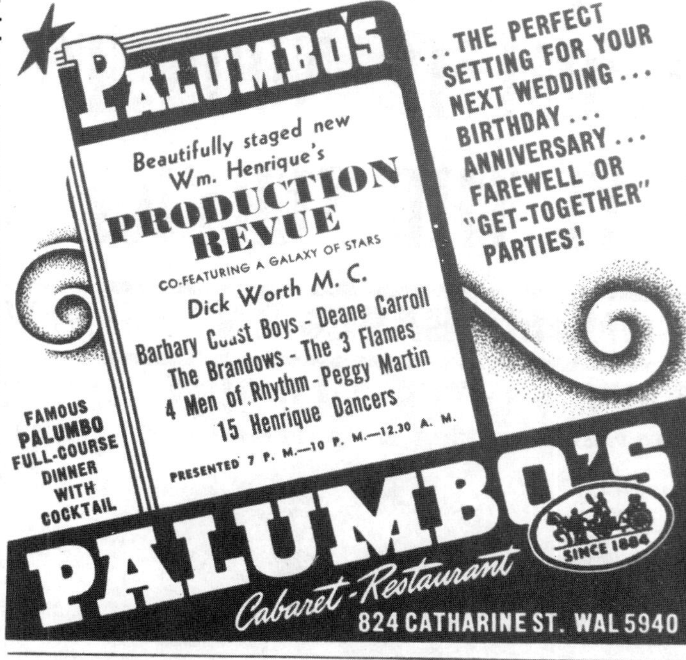

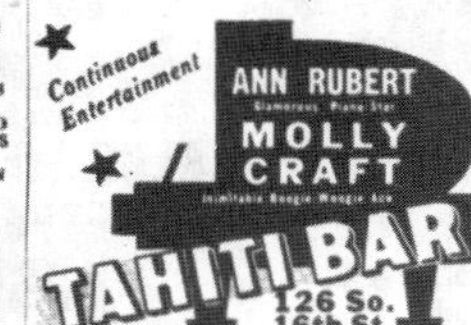

Officer to Speak At P. M. C. Tonight

Lieutenant Frank W. Jakob, a graduate of the 1941 class of Pennsylvania Military College, Chester, who recently returned from North Africa, where he served with the U. S. First Division, will be the speaker before the cadets and trainees in the Army Specialized Unit at the college tonight.

The officer was a star player on the college football team during his junior year and was battalion commander of the Cadet Corps. After receiving his commission he was stationed at Camp Devens and Fort Jay.

Entire Block, Market, 11th to 12th Streets, Through to 1125-27-29 Chestnut Street, Phila. 5, Pa.—Mail and Phone Orders Filled—Call LOCust 5200—Philadelphia Suburbs, Enterprise 1-0160—Camden and Suburbs, WX-1150

FROM 12 NOON TO 9 TONIGHT Snellenburgs IS AT THE SERVICE OF THRIFTY CHRISTMAS SHOPPERS

ECONOMY BASEMENT *Thrift* VALUES!

HEAVY WINTER CLOTHES
For Outdoor Men & Sportsmen

HEAVY MELTON JACKETS $6.95

Warm blue wool melton . . . 100% reprocessed wool just as sturdy as can be for the outdoor man! 32 oz. of real protection. 38 to 50.

LEATHER JACKETS $12.95

Hardy capeskin, fully lined for warmth protection. Seal out winds with a fly front. 38 to 48. Others from $8.95 to $15.95.

BLUE MELTON REEFERS $10.95

Heavy blue melton cloth makes reefers for real service. Of 100% reprocessed wool, and double-breasted, with 4 roomy pockets. 42-48.

SNELLENBURGS Economy Basement

Famous "Collarite"
SHIRTS $1.95

White, gray, and blue. Fancy patterns. Finely tailored of quality fabrics by Phillip-James, makers of Van Heusen shirts. Fully cut for comfort. An unusually good assortment of better shirts. Grand gifts are the ever popular collar attached style! Sizes 14 to 17.

Shaker Knit
COAT SWEATERS $4.95

Closely knit for warmth, with deep-ribbed cuffs for extra wear. Sturdily tailored for all outdoor activities . . . work or play. Navy only. Sizes 36 to 46.

SNELLENBURGS Economy Basement

Action Loving Shoes for Action Loving Women
CASUAL OXFORDS $3.45

A Cuban Heel Oxford—Leather sole
B Loafer—Rubber sole
C Moccasin—Rubber sole

Put your foot down . . . solidly! In antique tan leather uppers with Goodyear welted soles. A width 5 to 9, B and C widths 4 to 9. Bring Ration Book so we can detach shoe coupon.

SNELLENBURGS Economy Basement

Indian Design
BLANKETS $1.98 each

Colorful Indian designs and colors borrowed from the blankets used in the pueblos of our American Indians. Slightly imperfect. Mail and phone orders can only be filled while the lot lasts.

SNELLENBURGS Economy Basement

Cleanable
WINDOW SHADES 39c

So easy to clean—just lay the shade flat and whisk with a damp cloth. Perfect rollers. Made of strong composition.

SNELLENBURGS Economy Basement

Glass Door
UTILITY CLOSETS $29.95

Attractive gleaming white enamel with black pulls. 11x29x68 inches.

Sold on Deferred Payment Plan Plus Small Carrying Charge

SNELLENBURGS Economy Basement

24 Inches Long

MIRROR-TOP RADIATOR COVERS $2.98

The unsightly radiator comes into its own at last! Almost a piece of furniture now with a mirror top. Insulated unpainted frame.

30-INCH LENGTH . . . . $3.49 36-INCH LENGTH $3.98

SNELLENBURGS Economy Basement

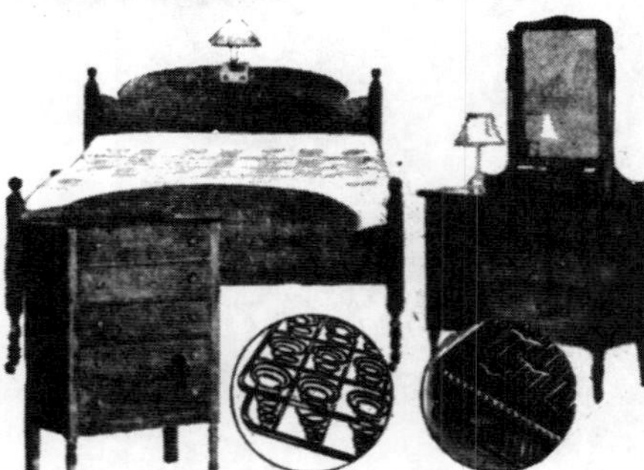

5-Pc. Bedroom ENSEMBLE
Walnut or Maple Finish Hardwood

$69.98 *Sold on Deferred Payment Plan*

- 4-drawer dresser with attached swinging mirror.
- 5-drawer chest of drawers.
- Panel-type bed, solid head and foot board. Full size (54 inch) or twin size (39 inch).
- Victory-type coil spring by "Bunting," with enamel finished coils and hardwood base.

SNELLENBURGS Economy Basement

Heavy
TOWELING
10 yds. $1.69

Heavy quality cotton toweling for hand or roller towels. Blue borders only. Make your own.

SNELLENBURGS Economy Basement

CONGOLEUM NAIRN *Gold Seal* RUGS
9x12 ft.
$5.98

HARDWOOD RUG BORDER 36" 29c

Cover your old floors and it looks like real hardwood. Smooth finished, and easy to clean. 24", 25c yd. 72", 29c sq. yd.

ARMSTRONG INLAID LINOLEUM 98c sq. yd.

Colorful design and marbleised effects. Wide selection of newest patterns by the famous Armstrong. 2 yds. wide.

ARMSTRONG'S RUGS

12x12 ft. $10.98 12x15 ft. $12.98

Just the size for that extra large room without a seam. Completely bordered rugs.

RUBBERLIKE RUNNERS 36" 39c yd.

Use on halls, offices, stores and porch. Large lengths.

SNELLENBURGS Economy Basement

Make Your Holiday Table Festive and Gay With One of These Cloths of

Irish Linen Double Damask

70x88 inches **$10.75** 70x106 inches **$12.75**

Dinner cloths that lend an air of festive elegance, befitting the importance of holiday occasions—snowy white Irish linen, in beautiful double damask weave—handsome floral or conventional patterns—perfect settings for a lifetime of gay entertaining and lasting service.

Matching Dinner Napkins, 22x22 Inches . . . . . . dozen $10.75

Linen Dish Toweling, 49c yard

Firmly woven toweling that will prove extra absorbent and durable. Colored striped borders of blue, gold, red or green.

Printed Cotton Table Cloths, $2.50

Cheerful cloths in that grand size, 52x70 inches. Sparkling in their gay color combinations and patterns—serviceable in their firm, close weave.

Snellenburgs Linens, Second Floor

Sparkling Reflectors of Holiday Scenes!

Large Gilt Frame Mirrors

Think how your home will be improved by one of these in a strategic position above the mantel, over the davenport, in a spot that needs a bit of stepping-up. Offered in time for your holiday entertaining or to select for some lucky person as a gift. Genuine plate glass with ornamental frame of rare beauty.

$12.95 34x36 Inches

Snellenburgs Mirrors, Fourth Floor

Long Lasting, Fine Quality Bedmuslins for Proud Homemakers! Extra Heavy! Extra Strong!

Perfect Muslin Sheets

Size 72x108 Inches
Size 81x99 Inches **$1.98**

Size 72x99 Inches $1.89
Size 81x108 Inches $2.19
Pillow Cases, size 42x36 Inches . . . 49c

SEECO COIL SPRING PROTECTORS—So popular with careful housekeepers, for keeping dust out of mattresses. Prevent rusting of springs and tearing of bedding. Chemically treated. Full, twin and three-quarter sizes, each **$1.00**

"TEX - KNIT" MATTRESS PROTECTOR—Made of waffle-weave cotton, firmly stitched and bound with 2-inch bias tape. Ample size. 54x76 inches **$2.98**

Flowered Pillow Ticks, 69c

NON - ALLERGIC PILLOW COVERS—To keep dust from pillows — a relief to sleepers with allergy to dust or feathers. Easily cleaned with a damp cloth **$1.29**

Snellenburgs Bedmuslins, Second Floor

Fine Table Lamps
Give Bright Meaning to Practical Gifts

$9.95 each

Lamps that will be the light of her life—practical, and yet so charmingly decorative on her favorite table. Tall and graceful stems of gleaming crystal—soft, glowing shades of lovely multifilament rayon, beautifully lined, in three styles. Gay ruching adds the finishing touch. Warm, friendly gifts for the home-lover on your list.

Snellenburgs Lamps, Fourth Floor

Smartly Efficient Four-Burner Gas Range
$49.98

A grand value, sold under Government regulations. Rigid frames are made of structural steel, the front of porcelain. Complete with oven and broiler. A favorite style and size. Deferred payment plan, plus small carrying charge.

Snellenburgs Housefurnishings, Third Floor

Health Food Suggestions From Our Chestnut Street Food Store

Carnation Malted Milk
1-lb. jar **43c**

How the children will go for their milk when this delicious flavoring is added . . . and it's an extra nourishment.

Schindler's Peanut Butter 1-lb. jar 33c

Everyone from the kiddies to Grandpa will love this fine peanut butter spread. Nutritious and delicious in both its coarse and fine grinds.

WE CARRY DIABETIC FOODS. We recommend the famous Celiu line of fruits packed in either juice or water.

Snellenburgs Food Store, First Floor, Chestnut Street

The Philadelphia Inquirer

PUBLIC LEDGER

An Independent Newspaper for All the People

FINAL CITY EDITION

CIRCULATION: October Average: Daily 487,836; Sunday 1,266,718

MONDAY MORNING, NOVEMBER 22, 1943
Copyright, 1943, by The Philadelphia Inquirer Co. Vol. 229, No. 145

abdefgh

THREE CENTS

U. S. Troops Invade 2 Gilbert Islands

Rep. Ditter Killed in Crash of Navy Plane

Inflation

Spiral Starts With Drop In Supply and Loss Of Wage-Price Control

By Irwin S. Hoffer

Professor of Economics and Statistics, School of Business and Public Administration, Temple University, As Told To

Rose McKee

(First in a series)

INFLATION, which could boost the price of a five-cent cigar to $500, is little understood simply because in talk of it, people lose sight of basic economic facts.

Everyone of us plays two roles on the stage of economic, that of producer and consumer. Because of our division of labor, we as producers consume very little of what we produce. The results of our labor are sold for a price and what we buy is bought for a price. The exchange would present very little of a problem were it not for the large number of steps required in modern production and the large number of people involved.

When the demand for any article or all articles exceeds the supply, prices rise. That is basic.

The complicating feature of our present situation is the fact that about 70 percent of our production this year is for the prosecution of the war. Consequently the supply available to civilians is relatively small. At the same time civilians have an unusually large amount of money to spend. The result: tremendous pressure on the curtailed supply and rising prices.

• • •

ANOTHER complication in today's economic drama is the great disparity between relative increases in purchasing power. Some groups feel the rising prices less because their wages or incomes have been increased and they can keep up to the soaring prices. Others, whose purses are no fatter than they were in 1941, are having to pinch to make both ends meet. The cost of living has risen about 25 percent in the last two years.

When changes in supply, demand and prices take place slowly over a period of years, there are no serious difficulties. It is when changes in supply, demand and price take place quickly that disaster impends. For in sudden change, the three do not keep the same pace nor do they even head in the same direction, as we see today in a supply that is plunging downward and a demand that is zooming upward. In sudden change, too, the impact of these distortions on consumers is not equal.

Just when does inflation take place? When the demand for goods because of an unusual increase in purchasing power runs rapidly ahead of the goods available to meet those demands, prices tend to rise very sharply and inflation results. We have a mild form of inflation today.

• • •

VARIOUS attempts to halt the price climb have been made—rationing programs that equalize the distribution of available goods, price ceilings, the Little Steel formula to stabilize wages. If these or like measures can be continued until the supply of civilian goods is brought more nearly into line with the demand for those goods, serious inflation will be averted.

If on the other hand, pressure is brought to bear to force up wages and consequently consumers' incomes, and price controls are weakened, the tendency will be for the demand for civilian goods to run still further ahead of supply and drive up prices still more.

This would lead to the often described "spiral" of increasing wages and income and higher prices, which in turn would lead only to further demands for wage increases and still higher prices. The pattern would be repeated until there is tremendous distortion in our economic life, immense inequities between consumers and widespread, severe distress.

(Continued tomorrow)

PILOT ALSO DIES IN FLAMES AT COLUMBIA, PA.

Ship Forced Off Course by Weather; 7 Dead as Bomber Falls Near Tamaqua

Map and Picture on Page 10

Congressman J. William Ditter, Republican Representative from Montgomery county, was one of two men killed last night when a single-motored Navy Beachcraft plane crashed near Columbia in Lancaster county.

His companion in death was the pilot of the plane, Lieutenant Commander J. J. Mansure, executive officer of the Naval Air Station at Willow Grove, just north of this city.

THREE OTHER CRASHES

Their deaths came at 10.30 P. M., according to announcement early this morning by the Fourth Naval District, with headquarters here.

The crash was one of four involving service planes in the Pennsylvania area. Near Tamaqua an Army transport plane crashed against a mountain in a rainstorm, killing seven fliers and injuring two. Not far from Johnstown, Pa., five Army airmen set the automatic pilot and parachuted to safety from a Flying Fortress, which eventually crashed 80 miles away near Frostburg, Md. Near Altoona, Pa., a WASP bailed out safely from a service plane in trouble.

DRIVEN OFF COURSE

According to announcement made in this city, the plane carrying Representative Ditter had left the Naval Station at Squantum, Mass., earlier in the day, and was bound for the Willow Grove Station. However, it was driven off its course, presumably by bad weather, and crashed to earth while seeking a landing place in the vicinity of Columbia.

The plane was approximately 80 miles from its destination, the Navy said, when it crashed in a hilly, wooded section of Lancaster county, three miles from the Susquehanna River.

FLARES DROPPED

Residents of Columbia and the nearby community of Kinterhook said the craft flew low, dropping flares as though seeking a landing place. One man said he heard the motor sputtering.

The Navy was unable immediately to explain Ditter's presence on the plane, but members of Con-

Continued on Page 10, Column 3

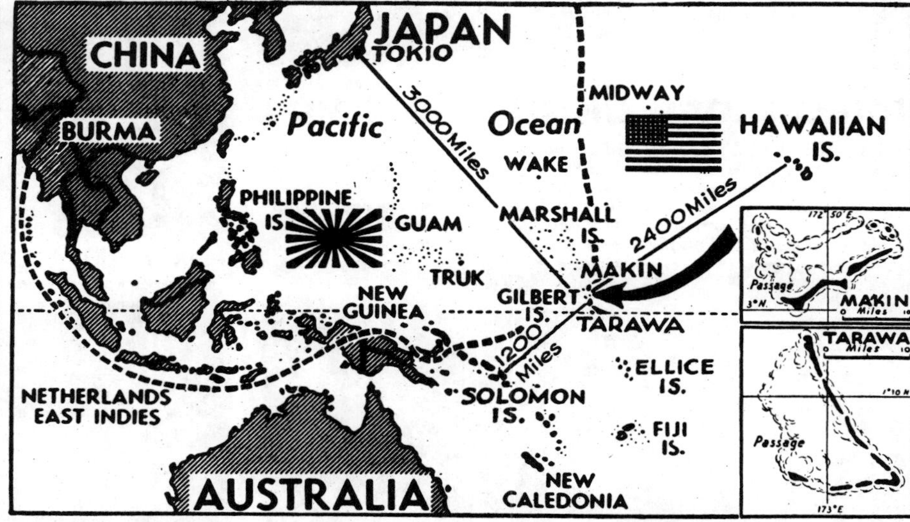

WHERE AMERICANS LANDED ON TWO ISLANDS IN MID-PACIFIC GILBERT GROUP

Arrow points to Gilbert Islands, in Central Pacific, which were invaded at dawn Saturday by U. S. troops who landed on Makin and Tarawa (insert maps show contour of isles and coral reefs which surround their lagoons). Dotted line marks limit of Japanese-dominated area. Distances to Tokio, Hawaiian and Solomon Islands are shown. The Gilberts provide key stepping stone for attack on major Jap base at Truk, to northwest.

Tarawa, Makin Attacked

Illustrated on Page 16

By WILLIAM F. TYREE

PEARL HARBOR, Nov. 21 (U. P.).—United States Marines and soldiers, opening the long-awaited offensive against Japan's mid-Pacific strongholds guarding the road to Tokio, invaded Makin and Tarawa atolls in the Gilbert Islands at dawn Saturday.

Hand-to-hand fighting was believed under way today as the Americans fought to extend their beachheads.

HEAVY FLEET COVER

Covered by powerful units of all types of the Pacific Fleet — battleships, aircraft carriers, cruisers and destroyers — the Americans splashed ashore to the tune of bursting naval shells and aerial bombs at opposite ends of a 180-mile north-south line, and quickly won beachheads.

The invasion, first of the war against the hundreds of coral islands forming Japan's easternmost Pacific ramparts, was announced at 11 A. M. (4.30 P. M. Philadelphia time) by white-haired Admiral Chester W. Nimitz, Pacific Fleet Commander, who had been predicting for several weeks that the Japanese soon would be dug from their island positions.

2400 MILES FROM HAWAII

The Gilberts, 16 atolls lying astride the Equator, are 2400 miles southwest of Hawaii and were seized from Britain by Japan on Pearl Harbor day, Dec. 7, 1941.

Admiral Nimitz's communique said:

"Marine Corps and Army forces, covered by powerful units of all types of the Pacific Fleet, established beachheads on Makin and Tarawa atolls, Gilbert Islands, meeting moderate resistance at Makin and strong resistance at Tarawa. Fighting continues.

"During these operations Army Liberators made diversionary attacks in the Marshalls."

VAST ENCIRCLEMENT

A successful invasion of Tarawa and Makin not only would neutralize nearby Japanese islands, it was said, but would represent a gigantic encirclement movement against the great Japanese naval base of Truk, 1600 miles to the west, and also pave the way for a stab northward into the Jap-held Marshall Islands.

Nimitz announced that more than 24 hours after the invasion began the doughboys and devil dogs were battling the Japanese on the beaches of Makin and Tarawa and in the coconut groves, fighting side by side as they are some 1200 miles southwest on Bougainville Island.

'MODERATE' AT MAKIN

It was believed that Marines led the way ashore at Makin, northernmost of the Gilberts, and Tarawa, 180 miles below Makin and the most important island of the group.

Nimitz announced that at Makin, where Lieutenant Colonel Evans F.

Continued on Page 3, Column 3

TWO SHIPS COLLIDE OFF CAPE HENLOPEN

Collision of two merchant ships in a dense fog off the Delaware Capes, with an undisclosed number of casualties, was officially announced yesterday by the Fourth Naval District.

The crash, according to the announcement, occurred approximately 58 miles south of Cape Henlopen, and resulted in one of the ships roaring up in flames.

BURNING IN PORT

Late last night a Navy spokesman said the burning ship had been towed into Cape May, with scattered fires still raging aboard her. He said the flames were under control and that the vessel would be salvaged.

Navy officials announced earlier that the other ship had made port under her own power. The port was not designated.

A Navy spokesman said the number of missing in the collision would be withheld pending a complete Navy check, and that their names would not be announced until the next of kin are notified.

SHIP NAMES NOT REVEALED

The collison was said to have occurred at approximately 2 A. M. yesterday, but the Navy did not disclose the names of the two ships involved, nor did the official announcement offer any speculation on the cause or causes of the collision.

It was announced, however, that 39 survivors had been rescued.

An unverified report indicated that the captain of one of the ships was among the survivors.

REPORT 3 BODIES RECOVERED

Unofficial reports at Lewes said they were brought ashore at 3 P. M. Britain.

Continued on Page 10, Column 3

8-Mile German Wedge Erased in Central Italy

Map on Page 2

By EDWARD KENNEDY

ALLIED HEADQUARTERS, ALGIERS, Nov. 21 (A. P.).—In sharp fighting Allied armies have captured four key points along the Italian front—Agnone, Archi, Castel San Vincenso and Rocchetta — straightening out their line and shortening it by some 20 miles, Allied Headquarters announced today.

In seizing Agnone, the veterans of General Sir Bernard L. Montgomery ironed out an eight-mile-deep German salient, which extended from Carovilli to Salcito in the central sector and which had prevented the Allies from using all of the lateral highway running from Vasto on the Adriatic to Isernia in the mountains.

FIFTH ARMY GAINS 3 MILES

Overrunning Agnone without meeting opposition, the Eighth Army plunged on beyond.

Near the Adriatic, the troops under Montgomery also pushed forward to capture Archi and nearby heights 13 miles from the sea.

Another three-mile advance was chalked up in the upper Volturno region where Lieutenant General Mark W. Clark's Fifth Army troops occupied Castel San Vincenzo and Rocchetta, northwest of Isernia, broadening their elbow room for a thrust toward the highway center of Castel di Sangro.

All these operations accomplished yesterday were carried out in extremely bad weather—so bad that virtually all Allied air operations were cancelled.

In previous advances the Allies, especially on the Eighth Army front,

Continued on Page 2, Column 3

War Summary

Monday, Nov. 22, 1943

American soldiers and Marines at dawn Saturday invaded Tarawa and Makin, two islands in the Japanese-held Gilbert group, astride the Equator 2400 miles southwest of Hawaii, in the first U. S. offensive in the Central Pacific. The landings, revealed yesterday, were achieved under a terrific bombardment by carrier-based planes and by heavy warships of the Pacific Fleet.

Admiral Nimitz reported several beachheads had been secured, although a fierce battle still was raging on Tarawa, largest of the Gilberts. The opposition was smaller but nonetheless determined on Makin.

The invasion was regarded as the second arm of a huge pincers aimed at the major Jap base of Truk, with the Solomons drive as the first arm.

Elsewhere in the Pacific, Australian infantry and tanks pressed closer to the Japs at Sattelberg, New Guinea, while Allied fliers dropped 138 tons of bombs on Gasmata, New Britain.

In the European theater Allied troops met with fairly general success. The Fifth and Eighth Armies in Italy wiped out an eight-mile German salient to straighten their line in the center, capturing four key towns.

The Russians widened two prongs of their wedge in the Dnieper River bend near Krivoi Rog and Nikopol, and held firm before determined German assaults against the vital Kiev bulge.

Heavy Nazi reinforcements in the Western Balkans also were checked by General Tito's Partisans, who struck back to capture Foca, on the Drina River in Bosnia.

MID-PACIFIC DRIVE AIMS AT TRUK BASE

WASHINGTON, Nov. 21 (U. P.). —The American landings in the Gilbert Islands are viewed by military experts as the second arm of a powerful pincers aimed at the Japanese bastion of Truk—the enemy's "Pearl Harbor" of the Pacific.

The Gilberts and the neighboring Marshall Islands to the north form the primary eastern defenses of the giant air and naval base which already is threatened by the U. S. drive through the Solomons. That drive now is closing in on Rabaul, strong Jap base on New Britain blocking the way to Truk.

MAY SPREAD DEFENSES

Truk lies 1600 miles west of Tarawa and Makin, the Gilbert Islands on which U. S. forces have landed, while Rabaul is about the same distance west-southwest.

The new offensive may force the enemy to spread his forces, particularly his air power, to meet the threats from both directions.

Some observers believe the operations are a big step in plans to reconquer the Philippines and are intended to isolate Truk and protect

Continued on Page 3, Column 4

Turk Envoy to Reich Returning to Ankara

ANKARA, Turkey, Nov. 20 (U. P.). —Nerlin Saffet Arikan, Turkish Ambassador to Germany, arrived at Istanbul today and entrained for Ankara.

There were unconfirmed reports at Istanbul that he might not return to Berlin.

HOUSE DEFEAT NEAR FOR FOOD SUBSIDIES

WASHINGTON, Nov. 21 (A.P.).—Caught in a storm of Congressional rebellion, the Administration's program to hold down the cost of living faces its worst buffeting of the session in the House this week.

Waiting for Administration leaders in Congress as they return from the week-end is this triple assault against the White House home-front strategy:

1. **Within 24 hours a House coalition of Democrats and Republicans is expected to swat the food subsidy program, No. 1 weapon in the Administration's fight against higher prices.**

2. **Before mid-week the House will take up a $2,140,000,000 revenue bill which snubs the Treasury's demand for $10,500,000,000 in new taxes to fight the war and inflation.**

3. **Gaining strength is a Congressional move to take control of oil and coal prices away from the Office of Price Administration, which has resisted stubbornly several attempts to boost the crude-oil ceiling. Sponsors said they had 200 of the necessary 218 names on a petition to get the bill out of committee and get the bill said they would get the rest tomorrow. The measure would give control to Secretary of the Interior Harold L. Ickes, who has recommended an oil-price increase.**

The House probably will reach a vote some time tomorrow on a double-edge bill to outlaw food subsidies while putting new life into the Commodity Credit Corporation, which, as one of its functions, has financed many of them. Opposition from both parties in two days of de-

Continued on Page 9, Column 7

U. S. Urged to Dismiss 300,000 Jobholders

WASHINGTON, Nov. 21 (U. P.).—The Joint Congressional Economy Committee, charging wasteful and extravagant use of Federal personnel, tonight demanded immediate discharge of at least 300,000 Government workers and advocated a survey of all departments and agencies to promote fuller utilization of manpower.

Its second report on Government personnel, submitted by Senator Harry F. Byrd (D., Va.), said September figures, the latest available, showed 2,964,405 paid civilian employes on the payroll—"more than necessary for the successful and effective prosecution of the war." It said 52.2 percent "are not engaged in

Continued on Page 9, Column 4

IN TODAY'S INQUIRER

SPECIAL DEPARTMENTS

FOOD WORKERS HERE ARE FROZEN IN JOBS

Effective today, some 22,500 employes in the food distribution industry in this area are to be frozen in their jobs for at least four months by a sweeping War Manpower Commission edict designed to correct "a serious manpower shortage and turnover in the food trades."

The drastic action, announced by Frank L. McNamee, WMC regional director, affects workers in 11,376 retail stores, 53 grocery warehouses and 10 produce warehouses in Philadelphia and Delaware counties and most of Montgomery, Bucks and Chester counties, but excludes family-operated shops.

MAY BE EXTENDED

The order, reached after a conference at which food distributors appealed for WMC aid in solving their acute manpower problems, will remain in effect four months, and probably will be renewed after the results are studied, McNamee indicated.

The WMC move specifically designated the food industry in the area as a "vital war service" covered by the provisions of the Area Employment Stabilization Plan, which means that no worker may leave the industry without a statement of availability.

The chief contribution of the food

Continued on Page 7, Column 2

WLB Allows Firm To Serve Free Food

The Regional War Labor Board has approved a request of Warren Webster & Co., 17th and Federal sts., Camden, makers of heating systems and artillery fuse parts, to serve its 500 employes, free of charge, hot coffee six days a week and hot soup three days a week at lunch time.

The company said it has furnished hot soup to its workers for a number of years, but discontinued the practice prior to last Oct. 1. It added that it wished to reinstate the practice to "reduce absenteeism and winter colds."

Ideas Wanted To Improve City

WHAT improvements are needed in Philadelphia now and in the future?

To get a broad opinion of this important civic problem, The Inquirer is asking its readers to write constructive suggestions in letters not longer than 200 words each. Several will be published each day. To the writer of each letter used, $10 will be paid.

The letters should be addressed to The Planning Editor, The Inquirer, Philadelphia 1, Pa.

For Details See Story on Page 19

COLUMNIST CHARGES PATTON HIT SOLDIER

WASHINGTON, Nov. 21 (U. P.).—Drew Pearson, columnist and radio commentator, said tonight in his broadcast that Lieutenant General George S. Patton, commander of the U. S. Seventh Army in the Sicilian campaign, had been "severely reprimanded" by General Dwight D. Eisenhower for mistreating an American soldier suffering from shock, or a nervous ailment, in a hospital in Sicily.

"I don't think he (Patton) will be used in combat any more," Pearson said.

Pearson's statement was without confirmation. The War Department said it had "no information and no comment."

WHEREABOUTS MYSTERY

"Here is a story which I don't like to tell," Pearson said, "But in wartime we have to let the chips fall where they may. The lowly private who gets punished for a mistake is not spared by his superior officers and so the general who makes a mistake should not be spared either.

"A great mystery has surrounded the whereabouts of General 'Blood and Guts' Patton. His pearl-handled revolver, his picturesque language, made headlines in the Tu-

Continued on Page 2, Column 6

Reds Hold Before Kiev, Gain in Dnieper Bend

By JUDSON O'QUINN

LONDON, Nov. 22 (Monday) (A. P.).—The Red Army withstood the mechanized might of massive German attacks against the vital Kiev bulge in bloody fighting in the Northern Ukraine yesterday and broadened two prongs of the Soviet wedge aimed at the iron wealth of Krivoi Rog and the manganese of Nikopol in the Dnieper River bend, Moscow announced early today.

In battles extending all the way from Rechitsa, west of almost-encircled Gomel, to the area southwest of Dniepropetrovsk the Russians killed 6100 Germans and destroyed or disabled 121 Nazi tanks, it was stated in the Soviet midnight communique recorded here by the Soviet monitor from a broadcast.

FORCE NAZIS BACK

Listing three violent German tank onslaughts against General Nikolai F. Vatutin's First Ukrainian Army in the Zhitomir-Korostishev battlefield, the communique said the Russian armies weathered these blows and forced the Germans to retreat. In another sector of the region Soviet

Continued on Page 2, Column 5

German Train Ferry Crippled by Bombs

ENEMY SOURCE

NEW YORK, Nov. 21 (A. P.).—The Nazi-controlled Danish radio said today that one of the two train ferries which ply the Storebaelt, the narrow stretch of water which separates the Danish islands of Sjaelland and Fyn, had been so severely damaged by time bombs that a full year would be required for repairs.

The ferry routes are important military links between Copenhagen, in Sjaelland, and Jutland.

U. S. WEATHER FORECAST

Philadelphia and vicinity: Colder today and tonight with partly cloudy weather. Tuesday fair and continued rather cold.

Sun rises 7.52 A. M. Sets 3.40 P. M.
Moon rises 2.27 A. M. Sets 3.18 P. M.

Other Weather Reports on Page 3

The Philadelphia Inquirer
WEDNESDAY MORNING, DECEMBER 1, 1943 a d e t k 22

Cannon-Armed Plane Blasts Jap Ship

A series of photos showing the first attack by a U. S. B-25 medium bomber, mounting a 75-mm cannon in its nose, on a large Japanese destroyer in the South Pacific. Word that these bombers are so armed was released two days ago. Above: the destroyer shown as the attack began. Below: clouds of smoke and geysers of water obscure the target as five shells strike home. Bottom: the enemy ship is left burning and in a sinking condition. The arrow points to damage caused by one shell. Hits were scored on a turret, the bridge, amidships and on the bow of the Jap destroyer.

FIRST AID A heroic Russian Army nurse (right) braving German fire to administer to a wounded Soviet soldier in the midst of a battle on the Ukrainian front. Around her are machine gunners and riflemen using the ruins of a peasant's home as cover while they battle the foe.

ENVOY DINES Lord Halifax, left, British Ambassador to the United States, is shown last night at 194th annual dinner of St. Andrew's Society of Philadelphia, where he warned that Germany will fight on even though hope of victory is gone. With him is Dr. Merle M. Odgers, president of the society and head of Girard College. More than 400 attended the gathering.

(A. P. Wirephoto)

MASCOT Barbara Lou Erlichman, five, being sworn in as official mascot of the SPARS by Lieutenant (j. g.) Dorothy Beckwith in Nev York as Lieutenant (j. g.) Mary Lynn and Ensign Henrietta Baker look on.

PILED UP Twenty-eight cars of a Pennsylvania Railroad train were wrecked in a derailment yesterday near Norristown. The battered cars blocked both tracks of the main freight route from Harrisburg to Trenton. The cars, fully loaded, contained lumber, cement, steel tubing and girders. No one in the train crew was hurt. Cause of the derailment is undetermined.

The Philadelphia Inquirer

PUBLIC LEDGER

An Independent Newspaper for All the People

FINAL CITY EDITION

CIRCULATION: October Average: Daily 487,836; Sunday 1,266,718

THURSDAY MORNING, DECEMBER 2, 1943

Copyright, 1943, by The Philadelphia Inquirer Co. Vol. 229, No. 155

a b d e f g h

THREE CENTS

Japan to Lose Her Whole Empire, Allies Decree at Cairo Conference; 1026 U. S. Troops Slain at Tarawa

Today

Jap Fangs Drawn
Soviet Gives O. K.
Policy Helps China
Reds Get Security
U. S., Britain Gain

—By Walter Lippmann—

THE Declaration of Cairo is a weighty confirmation of the view that the Moscow agreements inaugurated a genuine understanding.

The declaration is a commitment to destroy the modern Japanese Empire and to confine the Japanese to the island territory which they possessed before they began campaigns of conquest a century ago. When ... nounced at Cairo ... to effect, Japan ... a great Power ... aggressive war. ... been ousted ... of Asia— ... uria and ... lost the ... stra- ... ting a ... ussia

2557 OTHERS WOUNDED IN ATOLL BATTLE

Total Casualties In 76-Hour Attack On Gilbert Isles Is Placed at 3772

By JOHN M. McCULLOUGH

Inquirer Washington Bureau

WASHINGTON, Dec. 1.—The 76-hour conquest of Tarawa, one of bloodiest battles in the proud history of the Marine Corps, cost the American victors 1026 dead and 2557 wounded.

In announcing the casualties suffered by American forces in the Gilbert Islands, the Navy revealed tonight that they totaled 3772. Sixty-five were killed and 121 wounded at Makin and one was killed and two were wounded at Abemama.

BLOODIEST OF BATTLES

The casualties sustained at Tarawa, announced simultaneously here and at Pearl Harbor, are believed to constitute the heaviest in a single American action in World War II.

Although Admiral Chester W. Nimitz' communique did not specify, it is assumed that the bulk of the Tarawa casualties were suffered by the Second Marine Division.

If so, Tarawa ranks second in to... casualties only to Belleau Wood, ... 3-9, 1918, as the heaviest single ... sustained by the Marine Corps.

...ST IN 1918

...ing to official Marine Corps ...56 officers and men were ...3037 wounded in the grim ...18 upon the right flank ... German drive to cross ... invest Paris.

(A. P. Wirephoto)

THREE ALLIED LEADERS PLANNING TO STRIP JAPAN OF HER EMPIRE

Generalissimo Chiang Kai-shek, President Roosevelt and Prime Minister Winston Churchill shown during a recess in their five-day conference in North Africa. The leaders decided to strip Japan of all her imperialistic gains of the last 50 years. (Map on Page 2; other conference photos on Pages 3 and 18).

F.D.R., Churchill Now Believed in Iran With Stalin

Official Communique of Three-Power Parley on Page 2

By JOHN F. CHESTER

CAIRO, Dec. 1 (A. P.).—President Roosevelt, Prime Minister Winston Churchill and Generalissimo Chiang Kai-shek have held an historic five-day conference, have bound their nations in an agreement to beat Japan into unconditional surrender and to strip her of all her imperialistic gains of the last half century and have left for unannounced destinations.

It was also considered probable that the Allied leaders had concluded details for a new front in Europe and for actions concerning Mediterranean and Middle East affairs. A reliable source tonight confirmed reports that British-American general staffs had gathered in greater strength than ever before in a separate session, with the Chinese not participating.

(In Washington it was assumed that an even more important meeting, particularly on the European phases of the war, would be held with Premier Josef Stalin. Reuters dispatches from Lisbon, Portugal, said the three had left for Teheran, capital of Iran, there to meet Stalin in the biggest United Nations conference of the war.

PARLEY REPORTED UNDER WAY IN IRAN

(Berlin broadcasts said the conference already was under way in Teheran—on the Russian supply corridor where British-American-Russian war-time cooperation has had its most conspicuous success.)

In an extraordinary atmosphere of secrecy and precaution, the three leaders of the United States, Britain and China, representing more than 1,000,000,000 people, counting all those of the British Empire, met for five days—from Nov. 22 through Nov. 26—while surrounded by the highest galaxy of military, supply and political advisers, and departed at least three days before the news was given to the public.

The conferences were held in a strictly guarded zone which restrictions even yet will permit only to be described as in North Africa. (In Washington it was presumed that the meeting took place in Cairo or nearby, since the news came under that dateline, and the principal participants visited the Sphinx and Pyramids, which are in the vicinity.)

ALLIES PLEDGE 'UNRELENTING PRESSURE'

A communique issued at the close declared they had agreed upon a plan of military operations against Japan which would "bring unrelenting pressure against their brutal enemies by sea, land and air."

Declaring their purpose to drive Japan back into her home islands, the three powers outlined this specific four-point program:

1. Japan must disgorge all the islands she has seized in the Pacific since the beginning of the first World War in 1914 (from which she gained, from Germany, the Mar-

Continued on Page 2, Column 3

2 JAP BASES SHELLED IN BOLD NAVY RAID

By MURLIN SPENCER

ALLIED HEADQUARTERS IN THE SOUTHWEST PACIFIC, Dec. 2 (Thursday) A. P.). — Carrying the naval war to the Japanese, American light naval craft shelled Gasmata, New Britain, and Madang, New Guinea, during the night and dawn hours of Nov. 29 and 30 in the first sea bombardment of these enemy strongholds.

The naval vessels—probably destroyers—sought to blast out Japanese shore installations at Gasmata and aerial spotters, a headquarters spokesman said, termed their marksmanship "effective."

...AP VESSEL SUNK

The attack on Madang, strong ...my aerial and barge point on ...labe Harbor. Northeast New ...a, was a foray deep into ...se territory. Shells were ...into shore installations and ... unidentified enemy vessel ...in Dallman Passage.

...ld naval strokes not only ... the action against the ... New Guinea-New Brit-

...Page 6, Column 6

3-Mile U. S. Gain Rips Center of Nazi Line

Map on Page 6

By NOLAND NORGAARD

ALLIED HEADQUARTERS, ALGIERS, Dec. 1 (A. P.).—Under the heaviest tactical air support of the entire Italian campaign, the British Eighth Army smashed through German defenses beyond fallen Sangro Ridge today while American troops of the Fifth Army fought forward three miles in the central sector, possibly heralding the start of an all-out Allied drive on Rome.

At every point the Germans fought with desperation to stem the attack. Despite the demoralizing onslaught by hundreds of Allied fighters, fighter-bombers and bombers, the enemy troops clung to their positions until they were killed or captured in bloody hand-to-hand fighting. An Allied communique described Nazi losses as "very heavy."

EXPECT COUNTER-DRIVE

"The Germans are offering very fierce resistance for every inch of ground," a military commentator said. He predicted they would make violent efforts to retake Sangro

Continued on Page 6, Column 2

War Summary

Thursday, Dec. 2, 1943

President Roosevelt, Prime Minister Churchill and Generalissimo Chiang Kai-shek were reported conferring yesterday with Premier Stalin in Teheran following a five-day conference — presumably in Cairo—in which it was agreed to strip Japan of all her imperial gains of the last half-century.

Surrounded by the highest galaxy of military and political advisers, the three leaders issued an unconditional surrender declaration which may be the signal for a vast land offensive in Asia.

As a grim reminder of battles to come, the Navy disclosed that 1026 American troops were killed and 2557 wounded in the 76-hour battle for capture of Tarawa.

On the Pacific battle front, American light naval craft, in a bold foray in Jap waters, shelled Gasmata, New Britain, and Madang, New Guinea.

In Western Europe, American heavy bombers raided the Rhineland industrial city of Solingen for the second time in two days, and 27 of the big craft were lost.

The struggle in Russia was rapidly becoming a test of reserve strength as reinforced German armies fought back vigorously on every front in some of the heaviest battles of the war. Red troops northwest of Gomel captured Narovl on the Pripet River and several towns in the Dnieper bend.

U.S. HITS SOLINGEN, 27 BOMBERS LOST

By ROBERT N. STURDEVANT

LONDON, Dec. 2 (Thursday) (A. P.).—Large formations of United States heavy bombers with their fighter escorts overcame stiff German fighter opposition to attack the Rhineland industrial city of Solingen yesterday as U. S. Marauders blasted German-controlled airfields in northern France and Belgium, it was announced early today.

Other allied craft attacked a German aircraft works at Albert in France, targets in Holland and enemy shipping off the Brest peninsula. A total of 42 Allied planes were missing from the operations, including 27 American flying Fortresses and Liberators, one light bomber and 14 fighters. The Allied forces accounted for 33 German planes in aerial combat while two others were believed destroyed on the ground.

2D RAID IN 2 DAYS

It was the second attack in two days for Solingen, site of Europe's largest light metal foundry. In the first attack on this Rhineland city of 150,000 persons Tuesday the Amer-

Continued on Page 6, Column 4

...ctions ...day

RED DRIVES STALLED, HUGE BATTLES RAGE

By JAMES M. LONG

LONDON, Dec. 1 (A. P.).—A strongly reinforced German army fought back on every sector of the Russian front with new-found vigor today as some of the heaviest fighting of the war brought the great Russian summer-autumn offensive almost to a halt.

The swirling conflict at three key-points—the White Russian road to ...and, the Kiev bulge and the ...per bend—was rapidly becom... test of reserve strength of both ...nd of the ability to get a ...low of reinforcements and ... first to the hottest sectors ...-about rail lines and sod-

...DVANCES

...s, having curtly re... from the railway ... Korosten on the Kiev ...terday, today briefly men...ed fighting in only three areas, with meager advances capturing less than a dozen populated places in the entire 600-mile active front.

The Moscow communique, recorded by the Soviet monitor, said the offensive northwest of Gomel had advanced slightly, overrunning the

Continued on Page 5, Column 1

Cairo Expense Item: 6 Fezzes for the FBI

CAIRO, Dec. 1 (A. P.).—One item listed under expenses of the big three-power conference was for "six fezzes for the FBI."

Apparently it was felt that agents guarding President Roosevelt and watching out for subversive activities could operate less conspicuously in the red native headdress.

Allied Pact to Make China a Major Power

By WILLIAM C. MURPHY, JR.

Inquirer Washington Bureau

WASHINGTON, Dec. 1.—Post-war Japan is to be a second-rate Asiatic Power occupying a string of islands off the mainland and holding about the same status as when her ports were opened to the western world by the American Commodore Matthew C. Perry 90 years ago.

That in plain words is the apparent meaning of the joint communique issued here and in Cairo tonight following the personal meeting of President Roosevelt, Prime Minister Winston Churchill and Generalissimo Chiang Kai-shek.

MUST DISGORGE LOOT

The language of the communique was clear on that point. Not only is Japan to be stripped of all the territory she has stolen from other nations since Pearl Harbor, not only is she to be shorn of the islands and other territory which she acquired by conquest and treacherous adherence to the League of Nations during and following World War I—she is also to be deprived of such other territories as Formosa which she seized from China in 1895 and Korea which she annexed in 1910.

What will be left to the sovereignty of the Son of Heaven—or whoever may rule in Tokio after the war—will be just about what constituted

Continued on Page 3, Column 6

Of Special Interest

John M. McCullough, of The Inquirer Washington Bureau, continues his story of military medical miracles with the fourth installment of "Wounded in Action!"

Today on Page 19

A new ration point chart for meats, fats, fish and dairy products, and a table of ration point value changes for processed foods appear

Today on Page 8

DAVIS SAYS BRITISH VIOLATED SECRECY

WASHINGTON, Dec. 1 (A. P.).—Elmer Davis, director of the Office of War Information was reported tonight to have sent a note of protest to Brenden Bracken, British Minister of Information, over the premature publication by Reuters, British news agency, yesterday of the Cairo meeting of United Nations leaders.

This disclosure followed an earlier statement by Davis that he would "do everything feasible" to protect the American press from being scooped on inter-Allied news while holding to this country's censorship code. Asked specifically what he planned to do, Davis would not elaborate, but the fact that a stiff pro-

Continued on Page 3, Column 3

U. S. WEATHER FORECAST

Philadelphia and vicinity: Cloudy and warmer today, occasional light rain and warmer tonight. Rather windy.

Sun rises 8 02 A.M. Sets 5 36 P.M.
Moon rises 12 33 P.M. Sets 11 05 P.M.

Other Weather Reports on Page 2

Landis Grants Cox Hearing on Wagering Charge

NORTHEAST HIGH SCHOOL'S FOOTBALL TEAM WHICH DEFENDS ITS CITY CHAMPIONSHIP AT FRANKLIN FIELD THIS AFTERNOON

From left to right the Archive line includes Edward Olney, R. E.; John Werner, R. T.; William DiFrancisco, R. G.; John Witsch, C.; Robert Patterson, L. G.; Frank Lovrich, L. T.; John Lehman, L. E. In the backfield are Clayton Liddel, William Neamand, Norman Waldman and William Jones. Gus Geiges is coach of the Archives.

WEST CATHOLIC'S UNDEFEATED TEAM WHICH IS MAKING ITS THIRD APPEARANCE IN FOUR YEARS IN THE ANNUAL CLASSIC

Left to right the Burr line is Dan Brown, R. E.; Peter Murphy, R. T.; John McCoach, R. G.; Thomas VanKirk, C.; Charles Ward, L. G.; Joseph Topper, L. T.; Michael Bogan, L. E. The backfield is William Thomas, Robert Connor, John Tulskie and Thomas Graham. Bob Dougherty is now in his fourth year as coach of the team.

Ex-Phillies President Denies Old Testimony

Cox Tested Loyalty of Club Official, Says Lawyer; Meet in N. Y. Today

By STAN BAUMGARTNER

NEW YORK, Dec. 3.—Judge Kenesaw Mountain Landis, baseball high commissioner, whose dramatic rulings have often electrified baseball, dropped another bombshell into the major-minor league meeting here today.

Just when it appeared that the gathering would pass quietly into baseball history and many of the magnates as well as the writers had left the Roosevelt Hotel (the judge's headquarters), Landis announced to the assembled reporters:

COX ASKED HEARING

"William D. Cox, ex-president of the Phillies, whom I expelled from baseball for life on Nov. 23, has asked for and will receive a public hearing before me tomorrow morning at 10.30 o'clock.

"The request for the hearing was made by Lloyd Paul Stryker, Cox's attorney, a week ago Saturday. He asked that the original meeting scheduled for Dec. 4 and canceled by Cox be reinstated."

NEVER MADE WAGERS

Stryker is the attorney who defended Jimmy Hines, famous political figure who was convicted and sent to Sing Sing. The assistant prosecuting attorney at that time was Charles P. Grimes, previously personal counsel for Cox.

In asking the judge to hold the hearing Stryker said that Cox had told and convinced him that he had never made any bets on the Phillies.

"Stryker said," according to Landis, "that Cox hadn't told all the facts about the betting statement, and that he made his statement to test the loyalty of a 'man' in the Phils' organization. The attorney told me he is convinced Cox made no bets, and that Cox could convince me, if given a hearing.

JUDGE SPEAKS OUT

"If Cox can convince me," said Landis, "that his admissions of betting on ball games, admissions made to one of the directors of his club as well as Ford Frick, National League president, and me, were false and that he did not wager on the Phillies' games, I will make a public statement to that effect immediately after the hearing."

Bucky Harris, former manager of the Phillies, who was let out in July; Bill Phillips, public relations director; Jimmy Hagen, traveling secretary; Nathan Alexander, office employe; George P. Fletcher, secretary-treasurer, and possibly a director of the Phillies have been summoned to the meeting.

CARPENTER RETAINS CONTROL

Should Cox be exonerated there will be no change in the status of the Phillies, Judge Landis stat[ed]. Robert R. M. Carpenter, Sr., w[h]o purchased Cox's stock in the Ph[illie]s, will remain as owner his son, Ro[b]ert R. M., JJr., as president, and t[h]ere will be no change in arrange[me]nts that have already been made. This means that Herbert Pennocl will remain as general manager.

Cox, however, would be free to negotiate his way back into organized baseball, if he is vindicated.

COX EXPLAINS TESTIMONY

Cox explained the apparent contradictory testimony — and the admission to one of the directors of the club that he wagered — by declaring that he did so "to test the loyalty of this man."

Later in the evening of the day (Nov. 23d) on which he was expelled, Cox admitted over a Nation-wide hookup that he made 'several "sentimental" bets on the Phillies. At the time this was taken as proof that he had made wagers, wagers which Landis said he had admitted to him — from $25 to $100 on 15 or 20 games.

JUST SENTIMENTAL WAGERS

However, it appears that Cox now says that these sentimental wagers were hats and boxes of cigars — not money. When Cox was reached by telephone here today he declined to amplify his lawyer's request for a hearing.

The Cox story, never told before — in all of its ramifications from beginning to end, is most interesting.

It had its beginning late in Jul[y] shortly after Bucky Harris was u[n]ceremoniously fired by Cox. Ha[rris] came to Philadelphia to give his s[ide] of the case, explained the dismis[sal] etc., and then casually remarke[d]:

"That guy is no good. Why do[n't you] know, he bet on his own ball ga[mes]"

STATEMENT STUNS REPOR[TERS]

It was a statement that st[unned] the reporters gathered abou[t] Harris was asked to make a[n affi]davit to that effect but [...] Then he told us the story, [...] was in Cox's office when [...] the secretary receive the od[ds on a] game to be played that da[y].

Harris said he turned to [...] lady and said "you don'[t mean to] say that Mr. Cox bets o[n] games?"

"Oh, I thought you kn[ew]" said she replied. "I ke[ep] the wagers he makes [...]"

"If Landis ever hea[rs ...] will mean the end o[f ...]" Harris said he remark[ed].

LANDIS LEARNS D[...]

With Harris at th[...] in Cox's office was [...] traveling secretary [...] their way back in [...] hotel Harris said t[...]

Continued on Pa[ge ...]

Red Sox Buy Bob Johnson

Majors Say Each Club Entirely Free To Employ Negroes

NEW YORK, Dec. 3.—Although overshadowed by Judge Kenesaw Mountain Landis' dramatic announcement that he had granted a hearing to William D. Cox, deposed president of the Philadelphia National League baseball club, on charges that he made wagers on the team during the 1943 campaign, the National and American Leagues concluded their annual winter meeting here today with the usual amount of work.

Highlight of the day was the sale by the Senators of their hard-hitting outfielder, "Indian Bob" Johnson, to the Boston Red Sox in a straight cash deal. Johnson was a former member of the Athletics, but was traded by Connie Mack last winter when he announced he no longer would play for the Tall Leader after 10 years under his direction.

APPROVE NIGHT GAMES

The major league meet[ing approv]ed 21 night games for th[e St. Louis] Browns and Cardinals [in 1944, a] boost of seven each for t[he two] clubs; awarded the All-[Star game to] Pittsburgh and set the [date July] 11; granted the Senato[rs unlimited] night games after M[...] Sundays and holiday[s ...] also voted to open [...] schedule on April 1[...] Oct. 1.

Before the mee[ting a] delegation of spe[...] Negro ball players [...] organized baseb[all ...] speakers was Pa[ul Robeson, former] Rutgers athlete [...] pearing in Othe[llo].

No action w[...] O'Conner, secr[etary to Lan]dis, in summa[ry ...] the meeting [...] tirely free to [...] and all exte[...] matter is on[...] decide wit[...] whatsoever[...]

F. & [...] Ur[...] Be[...]

In[...] tha[...] spi[...] ke[...] nu[...] la[...] s[...] C[...]

Stryke[r ...] As Ha[...]

NEW YOR[K ...] Paul Stryker, [...] William D. [Cox ...] the Phillies, [...] Landis tom[orrow ...] years attor[ney ...] Medical So[ciety ...] and winni[ng ...] He resign[ed ...] work. Pre[...] assistant [...] the late [...]

The 5[...] was bor[n ...] Melanc[...] preside[nt ...] 25 yea[rs ...] ting t[...] Hami[lton ...] memb[...]

West Catholic, Northeast Clash Today for City Scholastic Title

By KEN HAY

No predictions would be made either by Coach Bob Dougherty or Coach Gus Geiges as West Catholic High's football team, undefeated champion of the Catholic League, and the Northeast High squad, Public High and defending City titlist, went through their final drills for the sixth annual championship playoff to be played before 50,000 fans at Franklin Field this afternoon.

When Referee Ken Simendinger blows the starting whistle at two o'clock, there looms one sure winner in this clash between two of the fastest lines in the State and a pair of all-round backfields. The certain winner is the School Milk Fund for the care of the City's needy school children. The fund will receive a goodly share of the proceeds.

AID ATHLETIC FUNDS

Another beneficiary will be the athletic funds of each and every school in the Catholic and Public High Leagues; all of whom share equally with the two top teams in a percentage of the receipts. As Mayor Bernard Samuel stated, "This game will be a godsend to the last place teams to carry on their athletic program and I cannot commend too strongly to the citizens of Philadelphia to support this worthwhile charity in the guise of the sixth annual football championship."

Both coaches will stand pat on the starting lineups that carried the Burrs and Archives to the top of their respective leagues. With no injuries reported, the teams will be at full strength and there is every promise that the service men and women, who will be admitted free, will witness the same type of team play and co-ordination that they find so important in their daily duties for the Army, Navy and Marines.

BANK ON TULSKIE

Bob Dougherty, West Catholic Mentor, will start the three players who gained All-Catholic recognition on the team picked for The Philadelphia Inquirer by the balloting of the League's nine coaches. Captain Dan Brown, who looms as a possible All-State nominee at end; John Tulskie, whose slippery running has been the spark which carried the Burrs victorious over eight opponents, and Pete Murphey, tackle who has the added ability of placement kicking will try to bring West Catholic its first City title.

Tulskie's teammates in the West Catholic backfield will be Bob Connor, one of the best blockers in schoolboy ranks; Bill Thomas, another excellent ball-carrier, and Tom Graham, the team's passer.

BROWN, BOGAN AT ENDS

Brown's running mate at end will be Mike Bogan, a standout as a pass receiver, while Joe Topper will be at the other tackle position. Charles Ward and John McCoach are slated for the Burrs' guard posts with Tom VanKirk at center.

City Title Game Line Up

WEST CATHOLIC						NORTHEAST			
Wt.	Ht.	Name	No.	Pos.	No.	Name	Ht.	Wt.
165	5-11	Bogan	(13)	L. E.	(15)	Lehman	5-10	155
180	6-00	Topper	(28)	L. T.	(13)	Lovrich	5-08	171
165	5-10	Ward	(22)	L. G.	(18)	Patterson	5-08	152
156	5-11	VanKirk	(30)	C.	(21)	Witsch	5-08	171
165	5-10	McCoach	(19)	R. G.	(14)	DiFrancisco	5-05	162
190	6-00	Murphey	(32)	R. T.	(22)	Werner	5-09	176
165	6-00	Brown	(47)	R. E.	(10)	Buehler	5-11	151
150	5-07	Conner	(29)	QB.	(12)	Beale	5-07	144
155	5-10	Graham	(27)	L. HB.	(20)	Jones	5-11	167
156	5-10	Thomas	(17)	R. HB.	(16)	Liddel	6-00	161
160	5-09	Tulskie	(11)	FB.	(17)	Waldman	5-07	167

Average Wt.: Line, 169 3-7; backfield, 155¼; team, 164 3-11. Average Wt.: Line, 162 4-7; backfield, 159¾; team, 161 6-11.

WEST CATHOLIC SQUAD: (10) James King, (11) John Tulskie, (12) Francis Kirkman, (13) Michael Bogan, (14) John Convery, (15) Donald Dougherty, (16) Francis Conway, (17) William Thomas, (18) Robert Kelly, (19) John McCoach, (20) Leonard Hope, (21) Joseph Dougherty, (22) Charles Ward, (23) John Diver, (24) Daniel Gallagher, (25) James Burke, (26) John Ciesulk, (27) Thomas Graham, (28) Joseph Topper, (29) Robert Connor, (30) Thomas VanKirk, (31) Francis Mullarkey, (32) Peter Murphey, (33) Raymond Devenney, (34) John Hennessey, (35) Donald Wickersham, (36) James McGrane, (37) George McAndrews, (38) James Dougherty, (39) Edward Kane, (47) Daniel Brown, (53) Lawrence Clark, (74) Francis McCartney.

NORTHEAST SQUAD: (7) Stan Greenwald, (10) William Buehler, (11) William Neamand, (12) Robert Beale, (13) Frank Lovrich, (14) William DiFrancisco, (15) John Lehman, (16) Clayton Liddel, (17) Norman Waldman, (18) Robert Patterson, (19) John Wisniewski, (20) William Jones, (21) John Witsch, (22) John Werner, (23) Edward Olney, (25) Thomas Quigley, (26) Harold Woodruff, (30) Samuel Handler, (31) Herbert Levin, (33) Edward Daly, (34) Jack Levin, (35) Hyman Gavrilovitch, (36) William Frederick, (37) Joseph Billkiewitz, (41) William Kommer, (42) Frank Szumski, (43) John Thompson, (44) William Rosser, (45) Fred Hauser, (48) Lawrence Roller, (50) Scaramusso, (56) Russell Kane, (63) Robert Sim.

OFFICIALS: Referee, Ken Simendinger, Holy Cross. Umpire, Joseph Shane, Swarthmore. Head linesman, John Oakes, St. Joseph's. Field judge, Charles Gault, Muhlenberg. Time of periods—12 minutes. Kick-off—2 P. M.

SEASON'S RECORDS

W. CATHOLIC		NORTHEAST	
44 La Salle	0	6 R. Catholic	13
44 St. Thos. More	0	6 Haverford S.	8
31 S. Catholic	0	31 Gratz	7
31 St. James	0	12 Southern	7
26 N. E. Catholic	13	6 Bartram	0
31 St. Joseph's	0	14 Frankford	7
33 St. John's	0	13 Central	0
21 West Phila.	0	14 St. Joseph's	12
261	13	144	66

Won 8, lost 0, tied 0. Won 7, lost 2, tied 0.

CHAMPIONSHIP SERIES

1938—St. Joseph's, 7; Central, 0.
1939—St. Joseph's, 27; Northeast, 0.
1940—Frankford, 13; West Catholic, 0.
1941—West Catholic, 0; West Phila., 0.
1942—Northeast, 14; St. Joseph's, 12.

Episcopal Honors Team

Honor after honor was heaped on Captain E. Newbold Smith and his Episcopal Academy teammates as parents and friends of the school feted the Interacademic League championship football team and the soccer team at the annual fall banquet in the Academy's dining hall at Berwick rd. and City Line last night.

Most coveted award was that received from Clifford F. Lincoln, representing the Lehigh University Club of Philadelphia. Lincoln presented to Greville Haslam, headmaster, the Lehigh Cup, emblematic of the Interacademic League championship. It marked Episcopal's first leg on the third cup since the presentations started in 1929. Haverford School won the first cup and the Churchmen retired the second trophy last year.

Gold footballs, gold medals and letters were given the 23 members of the squad that carried Episcopal to its fifth straight championship.

Speakers included George Munger, alumnus and head football coach at the University of Pennsylvania; Captain Thomas Ridgeway, U. S. Army Air Corps, who is home from action in China, and Byron Saam, radio sports commentator. The toastmaster was Thomas Hart, president of the Board of Trustees.

Football awards: Harry Alkar, Hugh Beahm, Robert Berdolett, Tony Blapham, Alfred Cancelmo, Jack Corey, Captain elect Joseph Cunningham, Robert De Coursey, Rodney Finkbiner, Philip Flanders, Harry French, Theodore Flannigan, Leonard Fulton, Austin Hepburn, James Hewson, Chester Ivory, Jr., Richard Lander, Donald Meenen, Ben Moore, Warren Nagle, Robert Simonin, Captain E. Newbold Smith, Charles Urban, Jr., Co-Manager H. Morell Bailey, Jr., Co-Manager W. F. Atlee Harvey.

Soccer awards: Thomas Brown, Mark Davidon, William Erwin, Thomas Harris, John Hepburn, Alan Hume, Robert Kane, William Kinard, Jr., George Kneass, Jr., David Knodel, Captain Douglas Raymond, Jr., Rufus Latts, Roland Roberts, Jr., Gardiner Rogers, William Sherrerd, III, Edward Snader, III, Andrew Stone, Warren Stone, James Thornington, II, Manager Robert Charles Venturi.

The Philadelphia Inquirer

14 g h ★ PHILADELPHIA, SATURDAY MORNING, DECEMBER 4, 1943

N. Catholic Wins; Verdeur Stars

Joe Verdeur unofficially beat the national interscholastic breaststroke swimming record yesterday when he paced North Catholic High to a 40-26 triumph over South Catholic High in a Catholic League meet in the North Branch Y. M. C. A. pool.

West Catholic High defeated St. Thomas More, 45-21, in another league meet at 52d and Sansom sts.

Verdeur, captain of Joe Kirk's Falcons and holder of the National A. A. U. breaststroke title, sped over the 100-yard course with his powerful overhand butterfly stroke to a Catholic League record of 1.03.4, which was also a new pool mark.

N. CATHOLIC, 40; S. CATHOLIC, 26.

40-YARD FREE STYLE—1. Jim McLaughlin, North Catholic; 2. Ed Connelly, North Catholic; 3. Dave McDonald, South Catholic. Time, 0.21.0.

100-YARD BREASTSTROKE—1. Joe Verdeur, North Catholic; 2. Bill Manley, South Catholic; 3. Tom Callahan, North Catholic. Time, 1.03.4. (New league record, old record, 1.05.6, set by Ed Geisz, North Catholic, in the Germantown Y. M. C. A. pool, January, 1942. New pool record, old record, 1.05.4, set by Verdeur, November, 1943.)

220-YARD FREE STYLE—1. Jack Ricks, North Catholic; 2. William Brash, North Catholic; 3. Ralph Carfogna, South Catholic. Time, 2.58.9.

100-YARD BACKSTROKE—1. Joe Staunton, North Catholic; 2. George Weakland, North Catholic; 3. William Bailey, South Catholic. Time, 1.12.8.

100-YARD FREE STYLE—1. Jim Kent, North Catholic; 2. John Lynch, South Catholic; 3. Larry Udry, North Catholic. Time, 1.13.5.

LOW BOARD FANCY DIVING—1. Dave McDonald, South Catholic, 82.8 points; 2. Frank Staunton, North Catholic, 72.3; 3. William Connelly, North Catholic, 67.5.

180-YARD MEDLEY RELAY—1. South Catholic (Bailey, Manley, Jim Green); 2. North Catholic (John Brady, Jack Bleuit, William Leahy). Time, 2.13.0.

180-YARD FREE STYLE RELAY—1. South Catholic (John McCaughan, John McDevitt, Carfogna, Lynch); 2. North Catholic (Dick O'Donnell, Gene Curran, Jack Kelly, Jim Sharkey). Time, 1.35.6.

W. CATHOLIC, 45; ST. THOMAS MORE, 21

40-YARD FREE STYLE—1. Zigvaitis, W. Catholic; 2. Collins, W. Catholic; 3. Cassidy, St. Thomas More. Time—22 seconds.

100-YARD BREAST STROKE—1. J. Mullin, W. Catholic; 2. Carr, St. Thomas More; 3. Gillane, W. Catholic. Time—1.20.3.

220-YARD FREE STYLE—1. Zigvaitis, W. Catholic; 2. Hadfield, St. Thomas More; 3. Becker, W. Catholic. Time—3.02.

100-YARD BREAST STROKE—1. W. Mullin, W. Catholic; 2. Evans, W. Catholic; 3. McKenna, St. Thomas More. Time—1.20.

100-YARD FREE STYLE—1. O'Neill, St. Thomas More; 2. Boudwin, St. Thomas More; 3. Scannipieco, W. Catholic. Time—1.08.3.

DIVING—1. Callahan, St. Thomas More; 2. Deserable, W. Catholic; 3. Lavelle, W. Catholic. Time—35.7.

180-YARD MEDLEY RELAY—1. W. Catholic (W. Mullin, J. Mullin, McAlear). Time 2.08.8.

160-YARD FREE STYLE RELAY—1. W. Catholic (McDermott, Collins, Swaan, Scannipieco). Time—1.29.

Navy Pleased With Elevens, Says Knox

WASHINGTON, Dec. 3 (A. P.).—Is the Navy satisfied with its policy of allowing its personnel to play football during pre-flight and college training programs?

"Very much so," says Secretary of the Navy Knox. He was asked for his comment as the first full season of the experiment came to a close.

PROBABLY PLAY NEXT YEAR

Whether the same program will be projected into next season is a matter depending on many things, so Knox isn't committing himself at this time.

But, Navy officials note, the order under which the policy came into existence has not been descinded. This, coupled with Knox's expression of satisfaction over the try-out, seems to give odds-on likelihood that next season will see Navy players on the field again.

More than 125 colleges were in the pre-flight and college training program (the Army didn't follow the same policy.) Big name coaches were recruited to teach the game. Navy-manned teams representing colleges and sailor trainees at the pre-flight schools turned in a creditable performance throughout the year.

St. Joseph's Five Trips Gratz, 26-23

The St. Joseph's High basketball team handed its new coach, Jocko Collins, an opening game victory by topping Simon Gratz High, 26-23, yesterday at Kenney Gym, 17th and Stiles sts. Collins, who coached St. Thomas More last year, took over for Cookie McCusker.

ST. JOSEPH'S	G.	F.	P.	SIMON GRATZ	G.	F.	P.
Jim Kane, f	5	0	10	Stoerrle, f	5	1	7
Bracken, f	1	0	2	Ragland, f	0	0	0
Joe Kane, f	1	0	2	Cathers, f	3	1	7
McGrath, f	0	0	0	Muhe, f	0	0	0
Cope, c	0	0	0	Koecher, c	2	2	6
Taney, c	0	0	0	Miller, g	0	1	1
Wilcox, g	0	0	0	Roland, g	1	0	2
Bailey, g	0	0	0				
Fanning, g	6	0	12				
Bailey, g	0	0	0				
Tracey, g	0	0	0				
Totals	13	0	26	Totals	9	5	23

Simon Gratz	3	6	9	5—23
St. Joseph's	4	6	6	10—26

Personal fouls: St. Joseph's 3 (Wilcox 3, Fanning 3, Cope, Bracken, Bailey); Simon Gratz 6 (Miller 2, Roland, Ragland, Koecher, Stoerrle). Missed fouls: St. Joseph's, 6; Simon Gratz, 5. Referee, Warren Weller, Temple. Umpire, Jimmy McCune, Frankford. Time of periods, 8 minutes.

Foley, Verdon In Tourney Ring

By JOHN WEBSTER

Popular belief is that post-war ring champions will come out of the service, and the case of Corporal Lewis Foley is definitely a point for the affirmative. He's done a lot of fist-fighting in the Army, is expected to do a lot more in The Inquirer A. A. Tournament, and should arrive at the spot where he can bargain in punches with any lightweight.

Foley, 21, whose home is at 5232 Vine st., in West Philadelphia had done little boxing, so far as one knows, when he went to join the colors. His father, Lew Foley, is a Democratic division leader in the 44th Ward. Young Foley was fortunate in being stationed at a camp where he had a pretty fair sort of boxing instructor, and he profited by his fistic lessons.

FOLEY VS. VERDON

Tournament fans will have their first peek at Corporal Foley on Monday night as the Diamond Belt and Middle Atlantic A. A. U. Championships start at the Cambria, Kensington ave. and Somerset st. They will see the pupil of Joe Louis, for it was, indeed, the Cold Slayer who schooled Foley at Fort Riley, Kan., pitted against Bill Verdon, a favorite of the Kensington neighborhood, in a special bout.

Tassel-topped Bill, an Army private at Camp Lee, Va., is arriving home tomorrow, and expects to compete in the tournament through his leaves. So does Foley, who current ly stationed at Fort George Meade, Md.

SCHOOLED BY LOUIS

A cavalryman, whose spurs figuratively jingle-jangle-jingle, Foley reported for his physical check-up this week, and announced that he could be present when he's drawn for tourney bouts. He gained, he said, a strong likeing for boxing while at Fort Riley, and is most anxious to fight in his hometown.

Stationed at the Kansas base for a year, he was, so Foley says, one of the four youngsters who were given special attention by the world's heavyweight boxing champion. Blond, trim youth, the Corporal confesses he learned a lot from Louis.

Continued on Page 15, Column 7

Central Rallies, Defeats La Salle

A fourth period rush carried Central High to a 36-25 triumph over LaSalle High in a non-league game yesterday at 20th and Olney ave.

Central	G.	F.	P.	LaSalle	G.	F.	P.
Goldsbor'h,f	1	0	2	Davis,f	2	0	4
Stoloff,f	3	0	6	Williams,f	0	0	0
Cohn,c	6	5	17	Gaynor,c	3	0	6
Barish,g	0	1	1	Reagen,g	0	0	8
Siegel,g	2	1	5	Byron,g	0	0	0
Sabatine,f	0	0	0	Thompson,f	1	1	3
Dodies,f	0	0	0	Wiglicki,f	0	4	4
Garett,g	1	3	5	Leo,c	0	0	0
Silverman,g	0	0	0				
Shapiro,g	0	0	0				

Central	7	8	7	14—36
LaSalle	6	9	9	1—25

Officials—Jimmy Osborne and Harry Barfoot. Time of periods—8 minutes.

Expansion Plan for A.A.U.

COLUMBUS, O., Dec. 3 (U. P.).—The rehabilitation program of the Army Air forces for wounded soldiers has "paid high military dividends" and points the way to a post-war physical fitness program which would lift the health of the Nation's civilian population, Captain Alfred Fleishman, Medical Services Division of the AAF, told the 55th convention of the Amateur Athletic Union today.

Dan Ferris, secretary of the organization, presented a program to expand the A.A.U.'s general physical fitness program by organizing clubs in all cities of more than 3000 and spurring inter-city competition.

The swimming committee refused to recognize the 200-meter and 200-yard breaststroke marks of Emmett J. Cashin, Stanford U., because of a question regarding the leg action used.

Among the 1944 championship events tentatively awarded, subject to approval of the convention, were: Senior boxing, Boston, Mass., April 10-11; walking, 10 kilometer, Philadelphia, July 4; 20 kilometer, Philadelphia, Oct. 10.

PHILADELPHIA
ARDMORE
JENKINTOWN

We Buy from Thousands of Sources to Make Your Gift Buying Easy

U. S. War Stamps and Bonds Make Fine Christmas Gifts

Whether presented alone or wrapped together with some other pretty or useful gift, War Stamps or Bonds will be highly appreciated. We know the fate of our enemies is sealed, but our leaders know the hardest and most costly fighting is ahead. It would be dangerous to hope for final VICTORY without pouring more and more war materiel into the fight! And that means, MORE AND MORE WAR BONDS must be bought—and soon! Why not add to your own investment NOW—and buy Stamps and Bonds for gifts. Complete facilities for selling them at all our stores.

Gift Certificates a Happy Solution When in Doubt

Strawbridge & Clothier Merchandise Bonds are as good as gold to the lucky persons who receive them—and if you have someone on your gift list for whom you are not sure of making a suitable selection of merchandise (an employee for example), just come to our desk in the first floor elevator lobby for Merchandise Bonds in denominations of $1, $5 and $10 or neatly printed Gift Certificates filled out for any amount desired. A miniature hat for a man or dress for a woman with certificate allowing recipient to choose size and style is a clever idea, too. These may be charged if you have an account.

Federal Bouquet Print on Handsome Spun Rayon
Overdraperies

$15.65 pair

There's a richness of design and a depth of color in this beautiful print that build up to great distinction every room you hang it in! The floral motif is in full color, printed sharp and clear and true, and stands out most effectively on the handsome weave with its shell-like lustre and lovely draping qualities. Each side has a full 50" width of material in it, and is fully lined; 2¾ yards long. On rose, blue, turquoise and natural backgrounds.

STRAWBRIDGE & CLOTHIER—*Draperies, Sixth Floor*
Also at Ardmore and Jenkintown

Gifts That Tell the Weather

Swan Forecaster, predicts weather conditions from 8 to 24 hours in advance; it's colorful, decorative and useful, **69c**

Wet-or-Dry Hygrometer, a scientific instrument that gives both the temperature and the comparative moisture in the air ---------------------- **$2.50**

Mail and Telephone Orders Filled
Call Walnut 4500 Monday

STRAWBRIDGE & CLOTHIER
Dispensing Opticians, First Floor

Our TOY STORE is Santa's Happy Hunting Ground And a Time-and Effort-Saver to Grown-Up Shoppers

Express Wagon
The AMC Flash, made entirely of hardwood with oak bolsters and strong hardware exclusively for us; measures 36" x 15½", 13" high. **$7.95**

Snoozie Sleepy Head Doll, as cuddly as a real baby; covered in handsome pastel rayon plush, with zipper pocket in back; measures 24" long--- **$4.98**

Wood Scooter, for older boys; strong and firm and swift; streamline model measures 32" from wheel hub to wheel hub; well varnished and painted. **$5.59**

Kiddie Kar, a fine, strong, easy-rolling exerciser, made entirely of wood, nicely varnished; measures 20" long, 11" wide, 13" high to handlebars **$3.45**

Doll Coach
Smart modern design in wood and imitation leather; 36" long, 29½" high, 12" wide; a beauty to carry many dolls at once. **$11.95**

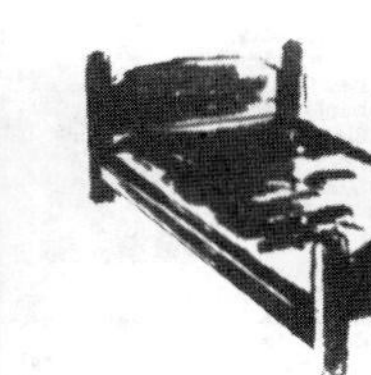

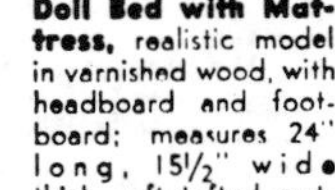

Doll Bed with Mattress, realistic model in varnished wood, with headboard and footboard; measures 24" long, 15½" wide thick, soft tufted mattress ----------- **$6.95**

Double Header Baseball Game, with real pitching, base-running, hitting and fielding; with bat, 3 balls, etc.; 24" square; for two or more players. **$4.95**

Set of Four Games, neatly boxed, very compact and space-saving; two different assortments, all the favorites for service men and women, travelers. **98c**

STRAWBRIDGE & CLOTHIER—*Toy Store, Fifth Floor. Also at Ardmore and Jenkintown*

Boudoir Chairs
for Lovely Lounging

Gifts she'll have to enjoy all for her very own—charming additions to her dressing room that build up its atmosphere of daintiness and femininity, and are most practical and useful besides as potent helps to relaxation and rest.

A darling chair with tufted seat and back; softly padded all-over, and nice and roomy, too; covered in nice quality printed sateen on rose, blue or natural backgrounds-- **$14.95**

Luxurious boudoir chair with channel back and reversible separate seat cushion; the covering is a very handsome rayon stripe woven in two rich contrasting colors------ **$27.50**

Beautiful boudoir chair with reversible separate seat cushion and tufted back; the covering is lustrous glosheen with handsome floral motif in full color on gold, green or natural back grounds----------------------------- **$19.95**

STRAWBRIDGE & CLOTHIER—*Furniture, Eighth Floor. Also at Ardmore and Jenkintown*

Case Cutlery of Chrome-Vanadium Steel

$3 to $14

Made by the famous Case works, and, of course, unobtainable now after present stocks are exhausted. Cutlery for perfectionists; every blade fine and true, every handle beautifully balanced.

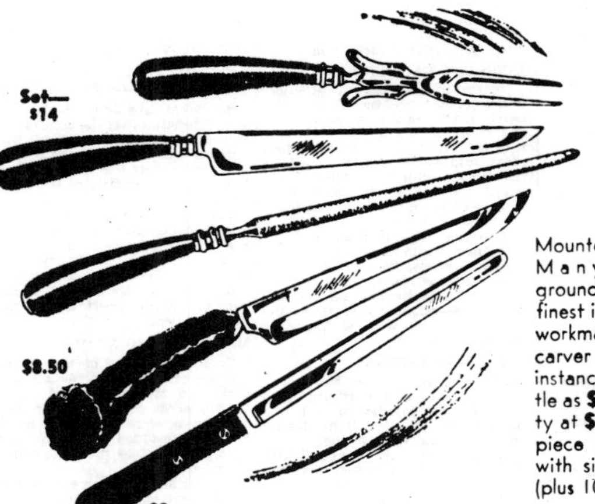

Mounted in the newest ways. Many blades are hollow-ground, and all represent the finest in materials, design and workmanship. An excellent carver 9½" or 10" long, for instance, can be had for as little as **$3;** a stag handle beauty at **$8.50;** the lovely three-piece carving set sketched with silver mountings is **$14** (plus 10% tax).

Gaily Painted Chairs Just in from Mexico

$4.95

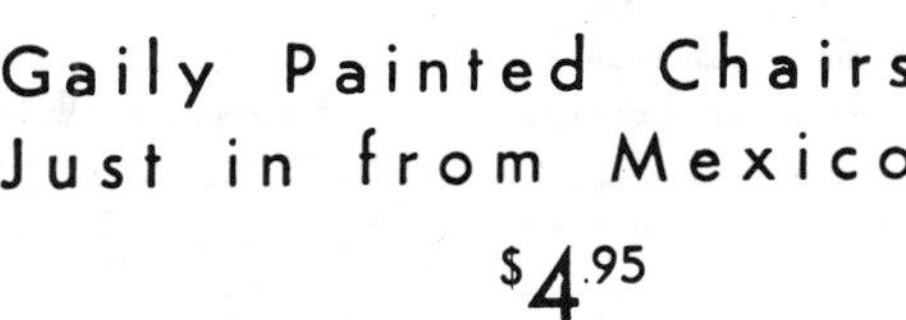

A world of style in their simple rustic effect, in their bright colors, in their peasant handiwork. And a world of practical usefulness, too, in their strong construction and comfortable proportions. The artistic decorative painting is hand-done; the palm-leaf seat is hand-woven. In red, yellow, blue, light or dark green, ivory. Seat measures 15½" by 18", and is 18" high.

STRAWBRIDGE & CLOTHIER
Homewares, Fifth Floor
Also at Ardmore and Jenkintown

Former Phila. Athlete Tackles English Thief

Staff Sergeant William J. Ferguson, 23, of 7824 Nixon st., Roxborough, who was well known as a sand-lot football player in his neighborhood before he enlisted in October, 1941, used his tackling ability to capture a thief in England last Saturday, a dispatch from London revealed yesterday.

Ferguson brought the thief down with a flying tackle after detectives had chased the man into a U. S. Army garage where Ferguson is stationed, as a dispatcher, the story from abroad related. It added that the sergeant said, after his feat: "It sure felt good; I haven't tackled a man in years, and it was worth a couple of bruises."

SGT. FERGUSON

He is the son of Mr. and Mrs. Peter Ferguson. He attended Roxborough High School and Roman Catholic High School, and was on the latter's baseball team. He was being considered for a tryout by a major league club, his parents said, when he enlisted. His father is a patrolman attached to the 43d district police station, Leverington ave. west of Ridge.

Sergeant Spreads Amity in England

Staff Sergeant William Johnson, 28, of 2004 E. Birch st., spent last Thanksgiving Day in England in a manner which "probably did more good for Anglo-American relations than a dozen diplomats," a dispatch from the Eighth Army Air Force headquarters disclosed yesterday.

Sergeant Johnson contributed to international amity when he paid a holiday visit to the 25 school children of Sudborough, a village in the English Midlands, and told them about America's Thanksgiving and many other things about this country, the dispatch said.

"It would have been swell to have been home for Thanksgiving in Philadelphia, but I got a big kick out of telling those kids about the States. It made me feel good to realize they are interested in us," Johnson said.

In this city, his mother, Mrs. Mary E. Metzger, said he remarked in a recent letter that he "had a great time at the little school." Mrs. Metzger said her son enlisted Oct. 26, 1940, after working here for a janitorial supply concern. At present, he is an Air Force's supply clerk.

"By picking up the baby now and then when he is awake and lying quietly in his crib, you will teach him that he can have attention when he is good." Carolyn Randolph's sage advice on child care is a regular and helpful feature of The Inquirer.

With the Armed Forces

News of Philadelphians in Service

PRIVATE FIRST CLASS DOMINIC A. PIRONTI, 538 E. Walnut lane, serving in the South Pacific, is ready to believe the world is a small place. For, while he was stationed in Guadalcanal he "bumped into" his brother, Seaman Vincenta Pironti, a member of a naval construction battalion. The brothers had not seen each other for more than a year.

Sergeant Ruth D. Waggner, who is a clerk in the officers personnel branch, Post Headquarters, Fort Belvoir, Va., also acts as a platoon sergeant in the WAC Detachment there. Prior to entering the service in October, 1942, she was employed in the executive department of the Bell Telephone Co. here. She is a former president of the Women's Traffic Club of Philadelphia.

SGT. WAGGNER

With 14 strikes against Jap-infested island bases in the central and northern Solomons to his credit, Second Lieutenant Paul O. Nadler, bomber pilot, of 5410 Saul st., has been awarded the Air Medal "for meritorious achievement while participating in aerial flights on combat missions."

Arthur Samuel, 7316 Passyunk ave., serving with the Army engineers in the European theater of operations, has been promoted to staff sergeant. He also has seen service in the Marine Corps, from November, 1937, to June, 1940.

• • •

John Francis McGovern, of 247 Paxon st., serving with a "Lightning" fighter unit in New Guinea, has been promoted to first sergeant. The 26-year-old flier has been overseas 22 months.

• • •

Corporal William W. Quinn, son of Mr. and Mrs. Edward J. Quinn, Jr., 5119 Cedar ave., is serving with the Eighth Air Force somewhere in England. He entered the Army last February and finished his training in Florida and California before going overseas.

CORP. QUINN

Andrew Megeish, serving at an Eighth Air Force bomber station in England, has been promoted to corporal. His wife, Cecelia, and their child live at 901 New Market st.

Technical Sergeant Philip E. Betz, 27, of 2833 Belgrade st., serving at an Eighth Army Air Force fighter station in England, has been awarded the Good Conduct Medal.

Captain Leon Spector, 25, of 822 N. 2d st., attached to the administrative branch of the 14th Air Force in China, recently was promoted to that rank from first lieutenant. He entered the service in July, '41, and received basic training at Ellington Field, Tex. He went overseas last February. He has a brother, Jules, 32, attached to an armored unit at Ft. Knox, Ky.

CAPT. SPECTOR

Second Lieutenant Stanley C. Peltzman, of 4300 Westminster ave., stationed at Fort Knox, Ky., recently married Miss Shirley Friedman, of 42d and Ogden sts., a metallurgist research worker at the Philadelphia Navy Yard.

• • •

Private First Class Anthony De Francesco, 636 Wynnewood road, is a member of a regimental Army band in Great Britain.

NAVY

William J. Phillipo, 24, seaman first class, of 528 S. Taney st., who enlisted in the Navy in December, 1942, is now serving in the South Pacific. A graduate of West Philadelphia High School, he attended La Salle College, and prior to entering the service he was a dispatcher for the Yellow Cab Co. His wife, Gertrude, and their 13-month-old son, William, Jr., reside at the Taney st. address.

SEAMAN PHILLIPO

Lieutenant (jg.) Philip N. Wainwright, of Ambler, pilot of a Catalina flying boat, has been awarded the Distinguished Flying Cross. He picked up a distress signal from a Liberator bomber which crashed into the water, and in spite of unfavorable landing conditions made a rough landing and administered first aid to eight members of the bombers' crew who had taken to life rafts and had been injured.

MARINES

It took a Japanese machine gun to stop Private George R. Metzler, of 4111 Walnut st., but months in Naval hospitals are bringing him back to health. Private Metzler, a veteran of the initial Marine landings on Tulagi in the Solomons in August, 1942, is now at the U. S. Naval Hospital, Oakland, Calif. At home in Philadelphia cheering Private Metzler's recovery are his wife, the former Ethel Hoover, and his three-year-old son, George R. Metzler, Jr.

Technical Sergeant Lewis (Jim) Slepin, son of Mr. and Mrs. William Slepin, of 65th ave. and 11th st., who recently was promoted to that rank, is on duty at the Marine Corps Air Station at El Centro, Calif. Slepin was rejected when he first tried to enlist in the Marines, but was accepted in May, 1941, following a major operation.

SGT. SLEPIN

Frank H. Fleer, U. S. M. C. R., 227 Narberth ave., Narberth, chairman of the Quantico, Va., Air Station Athletic Committee, has been promoted to major. He served in the Marine Corps from 1918 to 1922, and was recommissioned in July of last year. Prior to re-entering the corps, Major Fleer was associated with the Philadelphia Electric Co.

COAST GUARD

Among the SPAR officers commissioned at the Coast Guard Academy last Wednesday was Ensign Anne Francis Smith, daughter of Mr. and Mrs. Joseph M. Smith, of 5301 N. 10th st. Prior to entering the service she was engaged in secretarial work and banking and is a member of the Philadelphia Chapter of the American Institute of Banking. She enlisted in the WAVES in November, 1942, and was transferred to Coast Guard last March 15. Her brother is First Lieutenant Frank M. Smith, U. S. Army.

The third and last of her family to enlist in the armed forces of the United States, SPAR Clara C. Leinhauser, seaman second class, daughter of Mr. and Mrs. Otto Leinhauser, 222 Sharon ave., Sharon Hill, has a brother serving in the Army Air Corps and a sister in the WAC.

SPAR LEINHAUSER

Her brother, Otto P., Jr., is an Aviation Cadet at the University of Akron, Akron, Ohio. Her sister, Ruth M., is a first sergeant in the WAC, stationed at Camp Edwards, Mass.

Byrd Seeks Refund Of Hundred Billions

WASHINGTON, Dec. 19 (U. P.).—The Joint Congressional Economy Committee disclosed tonight it would ask Senate Appropriations Committee co-operation in a move to return almost $100,000,000,000 of uncommitted War and Navy Department, Maritime Commission and War Shipping Administration appropriations to the Treasury.

The committee, headed by Senator Harry F. Byrd (D., Va.), said unexpended balances of the four agencies totaled $186,785,383,797 in September, of which $92,000,000,000 had not been committed.

INVESTIGATION SOUGHT

"The committee will urge an investigation to determine whether additional appropriations will be needed until such time as all the outstanding balances have been encumbered," the statement said.

In other projected inquiries the committee will seek:

1. Curtailment of non-war functions of agencies assigned to war work.

2. Elimination of an additional 400,000 employes from the Federal payroll.

3. Reduction of travel and communication expenses.

4. A curb on creation of new agencies to handle work which could be done by existing agencies.

5. Equitable promotion policy.

6. An end to abuse of the franking privilege.

The committee said it has been instrumental in saving the Government $2,117,543,231 since its inception in September, 1943.

Today

—By Mark Sullivan—

Continued From First Page

the Senate will not need to be acted upon by the House at all.

In the Senate was debated, early this month, a measure to give soldiers opportunity to vote, largely by Federal action. After six days of debate the Senate voted down the original measure, passed a substitute putting soldier voting almost wholly in the hands of the States, with co-operation by the Army and Navy.

The measure as passed went to the House, will be acted upon by the latter body after recess.

About this measure, violent controversy has arisen, including epithets and charges which imply that some Senators do not support soldier voting. This is not true—there is not a man in House or Senate but wishes every soldier to have an opportunity to vote.

What happened was that the Senate, after six days of careful and intelligent consideration—a legislative body at its best—discovered that giving all soldiers the opportunity to vote is an extremely intricate task.

It entails setting up formidable mechanisms, and involves delicate questions of law and constitutional procedure which, unless carefully solved, might lead to a contested Presidential election.

Opportunity to vote means opportunity to vote for every candidate, from local school directors up to President. In the end this will be done, by the measure which will be passed in the House, and adjustment of this to the measure already passed by the Senate.

The process must include a large measure of action by the individual States. Steps toward this, by the States, will begin during the recess of Congress.

Phila. Ensign Killed In Plane Crash

SEATTLE, Dec. 19 (A. P.).—The Navy today identified Ensign Edmund T. Lilly, of Philadelphia, and Ensign H. L. Jackson, Peninsula, O., as the two naval officers killed yesterday in a plane crash.

Ensign Lilly is survived by his wife, Mrs. E. T. Lilly.

Ration Dates

MEATS, BUTTER, FATS: Brown stamps, L, M, N, P and Q now in use, this series expiring Jan. 1. Stamp R will be good Dec. 26; S, Jan. 2; T, Jan. 9, and U, Jan. 16. Stamp Q expires Jan. 1, the others Jan. 29.

PROCESSED FOODS: Green stamps A, B, and C in ration book No. 4 are good through today. Stamps D, E and F are effective through Jan. 20.

SUGAR: Stamp 29 in ration book No. 4 is valid through Jan. 15.

SHOES: Coupon 18 of Book No. 1 and coupon 1 on the "airplane" sheet in Book No. 3 are valid for an indefinite period.

FUEL OIL: Period 1 coupons, valid through Jan. 3, Period 2 coupons, effective through Feb. 7, and Period 3 coupons, valid on Jan. 4 through March 13, are all good for 10 gallons per unit.

GASOLINE: A8 gas coupons, good for three gallons, are valid through Feb. 8; B1 and C1 coupons now worth two gallons; B2 and C2 are good for five gallons.

HOME CONSUMERS TO GET MORE FOOD

WASHINGTON, Dec. 19 (U. P.).—Larger rations of meat and processed foods for those who eat at home were envisaged tonight by Price Administrator Chester Bowles in announcing major rationing revisions for more than 400,000 restaurants, hotels and other commercial and institutional eating establishments.

Bowles said the new program, effective March 1, provides that food rations for eating establishments will be based only on the number of persons to whom food and not refreshments only is served. Allotments now are made on the number of customers.

TO REDUCE RATIONS

He said it would reduce the rations of soda fountains, roadside stands and taverns which, in many instances, have been able to get larger allotments than restaurants whose chief business is food.

These savings, he said, will be added to the national supply, increasing the ration share of those who eat at home.

Actual servings of refreshments—soft drinks, coffee, milk drinks, alcoholic beverages and the like will be used as the basis for computing refreshment allotments.

THOROUGH OVERHAULING

He described the change as a "thorough overhauling" of the program in co-operation with representatives of the hotel and restaurant industries. OPA was required to invoke the present plan "under pressure of an emergency" and inequalities now are corrected in a "practical system that is fairer all around," he said.

Only two alternatives were possible—standardization of meals and collection of ration coupons for meals eaten out—and both were turned down, he said.

BACKERS CONVINCED M'ARTHUR WILL RUN

WASHINGTON, Dec. 19 (A. P.).—General Douglas MacArthur's failure to say specifically that he would not accept a Presidential nomination if it were offered, has convinced his supporters the Republicans could draft him as a nominee.

Senator Arthur H. Vandenberg (R., Mich.), looked upon as the father of the MacArthur boom, said today he is proceeding on the theory that the Southwest Pacific commander would not refuse the Republican nomination.

"I shall continue to assume that he will accept unless he says he would not," Vandenberg said.

INTEREST HEIGHTENED

Interest in this aspect of the situation was heightened by a Dec. 17 dispatch from Southwest Pacific Allied Headquarters in which Arthur R. Ford, president of the Canadian press, said MacArthur "touched on the delicate subject of United States politics" in an off-the-record conference with a visiting Canadian newspaper party.

Although Ford said MacArthur's utterances would have to remain secret, it is viewed here as significant that the general—who has said in the past that he had no political ambitions—would spend time discussing politics with a Canadian group.

AWARE OF EFFORTS

The inference is that MacArthur is fully aware of the efforts being made in this country to launch a draft campaign, even if he doesn't care to discuss them publicly.

MacArthur's friends noted with satisfaction Ford's report that the general wound up his press conference with a discussion of his philosophy of war and life, quoting from such solid sources as the Bible, Adam Smith, the economist, and Abraham Lincoln.

Murray, Rankin Assail Colleagues On Soldier Vote

WASHINGTON, Dec. 19 (A. P.).—Two Southern Democratic Congressmen strongly denounced today the action of a group of 25 colleagues in circulating a petition criticizing a Senate-passed bill to leave with the States, instead of the Federal Government, supervision over soldier voting in next fall's elections.

The petition, declaring the measure a "substitute for democracy" and "a slap in the face" for members of the armed forces, drew from Representative Thomas Murray (D., Tenn.) a statement that he was "utterly shocked."

RANKIN ASSAILS 'LEFTISTS'

Representative John Rankin (D., Miss.) declared that the signers constituted "a small group of left wing Congressmen" and that the petition "does not reflect the views of a majority of the members of the House on either side."

The petition pledged united effort to obtain Congressional approval of a bill assuring a Federal guarantee of a vote to all service men and termed the Senate measure "an insult to the intelligence of these millions of gallant Americans whom it disfranchises."

MARCANTONIO NAMED

Referring to one of the signers, Murray asserted that "we all know that Vito Marcantonio (A. L. P., N. Y.), wants to bring about social equality between the races in the South." He added that the petitioners would "destroy the State control of the franchise."

Signers of the statement included six Pennsylvania Democrats: Grant Furlong, Michael J. Bradley, Thomas E. Scanlon, Augustine B. Kelly, Francis E. Walter and Herman P. Eberharter.

CONGRESS THINS OUT ON EVE OF HOLIDAYS

WASHINGTON, Dec. 19 (U. P.).—Congress, its ranks already greatly diminished by holiday departures, will give only perfunctory attention this week to taxes and the rail wage issue before starting a Christmas adjournment Tuesday that will continue until Jan. 10.

Tuesday was chosen so Congress would be technically in session when the Senate Finance Committee formally reports its $2,284,000,000 tax bill to the floor. The measure will not be taken up, however, until after the recess.

MAJOR ISSUES DEFERRED

The House Interstate Commerce Committee is scheduled to meet tomorrow for further consideration of the Senate-approved Truman Resolution validating an eight-cent-an-hour wage increase for non-operating railway workers, but President Roosevelt's intervention in the explosive rail situation and the absence of several committeemen will reduce the session to a mere formality.

All other pending major topics will be deferred until mid-January or later. They include the hotly contested subsidy fight, the soldier vote bill and legislation to provide mustering-out pay for the armed forces.

The subsidy question has been put off until Feb. 17 by temporary extension of the Commodity Credit Corp.'s life beyond its scheduled expiration Dec. 31. Administration Senate leaders plan to use the breathing spell to devise a workable compromise as an alternative to the House-indorsed outright ban on subsidies which is before the Senate Banking Committee.

SOLDIER BILLS HELD UP

The Senate passed a bill to provide the armed forces with mustering-out pay ranging from $200 to $500, but the House Military Affairs Committee thus far has been unable to agree on its own version and expects no decisive action until next year.

Likewise in a state of suspension is the controversial soldier vote issue. The House Elections Committee is considering a Senate-adopted bill placing overseas balloting administration in State hands.

Censorship No Threat To Free Press, 2 Say

Speaking during the University of Pennsylvania Forum of Public Opinion on Radio Station WIP, two newspaper men yesterday expressed the opinion that there was no serious threat to freedom of the press under the present voluntary censorship code for wartime news.

Richard A. Thornburgh, of The Inquirer, and Alexander R. Griffin, of The Record, agreed that the only actual "gag" on news had been in cases where military authorities felt security was in danger.

Dr. Reese D. James, professor of English at the University, in opening the discussion, raised the question of the "muzzling" of correspondents during the Teheran conference and cited other instances which he felt might threaten freedom of the press. Dr. Scully Bradley, also an English professor at Pennsylvania, was the moderator during the discussions.

Service Entertainment

Tickets for service men and women to various types of shows—the theaters, sports events—may be obtained at the Philadelphia Hospitality Center for Service Men, 18 S. 15th st. There you can learn of special affairs each night.

MEN AND WOMEN

USO-Labor Plaza, Town Hall, Broad and Race sts.—Dancing, refreshments, 6 P. M. to midnight, daily except Sunday.

Y. M. C. A., 117 N. 15th st.—Lodging, pool, special recreation, gym, showers.

Jewish Welfare Board Club and Canteen, 401 S. Broad st.—Dancing and food.

Travelers' Aid Lounge, 30th St. Station—Open 24 hours a day. Broad St. Station—Open 10 A. M. to 10 P. M.

Philadelphia Hospitality Center, 18 S. 15th st.—Information and referral service; limited number of free entertainment tickets; free mending shop for men.

Benedict Club (National Catholic Community Service), 157 N. 18th st.—Dancing and food.

Y. W. C. A., 1800 Arch st.—Hospitality and dancing.

Salvation Army Red Shield Club, 703 N. Broad st.—Entertainment, music, lodging and food.

Lutheran Service Center, 1218 Walnut st., lounges, writing and recreation room, snack bar, lounge for service women.

Baptist Hospitality Center, 17th and Sansom sts., facilities for service men and women.

Zoological Gardens, 34th st. and Girard ave.—Open 9 A. M. to 5 P. M.

Franklin Institute, 20th st. and Parkway—Open 1 P. M. to 6. Closed Monday.

Pennsylvania Academy of the Fine Arts, Broad and Cherry sts.—Exhibits free to service men and women in uniform, daily 1 P. M. to 5 P. M.

University Museum, 33d and Spruce sts.—Admission free. Exhibition of current interest. Open weekdays, except Mondays, 10 A. M. to 5 P. M.; Sundays 1 to 5 P. M.

Free Museum of Natural History, Academy of Natural Science, 19th st. and the Parkway, weekdays, 9 A. M. to 5 P. M.; Sundays, 1 P. M. to 5 P. M. Admission free.

Philadelphia Museum of Art, 26th and Parkway—Open daily, 10 A. M. to 5 P. M., current exhibition of interest.

MEN

United Service Club, 17th and Locust sts.—Music, dancing, refreshments. Open 24 hours.

USO Date Club, Broadwood Hotel, 320 N. Broad st.—Dancing. Open 5 to 12 P. M.

South Broad St. USO Club, 510 S. Broad st.—Dancing, open 10 A. M. to 11 P. M.

United Merchant Seamen's Club, 321 S. Fourth st.—Dancing, snack bar.

Navy Mother's Club, 246-48 S. Quince st.—Dancing and refreshments for Navy men, 10 A. M. to midnight.

Stage Door Canteen, Broad and Locust sts.—Entertainment and dancing.

St. Stephen's Service Club, 10th st. below Market—Library, gymnasium, free refreshments. Open 3 to 12 P. M.

Bellevue-Stratford—Officers' Club. Open daily from 10 A. M. to midnight.

Presbyterian Hospitality House, 2200 Locust st.—Recreation, refreshments, sleeping quarters.

Church Door Canteen of Jenkintown, Homestead road, snack bar and lounge, open every night, 6 P. M. to 12.

Open Door Canteen of Upper Darby, 7053 W. Garrett road—Tuesday, Wednesday and Thursday, dances for service men, 8 P. M.

WOMEN

Service Women's Club, USO—Emergency Aid, 245 S. 15th st., home facilities, information, tea service. Open weekdays, 9 A. M. to 11 P. M.; Sunday, 4 to 8 P. M.

Women's Officers' Club, 1521 Walnut st.—Club facilities, 11 A. M. to 11 P. M.

More Victory Gardens in 1944 Urged

By Jane Leslie Kift

The call has been sounded: "Bigger and better Victory Gardens in 1944 will be part of the answer to the Nation's need for at least 28 percent more fresh vegetables in the coming year."

While commercial growers throughout the nation are doing a splendid job, we cannot depend on them to produce this tremendous increase, as they have both transportation and machinery problems that limit expansion.

This past summer, the Victory Gardeners of America did an amazing piece of work when they established 20,000,000 vegetable gardens, in many cases on the poorest types of soil, which produced 8,000,000 tons of food worth at least one billion dollars and 4,400,000 jars of canned goods valued according to the Department of Agriculture at $880,000,000. This all-time record achievement was even more amazing when we consider that many of these gardeners had never grown a row of radishes and some had never had any flower garden experience.

The need for food next year will be even more pressing. The goal for 1944 has been set at 22,000,000 home and community gardens. The Victory Garden Institute, which was organized the early part of this year, reports that the War Food Administration has stated: "Even if farmers and Victory Gardeners break all production records in 1943 and 1944, it won't be enough. We'll need more."

December is a good month to take notes on garden plans for next year so that a practical idea of garden operations for 1944 will be ready when seed-ordering time comes in late January. We all know at this time which crops the family prefers, which ones deserve extra space next year.

The many novice gardeners expected next year also will be able to benefit from our experience. County agents, Victory Garden Coordinators, Garden Club members, Departments of Agriculture in the various sections of the country will know the type of help needed by the amateur. With the work so well organized, there is no limit to what we can accomplish.

Girls Turn to Bouffante Formals For Gala Moments in Busy Life

Styles Feature Flounces and Double Ruffle

By Cynthia Cabot

BUSY as they are, these junior stage stars still find the time for dance dresses. Which seems little short of a miracle, as jam-packed with activity as their lives are.

Betty Anne Nyman at the left is continuing her studies at Temple while she is in Philadelphia. Besides six evening performances a week and two matinees, both she and Gloria Stroock are frequently entertaining at the Stage Door Canteen and with the traveling unit that visits nearby Service hospitals.

When their thoughts turn to gala moments, you will find them in the sweet, bouffante formals that every girl loves. Black moire and layers of black tulle are combined in this beau-catcher. Its off-the-shoulder neckline has a double ruffle of the tulle and a big red rose plays hide-and-seek at one side of the skirt.

Scarlet taffeta is used for the young bare shoulder gown at the right. The bodice is softly shirred and accented by a cabbage-size rose while deep V's of shirring give a flounce to the ankle-length skirt.

Call Cynthia Cabot at Rittenhouse 1600 for the name of the store.

* * *

Pets in Home Helpful In Raising of Children

By Carolyn Randolph

There is always a question of pets in the home where there are small children. Almost all children want pets and their parents, for one reason or another, do not feel they can have them.

Whenever animals are part of a household the children must be taught how to handle them. The animals must not be mistreated by unguided children.

Mrs. Louis Bloch, Philadelphia, expressed her opinion on the question of pets in the home and their effect on little children in her letter which follows. She will receive two dollars.

PETS OFFER REAL PROBLEM

"The problem of pets is a real problem, but not in the sense that it is generally considered. Most children beg for a kitten or puppy and are deprived of them because their parents have been taught to fear them or consider them too much bother.

"My baby has been brought up with cats and dogs. He was taught to respect them, never to approach them while they eat, never to tease them. He has grown up to be a real Indian, but doesn't hit or grab other children or their possessions.

"This I attribute to his lessons and experiences with the pets he has had."

Two dollars is paid for each Child Care letter published. Write to Carolyn Randolph, The Philadelphia Inquirer.

CHILD CARE QUERIES

Carolyn Randolph, whose commonsense column on Child Care is a regular feature of The Inquirer, will answer your child care queries. Address your queries to Carolyn Randolph, The Philadelphia Inquirer.

Child Lonesome

Q. My baby will soon be a year old and until now he has been a perfect baby. He rarely cried and when he did there was a reason. But for the past month he will not play alone in his pen as he used to. As soon as I leave the room, he starts crying and keeps this up until I return or just lays on his tummy and sucks his thumb. As long as I am in the room he will play quietly. I don't think he is spoiled as we have never picked him up when he cried. He is teething, but I don't think that would account for his behavior. MRS. J. J. B.

A. It sounds as if your baby were lonesome. He is getting old enough to enjoy company and he is unhappy without it. Also he is at the age where he is outgrowing a play pen. His interests cover a wide field now and he needs more space than that afforded by a play pen.

I would suggest that you discontinue using the pen except at times when you can not be on hand to watch the baby. Also play with him more so that he will not be lonesome. Be sure to start playing with him when he is in a happy mood so he will not learn to cry for attention. An hour is a long time for a child of one year to entertain himself, so break it up by frequently talking to him or handing him a different toy.

Your Fashion Query Box

Cynthia Cabot, Fashion Editor of The Inquirer, will help you with your personal style problem through the columns of this newspaper. Address all queries to Cynthia Cabot, The Philadelphia Inquirer.

Mixed Wedding

Q. At my daughter's 4 o'clock wedding on Jan. 15 there will be three civilians, three Army men and one Naval officer in the bridal party. The bride will wear a white satin gown and veil. Would dark blue business suits or cutaways with striped trousers be the correct dress for those not in uniform? C. L. S.

A. The civilian ushers at an afternoon wedding would be correctly attired in dark blue business suits with blue ties, small boutonnieres and no gloves. Such apparel is a safe choice for all civilians at semi-military weddings even though the hour of the day and the bride's attire would call for more formal dress.

It's 4 o'clock in the morning and time for the Marine Bombing Squadron to get going. Capt. Armon Christopherson, of Grand Rapids, Mich., hits the deck.

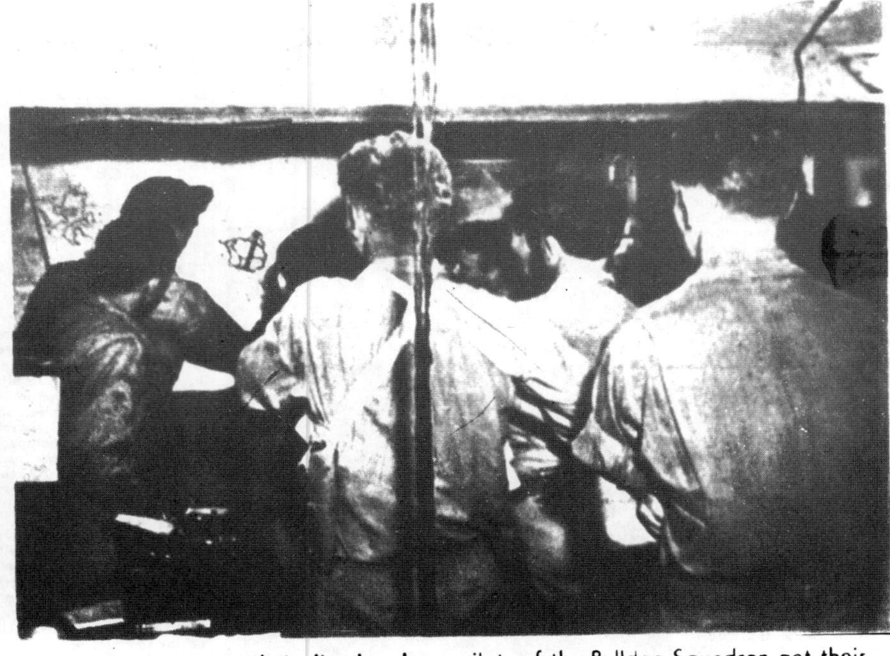

Before scattering to their dive bombers, pilots of the Bulldog Squadron get their targets and final instructions in front of a large map of the Solomons.

Log of a Marine Bombing Raid in the Pacific

A TYPICAL day in the life of a Marine Corps bombing squadron in the Southwest Pacific is outlined by the pictures on this page. They show members of the Bulldog Squadron from the time they arise before dawn, through their briefing and take-off in the early morning light to their safe return after a successful mission. The target in this instance was the Vila Plantation Airdrome on Kolombangara Island in the Central Solomons, since captured from the enemy. Of the 32 planes taking part, all returned to Guadalcanal. A day's work like this is strictly routine, but never monotonous.

'Raring to go, planes taxi down the ramps toward the runways on Henderson Field to take off for their raid. Another unhealthy surprise is due for the Japs.

With wing tips almost touching, so close is the formation, the planes speed toward the target. Each carries a bomb plainly visible beneath the fuselage.

Nearing the target, the planes start their bombing runs. Softening up expeditions like this greatly aided the Marines in capturing the island later.

Back at their base, pilots report on the results of the mission to Capt. W. G. Pederson (with glasses), intelligence officer of the Bulldog Squadron.

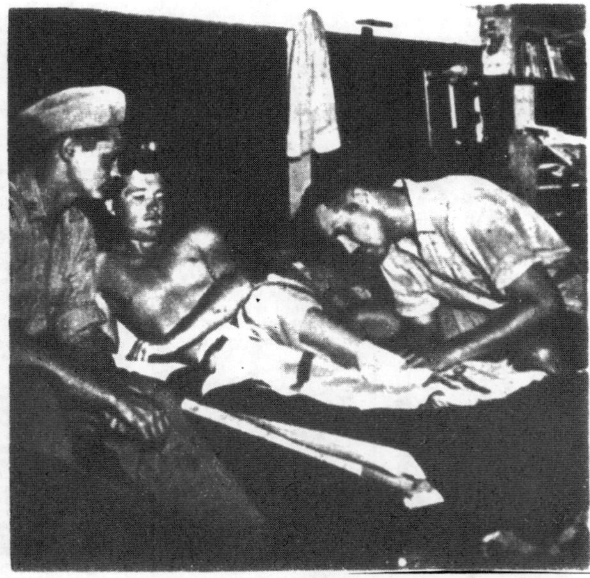

Official U. S. Marine Corps Photos

Only casualty was Staff Sergeant Ward F. Keevert, of Billings, Mont., whose left leg was cut by shrapnel from anti-aircraft fire. He was up in three days.

The Philadelphia Inquirer

PUBLIC LEDGER

An Independent Newspaper for All the People

FINAL CITY EDITION

CIRCULATION: January Average: Daily 474,418; Sunday 1,262,751

THURSDAY MORNING, FEBRUARY 3, 1944

Copyright 1944 by The Philadelphia Inquirer. Vol. 230 No. 34

a b d e f g h

THREE CENTS

Yanks Win Main Marshall Air Base; Allies Storm Into Cassino Outskirts

Today

Where Is Jap Fleet?
Missing at Marshalls
Not Eager for Action
Bitter Choice Ahead
'Face' Versus Fact

By John M. McCullough
Inquirer Washington Bureau

WASHINGTON, Feb 2.

JAPAN apparently is deliberately avoiding a major show of strength with the tremendously expanded United States fleet in the Pacific, pursuant to a pre-determined policy of steady withdrawal to Japanese home waters.

There has been no evidence whatever of major elements of the Japanese fleet in the vicinity of the Marshalls, and some well-posted observers here do not expect that the enemy will undertake a major counter-offensive by surface units against the mightiest naval armada which has ever sailed under the Stars and Stripes.

Indeed, on the basis of the history of the past 19 months of the war in the Pacific, the prophecy is hazarded in some quarters that the Japanese fleet will be held for a final showdown in the home waters of the Japanese Empire itself.

If Japan is not prepared to gamble her fleet, whose main strength never has been committed to action, in defense of the vital Marshall Islands, it is argued—islands which form an inestimably valuable bulwark to her entire central Pacific position—she will not gamble them on any purely defensive operation short of the immediate vicinity of the Japanese islands.

Naval observers admit that this is conjecture, but it has much to recommend it. Among the points supporting the view are these:

1. Japan has not attempted a real surface engagement since the catastrophic reverse in the Battle of Midway Island, exactly 19 months ago.

2. Japan has consistently refused to commit any of her capital ships in large-scale action since the greater task force raids of November-December, 1942, when the enemy strove unsuccessfully to break the Allied deadlock on the southeastern Solomons.

3. Repeated reconnaissance has not resulted in report of heavy assemblage of the Jap fleet in any of the forward defense bases, such as Rabaul, Wotje or Jaluit, within recent months.

It is estimated that approximately 40 percent of the Japanese fleet, normally based on Truk, the big stronghold in the mandated Caroline Islands, only 1075 statute miles east of Kwajalein in its general conformation, will be evacuated by the enemy

Continued on Page 12, Column 4

DRIVE BEGUN FOR ACCORD ON SOLDIER VOTE

Compromise Plan Offered as Senate Rejects Changes in U. S. Ballot Bill

By HERMAN A. LOWE
Inquirer Washington Bureau

WASHINGTON, Feb. 2. — There were indications tonight that Congress, having entangled itself and the public in confusion, intemperate oratory, charges and counter-charges on the soldier vote issue, was beginning to grope for a compromise path out of the morass.

The most important development was in the Senate, where an amendment jointly sponsored by eight Democrats and six Republicans was offered. It is a middle-of-the-road measure about halfway between the Green-Lucas (Federal ballot) and the Eastland-Rankin (State's rights) bills.

APPEASEMENT PROGRAM

There was still another amendment ready in the Senate to limit Federal ballots to service men overseas and require those in this country to follow the regular State absentee voting procedures.

In both chambers, Administration leaders launched an appeasement program, insisting they disagreed with the President and did not feel that the Eastland-Rankin bill was a "fraud" upon service men. Several leading House Republicans admitted privately that something in the way of a compromise would probably come.

The new Senate amendment provides (1) a definite termination date, Dec. 31, 1945, for the legislation;

Continued on Page 4, Column 3

OPA SAYS HOTELS GOT STOLEN MEAT

Illustrated on Page 6

Criminal prosecution was being prepared yesterday against restaurants and hotels which, it was asserted, bought meat stolen from a large wholesale meat house here at black market prices and without the required ration stamps.

The Office of Price Administration, which said it was making a sweeping investigation of restaurants and cafes which purportedly received the stolen meat, announced that maximum penalties would be sought.

FACE 5 YEARS IN JAIL

Those found guilty are subject to five years in prison and $10,000 fine.

OPA said its investigation already disclosed that 100,000 ration points were involved in the sale of the meat, which was stolen from Lorch & Co., suppliers of restaurants and hotels, at 122 N. Delaware ave.

Two more arrests were made yesterday as city detectives began

Continued on Page 6, Column 4

Gustav Line Broken

Map on Page 2

By RICHARD G. MASSOCK

ALLIED HEADQUARTERS IN ITALY, Feb. 2 (A. P.).—American troops, after smashing with French forces through the entire width of the bitterly-defended Gustav Line, battled their way through German "sacrificial squads" today into the outskirts of Cassino, gateway key to a broad highway to Rome.

The Americans' progress on this front 80 miles below the capital was slow but steady in the face of a heavy tank, artillery, mortar and small arms fire put up by the German defenders in a bloody last-ditch stand, it was disclosed by Hal Boyle, Associated Press correspondent, in a dispatch dated 'at the edge of Cassino.'

TOWN HEAVILY MINED

Cassino, which has been under Allied siege for three weeks, still was filled with snipers, and its streets and buildings were heavily mined, Boyle related.

American patrols had battled to within 300 yards of Cassino last night, but were thrown back by the Nazi "sacrificial squads" which gave no quarter in their death-defying tactics to delay the Allied advance every moment possible. They resumed the push today, some infantrymen fighting for as much as 20 hours without rest, encountering still more of these determined German rear guard units.

PRISONERS TAKEN

Some German prisoners were taken in the advance.

Despite the imminent loss of Cassino, principal bastion of their southern defenses, the Germans continued to draw back crack troops both from that front and from northern Italy as they assembled a powerful force around the Allied beachhead on the west coast, one of whose tentacles was within 16 miles of the Eternal City.

ATTACK IMMINENT

Information received here indicated that a strong counter-offensive might be flung against the beachhead at any hour. A field dispatch

Continued on Page 2, Column 6

14 Italian Nuns Killed In Attack, Nazis Say

ENEMY SOURCE

LONDON, Feb. 2 (A. P.).—The German-controlled Rome radio said tonight that 14 nuns were killed yesterday in "an attack" on Castel Gandolfo, the Pope's summer residence south of Rome.

The broadcast did not say who made the attack.

"A convent at the outskirts of the Papal residence was hit and the bodies of 14 nuns have been recovered so far," the radio said.

There has been no report of such an incident from Allied sources.

MARSHALL ISLAND TAKEN BY U. S. MARINES

Roi Island, site of the most important airfield in the Marshall Islands, was taken by U. S. Marines yesterday as other invasion forces fanned out over the Kwajalein atoll. In addition, the Marines have cornered the Jap defenders on nearby Namur Island. The inset map shows the entire atoll, with Kwajalein and surrounding isles where the invaders have secured beachheads. (Pacific war pictures on Page 12).

ALL-OUT TAXATION ASKED BY WILLKIE

NEW YORK, Feb. 2 (U. P.).—Wendell L. Willkie tonight asserted that President Roosevelt's request for more than $10,000,000,000 in new taxes should be doubled, and urged the Administration and Congress while the Nation is at war to "ruthlessly tax every dollar in every income group for the preservation of the American future."

Willkie, the 1940 Republican candidate for President, who leaves Friday on a speaking tour of Western States in connection with his drive to win the Republican nomination again this year, spoke at a meeting sponsored by the New York Times which was one of a series on the general subject: "America Plans and Dreams."

He blamed both the Administra-

Continued on Page 4, Column 6

Nazis in Reprisal Raze French Town

BERN, Switzerland, Feb. 2 (A. P.).—An Annemasse dispatch to the Journal de Geneve said today that the Germans had turned flame throwers on the tiny village of Poully near St. Jeoire in Haute-Savoie, France, burning it to the ground in reprisal for attacks on the Nazi garrison.

Partisans fired through windows to defend the village and the Germans had to call reinforcements from Annemasse before being able to burn it.

Soviets Inside Estonia, Close On Rail Center

By JAMES M. LONG

LONDON, Feb. 3 (Thursday) (A. P.).—The Russians have smashed across the old Estonian border near the mouth of the Narva River, capturing more than 40 towns on the approaches to the rail city of Narva, Moscow announced today.

Berlin reports, meanwhile, told of a new Soviet break-through in the Dnieper Bend and a new Red Army drive upon Rovno, 30 miles inside old Poland.

One Soviet spearhead yesterday reached to the town of Venkule, five miles across the pre-war frontier north of Narva and about a mile from the Narva River mouth.

"There was some confusion over the Red Army's exact position at the Estonian border. The communique announced the capture of Venkule (or Vanakyula). A town of this name is five miles across the pre-war frontier in Estonia near the mouth of the Narva River. However,

Continued on Page 3, Column 3

King Makes Spaatz A Knight Commander

LONDON, Feb. 3 (Thursday) (A. P.).—Lieutenant General Carl A. Spaatz, chief of the U. S. Strategic Air Forces in Britain, has been made a Knight Commander of the Order of the British Empire (K. B. E.) military division, by King George VI at an investiture in Buckingham Palace, it was announced today.

War Summary

Thursday, Feb. 3, 1944

Sweeping ahead against feeble resistance, U. S. Marines and Army troops have captured Roi Island, site of the biggest airdrome in the Marshall Islands, and have won beachheads on Kwajalein and Namur Islands, Admiral Nimitz announced yesterday. American casualties have been moderate and there have been no naval losses.

In Italy, Allied troops smashed through the Gustav Line into the outskirts of Cassino. The Germans battling against the Allied advance south of Rome were reported ready to launch a powerful counter-offensive.

Russian troops surged over the old frontier of Estonia and captured 40 more towns as they sped toward the Estonian railway city of Narva. Berlin reported a new Soviet break-through in the Dnieper Bend and a revived drive upon Rovno in old Poland.

R. A. F. bombers struck at Europe last night following daylight raids by U. S. Liberators on the invasion coast of northern France.

U. S. Seizes Roi, Corners Japs on 2 Major Islands

By WILLIAM F. TYREE

PEARL HARBOR, Feb. 2 (U. P.).—The Fourth Marine and Seventh Infantry Divisions have captured Roi Island, site of the biggest airdrome in the Marshall Islands, and have stormed ashore to win beachheads and to drive inland on Namur and Kwajalein Islands, Admiral Chester W. Nimitz announced today.

The Marines took Roi, dragging their own artillery through the surf, and moving swiftly to extend their victory. They have already forced the Japanese back into the extreme northern end of adjoining Namur.

The infantrymen also are making good progress on Kwajalein, Nimitz reported.

LOSSES LIGHT, JAP RESISTANCE FEEBLE

Losses among the American troops have been moderate so far and Japanese resistance, although increasing, has not been strong, Nimitz said.

No naval losses have been suffered to date, two days after the first landings, Nimitz reported.

The American troops now hold beachheads on at least 12 Kwajalein atoll islets, in addition to captured Roi, and advices from the Central Pacific indicated that men and equipment were pouring into other islets from landing craft.

Warships, planes and land-based artillery, firing from beachheads won by the American shock troops in the first hours of their bold operation, enabled the Marines and the infantry to effect landings on Roi, Namur and Kwajalein with little resistance.

FOE TAKEN BY 'COMPLETE SURPRISE'

"It is now apparent that the attack took the enemy completely by surprise," Nimitz said.

But now the Japanese, recovered from their surprise and aware that they faced annihilation, were stiffening their resistance, and the infantrymen at the southern end of Kwajalein, especially, met brisk rifle and machine gun fire and mortar bombardment.

But there was an unmistakable atmosphere of optimism here as the most ambitious American operation of the Pacific war, an attack on islands which the Japanese had been fortifying for more than 20 years, entered its third day.

The Americans, the Marines with their nucleus of Solomons veterans, the tough Seventh infantrymen who had given the Japanese their disastrous defeat on Attu in the Aleutians, were moving swiftly against an enemy calculated to be nearing demoralization under one of the most terrible bombardments ever made.

LAND-BASED ARTILLERY AIDS DRIVE

Within 48 hours, one of three important objectives had been captured and the Japanese were fighting for life on the other two, against Marines on Namur at the northern end of Kwajalein, and against the infantrymen on Kwajalein Island at the southern end.

From their beachheads flanking Roi, the Marines stormed across the shallow water onto the heavily fortified Japanese base under cover of a pulverizing land-based artillery barrage which whistled over their heads and crashed just before them, rolling forward as they advanced.

In capturing Roi the Marines had taken an important

Continued on Page 2, Column 1

Bomb-Like Package Found on Ship Here

A package resembling a home-made bomb was discovered last night in the hold of a merchant ship docked at Pier 82, S. Wharves, at the foot of Wolf st.

Detective Sergeant Charles Brown and Detective Letcher Carruthers of the Detective Bureau's bomb squad immediately subjected the object to examination, but announced that no time mechanism or detonating element could be found.

FOUND BY CARPENTER

The package was discovered by a carpenter as he walked through the hold of the ship, Brown said. U. S. Customs guards first were notified and they in turn called in the city police.

Brown described the object as of light metal in the form of a food can. It was said to be about four inches long, rounded at both ends and about two and one-half inches in diameter. The metal, Brown said, was wrapped with what appeared to be heavy tin foil.

POLICE CONVERGE ON SPOT

Squads of police, including officials of the 4th st. and Snyder ave. station, and detectives from City Hall converged on the scene when

Continued on Page 9, Column 2

IN TODAY'S INQUIRER

SPECIAL DEPARTMENTS

COLUMNS AND FEATURES

TRUTH SERUM TEST PLANNED IN KILLING

CHICAGO, Feb. 2 (U. P.).—Constant questioning of Mrs. Ellen Bennett in the Drake Hotel murder of Mrs. Frank Starr Williams was "beginning to pay off," authorities said tonight as they asked permission to use a "truth serum" to break further her reluctance to discuss the slaying.

MRS. BENNETT

During the 48 hours she has been held in custody, Mrs. Bennett, a red-haired room clerk and resident of the Drake, first denied any knowledge of the shooting and claimed she was on a shopping trip when an unidentified woman entered Mrs. Williams'

Continued on Page 9, Column 3

First Taste of Action

Phila., Reading Men Blast London Raiders

By Paul W. Ramsey
Inquirer War Correspondent
By Wireless
(Copyright, 1943)

LONDON, Feb. 2.

AS THE rising wall of hundreds of sirens warned Londoners of German bombers approaching the city, there was one battery of anti-aircraft gunners who reacted with greater inner excitement and eagerness for fight than all the thousands of soldiers who man the mighty weapons of London's defenses. They were the youngsters from Reading and Philadelphia, Chicago and Main Street, who man the only American anti-aircraft battery taking part in the defense of Greater London. And they have been at it only since Jan. 1.

For two years they had been training to get a shot at enemy planes. Over here they get lots of shooting. It's old stuff to blitz-hardened gunners, but to the Amer-

Continued on Page 3, Column 2

2,515,000 Tons Sunk By Allies in Year

LONDON, Feb. 2 (U. P.).—The Admiralty announced today that 2,515,000 gross tons of enemy merchant shipping had been sunk, captured or damaged in 1943 by Allied surface ships, submarines or mines. This figure raises the total for the war to 10,056,000 gross tons.

The figures released are exclusive of Japanese losses and of damage inflicted by Russian naval forces.

'Your Income Tax Guide'

THE Picture Parade section of the Sunday Inquirer will provide you with a 20-page Income Tax Guide by Joseph A. Wilson, former Chief of the Income Tax Division, Philadelphia Office of the Collector of Internal Revenue.

This supplement will give you simplified, easy-to-understand explanations of the most bewildering income tax blank ever issued and will include specimen tax forms completely filled out for your guidance. Don't fail to get a copy of "Your Income Tax Guide" in

The Inquirer Sunday

So Sorry, Please!

7th Division Exceeds Goal, Takes Isle by Mistake

By Philip G. Reed
Representing Combined U. S. Press

ABOARD JOINT EXPEDITIONARY FLAGSHIP, KWAJALEIN ATOLL, Feb. 1 (Delayed) (U. P.).

WAVES of the veteran Seventh Army Division today exceeded their first day's objective when they swarmed across the islets of Gehh, Ninni, Ennylabegan and Ennujubi in the Marshall Islands invasion.

The Seventh Division, before the attack on Kwajalein proper, exceeded the day's goal by reaching the islet of Gehh first, due to a mistake in the darkness, but rectified the situation by simply crossing the narrow channel and also occupying the designated objective of Ninni.

Ennylabegan and Ennujubi were expected to be tough nuts to crack, but they proved pushovers as the Japs withdrew their meager garrisons to Kwajalein for a last-ditch stand.

* * *

MEANWHILE, the Fourth Division Marines under Major General Harry Schmidt quickly captured Mellu and Boggerlap on the west side of the northern peak of the lagoon, then unhesitatingly crossed the lagoon to take Ennugarret, Unnumennet and Ennubirr in a matter of minutes.

In contrast to the Gilbert invasion and other earlier Pacific operations, things here began by breaking right for the Americans.

Even the huge radio tower, an

Continued on Page 2, Column 4

THE WEATHER

Philadelphia and Vicinity: Light snow changing to rain and warmer today. Occasional rain and warmer tomorrow.

Sun rises 8 08 A.M. Sets 6 20 P.M.
Moon rises 1.56 P.M. Sets 3.36 A.M.

Lady Leathernecks Round Out a Year Of Useful Service

A YEAR of achievement marks the first anniversary of the U. S. Marine Corps Women's Reserve. Since February 13, 1943, when an Act of Congress established the Reserves as an integral part of the U. S. Marine Corps, women Marines have gone far to fulfill their purpose—freeing fighting men for combat. In a six-week "boot" training period of incessant study and drill at Camp Lejeune, New River, N. C., girls were turned from soft living and hardened for the job ahead. These jobs, every one of which was done by a Fighting Marine a year ago, cover almost every field of endeavor. Some of them are pictured here. By sheer ability, the Lady Leathernecks have won the respectful approval of their commanding officers and fellow Marines.

Photographer

Aviation Machinist's Mate

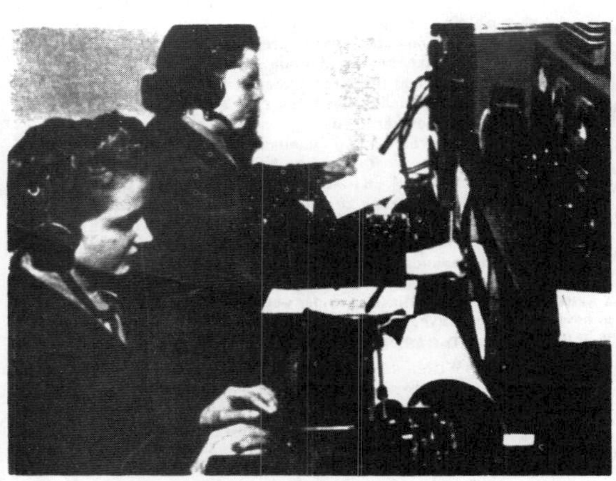

Radio Operator

Clerk

Radial Drill Operator

Radio Technician

Lineman

The Philadelphia Inquirer

PUBLIC LEDGER

An Independent Newspaper for All the People

FINAL
CITY EDITION

CIRCULATION: January Average: Daily 174,418; Sunday 1,262,751 | MONDAY MORNING, FEBRUARY 21, 1944 | Copyright, 1944, by The Philadelphia Inquirer Vol. 230 No. 52 | a b d e f g h | THREE CENTS

Japs Lost 19 Ships, 201 Aircraft At Truk; 2000 American Planes Batter Germany in Greatest Raid

Today

The Baruch Report
Fundamentally Sound
But Questions Arise
Congress on Guard
Baruch as a Symbol

—By Mark Sullivan—

WASHINGTON, Feb. 20.

ABOUT the Baruch plan as written, there was no question and could be none. On the basic question — whether America after the war is to go in the direction of private ownership of industry, or toward collectivism—on that, the Baruch report is four-square. It assumes that America, when peace comes, is to pass from the necessary regimentation of war, and return to the principle of private ownership.

The report itself says so, and any statement signed by Mr. Baruch is universally accepted. Even if Mr. Baruch had not made the statement explicit in his report, his mere association with it would have been enough. Mr. Baruch is a thorough believer in the private ownership of industry as America's salvation.

But about the Baruch plan as it might be administered, questions arose, and these are the cause of current agitation. The questions arise from the fact that the administration of the Baruch plan would be in the hands of appointees of the executive branch of the Government.

The nature of the questions thus arising can be understood from a criticism of the New Deal once made by Mr. Wendell Willkie. He said that the New Deal is not Socialism nor any other form of collectivism—it is not any consistent philosophy or plan of society at all; but in its inconsistencies and eccentricities, it amounts to such distortion of the system of private ownership as to make it unworkable.

This is the apprehension that arose about administration of the Baruch plan—that it might be put in the hands of men who, through zeal for some features of collectivism, or mere lack of understanding, might so operate it as to muddle the purpose of having America go forward on the basis of private ownership. Such a muddle, if it should occur, would not merely make private ownership unworkable but leave

Continued on Page 10, Column 1

Day Blows Raze 25 Pct. of Nazi Fighter Output

Map on Page 2

By WALTER CRONKITE

LONDON, Feb. 20 (U. P.).—In the greatest daylight assault of the war, 2000 United States planes destroyed 25 percent of German's fighter plane production in vital Nazi aircraft cities as they penetrated confused Nazi defenses to within sight of Berlin today, following a Royal Air Force attack on the great plane center of Leipzig last night in which 2300 long tons of bombs were dropped.

Allied fighters accompanying the U. S. bombers shot down 61 enemy fighters while Allied losses were 22 heavy bombers and four fighters, headquarters of the European Theater announced. R.A.F. losses in the Leipzig attack were 79 planes—a record.

The enemy losses do not include planes shot down by the U. S. heavy bombers, which have not been determined, the announcement said.

BIGGEST U. S. ATTACK

The cities struck in today's record-breaking daylight blows at the vitals of German aircraft production included Leipzig, Oschersleben, Bernburg, Brunswick, Gotha and Tutow.

Late tonight a big force of R. A. F. night bombers, taking an hour to pass one point, crossed the east coast headed for the continent, while Nazi raiders struck London again, dropping bombs and incendiaries and causing widespread damage and some casualties.

General Henry H. Arnold, chief of the Army Air Forces, said in Washington tonight that today's day attacks were "the biggest United States air mission in history" and that the American losses must be considered light.

AT LEAST 2500 TONS

General Arnold's statement helped to lift the usual veil of secrecy which surrounds bombing operations and permitted European headquarters to reveal that more than 1000 heavy bombers and almost an equal number of fighters participated in the daylight drubbing of Nazi cities. If each bomber carried only a two-

Continued on Page 2, Column 5

LONDON SET ABLAZE AS NAZI FLIERS RAID CITY TWICE IN NIGHT

LONDON, Feb. 21 (Monday) (A. P.).—German planes set some sections of London blazing last night with tons of oil bombs and incendiaries, and for some time after the all-clear sounded the sky still glowed red.

This latest Nazi air blow against the British capital was a follow-up to the huge fire raid made by the Germans early Saturday morning, which was the heaviest attack London had received since the campaign of 1940-41.

SIRENS SOUND AGAIN

Early today the air raid sirens in London sounded for a second time within a few hours but the all clear came soon afterwards.

The sirens blared the second warning at 3 26 A. M. (10.26 P. M. Eastern War Time). The all-clear for the first raid had come at 11 P. M.

The second alert apparently was caused by enemy reconnaissance planes.

INDISCRIMINATE BOMBING

In the short, fierce raid last night the German fighter-bombers fanned out over London after winging up the Thames. They scattered incendiaries indiscriminately, causing fires in many areas. There were a number of casualties.

Three schools and a convent of the Roman Catholic Church, a ho-

Continued on Page 3, Column 1

TRUK ISLANDS

North Pass — 0 10 STATUTE MILES — LAMOIL — FALALU — TO TOKIO — TO MANILA 2100 MILES — MAIN JAP ANCHORAGES AIR STRIPS AND INSTALLATIONS — NORTHEAST IS — Coral Reef — FALAS — Northeast Pass Main Passage — Lelom Pass — ULALU — UDOT — MOEN — PARAM — DUBLON — TRUK — ETEN — Plaanu Pass — FEFAN — TOL — TSIS — UMAN — OLLAN — Coral Reef — Otta Pass — GIVRY — KUOP ISLANDS

19 JAP SHIPS SUNK	201 JAP PLANES DESTROYED
7 PROBABLY SUNK	50 PLANES DAMAGED
1 U.S. SHIP MODERATELY DAMAGED	17 U.S. PLANES LOST

U. S. NAVY PARTIALLY AVENGES PEARL HARBOR

The American Pacific Fleet gained at least partial revenge for the Japanese sneak attack on Pearl Harbor in two-day U. S. assault on Truk (above) last week. Inset compares losses suffered by the Japs at Truk and minor damage sustained by the U. S.

Nimitz Acclaims Partial Revenge For Pearl Harbor

Today's War Summary on Page 3

By CHARLES H. McMURTRY

PEARL HARBOR, Feb. 20 (A. P.).—The United States Pacific Fleet has sunk 19 Japanese ships, destroyed 201 enemy planes and wrought other heavy damage at the Nipponese island bastion of Truk, in "partial settlement" for Pearl Harbor.

Admiral Chester W. Nimitz, Pacific Fleet Commander, today lifted the five-day silence cloaking the attack against Japan's own "Pearl Harbor" and disclosed in a communique that the great thrust was carried out at a cost of one ship damaged and 17 planes lost.

Great as was the devastation at the enemy's Central Pacific fortress, Admiral Nimitz did not consider it full payment for the Japanese sneak attack of Dec. 7, 1941, when 18 American warships and 177 planes were knocked out at Pearl Harbor and more than 3300 persons were killed and left missing.

ALL JAP PLANES KNOCKED OUT FIRST DAY

Apparently American forces made no landing at Truk, as was reported by the Tokio radio. Admiral Nimitz made no mention of any such operation. Instead, his communique indicated, it was a sort of merry-go-round attack by hundreds of carrier planes, each of which struck repeatedly after Japanese aerial opposition had been knocked out early in the fight.

"The Pacific Fleet has returned at Truk the visit made by the Japanese on Dec. 7, 1941, and effected a partial settlement of the debt," Admiral Nimitz said at the outset of the triumphant communique.

Significantly, Admiral Nimitz reported the initial approach of the United States forces was not detected, and "there was no enemy air opposition on the second day of the attack."

NO CAPITAL SHIPS MENTIONED

These ships were listed as sunk at Truk:

Two light cruisers, three destroyers, one ammunition ship, one seaplane tender, two oilers, two gunboats and eight cargo ships.

Listed as hit and probably sunk were: One cruiser or large destroyer, two oilers and four cargo ships.

Failure to mention capital ships in the communique possibly indicated the Japanese had withdrawn their heavy units from Truk. A reconnaissance flight over Truk Feb. 4 by two Liberators revealed at least two carriers anchored in the Truk lagoon.

Our carrier-based planes shot down 127 enemy planes

Continued on Page 2, Column 3

KIRK TO COMMAND U.S. INVASION FLEET

WASHINGTON, Feb. 20 (A. P.).—The Navy tonight disclosed further details in the plans for the European invasion with announcement that Rear Admiral Alan Goodrich Kirk had been named commander of the United States task force operating as part of the combined naval force in England.

Also assigned to command of units of the task force are Rear Admiral John Lesslie Hall, Jr., and Rear Admiral John Wilkes.

SERVING UNDER STARK

Admiral Harold R. Stark is commander of all United States naval forces in the United Kingdom area.

The Allied commander-in-chief of naval forces for the western theater is Sir Bertram Ramsay.

A native of Philadelphia, Admiral Kirk formerly was commander of amphibious forces of the Atlantic Fleet and at one time served in London as chief of staff to Admiral Stark. He commanded task forces that backed up Allied troops who stormed ashore in North Africa and in Sicily.

SUBMARINE VETERAN

Admiral Wilkes, a native of Charlotte, N. C., is a veteran of submarine service. He was decorated with the Distinguished Service Medal for his work as commander of a submarine squadron operating first in the defense of the Philippines and later in Dutch East Indies waters at the beginning of the present war. His submarine squad-

Continued on Page 3, Column 3

Allies Advance 2 Miles, Halt Nazis Above Anzio

By EDWARD KENNEDY

ALLIED HEADQUARTERS, NAPLES, Feb. 20 (A. P.).—American armored columns smashed into the German flank today, and drove two miles toward Carroceto in a fierce counter-attack sprung after invasion beachhead forces had withstood an all-out, reckless onslaught by nine Nazi divisions.

The tide of battle has turned, and "the beachhead was never more secure than today"—the date reportedly set by the Germans for its extinction—Daniel De Luce, Associated Press correspondent, said in a front dispatch written at 12.30 P. M today.

The mauled Germans relaxed the initiative, he declared, and the United States armored thrusts, biting into the eastern flank of the Nazi salient, gained "as much as three kilometers (two miles) in the direction of Carroceto." These blows by tanks and infantry began at 6.30 A. M. Saturday, and continued today.

Thus the ground lost below Carroceto to the intense German charges was being recovered, and De Luce said the Germans may have lost so heavily "that another attack can not be mounted on a similar scale."

More than 500 prisoners have

Continued on Page 3, Column 4

Harriman's Daughter 4th in Soviet Ski Race

MOSCOW, Feb. 20 (A. P.).—Kathleen Harriman, with her father, Ambassador W. Averell Harriman in the gallery, placed fourth today in the women's slalom race of the Russian Republic ski championship.

She covered the course on Lenin Hills, outside of Moscow, twice in 49 and 50 seconds. The times of the winner, who is a skiing instructress, were 42 and 43 seconds, respectively.

Fiance of Ex-WAVE Has Wife and Child

The romance and wedding plans of a former member of the WAVES and her fiance, both held without bail in Norristown on charges of looting the Ashbourne Country Club in Cheltenham township, received a rude jolt yesterday when a police teletype message from Massachusetts reported that the prospective "bridegroom" has a wife and child.

The accused man, James B. Kalbeck, denied he was married. "That's my brother," he said. "He's married and has a child. The police have us mixed up, that's all."

But County Detective Harry Rankin said the description of Kalbeck fitted "in every detail" and he was the right man.

'I DON'T BELIEVE IT'

"I don't believe that he's married," cried the prospective bride, Ruby Thorpe, former WAVE, on learning the news.

"He told me he was single. He always told me so. I still want to marry him as soon as possible."

Authorities here said the message, from a lieutenant of detectives of the Massachusetts State Police, not only disclosed that Kalbeck, 28, of Richmond, Vt., has a family in Clinton, Mass., but that he also is wanted on a larceny charge in the New Eng-

Continued on Page 7, Column 4

IN TODAY'S INQUIRER

SPECIAL DEPARTMENTS

COLUMNS AND FEATURES

MAY URGES DRAFT FOR MEN OVER 38

WASHINGTON, Feb. 20 (A. P.).—Chairman Andrew J. May (D., Ky.) of the House Military Committee suggested today that the existing top of 38 years on the draft be raised "a few more years."

At the same time he told reporters that his committee would never approve legislation to lower the minimum draft age from 18 to 17.

Mr. May advocated raising of the top limit as a means of slowing down the drafting of pre-war fathers.

NOTICES 'MOVEMENT'

He said he had noticed a movement in some newspapers and among some members of Congress in behalf of legislation to permit the armed services to draft 17-year-olds, with the understanding they would not be sent into combat until they were at least 18.

"The Army hasn't asked for it," he said, "and I doubt if they willl. When they asked us to lower the draft age to 18, and we did it, they assured us that would care for the situation."

'NOT OLD ENOUGH'

Seventeen-year-old boys, Mr. May contended, "are not old enough to be drafted, and if I had my way about it, the Army would be pro-

Continued on Page 4, Column 4

Finnish Peace Envoy To Return to Helsinki

STOCKHOLM, Feb. 20 (A. P.).—Juhu K. Paasikivi, the Finnish diplomat, plans to return to Helsinki tomorrow or Tuesday to report on his efforts to obtain terms for cessation of hostilities between Finland and the Soviet Union, the Swedish newspaper Dagens Nyheter reported today.

Dr. Paasikivi ostensibly came to Stockholm recently for a vacation but his continued presence here has been interpreted as meaning that preliminary negotiations looking toward a Finnish-Russian armistice may have been taken.

RED DRIVES CLOSING ON BALTIC GATEWAY

By JAMES H. LONG

LONDON, Feb. 21 (Monday) (A. P.).—Three Russian armies fighting through blizzards toward the Baltic gateway of Pskov yesterday captured points within 30 miles of the important rail junction of Dno, seizing 114 villages in gains of two to 12 miles and kiling more than 2000 Germans, Moscow announced today.

The swift Russian advance, facilitated by soil hardened by sub-zero temperatures, threatened to outflank another 100-mile section of the crumbling German northern front between Dno and Novosokolniki.

MINSK DRIVE REPORTED

"The Germans retreating under the blows of Soviet troops are abandoning equipment and arms," a midnight communique said.

Berlin broadcasts also said the Russians had flung 100,000 more troops into a renewed drive toward Minsk in White Russia far to the south, and also declared the Red Army of the Ukraine was attacking with mounting fury toward the bastion of Krivoi Rog, last big city still held by the Germans in the Dnieper River bend.

Dno, 60 miles east of Pskov, is a

Continued on Page 3, Column 7

WACS' Work Pleases

Girls Serving Overseas Prove to Be Good Soldiers

Exclusive pictures of WACS and soldiers from the Philadelphia area, on duty in England, appear on Page 10.

By Paul W. Ramsey

Inquirer War Correspondent

LONDON, Feb. 20.

In the wake of Colonel Oveta Culp Hobby's recent whirlwind visit to the United Kingdom, correspondents were invited by Army public relations officers to do some stories on the WACS who are serving over here. WAC recruiting, it was explained, is not what it ought to be, and would the correspondents lend a hand? It was a fair request and no suggestion was made that the stories be "slanted." So here goes:

There are now some 63,000 women in the corps, although the authorized strength is 200,000. At present about 5000 WACS are serving overseas, 1200 of them in this theater. But there will be more. A lot of high-placed officers, pleased with the work the WACS have done, are demanding more of them.

A brigadier general is known to have remarked that one WAC is worth two-and-one-half GIs in the particular jobs they have taken over in his command. They are working as secretaries, stenographers, teletype and telephone operators, in aircraft control rooms and as file clerks.

• • •

YES, their jobs are routine. At least most of them are. And perhaps that explains why they can do the work better than most men.

Continued on Page 4, Column 3

U. S. WEATHER FORECAST

Philadelphia and vicinity: Cloudy and slightly warmer today. Partly cloudy and moderate temperature tomorrow.

Sun rises 7.49 A.M. Sets 6.42 P.M.
Moon rises 5.56 A.M. Sets 3.58 P.M.

NEW LANDING WINS HALF OF ENIWETOK

By CHARLES McMURTRY

PEARL HARBOR, Feb. 20 (A. P.).—Infantry and Marine troops have landed on Eniwetok Island, capturing the western half, and now have seized all of Eniwetok Atoll except the Japanese base on Parry Island.

The new landings on Einwetok, made yesterday, were announced in a communique tonight by Admiral Chester W. Nimitz, who said "casualties continue to be light."

AIRFIELD ALREADY TAKEN

The Marines already had seized Engebi Island, with its important mile-long airfield, and all other islands on the northern tip of the atoll.

Admiral Nimitz still has not reported the extent of resistance the 22d Marines or 108th Infantry met on Engebi or are meeting on Eniwetok. The rapid progress made across Eniwetok Island, however, indicated the terrific aerial and warship bombardment which preceded the invasion, knocked out many Japanese installations and rendered the shell-shocked Japs incapable of as stiff opposition as our forces encountered on Tarawa. The Marines required only six hours to capture Engebi.

Eniwetok Island is 6000 yards

Continued on Page 2, Column 4

The Philadelphia Inquirer

PUBLIC LEDGER

An Independent Newspaper for All the People

VOL. 230, NO. 58 abcdefg PHILADELPHIA, SUNDAY MORNING, FEBRUARY 27, 1944 B PRICE, TWELVE CENTS

Official Navy Photos Depicting Mighty U. S. Attack on Jap Base at Truk

(U. S. Navy Photos from A. P. Wirephoto)

JAPANESE WARSHIPS CAUGHT IN DARING RAID BY U. S. CARRIER PLANES ON HARBOR AT TRUK

Caught in the harbor at Truk when the Americans unleashed their surprise attack on that Central Pacific bastion, these Jap warships are seeking to escape the bombing planes. Two of the vessels, and probably three, are burning from bomb hits. Eten Island is in the foreground, Moen Island in the background. The Japanese lost 19 ships and 201 planes in the attack, which Admiral C. W. Nimitz called partial revenge for Pearl Harbor.

JAPS' TRUK SEAPLANE BASE BOMBED BY AMERICAN FLIERS

Bombs from attacking U. S. Navy carrier-based planes (upper center) speed toward the Japanese seaplane base on Dublon Island, Truk group in the Carolines, during the Feb. 16 attack. Hangars, repair and supply buildings are among the objectives set ablaze by explosives dropped by a previous wave of planes.

SMOKE BILLOWS FROM ETEN ISLAND EARLY IN OFFENSIVE

Explosives dropped from early arriving U. S. bombers already have started fires on Eten Island (left) as other Yank fliers come in for a smash at the foe's stronghold at Truk. The great thrust was carried out at a cost of only one American ship damaged and 17 planes lost.

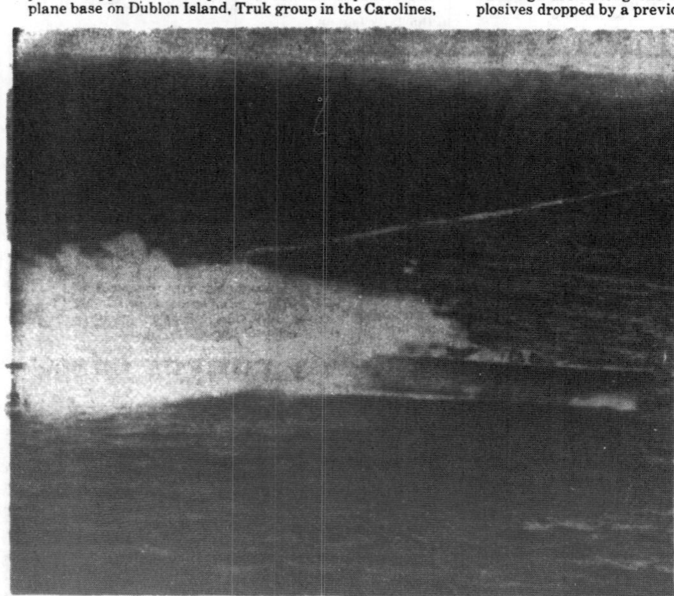

ONE OF FOE'S CRUISERS BURNING DURING ATTACK

Cornered and blasted by Navy planes during the attack on Truk, this enemy cruiser burns and lists. The thin line is the wake of an American torpedo.

JAP AMMUNITION SHIP IS BLOWN UP IN ASSAULT AT TRUK

Hidden by the smoke of the explosion, and showering debris over a wide area, a Jap ammunition ship blows up in Truk harbor. The men on the Navy dive-bomber that made the attack are presumed lost as their plane was caught in the terrific blast.

U. S. Strategy Scores Again in the Pacific

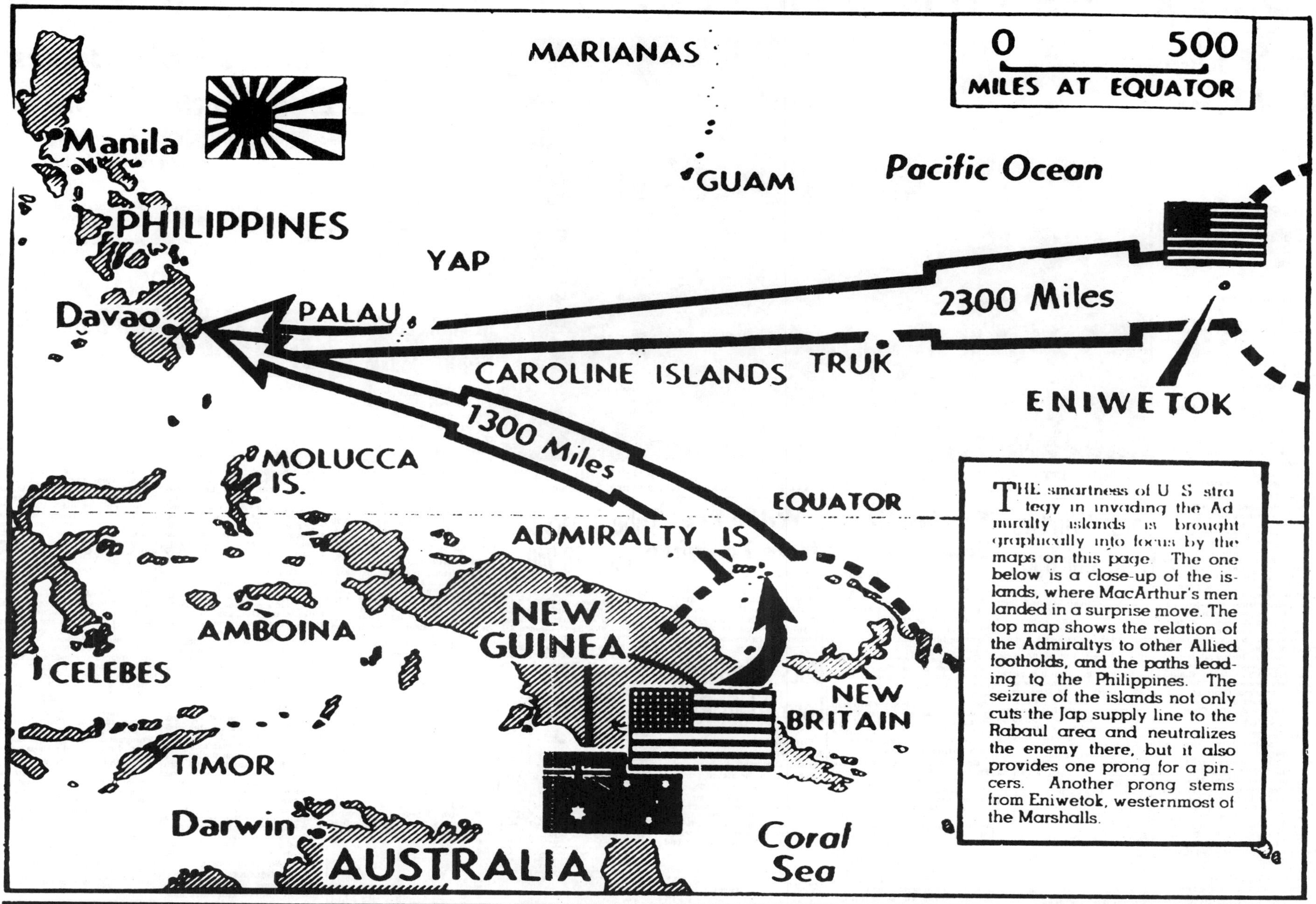

THE smartness of U. S. strategy in invading the Admiralty islands is brought graphically into focus by the maps on this page. The one below is a close-up of the islands, where MacArthur's men landed in a surprise move. The top map shows the relation of the Admiraltys to other Allied footholds, and the paths leading to the Philippines. The seizure of the islands not only cuts the Jap supply line to the Rabaul area and neutralizes the enemy there, but it also provides one prong for a pincers. Another prong stems from Eniwetok, westernmost of the Marshalls.

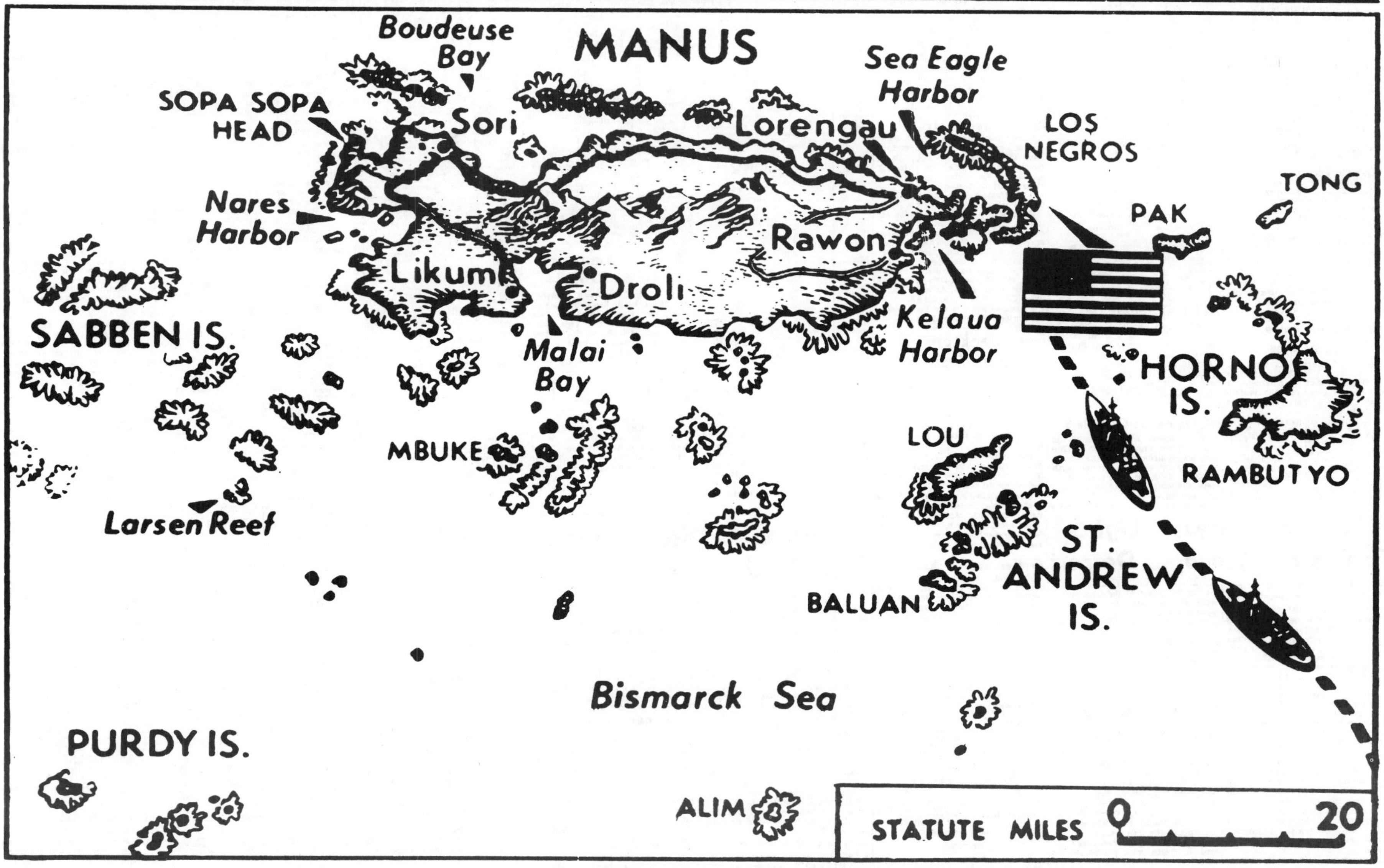

30,392 See Phils Win, 2-1, in 14th; Curfew Halts 2d

McSpaden And Platt Victors

Dudley-Fraser Beaten, 6-5, in Bala Charity Golf

By DORA LURIE

Harold (Jug) McSpaden, leading winter circuit professional golf money player, clipped two strokes off par as he and J. Woody Platt, Aronimink Country Club amateur, defeated big Ed Dudley and Sonny Fraser, Country Club of Atlantic City pro-amateur duo, 6-up, in a best ball foursome match for the benefit of the Salvation Army War Fund yesterday at the Bala Golf Club.

A gallery of 400 followed McSpaden's every stroke as the Philadelphia Country Club pro tabbed 32-34—66 slicing one stroke off par going out and another coming home. Although the match ended on the 13th the players finished the round to the delight of the gallery.

NET $2350.50 OVER ALL

The match, originally scheduled for the previous Sunday, had been washed out by rain. But the Salvation Army was enriched by another tidy sum yesterday as Mrs. Joseph M. Patterson, Main Line campaign chairman, announced that the total netted $2350.50 over-all. She was aided by Mrs. Frederick W. Graham, Jr., chairman of the Bala sponsors.

McSpaden plainly indicated that he is ready to continue his winter circuit wizardry in the summer campaign. He has been granted a leave of absence by his club to compete in a series of War Bond and charity matches from June to September which opens with the first annual $17,500 War Bond invitation tournament sponsored by The Philadelphia Inquirer Charities, Inc., the week of June 5 at the Torresdale-Frankford Country Club.

McSPADEN HOT

McSpaden, 36, and a Kansas native, set a hot pace yesterday. Fraser matched strokes on the incoming nine, scoring 37-34—71; Platt carded 37-36—73 and Dudley, P.G.A. president, tabbed 38-36—74.

McSpaden birdied the 391-yard seventh with a 3 and the subsequent 335-yard unit with another 3 to win those holes. He blasted out of traps right close to the pins for one-putts to par the third, fourth and ninth. Against this kind of shooting the Dudley-Fraser pair, who had started out by halving the first hole with 4s by all, could not win.

Taking a 5-up lead at the turn, they halved the 10th and then Fraser came through with a birdie 3 on the 367-yard 11th to cut the lead as the losers gained their only hole of the match. Then, Platt, stepped into the picture and proved why he held the Philadelphia championship seven times, by winning the 12th with a sub-par 3 and the 13th with a par 3 to clinch victory. Jug's card:

Par out [illegible]—33
McSpaden out [illegible]—32
Par in [illegible]—35—68
McSpaden in [illegible]—34—66

KAYOED: WIETELMANN, BOSTON, FLATTENED IN COLLISION WITH PHILS' FORD MULLEN
On force-play at second, Mullen jumps for wild throw, and knocks Brave unconscious (third inning, first game).

Nieman's Homer Enables Braves To Tie, 2-2, in Ninth of Final

Rookie Pitcher Covington Gets Credit for Victory In Opener as Northey Scores on Wietelmann's Error

By STAN BAUMGARTNER

Before 30,392, the largest crowd that ever watched the Boston Braves play in this city, the Phillies won the first game and tied the second at Shibe Park yesterday in a spectacular 23-inning double-header.

They won the opener, a thrilling, nerve-tingling 14-inning game, 2-1, and then battled on even 2-2 terms for nine innings in the second until Umpire Lou Jorda called a halt because of the Sunday curfew law.

ERROR AIDS VICTORY

An error by the usually reliable Bill Wietelmann, Brave shortstop, gave the Blue Jays a victory in the first game.

With Ron Northey on second base and one out in the 14th, Wietelmann made a wild throw of Bob Finley's slow roller and Northey tallied the winning run.

HOMER TIES NIGHTCAP

In the second game, Dick Barrett had the triumph apparently completely in his grasp when he drove home the run which gave the Phils a 2-1 lead in the eighth, but in the next inning Butch Nieman, slugging left fielder of the Braves, hit a homer into 20th street to tie the score. Jim Tobin then came in to pitch the ninth for the Braves and keep the score a tie.

The first game was a sensational scrap which had the vast throng on edge from the first pitch to the last. It was a magnificent pitching battle between Al Javery, fireball righthander of the visitors, and Al Gerheauser and Chet Covington, two Phil southpaws.

ROOKIE GETS CREDIT

Gerheauser stood toe to toe with Javery until relieved for pinch hitter in the 11th, and Covington, recently purchased from Louisville, finished and received credit.

Neither team scored in the first nine innings, although there were plenty of sideline fireworks. In the third inning Bill Wietelmann was knocked unconscious in a collision at second base, but remained in the game.

WASDELL EJECTED

In the ninth, Jimmy Wasdell was called out on strikes with the winning run on third and was so annoyed at Umpire Stewart's decision that he kicked dirt on the arbiter's shins. He also tossed his bat high in the air. For this display he was ejected from the double-header.

Boston drew first blood in the 11th after two out when Connie Ryan singled to center, stole second and scored on Tommy Holmes' hit. The Phils tied it in their half when Ford Mullen singled, Buster Adams doubled and Lee Riley (who had replaced Wasdell) hit a long fly to Chuck Workman in right.

THRILLS GALORE

It remained, 1-1, until Ron Northey opened the 14th with a short single to left. Tony Lupien sacrificed him to second and Finley followed with the slow roller that Wietelmann threw wild past Max Macon.

The second game was equally exciting, but the fans were thrill weary. The Braves scored a run in the first after one out on successive singles by Holmes, Workman and Roland Giadu. The Phillies tied it in the second on a double by Riley and Dick Barrett's single.

BARRETT GETS HIT

Barrett then apparently won his own game in the eighth when, after Hamrick doubled to left, he hit a curve ball to right for a single that sent the shortstop over. But he let a fast ball get away from him in the ninth and Nieman parked it in 20th st. By the time Tobin erased the Phils it was after 6.50 P. M. and the game was called.

Ted Cieslak hit safely in both games, sending his streak to seven.

Before the game, General Manager Herb Pennock's Kennett Square

Continued on Page 18, Column 2

Giants Win, 26-8, In First, Lose 2d Before 58,068

NEW YORK, April 30 (A. P.).—The New York Giants and Brooklyn Dodgers divided a double-header today before the season's record crowd of 58,068, of which 52,037 were paid.

Hal Gregg won his first major league game as the Dodgers won the final, 5-4, which was shortened to seven innings by darkness. The Giants won the opener, 26-8, to tie a run record for a major league scoring mark.

The St. Louis Cardinals scored 28 runs against the Phillies, July 6, 1929. The American League mark is 27, made by Cleveland, July 7, 1923.

WEINTRAUB NEAR MARK

Phil Weintraub, Giants first baseman, batted in 11 runs with a homer, triple and two doubles just to miss tieing the major league record of 12, set by Jim Bottomley of the St. Louis Cardinals, Sept. 16, 1924. Ernie Lombardi, Giant catcher, drove in seven runs.

Mel Ott added two records to his all-time marks when he received five walks for the fourth time of his career, and scored six runs, a feat he has accomplished once before.

GIANTS TIE RECORD

The Giants tied the league record for receiving the most bases on balls in a game, 17, from five Brooklyn pitchers. The Dodgers also received 17 bases on balls August 27, 1903.

Hal Gregg issued eight walks in the second game but tightened in the pinches. Howard Schultz, besides hitting two homers in the opener, drove in three runs in the second game to increase his league leadership to 14 runs batted in.

Brooklyn Manager Leo Durocher was hit by a flying pop bottle near the club house after the first game was over and didn't play in the nightcap.

FIRST GAME

Brooklyn	ab	r	h	o	a	New York	ab	r	h	o	a
Borda'ay,rf	[illegible]					Rucker,cf	[illegible]				
Walker,lf	[illegible]					Hausm'n,2b	[illegible]				
P.Waner,rf	[illegible]					Ott,rf	[illegible]				
Olmo,2b	[illegible]					Medwick,lf	[illegible]				
Galan,cf	[illegible]					Weintr'b,1b	[illegible]				
Schultz,1b	[illegible]					Lombardi,c	[illegible]				
Hart,ss	[illegible]					Luby,3b	[illegible]				
Bragan,3b	[illegible]					Kerr,ss	[illegible]				
Owen,c	[illegible]					C.Melt'n,p	[illegible]				
Jarvis,c	[illegible]					Feld'n,p	[illegible]				
F. Melton,p	[illegible]										
a-Wyatt	[illegible]										
Webber,p	[illegible]										
Zachary,p	[illegible]										
Osterm'r,p	[illegible]										
b-Moore	[illegible]										
Warren,p	[illegible]										
Totals	39	8	12	24	6	Totals	42	26	18	27	10

a-Batted for F. Melton in 2d.
b-Batted for Ostermueller in 4th.

Brooklyn [illegible]—8
New York 3 4 4 5 0 2 0 8 x—26

Errors—C. Melton, Kerr, Olmo, Walker. Runs batted in—Galan, Weintraub 11, Luby 2, Medwick, Lombardi 7, Schultz 2, Owen, Bordagaray, Olmo 2, Kerr, Feldman, Hausmann 2, Ott. Two-base hits—Weintraub 2, Owen, Rucker, Lombardi 2, P. Waner, Feldman, Hausmann, Medwick. Three-base hits—Rucker, Weintraub. Home runs—Schultz 2, Kerr, Weintraub. Stolen bases—Schultz, Hart, Ott. Sacrifices—Hausmann. Double plays—Feldman, Kerr and Weintraub; Hausmann, Kerr and Weintraub. Left on bases—New York 10, Brooklyn 8. Bases on balls—Off F. Melton 3, Webber 4, Zachary 2, Ostermueller 2, Warren 6, Feldman 4. Strikeouts—C. Melton 2, F. Melton 1, Webber 1, Ostermueller 1, Feldman 3, Warren 2. Hits—Off F. Melton 2 in 1 inning; Webber, 1 in 1-3; Zachary, 0 in 0 (pitched to 2 batters); Ostermueller 2 in 2 2-3; Warren, 13 in 4; C. Melton, 7 in 3 1-3; Feldman, 5 in 5 2-3. Wild pitches—C. Melton, F. Melton, Warren. Winning pitcher—Feldman. Losing pitcher—F. Melton. Umpires—Reardon, Dunn and Goetz. Time—2:58.

SECOND GAME

New York	ab	r	h	o	a	Brooklyn	ab	r	h	o	a
Rucker,cf	4	1	1	2	1	Bordag'y,rf	3	1	2	2	0
Hausm'n,2b	3	0	1	2	1	Walker,lf	3	2	2	1	0
Ott,rf	3	0	1	3	1	Olmo,2b	4	1	0	2	5
Mead,lf	3	1	0	1	0	Galan,cf	2	0	1	0	0
Weintra'b,1b	3	1	1	5	1	Schultz,1b	4	0	2	7	2
Luby,3b	4	1	1	2	3	Bragan,3b	3	0	1	2	0
Mancuso,c	2	0	0	2	2	Hart,ss	3	0	1	2	2
a-Lombardi	1	0	0	0	0	Owen,c	4	0	0	3	0
Kerr,ss	2	0	0	3	2	Gregg,p	3	1	1	2	4
Pyle,p	0	0	0	1	0						
b-Sloane	0	0	0	0	0						
Fischer,p	0	0	0	0	0						
Totals	25	4	5	21	11	Totals	29	5	10	21	13

a-Batted for Pyle in 6th.
b-Batted for Mancuso in 7th.

Brooklyn 0 0 1 0 2 0 2—5
New York 0 0 1 1 0 1 1—4

Errors: Hausmann, Olmo. Runs batted in: Mancuso, Schultz 3, Rucker, Galan, Luby. Two-base hit, Bordagaray. Three-base hit, Hart. Stolen bases: Olmo, Rucker. Sacrifices: Bordagaray, Hart, Mancuso. Double play, Gregg, Hart and Schultz. Left on bases: Brooklyn 9, New York 9. Bases on balls: off Gregg 8, Pyle 2, Fischer 2. Strike-outs: by Gregg 1, Pyle 1. Hits: off Pyle 7 in 6 innings; Fischer 3 in 1. Wild pitches: Pyle 2, Gregg. Losing pitcher, Fischer. Umpires: Dunn, Goetz and Reardon. Time, 2:01. Attendance, 58,068.

25,645 See A's Beat Boston, 3-1, After Losing, 3-2

Special to The Inquirer

BOSTON, April 30.—The Athletics divided a double-header with the Red Sox today before 25,645 (including 2288 servicemen) in earning a 3-1 victory behind Luman Harris' brilliant pitching after losing the first game, 3-2. Tex Hughson was Boston's winning pitcher.

Although outhit by the Sox in the nightcap, the A's put some heads-up base-running and a Boston error to use in the seventh inning for their three runs. The visitors were blanked to that point by Emmett O'Neil, but they loaded the bases with none out. O'Neil hit Bill Burgo, missed Bob Wilkins' bunt, which went for a single, and then walked Harris.

NEWSOME ERRS

Jo Jo White then popped to short, but Irv Hall hit a possible double play roller down to Bobby Doerr at second. Doerr scooped up the ball and tossed to Newsome on second for the force out. Newsome, however, dropped the ball and before he could recover it, Burgo and Wilkins both crossed the plate.

Harris, safe at second, moved to third on Lew Flick's grounder to Doerr and scored on O'Neil's wild pitch. These three runs erased a one-run advantage chalked up by the Sox in the second inning. Bill Conroy's single brought home Doerr, who had singled and stole second.

JOHNSON HITS HOMER

Although Bob Johnson clouted a none-on homer in the fifth of the first game which provided the winning Boston margin, Don Black, the A's pitcher, deserved a better fate. Not only were the first two Sox runs a bit tainted, but Don drove in both of the A's markers.

In the fifth, Black singled to score Wilkins from second and in the seventh repeated the performance, this time coming through with a single to short right, again scoring Wilkins from second.

WIDE TOSS COSTLY

Boston scored one run in the first inning. George Metkovich doubled to right center and scored. Black and Dick Seibert got mixed up on Doerr's grounder between them. Siebert finally took the roller but tossed widely to Black covering first. In the fourth, [illegible] against Black. Jim Tabor singled, stole second and made home when Edgar

Continued on Page 18, Column 1

Cards Win Two From Chicago

ST. LOUIS, April 30 (A. P.).—The St. Louis Cardinals retained their top-of-the-heap National League standing in a double victory, 5-0 and 7-5, over the Chicago Cubs today before 11,498, thus amassing nine triumphs in 11 starts this season.

In the more violent second game, the Cubs grabbed an early lead in the fourth inning when they picked up two runs. The Cards gleaned a single counter in the same inning and then the pressure seemed relaxed until the last of the seventh when the St. Louis club opened up with a barrage of heavy hitting that smashed in six runs and knocked Wyse out of the box.

FIRST GAME

Chicago	ab	r	h	o	a	St. Louis	ab	r	h	o	a
Shuster,ss	4	0	0	4	3	Verban,2b	4	0	1	3	4
Johnson,2b	4	0	1	1	5	Hopp,cf	4	1	3	0	0
Cav'etta,1b	3	0	1	11	1	Musial,rf	4	1	1	4	0
Nich'son,rf	3	0	0	0	0	O'Dea,c	3	0	0	4	0
Pfako,cf	3	0	0	2	0	Sanders,1b	3	2	0	12	1
Sauer,lf	3	0	1	1	0	Ku'ski,3b	4	1	1	0	4
Hughes,3b	3	0	0	2	3	Litw'ler,lf	3	0	2	2	0
Holm,c	2	0	0	2	0	Marion,ss	4	0	2	1	4
Hanyz'ki,p	2	0	0	0	1	Lanier,p	2	0	0	1	2
a-Ostrowski	1	0	0	0	0						
Kreitner,c	0	0	0	1	1						
Fleming,p	0	0	0	0	1						
b-Stanky	0	0	0	0	0						
Totals	28	0	3	24	18	Totals	31	5	10	27	15

a-Batted for Holm in eighth.
b-Batted for Fleming in ninth.

Chicago 0 0 0 0 0 0 0 0 0—0
St. Louis 0 1 0 0 1 0 0 3 x—5

Error—Johnson. Runs batted in—Marion 2, Hopp, Kurowski, Litwhiler. Two-base hit—Sauer. Home run—Hopp. Sacrifice—Lanier. Double plays—Johnson, Schuster, Cavarretta; Lanier, Marion, Sanders; Kurowski, Verban, Sanders. Left on bases—Chicago, 2; St. Louis, 6. Bases on balls—Hanyzewski, 3; Lanier, 1. Strikeouts—Hanyzewski, 1; Lanier, 4. Hits—Off Hanyzewski, 10 in 7 2-3 innings; Fleming, 0 in 1-3. Umpires—Sears and Conlan. Time, 1.44.

SECOND GAME

Chicago	ab	r	h	o	a	St. Louis	ab	r	h	o	a
Schuster,ss	5	1	2	1	2	Verban,2b	4	1	1	2	1
Johnson,2b	5	0	2	0	3	Hopp,cf	4	1	1	11	1
Cavar'tta,1b	4	1	1	11	0	Musial,rf	4	1	2	1	0
Nicholson,rf	4	1	3	0	0	O'Dea,c	4	1	2	3	1
Pafko,cf	3	0	1	3	0	Sanders,1b	4	1	1	6	0
Sauer,lf	4	0	1	1	0	Kurowski,3b	4	1	1	1	2
Hughes,3b	4	0	0	1	2	Litwhiler,lf	3	1	1	3	0
Holm,c	3	0	0	7	0	Marion,ss	2	0	0	0	0
Wyse,p	3	0	0	0	2	Wilks,p	3	0	0	0	0
aDall'sandro	1	1	1	0	0						
Vandenb'g,p	0	0	0	0	1						
bGoodman	0	1	0	0	0						
Totals	36	5	11	24	10	Totals	32	7	9	27	5

a-Batted for Holm in 9th.
b-Batted for Vandenberg in 9th.

Chicago 0 0 0 2 0 0 0 0 3—5
St. Louis 0 0 0 1 0 0 6 0 x—7

Errors: Johnson, Pafko. Runs batted in: Nicholson, Sauer, Schuster 3, Musial 3, Sanders, Litwhiler 2. Two-base hits: Cavaretta, Sauer, Musial, Hopp, Nicholson, Dallessandro. Three-base hits: Nicholson, O'Dea. Home runs: Musial, Litwhiler, Schuster. Stolen base: Johnson. Sacrifice: Pafko. [illegible] Umpires: Conlan and Sears. Time, 1:56. Attendance, 11,498.

Feather Champ Willie Pep Boxes Leamus Here Tonight

By JOHN WEBSTER

Back to the boxing rings after having been given an honorable discharge from the Navy, Willie Pep, champion of the featherweights, tonight meets Jackie Leamus, hot from Harlem, in a 10-round non-title contest at the Arena. It is Pep's third start since his return to civilian life, and his young opponent's chance of pressing him should depend largely upon the titleholder's current ability.

One of the more remarkable figures in modern ring annals, Pep, 21, won his first 62 professional fights, and has lost only one decision—to Sammy Angott, a lightweight. He won the feather title in his 54th fight by defeating ageless Chalky Wright at the Garden on Nov. 20, 1942, and drew a record gate for an indoor 126-pound championship—$71,868.

MAY FIGHT WILLIAMS

Unextended winner over Leo Francis and Shooks Lacey in recent weeks, Pep, who lives in Hartford, Conn., tonight wages his 71st battle in his first Philadelphia showing. He will be heavily favored in Herman Taylor's ring to gain his 70th victory and qualify for a summer showing with Ike Williams, sensational Trenton lightweight.

Still, the fact that Willie the Wisp was out of action for eight months gives the fledgling Leamus a fighting chance. In his favor are high speed and greater recent activity. Should Pep, who at 128 will spot seven pounds to the Negro, prove slower than usual, and deficient in timing and judgment of distance, there's a possibility for upset.

An undefeated amateur, Leamus is an improving ringman. He has lost only to Southwark's Sante Bucca in his pro campaign of 15 bouts. He lost two close decisions to Sante, gained a draw with him in their third meeting by slugging him into a late-round fog.

GIOSA BOXES COLLINS

Victor once since a bloody brow snapped his 21-bout winning streak, Eddie Giosa, Southwark lightweight, strives to continue his winning streak in an eight-rounder with Jimmy Collins, Baltimore boxer. The latter defeated Al Guido, only man to beat Giosa.

Waging his first battle since he lost to Gus Dorazio, Dusty Wilkerson, local Negro heavy, faces Herbert Marshall, New York, in one eight, and Bob Smith, bustling little North Philadelphian, opposes Jimmy Phillips, lanky Baltimorean, in another. Billy Furrone, who went eight rounds with Billy Arnold, meets Tony Grey, New York, for six.

Picked as winners are Pep, Giosa, Wilkerson, Smith and Furrone.

Bucs Win First, Lose 2d to Reds

CINCINNATI, April 30 (A. P.).—Bucky Walters' three-hit pitching enabled Cincinnati to beat Pittsburgh, 4-1, in the second game of a doubleheader before 16,060 today. The Pirates won the first game, 7-1, hitting Elmer Riddle, starting hurler and his successor, Clyde Shoun, freely. Eric Tipton, Reds' outfielder, hit his first home run of the season in the eighth inning of the second game.

FIRST GAME

Cincinnati	Ab	r	h	o	a	Pittsburgh	Ab	r	h	o	a
Criscola,rf	4	0	1	3	0	Barrett,rf	5	1	1	2	0
Williams,2b	4	0	1	3	2	Handley,2b	5	1	3	4	6
Crabtree,cf	4	0	0	0	0	Russell,rf	5	0	1	1	0
McC'm'k,1b	3	0	1	12	0	Elliott,3b	5	1	1	1	1
Tipton,lf	4	0	1	5	0	Gustine,ss	4	0	2	2	6
Faussett,3b	4	0	0	2	5	Dah'en,1b	3	0	0	16	0
Miller,ss	3	1	1	1	5	DiM'io,cf	3	2	1	1	0
Mueller,c	2	0	1	1	0	Lopez,c	3	2	1	0	0
Rice,c	1	0	0	0	0	Str'vich,p	2	0	0	0	5
Riddle,c	2	0	0	0	3						
Malloy,p	0	0	0	0	0						
a-Marshall	1	0	0	0	0						
Shoun,p	0	0	0	0	0						
Totals	32	1	6	27	15	Totals	35	7	10	27	18

a-Batted for Malloy in eighth.

Pittsburgh 0 0 2 1 0 1 1 0 2—7
Cincinnati 0 0 0 0 0 0 0 1 0—1

Error: Russell. Runs batted in: Barrett 2, Handley, Russell, Gustine, Dahlgren, Lopez, Criscola. Two-base hits: Handley, Gustine, DiMaggio, Lopez. Sacrifice: Strincevich. Double plays: Handley, Gustine and Dahlgren; 2; Faussett and McCormick. Left on bases: Pittsburgh, 6; Cincinnati, 5. Bases on balls: Strincevich, 1; Riddle, 1; Malloy, 1; Shoun, 2. Struck out: By Riddle, 1. Hits: Off Riddle, 8 in 7 innings; Malloy, 0 in 1; Shoun, 2 in 1. Losing pitcher: Riddle. Umpires: Boggess, Pinelli and Ballanfant. Time, 1.45.

SECOND GAME

Pittsburgh	ab	r	h	o	a	Cincinnati	ab	r	h	o	a
Barrett,rf	4	0	2	3	0	Clay,rf	4	0	0	1	0
Handley,2b	4	0	0	3	1	Will'ms,2b	4	0	1	0	5
Russell,lf	4	0	0	4	0	Crisc'a,rf	3	1	2	5	0
Elliott,3b	2	0	0	0	3	McC'o'k,1b	4	0	11	0	1
Gustine,ss	3	0	0	0	2	Tipton,lf	4	1	1	3	0
Dahlg'n,1b	3	0	0	7	1	Fausett,3b	[illegible]				
DiMag'o,cf	[illegible]					[illegible]					
Lopez,c	[illegible]					[illegible]					
Camelli,c	[illegible]					[illegible]					
a-Rubeling	[illegible]					[illegible]					
Davis,c	[illegible]					[illegible]					
Rescigno,p	[illegible]										
Totals	29	1	3	24	7	Totals	[illegible]				

a-Batted for Camelli in 8th.

Pittsburgh [illegible]—1
Cincinnati [illegible]—4

Errors—Elliott. Runs batted in—Handley, Williams, McCormick, Mueller, Tipton. [illegible] Time—1.34. Attendance—16,060.

Tribe, Tigers Split Before 38,940

DETROIT, April 30 (A. P.).—The Cleveland Indians clinched their series with the Detroit Tigers today before 38,940 spectators by winning the opener of a double-header, 2-1. Detroit won the nightcap, 4-2, on Chuck Hostetler's two-run single in the seventh. Don Ross of Detroit and Ken Keltner of Cleveland homered in the nightcap.

FIRST GAME

Cleveland	ab	r	h	o	a	Detroit	ab	r	h	o	a
Peters,2b	[illegible]					Hoover,ss	[illegible]				
Rocco,1b	[illegible]					Mayo,2b	[illegible]				
Cullen,rf	[illegible]					Cramer,cf	[illegible]				
Heath,lf	[illegible]					Ross,rf	[illegible]				
Keltner,3b	[illegible]					York,1b	[illegible]				
Boudr'u,ss	[illegible]					Outlaw,lf	[illegible]				
Seerey,cf	[illegible]					Hostet'r,rf	[illegible]				
Susce,c	[illegible]					Rich'ds,c	[illegible]				
Kennedy,p	[illegible]					Overm'e,p	[illegible]				
Totals	35	2	10	27	19	Totals	29	1	8	27	13

Cleveland [illegible]—2
Detroit [illegible]—1

[illegible]

SECOND GAME

Cleveland	ab	r	h	o	a	Detroit	ab	r	h	o	a
Peters,2b	[illegible]					Hoover,ss	[illegible]				
Rocco,1b	[illegible]					Mayo,2b	[illegible]				
Cull'ne,cf	[illegible]					Cramer,cf	[illegible]				
Heath,lf	[illegible]					Higgins,3b	[illegible]				
Keltner,3b	[illegible]					York,1b	[illegible]				
Boudreau,ss	[illegible]					Ross,rf	[illegible]				
Grant,2b	[illegible]					Outlaw,lf	[illegible]				
Seerey,cf	[illegible]					Swift,c	[illegible]				
Susce,c	[illegible]					Gorsica,p	[illegible]				
a-Hockett	[illegible]					c-Richards	[illegible]				
McDonald	[illegible]										
Reynolds,p	[illegible]										
Naymick,p	[illegible]										
b-O'Dea	[illegible]										
Klieman,p	[illegible]										
Totals	31	2	7	24	9	Totals	30	4	9	27	19

[illegible]
Cleveland [illegible]—2
Detroit [illegible]—4

Errors: Borom and Gorsica. Runs batted in: Keltner, York, Ross, Hostetler 2. Two-base hits: Peters, York, Gorsica. Three-base hit: Heath. Home runs: Ross, Keltner. [illegible] Umpires: Rommel and Weafer. Time, 1.56. Attendance, 38,940.

Major Leagues Draw 218,262

With ideal baseball weather prevailing, eight doubleheaders in the major leagues yesterday attracted 218,262 fans. This compares with 165,189 on the corresponding Sunday last year, an increase of 53,073.

NATIONAL LEAGUE

Brooklyn at New York	58,068
Boston at Philadelphia	30,392
Pittsburgh at Cincinnati	16,060
Chicago at St. Louis	11,498
Total	116,018

AMERICAN LEAGUE

Cleveland at Detroit	38,940
New York at Washington	31,057
Athletics at Boston	25,645
St. Louis at Chicago	6,602
Total	102,244
Grand total	218,262

Picard Slashes 5 Strokes Off Par

HARRISBURG, Pa., April 30.—Henry Picard, new golf pro at Harrisburg Country Club, today showed he is ready for major tournaments when he sliced five strokes off par with a dazzling 67 on the Fort Hunter course.

Picard teamed up with Ed Tabor, new West Shore pro, to defeat Sandy Heron, Blue Ridge pro, and George Morris, Colonial Club veteran, 3 and 2. Morris and Heron shot 78s. Tabor had 80. Picard showed all his former links cunning in shattering par today.

DeBerardinis, Boyle Tie at Tully-Secane

Joseph A. DeBerardinis, top amateur, tied with T. C. Boyle at 75 in the "Old Golf Ball" tournament at Tully-Secane Country Club yesterday in a field of 250, as 1500 balls were collected.

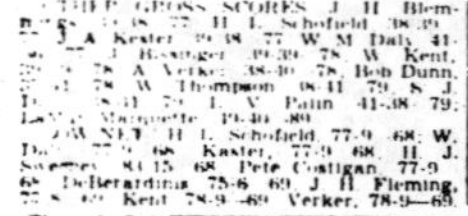

Defense Golfers Tie

Paul Brown and Charles Frazier tied with 75s in the Sun Shipbuilding Co. golf yesterday at Springhaven Country Club.

OTHER SCORES: P. Martin, 41-38—79; Walter Maykut, 38-41—79; Joe Kesler, 41-38—79; Ed Cassidy, 40-39—79; R. Sweeney, 40-41—81; G. McFarland, 43-41—84; Al Sweet, 41-43—84; Frank Reitz, 41-45—86; A. Kershaw, 45-42—87; F. Warburton, 45-41—86; T. Leavy, 41-48—89.

Myers Leads Qualifiers

Milord Myers led the qualifying round in the annual Vogelson Cup handicap tournament of the Green Valley Country Club yesterday with 44-43-87-14-73. Milton Lichtenstein, defending champion, was second with 40-42-82-8-74.

WPB May Release Lights To Boston, Chicago, Detroit

WASHINGTON, April 30 (A. P.).—The War Production Board is considering the possibility of releasing materials for the construction of lights in major league parks not now equipped for night games, George W. McMurphey, chief of WPB's recreation division, said tonight.

McMurphey said the two Boston clubs and the Chicago Cubs had expressed an interest in installing equipment for night games and that he understood the Detroit Tigers were considering it. The New York Yankee management advised him, he said, that the club is not in a position now to light their field.

Some of the materials, such as wire, reflectors and utility connectors, are available now, McMurphey said, adding that the questionable items included panel boards and transformers. The clubs, he said, have been asked to apply for the lighting and a decision will be made on an individual basis if it is determined that the materials can be spared.

McMurphey said the "official feeling" at WPB is that lighting equipment at the parks would provide more night games and greater opportunity for war workers to see them.

In addition, he said, more night games will tend to relieve congestion of traffic facilities during the day and help curb absenteeism by war plant workers.

Colter Captures Archery Opener

William B. Colter won the Double American round with 1198 and also scored six perfect goals to feature the Philadelphia Archery Association's opening tournament of the season yesterday. The matches were held at Cedar Grove Driving Range, Fairmount Park, and marked the start of the 18th season.

Colter had a wide lead over Clifford B. Herts, who placed second with 1105.

Fort Jackson Cancels Schedule

FORT JACKSON, S. C., April 30 (A. P.).—Fort Jackson's powerful baseball team, winner of three one-sided victories over Atlanta (Southern Association), has cancelled its schedule, Brigadier General Duncan G. Richart, post commander, said today.

The move dictated because of the Army's speed-up in transfers of men fit for general service from post detachments to active units.

The post's two best pitchers, Kirby Higbe, former Brooklyn and Phillies star, and Jimmy McClure, ex-Memphis Chick, already have been transferred and other former pro players are scheduled to go soon.

Johnson Aids Victory

WEST HAVEN, Conn., April 30 (A. P.).—Bill Johnson, last year's rookie third baseman for the New York Yankees who is now stationed with the U. S. Merchant Marine at New London, made his debut with the West Haven sailors today and punched out a single that drove in his team's fourth run in a 4-1 victory over the Chance Vought Flyers, Stratford.

Golfer Scores Ace

The first hole-in-one of the Ashbourne Country Club season was registered yesterday by Dr. Abe Lubowitz on the 235-yard par 35 seventh. He was in a foursome with Harry Goldenberg, Harry Ross and Arthur Grossman.

Sports Results

Professional

SOCCER

LEWIS CUP PLAYOFFS

Phila. Nationals, 4; Brooklyn Hispanos, 1.
Kearny Celtics, 4; Phila. Americans, 2.
Brooklyn Wanderers, 4; N. Y. Americans, 1.
Brookhattan, 7; Kearny Scots, 3.

STANDINGS

Team	W.	L.	T.	P.	Team	W.	L.	T.	P.
Bro'lyn W.	2	0	0	4	Phila. Amns	[illegible]			
Kearny C.	2	0	0	4	N.Y. Amns	[illegible]			
Brookhattan	1	0	1	3	Kearny Scots	[illegible]			
Phila. Nats	1	1	0	2	Brooklyn H.	[illegible]			

EXHIBITION BASEBALL

Binghamton 2; Scranton [illegible]
Allentown 4; Lansdale [illegible]
Wilkes-Barre 5; Wilmington 5 (called end of 9th)
Merchant Marine (New London) 4; Chance Vought Flyers 1

Amateur

SOCCER

National Cup

Morgan Strassers 3; Milwaukee Falls 1

Princeton-to-Discontinue-Football Rumor Finds Bushnell, Athletic Director, Silent

By LEO RIORDAN

The most persistent gossip among the college athletic officials and coaches gathered here over the week-end for the Penn Relay Carnival centered around a rumor that Princeton University, co-pioneer of American football with Rutgers University, has decided to abandon the game for 1944.

Reached yesterday at his home on the Princeton campus, Asa Bushnell, graduate manager of athletics, said: "I have no statement."

Observers, knowing Mr. Bushnell, an outstanding athletic official, could only construe this reply as a reluctant refusal to deny the rumor. Presumably, announcement of any such sweeping policy change might be expected to come from Dr. Harold W. Dodds, president of the University, or from a policy board of which Mr. Bushnell would probably be a member.

EXPECT ANNOUNCEMENT

Talk around the select Philadelphia men's clubs yesterday was that such an announcement was in preparation.

When Harvard University withdrew from the football shortly after the 1942 season, observers first assumed that the game would stop as it had in 1918. This assumption was based on the expectancy that Princeton and Yale University would follow Harvard's lead. These Big Three institutions had previously scheduled for 1943.

TRANSPORTATION PROBLEM

Princeton's continuance in football was generally credited to Mr. Bushnell. When war broke he was spokesman for Eastern college football in his capacity as executive director for the central office of Eastern Intercollegiate athletics. He promptly returned to Princeton to take over its sports program, meanwhile continuing in his directorship. He remained a constant source of support to colleges attempting to continue athletics.

Princeton, which last year was defeated by both Pennsylvania and Villanova, has a peculiar problem. Under war-time restrictions, Princeton is inaccessible for football games. In peacetime, special trains jam the sidings in the Colonial village and cavalcades of motor cars bring a large percentage of the crowds which total 50,000 for big games.

Despite adjustments like switching games to Philadelphia (the Pennsylvania game was originally scheduled for Princeton) and to New York City—few Princeton alumni were able to follow their team regularly last year.

CUSHIONED BLOW

Observers are inclined to believe that if Princeton drops football now, the blow generally will be cushioned. Had it done so for 1943, the effect would have been widespread. Many colleges which abandoned the game last year have already announced 1944 schedules.

Officials at both Penn and Villanova yesterday said that games with Princeton were "under negotiation" for 1944.

Baseball Facts

NATIONAL LEAGUE

Yesterday's Results

PHILLIES, 2; Boston, 1, 1st game, (14 innings).
PHILLIES, 2; Boston, 2, 2nd game, (called 9 innings).
Pittsburgh 7; Cincinnati 1, 1st game.
Cincinnati 4; Pittsburgh 1, 2nd game.
New York 26; Brooklyn 8, 1st game.
Brooklyn 5; New York 4, 2nd game, (7 innings, called).
St. Louis 5; Chicago 0, 1st game.
St. Louis 7; Chicago 5, 2nd game.

Standing of the Teams

	W.	L.	P.C.
St. Louis	9	2	.818
New York	7	3	.700
Cincinnati	7	4	.636
PHILLIES	6	4	.600
Brooklyn	5	6	.455
Pittsburgh	3	5	.375
Boston	3	8	.273
Chicago	1	9	.100

Today's Schedule

No games scheduled.

AMERICAN LEAGUE

Yesterday's Results

Boston, 3; ATHLETICS, 2, 1st game.
ATHLETICS, 3; Boston, 1, 2d game.
New York, 2; Washington, 1, 1st game.
New York, 3; Washington, 2, 2d game.
Cleveland, 2; Detroit, 1, 1st game.
Detroit, 4; Cleveland, 2, 2d game.
Chicago, 6; St. Louis, 5, 1st game, 10 in.
St. Louis, 5; Chicago, 4, 2d game.

Standing of the Teams

	W.	L.	PC.
St. Louis	10	2	.833
ATHLETICS	5	4	.556
New York	5	4	.556
Boston	5	5	.500
Cleveland	4	6	.400
Washington	3	5	.375
Detroit	4	7	.364
Chicago	3	6	.333

Today's Schedule

Probable Pitchers and their Records

Washington at Boston, Wolff (0-0) vs. V. Johnson (0-0).
Chicago at Cleveland, Lee (0-2) vs. Kleine (0-0).
Only games scheduled.

INTERNATIONAL LEAGUE

Yesterday's Results

Montreal, 10; Syracuse, 5, 1st game.
Syracuse, 4; Montreal, 3, 2d game.
Baltimore, 8; Toronto, 2, 1st game.
Toronto, 1; Baltimore, 0, 2d game.
Jersey City, 5; Buffalo, 0, 1st game.
Jersey City, 6; Buffalo, 4, 2d game.
Newark, 6; Rochester, 4, 1st game, 11 in.
Newark, 4; Rochester, 3, 2d game.

Standing of the Teams

	W.	L.	PC.		W.	L.	PC.
Toronto	3	2	.600	Syracuse	3	3	.500
Baltimore	4	3	.571	Jersey C.	4	4	.500
Buffalo	4	4	.500	Montreal	3	4	.429
Rochester	4	4	.500	Newark	3	4	.429

TODAY'S SCHEDULE — Montreal at Syracuse; Buffalo at Jersey City; Rochester at Newark. Only games scheduled.

AMERICAN ASSOCIATION

Louisville 6; Toledo 4, 1st game.
Toledo 6; Louisville 2, 2nd game.
Columbus 8; Indianapolis 7, 1st game.
Columbus 11; Indianapolis 6, 2nd game.
Kansas City at St. Paul, postponed.
Milwaukee at Minneapolis, postponed.

Continued on Page 18, Column 1

Yanks Defeat Griffs Twice Before 31,057

WASHINGTON, April 30 (A. P.).—The New York Yankees twice defeated the Washington Senators 2-1 and 3-2, in a twin-bill today before 31,057, largest turnout of the season.

Ernie Bonham turned in a five-hit masterpiece in the opener.

PAGE BLASTED

The Yanks counted both their runs in the first inning on hits by George Stirnweiss, Tuck Stainback and Don Savage and Johnny Lindell. A New York error, a stolen base by George Case and George Myatt's blow gave Washington a run in the ninth.

The Senators blasted Joe Page, southpaw, from the mound in the seventh inning of the nightcap during a two-run rally. Hank Borowy quelled the uprising.

FIRST GAME

Washington	ab	r	h	o	a	New York	ab	r	h	o	a
Case,lf	4	1	0	2	1	Stir'w's,2b	3	1	1	2	4
Myatt,2b	4	0	2	2	0	Sta'nb'k,rf	4	1	3	4	0
Spence,cf	3	0	0	5	0	Etten,1b	2	0	1	8	0
Ortiz,rf	3	0	1	1	0	Savage,3b	4	0	2	1	1
Kuhel,1b	3	0	0	13	0	Meth'y,lf	0	0	0	1	0
Torres,3b	3	0	0	0	6	Levy,lf	4	0	0	2	0
Ferrell,c	3	0	0	3	0	Lindell,cf	4	0	1	4	0
Sul'v'n,ss	3	0	2	1	5	Milose'h,ss	4	0	0	4	3
Haefner,p	2	0	0	0	3	Hemsley,c	4	0	0	1	1
aWynn	1	0	0	0	0	Bonham,p	3	0	1	0	3
Totals	29	1	5	27	15	Totals	34	2	9	27	12

aBatted for Haefner in 9th

New York 2 0 0 0 0 0 0 0 0—2
Washington 0 0 0 0 0 0 0 0 1—1

Errors—Milosevich. Runs batted in—Savage 2, Myatt. Stolen base—Case. Sacrifices—Etten (2). Double plays—Bonham, Milosevich and Etten (2), Milosevich, Stirnweiss and Etten. Left on bases—New York 6, Washington 1. Base on balls—Haefner 1. Strikeouts—Haefner 2. Umpires—Rue, Boyer and Summers. Time—1.27.

SECOND GAME

New York	ab	r	h	o	a	Washington	ab	r	h	o	a
Stirn'ss,2b	4	0	1	1	7	Case,lf	4	0	1	5	0
Stain'ck,cf	4	1	0	7	1	Myatt,2b	3	0	1	2	2
Metheny,lf	4	2	3	0	0	Spence,cf	1	0	0	1	0
Etten,1b	4	0	1	7	0	Powell,lf	3	0	0	3	0
Savage,3b	4	0	1	2	1	Ortiz,rf	4	1	1	1	0
Rosent'l,rf	2	0	1	2	0	Butka,1b	3	0	2	5	0
Milose'h,ss	3	0	1	3	5	Kuhel,1b	1	0	0	3	0
Garbark,c	3	0	0	3	1	Torres,3b	4	1	0	2	3
Hemsley,c	1	0	0	2	0	Guerra,c	4	0	2	2	0
Page,p	3	0	0	0	0	Sullivan,ss	3	0	1	3	3
Borowy,p	1	0	0	0	0	Wynn,p	3	0	0	0	3
Totals	33	3	8	27	15	Totals	33	2	8	27	11

New York 2 0 0 0 1 0 0 0 0—3
Washington 0 0 0 0 0 0 2 0 0—2

Errors—Etten, Savage, Sullivan. Runs batted in—Etten, Milosevich, Rosenthal, Torres, Guerra. Two-base hits—Milosevich, Guerra, Sullivan. Double plays—Sullivan, Myatt and Kuhel. Left on bases—New York 7, Washington 5. Base on balls—Off Wynn 4, Borowy 1. Strikeouts—By Wynn 2, Page 3, Borowy 2. Hits—Off Page, 8 in 6 2-3 innings; Borowy, 0 in 2 1-3. Winning pitcher—Page. Umpires—Boyer, Summers and Rue. Time—2.00. Attendance—31,057.

Leahy Gets Commission

CHICAGO, April 30 (U. P.).—Frank Leahy, head football coach and athletic director at Notre Dame University, will be commissioned a Navy lieutenant tomorrow.

The Philadelphia Inquirer

PUBLIC LEDGER

An Independent Newspaper for All the People

FINAL CITY EDITION

CIRCULATION: May Average: Daily 496,780; Sunday 1,097,774

MONDAY MORNING, JUNE 5, 1944

Copyright, 1944, by Triangle Publications, Inc. Vol. 230, No. 157

a b d e f g h

THREE CENTS

ROME CAPTURED BY ALLIES

Germans Flee to North Under Fierce Bombing; 1200 U. S. Planes Pound West Wall, Riviera

NAPLES, June 4 (U. P.).—Triumphant Fifth Army troops tonight captured Rome, bringing liberation for the first time to a Nazi-enslaved European capital, and German rear guards were fleeing the Eternal City in disorganized retreat to the northwest. Except for the rail yards, smashed by Allied bombs, the city is 95 percent intact, Reynolds and Eleanor Packard of the United Press reported after their arrival in the city with the Allied occupation forces.

(The Berlin radio announced the Nazi evacuation of Rome and, quoting an order from Adolf Hitler's headquarters, said German troops had been ordered to take up new positions to the northwest to avoid bringing the city under the peril of destruction.

KESSELRING ACTS THROUGH VATICAN

(The evacuation was ordered after Field Marshal Albert Kesselring, German commander in Italy, proposed through the German Ambassador to the Vatican that both sides recognize Rome an open city, Berlin said.)

Late tonight the British Eighth Army, rushing into Rome from the southeast along the Via Casilina, was reported joining the Fifth Army in close pursuit of the hard-pressed enemy remnants, under orders to destroy them to a man if that were possible.

Only enough troops to maintain order and ferret any German snipers or suicide nests were to be left in Rome as the main Allied armies pounded on without pausing to celebrate their greatest triumph, coming 270 days after the start of the Italian campaign.

At the very gates of Rome, the Germans had made a final stand but Lieutenant General Mark W. Clark, after waiting three hours for the enemy troops to withdraw in accordance with their own avowal of Rome as an open city, ordered a violent anti-tank barrage.

FIFTH ARMY SMASHES INTO CITY

Then masses of Fifth Army men and weapons crashed into the city, and began mopping up enemy snipers and a few tanks and mobile guns which were trying to cover the retreat.

(Daniel De Luce, Associated Press correspondent, said that mopping up of the heart of the city was completed when a Fifth Army force knocked out an enemy scout car in front of the Bank of Italy, near the column erected to the Emperor Trajan. De Luce reported the Germans earlier had begun a frenzied series of demolitions inside Rome.)

The Allies' work was completed tonight except for isolated nests of resistance in the northwestern outskirts—and the capture of the city, the great capital of the Caesars and administrative seat for a large part of the Christian world, was an accomplished fact.

(Hitler's order as quoted by the German D. N. B. agency

Continued on Page 2, Column 1

(Official Signal Corps Radiophoto from A. P. Wirephoto)

VICTORIOUS ALLIED TROOPS ENTER ROME IN DRIVE TO WIPE OUT NAZIS

This radiophoto shows some of the first Allied troops to enter Rome, near the "Roma" sign at the gates of the city, which was captured after a brief fight. (Other pictures and maps on Pages 2, 3 and 8.)

Today

Great Allied Victory

Nazi Hopes Dashed

Retreat Route Lost

5th Army Superior

New Disaster Looms

By John M. McCullough

Inquirer Washington Bureau

WASHINGTON, June 4.

THE importance of the military, political and psychological consequences of the Allied occupation of Rome can hardly be exaggerated.

There is no question whatever, competent sources here maintain, that Field Marshal Albert Kesselring fully anticipated holding the Velletri-Valmontone defenses in front of Rome while the main elements of his 10th Army, located further to the east, withdrew in order over the superb road net of which Rome is the hub.

The encouraging fact is that the 5th Army both outfought and outgeneraled the German commander holding that line, pierced it, flanked its strong points, and sent the entire hinge swinging back in broken disorder upon Rome.

That road net now is no longer available to Kesselring, who must extricate the main body of his troops over good but narrow, circuitous and extremely vulnerable highways of retreat.

It is too early, observers here insist, to fully assess the military future, but it is certain that there is at least a possibility of further disaster for the Nazi forces.

If—leaving only a garrison force in Rome — General Sir Harold Alexander, Allied ground forces commander, can detach a group of fresh, highly mobile divisions to smash at Kesselring's exposed right flank as he withdraws northward and northwestward, decisive events may interpose long before the enemy can reach his next obvious defense line—the Rimini-Florence-Leghorn line astride the Etruscan Apennines.

Since late March, German reinforcements and supplies have not dared to move except after nightfall because of the absolute Allied command of

Continued on Page 8, Column 1

R.A.F. Fleet Hits Continent In Night Raids

American Bombers Attack Europe From West and South

By W. W HERCHER

LONDON, June 5 (Monday) (A. P.).—Royal Air Force bombers battered targets in enemy-occupied Europe again last night, the British announced today, taking up the burden of the non-stop offensive after 1200 American heavy bombers had struck the continent twin daylight blows from bases in Britain and Italy yesterday.

Specific objectives of the overnight assault were not immediately announced, but the R.A.F. has been concentrating for the most part of late on vital communication centers which supply the Nazi West Wall defenses.

TWIN BLOWS

In yesterday's assaults, some 500 U. S. bombers pounded German strongholds along the French invasion coast, while another armada from the Mediterranean made a strong attempt to sever two main rail lines between Italy and France.

(Four American heavy bombers and three fighters were missing from the raids against Nazi transport lines and airdromes in occupied France, the U. S. Army Air Forces announced early Monday. One German plane was reported shot down.)

DEFENSES SATURATED

Swarms of medium bombers and fighter bombers from Britain kept the thunderous assaults going after the Flying Fortresses and Liberators had saturated defenses around Boulogne with 1500 tons of bombs.

Spitfire bombers and fighters

Continued on Page 3, Column 2

Radio Talk Tonight By F.D.R. on Rome

WASHINGTON, June 4 (A. P.).—President Roosevelt tomorrow night will talk to the people of the United States on the fall of Rome, the White House announced tonight.

The President's 15-minute talk will be carried over the four major networks between 8.30 P. M. and 8.45 P. M. (E. W. T.).

Two Subs Launched In Honor of Detective

Illustrated on Page 8

Before an audience of nearly 8000 persons, two new submarines, dedicated to the memory of Detective George H. Muhs, and paid for with $16,500,000 in War Bonds sold by Philadelphia policemen in the Fourth War Loan drive, were launched yesterday at the yards of the Cramp Shipbuilding Co.

National, State and city officials, flanked by more than 800 members of the Bureau of Police, witnessed the impressive ceremonies held as a tribute to the first member of the department to give his life for his country in this war.

SLIDES INTO DELAWARE

The first fighting ship, the U. S. S. Sabalo, sponsored by Mrs. Charles M. Oman, wife of Rear Admiral Oman, commanding officer of the U. S. Convalescent Hospital for Officers, Harriman, N. Y., slid into the Delaware at 11.50 A. M.

Fifteen minutes later the U. S. S. Sablefish, the other new submarine, was launched from the same ways directly behind the berth emptied by the U. S. S. Sabalo.

Mrs. Edmund E. Burrough, wife of Captain Burrough, attached to the headquarters of the Commander-

Continued on Page 4, Column 7

Casualties

Ex-Swim Star Is Killed in Italy

A former University of Pennsylvania swimming star, who was commander of a Fifth Army tank unit, was killed in Italy on the day the Allied Armies started their big push on Rome.

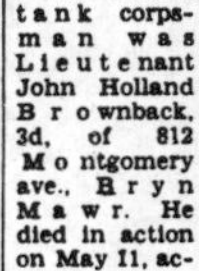

LIEUT. BROWNBACK

The dead tank corpsman was Lieutenant John Holland Brownback, 3d, of 812 Montgomery ave., Bryn Mawr. He died in action on May 11, according to a War Department telegram his parents, Mr. and Mrs. John H. Brownback, Jr., received yesterday.

An only son, Lieutenant Brownback enlisted in the Army in May, 1942, while he was a student at the University of Pennsylvania. Six months later he was graduated from the Officers' Candidate School at Fort Knox, Ky.

The 22-year-old officer saw action abroad with the armored forces in

Continued on Page 4, Column 4

135 Nazis Mutiny, Shoot 2 Officers

WITH THE FIFTH ARMY IN THE SUBURBS OF ROME, June 4 (A. P.).—One hundred and thirty-five German soldiers mutinied, shot two officers and surrendered to an American infantry company west of Lanuvio, as the final drive toward Rome got under way, it was reported today.

The Germans were said to have explained that their act was provoked when the officers shot two privates who were trying to desert.

Rome 95 Percent Intact Despite Bitter Fighting

Flowers Tossed In Path of Victors

(The following dispatch is from a famous man-and-wife team of war correspondents who were stationed in Rome until the United States entered the war. They describe their return to the Italian capital with victorious Allied forces, under assignment to reopen the United Press Rome Bureau at the earliest possible moment.)

By ELEANOR AND REYNOLDS PACKARD

ROME, June 4 (U. P.).—We returned to Rome tonight through shell, machine gun and snipers' fire to find the Italian capital almost unscarred.

Except for the complete wreckage of its railway marshalling yards, battered incessantly and accurately by Allied aerial bombs, we found the city almost 95 percent intact.

FIRES LEFT BURNING

A few fires had been left burning by the retreating Germans.

The last we had seen of Rome was after Benito Mussolini's declaration of war on the United States when we were sent to a diplomatic internment camp to await transfer to the United States, which finally occurred in June, 1942.

We entered Rome tonight along with the vanguard of American in-

Continued on Page 2, Column 6

Battle Is Waged To Forum's Edge

By DANIEL De LUCE

ROME, June 4 (A. P.).—Rome, the Eternal City, was liberated tonight by tanks and infantry troops of the Allied Fifth Army, which battled German rearguards to the edge of the ancient Forum.

A force from the old Anzio beachhead completed the mop-up of Nazi forces at 9.15 P. M. (3.15 P. M., E. W. T.) by knocking out an enemy scout-car in front of the Bank of Italy, almost within the shadow of the column erected to the Emperor Trajan, who ruled the Romans from A. D. 98 to 117.

BATTLE IN SUBURBS

The Fifth Army force fought its way into the heart of the city after a four-hour battle against German armor in the suburbs of the ancient capital.

In a dawn dash from Borgata Finocchio, 13 miles distant on the Via Casilina, a spearhead of 24 Sherman tanks, eight armored cars and 150 U. S. and Canadian infantrymen pushed beyond suburban Torre Spaccata before they ran headlong into a German road block.

Old men and young girls and toddling children were waving the Americans on when the fire of German 88-millimeter guns knocked out

Continued on Page 2, Column 3

$50,000 Transfer By Laval Reported

By United Press

Pierre Laval, chief of the Vichy government, recently tried to transfer $50,000 from Spain to Argentina, the Brazzaville radio said yesterday.

"A Madrid bank revealed to the Spanish authorities that a deposit of $50,000 had been made with them for transfer to an Argentine bank," the French radio said. "An inquiry was opened, and the person behind the depositor was discovered: He is Pierre Laval."

Pope Pius Prays In Private Chapel

LONDON, June 4 (A. P.).—Behind a double Swiss guard sealing off Vatican City, Pope Pius XII held urgent consultations today with the Papal Secretary of State, Luigi Cardinal Maglione, and prayed in his private chapel, the London Daily Mail's Madrid correspondent reported.

The Pope received frequent reports on the situation in Rome, it was stated. No one was allowed to leave or enter the Vatican without a special pass. The Pope has been a virtual prisoner in the Vatican since the Germans seized control of Rome last July.

Nazis Now Make Rome Open City

LONDON, June 4 (A. P.).—Adolf Hitler announced tonight in two special communiques — broadcast after Allied troops had liberated Rome — the withdrawal of German troops to the northwest of the city and said the Allies had been offered a plan whereby Rome would be regarded as an "open city."

In the first word from the Fuehrer's headquarters in several days, it was asserted the fight in Italy would continue and that measures were being taken "to force final victory for Germany and her allies."

HITLER CONFIDENT

"The year of the invasion," one communique said, "will bring Germany's enemies an annihilating defeat at the most decisive moment."

The order to evacuate German troops from the city, it was said, was intended "to prevent the destruction of Rome."

The proposals were said to have been advanced at 11 P. M. Saturday. This was less than 24 hours before Rome changed hands.

The German radio said Field Marshal General Albert Kesselring had submitted to the Vatican proposals to make Rome an open city with a request that they be conveyed to the Allies, but that "so far no reply has been received from the Anglo-American High Command."

German radio commentators im-

Continued on Page 2, Column 7

Canadian Soldiers, 'Zoot Suiters' Riot

MONTREAL, June 4 (U. P.).—Riot squads were called out here again tonight as a group of Canadian servicemen attempted to converge on a public dance hall, apparently in a renewal of a feud between soldiers and sailors and youthful "zoot suiters."

Police broke up the group, estimated to number some 200 soldiers and sailors, but later were called out again when the men attempted to reform their ranks.

More than a score of persons were injured in several clashes between the servicemen and "zoot suiters" in downtown Montreal last night and early today. Forty persons were arrested.

War Summary

Monday, June 5, 1944

ITALY — **Allied troops captured Rome yesterday, climaxing a 23-day-old drive in Italy. The Nazis offered stubborn resistance up to the gates of the city, but finally broke and fled. Allied bombers pounded the retreating foe along roads northwest of the city.**

In the final move on Rome the Allies drove 15 miles in 24 hours. There was sporadic resistance inside the city itself. Berlin said the defense of Italy would continue north of Rome, which Hitler belatedly had declared an "open city."

AIR OFFENSIVE — **About 1200 U. S. heavy bombers and swarms of medium bombers and fighter-bombers attacked Hitler's Europe from British and Mediterranean bases. The invasion coast, particularly the Boulogne area, was one of the chief targets. Other were rail lines, bridges and tunnels along the French-Italian Riviera. Allied planes again attacked enemy-held territory during the night.**

INVASION—**Start of shuttle bombing between Mediterranean bases and Russia was reported to have thrown the peoples under Axis rule into panic, with fleeing refugees jamming the roads of eastern Europe.**

RUSSIA — **Russians hurled back repeated new drives by the Germans north of Iasi in Rumania. Moscow reported that 1100 Nazis were killed.**

PACIFIC—**U. S. troops resumed their advance on Biak Island. The Kuriles were bombed for the fifth straight day, and Truk and Ponape also were blasted.**

BURMA-CHINA — **Spearheads of Chinese and American troops pushed toward the center of Myitkyina from two directions. Chungking said the Chinese had halted one of the Jap columns pressing toward Changsha, 25 miles from that city, and that other Chinese troops had recaptured three cities southwest of Loyang.**

U. S. WEATHER FORECAST

Philadelphia and vicinity: Partly cloudy and warmer today; showers and warmer tomorrow.

Sun rises 5.34 A.M. Sets 8.25 P. M.
Moon rises 7.19 P.M. Sets 4.57 A. M.

Marquis Childs

Allied Heads Differ in Attitude

WASHINGTON, June 4.

TWO men could hardly be more unlike each other than President Roosevelt and Prime Minister Churchill. To his associates F. D. R. presents an outward air of detachment and calm. Mr. Churchill, all through the past weeks, has been intensely preoccupied with the big event to come, brooding over its outcome and its consequences.

Completely absorbed in preparations for the great offensive, Mr. Churchill has brushed aside any talk about what is to happen after the war. He simply won't hear it.

That is the explanation given by those who have seen him recently for his "kind words" for "Franco Spain. They say that he was thinking solely of Spain today in relation to the supreme test of Allied arms. He knows—so the explanation goes—as well as anyone else that Dictator Franco cannot long survive the end of the war

• • •

FOR all his preoccupation with the events on which so much turns, Mr. Churchill's humanness comes out from time to time. Not long ago he told a story on himself which gave the War Cabinet a good laugh. It was a story which had already gained wide currency but Mr. Churchill furnished details that were new.

The Prime Minister had been impressed with the political reports from America, sent by Isaiah Berlin, a member of the British Embassy staff in Washington. Hearing that Mr. Berlin was on a visit to London, the Prime Minister told a reporter to ask him around to lunch at No. 10 Downing street. At the appointed time the two men sat down to lunch alone and Mr. Churchill began to quiz the embassy secretary on political developments in the United States.

The responses were remarkably weak. The great man was first puzzled and then a little irritated. Finally he said, half in reproof:

"You know, Mr. Berlin, I have studied your work very carefully."

Looking startled, Mr. Berlin replied: "Why, Mr. Prime Minister, I didn't know that you cared for light music." Through a mistake, Irving Berlin, who was also in London, had been invited to lunch instead of Isaiah Berlin. The Prime Minister could chuckle over that with the members of his cabinet.

• • •

HIS interest in American politics is a continuing one. He knows that any British interference, or even seeming interference, will do great harm in this country. No British official will breathe a word about our politics.

Nevertheless, with American visitors, Mr. Churchill finds it hard to keep back his own feelings. With one such visitor not long ago, he talked about "The Team"—The Roosevelt-Stalin-Churchill team—and the importance of keeping it together during the war and its immediate aftermath. His visitor, it happened, was a lifelong Republican who remonstrated a little at this. Mr. Churchill still insisted it was important for "The Team" to go on working together.

He has had some rather sharp disagreements with Mr. Roosevelt, some of them face to face, others by long distance. These have involved, on several occasions, Mr. Churchill's [illegible] of colonies and "subject peoples." The American President and the British Prime Minister have found themselves diametrically opposed.

• • •

AT TEHERAN there was something like a showdown. Whether the differences have since been reconciled, only the principals know. Mr. Churchill may stand pat on the question of colonies and the empire.

That would then give the vote of the third member of the team—Mr. Stalin—decisive importance. At Teheran Mr. Stalin was with Mr. Roosevelt, as Mr. Chiang Kai-shek had been at Cairo. It must always be remembered, however, that what Mr. Stalin wants above everything else is a peaceful, orderly world in which Russia can be rebuilt.

Uncle Joe might decide that there would be less confusion if everything was put back—for the time being, anyway—as it was before 1939. Therein, his views might coincide with Mr. Churchill's.

The British aristocrat and the Georgian peasant's son have had at least one major row—at the time Mr. Churchill visited Moscow in 1942. But they are both supremely realistic and they both know what they want.

Washington Background

Kimmel, Short Wait Trial As Sons Serve Country

WHILE Congress debates whether to attempt to force an immediate court-martial for Rear Admiral Husband E. Kimmel and Major General Walter C. Short, Pearl Harbor commanders on Dec. 7, 1941, Admiral Kimmel's three sons carry on as Navy officers and General Short's only son as an Army officer . . . Lieutenant Richard Barthelmess, U. S. N. R., was in town the other day, looking little changed from his days on the silent screen . . . Al Jolson bronzed by the African sun, showed up at the Mayflower lounge in khaki, planning a cross-country trip with Army camp shows en route . . . A June cloudburst during the garden party given the other day by the Chinese Ambassador, Wei Tao-ming, and Mme. Wei, sent 600 guests scurrying for cover . . . No less than 11 admirals were visible at a recent party in honor of Ira C. Copley, of Los Angeles, a former Congressman—who is a colonel in the Army . . . Senator and Mrs. Gerald P. Nye, of North Dakota, are receiving congratulations on the birth of a son.

•

The jury which acquitted Robert I. Miller, Washington attorney tried for the love-triangle slaying of a prominent capital psychiatrist, reached its "not guilty" verdict on the first ballot, 10 minutes after retiring, but stayed out more than an hour because the judge had told the jurors to consider the evidence carefully and slowly . . . Mason-Dixon notes: General Julius Franklin Howell, 98, was guest of honor at a dinner here the other evening, given by the District Daughters of the Confederacy and the Sons of Confederate Veterans. He's head of the United Confederate Veterans. Mississippi has "seceded" from the Nation-wide 35 mile-an-hour speed limit, making the limit in that State 40 for trucks, 50 for passenger buses, and 55 for automobiles.

•

This bureau's social climber, who not long ago rated an invite to Senator Joe Guffey's garden party, reports a new conquest: He recently was a guest at the John M. Cummings estate at Penllyn, near Philadelphia, which has an elaborate sign proclaiming that the name of the joint is "Horsefeathers" . . . The corridor at OWI leading to the offices of boss Elmer Davis and his right-hand men has been dubbed "King's Row" . . . Local note: Visitors to Washington last week included M. H. McCloskey, of Philadelphia; Dr. Max M. Strumia, of Penn Valley; Lewis W. Trayser, of Philadelphia, and H. F. Park, Jr., of Eddystone . . . Two sets of twin girls were baptized at a Washington church yesterday. One pair were the daughters of Mr. and Mrs. Harold E. Eberenz, of Wellsboro, Pa., and their grandmother and great-grandmother were on hand for the event.

•

Harrison E. Spangler, chairman of the Republican National Committee, stepped into a fast one at a Washington party the other day when he remarked that only politicians who keep their promises stay in office very long. "Is that why President Roosevelt has stayed in so long?" a feminine guest inquired. "You've got me there," Mr. Spangler confessed . . A Wave respectfully asked Admiral James O. Richardson the other morning whether he was "a full admiral." Said the admiral: "At this hour of the morning I am full—in only one respect." . . . A Frank Sinatra autograph went for $752.50 at a Washington War Bond auction—to two boys. Six bobbie-sox girls screamed in anguish when the well-heeled young men outbid them, but nobody swooned . . . At the same auction, however, a pair of nylons, a carton of tissues and an eight-ounce bottle of cologne brought bids of $2000 each. . . . Women operators of Washington trolleys get glamor tips at a "charm school" run by the Capital Transit Co.

•

A friend of this column sends an urgent request from Teheran for news of what happened to Flattop. The Dick Tracy comic strip there, he reports, is still laboring through the trials of Lois, the girl who took dope, and our newly-arrived friend is having a terrible time restraining the impulse to tip off the Army men in Teheran on how the Lois problem is solved. Our friend, incidentally, hasn't even heard about the Summer Sisters . . . Rocky Mountain spotted fever h: caused a third fatality in the Washington area. Latest victim was a five-year-old girl. Previously, a 53-year-old British officer and a woman of 35 died of the tick-borne disease . . . Lieutenant Colonel Edward P. Johnston, brother-in-law of the Canadian Postmaster General, was married here to Mrs. Dorothy Lee Ward . . . G. I. sweet tooth note: The Army bought 300,000,000 candy bars during the first quarter of this year for resale to soldiers overseas.

Edited by John C. O'Brien

Mark Sullivan

Forced Union Membership Exercised by Government

WASHINGTON, JUNE 4.

LAST week there was a debate on "Maintenace of Union Membership," carried by the Nation-wide radio hook-up of Town Hall. The debaters knew the subject. Both are members of the War Labor Board, which originated and enforces maintenance of union membership. One represented the majority of the board, which strongly insists that maintenance of membership is right and good. The other represented the minority of the board, which dissents.

The first step toward understanding is to divorce maintenance of union membership — which is carried on by a Government agency, WLB — from two other practices carried on by private parties, the "closed shop" and the "union shop."

The closed shop and the union shop, where they exist, are agreed upon by private parties, an employer and a labor union. Many private contracts stipulating the closed or union shop have been in existence for many years and have worked satisfactorily. There are arguments about them — but such arguments are totally foreign to consideration of maintenance of union membership.

• • •

IN MAINTENANCE of union membership, a Government agency, WLB, directs an employer and a labor union to sign a contract. Either or both may not like the contract, but they must sign it. The contract stipulates that any worker who is a member of a union on a specified date must remain a member throughout the life of the contract.

At first, this order of WLB descended upon the worker automatically, without option. Because of protests, WLB now gives the worker an escape period of 15 days during which the worker may resign from the union, without penalty. But afterward the worker must remain a member of the union, pay his dues and otherwise abide by union rules —or be discharged.

This, of course, is compulsory union membership. The compulsion is not exercised by the union, nor by the employer — it is exercised by a Government agency.

• • •

NOT only is the worker compelled, by a Government agency, to remain a member of a specified labor union. Through a recent development the worker may, in some cases, be required to remain a member of what is in effect a political movement. For one national labor organization, C.I.O., has set up what it calls its "Political Action Committee." This C.I.O. Political Action Committee has indorsed a candidate for President, Mr. Roosevelt; and has set up a Nation-wide organization with fourteen branch offices, to carry on direct activity for political objectives.

Thus workers belonging to C.I.O. unions, if covered by maintenance of union membership, are required to remain in a political movement. Without doubt, most of the members of C.I.O. agree in wanting Mr. Roosevelt to be President again; and many may agree with the other objectives of the C.I.O. Political Action Committee; but some do not. And these are required to remain in, and support, a political movement not of their own choosing.

• • •

THE compulsion, in some cases, may go the length of involuntary contributions to a political campaign fund. For, in some cases, maintenance of union membership is accompanied by the "check off." To understand this, follow the course of a given dollar.

The dollar is earned by the worker. But he never sees it. It is deducted from his pay check by the employer, who does so under the requirement of a Government agency. From the employer, the dollar is sent to the treasury of the labor union—this is part of the requirement. In the labor union treasury, the dollar becomes part of the union's funds for all purposes. Recently some large C.I.O. unions have given large amounts of money from their treasuries to the C.I.O. Political Action Committee for use in political work.

True, the union member is free to vote for whom he chooses and to act in politics as he chooses. But some workers might prefer not to belong to an organization which takes a partisan political position.

Today

By J. M. McCullough

Continued From First Page

the air. Now that the flow is reversed, congested and accelerated by the stark necessity of withdrawal, bottlenecks cannot help but develop—bottlenecks which will stand out as vulnerable to Allied tactical and strategic air attack missions as though lighted by flares.

If these routes of retreat can be blocked only partially during the daylight hours, even such masters of disengagement as the Germans have proved themselves may find the difficulties all but insuperable.

Military sources here, however, are counting on a stubborn, able and savage withdrawing action. The Germans, they know, will not permit any easy pursuit. All the tricks of blocking it—land mines, road blocks, demolitions, entrenched rear-guards—will be employed to their maximum.

The political and psychological consequences of the fall of Rome are fully as obvious, if not so readily reduced to formulas.

Rome is not only the seat of the Roman Catholic Church, to which at least 300,000,000 citizens of the world hold devout allegiance, but it is the first great capital of Europe to be recaptured from the Axis despoilers. Within hours, King Victor Emmanuel must redeem his promise of abdication, leaving the way clear for the organization of a liberal Italian Government.

The impact of these facts—the freeing of Holy Rome upon the millions of devout though enslaved European Catholics, and the conquest of one of the fountainheads of Axis ideology—not only is potent in its unadorned realism, but is certain to be exploited by Allied propagandists to the utmost.

Acquisition of the port of Rome, relieving the difficulties of supplying armies through the pitifully inadequate ports of Anzio and Nettuno; acquisition of airfields already in existence on the Roman Campagna—in brief, the general advancing of the lines against a Nazi now in full and avowed retreat — are further elements in the unfolding of the Mediterranean design which hardly could have been read into the North African landings of almost 17 months ago. But they make good and encouraging reading.

Westbrook Pegler

Coat, Tie Ban In Louisiana May Be Jest

THE New York Times is inclined to regard as a jest the proposal of a member of the Louisiana Legislature to forbid by law the wearing of coats and neckties between June 1 and October 1. This could be true. For times do change, old customs giving way to new.

But, had Raymond Daniel, of the Times, been consulted on the basis of his experience in Louisiana during the dictatorship of Huey Long, he might have told the editorial writer to turn the matter over and consider other possibilities, including the interests of the clothing and necktie trades which would be in jeopardy and worth saving at some cash outlay placed under a stone by a bayou bridge, five miles out of Baton Rouge.

This may, indeed, have been, as the Times suspects, a low-comedy bill, such as often drop into the hoppers of the State Assemblies every year, or even an honest, if unconstitutional, protest against discomfort imposed by convention.

Still another possibility, however, the Kingfish recognized when he said, in his day, that he could buy and sell the members of the Louisiana Legislature like sacks of potatoes, and not necessarily at the market price for good potatoes, and in the interests of efficiency, decreed that all strike bills were to clear through him.

• • •

THAT did simplify matters while the Kingfish lived, for the petroleum, shipping and soft drink interests relied on his discipline and thus were spared the need to haggle with individual up-country clay-and-acorn eaters and runners for books and cribs of New Orleans who, ordinarily would have gone after extra money in a manner honored by time and legislative practice, if not by ethics, the country over.

But Huey Long lies moldering in his grave; his speaker and legislative straw-boss, Allen Ellender, adorns, in an elaborate manner of speaking, the United States Senate; and the Legislature long ago broke discipline, whether for better or for worse we do not know. It is optimistic, to be sure, and good policy, to assume that this bill was offered as a protest against the heat of the Louisiana summer and those who cannot join in this assumption surely will not refuse to hope.

A realist of reminiscent mind may permit himself to speculate how much it would be worth to manufacturers and dealers in coats and ties to protect their market during one-third of each calendar year, bearing in mind that Huey would have reckoned this down to a fine figure and settled out of court for a free-will contribution to his Share-Our-Wealth-Society.

• • •

I HAVE sometimes wondered whether Huey was the cynic I thought he was, or I was at fault myself. He was utterly practical, knowing his statesmen as a small-scale farmer knows his swine, and he had reached the sensible conclusion that, with his superior intelligence, there was no sense in trusting them. It would be wasteful and disruptive to permit each threatened interest to deal individually with the members whereas he, a man of his word and with power to keep his pledge, could do business briskly in the Governor's office while that gentle servant played spit-for-a-crack with the commissioners and fly-cops down the corridor.

He rewarded the statesmen on a sort of week-pay basis the year round, through jobs for their indigent kinfolks, commissions on State purchases and per diem and mileage for the theoretical committee work. I thought otherwise, but I was thinking of ethics and ideals which had no place in the problem. So Huey surely was right to the extent that, under the known conditions, his way was more efficient and more profitable to all concerned.

He might not have permitted such a bill to come out of the box at all for, although Huey sometimes played the clown, he never played the fool Mussolini, in his early days, forbade the Austrians of his conquered lands to yodel but still they yodeled under their breath.

Huey would have realized that rebels in Louisiana, forbidden to wear coats and ties, would hold secret meetings in the woods to defy him in wholly unnecessary expression of his authority. Moreover, as a practical matter, he might have decided that because so few Louisiana men do wear coats and ties in summer the trade would have been unable to carry a pay-load on a negligible market.

Word Detective

Hyacinth

HERE is the poignant story of a youth whose blood was shed accidentally by his best friend. The youth's name was Hyacinthus. His friend was Apollo. The two were inseparable. Passionately fond of Hyacinthus, Apollo accompanied the youth in his sports, carried the nets when they were fishing, led the dogs during the hunt and followed the lad on his excursions in the mountains.

One day the two decided to play a game of quoits. Apollo threw first. He tossed the discus high and far. Hyacinthus was full of youthful excitement, and in his eagerness ran forward to obtain the missile so that he could make his throw. But it bounded, flying up and striking him in the forehead.

Apollo ran to his bleeding friend, who had fallen and fainted. In vain he tried to stanch the blood. Hyacinthus grew weaker and weaker. He finally died in Apollo's arms. With tears in his eyes, Apollo said, "Thou diest, Hyacinthus, robbed of thy youth, for me. Would that I could die for thee! But since that may not be, my lyre shall celebrate thee. My song shall tell thy fate, and thou shalt become a flower inscribed with my regret."

Immediately the blood on the ground ceased to be blood, and in its place sprang up a beautiful flower resembling a lily—the hyacinth.

ROME FALLS. Dotted lines on above map show the main routes by which the victorious Fifth Army forces entered Rome and smashed to the heart of the Eternal City to liquidate the Nazis' last point of resistance. This point is marked by arrow in photograph below. It was near the Emperor Trajan's Column—not far from the Colosseum, in background—that the Allies' final skirmish with the Nazis occurred.

ARROW SHOWS TRAJAN'S COLUMN, WHERE LAST NAZIS WERE ROUTED

U. S. SUB SABALO LAUNCHED

LAUNCHING At left is one of the two submarines launched at Cramp's Shipbuilding Co. yesterday. They were dedicated to the memory of Detective George Muhs, who lost his life in action with the Navy in 1942. A large number of policemen were invited to the ceremonies. Some are seen above with national, State and city officials.

The Philadelphia Inquirer

PUBLIC LEDGER

An Independent Newspaper for All the People

FINAL
CITY EDITION

CIRCULATION: May Average: Daily 496,780; Sunday 1,097,774

TUESDAY MORNING, JUNE 6, 1944

a b d e f g h ★★

THREE CENTS

FRANCE INVADED

Allied Troops Launch Mighty Offensive

Naval, Air Units In Giant Assault On Axis Europe

SUPREME HEADQUARTERS, ALLIED EXPEDITIONARY FORCE, June 6 (Tuesday), (A. P.). — General Dwight D. Eisenhower's headquarters announced today that Allied troops began landing on the northern coast of France this morning strongly supported by naval and air forces.

The Germans said the landings extended between Le Havre and Cherbourg along the south side of the bay of the Seine and along the northern Normandy coast.

Parachute troops descended in Normandy, Berlin said.

Berlin first announced the landings in a series of flashes that began about 6:30 A. M. (12:30 A. M., Philadelphia time).

The Allied communique was read over a trans-Atlantic hookup direct from General Eisenhower's headquarters at 3:32 (E.W.T.), designated "Communique No. 1."

A second announcement by the Supreme Headquarters said that "it is announced that General Sir Bernard L. Montgomery is in command of the army group carrying out the assault. This army group includes British, Canadian and United States forces."

The Allied communique did not say exactly where the invasion was taking place, but Berlin earlier gave these details:

Allied naval forces, including heavy warships, are shelling Le Havre. "It is a terrific bombardment," Berlin said.

Allied parachute troops floating down along the Normandy coast were landing and being engaged by German shock troops.

Other Allied units were streaming ashore into Normandy from landing barges.

LONDON, June 6 (Tuesday) (A. P.)—Three German news agencies tonight flashed word to the world that an Allied invasion of western France had begun with Allied parachute troops spilling out of the dawn skies over the Normandy peninsula and sea-borne forces landing in the Le Havre area.

There was no immediate Allied confirmation.

(The War Department in Washington said it had no information on any invasion.)

The Germans also said that Allied warships were furiously bombarding the big German-held French port of Le Havre at the mouth of the Seine River, 100 miles west of Paris.

German shock troops also were hurled against Allied troops rushing ashore from landing barges, tthe broadcasts said.

Le Havre lies 80 miles across the Channel from the British coast.

Dunkirk and Calais, just across the Channel coast from Britain, were under attack by strong formations of bombers, D. N. B., official German news agency, said.

BRITISH TELL DUTCH TO LEAVE HOMES

"The long-expected invasion by the British and Americans was begun in the first hours of the morning of June 6 by the landing of parachute troops in the area of the mouth of the Seine," declared the Transocean broadcast.

A spokesman for General Dwight D. Eisenhower, Supreme Allied Invasion Commander, told the people living on Europe's invasion coast early today that "a new phase of the Allied air offensive has started" and warned them to move inland to a depth of 35 kilometers (about 22 miles).

In a special broadcast, directed to France and other coastal countries, the spokesman said:

"A new phase of the air offensive has started. It will

Continued on Page 2, Column 2

WHERE ALLIES HAVE LAUNCHED INVASION OF EUROPE

Allied troops have opened their long-awaited invasion of Fortress Europe, General Dwight D. Eisenhower's headquarters announced this morning. The Germans report landings at Le Havre, at the mouth of the Seine River; Abbeville, at the estuary of the Somme; and other fighting on the Normandy Peninsula where parat-troops have also landed. Meanwhile, powerful Allied naval units are reported shelling Le Havre. The Germans report air attacks on Dunkirk and Calais.

Today

Solution for Germany
The Honorable Course
A People's Rebellion
Can't Draw Blueprint
Treatment as Adults

By Walter Lippmann

IN HIS address to the College of Cardinals just before the Allies entered Rome, the Pope spoke of "the courage of desperation" which is instilled into many Germans by their belief that we mean to "destroy national life to the very roots," and he asked that "this fear should give way to a well-founded expectation of honorable solutions."

The problem here is how deeply rooted in the national life of Germany are the power and the will to conquer. For this evil thing we must destroy to its very roots. Are the Germans right who say that if we uproot their militarism thoroughly, we shall thereby destroy not only Hitler's Reich, not only Bismarck's Reich, but the German nation?

If they are right, then there is no hope. If, as they argue, German nationality and German militarism are identical and inseparable, that they have the same roots, then how could an honorable solution be found?

An honorable solution must rest on the assumption that German militarism can be destroyed to its very roots without destroying the German nation. The corollary of that is the German nation must itself participate in the destruction of German militarism. If it does, it will not only make possible, but it will compel an honorable solution.

We should be deluding ourselves and the Germans as well if we pretended that we can know how to separate the peaceable Germans from the warlike. Only Germans by their own actions in uprooting militarism can draw this distinction.

If there is no German rebellion, if there is no German people's movement against their military institutions, the good and the bad Germans will all suffer together. For we shall be unable to tell them apart.

To destroy German militarism we cannot pause, as we did in 1918, when the occupied territories are liberated. We shall pursue the German army into Germany itself, and when

Continued on Page 12, Column 3

5th Army Chases Shattered Nazis North of Rome

By EDWARD KENNEDY

ROME, June 5 (A. P.).—Allied armor and motorized infantry roared through the Eternal City today—not pausing to sight-see—crossed the Tiber and proceeded with the grim task of destroying two battered German armies fleeing to the north.

Flashing forces of Allied fighter-bombers spearheaded the pursuit, jamming the escape highways northward with burning enemy transport and littering the fields with dead and wounded Nazis.

The enemy was tired, disorganized and bewildered by the slashing character of the Allied assault, which in 25 days had inflicted a major catastrophe on German forces in Italy and liberated Rome almost without damage to the historic city.

QUIT TIBER BANK

(The Vichy radio said Monday night the Germans had abandoned the entire left bank of the Tiber River from its mouth to Rome. Included in the area is the port of Ostia.)

Joining the relentless program of destruction, 500 American heavy bombers blasted rail yards at five points in northern Italy between Venice and Rimini through which the Germans might attempt to move reinforcements and equipment to bolster Marshal Albert Kesselring's beaten armies.

At 10 A. M. today Lieutenant General Mark W. Clark, commander of the victorious Fifth Army, entered Rome in a jeep and drove to the city hall, where he formally proclaimed the Allied occupation and praised the valor of his troops.

20,000 NAZI PRISONERS

Addressing his corps commanders and looking out over thousands of cheering Italians, General Clark declared that both the 10th and 14th German Armies had been at least partially destroyed, more than 20,000

Continued on Page 2, Column 4

Victor Emmanuel Yields Power To His Son

By CLINTON B. CONGER

NAPLES, June 5 (U. P.).—King Victor Emmanuel III of Italy today signed over his royal powers to Crown Prince Humbert as Lieutenant General of the Realm, carrying out his pledge to Allied officials that he would give up the royal authority he has held for nearly 44 years when Allied troops liberated Rome.

The King did not abdicate his throne. A formal statement said that he had turned over all his powers "without exception" to Humbert, who would hold them "irrevocably" as long as he lives, but that Victor Emmanuel would remain King of Italy and head of the House of Savoy.

KEEPS PLEDGE

The historic documents were signed at 3 P. M. in the King's closely-guarded villa at Ravello. The action carried out to the letter his April 12 pledge to the Allies that "this appointment (of Humbert as Lieutenant General) will become effective by a formal transfer of power on the day on which Allied troops enter Rome."

The swift transfer of power came as a surprise to Naples political

Continued on Page 2, Column 7

Italy Repudiates Pact With Vichy

NEW YORK, June 5 (A. P.).—The Algiers radio said tonight the Italian Council of Ministers had adopted unanimously today a decree "to declare null and void the armistice agreement between the Vichy regime of Petain and Mussolini."

British Cargo Ship Sunk by U-Boat

WASHINGTON, June 5 (A. P.).—A medium-sized British merchant vessel was torpedoed and sunk by an enemy submarine in the Atlantic early in May, the Navy announced today.

4th Term, C.I.O. Pins Found in Bond Buttons

LOS ANGELES, June 5 (A. P.).—Several "Roosevelt for Fourth Term" buttons and others indorsing the C. I. O. were found today in a shipment of lapel pins sent here to promote the Fifth War Loan drive, and immediately an "it-is-all-a-mistake" explanation was forthcoming.

Robert H. Moulton, War Loan Committee chairman, said "four or five" Roosevelt buttons, bearing the President's picture, and "one or two" C. I. O. pins were found in a shipment of 200 000 Bond buttons sent here from a Rochester, N. Y., factory.

GIRL MADE ERROR

Mr. Moulton communicated with W. J. Heinrich, local agent for the factory, who telephoned its vice president, Frank Brown, and then issued this statement:

"He (Brown) told me it is all a mistake and was due to some girl packer reaching in the wrong bin for buttons. We have been making buttons for anybody who wants them for the last 50 years. We are not interested in promoting anybody.

"We have all kinds of orders and the mistake was made in the packing room. We will replace all of them with Treasury Department buttons."

No comment was forthcoming from War Loan or Treasury Department officials.

2d Report Hinted On Pearl Harbor

By HUGH MORROW

Inquirer Washington Bureau

WASHINGTON, June 5.—Charges that a "second Roberts report" on the Pearl Harbor disaster was hidden away in the archives were aired on the House floor today as the greatest naval catastrophe in American history became a major election year issue.

Republicans spearheaded a drive to force court-martial proceedings within the next three months against Rear Admiral Husband E. Kimmel and Major General Walter C. Short, which they declared would reveal facts about Pearl Harbor said to be hidden away in the alleged "second report" by the investigating commission which was headed by Supreme Court Justice Owen J. Roberts.

REP. SHORT IS ACCUSER

On the other hand, Representative John W. McCormack (D., Mass.), House Democratic leader, declared the court-martial should be delayed until after the national election this fall because "we should eliminate as much emotional reac-

Continued on Page 6, Column 1

Hardest Fight Ahead, F. D. R. Warns Nation

Text of President Roosevelt's Address on Page 4

By WILLIAM C. MURPHY, JR.

Inquirer Washington Bureau

WASHINGTON, June 5.—President Roosevelt told the Nation tonight that the capture of Rome had placed the Allies "one up and two to go" in the matter of captured Axis capitals, but at the same time sounded a warning that much hard fighting remained before Germany was rendered incapable of starting a new war of conquest a generation hence.

"The victory still lies some distance ahead," Mr. Roosevelt said in a Nation-wide radio broadcast. "That distance will be covered in due time—have no fear of that. But it will be tough and it will be costly."

PROSPECT OF RELIEF

At the same time the President held out to the Italian people the prospect that no effort or expense would be spared to provide speedy relief and rehabilitation in Italy.

And, taunting Adolf Hitler on his announcement that the Nazi hordes had been withdrawn from Rome to spare the cultural and religious monuments of the Italian capital,

Continued on Page 4, Column 6

U. S. WEATHER FORECAST

Philadelphia and vicinity: Partly cloudy and warmer today and tomorrow.

Sun rises 5.33 A. M. Sets 8.26 P. M.
Moon rises 8.23 P. M. Sets 5.36 A. M.

Escort Carrier Lost in Atlantic

By JOHN M. McCULLOUGH

Inquirer Washington Bureau

WASHINGTON, June 5.—The Navy today announced the loss of the escort aircraft carrier Block Island in the Atlantic last month "as the result of enemy action."

Casualties in the sinking, which apparently was the result of U-boat action, were light, the communique said. Among the survivors was Commander Francis Massie Hughes, 45, of Alabama, commander of the "baby flat-top."

The Block Island was the first American aircraft carrier announced lost in the Atlantic in the war. However, a number of armed merchant

Continued on Page 3, Column 5

Gen. Clark Named 'Father of Year'

NEW YORK, June 5 (A. P.).—Lieutenant General Mark W. Clark, whose Fifth Army troops took Rome, was designated Father of the Year" today, the National Father's Day Committee announced.

1250 U. S. Planes Rip French Coast

By WALTER CRONKITE

LONDON, June 6 (Tuesday) (U. P.).—The French invasion coast, shaken by 13,000 tons of bombs in four days of Allied air attack, was hammered Monday by 1250 United States heavy bombers and fighters which concentrated on the Boulogne and Calais areas, and last night Royal Air Force heavy bombers went out unusually early on their regular nightly missions against Axis Europe.

The R.A.F. heavy bombers, in strength, bombed enemy-occupied territory, it was announced authoritatively.

Monday's operations generally were held down by poor weather.

At least 2500 Allied planes had preceded them toward Axis Europe during Monday despite weather conditions, most of them attacking targets in France. U. S. Flying Fortresses and Liberators dropped some 2250 tons of bombs. They encountered no enemy fighters, but six heavy bombers and two fighters were missing.

Throughout the day, these planes

Continued on Page 2, Column 1

Combat Troops To Garrison Rome

ROME, June 5 (U. P.).—The honor of garrisoning Rome will go to doughboys who have seen heavy combat throughout the Italian campaign, it was announced today by Major General Harry Johnson, who heads the Rome area.

General Johnson said he felt that only fighting men deserved the privilege and restful assignment of keeping order in Rome.

First Pictures of the Allied Invasion of Europe

(Official U. S. Coast Guard Photo from A. P. Wirephoto)

ON WAY The Allied invasion armada, guarded by barrage balloons, plowing through the English Channel to the northern coast of France for the long-awaited invasion of Hitler's "Fortress Europe." The large cables in the foreground are anchors for the balloons attached to the landing craft. This photo was radioed from England to New York yesterday.

(Official U. S. Army Photo from A. P. Wirephoto)

INVASION MARCH Carrying full packs and large allotments of ammunition, American soldiers march down the street of a British port to their waiting landing craft. This photo was radioed from England a few hours after the landings in France were announced.

(Official U. S. Army Photo from A. P. Wirephoto)

D-DAY SAILING Landing craft, loaded with American troops and guarded by barrage balloons, riding the calm waters of the English Channel as they put forth from the British coast for the invasion of France. Note the American flag flying from one of the ships.

(Official U. S. Army Photo from A. P. Wirephoto)

ON DECK Admiral Sir Bertram Ramsay (left), Allied naval commander-in-chief, watching from the deck of a ship as the invasion armada takes off from England for its trip across the Channel to beaches in France.

(Official U. S. Army Photo from A. P. Wirephoto)

PARATROOPS Smoking, chatting, smiling or just sitting wrapped in thought, these heavily-armed American paratroops are shown in a transport plane as they soared over the English Channel on their way to play a key part in the invasion of France. They are in thick of battle.

WILL STRIKE A NEW NOTE IN HER CINEMA CAREER
Deanna Durbin will be seen in her first dramatic role, the wife of a murderer, when "Christmas Holiday" becomes the feature at the Boyd Thursday.

AMUSEMENTS
STAGE, SCREEN AND MUSIC
The Philadelphia Inquirer

S O 8 SUNDAY, JULY 16, 1944 a e

CALL BOY'S CHAT

Mae West's Ornate Role As Empress

Offers History, Little Hilarity, As Catherine II

By Linton Martin

Considering the respective reputations of Mae West as actress and author, and Catherine the Great as empress, the combination of the two in a play certainly seemed a "natural" for bedroom farce.

Perhaps bedroom farce trimmed with the royal ermine of Russia's insatiably amorous empress, but basically bedroom farce. Especially since five of the 12 scenes of "Catherine Was Great," which the versatile Miss West wrote for herself, are up in Catherine's room, to say nothing of whatever implications might be taken from the title of the eyeful of an offering which Michael Todd opulently unveiled for the first time anywhere at the Forrest last Monday.

Even the prologue, which shows soldiers in a U. S. O. recreation center of today discussing the celebrated man-mad monarch, gives a broad hint of sultry scenes to follow, when one of the boys tells how his mother burned his book about Catherine, adding that "the kitchen stove has never been so hot since." But why the kitchen stove got so hot isn't apparent in the play, which certainly isn't so hot, or even tepid in its temperature.

Temperature Is Tepid

Leopards may not change their spots, but Miss West has certainly changed her style in "Catherine Was Great." The most amazing thing about it is that it was produced by the pen of the playwright who wrote "Diamond Lil," "Sex," "The Drag," "Pleasure Man," "The Constant Sinner," "The Wicked Age," and "I'm No Angel," as well as acting in them.

For one of those, the police tumbril, as was recently recalled in this column, backed up to the stage door and clamped Miss West in clink. On another occasion, one of Miss West's plays was abruptly banned after its opening in Washington, D. C., as genial Eddie Rosenbaum, now of the screen and once of the stage publicity departments, ruefully recounted to your Call Boy after the opening of "Catherine Was Great." That was when, said Eddie, he told Mr. Shubert he had done many things for him, but, by jimminy, he wouldn't risk going to jail by going on with the show by defying the order to close after the opening.

Whatever else happens to it, Miss West's present play will never create that kind of commotion. Nor will it ever land her in jail.

History the Hard Way

Even the more or less leering lines of "Catherine Was Great" sound almost primly self-conscious and coy, inhibited and artificial, as though Miss West felt she had to give her play the trademark tag expected of her as author and actress. Some remarks are deliberately made with a double meaning, it is true. And in one scene, one of her admirers scrambles into the already occupied royal couch. But ribald and rowdy the play is not. It's an overstuffed turkey of historical drama.

Obviously Miss West approached her play with lots of conscientious research. And also obviously, on the

Continued on Page 9, Column 1

THREE VAUDEVILLIANS POOL THEIR TALENTS FOR A SERVICE CANTEEN
Jimmy Durante, June Allyson and Gloria DeHaven, lifelong friends in show business, have a little rehearsal in "Two Girls and a Sailor," the current film feature on the Stanley screen.

HOLLYWOOD

Diana Lynn, Hollywood's 'Brat', Goes Glamorous

By Louella O. Parsons

HOLLYWOOD, July 15.—Diana Lynn, who has been everyone's kid sister in movies on the Paramount lot, has at long last gone glamorous. The dazzling young lady with the blonde curls and the black lace form-fitting dress looked anything but the awkward-age brat, when I paid her a visit on the set of "Out of This World."

She was all dolled up for her role of leader of a girl orchestra and loved it. Diana, aged 17, is young enough to get a kick out of looking pretty, and I think she can be pardoned if she preened a bit and acted grown up. My visit to Diana was made at the request of some 100 or more readers of my column, who demanded I do an interview with this very popular young lady.

I make it a point to please special requests from young people of 'teen age because these are the most avid motion picture fans. So here goes: Diana first made a place in the hearts of these youthful fans in "The Major and the Minor," and then again when she was Betty Hutton's kid sister in "The Miracle of Morgan's Creek."

Tired of 'Brat' Roles

"I have played so many brats," she told me, "that I want to get away from that type of role."

"What do you want to do?" I asked.

"Well," she said, "Helen Hayes is my favorite actress and I want to do serious plays—dramas—and not confine myself to comedy."

Diana believes she should have a season of summer stock and when she is older is going to try the stage via the "Cape Cod Route."

I asked what she did in her leisure time—if she danced or had dates.

She said, "Oh, of course I have dates, but I don't go to night clubs. I like to dance—not those rapid, crazy jitterbug steps, but calm dancing."

There is a great deal of dignity in this 17-year-old, who has spent most of her years studying the piano. Her mother, a piano teacher, saw to it she practiced five to six hours a day with the result that any time she tires of movies she can be a concert pianist. Few people realized what a finished musician Diana is until she played with the juvenile symphony orchestra last year.

"My music really brought me into pictures," she said. "When Susanna Foster was making 'There's Magic in Music' I was 13 and Paramount wanted some children who had musical background. I went to play the accompaniment for a girl violinist and remained to play a piano solo of my own."

Took New Name

"There's Magic in Music" was made under Diana's real name of Dolly Roehr. "I didn't like the name Dolly," she confided, "and I wanted a name that was easier to pronounce, so I became Diana Lynn."

This native Californian was born in Los Angeles and went to school there.

She said, "my last years in high school were spent with private teachers, but I did graduate with my class."

She didn't take a flying leap to fame. After one picture there was a long wait before any director would give her a chance.

"I was at the awkward age, all feet and hands, and I thought I had made a mistake to try to be a movie actress. Then, when Ginger Rogers made 'The Major and the Minor,' William Wyler had me play the tiresome sister with the highbrow notions—a sort of glorified brat."

Well, you know the rest. Diana had one of the top roles in "Our Hearts Were Young and Gay" and she is Dorothy Lamour's sister in "And the Angels Sing."

If the publicity department had its way she would be the biggest star on the lot. They are all pulling for her because, as one of them said, "she has never had her head turned, and she is just a regular girl."

THE PLAYBILL

'Lightnin'', Bucks; 'Catherine' Stays

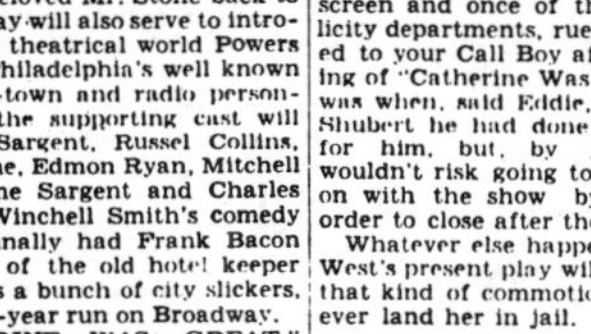

"LIGHTNIN'," starring FRED STONE will open at the Bucks County Playhouse in the Bellevue tomorrow night. Besides bringing the much beloved Mr. Stone back to town the play will also serve to introduce to the theatrical world Powers Gouraud, Philadelphia's well known man-about-town and radio personality. In the supporting cast will be Brent Sargent, Russel Collins, Viola Roache, Edmon Ryan, Mitchell Harris, Anne Sargent and Charles Parsons. Winchell Smith's comedy which originally had Frank Bacon in the role of the old hotel keeper who outwits a bunch of city slickers, had a three-year run on Broadway.

"CATHERINE WAS GREAT," with and by MAE WEST, produced by Michael Todd, continues at the Forrest. The cast includes Joel Ashley, Charles Gerrard, William Davis, Coburn Goodwin, Ray Bourbon and many others.

"LITTLE WOMEN," a dramatization of Louisa May Alcott's famous story, starring MADGE EVANS and featuring Julie Haydon, will be the attraction at the Bucks County Playhouse in the Bellevue beginning June 24.

"EARLY TO BED," a musical comedy with book and lyrics by George Marion, Jr., and music by the late Thomas "Fats" Waller, is scheduled for the Forrest July 31. Doris Patston and Joseph Macaulay, have the leading roles.

CONTINUES TO REIGN
Mae West in "Catherine Was Great," now at the Forrest Theater.

A DEAR OLD DARLING
Fred Stone, star of "Lightnin'", Bucks Co. in Bellevue tomorrow.

FILM TIMES TODAY

Movie Bills Of the Week; Future Films

ALDINE—"Snow White and the Seven Dwarfs," revival, Walt Disney cartoon-fairy tale. 2.35, 4.30, 6.20, 8.10, 10.

ARCADIA—"The Mask of Dimitrios," melodrama, with Sydney Greenstreet, Peter Lorre, Zachary Scott. 2.20, 4.15, 6.10, 8.05, 10.

BOYD—"Once Upon a Time," comedy-fantasy, with Cary Grant, Ted Donaldson, Janet Blair. 2.40, 4.30, 6.20, 8.10, 10.

CAPITOL — "Gambler's Choice," drama, with Chester Morris, Nancy Kelly, Russell Hayden. 3.05, 7.40, 10. Also "Attack!"

EARLE (Today only) "Two Girls and a Sailor," 2.50, 5.10, 7.30, 9.50 (Daily) "Take It Big," musical, with Arline Judge, Jack Haley, Harriet Hilliard, Patricia Morison, Glen Gray and orchestra on stage.

FOX—"Double Indemnity," melodrama, starring Barbara Stanwyck, Fred MacMurray, Edward G. Robinson. 2.10, 4.05, 6.05, 8, 10.

KARLTON—"Up In Arms," musical, starring Danny Kaye and Dinah Shore. 2.15, 4.15, 6.10, 8.05, 10.10.

KEITH'S—"Up in Mabel's Room," comedy, with Dennis O'Keefe, Gail Patrick, Marjorie Reynolds. 3, 4.45, 6.30, 8.15, 10.05.

MASTBAUM—"Going My Way," comedy, starring Bing Crosby, Barry Fitzgerald, Rise Stevens. 2.35, 5.05, 7.30, 10.

NEWS—"Love Is News," comedy, starring Tyrone Power, Loretta Young, Don Ameche. 2.10, 3.50, 5.25, 7, 8.35, 10.10, 11.50, all night.

STANLEY—"Two Girls and a Sailor," musical, with Gloria De Haven, Van Johnson, June Allyson, Jimmy Durante. 2.40, 5.10, 7.35, 10.

STANTON "Cobra Woman," melodrama, starring Maria Montez, Jon Hall, Sabu. 2.40, 4.30, 6.20, 8.10, 10.

STUDIO "A Bill of Divorcement," revival, starring John Barrymore, Katharine Hepburn, Billie Burke. 3.10, 5.40, 8.05, 10.30. Also "Winterset."

TRANS-LUX—Newsreels, shorts, hour-long bill, starting at 2.

TOMORROW

NEWS "Wake Up and Live," musical, with Alice Faye, Jack Haley, Walter Winchell.

WEDNESDAY

ALDINE—"The Canterville Ghost," drama, starring Charles Laughton, Margaret O'Brien, Robert Young.

CAPITOL—"The Monster Maker," chiller, with J. Carrol Naish, Ralph Morgan, Wanda McKay.

THURSDAY

BOYD — "Christmas Holiday," drama, starring Deanna Durbin, Gene Kelly, Richard Whorf.

FRIDAY

EARLE—"Song of the Open Road," comedy, with Jane Powell, Edgar Bergen, Charlie McCarthy, W. C. Fields, June Preisser, Lois Andrews, Ada Leonard and orchestra on stage.

KARLTON — "Gaslight," melodrama, staring Ingrid Bergman, Charles Boyer, Joseph Cotten.

KEITH'S—"Home in Indiana," drama, with Walter Brennan, Lon McCallister, Jeanne Crain.

ARCADIA—"The White Cliffs of Dover," drama, starring Irene Dunne, Alan Marshal, Frank Morgan.

SATURDAY

STANTON "Secret Command," melodrama, with Pat O'Brien, Carole Landis, Ruth Warrick.

UNDATED

STANLEY "The Story of Dr. Wassell," war drama, with Gary Cooper, Laraine Day, Signe Hasso, Dennis O'Keefe, Carol Thurston.

FOX—"Step Lively," comedy, with Frank Sinatra, Gloria De Haven, George Murphy, Adolphe Menjou.

MASTBAUM "The Adventures of Mark Twain," biography, starring Fredric March and Alexis Smith.

STUDIO—"Roberta," revival, starring Ginger Rogers, Fred Astaire, Irene Dunne. Also "Little Women," with Katharine Hepburn, Paul Lukas, Joan Bennett.

CAMERA ANGLES

Barbara Stanwyck Scores In Tale of Modern Borgia

By Mildred Martin

No one can accuse the movies of not having at least tried to do something about the heat wave. And if they weren't able to affect the mercury much, a couple of newcomers have certainly succeeded in taking a perspiring public's mind off its torrid troubles for an hour or so anyway.

Like "Gaslight," "Double Indemnity" carries its own cooling system with it in the form of melodramatic chills as it spins a yarn of murder which, according to one of the characters most deeply involved, "smelled like honeysuckle."

As for "Two Girls and a Sailor," this latest Joe Pasternak musical is such gay, gracious, good-humored entertainment, so packed with tunes and talent, that only the most determined crosspatch could fail to be charmed by it.

Fans with long memories will probably recall that just a few years ago Hollywood found James M. Cain's "The Postman Always Rings Twice" much too hot to handle. And after the screen rights had been acquired, too. Now, however, another of Mr. Cain's lethal ladies is on the prowl, and to our mind, she makes a sissy out of the wife who wanted to get rid of her Greek lunchroom proprietor spouse in "The Postman."

Fascinatingly Grisly

Billy Wilder, who directed and helped write the screenplay for "Double Indemnity," hasn't pulled any punches in turning this into one of the toughest, most hard-boiled and, in its way, one of the most fascinatingly grisly film excursions of many seasons. For here before one's eyes is a clinical study of a human female spider at work; at work and at play, one might say.

Just as Bette Davis is at her best when she gets the screen chance to be bad, so Barbara Stanwyck really swings into stride with a role that makes no concessions to sweetness and light. And certainly there is nothing either sweet or light about her playing of Phyllis Dietrichson, the monstrous heroine of this tale of a carefully, coldly planned murder for money.

Startling Portrait

With brassy hair to match the brassy nerve of this modern Borgia, and with a steely glitter in her eyes, Miss Stanwyck draws a startling portrait of a conscienceless killer who capitalizes on her feminine charms for her own devious ends. As a nurse, she had contrived the death of her patient in order to marry the woman's husband. As wife, she plots with a dazzled, weak-willed insurance salesman to take out an accident policy with a double indemnity clause in her husband's name and then, by seduction and threat, forces the agent to kill her unsuspecting victim.

As a sideline, Phyllis also does what she can to dispose of her uncomfortably suspicious step-daughter. And finaly, when the going gets tough and the net spun by a wily claims agent begins to tighten, she pulls a gun on the unhappy insurance man whom she had used and ruined in her murderous game.

Pungent Direction

It is, as you may imagine, a role into which Miss Stanwyck can sink her teeth and it is apparent, following a series of parts with no particular distinction or color, that Miss Stanwyck is enjoying herself immensely while counting on her fans to appreciate her recaptured and too long submerged gifts as one of the screen's better dramatic actresses.

Mr. Wilder's pungent direction and writing are not only extremely valuable in re-establishing Miss Stanwyck in the niche she never should have left, but they are of great assistance to Fred MacMurray and Edward G. Robinson. As the insurance salesman lost from the moment he meets the towel-clad heroine, Mr. MacMurray has what must have been the extremely welcome opportunity to do a right-about-face from his usual film characterizations.

And Mr. Robinson, whose recent pictures have been considerably less than memorable, strides back to power and the prominence he deserves with his playing of the stocky, stubborn claims agent whose tenacity and bulldog mind worry the threads of a presumably perfect crime until it falls apart.

That lighter side is amply taken care of, of course, by the already mentioned "Two Girls and a Sailor." Upon the slightest thread of fabulous romantic plot all about a pair of cute little night club sisters, a likeable sailor with a 60 million dollar fortune tucked away and the service canteen he anonymously backs for the girls, Producer Pasternak and Director Richard Thorpe have whipped up one of the season's most delightful musicals.

On the Lighter Side

Surrounded, but not submerged, by more varied talent than one might think could be crowded comfortably into a single film, Gloria De Haven, June Allyson and Van Johnson bring bubbling youth and charm to the title roles. And there's literally something for everybody in the assorted specialties and specialists fitted so deftly into the broad outline of the picture as a whole.

You pay your money and, since they're all there, you don't have to make any choice even if you could among such gifted people as Jimmy Durante, Lena Horne and Harry James; Jose Iturbi, Virginia O'Brien and Xavier Cugat; Gracie Allen, Albert Coates, Ben Blue and Maestro Iturbi's pianist sister, Ampara Novarro.

Shuffle them all together and you get "Two Girls and a Sailor." Who could ask for anything more?

AT THE DELL

3 Conductors, 5 Soloists Are Featured

This week Robin Hood Dell will present to its patrons three well known conductors and five popular soloists in programs of diversified appeal ranging from the classics to the operetta field.

Tomorrow night Dean Dixon, prominent young Negro conductor, will preside at the conductor's stand and Anne Brown, Negro soprano, and Todd Duncan, Negro baritone, will be the soloists. Mr. Dixon has had appearances with the N B C symphony orchestra, the New York Philharmonic and other major symphonic organizations. Miss Brown and Mr. Duncan will be remembered for their roles in the original production of George Gershwin's "Porgy and Bess" and they will sing several selections from this melodious work. Miss Brown will also be heard in the "Gavotte" from "Manon" and "Pleurez, pleurez Mes Yeux" from "Le Cid", both by Massenet, and Mr. Duncan will sing "Vision Fugitive" from Massenet's "Herodiade" and the spiritual "Walk with Me." The orchestral selections will include compositions by Gershwin, Bach-Franko, Tchaikovsky, and Wolf-Ferrari.

Vladimir Golschmann, conductor of the St. Louis Symphony Orchestra, will pay a return visit to the Dell beginning Tuesday night, and is scheduled to lead most of the concerts during the final three weeks of this season. An all-Russian program will be presented featuring the Symphony No. 5 in E minor of Tchaikovsky and including the Overture to "Russian and Ludmilla" by Glinka; Mussorgsky's "A Night on Bald Mountain" and the colorful "Capriccio Espagnole" by Rimsky-Korsakoff.

Romberg 'Pop' Concert

A program definitely on the melodious and popular beat will be heard on Thursday night when composer-conductor Sigmund Romberg will direct one of his typical "Pop"

Continued on Page 9, Column 4

TWO STARS IN A MURDER MYSTERY
Barbara Stanwyck and Fred MacMurray in "Double Indemnity," present screen feature at the Fox.

The Philadelphia Inquirer

PUBLIC LEDGER

An Independent Newspaper for All the People

FINAL CITY EDITION

CIRCULATION: June Average: Daily 507,034; Sunday 1,077,659

SATURDAY MORNING, JULY 22, 1944

Copyright, 1944, by Triangle Publications, Inc. Vol. 231, No. 22

abdefgh★

THREE CENTS

Rebellion Reported Raging in Germany, Navy Units Mutiny, 100 Generals Slain

Truman Wins Nomination on 2d Ballot

Today

Fighting in Normandy
St. Lo Flattened
Bad Tank Country
Discipline Is Vital
Foot Soldiers' Job

—By Ivan H. Peterman—
Inquirer War Correspondent
By Wireless
Copyright, 1944, The Philadelphia Inquirer

AMERICAN FORCES HEADQUARTERS IN NORMANDY, July 21.

"ST. LO is picturesquely situated on the Vire River and makes a pleasant center for excursions," says Muirhead's Blue Guidebook of Normandy. Mr. Muirhead can start revising his book any day now.

The beaten-up remains of this dairyland capital of 10,000 population, firmly held by elements of our 115th and 134th Infantry regiments, these days is like a score of other towns in the Allies' wake: It's flat. It has been flattened by our bombs and shells, and is taking an additional beating from German mortars and shells which pitch into the town hourly from heights to the south.

But St. Lo, like La Haye du Puits on the other flank, is ours, and the Allied position grows stronger daily. But the price paid hasn't yet been told.

Before passing to other sectors of the 50-mile American front, it might be interesting to review the type of fighting and the method necessary to seize St. Lo. As the Germans' vital crossroads and communication center, where troops were deployed for the defense of the Cotentin peninsula, St. Lo is possibly more important to the Allies than even Cherbourg or Caen. It certainly was defended fiercely.

To take it, not only the regiments mentioned but many others participated, for everyone now understands that battle is sometimes won at spots seemingly not related to the main objective.

Such was the case of the major general who philosophized at the lunch table under the tent of his far advanced headquarters the other day, recalling his old Central High School days in Philadelphia (his wife lives in Llanerch and his mother near Swarthmore, Pa.).

This commanding officer described his comparatively new but brilliant outfit, which was in

Continued on Page 8, Column 2

Wallace Buried Under Landslide Vote for Senator

Illustrated on Page 8

By WILLIAM C. MURPHY, JR.
Inquirer Convention Bureau.

CHICAGO, July 21.—Senator Harry S. Truman of Missouri was nominated by the Democratic National Convention tonight to be President Roosevelt's Vice Presidetnial running-mate in the fourth term campaign.

In a riotous all-day closing session of the convention, Senator Truman overcame a first ballot lead held by Vice President Henry A. Wallace and was nominated by the landslide vote of 1100 to 66 for Mr. Wallace. Other candidates received scattered votes on the second and final ballot tabulation.

Mr. Wallace, supported by a coalition of the so-called liberal wing of the New Deal and the C. I. O. Political Action Committee, had led on the first ballot by 429½ to 319½ for the Missouri Senator, with 589 required for nomination.

THANKS CONVENTION

Immediately after he had been declared the nominee "and next Vice President of the United States," in the words of Senator Samuel D. Jackson, of Indiana, the convention chairman, Senator Truman took the speakers' stand to announce his acceptance and to thank the convention for the honor.

It was an honor, he said, which carried with it "a very great responsibility which I am perfectly willing to assume."

PRIMARY OBJECTIVE

His primary objective, the Vice Presidential nomnee declared, would be "to help shorten the war and win the peace under our great leader, Franklin D. Roosevelt."

Senator Truman's victory was accomplished with the assistance of a coalition of anti-Wallace Southern Democratic delegates and the big city political machines from which the Democrats have drawn so much of their strength in recent elections.

Advocates of both Mr. Wallace and Senator Truman claimed that their candidates had the support of the President. The Wallace claim was based upon a letter written July 14 by the President stating that if he were a delegate he would vote for Mr. Wallace's renomination because he liked and respected the Vice President and was his personal friend.

NO DESIRE TO DICTATE

In that letter, however, the President added that he did not wish to dictate the choice of his running

Continued on Page 5, Column 1

Guffey Missed 'Truman Boat,' Delegates Say

By JOSEPH H. MILLER
Inquirer Convention Bureau

CHICAGO, July 21.—Pennsylvania's delegation to the Democratic National Convention tonight lost an opportunity to capture the credit for putting across Senator Harry S. Truman, of Missouri, as the party's Vice Presidential nominee.

And, throughout the entire delegation of 72 members, the blame was placed upon United States Senator Joseph F. Guffey, who failed to release 46 delegates backing Vice President Henry A. Wallace on the first two rollcalls in time to hop aboard the Truman bandwagon.

The Missouri Senator polled 23½ Pennsylvania votes on the first ballot and 24 on the second.

RULED OUT OF ORDER

Even when it was apparent that Senator Truman had more than a majority of 1176 delegates, the Pennsylvanians who had followed Mr. Guffey's leadership in supporting Vice President Wallace stood mute.

Only after the Truman stampede was so great that a child could have sensed the Missourian had been nominated, did Senator Guffey act.

Then Senator Guffey, spearhead of the Wallace drive, sought to make Senator Truman's nomination unanimous, but he was ruled out of order. A few minutes later he announced 70 Pennsylvania votes for Mr. Truman. Two were not

Continued on Page 5, Column 3

(A. P. Wirephoto)

WINS VICE PRESIDENTIAL NOMINATION

Senator Harry S. Truman (right), of Missouri, smiling broadly as he shakes hands with Senator Pat McCarran, of Nevada, when the balloting started for the Democratic Vice Presidential candidate at the convention yesterday. Senator Truman was nominated on the second ballot, defeating Vice President Henry A. Wallace.

Reds Capture Ostrov, Surge Over Bug River

Map on Page 2; Picture on Page 8

By ALEXANDER KENDRICK
Inquirer War Correspondent
(By Wireless)
Copyright, 1944, The Philadelphia Inquirer

Against a background denoting the increasingly serious condition in Germany, Soviet forces today climaxed their month-long summer offensive by capturing Ostrov, gateway to Latvia and Estonia and by developing Marshal Rokossovsky's breakthrough in the Kovel sector. The Polish-born marshal, whose troops reached and crossed the western Bug River, is heading directly for Warsaw via Lublin.

At the same time the great German fortresses at Lwow and Brest Litvosk are outflanked by Soviet forces streaming past on both sides. Both big cities may resist for some time, with bitter street fighting in prospect, but their fall is reckoned only a matter of days.

BACKGROUND OF REVOLT

The forward surge of the Red Army along the entire Eastern Front provides a proper perspective for what has happened in Germany in the past 24 hours.

Whether the so-called assassination plot against Hitler was real or merely a staged repetition of the Reichstag fire incident, this time with Junkers instead of Communists as the target, there is no doubt that a major purge—the most far reaching since June 30, 1934—is now taking place in the Reich.

Details are, of course, still sparse but whether the Junker generals are being purged for real or merely anticipated opposition to Hitler leadership, there is a definite connection between these internal develop-

Continued on Page 2, Column 4

Yanks Smash Inland to Ring Big Guam Port

Jap Resistance Stiffens as U. S. Troops Advance

Map on Page 3

By CHARLES H. McMURTRY

PEARL HARBOR, July 21 (A. P.).—The invasion of Guam is going well, Admiral Chester W. Nimitz reported tonight, and front line dispatches disclosed the invaders were moving in from beachheads on either side of Port Apra, one of the finest in the Pacific.

Admiral Nimitz, reporting only light casualties sustained in actual landings and stiffening resistance as the Marines and soldiers moved into the interior, made no mention of where the Yanks struck.

LAND ON WEST COAST

But from a warship at Guam, John R. Henry, representing the combined Allied Press, disclosed the landings were on Guam's west coast on either side of the fine harbor.

Henry said one beachhead was below the Orote peninsula which forms the southern arm of the port. In that area, the town of Agat was described as "shattered" by the 17 straight days of warship and plane attacks.

HINGED ON ASAM

The northern beachhead above the port was reported by Henry to be hinged on the town of Asan.

(The location of the beachheads indicated the invaders intended to sweep behind and pinch off the harbor area.)

Henry said the northern beachhead "stretched in an arc of several thousand yards" and that the southern beachhead was "substantial."

17-DAY POUNDING

The front line dispatch said the 17-day attack loosed 10,000 tons of explosives on Guam—battleships moved in close with their heavy guns in the final stages—and the preparation was so effective that the progress so far exceeded all expectations.

Rear Admiral Richard L. Conolly, commanding the operations, said this was the smoothest of all Pacific landings to date.

Tanks were on the beaches within a few hours after the dawn landings

Continued on Page 3, Column 2

'Mystery' Radio Calls on Army to Overthrow Hitler

War Summary on Page 2; Pictures on Pages 2 and 8

By ALEX SINGLETON

LONDON, July 22 (Saturday) (A. P.).—A self-styled rebel German officer insisted today that a full-scale revolt against Adolf Hitler's regime was continuing, while a welter of reports said the vengeful Gestapo had slaughtered some of the most illustrious figures in the Army, and the Nazis themselves admitted the broad scope of the conspiracy even as they claimed to be firmly in control.

(Swiss dispatches, quoted by the United Press, said German naval units had mutinied at the important bases of Kiel and Stettin, and that a virtual civil war was raging throughout the Reich where thousands of persons were said to have been arrested.

4 NAZI MARSHALS BELIEVED SHOT

The dead in a blood purge by which the shaken Nazi chiefs sought to retain power included Field Marshals Walther von Brauchitsch, Karl Gerd von Rundstedt, Sigmund Wilhelm List and Fritz Erich von Mannstein, according to reports via Switzerland from unconfirmed but usually reliable sources.

Travelers reaching Sweden also said there were many well-known names among at least 100 generals executed after the unsuccessful attempt to assassinate Hitler Thursday.

(The United Press reported the travelers were relaying rumors that whole German regiments had been shot in East Prussia for their attempts to mutiny. Some were quoted as believing that Germany's collapse could not long be delayed because of the desperate situation inside the country.)

MYSTERY RADIO VOICES WARNING

Early this morning, after the German home radio had shut down, a mysterious speaker on the Frankfurt station's wavelength called for attention and announced that "by order of the commander of the Army Group of Resistance" he was empowered to state that although Colonel Count Claus von Stauffenberg, the man who planted the bomb that almost killed Hitler, had paid with his life, this was only "the first blow," and declared:

"Let Hitler know this much for certain—there is more than one Stauffenberg. Stauffenbergs are here in the thousands."

'RELENTLESS BATTLE AGAINST HITLER'

He admitted the "initial action attempt against Hitler's life has failed," but insisted, "the general action continues. We German officers are waging a battle against Hitler and

Continued on Page 2, Column 6

Casualties

La Salle Athlete Killed in Action

Second Lieutenant Clarence A. Stearns, Jr., former La Salle High School athlete, was killed in action in France on June 10, his wife, the former Mary Elizabeth Birk, and his parents, Mr. and Mrs. Clarence A. Stearns, of 2467 78th ave., have been informed by the War Department.

The dead officer's wife, whose home is in Bethlehem, where Lieutenant Stearns attended Lehigh University, is living with his parents.

Both of the 22-year-old lieutenant's parents are veterans of World War I. His father was a major in the Army, while his mother served with the Army Nurses Corps.

Lieutenant and Mrs. Stearns were married Feb. 25, 1943, in Allentown.

Besides his wife and parents, he is survived by a brother, Private John Stearns with the Army at Indiantown Gap.

Other casualties:

KILLED

Albert Arthur Neely, Jr., aviation radioman, second class, U. S. N. R., of 2037 E. Fletcher st., who was reported missing since March 10, is now listed as dead by the Navy Department.

Aviation Radioman Neely, son of

Continued on Page 4, Column 1

British Win Firm Hold On Area Beyond Caen

By JAMES M. LONG

SUPREME HEADQUARTERS ALLIED EXPEDITIONARY FORCE, July 22 (Saturday) (A. P.).—British and Canadian infantry cemented positions below Caen to a depth of five miles yesterday and smashed back a heavy counter-attack as the Germans struck through rain and mud that mired the main Allied drive toward Paris.

The enemy counterattack developed near St. Martin de Fontenay, five miles south of Caen, which was reached by the Canadians in a blinding rainstorm. Early dispatches reported the town itself was captured, but Supreme Headquarters said later the town still was in enemy hands.

GERMANS USE TANKS

The Germans threw tanks into the bitter struggle, but were hurled back with losses, the midnight communique from Supreme Headquarters said.

Nearby St. Andre-sur-Orne was captured by the Allies in the day's most significant gain. The Germans also were forced into slow retreat on the west of Caen as the Allies fought for elbow room.

General Sir Bernard L. Montgomery's forces captured the village of Monts, only three and a half miles

Continued on Page 2, Column 3

IN TODAY'S INQUIRER

Hitler Reported Set to Flee by Air

NEW YORK, July 21 (A. P.).—N.B.C. said today that a clandestine German radio station had reported a four-engine transport plane, capable of flying 10,000 miles, was standing by at a secret air base in Germany at the disposal of Adolf Hitler.

The station "implied that Hitler may be preparing to flee the country, or at least is getting things in readiness for any eventual emergency," N.B.C. said. "The plane is the same craft that last year flew non-stop to Japan."

Germans Facing 2d Gruenewald

By ALEXANDER KENDRICK
Inquirer War Correspondent
By Wireless
Copyright, 1944, The Philadelphia Inquirer

MOSCOW, July 21.—The battle of Gruenewald was not a recent battle. It was not fought in this war. In fact it took place 534 years ago.

But, more than any other event in European history, it has deep and symbolic meaning for hundreds of millions of Slavs. For it was at Gruenewald—later called Tannenberg—in what is now East Prussia, that the Slav coalition of Poles, Russians, Lithuanians and others inflicted a final and lasting defeat upon the Teutonic Knights and

Continued on Page 2, Column 3

Newsie's Extra: 'Missed Him'

LONDON, July 21 (U. P.).—A London newspaper vendor chalked the following headline on the blackboard beside his stand of newspapers reporting the attempted assassination of Adolf Hitler:

"Missed him."

Gen. Koiso Is Named New Premier of Japan

By Associated Press

The Tokio radio announced today that General Kuniaki Koiso, former Governor-General of Korea, had been named Premier of Japan to succeed General Hideki Tojo, whose resignation followed a series of Japanese military setbacks.

The announcement was made in a Japanese wireless dispatch to the East Asia Press reported to the Office of War Information by the Federal Communications Commission.

SUMMONED BY HIROHITO

After the resignation of the Tojo Cabinet five days ago, Koiso was summoned by Emperor Hirohito, along with Admiral Mitsumasa Yonai, and instructed to form a new Cabinet "in co-operation."

An earlier Tokio broadcast said Koiso was expected to submit to the Emperor this morning a list of names for the new Cabinet.

The Tokio announcement said Admiral Yonai becomes minister of the Navy in Koiso's new cabinet and Field Marshal Gen. Sugiyama returns to a prominent military role as Minister of War.

SHIGEMITSU NAMED

Mamoru Shigemitsu remains Foreign Minister and takes over the

Continued on Page 3, Column 1

Stimson Returns From War Fronts

WASHINGTON, July 21 (A. P.).—Secretary of War Henry L. Stimson returned today from a trip to the battlefronts in Italy and Normandy and a visit to England.

Coming back with him were Major General Alexander D. Surles, chief of the Army's Bureau of Public Relations, and Harvey H. Bundy, special assistant to the secretary. Mr. Stimson had been out of the country about three weeks.

Spellman in Rome For Vatican Visit

ROME, July 21 (A. P.).—Archbishop Francis J. Spellman, of New York, arrived in Rome today by airplane from Africa, and was driven directly to the Vatican.

1000 Are Seized In Plot on Hitler

STOCKHOLM, July 21 (A. P.).—More than 1000 persons in Berlin, mostly from workers' districts, were arrested today by the Gestapo in widespread raids following up the attempt on Adolf Hitler's life, first eye-witness accounts from the German capital asserted.

All communications inside Germany—trains, planes and telephones—were cut off completely beginning late Thursday afternoon, the first air passengers from Berlin declared upon arrival in Stockholm. Essential communication services were resumed at 5.30 P. M. today.

SITUATION UNDER CONTROL

"When I left Berlin at about 6 P. M. today," said one Swedish traveler, "the impression was that the German government has the situation under full control.

"There was absolutely no enthu-

Continued on Page 2, Column 8

U. S. WEATHER FORECAST

Philadelphia and vicinity: Fair and continued cool today and tomorrow.

Sun rises 6.00 A.M. Sets 8.14 P.M.
Moon rises 7.59 A.M. Sets 10.04 P.M.

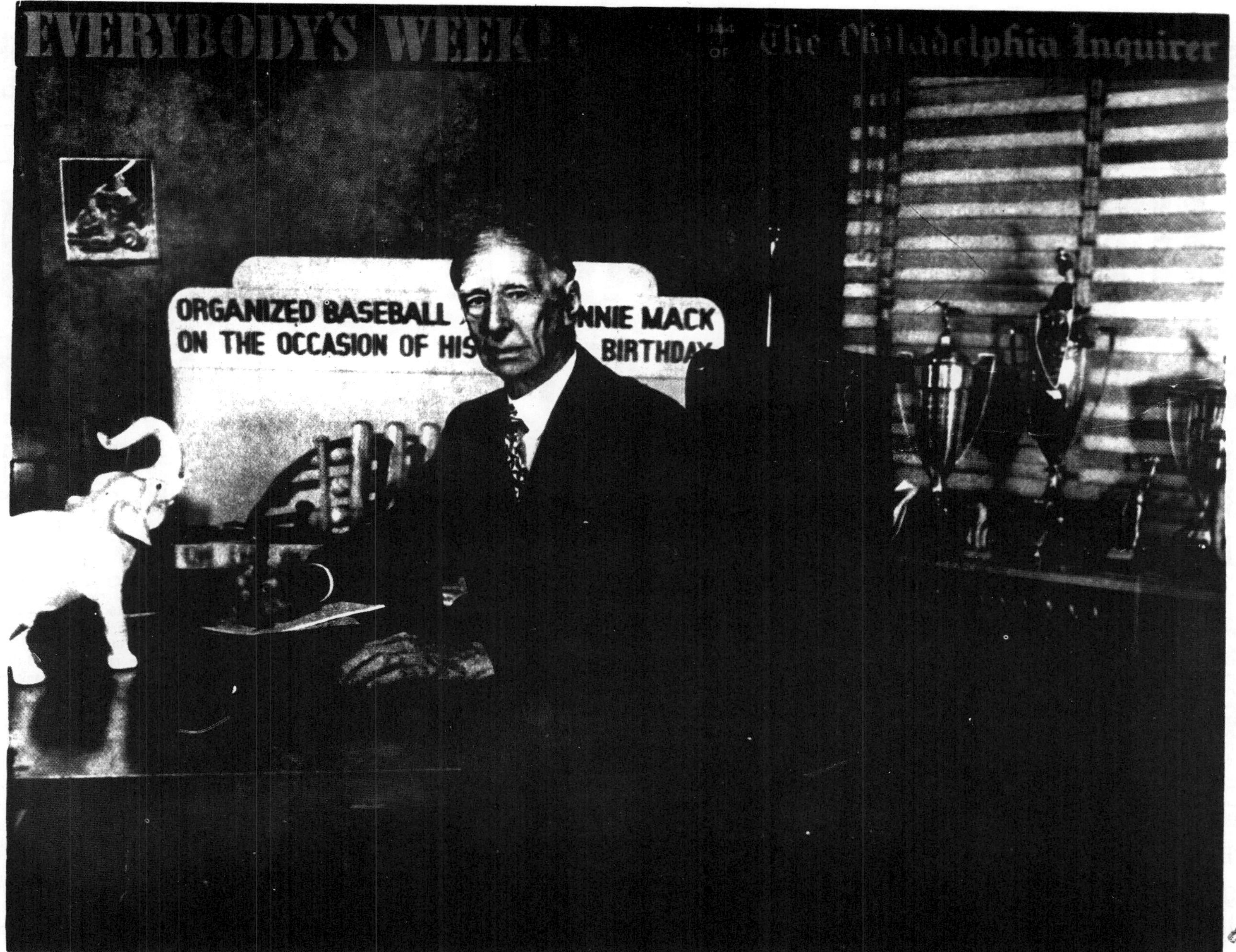

Inquirer Natural Color Photograph by William M. Irving

Connie Mack, celebrating his golden anniversary as manager, hopes to give Philadelphia another championship baseball team.

My 50 Years As Baseball Manager Have Been Happy

By Connie Mack

A HALF century of happiness is a great deal of happiness; especially it is a great deal for one man to claim. And yet as I look backward from this milestone of my golden anniversary as a manager, which occurs next Friday, I know that my fifty years in baseball have been happy. In any business fifty years is a long while, and in baseball with its thousands of thrills and headaches—we have those too!—it is truly a lifetime.

Naturally, I am proud of the championships my teams have won. But I have had another, more treasured reason for happiness throughout these years. It is the patience, the understanding and the support of the fans and press in Philadelphia in particular and the country in general when I most needed them.

The loyalty I have received is without a parallel in the history of sports. The fans—all of you who take an active, personal interest in our great national sport—have made me feel that we have grown up in baseball together. As one we have suffered its problems and shared its joys. Now, at eighty-one, I feel as if baseball has kept me young with the constant inspiration of youth.

I AM proud of the progress that baseball has made during the years we all have been together. I am proud of the record of our players in our armed services; also I am proud of the manner in which those players at home have carried on. And when the war is over, I look for better, more exciting baseball played by more skillful men before greater crowds than any we ever have known.

I do not believe I am exaggerating when I say that baseball is helping to win the war. More than 300 Major League players—seventy-five percent of the personnel of the teams two years ago—are in the service of their country. Eighty percent of the men were found physically fit. Those left at home as well as the hundreds of players in the Minor Leagues who have filled the vacancies are doing a splendid job in keeping baseball going.

And men who have seen action tell me they and their buddies want baseball to continue. They say they want something to talk about, to argue about, something to take away the horror of war.

A YOUNGSTER who returned recently from the South Pacific had this to say: "Mr. Mack, on the night before we were to land on Tarawa I thought I would go crazy. Thinking about it, worrying about my family, not knowing whether I ever would come back. Then someone started an argument about the Yankees and the Brooklyn Dodgers. I forgot my fears. I tired myself out talking and had a sound sleep."

I feel that baseball is doing its part at home, perhaps in a less spectacular manner, but achieving the same sound results by providing relaxation for workers. It is a diversion that lightens the burdens on relatives of men across the sea.

Partly because of the sustained interest in baseball and the vital factor it has become in our national life, I am convinced that its greatest years are to come after the war ends.

Thousands of young men who have learned to play baseball in the camps in this country and in England, on the fields of New Guinea and on diamonds all over the world will provide players for fifty—not a mere ten—minor leagues They may produce greater Bob Fe[illegible] Joe DiMaggios, Red Ruffings and Ted Williamses. It should be a truly golden age of baseball.

IT SEEMS only yesterday that I was called over to the Pittsburgh Athletic Club one afternoon in 1894 for a conference with William W. Kerr, William C. Temple and P. L. Auten. They were the owners of the Pittsburgh Club of the National League and they wanted me to become manager of the team.

I was only 31 then, and of course I was flattered and pleased. But I refused the offer. Three or four of our men including myself were not in the best of shape. I asked that Al Buckinberger, the manager, be given a fair chance until we got into condition to play.

Six weeks later they called me again. Mr. Kerr said they had released Mr. Buckinberger. "We want you to manage our club," he told me. "We know you are young but we have watched you carefully. We know you are smart and tricky."

Even then I hesitated. As a catcher, I had at least five more years in the Big League. As a manager I might last only five weeks. Mr. Kerr must have read my thoughts for he offered me a contract for the entire season. I accepted then. The job has turned out to be more permanent than I expected.

I had to break up my first great Athletics team in 1914 because of the high salaries offered my players by the outlaw Federal League when that organization tried to establish a third major circuit. My second great team, champions of 1929, 1930, 1931, I had to break up because the overhead was so great. Not one man on the Athletics was getting less than $10,000 a year. Al Simmons was paid $33,000. We were the highest salaried club in baseball including the Yankees with Babe Ruth.

SOME of the fans would be surprised to learn that salaries are only one-third of the expense attached to a ball club. Many persons think I am rich. I am not. I have to make baseball pay the same as any other business man. I wish I even could say that I am out of debt!

Baseball, like every other business, keeps step with the times. It keeps step with the progress in chemistry, physics and mechanics. When I was a boy, baseballs were wound by hand, covered with a bit of leather that was rough and uneven and that stretched out of shape under the slightest pressure.

Today balls are wound by machinery with uniform wool and sealed with a cover sliced to uniform thickness as well as stretched to a tightness no amount of pounding can loosen. Bats in those old days were hewn out of fence posts or turned on crude lathes. They were unbalanced and untreated. Today they are of the finest wood, carefully cut for perfect balance and maximum resiliency.

AS BATS and balls have changed, so have the men who play. When I first took hold of the Pittsburgh Club our players for the most part came from the dead-end streets. They were rough, tough and uncouth. We were not welcome in first- or second-class hotels. Third-class hostelries received us only when we promised not to eat with other guests. Now the finest hotels not only solicit our patronage but safeguard us from disturbance by other guests. Players have progressed in social acceptability;

Continued on Page Six

The Philadelphia Inquirer

PUBLIC LEDGER

An Independent Newspaper for All the People

FINAL CITY EDITION

CIRCULATION: July Average: Daily 519,422; Sunday 1,089,217

TUESDAY MORNING, AUGUST 15, 1944

Vol. 231, No. 46

abdefgh ★ THREE CENTS

SOUTHERN FRANCE INVADED

Germans Trapped West of Paris, Turn to Fight

'Major Victory' Can Be Won Now, Eisenhower Says

War Summary on Page 3

Map on Page 2

By JAMES M. LONG

SUPREME HEADQUARTERS ALLIED EXPEDITIONARY FORCE, Aug. 15 (Tuesday) (A. P.).—Triumphant Allied armies welded a trap of steel and artillery fire about the flower of the German Seventh Army today in the greatest victory of Allied arms in France, and from 100,000 to 200,000 enemy troops turned for a battle to the death.

Backing away from a hail of bombs and artillery shells sealing a 12-mile gap at the eastern end of their Normandy "coffin corridor," the Germans checked their rush and some forces swung around west in an attempt to plug their leaking lines.

Thus they invited destruction—a consummation which would mean a gigantic victory for the Allies in the battle for northwestern France, open the road to Paris, and clear the way for the final battles for northeastern and southern France.

For this stroke, General Dwight D. Eisenhower in a dramatic order of the day summoned his armies to drive ahead with every ounce of energy. For here, he said, was "a definite opportunity for a major Allied victory" after which Paris would fall with but little effort.

JAW OF PINCERS CLOSING

The southern jaw of the great Allied pincers was being closed by the U. S. Third Army—which the Germans said was being led by Lieutenant General George S. Patton, Jr.—battering up to within eight and a half miles of Falaise.

Canadian troops smashed to within three and one-half miles of Falaise on the north in a rolling offensive that jumped off Monday after clouds of Allied bombers obliterated a German anti-tank screen before the city.

EVERY ROAD RAKED

Between these two forces, Long Toms fr m north and south raked every road leading eastward to the Seine and Paris, and waves of bombers added to the hurricane of fire.

Before this gap vanished Germans had been streaming eastward in haywagons, bicycles and every other farm vehicle they could

Continued on Page 2, Column 1

WPB Opens Door For Making of 79 Civilian Items

By HERMAN A. LOWE

Inquirer Washington Bureau

WASHINGTON, Aug. 14.—The War Production Board took another step toward limited production of civilian goods late today in an order which would allow manufacturers to make 79 types of items, providing that material and labor are available and that there is no interference with war production.

Specifically excluded are automobiles, washing machines, and gas and electric refrigerators.

Some of the permitted items are now being made in limited quantity such as automotive replacement parts, hair and bobby pins, beds and bedsprings, cooking enameled and cast iron ware. Other things such as metal office and industrial furniture and musical instruments are expected to go into limited production for the first time since war shortages halted their manufacture.

OTHERS ON THE LIST

Still others on the list, such as outboard motors, automatic phonographs, gaming machines and vacuum cleaners, probably will not be made for some time, since, while manufacturers may apply, it is unlikely they will get either material from WPB or approval from the War Manpower Commission.

The order is bound around with a

Continued on Page 7, Column 3

Commando Kelly Punished by Army

FORT BENNING, Ga., Aug. 14 (U. P.).—Technical Sergeant Charles E. (Commando) Kelly, the one-man army from Pittsburgh, has drawn a $90 fine and a three-months restriction to quarters for overstaying a furlough.

Infantry School authorities said the 23-year-old Medal of Honor winner, whose heroism at Alatavile, Italy, is now a legend of the Army, testified at his court-martial that his tardiness in returning from a visit to his home was due to enthusiasm displayed by his well-wishers along the route back to camp.

Allies Drop Arms, Officers to Maquis

AT THE FRENCH FRONTIER NEAR ST GINGOL, Aug. 14 (A. P.).—Allied planes parachuted heavy arms and also dropped a half-dozen officers from headquarters into France's Maquis region, it was reported here tonight through reliable channels.

Anti-tank guns were included in some sectors this afternoon, whereas before only light arms have been dropped into the Haute-Savoie and Jura regions. The appearance of officers was taken to indicate a forthcoming Partisan drive of major proportions there.

Signal flares seen from the frontier tonight indicated that the provisioning still was going on.

WHERE ALLIED ARMIES MADE NEW LANDINGS

Strong Naval, Air Action Backs New Allied Landing

By JOHN M. McCULLOUGH

Inquirer Washington Bureau

WASHINGTON, Aug. 15 (Tuesday)—Powerful forces of American, British and French troops landed today on the southern coast of France.

The announcement was made here at 6.10 o'clock this morning in a brief communique simultaneously issued here and in Rome.

The communique, signed by General Sir Henry Maitland Wilson, Supreme Allied Commander in the Mediterranean, read as follows:

"Today, American, British and French troops strongly supported by Allied Air Forces are being landed by American, British and French fleets on the southern coast of France."

AIM TO JOIN TWO FORCES

In a separate announcement, likewise made public here, General Wilson said that the objective of the new invasion "is to drive out the Germans and join up with the Allied armies advancing from Normandy."

General Wilson's announcement revealed that French troops are participating in the operation and probably are landing for the first time in force on the soil of their native land.

The powerful forces, which landed 80 days after the great invasion of western France, are believed to have struck somewhere on the Riviera west of the Italian border.

The strength and the disposition were not disclosed in the official announcement. But it is assumed that the great naval base Toulon and the French Mediterranean harbor of Marseilles would be immediate objectives.

AIM TO DRIVE GERMANS OUT

The text of General Wilson's statement:

"The armies of the United Nations have landed in the south of France. Their objective is to drive out the Germans and join up with the Allied armies advancing from Normandy.

"French troops are participating in these operations side by side with their Allied comrades in arms, by sea, land and air. The Army of France is in being again, fighting on its own soil for the liberation of its country with all its traditions of victory behind it—remember 1918.

"All Frenchmen, civilians as well as military, have their part to play in the campaign in the south. Your duty will be made clear to you. Listen to the Allied radio, read notices and leaflets, pass on all instructions from one man and woman to another.

"Let us end the struggle as quickly as possible so

Continued on Page 2, Column 6

5 Coast Plants Seized by Navy

WASHINGTON, Aug. 14 (A. P.).—The Government today seized five San Francisco machine shops where an A.F.L. machinists union has balked at complying with a War Labor Board order to stop limiting union members to a 48-hour week.

President Roosevelt directed the Navy Department to assume nominal control of the plants, but to permit the managements to continue normal functions so far as possible.

OVERTIME WORK BANNED

The five shops were among 104 where the A.F.L. Machinists Lodge 68 imposed a prohibition against Sunday and overtime work. WLB Chairman William H. Davis, however, advised the President that these five employ the most workers and have been affected most by the union's refusal to withdraw the ban.

Mr. Davis said the WLB was hopeful that seizure of the five will bring about an end to the prohibition, which board officials have described as a "limited strike" because it restricts a union member to a 48-hour week.

The WLB order, which the union

Continued on Page 8, Column 4

87 Snow Victims Found

SANTIAGO, Chile, Aug. 14 (A. P.).—Eighty-seven bodies have been recovered from the snowslide which last Tuesday wrecked buildings in the copper mining town of Sewell.

Toscanini Daughter Saved From Nazis

ROME, Aug. 14 (U. P.).—The Communist newspaper Unito said today that Count Emanuele Castelbarco of Pindemonte Rezzonico and his wife, the daughter of Arturo Toscanini, the anti-Fascist orchestra conductor, had escaped the Nazis in Florence by living in a house in the city's working class section.

The poorer classes of the city, motivated by a common hatred of Fascism, threw open their doors to rich refugees.

Uprising in France Ordered by de Gaulle

By JUDSON O'QUINN

SUPREME HEADQUARTERS ALLIED EXPEDITIONARY FORCE, Aug. 14 (A. P.).—People of France were summoned today by General Charles de Gaulle's French Committee of National Liberation to strike for their own freedom with a general uprising against the German conquerors whose hold on the country is weakening under Allied blows.

Calling for a national uprising which would be "the prelude of liberation," the Committee statement said "there is not one Frenchman who does not feel and who does not know that it is his simple and sacred duty to take part immediately in the supreme war effort of his country."

The French were told to strike with all their might and to harass the enemy by joining the direct war with the Allied Armies, by laying down their tools in Nazi-held factories and by destruction of small German garrisons.

They were asked to prevent Germans from fleeing through the Pyrenees and east and north to Paris. Special instructions are to be issued for the Paris area, said the statement.

"In the field, in the factory, in the workshop, in the office, in the home and in the street, whether he be under arrest, deported or a prisoner of war, each Frenchman can harm the

Continued on Page 5, Column 5

U. S. 3d Army In France Battle

By HAL BOYLE

AMERICAN THIRD ARMY HEADQUARTERS, France, Aug. 14 (A. P.).—It was disclosed officially tonight that the American Third Army is fighting in France and had closed the Southern arm of the pincers movement that had trapped the German Seventh Army after one of the most spectacular armored surges in military history.

Supreme Headquarters has withheld publication of the name of the Third Army's commander.

LT. GEN. HODGES

(Another Supreme Headquarters announcement disclosed that Lieutenant General Omar N. Bradley was overall commander of the entire American fighting force in France which includes the First and Third U. S. Armies. General Bradley's place as commander of the First Army was taken by Lieutenant General Courtney H. Hodges, previously

Continued on Page 2, Column 3

Casualties

Missing Organist Killed in France

A former Philadelphia choir master, previously listed as missing in action, has now been reported killed in France on June 30, according to word received by his parents.

Before his induction, Private Wendell B. Lewis, 31, of 1316 W. Lycoming st., had also served as organist at the Trinity Episcopal Church, Swarthmore. He met his death six weeks after going overseas, while serving as an M-1 rifleman.

PRIVATE LEWIS

Private Lewis was graduated from the University of Pennsylvania in 1938 and received the Alumni Award in Music. While attending the university, he was a member of the Glee Club and the Mixed Chorus. He is the son of Mr. and Mrs. David Lewis.

Other casualties reported by the War Department and the Navy include:

KILLED

Sergeant John A. Callahan, Jr., son of John A. Callahan, Sr., of 6227 Buist ave., in the European area.

Private First Class Anthony F. Barone, son of Mrs. Jennie Barone, of 1335 S. Grove st., in the same area.

Private First Class Charles E. Connelly, U. S. M. C. R., son of Mrs. Annie Connelly, of 2022 Plum st., on Saipan June 17.

Sergeant Stanley S. Englert, U. S. M. C., son of Mrs. Kathryn Englert, of Lansdale, in the South Pacific.

WOUNDED

Private Raymond T. Rhodes, son

Continued on Page 5, Column 3

Forrestal Touring Italian Front

Illustrated on Page 12

WASHINGTON, Aug. 14 (A. P.).—Secretary of the Navy James V. Forrestal was disclosed today to be among the high Allied leaders present in Italy during recent days.

An Army Signal Corps picture showed Secretary Forrestal on an inspection tour of the Fifth Army front. Dispatches from Italy have mentioned the presence there of a number of leaders, including Prime Minister Winston Churchill, Lieutenant General Brehon Somervell, Chief of Army Service Forces, and Undersecretary of War Robert P. Patterson.

Richard Strauss Reported Arrested

AT THE GERMAN FRONTIER, Aug. 14 (A. P.).—Richard Strauss, the composer, has been placed under house arrest somewhere in Austria, travelers from Vienna report. This cannot be confirmed, but it is known that a number of his public appearances recently were cancelled.

French Name Juin Chief of Staff

ALGIERS, Aug. 14 (U. P.).—General Alphonse Juin, who has been commander-in-chief of French Expeditonary Forces in Italy, has been appointed Chief of Staff of the committee of national defense, it was announced tonight.

Parley Hints Army Will Quit P.T.C. Soon

Illustrated on Page 8

Return of Philadelphia's transit system to civilian management before the end of this week was foreseen last night as the result of a conference held here by Governor Edward Martin, Mayor Bernard Samuel and Major General Philip Hayes. General Hayes has been operating the lines for the War Department since Aug. 3.

Withdrawal of all troops would be a routine phase of return of the transit system's operation to the Philadelphia Transportation Co., it was understood.

Governor Martin and Mayor Samuel discussed with General Hayes at the conference, held in the Mitten Building, the role city and State police will play once the order is given for the withdrawal of the soldiers remaining on duty at P. T. C. depots and barns here.

At the close of the conference General Hayes issued this statement:

"I met with the Governor and the

Continued on Page 8, Column 2

IN TODAY'S INQUIRER

SPECIAL DEPARTMENTS

Mid-City Count Of Pollen Starts

The ragweed pollen count which is to be taken daily for The Philadelphia Inquirer by a recognized authority in the field of allergy appears for the first time today.

A low count of three granules per cubic yard of air was computed yesterday by the allergist who said that it was yet early for a concentration of pollen which would affect hay fever sufferers. A minimum count of 20 begins to affect most victims, he said.

The count will be taken over 24-hour periods ending at 4.30 P. M. of the day preceding publication, the allergist said, at central-city locations where an accurate average of pollen content may be measured.

Since hay fever sufferers in the greatest numbers live within the city limits, the allergist pointed out, they will be affected by the pollen which is in the air at their homes and offices and not at outlying locations.

In suburban areas heavier counts may be recorded, the allergist said, but such counts may be the result of nearby growths of the sources of pollen.

(See Pollen Count in Weather Table on Page 2.)

Victorious Reds Poised For East Prussia 'Kill'

Map on Page 3

By ALEXANDER KENDRICK

Inquirer War Correspondent

By Wireless

MOSCOW, Aug. 14.—The stage is fully set for what may be the great, conclusive battle of the war on the Eastern Front—the battle for East Prussia. Two mighty Soviet armies stand at the borders of the province, which is Germany's historical and sentimental heart.

One of the armies, led by youthful General Ivan Cherniakhovsky, has been battering at the East Prussian wall for two weeks against the stiffest and most desperate resistance by the Germans of the entire three years of conflict.

REDS SEIZE FORTRESS

The other Soviet army, led by Colonel General Zakharov, today captured the Biebrza River fortress town of Osowiec, in Poland, 17 miles from the German East Prussian border.

Berlin soberly warned the homeland that "a very great trial of strength" was at hand.

Osowiec, east-bank stronghold on the Biebrza, fell as thousands of attacking Russian troops sent the Germans fleeing across the river to roads slashed by the guns of swarming Soviet planes.

A Soviet communique also announced that Russian troops racing across southern Estonia toward the Gulf of Riga had captured 100 localities, including Antsla, only 80 miles from the Baltic coast.

Antsla fell in a 19-mile gain from

Continued on Page 3, Column 3

U. S. WEATHER FORECAST

Philadelphia and vicinity: Continued hot and humid with scattered evening thundershowers today and tomorrow.

Sun rises	6.11 A.M.	Sets 7.59 P.M.
Moon rises	3.06 A.M.	Sets 6.07 P.M.

The Philadelphia Inquirer

PUBLIC LEDGER

An Independent Newspaper for All the People

FINAL CITY EDITION

CIRCULATION: July Average: Daily 519,422; Sunday 1,080,217

THURSDAY MORNING, AUGUST 24, 1944

Copyright, 1944, by Triangle Publications, Inc. Vol. 231, No. 55

a b d e f g h

THREE CENTS

Rumania Surrenders and Joins Allies; Paris, Marseilles Freed by French; Americans Drive for German Border

Patriots Victors In 4-Day Battle To Win Capital

Paris and Marseilles—the first two cities of France—were wrested from German bondage yesterday as Allied armies surged forward with amazing rapidity.

The French capital fell to French partisans after four days of street fighting. The French Second Armored Division and some American troops later entered the capital. In the south of France, French troops battered into the great port of Marseilles and occupied most of the city.

American tank forces smashed 15 miles beyond Sens, 65 miles southeast of Paris, in their drive across France. Other U. S. and Allied forces tightened the noose about the tens of thousands of Germans trapped in the Seine loop northwest of Paris.

4-Year Nazi Rule Ends; All Public Buildings Occupied

By JAMES M. LONG

LONDON, Aug. 23 (A. P.). — French patriot forces battling in the streets as their forefathers did in 1789 have liberated Paris, the gay heart of France and historic symbol of freedom, bringing to an end four years and two months of Nazi bondage. General Charles de Gaulle's Headquarters announced today.

With a great force of American armored troops poised in an assault arc almost half way around the capital, 50,000 armed French patriots, aided by several hundred thousand citizens who wielded what arms they could find, defeated the Nazi occupation forces in a four-day battle ended last night.

VICHY AIDES SEIZED

The patriots occupied all public buildings and arrested all Vichy government representatives who did not flee, said a formal announcement signed by Lieutenant General Joseph Pierre Koenig, commander of the French Forces of the Interior and newly-named Military Governor of Paris under General de Gaulle.

C. B. S. reported Wednesday night that the French Second Armored Division, headed by Brigadier General Jacques Le Clerc, had entered Paris.

PART OF THIRD ARMY

(General Le Clerc's army is part of the American Third Army, under George S. Patton, Jr.)

(At the same time it was revealed that some American units had been ordered into Paris to work with

Continued on Page 2, Column 3

Grenoble Captured In 140-Mile Smash By Yank Columns

By GEORGE TUCKER

ROME, Aug. 23 (A. P.). — Marseilles, France's second city and greatest seaport, fell to the swift onslaught of French infantry and armor today as American forces swept 140 miles inland from the Mediterranean and captured Grenoble to within less than 240 miles of a junction with General Dwight D. Eisenhower's legions below liberated Paris.

Only eight days after the landings in southern France the inspired Poilus battered their way into the heart of Marseilles against slight Nazi resistance and tonight were cleaning out pockets of last-ditch defenders.

ASSURES SUPPLIES

The unexpectedly easy capture of the great port insures the Seventh Army of Lieutenant General Alexander M. Patch an adequate flow of supplies and reinforcements for speedy continuation of their thrust toward northern France. Prior to the city's fall, other French troops had cut the last escape route for the German garrison along the coast to the west.

The encircled and doomed Nazi force in Toulon, big naval base 27 miles east of Marseilles, still was holding out tonight, but French troops had fought their way within a few hundred yards of the docks and the city's fall was expected any hour.

TOULON FALL REPORTED

(Radio Atlantic, secret German-language station, was quoted Wed-

Continued on Page 2, Column 6

WHERE THE ALLIES ARE CLOSING IN ON HITLER'S GERMANY

With Rumania deserting Germany and coming into the war on the side of the United Nations, coincident with the liberation of Paris and Marseilles, this is how the European situation appears today. The shaded area is in Allied hands. Distances from major battlefronts to German frontiers and from Rumania to Germany are indicated. On the Russian front, Red Army units have been reported in sight of German soil in East Prussia.

Bucharest Army Reported Battling Hitler's Troops

War Summary on Page 3

By TOM YARBROUGH

LONDON, Aug. 24 (Thursday) (A. P.).—Rumania, Adolf Hitler's most useful satellite, abandoned him last night and announced she was joining the Allies in the war against the Axis—a turnabout suggesting the imminent collapse of the whole blood-bathed Nazi empire.

Moscow immediately afterward reported that fighting had broken out between German and Rumanian troops on the Eastern Front, with many Rumanians slain by Nazi security forces as they sought to retreat before the gigantic Red Army onslaught through Bessarabia and northeastern Rumania toward Ploesti and the Danube.

The Daily Express reported it had recorded a German military broadcast saying that the Rumanian Third Army had already turned around and was fighting alongside the Russians.

CAPITULATION DENOUNCED BY NAZIS

The German radio today violently denounced Rumania's capitulation to the Allies, declaring that a "clique of traitors has put aside Premier Antonescu, and King Michael has come to an understanding with Britain and America."

The broadcast, beamed to Rumania, asserted that a "national government"—presumably a puppet regime sponsored by the Nazis—had been formed to "prevent bolshevization" of the country, and told the Rumanian people:

"Obey only its orders and not those of the traitors."

The radio added that "Rumania is threatened with the greatest danger" and appealed to Rumanians to "fight together with the Germans against Russian bolshevism."

REDS SHATTER RUMANIA'S DEFENSES

The Russian advance already had broken through the last strongRumanian defenses. The Nation had been under a steady Allied air bombardment.

Young King Michael announced the capitulation and switch in a proclamation broadcast from Bucharest.

Indications were that Rumania would be a co-belligerent, like Italy, rather than a full ally, and that her main offensive intentions were against Hungary in the hope of recovering Transylvania.

The proclamation said "Rumania has accepted armistice terms offered by the Soviet Union, Great Britain and the United States."

There was no official confirmation by any of the Allies,

Continued on Page 3, Column 4

Dewey Aide Hits Parley Secrecy

Illustrated on Page 6

By JOHN C. O'BRIEN

Inquirer Washington Bureau

WASHINGTON, Aug. 23. — John Foster Dulles, mild-mannered foreign affairs adviser of Governor Thomas E. Dewey, Republican Presidential candidate, found himself today in disagreement with Secretary of State Cordell Hull over the secrecy imposed on the Dumbarton Oaks tri-power security conference which opened here Monday.

After a two-and-one-half hour exchange of views with the Secretary, Mr. Dulles told newspaper correspondents that he was "inclined to think that there could be more information given than is being given" concerning the history-making discussions involving the shape of the post-war world among the delegations representing the United States, Great Britain and Russia.

SECRECY CALLED FUTILE

Mr. Dulles took up the matter of secrecy at Dumbarton Oaks with Secretary Hull after the State Department Correspondents' Association had requested an appointment with Undersecretary of State Edward R. Stettinius, Jr., to protest against the meager and meaningless

Continued on Page 6, Column 3

U. S. Seizes Mines In Anthracite Strike

Government seizure of the mines and properties of the Philadelphia and Reading Coal and Iron Co., five of whose collieries have been closed by an unauthorized strike since June 29, was ordered yesterday by President Roosevelt.

The President's order directed Secretary of the Interior Harold L. Ickes to take over the mines "through and with the aid of such public and private instrumentalities as he may designate," to break a stoppage which Mr. Ickes recently estimated has cost the Nation 390,000 tons of vitally needed anthracite. The seizure takes effect "immediately."

More than 4000 Philadelphia and Reading miners at collieries in District 9, in the vicinity of Shenandoah and Mahanoy City, have been out for the last seven weeks, in protest against what they claim was a company violation of the Anthracite Agreement of June 17 in "docking" their $8-a-day wages.

The company, terming the walkout unjustified, has had the backing of John L. Lewis, president of the United Mine Workers, and other union officials. Mr. Lewis, after the local unions had disregarded his back-to-work order on Aug. 8, called the strike a "flagrant violation" of the union's word.

In addition to directing Secretary Ickes to make use of such instrumentalities as he might designate, the President's order specifically

Continued on Page 7, Column 1

Casualties

Phila. War Hero Killed in Action

A Philadelphia soldier, who captured 26 Germans single-handed in Italy shortly before he was reported missing, was killed in action, the War Department has notified his mother, Mrs. Edna Miller, of 3113 Robbins ave.

The infantryman, Private First Class Charles F. Miller, was awarded the Silver Star for capturing the Germans on April 26. A few days later, his mother received word that he was missing in action.

WAS P. R. R. CLERK

Employed as a clerk on the Pennsylvania Railroad prior to his induction in June, 1942, Private Miller was a graduate of Frankford High School. He trained at Fort Meade, Md.

Captain James H. Clement, 26, son of Martin W. Clement, president of the Pennsylvania Railroad, was wounded in action in France and is recovering in a hospital in England, according to a cable received by his wife, the former Ida Louise Larkin, of New York.

CAPT. CLEMENT

Captain Clement, a field artillery officer, who enlisted in the Army as a private in September, 1940, is a graduate of Princeton University.

He was awarded a commission of second lieutenant in February, 1941,

Continued on Page 5, Column 3

American Tanks Drive For German Border

Map on Page 2

By WILLIAM F. BONI

SUPREME HEADQUARTERS ALLIED EXPEDITIONARY FORCE, Aug. 23 (A. P.).—An American armored spearhead lanced on 15 miles virtually unopposed across the heart of France tonight—80 miles southeast of liberated Paris—cutting the ground steadily from beneath German armies now in retreat toward the Reich's frontier.

"The main battle for France is already over," declared Harold Boyle, Associated Press correspondent, who watched U. S. tanks drive 15 miles east of Sens to within 150 miles of the German border with no sign that the Germans were rallying for a stand.

MANY PRISONERS TAKEN

(A United Press dispatch, saying American tanks had gained 35 miles southeast of Paris, placed the U. S. spearhead only 125 miles from the German border.)

Truckloads of prisoners streamed back in the wake of the American advance, but there was not a single smoldering enemy vehicle to indicate the enemy had put up a determined

Continued on Page 2, Column 1

IN TODAY'S INQUIRER

Troop Call Ready In Freight Tieup

The Army threatened last night to move service forces into the Philadelphia Port of Embarkation to break a freight stoppage that is seriously curtailing shipment of war materials abroad.

At the same time, stevedore companies which purportedly caused the breakdown by pirating workers from car loading crews, were given 48 hours in which to clean up the situation or be subject to the sanctions of every possible Federal Government agency.

CONFERENCE IS HELD

The tieup, which has been developing for the past three weeks, was revealed at a conference of representatives of the Army, Coast Guard, stevedore companies and union, the War Manpower Commission and the War Shipping Administration yesterday in the WMC headquarters at the Stephen Girard Building.

It was revealed that stevedore companies, offering higher wages as the chief inducement, had pirated the ranks of the relatively low-paid car loaders until at present long lines of freight cars, bearing hundreds of thousands of tons of vital war materials, are lying on railroad sidings of the city's vast embarka-

Continued on Page 7, Column 5

Trust Suit Cites 47 Railroads

By NICHOLAS P. GREGORY

Inquirer Washington Bureau

WASHINGTON, Aug. 23. — The Department of Justice today opened its biggest anti-trust case since the famed Standard Oil proceeding, charging the Association of American Railroads, 47 Western carriers and their officers and two New York banking firms—J. P. Morgan & Co., and Kuhn, Loeb & Co., identified with railroad financing for more than 70 years—with violation of the Sherman anti-trust act.

The Justice Department's action against the Western carriers coincided with reliable reports that similar proceedings would be launched soon against several of the country's leading investment banking firms, also charging them with violating the Sherman anti-trust act in connection with the distribution of securities.

The monopoly charges leveled at the Western railroads are considered highly significant here and an official of the Association of American Railroads saw political implications in the action.

He pointed out that the Western

Continued on Page 9, Column 1

Nazi Gen. Hausser Hurt in Normandy

LONDON, Aug. 23 (A. P.).—Colonel General Paul Hausser, commander of the German Seventh Army, has been wounded in Normandy, the Berlin radio said tonight.

Hausser, under the overall command of Field Marshal General Guenther von Kluge, led the army which was battered heavily in the Falaise pocket and now is falling back upon the lower Seine, menaced with a new envelopment.

Carrier Planes Hit Tirpitz Again

LONDON, Aug. 23 (U. P.).—Carrier-based Barracuda planes of the British fleet air arm today delivered the third smashing attack on the German battleship Tirpitz, the Daily Telegraph's Stockholm correspondent reported.

Senate Confirms Promotion of Patch

WASHINGTON, Aug. 23 (A. P.).—The promotion of Major General Alexander M. Patch, Jr., to the temporary rank of lieutenant general was confirmed today by the Senate.

General Patch, commanding the American Seventh Army in southern France, is a native of Ft. Huachuca, Ariz.

Red Army Continues Offensive in Rumania

By W. W. HERCHER

LONDON, Aug. 24 (Thursday) (A. P.).—The two-fisted Soviet offensive that knocked Rumania out of the war roared through its fourth day yesterday, capturing Vaslui, 140 miles northeast of the Ploesti oil center, and toppling the two big Bessarabian bastions of Tighina and Cetatea-Alba on the west bank of the Dniester, and more than 400 other towns.

Disregarding developments on the political front, at least for the present, the Second and Third Ukrainian Armies deepened to as much as 60 miles the holes they have ripped in the German-Rumanian defenses and advanced within 167 miles of the capital city of Bucharest.

GARRISONED BY NAZIS

Rumania still was garrisoned with thousands of German troops, and the Russians were likely to continue their lightning campaign to drive the Nazis entirely out of the country, regardless of what Rumanian troops chose to do.

The Rumanians were attempting

Continued on Page 3, Column 3

Report Antonescu Fleeing to Reich

LONDON, Aug. 24 (A. P.).—A Swiss broadcast, quoting dispatches from Bucharest, declared today that Marshal Ion Antonescu, deposed Premier of Rumania, has fled to Germany.

The broadcast also asserted that Rumanian troops last night marched into the border province of Transylvania, which Rumania ceded to Hungary early in the war at German behest.

U. S. WEATHER FORECAST

Philadelphia and vicinity: Fair and rather warm today; fair and slightly cooler tomorrow.

Sun rises 6.19 A.M. Sets 7.47 P.M.
Moon rises 11.35 A.M. Sets 10.52 P.M.

The Pollen Count will be found with the Weather Tables on Page 2, Column 1.

The Philadelphia Inquirer
MONDAY MORNING, AUGUST 28, 1944 e f ß h 8

Mark Sullivan

Conditions Inside WPB Are Typical

WASHINGTON, Aug. 27.

THE explosion in the War Production Board last week was sensational, and more developments will follow. But to see it as merely a clash or series of clashes, or to think of it as something within one Government department, would be superficial. The condition is wider and deeper than that. Consider just what happened.

In one of the most important Administration departments, WPB, the No. 2 man, Mr. Charles E. Wilson, is out.

This No. 2 man is out, not because the No. 1 man wanted him out. The No. 1 man, Mr. Donald Nelson, chairman of WPB, did not fire Mr. Wilson; he assured Mr. Wilson that he was fully satisfactory.

• • •

NEITHER is Mr. Wilson out because the President wanted him out. The President received his resignation reluctantly, and on two previous occasions when Mr. Wilson wanted to resign, Mr. Roosevelt persuaded him to remain.

Why, then, is Mr. Wilson out? It is a remarkable reason. He said it in his letter of resignation, and amplified it in even stronger words at a press conference. Mr. Wilson is out because of "attacks" upon him "inspired by subordinate officials of the board." These attacks, inspired by subordinate officials, and circulated publicly, were without the "knowledge or approval" of the head of WPB, Mr. Nelson. Mr. Wilson believed that "instead of being discontinued, these attacks upon me . . . will be increased." So, Mr. Wilson got out.

• • •

HERE is a remarkable condition—the subordinates more powerful than the head of their own department—and more powerful than even the President, for in getting Mr. Wilson out, they achieve a result which the President did not want, which he acutely deplored.

To a large extent the Government has come to be operated by anonymous officials of subordinate rank. One reason is mere size, sprawling unwieldiness. In departments more things must be done than can be done by the head of the department.

And in the Administration as a whole, more things must be done than any President or any man can have adequate information or sufficient time for thought to do. Heads of departments, and even more the President, must take action on the basis of reports put up to them by subordinates, sometimes accompanied by judgments suggested by the subordinates.

Some remedies are in sight. The end of the war, by reducing the number of controls exercised by the Federal Government, will reduce the burdens on department heads and on the President, and reduce the number of subordinate officials.

Another remedy is decentralization, preventing the Federal Government from taking over functions now exercised by the States. That Congress has this in mind is shown by its insistence that the administration of unemployment benefits for war workers shall be carried on by the States, not by the Federal Government.

Today

—By Maj. Geo. F. Eliot—

Continued From First Page

direct from America and discharge their cargoes of men and stores without the labor of unloading in British ports, hauling across England on the overtaxed British railways, and then shipping once more across the Channel.

Brest is perhaps the best hope in this regard, because it is an excellent harbor and because, even though the German demolitions may be extensive, it will still be difficult for them to do enough damage to prevent the entry of ships and the discharge of cargoes in lighters.

Lorient is also a good harbor, though not as commodious as Brest and inferior to it in docking facilities. St. Nazaire, unfortunately, has an artificial harbor controlled by lock-gates, and injury to these lock-gates would render the harbor basins unusuable for a long time.

The fall of St. Nazaire would, however, open the estuary of the Loire and enable us to use the port of Nantes which, like Rouen, can take ocean-going vessels of medium size and which has extensive quayage.

In all these enterprises, we are racing against time. The main military effort must continue to be devoted to the pursuit and destruction of the German armies in northern France. But in order that this pursuit and destruction may be carried out, in order that the pressure shall never relax, it is essential that the flow of ammunition, stores and reinforcements to our troops should never be checked even for a day. . . .

The farther away the battle moves from the ports through which our armies were originally supplied, the heavier the demands on day-to-day movement from Britain and America. The more the originally assembled dumps in Normandy are depleted, the larger must be the flow across the Channel and across the Atlantic Ocean.

It is hard for the commander-in-chief to divert divisions to the capture of Brest and Lorient which are urgently needed at the front, and it is hard for him to divert to Brittany ammunition and airplanes for which he is receiving urgent calls from his armies along the Seine; but if ever a diversion were justified in war, it is this one.

Washington Background

Bowles' Home Town Irked By Low Price Ceilings

By Inquirer Washington Bureau Staff

WASHINGTON, Aug. 27.

WASHINGTON SOCIAL NOTES: President Roosevelt entertained Sveinn Bjornsson, first President of the Republic of Iceland, and 37 other guests from the Cabinet, Congress, services, White House and administration bureaus at dinner in the White House the other evening . . . Elmer Davis, Office of War Information chief, and Mrs. Davis, announce the engagement of their daughter, Anne, to Lieutenant Morris Kaplan, of the Army . . . Rowland Egger, general manager of the Bolivian Development Corp., was host at the Mayflower to 45 luncheon guests from the State Department, Petroleum Administration for War, Public Roads Administration, Foreign Economic Administration, Office of the Co-Ordinator of Inter-American Affairs, War Production Board, War Department, White House and Bolivian Embassy . . . Most Rev. Paul Yu-pin, Catholic Bishop of China, entertained 20 prominent guests at the Statler.

• • •

Rumania's capitulation brings to mind that George Boncesco, former financial counselor of the Rumanian Embassy here, and Emmanuel Dimitriu, former attache, are living in Washington. Both quit their country's diplomatic service because of their government's pro-Nazi policy. Radu Irimescu, Rumania's last envoy to Washington, is living in New York . . . Colonel Oldrich Spaniel, who has been serving as military and air attache of the Czechoslovakian Embassy here, is off for London to serve as head of President Eduard Benes' military cabinet . . . Wilhelm Munthe de Morgenstierne, the Norwegian Ambassador, has returned to the capital after a speaking tour through the Middle West . . . Miss Marion Crowley, niece of Foreign Economic Administrator Leo T. Crowley, christened a cargo ship at Superior, Wis.

• • •

Chester Bowles is hearing from his home town, and no fooling. The town is Essex, Conn., before the war a peaceful village of 3000 whose principal industry was a piano parts factory. Then the factory converted to glider-making, increasing the town's population to 6000. Now the Army has cut back its contract, and most of the plant's employes are out of work. The company says it would like to resume making piano parts, but that OPA's price ceilings are so low it can't. No wonder the Price Administrator is hearing from the home folks . . . A bureaucrat was dictating a letter to his stenographer. When he said "M-125," the stenographer stopped him and asked whether he said "M" or "N." "I said 'M'," her boss declared. " 'M' as in mnemonics." . . . At the Dumbarton Oaks peace conference, Undersecretary of State Edward R. Stettinius, Jr., calls Sir Alexander Cadogan, the correct British Permanent Secretary of State for Foreign Affairs, "Alex," and Russian Ambassador Andrei A. Gromyko, "Andrei."

• • •

Washington's air raid sirens, test-sounded every noon for the last two years, have been silenced except for Saturday tests . . . Another quietness note comes from the court of U. S. Commissioner Needham C. Turnage, in Washington, who conducted a case involving an estranged couple in two and one-half hours of almost complete silence. The warring man and woman were mutes . . . A 14-year-old Negro who looted 30 Georgetown homes was peddling filched whisky at prices ranging from 25 cents a fifth for a standard brand of rye to $1.25 for a fifth of "very rare" Scotch, when detectives caught up with him . . . The late Harry H. Billany, who was fourth assistant Postmaster General, left an estate of more than $400,000 . . . The District of Columbia commissioners have issued stringent fire regulations for any public meetings held in tents here, as a result of the Hartford, Conn., circus disaster.

• • •

Secretary of the Navy James V. Forrestal reports that when he polled war correspondents attached to General Dwight D. Eisenhower's headquarters in Normandy, their guesses as to when the European war would end ranged all the way from Sept. 30, 1944, to June 1, 1945 . . . Captain George Culver, of Mobile, Ala., who is six feet, six inches tall and weighs 355 pounds, is the largest skipper in the U. S. Maritime Service, but he commands the smallest ocean-going vessel built by the Maritime Commission—the Phineas Winsor, which is only half as long as a Liberty ship and one-fourth its deadweight tonnage . . . In Washington it's illegal to carry a beanshooter if you're less than 18; sales of lame mules are considered misdemeanors, and owners of talking birds are warned that if they (the birds) annoy their neighbors, the birds will be shot at once, according to police regulations.

Edited by John C. O'Brien

Wilfrid Fleisher

Rigid Control For Mandates Is Planned

AMERICAN peace planners, looking beyond the Four-Power conferences on post-war security at Dumbarton Oaks, envisage the creation of three regional councils to take their place under the central executive council of the new peace organization.

The regional councils would deal with three world areas. One, the Far East including India; two, Europe, the Near East and Africa, and three, North and South America.

The nations which would be represented in the regional councils would be those of the United Nations having direct interests in a particular region. The Far Eastern regional council would include the Big Four, the United States, Great Britain, Russia and China and probably The Netherlands, France, Australia, New Zealand, the Philippines, which will become free when the Japanese are driven out of the islands, and India, if it attains either dominion status or complete freedom at the end of the war.

• • •

THE regional council for the Far East will have more of a task before it than either of the other two councils for Europe and the Americas, because over half of the peoples of Asia were dependent or colonial nations up to the time of the outbreak of the present Pacific war and will have to be administered under some form of international trusteeship after the war

If the plans now being worked out take definite shape, the regional council for the Far East would act as trustee, supervising the administration of dependent territories, which would be under the direct rule of an "administering power," the new name to be given to mandatories.

• • •

AMERICAN peace planners envisaged the trusteeship as an improvement over the mandate system of the League of Nations since several of the mandatory nations, particularly Japan, acted as if they considered the mandated territories had been awarded to them rather than placed in their trust to administer.

It would be made plain in the future that the administering power of a colonial territory would be acting merely as trustees, and would be responsible for its administration to the Regional Council. This would mean it would have to make regular reports, not perfunctory ones, such as were made to the League of Nations, and which the League set aside when the issue was embarrassing or explosive, as was the case with Japan. It would have to submit to inspection and supervsion by the Regional Council and carry out its recommendations.

Streets of Paris Today

Excitement, Danger Lurk Everywhere

By Ivan H. (Cy) Peterman
Inquirer War Correspondent
By Wireless

PARIS, Aug. 27.

DO YOU remember during the World's Fairs, the Century of Progress, the Sesquicentennial, the Pan-American Exposition and the World of Tomorrow those popular sideshows called the Streets of Paris? And do you remember the tremendous business they did because sensation lovers preferred their lively human demonstrations to the arts, culture and farflung exposition of man's productive genius?

Well, the Streets of Paris today put that peepshow stuff to shame. If it's excitement you wish, just stick your head outdoors these days and somebody will have a shot at you. Perhaps you'd like to take a brief tour with me and get the feel of the fabled city as it tastes its first freedom in four years, amid the accompaniment of snipers.

You are driving along Boulevard Rue Martin near the Paris police prefecture, just a couple of squares from the Seine's turgid waters where a good many German bodies have lately washed. Even now, if you wish to wander there on a blacked-out night you may hear a splash and hurrying footsteps, but don't try to look into that. It's not done these Paris nights if you like to live.

• • •

LOOK about you and note the blast-scarred walls and pillars and someone says:

"Oh, that. The Germans had an unfortunate accident here one day last week. They ran out of grenades and tried throwing a teller mine at besieging patriots. Unfortunately they didn't throw it far enough—it finished them instead."

Now drive through the shuttered streets until you reach the Rue de Rivoli where every woman delights to shop. Remember those trick dress stores and the fancy millineries? There's not much on view these days, but there is some excitement in the street. They bring Germans down the Rue de Rivoli to prison and the crowd watches.

Look at that crowd for a moment. It isn't mob, nor is it as sullen and murderous as those of classic description. This isn't the Paris mob of 1789, although it is hungry. You remember the woman, frayed but neat, who approached your jeep an hour back.

"My stomach is empty," she said. "But my heart is full of gratitude. I am happy to see this day when you Americans have come."

• • •

THIS woman, and thousands like her, stands in the crowd and laughs and waves. Only in the partisans' faces do you see indications of passion. The guerilla fighters do not fool and the Germans fear them. Now we are in the Place de la Concorde, with its German headquarters at the Crillon.

It is full of trees here, and countrylike. The Germans like lots of trees and bucolic surroundings, and here they gravitated whenever they visited Paris. Here daily they gave band concerts, unattended by decent Frenchmen. They marched daily beneath the Arc de Triomphe. But now they're barricaded within the Crillon, what remains of the German holding forces.

They consist of about 50 high ranking officers—major colonels and a few equivalent to our one-star generals. They are now surrounded, and here, as if watching the last quarter of a big game, the crowd stands now in many thousands, packed so thick, roosting as if in bleachers, upon the esplanades and statuary commemorating the lost cities of Alsace and Lorraine dating back to 1870.

• • •

THE crowd is here for the kill and it surges gradually against the barricades.

Now the Germans are coming out —they see their motor cars burning and are startled. French Forces of the Interior ignited the cars, although they could have put the vehicles to good use. You will see more of that curious reaction in a moment. The German officers try to remain erect and unflustered, but while they're being searched many show signs of fear.

"Hitler assassins! . . . Hilter assassins! . . . robbers . . . murderers . . . thieves . . . pigs," the crowd cries.

Now people are pressed to the barricades—barbed wire and steel obstructions made by the Germans and erected by the French. It's a good obstacle but some scale it quickly and the 250 Nazis look nervous. You cannot know what this means to the German officers — this humiliation before the people so lately conquered. A German colonel in the Reichswehr regards himself as a super-leader among Herrenvolk, a demigod whose word is life or death and who never stoops to a menial task. The crowd applauds, clearing a space for the prisoner vans.

They are ordered forward presently, a loose unmilitary lot who don't keep ranks in this crisis and must lift and carry their own bags. Each put his belongings down at the door—fine looking valises. One made of chrome and aluminum glitters in the sunlight and seems full of an officer's personals.

• • •

NOW look about you where a dozen Frenchmen are standing on a jeep, kissing and hugging, young and old, and all intelligent looking people. This crowd is similar to one you'd find at an American game or race track. Mixed, to be sure, but well-dressed, cheerful and average. Nothing mean or surly individually, but they don't want those Germans to have that luggage. They know how they stole most of the stuff.

You see in their faces—Frenchmen have expressive faces—that they hate these Huns, but they won't touch property not theirs. The officers are pushed into the waiting vans as the crowd menacingly breaks through the barricade. They roll away amid imprecations, then suddenly the angry crowd laughs again and in turn cheers the Tricolor ascending while partisans fire a salute.

It is exactly like the end of a big game, with the crowd wending again toward their homes. You try to recall comparisons and remember a particularly tough ball game won by the home team. It was jeopardized by the umpire's decision and the crowd became sullen and got on him. Then, when victory was assured, the fans were pleasant and going home they were cheerful and satisfied.

That's the Paris crowd these turbulent days.

• • •

THEY have no fear except crowd panic. They don't flinch until bullets strike; they cheer the Yanks and boo the Germans and since they seem to have nothing to do, are always in the streets. One woman put it this way:

"Why should we be afraid now? You Americans are here. All is well."

That may be the answer. It may explain the rashness, too, of the F. F. I. boys, young wild-looking kids who roar down Paris boulevards shooting into windows as they ride.

You watch a tipsy Moroccan suddenly raise his tommygun and fire the whole magazine into an open window of a building although the streets are quiet except for him. He saw nothing. He just felt the urge to shoot.

You're wriggling your jeep among the mad, racing F. F. I. cars occupied by so many amalgamated Parisian partisans, united only in their hatred of the Boche. You wonder if they'll know friend from enemy after dark and decide to stay inside.

Again you're riding in the great procession which foolishly was staged over French General LeClerc's wishes, although the town still was full of collaborationists and Huns in civilian clothing wearing F. F. I. armbands, too. You suspect trouble and it begins, shooting from everywhere. You are in the square as General de Gaulle escapes into a building and is whisked to the Cathedral of Notre Dame where more trouble breaks.

• • •

ODD things occur. You see a Yank tank crunch over a dozen Paris bicycles so indispensable these days, and it makes you wince knowing they mean food, transportation, even life to their owners. But the snipers must be routed and the tank crushed them in the gutter where they were abandoned, while their helpless owners stand inside a building. Life is cheap in Paris today but not bicycles.

You notice the famous places locked and barred with chairs piled high—in Maxim's, Weber's and other famous cafes along Grand Boulevard. You learn Paris after dark is just that—lights go out and you go to bed. You will find small family celebrations, and it's difficult to resist their insistent hospitality but when darkness falls and bombers come and red flames from burning buildings light the skies, the streets of Paris are not gay, but dangerous.

And they are nothing whatever like those you saw at the World's Fair!

(Signal Corps Radiophoto from A. P. Wirephoto)

PARIS TRIUMPH The famed Arc de Triomphe in Paris, scene of many a grand military display in the past, became the focal point of a parade when American troops and the French Forces of the Interior retook the French capital from the Nazis. Cheering crowds are shown at the right and left.

RESCUER Coast Guard Radioman Charles J. Mulholland, of 4129 Taylor ave., Drexel Hill, was with rescuers who saved 1100 invaders from the Channel on D-Day.

(Signal Corps Radiophoto from A. P. Wirephoto)

STREET FIGHTING As the Germans evacuated Paris they left snipers who frequently fired into throngs of the citizenry. The above photograph records an incident on Saturday. French gendarmes are shown taking to the ground and the cover of vehicles while American troops seek to dislodge the snipers.

(Signal Corps Radiophoto from A. P. Wirephoto)

PARISIANS CELEBRATE For the first time since the beginning of the German occupation, there was gaiety in Paris last Friday when Allied troops entered the city. This big, cheering throng is gathered at the Hotel de Ville, the Paris city hall, shown in the background.

GETS CAPTAINCY First Lieutenant Hilton L. Goodman (left), of 457 E. Allegheny ave., gets captain's bars in Italy from Lieutenant General Mark W. Clark, on whose staff he is assigned. It was a field ceremony.

IN FRANCE Second Lieutenant Martha J. Thompson, a Wac from Philadelphia and daughter of Federal Judge J. Whitaker Thompson, is pictured with her chief, Major General Hoyt S. Vandenberg, at advance post. She is his secretary.

FEATURES FOR WOMEN

Crusade Group to Map Plans for Reveille Rally

By Jane Wister

For many the Labor Day week-end formed a fitting climax to the summer's gaiety, and now society is returning to resume committee meetings and duties preliminary to charitable undertakings which are a regular part of the annual autumn calendar.

Today Mrs. Thomas Biddle K. Ringe will entertain at luncheon at the Acorn Club for the members of what is known as the "events committee" of the Community Crusade of the United War Chest, to plan the Reveille Rally for early in October.

This occasion is the first get-together of the workers since the group scattered for the summer holiday. The members expected to attend the luncheon include Mrs. Charles C. Norris, Jr., Mrs. J. Howard Pew, Mrs. Kermit Fischer, Mrs. William Tefft Schwarz, Mrs. Harrison F. Flippin, Mrs. E. A. Roberts, Mrs. Sidney B. Dexter, Mrs. H. A. W. Myrin, Mrs. Frank A. Pfalzer, Mrs. Joseph N. Snellenburg, Mrs. S. Dana Weeder, Mrs. Francis R. Strawbridge, Mrs. Stephen C. Stephano and Mrs. Otto F. Bradley.

Time for another Starlight Dance at the Bellevue-Stratford and the talent for this evening's entertainment arranged by the Officers Club will be from the cast of the current stage hit, "Three Is a Family," with Emily Noble and Ruth McArthur contributing to the program.

The hostesses at the dance will be Mrs. Sidney S. Blake, Mrs. Clarence J. Lewis, Jr., Mrs. Roy Underdown, Mrs. Robert Greene, Miss Mary Anne Mechling and Mrs. Stephen Gimber. Plans for the next Sunday at Nine concert, another project of the Officers' Club, to be held this coming Sunday, sound attractive enough, with Frank Lynn scheduled to play the accordion for the square dances.

Invitations have just come for the card party to be given at the Philadelphia Cricket Club on Wednesday afternoon, Sept. 27, for the benefit of the Chestnut Hill Hospital. The benefit, which is being arranged by the War Relief Aid Committee, will be preceded by a buffet luncheon to be held on the club terrace.

The event is the first in this season's series sponsored by this group of energetic workers, who are headed by Mrs. John B. Hendrickson and Mrs. Joseph J. Hoffman, as co-chairmen.

The committee includes Mrs. Walter C. Bailey, Mrs. Thomas Hand Ball, Mrs. Walter D. Banes, Mrs. Chester Bidwell, Mrs. Charles Stanley Borton, Mrs. William Van Courtland Brandt, Mrs. Harry W. Butterworth, Jr., Mrs. Herbert E. Calves, Mrs. Harry Lippincott Cassard, Mrs. F. Stokes Coleman, Mrs. Edward G. Costello, Mrs. John N. Costello, Mrs. Richard H. DeMott, Mrs. James S. Dempsey, Mrs. Lawrence J. Fuller, Mrs. Arthur N. Goodfellow, Mrs. Russell L. Heberling, Mrs. Lee Harrar Heist, Mrs. John F. Keator, Mrs. Howard Ketcham, Mrs. M. H. Leister, Mrs. Bruce L. Lewis, Mrs. Horace M. Lippincott, Mrs. James H. Little, Mrs. T. Carlisle Mitchell, Mrs. John F. McCloskey, Mrs. Edward K. Moore, Mrs. Edward T. Newkirk, Mrs. Davenport Plumer, Mrs. Roland D. Pollock, Mrs. William A. Schnader, Mrs. Thomas M. Searles, Mrs. Stewart Smythe, Mrs. Edwin H. Stulb, Mrs. Joseph R. Stulb, Mrs. Dexter A. Tutein, Mrs. W. K. B. Urquhart, Mrs. R. Morris Urquhart, Mrs. Oliver Walker and Mrs. Jerome West.

3884
SIZES 12-46

The Suit Dress

Fashion has a pet these days—a two-piece suit that is a dress, but a dress that embraces all the qualities of fine tailoring and the suit-like look.

Style No. 3884 in size 36 requires 3¼ yards 54-inch fabric.

Send 16c for pattern. Write plainly, your name, address, postal zone number and style number. Be sure to state size.

Address: Pattern Department, The Philadelphia Inquirer, 121 West 19th street, New York 11, N. Y. If not delivered within two weeks, telephone Ruth Martin Rittenhouse 1000, or write.

The current Fashion Book, illustrating 175 pattern designs, is 15c with a pattern, 15c if ordered separately. Include two cents extra for mailing.

The Daily Recipe

Often spinach or other cooked greens are among the foods which are difficult to use as leftovers. Combining the cooked greens with chipped beef and cream sauce on toast makes a delicious luncheon dish.

Savory Spinach

- 4 tablespoons butter
- 2 tablespoons flour
- 1 cup milk
- ⅛ teaspoon pepper
- ½ teaspoon Worcestershire sauce
- ¼ pound chipped beef
- Cooked spinach or other greens

Make a white sauce of the butter, flour, milk, pepper and Worcestershire sauce. Drain the spinach and add to white sauce mixture. Add slivered chipped beef. Heat thoroughly. Serve on toasted slices of bread and garnish with diced egg yolk. Serves six.

Rationing Calendar

RATION TOKENS now in use: Red for beefsteaks, beef roasts and lamb, ham, pork loins, butter and cheese. Blue for processed foods.

MEATS, BUTTER, CHEESE: All meats except beef steaks, beef roasts and choice cuts of lamb, pork loins and ham are point-free. Utility grade lamb and utility grade beef roasts and beef steaks point-free. Book 4 red stamps A8 through Z8 and A5 through G5 now valid for 10 points each. Butter, margarine, cheese and canned fish require red ration stamps or tokens.

PROCESSED FOODS: Blue stamps A8 through Z8 and A5 through L5 good for 10 points each, are valid indefinitely.

SUGAR: Stamps 30, 31, 32 and 33 Book No. 4 are good for five pounds indefinitely. Stamp 40 is now valid until Feb. 28, 1945.

USED FATS: Each pound of waste fat is good for two red points and four cents.

SHOES: Airplane stamps 1 and 2 in Book 3 are valid for an indefinite period.

GASOLINE: A-11 coupons are valid until Nov. 8. B-3, B-4, B-5 and C-3, C-4, C-5 coupons are good for five gallons. T coupons marked "3 Qtr." are now valid.

FUEL OIL: Coupons for Periods 4 and 5 are good through Sept. 30. New period number 1 coupons may be used as soon as received from ration boards.

LIQUOR: War Ration Book No. 3 good for one-fifth gallon whisky until Sept. 23.

Along the Social Way

Miss Virginia R. Barton, daughter of Mr. and Mrs. Thomas C. Barton, of "Woodleave," Bryn Mawr, will entertain at a buffet supper on Wednesday evening, Sept. 20, in honor of Miss Sophronia M. Worrell, daughter of Mr. and Mrs. Granville Worrell, of "Hermstead," Gladwyne, and Midshipman Tyler Griffin, U.S.N.R., son of Mr. and Mrs. Frank H. Griffin, of "Old Orchard," Wawa, following the rehearsal for their marriage, which will take place the following afternoon, in the Church of the Redeemer, Bryn Mawr. The guests will include the members of the bridal party.

The date of the tea and shower planned in honor of Miss Nina Cooke, daughter of Lieutenant Colonel and Mrs. Jay Cooke, of "Brookfield," Chestnut Hill, for Sept. 23, has been changed to Thursday afternoon, Sept. 14, when the hostesses will be Miss Barbara Jane McDowell, daughter of Mr. and Mrs. William W. McDowell, of Chestnut Hill, and Miss Virginia C. Barba, daughter of Dr. and Mrs. Philip S. Barba, of Germantown.

The engagement of Miss Cooke to Mr. Alan L. Emlen, son of Mr. and Mrs. George W. Emlen, of "Awbury," Germantown, was recently announced.

On Cape May Visit

Mr. and Mrs. Gilbert A. Harvey, of the Cambridge Apartments, Germantown, are spending a short time at Cape May.

The marriage of Miss Sara Jane Snyder, daughter of Mr. and Mrs. Alfred J. Snyder, of Chestnut Hill, to Lieutenant Dyckman Ware Vermilye, U. S. Army Air Forces, son of Mr. and Mrs. Joseph W. Vermilye, of Staten Island, N. Y., will take place at 2.30 o'clock tomorrow afternoon in Grace Episcopal Church, Mt. Airy. Rev. Charles E. Eder, rector of the church, will officiate.

Miss Shirley Eder will be maid of honor and only attendant. Mr. Vermilye will act as best man for his son. A reception will follow the ceremony.

After a wedding trip Lieutenant Vermilye and his bride will reside at Grand Island, Neb., where he is stationed.

Daughter Is Born

Lieutenant and Mrs. William T. Arnold, Jr., are receiving congratulations upon the birth of a daughter, Sarah Elizabeth Arnold, on Aug. 31. Mrs. Arnold is the former Miss Elizabeth M. Hardt, daughter of Mr. and Mrs. Walter K. Hardt, of Haverford, with whom she is living while Lieutenant Arnold is in the service.

Mrs. John K. Strubing, of Chestnut Hill, returned recently from Longport, N. J., where she spent part of August.

Mr. and Mrs. Robert A. Hall, of Rosemont, are receiving congratulations upon the birth of a son, Charles Shipley Hall, on Sept. 6. Mrs. Hall is the daughter of Mr. and Mrs. Charles R. Shipley, of Rosemont and the Barclay.

Lieutenant Commander and Mrs. Robert P. Farrington are now living at 3634 Royal Palm ave., Coconut Grove, Miami. Mrs. Farrington is the former Miss Helen Brannen, of the Barclay and Longport, N. J.

Mr. and Mrs. Benjamin R. Bacon, of Mount Airy, announce the engagement of their daughter, Miss Margaret Collingwood Bacon, to Robert Earle DuBois, son of Mr. Earle DuBois, also of Mount Airy.

Select Stories To Lull Child At Bedtime

By Carolyn Randolph

Child Care Parents must take into consideration their youngsters' imaginations. When left alone children can imagine dreadful things, once they have been stirred by eerie tales.

Bedtime stories should be chosen carefully or they will rouse your youngster instead of quieting him. Don't select a book for its colorful cover or gay pictures—know the story yourself before you start reading it.

It's also important that stories be satisfactorily concluded before you put out the light at night. Don't stop reading at the most exciting part or your youngster will worry and fuss wondering what will happen next. You may forget it immediately, but the story is important to him and he thinks much more about it than you do.

Mrs. Gentry, of Philadelphia, will receive two dollars for her letter, which follows:

"While away on vacation I noticed that our little girl, who never was afraid at night, developed a sudden concern that her closet doors be closed and hall lights be left on. At first I blamed a strange bedroom for this, but it turned out to be her cousin's thriller comics.

"On reaching home she wanted to buy more of these, but I persuaded her to invest in good books, well-known children's classics. When she does get an occasional comic book I see to it that they're of the truly humorous type rather than the thriller kind, which in her case were certainly proving harmful."

Two dollars is paid for each Child Care letter published. Write to Carolyn Randolph, The Philadelphia Inquirer.

Carolyn Randolph, whose commonsense column on Child Care is a regular feature of The Inquirer, will answer your child-care queries. Address your queries to Carolyn Randolph, The Philadelphia Inquirer.

Comings and Goings—

Mr. and Mrs. Harry W. Fehr and their daughter, Mrs. William Gribbel, of "Cricket Heath," Whitemarsh, have returned from a visit with Mrs. John W. Watson, at the latter's summer home at Longport, N. J.

Mrs. William H. Horstman and Miss Josephine Fraley, of "Norwynden," Overbrook, who have been spending the summer at Northeast Harbor, Me., will return home the middle of this month. Dr. and Mrs. Frederick Fraley will remain at Northeast Harbor until early in October.

Mr. Thomas M. Scott, of Four Gables, Wynnewood, has returned from a short visit with his daughter, Mrs. M. LeBaron Hibbs, at Newport, R. I.

LIEUT. LEONARD STERLING, Toys · LIEUTENANT JOHN KELLY, Service Manager · CORPORAL ELSA PHILLIPS, Housefurnishings · CAPTAIN JESSE MERCY, Millinery Buyer · STAFF SERGT. JOSEPH REILLY, Toys · SERGT. GRACE DELGI UOMINI, 400 Aisle · STAFF SGT. HARRY DeMARCO, Pure Foods · SERGEANT FRANK HARTUSCH, Display

STAFF SERGT. NEAL LEHANE, Warehouse · CORPORAL JOHN BATTANYI, Flower Shop

Gimbels dedicates

PRIVATE THOMAS REEVES, Mail Room · SGT. WILLIAM NAPOLINE, Auto Accessories · SERGEANT LEWIS GREEN, Advertising · LIEUT. SAMUEL ROTNER, Sporting Goods · PVT. HYMAN WHITMAN, Boys' Clothing · CAPTAIN ALVIN GRAUER, Advertising · CPL. WM. KEYSER, Women's Shoes · SERGEANT CLAIRE WEBER, Telephone Service

STAFF SGT. A. CANNATARO, Subway Shoe Repair · CPL. PHILIP COSTELLO, Furniture warehouse · PVT. RICHARD ELFMAN, Santa Claus · LT. HENRY GOLDBERG, Subway Men's Furnishings · S 1/C STANLEY FINE, Display · LIEUTENANT NAT HANDLER, Sporting Goods · PFC JOHN TWITTY, Receiving · SGT. JACK COHN, Subway Coats

CPL. MILTON SEGAL, Fur Repairs · RAYMOND GALLAGHER, Delivery · MAJOR R. WARREN, Leather Goods Buyer · LT. COL. RICHARD FLEISHER, Men's Hosiery Buyer · CAPT. WARREN VANHOOK, Upholstery · PVT. FRANK KILCOYNE, Rugs · PVT. JOSEPH SUMMERS, Warehouse · CPL. HOWARD JAMIESON, Receiving

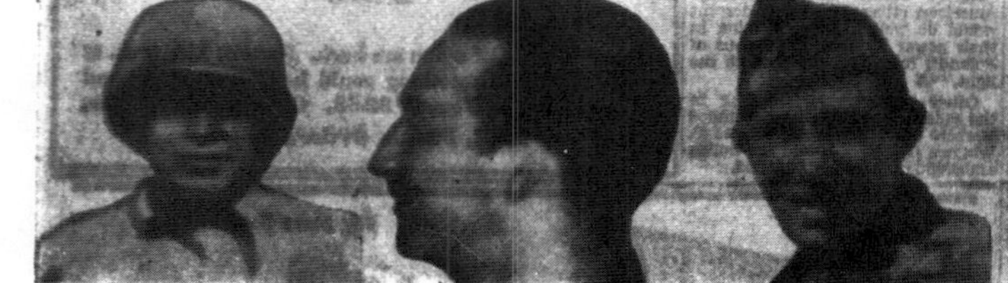

MAJOR ALLAN KING, Bedding · PRIVATE REUEL SIDES, Advertising · SGT. WILLIAM CHRISTY, Subway Dresses · PVT. FRANK ADER, Store Packing · S 1/C RALPH SESSO, Boys' Clothing · CPL. CHARLES PATTERSON, Delivery · PVT. JOHN DOODY, Receiving · DORIS MULFORD, A S, Advertising

not only those whose pictures we have, but these, whose names are just as valued:

SGT. HARRY C. ABELE, Jr. — Linens
CORPORAL RUSSELL ALLEN — Fountain
STAFF SGT. EDW. ANDRES — Service Manager
SGT. ADELE APFELBAUM — Accounts Receivable
PFC. PETER BACH — Men's Clothing
PRIVATE FRANK BAKER — Receiving
LIEUTENANT HARRY BALLEN — Upholstery
S 2/C NORMAN BARKER — Leather Goods
PRIVATE STANLEY BASS — Subway Rugs
ULLA E. BAUERS, Y 1/c — Subway Men's Clothing
CPL. JAMES J. BLACK — Subway Rugs
DALLAS BLACKWELL, S 1 c — Night Porter
PFC SIDNEY BLOCK — Radios
PFC VIOLA BOOKER — Accounts Payable
PRIVATE JOHN BOMBA — Receiving
CAPT. STANTON BONNEM — Furs
PRIVATE GEORGE BOYCE — Store Packing
PRIVATE THOMAS BRADY — Major Appliances
PVT. EDWIN BUCHNER — Reserve Stock
CORPORAL NORMAN BUCK — Pure Foods
WILLIAM J. BURNS, PHM 2 c — Carrier
CAPT. CHARLES CARROLL — Furniture
SERGEANT LOUIS CHALSON — Auto Accessories
LESTER CHEW, S 2 c — Store Packing
LT. J. G. GLADYS CHURCH — Advertising
HARVEY CLEVELAND — Restaurant
SERGT. WILLIAM CAMPBELL — Carpet Workroom

CAPTAIN BENJAMIN DESSEN — Store Dentist
CORPORAL FRANK DeTRANE — Sign Shop
LIEUTENANT WILLIAM DEVINE — Advertising
ALLEN DICKERMAN — Men's Clothing
ANTONI DINTINO, A/S — Subway Fountain
PRIVATE CHARLES DONNELLY — Scout Equipment
STAFF SGT. DAVID DORMAN — Misses' Coats
PRIVATE ROBERT DOYLE, Jr. — Men's Clothing
LIEUT. RAYMOND DRESSLER — Men's Hosiery
PRIVATE ARTHUR DUPIETRO — Silver Salon
PFC RONALD ENGLISH — Women's Shoes
PRIVATE MICHAEL FEENEY — Warehouse
GERALD FISHER, Y 1 c — Subway Luggage
CORP. JOSEPH FITZGERALD — Service Manager
LT. RICHARD FITZGERALD — Sewing Machines
PRIVATE JOSEPH FORD — Housefurnishings
LT. WILLIAM FRANKFURTER — Advertising
ROBERT FRITZ, S 2 c — Display
PRIVATE GEORGE FRIES — Night Porter
CPL. LILLIAN GABLE — Credit
HARRY GALLAGHER S 2 c — Shoe Clinic
PRIVATE PHILLIP GALLAGHER — Boys' Furnishings
PFC BERNARD GARRETT — Men's Hosiery
FRANK GASPENO, S 1 c — Infants' Furniture
STAFF SGT. F. GEISENHOFFER — Pure Foods
PRIVATE ISSY GERAS — Watch Repair
PFC JOHN GEORGE — Subway Boys' Clothing

S 2 C LEWIS GIBSON — Delivery
PFC DANIEL GOFFREDO — Receiving
ROBERT GOODWIN, ACOM. — Warehouse
ROBERT GOSLEE, S 2 c — Subway Toiletries
LEONARD GREENBERG, S 2 c — Men's Hosiery
PRIV. RUSSELL GRIENDLING — Subway Housefurnishings
PVT. EDWARD GROSSKOPF — Flower Shop
PFC. CHARLES HAMMES — Reserve Stock
SERGEANT ALBERT HARVEY — Receiving
PRIVATE JULIUS HECK — Toys
PRIVATE ROY HEMMINGER — Pure Foods
LESLIE HENDRICKSON, SK 3 c — Beauty Salon
PRIVATE JAMES HICKEY — Warehouse
SGT. LEON HOCKSTEIN, — Toys
PRIVATE HAROLD HODGES — Delivery
MAR. GUNNER FRANK HOLLORAN — Electrician
SERGEANT HARRY HORNER — Receiving
SERGEANT JAMES HOUCK — Subway Men's Furnishings
ENSIGN G. HOLLINGSWORTH — Receiving
LIEUT. WADE HOWELLS — Men's Hosiery
RICHARD HUBBARD S 1 c — Co-worker Cafeteria
PRIVATE WILLIAM HUTTON — Receiving
LIEUTENANT ALTA JOFFE — Personnel
SERGEANT WILLIAM JORDAN — Subway Shoes
STAFF SGT. ALBERT JONES — Sporting Goods
PVT. LARRY JUD — Reserve Stock
BENJAMIN KAETES, S 1 c — Subway Boys' Clothing

CAPTAIN CLARENCE KEISER — Subway Rug Buyer
PVT. WM. KIMBER — Fur Storage
LIEUTENANT ROBERT KINSEY — Furniture
SGT. CHAS. KLIEMAN — Men's Furnishings
PRIVATE BENJAMIN KOHN — Subway Coats
CPL. FRANCIS LAKE — Subway Rugs
JACK LAMARRA, SK 3 c — Beauty Salon
PRIVATE JULIA LAWLER — Furniture Office
ALLAN LEIGH, Y 3 c — Men's Furnishings
PRIVATE EDWARD LENTERS — Upholstery
PRIVATE ISADORE LERNER — Supply Room
PRIVATE BEULAH LEVY — Corsets
CADET BERNARD LIPS — Delivery
STAFF SGT. JAMES LLOYD — Watch Repair
CAPTAIN PAUL LORD — Display
STAFF SGT. THEO. LOWENSTEIN — Men's Hats
SERGEANT JAMES MAGEE — Yard Goods
T/4 CHARLES MAIER — Mail Room
PRIVATE JOHN MALLOY — Supply Room
THOMAS MALTESE, A S — Men's Clothing Workroom
ROBERT MANLEY, F 2 c — Furniture Stock
PRIVATE ALLEX MANUS — Carpet Workroom
PRIVATE CHARLES MILLOY — Supply Room
CECELIA MILLIGAN, WAAF — Subway Dresses
DONALD MONIAT, A S — Men's Clothing
GLEN MOTON, A S — Subway Shoe Repair
PRIVATE GEORGE MOORE — Flower Shop

PFC. FRANZ MORRISON — Beauty Salon
THOMAS MUDD — Delivery
PFC PAUL MULLER — Pure Foods
CPL. JOHN MURPHY — Subway Rugs
GEORGE MURRAY, A S — Furniture Workroom
HELEN MYERS — 800 Aisle
JOHN MYERS, S 2 c — Furniture Stock
CORPORAL THOMAS MacHALE — Controller's Office
AFC. MADELINE McBRIDE — Accounts Payable
PRIVATE MICHAEL McCANN — Young Budget Dress Buyer
PRIVATE JAMES McCONAGHY — Warehouse
LT. CLIFFORD McCORMICK — Carpenter
PVT. JOHN McFASSELL — Delivery
S 2/C BOYD McGRANAGHAN — Receiving
SERGT. HERBERT NELSON — Day Porter
GERALD NICOLINI, S 2 c — Pure Foods
PRIVATE ALBERT NOVIN — Advertising

STAFF SGT. JAMES O'REILLY — Rugs
WM. O'REILLY — Delivery
OLIVER PATTEN, S 1 c — Bank
S. SGT. HERMAN PERTOSOFF — Beauty Salon
PRIV. HOWARD PETERZELL — Subway China
JAMES PHINNEY, A S — Subway Stock
PAUL PRIEMAZON, A S — Flower Shop
PFC RUTH PROVENCE — Subway Luncheonette
JOHN PROVENCE, S 2/C — Carrier
HELENE ROBACZEK, A S — Yard Goods
SERGT. FRANK RODZIEWICZ — Subway Shoe Repair
FRANK ROSEN, SK 3 c — Men's Furnishings
CORPORAL MARIO ROSSI — Beauty Salon
PRIVATE LEONARD RUBER — Subway Furniture
PRIVATE HARRY RUBIN — Housefurnishings
PRIVATE VICTOR RUDINSKI — Receiving
CORP. PHILLIP SACCHETTI — Cameras

MICHAEL SAMMON, A S — Reserve Stock
CORPORAL FRANK SALANTRI — Budget Beauty Salon
PFC GEORGE SALTROFF — Reserve Stock
DAVID SCHEIN, SC 1 c — Lamps
PRIVATE RAYMOND SCHERB — Pure Foods
PRIVATE MARTIN SCHOLL — Subway Furniture
SERGT. NORMAN SCHMIDT — Men's Furnishings
CORPORAL GEORGE SCHULTZ — Contingent
PRIVATE HARRY SCHWARTZ — Reserve Stock
PRIV. JOSEPHINE SCHWINGER — 400 Aisle
CORPORAL HUGH SCOTT — Store Packing
PRIVATE JOSEPH SHEERAN — Reserve Stock
T/SGT. DAVID SIEGAL — Men's Gloves
LIEUTENANT AL SMITH — Advertising
PRIVATE FRANCIS SMITH — Receiving
PFC WILLIAM SMITH — Elevators
PRIVATE JOHN SNEDDEN — Flower Shop

HENRY SOLIDAY, A S — Subway Furniture
A S JEANNE STACKHOUSE — Subway Housefurnishings
CORPORAL THOMAS TARPEY — Auto Accessories
PRIVATE JOHN TASEL — Flower Shop
SERGEANT ROBERT TOOP — Display
CORPORAL FRANK TUCCI — Subway Men's Clothing
PVT. ADOLPH VanHOLLANDER — Display
PFC ANDREW VeTRONE — Subway Upholstery
AVC. THOMAS WALLACE — Carpet Workroom
WILLIAM WEISBERG, AM 3 c — Flower Shop
SGT. ALBERT WESSEL — Warehouse
SGT. IRVING WILSKER — Credit
PRIVATE JOHN WISBER — Furniture
PRIVATE ANNA WITTMAN — Hosiery
PRIVATE MAX WEINFIELD — Receiving
PRIVATE SOL WEINSTEIN — Men's Clothing

OCTOBER is

PFC. DANIEL SWEENEY
Delivery

PFC. WM. RIBELL
Accounts Receivable

PFC. EDWARD JAMIESON
Delivery

LIEUTENANT THEODORE FAIR
Sporting Goods

CORPORAL THOMAS MARSALA
Display

LIEUTENANT JAMES DOYLE
Men's Furnishings

PFC. WILLIAM KEARNEY
Subway Men's Furnishings

SGT. GEORGE ASHWORTH
Fur Storage

to these 245

COLONEL KARL BOWERS
Furniture

CPL. EDWARD WREEN
Receiving

LIEUTENANT DAVID ARONS
Advertising

SGT. WM. SLOSS
Subway Men's Clothing

PFC. HAROLD SIMPSON
Warehouse

PVT. ALLAN KAMM
Subway Rugs Asst. Buyer

PFC. GEORGE LAPUTKA
Delivery

SGT. B. RICHARD RUBIN
Smoke Shop

PVT. MORRIS POPOVER
Men's Furnishings

CPL. WM. MacMULLIN
Subway Upholstery

PVT. JOSEPH McCULLOUGH
Furniture Workroom

Our 102nd Anniversary message

WE'LL GIVE THEM BACKING IN THE FIGHT

—and the solemn assurance

of happy, profitable creative jobs

at Gimbels when it's over!

ANDY COOPER, S 2/c
Correspondence

PFC. ALEX SCHMERLING
Advertising

JOSEPH O'DONNELL, GM 3 c
Linens

T/3 SOL SCHWARTZMAN
Men's Hosiery

PVT. WILLIAM STREET
Toiletries

LT (jg) WM. F. BURNS
Personnel Director

CORPORAL WALTER SCOTT
Firm's Office

CPL. ANTHONY De VUONO
Contingent

ERNEST LoFURNO Ptr 1/c
Receiving

This is our Anniversary month, a time to honor the ideals which have carried this business through five generations of service to America. And in this year of decision we can honor them best by paying tribute to these 245—paying it not alone with words, but with deeds! To back the Gimbel men and women who left our ranks for the uniformed ranks of war, Gimbel co-workers have sold more than $11,000,000 worth of War Bonds, donated more than 1000 pints of blood for plasma, conserved more than 530 tons of paper, contributed thousands of dollars to Philadelphia's war funds. But we have an obligation beyond this, and we acknowledge it with proud and solemn acceptance.

It is our obligation, not only to back them while the fight is on, but to see to it that they come back to secure homes, and to good, creative, opportunity-filled jobs at Gimbels. Those of our former Gimbel workers who apply within 40 days after mustering out will be on our payroll immediately, either in the jobs they left, or comparable jobs (a lot of them have learned new skills in the service, and we'll help them make the most of them)! To these men and women we owe a tremendous obligation. And on this, our 102nd Anniversary, we want them to know we are resolved to discharge that obligation as faithfully as they have discharged theirs to all America.

GIMBELS 102nd ANNIVERSARY

Cardinals Beat Browns, 3-1, Win World Series

Football Follies

Deserts Bed For the Bench

Doctor Finds Ace, Hidden by Friends, Groggy But Game

By ART MORROW

A SHARP elbow to the jaw added to the complications of the University of Pennsylvania dressing room strategy between halves of Saturday's 20-6 victory over Dartmouth. Bob Kurtz, the 17-year-old guard, was still groggy. "Where am I?" he yelled. "What happened?"

He was sent to the infirmary. There doctors ordered him held for observation. He undressed; a nurse tucked him into bed . . . But a few moments later the nurse, returning to make sure the patient was comfortable and to pick up the discarded clothing, found the bed empty. Even the clothes were gone.

Hastily she summoned Dr. Harry Hoffman; in near panic confessed the bird had flown the coop . . . But Dr. Hoffman proved of such stuff as Sherlock Holmes was made. Off he went, through the northwest gate, into Franklin Field. One man among a crowd of 40,000, of course, is like the proverbial needle in the hay-stack—but Dr. Hoffman knew where to look.

And there, sure enough, sat Kurtz—huddling behind a screen of teammates on the Penn bench. The doctor marched the 210-pound youth back toward the infirmary. "What," he demanded indignantly, "was the idea?"

"I thought maybe they'd need me," the kid said, meek but serious. "I wanted to be there."

Line Coach Rae Crowther told George Munger all about it yesterday. "That," the head coach commented, "shows the spirit of our whole squad."

• • •

IT MAY never happen to them again, and a good thing for the blood pressure if it never does, but even the Eagles were excited during the 80-yard march that brought them a 31-31 tie in the last five seconds of Sunday's game with the Washington Redskins. The only cool head in Shibe Park, it seemed, belonged to little Al Sherman, the quarterback.

"The rest of us," a lineman confessed yesterday, "were plain mad—mad we hadn't got in there sooner. Then, with so little time left, we thought it was too late."

But Sherman didn't. "All right, now, guys," he said crisply, quickly, in huddle. "This is it—" he'd name the play—"let's go." And go they did. But when they got to the 30, only 30 seconds were left.

"We need a long pass," Coach Greasy Neale moaned along the sidelines. Sherman stepped back. "How about the screen pass, coach?" he hissed. "The screen pass!" But Greasy, who suffered a heart attack two years ago rooting his Eagles home, was beyond strategy. ". . . look a deep breath, waved Sherman away.

Sherman called the screen; Choo-Choo Maciowczyk grabbed it and reached the 8. Mike Mandarino, the tackle, looked up at the clock. There were more, but only one second showed. Mike started pounding the man next to him. "Fall down!" he yelled. "Fall down—pretend you're hurt. We gotta stop the clock."

• • •

THE final play was supposed to be an end run. Jack Banta started to his left. "I saw three Redskins in front of me." He ran back to his right. "Somebody crashed into me." But Banta refused to be held. Over he went for the touchdown—and, as he trotted back to the bench afterwards, Neale grabbed him, hugged him—held him, too, as none of those Washington tacklers could. But this was friendly.

It was complete reversal of Greasy's feelings of the first quarter. "I made a few mistakes," Banta tells it. Actually, he had received a kick; his right arm still was black and blue yesterday. He missed a couple of tackles. "Hit 'em—hit 'em!" Neale screamed from the sidelines. Banta heard him, waved his arm to indicate he was hurt. To Greasy it looked like a gesture of dismissal. He ranked Banta, glared at him as he sat down—and didn't put him back into the game until that final drive.

Old Blue—Bert Bell's nickname for Greasy—was pretty excited all right; but no more so than the Washington coaches. National League rules permit a coach to pace backward as he wants between the 40-yard lines, but Dud DeGroot and Turk Edwards were all the way down to the 25 on the Redskins' last two drives. "Look, look!" Neale kept screaming to the officials, pointing across the field. But the officials didn't see.

The beat of the afternoon, some half-cooked lamb chops eaten a couple hours before the game worked havoc with the players at times. Once Fullback Ben Kish rubbed his stomach, looked over at the bench and yelled he was sick. "Work it off—work it off" he was excitedly advised.

• • •

IT WAS like the time John Hober reported to Marty Brill at La Salle College with a bad ankle. "Can't practice today, Coach," he said. Brill looked at the ankle. "Walk it off," he ordered curtly. "Walk it out." . . The next day Hober missed practice; Brill was peeved, demanded the following afternoon: "Where were you?" Hober had the answer: "Out taking that five-mile hike you ordered me to take."

Hober, ex-Coast Guardsman who started the season as an Eagles' end, now represents a wholesale florist concern, also helps Heinie Miller coach Penn Charter. A couple weeks ago Hober went out to see the Friends Central team coached by Frank Fitts and Ben Kish in a game with Swarthmore. Kish spotted him. "What are you doing—working for a paper?" he asked. "Maybe," Hober replied, non-committal. Fitts and Kish graciously diagrammed some of their plays for him.

Penn Charter beat Friends Central last Friday, 26-6.

Earnshaw Decorated As Navy Hero

Inquirer Washington Bureau

WASHINGTON, Oct. 9.—Big George Earnshaw, who starred on the mound for the Philadelphia Athletics in the halcyon days of 1929 to 1931, turned up today as a hero in a bigger league.

COMDR. EARNSHAW

The Navy announced that Lieutenant Commander George L. Earnshaw, U. S. N. R., of Swarthmore, Pa., had been awarded the commendation ribbon by Admiral Chester W. Nimitz for helping to save an aircraft carrier from serious damage by Jap torpedo planes during an American attack on Truk Islands in the Pacific last April 29.

The Commendation disclosed that Commander Earnshaw, who has been on active duty in the Navy four years, was gunnery officer of an aircraft carrier during operations against Truk, and cited him for "meritorious conduct in the performance of outstanding service."

"With exceptional ability and judgment and commendable calmness he controlled and directed effective anti-aircraft fire against three, fast, low-flying enemy torpedo planes, and contributed directly in saving his ship from serious damage," the commendation said.

"One plane turned off and was shot down while under fire from the carrier. The other two planes continued and pressed their attacks against the carrier.

"Before coming within effective torpedo range, both were hit many times and flamed by the accurate, concentrated and unrelenting fire which apparently killed the pilots, since the planes crossed and crashed close aboard on the port side of the ship without dropping their torpedoes.

"His outstanding service and conduct throughout were in keeping with the highest traditions of the United States Naval service."

The Navy announced that Commander Earnshaw "at present is gunnery officer on an Essex class carrier."

Commander Earnshaw was a star baseball and football player at Swarthmore College.

William & Mary Tackle Returns

WILLIAMSBURG, Va., Oct. 9.—Johnny Clowes, 210-pound tackle and captain of William and Mary College's undefeated football team, returned to the squad today after being absent for two weeks to undergo an operation for removal of a loose piece of bone from his knee, but Coach R. N. (Rube) McRay said it is not certain whether Clowes will see action against unbeaten University of Pennsylvania at Philadelphia Saturday.

Fortunate in escaping serious injuries while beating Fort Monroe, 48-0, and Hampden-Sydney College, 38-0, the Indians are in a serious mood for the Penn game, realizing that victory over the Quakers, who have beaten Duke University and Dartmouth College, would catapult them into the nation's football spotlight.

McRay today expressed great satisfaction with the showing of several of his players, including Tom Mikula, stellar guard from Johnstown, Pa.

Temple Team Drills For N. Y. U. Contest

Temple University's football team, in fairly good physical trim following the defeat at the hands of Holy Cross Friday night, started drilling yesterday for New York University, Saturday at New York. It will mark the first time the two have met in football.

Jim Wilson, one of the veteran members of Temple, suffered no further injury to the arm he hurt in the Swarthmore game and the experienced left halfback is slated to start against the Violet.

Roman Catholic Victor in Run

Roman Catholic High School defeated Olney High School, 23-40, in a cross-country run yesterday over the Fairmount Park course at 33d and Dauphin sts.

The Catholic League system of counting only the first five runners to finish on each team was used, but the Public League system of scoring was substituted.

1. Walsh, Olney, 13 minutes 19 seconds; 2. Hannigan, Roman Catholic, 13:21; 3. McIntyre, Roman Catholic, 13:29; 4. Ingram, Olney, 13:32; 5. Fisher, Roman Catholic, 13:63; 6. Eichler, Roman Catholic, 14:07; 7. Lawlor, Roman Catholic, 14:08; 8. Martin, Roman Catholic, 14:09; 9. Stuart, Olney, 14:10; 10. Carpenter, Olney, 14:21; 11. Prendergast, Roman Catholic, 14:31; Mason, Roman Catholic, 14:34; 13. Kearney, Roman Catholic, 14:35; 14. Allison, Olney, 14:41; 15. Fahinger, Roman Catholic, 14:37; 16. Cooper, Olney, 15:02.

Arnold Stops Wills in First

Billy's 24th Knockout Thrills 5200 at Met; Wilmer, Jones Win

By KEN HAY

Readying his opponent with a left hook to the mid-section and crossing with a right hook to the left temple, in the first round, Billy Arnold, 145-pound Philadelphia fighter, scored his 24th knockout last night before 5200 fans, who paid $10,485.36 to see the opening boxing show at The Met.

Frankie Wills, 149½ pounds, from Washington, was the victim in the scheduled 10-round windup arranged by Jimmy Toppi. Two minutes, 51 seconds had elapsed when Arnold finished the Southern scrapper who had gone the limit against Henry Armstrong and Bob Montgomery.

ARNOLD GOES TO WORK

Wills simply couldn't withstand the whirlwind assault of Arnold. Arnold just sidestepped a few jabs and then went to work. He faked the left hook in one corner but just missed the cross. Less than a minute later it was a different story.

Wills dropped both arms to ward the dangerous hook. It was a mistake. Arnold just stepped lightly to the right and swung. The blow started slow and gained momentum quickly. To some of the more distant spectators it might have seemed a glancing blow but it hit the right spot and Wills went down for the count.

WILMER TRIUMPHS

In the semi-windup, Archie Wilmer, 128-pounder from Wilmington, pounded New York's Al Guido, 132, heavily in the final three rounds to gain an easy eight-round decision. Wilmer started slower than he has in his more recent fights and Guido took the early edge. Wilmer applied the pressure in the closing rounds, whistling rights and lefts on Guido during this spirited action.

McCoy Jones, 145, Philadelphia, easily gained a six-round decision over Irish Red Schultz, 140, Kensington, in the main preliminary.

T. K. O. FOR MORRIS

Ray Morris, 122½, Wilmington, scored a technical knockout over Jimmy Jerico, 128½, Chicago, in the opening preliminary, while in the other Lester (Cueball) Young, 139½, South Philadelphia, completely outclassed Harry Diduck, 141, Washington, in six rounds. Referee Willie Clark stopped the opening bout after 53 seconds, because Jerico's left eye was badly cut. In a special four-round bout Booker Robinson, 174, Philadelphia, outclassed Mickey Rocco, 171, West Philadelphia. Rocco took a count of nine in the first round.

SCRANTON, Pa.—Henry Jones, 207, New York, knocked out Danny White, 210, Newark, (8).

BALTIMORE—Vic Dellicurti, 160½, New York, decisioned Johnny Walker, 156⅛, Philadelphia, (10).

HARTFORD, Conn.—Red Doty, 149, Hartford, and Joe Malone, 149, Brooklyn, N. Y., drew (10).

NEWARK—Harold (Red) Green, 148½, Brooklyn, decisioned Henry Jordan, 145½, Philadelphia (8); Benny Cartagina, 142, New York, knocked out Russell Richter, 140½, Paterson (5); Charlie Fusari, 139½, Newark, knocked out Lloyd Lasky, 141, New York (4); Walter Cunningham, 163½, Newark, knocked out Mario Griffin, 171, Cuba (1); Vinnie Mellio, 131, Jamaica, knocked out Marty Bell, 136, Newark (1).

HOLYOKE, MASS.—Joe Bennett, 152, New York, decisioned Jerry Fiorello, 157, Brooklyn, (10).

Cardinals' Plans Preclude Series With Navy Stars

ST. LOUIS, Oct. 9 (A. P.).—Manager Billy Southworth of the World champion St. Louis Cardinals thinks a play-off with a winning all-star Navy team in Hawaii is a good idea but "all of my boys have made plans from now on."

"They should have thought of the idea six weeks ago. Then there might have been a chance to consider it," he said of a suggestion in Mid-Pacifican, a service men's newspaper in the Pacific, for an all-around-the-world championship series in Hawaii on Oahu Island.

The Navy's service publication admitted it is not customary for World Series winners to play post-season games, but said such games surely could be held in wartime.

The Navy team, which recently defeated the Army in a Service Series, includes such stars as Schoolboy Rowe, Peewee Reese, Johnny Mize, Phil Rizzuto, Dom Di Maggio, Joe Grace, Al Brancato and Hugh Casey.

$4334 Reward For Each Card

ST. LOUIS, Oct. 9 (A. P.).—Victory in the World Series today meant approximately $4534 for each of the 'St. Louis Cardinals, while the losing Browns will receive about $2842 per player. The total player pool of $309,590.91 was the smallest since 1933.

The winners' shares were the smallest since the New York Giants pocketed $4256.72 for beating Washington in 1933, while the Brownies profited less than any losers since each Brooklyn Dodger took home $2419.60 in 1920.

(A. P. Wirephoto)

BROWNS WORK PINCERS MOVEMENT ON WHITEY KUROWSKI

Second Baseman Don Gutteridge (behind ball, center) tosses to Pitcher Nelson Potter (24) for putout on Cardinals' third baseman in second inning of yesterday's game. Shortstop Vern Stephens (background) and First Baseman George McQuinn watch. Play started when pitcher picked runner off first base.

Sewell: Breaks Helped Cardinals to Win, But We've Still Got the Better Club

By CHARLES DUNKLEY

ST. LOUIS, Oct. 9 (A. P.).—There were lumps of emotion in the throats of Managers Billy Southworth of the Cardinals and Luke Sewell of the Browns as they met in the clubhouse after the Red Birds won the 1944 World Series championship today, four games to two.

Sewell was among the first visitors to reach the Cardinals dressing room to congratulate his conquerors. "You won it, Billy," he blurted, as they looked each other squarely in the eye.

PITCHING PRAISED

Southworth was lavish in his praise of the pitching in the Series, and the catching of both Myron Hayworth and Walker Cooper. "Those fellows did a remarkable job of controlling the pitchers."

"We beat a hell of a ball club," Southworth said. "Sewell is a fine, high class gentleman."

"The Cards got the breaks and won—that tells the whole story," said Sewell, "but we've still got the better ball club."

"We didn't hit the ball but the boys hustled and that's all I could ask of them," Sewell added.

"They never could have won a pennant in our league," said Milt Byrnes, Brownie outfielder.

The smiling Southworth was on the end of a receiving line as his grinning players filed past shaking his hand in congratulations. In popped Ford Frick, president of the National League, then Will Harridge, president of the American League, and finally, Sam Breadon, president of the Cardinals.

BILLY JR. ON HAND

Standing beside Southworth was his 27-year-old son, Billy, Jr., now a major in the Air Forces. Major Billy proudly wore campaign ribbons and decorations. He piloted a Flying Fortress out of England on 25 missions over Europe.

When Pitcher Max Lanier began showing signs of folding up, in the sixth inning, Southworth decided on the spot to relieve him.

"We already had the game won, but I didn't want to take any chances. I felt Lanier was forcing himself and possibly weakening after only three days rest. I told him 'We are winning this game for us, not for any one individual.'"

(A. P. Wirephoto)

BROWNS' 'ROOKIES' TRY ON EQUIPMENT

Chester Joe Laabs, six, and Vernon Stephens, III, 18 months, compare sports gear in St. Louis' Sportsman's Park where their fathers played on losing team in yesterday's World Series finale.

'Wild Hoss' Turns Seer

Wilks Fulfills Martin Prophecy

By F. W. CRAWFORD

SPORTSMAN'S PARK, St. Louis, Oct. 9 (A. P.).—Mike Kreevich, who tried for two shoestring catches in the third inning but dropped the ball both times, smashed a low liner to right in the seventh and watched Stan Musial make a fine running catch barely off the ground.

• • •

Tom Connolly, supervisor of American League umpires, went to the dugout to congratulate the Browns for "making a game bid" in the Series.

• • •

"You'll be out there again and it will be different," prophesied Pepper Martin in consoling Ted Wilks after he was batted off the mound in the third game. When Mike Chartak struck out to end the Series Wilks was doing the hurling.

• • •

An envelope containing Dewey-Bricker campaign literature was in each Cardinal clubhouse locker when the Redbirds arrived at the park. The players suspected Dr. Harrison Weaver, club physician and ardent Republican, of attempting to influence some baseball votes for the G. O. P.

• • •

Chet Laabs' three-bagger into centerfield fell 420 feet from the plate and bounced against the fence. It was the second longest hit of the Series. Only Walker Cooper's triple in the fourth game carried farther on the fly.

• • •

The Cards had hits to waste. Johnny Hopp apparently missed Coach Mike Gonzalez' signal, and rounded first after his seventh-inning single, and sped toward second. Laabs' throw to Stephens caught Hopp in a trap and he was an easy out when he tried to return to first.

• • •

Ray Sanders and Hopp tied for the number of strike-outs in the Series with eight each, but this was one short of the mark set by Jim Bottomley, also with the Cardinals, in the six-game Series against the Athletics in 1930.

• • •

Danny Litwhiler did not draw the hero role but he played fine ball in the field and made a valuable home run in the fifth game yesterday. "It was my mother's birthday," he explained, "and I had to do something for her."

• • •

Musial's error in Sunday's game deprived the Cardinals of a six-game Series fielding record for both leagues. Despite it the club did set a National League mark, but without it, would have bettered the Boston Red Sox of 1918.

Del Baker Likely To Coach Red Sox

BOSTON, Oct. 9 (A. P.).—The Boston Post said today in a copyright story from St. Louis that Delmar (Del) Baker, former manager of Detroit, has signed to coach the Boston Red Sox next season.

Baker, who resigned as coach of Cleveland at the close of the past season, will take the place of third-base Coach Bill Burwell, who will return to Louisville, Sox farm team, as manager, The Post said.

Nemo Leibold, present Louisville manager and the fellow Burwell would replace, said in Baltimore today that he "knew absolutely nothing about it."

Segura, Peggy Welsh Win In Pan-American Tourney

MEXICO CITY, Oct. 9 (A. P.).—Pancho Segura, Ecuador, defending champion, defeated Pancho Galvan, Mexico, 6-3, 6-1, today in the second round of the Pan-American Tennis Tournament.

Cuba's woman champion, Bertha Garcia, won the last match of the first round, defeating Maria Tapia De Roldan, Mexico, 6-8, 6-2, 6-2.

In other second-round matches:

Peggy Welsh, Lima, Pa., defeated Elvira de Ampudia, Mexico, 6-4, 6-1. Jose Aguero, Cuba, defeated Flavio Martinez, Mexico, 6-3, 7-5. Pauline Betz, Los Angeles, defeated Esther Reyes, Mexico, 6-1, 6-0. Margaret Osborne, San Francisco, defeated Esperanza de Chavez, Mexico, 6-0, 6-1. Eduardo Buse, Peru, defeated Alfredo Millet, Mexico, 6-2, 5-7.

Canadian to Fight Here

TORONTO, Oct. 9 (A. P.).—Jack Allen, manager of Dave Castilloux, Montreal, Canadian lightweight champion, said tonight he has accepted an offer from Promoter Herman Taylor to take Castilloux to Philadelphia for a bout Nov. 13 with Ike Williams.

Lanier, Wilks Check Losers With 3 Hits

31,630 See Verban Star as Potter Is Routed; Stephens' Error Costly

By STAN BAUMGARTNER

Continued From First Page

and the dash that had enabled them to outlast the Detroit Tigers simply did not flame today. So the Cards won and won convincingly.

The Cardinals were a better ball club. They were faster in the field, out-hit their American League rivals and for the most part they had better pitching. This was particularly evident today when relief hurler Ted Wilks stepped to the mound in the sixth inning to relieve Max Lanier with the score 3-1, Browns on second and third and one out, and retired 11 batters in succession.

BOTH IMPOTENT AT BAT

Neither side showed any power at the bat and the Series set a new negative record for strikeouts with 92. This broke all standards for any Series no matter how many games, and smashed the mark of 87 set by the Athletics and Cardinals in the seven-game Series in 1931. The impotence of the Browns attack was well illustrated by the fact that the last eight Browns' pinch-hitters, four yesterday and four today, struck out.

It was the National League's 16th victory in the fall classic against 25 by their rival American Leaguers. And it was the Cardinals' fifth World Series crown. They won in 1926, 1931, 1934, 1942 and 1944. Manager Billy Southworth has managed the club in the last two and became the first pilot to win two series in St. Louis.

There was nothing dramatic in their triumph today. In fact, only one of their three runs scored in the fourth inning was earned. The others were presents from Vernon Stephens—whose play during the Series fell far below the standard he set for the season.

COOPER STARTS RALLY

Walker Cooper started the rally with a walk after one out and Ray Sanders sent him to third with a single to center that might easily have been handled by a faster man than Don Gutteridge and would have been turned into a double play by Joe Gordon. Whitey Kurowski followed with a fast hopper to Stephens that might have been made into a double play, but the shortstop's throw was either wide of the bag or Gutteridge ran past the sack in his anxiety to take the relay, for when he received the ball he was three feet off the bag. Umpire George Pipgras correctly called Sanders safe as Cooper dashed over the plate with the tying run.

Gutteridge put up a feeble protest to Pipgras, but it was clear his heart was not in the "beef." For a moment it looked as if Nelson Potter might pull himself out of the hole his mates had dug for him when he forced Marty Marion to fly to left for the second out, but Emil Verban—an itch to the Browns the entire Series—broke the tie and sent Sanders over with what proved to be the winning run with a single to left.

VERBAN HITTING STAR

It was Verban's second of his three hits of the day and when the game was over he led all the Cardinals' batters with seven safeties in 17 times at bat. It was at second base last year—Verban's spot which was held down by Lou Klein—that the Cardinals lost the Series.

Lanier followed Verban's single with another safety—this time to center—and Kurowski scored the third and last run of the Series. Potter was then relieved by Bob Muncrief and all scoring ceased.

HOPP IN BONEHEAD PLAY

The Cardinals had two more chances to score. Johnny Hopp, Red Birds centerfielder, opened the seventh with a single to center, then won the title of "Bonehead" for the Series. He either thought the ball had been caught or was counting his share of the World Series money, for he jogged down to second base on his way to the bench—and was promptly tagged out.

In the eighth both Kurowski and Verban walked and went to second and third after one out on a wild peg by Myron Hayworth, but Wilks fanned and Danny Litwhiler rolled out.

LAABS TRIPLES

The Browns' run in the second which gave them a temporary lead was well earned. Chet Laabs lashed a triple against the right center-field fence and scored on the next pitch when George McQuinn lashed it for a single to center.

This was all for the Browns until the sixth, when Lanier suddenly got wild, walked both Laabs and McQuinn after one out, and then cut loose a wild pitch on the first ball to Mark Christman. Southworth then called on Wilks to relieve Lanier. Laabs was promptly caught at the plate when Christman rolled to Kurowski. The Browns' outfielder did not even try to slide—he merely bumped Cooper on his way to the Browns' bench. Hayworth then flied to Hopp for the third out.

UMPIRING EXCELLENT

It was a unique Series in that no one attempted to steal a base and the only complaint against the umpires was Gutteridge's feeble protest against Pipgras and his pantomime act of touching second base several times on a similar play an inning or two later.

McQuinn, the Browns' first baseman, led both clubs in hitting and drove in the most runs—five. The Browns did some feeble hitting but did not reach the all-time low of .161 established by the Athletics in the Series with the New York Giants in 1905—the year Christy Mathewson shut them out three times.

Series Facts

FIRST GAME

										R.	H.	E.
Browns	0	0	0	2	0	0	0	0	0	2	2	0
Cardinals	0	0	0	0	0	0	0	0	1	1	7	0

Batteries—Galehouse and Hayworth, Browns; M. Cooper (7), Donnelly (2) and W. Cooper, Cardinals.

SECOND GAME

												R.	H.	E.
Browns	0	0	0	0	0	0	2	0	0	0	0	2	7	4
Cards	0	0	1	1	0	0	0	0	0	0	1	3	7	0

Batteries—Potter (6), Muncrief (4 1-3) and Hayworth, Browns; Lanier (7), Donnelly (4) and W. Cooper, Cardinals.

THIRD GAME

										R.	H.	E.
Cardinals	1	0	0	0	0	0	0	1	0	2	7	0
Browns	0	0	4	0	0	0	2	0	0	6	8	2

Batteries—Wilks (2 2/3), Schmidt (3 1/3), Jurisich (2/3), Byerly (1 1/3) and W. Cooper, Cardinals; Kramer and Hayworth, Browns.

FOURTH GAME

										R.	H.	E.
Cardinals	2	0	2	0	0	1	0	0	0	5	12	0
Browns	0	0	0	0	0	0	0	1	0	1	9	1

Batteries—Brecheen and W. Cooper, Cardinals; Jakucki, (3); Hollingsworth, (4), Shirley (2) and Hayworth (7), Mancuso (2).

FIFTH GAME

										R.	H.	E.
Cardinals	0	0	0	0	0	1	0	1	0	2	6	1
Browns	0	0	0	0	0	0	0	0	0	0	7	1

Batteries—M. Cooper and W. Cooper, Cardinals; Galehouse and Hayworth, Browns.

SIXTH GAME

										R.	H.	E.
Browns	0	1	0	0	0	0	0	0	0	1	3	2
Cardinals	0	0	0	3	0	0	0	0	x	3	10	0

Batteries—Potter (3 2/3), Muncrief (2 1/3), Kramer (2) and Hayworth, Browns; Lanier (5 1-3), Wilks (3 2/3) and W. Cooper, Cardinals.

FINAL STANDING

	W.	L.	P.C.
Cardinals	4	2	.667
Browns	2	4	.333

FINANCIAL FIGURES

SIXTH GAME

Paid attendance, 31,630.
Gross receipts, $142,062.
X-War relief, $142,062.

SIX-GAME TOTALS

Attendance, 206,708.
Gross receipts, $906,122.
Players' share, $309,590.91.
Commissioner's share, $68,826.00.
Each club's share, $59,021.32.
Each league's share, $59,021.32.
X-War relief, $291,619.80.

X-All receipts of the third and fourth games, after deduction of players' share and the entire receipts of the sixth game go to the War Relief and Service Fund, Inc., which also received the $100,000 paid for radio broadcasting rights.

The players share in the receipts of the first four games only, while the commissioner's office, the competing clubs and the two leagues share in the first and second games and receive all receipts of the fifth game.

Official Series Box Score

SIXTH AND FINAL GAME

ST. LOUIS BROWNS

	ab.	r.	h.	2b.	3b.	hr.	tb.	rbi.	sb.	sh.	po.	a.	e.
Gutteridge, 2b.	3	0	0	0	0	0	0	0	0	0	3	2	0
Baker, 2b.	1	0	0	0	0	0	0	0	0	0	1	0	0
Kreevich, cf.	4	0	1	1	0	0	2	0	0	0	3	0	0
Moore, rf.	3	0	0	0	0	0	0	0	0	0	0	0	0
Stephens, ss.	4	0	0	0	0	0	0	0	0	0	3	3	1
Laabs, lf.	2	1	1	0	1	0	3	0	0	0	1	1	0
McQuinn, 1b.	2	0	1	0	0	0	1	1	0	1	6	1	0
Christman, 3b.	3	0	0	0	0	0	0	0	0	0	1	1	0
Hayworth, c.	2	0	0	0	0	0	0	0	0	0	5	0	1
Potter, p.	2	0	0	0	0	0	0	0	0	0	1	1	0
Muncrief, p.	0	0	0	0	0	0	0	0	0	0	0	1	0
a-Zarilla	1	0	0	0	0	0	0	0	0	0	0	0	0
Kramer, p.	0	0	0	0	0	0	0	0	0	0	0	1	0
b-Byrnes	1	0	0	0	0	0	0	0	0	0	0	0	0
c-Chartak	1	0	0	0	0	0	0	0	0	0	0	0	0
Totals	29	1	3	1	1	0	6	1	0	1	24	11	2

ST. LOUIS CARDINALS

	ab.	r.	h.	2b.	3b.	hr.	tb.	rbi.	sb.	sh.	po.	a.	e.
Litwhiler, lf.	5	0	0	0	0	0	0	0	0	0	2	0	0
Hopp, cf.	4	0	1	0	0	0	1	0	0	0	3	0	0
Musial, rf.	4	0	0	0	0	0	0	0	0	0	2	0	0
W. Cooper, c.	3	1	2	0	0	0	2	0	0	0	10	0	0
Sanders, 1b.	3	1	1	0	0	0	1	0	0	0	7	1	0
Kurowski, 3b.	3	1	1	0	0	0	1	1	0	0	0	1	0
Marion, ss.	3	0	0	0	0	0	0	0	0	1	0	2	0
Verban, 2b.	3	0	3	0	0	0	3	1	0	0	2	2	0
Lanier, p.	2	0	2	0	0	0	2	1	0	0	1	1	0
Wilks, p.	1	0	0	0	0	0	0	0	0	1	0	1	0
Totals	31	3	10	0	0	0	10	3	0	2	27	8	0

BROWNS	0	1	0	0	0	0	0	0	0	—1
CARDINALS	0	0	0	3	0	0	0	0	x	—3

a-Batted for Muncrief in seventh.
b-Batted for Christman in ninth.

Left on bases—Browns, 7; Cardinals, 10. Base on balls—Off Lanier 5 (Moore, Laabs, 2; Hayworth, McQuinn); off Potter, 1 (W. Cooper); off Muncrief, 1 (Sanders); off Kramer, 2 (Kurowski, Verban). Struck out—By Lanier, 5 (Kreevich, 2; Moore, Stephens, Potter), by Wilks, 4 (Zarilla, Baker, Byrnes, Chartak); by Potter, 3 (Litwhiler, 2; Hopp); by Kramer, 2 (Sanders, Wilks). Hits—Off Potter, 6 in 3 2-3 innings; Muncrief, 2 in 2 1-3; Kramer, 2 in 2; Lanier, 3 in 5 1-3; Wilks, 0 in 3 2-3. Wild pitch—Lanier. Winning pitcher—Lanier. Losing pitcher—Potter. Umpires—McGowan (A. L.), plate; Dunn (N. L.), first base; Pipgras (A. L.), second base; Sears (N. L.), third base. Time of game—2.06.

(Composite Box Score of Six Games on Page 22)

52,833 See Louisville Beat Baltimore, 5-4

BALTIMORE, Oct. 9 (A. P.).—The Louisville Colonels survived a ninth-inning rally tonight to defeat the Baltimore Orioles, 5-4, and square the Little World Series at two games apiece before a record minor-league crowd of 52,833 at Baltimore Municipal Stadium.

The Colonels got to Hal Kleine, Orioles' left-hander, in the first inning and scored a run to take the lead. Johnny Podgajny had to come in with two out to retire the side.

A single by Ben Steiner and homers into the left-field stands by Nick Polly and Steve Barath gave the Colonels three more tallies in the third. Louisville then picked up their last tally in the fourth on singles by George Savino, Steiner and an outfield fly.

Box Score

Baltimore (IL)	ab.	r.	h.	o.	a.	Louisville (AA)	ab.	r.	h.	o.	a.
Monaco,2b	3	0	0	3	4	Steiner,2b	4	0	2	2	0
Latshaw,1b	4	1	3	10	1	Geno'z,cf	4	1	1	3	0
Benjamin,lf	3	0	0	1	0	Browne,1b	4	1	1	5	0
Moss,rf	5	0	1	1	0	Polly,3b	3	1	2	2	0
Mack'cz,cf	5	0	1	3	0	Barath,lf	4	1	2	0	0
Skaff,3b	5	1	1	3	1	How'ton,lf	0	0	0	0	0
Lollar,c	5	0	3	2	1	Cotelle,lf	4	0	0	0	0
Braun,ss	3	1	0	3	2	Savino,c	4	1	1	14	1
Kleine,p	0	0	0	0	0	Shofner,ss	3	0	0	0	1
Podgajny,p	2	0	0	1	3	Patton,p	1	0	0	1	2
a-Riley	0	1	0	0	0	c-Piet	1	0	0	0	0
Lowry,p	0	0	0	0	1	Simonds,p	1	0	0	0	0
b-Kahn	1	0	0	0	0						
Van Slate,p	0	0	0	0	0						
Totals	36	4	9	27	13	Totals	33	5	9	27	4

a-Batted for Podgajny in 6th.
b-Batted for Lowry in 8th.
c-Batted for Patton in 6th.

Louisville (AA)	1	0	3	1	0	0	0	0	0	—5
Baltimore (IL)	0	0	0	0	0	3	0	0	1	—4

Errors—Polly.

The Orioles then came to life in the sixth and scored three runs. Singles by Frank Skaff, Sherman Lollar and a pass to Pat Riley, pinch-hitting for Podgajny, loaded the bases. A triple by Bob Latshaw cleaned them and Baltimore was only two runs behind.

Latshaw opened the ninth with a double, but Stan Benjamin and Howie Moss fanned. Felix Mackiewicz kept the rally alive by beating out an infield roller and then Latshaw tallied on Polly's wild throw on Skaff's bouncer. Dwight Simmonds, however, fanned Lollar.

The Philadelphia Inquirer

PUBLIC LEDGER

An Independent Newspaper for All the People

FINAL CITY EDITION

CIRCULATION: September Average: Daily 528,148; Sunday 1,087,044

SATURDAY MORNING, OCTOBER 28, 1944

Copyright, 1944, by Triangle Publications, Inc., Vol. 231, No. 120

abdefgh

THREE CENTS

Yanks Avenge Bataan Death March

F.D.R. Accuses G.O.P. of 'Politics' in War

President Asserts Republicans Hint Peace Plan Threat

Text of Mr. Roosevelt's Address on Page 5; Other Stories and Pictures on Pages 4, 5 and 10

By JOHN C. O'BRIEN

President Roosevelt, in a point-by-point reply to the campaign charges of his Republican opponent, Governor Thomas E. Dewey, declared last night the opposition was guilty of a "deliberate and indefensible effort to place political advantage above devotion to country" in intimating that Republicans "would not co-operate in establishing a world peace organization in the event of a Democratic victory."

"I do not think that the American people will take kindly to this policy of 'Vote my way or I won't play,' " the President said at a Democratic mass meeting in Shibe Park. His speech to 40,000 men and women followed a four-hour tour of Philadelphia and Camden during the afternoon. Mr. Roosevelt remained seated in his automobile while he delivered his speech.

The President also gave what he called his "once-and-for-all" answer to Governor Dewey's charge that the New Deal Administration had made "absolutely no military preparation for the events it now claims it foresaw."

HAILS NAVAL VICTORY

The answer to that charge, Mr. Roosevelt said, as well as to the charge that he had failed for political reasons to send enough forces or supplies to General Douglas MacArthur, was that the Japanese fleet had been defeated and General MacArthur had returned to the Philippines.

Of the battleships, cruisers and aircraft carriers, forming the backbone of Admiral William F. Halsey's powerful Third Fleet, which has just given the Japanese Navy the worst licking in its history, all but two cruisers had been authorized before Pearl Harbor and most of the ships were then under construction, the President said.

"ONCE AND FOR ALL"

"That is the answer—once and for all—" he added, "to a Republican candidate who said that this Administration has made absolutely no military preparation for the events it now claims it foresaw."

Describing the whole story of the country's vast effort in the war as "a story of incredible achievement," Mr. Roosevelt added, with another thrust at his Republican opponent, it was a story "of the job that has been done by an Administration which, I am told, is old and tired and quarrelsome."

The President's speech, his fourth of the campaign, was a hard-hitting bid for Pennsylvania's 35 electoral votes, which the New Deal campaign managers have heretofore carried on their doubtful list.

ALL SEATS FILLED

Shibe Park's grandstands, bleachers and temporary seats on the field were filled long before the President and his party arrived.

The crowd, mistaking the first car that entered the park at 8.50 P. M. for the President's broke into a frenzy of cheers. Then when they discovered that the early arrivals contained only members of the official party, a chant of "We Want Roosevelt" filled the park.

Five minutes before 9 o'clock, the President appeared, sitting beside Postmaster General Frank C. Walker in an open car. He was wearing

Continued on Page 4, Column 3

Dewey Summons Session to Keep Polls Open Later

By WILLIAM C. MURPHY, JR.

Inquirer Staff Reporter

ALBANY, Oct. 27. — Governor Thomas E. Dewey today called a special session of the New York Legislature to authorize an extension of the hours of voting in New York State on Nov. 7.

The legislators will meet on Monday and are expected to approve a recommendation by the Governor that the polls be kept open from 6 A. M. to 9 P. M. Present law provides for voting from 6 A. M. to 7 P. M.

SAME AS IN '36 AND '40

However, in the Presidential elections of 1936 and 1940 the Legislature in each instance authorized an extension to 9 P. M. So the net result of the anticipated action Monday would be that the voters of New York will have the same time for voting that they have had in the two most recent elections.

Governor Dewey issued his call for the special session after receiving a report from Charles D. Breitel, counsel to the Governor, which recommended such action.

3 REASONS GIVEN

Mr. Breitel based his recommendation for a special session upon three grounds: the desirability of enabling war workers to vote without taking time from their work, the large number of new voters, and inexperience of many election officials.

He rejected three other arguments advanced by proponents of an extension; namely, the alleged unusually heavy registration in New York City, the insufficient number of voting machines and the inadequacy of the number of election districts.

These three points had not been

Continued on Page 7, Column 1

Brownell Reports 'Irresistible Tide'

NEW YORK, Oct. 27 (A. P.).—Herbert Brownell, Jr., Republican National Chairman, said today that an "irresistible tide to the Republican ticket," would elect Governor Thomas E. Dewey as President and "assure an anti-New Deal Congress."

"There are only eleven days to go," Mr. Brownell told a press conference. "I see nothing in the wind to change the Republican trend. Governor Dewey's speeches should accelerate that trend."

IN TODAY'S INQUIRER

SPECIAL DEPARTMENTS

COLUMNS AND FEATURES

PRESIDENT WAVES TO CHEERING CROWDS ON CITY TOUR

Philadelphia throngs jammed the sidewalks yesterday to catch a glimpse of President Roosevelt during his motor tour of the city. The President is shown here waving to the crowds from the rear seat of his car at Allegheny and Kensington aves.

Roosevelt Hailed By 600,000 Here

By GEORGE M. MAWHINNEY

President Roosevelt made a campaign visit to Philadelphia yesterday, toured 43 miles of the city's streets in a canvass of military installations and major war plants, and waved from an open automobile to approximately 600,000 persons, according to an estimate of the committee which made arrangements for the visit.

The tour, which encompassed most of the city except the heavily populated areas of West Philadelphia and the Greater Northeast, and included a brief visit to Camden, was climaxed last night by a crowd scene at Shibe Park which almost reached the numerical gate of a good fight night there.

40,000 JAM SHIBE PARK

On a first-class fight night that baseball park can pack in perhaps 50,000 by setting up seats on the field.

Continued on Page 4, Column 1

2 Teeth Pulled, Hull Improves

WASHINGTON, Oct. 27 (A. P.).—Acting Secretary of State Edward R. Stettinius, Jr., said today that Secretary of State Cordell Hull, who is in Bethesda Naval Hospital, had two infected teeth pulled yesterday and is making favorable progress.

Greek Patriot Slain As Eden Tours Athens

By REYNOLDS PACKARD

ATHENS, Oct. 27 (U. P.).—A member of the EAM Party (National Liberation Front) was shot and killed on one of Athens' main streets today by a man uniformed as a Greek Army major while crowds were parading in honor of British Foreign Secretary Anthony Eden. Immediately extra police were stationed at strategic points in the restless city.

Crowds threatened to storm the temporary War Ministry where the alleged killer, identified as Major George Papadongas, 39, sought refuge. The police, and an officer of the Elas, fighting arm of the EAM, assured the crowd that the accused man would be given swift justice.

CONTINUE DEMONSTRATION

Although the crowds cleared from in front of the War Ministry building, members continued to parade menacingly.

I was walking along University st. watching the parade when the shooting occurred, about 20 yards ahead of me. I heard three shots and saw a man in civilian clothes fall to the sidewalk while a man in uniform bolted into a doorway.

Greeks who had been standing beside the man who was slain said he was a member of the EAM. They said he had recognized and pointed out a man, garbed in a Greek ma-

Continued on Page 3, Column 2

Casualties

3 Phila. Residents Killed in Action

A Marine sergeant major and a Navy enlisted man from Philadelphia were reported killed in action and eight other Marines from this area were listed as wounded in a Navy Department casualty list, released yesterday.

In addition, the death of a soldier killed in action was reported by his mother after she received a War Department notification. He was Private First Class Eugene F. Teti, 23, son of Mrs. Marion Teti, of 2022 Morris st.

PFC. E. F. TETI

Private Teti, member of a tank battalion, attended South Philadelphia High School. He was employed in a bronze foundry at Berwyn, Pa., when he enlisted on April 6, 1942. Besides his mother, he left five sisters and one brother.

Army and Navy Department casualty lists are subject to change.

Other casualties:

KILLED

Sergeant Major George Dyson, U. S. M. C. R., of 3413 G st.

Matthew Sierakowski, seaman second class, 23, of 2615 E. Indiana ave. The son of Mr. and Mrs. Michael Sierakowski, he previously had

Continued on Page 3, Column 6

2 Doctors Deny Wife Of Connors Was Slain

Special to The Inquirer

CINCINNATI, Oct. 27.—Testimony of two pathologists was introduced today in the second-degree murder trial of Robert J. Connors, Philadelphia Army captain, in a last-minute attempt by the defense to refute State charges that the Army officer killed his wife, Lois, 28, in a hotel room here July 8.

Dr. Ward Ventress, Hamilton county deputy coroner, and Dr. John Batte, Cincinnati doctor, were called to the stand by W. Foster Hopkins, defense counsel, as the trial entered its fifth day. The physicians declared that Mrs. Connors died of natural causes.

DISPUTE TESTIMONY

The State has hinged its whole case on the testimony of Dr. Lawrence Smith, of Temple University, and Dr. Benjamin A. Gouley, Philadelphia coroner's physician, that the young woman's death had been caused by a fractured larynx and a blow on the head.

In his opinion, Dr. Ventress said, Mrs. Connors, daughter of Mr. and Mrs. Robert E. Burns, of 5629

Continued on Page 18, Column 1

F.D.R. Pays Tribute To Canterbury

WASHINGTON, Oct. 27 (A. P.).—President Roosevelt, in a message of sympathy sent to King George VI of England after the death yesterday of the Archbishop of Canterbury, said the churchman "exerted a profound influence throughout the world."

"I am deeply grieved to learn of the death of the Archbishop of Canterbury," the message said. "He was rightly considered a good friend of the United States, and his efforts to promote Anglo-American understanding and co-operation were unceasing. As an ardent advocate of international co-operation based on Christian principles he exerted a profound influence throughout the world. The American people join me in extending this expression of sympathy."

Argentina Calls Parley of Critics

BUENOS AIRES, Oct. 27 (A. P.).—In a memorandum expressing concern over the situation "facing the concert of American nations because of the attitude assumed by some of its governments regarding Argentina," the Argentine Government tonight called for a conference of all foreign ministers in the Americas.

The Foreign Ministry here announced that the request for such a convocation was made in a note handed by the Argentine charge d'affaires in Washington, Rodolfo Garcia Arias, to the Pan American Union.

ENTIRE CONTINENT INVOLVED

"Argentina is accused of the alleged failure to observe its international commitments, which in view of the nature of the commitments involves a problem which interests not one country, or group

Continued on Page 3, Column 7

Nazis Threaten To Raze The Hague

NEW YORK, Oct. 27.—The British radio said today the German commander at The Hague had informed the burgomeister there that all public buildings were mined and would be blown up by the retreating Germans.

All civilians have been evacuated from the city, it added.

60,000 Nazis Trapped in West Holland

Enemy Resistance Collapsing Along Front of 75 Miles

By JAMES F. McGLINCY

ALLIED SUPREME HEADQUARTERS, Paris, Oct. 28 (Friday) (U. P.).—The British Second Army captured the big Dutch strongholds of Tilburg and 's Hertogenbosch today and raced for the mouth of the Meuse in two converging columns to close a corral around the greatest number of Nazis to be hemmed in since the Normandy break-through.

From 60,000 to 70,000 reeling Germans were reported caught in the trap, including the last 11,000 blockading Antwerp, who even now were being liquidated by a daring British amphibious landing on South Beveland Island in conjunction with a Canadian drive of 13 miles via the causeway from the Dutch west coast.

BRITISH GAIN SIX MILES

On a 75-mile front south of the Meuse, organized resistance was reported collapsing as the Second Army ripped off gains up to six miles and a high British field officer announced that "the enemy's efforts to stabilize a front have failed."

Desperate diversion attacks by four German columns, none of them stronger than a few companies of men backed by several tanks, against the eastern flank of the Allied salient were hurled back.

REPULSED BY U. S. TANKS

One advanced a mile to the village of Meijel, 18 miles southeast of Eindhoven, but quailed before the massed fire of American tanks operating on the Second Army's flank.

Breda, the third big Dutch city in the path of Lieutenant General Sir Miles C. Dempsey's oncoming tanks and infantry, was left high and dry when a British column thrust six miles due north across its communications with Tilburg midway between the two cities. This column captured or bypassed Gilze,

Continued on Page 2, Column 7

Australia Reveals 8 Attacks by Subs

CANBERRA, Oct. 27 (U. P.).—Prime Minister John Curtin today revealed hitherto unannounced details of eight attacks by enemy submarines in Australian waters between July, 1942, and December, 1943.

Of the eight vessels attacked, four were sunk and four reached port. Total casualties were given as 156 lost and nine injured.

A U. S. freighter was torpedoed and sunk off the coast of New South Wales with no casualties, and another was torpedoed and sunk off the same coast, with five of the crew killed and four injured. A U. S. tanker and a third freighter also were torpedoed off New South Wales, both making port, but the former had three of her crew killed and five injured and the latter had one of her crew killed.

War in Last Lap, Churchill Says

By PHIL AULT

LONDON, Oct. 27 (U. P.).—Prime Minister Winston Churchill, prophesying that the war was in "the last lap" and that Allied forces were now closing in to crush the life out of German resistance, told the House of Commons today that "the future of the world" depends upon the united action and friendship of Britain, Russia and the United States in shaping the peace.

Reporting on his recent Moscow conferences with Premier Josef Stalin and the Soviet Government, Mr. Churchill said:

SEEKS 'BIG 3' MEETING

"Other countries will be associated, but the future depends on the union of the three most powerful Allies. If that fails, all fails. If that succeeds, a broad future for all nations may be assured."

The Prime Minister hoped that he, President Roosevelt, and Premier Stalin could meet again before the end of 1944 to supplement the re-

Continued on Page 3, Column 1

14,000 Jap Killers Slain, Wounded In Leyte Battles

Map, Chart and War Summary on Page 2

Gaining virtual control of Samar Island and administering a smashing defeat to the Japanese on Leyte in the central Philippines, General Douglas MacArthur's troops have "completely defeated" the Japanese 16th Division, perpetrators of the infamous "march of death" on Bataan. General MacArthur revealed that 14,045 Japanese soldiers—half the enemy force on Leyte—have been killed or wounded in a week of fighting on the Philippines.

At sea, the United States Navy was still revising upward the number of Japanese warships sunk in the three-pronged naval battle off the Philippines. Latest figures, still incomplete, raised enemy losses from 39 to 41 ships sunk or damaged, including 11 battleships and three cruisers. American fleet losses included a light carrier, two ecort carriers, two destroyers and one destroyer escort.

American Victory In Pacific Cost Navy 6 Warships

By MAC R. JOHNSON

PEARL HARBOR, Oct. 27 (U. P.).—The United States naval triumph in the Philippines, in which three Japanese fleets were ripped to pieces, was achieved at the cost of six American warships sunk, in addition to several PT boats, it was made known today.

The estimated toll exacted from the enemy rose from 39 to 41 ships sunk or damaged, including 11 battleships and three carriers.

HAILED BY NIMITZ

Admiral Chester W. Nimitz in a Navy Day statement said the enemy losses were:

"So great as to render his fleet incapable of challenging any sizeable portion of ours for some time to come."

An upward revision of unofficial estimates of the Japanese losses was made on the basis of a statement by Rear Admiral Jesse Barret Oldendorf, commanding a battleship squadron of the Seventh Fleet.

U. S. LOSSES LISTED

American ships sunk in all three Philippines battles, including that between Formosa and Luzon, were the 10,000-ton light aircraft carrier Princeton, previously announced; two escort carriers, two destroyers and one destroyer escort.

Several escort carriers, destroyers and PT boats were damaged, General Douglas MacArthur had previously announced.

Admiral Oldendorf, in a statement to Ralph Teatsorth, United Press war correspondent, aboard Vice Admiral Thomas C. Kinkaid's Seventh Fleet flagship, said he believed the entire Japanese fleet of three battleships, five cruisers and six to eight destroyers was sunk in the battle of the Surigao Strait.

CAUGHT IN CROSS FIRE

Admiral Oldendorf caught the Japanese under cross fire in the 12-mile strait and took it apart with his

Continued on Page 2, Column 3

M'Arthur Forces, Aided by Guerillas, Win Samar Control

By C. YATES McDANIEL

GENERAL MACARTHUR'S HEADQUARTERS, Leyte, Philippines, Oct. 28 (Saturday) (A. P.).—Mud-caked Yanks, heroically aided by guerillas, have seized control of virtually all Samar Island, next to Luzon, captured its capital and killed or wounded 14,045 of Japan's hated 16th Division—the torturers of Bataan—on fast-falling Leyte.

General Douglas MacArthur, in a communique today, reported these great successes:

The enemy; 16th, perpetrators of the infamous "march of death" on Bataan, has been "completely defeated" on Leyte.

Nine more in a swiftly-mounting list of Leyte towns have been liberated. The total to date is more than 40.

HOLD 70 MILES OF COAST

Control of nearly 70 miles of Leyte's coastlines has passed into Yank hands—from captured Barugo in the north on Carigara Bay on around to Abuyog on the east coast, 14 miles below Dulag.

The Leyte valley has been bottled up on the north by 24th Division spearheads entering it through Santa Fe and Pastrana, west and northwest of Palo. At Pastrana these are less than 10 miles from juncture with a force of Seventh and 96th Division elements moving within two miles of Dagami.

Japan's 16th Division casualties are estimated to total half of Leyte's defenders. These were inflicted in the first week of fighting.

JAPS IN RETREAT

The 16th Division, which General MacArthur said he was particularly eager to meet, is in retreat from the east coast of Leyte and is completely disorganized.

American casualties were 518 killed, 139 missing and 1503 wounded.

In a field dispatch, Fred Hamp-

Continued on Page 2, Column 4

Red Army Completes Conquest of Ruthenia

By W. W. HERCHER

LONDON, Oct. 28 (Saturday) (A. P.). — A powerful Russian mountain army virtually completed the conquest of Hungarian-annexed Ruthenia in eastern Czechoslovakia yesterday by capturing Ungvar in a 15-mile advance, and also penetrated six miles into neighboring Slovakia.

In German East Prussia, where the Nazis were putting up one of the most savage defenses of the entire war, a Moscow communique announced the seizure of three more villages in two-mile gains in the Ebenrode area.

3000 MORE NAZIS KILLED

A midnight Soviet communique said the Russians, beating off numerous counter-attacks by large German infantry and armor, killed 3000 Germans, making a two-day total of 5800. Ninety-five enemy tanks, 11 armored carriers and 100 enemy trucks were wrecked or burned, it said.

In Jugoslavia other Soviet forces aided by partisan troops of Marshal Josip Broz (Tito) captured Novi Sad, Jugoslavia's seventh city of 64,000 on the north bank of the Danube 42 miles northwest of fallen Belgrade.

The toppling of Ungvar (Uzho-

Continued on Page 3, Column 4

Admiralty Head Hails U. S. Navy

LONDON, Oct. 27 (A. P.).—A. V. Alexander, First Lord of the Admiralty, hailed today the American Navy's "great and enduring victories in the Pacific."

In a Navy Day greeting to U. S. Navy Secretary James V. Forrestal, Mr. Alexander said the British Navy soon would be in the Pacific in force to join "the concentrated attack" upon Japan.

U. S. WEATHER FORECAST

Philadelphia and vicinity: Fair and continued cold today; fair and somewhat warmer tomorrow.

Sun rises 7.25 A.M. Sets 6.04 P.M.

Moon rises 4.49 P.M. Sets 3.33 A.M.

'Marriage Is a Private Affair' Stars Lana Turner at Boyd

By Mildred Martin

If just looking at Lana Turner makes you happy, by all means see "Marriage Is a Private Affair," at the Boyd. Back from her date with the stork, and looking prettier than ever, Lana holds the screen for 116 minutes—or almost.

At any rate, the camera focuses a hypnotized lens on the Turner torso, blonde tresses and lovely, unlined little face in nearly every one of the film's scenes.

LOTS OF NEW HAIR-DOS

Studio hairdressers have dreamed up dozens of new Turner hair-dos. Irene has supplied her with a wardrobe to knock your eye out, including a quaint bathing-suit-and-apron idea that, as filled by Lana, is definitely something for the boys.

In addition to the merely visual aspects, Lana melts into the arms of virtually every male in the cast who comes within melting distance. It's all quite chummy, overheated and, so far as plot goes, pretty incredible.

MARRIES IN HASTE

For "Marriage Is a Private Affair," based on a novel by Judith Kelly, deals with a vapid playgirl's fumbling efforts to find out just what sort of person she is and whether it's possible for her ever to become a good wife.

With just sense enough to suspect her own lack of mental stability, Theo marries in haste and spends a couple of years holding "Strange Interlude-ish" conversations with herself about her emotions, her husband, her former boy friends and the not-all-they-might-be friends of the family.

MENTAL MUDDLE THICKENS

The arrival of a baby and the fact that her husband is kept home for a while instead of being shipped right off to the South Pacific increase Theo's mental muddle. And, believe it or not, the war has to be held up while a long distance call is put through to New Guinea, before Theo can be induced to cancel her Reno reservations.

John Hodiak has the ungrateful role of the flier who doesn't fly soon enough, apparently, to keep his pretty little wife happy; while poor John Craig marks time as the other man in Theo's life.

'Iolanthe' Is Presented

"Iolanthe," loveliest and most lyric of the Gilbert and Sullivan operettas, was the offering at the Forrest Theater last night. It was given as the fourth work in the Savoyard series by the able and efficient Gilbert and Sullivan Opera Company under the direction of R. H. Burnside.

The fanciful tale of fairyland was notable, in this presentation, for its absence of exaggeration, and for its fidelity to the true spirit of the book and music.

CAREFULLY PRESENTED

Every member of the cast obviously realized that any element of burlesque or the introduction of a gag would injure the effect of the story of the Peer and the Peri, which has its gay spirit and its sly satire but lacks the broad strokes and comic characters of the others.

Ralph Riggs gave a consistent characterization as the Lord Chancellor. It was free from inappropriate exaggeratiton, but not lacking in humor.

Catherine Judah displayed authority, vocally and dramatically, as the Fairy Queen, though her singing misses something of the sensuous quality of the music written for that role. Lewis Pierce played Strephon with ease and individuality of style. In the brief part of Private Willis, Robert Eckles was commendable for his comic dignity. Kathleen Roche was charming as Phyllis, and Kathryn Reece as well cast as Iolanthe.

'Dark Hammock' To Open Nov. 15

Mary Wickes, who is featured with Elissa Landi in "Dark Hammock," the new Mary Orr-Reginald Denham play which opens Nov. 15 at the Locust Street Theater, has spent so much of her professional life in a nurse's uniform that she actually feels like one.

Such were her duties in "Hitch Your Wagon," "The Man Who Came to Dinner," in which she played in both the stage and movie versions, and "Now, Voyager."

FORREST Wal., 11th & 12th — TONIGHT at 8.30 "GONDOLIERS" — GILBERT & SULLIVAN OPERAS — ALL-STAR NEW YORK CAST — Tomor. Mat. & Eve.—"The Mikado." Next Wk., Mon.—"Pirates of Penzance." Tues. Eve. & Wed Mat.—"Trial by Jury" & "Pinafore." Wed. Eve.—"The Mikado." Thurs.—"The Sorcerer." Fri.—"Iolanthe." Sat. Mat. & Eve.—"The Mikado."

SHUBERT Evgs. 8.30 | MAT. TOMOR. AT 2.30 — A ROUBEN MAMOULIAN Production — SADIE THOMPSON — Lyrics by HOWARD DIETZ, Music by VERNON DUKE, with JUNE HAVOC, LANSING HATFIELD, Cast & Chorus of 70

"UNFORGETABLE EVENT" —Inquirer. "SWIFT WITH DRAMA" —Record. TRIO — LOCUST LAST 2 Evgs. 8.30 LAST MAT. TOMOR., 2.30

Wk. Beg. Only Mon. JOHN C. WILSON presents LAURENCE STALLING'S New Play THE STREETS ARE GUARDED — Directed by JOHN HAGGOTT

TROC 10th & Arch Wal.9697 — BURLESQUE — SCARLET KELLY plus BENSON & RYAN

LEW TENDLER'S RESTAURANT 227 S. BROAD ST. FINEST FOOD IN PHILA. LUNCHEON • DINNER SUPPER — FAMOUS FOR SEA FOOD

"SADIE THOMPSON" HELD OVER — MOVES MONDAY TO WILLIAM GOLDMAN'S ERLANGER 21st & Market RIT. 9980 — 3RD BIG WEEK — A. P. WAXMAN Presents A ROUBEN MAMOULIAN PRODUCTION "SADIE THOMPSON" SENSATIONAL MUSICAL SUCCESS BY HOWARD DIETZ, ROUBEN MAMOULIAN, VERNON DUKE BASED ON "RAIN" BY SOMERSET MAUGHAM AND JOHN COLTON — JUNE HAVOC — LANSING HATFIELD — CAST AND CHORUS OF 70 — Seats Now at Erlanger Theatre Box Office, Gimbel Bros., Central Ticket Office, Crosier Arcade—1420 Chestnut. Rit. 6920, and all hotels.

TONIGHT — DR. DANIEL A. POLING — "WINNING THE WAR AND THE PEACE" — 11:15 P.M. KYW — Sponsored by the Independent Republican Committee For Roosevelt

★ ROOSEVELT licked a Hoover depression ★ and a Hitler war. ★ Keep F.D.R.! — BUSINESS MEN FOR ROOSEVELT, INC.

TONIGHT 8 P.M. ACADEMY OF MUSIC — Norman THOMAS — Darlington HOOPES — Brig. Gen. H. C. HOLDRIDGE U. S. Army Ret. — SOCIALIST CAMPAIGN MEETING — ADMISSION FREE

IT'S TIME TO CHANGE — Tune in — Hugh D. Scott, Jr. Congressman, 6th District — "Teamwork Wins" — Tonight—WFIL 6:45 P.M. — LISTEN BEFORE YOU VOTE — Sponsored by Republican Congressional Committee

Don't Miss a Word of It! LISTEN TO Honorable HAROLD L. ICKES SECRETARY OF INTERIOR — TONIGHT — TUNE IN WFIL 11.15 P.M. — Sponsored by Pennsylvania Democratic State Committee

STANTON 16th & MARKET TOMORROW DOORS OPEN 10:45 A.M. — JAMES CAGNEY — OLIVIA deHAVILLAND — RITA HAYWORTH are back — STRAWBERRY BLONDE — RE-RELEASED Warner Hit! — with ALAN HALE • JACK CARSON • GEORGE TOBIAS — Directed by RAOUL WALSH

DEWEY BRICKER — SEE HIM! HEAR HIM! TONIGHT Gov. JOHN W. BRICKER OF OHIO OUR NEXT VICE-PRESIDENT — Brings the Republican Campaign to a fighting climax! — GLORIA SWANSON, ADOLPH MENJOU, EDDIE BRACKEN and other Hollywood Stars will appear in Person — METROPOLITAN OPERA HOUSE Broad and Poplar Streets, Philadelphia — 8:15 P.M. ALL WELCOME — Rally sponsored by the Republican Central Campaign Committee of Philadelphia and the Republican State Committee of Pennsylvania

Today's Service Entertainment

Tickets for service men and women to various types of shows can be obtained at the Philadelphia Hospitality Center for Service Men, 18 S. 15th st. There you can learn of special affairs each night.

MEN AND WOMEN

USO-Indoor Labor Plaza, Town Hall, Broad and Race sts.—Dancing and refreshments, 6 P. M. to midnight, daily except Sunday.

Y. M. C. A., 117 N. 15th st.—Lodging, pool, special recreations, gym, showers.

Jewish Welfare Board Club and Canteen, 401 S. Broad st.—Roof Garden, dancing and food.

Travelers' Aid—Pennsylvania Railroad Lounges—Broad St., 30th St. and North Philadelphia Stations, open 24 hours.

Travelers' Aid—Baltimore and Ohio Station, 24th and Chestnut sts.—Open 9.30 A. M. to 5.30 P. M.

USO—Reading Terminal Lounge, 12th and Market sts., open 10 A. M. to 10 P. M. daily.

Canteen for Service Men and Women, Baltimore and Ohio Station, 24th and Chestnut sts.—Open 9.30 A. M. to 4.30 P. M. Books, magazines, sandwiches, coffee served without cost.

Philadelphia Hospitality Center, 18 S. 15th st.—Information and referral services; limited number of free entertainment tickets; mending shop for men.

Benedict Club (National Catholic Community Service), 157 N. 15th st.—Dancing and food.

Y. W. C. A., 1800 Arch st.—Hospitality and dancing.

Salvation Army Red Shield Club, 703 N. Broad st.—Entertainment, music, lodging and food.

Lutheran Service Center, 1215 Walnut st.—Open daily, 11 A. M. to 11 P. M. Lounges, writing room, showers, recreation, lunches—Sunday evening suppers.

Baptist Hospitality Center, 17th and Sansom sts.—Facilities for service men and women.

Methodist Service Center, Erie ave. east of Broad st.—From noon to midnight daily. Lounge, writing room, shower room, game room, snack counter.

Morning Cheer Victory Center, 1511 Walnut st.—Open 24 hours daily. Writing and recreation room, lounge, lodging and food.

Church Door Canteen of Jenkintown, Homestead Road—Snack bar and dancing. Open every night, 6 P. M. to midnight.

Willow Grove Service Center, Legion Building, Easton Road—Meals, dancing, games, daily 6 P. M. to 12.

Zoological Gardens, 34th st. and Girard ave.—Open 9 A. M. to 5 P. M.

Franklin Institute, 20th st. and the Parkway—Open 1 to 6 P. M. Closed Monday.

Pennsylvania Academy of the Fine Arts, Broad and Cherry sts.—Exhibits free to service men and women in uniform, daily 1 P. M. to 5 P. M.

University Museum, 33d and Spruce sts.—Admission free. Exhibits of current interest. Open weekdays, except Monday, 10 A. M. to 5 P. M.; Sundays 1 to 5 P. M.

Academy of Natural Sciences, 19th st. and the Parkway—Weekdays, 9 A. M. to 5 P. M.; Sundays, 1 to 5 P. M. Admission free.

Philadelphia Museum of Art, 26th st. and the Parkway—Open daily, 10 A. M. to 4 P. M.—Current exhibition of interest.

The Philadelphia Art Alliance, 251 S. 18th st.—Exhibits. Daily, 10.30 A. M. to 9 P. M.; Sundays, 1 to 6 P. M. Exhibits changed weekly.

Aquarium, 26th and Green sts.—Open daily, 8.30 A. M. to 4.30 P. M. Sundays, 9 A. M. to 5 P. M.

MEN

United Service Club, 17th and Locust sts.—Open 24 hours. Sleeping and shower accommodations, lounge, library, hobby room. Breakfast and dinners served. Dancing and refreshments nightly.

USO Date Club, Broadwood Hotel, 320 N. Broad st.—Dancing. Open 5 to 12 P. M.

South Broad St. USO, 510 S. Broad st.—Dancing, snack bar.

United Seamen's Service Club, U. S. S. Hotel Tracy, 36th and Chestnut sts.—Dancing, snack bar.

Navy Mothers Club, 246-48 S. Quince st.—Dancing and refreshments for Navy men, 10 A. M. to midnight.

Stage Door Canteen, Broad and Locust sts.—Open daily, 11 A. M.; dancing, with refreshments, 5 P. M. to midnight; Sundays, 2 P. M. to midnight.

The Military Order of the Loyal Legion, 1805 Pine st.—Museum of Civil War weapons, flags and pictures. Open 9 A. M. to 5 P. M.

Bellevue-Stratford—Officers' Club. Open daily from 10 A. M. to midnight. Free tickets for amusements.

St. Stephen's Service Club, 10th st. below Market—Library, gymnasium, free refreshments. Open 10 A. M. to 11 P. M.

Presbyterian Hospitality House, 2200 Locust st.—Recreation, refreshments, sleeping quarters, laundry facilities.

Open Door Canteen of Upper Darby, 7058 W. Garrett Road—Tuesday, Wednesday and Thursday, dancing for service men, 8 P. M.

WOMEN

Service Women's Club, USO-Emergency Aid, 254 S. 15th st.—Home facilities, information, tea service. Open weekdays, 9.30 A. M. to 10 P. M., Sundays 4 to 8 P. M.

Women's Officers' Club, 1521 Walnut st.—Many facilities, 9 A. M. to 9 P. M.

Amusement Guide

THEATERS

FORREST—"Iolanthe," 8.30.
LOCUST—"Trio," 8.30.
SHUBERT—"Sadie Thompson," 8.30.

MOTION PICTURES

ALDINE—"Abroad With Two Yanks," 11.45, 1.40, 3.50, 5.50, 7.50, 10.
ARCADIA—"The Seventh Cross," 11.10, 1.20, 3.30, 5.40, 7.50, 10.
BOYD—"Marriage Is a Private Affair," 11, 1, 3, 5.05, 7.05, 9.10, 11.15, 1.15 A. M., 3.15.
CAPITOL—"Strangers in the Night," 10.30, 12.25, 2.20, 4.15, 6.10, 8.05, 10.
EARLE—"Minstrel Man," 10.40, 1, 3.25, 5.45, 8.10, 10.25. Jimmy Dorsey and orchestra on stage, 12, 2.20, 4.45, 7.05, 9.30.
FOX—"Till We Meet Again," 11, 12.50, 2.40, 4.30, 6.20, 8.10, 10.
KARLTON—"Maisie Goes to Reno," 11, 12.50, 2.45, 4.35, 6.20, 8.05, 9.55.
KEITH'S—"Wilson," 11, 1.40, 4.20, 7.05, 10.
MASTBAUM—"Since You Went Away," 10.15, 1.10, 4.05, 7, 10.
NEWS—"A Farewell to Arms," 8.15, 9.50, 11.20, 12.55, 2.30, 4.05, 5.40, 7.10, 8.45, 10.20, all night.
STANLEY—"An American Romance," 11.10, 1.25, 3.50, 5.40, 7.45, 10.
STANTON—"Are These Our Parents?" 11.10, 1, 2.50, 4.35, 6.20, 8.10, 10.
STUDIO—"Rain," 12, 2.30, 5, 7.35, 10.10.

2 DRAMAS OF TORRID LOVE — JOAN CRAWFORD as SADIE THOMPSON in "RAIN" with WALTER HUSTON — CHARLIE RUGGLES in "FALSE RAPTURE" — MIDNIGHT SINNERS — STUDIO

A WILLIAM GOLDMAN THEATRE KARLTON BROAD & CHESTNUT — ANN SOTHERN — MAISIE GOES TO RENO

Doors Open 10 A. M. — TODAY — STANLEY-WARNER Earle

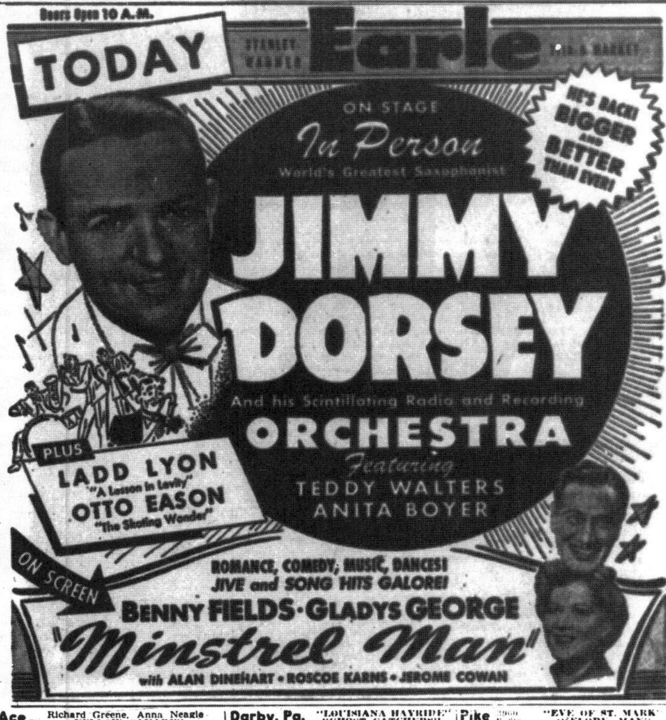

PLUS LADD LYON "A Lesson in Levity" — OTTO EASON "The Skating Wonder"

ON SCREEN — ROMANCE, COMEDY, MUSIC, DANCES! JIVE and SONG HITS GALORE! — BENNY FIELDS • GLADYS GEORGE — "Minstrel Man" — with ALAN DINEHART • ROSCOE KARNS • JEROME COWAN

DOORS OPEN 10:45 A.M. — STANLEY-WARNER MASTBAUM 16th & MARKET — 5th and... FINAL WEEK! — DAVID O. SELZNICK presents his first production since "Gone with the Wind" and "Rebecca" — SINCE YOU WENT AWAY — United Artists Release Starring CLAUDETTE COLBERT, JENNIFER JONES, JOSEPH COTTEN, SHIRLEY TEMPLE, MONTY WOOLLEY, LIONEL BARRYMORE, ROBERT WALKER

STANLEY-WARNER CENTRAL CITY THEATRES

WAR BONDS & STAMPS CAN BE PURCHASED AT ALL STANLEY-WARNER THEATRES

BOYD — DOORS OPEN 10:45 A.M. — LANA TURNER — "MARRIAGE IS A PRIVATE AFFAIR" — JAMES CRAIG • JOHN HODIAK — TONIGHT LATE SHOWS CONTINUOUS LAST FEATURE 3:15

STANLEY — DOORS OPEN 10:45 A.M. IN TECHNICOLOR — "AN AMERICAN ROMANCE" IN TECHNICOLOR — Brian DONLEVY • Ann RICHARDS • Walter ABEL

ALDINE — DOORS OPEN 10:45 A.M. — WILLIAM BENDIX, Helen WALKER, Dennis O'KEEFE — ABROAD with TWO YANKS

FOX — DOORS OPEN 10:45 A.M. — "TILL WE MEET AGAIN" — Ray MILLAND • Barbara BRITTON — WALTER SLEZAK, LUCILE WATSON

STANTON — LAST DAY — Doors Open 10.45 A.M. — "ARE THESE OUR PARENTS" — HELEN VINSON • LYLE TALBOT

STANLEY-WARNER NEIGHBORHOOD THEATRES

U. S. BONDS AND STAMPS ON SALE EVERY DAY AND NIGHT—IMMEDIATE DELIVERY

PALACE: LATE SHOWS TONIGHT, LAST COMPLETE FEATURE 3.30 A. M.

CAPITOL 8th & Mrkt. "STRANGERS IN THE NIGHT" — Terror Strikes With Evil Vengeance When a Murderess Traps Her Victims!

PALACE 12th & Market — SPENCER TRACY, SIGNE HASSO "SEVENTH CROSS" | VICTORIA 9th & Market — DON AMECHE, CARMEN MIRANDA "Greenwich Village" in Tech.

CIRCLE, TOWER, MIDWAY, UPTOWN, STATE, BROADWAY, YORKTOWN, ORPHEUM — CARY GRANT, PRISCILLA LANE "Arsenic and Old Lace"

COLONIAL, NEW 69th, NIXON, SAVOIA, ROOSEVELT — WALLACE BERRY, BINNIE BARNES "Barbary Coast Gent"

VERNON — JOAN DAVIS, BOB CROSBY "KANSAS CITY KITTY"

THIS MARK (*) INDICATES RE-ISSUE PICTURE

FAMILY, 333 MARKET, PRINCESS, SAVOY, CENTER, ALHAMBRA, COMMODORE, OXFORD, LIBERTY, MODEL, COLNEY, PLAZA, PARK, ASTOR, SEDGWICK, BROMLEY, FORUM, AVON, COLUMBIA, LINDLEY, ORIENT, OGONTZ, GADET, DIAMOND, IMPERIAL, LIBERTY, LINDY — "DRAGON SEED", "MR. SKEFFINGTON", "GOING MY WAY", "PINTO BANDIT", Esther Williams, Red Skelton "BATHING BEAUTY", BENN, KENT, STRAND, FAIRMOUNT, BETTE DAVIS, CLAUDE RAINS "Mr. Skeffington", HARROWGATE, Katharine Hepburn, Walter Huston "Dragon Seed", LEADER, GARY COOPER "STORY OF DR. WASSELL" in Tech.

ALLEGHENY, LANE, LOGAN, CROSS KEYS, EARL, FELTON, FERN ROCK, GRANGE, FRANKFORD, IMPERIAL, KEYSTONE, NORTHEASTERN, REXY, RICHMOND, WISHART, WYNNE — SUBURBAN — AMBLER, ARDMORE, GROVE, HIWAY, LANSDOWNE, MANOR, PARKER, WAVERLY

Ace, Adelphi, Admiral, Airport, Alden, Allegheny, Ambassador, Anthony Wayne, Apollo, Avenue, Band Box, Belgrade, Belmont, Benner, Benson, Berwyn, Pa., Bluebird, Boro, Boyd-Chester, Breeze, Broad, Broadway, Byrd, Cambria, Cameo, Carman — WALLACE BEERY, BINNIE BARNES "Barbary Coast Gent" PLUS—STAGE SHOW — Casino, Cayuga, Cedar, Century, Chelten, Clearfield, Clifton, Colonial — BUD ABBOTT, LOU COSTELLO "IN SOCIETY" — Crest — BING CROSBY "GOING MY WAY" — Dante

Darby, Pa., Doris, Edgemont, Egyptian, Erlen, Eureka, 56th, Frolic, Girard, Glenside, Pa., Grand, Grant, Gt. Northern — "SENSATIONS OF 1945" — Greenway, Hamilton, Hill, Hollywood, Howard, Iris — "BLACK MAGIC", "SONG OF NEVADA" — Jackson — "WATERLOO BRIDGE" — Jeffries, Joy, Jumbo, Keswick-Glenside — "Hail The Conquering Hero" — Lawndale, Lenox, Locust, Mayfair, Media, Pa., Narberth, New Jewel, New Lyric, New Penn, Overbrook, Palm, Park, Pearl, Penn, Pennypack — "SONG of the OPEN ROAD"

Pike, President — Katharine HEPBURN, WALTER HUSTON "DRAGON SEED" — Regal, Regis, Renel, Rex, Rialto, Riant, Ridge, Ritz, Riviera, Rivoli, Rockland, Roxy — "MARINE RAIDERS" — Royal, Senate, Seville, Sherwood, Southern, Spruce, Star, Stonehurst, Stratford, Suburban, Tempo, Terminal — "ATLANTIC CITY" — Tioga — BING CROSBY, BARRY FITZGERALD "GOING MY WAY" — Towne, Tyson, Unique, Upsal, Venice, Victory, Viola, Vogue, Walton, Wayne, Yeadon, Pa., York — HATBORO, PA. — Hatboro

The Philadelphia Inquirer

PUBLIC LEDGER

An Independent Newspaper for All the People

FINAL CITY EDITION

CIRCULATION: October Average: Daily 522,247; Sunday 1,095,035

WEDNESDAY MORNING, NOVEMBER 8, 1944

Copyright, 1944, by Triangle Publications, Inc., Vol. 231, No. 131

abdefgh ★★

THREE CENTS

ROOSEVELT WINS

Leads Dewey in 34 States With 395 Electoral Votes

30 Jap Ships, 440 Planes Hit at Manila

Two War Vessels Among Those Sunk By U. S. Fliers

War Summary on Page 14

By CHARLES H. McMURTRY

PEARL HARBOR, Nov. 7 (A. P.).—Carrier-based Helldivers, Hellcats and Avengers destroyed 440 Japanese planes, sank two enemy warships, probably sank a third and damaged eight others in a two-day raid on the Manila area of the Philippines, the Navy disclosed today.

Additionally, three cargo vessels and an oil tanker were sunk, a trawler and 14 others were damaged and heavy destruction was spread among airfields, oil stores and installations.

THIRD FLEET PLANES

The raids by planes of the U. S. Third Fleet were made Saturday and Sunday. An enemy sub chaser went down Saturday and a heavy cruiser probably sank. An enemy destroyer was sunk Sunday.

A light cruiser and three destroyers were damaged Saturday. Two destroyers and two destroyer escorts were hit Sunday.

At least 191 enemy planes were wiped out Saturday, the bulk of them on the ground. Another 249 were accounted for Sunday.

TOLL MOUNTS TO 72

The enemy warship score increased to at least 72 the total sunk, probably sunk or damaged in actions related to General Douglas MacArthur's invasion of Leyte Oct. 20.

Admiral Chester W. Nimitz announcing the continued neutralization of the Manila area in a communique today, reported additional "heavy damage" was inflicted on ground installations.

Three oil storage areas were set afire on the north strip at Clark Field and a tremendous explosion started another large fire in the

Continued on Page 17, Column 2

F.D.R. Loses Home District

HYDE PARK, N. Y., Nov. 7 (U. P.).—President Roosevelt lost his home district of Hyde Park to Governor Dewey by approximately 375 votes, the election board reported tonight.

President Sweeps Penna.; Big Cities, Coal Areas Decide

By JOSEPH H. MILLER

Piling up big leads in Philadelphia, Allegheny county and the soft coal fields, President Roosevelt early this morning appeared certain of winning Pennsylvania and its 35 electoral votes.

On the basis of returns from more than three-fourths of the State's 8208 precincts, Mr. Roosevelt held a comfortable lead over Governor Thomas E. Dewey, his Republican opponent, in his successful fourth-term drive.

Returns from 7374 precincts, including virtually all in Philadelphia, gave:

Roosevelt	1,607,532
Dewey	1,547,755

Unofficial returns from the 52 Philadelphia wards gave Mr. Roosevelt a 132 028 lead in the city. The vote was:

Roosevelt	460,613
Dewey	328,585

Despite the President's margin, Republican State Chairman M. Harvey Taylor at 3 A. M. would not concede defeat in the State, asserting it would be found in the Dewey column when final returns came from rural counties.

CLOSES OFFICE

Shortly thereafter he closed his headquarters office in Harrisburg and departed without further comment.

It was doubtful whether Mr. Dewey could gain sufficient strength in the remaining returns to upset the civilian voting results when approximately 240,000 soldier ballots are computed on Nov. 22.

Mr. Roosevelt's Democratic running mates for State-wide offices were not doing so well, according to the returns. Only one, Congressman Francis J. Myers, of Philadelphia, who opposed Senator James J. Davis, Republican incumbent, for re-election held a lead.

Returns from 6793 precincts gave Mr. Myers 1,441,694 to 1,373,700 for Senator Davis. The Senator, however, was expected to gain some strength in further reports from rural counties.

The remainder of the Democratic

Continued on Page 2, Column 1

Roosevelt Takes Philadelphia by 132,028 Plurality

By GEORGE M. MAWHINNEY

President Roosevelt led the Democratic slate to victory in Philadelphia yesterday, taking all but 14 of the city's wards, and sweeping the city for a majority of 132,028.

The city-wide tally, vitally important in carrying Pennsylvania's 35 electoral votes, was 460,613 for the President and 328,585 for his Republican opponent, Governor Thomas E. Dewey.

VOTING HEAVY

It was piled up during a day in which the voting in every ward was heavy, but not so great as the total vote cast in the Presidential race of four years ago, when President Roosevelt overcame Wendell L. Willkie within the city limits by a majority of 177,000.

The decrease in the Roosevelt vote in the four-year period struck a sharp blow to the early hopes of Democratic leaders for a Philadelphia majority of up to 200,000. Early this morning, however, James P. Clark, Democratic city leader, said he believed that when the soldier vote is counted, the Democratic majority will be brought up to 150,000.

AHEAD OF TICKET

President Roosevelt ran well in the lead of the State-wide Democratic candidates, but these followed close behind and achieved substantial city majorities over their Republican opponents for the U. S. Senate, the State Supreme Court, State Treasurer and Auditor General.

With the completion of the vote count early this morning, Republican City Chairman David W. Harris telephoned congratulations to Democratic Chairman Clark.

"You've done a swell job," the Republican leader told the leader of the opposition. "You have one fine committeeman. His name is Roosevelt."

Slightly earlier, Mr. Harris issued

Continued on Page 5, Column 1

Sen. Davis Hurt In Fall on Stairs

PITTSBURGH, Nov. 8 (A. P.).—Senator James J. Davis suffered a wrenched ankle in a fall down stairs last night after making a last-minute appeal at a local radio station.

Later, he received election returns alone in his Hotel William Penn room but turned off his radio at 11 P. M., saying:

"I want to get some rest. The returns so far don't mean a thing."

(A. P. Wirephoto)

PRESIDENT ROOSEVELT ELECTED FOR A FOURTH TERM

President Franklin D. Roosevelt, who has been re-elected to the Presidency for a fourth term. This portrait was made a few days before the election.

East and Far West Carry F. D. R. to 4th Term Victory

Additional Election News and Pictures on Pages 2, 3, 4, 5, 6, 7, 8, 9, and 22

By WILLIAM C. MURPHY, JR.

Franklin D. Roosevelt won a fourth term in the White House in yesterday's record-smashing turnout of voters in which, apparently, more than 50,000,000 electors marched to the pools for the nation's first wartime election in 80 years.

The President defeated his Republican opponent, Governor Thomas E. Dewey of New York, by an overwhelming plurality in the Electoral College but his popular vote percentage margin apparently was less than that by which he defeated the late Wendell L. Willkie four years ago.

Mr. Dewey, from his headquarters in New York conceded the election to Mr. Roosevelt at 3.15 A. M. with a statement saying:

"It is clear that Mr. Roosevelt has been elected and every good American agrees with me in the spirit of my greeting him. I extend my hearty congratulations and my wishes for a speedy victory and a lasting peace . . ."

ROOSEVELT LEADS IN 34 STATES

At the time Mr. Dewey conceded, Mr. Roosevelt had a lead in 34 States with a total of 395 electoral votes while Mr. Dewey was ahead in 14 States with 136 electoral votes.

At the same hour, however, Mr. Roosevelt's percentage of the then tabulated popular vote was 53.8 to 46.2 for Mr. Dewey, while at a comparable hour four years ago Mr. Roosevelt led Mr Willkie by 55 to 45. Returns from 77,359 of the country's 130,810 voting units showed the popular vote:

Roosevelt	15,771,666
Dewey	13,594,710
Total	29,366,406

The results in several large States still were mathematically in doubt, but Mr. Roosevelt, building upon the traditional Democratic backlog of votes in the South, had piled up enough votes along the industrialized North Atlantic Seaboard to insure his victory—even without the votes of several inland States which appeared to be swinging into his column after giving the New York Governor early leads.

PLURALITY MOUNTS IN FAR WEST

Mounting returns from the Far West apparently were increasing Mr. Roosevelt's pluralities at the time pre-dawn tabulations were made.

Final results may not be available for several weeks, since 11 States provide for delayed counting of service ballots, and an estimated 800,000 votes are involved in those States. It appeared improbable, however, that the late votes would have any substantial effect upon the outcome.

The story of Mr. Dewey's defeat was told in the figures showing Mr. Roosevelt's pluralities in half a dozen or more "key" States—margins which were comparatively small in some instances but sufficient to swing substantial blocs of votes in the Electoral College.

NEW YORK SWINGS TO ROOSEVELT

In New York State, for example, with a total vote of approximately 5,000,000 tabulated at an early hour this morning, Mr. Roosevelt was leading Governor Dewey by something in excess of 250,000 votes, which meant that New York's 47 electoral votes had been switched into the Roosevelt column.

In Connecticut, with eight electoral votes at stake, Mr. Roosevelt at approximately the same time was leading Mr. Dewey, 434,841 to 391,349.

Massachusetts' 16 electoral votes were headed for the Democratic column by a margin of about 50,000 with something more than 700,000 votes counted.

SIZEABLE F. D. R. LEAD IN ILLINOIS

At the same time the 28 electoral votes of Illinois—which had given Mr. Dewey a substantial margin in the early returns—were being switched to Mr. Roosevelt who had piled up 1,508,618 votes to 1,276,425.

In Missouri, another State in which Mr. Dewey was well ahead in the early tabulations, Mr. Roosevelt had moved out in front, 492,445 to 474,741, with 15 electoral votes at stake.

California, with 25 electoral votes, also was headed for the Roosevelt column with the President leading Mr. Dewey

Continued on Page 2, Column 6

N.J. Gives Dewey Lead of 24,000

Returns from 2458 of New Jersey's 3657 voting precincts early today gave Thomas E. Dewey a 24,000 lead over President Roosevelt, his margin falling off from an early pace that saw him at times leading his Democratic opponent by more than 60,000.

The unofficial count from 2458 precincts was:

Roosevelt	612,093
Dewey	636,140

In the race for U. S. Senator, H. Alexander Smith, Republican, held a comfortable lead of 67,000 votes over Representative Elmer H. Wene in 2316 of the State's precincts. The vote was:

Wene	523,574
Smith	590,091

The tabulation in three counties was complete by 2 A. M. Observers were startled by the absence of an overwhelming majority for the Pres-

Continued on Page 2, Column 2

Democrats Hold Senate, Expected to Rule House

By HERMAN A. LOWE

The Democrats apparently retained control of both chambers of Congress yesterday, on the basis of incomplete national returns. There was no question about the Senate, but the House race was close, with a number of western districts whose final returns will not be reported until later today.

Republican hopes for a substantial gain in the Senate went glimmering as the early returns piled up.

Of the 35 Senate seats before the voters, 22 are now held by Democrats. Only three of these appeared headed toward the Republican column—in New Jersey, Missouri and Iowa.

On the other hand, the Democrats had captured one Republican seat in Connecticut, and had a chance to win others in Pennsylvania and North Dakota.

In New Jersey, H. Alexander

Continued on Page 2, Column 8

Yanks, Germans Battle For Reich Forest City

By HOWARD COWAN

LONDON, Nov. 7 (A. P.).—American and German troops were locked tonight in a swaying, bitter struggle for the center of the German town of Vossenack in Hurtgen Forest, with powerful Nazi reinforcements battling fiercely to bar the road to Cologne and the rich Rhine Valley only 30 miles away.

After five days of see-saw fighting, Lieutenant General Courtney Hodges' First Army doughboys tonight held half of the mile-and-a-half-long town, and the Germans were solidly entrenched in the other half. Shock troops of both sides actually were fighting from opposite wings of the church in the heart of the town.

13 MILES FROM AACHEN

Vossenack, 13 miles southeast of Aachen, was captured by General Hodges' forces at the outset of their new offensive last Friday, but repeated counter-attacks by German reserves rushed down from the Arnheim sector in Holland knocked the Americans back.

A front dispatch tonight described the fight for Vossenack as "savage as was the struggle for Aachen—and one of much greater scope." It

Continued on Page 10, Column 8

IN TODAY'S INQUIRER

SPECIAL DEPARTMENTS

COLUMNS AND FEATURES

Fish Concedes Defeat by Bennet

ALBANY, N. Y., Nov. 7 (A. P.).—Republican Representative Hamilton Fish conceded tonight that Augustus W. Bennet had won his seat in the 29th Congressional District, to which Representative Fish was seeking re-election for a 14th term.

"I believe in the will of the majority, cast in the American way," Representative Fish said in a statement at his headquarters in Newburgh.

WINNER 'GRATIFIED'

Mr. Bennet, a lifelong Republican who ran on the Democratic, American Labor, Liberal and Good Government tickets after Representative Fish had defeated him in the primary for the Republican nomination, also issued a statement in which he said his first reaction was "one of gratification at the outcome of the long and hard battle."

Representative Fish, who previously had represented the 26th District, President Roosevelt's home district, added in his statement:

"From the reports received to date

Continued on Page 3, Column 1

City Vote At Glance

PRESIDENT	
F. D. Roosevelt, D.	460613
Thomas E. Dewey, R.	328585
Norman Thomas, Soc.	2030
Edward Treichert, Ind. G.	237
Claude Watson, Proh.	453
U. S. SENATOR	
Francis J. Myers, D.	457323
James J. Davis, R.	325859
STATE SUPREME COURT	
Charles A. Jones, D.	448493
Howard W. Hughes, R.	326293
SUPERIOR COURT (Two to be elected)	
F. Clair Ross, D.	450813
Chester H. Rhoades, D.	446380
Arthur H. James, R.	328222
J. Frank Graff, R.	325357
STATE TREASURER	
Ramsey S. Black, D.	443985
Edgar W. Baird, R.	329807
AUDITOR GENERAL	
G. Harold Wagner, D.	451437
G. Harold Watkins, R.	330139

Roosevelt Wires Thanks to Dewey

By JOHN C. O'BRIEN

Inquirer Staff Reporter

HYDE PARK, N. Y., Nov. 8 (Wednesday)—President Roosevelt, 15 minutes after hearing Governor Thomas E. Dewey's radio statement conceding defeat, sent the Republican candidate a telegram of appreciation.

The text of the President's telegram follows:

"His Excellency, Thomas E. Dewey, Governor of New York, Hotel Roosevelt, New York.

"I thank you for your statement which I have heard over the air a few minutes ago.—Franklin D. Roosevelt."

After greeting several hundred of his Hyde Park neighbors from the front porch of his home about half an hour before midnight, the President returned to his tally sheets and continued to follow the returns with close attention.

Forty minutes after he sent his message to Governor Dewey at 3.50

Continued on Page 3, Column 2

Dewey Accepts 'Will of People'

By WALTER HAZLETT

Inquirer Staff Reporter

NEW YORK, Nov. 8 (Wednesday).—Governor Thomas E. Dewey conceded at 3.15 A. M. today that Franklin D. Roosevelt had been re-elected for a fourth term and called on all good Americans to accept the will of the people.

Governor Dewey, with Mrs. Dewey standing by his side, held his emotions under complete control as he read his statement in the main ballroom of the Roosevelt Hotel, here.

PARTY REVITALIZED

He declared that the campaign conducted in his behalf had revitalized the Republican Party, and expressed his earnest hope that President Roosevelt's next term will see speedy victory in the war, the

Continued on Page 3, Column 5

U. S. WEATHER FORECAST

Philadelphia and vicinity: Fair today and tomorrow, with moderate temperatures.

Sun rises 7.36 A.M. Sets 5.52 P.M.
Moon rises 12.36 A.M. Sets 2.44 P.M.

34 Schoolboy Athletes Feted at Inquirer Banquet

ALL-PUBLIC, ALL-INTERACADEMIC, ALL-CATHOLIC FOOTBALL TEAMS HONORED BY INQUIRER LAST NIGHT AT WARWICK

Top row—left to right—All-Public High School Conference Team: Thomas Sabol, Southern; James Seifert, Frankford; Uriel Wallace, Jr., Benjamin Franklin; Theodore Zygmont, Roxborough; Milton Komarnicki, Southern; Victor Frank, Jr., Central; William DiFrancesco, Northeast; Edwin Carr, Olney; Anthony Colletta, Southern; Norman Waldman, Northeast; William Jones, Northeast. Middle row — All-Interacademic League Team: A. Wallace Schofield, Jr., Germantown Academy; Robert McIlwain, Haverford; John Russell, Jr., Haverford; Douglas W. Crate, Jr., Friends Central; John B. Kelly, Jr., Penn Charter; Norman Moore, Penn Charter; Rodman B. Finkbiner, Episcopal; Victor Mauck, Jr., Haverford; Thomas L. Hogan, Jr., Friends Central; Ralph Knode, Jr., Episcopal; William S. Schofield, Jr., Penn Charter. Bottom row—All-Catholic League Team: Walter Buckley, Northeast; Michael J. Bogan, Jr., West; Thomas J. Donnalley, St. Joseph's; William M. Gaynor, Jr., LaSalle; James J. Burke, Jr., West; Walter Kolanko, Northeast; George McAndrews, West; John Fanuka, LaSalle; Joseph A. Byers, St. Joseph's; Robert Connor, West; Joseph Dougherty, West; James Sundstrom, LaSalle. The 34 players received gold awards from The Inquirer, emblematic of their outstanding achievements.

Col. Larson Praises 'Forgotten' Parents

Gold Footballs Awarded 'All' Teams; Holcomb Speaks; Coaches Introduced

By ART MORROW

It is hardly likely that the 34 members of the All-Interacademic, All-Catholic and All-Public High School teams would have been recognized by even their bitterest opponents in the main ball room of the Warwick Hotel last night. The occasion was the second annual dinner in honor of The Philadelphia Inquirer Gold Football Award winners, and opponents never found them in a mood like this.

All were dressed in holiday best, faces scrubbed clean. Some were beet red. Some glowered. Some stared steadily at their polished shoes. Some gazed vacantly out into space, never seeing the bright and shining expanse of older faces in the room before them. The boys looked embarrassed. The parents looked proud.

PARENTS PRAISED

Colonel Emery Ellsworth Larson—medals and decorations gleaming on a chest of olive drab, the very personification of all that has been fought from the Shores of Montezuma to the Halls of Tripoli, and now to the Beachheads of Tarawa, too—big smiling Swede Larson of the United States Marines looked out on the gathering and struck the keynote of the evening:

"I am happy to see so many mothers and fathers here, and I think The Inquirer has done a wonderful thing in bringing them together at a banquet in honor of their boys. For in the swift passage of time parents too often are forgotten. I remember my own years at the Naval Academy, and my mother and father never saw me play until the final game of my last year.

LARSON REMINISCES

"That was 1921—I was captain of the team that year — and my parents came on from Minnesota to see us play the Army. The game was in New York, at the Polo Grounds, and Bob Folwell, our coach, asked my father to sit on our bench. We won the game, 7-0, and I left with 45 seconds to play.

"I'll never forget my father then. It was late afternoon, and not yet dark; but it wouldn't have mattered if it had been inky night. The light on my father's face would have guided me as he stood there, on the sidelines, with a big Navy blanket. He threw it around my shoulders as I came off the field, threw his arm around me. And I'll never forget how I felt when he said, 'You looked like a football player out there today, son.'"

BRILLIANT PLAYER

Naval Academy history records that the Swede looked like a football player on many another day, too, for in his three years as a player—1919, '20, '21—and in three subsequent seasons as head coach—'39, '40, '41—the Navy never lost to the Army team. And in '21 Swede was on the All-America.

Swede, presenting the Gold Footballs to the players in behalf of The Inquirer, was one of five speakers at the Warwick, and many a stirring word was heard, too, from Lieutenant Ralph E. Harcourt of the U. S. Coast Guard, Private Stuart K. Holcomb, the end coach of the U. S. Military Academy's national championship team; Francis T. Murray, director of The Philadelphia Inquirer Charities, Inc., and Leo Riordan, the executive sports editor who served as toastmaster at a unique affair instigated and brought together with Walter H. Annenberg, the publisher, as host.

COACHES INTRODUCED

Many another notable was introduced — Captain Lemuel M. Stevens, U. S. N., retired, commandant of the Naval V-12 training program at the University of Pennsylvania; Jordan Olivar, head coach at Villanova College; Paul Riblett, the Penn end coach; Lieutenant Colonel J. Howard Berry, U. S. M. C. R., one of the U. of P.'s greatest athletes of all time; Dr. Jonathan K. (Poss) Miller, 1922 Red and Blue captain; DeBenneville (Bert) Bell, president of the Maxwell Memorial Football Club and co-owner of the professional Pittsburgh Steelers; John B. (Jack) Kelly, chairman of the National Committee on Physical Fitness, whose son was among the players honored; Donald E. MacCormick and Henry Heine, Interacademic officials, and, of course, all the coaches who participated in the selection of the three all-star teams.

NIGHT FOR PARENTS

But the night belonged to the parents. The boys looked embarrassed. But Dad's vest was strained, and Mother's face was flushed. The boys were introduced individually, but applause was withheld until his whole outfit was assembled in front of the speakers' dais; "for," in the words of Toastmaster Riordan, "the boys are being honored not as individual stars, but as great team players."

"When Japan started this war on

Continued on Page 23, Column 5

'43 All-Stars Now in War

Inquirer Standouts In All Branches Of Armed Forces

By KEN HAY

The wartime aura that prevailed at the second annual Inquirer Gold Football Award dinner last night at the Warwick Hotel, with speakers from four branches of the United States Armed Forces, brought memories of the similar occasion last December.

With those memories was the realization that these are serious times, a theme used by the speakers with theories based on fact. Last December, as last night, 34 boys were feted for outstanding work on the football field—many of these boys are now with the United States Armed Forces.

At least four of last year's stars are serving on the far-flung battle fronts of this war. Ed Lanigan, Northeast Catholic, is overseas with the Navy; Tom Kelleher, Northeast Catholic, is with the Marines in the South Pacific; Albert Sigel, Germantown Academy, is in the South Pacific with the Navy, and his teammate, Charles Smith, is somewhere in the Atlantic with the Navy.

MANY IN V-12 UNITS

Navy V-12 units have claimed many of these players who gained the city's outstanding scholastic honors. At Ursinus College are William Carlin, St. Joseph's, and Charles Reinhart, Germantown Academy. Swarthmore College is the base for Ed Marshall, Penn Charter, and Art Littleton, Haverford School. Starring on the basketball team at the University of Louisville is George Hauptfuhrer, Penn Charter.

Ed Veith, Central, is at North Carolina Pre-flight School, while Don Katz, his teammate, is at the Bainbridge Naval Training Station. Norfolk is the base of Al Papa, Overbrook, while John Sandusky, Southern, is taking his training at Fort Benning, Ga.

TWO MORE TO ENLIST

Sam Baird and Homer Hungerford moved from Haverford School to Princeton University as civilians but both will enter the service within a month. Baird is joining the Marines while Hungerford is listed with the Army Air Force.

A civilian student at Holy Cross College, LaSalle's Ed Reilly achieved distinction this fall with the Crusaders. He has received honorable mention on several All-American teams as guard. Another civilian student is Southern's Lloyd Eisenberg who will be a starter for Duke University in the Sugar Bowl game.

KURTZ, LAWLESS AT PENN

John Begley, crashing fullback at Northeast Catholic, is with the Army at a base in South Carolina. All three of the boys selected last year at West Catholic are in the service. Dan Brown and John Tulskie are in the Army, while Pete Murphy is with the Navy.

Bob Kurtz, Frankford, and Ed Lawless, Roman Catholic, were civilian members of the University of Pennsylvania team this past fall. Vince McPeak, St. Joseph's, played with Villanova College where he is a Navy trainee taking a pre-medical course. E. Newbold Smith, the all-around athlete at Episcopal Academy, is at Annapolis.

Elmer Green, Overbrook, starred for the University of Nevada this past season. John Witsch, Northeast, is in the Merchant Marine and Joe Quigley, St. Thomas More, is awaiting call for the service.

SOME STILL IN SCHOOL

Several of the boys are still finishing their high school work. These include Bill Jones, Northeast; Jim Seifert, Frankford; Lou Sciascia, Frankford; Ed Carr, Olney; Charles Pearson, Penn Charter, and Joe Cunningham, Episcopal Academy.

Because of the war, there was an absentee last night in the parents' ranks. He was Captain Douglas W. Crate, Sr., U. S. M. C. Captain Crate, former coach at Friends Central and Roxborough, is on duty in the Southwest Pacific. His son, Douglas, Jr., was named All - Interscholastic League tackle from Friends Central.

Interacademic League coaches present included, Raymond Keegan, Episcopal Academy; Frank Fitts, Friends Central; Cooper French, Germantown Academy; Fred R. Wallace, Haverford School, and Henry Miller, Penn Charter. In attendance also were Henry Heine, Penn Charter, president of the League, and Donald E. MacCormick, Penn Charter, secretary of the League.

Catholic League coaches present included, Bernard Bradley, LaSalle; John Gillespie, Northeast Catholic; Joseph Graham, Roman Catholic; Stanley Jaworowski, St. John's; Jack Shields, St. Joseph's; Val Hartman, St. Thomas More; John McGarry, Southeast Catholic, and Robert Dougherty, West Catholic.

Public High Conference coaches present included, John (Tex) Flannery, John Bartram; David Patchell, Central; Theodore Doering, Frankford; John Hinkle, Simon Gratz; Harold Geiges, Northeast; A. M. (Bert) Barron, Olney; John Rau, Overbrook; Benjamin Weinstein, Roxborough; Joseph Pitt, Southern, and Wesley Hackman, West Philadelphia.

Criswell, McCormick Win Inquirer Bouts

Wirtzschafter, Kelly, Trader, Thomas Kayo Victors; Grantano Is Outpointed

By JOHN WEBSTER

In spite of a drenching, windswept night, a near-capacity crowd jammed into the Cambria last night to whoop and roar as another group of hard-hitting victors emerged from the Diamond Belt and Middle Atlantic A. A. U. eliminations, and moved up the glory road that leads to February's classic Tournament of Champions.

Sub-Novice featherweights opened the tournament program, sponsored by the Northeast A. A., with three punch-packed battles that had the 1500 spectators in wild uproar. From that point every contest seemed to hold its quota of thrills.

McCLOSKEY KAYOED

Looking very good for a novice laddie (they're the 16-17-year-old group), taffy-haired John Wirtzschafter, Eastside, registered a second-round knockout in his 126-pound test. Hard pressed by Robert McCloskey, unattached, the cool Eastsider brought down his man with a volley of left hooks to the head at 39 seconds of the second round.

Previously in this bracket, Elmer Criswell, unattached, came off the floor twice in the opening period, and outpunched Charles Lenoir, stocky Eastside product, in a duel of unskilled but high-powered punchers, and Frank McCormick, Dunbar curlytop, jabbed and slapped tall, slatty Elmer Schroeder, an unattached youth to defeat across the usual three-round route.

WELTERS IN SLUGFESTS

Even more dramatic walloping was on view when the welterweight young-timers swung into action. Two crashing, first-round knockouts abbreviated the slugging in this bracket.

Fastest worker of the night was Charles Kelly, from Burlington—Jersey lightning hit Charles Singer, Bear's gym, at 54 seconds of the first round. A gaudy right to the jaw smashed Singer into a fog on the floor, and Referee Ed McGinn said "enough."

GILL STOPPED

But Leonard Trader, a brother of Pro Fighter Earl Trader (who fights at Convention Hall tonight) came out of Wilmington to stretch Dunbar's John Gill at 1.44 of the first. It was hammer-and-tongs from the bell with honors even for a minute

Continued on Page 23, Column 4

Tourney Bouts In South Phila.

South Philadelphia's first elimination bouts in the 1944-45 Diamond Belt and Middle Atlantic A. A. U. Boxing Championships will be staged tomorrow night at the Olympia, Broad st., below Bainbridge. Sub-novices are assigned for 135- and 147-pound bouts; open division tests are listed in the 147- and 160-pound classes.

The tournament show is to be staged under the auspices of the South Philadelphia A. A., a group of clubs which will conduct the downtown programs, including one city final card, on Wednesday nights.

Bar Bowl Games To A.A.F. Teams

WASHINGTON, Dec. 11 (A. P.).—Any chances that Army Air Forces football teams would be permitted to play beyond Saturday's Randolph Field-Second Air Force Sixth War Loan game in New York were squelched today by a War Department announcement.

"The thing that really put the quietus on this bowl business," a spokesman said, "is that the department does not want to do anything that might be interpreted as encouraging absenteeism when production demands are at a peak."

Saturday's game, it was pointed out, will decide the Army service championship and is "not a special, added or post-season game."

The announcement sent promoters of the January 1 Oil Bowl game in Houston and the Sun Bowl game in El Paso scurrying for new participants. The former had listed the Ramblers as one-half of its attraction and the latter similarly announced the Superbombers.

Navy authorities, whose permission was similarly sought for Bainbridge and Norman, Okla., have consistently refused.

OIL BOWL GAME CANCELED

HOUSTON, Tex., Dec. 11 (A. P.).—There'll be no Oil Bowl football game New Year's Day.

It was disclosed today the game had been canceled as the result of the War Department ruling. More than $40,000 in tickets had been sold, the committee said, and the work of returning checks and money orders would start immediately.

Valley Forge Wins 8th in Row, 72-39

PHOENIXVILLE, Pa., Dec. 11.—Valley Forge General Hospital chalked up its eighth straight basketball victory tonight by trouncing the U. S. Coast Guard of Philadelphia, 72-39, at the hospital gymnasium.

Stan Szukala, former All-America ace at DePaul University, continued his scoring rampage with 18 points.

Wally Tenana, former Detroit Eagle professional ace, tallied 14 points for the Coast Guard.

Valley Forge G. H.	G.	F.	P.	U. S. Coast Guard	G.	F.	P.
Craddock,f	4	1	9	McCollom,f	2	0	4
Schwille,f	4	1	9	Sweeney,f	1	3	5
Niemiera,f	1	3	5	Belover,f	0	0	0
Di Gioia,f	[illegible]	[illegible]	[illegible]	Tenana,c	4	6	14
Davis,c	6	3	15	Cody,c	1	0	2
Porter,c	0	0	0	Holden,c	0	0	0
Graf,g	2	1	5	Mil'vics,g	2	2	6
Tanitsky,g	4	1	9	Smith,g	2	1	5
Motsen,g	1	0	2	Mucci,g	1	0	2
Szukala,g	8	2	18	McEnroe,g	1	0	2
Totals	30	12	72	Totals	14	11	39

Halftime—Valley Forge, 37-21. Officials—Devlin and Stackowski.

Ray Robinson Faces Rangel

Returning to a Philadelphia ring after an absence of two years almost to the day, Ray Robinson, Harlem's carbon copy of the great old boxing masters, punches with Richard (Sheik) Rangel, a leather-tough Mexican from Fresno, Calif., in a 10-round welterweight contest tonight at Convention Hall. Heavy advance sales indicate a crowd of 12,000 and a gross gate of $26,000; favorable weather might bring a sellout, however, so eager are fight fans to learn whether Sugar Ray has recaptured his pre-service form.

Needless to say, Robinson, probably the most outstanding ringman of the times, is heavily favored. He would be rated over any man he might meet and, since Rangel is a newcomer here, it remains to be seen how he will fare with the rangy Negro boxer-hitter. In the Sheik's favor are his ruggedness and his style of milling.

RAY BEATEN BUT ONCE

Rangel fights a crouching, crowding, chucking-gloves sort of battle. He comes a-winging out of a weave, which might prove very troublesome for the Harlemite — who will be waging his fourth bout since his return to civilian life. Jake LaMotta, only man to outfight Ray in the latter's 49 bouts, and Marty Servo, who twice extended him, operated in that manner. Ray is the national selection.

Jimmy Hatcher, Lake City, Fla., meets Gene Burton, New York, who recently stopped Billy Nixon here in Herman Taylor's eight-round semi. Hatcher, who often has fought here, is picked to win.

ARNOLD IN TRENTON RING

Frankie Jamison, New York, a rough, rude fellow in action, is selected to thrash Rudy Richardson, a Clevelander of similar type, in the second eight, a middleweight affray. Joey Puig, New York, should hit too sharply for Earl Trade, local Negro, when they bargain in bantam punches for eight rounds.

Billy Arnold, Philadelphia's specialist in ring refrigeration, goes into action tonight with Johnny Finnazzo, Baltimore, for eight rounds at Trenton—not last night, as previously reported. The ex-Diamond Belter, a ripe old 18, is favored to score his 31st straight, his 29th by knockout. Billy then will resume training for his ten-rounder with "Broadway Johnny" Jones at the Met here next Monday night.

JOHN WEBSTER

Munger Speaker At Bryn Mawr

George Munger, University of Pennsylvania football coach, was the guest of honor and principal speaker last night at the first annual "Dad 'n' Son" dinner sponsored by the Men's Union of the Bryn Mawr Presbyterian Church. He showed movies of highlights of Penn's recent football season.

Other speakers at the dinner, held in the Church Rooms, included Fred R. (Doc) Wallace, director of athletics at Haverford School; Lou Young, former Penn star and coach, and Ed Pollock.

Cochran Leads Hoppe In Billiard Tournament

NEW YORK, Dec. 11 (A. P.).—Welker Cochran, San Francisco, won his eighth straight match in the national three-cushion billiard championship tourney tonight by beating Jay Bozeman, Vallejo, Cal., 50-39, in 47 innings.

The victory kept Cochran a full game ahead of defending champion Willie Hoppe. The two play tomorrow night. If Hoppe wins to end the 10-day round-robin competition in a tie, a playoff will be held Wednesday night.

Chicago Wins Fourth

CHICAGO, Dec. 11 (A. P.).—Chicago University, back in sports again this year, won its fourth basketball game in eight starts tonight, beating Wheaton College, 48-44.

Sports Results

College

BASKETBALL

Rider 42 ... Villanova 27
Iowa U. 87 ... S. Dakota State 37
Chicago 48 ... Wheaton 44
Emory & Henry 74 ... Lynchburg 29
Kansas State 33 ... Washburn 29
Davidson 54 ... U. S. Rubber 46
Concordia (Moorhead) 46 ... Moorhead Tchrs. 34
DePaul 66 ... Illinois Wesleyan 44
New Mexico 78 ... Hardin-Simmons 27

School

BASKETBALL

Haverford School 46 ... Overbrook 39
La Salle 30 ... Central 21
Tremont 43 ... Lykens 33
Pottsville Catholic 36 ... Orwigsburg 21
St. Clair 41 ... Schuylkill Haven 21

SWIMMING

La Salle 50 ... Camden Voc. 16

CATHOLIC LEAGUE

Roman 34 ... St. Joseph's 32

Service

BASKETBALL

Floyd Bennett Field 40 ... Union Temple 42
Great Lakes 62 ... Lincoln A.A.F. 57
Valley Forge G.H. 72 ... U.S. Cst. Guard 39
Ft. Worth A.A.F. 54 ... Texas Christian 40

Independent

BASKETBALL

MAIN LINE LEAGUE

Wayne 42 ... Brookline 36

GIRLS' NATIONAL INDUSTRIAL LEAGUE

Spars 42 ... Radio Condenser 28
I. T. E. 16 ... Hospital Waves 10
Marines 41 ... Quartermaster 35

OLDER BOYS' LEAGUE

Neighborhood 53 ... Rodney 27

INTERMEDIATES

Neighborhood 38 ... Rodney 18

PHILADELPHIA BOYS' CLUB LEAGUE

Northeast K 33 ... German-Hungarians 34

JUNIORS

Northeast K 37 ... German-Hungarians 4

GIRLS' KENDRICK RECREATION LEAGUE

Eddystone 28 ... Hallahan 20
Rovers 28 ... Central 23

CENTRAL Y INTRAMURAL LEAGUE

Sports 22 ... Penna. Salt 16

OTHER GAMES

Phila. Induction Station 37 ... Disston Saw 29
North Branch 65 ... Bayard 37

Majors Name Advisory Council, Terminate Commissioner's Pact

Frick, Harridge, O'Connor to Serve; Boston Gets All-Star Game July 10; Wade Traded to Yankees

By STAN BAUMGARTNER
Inquirer Sports Reporter

NEW YORK, Dec. 11.—The National and American Leagues today terminated the agreement under which the office of Commissioner of Baseball was created on Jan. 12, 1921, and appointed an advisory council to rule the game.

Meeting in separate sessions but taking joint action, they declared that whereas the office of Commissioner has become vacant due to the death of Judge Kenesaw M. Landis all the duties and powers of the office shall be exercised hereafter by a major league advisory council to consist of Ford Frick, president of the National League; Will Harridge, president of the American League, and Leslie M. O'Connor, secretary of the late Commissioner.

MEET IN FEBRUARY

At the same time, however, the two bodies made it clear that a Commissioner would be named as soon as they could draw up a new major-league agreement. A preliminary meeting will be held in February to take the first steps and while nothing definite was forecast, it was generally felt that when the two circuits canceled the present pact they also killed the arbitrary powers which Landis exercised and that in the new document the Commissioner would be well fenced in.

Provisions were also made for any contingencies that might arise until a permanent commissioner is selected. It was decreed that in case of a division of opinion within the council the decision of the majority shall be controlling, except in any case involving a player's claim against a club or league. In that case the two presidents shall have no vote, but the question will be decided by the third member of the council—O'Connor.

ESTABLISH AWARDS

In case O'Connor shall at any time be unwilling or unable to serve as a third member of the council, the selection of his successor shall be made by the two league presidents.

Harridge and Frick also announced that the two circuits voted to establish what is known as the Landis Memorial Award, in memory of the late Commissioner. The awards, one for each league, will go to the most valuable player selected for each league by a committee appointed by the Baseball Writer's Association of America.

FRICK RE-ELECTED

Previous to the start of their annual confab, the National League owners re-elected Frick president for another four-year term, the maximum permitted by the league constitution.

The 1945 All-Star game will be played on July 10 at Fenway Park, home of the Boston Red Sox. Clark Griffith, Washington, and Sam Breadon, St. Louis Cardinals, were elected vice presidents of their respective leagues while both leagues also elected boards of directors.

Named to the American were Don-

Continued on Page 23, Column 5

Set Race Dates For Garden State

TRENTON, N. J., Dec. 11 (A. P.).—The State Racing Commission announced today that the 1945 season at Garden State Park near Camden would open July 13 and run to Sept. 8, with 50 days of horse racing scheduled.

The track will resume operations on Mondays, a practice it had dropped during the past two years.

Villanova Halted By Rider, 42-27

Special to The Inquirer

TRENTON, N. J., Dec. 11.—Rider College snapped the four-game winning streak of Villanova College's basketball team tonight, 42-27, with Al Rossi and Ken Kunsch combining their scoring efforts for 26 points.

Rossi, a freshman from Hun Trenton High School, dropped in seven field goals and a foul as Rider, which had broken even in four previous starts, took command early and piled up a 29-16 halftime lead.

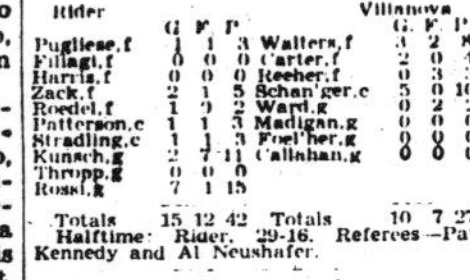

Rider	G.	F.	P.	Villanova	G.	F.	P.
Puglies,f	1	1	3	Walters,f	[illegible]	[illegible]	[illegible]
Fillagi,f	0	0	0	Carey,f	[illegible]	[illegible]	[illegible]
Harris,f	0	0	0	Keeher,f	[illegible]	[illegible]	[illegible]
Zack,f	2	1	5	Schau'gee,c	[illegible]	[illegible]	[illegible]
Roedel,f	0	0	0	Ward,g	[illegible]	[illegible]	[illegible]
Patterson,c	1	1	3	Madigan,g	[illegible]	[illegible]	[illegible]
Stradling,c	3	1	7	Foelber,g	[illegible]	[illegible]	[illegible]
Kunsch,g	2	7	11	Callahan,g	0	0	0
Thropp,g	0	0	0				
Rossi,g	7	1	15				
Totals	15	12	42	Totals	10	7	27

Halftime: Rider, 29-16. Referees—Pat Kennedy and Al Neushafer.

Haverford School Wins, Mauck Scores 17 Points

Haverford School's basketball team defeated Overbrook High School, 46-39, yesterday at Haverford. Victor Mauck, Jr., led the winners with 17 points.

Haverford	G.	F.	P.	Overbrook	G.	F.	P.
Thornton,f	5	1	11	Stone,f	6	1	13
Boyd,f	0	0	0	Aspen,f	2	0	4
Hanson,f	0	0	0	Duckett,f	5	1	11
Diamond,f	3	1	7	Rosenbaum,f	0	0	0
Smith,f	0	0	0	Graboyes,c	2	0	4
Cozens,c	3	1	7	Becker,g	0	0	0
Curran,c	0	0	0	Seltsher,g	1	0	2
Fritz,c	0	0	0	Jacobs,g	1	3	5
Mauck,g	6	5	17	Love,g	0	0	0
Esrey,g	0	0	0				
Yarrow,g	2	0	4				
Grosecl'e,g	0	0	0				
Totals	19	8	46	Totals	17	5	39

La Salle Beats Central For Fourth Triumph

La Salle High School won it's fourth straight basketball game yesterday by defeating Central High School, 30-21, at Ogontz and Olney aves.

LA SALLE	G.	F.	P.	CENTRAL	G.	F.	P.
Williams,f	1	2	4	Stoloff,f	1	1	3
Delaney,f	0	1	1	Gecker,f	2	1	5
Weglicki,c	5	1	11	Riley,c	2	2	6
Thompson,g	3	1	7	Parrish,g	1	1	3
Reagan,g	2	2	6	Sabatini,g	1	2	4
Phelan,f	0	1	1				
Totals	11	8	30	Totals	7	7	21

Half-time score: La Salle, 14-12.

Neighborhood Wins

Neighborhood made it two straight in the Older Boys Basketball League last night by defeating Rodney, 53-27. Neighborhod Intermediates also were victors over Rodney Intermediates, 38-18.

Rodney	G.	F.	P.	Neighborhood	G.	F.	P.
Brower,f	4	0	8	Cech,f	1	1	3
Barnard,f	0	0	0	Roz'ski,f	1	1	3
Leonard,c	2	0	4	Jar'wiecz,f	4	0	8
Diamond,g	0	1	1	Welde,c	6	2	14
Skonsky,g	0	1	1	Przy'ski,g	5	1	11
House,g	3	2	8	Guzak,g	0	0	0
				Kolodzey,g	3	2	8
				Levin,g	1	1	3
				Soda,g	0	1	1
Totals	11	5	27	Totals	22	9	53

Halftime score—Neighborhood, 20-15.

Lieutenant Wilson Reported Missing

Lieutenant Robert Wilson, 21, son of Jimmy Wilson, former manager of the Phillies and now a coach for the Cincinnati Reds, has been reported missing in action in the Asiatic area.

Lieutenant Wilson, a bombardier in the Army Air Forces, was graduated from Lawrenceville School and attended Princeton University.

Williams Stops Castilloux in 5th

BUFFALO, Dec. 11 (U. P.).—Ike Williams, 135, of Trenton, N. J., won a technical knockout over Dave Castilloux, 135½, Montreal, in one minute 53 seconds of the fifth round before 3800 in Memorial Auditorium tonight.

By United Press

NEWARK.—Bert Lytell, 152½, Fresno, Calif., stopped Johnny Brown, 159, New York, (7).

NEW YORK (St. Nicholas Arena).—Billy Grant, 170½, Orange, N. J., knocked out Roberto (Lotario) Ramirez, 185½, Mexico City, (7); Sal Scalabra, 125, Greenwich, Conn., knocked out Mickey Polo, 126½, Paterson, N. J., (1); Orlando Ferraro, 133, Stamford, Conn., drew with Gene Gregory, 133, New Haven, Conn., (6); Bobby Giles, 167, Buffalo, N. Y., stopped Danny Devlin, 173, Allentown, (3); Tommy Gargano, 136, Brooklyn, knocked out Carl Olson, 139½, New Haven, (1); Eddie Sanders, 160½, New York, stopped Steve Kish, 164 (3).

PROVIDENCE, R. I.—Sammy Mammone, 143, Stamford, Conn., decisioned Charlie Smith, 139, New York, (10).

HOLYOKE, Mass.—Indian Gomez, 159½, Havana, drew with Jerry Fiorello, 158, Brooklyn.

BALTIMORE.—Walter Woods, 165½, New York, technically knocked out Ellis Stewart, 164, Baltimore (7); Bobby Thompson, 190½, decisioned Matt Hines, 185½, Philadelphia (6).

WASHINGTON.—Melio Bettina, 184, New York, decisioned Georgie Parks, 184, Washington (10).

Pete Virgin, 125, New York, knocked out Willie Alexander, 123, Chester, Pa.; Foots Jackson, 153, Atlanta, drew with Lee Datta, 159, Philadelphia.

Horvath, Hackett Hurt In Traffic Accident

COLUMBUS, O., Dec. 11 (A. P.).—Les Horvath and Bill Hackett, Ohio State University All-America football players, were injured slightly tonight in a head-on auto collision in an icy suburban street.

Horvath suffered a facial laceration while Hackett sustained knee and head injuries, assistant coach Dan Dillon reported. They were admitted to University Hospital.

All-Star Football Teams Honored at Dinner

ALL-CATHOLIC	ALL-INTERACADEMIC	ALL-PUBLIC HIGH
E. Michael J. Bogan, Jr., West Catholic H. S.	E. Robert McIlwain, Haverford School	E. Thomas Sabol, Southern H. S.
E. Walter Buckley, Northeast Catholic H. S.	E. A. Wallace Schofield, Germantown Academy	E. James Seifert, Frankford H. S.
T. Thomas J. Donnalley, St. Joseph's H. S.	T. John Russell, Jr., Haverford School	T. Uriel Wallace, Jr., Benjamin Franklin H. S.
T. William M. Gaynor, Jr., La Salle H. S.	T. Douglas W. Crate, Jr., Friends Central School	T. Theodore Zygmont, Roxborough H. S.
G. John Fanuka, La Salle H. S.	G. Norman Moore, Penn Charter School	G. William DiFrancesco, Northeast H. S.
G. George McAndrews, West Catholic H. S.	G. Rodman Finkbiner, Episcopal Academy	G. Victor Frank, Jr., Central H. S.
G. Walter Kolanko, Northeast Catholic H. S.	C. John B. Kelly, Jr., Penn Charter School	C. Milton Komarnicki, Southern H. S.
C. James J. Burke, Jr., West Catholic H. S.	B. Victor Mauck, Jr., Haverford School	B. William Jones, Northeast H. S.
B. Robert Connor, West Catholic H. S.	B. William S. Schofield, Jr., Penn Charter School	B. Edwin Carr, Olney H. S.
B. Joseph A. Byers, St. Joseph's H. S.	B. Thomas L. Hogan, Jr., Friends Central School	B. Anthony Colletta, Southern H. S.
B. James Sundstrom, La Salle H. S.	B. Ralph Knode, Jr., Episcopal Academy	B. Norman Waldman, Northeast H. S.
B. Joseph Dougherty, West Catholic H. S.		

Indiantown Gap Wins

INDIANTOWN GAP, Dec. 11 (A. P.). — The Indiantown Gap basketball team nosed out Olmsted Field, 33-21, tonight. Hillery Brown tallied the winning field goal in the final 23 seconds.

The Philadelphia Inquirer

PUBLIC LEDGER

An Independent Newspaper for All the People

FINAL CITY EDITION

CIRCULATION: November Average: Daily 519,378; Sunday 1,096,611

THURSDAY MORNING, DECEMBER 28, 1944

Copyright, 1944, by Triangle Publications, Inc., Vol. 231, No. 181

a b d e f g h ★

THREE CENTS

Yanks Take Offensive in Belgium; Heroic Bastogne Garrison Rescued

Today

The German Offensive
Allies More Hopeful
Aerial Blows Telling
Nazis Short on Fuel
Next Move Awaited

By John M. McCullough

Inquirer Washington Bureau

WASHINGTON, Dec. 27.

A DEFINITELY favorable turn in the fighting on the Western Front in Europe was noted here today by military observers.

While it is still too soon to conclude that the great German counter-offensive through Belgium and Luxembourg has reached its peak, Field Marshal Gerd von Rundstedt is directly faced with two alternatives.

They are

1. Shall the German offensive be continued at full speed, feeding more and more reserves and supplies into the salient of penetration, in an effort to drive ahead and fan out, or

2. Shall a withdrawal be attempted, accepting the limited success which the offensive already has achieved?

That these alternatives face the Nazi commander on the Western Front arises, it is argued here, out of the definitely favorable situation of the American counter-action.

The elements in this situation are:

1. The American north flank has definitely driven in, sharply restricting the German advance to the northwest in the general direction of the line of the Meuse between Namur and Liege.

2. Not only has the American south flank held firm, anchored on Echternach, but the forces there have begun a drive which has relieved Bastogne, thereby threatening the rear of German advance elements attempting to break the line of the Meuse east of the area from Dinant north to Namur.

3. Aided by spotty but at least moderately good flying weather, Allied air forces have given German troop and supply areas terrific punishment.

4. The German drive has been slowed down if it has not been halted in its advance to the Meuse, the conclusion being that very strong American elements have advanced to the river and are fully deployed.

In the whole picture, it is conceded, the continuance of at least reasonable flying weather, in which Allied strategic and tactical air forces can be employed to their fullest, is vital.

If the weather were to continue fair, one observer pointed out, "it is not over-optimistic to believe that eventually the Ger-

Continued on Page 10, Column 1

War Output Slowed Here By Absentees

Shipyards, Plants Hampered; Cargoes Pile Up on Piers

The absence of thousands of workers, suffering from a "holiday hangover," from war production plants in the Philadelphia and Wilmington areas, was revealed yesterday as employers and Government agencies combined in an urgent plea to the men and women to report back to work immediately.

Company spokesmen expressed alarm over the soaring absenteeism rate and feared the condition would carry over the coming New Year week-end.

SUPPLIES PILE UP ON PIERS

Meanwhile, supplies for the fighting fronts in Europe were piling up on piers here as longshoremen joined the other workers in taking an unwarranted "holiday."

An Army spokesman said the situation was "extremely grave" and declared that "it would be a shame for the longshoremen to do anything that would cause cargo to arrive late just because a holiday season is here, when the boys in the battle areas who need the cargo cannot take a holiday."

It was explained that absenteeism has not caused any delay in scheduled departures of cargo vessels, but that the current slowdown "in all probability" would affect sailings in the next two or three weeks.

50 PCT. ARE ABSENT

The Dravo Shipyard, largest in the Wilmington area and employing a total of 6000 workers, reported that 50 percent of its employes were absent yesterday.

A check through the various departments of the yard, according to a spokesman, revealed only 25 percent of the regular personnel at work in one shop, while two other departments showed 65 and 70 percent at work.

The Philadelphia area office of the War Manpower Commission said it made a quick survey of the situation here and found absenteeism heaviest in metals plants, although the Sun Shipbuilding and Dry Dock Co., Chester, reported a "pretty heavy" total of workers missing from their jobs.

Officials of the Pusey & Jones Corp. Shipyard in Wilmington said work there had been "curtailed and

Continued on Page 4, Column 3

186 More Ships Ordered for 1945

WASHINGTON, Dec. 27 (A. P.).—James F. Byrnes authorized the Maritime Commission late today to begin construction immediately of 186 commercial vessels for delivery in the last half of 1945.

The War Mobilization Director said in a statement he hoped this additional authorization, together with available shipping, would "meet essential military requirements and still leave a balance for other purposes."

He did not name those other purposes, but Anglo-American conferences on problems of getting supplies to liberated civilians in Europe have stressed the need for shipping.

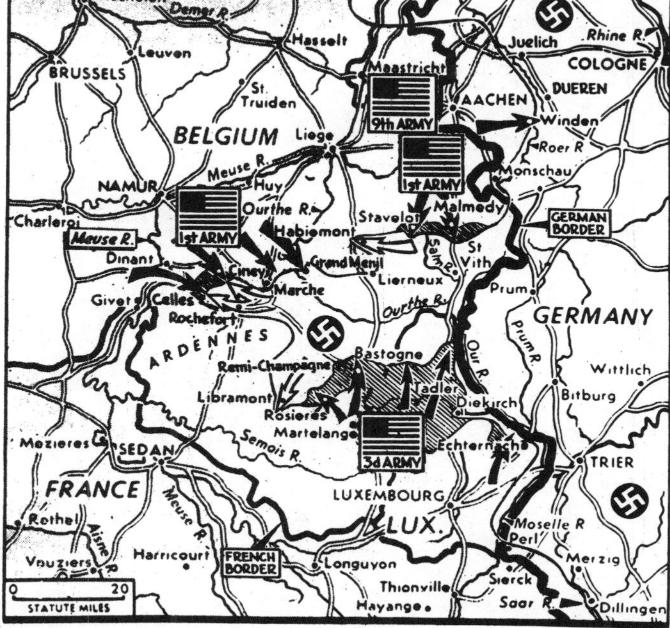

WHERE YANKS CUT INTO NAZI SALIENT ON WESTERN FRONT

American troops yesterday were reported to have narrowed the neck of the Nazi salient in Belgium to 20 miles. Striking from both north and south, the Yanks are reported to have taken back the sectors indicated on the map with lines, while the Nazis have admitted withdrawing from some Luxembourg positions to the Siegfried Line. Bastogne, which was isolated by the enemy, has been relieved. Ciney and Celles, points of the enemy's deepest penetration, have been recaptured.

3 Jap Destroyers Sunk at Mindoro

GENERAL MacARTHUR'S HEADQUARTERS, Philippines, Dec. 28 (Thursday) (U. P.).—United States warplanes and torpedo boats sank three Japanese destroyers and scored hits on a battleship and a heavy cruiser Tuesday night in putting to flight an eight-ship enemy task force which inaccurately shelled American positions on southwestern Mindoro for 20 minutes, it was announced today.

The enemy force, first major one to venture out to battle since Japan's disastrous defeat in the Philippines Sea in October, comprised a battleship, a heavy cruiser and six destroyers, and was kept under steady attack from dusk until midnight.

SPOTTED BY NAVY PLANE

A Navy Liberator bomber observed the task force as it was steaming through the South China Sea off Mindoro at a speed of 20 to 25 knots and fighter planes and medium bombers, as well as torpedo boats, swarmed out from the American base on Mindoro Island, 150 miles south of Manila.

The Navy bomber returned and hit the battleship. The fleet was under attack until it reached a point off the American Mindoro position shortly before midnight. The Japanese shelled Mindoro for 20 minutes but the American commander, Brigadier General William

Continued on Page 3, Column 7

Greek Factions Agree On Immediate Regency

ATHENS, Dec. 27 (U. P.). Greek representatives, seeking to end the three-week-old civil war in Greece, voted unanimously tonight to form a regency under King George immediately, and Prime Minister Winston Churchill disclosed he would meet soon with President Roosevelt and Premier Josef Stalin to discuss the Greek situation.

Mr. Churchill, speaking at a press conference a few hours after two sniper bullets had whizzed near him, said the "Big Three" might set up an "international trust" for Greece, which is expected to operate under a regency until the Greek people are able to select their own government in an orderly manner.

FEARS DRIFT TO ANARCHY

Speaking of the prospective "Big Three" conference, Mr. Churchill said, "We can't see this place drifting into anarchy."

There was no discussion of a truce pending appointment of a regency, so the fighting continued.

Gunfire made the British Embassy building tremble during the press conference, and Mr. Churchill said if the anti-government ELAS forces did not yield and evacuate Attica, "the guns will continue firing."

He disclosed that the Greeks then were discussing the problem of a regency, and warned that "we will use whatever force is necessary" to clear Attica, and "we do hope some

Continued on Page 3, Column 3

U. S. Subs Sink Big Jap Carrier

By JOHN M. McCULLOUGH

Inquirer Washington Bureau

WASHINGTON, Dec. 27.—Twenty-seven Japanese vessels, including a large aircraft carrier and a light cruiser, have been sunk in recent operations by United States submarines, Secretary of the Navy James Forrestal announced today.

He said 99 enemy combat vessels and 835 merchant ships had been sunk by American submarines alone since the outbreak of the war, and that these sinkings represent "more than 3,500,000 tons of Japanese shipping."

LOSS OF 43 PERCENT

This is more than 43 percent of the total estimated shipping with which Japan began her conquest of the Pacific and the Far East slightly over three years ago.

At the same time, the Navy Department announced the loss of the 2200-ton destroyer Cooper and the 200-foot LSM-20 (Landing Ship Medium) in operations in the Philippines.

COMMANDERS RESCUED

Commander Mell A. Peterson, 36, of Algona, Iowa, who commanded the Cooper, and Lieutenant John R. Bradley, 28, of Oak Creek, Col., who commanded the LSM-20, both survived, but Lieutenant Bradley was wounded, the Navy announced.

Casualties in the two sinkings, previously reported in communiques issued by General Douglas MacArthur's Headquarters in the Philippines, were not estimated. The normal complement of a destroyer of

Continued on Page 3, Column 6

U.S. Column Cuts Way to Trapped Men

Americans Refused To Yield, Took Big Toll of Foe's Tanks

Illustrated on Page 2

LONDON, Dec. 27 (A. P.).—American armored columns, in a five-mile drive from the south, have broken through to relieve the American garrison at Bastogne which had been cut off for more than a week by the German advance.

Supreme Headquarters confirmed an earlier report that relief units had reached the heroic defenders of Bastogne and that the German siege had been lifted.

TOOK HEAVY TOLL

Having rejected a Nazi ultimatum for surrender, the trapped doughboys have been holding out against tremendous enemy pressure and were reported to have taken a large toll of German armor in their defense of the town. The American force is described as sizable, but its number has not been disclosed.

The besieged troops received hundreds of tons of supplies, principally ammunition, today. They were dropped from trains of C-47 transport planes which flew from both Britain and France with their cargoes.

PARATROOPS DROPPED

The first transport slipped over the German lines at dawn and dropped a unit of paratroopers to guide the other C-47's to the scene.

Half an hour afterward they radioed back that they had landed safely and that bundles of ammunition, food and medicine were being dropped to the surrounded Americans.

NO AIR OPPOSITION

The transport pilots encountered no opposition from German planes, but flew through heavy ground fire. They saw four tanks, which they believed were German, burning in the Bastogne area, spotted an enemy tank column resting by the road and notified Air Force Headquarters that it was a perfect target for fighter bombers.

The C-47 mission was carried out without any fighter escort.

More than 200 of the big transports, unarmed and unarmored, took part in the supply operation and Headquarters of the troop carrier forces reported losses were "far lower than might have been expected."

YANKS TAKE INITIATIVE

One observer who made the flight said he saw American columns pushing near Bastogne and that "now it appeared our men were resuming the offensive. This was an entirely different ground situation than our first mission Saturday. Then it seemed a situation of impending disaster."

The majority of the parachuted cargo consisted of artillery shells, rolls of telephone wire for restoring communications and cases of rations. There was room also for cigarets, gum, candy and G.I. messages of Christmas cheer.

Pope Voices Fear Of More Wars

VATICAN CITY, Dec. 27 (U. P.).—Pope Pius voiced the question today whether after the war it would be possible to achieve a peace which did not contain the seed of new wars. He spoke briefly when the new Ecuadorian ambassador to the Holy See, Manuel Sotomayer, presented his credentials

"Terrible is the pain caused us by the errors of war, but no less is that provoked by the uncertain outlook for a final solution," the Pope said.

"Will the new order of international relations be able to solve the conflicts and asperities which follow the cessation of hostilities? Will it be possible to attain a peace which does not have in its bosom the seeds of new wars?"

2 Drives Narrow Neck of Salient To Only 20 Miles

War Summary on Page 2

By EDWARD KENNEDY

PARIS, Dec. 28 (Thursday) (A. P.).—German broadcasts acknowledged tremendous Allied counter-attacks on both flanks of the Nazi offensive into Belgium last night. The Luxembourg radio asserted the enemy salient had been narrowed to 20 miles and Supreme Allied Headquarters announced relief troops had reached the heroic American garrison at Bastogne.

The information, coming from assorted sources, could be pieced into a picture cheering to the Allies.

The beleaguered doughboys at Bastogne, who had been encircled since Dec. 20 and had gallantly smashed back every German attempt to wipe out their position since then, were reached by a hard-hitting column of American armor which drove up from the south.

COLUMN DRIVES FIVE MILES IN DAY

The official announcement telling of the garrison's relief gave no details, not even the exact time, but field dispatches reporting events more than 24 hours old said the American forces were within five miles of the besieged Belgian town yesterday.

Dispatches from correspondents at the front said this thrust was by "heavy American forces," declared they had "punched a deep salient into the German southern flank," and made gains of two to four miles.

The forces hammering at Field Marshal Gerd von Rundstedt's armies from the south were not officially identified, but German broadcasts last night declared that "practically the whole American Third Army" was battering at the southern sector.

FOE RETREATS IN LUXEMBOURG AREA

Berlin said some German forces in the frontier region of Luxembourg had withdrawn into pillboxes at the approaches to the West Wall (Siegfried Line) and also told of powerful counter-attacks being thrown against von Rundstedt from the north.

The German account said one of Field Marshal Sir Bernard L. Montgomery's crack British divisions along with "still another American division withdrawn from the Aachen sector" were making "particularly grim counter-attacks in the north."

At the same time these reports of Allied attempts to choke the neck of the German offensive were coming from enemy sources, the Allied-controlled Luxembourg radio said "von Rundstedt's supply funnel through Belgium has been narrowed to less than 20 miles in width tonight." This mileage coincides with the distance from Bastogne northward to last reported Allied positions near Lierneux.

SITUATION REPORTED 'WELL IN HAND'

Premier Hubert Pierlot told the Belgian Parliament he had word from "the highest Allied authority that the situation at the front is well in hand," the Brussels radio said.

All along the northern flank of the 35-mile-wide salient there were indications that the Nazis were on the defense for the moment, said Wes Gallagher, Associated Press correspondent. With hundreds of American and British planes searching the roads, he said von Rundstedt could not use his tanks on a big scale without risking a massacre.

News that General Dwight D. Eisenhower had struck

Continued on Page 2, Column 1

Less Food in '45, Civilians Warned

Philadelphia consumers were warned yesterday by Frank J. Loftus, district OPA director, that they could expect less meats, processed foods, canned vegetables, fruits and fruit juices and sugar during 1945.

At the same time he cautioned food retailers in the city against accepting from customers ration stamps cancelled under the new program. He said those found guilty of taking these stamps would lose the privilege of selling rationed foods.

REASONS OUTLINED

Mr. Loftus issued the warning to the consumers and storekeepers in a detailed statement outlining the reasons for the revision of the point values on meat, canned foods, sugar and butter which became effective 12.01 A. M. Tuesday.

Basing his estimate on an average per capita allotment for the Nation, Mr. Loftus said Philadelphians will

Continued on Page 6, Column 3

Magistrate Relieved Of Short-Weight Cases

Expressing dissatisfaction with recent handling of alleged shortweight violations, County Commissioner Morton Witkin announced yesterday that he had relieved Magistrate Benjamin Schwartz of further responsibility for handling such cases.

The Commissioner's action, announced in what he said was a "sharp" letter to the Magistrate, followed a series of disagreements over the latter's dismissal or lenient treatment of coal, food and meat dealers brought before him on short-weight charges.

SEEKS BETTER ENFORCEMENT

"What we are after is better enforcement of the weights and measures laws so that offenders are brought to justice," Mr. Witkin declared, indicating that he might propose a transfer of these cases to Quarter Sessions Court.

At his 5th and Green sts. office, where a majority of weights and measures hearings has been held since early in November, Magistrate Schwartz commented yesterday that court hearings "might be a good thing. To me they're just a headache." He said he had already received Commissioner Witkin's letter relieving him.

"I took the cases away from Mag-

Continued on Page 26, Column 4

IN TODAY'S INQUIRER

'Nuts' Is Yank Reply To Nazi Ultimatum

WITH AMERICAN FORCES, Dec. 27 (A. P.).—A German commander who should have known better sent an ultimatum to surrender to the Americans besieged in the Bastogne pocket.

"Nuts," answered an American officer commanding one of the surrounded units.

The German commander's ultimatum was dated Dec. 22 and gave the Americans two hours in which to reply. He got it in 30 minutes.

Casualties

Five Men Killed, 10 Are Wounded

A Navy Department casualty list released yesterday and notices to next of kin reported the names of 10 men from the Philadelphia area wounded, five killed and two listed as missing in action.

Private First Class Joseph J. Hudome, Jr., U.S.M.C.R., of 5618 Halfield st., who outwitted the Japs on Saipan in the Marianas Islands last July, has been wounded, the Navy Department announced.

During a dawn attack staged by 70 Japs on a Marine unit, the Marines ran out of hand grenades. Private Hudome led the defense with clods of dirt and sound effects to fool the enemy until more munitions arrived.

Private Curtis Koerner, 38, of Berwyn, was killed in action in Germany Dec. 7, his wife, the former Ellen Brown, of Berwyn, has been notified.

INDUCTED LAST YEAR

Formerly of Phoenixville, Private Koerner was inducted into the Army in November, 1943. Before his induction, he was employed by the Budd Manufacturing Co. Besides

Continued on Page 4, Column 2

Japs Threaten To Raze Shanghai

CHUNGKING, Dec. 27 (U. P.).—The Japanese have threatened the complete destruction of Shanghai if and when they are forced to evacuate, a Chinese military spokesman said today.

He said the threat was voiced by the Japanese garrison commander recently to a mixed Chinese and Japanese audience at Shanghai.

Japanese are preparing to strengthen defenses on the China coast as a precaution against Allied landings, the spokesman said.

Breakthrough Blamed On Allied Command

Bad Judgment Is Indicated

By JAMES M. LONG

SUPREME HEADQUARTERS ALLIED EXPEDITIONARY FORCE, Paris, Dec. 27 (A. P.).—An outright under-estimation of German striking power coupled with either a failure to learn of, or to appreciate Field Marshal Gerd von Rundstedt's mobile reserve movements behind the lines, appeared more than ever today to be the major factors behind the first serious Allied setback since the successful invasion of Europe.

That would seem to place the responsibility for the Nazi breakthrough high up in the Allied staff and to suggest that any important shakeup in the command—none has materialized as yet—would amount to finding a scapegoat.

NO SCAPEGOAT APPEARS

However, the forthright Allied commander, General Dwight D. Eisenhower, has shown no inclination to hunt for scapegoats, either

Continued on Page 2, Column 6

Gen. March Hits Army Intelligence

Illustrated on Page 10

By JOHN C. O'BRIEN

Inquirer Washington Bureau

WASHINGTON, Dec. 27.—General Peyton C. March, Army Chief of Staff in the First World War, who said on his birthday a year ago that victory in 1944 "was not in the cards," today declared a complete failure of American military intelligence was responsible for the success of the German breakthrough on the Western Front.

Erect and vigorous, the man who directed the transportation of 2,000,-

Continued on Page 2, Column 7

U. S. WEATHER FORECAST

Philadelphia and vicinity: Rain ending this afternoon with somewhat warmer temperatures today. Fair and colder tomorrow.

Sun rises	8.22 A.M.	Sets 5.43 P.M.
Moon rises	5.06 P.M.	Sets 7.15 A.M.

BLONDIE
By
CHIC YOUNG
GREAT SCOTT! THEY SENT THE STRAGUSCOPE UNASSEMBLED!

IF I DON'T GET IT PUT TOGETHER FOR THE BOARD MEETING TONIGHT, I'LL LOSE OUR BIGGEST ORDER IN YEARS
BUMSTEAD IS THE ONLY MAN IN THE FIRM WHO CAN ASSEMBLE THE STRAGUSCOPE AND HE'S AT HOME

DAGWOOD, FOR FIFTEEN YEARS I'VE PUT UP WITH THAT PEA-SIZED BRAIN OF YOURS
YES, BOSS

AND THEN, THERE HAVE BEEN TIMES YOU'VE BEEN A HELP FOR WHICH I'M DEEPLY GRATEFUL--BLESS YOU, MY BOY
THANKS, CHIEF

AND THEN, THERE HAVE BEEN TIMES I'VE WANTED TO MURDER YOU
I'M SORRY, BOSS

TONIGHT, I COME TO YOU ON BENDED KNEES DEAR, DEAR, DAGWOOD
HUH?

IF YOU'LL ASSEMBLE THAT STRAGUSCOPE FOR ME, I'LL BE ETERNALLY GRATEFUL --I'LL GRANT ANY REQUEST
REALLY?

AFTER FIFTEEN YEARS, I FINALLY GOT THE OLD BOY WHERE I WANT HIM
IT'S A PERFECT TIME TO ASK HIM FOR A RAISE

BUMSTEAD, YOU DRIVE A HARD BARGAIN, BUT I'LL DO WHATEVER YOU SAY
IT'S A DEAL!

THE STRAGUSCOPE IS ASSEMBLED, BOSS
OKAY, I'LL KEEP MY END OF THE BARGAIN

DAGWOOD, DIDN'T YOU DEMAND THE RAISE?
Copr. 1944, King Features Syndicate, Inc., World rights reserved

NO--- I MADE HIM PROMISE TO LET ME GIVE HIM A GOOD SWIFT KICK IN THE PANTS
CHIC YOUNG

PANCHITO
By
WALT DISNEY

WHERE THE LEETLE MICE COME FROM I DON' KNOW THEY HAVE OVERRUN THE TOWN!
WHY, MAYOR... DEEDN'T YOU KNOW HOW TO GET RID OF THEM?

YOU REMEMBER THE LEETLE CHEELDREN'S STORY OF THE PIEDS PIPER...? HE PLAY 'APPY MUSIC AND ALL THE RATS FOLLOW HEEM OUT OF TOWN!

PANCHITO... DON' STAN' THERE TELLING ME CHEELDREN'S STORIES! I'M EEN TROBBLE!

THE TROBBLE EES, MAYOR.. YOU DON' 'AVE FAITH IN CHEELDREN....AND IN CHEELDREN'S STORIES!

WEETH THE FINES' VOICE IN MEXICO, WHICH IS MINE... I WEEL STAND OUTSIDE THE TOWN AND ATTRACT THE LEETLE ONES!

HOURS LATER..
COME LEETLE MICE 'APPY LEETLE MICE!

MUCHO HOURS LATER..
YOU ARE THE RIGHT ONE, MAYOR...... THE LEETLE MICE DON' BELIEVE IN CHEELDREN'S STORIES EITHER!

DO NOT MIND, PANCHITO... WE LIKE YOUR VOICE! WEEL YOU SEENG SOME MORE?

GRACIAS, MAYOR! I AM THE 'APPY CABALLERO!

I AM THE 'APPY CABALLERO... I... AY....

WE ARE PLEASE TO HONOR THE MOS' MOVING VOICE IN ALL MEXICO!
HMMMMMMPH!
SMACK

The Philadelphia Inquirer

PUBLIC LEDGER

An Independent Newspaper for All the People

FINAL CITY EDITION

CIRCULATION: November Average: Daily 519,378; Sunday 1,096,611 — FRIDAY MORNING, JANUARY 5, 1945 — Copyright, 1945, by Triangle Publications, Inc.; Vol. 232, No. 5 — abdefgh — THREE CENTS

Yanks Cut Deep Into Nazi Bulge, Patton Repels 100 Enemy Tanks; Planes Continue Formosa Attack

Today

If Dewey Had Won
Some Call Him Lucky
Many Disillusioned
Leaders No Messiahs
Public Not Blameless

—By Mark Sullivan—

WASHINGTON, Jan. 4.

MUCH talk says that Governor Dewey was lucky to lose the Presidential election, that if he had won, he would have been blamed for the unfortunate developments since Election Day.

In spirit, much of this talk is political; it is the spirit of Republicans saying, "Roosevelt won, and now look." But it will be wiser to dismiss that and look upon a larger lesson which the condition contains.

It is true that during the campaign, supporters of Mr. Roosevelt argued that defeat of the President would have certain consequences, Mr. Dewey would not get along so well with Prime Minister Churchill, or with Premier Stalin. This impaired co-operation would encourage the Germans to fight harder, the war would be prolonged.

The Atlantic Charter, as a program for peace settlements, would be impaired by the defeat of Mr. Roosevelt as one of the charter's authors. The hope of a world organization to prevent war would be reduced, because Britain and Russia would doubt the possibility of co-operation with the new American President.

These things were predicted as consequences if Mr. Roosevelt should be defeated. It was to avert these things that Candidate Roosevelt was called by some "the indispensable man." Accepting the "don't change horses" argument, many persons voted for Mr. Roosevelt who otherwise would not have.

But Mr. Roosevelt was elected, and these things have happened anyhow. Human psychology being what it is, the disillusioned are reproachful. Mr. Roosevelt as a solicitor of popular support, which every President must be, is not as strong as he would have been had things gone better.

It is true that had Mr. Dewey been elected, these things would have happened anyway. As a new President, beset with many difficulties, he would have been handicapped. This is what people mean when they say he was fortunate not to win.

But this sort of thing is trivial. There is a more important point of view. The lesson is for the people themselves to take to heart, not only in the United States, but to a greater extent in other countries.

The mistake of peoples everywhere has been to attribute to leaders responsibility for what leaders cannot control. In some cases it is illogical blame, in other cases illogical credit.

All of it is part of a condition that has increased throughout the world during several years past.

It is a disposition on the part of peoples to think of leaders as messiahs, and a disposition on the part of some leaders to play upon this weakness and accept the role of messiah.

Of all the problems the world ponders, the underlying one is, how can wars be prevented, and, associated with that, what causes wars. There is no single answer. But any study of how the present war started will say that part of the cause was a too

Continued on Page 12, Column 1

2 School Aides Held in Ration Point Thefts

3d Suspect Caught With Stolen Books By Director Malone

Illustrated on Page 7

The arrest of two trusted employes of the Philadelphia Board of Education and of a police character yesterday disclosed that ration stamps worth millions of points had been stolen in recent weeks from the board's storerooms to supply the black market along the Eastern seaboard.

The disclosure, brought about through the personal vigilance of Director of Public Safety James H. Malone, was credited by officials of the Office of Price Administration here with "knocking the pegs out from under a black market in food and gasoline stamps that has spread throughout the East."

In custody at City Hall last night were:

Samuel Bailey, 46, of Drexel road near 64th st., Overbrook, $4200-a-year assistant to Add B. Anderson, secretary and business manager of the Board of Education.

Thomas Wagner, 40, of Brill st. near Bingham, Frankford, $2200-a-year assistant to Bailey, who has been a board employe for the past 23 years.

James (Jimmy) Bailey, 40, of 905 Church lane, Yeadon, not related to Samuel Bailey, but a police character with a record going back to 1922. He is said to be a brother of the notorious Frankie Bailey, underworld figure of Prohibition days.

FORMAL CHARGES FILED

The three men were formally charged last night, after several hours of questioning by police, with conspiracy and larceny, and will have a hearing in Central Police Station this morning. They were released last night in bail of $10,000 each, on copies of the charge signed by Magistrate George Levin.

Myron M. Caffey, chief enforcement agent of the OPA here, said that since Federal property was involved in the thefts, additional Federal charges would be lodged against

Continued on Page 7, Column 1

2d Raid Also Hits Ryukyus

PEARL HARBOR, Jan. 4 (A. P.)—Official silence screening the American carrier plane attack on Formosa and Okinawa Islands guarding Japan's southern flank was lifted briefly today to announce that the assault extended into the second day but that details still were not available.

A Navy communique said the carrier-borne typhoon which hit the enemy strongholds Tuesday continued to sweep the two islands the following day.

BRIEF REPORT ISSUED

"Details of this strike and that of the previous day are not yet available," said the brief announcement.

The possibility was advanced here that the carrier force, a part of Admiral William F. Halsey's Third Fleet, may have spotted a large concentration of enemy shipping which it desired to destroy before retiring. Neutralization of enemy airfields on the two islands also may have lengthened the foray.

Today's announcement confirmed earlier broadcasts by the Tokio radio that the Yank naval aircraft had struck Formosa and Okinawa, the latter one of the Ryukyu group, for the second straight day.

900 PLANES, TOKIO SAYS

The enemy reports said 500 planes participated in the first day's attack and 400 in the second. Claims were made that 20 of the raiders were shot down in the two days and a number damaged.

For the first time in nearly a month, the daily communique failed to report a raid on Iwo Jima, in the Volcanos 750 miles south of Tokio. That enemy base, springboard for air attacks on the American Superfortress base in the Marianas to the south, had been hit for 26 consecutive days, starting with Dec. 7. It was last reported raided on Jan. 1.

35 MORE SHIPS BLASTED

GENERAL MacARTHUR'S HEADQUARTERS, Philippines, Jan. 5 (Friday) (A. P.).—Vital Japanese shipping around Luzon, main Philippines' island, took a body blow from American bombing and attack planes the first three days of 1945, General Douglas MacArthur disclosed today.

The Headquarters communique announced sinking or damaging of 35 ships at Subic Bay and in Lingayen Gulf Jan. 2 and 3. Yesterday General MacArthur reported 25

Continued on Page 3, Column 3

(Official U. S. Army Photo by A. P. Wirephoto)

PATTON DECORATING LEADER OF BASTOGNE HEROES

Lieutenant General George S. Patton, Jr. (left), commander of the U. S. Third Army, chatting with Brigadier General Anthony C. McAuliffe after awarding him the Distinguished Service Cross. General McAuliffe, leader of the 101st Airborne Division, replied "nuts" when Nazis demanded he surrender Belgian city of Bastogne.

Hodges Advances More Than 3 Mi. Despite Blizzard

Map and War Summary on Page 2

By AUSTIN BEALMEAR

PARIS, Jan. 4 (A. P.).—U. S. First Army armor and infantry struck through a raging blizzard today on a 17-mile front, grinding out gains up to three and a half miles which put them scarcely 12 miles from where the Third Army was hammering back an enemy onslaught led by 100 tanks.

(Berlin broadcasts said British tanks and the U. S. Ninth Army had joined the offensive on the north, and the U. S. Seventh entered the struggle from the south, indicating General Dwight D. Eisenhower was throwing such powerful forces into the battle that he had abandoned his winter drive into Germany.)

THREE BELGIAN TOWNS CAPTURED

The fury of the doughboy attack matched the fury of the elements. Three Belgian towns were engulfed, at least six others were entered, and the battle to drive the enemy from Belgium for the second time in four months was breaking inside the main German northern defenses.

On the south, Lieutenant General George S. Patton, Jr.'s Third Army stood up under great enemy blows without losing an inch of ground, then lashed out with half-mile gains both east and west of Bastogne, which cut to three and a half miles the neck of a five-mile-deep box between Bastogne and Wiltz, 10 miles to the east.

American artillery fire was bursting in the ranks of the Germans massed within the box, and dazed prisoners emerging from this mountainous inferno in northern Luxembourg told of company casualties as high as 75 percent.

ENEMY APPEARS TO BE RETIRING IN WEST

The enemy lines at the tip of the Belgian triangle were giving way, the village of Bure, four miles southeast of Rochefort, was overrun, and a field dispatch said the enemy appeared to be pulling out of his dearly won apex running westward from Bastogne.

There was little sign of enemy armor anywhere west of a line running north from Bastogne, and Allied forces driving in from the northwest between Marche and Rochefort found the Germans were pulling back.

Diversionary enemy assaults spreading from the western Saar 70 miles east to the Rhine were blunted after the U. S. Seventh Army had given up all footholds in the Reich's Palatinate and the enemy had penetrated seven miles into the doughboys' northern Vosges Mountain line.

(The Paris radio said the Americans had quit the French border city of Wissembourg, north of Strasbourg, and were falling back toward the Maginot Line in retreats up to five miles. Swiss dispatches said German attempts to cross the Rhine just north of the Swiss border had been repulsed.)

VISIBILITY CUT TO ONLY 100 YARDS

In a blinding blizzard that cut visibility to 100 yards, Lieutenant General Courtney H. Hodges' vengeance-bent First Army, scoring gains averaging two miles on the second day of its offensive, was less than two miles from Field Marshal Gerd von Rundstedt's main northern highway of supply.

The Third Army was the same distance away from the only other good all-weather east-west highway on the south,

Continued on Page 2, Column 4

Killer of Girl, 9, Eludes Search

Illustrated on Page 8

Special to The Inquirer

SCRANTON, Jan. 4.—State police and Lackawanna County authorities today were utilizing the process of elimination in their search for the slayer of nine-year-old Mae Barrett, whose battered body was found yesterday in the basement of a vacant house at Vandling, 15 miles northeast of here.

Convinced that the killer is a "perverted sex maniac" familiar with the community of Vandling, more than 20 State troopers and the entire force of county investigators under District Attorney James F. Brady, spent the day checking the movements of known and suspected moral degenerates.

SEVERAL QUESTIONED

Mr. Brady declared that "several" persons had been questioned, but admitted that up to that moment there was no individual suspect under surveillance. He said he did not expect a "break" in the case until tomorrow at least.

Early today investigators reconstructed the child's last movements before she was bludgeoned to death beside a garage in the rear of the vacant house on Clinton st., only a

Continued on Page 8, Column 2

Chicago Drops Petrillo Bodyguard

CHICAGO, Jan. 4 (U. P.).—A 13-year practice of assigning two detectives to serve as bodyguards to James C. Petrillo, president of the American Federation of Musicians, was abandoned today on the order of Police Commissioner James Allman.

Detectives John Pine and William Ricker, who have had the assignment for two years, were ordered to report to the Detective Bureau for reassignment today because Mr. Petrillo now spends most of his time in New York.

4-F Draft Plan Gains in Capital

By DOROTHY ROCKWELL

Inquirer Washington Bureau

WASHINGTON, Jan. 4.—Sentiment favoring the forced draft of 4-F's into war jobs mounted today on Capitol Hill and in the war agencies.

Following the statement Monday by James F. Byrnes, Director of the Office of War Mobilization and Reconversion, that he planned to ask Congress for legislation to bring 4-F's into the war effort, Senator Harley M. Kilgore (D., W. Va.) called for the replacement of 500,000 civilian Army and Navy employes by uniformed 4-F's to halt what he termed a "wasting of manpower."

Other developments were:

1. Representative Clare Booth Luce (R., Conn.) reintroduced her 1943 bill calling for use of 4-F's in war jobs.
2. J. A. Krug, Chairman of the War Production Board, told a press conference he favored legislation putting 4-F's "where they're needed if they won't do it under their own power."
3. Mr. Krug also revealed that the Army is now perfecting plans to re-examine "borderline"

Continued on Page 4, Column 4

Casualties

Flier Killed, 50 Soldiers Wounded

War Department casualty lists and notifications to next of kin yesterday reported one soldier from the Philadelphia area killed in action, one missing and 50 wounded.

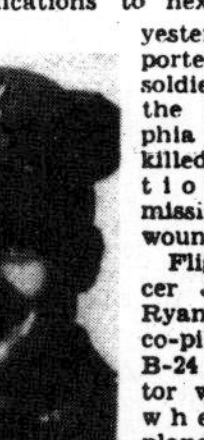

FLT. OFFICER RYAN

Flight Officer James F. Ryan, 19, a co-pilot of a B-24 Liberator was killed when his plane crashed somewhere in Italy Dec. 15, according to a War Department telegram received by his parents, Mr. and Mrs. James Ryan, of 1426 Vankirk st.

Flight Officer Ryan entered the Army Air Forces in February, 1943, and had been overseas one month when he was killed. He was a

Continued on Page 4, Column 2

Nazi Drive Halted Above Budapest

LONDON, Jan. 5 (Friday) (U. P.).—The Red Army, destroying 171 German tanks and 76 planes in the first three days of Germany's first major counter-offensive on the Eastern Front in a year, yesterday repelled continuing enemy attempts to break through to encircled Budapest and expand small initial gains.

The great mechanized battle some 30 miles northwest of Budapest was increasing in ferocity.

BOTH SIDES REINFORCED

Both sides were reported rushing reinforcements into the struggle which may decide the fate of Budapest and of the Red Army's stalled push toward Vienna.

Moscow's midnight communique said units of six tank divisions and many infantry divisions were taking part, and described the German forces as "superior."

Within Budapest battles for the annihilation of the remnants of an estimated 80,000 Nazi troops were

Continued on Page 3, Column 2

Devers Predicts 'Decisive Victory'

WITH THE U. S. SEVENTH ARMY, France, Jan. 4 (U.P.).—Lieutenant General Jacob L. Devers, in a message to Franco-American troops of his Sixth Army Group, declared today that "decisive victory is in your hands" despite changes in Allied operations which have forced them to halt and regroup "before again advancing to the attack."

"The enemy is probing our lines," the order of the day said. "He's looking for a weakness. I'm confident your strength and courage, which have triumphed over him on every battlefield from the beachhead to the Rhine, will not fail.

"Our objective is to destroy the enemy. . . ."

Chaplin Jury Divided, Case Ends in Mistrial

Illustrated on Page 12

HOLLYWOOD, Jan. 4 (U. P.).—Joan Berry's paternity suit against Charles Chaplin was declared a mistrial today after a Superior Court jury, which had deliberated for a day and a half, failed to agree on whether the white-haired actor was the father of Miss Berry's baby daughter, Carol Ann.

Superior Judge Henry M. Willis had no more than dismissed the jury of seven women and five men when Joseph E. Scott, Miss Berry's attorney, announced he would go to court tomorrow to ask for a retrial of his client's charges that her intimacies with Chaplin in December, 1942, led to the birth of her baby.

NEW TRIAL TO BE ASKED

"We are going right back to the calendar court and ask for a new trial," the indignant Scott said. "The outcome is just as I thought it might be, with the women throwing the rocks at Carol Ann."

Judge Willis dismissed the jury, which had listened to almost two weeks of vivid testimony and emotional oratory, when it reported that it was deadlocked at 7 to 5 in favor of Chaplin after six ballots

Continued on Page 9, Column 5

IN TODAY'S INQUIRER

'Work or Move,' New War Order

Government pressure on Philadelphia war workers who have transferred to non-essential jobs increased yesterday, with a threat to deprive low-cost housing tenants of their homes.

"Work or move," was the tenor of an order that J. Griffith Boardman, recently appointed regional director of the War Production Board, asked the Philadelphia Housing Authority to serve on hundreds of tenants who moved into seven big housing developments on the understanding that they were war workers and would continue to be for the duration.

SOME ALREADY INELIGIBLE

Simultaneously, J. B. Kelly, executive director of the Housing Authority, disclosed that a survey had revealed more than five percent of the occupants of the seven projects already had become ineligible for occupancy by transferring from highly essential jobs.

Unless they get back to war production quickly, the Authority will declare they have abrogated their leases and will order them out to make way for war workers.

Another phase of the drive to put every available worker at a job in

Continued on Page 5, Column 3

'This Is the Pacific!'

Jungle Becomes Base Under Seabee Magic

(Fifth of a Series)

By John M. McCullough

Inquirer Washington Bureau

NINE months ago, Manus, in the Admiralty Islands, was a mangrove swamp infested with Japanese.

Today—by virtue of the fighting spirit of the First Cavalry Division and the incredible ingenuity of the Seabees—it is one of the most powerful naval bases in the world.

Nowhere in the Pacific, with the possible exception of Guam, is the fantastic power which the United States Navy is marshaling to crush Japan so astoundingly exemplified.

Get out your map. If it is a fairly recent one you will see a few little dots in the Bismarck Sea, about half way between Dutch New Guinea and the upper end of New Ireland island just south of the Equator.

That's Manus.

Properly speaking, "Manus" is Navy terminology for vast Seeadler Harbor, encircled by Manus and Los Negros islands, sheltered to windward by a chain of palm-fringed atolls.

• • •

ASIDE from Momote air-strip on Los Negros—taken last March by the First Cavalry and by whose coral sweep the First buried its dead—the Japanese did very little to develop Manus-Los Negros as a fleet anchorage. They had an embarrassment of naval riches, anyway.

But some shrewd eye in the United States Navy—we were told here it was Admiral William F. Halsey, Jr., frosty-eyed Nemesis of Nippon—

Continued on Page 12, Column 3

Girls in Congress Won't Pull Hair

WASHINGTON, Jan. 4 (A. P.).—Representative Clare Boothe Luce (R., Conn.) and Representative Helen Gahagan Douglas (D., Calif.), Congressional glamor girls, shook hands tonight and agreed they wouldn't get into a fight with each other.

Both appeared at a dinner of the Women's National Press Club in honor of newly elected Congresswomen.

Mrs. Douglas, a former screen actress, said she resented "attempts of some people to jockey Mrs. Luce and myself" into a feud. Mrs. Luce, sitting nearby, shook hands with Mrs. Douglas and said, "I do too."

U. S., Britain in Accord On Italy, Stettinius Says

By JOHN C. O'BRIEN

Inquirer Washington Bureau

WASHINGTON, Jan. 4.—Secretary of State Edward R. Stettinius, Jr., said today that the United States and Great Britain were in "basic agreement" on a policy of feeding the Italian population and aiding Italy to rebuild its economic life and thus make a maximum contribution to the war effort.

The Secretary's statement was prompted by a quotation in a Washington column from a memorandum of Lord Halifax, British Ambassador, under date of Aug. 22, indicating a seeming divergence of views between the two Governments on the bread ration to be supplied the Italian people.

DEPLORES PUBLICATION

Asserting that the "unauthorized publication" of the document, "a part of the confidential records" of the State Department, created an "erroneous" impression and was "in the highest degree regrettable," Mr. Stettinius made public other quotations from the exchange of memoranda between the two Governments

Continued on Page 2, Column 7

French Air Chief Missing on Flight

PARIS, Jan. 4 (A. P.).—Captain Lionel de Marnier, manager of all French air lines, is missing on a flight from Algiers to Paris. Eight others were said to have been aboard the plane, which took off three days ago.

Captain de Marnier, decorated in the First World War and a pioneer in French commercial aviation, commanded the first Fighting French bombing squadron under General Charles de Gaulle and accompanied the French leader to Moscow last month.

U. S. WEATHER FORECAST

Philadelphia and vicinity: Cloudy with moderate temperatures today. Fair and colder tomorrow.

Sun rises 8 22 A. M. Sets 5 49 P. M.
Moon rises ——— Sets 12 37 P. M.

TERRY AND THE PIRATES

By Milton Caniff

CANDY

By Goggin and Sahle

WELL, BEAT ME, DADDY! WHY THE DARK BROWN LOOK? DOESN'T ALL THE CLAPTRAP ABOUT THE HOP CLUB SEND YOU?
IN A WORD, NO! IT LEAVES ME COLD—BUT DEFINITELY!
TED, YOU'RE STRICTLY A SLUG. LUG! NO ZIP! NO GET-UP-AND-GET!
COMING, CANDY! LET'S BEAT FEET! I HATE TO TELL YOU, BUT YOU'RE COLD, HE SAYS!
AW, CUT THE CACKLE! I AM, TED! YOU RAISED THE STUFF BEFORE— WHY NOT NOW?
BUT THAT WOULD BE STRICTLY GOOD-BYE STRATEGY!
WE'D LOOK POSITIVELY WHACKY DOING A LINDY HOP WITHOUT A DANCE FLOOR!

LITTLE ORPHAN ANNIE

By Harold Gray

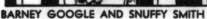

BARNEY GOOGLE AND SNUFFY SMITH

By Fred Lasswell

THEY'LL DO IT EVERY TIME

By Jimmy Hatlo

THRILL THAT COMES ONCE IN A LIFETIME

DONALD DUCK

Distributed by King Features Syndicate

Twistagram

(Copyright, 1934-36-37-42, by J. Langdon-Sullivan.)

2. Of (French).
3. A zone at Franklin Field.
4. Generous people ---- their things frequently.
5. Loaded.
6. What many a waiter has done against a bus stop pole.
7. He crossed the Hellespont under his own power.
8. Evergreen shrub with fragrant flowers.

Solution Monday

Yesterday's Twistagram

L A
F A L
S L A P
C L A S P
P L A C E S
S P E C I A L
R E P L I C A S

DIVORCES GRANTED

Fanelli—Ruth N. from Victor L.
Gallagher—Leona from George.
Gaitzia—Alma from Robert.
Gantz—Ada from Sidney.
Rosenheck—Elsie from Morton.
Swain—Mattie from Joseph.
Schulgen—Rose from George.
Tarracchio—Theresa from Anthony.
Welischek—Mary from Wenzel J.
Kaufmann—Kathryn E. from David.
Weingarten—Benjamin from Alice.
Ferber—Sidney from Lillian.
Richards—Sophie B. from Merritt.
Mock—Lillian from George.
DeHaan—Helen from Jule.
Crouch—Sylvia from William H.
Olivie—Marie D. from Jesse T.
James—Edward T. from Laura N.
Orr—Demalia K. from James H.
DeRosa—Theresa from Romaldo H.
Keough—Elva from John C.
Mattesini—Theresa from Joseph.
Lofland—David from Margaret.
Jeffries—George G. from Mildred G.
Culbertson—Edward J. from Mary A.
Marquette—Mary C. from George H.
Jacobson—Irma from Harold H.
Nicholas—Helen from Edmund.
Cleary—Barbara from David.
Lauck—Adele from William S.
Salvi—Helen from Samuel.
Shumweller—William G. from Lillian.
Pearlstein—Bertha from Nathan.
Bauer—Grace M. from William H., Jr.
Nemitz—Abraham from Minnie.
Hitt—Ina M. B. from Lonel G.
Ramsey—Elsie from Frank D.
Wolf—Henry R. from Betty C.
Robinson—Oliva from Clenton.
Sturm—Mary from Fred.
Kessler—Helene from Melville C.
Sipers—Frances S. from Joseph.
Kasky—Sidney from Lillian.
Ebersold—Vera from Louis.
Hall—Mary from William.
Klinger—Herman from Ruth.
Hoffman—Helen from Frank, Jr.
Downing—Merle C. from Earl H.
Gibson—Mary E. from Franklin A.
Lawrence—Harold from Mabel.
Martin—Florence from Vernon.
Stieb—Walter W. C. from Helen L. E.
Tomeo—Hester A. from Joseph [illegible]
Marshall—Samuel E. from Martha F.
Edwards—John W. from Eva P.
Freed—Rose M. F. from Robert.
Rizzo—Helen from Anthony.

SUITS FOR DIVORCE BEGUN

Steinberg—Simon vs. Sophie.
Henderson—Helen E. vs. Fred H.
Kurz—Kathryn M. vs. Frank F.
Sinter—Arthur R. vs. Margaret M.
Pushinsky—Benjamin vs. Marie.
O'Donnell—Harry vs. Nora.
Ledger—[illegible]ene G. T. vs. Henry, Jr.
Ma[illegible]—Daniel A. vs. Mabel A.
Mullen—Josephine F. vs. Joseph.
Rossi—[illegible]ith vs. Domenic.
Meredith—Jack C. vs. Helen.
Dencer—George R. vs. Nora A.
Bailey—Doris E. vs. Roland M.
Tobin—Florence, by her guardian Mary Childs, vs. Samuel.
Lutz—Lillian C. vs. Harry, Jr.

Louella O. Parsons

HOLLYWOOD, Jan. 5.

IF YOU think "Tarzan" has run his course, think again. As the result of a deal between Sol Lesser and Edgar Rice Burroughs' office (he's in Honolulu), there will be 20 years more of "Tarzan" movies. Brother, has he been a hearty boy? It was 1918 when Burroughs wrote his first jungle hero story and it's been going good, both in fiction and on the screen, ever since.

Bet you can't remember the first actor to play "Tarzan" 27 years ago? I wouldn't have remembered, either, if Sol hadn't reminded me that it was Elmo Lincoln. In the meantime, 10 other players have been cast in the part, including Buster Crabbe, but the best known is Johnny Weissmuller. Yes, Johnny has also been signed to do at least two years more of "Tarzan." Even he can't hold out for the full 20 years to go.

• • •

The breaks are coming to Jane Wyman fast and furious. Jack Warner told me that he has put her into the lead of "When Old New York Was Young," the role that brought on Anne Sheridan's suspension when she refused to do it. Jane waited for years to get a chance and ate her heart out when she had only small parts. Now she has just finished "The Lost Week-End" and, according to her boss, this is going to be a big year for her. She will have Dennis Morgan and Jack Carson as her co-stars and Jerry Wald as her producer in her present musical assignment.

• • •

Greer Garson has always wanted to do a comedy. She has played so many heavy roles—sad ones—but you'll admit she's done them well. Now they are all talking at the M-G-M studio about "Yama Yama Girl" for her, the romance of Richard Harding Davis and Bessie McCoy. And who do you think is being discussed for the Richard Harding Davis role? Clark Gable, no less. Mind you, this is just at the talking point, but wouldn't it be something—Greer and Clark?

• • •

Lana Turner has been almost sick over Susan Peters' tragedy. She told me that she and Turhan Bey had planned to go with Susan and Lieutenant Richard Quine to San Diego for the hunting when Turhan was taken sick. He was sick all through the holidays and so she didn't go. She said the thing that upset her so is that Susie was just beginning to feel a little better and like herself, and that she and Dick Quine have been so happy together. If she can have any visitors, Lana will go down over the week-end to see her.

• • •

Snapshots of Hollywood Collected at Random: Joan Blondell has been in bed with a bad attack of ptomaine poisoning . . . Betty Hutton, too, has been ill ever since the holidays . . . Veronica Lake tells me since I printed the story of her little daughter Elaine's dog being killed they have been flooded with letters offering to give the little girl another dog. But Andre De Toth has bought her a full sister to the St. Bernard she lost . . . Sabu has now been made a sergeant and is in the South Pacific with a bomber squadron . . . Paulette Goddard and Burgess Meredith entertained 18 at a "beachcomber" dinner at their home in Santa Monica . . . It's now definite that Anne Shirley and Adrian Scott, RKO producer, will wed Feb. 25 . . . June Allyson and Dick Powell, who had a tiff last week-end, are all love and sweetness again . . . Lorraine Miller, Warner starlet, is out of the hospital following a serious operation . . . Ben Blue has a movie job, so Slapsie Maxie is in need of a comedian to take his place temporarily.

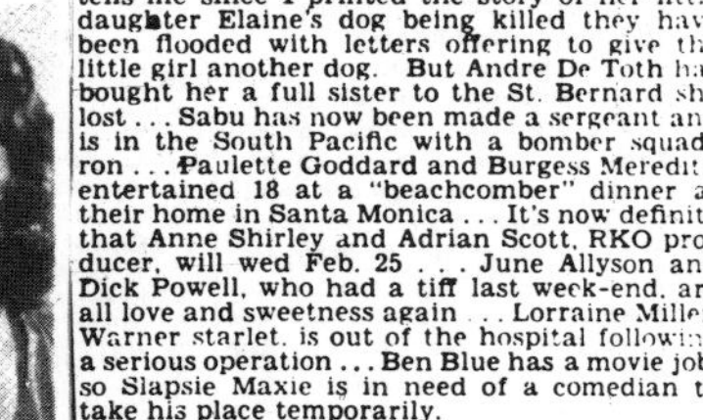
JOAN BLONDELL

• • •

It sure is love with Xavier Cugat, rumba king. He was booked in the Copacabana in New York, and in Miami, as well as one of the theaters, the amount totaling over $100,000, but the girl friend, Ann Marshall, wanted to stay in Hollywood for a career, so, poof, right out the window went Cugat's many contracts. He is opening instead at the Trocadero.

Service Entertainment

Tickets for service men and women to various types of shows can be obtained at the Philadelphia Hospitality Center for Service Men, 18 S. 15th st. There you can learn of special affairs each night.

MEN AND WOMEN

USO-Indoor Labor Plaza, Town Hall, Broad and Race sts.—Dancing and refreshments, 6 P. M. to midnight, daily except Sunday.

Y. M. C. A., 117 N. 15th st.—Lodging, pool, special recreation, gym, showers.

Jewish Welfare Board Club and Canteen, 401 S. Broad st.—Roof Garden, dancing and food.

Travelers' Aid—Pennsylvania Railroad Lounges—Broad St., 30th St. and North Philadelphia Stations, open 24 hours.

Travelers' Aid—Baltimore and Ohio Station, 24th and Chestnut sts.—Open 9.30 A. M. to 5.30 P. M.

USO—Reading Terminal Lounge, 12th and Market sts. Open 10 A. M. to 10 P. M.

Canteen for Service Men and Women, Baltimore and Ohio Station, 24th and Chestnut sts.—Open 9.30 A. M. to 4.30 P. M. Books, magazines, sandwiches, coffee served without cost.

Philadelphia Hospitality Center, 18 S. 15th st.—Information and referral services; limited number of free entertainment tickets; mending shop for men.

Benedict Club (National Catholic Community Service), 157 N. 15th st.—Dancing and food.

Y. W. C. A., 1800 Arch st.—Hospitality and dancing.

Salvation Army Red Shield Club, 703 N. Broad st.—Entertainment, music, lodging and food.

Lutheran Service Center, 1215 Walnut st.—Open daily, 11 A. M. to 11 P. M. Lounges, writing rooms, showers, recreation, lunches—Sunday evening suppers.

Baptist Hospitality Center, 17th and Sansom sts.—Facilities for service men and women.

Methodist Service Center, Erie ave. east of Broad st.—From noon to midnight daily. Lounge, writing room, shower room, game room, snack counter.

Morning Cheer Victory Center, 1511 Walnut st.—Open 24 hours daily. Writing and recreation room, lounge, lodging and food.

Church Door Canteen of Jenkintown, Homestead Road—Snack bar and dancing. Open every night, 6 P. M. to midnight.

Zoological Gardens, 34th st. and Girard ave.—Open 9 A. M. to 5 P. M.

Franklin Institute, 20th st. and Parkway—Open 1 to 6 P. M. Closed Monday.

Pennsylvania Academy of the Fine Arts, Broad and Cherry sts.—Exhibits free to service men and women in uniform, daily 1 P. M. to 5 P. M.

University Museum, 33d and Spruce sts.—Admission free. Exhibits of current interest. Open weekdays, except Monday, 10 A. M. to 5 P. M.; Sunday, 1 to 5 P. M.

Academy of Natural Sciences, 19th st. and the Parkway—Weekdays, 9 A. M. to 5 P. M.; Sundays, 1 to 5 P. M. Admission free.

The Philadelphia Museum of Art, 26th st. and the Parkway—Open daily, 10 A. M. to [illegible] M.—current exhibition of interest.

[illegible] Art Alliance, 251 S. [illegible] Exhibits. Daily, 10.30 A. M. to [illegible], 1 to 6 P. M. Exhibits [illegible]

[illegible], 28th and Green sts.—Open [illegible] A. M. [illegible] 30 P. M.; Sundays, 9 A. M. to 5 P.

MEN

United Service Club, 17th and Locust sts.—Open 24 hours. Sleeping and shower accommodation, lounges, library, hobby room. Breakfast and dinners served. Dancing and refreshments nightly.

USO Date Club, Broadwood Hotel, 320 N. Broad st.—Dancing. Open 5 to 12 P. M.

South Broad St. USO, 510 S. Broad st.—Dancing, snack bar.

United Seamen's Service Club, U. S. S. Hotel Tracy, 36th and Chestnut sts.—Dancing and restaurant.

Navy Mothers' Club, 1718 Spruce st.—Dancing and refreshments for Navy men. 10 A. M. to midnight.

Stage Door Canteen, Broad and Locust sts.—Open daily, 11 A. M. Dancing, with refreshments, 5 P. M. to midnight; Sunday, 2 P. M. to midnight.

Bellevue-Stratford—Officers' Club. Open daily from 10 A. M. to midnight. Free tickets for amusements.

Women's University Club, Hotel Sheraton, 19th and Walnut sts.—Open house for officers every Thursday evening from 7 P. M. to 11 P. M.

The Military Order of the Loyal Legion, 1805 Pine st.—Museum of Civil War weapons, flags and pictures. Open 9 A. M. to 5 P. M.

St. Stephen's Service Club, 10th st. below Market—Library, gymnasium, free refreshments. Open 10 A. M. to 10 P. M.

Presbyterian Hospitality Hou[illegible], 1200 Locust st.—Recreation, refreshments, sleeping quarters, laundry facilities.

Open Door Canteen of Upper Darby, 7058 W. Garrett Road—Tuesday, Wednesday and Thursday, dancing for service men, 8 P. M.

WOMEN

Service Women's Club, USO-Emergency Aid, 254 S. 15th st.—Home facilities, information, tea service. Open weekdays, 9.30 A. M. to 10 P. M.; Sundays, 4 to 8 P. M.

Women's Officers' Club, 1521 Walnut st.—Many facilities, 9 A. M. to 9 P. M.

APPLICATIONS FOR MARRIAGE LICENSES

Helen V. Aikens, 33, 2611 E. Lehigh ave., and Thomas J. Grady, 33, 217 S. [illegible]
Ethel Morin, 21, 1410 68th ave., and Milford E. Kaplan, 23, 5721 Spruce st.
Ethel R. Chinery, 24, 5107 [illegible] ave., Leonard J. Evans, 26, [illegible] ton ave.
Doris M. Syphard, 21, [illegible], and William E. Hurley, 23, [illegible] ave.
Mariette Schobert, 19, Elizabeth, N. J., and Raymond L. Sweet, 27, Hillside, N. J.
Anna McKenna, 23, 2715 Almond st., and Gerard A. Fenerty, 22, 2506 E. Clearfield st.
Helen Coles, 21, 1637 French st., and Conell Murray, 18, 1637 French st.
Helen E. Williams, 25, 7540 Fayette st., and John L. Wellings, 22, 7741 Temple [illegible]
Evelyn Rosenberg, 21, 701 E. [illegible] st., and Karl Goldberg, 21, 3123 W. Huntingdon st.
Marie Young, 26, 1301 Sellers st., and Joseph J. Perry, 24, 4326 Leiper st.
Elizabeth I. Morano, 22, 3659 Stanton st., and Salvatore M. Cavoto, 24, 4806 Princeton ave.
Norine M. Long, 23, Brooklyn, N. Y., and Paul F. Timmer, 24, Hamilton, Ohio.
Helen I. McLaughlin, 19, 360 E. Chelten ave., and William C. Heist, 20, 260 W. Haines st.
Stella J. Meyers, 23, 175 E. Ontario st., and Jack E. Mintzer, 26, 175 E. Ontario st.
Edith M. Kopatz, 23, Plainfield, N. J., and Harold F. Ross, 36, 3541 Kensington ave.
Nancy M. Geraghty, 21, [illegible], and Thomas F. Hills, 24, 532 W. [illegible] ave.
Anne B. Leyden, 24, 2437 E. Hazzard st., and Leonard J. Nellinger, 26, 2126 E. Clearfield st.
Merle L. Carnelix, 28, 1320 71st ave., and Albert L. McDonnell, 47, 1320 71st ave.
Beatrice Sosnove, 20, Audubon, N. J., and Joseph M. Foster, 25, Brookline, Mass.
Elizabeth L. Hostetter, 21, [illegible] st., and William J. Beckfield, 24, Ber[illegible], Pa.
Mary T. Cousins, 20, 828 N. 43d st., and Herman L. Eldridge, 21, 826 N. 43d st.
Theresa Altomura, 32, 935 W[illegible] st., and Charles L. Michael, 24, 936 Em[illegible] st.
Anne G. Carney, 19, 5519 Pulaski ave., and Albert F. Cervino, 24, 6201 Baynton st.
Madeline M. Hagerman, 23, 2041 S. Hutchinson st., and Albert M. Pratt, 41, 1326 Harrison st.
Viola D. Reimann, 21, 426 E. Sentner st., and Robert V. Heinle, 26, 5441 Westford road.
Edith Judelson, 23, 131 Porter st., and William Needle, 30, 1328 S. Lawrence st.
Lucia C. Narcisi, 21, 1732 S. 29th st., and Anthony R. D'Annibale, 21, 1546 S. Dorrance st.
Mary A. Belinsky, 21, 5963 Lebanon ave., and Milton Levenberg, 26, 3107 D Mountain Drive.
Minnie Downing, 40, 5910 Haverford ave., and Clarence W. Clay, 56, Camden, N. J.
Betty Freedman, 20, 5932 [illegible] st., and Morey H. Goodinsky, 2[illegible], Highlands, N. J.
Virginia L. Wallace, 19, 439 E. Haines st., and William C. Taylor, 21, 521 E. [illegible] cott st.
Gertrude W. Reno, 24, 3302 N. 10th st., and Henry C. Petzel, 24, Jerkintown, Pa.
Dorothy R. Nagel, 24, 551 Graham st., and William J. Kaiser, Jr., 26, 627 M[illegible] st.
Cecilia H. Muldoon, 34, 726 N. De Kalb st., and Charles E. Etzler, 34, Rochester, N. Y.
Betty J. Gordon, 23, Upper Darby, Pa., and Edward F. Mucha, 22, 4358 N. 19th st.

Network and Local Radio Features on the Air Today

All Schedules in Eastern War Time—Subject to Last-Minute Changes by Stations—Saturday, January 6, 1945

(Copyright, 1945, The Philadelphia Inquirer)

WIP	610	KYW	1060
WABC	880	WHAT	1340
WJZ	770	WTEL	1340
WFIL	560	WIBG	990
WEAF	660	WCAU	1210
WOR	710	WCAM	1310
WPEN	950	WDAS	1400

9 A. M.
WFIL-Breakfast Club
WFIL-News: Moments for Mothers
WDAS-News: Variety
WIBG-News: Zella Harper
KYW-News: Dorothy Derby
WOR-Cleveland Orchestra
WCAU-Show Time
9.15—KYW-Voice of the Army
WIP-Housewives Serenade
WABC-Garden Gate
WCAU-Showtime
WPEN-Morning 950 Club
9.30—WEAF-Encores
WIBG-Music Old and New
WIP-[illegible] with Coupons
WABC-Country Journal
WCAU-Farm Weekly
9.45—WIBG-Radio Party
KYW-Let's Visit the Zoo
WCAU-Treasury Program
W[illegible]-Rise 'n' Shine
WEAF-Girl Scout Program
WFIL-Treasury Program

10 A. M.
WFIL-What's Cookin'
WCAU-Youth on Parade
KYW-Sports Comment
WDAS-News: Stars on Parade
WIBG-News: Novelty
WOR-WPEN-News
WIP-Mystery Melodies
10.15—WOR-Rainbow House
WIP-News
WPEN-Morning 950 Club
WDAS-Woman's Club
10.30—WIBG-Danceland
WIP-Calling All Girls
WCAU-Mary Taylor
WJZ-Dick Platt Orchestra
WDAS-Melodies
WFIL-Salvation Army
KYW-Yours Truly Julie
10.45—WIP-Music
KYW-Comment
WPEN-Pennsylvania State Police
WDAS-Music Hour

11 A. M.
WCAU-News: Let's Pretend
WOR-News
WIP-Midday Melodies
WIBG-News: Danceland
WDAS-News: Music Hour
WJZ-Piano Quartet
WPEN-Children's Bible
WFIL-Canteen
KYW-Piano Quartet
11.15—WOR-Music
WJZ-Transatlantic Quiz
11.30—KYW-Ed McConnell
WJZ-Land of the Lost
WIP-Hobby Hookey
WCAU-Danceland
WDAS-Music Hour
WFIL-Treasury Program

12 Noon
KYW, WIBG, WPEN-News
WCAU-Theater of Today
WDAS-News: Variety
WFIL-News: Show Music
WEAF-Music Room
WIP-Soldiers of the Press
WOR-Man on the Farm
WJZ-Kay Armen
12.15—WIP-Musical
WIBG-Front Page Drama
KYW-Consumer Time
WPEN-Tune Shop
WJZ-Frolics
12.30—WCAU-Drama
WEAF-Atlantic Spotlight
WIBG-Alpha Baptist Church
WFIL-Coast Guard Band
WABC-Stars Over Hollywood
12.45—WOR-Album
KYW-News: Music

1 P. M.
WDAS-News: Variety
WCAU-Grand Central Station
WIP-Jazz Contest
WIP-One O'Clock Express
WIBG-Front Page
WFIL-Metropolitan Opera
WPEN-News: Waves Programs
WPEN-News: Tune Shop
WOR-Vincent Lopez
1.15—WFIL-Guest Book
WIBG-Novelty
1.30—WFIL-Front Page Drama
WCAU-Report to the Nation
WIBG-Music
WOR-Rev. H. B. Rittenhouse
WABC-The Baxters
WOR-Luncheon with Lopez
WJZ-News
1.45—WJZ-Saturday Serenade
WOR-News: Comment
WFIL-Pianist

2 P. M.
KYW-Those Are Our Men
WCAU-Men and Books
WFIL-Metropolitan Opera "Lucia di Lammermoor"
WABC-Syncopation Piece
WDAS-News: 950 Club
WOR-News: Theater Time
WJZ-News
2.15—WCAU-Adventures in Science
WIP-Treasury Salute
2.30—WDAS-Voice of the Army
WCAU-Mixed Chorus
WIP-Quaker City Brevities
WABC-Carolina Hayride
WOR-News

3 P. M.
WABC-Syncopation Piece
WDAS-News: Slovak Hour
WCAU-Mitchell Melodies
WCAU-[illegible]
3.15—WPEN-Melodic Moments
3.30—WEAF-Rhapsody of the Rockies
WCAU-Handstand
3.45—WABC-Job for Tomorrow
WABC-Syncopation Piece

4 P. M.
WDAS-News: Polish Hour
WPEN-News: 950 Club
WCAU-Report From Washington
4.15—WCAU-Report From Overseas
WIBG-Jive Time
4.30—WCAU-Assignment Home
WFIL-Horace Heidt
KYW-Music on Display
4.45—WPEN-Your Neighbors
WFIL-Tea for You

5 P. M.
WPEN-News
WCAU-Philadelphia Orch.
WIP-Sports Parade
WIBG-News: Cowboy Tunes
5.15—WDAS-Bandwagon
WIBG-Uncle Jim Willard
WIP-Trio
5.30—KYW-News
WIBG-Islanders
WDAS-Interlude
WOR-Sports Parade
WCAU-Philadelphia Orch
WFIL-All-Star Band
WJZ-Paul Lavalle
WEAF-Commentator
WIP-Carmen Cavallero
5.45—WIBG-News
WDAS-Phila. Program
KYW-Curt Massey
WOR-Shirley Eder
WIP-Christian Science Program
WFIL-Hello Sweetheart

6 P. M.
WIBG-Danceland
WCAU-News Comment
WDAS-News: Hits of the Day
KYW-Commentator
WEAF-I Sustain Wings
WPEN-War Bond Give Away
WOR-Headlines
WJZ-News and Comment
WFIL-Hot Spot on the Map
WIP-War Extra
6.15—WABC-People's Platform
WPEN-Records
WIP-Music
WFIL-News: Music
WJZ-Sports
WOR-Newsreel
KYW-Friendship Ranch
WCAU-Warrington's Orch.
6.30—WFIL-Sportscaster
WOR-News
WEAF-People's War
WIP-Sports
WPEN-Church of Christ
6.45—WCAU-World Today
WFIL-Meet Your Navy
WIP-Uncle Wip
WDAS-Column of the Air
WEAF-Religion in the News
WJZ-Singer

7 P. M.
WCAU-Mayor of the Town
KYW-The Great Gildersleeve
WOR-Guess Who?
WDAS-Children's Church
WOP-Reflections in Rhythm
WPEN-Records
7.15—WIP-News
WFIL-Comment
7.30—WCAU-America in the Air
KYW-The Saint
WIBG-Franny Murray
WJZ-Meet Your Navy
WDAS-The Mallovs
WIP-Confidentially Yours
WFIL-School Sports
WPEN-Youth Center
7.45—WIP-Music and Lyrics
WDAS-Interlude
WIBG-News
WFIL-Chester Bowles
WPEN-News
WEAF-Great Novels

8 P. M.
WPEN-Gospel Program
KYW-Gaslight Gayeties
WIBG-Music at Eight
WDAS-Commentator
WFIL-Early American Dance Music
WCAU-Danny Kaye Show
8.15—WDAS-Jewish Program
8.30—WIP-Detroit Symphony
WCAU-FBI in War and Peace
WFIL-Boston Symphony
WIBG-Eric Wilkinson Organ Music
WPEN-The Pilgrims
KYW-Truth or Consequences
8.45—WIBG-Sports

9 P. M.
KYW-National Barn Dance
WDAS-News: Italian Hour
WIBG-News: Music
WOR-Chicago Theater
WPEN-Rev. Robert Fraser
WCAU-Hit Parade
9.30—WFIL-Spotlight Bands
KYW-Can You Top This
WIP-Nick Carter
WIBG-News: Glee Club
9.45—WCAU-Treasury Program
WIBG-Temple vs. Syracuse basketball

10 P. M.
ALL STATIONS President Roosevelt
10.30—WFIL-Mr. X. drama
10.45—WIP-C'mon 'n' Dance
WCAU-Caballeros
WPEN-Mirror Room
WIBG-Music

11 P. M.
WIP-Dance Music
KYW-News, Caravan
WIBG-Newsreel
WDAS-News: Nocturne
WCAU-News: Major George Fielding Eliot
WPEN-News and Music
WEAF-News: Comment
WFIL-News: Weather
11.15—WFIL-Barn Dance
WCAU-At Your Service: Sports
WPEN-Night Club
WEAF-News
WDAS-Nocturne
WABC-George Olson
11.30—WPEN-Disc Review
WEAF-I Sustain Wings
WOR-Shady Valley Jamboree
WCAU-Les Brown's Orch.
WJZ-George Paxton
11.45—WFIL-News
WOR-Harry James

12 Midnight
WFIL-Midnight Mosaic
WCAU-News: Weather
WJZ-Midnight Extra
WIBG-Here's Everything
WIP-Midnight Bandwagon
WOR-George Barry
12.05—WCAU-Orch.
WJZ-Gay Claridge
WABC-Count Basie
12.15—WOR-Trio
KYW-Thomas Peluso
12.30—WJZ-Orch.
KYW-Trio
WOR-Hal McIntyre
WCAU-Sammy Kaye

Letter Out

FORGET It's fungus of rye.	
DILATE It's what many bathrooms are.	
WELCHES It's to go on the wagon.	
RANTERS It's a wandering knight.	
STEER It's once upon a time.	

Remove one letter from each word and rearrange to spell word called for. Print letter in block opposite word from which you removed it.

If you have Lettered Out correctly IT'S NOT TRUE.

Solution on Opposite Page

Word Game

Today's Word ——Liliaceous

(Liliaceous: Lil a' shus. Like, or pertaining to lilies.)

Average mark ——48 words

Time limit ——30 minutes

Can you find 52 or more English words of four or more letters in LILIACEOUS? The list will be published Monday.

BEST LAUGHS OF 1945

"Do I sound like that?"

Cryptogram

CONVERTS

OMAR JH JKG
LJCPDNGL
IKMGUNGNP DA
FGDUMDA MGN
FNTJODAB UNM
PGDAQNGL.

Solution Monday

The Philadelphia Inquirer

PUBLIC LEDGER

An Independent Newspaper for All the People

FINAL CITY EDITION

CIRCULATION: December Average: Daily 501,385; Sunday 1,069,184

WEDNESDAY MORNING, JANUARY 10, 1945

Copyright, 1945, by Triangle Publications, Inc., Vol. 232, No. 10

abdefgh

THREE CENTS

MacARTHUR INVADES LUZON

Deep 15-Mile Beachhead Won North of Manila; Allies Gain on Both Flanks of Belgian Salient

F.D.R. Asks Budget of 83 Billions

Congress Is Told To Defer Any Plans For Tax Reductions

By NICHOLAS P. GREGORY

Inquirer Washington Bureau

WASHINGTON, Jan. 8.—President Roosevelt in his 13th annual budget message today bluntly told Congress to shelve any plans for a reduction in taxes, despite the fact that estimates of overall expenditures—war and non-war—had been cut to $83,000,000,000 for the 1946 fiscal year, a drop of $17,000,000,000 from 1945.

Of the $83,000,000,000, approximately $70,000,000,000 is earmarked for war expenditures, as compared with $90,000,000,000 of the $100,000,000,000 budget for 1945.

HUGE DEBT IS CITED

Warning that debt mismanagement must not take place after the defeat of Germany and Japan, the President said high taxes must be maintained after total victory for an orderly liquidation of the Federal debt, which is expected to exceed $252,000,000,000 at the end of the 1945 fiscal year which closes next June 30.

As if to emphasize the tremendous cost borne by the United States, the President's message highlighted the fact that from 1941 through 1946 the total war program measured by appropriations and authorizations, together with net commitments, will total $450,000,000,000. If all of this money were spent it would represent an expenditure of $3116 for war on a per capita basis, according to the latest census.

Highlights of the budget message:

1. Estimated expenditures for 1946 will total $87,000,000,000, of which $83,760,000,000 will rep-

Continued on Page 8, Column 2

U. S. Tanks Battle German Armor in Raging Blizzard

By AUSTIN BEALMEAR

SUPREME HEADQUARTERS ALLIED EXPEDITIONARY FORCE, Paris, Jan. 9 (A. P.).—American tanks clashed with German armor in a battle that raged all day today in a blinding blizzard as Field Marshal Sir Bernard L. Montgomery's two-army team whittled another mile off the northern side of the Belgian bulge and closed within three-fourths of a mile of the important communications hub of Laroche.

The U. S. Third Army, which had been forced to give ground late yesterday under repeated counter-attacks on the southern side of the salient, roared back today with gains up to a half-mile at several points despite the worst weather of the winter and continued fierce enemy resistance.

STRASBOURG SHELLED

As the Allies in Belgium pinched Marshal Gerd von Rundstedt's salient to a width of 9 miles between the areas of Laroche and Herbaimant, the Germans increased their pressure in Alsace and shelled Strasbourg with heavy artillery from the east bank of the Rhine.

American forces on the northern flank of the German bulge drove to within four miles of the last main escape and supply highway and von Rundstedt was reported hurriedly shifting tanks from the Bastogne area northward to meet this threat to his lifeline.

FOE MAY FACE DISASTER

Should the smashing Yank drive from the northern waist of the bulge sever the Houffalize-St. Vith highway, all German forces in the western half of the salient would be placed in a precarious position—perhaps faced with a second Falaise disaster.

A field dispatch from Roger Greene, of the Associated Press, tonight declared that "the next 12 to 24 hours may provide the turning point in the great battle that began Dec. 16 when von Rundstedt launched his surprise blow."

The American forces threatening

Continued on Page 2, Column 6

Corcoran Aided Firm With Nazi Link, Littell Says

By HERMAN A. LOWE

Inquirer Washington Bureau

WASHINGTON, Jan. 9.—Thomas G. (Tommy the Cork) Corcoran, former White House adviser, again was accused today of "dominating" actions of Attorney General Francis Biddle, as former Assistant Attorney General Norman M. Littell opened the second round of the Biddle-Littell feud.

Mr. Littell, in a second statement to the Senate War Investigating Committee, alleged that Mr. Corcoran choked off what should have been criminal action by the Justice Department against the Sterling Drug Co., formerly Sterling Products Corp., international drug firm.

LINKED TO NAZI FIRM

The company, whose vice president was David Corcoran, brother of "Tommy the Cork," and which was represented by Thomas G. Corcoran himself, was accused by the anti-trust division of the Justice Department with operating in a cartel agreement with I. G. Farben, German drug trust, even after Pearl Harbor.

"Beyond all shadow of a doubt," declared Mr. Littell in his statement, "this case is one of the most significant, not only in the history of the Department of Justice, but in the history of the country, and its settlement without submission of all the evidence to a grand jury marks the lowest point in the history of the Department of Justice since the Harding Administration.

"I state as a fact that the settle-

Continued on Page 7, Column 4

Victor Emmanuel Stricken, Nazis Say

By Associated Press

The Berlin radio said yesterday that King Victor Emmanuel of Italy had suffered a light stroke "which, however, was not fatal."

The broadcast by Transocean News Agency said "it was officially declared Tuesday that all rumors concerning his death were entirely unfounded."

The King is 75.

WHERE AMERICANS HAVE LANDED ON LUZON ISLAND

General Douglas MacArthur's troops have pushed ashore at four points on the south and east coasts of Luzon Island's Lingayen Gulf. One beachhead is 15 miles long. The blackened areas on the other Philippines are under American control. Inset map shows the relation of Luzon, chief island of the group, to other Pacific areas.

800-Ship Armada Lands Americans At Lingayen Gulf

Picture on Page 2; War Summary on Page 3

By WILLIAM C. WILSON

GENERAL MacARTHUR'S HEADQUARTERS, Philippines, Jan. 10 (Wednesday) (U. P.).—Veteran United States Sixth Army troops invaded the main Philippine island of Luzon yesterday from an 800-ship armada, establishing a 15-mile beachhead on Lingayen Gulf against Japanese resistance so beaten down by a three-day bombardment that not a single American in the first assault wave was reported killed.

The Americans, under the personal command of General Douglas MacArthur, who went ashore with his men, quickly seized several coastal towns, among them San Fabian, on the southeastern corner of the Gulf 109 miles northwest of Manila. A Headquarters spokesman said some forces had reached points within 107 miles of Manila on the south coast.

LANDING FORCE MEETS LITTLE FIRE

The Americans went ashore at 9.30 A. M. and encountered only a few bursts of artillery and mortar fire. Front dispatches said that there were so few Japanese defending the beaches that only a handful of enemy troops were killed.

"The Japs refused to fight," said one dispatch from the front.

The dispatch said the Americans encountered only light artillery and mortar fire on their left flank and that not a man in the first wave to hit the beaches was reported killed.

The Japanese had offered stubborn resistance to the preliminary three-day air and sea bombardment—one American admiral said it was worse than at Saipan. They inflicted some losses on our ships.

But yesterday morning the warships encountered virtually no opposition as they unleashed a two-hour bombardment which smashed shore defenses.

SHIPS 'SUNK' AT PEARL HARBOR AID YANKS

Some of the veteran battleships which the Japanese thought they had sunk at Pearl Harbor participated in the bombardment.

Then a fleet of more than 2500 landing barges, amphibious tanks and other craft moved in toward the same Lingayen beaches where the Japanese made their main landings on Luzon, Dec. 22, 1941. Their way was made easier by gallant minesweeper crews which had swept the big gulf of mines during the three preceding days.

The landing barges and 800 major craft, many of which had sailed all the way from New Guinea, comprised the greatest invasion fleet in the history of the Pacific war. It stretched for 100 miles along the China Sea.

Dispatches said the Japanese had no appreciable beach defenses and that they made half-hearted attempt to wreck bridges as they withdrew inland. A Headquarters spokesman

Continued on Page 2, Column 1

Nazis Step Up U-Boat Warfare

By JOHN M. McCULLOUGH

Inquirer Washington Bureau

WASHINGTON, Jan. 9.—The sinking of Allied merchant ships by German submarines increased in December, the monthly Anglo-American communique revealed today, adding that "this is but another index that the European war is far from over."

Despite the increased U-boat activity, which was forecast in the communique issued under the authority of President Roosevelt and Prime Minister Winston Churchill last month, it has not interfered with the supply of Allied combat forces throughout the world, today's announcement asserted.

ROBOT LINK HINTED

Although the statement made no reference to it, there was considerable speculation that the renewed submarine activity during last month, which presumably is continuing, is directly related to the warning concerning the probability of robot bomb attacks upon the North Atlantic coast made yesterday by Admiral Jonas Ingram, commander-in-chief of the United States Atlantic Fleet.

The communique did point out, however, that "the announcement of the recent landing of enemy agents from a U-boat on the Maine

Continued on Page 2, Column 5

Tokio Admits Luzon Invasion

By United Press

Tokio radio admitted the American invasion of Luzon Island Tuesday night and announced that U. S. forces had "started" landing operations at San Fabian and "other points on Lingayen Gulf."

"Japanese air units and ground forces are now engaging the enemy forces in sanguinary fighting," the brief enemy announcement said.

Casualties

64 Service Men Killed, 52 Hurt From City Area

Army casualty lists released yesterday and official notifications to relatives contained the names of 64 men from the Philadelphia area reported killed in action and of 52 wounded and two missing.

The deaths in action represent the greatest number reported in one day here since the war started.

Edward James Dooner, 22, aviation chief ordnance man, who was reported missing last Sept. 21 in the Southwest Pacific, has now been listed as killed, according to a Navy notice sent to his parents, Police Inspector and Mrs. John T. Dooner, of 3265 Cottman st.

The youth was the second of the couple's two sons to lose his life in the armed service. Private John J. Dooner, 25, was killed in the sinking of an Army troopship in the North Atlantic last February. Edward, who entered the Navy at the age of 18, had served as a bombardier on an aircraft carrier after becoming a chief petty officer. Their father is stationed at the 19th and Oxford sts. police station.

Staff Sergeant Ignatius J. Ricciardi, 33, was killed in action in Germany Dec. 22, his wife, Mary,

Continued on Page 4, Column 3

Man Kills Mother of 3, Shoots Self to Death

Illustrated on Page 10

While two young children clung to her skirt, a 25-year-old mother of three was shot and killed in Camden last night by a man nearly twice her age who then turned the gun on himself, according to police.

Mrs. Margaret Geraldine Deal, in whose home at 2018 Arlington st. the tragedy occurred shortly after 7 o'clock, died on the way to West Jersey Homeopathic Hospital, and the man, James Sherlock, 48, of 4th and Jackson sts., Camden, succumbed nearly three hours later.

Police responding to two simultaneous telephone calls found the woman lying at the foot of the first floor stairway of the tiny home and the man crumpled nearby in the arch between the hall and the dining room.

CHILDREN SOB NEARBY

Over their mother's form stood the two sobbing children, Marie, 4, and Arlene, 18 months. A third child, Patricia, three months old, lay in her coach a few yards away.

The woman's husband, Elmer, 29, summoned from his job at the RCA Victor Division of the Radio Corporation of America, told detectives that Sherlock had lived with them

Continued on Page 10, Column 5

IN TODAY'S INQUIRER

SPECIAL DEPARTMENTS

COMICS AND FEATURES

Airport to Open For Mercy Plane

An errand of mercy will open Philadelphia's long-closed Municipal Airport to a commercial airliner this morning for the third time since December, 1943.

At about 10.30 A. M., an Eastern Air Lines plane en route from Houston, Tex., will land at the big field here to take aboard eight-month-old Thomas Magill, victim of an intestinal obstruction for which he must undergo treatment at a hospital in Boston, Mass.

SPECIAL PERMISSION GRANTED

The child, son of Mr. and Mrs. Richard Magill, of Leola, Pa., near Lancaster, was brought recently to Children's Hospital here to undergo treatment by Dr. Mitchell I. Rubin.

When Dr. Rubin determined that the only hope for the child lay in an operation such as could be performed only at Children's Hospital in Boston, permission had to be obtained from the Civil Aeronautics Authority in Washington to land a civilian plane here for the flight.

Continued on Page 10, Column 1

Plane Spans U. S. In 6 Hrs., 9 Mins.

WASHINGTON, Jan. 9 (U. P.).—An Army Boeing Stratocruiser established a new transcontinental speed record tonight, flying from Seattle, Wash., to Washington in six hours and nine minutes for an average speed of about 380 miles an hour.

The huge plane, transport counterpart of the B-29 Superfortress, took off from Seattle at 2.38 P. M. (E.W.T.) and landed at Washington National Airport at 8.47 P. M., covering a distance of 2340 airline miles. It was flown by Dick Merrill, Boeing test pilot, and carried Army and Boeing officials.

Nurse Draft Bill Offered in House

By HUGH MORROW

Inquirer Washington Bureau

WASHINGTON, Jan. 9.—A bill to draft registered nurses between the ages of 18 and 45 into the armed forces was introduced late today by Chairman Andrew J. May (D., Ky.), of the House Military Affairs Committee.

Hearings were scheduled for next week amid indications that the principal resistance to such a measure would be based upon the belief that it would be unconstitutional to draft women into the Army and Navy.

LEGAL, PRESIDENT SAYS

President Roosevelt declared at his press conference this afternoon that lawyers had told him it was constitutionally legal to draft nurses to fill the urgent needs of the armed forces.

"Under what law?" Mr. Roosevelt was asked.

The President referred this question to Attorney General Francis Biddle, remarking that he, himself, only used to be a lawyer.

Mr. May said he hoped it would be unnecessary to use the legisla-

Continued on Page 3, Column 6

U.S. Navy Planes Blast 73 Jap Ships in 3 Days

Illustrated on Page 14

PEARL HARBOR, Jan. 9 (A. P.).—U. S. Naval fliers, slashing at Japan's sea-air strength within the Luzon defense orbit, sank or damaged 73 ships and destroyed or damaged 262 planes in a three-day sweep over the Luzon-Formosa-Okinawa area.

(It was announced in Washington, meanwhile, that thunderous new Superfortress raids had battered Tokio itself and the great Japanese base of Formosa.

(The Army, announcing results of the Tokio attack, said flames seared the heart of the target area. No mention of any losses was made on the Tokio flight. All planes returned from the Formosa raid.)

MORE DAMAGE LISTED

A Navy communique today listed additional damage to the enemy on Luzon in the carrier based strikes of Jan. 5 and 6 and ship-plane casualties in the far ranging raids Jan. 8 on Formosa, Okinawa and other islands in the Formosa area.

Hellcat fighters shot down a total of 18 Japanese planes and joined dive bombers and torpedo planes in destroying 74 more aircraft and damaging 103 on the ground at

Continued on Page 2, Column 1

Japs' Aim Poor

2 Torpedoes Miss M'Arthur

GENERAL MACARTHUR'S HEADQUARTERS, Philippines, Jan. 10 (Wednesday) (A. P.).

TWO torpedoes from a Japanese midget submarine missed the ship which took General Douglas MacArthur to Luzon Tuesday morning. The sub was rammed and sunk.

Wearing his famed campaign cap and calmly smoking a corncob pipe, General MacArthur rode upon the engine box of a landing craft and waded knee-deep in water on to the soil of Luzon. He hit the shore about two hours after the first wave.

General MacArthur talked with privates and generals alike and expressed himself pleased with the way the operation was proceeding.

Japs Refused To Fight Landing

By RALPH TEATSORTH

ABOARD ADMIRAL KINKAID'S FLAGSHIP, OFF LUZON, Jan. 10 (Wednesday) (U. P.).—The Japs refused to fight.

That sums up the first day's action on Luzon, where the American casualties have been virtually nonexistent Tuesday and hardly more than a handful of enemy defenders have been killed.

NO MAJOR OPPOSITION

There was no major opposition and only light artillery and mortar fire on our left flank. The enemy's air reaction was also comparatively light.

The "Venice-like" character of this terrain in Lingayen Gulf—with its miles and miles of swamps and rice paddies—might have been a

Continued on Page 2, Column 3

U. S. WEATHER FORECAST

Philadelphia and vicinity: Fair and cold today; increasing cloudiness and not so cold tomorrow.

Sun rises 8.22 A.M.	Sets 5.54 P.M.
Moon rises 4.47 A.M.	Sets 3.04 P.M.

The Philadelphia Inquirer

PUBLIC LEDGER

An Independent Newspaper for All the People

FINAL CITY EDITION

CIRCULATION: January Average: Daily 513,909; Sunday 1,099,766 — TUESDAY MORNING, FEBRUARY 13, 1945 — Copyright, 1945, by Triangle Publications, Inc.; Vol. 232, No. 44 — a b d e f g h — THREE CENTS

Big Three Agree on Post-War Europe, Doom German Militarism Forever; Kleve, Pruem Fall; Reds Cross Bober

Today

Big 3 Doom of Nazis
Threat of New Blows
A Foreboding Future
Allied Armies Moving
Drive From the North

—By John M. McCullough—

Inquirer Washington Bureau

WASHINGTON, Feb. 12.

ASSERTION today by the Big Three that Nazi Germany is doomed, and that further German resistance is "hopeless" is not, as military sources here see it, an exercise in threatening rhetoric.

Rather, it is the blunt statement of unavoidable military fact.

It is significant that military opinion generally holds this to be true quite aside from the "new and even more powerful blows" to which reference is made in the Yalta communique.

It is inconceivable, military men assert, that Germany's career militarists, raised upon the doctrine of Clausewitz, Von Moltke and Von Schlieffen, can entertain any hope whatever for the military future of the Reich.

This, it is emphasized, is not a matter of drawing inferences from possible repercussions inside Germany, nor of weighing in the balances possible future military developments. It is implicit in the scheme of things as they exist today, and this scheme comprises, among others, these foreboding aspects:

1. The progress of the Russian flanks northeast and southeast of Berlin, like all-engulfing floodwaters, have dimmed almost to the vanishing point any long-range success which the German General Staff might hope to win with an "all-or-nothing" counter-attack.

2. Major fighting has broken out on the Western Front as a result of Allied initiative, although still relatively local in character. The attack by the Canadian First Army is progressing steadily toward the first objective of clearing the western bank of the upper Rhine southeastward from the Dutch border, and is a direct and imminent threat to the security of the Ruhr.

3. It may be assumed that General Dwight D. Eisenhower has fully completed the regroup-

Continued on Page 12, Column 1

Canadians Take Gennep in Drive For Ruhr Valley

War Summary on Page 5

From both west and east, Allied armies dealt the crumbling German defenses severe blows yesterday.

The Canadian First Army completed the conquest of Kleve, northern terminus of the vaunted Siegfried Line, and plunged ahead toward Wesel and the vital industrial Ruhr Valley less than 22 miles away. The American Third Army seized Pruem, 115 miles to the south, meeting surprisingly little opposition.

The Russians captured Bunzlau, on the Bober River and a great 12-way road center on the Breslau-Leipzig highway, as they smashed forward 15 miles to within 74 miles of Dresden, capital of Saxony. Berlin reported the Russians had crossed the Bober at two points near Bunzlau.

Patton Army Meets Little Opposition; Roer Flood at Crest

Map on Page 4

By AUSTIN BEALMEAR

PARIS, Feb. 12 (A. P.).—Kleve and Pruem—fortresses of western Germany's front line of defense—fell today before the onslaught of two Allied armies striking 115 miles apart in the forefront of an expected big push from the west.

The Canadian First Army engulfed devastated Kleve, northern anchor linking the West Wall with the Rhine; captured Gennep, on the Meuse, then pressed on two miles southeast within 22 miles of Wesel, in the northwest corner of the Ruhr industrial basin, last great source of German war power.

FIRST MAJOR PRIZE

Kleve, a city of 20,000, was the first major prize taken in the five-day-old Canadian-British offensive. Its capture threatened to turn the Allies loose around the north flank for a slashing drive behind enemy forces defending the Rhine River plain.

Pruem, a stronghold in the Eifel Mountains 115 miles south of Kleve, was captured with surprising ease by the United States Third Army, which thereby seized control of the entire highway network east of its 10-mile breach in the Siegfried Line.

STRONG DEFENSE AHEAD

Only a few isolated snipers along the Pruem River still contested American control of this highway hub with a peacetime population of 10,000. Heavy fire east of the river showed the enemy meant to contest any attempt to plunge deeper

Continued on Page 4, Column 2

Russians Capture Bunzlau; Siege of Budapest Nears End

Map on Page 6

By W. W. HERCHER

LONDON, Feb. 13 (Tuesday) (A. P.).—Russian troops swept to within 74 miles of the Saxony capital of Dresden yesterday, capturing the Bober River stronghold of Bunzlau in a swift 15-mile drive in Silesia which slashed one Berlin-Prague highway and threatened to outflank Berlin on the south.

Simultaneously, Moscow announced that the end of the long, bloody siege of Budapest, Hungarian capital, was very near. Russian troops captured the Royal Palace and the ancient fortress on the high bluff on the west bank of the Danube River in the Buda section, smashing the core of organized enemy resistance and taking 30,000 more prisoners Sunday and Monday.

UNDER SIEGE 47 DAYS

Final figures for prisoners alone are expected to exceed 100,000, and German dead also will run into the thousands. Budapest, gateway to Vienna and Bratislava on the plains to the west, has been under direct siege 47 days since Dec. 27, when the Russians surrounded the city and broke into its streets. Soviet planes and artillery had been bombarding it since the first week in November.

Fresh Russian gains were made in Pomerania and in the Polish Corridor during the day. Colonel General Ivan Petrov's Fourth Ukrainian Army drove to within 20 miles east of Moravaska Ostrava, Czechoslovakia's third city which guards the northern gateway to the Moravian Gap leading to Vienna and Prague,

Continued on Page 6, Column 2

(A. P. Wirephoto)

ALLIED LEADERS AT HISTORIC CRIMEA CONFERENCE

Gathered at Livadia Palace during the Big Three parley near Yalta are these United Nations leaders. Standing behind Prime Minister Churchill, President Roosevelt and Premier Stalin are (left to right) Admiral Sir Andrew Cunningham, Admiral Ernest J. King, Air Marshal Sir Charles Portal, Admiral William D. Leahy, General George C. Marshall, two unidentified Russians. This is an official British radio photo.

3 U. S. Divisions Join in Manila

By C. YATES McDANIEL

MANILA, Feb. 13 (Tuesday) (A. P.).—As American forces sliced Luzon Island in two, three United States divisions linked forces Monday in a solid line which hemmed a furiously fighting Japanese suicide garrison against the shell-wrecked bay front of Manila south of the Pasig River.

The enemy's only possible means of escape would be across the bay to Corregidor and Bataan, which some 500 planes of all types battered with a record weight of nearly 1000 tons of explosives in a 48-hour period ending Sunday night.

35 TROOP BARGES SUNK

The hazards of such a flight were emphasized in today's communique, which reported American fighter planes sank 35 barges, loaded with 2500 Japanese, off the shores of Bataan Peninsula Sunday.

It appeared more likely the Nipponese in South Manila would stand and die in the rubble-strewn area they hold, already compressed to less than five square miles. There they were carrying out a carefully calculated plan to set the price of the city's capture as high in lives and property as possible.

They fought behind thick walls. They used every known type of mine and explosive. They still poured artillery shells on vital pontoon bridges over the Pasig across which

Continued on Page 8, Column 2

Communique Of Big Three

WASHINGTON, Feb. 12 (U. P.).—Text of the White House communique on the Big Three meeting:

For the past eight days, Winston S. Churchill, Prime Minister of Great Britain; Franklin D. Roosevelt, President of the United States of America, and Marshal J. V. Stalin, Chairman of the Council of Peoples Commissars of the Union of Soviet Socialist Republics, have met with the Foreign Secretaries, Chiefs of Staffs and other advisers in the Crimea.

The following statement is made by the Prime Minister of Great Britain, the President of the United States of America, and the Chairman of the Council of Peoples Commissars of the Union of Soviet So-

Continued on Page 2, Column 3

Polish Regimes To Be Merged

Inquirer Washington Bureau

WASHINGTON, Feb. 12.—Russia has agreed to drop recognition of the present Lublin-Warsaw regime in Poland, in favor of a new provisional government of national unity, which will include democratic members of the Polish Government-in-Exile in London and underground leaders in Poland itself.

In return, the United States and Great Britain have agreed to adopt the Russian solution of the Polish territorial question, namely the Curzon Line.

This is the evident quid pro quo contained in the settlement to the Polish boundary problem announced today by the Big Three.

But whether the solution includes

Continued on Page 3, Column 3

Parley April 25 In U. S. to Plan Enduring Peace

Map of Parley Sites on Page 2; Other Pictures and Stories on Pages 2, 3 and 12

By WILLIAM C. MURPHY, JR.

Inquirer Washington Bureau

WASHINGTON, Feb. 12.—The Big Three of the United Nations have agreed on plans and terms for unconditional surrender to be enforced on Germany and have served notice on the German people that continuance of "hopeless resistance" would only increase the costs of defeat.

A White House announcement late today gave the official results of the eight-day meeting of President Roosevelt, Prime Minister Winston Churchill and Premier Josef Stalin near Yalta in the Crimea, and revealed the Allied war leaders had reached agreement on the following points:

1. Full understanding among the United States, Britain and Russia on military plans against Germany which "will result in shortening the war."

2. Joint military occupation of the Reich following the collapse of German resistance, with each of the three Powers occupying separate agreed zones, the occupation to be co-ordinated through a Central Control Commission with headquarters in Berlin. France will be invited to share in the occupation and if she accepts will be assigned a zone. German militarism is to be destroyed. All German armed forces are to be disarmed and disbanded, all German military equipment removed or destroyed, all German military production eliminated and the German General Staff broken up "for all time."

3. The collection from Germany of compensation "in kind" for damage done in occupied nations, this provision to be enforced through a commission with headquarters in Moscow.

4. Establishment "at the earliest possible moment" of a general international organization to maintain peace and security, and as a step toward that end the convening of a United Nations conference in San Francisco on April 25 to prepare the charter for the organization along the lines of the informal Dumbarton Oaks agreement. France and China will be invited to join with the United States, Russia and Britain in sponsoring this meeting.

In this connection it was revealed that the Big Three had reached an agreement on the controversial question of voting procedure within the Council of the proposed organization—left unsettled at Dumbarton Oaks—and that the text of this agreement would be made public as soon as

Continued on Page 2, Column 1

Germantown Hospital Building Razed by Fire

Illustrated on Page 17

A three-alarm fire early today wrecked the three-story brick dispensary and out-patient building of Germantown Hospital, the original hospital building of the installation at Penn and Chew sts., driving 22 orderlies from their quarters on the third floor and 20 cadet nurses from an adjoining structure. No one was injured.

The first alarm was turned in at 12.09 A. M., followed by two others at 12.20 and 12.31. William F. Cowden, chief engineer of the Fire Bureau, declared the fire officially out at 1.20 A. M.

FLAMES SHOOT 20 FEET

Drafts, created by four cupolas in the roof, caused flames to shoot 20 to 30 feet above the building, which stands on a hill, and rendered the blaze visible in the entire Germantown area.

Crowds attracted by the red glow jammed traffic momentarily but later helped firemen lay hoselines from the nearest water hydrants, 100 yards away, on Wister st., and 300

Continued on Page 17, Column 4

IN TODAY'S INQUIRER

SPECIAL DEPARTMENTS

COLUMNS AND FEATURES

Casualties

27 Are Killed And 52 Wounded

War and Navy Department casualty lists released yesterday and official notifications to relatives contained the names of 27 men from the Philadelphia area reported killed in action, 52 wounded, five missing and two prisoners of war.

PFC. STURGES

Private First Class James H. Sturges, son of Mr. and Mrs. William Sturges, of 2226 S. 15th st., was wounded in action in Germany, according to a War Department telegram received by his parents.

A former shoe salesman employed by the A. H. Geuting Co., Private Sturges entered the Army three years ago and has been overseas for a year. He graduated in 1941 from

Continued on Page 8, Column 4

War Casualties Set at 8,000,000

NEW YORK, Feb. 12 (A. P.).—The Metropolitan Life Insurance Co. announced in a report made public today that company computations showed approximately 8,000,000 men lost their lives in the second World War up to the end of 1944.

The American fatality toll exceeds 200,000, as compared with 53,000 in the first World War, the report said. Steadily mounting Japanese fatalities have passed the 600,000 mark.

Wider Jap War Mapped at Malta

VALLETTA, Malta, Feb. 12 (A. P.).—Plans for stepping up the war against Japan as well as finishing off the conflict in Europe were discussed on this war-torn Mediterranean island by President Roosevelt and Prime Minister Winston Churchill.

They and members of their staffs then flew to their Crimea meeting with Premier Josef Stalin.

ONLY MENTION OF JAPAN

This information came from a high-ranking U. S. officer and constituted the only mention of Japan in connection with the Big Three meetings.

Meeting here with President Roosevelt and Prime Minister Churchill were many of the chief figures upon whom the final cleanup of Japan may rest.

The Prime Minister had with him Admiral Sir Andrew Browne Cunningham, First Sea Lord; Air Chief Marshal Sir Charles Portal and Field Marshals Sir Henry Maitland Wilson, Sir Alan Brooke and Sir Harold Alexander.

The President's party included

Continued on Page 3, Column 5

Blueprint for Peace Laid Down at Parley

By ALEXANDER KENDRICK

Inquirer Washington Bureau

WASHINGTON, Feb. 12.—The blueprint for a lasting piece was laid down before the free peoples of the world today by the Crimea conference of President Roosevelt, Premier Josef Stalin and Prime Minister Winston Churchill.

It has three parts:

1. The setting up of a permanent international organization on the Dumbarton Oaks plan, to be effected at a United Nations' conference in San Francisco, beginning April 25.

2. Interim action by the Big Three Allies to re-establish order and economic life in all the liberated areas of Europe, including the sponsoring of temporary governments.

3. Quarterly meetings of the three Allied Foreign Secretaries, for regular consultation on all questions.

The last barrier to the creation of joint peace machinery was hurdled at the Crimea meeting by an understanding on the question of voting procedure in the new League of Nations, the Big Three communique revealed.

This was taken here to mean that

Continued on Page 3, Column 4

Bill Asks Full Tests Before Operations

Inquirer Harrisburg Bureau

HARRISBURG, Feb. 12.—State Senator John J. Haluska of Cambria county, whose eight-year-old son died last July following an operation, tonight introduced a bill into the Legislature making obligatory a thorough physical examination of any patient about to undergo a surgical operation.

Senator Haluska asserted that no temperature reading, blood count or other physical examination was made when his son was operated on for removal of a birthmark

World Bank Bills Urged by F.D.R.

By NICHOLAS P. GREGORY

Inquirer Washington Bureau

WASHINGTON, Feb. 12.—President Roosevelt asked Congress today in a special message to take the lead in post-war monetary stabilization and world reconstruction by enacting legislation to appropriate $5,925,000,000 for United States participation in the Bretton Woods monetary and bank agreement signed last July by 44 nations.

The Bretton Woods agreement proposes the establishment of an $8,800,000,000 international monetary fund and an international bank for reconstruction and development with a capital of $9,100,000,000.

Pleading that the Dumbarton Oaks international political co-operation

Continued on Page 23, Column 6

U. S. WEATHER FORECAST

Philadelphia and vicinity: Increasing cloudiness and mild today with rain beginning this afternoon or evening. Tomorrow, occasional rains.

Sun rises	7.56 A.M.	Sets 6.33 P.M.
Moon rises	8.49 A.M.	Sets 7.50 P.M.

Phila. Team Vies For Bridge Crown

Special to The Inquirer

NEW YORK, Feb. 21.—The team of Charles J. Solomon, Mrs. Benjamin M. Golder, Stanley O. Fenkel and Simon Becker, of Philadelphia, and Miss Ruth Sherman, of New York, were matched tonight against the all-New York foursome of Harold B. Karp, Milton Jones, Charles Whitebrook and Lawrence Hirsch in the first knockout round of the Eastern Team of Four Contract Bridge championship.

Charles H. Goren, the only other Philadelphian entered, was playing with Leo and Peter Leventritt, of New York; Bertram Lebhar, of New Rochelle, and Samuel Katz, of Millburn, N. J., who are meeting the team of Mr. and Mrs. Louis Jaeger, Joseph Low, Henry Sonnenblick and Mason Lichtenstein, all New Yorkers.

WINNERS MEET TOMORROW

The winners of these two matches will meet in the semi-finals tomorrow night.

In the other bracket, the titleholders, Harry J. Fishbein, Charles S. Lochridge, Lee Hazen and Waldemar von Zedtwitz will play against an all-New York team.

The finals of this event will be played Friday night between the two teams which win their matches Thursday.

OTHER EVENTS LISTED

The first of two sessions of play to decide the Eastern women's open pair championship will be played tomorrow afternoon.

The other remaining event on the program of the 18th annual Eastern tournament of the American Contract Bridge League is the open pairs, in which Mrs. Golder and Mr. Solomon will play as partners and Mr. Goren is paired with Mrs. A. M. Sobel, of New York, with whom he has won many national bridge titles.

6 Given Prison Terms For Fatal Circus Fire

Continued From First Page

the administration of criminal law. The sentence imposed is not an expiation or an atonement for the offenses, but to prevent their recurrence."

Their attorney, William L. Hadden, appeared no less astonished than his clients.

ASKS 2-MONTH STAY

By permission of the court he conferred with them briefly in an anteroom, then asked for a two months' stay on the ground that the circus was about to start its annual tour and the men were essential to its operation.

Justice Shea ruled that William Caley, boss seatman, was not essential and he would have to begin his one-year jail term at once.

The court stayed execution of the other sentences until April 6. The circus opens its season in Madison Square Garden, New York City, April 4.

SENTENCES LISTED

The sentences were:

Haley: One to five years on each of 10 counts of manslaughter.

Smith: Two to seven years on each count.

Leonard S. Aylesworth, chief canvasman, two to seven years on each count.

David W. Blanchfield, rolling stock superintendent, six months on each count.

Edward R. Versteeg, chief electrician, one year on each count.

Caley: One year on each count.

LITIGATION AVOIDED

Nolo contendere is a technical plea by which a defendant is permitted to accept the penalty for the offense with which he is accused without either acknowledging guilt or being convicted by a jury of his peers.

Mr. Hadden, the defense attorney, told the court in two days of argument before the sentencing that his clients did not acknowledge guilt, but pleaded nolo contendere to avoid prolonged litigation and to restore the circus to full operation.

'TERRIFYING HAZARD'

The court found the defendants and the circus corporation negligent in the particulars specified in the indictments—the Big Top had been waterproofed with a mixture of gasoline and paraffin, creating "a terrifying fire hazard"; the exits had been blocked by runways for animals, and the electrical setup had been faulty.

In addition, the indictment said, the fire-fighting equipment was inadequate and had not been properly set up, and that the seatman, Caley, was absent from his post, though he was charged with the duty of fire detection.

Holmes Film At the Capitol

By Mildred Martin

Sherlock Holmes shows off once too often and right at the start of his latest adventure, "The Pearl of Death." But is the old boy's face red? Not at all.

On the contrary. For if he hadn't temporarily disconnected the museum's electrical protective system, the Borgia pearl wouldn't have been stolen a second time and, consequently, the Capitol wouldn't have had its entertaining new Holmes hair-raiser based on Sir Arthur Conan Doyle's "The Six Napoleons."

Having unwittingly assisted the crook, it's up to Holmes and the faithful Dr. Watson to locate the blood-stained jewel. They do it neatly, too, at considerable risk and to the accompaniment of broken crockery, broken backs and the ghastly menace of a hulking killer called "The Creeper." It seems the thief hastily hid the pearl in one of six plaster busts of Napoleon—and that as any one can see leads to plenty of violence and confusion.

Basil Rathbone and Nigel Bruce, as usual, offer their perfect teamwork as the great detective and his bumbling companion. Miles Mander and Evelyn Ankers do well as the jewel thieves; while Rondo Hatton is far more frightening than any Karloff or Chaney monster as the pathological Creeper who dotes on Miss Ankers and always snaps a back at the third vertebrae.

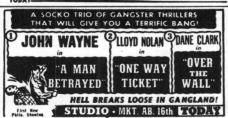

Amusement Guide in Philadelphia

MUSIC

ACADEMY—"La Forza del Destino," Phila. La Scala Opera Co. 8.15.

THEATERS

LOCUST ST.—"Calico Wedding," 2.30, 8.30.
SHUBERT—"One Touch of Venus," 2.30, 8.30.

MOTION PICTURES

ALDINE—"Meet Me in St. Louis," 11.15, 1.20, 3.30, 5.40, 7.50, 10.
ARCADIA—"Thirty Seconds Over Tokyo," 11.20, 2, 4.40, 7.20, 10.
BOYD—"Guest in the House," 11, 1.10, 3.20, 5.30, 7.45, 9.55.
CAPITOL—"Pearl of Death," 10.30, 12.25, 2.20, 4.15, 6.10, 8.05, 10.
EARLE—"Lake Placid Serenade," 10.55, 1.55, 4.50, 7.50, 10.30. Ina Ray Hutton and orchestra on stage, 12.35, 3.35, 6.35, 9.35.
FOX—"I'll Be Seeing You," 11, 12.50, 2.40, 4.30, 6.20, 8.10, 10.
KARLTON—"Wuthering Heights," 11, 12.50, 2.40, 4.30, 6.20, 8.15, 10.05.
KEITH'S—"The Keys of the Kingdom," 11, 1.55, 4.30, 7.05, 9.55.
MASTBAUM—"Objective Burma," 11.15, 1.55, 4.35, 7.15, 10.
NEWS—"Sun Valley Serenade," 8.15, 9.55.
... 11.40, 1.20, 3.05, 4.45, 6.25, 8.10, 9.50, 11.35, all night.
STANLEY—"Here Come the Waves," 11.25, 1.35, 3.40, 5.45, 7.50, 10.
STANTON—"Sunday Dinner for a Soldier," 11, 12.50, 2.40, [illegible] 6.20, 8.10, 10.
STUDIO—"A Man Betrayed," 11.15, 2.05, 1.45, 7.30, 10.20.

No piece of paper or cardboard is too small to save for the salvage collections—the torn grocery bag, yesterday's newspapers, unusable cardboard boxes.

Greatest Sea Search Under Way for Harmon

U. S. ARMY HEADQUARTERS, Pacific Ocean Areas, Honolulu, March 3 (A. P.).—The Pacific's greatest aerial and surface ship search was on today for Lieutenant General Millard F. Harmon, commander of Army Air Forces in the Pacific, and nine other officers and men reported missing on an trans-ocean flight.

The announcement that General Harmon's plane was overdue and that the search had been ordered was made here by Lieutenant General Robert C. Richardson, Jr., Army commander of the Pacific Ocean Areas.

FUEL AMPLE, WEATHER GOOD

No information was given as to time or place, but it was disclosed that the last message heard from the converted bomber used by General Harmon was a radio report saying the plane had plenty of fuel and was traveling in good weather over calm seas.

The others aboard were:

Brigadier General James R. Andersen, of Washington, D. C., General Harmon's chief of staff.

Colonel William Ball, of Washington, D. C., executive officer for the deputy commander of operations, Army Air Forces, Pacific Ocean Areas.

Major Francis E. Savage, of Tioga, Tex., pilot.

Major Archibald D. Anderson, of Brookings, S. D., navigator.

Lieutenant Jack M. West, of Chicago, co-pilot.

Master Sergeant Douglas Anderson, of La Center, Wash., engineer.

Technical Sergeant Steve Geist, of Brooklyn, N. Y., radio operator.

Private First Class Arthur Oscar, of Kansas City, Mo., assistant engineer.

Technical Sergeant McInerney (first name and home not available) was a passenger.

General Harmon, 57, a native of San Francisco, also is a deputy commander of the 20th Air Force, operating the B-29 raids against Japan.

DEPUTY OF B-29 FORCE

The search recalled one made in 1942 south of Hawaii for Captain Eddie Rickenbacker, whose plane was forced down in the sea while he was on a tour of the war fronts as a representative of the War Department. He and most of the plane's crew were rescued from rafts after being lost three weeks.

(Official U. S. Navy Photo by Acme Telephoto)

TOKIO PLANT BURNS AFTER NAVAL PLANE RAID

The huge Tachikawa engine plant in Tokio pictured while fires burned fiercely after the buildings had been bombed by planes sent up from U. S. Navy carriers.

Fleet Rips Jap Outpost Isle After Planes Blast Ryukyus

Continued From First Page

stretching across a 275-mile north-south arc, the fleet steamed southeast to batter Okino Daito under the cover of darkness.

The carrier planes, in their third major strike in two weeks, swept from Amami O Shima, 225 miles south of the big Kyushu naval base of Kagoshima, southward through Toku No Shima, Okinoerabu, Okinawa, Minami Daito and Kume.

FOLLOWS HACHIJO RAID

The attacks were made in an area 800 miles southwest of Tokio three days after the same fleet had finished battering the island of Hachijo, just south of Tokio, on Monday.

The carrier planes caught the Japanese by surprise. Only four enemy planes were shot down, and they were bombers or reconnaissance planes which just happened along.

Admiral Nimitz announced that 37 planes definitely were destroyed on the ground and about 50 destroyed or damaged, some of which may have been incapable of flight.

SHIPPING TOLL LISTED

The shipping toll was:

Sunk: One destroyer; one motor torpedo boat; six small cargo craft; two medium cargo craft; one ocean-going tug; two luggers—13.

Damaged: Four destroyer escorts or patrol craft; one medium transport; four medium cargo vessels; nine small coastal cargo ships; one small freighter; 10 luggers—29.

Probably Sunk: One medium cargo vessel; six small coastal cargo craft; six luggers—13.

U. S. LOSSES SMALL

American losses in the Ryukyu strike were 13 planes, five pilots and three aircrewmen. Total American losses now are 71 planes.

Admiral Nimitz announced that the planes also damaged airfield installations, barracks, administration buildings, mills, lumber yards, warehouses, radio and radar installations in the six islands and did not encounter any Japanese air opposition. Since such a heavy toll was taken of grounded Japanese air planes, it was speculated that the Japanese either might be hoarding planes or their air force is so depleted it is no longer able to make a substantial defense of the homeland.

The attack was the fourth major one on the Ryukyus by carrier planes. They were hit by Admiral William F. Halsey's Third Fleet on Oct. 10, 1944, and Jan. 3-4-9 and Jan. 22.

KOREA JAPAN CHINA Moppo Nagasaki KYUSHU KAGOSHIMA SHANGHAI AMAMI O SHIMA Kinghsien TOKU NO SHIMA OKINOERABU OKINAWA KUME OKINO DAITO FORMOSA RYUKYU ISLANDS Pacific Ocean PHILIPPINE ISLANDS LUZON MANILA MILES 0 200 400 MAP BY INQUIRER STAFF

FLEET IN ACTION

U. S. Pacific Fleet Thursday night shelled the Jap outpost island of Okino Daito, 460 miles south of Kyushu, after U. S. carrier planes attacked six islands in the Ryukyu group.

War Summary

Sunday, March 4, 1945

WESTERN FRONT—The U. S. Ninth Army yesterday widened its hold on the Rhine to 13 miles, entering Uerdingen, and by forming a juncture with the Canadian First Army between Geldern and Kevelaer trapped big portions of three German armies, to form a solid Allied front west of the river. The Germans blasted all the bridges in the Duesseldorf area. Farther north, the Yanks were within eight miles of the Homberg bridge. Continued reports of Yank patrols crossing the Rhine were unconfirmed. The U. S. First Army drove within four miles of Cologne and within 12 miles of Bonn.

EASTERN FRONT—The Red Army captured the Pomeranian strongholds of Pollnow and Rummelsburg in a drive which Berlin said reached the Baltic Sea, severing all communications between Danzig and the west. Parts of 20 German divisions were believed trapped.

AIR OFFENSIVE — As 850 Allied dive bombers attacked the enemy along the Rhine, 1800 Eighth Air Force planes raided central and southern Germany for the third straight day. The R.A.F. hit Berlin Friday night.

ITALY—Sharp fighting flared up on the Senio River front.

FINLAND — Finland formally declared war on Germany.

JAPAN—A big force of B-29's raided the Tokio area for the 11th time. Pacific Fleet warships shelled Okino Daito island south of the main Jap island of Kyushu, after U. S. carrier planes attacked six islands of the Ryukyu chain.

PACIFIC—U. S. Marines in a 400-yard advance, were within 500 yards of the north end of Iwo Jima. Jap resistance continued heavy.

In the Philippines, U. S. troops seized Ticao and Burias Islands in the Sibuyan Sea. Americans continued to fan out on Palawan Island.

Guerilla's Wife Freed in Manila

Mrs. Gertrude Wilson, wife of Commander Samuel J. Wilson, who led the guerilla fighters after the fall of Manila, was liberated from Santo Tomas prison camp where she had been interned in 1942, her sister-in-law, Miss Katheryn Wilson, of 3106 S. Congress rd., Camden, has been officially notified.

MRS. WILSON

A resident of Manila, Mrs. Wilson and her two sons, Samuel J., Jr., 17, and William, 14, were captured by the Japs soon after their return home from two years in California, where Mrs. Wilson received her naturalization papers. No word has been received of the children.

150 Superforts Smash at Tokio

Continued From First Page

er Command of Major General Curtis E. LeMay.

The tenth B-29 raid on Tokio was staged by more than 200 Superforts.

TOKIO REPORTS ATTACK

By Associated Press

Superfortresses opened an attack on Tokio and surrounding areas at 7:30 A. M. today (Japanese time) the Tokio radio said, and more than an hour later the raid was continuing.

"Our air forces are presently in the process of enemy interception," said the Tokio broadcast, recorded by the Federal Communications Commission.

The raid occurred one week to a day after more than 200 B-29's burned out 240 city blocks in the heart of Tokio, including business and factory sections.

The enemy said targets of today's attack included the Kanto area, comprising the Tokio-Yokohama metropolitan sector.

TOKIO AREA IS TARGET

The broadcast, beamed in English to the United States, charged the Superforts were "carrying out indiscriminate bombings at various points."

The Tokio area, south of the Kanto, including the industrial cities of Nagoya and Shizuoka, also was specified as a target.

The enemy announcer said the big bombers appeared in "formations comprised of two to 10 planes."

The raids of the B-29's now are aided by the Marine invasion of Iwo Island, 750 miles south of Tokio, thus blotting out what had been a warning station for the enemy.

Last Sunday's raid, made at a time when the Marine invasion of Iwo was a week old, was one of the most effective to date on Tokio.

The bombardiers strung out their explosives from a point just east of the Emperor's Palace all the way to the waterfront. They bombed by instrument because of a snowstorm.

MacArthur to Broadcast

NEW YORK, March 3 (A. P.).—N. B. C. announced tonight that General Douglas MacArthur would be heard from Corregidor on the Army Hour program Sunday between 3:30 and 4:30 P. M., Eastern War Time.

2 Phila. Airmen Saved After B-29 Explodes

Continued From First Page

area for five hours while picking up five of the men, while the submarine rescued the remaining four. Neither rescue crew knew of the other's action until the next day.

ENGINE WAS SHOT OUT

The Catalina was sent out by the Eastern Air Command in India after it had picked up the B-29's distress signal, and it reached the vicinity in time to rescue the group containing Sergeant Peleckis.

The Superfortress ran into difficulty over Singapore, according to crew members, when a Jap fighter plane shot out one of its engines and set fire to a wing. A few minutes later the enemy plane made a second pass at the crippled giant, destroying its hydraulic system.

Two more fires broke out, but the plane kept flying for three hours before Captain James E. Lyons, of Stockton, Calif., the pilot, ordered his crew to bail out.

EMPLOYED AS SHIPFITTER

Lieutenant Teplick entered the Army in April, 1941, and, according to his mother, was in the first Superfortress group sent overseas. Before his induction he was a partner in a firm manufacturing men's clothing at 321 Marketst.

Sergeant Peleckis, a graduate of Northeast Catholic High School in 1941, was employed as a shipfitter at the Cramp Shipbuilding Co. before entering the service.

Phila. Lieutenant Wins Silver Star

First Lieutenant Jay D. Boone, son of Mr. and Mrs. Thomas S. Boone, Jr., of 123 Gay st., has been awarded the Silver Star for gallantry in action with an infantry unit in Italy.

LIEUT. RAY D. BOONE

According to the citation, he led his platoon in two assaults on enemy positions near Casoni, Italy, on Oct. 7, 1944, and took both positions after a "fierce three - hour battle."

A graduate of Admiral Farragut Academy in Toms River, N. J., Lieutenant Boone attended Lafayette College, where he was a member of the R.O.T.C. He entered the Army as a second lieutenant about five years ago. He has been overseas 18 months. His wife, Josephine, and two-year-old twins, a boy and a girl, live in Phillipsburg, N. J.

Yungsin Retaken In Chinese Drive

CHUNGKING, March 3 (A. P.).—Chinese troops surging forward from three directions have recaptured Yungsin, 120 miles east of Hengyang, and severed Japanese contact with the Kwangsi province cities of Suichwan and Wanhsien, the Chinese High Command announced tonight.

Yungsin fell on March 1 before a Chinese counter-attack launched at dawn the day before. Defeated Japanese troops escaped through the South Gate and were being pursued by the Chinese.

The High Command also announced that Chinese troops had reoccupied Lienhwa, 30 miles farther east.

Consent Required For Recruits of 17

A 17-year-old youth who desires to enlist in the Marines must have the consent of both parents, if they are living, the U. S. Marine Corps recruiting office emphasized yesterday.

If it is impossible to obtain the mother's signature on the enlistment papers, the father's name will be sufficient. In any case, the father's consent is mandatory, it was pointed out.

The Philadelphia Inquirer

PUBLIC LEDGER

An Independent Newspaper for All the People

FINAL CITY EDITION

CIRCULATION: March Average: Daily 530,157; Sunday 1,106,619 — FRIDAY MORNING, APRIL 13, 1945 — THREE CENTS

ROOSEVELT DEAD

Succumbs to Stroke at 63; Truman Takes Oath as President

Organized Fighting in Reich Over in Few Days, Army Says

By WILLIAM C. MURPHY, JR., Inquirer Washington Bureau

WASHINGTON, April 12.—President Franklin Delano Roosevelt died today and Vice President Harry S. Truman succeeded to the office of Chief Executive and Commander-in-Chief of the armed forces of the Nation at war. The President died in the "Little White House" at Warm Springs, Ga., at 4.35 P. M. (E.W.T.) of a cerebral hemorrhage.

Formal announcement of the passing of the President was made by White House Secretary Stephen T. Early shortly before 6 P. M.

Vice President Truman was immediately summoned to the White House by Mrs. Roosevelt. He convoked the Cabinet within a few minutes after his arrival. Shortly afterward Chief Justice Harlan Fiske Stone arrived at the White House, and Mr. Truman was sworn in by the Chief Justice at 7.08 o'clock tonight.

ASKS CABINET AIDES TO KEEP POSTS

President Truman's first official act was to request members of the Cabinet to remain in their present offices. An hour later Mr. Truman issued a brief statement assuring the world that the United States would prosecute the war on all fronts.

"The world may be sure that we will prosecute the war on both fronts, east and west, with all the vigor we possess to a successful conclusion," he said.

Mr. Roosevelt, 63, had completed a record-breaking tenure of more than 12 years in the White House when he died—slightly more than five months after he had been elected for another record-breaking fourth term.

In accordance with the Constitution, Mr. Truman will serve as President until Jan. 20, 1949. No provision exists for filling the Vice Presidential office meanwhile.

COMPLAINS OF 'TERRIFIC HEADACHE'

Death came to the President at his Warm Springs, Ga., cottage atop Pine Mountain. He was reading official papers which had been sent to him from Washington, and an artist was sketching him as he worked.

"I have a terrific headache," the President remarked suddenly. Those were his last words. He fainted and did not regain consciousness.

Two attendants carried him to the small bedroom just to the left of the entrance to the Little White House.

Tonight messages were speeding to the President's four sons in the armed services. The messages were signed "mother" and informed her sons that the President had "slept away," that he had done his duty to the end.

WHITE HOUSE FUNERAL SATURDAY

The funeral will be held at 4 P. M. Saturday in the East Room of the White House. Burial will be at the Roosevelt ancestral home at Hyde Park, N. Y., Sunday. The body will not lie in state.

Meanwhile, Washington was struggling with the terrific international and governmental implications of the passing of a President and Commander-in-Chief while the Nation was waging global war and preparing for the establishment of a new world order to insure future peace.

There was no expectation that the change in the Presidency would bring any change in the top military direction of the war. It is known that Mr. Truman has every confidence in General of the Armies George C. Marshall, the Army Chief of Staff; and in Admiral of the Fleet Ernest J. King, Commander-in-

Continued on Page 2, Column 2

A complete sketch and pictorial history of the late President on Pages 3, 4, 5 and 6. Other

PRESIDENT HARRY S. TRUMAN

A recent, formal portrait of Vice President Harry S. Truman, who became 32d President of the United States yesterday after the death of President Roosevelt.

THE LATE PRESIDENT ROOSEVELT IN HIS FAMILIAR CAPE

One of the most recent pictures of the late President Franklin D. Roosevelt showing him wearing his favorite cape that saw him through Presidential campaigns and conferences abroad. The photo was taken after his return from the Yalta parley.

End of War Is Imminent, Senators Told

WASHINGTON, April 12 (A. P.).—High Army officials told Senators today the end of organized fighting in Germany probably will come within a few days.

Describing the pell-mell dash of American armies across Germany, General Staff officers expressed the opinion to members of the Senate Military Committee that a collapse of Nazi arms is imminent.

ORDERS PREPARED

Those who attended the conference said the Army chiefs said:

Only pockets of resistance will remain to be cleaned up after this collapse.

They feel so sure of results that orders have been drawn drastically reducing the shipments of durable equipment to Europe in preparation for reversing the flow toward the Pacific.

HOPE TO SEIZE HITLER

They hope that Hitler and his Nazi leaders will be captured, although they did not discount the possibility of escape by some.

In a review of problems developing with the imminent shift of major war activity to the fight against Japan, the Senators also were told by General Brehon B. Somervell, chief of the Army's Service of Supplies, and other military leaders that the Nation again is scraping the bottom of the barrel on steel.

NEW CRISIS IN STEEL

This new crisis in steel production has developed, it was disclosed, because of the increased weight of bombs, plus needs for heavy equipment in the Pacific.

The civilian pinch in the Pacific war will be felt primarily in steel, cotton goods and shoes, the Senators heard. Steel lack may hamper the reconversion of the auto industry. Cotton is needed for lightweight uniforms. Shoes rot fast in the Pacific fighting areas. Civilians may be cut to one pair a year.

THREE-WAY TRAIL

Plans have been worked out, the Senators were told, for a three-way trail of men and supplies from Europe to the Pacific. Some will go direct to the Orient. Some will come back to the United States and then go to the Pacific. Some will go direct from this country to the Japanese war zone.

The legislators were informed that the Army intends to adhere rigidly to a point system in deciding which of the fighting men in Europe shall

Continued on Page 9, Column 8

England to Stop Draft of All Over 30

LONDON, April 12 (A. P.).—Britain plans to discontinue conscription of men of 31 years and older for the armed forces after May 1 except where there is a need for specialists or other special factors, Labor Minister Ernest Bevin announced today.

With the same exceptions, conscription of men and women for war jobs under Britain's national service law also will be discontinued, Mr. Bevins told Commons. No British women have been called up for a considerable time.

THE WEATHER

Philadelphia and vicinity: Mostly cloudy and mild today. Fair and

U. S. 9th Reported Near Suburbs of Berlin

Map on Page 9

By AUSTIN BEALMEAR

PARIS, April 13 (Friday) (A. P.).—U. S. Ninth Army tanks smashed across the Elbe River on a six-mile front just 57 miles from Berlin yesterday and U. S. First and Third Armies in sweeps of nearly 50 miles thundered at the gates of the great city of Leipzig, 75 miles southwest of the capital.

A field dispatch said only orders from Lieutenant General William H. Simpson were needed to send the Second Armored Division dashing on into Berlin, which could possibly be reached today.

REPORTED NEAR SUBURBS

(United Press dispatches reported Ninth Army tank columns were approaching the suburban area of Berlin. One semi-official account placed the Yanks within 49 miles of the Reich capital.)

Wholly unconfirmed French reports said Allied parachute troops had been dropped at Brandenburg, barely 20 miles from greater Berlin.

The electrifying crossing of the

Continued on Page 9, Column 1

Goebbels Admits Finish Is Near

LONDON, April 12 (A. P.).—Nazi Propaganda Minister Paul Joseph Goebbels declared today that "the war cannot last much longer, in my opinion," a German broadcast said.

In an article in his weekly "Das Reich," Goebbels said, "We have sunk very low."

Although conceding that Germany's enormous "losses of territory in the east, west and south" had brought the nation to a crisis, the propagandist still tried to hold out hope over salvaging something from the Reich's military collapse.

HOPES FOR ALLIED SPLIT

"On the other hand," he said, "our enemies must finish this war quickly or they will stand no chance of winning this to-be-or-not-to-be struggle at all."

Harping his familiar theme that the Allied coalition was tottering, Goebbels said "the alliance can only be kept up because the peoples know

Continued on Page 9, Column 7

LADY, WANT YOUR MAN BACK SOON-

Civilian Bomb Toll 146,742 in Britain

LONDON, April 12 (A. P.).—Britain has suffered 146,742 civilian casualties—60,583 killed and 86,159 injured—from enemy air action since the beginning of the war, the Air Ministry announced tonight.

The figures included 792 killed and

Parley Opening Kept Unchanged

Inquirer Washington Bureau

WASHINGTON, April 12.—The United Nations Security Conference will be held at San Francisco as scheduled, despite the sharp impact of the death of President Roosevelt, it was announced tonight.

President Harry S. Truman, in his first official act after taking the oath of office, authorized the announcement, putting an end to two hours of speculation that the conference would be postponed.

PLANS REVEALED

Secretary of State Edward R. Stettinius, Jr., in a brief statement issued after the Cabinet meeting at which Mr. Truman was sworn in, revealed the plans to go ahead with the conference.

"With the authorization of Presi-

Continued on Page 2, Column 5

Roosevelt's Son Off Okinawa

GUAM, April 13 (Friday) (A. P.).—Word of President Roosevelt's death reached his son, Lieutenant Commander Franklin Roosevelt, Jr., off Okinawa this morning after a suicidal Japanese air attack on American invasion forces.

Young Roosevelt commands a destroyer escort on a screening assignment with the Okinawa force and was on the bridge directing his ship's anti-aircraft fire in a hot battle in which 118 Japanese planes were destroyed.

Another Roosevelt son, Lieutenant John Roosevelt, is supply officer on

'Terrific Headache,' F.D.R.'s Last Words

WARM SPRINGS, Ga., April 12 (A. P.). President Franklin D. Roosevelt's last words were: "I have a terrific headache."

He spoke them to Commander Harold Bruenn, naval physician.

Mr. Roosevelt, 63, was sitting in front of a fireplace in the "Little White House" here atop Pine Mountain when the attack struck him. Dr. Bruenn described it as a massive cerebral hemorrhage.

CARRIED TO BEDROOM

The President's Negro valet, Arthur Prettyman, and a Filipino messboy carried him to his bedroom. He was unconscious at the end. It came without pain.

Dr. Bruenn said he saw the President this morning, and that he was in excellent spirits at 10.30 A. M. (E. W. T.).

"At 2 o'clock," Dr. Bruenn added, "he was sitting in a chair while sketches were being made of him by an artist. He suddenly complained of a very severe occipital headache (back of the head).

"Within a very few minutes he lost consciousness. He was seen by

Continued on Page 2, Column 4

Roosevelt's Death Saddens Pope

ROME, April 13 (Friday) (A. P.). Pope Pius XII received the news of President Roosevelt's death with visible sorrow early today and immediately telegraphed condolences to the President's family and the United States Government.

The news of the President's sudden passing was communicated to the Pontiff in his private quarters

Mrs. Roosevelt Sorry for People

By JOHN C. O'BRIEN

Inquirer Washington Bureau

WASHINGTON, April 12.—Mrs. Eleanor Roosevelt received the news of her husband's death tonight with the fortitude she has always shown in family crises.

Those who know her best were not surprised that her first words after she had been told the sad news by Stephen T. Early, White House secretary, were an expression not of personal grief but of sorrow for the people of the country and the world who had lost a leader.

She was in the sitting room adjoining the President's study on the second floor of the White House when Mr. Early told her the President had "slept away."

She seemed stunned for a moment and then she said quietly:

"I am more sorry for the people

Continued on Page 2, Column 8

Eisenhower Gets The News at Front

PARIS, April 13 (Friday) (U. P.)

The President Who Guided Nation in Peace and War

THE MAN One of the finest camera studies ever made of Franklin D. Roosevelt, only man in U. S. history to become President for four terms. This photo was made on his 60th birthday, Jan. 30, 1942

FIRST TERM Mr. Roosevelt being inaugurated for his first term as President on a cold, gray day, March 4, 1933. Charles Evans Hughes (left), then Chief Justice of the U. S. Supreme Court, is administering the oath. To the right of the President is his oldest son, James, and at the extreme right is Ex-President Herbert C. Hoover, defeated for re-election by an overwhelming majority.

He Was Elected for 4 Terms

Franklin Delano Roosevelt, 63, the Hyde Park squire, is the only man in the Nation's history to be elected President for four terms. He reached the White House after bounding back from an overwhelming defeat for the Vice Presidency in 1920 and from a crippling attack of infantile paralysis a year later. He was elected New York's Governor in 1928 and in 1930, then was inaugurated President on March 4, 1933, during the depression. He galvanized a discouraged people into action with his measures to stabilize domestic economy. His gravest responsibility came with World War II when he set the Nation on the road to victory.

CANDIDATE

Mr. Roosevelt at 38, candidate for the Vice Presidency on the Democratic ticket in 1920. Prior to this, he had served as Undersecretary of the Navy in World War I.

FRIENDS Three close friends and staunch political associates back in 1932 were Mr. Roosevelt, the late Alfred E. Smith (center) and James A. Farley. They are shown in Albany when Mr. Smith nominated Herbert Lehman for Governor of New York and Roosevelt seconded the motion. In later years both Mr. Smith and Mr. Farley became less friendly with President Roosevelt.

SECOND TERM Mr. Roosevelt and John N. Garner acknowledging cheers of the delegates as they were nominated President and Vice President by the Democrats in Philadelphia, June, 1936, for a second term.

HOBBY The President had a wide assortment of hobbies. The most dear to him was his magnificent stamp collection that he seldom neglected even in his busiest days. His most enjoyable evenings were spent keeping his albums in shape. He also loved fishing, but duties limited this sport.

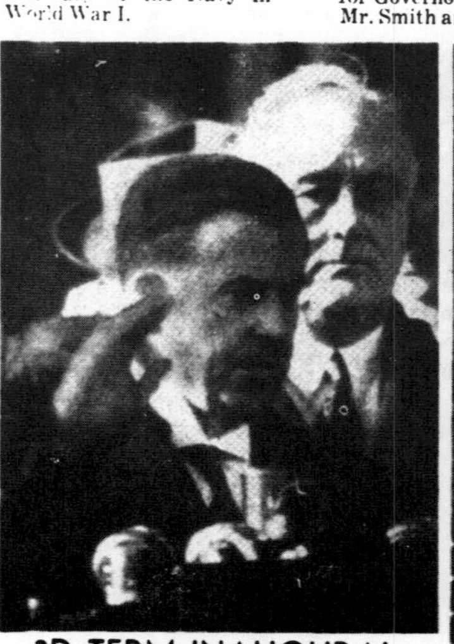

3D TERM INAUGURAL

President Roosevelt watching Henry A. Wallace become Vice President for the first time after Mr. Roosevelt had been sworn in as President for the third time on Jan. 20, 1941.

FOURTH TERM President Roosevelt delivering the briefest of his inaugural addresses after he had become President for the fourth time on Jan. 20, 1945. Others on the porch of the White House include Vice President Harry S. Truman (right) and Colonel James Roosevelt, the President's son.

FAMILY MAN One of the highlights of President Roosevelt's life was the annual gathering of his family for Christmas at Hyde Park. Pictured is one such wartime homecoming. In this group of his children and grandchildren are (left to right) Curtis Boettiger, Lieutenant Franklin D. Roosevelt, Jr., Mrs. Franklin Roosevelt, Jr., holding Christopher, her son; Franklin Roosevelt, 3rd, the President, Ann Boettiger on the floor with her son, John, and Havener, son of John Roosevelt. Standing (left to right) are Eleanor Boettiger, Mrs. John Roosevelt, holding daughter, Ann Sturgis; Mrs. Roosevelt and Lieutenant John Roosevelt. Two sons, James and Elliott, were both on war duty when

Complete Story, Pictures of European War—Pages 2, 3, 4, 5, 6, 7, 8, 9, 10, 11, 12, 18

The Philadelphia Inquirer

PUBLIC LEDGER

An Independent Newspaper for All the People

FINAL
CITY EDITION

CIRCULATION: April Average: Daily 546,961; Sunday 1,104,259

TUESDAY MORNING, MAY 8, 1945
Copyright, 1945, by Triangle Publications, Inc. Vol. 232, No. 128

a b d e f g h

THREE CENTS

NAZIS SURRENDER, END EUROPEAN WAR

LONDON, May 7 (A. P.).—Germany surrendered unconditionally to the Allies today, completing the victory in the European phase of the Second World War—the most devastating in history. Prime Minister Winston Churchill will proclaim the historic conquest at 9 A. M. (Eastern War Time) tomorrow from 10 Downing Street and simultaneous announcements are expected from President Truman in Washington and Premier Josef Stalin in Moscow.

Mr. Churchill then will report directly to Commons and ask for adjournment to Westminster Abbey for a service of thanksgiving.

The whereabouts of such war criminals as Heinrich Himmler, Hermann Goering, even Adolf Hitler himself, although he had been reported dead, were unknown or if they were known they had not been officially announced.

YIELD IN RHEIMS SCHOOLHOUSE

Germany's formal capitulation came at 2.41 A. M. (French time) in the red schoolhouse at Rheims, headquarters of General Dwight D. Eisenhower, Supreme Commander of the Allies of the West.

The crowning triumph came just five years, eight months and six days after Hitler invaded weak but proud Poland and struck the spark which set the world afire.

It marked the official end of the war in Europe, but it did not silence all the guns, for battles raged on in Czechoslovakia.

SCHOERNER DEFIES DOENITZ ORDER

There, Nazi General Ferdinand Schoerner, who has been designated a war criminal, defied the orders of Grand Admiral Karl Doenitz, successor to the dead or missing Hitler, to lay down arms.

But this force—all that remains of what once was the mightiest military machine on earth—faced inevitable liquidation or surrender.

Presumably, the victorious powers soon will label these troops guerilla outlaws, subject to execution unless they yield.

The only details of Germany's ignominious end came from Edward Kennedy, chief of the Associated Press staff on the Western Front, who was the first to flash the word the world had long awaited.

GENERAL JODL SIGNS FOR GERMANY

His story said:

"Germany surrendered unconditionally to the Western Allies and Russia at 0241 (French time) today in the big red Rheims schoolhouse which is the headquarters of General Dwight D. Eisenhower.

"The surrender which brought the war in Europe to a formal end after five years and eight months of bloodshed and destruction was signed for Germany by Colonel General Gustaf (Alfred) Jodl. Jodl is the new chief of staff of the Wehrmacht.

"It was signed for the Supreme Allied Command—the United States and Britain—by Lieutenant Gen-

Continued on Page 2, Column 2

In This Great Hour Let Us Thank God!

[EDITORIAL]

Thank God!

Out of hearts full of rejoicing, there pours today this fervent prayer.

Thank God the war in Europe is ended, our arms have triumphed, the Nazi abomination has been crushed.

Here is the glorious news we have been longing for. Let us receive it exultantly, but prayerfully.

Brave men have died to give us this day; many others may yet die before our other war is won.

Let us not forget them, or their deeds, or the things they fought and died for. Let us not forget the heavy tasks still ahead in carrying the war against Japan to a victorious conclusion.

And let us not fail, in our relief and joy over the collapse of Hitlerism, to offer to Divine Providence our humble thanksgivings.

Thanks be to God!

Joy, Prayer Mingle as City Hails Victory

Gathering slowly at first, and revealing all degrees of emotion from boisterousness to soberness and tearful thanksgiving, a large segment of Philadelphia's two-million-plus population appeared in central-city streets yesterday to hail the victory in Europe.

Word of the Nazi surrender, announced shortly after 9.30 A. M., seemed to spread slowly through this area at the outset, but gained momentum with each passing hour, reaching its climax at lunchtime in the downtown section.

CROWDS FLOCK TO SHRINE

Within a few minutes past noon, tens of thousands milled quietly but excitedly in the vicinity of City Hall, while other thousands flocked to Independence Square, in anticipation of a formal victory celebration there.

But the excitement—tempered to a great extent by the "false" peace report of April 28, Hitler's death, the fall of Berlin and the general knowledge that the Nazi hordes were licked—quickly subsided. The letdown became noticeable shortly after 1 P. M., and pronounced after 2 P. M., when it became known that President Truman probably would not announce V-E Day officially until later.

MAY CELEBRATE TODAY

It was reported, however, that Mayor Bernard Samuel and other city officials—who had been ready at noon to sound the air raid sirens to proclaim the great event officially—were prepared to set off the sirens at 9 A. M. today and stage Philadelphia's formal victory celebration three hours later at Independence Hall.

Service men and women on leave

Continued on Page 12, Column 3

READING OF VICTORY IN SHADOW OF INDEPENDENCE HALL

Independence Hall, shrine of American liberty, looks down on a trio of Philadelphians as they read of the historic victory of Allied arms over Nazi Germany. They are Private First Class John J. Falcone, a Marine who served in the Pacific for 18 months; his sister, Mrs. Daniel Bottler of 1536 Emily st., whose husband has been fighting in Germany and has been overseas for 15 months, and her son, Daniel, Jr.

New Unity Is Achieved At Security Conference

By ALEXANDER KENDRICK
Inquirer San Francisco Bureau

SAN FRANCISCO, May 7.—The end of the war in Europe burst upon the world security conference today in the midst of its labor of organizing the peace, and turned its eyes to the Pacific, where another war is yet to be won.

And, speaking significantly enough in the city which will be the principal mainland base for intensified Allied warfare in the East, Soviet Foreign Commissar Vyacheslav Molotov declared that his powerful and victorious country has "already" expressed its attitude toward Japan by abrogating the Moscow-Tokio neutrality pact last month.

HIGH PRAISE FOR UNANIMITY

Mr. Molotov at the same time bestowed high praise upon the Big Four unanimity achieved at the security conference—unanimity which if continued in the East as hostilities cease in the West will introduce an important new factor in the Pacific conflict.

Big Four agreement has even been

Continued on Page 15, Column 3

All U. S. Forces Gain on Okinawa

GUAM, May 8 (Tuesday) (A. P.).—American troops, scaling steep cliffs with rope ladders and rooting out entrenched Japanese with flame-throwing tanks, pushed ahead all along the tough southern Okinawa line yesterday.

In five weeks' fighting the Yanks have killed 36,535 Japanese, a ratio of 15 for every American slain.

LED BY FLAME-THROWERS

Major General Andrew D. Bruce's 77th Infantry Division, in the rugged central sector, threw flame-throwing tanks against Japanese cave positions before the fortress city of Shuri. The doughboys scaled heights with cargo nets and rope ladders.

Major General Pedro A. Del Valle's First Marine Division, on the

Continued on Page 14, Column 4

No Victory Salute At F. D. R.'s Grave

HYDE PARK, N. Y., May 7 (A. P.).—There was only silence today at the grave of Franklin D. Roosevelt, the President whose pledge of complete victory over Nazi Germany was fulfilled at last.

Soldiers with rifles quietly patrolled the rose garden in which Mr. Roosevelt was buried April 15—three weeks before the unconditional surrender he had demanded and confidently predicted.

The guards smiled when they heard the news, exchanged a few murmured words and resumed their slow pace along the evergreen hedge that surrounds the still unmarked grave.

Yanks Liberate Leopold and Wife

WITH THE U. S. SEVENTH ARMY, May 8 (Tuesday) (A. P.).—Leopold III, King of Belgium, and his wife have been liberated by the U. S. Seventh Army, it was announced today.

The Americans had been told of the whereabouts of the royal party by civilians. With the King and Queen were 18 members of their staff and four children. All were in good health.

Elements of the American 106th Cavalry Group had to overpower German SS (Elite Guard) troops to make the rescue.

TODAY IS B-Day —6

King Felicitates Gen. Eisenhower

LONDON, May 8 (Tuesday) (A. P.).—King George VI today sent a message to General Dwight D. Eisenhower congratulating him and his armies on the "complete and crushing victory" in Europe.

Text of the King's message:

"Eleven months ago you led the Allied Expeditionary Force across the English Channel, carrying with you the hopes and prayers of millions of men and women of many nations.

"To it was entrusted the task of

Continued on Page 2, Column 6

Truman Marks 61st Year Today

WASHINGTON, May 7 (U. P.).—When V-E Day comes tomorrow, it will fall on President's Truman's 61st birthday.

The Chief Executive was born in Lamar, Mo., on May 8, 1884.

Truman to Proclaim V-E Day in 9 A. M. Talk

By WILLIAM C. MURPHY, JR.
Inquirer Washington Bureau

WASHINGTON, May 7.—President Truman will address the Nation by radio at 9 A. M. (E.W.T.) tomorrow, presumably to proclaim complete victory over Germany. Jonathan Daniels, White House Press Secretary, said late this evening that unless "unforeseen developments" cause a change in plans the President "confidently expects to make an announcement to the Nation by radio at 9 o'clock tomorrow morning."

Preceding the radio address, Mr. Daniels said, the President plans to hold a press conference at 8.30 A. M., at which he will give to the press and to radio commentators, in confidence, the text of the statement.

V-E DAY PROCLAMATION

Although Mr. Daniels declined to give a categorical reply when asked whether this was the official announcement that V-E Day would be proclaimed tomorrow, there appeared to be no reason to doubt that

Continued on Page 2, Column 3

Casualties

10 Die in Action, 17 Are Wounded

The War and Navy Department casualty lists released yesterday named 10 Philadelphia area men killed in action, 17 wounded, six missing and two prisoners in the German area.

In case of differences between the following list and messages sent to next of kin, the latest notification to the

Continued on Page 14, Column 5

Bohemia Nazis Yield to Czechs

Map on Page 2

By ROMNEY WHEELER

LONDON, May 8 (Tuesday) (A. P.).—The Czech-controlled Prague radio announced today that the Germans in Prague and throughout Bohemia, a last major holdout pocket of Nazi resistance, had accepted unconditional surrender.

The announcement came as the U. S. Third Army battled to the outskirts of the Czech capital and three Russian armies hammered toward the same goal from the east and north.

LAST BIG NAZI FORCE

"The German military plenipotentiary is negotiating with the Czech National Council on the modalities

Continued on Page 2, Column 5

THE WEATHER

Philadelphia and vicinity: Showers followed by cooler today; partly cloudy and cooler tomorrow.

Full Weather Data on Page 2

Special Victory Features

The Philadelphia Inquirer

PUBLIC LEDGER

An Independent Newspaper for All the People

FINAL CITY EDITION

CIRCULATION: March Average: Daily 530,157; Sunday 1,106,619

WEDNESDAY MORNING, MAY 2, 1945

Copyright, 1945, by Triangle Publications, Inc. Vol. 232, No. 122

a b c d e f 8 B ★★

THREE CENTS

HITLER IS DEAD

Nazi Radio Reports Fuehrer Killed Fighting Russians, Doenitz Takes Over Rule; Resistance Fading in Berlin

By IVAN H. (CY) PETERMAN, *Inquirer War Correspondent*

SOMEWHERE IN GERMANY, May 1 (By Wireless)—Adolf Hitler has been killed fighting the Russians in Berlin, according to a dramatic announcement at 10.27 o'clock tonight (4.27 P.M., E.W.T.) over the Hamburg radio. Admiral Karl Doenitz, chosen by Hitler as his successor, has taken command of the crumbling Reich, the radio added.

"The military struggle continues," said the first proclamation of the new Fuehrer, whose elevation came as a complete surprise. "It is my first task to save Germany from destruction."

The announcement of Hitler's death was preceded by playing of passages from Wagner's "Goetterdaemmerung"—The Twilight of the Gods—interrupted periodically with:

"Achtung! Achtung! An announcement of utmost importance to the German people will soon be made."

REPORTED SLAIN IN CHANCELLERY

Precisely at 10.27 P. M., monitoring radio specialists at Army and other Allied listening posts throughout Europe heard the announcer's voice again:

"It is reported from the Fuehrer's headquarters that our Fuehrer Adolf Hitler, fighting to the last breath against Bolshevism, fell for Germany this afternoon in his operational headquarters in the Reichschancellery.

"On April 30 the Fuehrer appointed Grand Admiral Doenitz his successor. The Grand Admiral and successor of the Fuehrer now speaks to the German people."

Doenitz' speech called for continued resistance to Bolshevism, after citing Hitler's death as closing a lifelong battle against Communism. He conceded the "great responsibility of the hour."

HECKLING PERSISTS THROUGHOUT TALK

Even as the Admiral told of Hitler's dying "a hero's death," a powerful ghost voice interrupted him, shouting, "This is a lie!"

The heckling continued throughout Doenitz' address. When he referred to the Fuehrer as "one of the greatest heroes in German history," the voice added, as if in an aside:

"The greatest of all Fascists!"

Doenitz continued, apparently unaware of the interruptions:

"Filled with proud respect and mourning, we lower the banners before him."

"His death calls upon us to act," the ghost voice challenged. "Strike now!"

CALLS FOR ORDER AND DISCIPLINE

The 53-year-old Admiral, commander of the German Fleet who made his reputation in submarine warfare, pleaded for order and discipline, in towns and countryside alike. He

Continued on Page 2, Column 2

GERMANY'S DEAD FUEHRER AND ADMIRAL DOENITZ, WHO SUCCEEDED HIM

Adolf Hitler, who brought Germany under the control of his Nazi party and then plunged the world into its most terrible war, has been reported by the Germans to have been killed in the Reichschancellery among the ruins of Berlin. Admiral Karl Doenitz (left), commander of the German Fleet, has succeeded him as Germany's ruler.

A full page of Hitler pictures on Page 3; other stories and pictures on Pages 2 and 18, a sketch of his life on Page 4

Von Rundstedt Is Captured by U. S. 7th Army

WITH THE U. S. SEVENTH ARMY, May 2 (Wednesday) (U. P.).—Field Marshal Karl Gerd von Rundstedt, former commander of German troops on the Western Front, has been captured, it was disclosed today.

Map on Page 5

Their leader, Adolf Hitler, reportedly slain in battle, the die-hard defenders of Berlin began laying down their arms yesterday as German resistance in the capital's center neared collapse. The Russians took 14,000 captives and overran 100 blocks in the heart of the city as they drove for the Reichschancellery—where Hitler reportedly died—and the underground fortress in the Tiergarten.

Tanks of the U. S. Third Army meanwhile captured Hitler's birthplace of Braunau, Austria, on the Inn River, after a 25-mile dash across southern Germany.

14,000 Die-Hards Surrender in Berlin; Brandenburg Taken

By ROMNEY WHEELER

LONDON, May 2 (Wednesday) (A. P.)—German resistance in the heart of ruined Berlin neared total collapse today as 14,000 fanatical Nazi die-hards surrendered to the Red Army after reportedly losing their leader, Adolf Hitler.

Moscow's nightly communique announced last night that Soviet troops had overrun more than 100 blocks of buildings in the city's administrative core as they smashed toward the Reichschancellery and the Germans' underground fortress in the Tiergarten.

TWO DISTRICTS CLEARED

The Soviet High Command did not announce the capture of any specific buildings in Berlin's center and it was not known whether the Russians had reached the Reichschancellery, where the Hamburg radio asserted Hitler had died in the afternoon.

Soviet assault troops also cleared the city districts of Charlottenburg and Schoeneberg.

Some days ago the Russians said they believed that Hitler had fled Berlin, probably leaving a double who would die "heroically" and be

Continued on Page 5, Column 1

Patton Army Seizes Hitler's Birthplace In 25-Mile Drive

By ROBERT EUNSON

PARIS, May 2 (Wednesday) (A. P.).—Tanks of the U. S. Third Army, hurtling 25 miles across southern Germany, captured Hitler's birthplace at Braunau on the Inn River in Austria last night, shortly before the German radio announced that the Nazi Fuehrer was dead.

A field dispatch said General George S. Patton, Jr.'s forces had established radio contact with Russian columns pounding westward from Vienna and that the two armies were probably less than 40 miles from a junction which would trap all Germans in Czechoslovakia and isolate Nazi forces in the Alpine redoubt below Munich.

EISENHOWER SILENT

The broadcast report of Hitler's death brought no comment from General Dwight D. Eisenhower, whose several million fighting men had crushed the Nazi foe on the battlefields of France, Belgium, Holland and Germany and broken into the sanctuary of his long-planned southern redoubt.

Military observers here did not overlook the possibility that the dramatic announcement of Hitler's death might be a mask and recalled

Continued on Page 5, Column 5

Graziani Surrenders His Army in North Italy

ROME, May 1 (A. P.).—Marshal Rodolfo Graziani, Fascist commander, announced the unconditional surrender tonight of his Ligurian army as New Zealand units linked up with Jugoslav forces near Trieste at the head of the Adriatic Sea and American units raced for the southern end of the Brenner Pass into Austria.

Graziani told his troops in a broadcast that "the time has arrived when further resistance would be useless and inhuman, and, as far as I am concerned, criminal."

CONFIRMED BY NAZI

Lieutenant General Pemsel, German chief of staff to the Ligurian army, followed Graziani on the air and declared: "I confirm without reserve the words of my commander, Marshal Graziani. You must obey his orders."

Thus the two and a half-year-old Italian campaign was rapidly drawing to a close. Only skirmishes were reported as the Allied troops spread over the northern end of the peninsula to engulf the few knots of German soldiers offering a demoralized resistance.

The bag of prisoners continued to grow, with the British Eighth Army taking 10,000 yesterday and the U. S. First Armored Division rounding up 12,000, including four German major generals.

British troops entered Udine, 33

Continued on Page 5, Column 3

Fierce Fighting Rages in Borneo

MANILA, May 2 (Wednesday) (U. P.).—An official Australian announcement said today that Allied troops had invaded Borneo, world's second largest island, but General Douglas MacArthur's communique reported only that heavy bombers were neutralizing enemy bases and airdromes on the oil-rich island.

Tokio also reported the landings and said they were made off the 10-square-mile Island of Tarakan on the northeast coast, a region rich in oil wells, which the Dutch destroyed before the Japanese captured them in 1942. The enemy broadcast said "fierce fighting" was in progress.

YANKS GAIN ON MINDANAO

General MacArthur announced that on Mindanao Island the 24th Division, in another swift drive, had

Continued on Page 8, Column 3

Pay Tax Repeal Killed by Senate

By JOSEPH H. MILLER

Inquirer Harrisburg Bureau

HARRISBURG, May 2 (Wednesday).—The State Senate Finance Committee early this morning killed a bill repealing Philadelphia's one percent wage tax and another measure exempting non-residents working in the city from payment of the levy.

Action of the committee was taken following a public hearing on the Legislative proposals yesterday at which Mayor Bernard Samuel of Philadelphia, other city officials and civic leaders opposed approval of the bills on the grounds that they would wreck the municipal financial structure and bankrupt the city.

NO SUBSTITUTE PROGRAM

Responsible for the death of the two measures was the fact that proponents of the tax repealers failed to present a concrete program of substitute revenue-raisers so the city could carry on its normal functions. Both measures had previously been passed by the House.

Leading the fight for enactment of the House-approved proposals were State Representative Benjamin F. James (R., Delaware), sponsor of the measure exempting

Continued on Page 14, Column 4

Adequate Diet Assured In U.S. Despite War Aid

By HUGH MORROW

Inquirer Washington Bureau

WASHINGTON, May 1.—High Government authorities are doing their best to put Americans on notice that they must expect to tighten their belts this year so that Europe will not starve.

What does this mean? Whom are we feeding and planning to feed? Why? How much? What will America have left? Will Americans go hungry?

ADEQUATE DIET PLEDGED

These questions naturally arise. And these are the questions which The Inquirer asked today of Government officials most intimately concerned with the food problem. Herein it is hoped to give the answers.

At the outset, it is emphasized that by "tightening our belts," no one in Washington is thinking of impairing the American standard of nutrition. Americans will continue to have adequate nourishment. They may not get the variety of foods to which they are accustomed, but even then the bill of fare will be nothing even remotely approaching the gastronomical monotony which the British have endured through five and one-half years of war.

In broad statistics—and Washing-

Continued on Page 12, Column 3

Casualties

22 Die in Action, 38 Are Wounded

War and Navy Department casualty lists yesterday named 19 men from the Philadelphia area killed in action, 38 wounded, seven missing and eight prisoners of the Germans.

In addition, official notification to their families disclosed the deaths of three others, increasing the number of killed to 22.

Major Victor J. Maleski, a 25-year-old field artillery officer serving with the Ninth Army, was killed in action in Germany, according to word received by his wife, Marjorie, of 30 Lodges lane, Cynwyd.

Major Maleski who had been

Continued on Page 8, Column 2

Security Parley Appoints Boards

Illustrated on Page 18

By ALEXANDER KENDRICK

Inquirer San Francisco Bureau

SAN FRANCISCO, May 1.—The World Security Conference finally organized itself into commissions today and buckled down to the task of writing a new international charter, with Big Four harmony apparently well restored.

Fundamental differences among the sponsoring great powers, which had made themselves apparent in the deadlock over the conference presidency and in yesterday's heated debate over the admission of Argentina, have been sufficiently ironed out by the Big Four Foreign Ministers to give the go-ahead signal to the security session, it was learned.

As a result the following developments today marked the conference progress:

1. In commission assignments, Norway, which had yesterday aligned itself with Russia on

Continued on Page 10, Column 3

THE WEATHER

Philadelphia and vicinity: Fair with slowly rising temperature today and tomorrow.

Full Weather Data on Page 3

Promotion of Doenitz Puzzles U.S. Army

By JOHN M. McCULLOUGH

Inquirer Washington Bureau

WASHINGTON, May 1.—The reported promotion of Grand Admiral Karl Doenitz, 53-year-old Wuerttemburger, to the post of commander-in-chief of German armed forces and Reich chancellor by Adolf Hitler's dying direction came as a total surprise to War Department sources here.

The first reaction, following surprise, was that much more of the circumstances of Doenitz' succession should be known before any positive conclusions could be drawn.

However, these possibilities suggest themselves as the most logical consequences:

1. A shift in the center of gravity of Germany's [illegible]

Continued on Page 2, Column 4

Shakespeare Line Applied to Hitler

By United Press

The B. B. C., commenting on the reported death of Adolf Hitler, read a line [illegible] from the last scene of William Shakespeare's Richard III:

[illegible] "The bloody dog is dead."

Adolf Hitler: He Plunged the World Into War

MUNICH Adolf Hitler, the Austrian paperhanger who rose to control Germany and for a time most of Europe, shown at the moment of his greatest diplomatic triumph, Sept. 9, 1938, in Munich, where he forced England and France to abandon much of Czechoslovakia to him on the threat of war. Participating in that appeasement of the Axis, which did not prevent war a year later, were (left to right) Neville Chamberlain, Prime Minister of Great Britain; Edouard Daladier, the French Premier; Hitler and Benito Mussolini. Prior to Munich, Hitler, who was born in Braunau, Austria, April 20, 1889, had taken control of Germany, had occupied and remilitarized the Rhineland and had seized Austria without Europe's democratic nations raising a hand to stop him. Mr. Chamberlain, Hitler and Mussolini are now dead. M. Daladier is a Nazi prisoner.

BOTH DEAD NOW Hitler and his junior partner, Benito Mussolini, riding through the streets of Rome in 1938 when the Axis was enjoying its heyday. The wheel of fortune has turned with Hitler dead a few days after Mussolini was executed by Italian patriots. The former Duce's body was hung in a Milan square for his countrymen to abuse and revile.

BLUNDER

One of Hitler's most colossal blunders was his sudden attack on Russia, June 21, 1941. To add to the gravity of his decision, Hitler planned much of the strategy which led to such a disaster to the German arms as Stalingrad. The Nazi leader is shown on the Russian front.

POLITICIAN Hitler wearing the uniform of his brownshirted followers during a harangue before he seized control of Germany in 1933. The violence of his oratory was matched only by the fists of his strong-arm squads.

TRIUMPH Hitler, in the conqueror's role, striding along the streets of Paris with the familiar Eiffel Tower looming up behind him. His visit to Paris, after France was forced to ask for an armistice June 22, 1940, marked the end of one of the fastest conquests of a major nation in history. His armies were victorious after only 39 days of battle. Hitler and his ally, Italy, were then opposed only by England, whose fall Der Fuehrer confidently expected within a short time as he made his Paris visit. At Paris, Hitler was at his military peak.

ANNEXATION Hitler riding in triumph through the gaily decorated streets of Vienna on the eve of the plebiscite in which Austrians voted to be included in the "Greater German Reich." The voting was held April 9, 1938—a month after Nazi troops occupied the country.

CHANCELLOR Hitler seated with Paul von Hindenburg, then President of the Reich, after von Hindenburg had named him Reich Chancellor on Jan. 30, 1933. Two months later Hitler seized entire power over Germany and forced the Reichstag to proclaim him dictator.

The Philadelphia Inquirer

PUBLIC LEDGER

An Independent Newspaper for All the People

FINAL CITY EDITION

CIRCULATION: March Average: Daily 530,157; Sunday 1,106,649

MONDAY MORNING, APRIL 30, 1945

Copyright, 1945, by Triangle Publications, Inc. Vol. 232, No. 120

abdefgh

THREE CENTS

Mussolini Slain by Italian Patriots

Munich Captured by U. S. 7th Army

Today

How to Handle Nazis
Russians' System
Mailed Fist Tactics
Lend-Lease Praised
Secretive on Arms

—By Ivan H. Peterman—

Inquirer War Correspondent

By Wireless

Copyright, 1945, The Philadelphia Inquirer

TORGAU, Germany, April 29.

LIFE is real and rugged, and there is no red tape or lost time for ceremony on this rolling Russian front line where fraternization is more or less up to the Red Army man himself, I have discovered after visiting an advanced element of the Russian Army and listening to Soviet soldiers, officers and three top war correspondents these last few days.

While the American military people are inclined to kid-glove the conquered and conduct themselves as if they are afraid they will be handed the bill for damages, Russians take what they like, frighten the German civilian out of his boots and live, in a large degree, off the land.

Once the Cossack vanguards whip, on horseback, through a village street firing pistols and carbines and yelling at the top of their lungs, there is little need for a whole lot of military government.

The Russians call on the burgomeister, or a reasonable facsimile thereof, tell him what's cooking and go their way. If it is not done on the dot, there is room for no burgomeister until the job is done.

This matter of fraternization is typical. If a Russian has the inclination to talk with the Germans he can talk. If they get tough he shoots them. If he wants food or drink, they bring it or it is just too bad. A short blast from a Russian's tommy gun gets almost anything in Torgau.

An American sergeant told me that he was appalled when one Kraut began to argue, as per custom, with Russian troops and was liquidated where he stood.

So was a drunken Russian doughboy who refused to surrender his weapon to a superior officer. Upon obtaining possession, the officer pulled his pistol and with a well-placed bullet precluded the need of a court-martial.

Captured German towns are fairly beaten up, Allied prisoners filtering through our front report. Some of our people who got several miles behind the Russian lines said some places were quiet and deserted as though the residents had moved out or were in hiding.

The German dead, soldiers and civilians alike, are left lying long after the Russian casual-

Continued on Page 4, Column 3

Patton Liberates 27,000 Captives In German Camp

Map on Page 2

By ROBERT EUNSON

PARIS, April 30 (Monday) (A. P.).—Tanks and infantry of the U. S. Seventh Army took over Munich last night, meeting practically no opposition as they rolled into the birthplace of Nazism.

The entire city of 825,000 was not completely occupied by the American troops but front line dispatches said that lack of opposition indicated it was as good as captured.

General George S. Patton, Jr's., U. S. Third Army tanks dashing northeast of Munich liberated 27,000 Allied prisoners of war, mostly American airmen, at Moosburg. It was one of the largest if not the largest group yet liberated on the Western Front.

The final battles in Europe raged on unabated as General Dwight D. Eisenhower announced he knew nothing of an unconditional surrender offer from Germany or of any peace negotiations.

125,000 NAZIS YIELD

More than 125,000 German soldiers have surrendered in the past 48 hours to American, British and French troops, Allied Headquarters announced.

The British Second Army crossed the Elbe and captured Lauenberg 20 miles east of Hamburg. The U. S. Ninth Army lashed out from its own bridgehead in another blow at what remains of Nazi Germany in the north.

The Canadian First Army in a surprise crossing of the Ems River drove north to within seven miles of the German North Sea port of Emden.

ENTERED ON 3 SIDES

The 42d Infantry Division raced into the city first from the north, using a broad military highway. Then the 12th Armored Division hit Munich from the southwest, and the new 20th Armored Division—disclosed for the first time to be in action, roared in from the west.

These outfits had traveled at least 20 miles to reach this city where in 1938 the statesmen of France

Continued on Page 2, Column 6

Nazi Remnants Trapped by Reds In Berlin Center

LONDON, April 30 (Monday) (U. P.).—The Red Army jammed Berlin's suicide garrison into a 10-square-mile area around the Tiergarten and Unter den Linden yesterday after capturing 177 blocks of the inner city, including the ruined Anhalter station and the notorious Moabit prison.

Moscow dispatches said that Marshal Gregory K. Zhukov's vengeful veterans of Stalingrad already had broken across the Landwehr Canal on the southwestern edge of the Tiergarten and were fighting their way through a maze of sunken forts and casemented hillocks in Berlin's central park.

40,000 SEIZED IN POCKET

German broadcasts said the Russians had broken through to the Lustgarten court yard fronting the Royal Palace, the Berlin Cathedral and the old Museum at the eastern end of the Unter den Linden.

The Battle of Berlin entered its waning hours with approximately 156,000 Germans killed or captured in a desperate but futile defense of the city. More than 40,000 were captured Saturday and yesterday alone in a pocket southeast of Berlin which was all but eliminated, and 11,000 others gave up inside the city.

While his first White Russian Army mopped up Berlin in co-ordi-

Continued on Page 2, Column 7

Moscow Will End Blackout Today

MOSCOW, April 29 (U.P.).—After a four-year blackout, this city's lights will be turned on again beginning tomorrow—one of the numerous events marking the final days of the European war.

Moscow is being rapidly garbed in red b[illegible]ting and victory posters, in preparation for the May Day celebration.

Reds Report Wave Of Berlin Suicides

MOSCOW, April 29 (A. P.).—Izvestia said today that waves of suicides, including many of the elite Hitler guards, were sweeping Berlin.

Another dispatch said the Nazis, in an effort to combat mounting desertion among the city's defenders, had ordered wheels removed from every private automobile.

"We found in many courtyards this morning many automobiles in good order but minus their wheels," said Izvestia correspondents Bratya Tur and Lef Sheinin. "In some districts there were great stacks of these wheels only just removed."

SLAIN EX-DICTATOR AND HIS SWEETHEART

Benito Mussolini and his sweetheart, Claretta Petacci, who was executed Saturday with 16 other Fascists. The bodies of the former dictator of Italy and his followers were placed on exhibition before a huge crowd in a public square in Milan. Mussolini and the young woman were executed Saturday at Lake Como, near Milan.

16 Top Fascists, Sweetheart of Ex-Ruler Killed

A picture story of the rise and fall of Benito Mussolini on Page 10, with a sketch of his life on Page 2.

By JAMES E. ROPER

MILAN, April 29 (U. P.).—Italian patriots executed Benito Mussolini yesterday, and today a howling mob is kicking and spitting on his remains lying in the center of this city where Italian Fascism was born.

Mussolini's face wears a disdainful snarl. He died shouting "No! No!" to a firing squad which took his life, and that of his mistress, Claretta Petacci, near the village of Dongo on Lake Como at 4.10 P. M.

The body was taken by truck to Milan and dumped in the city's square.

(An Allied Headquarters announcement in Rome said the executions had taken place in the town of Guliano di Mezzegere near Como and that the bodies were placed on display in the Piazza Quindici Martiri (Fifteen Martyrs Square), formerly the Piazza Loreto, where 15 patriots were executed by Fascists a year ago.)

MOB OF 5000 SETS ON CORPSES IN MILAN

A bullet penetrated Mussolini's bald head through the left forehead and passed entirely through it. The man who took Fascist Italy into the war lay dead in the filth of a dirt plot in the center of Milan.

Along with Mussolini and his mistress, the patriots killed 16 other Fascists, many of them members of his Cabinet.

The bodies of all were brought to Milan, which American Fifth Army troops entered today. A mob of over 5000 persons immediately set upon the corpses, marking the final end to the Fascism which carried Italy to its doom.

All bodies were strewn about a small area. A few patriot guards tried to hold the crowds back, but the guards were shoved back so that they stepped on the bodies.

While I was examining the remains today, the crowd surged forward and almost shoved me atop the body. Partisan guards began firing into the air and some semblance of control was regained.

REJOINED EX-DUCE AFTER NAZIS FREED HIM

Early in the morning, when the bodies were dumped into the square, Mussolini's head had rested on the breast of his dead mistress. Her body had several bullet holes in the chest. Bloodstains showed crimson on her dainty white blouse with lace ruffles, which miraculously had escaped most of the muck and filth.

Her dark, curly hair had been dragged in the wet soil.

The Petacci woman was about 25 years old. Mussolini was 61. She was the daughter of a Rome doctor. Mussolini met her on a beach in 1939 and built a large villa for her outside Rome. She was arrested after Mussolini was ousted as Premier in July, 1943, but the Germans rescued her and she joined Mussolini in northern Italy.

(News of Mussolini's execution was received with grim satisfaction in Rome, where Claretta Petacci was described

Continued on Page 2, Column 2

Rumors of Surrender Of Germany Persist

By WILLIAM C. MURPHY, JR.

Inquirer Washington Bureau

WASHINGTON, April 29.—Washington this evening was still seething with the after-effects of last night's premature celebration of the reported surrender of Germany—a celebration halted abruptly when President Truman personally denied that there was any foundation for the rumor.

Reports from widely scattered sources, however, combined today to give the impression that, despite last night's denial, the official collapse of organized resistance in Europe could not be more than a matter of days—perhaps of hours—away.

And a new crop of surrender rumors sprouted today when the President, after attending church services this morning, paid a Sunday visit to his offices in the west wing of the White House, where he was joined by Admiral William D. Leahy, Chief of Staff to the Commander-in-Chief.

A BINGE OF RUMORS

Jonathan Daniels, White House press secretary, and his assistant, Eben Ayres, as well as a few members of the clerical staff, were also in the executive offices—leading to the impression that an important announcement might be forthcoming.

This particular crop of rumors subsided for the time being when the President, after spending about 25 minutes in the executive offices, returned across Pennsylvania ave. to the Blair House, his temporary living quarters while the White House living apartments are being redecorated.

What has turned out to be Washington's greatest binge of rumor-mongering started last Wednesday, April 25, when the President paid an unscheduled and, apparently, unexpected visit to Army headquarters in the sprawling Pentagon Building across the Potomac.

The President spent about an hour

Continued on Page 12, Column 2

Casualties

11 Killed, 34 Hurt, 14 Are Missing

War and Navy Department casualty lists released yesterday named 11 men from the Philadelphia area killed in action, 33 wounded, 14 missing and 17 prisoners of war of the Germans.

One other service man was reported wounded in an official notification to his parents, bringing the number of wounded to 34.

The notification stated that Private Leon Lyman, 24, son of Mr. and Mrs. Ernest Lyman, of 1003 N. 43d st., was wounded in March in the fighting on Okinawa. A brother, Signalman Second Class Albert Lyman, is serving in the Navy.

IN ARMY SINCE 1942

Private Lyman, a former employe of Sears Roebuck & Co., entered the Army in October, 1942, and was sent overseas in February, 1944.

(In case of differences between this list and messages sent to next of kin, the latest

Continued on Page 6, Column 3

Prison Horrors Of Nazis Detailed

By JOHN M. McCULLOUGH

Inquirer Washington Bureau

WASHINGTON, April 29.—Nazi concentration camps such as that at Buchenwald, a short distance from Weimar, were employed systematically as "extermination factories" for "many tens of thousands of the best leadership personnel of Europe."

That statement is made in a formal report prepared by United States Army officers for Supreme Headquarters Allied Expeditionary Forces.

BOARD PREPARED REPORT

The report, released by the War Department today, was prepared by a commission headed by Brigadier General Eric Fisher Wood, former chairman of the Pennsylvania Republican State Executive Committee and well-known Pittsburgh architect.

In terse, unemotional phrases, the 3000-word report confirms in every detail the horror of the infamous camp liberated by American troops, including the systematic strangling, clubbing and incineration of helpless civilians.

Buchenwald, Dachau, Kleine

Continued on Page 3, Column 3

Reds Offer Deal to Seat Both Poland, Argentina

SAN FRANCISCO, April 29 (A. P.).—Russia has revived the Polish problem before the United Nations conference, it was learned today, insisting anew that the Soviet-recognized Provisional Government in Warsaw be invited to send delegates and confronting the conference with another deadlock.

Soviet Foreign Commissar Vyacheslav M. Molotov has agreed to admit Argentina to the World Security sessions, it was learned, but made his acceptance conditional on an invitation to Poland.

The United States and Britain are understood to oppose firmly admitting the Polish Government as now constituted.

BIG FOUR CONFER

The United States position is that the Polish and Argentine problems are not connected, and that if a majority of the 46 United Nations delegations wish to invite Argentina, they may do so—without Soviet approval.

The question of inviting Poland came up again last night when the Big Four Foreign Ministers—Edward R. Stettinius, Jr., of the United

Continued on Page 12, Column 6

Communists Lead French Elections

PARIS, April 29 (A. P.). — Communist candidates for municipal office in Paris held a commanding lead on the basis of nearly complete returns from today's first election in France since the country fell to the Germans.

Election returns from other French metropolitan centers indicated their voters, too, had supported candidates of the leftist parties in contests for municipal offices, the only ones at stake in today's voting.

Edouard Herriot, former president of the Chamber of Deputies, who has just reached Switzerland from a German prison camp, was elected to the municipal council of Lyons by a four-to-one margin.

Austria Forms New Government

MOSCOW, April 29 (A. P.).—Austria, swallowed by Germany seven years ago as the first pawn of Nazi expansion, formed a new provisional government in Vienna Saturday under Dr. Karl Renner, a Social Democrat, as Chancellor and Foreign Minister.

DR. KARL RENNER

Dr. Renner, who is 75, was chancellor in 1919-20, and author of the constitution of the Austrian Republic. He strongly opposed Communism in Austria after the last war, and his policies are criticized in a Soviet encyclopedia published in 1941.

The coalition government intends "to restore an independent Austrian Republic," and was formed accord-

Continued on Page 2, Column 7

Superforts Blast Air Base at Tokio

GUAM, April 30 (Monday) (A. P.).—More than 100 Superfortresses today attacked the Tachikawa army air arsenal, 24 miles west of Tokio, while six small fleets of B-29's showered bombs on airfields at Kyushu, southernmost of the Japanese home islands.

Tachikawa arsenal, actually an air depot, borders the Tachikawa airfield and covers about 460 acres. It is near the Hitachi aircraft plant, which was blasted by B-29's Tuesday in the last previous flight to Honshu island.

The raids on Kyushu put that island under Superfortress bombsights for the fifth consecutive day.

British, Japs Battle At Burma Rail City

CALCUTTA, April 29 (A. P.).—Forward British armored spearheads driving toward Rangoon clashed today with Japanese at Pegu, at the head of the last rail escape route to the east, and 60 miles north of the Burma capital.

After a 56-mile dash yesterday, the column wheeled and struck toward the 12-mile eastward gap left between them and the sea at the Sittang River estuary, protected by reinforced Japanese.

Allied infantry was moving down the main Burma trunk road to catch up with the armor and seal off a large Japanese column isolated to the west. To the east units of the 15th and 33d Japanese armies already were fleeing toward the Thailand border pursued by British detachments.

U.S. Hospital Ship Hit By Jap Suicide Plane

ABOARD ADMIRAL TURNER'S FLAGSHIP OFF OKINAWA, April 29 (A. P.).—In one of the most dastardly actions of the war, a Japanese suicide pilot dove upon the fully-lighted and unescorted Navy hospital ship Comfort, bound for rear areas with a full load of Okinawa battle casualties, last night.

At least 29 persons were killed and 33 seriously injured. The plane plunged into the ship's stern after making several runs.

NO CHANCE FOR MISTAKE

There was no chance for any kind of mistake, as the attack on the unarmed vessel was in bright, full moonlight. The ship was brightly lighted and had clear markings identifying her as a hospital ship.

The raid occurred 50 miles south of Okinawa. No other American vessel was within many miles.

Loaded to capacity with wounded, the Comfort departed from rear areas late yesterday afternoon. She was hit less than four hours after sailing.

ABLE TO PROCEED

She at first was reported abandoning ship, but it soon was determined she was able to proceed under her

Continued on Page 3, Column 5

Churchill Hails Victories in Italy

LONDON, April 29 (A. P.).—Prime Minister Winston Churchill today congratulated Field Marshal Sir Harold Alexander on the "magnificently planned and executed operations of the 15th Group of Armies which are resulting in the complete destruction or capture of all enemy forces south of the Alps."

"That you and General Mark Clark are able to accomplish these tremendous and decisive results against a superior number of enemy divisions, after you have made great sacrifices of whole armies for the Western Front, is indeed another proof of your genius for war and of the intimate brotherhood in arms between the British Commonwealth and imperial forces and those of the United States," the Prime Minister said.

Milan, Venice Seized by Allies

ROME, April 29 (U. P.).—Allied troops today captured Milan, cradle of Fascism, seized ancient Venice and broke through to the Swiss border in a lightning thrust that completely split the disorganized Nazi remnants in northern Italy.

Milan was formally occupied by troops of Lieutenant General Lucian K. Truscott's American Fifth Army after it had been cleared by Italian patriots. Troops of Lieutenant General Sir Richard L. McCreery's British Eighth Army, in a 47-mile advance that smashed the Nazi Adige and Brenta River lines, took Venice under similar circumstances.

GAIN UP TO 50 MILES

Both armies gained up to 50 miles as they swept forward on a 150-mile front from the Adriatic to the Alps

Continued on Page 2, Column 5

THE WEATHER

Philadelphia and vicinity: Partly cloudy and slightly warmer today; tomorrow, fair and somewhat cooler.

Full Weather Data on Page 2

Stymie Triumphs; 14,927 See Rounders Win in Upset

Gardens Financial

The Philadelphia Inquirer
PUBLIC LEDGER

Sports Resorts

PHILADELPHIA, SUNDAY MORNING, JUNE 3, 1945 abcdefg S

Boy Knight Second In Brandywine 'Cap

Helis Entry Sets Delaware Stake Mark; Jockey Fiocchi Suffers Brain Concussion

Other Race News, Page 4

By JOHN WEBSTER
Inquirer Sports Reporter

STANTON, Del., June 2.—Lying off Ariel Flight's pace until deep into the final turn, William Helis' Rounders whistled to the front when Jockey Fred Remerscheid took off the wraps, and rapidly went away from all opposition for a record-shattering triumph in the eighth running of the $7500 Brandywine Handicap today before 14,927 spectators who poured $1,029,626 into Delaware Park's mutuels during the afternoon.

At the finish of the mile and a 16th, the big Irish-bred horse, a son of Colorado Kid-Short Run, was a surprising five lengths before Crispin Oglebay's Boy Knight in 1.44, a new mark for the stake. Steadily-closing Lord Calvert, bearing the colors of W. Pinckney Wetherall, was third, two lengths off the runner-up. Edgehill Stable's He Rolls rolled into the fourth slot, just a head behind Lord Calvert.

Jockey R. Fiocchi was seriously injured in the eighth race when Strolling Don stumbled and fell. Dr. W. H. Speer, at Delaware Hospital, said the jockey suffered a brain concussion. At a late hour tonight hospital officials said he was still unconscious and that he failed to respond to treatment.

VICTORY GAINS $6675

Rounders, whose victory was witnessed by Mr. Helis, New Orleans sportsman, known as the Croesus of the turf, paid $22.20, $11.30 and $7.90 across the board. Rounders efforts were worth $6675 to his owner, who also is the master of the Rancocas Farm in South Jersey, and really doesn't need the money.

Boy Knight, also an outsider, paid $8.90 place and $6.20 to show. Lord Calvert, the third long shot in the payoff group, returned $8.30 to holders of show tickets.

Carrying 115 pounds, 11 less than Bon Jour's top burden and running on a fast track, the six-year old outlander shaved one-fifth of a second off the Brandywine mark set by Tatterdemalion in '38. Still he was some short of the track mark, a nifty 1.42 4-5, set here last Summer by Bon Jour, later Trenton Handicap victor, who never was prominent in the stake today.

MEGOGO POOR FIFTH

Major disappointment of the event was the showing of Christiana Stable's Megogo, who closed as favorite on the board at 4-1. Away last of all the 11 starters, Megogo appeared to lack excuses and suffered only from lack of speed. He wound up fifth, preceding Alfios, Ariel Flight, Bon Jour, Harford, Gay Bit and Dare Me to the wire.

When the seasoned routers slashed into action, Ariel Flight, with Dante Scocca in the irons, winged to the

Continued on Page 4, Column 4

Penn Charter Crews Gain Three Scholastic Crowns

Jack Kelly, Jr., Takes 3d Title

W. Catholic Annexes Two Junior Crowns; North Catholic Wins

By FRANK B. [illegible]TES

Sweeping to three out of six Philadelphia schoolboy rowing championships, Penn Charter School crewmen took major honors in the year's scholastic finals on the Schuylkill in Fairmount Park yesterday.

The near sweep of top honors formed a fitting climax to the coaching efforts of Jack Kelly, who a quarter century ago won the Olympic single sculling crown, and this year launched forth as a crew coach.

Here was the crop:

1. Penn Charter's powerful eight, stroked by Jim Luscombe, turned back the Catholic League champions, Northeast Catholic, and two other rivals, to win the eight-oared crown by just a length in 5.10 3/5. La Salle was second; Northeast Catholic, third, and St. Joseph's High, fourth.

2. Al Bishop, bow, and Tony Loughran, stroke, won the double sculling title for Penn Charter by two lengths, when the leading La Salle High crew stopped rowing near the finish line. St. Joseph's High was second.

3. Jack (Kel) Kelly, Jr., 18-year-old son of the coach, won his third single sculling title in three weeks, when he led all the way to win by three lengths from Joe McIntyre, of West Catholic. Kelly may row in the Central States Regatta at Detroit next week.

BURRS ANNEX TITLES

West Catholic High School crews won two junior varsity crowns, while Northeast Catholic followed up its double Catholic League conquest of Memorial Day by taking the senior four-oared title, sixth championship at stake in the regatta.

George Mattson's Burrs took the junior eight-oared title by three lengths from LaSalle and Northeast Catholic juniors, who finished in the order named; then the West Catholic second four took the junior

Continued on Page 3, Column 8

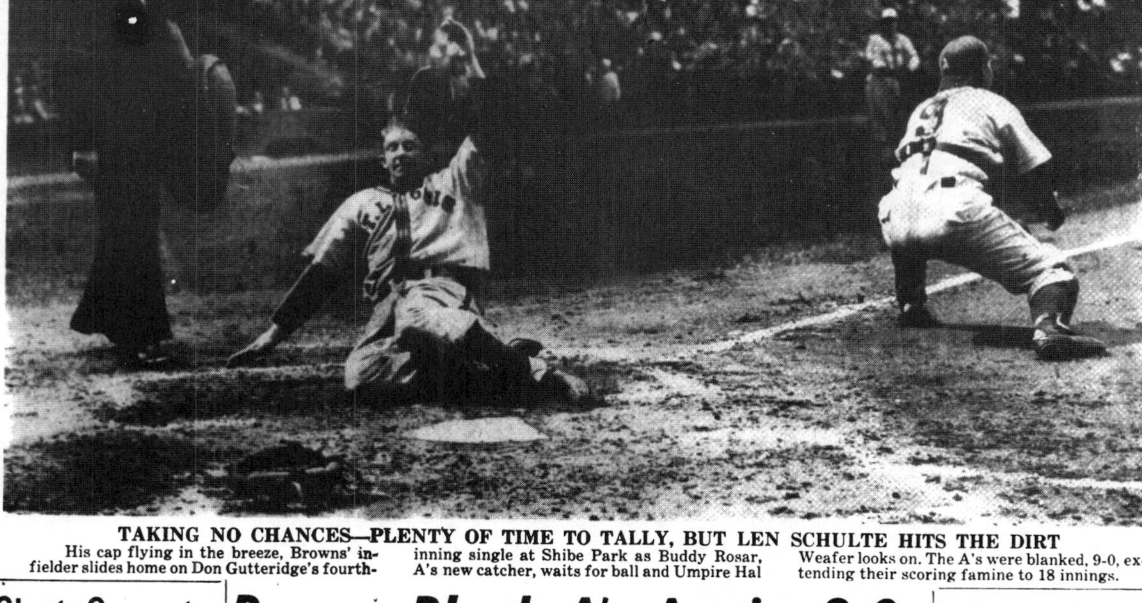

TAKING NO CHANCES—PLENTY OF TIME TO TALLY, BUT LEN SCHULTE HITS THE DIRT
His cap flying in the breeze, Browns' infielder slides home on Don Gutteridge's fourth-inning single at Shibe Park as Buddy Rosar, A's new catcher, waits for ball and Umpire Hal Weafer looks on. The A's were blanked, 9-0, extending their scoring famine to 18 innings.

Giants Consent To Tigers' Shift

NEW YORK, June 2 (U. P.).—The National Football League solved its most pressing post-war problem today when the New York Giants consented to the transfer of the Brooklyn Tigers to Yankee Stadium, effective in 1946.

The action was announced by Commissioner Elmer Layden.

Captain Dan Topping, U.S.M.C., owner of the Tigers and a part-owner of the New York Yankee baseball team, had threatened to withdraw from the league and join the All-America League, a projected post-war professional football loop, unless the Giants consented to the shift.

"Territorial rights were involved and the Giant owners for some time had balked the efforts of the league to get them to agree to the transfer.

WILL MERGE WITH YANKS

This fall the Tigers will merge with the Boston Yanks with all home games except one played at Boston. The exception will be a game against the Giants at Yankee Stadium.

The Tigers would have been without a home, for Branch Rickey, president of the Brooklyn Dodgers, had refused to lease them Ebbets Field beyond the 1945 season. Rickey plans on obtaining a franchise in one of the proposed post-war leagues.

Layden and some league club owners came here for an off-the-record conference at which the Giants' owners finally gave in to league pressure and consented to the transfer. The club owners also reportedly were discussing the status of Layden, whose contract as commissioner expires next year. Several owners are opposed to renewing his contract.

Browns Blank A's Again, 9-0; Phils Hand Another to Bucs, 7-6

Special to The Inquirer

PITTSBURGH, Pa., June 2.—One of the greatest baseball stories of the year was developed and spoiled at Forbes Field today, all because the Phils are too liberal.

A story book home run by former Pirate, Vince DiMaggio, the fellow the Buccos sold down the river, put the Quakers out in front in the sixth, but in the Bucco's half of this frame the Phils donated the necessary three runs for Pittsburgh to win, 7-6. It was the second victory for Pittsburgh and the Phils' sixth loss in a row.

Practically every Pittsburgh fan in the park clamored for a chance to see DiMaggio in action. With the bases full and two out and the Phils two runs behind Vince was called upon to hit for pitcher Charley Sproull.

Everybody sensed the possibilities of the occasion, what with Al Gerheauser on the mound for Pittsburgh. The southpaw was obtained in exchange for DiMaggio, who isn't playing regularly because he has a bad foot. Gerheauser tossed two strikes, then lost control. To make the situation as tense as possible, the count was run up to 3 and 2.

CLEARS 406 FT. MARK

As soon as it was hit there wasn't any doubt about where the next pitch was going. Jimmy Russell backed up against the left center wall but had to stand there as the ball sailed over the wall near the 406 foot mark. Everybody in the ball park applauded DiMaggio. His three mates, Vance Dinges, Gus Mancuso

Continued on Page 2, Column 6

By STAN BAUMGARTNER

For the second straight day a veteran St. Louis moundsman wove a wand of mystery around the Athletics bats as the American League champions romped over the last-placers to win the second game of the series, 9-0, yesterday at Shibe Park.

Jack Kramer, who had been knocked out of the box in his two previous starts, held the Macks to four measley hits and was never in danger of being scored on. Friday night Jack Jakucki blanked the A's with three hits, winning, 4-0.

BROWNS MAKE 14 HITS

While Kramer was doing his stuff, the Browns, who have been hitting mostly air on their Eastern invasion, came out of their batting slump with a bang against Southpaw Charles Gassaway and Righthander Don Black. They pushed over one run on Gassaway in the first, knocked him out of the box with five in the fourth and then completed the merry-go-round with three more off Black in the seventh—making a total of 14 hits.

Hoping to change his luck Connie Mack sent Buddy Rosar, recently obtained from Cleveland in the swap for Frankie Hayes, behind the bat, but the alteration in the batting order made no difference in the number or character of goose-eggs which the Mackmen put on the scoreboard.

With no reinforcements in sight and Larry Rosenthal and Hal Peck on the bench nursing muscle injuries, there does not appear to be much hope of the A's launching a batting drive.

Russ Christopher and Bobo Newsom will face the Browns in the

Continued on Page 2, Column 3

Baseball Facts

NATIONAL LEAGUE
Yesterday's Results

Pittsburgh, 7; PHILLIES, 6.
Boston, 5; Chicago, 4, 10 innings.
New York, 3; St. Louis, 2.
Brooklyn at Cincinnati, postponed.

Standing of the Teams

	W.	L.	Pc.
New York	27	12	.692
Pittsburgh	21	16	.568
Brooklyn	21	17	.553
St. Louis	21	18	.538
Chicago	18	17	.514
Cincinnati	16	18	.471
Boston	[illegible]	20	.412
PHILLIES	10	30	.250

Today's Schedule
Probable Pitchers and Their Records

PHILLIES at Pittsburgh—Schanz (1-6) and Kennedy (0-3) vs. Sewell (6-4) and Cuccurullo (0-1).

Boston at Chicago — Tobin (3-6) and Logan (1-1) vs. Wyse (5-3) and Passeau (2-2).

Brooklyn at Cincinnati—Davis (4-3) and Chapman (2-2) vs. Dasso (2-3) and Carter (2-3) or Bowman (0-2).

New York at St. Louis — Feldman (5-1) and Hansen (4-2) vs. Barrett (4-3) and Wilks (2-4) or Brecheen (3-1).

AMERICAN LEAGUE
Yesterday's Results

St. Louis, 9; ATHLETICS, 0.
Washington, 8; Chicago, 1.
Boston, 5; Detroit, 1.
Cleveland, 4; New York, 0.

Standing of the Teams

	W.	L.	P.C.
New York	23	14	.622
Detroit	19	14	.576
St. Louis	18	16	.529
Chicago	18	17	.514
Boston	18	19	.486
Cleveland	15	18	.455
Washington	16	20	.444
ATHLETICS	14	23	.378

Today's Schedule
Probable Pitchers and Their Records

St. Louis vs. ATHLETICS at Shibe Park, 1.30 P. M.—Potter (4-3) and Shirley (2-3) vs. Christopher (7-2) and Newsom (1-5).

Cleveland at New York — Reynolds (4-3) and Gromek (5-1) vs. Borowy (6-1) and Dubiel (4-3).

Detroit at Boston — Newhouser (5-4) and Overmire (3-1) or Trout (4-3) vs. Terry (0-0) and Wilson (1-5).

Chicago at Washington — Lee (5-2) and Humphries (1-1) vs. Wolff (4-2) and Pieretti (4-3).

Continued on Page 2, Column 3

Palmyra Keeps Title in Track

MONTCLAIR, N. J., June 2.—Trenton, Plainfield, Palmyra and Verona retained their crowns in the 27th annual State Interscholastic Athletic Association track meet today under adverse weather conditions. Despite a heavy rainstorm all events were completed, with only three new records established.

Coach Pete Smith's Trenton High kept its Group 4 championship with a total of 40 points. For the second and straight year Montclair High finished second with 25 points. Trenton gained but two first places, Fisher capturing the 880-yard run in a driving rain in 2:06.4, and Don Ray skirted over the 120-yard high hurdles to victory in 15.6, the best time of the day for the high timbers.

HADDON HEIGHTS SECOND

Picking up 36 points, Harold Brugerger's Plainfield High aggregation kept its Group 3 diadem, with Haddon Heights second with 25 markers. The Group 2 championship was taken by Mel Kreps' Palmyra High squad for the fourth straight year. Palmyra amassed 40 1-3 points, with Cranford in the runner-up spot with 28 5-6 points.

Verona High captured the Group 1 championship for the third straight year, collecting 43½ points, Glen Ridge, with 35¾, placed second.

A new division for Catholic high schools was conducted in conjunction with the titular State meet for the first time. A powerful St. Michael's squad from Jersey City won with 74½ points, with Trenton Catholic High the runner-up, with 55 1-3 points. Jack Moody, Plainfield High star, chalked up the only new record in the four regular divisions. He captured the high jump with a leap of 6 feet, 3¼ inches, bettering his own mark of last year

Continued on Page 3, Column 5

Bucs' Salkeld 4-F

PITTSBURGH, June 2 (A. P.).—Bill Salkeld, hard-hitting second-string Pirates' catcher, was rejected for military service today and classified 4-F because of an ailing right knee.

36,948 Watch Jamaica Race

Alex Barth Second, Bounding Home 3d; $3,164,363 Wagered

Race Chart on Page 4

JAMAICA, N. Y., June 2 (A. P.).—The "second" jinx that p[illegible] Alex Barth last year caught up with the Millbrook Stable's star again today when he bowed by a half length to Mrs. Ethel D. Jacobs' Stymie in the fifth Grey Lag Handicap, mile and a furlong main attraction on the final program of Jamaica's abbreviated 12-day meeting before 36,948 who wagered $3,164,363 on seven races.

Four straight favorites won before Alex Barth, at 55 cents on the dollar, went down to defeat. William Ziegler, Jr.'s Bounding Home was third, seven lengths out of it, while Olympic Zenith took fourth money and Great Rush completed the small field. Stymie, an $8.80 for two shot, earned a purse of $10,700 and his time of 1:49 4-5 missed tieing the track record by only one-fifth of a second.

WON SIX EVENTS

Just before the Grey Lag, thunder, lightning and rain broke out from leaden skies but the track remained fast for the headliner.

Last season, Alex Barth ran 24 times, won six events but was second on nine occasions. In most of his "seconds" he missed out on big stakes purses by narrow margins, but he managed to earn $99,560 during the year. He is now jointly owned by M. B. Milberg and the estate of the late Lou Nikoff.

Hirsch Jacobs, leading American trainer for 11 of the past 12 years, had Stymie in peak form and Bobby Permane gave the colt a faultless ride.

STYMIE GAINS

Olympic Zenith stole an eight lengths lead in the first quarter mile, with Bounding Home and Alex Barth virtually locked for the runner-up position. The latter pair cut down the gap along the backstretch and midway of the final bend, Alex Barth took the lead. Stymie meanwhile had remained in fourth position.

They began the stretch run with Alex Barth a length or more in front, but Stymie gained with every stride once straightened for home. He wore down the jinx horse—which carried 126 pounds to the winner's 120—through the last sixteenth of a mile.

Busher Triumphs In Santa Susanna

ARCADIA, Calif., June 2 (A. P.).—Louis B. Mayer's three-year-old filly, Busher, merely went through the motions today in winning the Santa Susanna handcap at Santa Anita Park, with a purse of $2[illegible],000 added. Busher, paying $2.30, $2.[illegible]0 and $2.10, won by seven lengths before 28,600 who wagered $2,502,014 during the day.

Mist finished second, followed by Glory Time, and Firstbourne, fourth. Mist paid $3.60 to place, Glory Time $2.40 to show

A secondary feature, the San Bernardino Handicap at six furlongs, with a $7500 purse, was won by Appleknocker, of the Coward and Dupuy stable, beating favored Ariel Lad by a stride and paying $21.90, $8.50 and $5.40.

Annapolis Takes 10 Events, Wins Heptagonal, Penn 4th

By ART MORROW
Inquirer Sports Reporter

ANNAPOLIS, Md., June 2.—In a meet conducted in an Olympic atmosphere the U. S. Naval Academy's track team all but chased rivals into the adjacent Chesapeake at the west end of Thompson Field, today, in the 11th annual heptagonal games.

It was the first time the Middies competed in the meet, and they made the occasion a memorable one. Led by football fullback Clyde L. Scott, Coach Earl Thomson's athletes won 10 events and tied for first in one of the five others as they rolled up 87½ points, 17½ more than the combined total of their nearest rivals, Cornell and Dartmouth, which shared second place with 35 apiece.

The University of Pennsylvania, scoring in 11 events, finished fourth with 33½, followed by the University of Virginia, 27; Columbia 17 and Princeton 5.

ONE RECORD FALLS

Twice during the afternoon the program was interrupted, victors and place winners called to the center of the field in front of the stands. They stood, then, on steps, Olympic fashion, to receive medals from Admiral John R. Beardall, Superintendent of the U. S. Naval Academy, and applause from the word go.

But if the atmosphere were Olympian, the performances were not particularly so. However, they were better than expected and during the course of the 2-hour festivities, one meet record fell. Cornell's 17-year-old John F. Kandl, I. C. 4-A and Penn Relay two-mile champion, hoofed over his favorite distance in 9 minutes, 34.1 seconds, three and a half seconds under the heptagonal criterion established at Harvard University in 1937 by another Cornell distance runner, William V. Bassett.

Nevertheless, the occasion must have been a pleasant one for Admiral Beardall. Practically every time he stepped up to make an award, he found a Navy man [illegible] receive it. The I. C. 4-A high hurdles' champion, was there twice for winning the low as well as the high barriers. Six other individual Middies received medals and Navy also won both the 440-yard and one-mile relay races.

SMITH WINS SHOT PUT

The Middies' winners were John Van Velzer, the Intercollegiate 100-yard dash champion, [illegible]

Continued on Page 3, Column 7

3 Jockeys Injured At Charles Town

CHARLES TOWN, W. Va., June 2 (U. P.).—Three jockeys were injured, perhaps seriously, when the eighth race at Charles Town today wound up in a five-horse spill.

Jockey J. Beedle suffered a possible broken neck when he was thrown from Miss Mary R. Fox's Broomoria. R. Gustin's Running Riot was well up when she fell, hurling Jockey G. Franklin into the path of the field. Broomoria and James Hamilton's Gay Victory piled up on her, followed by Colonel Scott and Great Play.

Beedle, Franklin and S. Palumbo, Gay Victory's rider, were rushed to a hospital. J. Hernandez, on Colonel Scott, and Apprentice Bobby Edens, on Great Play, were said to have jumped from their saddles and suffered only bruises.

171,240 Turf Fans Wager $10,439,185 For Saturday Mark

NEW YORK, June 2 (A. P.).—In the wake of Memorial Day's largest one-day wagering spree of $13,476,-021, a total of 171,240 turf followers wagered $10,439,185 at 11 tracks today for a new Saturday record.

Track.	Attendance.	Wagered.
Jamaica	36,948	$3,164,36[illegible]
Santa Anita	38,000	2,502,10[illegible]
Narragansett	22,000	1,554,874
Delaware	14,917	1,029,626
Hawthorne	15,175	963,213
Churchill	15,000	[illegible]
North Randall	8,000	208,[illegible]
Charles Town	5,000	180,000
Fairmount	6,500	110,[illegible]
Wheeling	4,200	82,37[illegible]
Beulah	5,500	est. 80,000
Totals (11)	171,240	$10,439,185
Memorial Day (11)	333,195	13,476,021
Week ago (7)	178,171	10,006,076
Year ago (11)	129,103	8,190,892
Year ago (11)	129,103	8,190,892

Overbrook Blind School Triumphs in Track, 45-18

The Overbrook School for the Blind remained undefeated yesterday when it triumphed, 45-18, over the Perkins School for the Blind in a track meet held at Overbrook, 54th and Malvern.

Fred Barkovich, victors coach, was graduated from the Overbrook School for the Blind and is now taking Physical Education at the University of Pennsylvania.

Burke's Homer Wins

Donald Burke's home run in the last inning with a teammate on base gave the Feltonville Trojans a 7-6 baseball victory over the Logan Eagles yesterday at Hunting Park in the Connie Mack Boys League.

Sport Results

College

BASEBALL

EASTERN INTERCOLLEGIATE LEAGUE

Penn 3 .... Columbia 2
Princeton 5 .... (1st game) .... Cornell 2
Princeton 3 .... (2d game) .... Cornell 1

STANDINGS

	W.	L.	P.C.		W.	L.	P.C.
Princeton	5	2	.714	Dartmouth	3	3	.500
Columbia	3	2	.600	Cornell	1	5	.167
Penn	2	2	.500				

WESTERN CONFERENCE

Northwestern ... (canceled) ... Minnesota
Michigan 9 ...... (1st game) ...... Purdue 2
Michigan 4 ...... (2d game) ...... Purdue 3

STANDINGS

	W.	L.	Pct.		W.	L.	Pct.
Michigan	8	0	1.000	N'hwestern	4	6	.400
Wisconsin	8	4	.667	Iowa	3	5	.375
Indiana	5	3	.625	Minnesota	2	4	.333
Illinois	6	5	.545	Purdue	2	10	.167
Ohio State	4	5	.444				

OTHER GAMES

Swarthmore 4 .... Muhlenberg 0
Pitt ...... (canceled) .. U. S. Military A.
Villanova 3 .... Bucknell 0
Yale 6 .... Dartmouth 1
Iowa Pre-Flight 5 .... Notre Dame 4
U. S. Merchant Marine A 7 ... Fordham 3

TRACK

HEPTAGONAL MEET

U. S. Naval A., 87½; Cornell, 35; Dartmouth, 35; Penn, 33½; Virginia, 27; Columbia, 17; Princeton, 5.

CENTRAL COLLEGIATE MEET

Great Lakes NTS, 48; Purdue, 30; Marquette, 27; Notre Dame, 20; Drake, 15; Idaho, 12; Illinois Tech., 10; Wright Field, 10; Wisconsin, 8¼; Minnesota, 8; Ohio State, 7; St. Thomas (Minn.), 5; Michigan State, 1; Iowa, ¼.

TENNIS

Cornell 7 .... Columbia 2
Notre Dame 5 .... Purdue 2

School

BASEBALL

Washington 2 .... Somerville 0

TRACK

N. J. STATE CHAMPIONSHIPS

GROUP FOUR
Trenton 40 .... Montclair 25

GROUP THREE
Plainfield 36 .... Haddon Heights 25

GROUP TWO
Palmyra 40 1/3 .... Cranfield 28 5/6

GROUP ONE
Verona 43½ .... Glen Ridge 35¾

CATHOLIC GROUP
St. Michael's 74½ Trenton Catholic 55 1/3

DUAL MEETS
Overbrook Blind 45 Perkins Blind School 18

TENNIS

Perkiomen 5 .... B. M. I. 1

Continued on Page 2, Column 6

GI's Not to Be Signed Until Discharged

CHICAGO, June 2 (U. P.).—Major and minor league club owners were warned today by baseball's Advisory Council not to sign players until they have been discharged from service and removed from the National Defense Service list.

In an open letter to all organized baseball clubs, Leslie O'Connor, chairman of the Advisory Council, wrote:

"Penalties will be imposed if any such contracts are made and incorrect dates are inserted for the purpose of concealing the fact that such player was in the Armed Forces or on the National Defense Service list at the time of contracting or accepting terms."

Yanks Blanked Second Time in 3 Days; Indians Win, 4-0; Red Sox, Braves Victors

By JOE TUMELTY

Shut out for the second time in three days, the Yankees probably make Marse Joe McCarthy long for his pre-war clubs of Babe Ruth, Joe DiMaggio & Co. that went through an entire season under the stigma of only a blanking or two.

Yesterday Ed (Specs) Klieman, Cleveland's sophomore hurler, kalsomined the American League leaders with six hits in a 4-0 victory; Thursday Detroit's Les Mueller did the trick, a two-hitter, 2-0. Adding insult to injury both hurlers were making their first starts of the season—and achieving their first triumphs.

TIGERS GO DOWN, 5-1

The second-place Tigers, however, failed to take advantage of the Yankee slip, since they could do little more with Clem Hausmann of the Red Sox than the Bronx Bombers could with Klieman. Hausmann also fired a six-hitter in a 5-1 success, and would have had a shutout had not Eddie Lake erred in trying for a double play in the fourth inning. The loss kept the Bengals two

Continued on Page 2, Column 4

Inquirer Golf Tickets on Sale

Tickets are now on sale for the second annual Philadelphia Inquirer Invitation Golf Tournament, Thursday, June 14, through Sunday, June 17, at Llanerch Country Club, Manoa, Pa., which is only 11 minutes from 69th Street Terminal on both the West Chester and Larchmont trolleys, stopping in front of the club.

The Inquirer Charities, Inc., sponsor, again offers the attractive $5 season ticket (tax included), but it must be purchased before Sunday, June 10. Daily tickets, all tax included, are: June 14—$1.50; June 15—$1.50; June 16—$2, and June 17—$2. Season tickets also admit to the pro-member tournament and the special match between Mrs. Mildred (Babe) Didrikson Zaharias and Lieutenant Patty Berg, U. S. M. C. R., and Dorothy Germain and Helen Sigel, June 13, for which daily admission is $1.

Tickets are on sale at Gimbels, Llanerch Country Club and The Inquirer, 400 N. Broad st., Philadelphia 1, and all District P. G. A. golf shops. The Inquirer will accept mail orders until Thursday, June 7. Add 30 cents for registration and mailing.

Inquirer Tournament, Llanerch C. C., June 14, 15, 16, 17

Craig Wood, Open Titlist, Jimmy Hines Join Nelson, Snead, McSpaden in Test

By ART MORROW

Blond Craig Wood, the Adonis of the fairways and reigning U. S. Open king by virtue of his triumph at Fort Worth in 1941, plans again to demonstrate in the second annual Inquirer Invitation Golf Tournament that consistency pays. He has already proved his point, of course, but at the Llanerch Country Club from June 14 through June 17 he hopes to provide an example even more convincing than his second place of a year ago. This time he aims to convince Sammy Byrd, in addition to the others in the $17,500 War Bond classic. Byrd, also due back, beat him for the big prize in '44.

HINES TO COMPETE

Wood was one of two veteran stars whose names yesterday were added to the lost of entrants in the four-day, 72-hole event being staged by The Philadelphia Inquirer Charities, Inc., in the interests of the P. G. A. Rehabilitation Fund for the purchase of supplies and equipment for wounded service men. The other was Jimmy Hines, former Amsterdam (N. Y.) Country Club pro now playing out of Chicago.

The additions of Wood and Hines add glitter to the already coruscating field in the June 14-17 links extravaganza—a field that includes, besides ex-Yankee ball player Byrd, the winter circuit's three top money-winners, Byron Nelson, Sammy Snead and Jug McSpaden, not to mention such clubhouse names a long-driving Jimmy Thomson, Big

Continued on Page 3, Column 2

CRAIG WOOD

JIMMY HINES

The Philadelphia Inquirer
SATURDAY MORNING, JUNE 23, 1945 Page 10

Washington Background

Jap-Americans in Hawaii Are Loyal U. S. Citizens

By Inquirer Washington Bureau Staff

WASHINGTON, June 22.

GOVERNOR INGRAM STAINBACK, of Hawaii, who has been a Washington visitor the last few days, tells us that the Americans in Hawaii of Japanese descent have a perfect loyalty record.

"Those Japanese-Americans," he said, "don't think of themselves as Japanese at all. In fact, it is a common thing to hear Japanese-Americans in Hawaii speak of 'our Puritan forefathers.'"

• • •

A friend of this column reports to us that the Pennsylvania Railroad seems to take a rather narrow view of ginger ale as a beverage.

Traveling to New York last week on the Pennsy—on one of those days when the thermometer was hovering around 96 degrees—our friend asked the porter in the chair car for a cola drink for his wife and some ginger ale for himself. The porter shook his head doubtfully.

"I don't think they serves ginger ale except as a setup for a highball," he said.

Our friend protested that it was too hot—the air-conditioning hadn't got working yet—for a highball. Nevertheless, the porter came back and reported he couldn't get the ginger ale—straight.

We suppose another friend of this column—Gus Payne—must have the answer to this one.

• • •

Here's a veteran of World War I who thinks that the Army's point system of discharging soldiers is a promise of OPA ration points to discharged members of the armed services, and he is burned up about it.

"I believe you should make a protest of this racket of the armed forces commercializing war expecting members of the armed forces to get ration points on their service in the Army to get their discharge from the Army," he wrote to the Veterans of Foreign Wars.

"OPA racket shouldn't run the armed forces," he added, suggesting that the V. F. W. should take the matter up with President Truman.

• • •

The ramifications of international relations are more extensive than we had supposed. It now turns out that efforts of Fisher Brothers to purchase the Hudson Motor Co. are temporarily stymied because the Hudson people have not yet been able to find out whether Queen Wilhelmena of The Netherlands, who owns 12 percent of Hudson's stock, wants to sell.

• • •

The fate of Washington's pigeons, it appears, is to be decided in Philadelphia.

Dr. George C. Ruhland, District of Columbia health officer, is studying Philadelphia's steps toward the humane extermination of the birds before opening an offensive on the capital's.

• • •

Parents who used to read—it seems only a few years ago—their children to sleep from A. A. Milne's "When We Were Very Young" and "Winnie the Pooh" will be taken aback to learn that Christopher Robin Milne, for whom the verses originally were written, was badly wounded in Italy while serving with the royal engineers.

• • •

One of the Government officials recently returned from Germany reports passing through a place named Dueren, on the east side of the Roer River and seeing a G. I. pacing up and down on a solemn patrol, passing and re-passing a sign marked "Columbus Circle."

There wasn't a whole building in sight, or even a piece of a whole building, or even a street, our friend reports—just the dust and rubble of a small town completely bombed off the map.

Edited by John C. O'Brien

Military Expert's Views

U. S. Landing on China Coast Seems Unlikely at This Time

By Maj. George Fielding Eliot

THE appointment of General Joseph W. Stilwell to command the 10th Army on Okinawa has been widely accepted as indicating an early landing on the Chinese coast. This is because of General Stilwell's experience in warfare in China and his knowledge of the Chinese people and army.

The idea is the more plausible, because Okinawa lies within easy striking distance of a part of the Chinese coastline where the Chinese forces have just succeeded in recapturing two important seaports—Foochow and Wenchow—from the Japanese.

We should, however, generally be hesitant to accept the idea of any major strategical move which is eccentric—that is, which diverts considerable forces from the main objective.

On the face of it, a large-scale landing in the immediate future on the coast of China would be eccentric. The main objective of our war in the Pacific is the destruction of Japanese military power in the Japanese main islands, the source of all Japan's strength. The base at Okinawa is in striking distance of these main islands. Therefore to go elsewhere from Okinawa than to the main islands is a diversion of strength from the main objective.

• • •

BUT that is to assume that the time is ripe for such a move. Has Japan been sufficiently "softened up" by bombing and blockade to permit a direct invasion to be attempted? That is one consideration. It must be considered in connection with the enemy's distribution of forces. Not very long ago, there were comparatively few combat divisions in the Japanese main islands, and they were not of the best quality.

Shifts of strength have probably taken place since then—to what extent it is impossible to say, though doubtless our intelligence officers are well enough informed on the subject.

Can we gain an advantage by striking now? Will we catch the Japanese unprepared to meet us by reason of not having enough troops in home garrisons? Obviously, the major objective of the Japanese, if they have reason to think an invasion of their homeland is imminent, will be to get every available soldier from the mainland into Japan itself for home defense, and especially their better combat divisions. If we can hit them at home before the moves are completed, or while they are in progress, then the sooner we strike the better for us.

As the official War Department release on the redeployment from Europe observed, the Japanese forces are divided and we hope to keep them that way, so as to destroy them in detail. The fall of Okinawa will enable American air and naval forces to close the Yellow Sea and the Strait of Korea to Japanese shipping, except for a few ships which may sneak along the coast.

• • •

INDEED, a great deal has already been done to interrupt Japanese ship movements in these waters. It is not, however, possible to stop large-scale movements from the ports of Eastern Korea across the Sea of Japan to Japanese west coast ports, even though the entrance to the Inland Sea can be partially blocked by mines.

Hence, it is still possible, even likely, that the Japanese may be carrying on a partial redeployment of their own, moving troops from various mainland locations to Japan proper. There is not much we can do to pin down the Japanese troops on the mainland, as there are not enough American troops there and there has not been time since the reopening of the Burma Road to build up and equip a powerful Chinese army.

These considerations might seem to urge a move into Japan now, instead of a move to China first. The Japanese, at any rate, seem to be convinced that we shall shortly invade the southernmost of their main islands, Kyushu, which lies only 325 miles from Okinawa. If they really mean what their radio keeps saying about this, it would follow almost certainly that they have concentrated all the good troops in Japan for the defense of Kyushu.

It would not necessarily follow, under these circumstances, that we would go to Kyushu at all. There are other possible locations for a landing which are within our reach from Okinawa.

• • •

ONE other consideration should be kept in mind: an invasion of the Japanese home islands would be the most serious military enterprise we have yet undertaken in the Pacific. The seven divisions we used on Okinawa will have a considerable period of rest and refitting before they can be used again; and three or four divisions are still busy in the Philippines.

It is not at all certain that we have enough troops in the Pacific area over and above these two groups of divisions to undertake an invasion of Japan right now. If that is so, then there would seem to be no reason why we should not, while assembling more forces, undertake a secondary operation on the Chinese coast if it offers compensatory advantages and does not seriously interfere with the build-up of the main effort.

Time is certainly of first importance, however. "Economy in lives and material," General Marshall told Congress, "demand that we mount a swift, powerful offensive, forcing a victory at the earliest possible moment. I hope that successive victories will enable us to reduce the size of our Army very soon."

It is only necessary to add that there is only one place where the final defeat of Japan can be accomplished — Japan itself. Sooner or later we must go there. The sooner we are able to go there, the sooner the war will be over.

Today

—By Walter Lippmann—

Continued From First Page

Secretary of State could stand by to be, in case of emergency, Acting President until the election of the new Vice President.

There is some reason to think, though the language is obscure, that something like this may have been the original intent of the authors of the Constitution.

In any event, we must bear in mind that nothing is so essential to orderly Government as an undisputed and universally accepted line of succession to the highest office in the land.

FIREMAN CARRIED FROM LU LU TEMPLE AMID HOSE SPRAY

ANOTHER FIREMAN WHO WAS CAUGHT IN ROOF COLLAPSE

FIVE ALARMS Flames roaring out of the great copper dome surmounting Lu Lu Temple, the Shrine headquarters on Spring Garden st. near Broad, yesterday. Firemen, responding to five alarms, poured tons of water onto the blaze, which destroyed the interior of the building. Photos at left show two firemen, trapped when part of the roof collapsed, being carried from the building.

Hammering on Gates of Nippon

Okinawa to Be Springboard For Final Attack on Japan

By John M. McCullough
Inquirer Washington Bureau

WASHINGTON, June 22.

OKINAWA, purchased at the heaviest price in lives and material yet paid in an assault upon a single island by America's land and sea forces in the Pacific, will be developed as the major base for the attacks preparatory to the actual land invasion of Japan.

It may be that the bomb and shell-desolated island may become the major springboard for the final operations themselves—attacks upon Japan, or upon both Japan and the China coast.

The Navy Department, which has not been distinguished during the war years for its loquacity concerning future operations, has become almost garrulous during the past few days on the subject.

• • •

A STATEMENT issued by the Navy Office of Public Information today, quoting Rear Admiral Carl H. Cotter, director of the Pacific Division of the Bureau of Yards and Docks, is typical:

"When finally accomplished, the work planned for this island will enable us to really pour the heat on the Japanese homelands. I believe that when this base is finished, the end of the war will be in sight—not around the corner, but in sight."

He declared that the base development of Okinawa was "by far the largest operation yet undertaken, the closest to the Japanese home islands."

This certainly means that the largest number of naval construction battalions (Seabees) ever assembled in the Pacific are industriously at work, building airfields, docks, roads and shore installations.

• • •

ONLY yesterday, Fleet Admiral Chester W. Nimitz's headquarters on Guam—itself a dizzying monument to Seabee construction ingenuity and speed—officially had this to say:

"It must be obvious to the Japanese general staff that American amphibious operations forces, using Okinawa for providing air cover and a forward supply base, will be enabled to assault Japan or China or both.

"To defend both positions, the enemy is now forced to split his strength. By driving directly into the heart of the Ryukyu Islands, the United States forces have gained, strategically, the interior position."

Yesterday, too, Lieutenant James H. (Jimmy) Doolittle declared that, with acquisition of Okinawa, the Army Air Forces would have abundant Pacific base areas upon which to mount their final annihilating air attack upon the enemy's war industry.

SUCH statements, it is obvious, are neither "the frantic boast and foolish word," on one hand, nor an effort on the part of America's military men to sugarcoat the serious casualties and injuries accepted as necessary and sustained in the Okinawa operation.

Yet it is equally true that the War and the Navy Departments, on the same day—literally in the same breath—are giving public voice to statements which are both optimistic and pessimistic.

The important fact about this apparent contradiction, which has led some cynics to accuse the Nation's military leadership of crying "Wolf, Wolf!" in the market place, is that it is not contradiction.

On the one hand, military men point out, there is no reason for hiding the tremendous strides which the United States has taken in the Pacific, nor the completely irresistible power which is being assembled for the final annihilation of Japanese resistance.

But on the other hand, that irresistible power is being met by a steady concentration of inferior but fanatic and lethal enemy resistance.

• • •

OKINAWA, which, competent authority insists, had to be taken, caps the price paid for a long series of other positions that had to be taken, and whose once seemingly impressive sacrifices now seem almost puny.

It is startling, and definitely dampening to excessive optimism, to realize that United States armed forces paid only one-seventh the price in casualties to seize Guadalcanal in a campaign lasting 186 days that were paid two and one-half years later to conquer Okinawa.

Okinawa, one hears—not merely from responsible sources here, but from the men who actually have done the fighting—must be interpreted in any realistic appraisal of what lies ahead, as a mere token of the fanaticism which must be met when American troops at last spill ashore from their landing craft upon Honshu or Shikoku or Kyushu.

Okinawa, though pounded from land, sea and air by the heaviest weight of high explosives ever expended upon a target of comparable size in World War II, was a formidable fortress where at least 11,260 Americans laid down their lives to exterminate 90,000-odd Japanese cave-dwelling fanatics.

GIFT Charles A. Tyler (left), General Manager of The Philadelphia Inquirer, presenting to William C. Hunneman, Jr., Chairman of the Red Cross War Fund Drive, a gift of $25,000 from The Philadelphia Inquirer Charities, Inc., proceeds from the recent Music Festival, which was held at the Municipal Stadium.

CUSTOMS Some of the passengers who arrived on the S. S. Magallanes, a Spanish vessel, being cleared through customs here yesterday. The ship is the first neutral vessel to dock at Philadelphia since the travel restrictions were lifted.

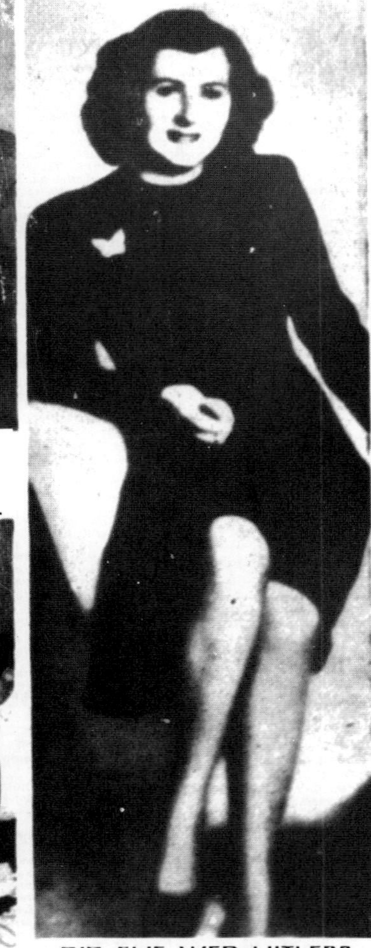

DID SHE WED HITLER?

A new picture of Eva Braun, who is reported to have married Adolf Hitler shortly before the end of the war and is said to have died with him amid the ruins of Berlin. They were friends for years.

Phila. G. O. P. to Back Cooke for Governor

By JOSEPH H. MILLER

Continued From First Page

ever, are reported to have other ideas. They are planning to slate Governor Edward Martin for the Senatorial nomination, although the Chief Executive of the Commonwealth has repeatedly asserted he is not a candidate for any further political honors.

COOKE BETTER KNOWN

The party leadership, which originally considered Lieutenant Colonel Dan (Dangerous Dan) Strickler, former member of the Legislature from Lancaster, for Governor, now is said to have switched to Mr. Cooke.

Party leaders are of the opinion that Mr. Cooke, who was seriously wounded and lost an eye on the battlefront, is better known throughout the State and would make an excellent running mate for Governor Martin if the latter consents to stand for the Senate.

Mr. Cooke is popular with the rank and file of the Philadelphia Republican organization and in the event of a primary contest for Governor would pile up a sizeable majority over any opponent.

He is well known throughout the State, having been a candidate for Senator against Mr Guffey in 1940, but lost as a result of the Roosevelt landslide.

Mainspring of the Cooke-for-Governor boom, as evidenced by Mr. Harris' efforts in that direction, is Joseph N. Pew, Jr., oil company executive who is influential in the State organization. It is believed that the faction headed by former Senator Joseph R. Grundy also is ready to accept Colonel Cooke for Governor.

Mr. Pew is said to have an "ace-in-the-hole," for Governor—Lieutenant Governor John C. Bell, Jr.—in the event Colonel Cooke refuses to aspire for the post.

The Grundy forces, however, do not look kindly toward the Bell candidacy in view of his pronounced political independent actions. They would favor Secretary of Internal Affairs William S. Livengood, Jr., if Mr. Cooke eliminated himself.

MARTIN DRAFT LIKELY

Colonel Cooke and Mr. Livengood are close personal friends and would like to tie up in a political race, the retired Army officer for Senator and the State official for Governor.

If Governor Martin persists in his stand that he will not seek the Senatorial nomination, there is a possibility Colonel Cooke might be slated for the post, opening the way for a Cooke-Livengood ticket. But most political observers believe the Governor will yield to a "draft" movement.

Truman Names Draper

WASHINGTON, June 30 (A. P.).—President Truman today named Earle S. Draper to serve as acting commissioner of the Federal Housing Administration until a commissioner is appointed. He succeeds Abner H. Ferguson, whose resignation as commissioner becomes effective today.

FIRST PICTURE OF THE POST-WAR LINCOLN CAR

This is the 1946 Lincoln car which the Ford Motor Co. expect to put into production in a few months. The car, a hand-built model, features wide bumpers and a new front grille, which gives it a broader appearance. Electrically operated hydraulic mechanism for opening the windows will be standard equipment on all cars.

Martin Setting Mark in Progress of State

By GERSON H. LUSH

Continued From First Page

tion, farmers, veterans, industry and labor.

At the same time, the Governor has practiced rigid economy and his Administration has the distinction of amassing the greatest surplus in the history of the Commonwealth—$166,000,000 on May 31 and reducing the State's indebtedness to $53,035,083.80, the lowest point since 1925. The $48,870,000 indebtedness of the General State Authority was liquidated last week.

Attempting to hold controversy in the Legislature to a minimum, the Governor innovated a program of bi-partisan co-operation at the 1944 special session, convened for the specific purpose of enacting a soldier vote law.

MODEL G. I. VOTE LAW

As a result of the two-party conferences the Legislature adopted in record time a bill hailed as the "Model G. I. Vote Law."

The bi-partisan conferences continued at this year's session, and although the Governor declined to discuss party issues at the meetings, misunderstandings were ironed out and some legislation was agreed upon.

At the outset of the Administration in 1943, the Governor carried out one of his first campaign pledges—reduction of taxes.

Despite increased appropriations, the Governor approved tax reductions totaling $45,000,000 and additionally agreed to the institution of a wartime merit rating system for unemployment compensation contributions, estimated to save Pennsylvania businessmen about $65,000,000 annually.

With the State's solid financial condition continuing, the Governor made new reductions this year. The Commonwealth's four-mill tax on municipal bonds was repealed to assist political subdivisions in financing operations. The levy on bank and trust company shares was reduced.

GAS TAX TRANSFERRED

The emergency one-cent gasoline tax was transferred from the general fund to the motor license fund and $17,000,000 of its receipts earmarked for distribution to counties, cities, towns, townships and boroughs.

School subsidies and teachers' salaries, always knotty problems, have received special consideration by the present Administration. The 1945 stabilization law, increasing school grants $51,000,000, has been described as the "greatest advance in Pennsylvania education in more than 100 years."

The new Act, revising the system of State subsidies and increasing teachers' salaries, provides a $127,000,000 appropriation for 1945-47, more than double the Commonwealth's share of education expenses in the Earle Democratic regime, and the high point in contributions by the State toward the support of public education.

Soon to go into effect is a new law providing for a thorough medical examination, at State expense, of all children in both public and private schools. The examinations are to continue at specific intervals.

LABOR LAWS LIBERALIZED

Labor has not been forgotten by the Governor. Failing in his attempt to effect a compromise between representatives of organized labor and industry, Mr. Martin made his own recommendations to liberalize labor laws.

As a result, workmen's compensation, unemployment compensation and occupational disease benefits were all increased this year. The State also established a second injury fund to enable physically handicapped veterans to obtain employment.

The huge post-war program involves expenditures of approximately $137,000,000 in highway improvements and more than $61,000,000 in other projects, including new buildings, anti-pollution and reforestation work, and improvements to the ports of Philadelphia, Chester, Erie and Pittsburgh.

Five Get Jobs In Federal Courts

Five official court reporters at a salary of $5000 a year each, have been appointed to the Federal District Courts here, it was announced yesterday by U. S. District Judge William H. Kirkpatrick.

The appointments are the first in this district since the courts were created 56 years ago. Everett G. Rodebaugh, of Pughtown, near Pottstown, was named "chief" reporter. The others are H. A. B. Schwartz, of 420 W. Chelten ave.; Harold Hanover, of 1017 Duncannon ave.; and Ephraim H. Roman and John H. Nicholls, both of 4819 Chester ave.

Girl's Body Found Under Her Bed

DETROIT, June 30 (A. P.).—A murder mystery as baffling as any plot ever conceived in a detective thriller confronted police today in the death of pretty 21-year-old Marie Beavers, whose body was found last night stuffed under her bed in a midtown rooming house.

Dressed in a blouse, skirt and bedroom slippers, the girl was found lying on her back with a deep gash over her left eye. She was gagged. A few feet from her head was a pool of dried blood, but police said there was no blood on her clothing and no sign of a scuffle in the room.

Police believe Miss Beavers, whose background remains a complete mystery, had not left her room since she was last seen by her landlady, Mrs. Marie C. Irwin, 53, last Tuesday between 4 and 5 P. M.

Mrs. Irwin said the girl, who police learned last worked as a waitress, came to live in the rooming house in March, and never had any men visitors. In the girl's room, however, were several letters written to service men.

Athletics, Tigers Play Record 24-Inning, 1-1 Deadlock

25,734 See Bobanet Triumph by Head; Turbine 2d

Radio. Resorts

The Philadelphia Inquirer

PUBLIC LEDGER

Financial Sports

PHILADELPHIA, SUNDAY MORNING, JULY 22, 1945 — a b c d e f g S

A's Tie Own Mark; Umpire Halts Game

Buzfuz 3d In Camden Feature

Wagering Record For 1 Race Set; $280.30 Double

By JOHN WEBSTER

On a blazing, record-shattering afternoon at Garden State Park, four horses drove for the wire and Bobanet charged on the rail to win the fourth running of the $10,000 Benjamin Franklin Handicap yesterday in a finish that left the 25,734 race-goers breathless. This was a record crowd for the current season.

Winner in the photographic manner, Bobanet, owned by R. Bruce Livie's Bobanet establishment of Baltimore, was a head before another longshot, Morton Newmeyer's Turbine, for the lion's share of the purse—$10,075. Just a neck off the runner-up was the favorite, Sunshine Stable's Buzfuz, who was in tight quarters right at the finish, but third at the line.

$282,505 WAGERED

Finishing fastest of all from a laggard's beginning was Mrs. W. E. Snell's Pentin, still another rank outsider, to be fourth.

When $282,505 poured into the mutuels on the six-furlong fixture for three-year-olds, a new wagering standard was set. The previous one-race high had come last Labor Day with a $268,601 handle.

Early expectations of a brand new eight-race record fell short when $1,811,069 was wagered. The high-water mark for the track is $1,881,336 which came on the '44 Labor Day.

Highweight in the field of 11, Bobanet, hero of last summer's Walt Whitman in South Jersey's flatlands, shouldered 119 pounds and ran the three-quarters of a mile in 1.14 over footing that was drying out but still termed slow. The son of Cohort-Flying Pennant was smartly handled by Shelby Clark.

BOBANET PAYS $17.40

Given scant regard in the wagering rings as the thousands rushed in to back Buzfuz, a winning invader from Long Island, Bobanet paid $17.40, $8.80 and $4.80 across the board.

Turbine, the Havre de Grace-owned son of Burning Star, a winner at the track on Wednesday, was so lightly played he returned $24.30 and $8.60. Show tickets on the favorite, owned by the Miami attorney, Dan Chapell, paid just $2.60.

RAMPART SHAKEN OFF

Bobanet, who was away from the starting gate no faster than he should have been, was sent into contention by Clark on the turn. On the head end, Buzfuz, ridden by the skilled veteran, Tommy Luther, was dueling with the flying grey, William Helis' Greek Warrior, who had been rushed through on the rail to take the lead at the half-mile pole from a sluggish beginning.

Rampart, the shimmering black filly, had been shaken off on the far turn as the two speed horses fought it out. Turbine, taken to the outside by Sterling Young, was in the thick of action as Bobanet began to roll.

Greek Warrior, with Freddy Rem-

Continued on Page 4, Column 4

176,833 Race Fans Wager $11,035,375

NEW YORK, July 21 (A. P.).—A huge gathering of 42,760 packed the little Jamaica race course today and set a new track wagering record for a seven-race program by sending $3,704,466 through the mutuel machines. The old mark was $3,564,151.

The heavy New York wagering set the pace for the other tracks throughout the country and a total of $11,035,375 was wagered at 10 tracks by 176,833 spectators.

Today's breakdown:

Track	Attendance	Wagered
x-Jamaica	42,760	$3,704,466
Garden State	25,734	1,811,069
Washington Park	25,000	1,656,887
Suffolk Downs	26,681	1,428,239
x-Del Mar	12,965	911,374
Detroit	17,169	586,196
Pascoag	5,000	336,668
Hagerstown	4,500	275,923
River Downs	11,974	211,709
Ascot Park	4,900	113,744
Totals	176,833	$11,035,375
A Week Ago (11)	186,875	10,524,195
A Year Ago (11)	127,124	7,364,654

x—Denotes new track wagering record.

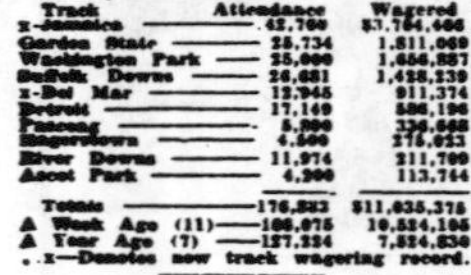

Wooderson Wins Army Mile Title

ALDERSHOT, Eng., July 21 (U. P.).—Corporal Sidney Wooderson, former world mile record holder, won the Army mile title today in 4.14.8 from a field of 16 to set a new record for the meet.

He announced after the race that he would run against Sweden's Arne Andersson in London's White City Stadium next month.

ED BUSCH BREEZES ACROSS FIRST BASE, SPLIT SECOND AHEAD OF SKEETER WEBB'S THROW

Athletics shortstop beats out hard smash to Tigers' shortstop in third inning of yesterday's game. Rudy York awaits belated toss in background.

Marathon Consumes 4 Hrs., 48 Mins.; Christopher Hurls 13, Mueller 19 2-3

By STAN BAUMGARTNER

In an amazing marathon that lasted four hours and 48 minutes to set a new American League record for time consumed and to tie that circuit's innings-played mark, the Athletics and Detroit Tigers battled to a 1-1 tie yesterday in Shibe Park. It was 7.48 o'clock and deep shadows lay across the field when Umpire-in-Chief Bill Summers called the game.

At the rate the teams were battling, they might have set who knows what records, but the rules state that no day game can be continued under lights. The record they tied recalled an earlier chapter in Connie Mack's career—the 4-1 Athletics victory at Boston, Sept. 1, 1906, in a game that went four hours and 47 minutes. The record they might have caught was the legendary 1-1 tie at 26 innings between Brooklyn and the Braves at Boston, May 1, 1920. However, yesterday's game, while a league record for time consumed, did not approach the major mark of five hours, 19 minutes set July 5, 1940, when Brooklyn defeated Boston, 6-2, in 20 innings.

SHORT IN ENDURANCE

Nor did yesterday's game approach either the A's-Red Sox or the Boston-Brooklyn 1920 classic in the matter of pitching endurance. Leon Cadore, Brooklyn, and Joe Oeschger (former Phil) both went 26-inning routes. And Jack Coombs of the A's and Joe Harris of the Red Sox both battled the entire 24 innings together.

Yesterday each club used two hurlers. Russ Christopher twirled the first 13 frames for the Athletics and Joe Berry the final 11. For the Tigers, Les Mueller, a big right hander who looks and pitches with the same motion but with triple the stuff of Boom Boom Beck, worked the first 19 and 2-3 innings. Dizzy Trout came to the mound in the 20th inning with two on base and two out—blanked the A's and hurled the rest of the way.

TIGERS' RUN TAINTED

All the scoring was done in the first seven innings. The Athletics took a 1-0 lead in the fourth after one out when Dick Siebert reached first on Rudy York's wild toss, went to third on a double by Roberto Estalella and scored on a single by Buddy Rosar.

The Tigers tied it, 1-1, in the seventh (a lucky run) and again the tally was made with one out. Roy Cullenbine worked Christopher for a walk and went to third when York sent a sizzling single to left-center. Roger Cramer then hit directly back to Siebert. The first baseman could have thrown Cullenbine out at the plate or he could have started a double play (3-6-3) to second and to first, but Dick hesitated—hesitated too long, finally stepped on first to get Cramer but tossed home too late to get Cullenbine and the score was tied.

A's MUFF CHANCES

Previous to this inning the Athletics had several chances to put the game on ice for Christopher who tried desperately to break a losing streak which had reached four straight and sent his pitching percentage down the ladder from 11 and 2 to 11 and 6. But they could not come through. In the fourth—the inning in which they scored—they had the bases loaded and only one out but George Kell hit into a double play.

Again in the sixth they had men on first and third and only one out after Hal Peck and Estalella had hit safely but Mueller put on the steam, fanned Rosar and forced Bill McGhee to pop up to Skeeter Webb at short.

DOUBLE PLAY ENDS THREAT

After the Tigers tied the score the A's had only one real chance to break the deadlock and this came in the 10th inning—and was spoiled by a magnificent peg to the plate by Jimmy Outlaw.

Irv Hall opened with a single to left but was forced at second by Peck. Siebert then flied out to Cullenbine but Estalella singled to left

Continued on Page 2, Column 7

(A. P. Wirephoto)

LES MUELLER

Detroit Tigers' right-hander who pitched 19 2-3 innings against the Athletics at Shibe Park yesterday in a game that was called after the 24th with the score 1-1.

Chester Soldier Wins Manila Bout

MANILA, July 21 (A. P.).—Pat. Gadson, 128, Chester, Pa., won a close decision over Joe Mosquida, 129, Manila, in the three-round main event of weekly service boxing bouts before 7000 spectators in Rizal Arena today.

Other results, all scheduled for three rounds: Clifford Cousins, 174, Fort Ott, Ohio, kayoed Eddy Elton, 174, Chicago, first round; Jerry Mason, 165, Brooklyn, kayoed Raleigh Batiste, 160, New Orleans, first; Joe Padilla, 118, Manila, TKO over Caspar Sealy, 118 (address not given), third; Joe Brown, 171, Galveston, Tex., TKO over William Grew, 175, Hewitt, Minn., first; Victor Cabrera, 141, Manila, defeated Bruno Kasiewicz, 138, Scottdale, Pa.; Felix Dolor, 120, Manila, decisioned Lowell Beatty, 120, Pittsburgh; George Williams, 126, New York, kayoed Diego Po, 126, Manila, second.

42,700 See Pavot Lose to Gallorette

By JACK GRIFFIN

NEW YORK, July 21 (U. P.).—Gallorette, a fleet little filly from the stables of W. L. Brann, looked like a carbon copy of the famed Twilight Tear today when she ran the mighty Pavot and nine other colts into the track to win the $50,000-added Empire City Stakes at Jamaica before 42,700 who wagered $3,704,466 during the day.

Held well up all the way under a sweet ride by Ted Atkinson, the fast little lady collared Pavot when they straightened out in the run for home and led him to the wire by three-quarters of a length to finish the mile and three-sixteenths romp in the fast time of 1.56.4. Her time was only four-fifths of a second off the track record.

RECORD DOUBLE HANDLE

A world record daily double handle was established when $202,800 was wagered on the two-race combination today. The former mark was $202,216. For the third time in four days long shot players had their inning in the double play when Sam Bernard, $88.30, and Darby Delilah, $12.50, won the first and second

Continued on Page 4, Column 7

Dot Head Wins From Peg Welsh

By DORA LURIE

Dorothy Head, Alameda, Calif., ranked 10th nationally, had to produce her best tennis foot in order to turn back Peggy Welsh, Philadelphia's top-ranking star, 7-5, 6-3, in the quarter-final round of the Pennsylvania and Eastern States women's grass court championship tennis tournament yesterday at the Merion Cricket Club, Haverford.

Miss Welsh played her best tennis in local history, but her efforts were not quite enough to turn in the biggest upset of the current season. She ranks 30th nationally.

CLOSE TO UPSET

The scores do not indicate the brand of magnificent tennis played by Miss Welsh, recent college graduate, who needed one point only twice at 40-15 to take a 5-2 game lead in the first set. But the blonde Philadelphian, daughter of Federal Judge George A. Welsh, recent college graduate, manufacture the points when she wanted them for game victory. And the result in no way indicates the pulsating duel between the pair throughout the match.

In one particular game, alone, the 10th of the first set, when Miss Welsh trailed 4-5 in games and warded off two set points, the pair played through 24 points, nine deuce scores, before the Quaker City favorite won

Continued on Page 3, Column 3

Dodson Keeps St. Paul Lead

By MAURICE PUTNAM

ST. PAUL, Minn., July 21 (A. P.).—Leonard Dodson, of Kansas City, the nonchalant "Clown Prince" of professional golfers, continued to lead qualifiers at the end of the second round of play in the $10,000 St. Paul Open today.

Dodson carded a 70 today which, with his Friday 67, gave him a 137 total for the two days. Five pros with 139 totals pressed close on his heels.

68 FOR SGT. HARRISON

They were Dick Metz, of Arkansas City, Kans., with a 71 today and a previous 68; Ky Laffoon, Chicago, who cut one stroke off his opening round 70; Sergeant E. J. (Dutch) Harrison, of Wright Field, O., who chopped three strokes off his earlier 71; Virgil Shreeve, San Francisco, down one stroke from an opening 70, and Toney Penna, Dayton, O., whose cards for the two days read 69-70.

Johnny Bulla, of Chicago, who lopped four off his initial 72 and Joe Coria, St. Paul, with a 69 today—two below his first card—were next with 140s.

PROTEST UPHELD

Bulla protested a 69 scorecard, contending a penalty stroke called on him at the 14th green because he

Continued on Page 3, Column 6

Sailor Feller Hurls No-Hitter

GREAT LAKES, July 21 (A. P.).—Chief Specialist Bob Feller, former fireball ace of the Cleveland Indians and present pitcher and coach of the Great Lakes Naval Training Station's team, hurled a no-hitter for the Sailors today, enabling them to trim the Ford All-Stars, Dearborn, Mich., 13-0, before 10,000 bluejackets.

Feller's perfect game gave the Great Lakes team its 19th victory of the season and his service strikeout record soared to 110 for 11 games. His last no-hitter in the major leagues resulted five years ago, when Feller blanked the White Sox, 1-0, on the opening day of the season for the first opening-day no-hit contest in the American League since 1900. Feller's catcher today was Walker Cooper, former Cards' star, whose 2-run homer in the fourth sparked the Sailors' five-run splurge.

Tom Raleigh, Jr., Takes New York Tennis Title

SYRACUSE, N. Y., July 21 (U. P.).—Tom Raleigh, Jr., Syracuse, won the New York State junior singles title today by defeating Fred Scribner, Forest Hills, N. Y., 7-5, 6-1, 6-0.

Later Raleigh paired with Walter Dockerill, of New Rochelle, N. Y., to capture the junior doubles title from Scribner and Stuart Robinson, of New York, 12-10, 6-1. Joseph Friedman, Woodmere, L. I., annexed the boys' singles title by beating Thomas Lewyn, New York, 1-6, 6-1, 6-1.

Senators, Browns, Yanks, Giants Win

By LOWELL REIDENBAUGH

A familiar and nostalgic ring reverberated through Yankee Stadium yesterday. It was the Yanks' once-stereotyped habit of home-running the opposition to earth, in this case the Chicago White Sox, bludgeoned, 12-3, with three circuit smashes.

Nick Etten, connecting with the runways congested, Herschel Martin delivering with one aboard, and Bud Metheny guided Ernie Bonham to his second conquest of the year, a seven-hitter that unseated Earl Caldwell and Johnny Johnson.

CALDWELL IS ROUTED

A crowd of 13,307—they saw Red Ruffing, ex-Army Sergeant, and Aaron Robinson, ex-Coast Guardsman, display the discharge emblem on their left sleeve for the first time in the Stadium—watched Caldwell make his first daylight start of the year and, after one inning, saw him tramp out under the home run barrage as the White Sox started their descent into sixth place.

The Washington Senators tightened their second-place post, trampling the Cleveland Indians, 7-4, behind Alex Carrasquel. Four Tribal runs in the second round chased starter Johnny Niggeling and introduced Carrasquel, who hurled shutout ball for the remainder of the game in addition to bashing a two-run single in the fifth that blotted out a 4-4 tie and routed Al Smith.

ERRORS HELP BROWNS

St. Louis' Browns hurdled into fifth place, whipping the Boston Red Sox, 4-1, with the assistance of two first-inning misplays. Nelson Potter with a six-hitter, won; Jim Wilson, though allowing but seven hits, lost.

Van Lingle Mungo strong-armed the Giants into fourth place, 6-3, spacing nine Cincinnati safeties for

Continued on Page 2, Column 7

Cubs, Merullo Beat Phils, 5-3

Special to The Inquirer

CHICAGO, July 21.—Len Merullo, a former Villanova College star, pounded out his first homer of the season with Mickey Livingston, one-time Phil, on base to give the Cubs a 5-3 victory over the Phils today in the opener of a four-game series.

The homer proved the payoff wallop in a 10-hit attack off Dick Mauney, who was doing very nicely until the late innings in a duel with Paul Derringer.

HOMER DECIDES

Stan Hack had paced the Cubs to a run with a double in the first and that was the lone tally until the sixth. Then the Cubs racked up another via doubles by Don

Continued on Page 2, Column 6

Magerkurth Freed Of Assault Charges

CINCINNATI, O., July 21 (U. P.).—Assault and battery charges against National League Umpire George Magerkurth, accused of striking a fan at Crosley Field Thursday, were dismissed today by Judge W. D. Alexander.

Magerkurth and the complainant, Thomas J. Longo, Dayton, shook hands in court and Magerkurth paid him $100 for "expenses."

The umpire complained that Longo had been "riding" him all season. Longo contended Magerkurth had mistaken him for the real heckler.

"Being an old baseball fan myself I know there's nobody so nutty as a fan in a close game," Alexander said in closing the case.

Baseball Facts

NATIONAL LEAGUE

Yesterday's Results

Chicago, 5; PHILLIES, 3.
New York, 6; Cincinnati, 3.
Boston, 5; Pittsburgh, 1, 1st game.
Pittsburgh, 3; Boston, 1, 2d game.
St. Louis, 8; Brooklyn, 7.

Standing of the teams

	W.	L.	P.C.	G.B.
Chicago	51	31	.622	—
St. Louis	49	36	.576	3½
Brooklyn	47	38	.553	5½
New York	46	43	.517	8½
Pittsburgh	44	42	.512	9
Boston	41	43	.488	11
Cincinnati	38	41	.481	11½
PHILLIES	24	66	.267	31

G.B.-Games behind.

Today's Schedule
Probable Pitchers and their Records

PHILLIES at Chicago (2)—Kraus (1-1) and Schanz (1-8) vs. Prim (6-4) and Wyse (13-5).

New York at Cincinnati (2) — Brewer (3-3) and Fischer (2-5) vs. Walters (4-4) and Bowman (7-4).

Brooklyn at St. Louis (2)—Gregg (11-6) and Lombardi (5-7) or Branca (0-0) vs. Barrett (12-6) and Donnelly (5-6).

Boston at Pittsburgh (2)—Andrews (6-9) and Tobin (9-11) vs. Roe (6-7) and Butcher (8-7).

AMERICAN LEAGUE

ATHLETICS, 1; Detroit, 1, 24 ings, called

Yesterday's Results

Washington, 7; Cleveland, 4.
St. Louis, 4; Boston, 1.
New York, 12; Chicago, 3.

Standing of the teams

	W.	L.	P.C.	G.B.
Detroit	46	34	.575	—
Washington	43	36	.544	2½
New York	42	38	.525	4
St. Louis	40	38	.513	5
Boston	42	40	.512	5
Chicago	42	41	.506	5½
Cleveland	37	42	.468	8½
ATHLETICS	28	51	.354	17½

G.B.-Games Behind.

Today's Schedule
Probable Pitchers and Their Records

ATHLETICS vs. Detroit at Shibe Park (2, 1.30 P. M.)—Gerkin (0-9) and Black (1-3) vs. Newhouser (11-8) and Benton (8-1).

Chicago at New York (2)—Grove (9-6) and Humphries (4-6) vs. Borowy (10-5) and Ruffing (0-0).

St. Louis at Boston (2)—Kramer (8-7) and Shirley (4-6) vs. Ferriss (16-2) and Heflin (0-3).

Cleveland at Washington (2) — Gromek (11-5) and Bagby (3-8) vs. Pieretti (9-6) and Haefner (6-9).

Continued on Page 2, Column 7

A's, Tigers' 24-Inning Box Score

DETROIT TIGERS

	*B.Av.	Ab.	R.	H.	2bh	3bh	hr	tb	rbi	sb	sh	po	a	e
Webb, ss	.179	10	0	2	0	0	0	2	0	0	0	7	11	1
Mayo, 2b	.275	9	0	0	0	0	0	0	0	0	0	7	9	1
Cullenbine, rf	.262	7	1	2	1	0	0	3	0	0	0	8	0	0
York, 1b	.272	9	0	3	0	0	0	3	0	0	0	28	6	1
Cramer, cf	.271	10	0	1	0	0	0	1	1	0	0	2	0	0
Outlaw, lf	.263	8	0	1	0	0	0	1	0	0	0	2	1	0
a-Greenberg	.239	0	0	0	0	0	0	0	0	0	0	0	0	0
b-Hostetler, lf	.156	0	0	0	0	0	0	0	0	0	0	0	0	0
Maier, 3b	.255	10	0	1	0	0	0	1	0	0	0	3	7	0
Swift, c	.223	9	0	0	0	0	0	0	0	0	0	12	0	0
Mueller, p	W3-L4	7	0	1	0	0	0	1	0	0	0	2	3	0
Trout, p	W8-L11	2	0	0	0	0	0	0	0	0	0	1	1	0
Totals		81	1	11	1	0	0	12	1	0	0	72	38	3

ATHLETICS

	*B.Av.	Ab.	R.	H.	2bh	3bh	hr	tb	rbi	sb	sh	po	a	e
Hall, 2b	.257	11	0	2	0	0	0	2	0	0	0	6	8	0
Peck, rf	.285	8	0	2	0	0	0	2	0	0	0	1	0	0
Siebert, 1b	.259	9	1	1	0	0	0	1	0	0	1	31	2	0
Estalella, cf	.313	10	0	5	1	0	0	6	0	0	0	5	0	0
Rosar, c	.205	9	0	2	0	0	0	2	1	0	1	13	2	0
McGhee, lf	.220	8	0	2	0	0	0	2	0	0	0	9	0	0
Kell, 3b	.231	10	0	0	0	0	0	0	0	0	0	2	6	0
Busch, ss	.213	10	0	1	0	0	0	1	0	0	0	3	12	1
Christopher, p	W11-L6	5	0	0	0	0	0	0	0	0	0	1	2	0
Berry, p	W4-L4	3	0	0	0	0	0	0	0	0	0	1	2	0
c-Burns	.247	0	0	0	0	0	0	0	0	0	0	0	0	0
d-Metro	.220	1	0	1	0	0	0	1	0	0	0	0	0	0
Totals		84	1	16	1	0	0	17	1	0	2	72	34	1

Detroit — 0 0 0 0 0 0 1 0 0 0 0 0 0 0 0 0 0 0 0 0 0 0 0 0—1
Athletics — 0 0 0 1 0 0 0 0 0 0 0 0 0 0 0 0 0 0 0 0 0 0 0 0—1

a-Batted for Outlaw in 22d.
b-Ran for Greenberg in 22d.
c-Batted for Berry in 24th.
d-Batted for Burns in 24th.

Two-base hits—Estalella, Cullenbine. Sacrifices—Siebert, Rosar. Double plays—Maier, Mayo and York; York, Webb and York; Webb, Mayo and York; Busch, Hall and Siebert. Left on bases—Detroit, 15; Athletics, 18. Bases on balls—Off Mueller, 5; Christopher, 2; Berry, 5. Struck out—By Christopher, 7; Mueller, 6; Berry, 2; Trout, 2. Hits—Off Christopher, 5 in 13 innings; Berry, 6 in 11 innings; Mueller, 13 in 19 2-3 innings; Trout, 3 in 4 1-3. Umpires—Summers, Rue and Boyer. Time of game—4.48. Batting average 1945.

25,000 See Devalue, Bought Month Ago, Nip Thumbs Up By Nose in $50,000 'Cap

By CHARLES DUNKLEY

CHICAGO, July 21 (A. P.).—Devalue, a 7-year-old thoroughbred owned by a Chicago housewife, scored a terrific upset in Arlington's $55,100 Stars and Stripes Handicap at Washington Park today by defeating the 3 to 5 favorite, Thumbs Up, by a nose before 25,000 astonished fans.

The winner is owned by Mrs. James Nemecek, whose husband is a tailor's manufacturer. She wasn't even present to witness the triumph.

PURCHASED LAST MONTH

Devalue had won only $5850 in one victory out of six starts this season, compared to the lump of $110,245 earned by Thumbs Up, winner of the $100,000 Santa Anita Handicap three weeks ago. Devalue never before had won an important stake and was just purchased by Mrs. Nemecek's Happy Hour Farms last month.

Devalue, trailing last in the field

Continued on Page 4, Column 1

Empire City Stakes Chart

JAMAICA, L. I., N. Y., JULY 21.—WEATHER CLEAR, TRACK FAST

FIFTH RACE—One and three-sixteenths miles; three-year-olds; Empire City Stakes. Purse—$50,000 added. Net values—$39,560, $10,000, $5000, $2500. Winner—Ch. f., 3, by Challenger 2d-Gallette. Owner—W. L. Brann. Trainer—E. A. Christmas.

Starters	Wt.	P.P.	St.	¼	½	¾	Str.	Fin.	Jockey	Win	Place	Show	Odds
Gallorette	116	9	4	3²	3¹½	2³	1nk	1¾	Atk'n	8.00	3.50	2.90	3.00
aPavot	126	1	1	1⁴	1²	1¹	2²	2²	Snider	—	4.60	4.10	2.65
Post G'duate	116	4	6	5³	4½	3⁴	3⁴	3²	Lindberg	—	—	14.70	64.90
Rick's Raft	116	3	5	7¹½	6hd	5hd	5²	4nk	Jemas	—	—	—	72.25
Darby Dieppe	116	11	3	6hd	7¹½	6¹¼	4hd	5²	M'Cr'ry	—	—	—	7.95
Esteem	116	10	7	11	9½	8hd	7½	6²	Wright	—	—	—	3.75
Bob Mann	111	5	8	4½	5²	4½	6¹½	7nk	Kirkland	—	—	—	31.10
Michaelo	111	7	11	8½	8½	9¹	8²	8²	Longden	—	—	—	15.50
War Trophy	111	6	10	9hd	11	10¹	9²	9⁴	Hearn	—	—	—	62.65
aRed Stick	111	8	9	10hd	10²	11	10⁴	10¹⁰	Permane	—	—	—	2.65
Coincidence	112	2	2	2¹½	2½	7hd	11	11	Arcaro	—	—	—	6.10

a-W. M. Jeffords and Mrs. W. M. Jeffords entry. Time: 1.56 4-5. Post: 4.06. Off: 4.07. Start poor from gate, won driving, place same. Overweight: Coincidence 1. Scratched: Pindus. Handle: $563,627.

Stars and Stripes Handicap

WASHINGTON PARK, JULY 21.—WEATHER CLOUDY, TRACK FAST

SEVENTH RACE—One and one-eighth miles; three-year-olds and up; Stars and Stripes Handicap. Purse—$50,000 added. Net values—$40,000, $10,000, $5000, $2500. Winner—B. h., 7, by Espino-Off Gold. Owner—Happy Hour Stable. Trainer—R. Salvino.

Starters	Wt.	P.P.	St.	¼	½	¾	Str.	Fin.	Jockey	Win	Place	Show	Odds
Devalue	108	5	10	9hd	8½	7½	5¹	1no	Br'ks	19.20	5.20	3.80	8.60
Thumbs Up	130	2	2	4hd	4hd	3hd	1½	2¹¾	Woolf		2.80	2.40	60
Sirde	115	1	1	1hd	1¹½	1hd	2½	3¹¾	Dodson		-	5.00	11.10
St. Jock	105	9	6	8²	5²	4½	3²	4no	Skor'ski				15.80
aOld K'utck	111	4	9	7½	7½	6¼	6²	5²	Bodiou				5.30
V'dina L'mar	106	7	4	3¹½	2¹½	2¹½	4hd	6½	Higley				25.00
Sigma Kappa	104	6	3	2½	3½	5²	7½	7½	Bates				148.60
Fire Dust	100	8	8	10	10	9¹	8²	8²	Fay				26.70
aDaily Tr'ble	121	10	7	6hd	9²	10	9½	9²	Adams				5.30
Good Bid	108½	3	5	5¹	6½	8²	10	10	Gardner				66.60

a-Walmac Farm and David Straus entry. Time: 1.51 3-5. Post: 5.18. Off: 5.18. Start good from gate, won driving, place same. Overweight: Devalue 2, Good Bid 4½, St. Jock 2. Scratched: Take Wing. Handle: $236,293. Attendance about 25,000.

The Philadelphia Inquirer

PUBLIC LEDGER

An Independent Newspaper for All the People

VOL. 233, NO. 29 | a b c d e f g | PHILADELPHIA, SUNDAY MORNING, JULY 29, 1945 | B | Copyright, 1945, by Triangle Publications, Inc. | PRICE, TWELVE CENTS

Bomber Hits Empire State Building, 13 Killed in Explosion and Flames

(Acme Telephoto)

DISASTER

Flaming death and destruction which visited the upper floors of the Empire State Building, world's tallest structure, when a bomber crashed into it yesterday, are shown graphically in these pictures. Above, the gaping hole torn in the building's 79th floor by the crash. At right, smoke billowing above the skyscraper as fires rage in 10 of the upper floors. Below left, photo-diagram of key areas involved in crash, located in a view looking south, with north side of structure shown. Below right, part of the B-25 bomber wreckage lying where it fell in 34th st., killing two Army airmen and a Navy passenger. At least 10 others were killed in the crash and 20 injured.

(A. P. Wirephoto)

PHOTO-DIAGRAM SHOWS WHERE BOMBER STRUCK

(Acme Telephoto)

SMOKE HIDES EMPIRE STATE TOWER

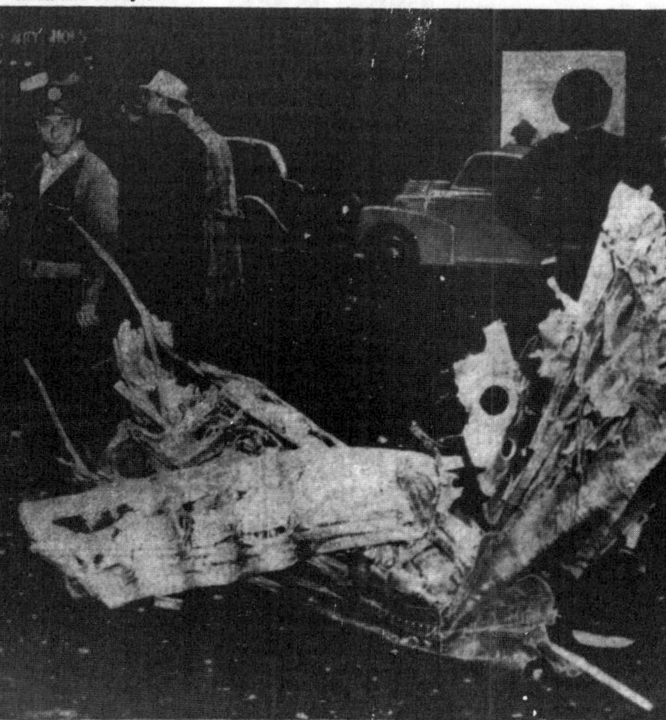

(A. P. Wirephoto)

FRAGMENT OF PLANE WRECKAGE IN BUSY 34TH ST.

10 Floors Burn As Plane Shears Through Edifice

Other stories and pictures on Pages 2 and 3.

NEW YORK, July 28 (U. P.).—A B-25 Billy Mitchell bomber rammed into the 78th story of the Empire State Building at 9:52 A. M. today, exploding in a cone of flames that turned the world's tallest skyscraper into a pillar of horror and brought death to at least 13 persons and injury to 20 more.

A searing envelope of gasoline flames shrouded 10 stories of the spire-like tower of the 1250-foot building.

The flames trapped hundreds of persons within fire and gas-filled rooms more than 1000 feet above the street.

Three elevators plunged out of control from the 80th floor to the basement.

Broken glass and debris rained down over several blocks. Half an hour after the explosion particles still sifted down.

EVEN FOG RIPPED AWAY BY BLAST

So tremendous was the explosion that it ripped away the fog which had hidden the topmost stories of the skyscraper from the vision of the B-25 pilot.

For two minutes the pinnacle of the chromium-girt Empire State stood out sharp and clear in the drizzle, while orange-red flames licked around.

Then the soft fog closed in again to hide the scene from the horrified sight of thousands of mid-town office workers who had rushed to windows at the sound of the blast which echoed over central Manhattan like a block-buster

Inside the building there was pandemonium.

PLANE ON FINAL LAP OF TRIP

The plane was en route to Newark, N. J. from Bedford, Mass., on the final lap of a cross-country flight which started at Sioux Falls, S. D.

It was piloted by Lieutenant Colonel William F. Smith, Jr., 27, of Watertown, Mass. He and his crew member, Staff Sergeant Christopher S. Domitrovich, 31, of Granite City, Ill., were instantly killed.

A Navy chief petty officer, riding in the plane as a passenger, also was killed.

A few minutes before the crash, the plane had inquired of LaGuardia Field by radio for instructions on landing conditions at Newark.

ROAR OF APPROACHING DISASTER

Suddenly, scattered observers near the Empire State tower heard the deep-throated roar of its motors. It was flying in the overcast at about 1000 feet and headed straight for the fog-hidden skyscraper.

A moment later it struck the north side of the building, between the 78th and 79th floors, penetrating with such force that one motor drove straight through the building to land on the roof of the 12-story Waldorf Building adjoining the Empire State on 33d st.

The fact that the disaster occurred on a Saturday morning, when many Empire State offices are closed, kept down the toll of the dead and injured. Casualties among pedestrians outside the building were reduced because mid-town streets are not crowded on Saturdays as they are during the week, and rain and drizzle held down the number out-of-doors.

EXACT DEATH TOLL STILL UNKNOWN

The force of the impact and explosion was such that many of the bodies were blown to bits. Hours after the tragedy, police, firemen and emergency workers were still trying to establish the exact death toll.

The plane struck near the ceiling of the 78th floor. The

Continued on Page 2, Column 3

Coast Guard Aide, 17, Tells of Victims' Agony

Illustrated on Page 2

By DONALD MOLONEY, U. S. C. G.

As Told to Mary Harrington

NEW YORK, July 28 (U. P.).—I'm just a hospital apprentice, second class, and I'm still in training. I suppose I could get prosecuted for what I did. I was on 34th st. and saw the B-25 crash into the Empire State Building.

There was a Walgreen's drug store across the street. They gave me syringes, two dozen needles, eight grains of morphine, bandages, 10 tubes of burn ointment and sterile water and alcohol.

GIRL STILL ALIVE

I ran first to the sub-basement. Somebody shouted that help was needed there. I'm 17 years old and I'm little, so the firemen let me climb down into the elevator, where the elevator girl was trapped. I had heard the elevator shoot down about 70 floors.

She was still alive and screaming. She hung on to me so I could hardly help her. I gave her morphine to ease the pain, and marked the dosage on her arm, where it wasn't burned, with her lipstick. I put oil on her burned face.

That was the only part of her I dared treat, the rest of her body was burned so badly. I put on sterile bandages, though. We carried her out. A priest and a rabbi helped me. The morphine didn't help her much. Her legs were crushed, and I think her back was broken.

There was another elevator operator in the basement, in the same shape. I helped him too.

Then I went up to the 79th floor. I picked up parts of four bodies and helped stack them on a table.

ELEVATOR FIXED

They called me down to the 70th floor, and I carried three women from there to the 67th floor. They had fixed the elevators.

I guess I must have carried and treated about 20 people. All of them were burned, and suffering terribly from shock. I gave morphine to 14 people.

We've been told in school for eight months, at Manhattan Beach and Groton, Conn., how to treat people suffering from burns and shock.

On the 69th floor I treated five in-

Continued on Page 2, Column 6

The Philadelphia Inquirer

PUBLIC LEDGER

An Independent Newspaper for All the People

FINAL CITY EDITION

CIRCULATION: July Average: Daily 569,159; Sunday 1,102,515

TUESDAY MORNING, AUGUST 7, 1945

Vol. 233, No. 38

a b d e f g h

THREE CENTS

Atomic Bomb, World's Most Deadly, Blasts Japan; New Era in Warfare Is Opened by U. S. Secret Weapon

Today

Key to Atomic Power Must Help Mankind

Trusteeship Set Up Bar to New Wars

World Balance Upset

By Alexander Kendrick

Inquirer Washington Bureau

WASHINGTON, Aug. 6

HOW to control atomic power, the greatest force for both war and peace ever placed in the hands of mortal men, automatically becomes the topmost problem of this Nation's Government, its military leaders, and its scientists.

For the revolutionary aspects of atomic energy are such that they unceremoniously upset the whole balance of world political, economic and military power, and present the key to the future development of all industry and agriculture.

The control of the world's basic source of energy, it is not too much to say, makes the United States, Great Britain and Canada a triumvirate in full charge of the harnessing of the universe.

And although the secrets of the atom will undoubtedly be shared eventually by other countries, the headlong start which the Anglo-Saxon nations have made on a road which leads where no one may imagine, imposes upon them a grave responsibility.

They must, as Secretary of War Henry L. Stimson said today, make sure that the new instrument "will be employed wisely in the interests of the security of peace-loving nations and the well-being of the world."

To this end, they have taken several important steps, within the limited compass of men confronted by a phenomenon surpassing all their understanding.

The most important is the creation of what is in effect a solemn international trusteeship to decide upon the application and development of atomic energy.

This trusteeship, with its perfunctory name of the Combined Policy Committee, must make sure that the use of atomic energy does not dislocate beyond dream of repair all the economic and industrial processes which have been the foundation of the world's material progress through recorded history.

In addition to this joint operation of policy-making, the three Anglo-Saxon nations have taken other neces-

Continued on Page 12, Column 4

Bong Killed Testing New Jet Plane

Leading Air Ace Burns to Death In Crash on Coast

BURBANK, Calif., Aug. 6 (U. P.).—Major Richard Bong, America's greatest air ace, died today in the flaming wreckage of a jet-propelled fighter plane which crashed while he was testing it.

MAJOR BONG

Only 24 years old, he wore 26 decorations, including the Nation's highest award, the Medal of Honor. He had survived countless air battles and shot down 40 Japanese planes without a scratch.

The knowledge he gained in those battles was too valuable to risk, so he was brought home to "safe" duty. He was on that "safe" duty today when his P-80 Shooting Star hurdled over a clump of trees and burst like a bomb in a bare field.

OVERSHOT THE FIELD

Witnesses did not agree on the cause of the crash. One Army flier said Major Bong overshot the field. Another witness said something appeared to fall out of the tail of the rocket-like ship.

Major Bong was trying to get out of the ship when it crashed. He had released the escape hatch and was partly clear when the tiny ship struck and boomed into flame. He was thrown clear.

Major Bong had pulled the rip-

Continued on Page 7, Column 3

Mackenzie King Wins By-Election

ALEXANDRIA, Ont., Aug. 6 (A. P.).—Prime Minister W. L. Mackenzie King was elected to the House of Commons tonight, defeating Dr. Richard Monahan, Independent Liberal, by a landslide majority in the Glengarry by-election.

Complete returns gave Mr. Mackenzie King 4623 votes against 327 for the 64-year-old doctor of Sharbot Lake, Ont.

Mr. Mackenzie King, defeated at Prince Albert in the June 11 general election, received the Liberal nomination in Glengarry.

(Acme Telephoto)

WHERE ATOMIC BOMBS ARE BEING MADE IN A TENNESSEE FACTORY

A view of a small portion of the Clinton Engineering Works, Oak Ridge, Tenn., where atomic bombs are being made. The works cover a Government reservation of 59,000 acres. Buildings are windowless except at the top.

Casualties

2 Die in Action, 18 Are Wounded

A Navy Department casualty list released yesterday named two men from the Philadelphia area killed in action and 18 wounded.

(In case of difference between this list and official information sent to the next of kin, the latest notification is always the final authority.)

NAVY DEAD

Malaby, Radarman Second Class Ira Bertram, Jr., son of Ira Bertram Malaby, Sr., of 1816 Ruscomb st.

Vahey, Fire Controlman Third Class John Albert, son of Mr. and Mrs. John F. Vahey, of 1522 S. Wilton st.

NAVY WOUNDED

Chiadek, Marine Assistant Cook Joseph Peter, son of Mr. and Mrs. George Chiadek, of 442 Olive st.

Cripps, Pharmacist's Mate Robert Lewis, son of Harry Muller Cripps, of 6724 Ditman st.

Dorsey, Radioman Third Class Bernice Leon, husband of Mrs. Dorothy Mae Dorsey, of 2214 Aspen st.

Freeman, Marine Platoon Sergeant Geoffrey

Continued on Page 7, Column 5

Japs Halt All Trains In Atomic Bomb Area

WASHINGTON, Aug. 6 (U. P.).—The Osaka radio—without referring to the atomic bomb dropped on Hiroshima—hinted tonight at the terrific damage it must have caused by announcing that train service in the Hiroshima and other areas had been cancelled.

First mention of the bomb itself came in a Japanese Domei agency dispatch announcing that President Truman and Prime Minister Clement R. Attlee had disclosed that the new missile had been dropped on Hiroshima, a leading Japanese port of embarkation.

HIT COMMUNICATIONS

The Osaka radio noted that the B-29's had begun a campaign against Japanese communication centers and warned that such assaults would be intensified. The broadcast did not mention any unusual form of explosive dropped by B-29's.

The Domei dispatch recorded by FCC carried this brief announcement:

"Tokio, Aug. 7 (Japanese Time).—President Harry Truman and Prime

Continued on Page 2, Column 5

Even a Penthouse

U. S. to Sell Mouse Works

Inquirer Washington Bureau

WASHINGTON, Aug. 6.

THE United States Government, which has always proceeded on the theory that if you make a better mouse the world will beat a path to your door, finds itself trapped today with too many mice.

It is desperately trying to auction off its $150,000 air-conditioned mouse factory, which has been turning out mice at the whisker-bristling rate of 15,000 per week all through the war, but which is now in danger of extermination as surplus property.

The big mousarium, the Nation's giddiest secret weapon of the war, is offered by the Reconstruction Finance Corp. to any would-be rodent magnate with a nose for a bargain.

The RFC tells its mouse tale in a handsome brochure issued by the Office of Defense Plants, with pictures and prospectus. It is a tale right out of an animated movie cartoon.

• • •

WHEN war came, it can now be told, the United States was in the midst of a crucial mousepower shortage. Research laboratories needed the white-furred, blue-

Continued on Page 8, Column 3

Stimson Predicts Shorter War Now

WASHINGTON, Aug. 6 (A. P.).—Secretary of War Henry L. Stimson predicted today that the atomic bomb would "prove a tremendous aid" in shortening the war with Japan.

Mr. Stimson said in his statement that the explosive power of the bomb is such as to "stagger the imagination." He added that scientists are confident of developing even more powerful atomic bombs.

MORE DATA PROMISED

Mr. Stimson promised that further statements will be released in the future to give additional details concerning scientific and production aspects.

He disclosed that development of the bomb was carried out by thousands of persons "with the greatest secrecy." The work has been so divided, he said, that no one has been given more information concerning the bomb than was absolutely necessary to his particular job.

The possibility of using atomic

Continued on Page 3, Column 4

Terrific Missile Unleashes Basic Force of Universe

Text of President Truman's Announcement on Page 3; Other Stories and Pictures on Page 2, 3, 4, 5 and 12.

By JOHN C. O'BRIEN

Inquirer Washington Bureau

WASHINGTON, Aug. 6.—A terrifying new weapon—an atomic bomb with a destructive force that staggers the imagination—has been loosed upon Japan, President Truman revealed today.

Called the greatest achievement of organized science, the explosive crashed with annihilating force Sunday on Hiroshima, Japanese army base with a population of 318,000.

EXCEEDS 20,000 TONS OF TNT

Developed at a cost of $2,000,000,000 by the Army with the assistance of American and British scientists, the new bomb, which harnesses the basic power of the universe (the force from which the sun draws its power) has more power than 20,000 tons of TNT and more than 2000 times the blast power of the largest bomb ever used in the history of warfare—although, according to London reports, it weighs only 100 pounds.

Results of the initial use of th[illegible] on Hiroshima were not immediately available. The War Department reported that reconnaissance planes found an impenetrable cloud of dust and sm[illegible] the target area.

WIDE AREA BELIEVED WIPED OUT

On the basis of tests in this countr[illegible] informed sources reported that the bomb would obli[illegible], not merely raze, everything in its path for a probable radius of 40 blocks from the point of detonation, wiping out all life within this area.

Dreadful as the new atomic bomb is in its present form, President Truman announced that "even more powerful forms are in development."

Perfection of the new secret weapon represented a victory for the United States and Great Britain in an anxious nip-and-tuck race with the Germans, who, it was learned, were working feverishly on a scheme to harness the explosive force of the atom for war purposes as early as 1942.

TRUMAN WILL ASK CONGRESS ACTION

"We may be grateful to Providence," the President said, "that the Germans got the V-1's and the V-2's late and in limited quantities and even more grateful that they did not get the atomic bomb at all."

Foreseeing vast possibilities for beneficial use of the Army's discovery in the world's peacetime economy—the use of atomic energy as a supplement to the power that now comes from coal, oil and falling water—the President was, nevertheless, so alarmed over its sinister implications (the bomb could conceivably wreck civilization) that he planned

Continued on Page 2, Column 2

Firm Opposes Draft of Strikers

A plea to the Ambler draft board to reclassify 42 former striking employes back into war worker status was made yesterday by an official of Keasbey & Mattison Co., as the men left for their pre-induction physical examinations.

The official said: "We want these men back—we can't afford to lose them."

ALL TAKE PHYSICALS

At the 32d st. and Lancaster ave. induction center, Army officials said the men went through the processes of physical examination and those who passed would be subject to Army call.

Meanwhile, in Harrisburg, the men were described at Selective Service headquarters as not of an age group, generally, or family status which the Army is eager to have inducted.

Lieutenant Colonel Clarence M. Hartman, acting Selective Service

Continued on Page 8, Column 6

Johnson Death May Put Hoover in U.S. Senate

Inquirer Washington Bureau

WASHINGTON, Aug. 6.—The name of Herbert Hoover has been discussed by Republican Party national leaders for the Senatorial vacancy caused by the death today of Senator Hiram W. Johnson (R., Calif.), The Inquirer has learned.

Governor Earl Warren, of California, is seriously considering the former President, who lives at Palo Alto, for the 18-month unexpired term of the veteran isolationist, it was said.

GOVERNOR MAY RUN

Whether Mr. Hoover, if seated in the Senate, would run for election next year, or whether Governor Warren himself would be the G. O. P. candidate, has not yet been decided. But the former President, it is believed, would welcome the opportunity to serve as a key figure in the Senate in what is expected to be a crucial election year in 1946.

If Mr. Hoover does not accept the seat, it was asserted, the new Senator from California may be chosen from two other logical candidates, Ray Haight, Republican National

Continued on Page 23, Column 7

Argentina Lifts State of Siege

BUENOS AIRES, Aug. 6 (U. P.).—The Government tonight lifted the state of siege which has prevailed since shortly after Pearl Harbor, in what was regarded as the most important single step possible towards a restoration of constitutional normality and the holding of free elections.

The action meant that repressive powers wielded by the Government under the state of siege decree were ended. Political leaders and newspapers had maintained that no free elections were possible under the state of siege. President General Edelmiro Farrell promised some time ago that before the end of the war he would call elections.

'Inside Spain'

IN VIEW of the Potsdam agreement, combined with the new British Labor Government's attitude toward Franco, the world spotlight is focused on Spain today. John Chabot Smith, War Correspondent, has just completed a tour of that country and tells what goes on INSIDE SPAIN in a timely series of articles which begin in

Tomorrow's Inquirer

50 Atomic Bombs Could Raze City

"Twenty to 50" atomic bombs, of the type which President Truman announced was dropped on Hiroshima, "probably would obliterate a city of this size and make Philadelphia worse than Berlin was after months of ordinary bombing."

That opinion of the terrific destructive powers of the newest and most deadly kind of military weapon was expressed yesterday by Dr. Roy K. Marshall, director of the Fels Planetarium and associate director of the Franklin Institute.

WEIGHT REPORTED 1000 LBS.

Dr. Marshall, a noted astronomer and astro-physicist, expressed the belief that the atomic aerial explosive hurled at the ill-fated Japanese city "weighed no more than 1000 pounds, due to the concentrated nature of its charge," and asserted that in view of that fact, "20 to 30 B-29's can now do the work of thousands of the giant American bombers."

He also said he believed that a substance known as Uranium 235,

Continued on Page 5, Column 1

Blast Vaporizes Tower, Test Felt for 250 Miles

LOS ALAMOS, N. M., Aug. 6 (A. P.).—The first man-made atomic explosion, a preview of the deadly destruction to be rained upon Japan, was set off in the New Mexico desert July 16, causing earthquake-like tremors for a radius of 250 miles.

Scientists and military authorities who lay face down nearly 10 miles away, their heads turned away from the blast area, peered through dark glasses to see a ball of fire "many times brighter than the midday sun," followed by an explosion that sent a cloud rolling 40,000 feet into the stratosphere in five minutes.

STEEL TOWER VAPORIZED

Two men were knocked down while standing outside the control center more than five miles from a steel tower where the blast was set off. The tower itself was vaporized and only a huge sloping crater left in its place.

The test of the $2,000,000,000 experiment occurred at 5.30 A. M. at a remote location on the Alamogordo, N. M., military reservation, 120 miles south of Albuquerque. It had been delayed an hour and a

Continued on Page 2, Column 4

Canadian Troops Arrive at Guam

GUAM, Aug. 6 (U. P.).—The first contingents of Canadian troops, ships and planes have arrived in this area, marking Canada's all-out entry into the Pacific war, it was disclosed today.

Colonel Richard S. Malone, director of public relations for the Canadian Army, said Canada would field 30,000 troops, all trained in Kentucky. They will use American arms.

The troops will be supplemented by squadrons of the Royal Canadian Air Force in addition to as least 60 Canadian Navy ships, including two aircraft carriers, two cruisers and numerous destroyers and frigates.

Churchill Bares Race With Nazis

LONDON, Aug. 6 (A. P.).—Former Prime Minister Winston Churchill said tonight it was "by God's mercy" that American and British—instead of German—scientists, discovered the secret of atomic power "long mercifully withheld from man."

The success of the historic achievement, he added, stood "to

Continued on Page 3, Column 5

THE WEATHER

Philadelphia and vicinity: Showers early this morning, followed by clearing. Fair with moderate temperature tomorrow. Moderate to fresh northwesterly winds.

Eastern Pennsylvania and Maryland: Fair with moderate temperature today.

New Jersey and Delaware: Clearing this morning. Moderate temperature.

Full Weather Data on Page 3

The Philadelphia Inquirer

PUBLIC LEDGER

An Independent Newspaper for All the People

FINAL CITY EDITION

CIRCULATION: July Average: Daily 569,159; Sunday 1,102,515

THURSDAY MORNING, AUGUST 9, 1945

Vol. 233, No. 40

abdefgh

THREE CENTS

REDS HURL ARMY AT JAPS

ATOM BOMB HITS NAGASAKI

Today

March of Jap Doom
July 26 Ultimatum
Atomic Bomb Raid
Red Entry Into War
End in Sight Now

—By Maj. Geo. F. Eliot—

EITHER the Japanese war is very near its end, or the Japanese are something more (or less) than human beings. It seems impossible to suppose that any people can longer sustain the terrific succession of physical and psychological blows which have been launched against the Japanese, by well-calculated design, beginning with the British-Chinese-American surrender demand of July 26 and continuing in unbroken succession at two or three-day intervals from that time onward.

The proclamation of July 26 was, as I suggested in a column, "only the first move in a calculated major operation of psychological warfare designed to bring about the collapse of Japanese morale; an operation undertaken with full Russian concurrence and indeed participation."

The next move was the announcement of a list of Japanese cities to be bombed "by roster" and immediately thereafter the attacks came as per schedule. This was followed by the Potsdam communique itself, which by the example of Germany's fate showed the Japanese what happened to a nation which stubbornly held out after all hope was gone, and drew upon itself the converging, irresistible power at the disposal of the United Nations.

The Potsdam communique was made public on Aug. 2; on Aug. 5 the first atomic bomb ever launched in war wiped out the Japanese city of Hiroshima. Now, on Aug. 8, the Soviet Union declares war on Japan. The mere recital of these successive events rules

Continued on Page 12, Column 1

By MURLIN SPENCER

GUAM, Aug. 9 (Thursday) (A. P.). — The world's second atomic bomb, most destructive explosive invented by man, was dropped on strategically important Nagasaki on western Kyushu Island at noon today.

Crew members radioed that results were good, but General Carl A. Spaatz said additional details would not be disclosed until the mission returned.

The first atomic bomb destroyed more than 60 percent—4.1 square miles—of Hiroshima, city of 343,000 population, Sunday (U. S. time), and the Tokio radio reported "practically every living thing" there was annihilated.

NAGASAKI MORE VULNERABLE CITY

Use of the awesome atomic bomb on Nagasaki came just after Japan had had time to assess the damage wrought at Hiroshima, which was one of the enemy cities best prepared to fight fires caused by bombing.

Nagasaki, with its closely packed houses, was believed to be more vulnerable. It has a population estimated at 255,000, and is an important shipping and railway center. It was hit first by China-based B-29's a year ago this month and was heavily attacked by Far East Air Forces bombers and fighters last July 31 and on the following day.

Although but two-thirds as large as Hiroshima in population, Nagasaki is considered more important industrially. Its 12 square miles are jam-packed with eave-to-eave buildings which won it the name "Sea of Roofs."

RANKS AS IMPORTANT WAR PORT

Nagasaki was vitally important as a port for transshipment of military supplies and the embarkation of troops in support of Japan's operations in China, Formosa, southeast Asia and the southwest Pacific. It was also highly important as a major shipbuilding and repair center for both naval vessels and merchantmen.

The city includes the industrial suburbs of Inase and Akunoura on the western side of the harbor and Ura-

Continued on Page 4, Column 6

By ALEXANDER KENDRICK *Inquirer Washington Bureau*

WASHINGTON, Aug. 8 — Russia today declared war against Japan and two hours later the crack Far Eastern Red Army launched a sudden attack on the Japanese Kwantung Army, on the eastern section of the far-flung Manchurian border.

At the same time, Red Air Force bombers opened attacks on Japanese military and economic concentrations in Manchuria.

The second war in 40 years between the two nations, traditional Far Eastern foes, became a reality shortly after midnight Soviet time (5 P. M., E. W. T.).

HUGE WAR MACHINE SET IN MOTION

Two hours before, at 3 P. M. (E. W. T.), the Moscow decision to enter the Pacific conflict had been announced in this country by President Truman, and in Europe by the Moscow radio.

The immediate Soviet attack made clear the fact that a gigantic Far Eastern military machine had been set in motion by the Russians, as part of an Allied master plan to bring the long Pacific War to a swift end with the unconditional surrender of Japan.

The Soviet declaration of war, delivered with the shattering effect of an atomic bomb, was made public here by President Truman after his return from the Potsdam Conference, where he was successful in the primary purpose of his trip—persuading Premier Josef Stalin to give up Russia's neutrality pact with Japan as a means of implementing the new World Security Charter.

REDS ATTACK FROM MARITIME PROVINCES

The exact location of the first Soviet assault on Japanese-held territory on the Asiatic mainland was not revealed by the Hsinking (Manchuria) radio, which told the world of the start of hostilities.

However, the announcement that the attack came on the eastern sector of the Manchurian border indicated that it was made from the Soviet Maritime Provinces, either from Khabarovsk or Blagoveschensk, into the extreme northeastern part of Manchuria.

Simultaneously, Soviet seizure of the southern Japanese-held half of strategic Sakhalin Island seemed likely,

Continued on Page 2, Column 3

MAP BY INQUIRER STAFF

WHERE RUSSIAN TROOPS AND ATOM BOMB HIT JAPS

Soviet forces (open arrow, A) were reported attacking the eastern frontier of Manchuria a few hours after the Russian declaration of war yesterday against Japan, while U. S. airmen dropped a second atomic bomb on Nagasaki (B). The black arrows show how Japan now is surrounded by Allied forces. Also indicated are distances to Jap home islands from various Allied bases. Enemy controls shaded area.

Temple Seeking 175-Acre Club

Negotiations for the purchase of the 175-acre tract of land belonging to the Cedarbrook Country Club on Cheltenham ave. in Cheltenham township, as a site for the undergraduate schools of Temple University has been authorized by the board of trustees of the university, it was announced yesterday.

The board authorized Robert L. Johnson, president of the university, to negotiate for suitable terms of purchase of the country club as part of the post-war plan of building construction contemplated by the university.

OTHER TRACTS UNSUITABLE

The site at Cedarbrook, across Cheltenham ave. from the eight-acre tract which houses the Temple Stadium and locker rooms, was chosen after officials of the institution were unable to purchase Hunting Park. Other tracts of land were offered a Temple University spokesman reported yesterday, but they did not meet the rigid requirements set down.

The university would build an administration building, college of arts and sciences, teachers and business college, a public administration and

Continued on Page 28, Column 2

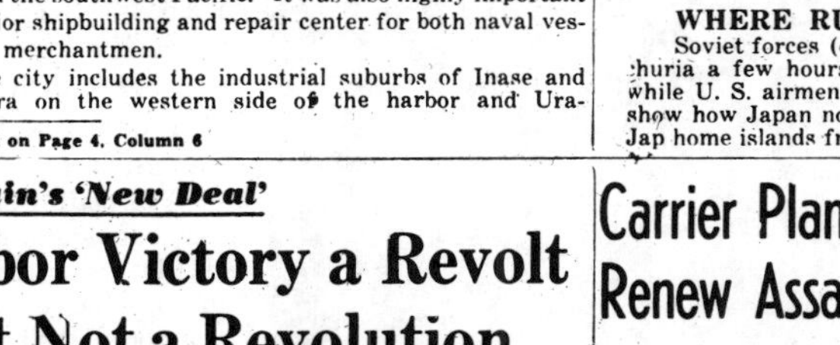

Britain's 'New Deal'

Labor Victory a Revolt But Not a Revolution

(In order to find out just what the new Labor Government means in Great Britain, The Inquirer last week sent Richard A. Thornburgh, an assistant managing editor, to London to talk with the man-in-the-street as well as with British leaders. Herewith is the first of his series of articles on "Britain's 'New Deal.'")

By Richard A. Thornburgh

LONDON, Aug. 8.

THE British election was a revolt, but not a revolution, and changes which may be brought about by the new Labor Government are not likely to upset the normal way of life in the United Kingdom.

That is the consensus of men and women in all walks of life in London and includes the studied opinions of some of the best minds on both sides of the British political fence.

There are exceptions, of course—Tories, who believe the end of the Empire is just around the corner, and working people who believe they soon will be living like aristocrats. But for the most part the British expect nothing very drastic, although there was disagreement on some of the details.

Frankly speaking exponents of the Conservative and Labor theories of government agreed that the basis of

Continued on Page 12, Column 2

Truman Breaks Three Big Stories

WASHINGTON, Aug. 8 (A. P.).—President Truman has electrified the world on three distinct occasions since he entered the White House 119 days ago.

Less than a month after taking office on April 12, he announced Germany's unconditional surrender and the end of the war in Europe.

Last Monday he released the epoch-marking story of the atomic bomb.

And today he announced that Russia had declared war on Japan.

In between, the President has kept news wires humming with statements on both domestic and international affairs.

Carrier Planes Renew Assault

GUAM, Aug. 9 (Thursday) (A. P.).—Admiral William F. Halsey's Third Fleet returned to its terrific carrier plane devastation of the Japanese homeland today, adding its weight to 400-plane B-29 raids, the wrecking of Hiroshima and Nagasaki with the world's first two atomic bombs, and entry of Russia into the war against Japan.

Admiral Chester W. Nimitz' communique reported that American and British carrier pilots launched "strong attacks" on shipping, air installations and other military targets on the northern part of Honshu Island at dawn.

ATTACKS CONTINUING

The attacks are continuing, Admiral Nimitz added. He announced that a battleship and lesser fleet units shelled Wake Island yesterday, destroying ammunition dumps and anti-aircraft emplacements and inflicting other damage.

Admiral Halsey's force was swinging into action for the first time in 10 days, during which it rode out a typhoon in the Western Pacific and undoubtedly refueled and resupplied itself for renewed efforts to attempt to knock Japan out of the war in

Continued on Page 5, Column 6

War Decree By U. S. S. R.

LONDON, Aug. 8 (U. P.).—Text of the Moscow radio announcement of the Russian declaration of war on Japan.

On Aug. 8, Foreign Commissar of the U. S. S. R. Comrade Molotov received Japanese Ambassador Sato and in the name of the Soviet Government made to him the following statement for transmission to the Government of Japan:

After the rout and capitulation of Hitlerite Germany, Japan remained the only great Power which still stands for continuation of war.

The demand of the three Powers, United States, Great Britain and China, of July 26, this year

Continued on Page 2, Column 2

Of Special Interest

Other stories and pictures concerning Russia's war declaration on Pages 2, 3, 4 and 12.

Other stories and pictures concerning the atomic bomb on Pages 4, 5 and 12.

Truman to Speak On Air Tonight

Illustrated on Page 4

By JOHN C. O'BRIEN

Inquirer Washington Bureau

WASHINGTON, Aug. 8. — President Truman will broadcast his report to the Nation on the recent Potsdam Conference at 10 o'clock tomorrow night. The 30-minute speech, the President's longest since he took office, will be carried on all radio networks and presumably will be short-waved to the rest of the world.

Back at his desk piled high with accumulated official business, the President took time out from interviews with callers and the preparation of his speech to sign, with Secretary of State James F. Byrnes, the Senate document ratifying the United Nations Charter and, a short time later, to announce that Russia had entered the war against Japan.

FIRST TO CARRY THROUGH

The United States became the first of the 50 nations which subscribed to the charter at the San Francisco Conference to complete action necessary to bring the United Nations organization into being.

White House Secretary Charles G.

Continued on Page 4, Column 3

Japs Still Have Time To Yield, Byrnes Says

Inquirer Washington Bureau

WASHINGTON, Aug. 8.—Secretary of State James F. Byrnes tonight hailed Russia's entry into the Pacific war as an action that should "save the loss of many lives," and warned the Japanese that they still had time—"but little time"—to avert destruction by surrendering.

Simultaneously, the Secretary, just returned from the Potsdam conference, revealed that President Truman had prevailed upon Generalissimo Josef Stalin there to give up Russian neutrality with Japan for the sake of United Nations' co-operation through the new World Charter.

CHARTER INVOKED 1ST TIME

Thus the Charter, although not yet in effect by ratification, was invoked for the first time as a means of curbing aggression and restoring peace.

Mr. Byrnes expressed his pleasure that "the Allied Powers that co-operated in Europe to defeat the enemy will continue their co-operation in the Far East, and will bring peace to the world."

Russia's decision to fight Japan,

Continued on Page 2, Column 8

Jap Announcement Quotes Red Radio

SAN FRANCISCO, Aug. 8 (A. P.).—Japan's first recorded wireless reaction to Russia's war declaration was a brief factual announcement of that action by the Domei Agency in an English language transmission to Europe.

The words "flash! flash!" preceded the dispatch, which quoted the Moscow radio.

THE WEATHER

Philadelphia and vicinity: Fair today and Friday with moderate temperatures; gentle to moderate winds, north to northeast.

Eastern Pennsylvania, New Jersey, Delaware and Maryland: Sunny and pleasant, with moderate temperatures and rather low humidity.

Full Weather Data on Page 2.

Let Us Thank God

TO ALMIGHTY GOD, for this blessed peace restored to a war-torn world, a grateful people offer devout thanksgivings.

Thank God, we say, the war is over at last. The guns are stilled. The bombs plunge no longer on their missions of death. Mothers and wives and sweethearts can breathe with unfettered hearts. Our loved ones will be coming home. An evil enemy has been crushed.

But there are many who are not here to rejoice with us this great day—because they gave their lives so we could have this day. Give them our prayers, our undying gratitude, our promise to cherish forever the ideals they freely died for. And for peace with victory, let us thank the All-Merciful God. (AN EDITORIAL)

Complete War History, Maps, Pictures: Pages 3, 5, 6, 7, 8, 9, 10, 11, 12, 13, 14, 15, 16, 26

The Philadelphia Inquirer

PUBLIC LEDGER

An Independent Newspaper for All the People

FINAL

CIRCULATION: July Average: Daily 569,159; Sunday 1,102,515 | WEDNESDAY MORNING, AUGUST 15, 1945 | abdefgh VJ | THREE CENTS

 Vol. 233, No. 46

PEACE

Truman Announces Jap Surrender, Ends Fighting; MacArthur Named Chief; Draft Calls Are Slashed

By ALEXANDER KENDRICK *Inquirer Washington Bureau*

WASHINGTON, Aug. 14.—The war is over. Japan has surrendered unconditionally, and Allied forces on land and sea and in the air have been ordered to cease firing. President Truman broke the news to a tensely waiting Nation at 7 P. M. today, just one hour after the Japanese acceptance of the final Allied terms had been delivered to the State Department by the neutral Swiss Government.

The acceptance included submission of Emperor Hirohito to the authority of an Allied Supreme Commander, and the President named General Douglas MacArthur as that commander. General MacArthur will receive the formal surrender. He promptly radioed Emperor Hirohito demanding that Japan begin arrangements for cessation of hostilities "at the earliest practicable date."

44 MONTHS OF WAR

The President's announcement, delivered with a smile as he stood in his White House office flanked by the members of his Cabinet, ended the bloodiest conflict in all history. It came 44 months after Pearl Harbor, when the Pacific War began, and three months after the unconditional surrender of Nazi Germany.

The matter-of-fact statement that the war was over, announced simultaneously in London, Moscow and Chungking, brought in its wake a world-wide celebration which drowned out in noise, revelry, tears and laughter all the premature celebrating of the last few days.

RECONVERSION PUT INTO MOTION

It also set into rapid motion this Government's machinery for reconverting from war back to a normal peacetime economy.

The draft was immediately reduced to 50,000 in-

Continued on Page 2, Column 2

GENERAL MacARTHUR NAMED SUPREME COMMANDER IN JAPAN
General Douglas MacArthur, who scored a brilliant series of victories against the Japs, has been named Supreme Allied Commander to rule conquered Japan.

U. S. Cruiser Sunk, All Men Are Casualties

By JOHN M. McCULLOUGH *Inquirer Washington Bureau*

WASHINGTON, Aug. 14.—The 10,000-ton United States heavy cruiser Indianapolis, flagship of the powerful Fifth Fleet, was sunk recently in the Philippine Sea, with the heaviest casualties sustained by an American warship in high-seas combat in this war.

The Indianapolis was lost on her return trip from Guam, after delivering "atomic bomb material"—presumably parts of the awesome weapon which destroyed Hiroshima.

Every one of the powerful cruiser's complement of 1196 men is listed as dead, missing or wounded. The Navy Department, in a special communique, listed the casualties as follows:

Dead: 5.
Missing in action: 875.
Wounded: 316.

This casualty list is exceeded only by that sustained by the battleship Arizona, which was torpedoed and sunk at her berth off Ford Island in Pearl Harbor on Dec. 7, 1941.

Listed among the wounded is Captain Charles Butler McVay, III, a native of Ephrata, Pa., the Indianapolis' skipper.

HOUSTON LOSS RECALLED

The United States heavy cruiser Houston, lost in the closing phase of the disastrous Battle of the Java Sea in late February, 1942, is not believed to have had as heavy a complement, although none of her personnel officially has been reported as surviving.

The manner in which the big cruiser met her end was not disclosed, aside from the usual Navy Department phrase "enemy action." However, it was disclosed that she was lost after having delivered "essential atomic bomb material" to Guam late in July.

"She delivered her unusual cargo,"

Continued on Page 4, Column 3

THE WEATHER

Philadelphia and vicinity: Showers this morning, followed by clearing and cooler tonight. Thursday, fair with moderate temperatures. Moderate southerly winds shifting to northwest this morning.

Eastern Pennsylvania: Showers and thunderstorms today with cooler temperatures.

New Jersey, Delaware and Maryland: Thundershowers, cooler in the interior.

(Full Weather Data on Page 2)

POLLEN COUNT

The pollen count for the 24-hour period ended at 4.30 P. M. yesterday taken in the central city by a recognized authority on allergy: one pollen granule per cubic yard [illegible]

Petain Gets Death; Jury Urges Mercy

PARIS, Aug. 15 (Wednesday) (A. P.). — Marshal Henri Philippe Petain was convicted and sentenced to death early today by three judges and a 24-man jury who deliberated almost seven hours.

The high court of justice added it "hoped the sentence would not be executed."

(This recommendation for clemency presumably will be considered by General Charles DeGaulle, President of the French Provisional Government.)

PROPERTY CONFISCATED

Besides condemning the 89-year-old former chief of the Vichy State to death for "plotting against the internal safety of France," the court also sentenced him to national in-

Continued on Page 6, Column 1

Drafting Halted On Men Over 26

By JOHN C. O'BRIEN *Inquirer Washington Bureau*

WASHINGTON, Aug. 14.— The Selective Service system tonight ordered cancellation of inductions of all registrants who are 26 years of age or older, after President Truman had directed an immediate cutback of selective service inductions from 80,000 to 50,000 a month.

The Selective Service order, signed by Major General Lewis B. Hershey, was sent tonight to all State directors.

The directors were instructed to postpone induction, assignment to work of national importance, or pre-induction examination of every registrant who had reached the age of 26, except volunteers.

YOUTHS TO FILL QUOTA

The local boards also were directed to fill the 50,000 monthly quota set by the President from registrants between the ages of 18 and 25 who were not eligible for deferment.

The result of this order, it was ex-

Continued on Page 6, Column 3

Nimitz Issues Cease-Fire Order

GUAM, Aug. 15 (Wednesday) (A. P.).—Orders have been issued to the U. S. Pacific Fleet and to other forces under command of the commander-in-chief of the U. S. Pacific Fleet to cease offensive operations against the Japanese, Admiral Chester W. Nimitz announced today.

The announcement was made in a very brief communique issued at 11 A. M.—exactly three hours after President Truman's announcement that Japan had accepted surrender terms.

Philadelphia Roars Salute To Victory

By WILLIAM C. FARSON

Philadelphia gave vent to its elation over Japan's surrender last night with the wildest, noisiest, most joyous celebration this old city has ever seen.

Around City Hall the tumult was terrifying in its intensity. Women and girls clutched at their throats, as if in fright, as the voices of countless thousands rose in a great, triumphant crescendo and echoed in what seemed still greater volume from the walls of the tall midcity structures.

HUGGING AND KISSING

Girls and service men hugged and kissed one another—and danced.

In an incredibly short time, the hundreds who had been streaming through the City Hall section on foot when the surrender flash was received had been joined by thousands of others. They dashed into the streets from office buildings. They abandoned meals in restaurants. They leaped from trolley cars to join the milling mob about City Hall.

Meanwhile, Broad st. and Market st. were beginning to fill up with the heaviest automobile traffic in their history, according to police, as the big parades toward City Hall from all parts of Philadelphia and its environs gained momentum.

TWO-DAY HOLIDAY

While the celebration here was at its ear-splitting peak, Governor Edward Martin at Harrisburg proclaimed today and tomorrow legal holidays throughout Pennsylvania.

This means banks will be closed and most stores and industrial plants will be shut down today—some both today and tomorrow. None of the big department stores here will be open today.

While the riotously happy throngs

Continued on Page 4, Column 2

Navy Contracts Cut 6 Billions

Inquirer Washington Bureau

WASHINGTON, Aug. 14.—Within 15 minutes after President Truman announced Japan's acceptance of surrender terms, the Navy Department announced cancellation of prime Navy contracts totaling $6,000,000,000.

This sum, which includes contract termination costs, is in addition to the $1,200,000,000 cut in ship construction announced last Saturday, involving the planned building of 95 combat ships.

Among the prime contracts, it was

Continued on Page 32, Column 1

Truman Statement

WASHINGTON, AUG. 14 (U. P.)—The text of the President's statement on Japanese surrender:

I HAVE received this afternoon a message from the Japanese Government in reply to the message forwarded to that government on Aug. 11. I deem this reply a full acceptance of the Potsdam Declaration which specifies the unconditional surrender of Japan. In the reply there is no qualification.

Arrangements are now being made for the formal signing of surrender terms at the earliest possible moment.

General Douglas MacArthur has been appointed the Supreme Allied Commander to receive the Japanese surrender. Great Britain, Russia and China will be represented by high-ranking officers.

Meantime, the Allied armed forces have been ordered to suspend offensive action.

The proclamation of V-J Day must wait upon the formal

Continued on Page 2, Column 4

Jap War Chief Commits Suicide

NEW YORK, Aug. 15 (Wednesday) (A. P.).—Japanese War Minister Korechika Anami has committed suicide, the Japanese Domei agency reported today. The English-language wireless broadcast was recorded by the Federal Communications Commission.

The Domei dispatch, directed to the American zone, said Anami had taken his life at his "official residence" to "atone for his failure in accomplishing his duties as his majesty's minister."

Anami had held the rank of general since May 1, 1943.

Hirohito Says He Quit To Save Civilization

By The Associated Press

A Domei dispatch broadcast by the Tokio radio said last night that Emperor Hirohito had told the Japanese people by radio that "the enemy has begun to employ a new and most cruel bomb" and should Japan continue to fight "it would lead to the total extinction of human civilization."

The dispatch was recorded by the Associated Press in New York.

"The enemy has begun to employ a new and most cruel bomb, the power of which to do damage is indeed incalculable, taking the toll of many innocent lives," the Emperor was quoted as saying.

"Should we continue to fight, it

Continued on Page 2, Column 6

All Censorship To End on V-J Day

WASHINGTON, Aug. 14 (A. P.).—Newspaper, radio and mail censorship all are due to die with the official coming of V-J Day.

The Office of Censorship said tonight that it was getting ready to announce its going out of business when President Truman proclaims the day.

Joyous Thousands Celebrating the End of the War

JOYOUS Jubilant crowds waving and shouting on the sidewalks and overflowing into the street near City Hall to welcome peace. Scenes like this were repeated in every section of the city, the State and throughout the Nation.

TEEMING

Thousands upon thousands of Philadelphians, wild with joy, jamming Market st. from sidewalk to sidewalk enthusiastically to celebrate the arrival of peace last evening. The celebration was one of the greatest in city's history.

A JUBILANT PARADE ON MARKET ST., EAST OF BROAD

STREET DANCE A couple dancing in the streets in the 1700 block of Chadwick st., during the city's joyous celebration.

A STORM OF PAPER COVERING AUTOS OPPOSITE THE EAST SIDE OF CITY HALL AS CITY WENT WILD OVER WAR'S END

SHARE JOY A sailor, his wife and his son savoring the joy of peace as together they read of the war's end yesterday. There will be no more journeys away from family into battle for him. They are Seaman and Mrs. Fred Brer and Fred, Jr.

PRAYER AT ST. JOHN THE EVANGELIST CHURCH

GOING WILD WITH JOY ON MARKET ST., NEAR BROAD

THE WEATHER
Philadelphia and vicinity: Fair and slightly colder today. Mostly cloudy and quite cold tomorrow with occasional snow. Moderate northerly winds today becoming easterly tomorrow.
Full weather data for Eastern Pennsylvania, New Jersey, Delaware and Maryland on Page 2.

The Philadelphia Inquirer

PUBLIC LEDGER

An Independent Newspaper for All the People

FINAL
CITY EDITION

CIRCULATION: November Average: Daily 581,739; Sunday 1,122,571

SATURDAY MORNING, DECEMBER 22, 1945

116th Year

abdefgh

THREE CENTS

Today

Publicity at Moscow
Silence Is Justified
'Open Covenants'
Wait for Results
Prejudice Unfair

—By Walter Lippmann—

IT DOES not seem to me fair and reasonable, or a service to the freedom of the press, or in the public interest, to cast discredit on the Moscow Conference because the negotiations are being conducted without publicity.

I know that this is not the prevailing view in this country, especially among my fellow newspapermen. So I should like to state the reasons why I believe that Secretary of State James F. Byrnes is quite justified, in so far as he deems it likely to produce satisfactory agreements, to treat the negotiations as confidential.

All negotiation, in fact, any process by which men make up their minds, is bound to be private at some stage.

We argue that when Messrs. Ernest Bevin, Vyacheslav M. Molotov and Byrnes meet face to face, they should tell us within a few hours what they were saying. Do we also insist that the three Foreign Ministers tell us what they say to each other when they are not meeting face to face? Hardly.

They may talk by telephone, by letter, through their ambassadors. They do this more or less every day of the year, and no one insists on a running current record of what they say.

Why then do we act as if some new vital principle were at issue if, having communicated at a distance, they then find it expedient to communicate face to face?

I can see how in theory one might ask, though it would be silly to do so, for full and current publicity on all communications between our Government and any other Government, be it by letter, cable, through envoys, or face to face.

But I cannot see why when Messrs. Bevin, Molotov and Byrnes are talking in the same room we demand a kind of publicity which we do not demand when they are talking at a distance.

President Wilson was the author of the first of the 14 points, which called for:

"Open covenants of peace openly arrived at after which there shall be no private international understandings of any kind but diplomacy shall proceed always frankly and in the public view."

When the fourteen points were accepted by the German Government in October, 1918, the Allies asked Colonel House, who had come to Paris to arrange the armistice, for an official commentary on each of the points. Colonel House directed Frank I. Cobb, then the editor of the New York World, and me to write the commentaries. The texts were cabled to President Wilson, and after he had approved them, they became official.

This is the substance of the official commentary on the first point: "The President explained to the Senate last winter that the phrase ('Openly arrived at') was not meant to exclude confidential diplomatic negotiations involving delicate matters. The intention is that nothing which occurs in the course of such confidential negotiations shall be binding unless it appears in the final covenant made public to the world."

By this test, which I submit is the correct test, neither Mr. Byrnes nor the other Foreign Ministers are subject to criti-

Continued on Page 10, Column 3

Council Votes For Widening Vine Street

Sunken Highway Plan Dropped After Shroyer Warning

Alarmed at the State Highway Department's threat to divert funds for the improvement of Vine st. elsewhere, City Council, it was learned yesterday, has voted secretly to proceed with city-State approved plans calling for the widening of that thoroughfare.

Council, at a meeting of Republican members of that body, pushed aside proposals for a sunken highway along Vine st. from the Delaware River Bridge Plaza to 22d st. and agreed to adhere to the original plan to construct a multi-lane boulevard from 7th to 18th sts.

STATE WARNED CITY

Council's behind-the-scenes action came on the heels of a virtual ultimatum from State Secretary of Highways John U. Shroyer warning Mayor Bernard Samuel that unless the municipality acted quickly on final plans for the improvement of Vine st., the State would be forced to allocate about $12,000,000 of State funds for other purposes.

Council's move has the support of officials of the city's Department of Public Works, which last month lined up in favor of the State plan to widen Vine st. at a cost of about $8,000,000.

Director of Public Works Martin J. McLaughlin at that time attacked the proposal to construct a submerged express highway in Vine st. on the grounds the cost would be prohibitive and added that the State plan was entirely feasible with slight changes.

The sunken highway plan was advocated both by the City Planning Commission and the Philadelphia Committee for the Relief of Traffic Congestion. Representatives of both organizations, at a meeting of Council's Public Works Committee last month, warned that the State plan was inadequate and would result in

Continued on Page 22, Column 1

Jury Discharged In Ration Thefts

The jury in the case of Samuel M. Bailey and Thomas M. Wagner, charged with the theft of 16,000 No. 4 ration books, was unable to agree after six and one-half hours deliberation in U. S. District Court late yesterday, and was discharged.

Judge Guy K. Bard, who presided at the six-day trial, released each defendant under $10,000 bail and directed that their cases be continued until the next term of court.

HOPELESSLY DEADLOCKED

Retiring at 11.45 A. M. yesterday, the eight men and four women on the jury were closeted until 6.15 o'clock last evening. Then their foreman, Rev. Alfred M. Rahn, of 309 Main st., Souderton, sent word to the court that they were hopelessly deadlocked. It was reported after they were dismissed that the jury members stood nine to three for acquittal.

The two defendants are former employes of the Board of Education

Continued on Page 22, Column 2

Enlistment Drive Nets One Private

CHUNGKING, Dec. 21 (A. P.).—An intensive re-enlistment campaign by the U. S. Army in Chungking has produced the following results:

Private First Class Jesus P. Rivers, of Harlingen, Tex., signed up for another two years.

The campaign is continuing.

G. M. to Resume Negotiations With Striking Employes

Management Agrees to Bargain After Session With Fact-Finding Committee in Washington

Illustrated on Page 2

By DOROTHY ROCKWELL
Inquirer Washington Bureau

WASHINGTON, Dec. 21.—General Motors Corp. agreed tonight to resume bargaining with the United Auto Workers (C. I. O.) next Wednesday in Detroit, as the President's fact-finding panel slowly applied the full pressure of its expanded authority.

Panel Chairman Lloyd K. Garrison, at the end of a long day of conferences with G. M. officials, announced that the hearings, which started yesterday, had been recessed until Dec. 28 "unless the parties mutually agree to a postponement."

He added that the panel members were "definitely hopeful that collective bargaining will go forward in the light of the meeting that was held this morning," referring to a G. M.-U. A. W. conference at which it had been decided to resume bargaining on local non-wage issues and to discuss methods for resumption of wage bargaining.

The panel also announced that if the strike were not settled by Dec. 28, and no postponement were requested—in other words, if bargaining once more broke down—it would then wade into the question of ability of the company to pay the demanded 30 percent wage increase.

MAY CALL FOR BOOKS

"Future developments in the case" would determine whether the panel "will call upon the company to submit books or records germane to the case for examination by the board," the announcement continued.

In any event, the company will be required to submit "exact and de-

Continued on Page 2, Column 3

Turner Denies U. S. Tricked Japan Into War

By HERMAN A. LOWE
Inquirer Washington Bureau

WASHINGTON, Dec. 21.—No one in the United States Government did anything in the fall of 1941 to try to trick Japan into war, Admiral Richmond Kelly Turner testified today at the Pearl Harbor inquiry.

Admiral Turner, who was chief of the Navy war plans division then, said that on the contrary efforts were made to stall for time because we were not ready.

REPLIES TO LUCAS

His answer was an emphatic one in reply to a query by Senator Scott W. Lucas (D., Ill.). Before the investigation got under way, charges were whispered that this nation tricked the Japs into a war that Japan did not want.

"Do you know anyone in our Government who tricked Japan into war?" was the question.

"No, sir," he replied, "far from it. We wanted to hold it off as long as we could. There was never the slightest tendency to do anything but what I believe was honest and sound."

'STEP BY STEP' TASK

Admiral Turner was asked whether the Fleet would have been able to relieve General Douglas MacArthur in the Philippines if it had not been damaged by the sneak attack.

"No, sir," he answered. "It would have been completely impossible. The only way was to do it the way it was done—step by step—and it took two years."

The committee recessed late this

Continued on Page 2, Column 6

Freight Rate Rule Stayed by Court

UTICA, N. Y., Dec. 21 (A. P.).—Federal Judge Stephen W. Brennan tonight filed an injunction staying an Interstate Commerce Commission order equalizing class freight rates of northern and southern railroads.

The injunction granted by a three-judge Federal District Court had been sought by nine Northeastern States.

The ICC order, which had been scheduled to take effect Jan. 1, required a 10 percent increase in class freight rates in the North and a 10 percent cut in class freight rates in the South and West.

Congress Recess Ends Session

By ROBERT BARRY
Inquirer Washington Bureau

WASHINGTON, Dec. 21.—The first session of the 79th Congress passed into history this afternoon with a measure of confusion in the Senate and an equal proportion of self-congratulation in the House. Both chambers adjourned sine die until Jan. 14, on which date the second session will convene.

The Senate struggled through nearly four hours with the constant threat of a quorum call over its head. There obviously was no quorum, and the lack of one would have meant automatic adjournment, with all the tags and tatters of year-end business hanging loose.

FILIBUSTER THREATENED

In addition, notice was served privately if not publicly that the new session would start off with a full-dress filibuster over the Fair Employment Practice Committee, which very likely will be the first subject of proposed legislation after the holidays.

The House spent some time joining the Senate in eulogizing General

Continued on Page 2, Column 2

Man Falls 40 Feet In N. Y. Manhole

NEW YORK, Dec. 21 (A. P.).—Firemen today rescued a 45-year-old man who slipped while running for a bus in crowded, snow-clogged Madison ave. and plunged 40 feet down a sewer manhole opened to aid snow removal.

Carried 25 feet through an accumulation of snow and slush at the bottom of the sewer, Hans P. Herz, of Chappaqua, N. Y., managed to cling to a wall projection and remain conscious during his 20-minute ordeal.

Three firemen extricated him as he was about to be swept along a main to the East River. Mr. Herz suffered back, leg and internal injuries.

Big 3 Envoys Make Gains In Conference

Ministers Dispel Cloud of Suspicion, Moscow Reports

MOSCOW, Dec. 21 (A. P.).—Informed sources close to the Big Three Foreign Ministers said tonight a "positive stage" had been reached in their talks, and that Russia, the United States and Great Britain appeared closer now on vital international issues than before the conference opened.

Considerable suspicion appears to have been dispelled on all sides, these informants said, as a result of the talks between U. S. Secretary of State James F. Byrnes, British Foreign Secretary Ernest Bevin and Soviet Foreign Commissar Vyacheslav Molotov, who met for their sixth session today.

SOME OBSTACLES REMAIN

Observers said that this does not mean that all obstacles to understandings on international issues had been removed, but that there were good reasons for believing some agreements were going to be reached.

Both Mr. Byrnes and Mr. Bevin were said to be anxious not to raise the expectations of their people too much in regard to definite results from the conference.

ATOMIC ENERGY ON AGENDA

There was no official word on progress of the ministers' conference, which had been slated to discuss control of atomic energy and other subjects held vital to the maintenance of world peace. Some sort of communique or announcement is anticipated when the conference closes.

In this connection it was suggested in American circles again that Secretary Byrnes still hoped to leave Moscow by Christmas, but observers said it was unlikely that the ministers would conclude their meetings by then. Mr. Byrnes plans to return to the United States before attending the General Assembly of the United Nations Organization in London scheduled to begin Jan. 10.

Foreign quarters said the foreign ministers of the Big Three have no intention of dominating the United Nations Organization, nor is there any move afoot to dissolve the Council of Foreign Ministers, which includes France and China in addition to Russia, Britain and the United States.

MAY BE DISSOLVED

The United Nations Organization will soon begin to take over some of the functions of the ministers' council, however, and it may eventually be dissolved.

While there is no daily channel of information being supplied to the French and Chinese representatives in Moscow, Mr. Byrnes and Mr. Bevin have consulted with them and it was believed they will be kept informed of anything of interest to them.

The French and other embassies protested when Mr. Byrnes held a press conference only for Americans.

Continued on Page 2, Column 6

Hemingway Wins Divorce in Cuba

HAVANA, Dec. 21 (A. P.).—Ernest Hemingway was granted a divorce today from Martha Gellhorn, also a writer, on grounds of abandonment.

Havana's East Court of First Instance accepted Mr. Hemingway's contention his wife "voluntarily abandoned" their home in London for six consecutive months. The suit was uncontested.

The Hemingways were married in Wyoming in 1940.

Camden Fire Perils Waterfront Area

The Camden waterfront was illuminated early today by flames from a three-alarm fire which, raging out of control, swept through several vacant buildings in Federal st. near Front.

Wintry winds fanned the blaze, impeding firemen battling to bring the flames under control. The fire apparently started shortly before 2 A. M. in the building at 113 Federal st., until recently occupied by the Camden Machine Co. It spread rapidly to 115 to 117, flaring through the roofs of the unoccupied buildings.

Patton Dies in Sleep; Hero to Be Buried on European Battlefield

General George S. Patton, Jr., who died in Heidelberg, Germany, yesterday.

Blood Clot Fatal To Tank Strategist; Wife at His Bedside

A Sketch of General Patton's Life on Page 18
Picture Story on Page 10

HEIDELBERG, Germany, Dec. 21 (A. P.).—America's great master of tank warfare, General George S. Patton, Jr., died in his sleep today of a blood clot which developed gangrene in his lungs and weakened his heart.

Mrs. Patton, who was at his side, decided immediately that the general would be buried in Europe, along the storied route of the powerful Third Army he drove to victory.

FUNERAL EXPECTED TO BE HELD MONDAY

"The exact place of burial has not been decided, but presumably it will be in France," U. S. Headquarters announced. The funeral probably will be held Monday.

The acid-tongued general, one of the greatest in American history, died at 5.50 P. M. (11.50 A. M., E. S. T.), 12 days after an automobile accident.

"He went down fighting," said General Joseph T. McNarney, commander of U. S. forces in Europe. Flags were ordered at half-staff across the American-occupied zone of Germany.

HISTORIC DRIVE OF 3D ARMY RECALLED

"The cause of death was pulmonary (lung) embolism, followed by cardiac failure," said the Army medical specialist who attended him.

General Patton, 60, died almost a year to the day after one of the greatest military feats in history—the 78-mile plunge by his Third Army to the relief of the battered men of Bastogne in last winter's Battle of the Bulge.

General Patton's neck was broken Sunday, Dec. 9, and he suffered paralysis from the shoulders down. He was injured in a collision between a truck and the motor car in which he was going pheasant hunting.

"This is a hell of a way to die," General Patton said then as he was lifted into an ambulance.

CONDITION IMPROVED BEFORE COMPLICATIONS

But his condition steadily improved, and last Wednesday he sat up in bed. Then, 48 hours ago, bronchial secretions brought on congestion of the lungs, and today his heart became affected.

Colonel R. Glen Spurling, War Department medical specialist, said the blood clot which caused death occurred when General Patton was well on his way to recovery from partial paralysis. The clot developed early today.

The medical facts, said Colonel Spurling, were these:

"Until the morning of Dec. 19, Patton made very satisfactory progress. His general condition was good, and he was confident he would recover.

STRICKEN BY PALLOR AND BREATHLESSNESS

"The first untoward sign was when he had difficulty raising secretions from his bronchial tubes.

"At approximately 2 A. M. yesterday he had an acute attack of breathlessness and pallor. The attack lasted about an hour, and he was relieved by medication. At that time we felt relatively sure the general had pulmonary (lung) embolism."

Colonel Spurling explained the blood clot probably originated in his injured neck and was pumped by the heart to the right lung, causing "a spot" of gangrene in the lung.

PARALYSIS AND AGE FACTORS IN DEATH

"Anybody, particularly an older person and especially one who is paralyzed, is liable to develop such a 'spot,'" Colonel Spurling said.

The specialist explained that the clot clogged up the vessels in Patton's lungs, and that though he recovered from the

Continued on Page 18, Column 4

British, Danes Clash at Frontier

LONDON, Dec. 21 (A. P.).—The Moscow radio tonight broadcast a Tass dispatch from Copenhagen saying "clashes" involving British and Danish frontier troops have occurred on the Danish-German frontier and that a German lieutenant who said he was attached to British troops was seriously wounded. No other casualties were given.

No comment was available immediately from the British War Office nor from official sources in Copenhagen.

SEARCH FRICTION

The broadcast, recorded by the Soviet monitor, said "a number of clashes took place . . . caused by the fact that the British do not permit the Danes to search the luggage of soldiers of the German army who are sent from Denmark to Germany.

"A former senior lieutenant of the Hitlerite army, Gerhardt Martin, categorically refused to open his (luggage) cases, maintaining that he was a signals officer attached to the British troops," the radio added. "The Danish frontier guards were compelled to use arms. The German Martin was seriously wounded."

'SPECIAL PROTECTION'

The broadcast said the Germans "considered themselves under a regime of special protection and do not wish to submit themselves to the demands of the Danish frontier troops."

"On Dec. 19 alone, Danish frontier troops confiscated several tons of Danish goods from German soldiers and officers," the radio added.

HusbandAccused Of Double Killing

Special to The Inquirer

ALLENTOWN, Pa., Dec. 21.—Authorities announced late today that a formal charge of murder would be made tomorrow against John Barnak, estranged husband of a 21-year-old mother of two children who was slain with a male companion shortly after last midnight outside her parents' home in East Allentown.

Detective Captain Wallace Yeager disclosed that Barnak, an employe of the Bethlehem Steel Corp., would be arraigned before Alderman Thomas Miller.

HOME NEAR MURDER SCENE

Captain Yeager added that the information in connection with the charge would be sworn to by Police Captain E. C. Sperling. The latter arrested Barnak at his home, about six blocks from the murder scene, a short time after the slayings.

Captain Yeager and, District Attorney Theodore R. Gardner revealed that witnesses had placed the 30-year-old husband at the scene of

Continued on Page 22, Column 3

N. J. Man, 79, Shoots In-Law, 74; Kills Self

Cracking under the strain of ill-repressed anger over his daughter's marriage to a man almost as old as himself, William Thornley, 79, fired a pistol at his son-in-law in his home at Lake and Maple aves., Laurel Springs, N. J., yesterday morning, then killed himself.

The bullet which, according to Camden County Coroner Edward C. Gardner, Mr. Thornley fired at Charles Shoffner, 74-year-old rural radio program broadcaster, penetrated one of Mr. Shoffner's ears and grazed his scalp. The wounds were not considered serious, the coroner said.

FIRES WITHOUT WARNING

"Mr. Shoffner told me," Mr. Gardener said last night, "that his father-in-law stepped into the first floor studio from which Mr. Shoffner broadcast a farm program each morning and, without a word, fired a shot at him, then strode from the room. Mr. Shoffner said Mr. Thornley hated him because of his marriage to Mr. Thornley's 40-year-old daughter, Martha, and had 'con-

Continued on Page 22, Column 3

British Shelve Demands on Siam

BANGKOK, Dec. 21 (U. P.).—Major British demands on Siam in current armistice negotiations have been struck out of preliminary treaty drafts, it was reliably reported today, but the reports did not specify what demands had been dropped.

Siam's Prime Minister, Mom Rajawongse Seni Pramoj, said "the Thai people feel grateful to America. The country descended on us in time of trouble and we've taken due note of the statement of Dean Acheson."

Acheson, acting United States Undersecretary of State, said Wednesday that the U. S. objected to Britain's terms and hoped that the British would sign no agreement with the Siamese until exchanges are finished with the United States.

What Job Fits YOU?

TOMORROW The Inquirer will answer the Number I question of the day for returning service men and civilians alike:

"WHAT JOB SHALL I LOOK FOR?"

It is a simple Occupational Interest Test that has been tried and approved at an Army Air Forces Separation Center and one which overseas veterans are finding of great assistance in determining the type of work for which they are best suited in peacetime employment.

Designed to help GI's reconvert to civilian life, it should be mailed to your man in the service wherever he is stationed. Don't miss the Occupational Interest Test

In Everybody's Weekly Section of Tomorrow's Sunday Inquirer

Priority for Veterans On Housing Granted

WASHINGTON, Dec. 21 (U. P.).—The Government today announced a building priorities program that gives veterans first chance to buy or rent new homes built for $10,000 or less. The priorities, effective Jan. 15, will reserve 50 percent of 10 scarce materials for such housing.

LIMIT ON SALE OR RENTAL

Only veterans who wish to build for themselves, or builders who agree to sell or rent to veterans, will be eligible for priorities.

Each house built must sell for not more than $10,000, including land and improvements, or must rent for not more than $80 a month. The builder must give veterans preference in buying or renting during the period of construction and for 30 days after the dwelling is completed.

FIGURE PUT AT 400,000

After that, the house may be sold or rented to a non-veteran. Sale or re-rent must be within the established ceiling price as approved by the Federal Housing Administration.

It was estimated that 400,000

Continued on Page 2, Column 5

In The Inquirer

SATURDAY, DEC. 22, 1945

Departments and Features

Pound Is Insane, Unfit for Trial

WASHINGTON, Dec. 21 (U. P.).—Ezra Pound, 60-year-old poet accused of treason, today was adjudged insane and mentally unfit for trial.

The ruling was made by District Judge Bolitha J. Laws on the basis of a report by four psychiatrists. Pound was committed to St. Elizabeth's Federal Hospital for observation and treatment.

PERSONALITY ABNORMAL

The treason charge was based on allegedly pro-Axis radio broadcasts while he was in Italy. Italian witnesses had been brought to this country to testify.

The psychiatrists said that Pound's personality had been abnormal for many years. They added that it "has undergone further distortion to the extent that he is now suffering from a paranoid state which renders him mentally unfit to advise properly with counsel or to participate intelligently and reasonably in his own defense."

They said that he "exhibits ex-

Continued on Page 2, Column 2